170110

AN INTRODUCTION TO SHORT FICTION

The Writer's Path

EDITED BY

CONSTANCE
& LEON ROOKE

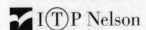
ITP Nelson

an International Thomson Publishing company

Toronto • Albany • Bonn • Boston • Cincinnati • Detroit • London • Madrid • Melbourne
Mexico City • New York • Pacific Grove • Paris • San Francisco • Singapore • Tokyo • Washington

I(T)P® **International Thomson Publishing**

The ITP logo is a trademark under licence

www.thomson.com

Published in 1998 by

I(T)P® **Nelson**

A division of Thomson Canada Limited
1120 Birchmount Road
Scarborough, Ontario M1K 5G4
www.nelson.com

Canadian Cataloguing in Publication Data

Main entry under title:
The writer's path : an introduction to short fiction

ISBN 0-17-606966-6

1. Short stories.   2. Short story.   I. Rooke, Constance, 1942–   .
II. Rooke, Leon.

PN6120.2.W74 1997   808.3'1   C97-932635-4

Team Leader and Publisher	Michael Young
Acquisitions Editor	Nicole Gnutzman
Production Editors	Tracy Bordian and Marcia Miron
Production Coordinator	Brad Horning
Editorial Assistant	Mike Thompson
Art Director	Sylvia Vander Schee
Cover and Interior Design	Stephen Boyle
Cover Illustration	Murray Kimber
Senior Composition Analyst	Marnie Benedict

Printed and bound in Canada

1 2 3 4 (WC) 01 00 99 98

CONTENTS

PREFACE

This book contains 64 extraordinary short stories—enough so that if some do not satisfy a particular taste, there will be plenty of others from which to choose.

It wasn't easy to decide on the stories, primarily because there was such a plethora of riches from which to choose, and secondarily because there were *two* of us. We knew that we wanted to include both famous, frequently taught stories and others that would be less familiar. For the first category, we each made a long list of favourites, discovering a fairly comfortable degree of overlap, and then set it aside. For the second category, we began by developing a list of stories that had made a lasting impression on one or both of us, the idea being that surely many of these would have "stuck" for good reason. Sometimes, they were stories we hadn't looked at for years and had considerable difficulty finding again. But we rounded them up and began the fascinating process of renewing acquaintance with these more or less deeply buried personal treasures.

Many "held up," their merits still radiant in our eyes, and some did not; or they worked splendidly for one of us, but not the other. (The "other" in this case was often judged sorely mistaken by the story's champion.) The first list of more familiar stories became a problem as well when we realized that we had chosen far too many stories. And so our highly animated quarrels began. Why we should have expected perfect unanimity it is hard now, with our tempers cooled and the last decisions made, to imagine; and, in fact, more often than not we did agree. We are confessing here to some discord not only to suggest the passion that went into the making of this anthology, but also—primarily—to make the point that readers do disagree. It would be a much less interesting world, and literature would be a terribly barren enterprise, if they did not.

How, though, did we resolve our disagreements? We entertained for a time, and then dismissed, the rule that no story would be included unless we both wanted it badly. That approach, we felt, would have led to a less exciting and, ultimately, a less useful book. Instead, we drew up a single list of stories that one or the other or both of us wanted very much to include, and then winnowed it down on the basis of representation or balance, taking into account such issues as form and technique, nationality and place in the tradition, links between stories, and the areas of human experience being addressed. This approach allowed each of us to ensure that a fair number of the stories we found indispensable simply on the basis of how deeply they affected us would not be left out. We were also guided very strongly by the desire to use stories we believed, or knew from our own experience of teaching them, could ignite a strong response in students and provoke interesting discussions in the classroom.

The anthology is international in scope and it places special, roughly equivalent emphasis on the United States and Canada. Stories from Latin America and from Italy receive emphasis among those that appear in translation, so that at least in the literature of these two parts of the world, the reader might have enough samples to glimpse a tradition. Some stories take us back to the nineteenth century; the majority were written in the twentieth century, and a large proportion of these are contemporary. Some of the stories—by Margaret Atwood and Jorge Luis Borges, for example—are very short. Others—Jane Bowles' "Camp Cataract," Kafka's "Metamorphosis," Melville's "Bartleby, the Scrivener," and Tillie Olsen's "Tell Me a Riddle"—are long enough to be called novellas. We have made a concerted effort to include here stories of many kinds, arising from very different authorial sensibilities and ideological or aesthetic persuasions.

Some interesting (and more or less significant) links exist among the stories. For example, Doris Lessing's "Out of the Fountain" and Donald Barthelme's "The Emerald" are wildly dissimilar stories that both focus on jewels; James Joyce and Dylan Thomas write about drinking; and Dionne Brand, Githa Hariharan, Tillie Olsen, and Eudora Welty have all chosen grandmothers as their heroines. There are stories that raise troublesome questions about the first person point of view, such as Russell Banks' "Sarah Cole: A Type of Love Story" and Adolph Muschig's "The Scythe Hand, or the Homestead." There are, of course, hundreds of other ways in which the stories might be grouped—by date of publication, country of origin, theme, tradition, or whatever. In order not to force such associations, or to privilege any one of them, we have chosen to print the stories simply in alphabetical order, by their authors' names.

As the title indicates, our special concern in this anthology has been to illuminate "the writer's path"; in the Introduction to the anthology, Constance Rooke develops this idea of the writer's path. Each of the stories included in the book is a journey taken by the writer—and if each writer may be said to blaze his or her own trail, it is also the case that they are in some sense *together* creating our map. They are helping one another along, writing in the light of what has gone before, and well aware of this, as the writers' own comments should make amply clear. Stories that show writers speaking directly to one another in their fiction—Raymond Carver's story about Chekhov and the three Australian stories called "The Drover's Wife"—enforce this point.

The Symposium on Stories section includes statements on the art of the story by a number of the writers whose stories are included here, as well as by a number of other important fiction writers. The Symposium section also contains some commentary on particular stories included in the anthology, by both fiction writers and literary critics. Many of these selections are cross-referenced in the Stories section of Table of Contents; several others of general interest (such as Clark Blaise's essay on the critical importance of the beginnings of stories, or John Gardner's remarks on the importance of rhythm in prose fiction) are not. The items included in the Symposium are again printed in alphabetical order, by the authors' names.

The Writer's Path also contains three Casebooks. The Casebook on Alice Munro collects statements about her art by this great Canadian practioner of the short story form, who is represented in the anthology by two full-length stories. The Chekhov and Carver Casebook is an odd hybrid. On both of these important writers, we have selected enough supplementary material not to wish to see it dispersed in the Symposium section; Carver's story about Chekhov's death, marking his intense admiration of Chekhov, creates the necessary link between them. The Casebook on "The Drover's Wife" brings together Murray Bail's and Frank Moorhouse's intertextual take-offs on the Henry Lawson story, which is included in the "Stories" section, and the painting by Russell Drysdale, which was also inspired by Lawson's story; together, these works address the rise and fall of a potent Aussie myth.

In the Appendixes, we provide a brief history of the short story form, a comment on the impossibility of "defining" the story, a section on the elements of fiction (plot and structure; character; point of view; setting, voice, style, and tone; imagery and symbolism; and theme), some advice on essay writing, and a sample essay on Eudora Welty's "A Worn Path," which is taken through several iterations from a failing paper to an "A" paper.

The Writer's Path could not possibly have been pulled together without the gargantuan efforts, learning, and intelligence of our two editorial assistants, Lin Coburn and Mark McCutcheon. We are very deeply indebted to them.

Thanks must go to those who took the time to review the text: Jean Clifford (Capilano College), Ingrid Hutchinson (Fanshawe College), Antanas Sileika (Humber College), and Ari Snyder (Vanier College).

We would also like to thank the team at ITP Nelson: Nicole Gnutzman, Tracy Bordian, Marcia Miron, and Mike Thompson.

—*Constance and Leon Rooke*

CONSTANCE ROOKE

INTRODUCTION TO THE SHORT STORY

I. THE WRITER'S PATH

To read a story is to follow the writer's path. The words of the story are stepping stones selected and laid by the writer on that path. The first word of the story is the first step on the writer's (and subsequently on the reader's) path, and so on through to the end. Yet what one sees along the way and how one sees it will vary at least slightly with each reader. Because readers respond differently to those words on the page, each reader takes a different path through the text.

But the writer's path that serves as the title of this anthology is intended to suggest something more than the finished story, or the path that has been laid out for readers to follow as they will. We want also to consider how the writer got there—how and why the path of a story is made. We want you to imagine walking in the writer's shoes. The point here is not to induce authorial ambitions or to assert the godlike authority of the writer or to suggest that good reading is a "tracking" of authorial intentions. It is simply that closing the gap between writer and reader can help us to become better readers. If you have some feeling for the imaginative and technical challenges faced by the writer, and also for the passion that goes into the production of literature, you will be better equipped both to appreciate stories and to engage in a critical analysis of them.

The chance to walk for a while in the shoes of someone else, to feel in one's bones the circumstances and ambitions of another human being, is a large part of what fiction, through its creation of compelling characters, offers to us. The recognition that there is also a human being behind the scenes who is fired by ambition, taking risks, working alone and within particular social and literary contexts, somehow raises the stakes of the reading experience. Both emotionally and intellectually, we become more engaged. If we like the story, we feel excitement about how well the thing is done, and this adds to our pleasure in the journey.

Any made thing implies a maker who intended this thing to be used. But when the made thing is a work of art, we use it best and gain vastly more from it by devoting some share of our attention to how it is made and how it generates

I

various responses in us. The analysis of literary texts is humanized when behind the how and the what we can also feel (even if we cannot really know) the who and the why. Understanding what compels writers to make stories and how a story typically gets written can help us along the reading path.

II. Story telling

A story is told at a specific time by a particular person; presumably this person—the writer—has something to say that she or he judges worthy of being said. Or does the writer simply feel like talking to someone? Is it, perhaps, not what is said that matters most to the writer but how it is said? Is it the sheer ability to write—to create a fictional world that must be exercised and established to the writer's own satisfaction? Or is the writer concerned primarily with gaining the admiration of others? To get at what a short story is, and what causes it to be written, it may be helpful to think first about the stories we tell people in daily life, and what prompts their telling. The mystery of the short story becomes even more complicated once we consider the fact that it is invented or "made up" and written, rather than merely said. But let's start there, with the story I might tell someone seated next to me at dinner.

Do I think of a story just to be sociable? Maybe I dredge up some story to tell as a way of getting acquainted or deepening my acquaintance with the woman on my right. The story I choose to tell, the way I tell it, and the personal history or attitudes I reveal through my story will all be means of communicating who I am to this other person—and also, perhaps, of signalling to her that I'm worth knowing. How she responds may tell me something about her and whether she is worth knowing. The story, in this sense, is a tool we use to explore the possibility of intimacy, and it is a bridge across which we may both travel (I from the teller's shore, she from the listener's) in order to know each other better.

But the story itself should matter to me. It is my interest in the story, and the quality or nature of that interest, that should establish whether I am worth knowing. Perhaps the story that I choose to tell is a fake story. An example of a fake story would be a story about my rich and crazy uncle Harry, the whole point of which is to smuggle across that bridge to my dinner partner the information that I come from a rich and distinguished family. The story is fake because I am merely pretending to be interested in Harry. The facts of the story might be true, but it's not true as a story if the teller has no real interest in it.

A genuine story is one that the teller is moved to tell for its own sake, because it is worth telling. When I tell a story, I am implicitly claiming that something about this story interests me; the story provides a window on my view of the world. In a sense, I am putting my own authenticity on the line. I may know that I am revealing something about myself in the process of telling the story; I may also want to impress you. The teller's motives need not be pure. But if we connect on the storyteller's bridge in a real way, it is because we share a belief that there is something of interest (apart from hints at my bank account or my pedigree) in the story.

Perhaps I tell a certain story because it's on my mind—because it matters to me for some reason, and I'm still trying to figure out why it matters and what it means. I may be thinking out loud, in the hope that telling it will clarify things for me, or I may hope that it will prompt my companion to say something useful in response. The story rather than the person I'm telling it to seems to be the real issue. Even so, it will have the effect of revealing me to my listener; it can serve as a bridge between us. The story could also start casually, as an attempt to be sociable, and then, to my surprise, become significant. I will feel suddenly that I'm on the track of something, that I'm not just engaged in idle chit-chat anymore. It might be a story I've told before, but this time I'm telling it a little differently, and so I find that I'm teaching myself something even as I speak.

Human beings are story-telling animals. A story may be defined as *words that serve to depict or interpret some portion of human experience.* Stories are supposed to be interesting; that's why we tell them. But why do we feel compelled to tell stories? One common answer is that stories help us to make sense of our lives. As we shape the story, deciding what to leave in, what to take out, and what to emphasize, we are building or setting the stage for an interpretation. This is true for short-story writers, who select and arrange the words that will subsequently be interpreted by readers, and for people telling stories at the dinner table. In both cases, we might say that the teller is trying first to make sense to himself.

But we don't tell stories only to create meaning for ourselves. A story also implies an audience and a desire to reach or connect with that audience. Why do we ask others to hear our attempt to record and shape human experience? I think this impulse arises from a duality in the nature of human beings. Which am I, this solitary tower-like creature enclosed by skin, an echoing consciousness that runs on and on, or part of something more? And if there are others out there, who are also part of this larger whole, shouldn't we be signalling to one another? Shouldn't we be figuring this thing out? Getting together?

The seventeenth-century English poet John Donne said "No man is an islande. We are all a part of Mankinde." But we may feel both things: alone on the island of the self, and also connected to something larger. Donne's metaphor suggests that although we may imagine the self as an island, each of us is in fact a *peninsula.* (An island is completely surrounded by water; a peninsula may look like an island, but at one end it is connected to a larger land mass.) Thus, we apparently insular human beings are in fact connected to the mainland of "mankinde." The story may be thought of as occurring at the point where the island is shown to be in fact a peninsula; and so the bridge across which the storyteller sends messages to another human being functions as a passage to the mainland of humankind.

Human beings are both solitary creatures and creatures of society. We are creatures of society in the sense that we are made—our attitudes and behaviours are shaped—by society, of which we are all, inevitably, constituent parts. Without us, society cannot be. Delete it, and we are no one; all that has made us who we are disappears. And we are driven to connect with others in part as a means of coming home to the communal self, to that fundamental dimension of our being of which, strangely enough, we often feel deprived.

Simultaneously, however, we are attempting to gain recognition for the solitary self, or to make our individuality manifest. We feel more or less alienated, unseen, alone, and undervalued. We are unsure of both dimensions of our being (the solitary—or the unique—and the communal), and telling stories allows us to assert the value of both, restoring the self to the context of the human family, in which it truly belongs, or to an even larger whole. Storytelling also helps us to explore these two dimensions of our being; in making both of these more real, or more explicit, we grow as human beings.

The philosopher Descartes is famous for having said "I think; therefore, I am." He takes thinking as the proof of his own existence. Story-telling, however, confirms more than the storyteller's existence; it is also a testimony to the existence of a world beyond the self and to the reality of other people: both the audience and the people the story is about.

III. THE WORLD BEYOND THE SELF

The American writer and Nobel laureate Saul Bellow has said that "novels are about other people. They lack everything if they lack this sympathetic devotion to the life of someone else." It is a wonderful claim, and perhaps a surprising one, given the common assumption that writers generally write about themselves and that fiction is more or less thinly disguised autobiography. Is Bellow wrong, then, in his assertion? Are all the stories we write or tell to others in daily life really just self-investigation (a kind of therapy, perhaps) or self-display? A story always has some element of this, but a good story has something more, some "sympathetic devotion" to something beyond the self.

Society, or Donne's "mankinde," often disappoints or angers us. It falls short, sometimes wildly short, of the ideals we are haunted by. We have complaints and wish to make them to someone, perhaps in hope of reform or redress. Such complaints may take the form of stories that try to capture what what we feel when a woman screams at her child in the supermarket, when a husband and wife cease to speak to each another, or when a white police officer beats up a young black man on the streets of Toronto. We have concerns about how people behave toward one another and about how the world is run. Sometimes, too, we see things that seem marvellous or that demonstrate for us how the world ought to be; we catch sight of the ideal and wish to record it. Whether the storyteller's impulse is one of protest or celebration or, as is often the case, some mix of the two, the story says "I care—that's why I'm telling you this." Maybe the story says that I, or we, have a responsibility to get to the heart of things, to appreciate what's good, and to change what needs changing.

The words we speak or hear with serious attention can lead to heightened consciousness, stripping away what the great British novelist Virginia Woolf has called the "cotton wool" that separates us from moments of being, or from a true appreciation of reality. Woolf is talking about the fact that we waste a lot of our lives by not really feeling our own aliveness or the aliveness of the world; it is as if we are insulated from the beauty or the pain around us by cotton wool. Perhaps we are too busy putting one foot in front of the other to look around us, too preoccupied to smell the flowers (or, for that matter, the poison gas), to hear either the music or the gunfire. Perhaps we are half asleep. If so, one purpose of the story is to help us wake up. Woolf's "moments of being" do not depend on art; they can obviously happen without it. But the desire for such moments—for greater *intensity* of being—is one of the principal reasons we turn to art, as makers or as audience.

Poor, formulaic stories, such as Harlequin romances, can sometimes entertain us sufficiently to "kill the time"; we're half asleep as we experience them, and nothing more than that is called for. But good, surprising, somehow different stories can wake us up. "Aha!" we say, "here is something I should pay attention to." Instead of "killing" time, such stories redeem time; they make it count by giving us access, in Virginia Woolf's words, to "moments of being."

What happens, though, when we do wake up? Does the story do any good beyond the moment? Perhaps we feel something intensely for awhile, but does the experience of the story change us? Can it change the world? The German poet Rilke has a poem in which the speaker sees a beautiful statue of the god Apollo, and what it says to him—what the splendour of this work of art makes him feel—is "You must change your life!" To extend this challenge to the observer or listener is, for Rilke, the purpose of all art. And he has chosen a particularly difficult or unlikely example to make his point. The work of art in question is as far from the didactic, or the moralizing, as one could imagine: he chooses the figure of a beautiful young man, as opposed, for example, to a depiction of the horrors of a Nazi death camp. It does not say: do this, stop that. But still it moves him. Rilke is suggesting that all art is kinetic: it causes something else to happen. The figure of Apollo, if only for a moment, makes the poet want to change his life, perhaps to be closer to or more worthy of this beauty. Similarly, when we say that music soothes the savage beast, we mean not that music puts him to sleep, but that it reminds him of some better way of being.

The moment of being may pass. Our attention and our resolve to seize the day—to smell the flowers, be kinder to our mothers, or do something about racism—may lapse. Because art has not fixed the world yet, we might ask what use it is. How can we claim for art a redemptive power? We might reply that art makes the world better simply by giving pleasure or moments of intense feeling to human beings, and that this is redemption enough. Yet for many centuries, we have also heard more expansive claims for the power of art. For example, Cicero, the Latin poet, said that the purpose of poetry is to please and instruct. On one level, at least, it seems clear that poetry and art in general are often, or maybe always, meant to teach us something. Perhaps the real question is whether we actually learn from it.

The change occurring in an individual or in society as a consequence of art is difficult to prove. Yet we know that the words of others have some degree of power, for good or ill, to change how we think and ultimately how we behave. The rhetorical skill of both Martin Luther King and Hitler moved thousands to adopt their points of view; the words of friends may influence us. The change does not always happen, and even if there is some kind of impact, there is no guarantee that it will be a positive one, or indeed that it will last. But we may conclude that stories, and art generally, can have some lasting influence; they contribute to making us who we are, and therefore to making the world beyond the self what it is. I may not be able to attribute a certain change in myself to a particular story I've read, or film I've seen. But some things do stick. They combine over time with other things that stick to displace or revise previous conceptions of the world around us. Gradually, for example, they may change the way we look at women or homosexuals or old people—and also change the way we behave.

IV. WRITING AGAINST DEATH

Another psychological or philosophical issue underlying the creation of fiction and linking writer and reader is the fact of our mortality. We may or may not believe in some form of life after death, but in either case we are haunted by the knowledge that we will die. We are born and begin to take shape as individuals who are invested, to varying degrees, with a sense of mission; we think we are supposed to "make something" of our lives, perhaps to grow in understanding or to accomplish some good in the world. But all of our lives are a work-in-progress that is interrupted by death. We worry that we are wasting time, or wasting the potential that is in us—to have a great love, perhaps. The clock is ticking. Even before we die, we may find suddenly that it is too late. Our powers have diminished; our mistakes are entrenched; our chances are lost. And when death does come at last, it may seem to set the stamp of failure on our lives. Even if things are going well, and we think that on the whole we are making good progress, we rarely, if ever, feel that we have achieved all of our goals before death makes us stop.

For the writer, writing fiction well—conveying the truth of experience, extending the limits of what fiction has been able to achieve in the past— becomes a consuming goal. This ambition may be linked to the desire for immortality through fame—the hope that one will be remembered and have some continuing power to affect the lives of others, even after death. In this sense, the writer may be said to write against death, sending out filaments of the self in words that will survive the body's dissolution. But the writer's mission is not so simply egotistical; it mirrors the desire we all have to grow and to use our time well.

Perhaps more importantly, the writer writes against death on behalf of other people. Bellow's "sympathetic devotion to the life of someone else"— that quality he considers essential to fiction—means, quite simply, that the writer cares about the life or lives that are represented in the story. The writer devotes sympathetic energy to the task of expressing this life, as if to preserve it or keep it from disappearing into the shadow of death. The character can be entirely made up and still compel this sympathetic devotion from the writer. This sort of passion or commitment to an imaginary being may seem strange. But it stands for a commitment to humanity, and for an affirmation of the value of human life.

When asked for whom they write, a surprising number of writers will answer that they write for the dead. This may seem a strange or even a pretentious reply. But what such writers are saying is that they write to commemorate human life—as if to say to the dead, you have not disappeared; it is not all for nothing; we are still here, trying. Cumulatively, the dead are all the people who have gone before us on this journey; and writers who may think of themselves as writing for the dead are the descendants or heirs of these dead, carrying on their work, performing a kind of ritual of respect. "The dead" could be a particular group of people with whose history the writer feels a special bond—black women, perhaps. They might also be other writers. The dead might even be constructed as an ideal audience, since only they are positioned to know (if by chance they do) the whole of the human story.

This phrase, "the human story," has two levels of meaning that may recall those two dimensions of our being discussed earlier: the solitary and the communal. The human story is the story of us all—the story of the human race, or Donne's "mankinde"—as well as the story of a single human life; and when we say "the human story" we are implying a link between the two. It is striking that for many centuries, and in all parts of the world, human beings have tended to conceive of their lives as stories. A human life, like a story, has a beginning and an end, and each is "written" in the desire to get it right, to grasp some meaning, to achieve something of value in the time available. I may think of myself as the author of my life story, and also as its central character. The fact that I am in some sense both of these—author and protagonist of my own life—explains something of the curious bond that exists between writers and readers, as well as the feeling so many people have that they are themselves writers at heart or that someone should write their story, because— really, if you only knew—it is a story worth telling.

All of us—old people especially—want our stories told before we disappear. We want to believe that our stories are worth telling, as our lives, in spite of all that has gone wrong or been left undone, have been worthy of being lived. That is what writers do for us, even though the story is "made up"; that is the sense in which writers may be said to write against death.

V. MAKING SHORT STORIES

Short stories differ from the stories we tell about our lives most critically in being—or, perhaps, in attempting to be—works of art. They are written works of the imagination. They are, first of all, "made up" and, secondly, made out of words. Although the story, or indeed any work of art, may be said to express in more or less obvious ways the human experience that exists outside the work of art, and although art exists in life, it is also something quite different from the rest of life. (What exactly a work of art is and what the relationship is between art and life are questions that have been debated intensely through much of human history.)

The fact that the story is made up does not reduce its imaginative truth. For example, the people we come to know in short stories are not more or less real for us according to whether they have been modelled on living people or have arisen from the writer's imagination. Indeed, this may be an impossible distinction. Even a story that is based closely on actual events and real people depends on the imagination of the writer to filter it, to fill it out, to give it shape; if it is a real story, it still has to be "made" by the imagination. And even an entirely made up story must originate somehow in the writer's experience. The central character may or may not resemble the author's father; in most cases, we won't know. This character might be an amalgam of the author's father and aspects of half a dozen other people the author has known, together with much more that seems simply to have been invented. Ultimately, it doesn't matter. What matters is whether the story works.

In writing a story, the author often will use bits and pieces of real life—the oxodized copper nailpolish she bought yesterday afternoon at Eaton's, her husband's insistence on singing Leonard Cohen tunes at breakfast, something she has read in the newspaper about a place in California called "Conversation," where people will converse with you on any subject for thirty dollars an hour. Or she may just invent these things as needed and put them in her story; again, it doesn't matter. Many writers describe themselves as magpies or packrats, busily collecting things, storing them in journals, all in the hope of eventually finding some ideal point at which to insert them in a story. Other writers do this less consciously. Details that find their way into a story may be resurrected from the writer's journals or culled from research, or they may appear suddenly like a gift outside the window as the writer looks away from her computer screen. (Perhaps a woodpecker appears, or the Goodyear blimp.) Most often, these details arise from memory or imagination; at their root these two are almost impossible to distinguish from each another, since the imagination is fed by memory.

The word "fiction" comes from a Latin verb meaning "to make or shape"; and the imagination is sometimes called "the shaping imagination," since this is its task. The imagination takes fragments of reality (or memory), combines them, and creates a new shape. These pieces vary greatly in size—say, from the story of Kennedy's assassination to the glint of light on a raven's wing. The writer might use the whole of the design of her own kitchen for a story, or she might use only how the refrigerator stands in relation to the sink. The rest of the story's kitchen she makes up from a thousand other kitchens she has seen— so many, in fact, that she could not possibly track these sources down. But where these fragments of reality come from is not usually the point; the question for the writer is how they fit into the new whole—the new reality—that the imagination creates.

An autobiographical or historical work of fiction contains large pieces of extra-textual "story"; the author's stringing together of small fragments is substantially influenced by how those fragments were combined in some reality lying outside the text. A work of fiction that is only minimally autobiographical or historical will have fewer and smaller extra-textual pieces. (It might, however, actually feel more "true to life," and it might have an enormous amount of real stuff in it, such as familiar song lyrics, Reebocks, and the smell of coffee.) In any fiction, each element whether recognizable has some connection to the real; and each element, whether large or small, whether recognizable as "real" or not, must find its proper place within the larger imagined thing—the shape that the story makes—or the story will suffer.

Some stories, of course, are much more "realistic" than others. We might think of a continuum with history (the real) at one end and fantasy (the unreal) at the other; stories that might have really happened are closer to history and may be called realistic, meaning like the real. Stories that we say could not have happened, containing creatures or events that seem impossible on any literal level, we call fantasy. Stories that distort or exaggerate the real, without actually violating what we regard as the laws of nature, occupy a position on this continuum somewhere between realistic stories and fantasy; romance (in which reality is idealized or made more marvellous) and satire (in which the faults of reality are writ large) may be positioned here. An individual story might be described as realistic, romantic, satirical, or fantastic, but it could also mix these types, containing elements of more than one.

How does a story begin? Does the writer have a story in mind and then sit down to write it? Is it planned, outlined, or "imagined"—so that a reasonably complete picture of the whole exists in the writer's head—before the writing begins? The analogy of the completed story as a path that the writer has laid down may be of use in framing this question. Does the writer see the path through the woods before he creates that path? Does he know where he's going? Does he, perhaps, work from a sort of blueprint? The answer to these questions will vary with the story and also with the writer. Some writers typically begin "blind," or with very little, and others prefer a more substantial anticipation of the path that remains to be taken.

Often, however, and perhaps in its purest or most miraculous form, the story simply begins. Imagine a pile of blank paper. Or imagine that it's morning, and the writer goes to her computer to start something new. She doesn't know what this might be. The screen is empty. She types a few words: "Alice woke up with what she understood at once was going to be the very worst hangover of her life so far." Now where did *that* come from? The writer doesn't care. (She may or may not have a hangover herself.) What she cares about is whether anything in that sentence might lead her to an interesting *second* sentence, whether, to use still another analogy, she's had a nibble; she has cast out her line with that first sentence, and her question is whether a fish (something alive, the possible start of a new story) has attached itself to that line. If not, she hauls it in, by pressing delete, and starts again.

But say she stays with the hangover sentence, having, perhaps, some faint glimmer of interest in what Alice was up to the night before. For example, is there going to be anyone else in Alice's bed? The way this often works is that the writer decides to give it a bit more time—a few more sentences—in the hope that down the page she will feel a major tug, and know that she has indeed got a fish on her line, a possible story.

Returning to the path analogy, we might say that she is out in the woods thrashing around, when suddenly, if she's lucky, she recovers her sense of direction. She has caught the scent of something that is worth pursuing; it is time to start tracking in earnest. THAT WAY, she thinks. She may race ahead, cutting only a crude path through the underbrush, anxious to get through to the end. She may go back to where she started (the blank page) to approach the thing she now supposes herself to be after in another, more efficient way. She may pause to plot out a strategy, or to mull over the possible features of the terrain that lies ahead. The relationship of writing and rewriting varies. Some people polish each sentence—each jewel-like stepping stone of the writer's path—carefully before moving on to the next; they feel they can't go on until they are sure that this bit is right. Others fear that too much fussing now will mean they lose the scent. Either way, the writer almost always finds that the path must be revisited—gone over, reshaped, rewritten to some degree—once the end has been attained.

No matter how carefully the writer may plan her next steps, surprises always lie ahead. Indeed, this is one of the great delights in writing fiction. A writer might intend that some character will just nip into the supermarket to buy a single pork chop, when something about how the writer has turned a phrase, or some detail she threw in to establish the setting, perhaps, suddenly takes her in a new direction. This is how a story grows, or deepens. Characters start to reveal new sides of themselves; some thematic element of the story suddenly becomes more complex; an image unleashes a surprising new pattern of imagery.

Because such new elements seem to have come out of nowhere, unwilled, a writer will sometimes say that the story has a mind of its own, or that the characters do. This sort of experience makes the writer feel "inspired," as if something else is speaking through him. (The "dead," perhaps. This might be another reason that writers sometimes speak of writing for the dead!) To be "inspired" is, if we go back to the root of that word, to have one's breath taken over or enlarged. Historically, this idea of inspiration has often been connected with the idea of divinity, or with the breath of God.

It is possible to feel "inspired" from the very start all the way through to the end. (In this case, there may be very little need for revision.) The feeling of inspiration, whether it is continuous or occurs in fits and starts, with occasional wrong turns, might be compared to moving across the ground with a divining rod in search of water. The water is there, underground; you just have to find it. Similarly, it may seem to the writer who feels inspired that the whole of the path she is creating word by word is in some sense already there, awaiting discovery. (The Canadian writer Margaret Laurence called one of her novels *The Diviners* for this reason.) But there is also an important difference between the water witch, or diviner, and the writer of fiction. The diviner does not need to worry about what path he takes to arrive at the place where a well can be dug; he just has to get there eventually. What the writer must divine is the path itself; the end of the path, the conclusion of the finished story, is just the place where the writer can look back and say, yes, it's finished—it is right, or as right as I can make it.

Because the path itself is the goal, each step of that path must also be right. At some point along the way, possibly not until the end of a first draft, the writer may recognize that a certain character, element, or passage of the story is extraneous. This part fails to contribute to the vision of the whole, or it is misleading; it may be interesting to the writer in itself, it may even be usable in some other work of fiction, but for this story it amounts to a wrong turn. Such things are removed in the process of rewriting. Other things may have to be added. A new element of the story that makes a sudden appearance may well require the writer to revise earlier portions of the story. To set up this new element more effectively, the writer adds signposts anticipating its appearance and prunes away the bits that work against it.

So the writer's path on the way to a finished story often involves a good deal of scouting around, detours that run into dead ends, retracing of steps, and so on, before the story's path is judged worthy of inspection by the reader. Revisions can be made at any stage before completion, and they can occupy an enormous amount of the writer's time. Some passages in a story might be revised a hundred times. Revision can involve drastic structural adjustments, or the recrafting of any number of individual sentences. But even a minute change, one that takes just a moment for the author to effect, can make a critical difference. One detail, say the fact that Leonard's face looked gleeful as he was skinning the squirrel, may set off tremors that shift a story's whole meaning.

The word "revison" means re-visioning, or seeing again; the writer revises to see better, to get it right. There is also, however, the question of refining and ordering the various elements of the story with a view to creating a particular experience for the reader. For example, something that the writer saw early may be better discovered by the reader later in the story, or vice versa. The degree to which a writer is conscious at any stage of designing the path of a story for the reader will vary greatly, and can probably never be disentangled from the writer's pursuit of her own vision. But it is often in the process of revision that the writer is most keenly aware of those others who follow on the writer's path, of what they will see and when it will be best for them to see it.

This emphasis on "getting it right" may seem to imply that the writer is a visionary who cannot quit until she has attainted some pitch of perfection or truth. This is a romantic conception of art, which exaggerates or distorts the plain facts of literary performance; but it is also an ideal that continues to torture or inspire the working writer, and that helps to reveal the creative process. In any case, it is important to acknowledge that all attempts to create a fictional world are not perfectly realized, all stories are not great or even good, all great stories are not perfect, and perhaps none is perfect.

The whole question of greatness or perfection, even the question of whether it is possible to say that one story is better than another, is hotly disputed in our time. Both "truth" and aesthetic value (the quality of a work of art) are increasingly considered relative, a matter of opinion. Thus, "work of art" itself becomes a problematic term. Historically, to call something a work of art has been to praise it, indeed to suggest that it has some kind of lasting or eternal value. Now the term is often used simply to describe the product of a certain kind of human activity, without regard for questions of value.

Still, I would argue that the artist is concerned with discovering and expressing a vision of some kind, and has a passionate wish to get it right. (How we as audience understand the making of art or evaluate a particular work of art is an entirely different question.) Both the vision and getting it right must also be understood in terms of language—the material with which a writer builds the story's path. A story is made out of words, and these words are not only windows onto the world. There is an important level on which the story is also about words and what words can be made to do. The writer is concerned not only with what one sees from the path, but with the path itself. These two things, words and what they refer to in the world, cannot be separated as easily as this use of the path analogy suggests. But both are critical for the writer, whose devotion to language itself requires more thought.

What makes a writer, apart from some particularly strong and lasting experience of the story-telling impulse that exists in us all? This question has many possible answers. But often the determination to become a writer oneself arises from reading the work of others well, with real attention. (In an oral culture, it may begin with an appreciation of the power of stories that are told especially well.) What the would-be writer sees and becomes excited by is the skill with which others have selected and combined their words. The words themselves, turned with such skill, seem wonderful as well; and so the love affair with language begins. If this potential writer becomes a writer in earnest, a substantial part of the vision expressed will be an exploration and discovery of what language can do.

Admiring how well others have written, the aspiring writer sets out to discover whether he also might be able to write well. If he discovers in himself some ability, the desire to exercise and develop it is likely to grow; ultimately, the exercise of this skill may become a kind of necessity. The need to be a writer—to spend a considerable portion of your time working with language, finding out what it can do, or what you can do with it—may become overwhelming. But in the background, there is always the writer's knowledge of what other writers have done. This is a critical point. The writer is almost always a reader, usually a very good reader, and for this reason stories are written very much within the context of other stories.

Much is made of the question of literary influence, which may be more or less difficult for the writer, or indeed the reader, to trace. But it is there nonetheless. The pre-existing reality from which the writer's imagination discovers those fragments that will be combined to make a new story includes other stories, and it includes all other experiences of language. The writer may be understood as a person who experiments with language and who conducts his experiments in the light of countless experiments and discoveries that have preceded his own work. For example, if a writer's characters are about to make love, the way that activity and the feelings associated with it will be described may be as much a function of how other writers have written sexual scenes as of the writer's own experience.

The writer's path is haunted by the ghosts of other writers, both living and dead. This can be a curse if the presence of those other writers is too forceful, steering the would-be pathfinder in the same old directions. Often, the task of liberating oneself from these too potent influences is called "finding one's own voice." But other writers are also crucial guides. The torch gets passed on. One writer helps another to move along on the larger "writer's path" which is literature. Indeed, the individual story might be thought of as living in a kind of great library, where the books can whisper to one another. In some sense together, these stories are telling both the story of what language can do and the human story; together, they are trying to get it right.

VI. THE READER'S PATH

Reading is a transaction between the reader and the text, and also between the reader and the writer. The word "transaction," applied to the act of reading, should suggest both the complex interaction of text and reader, and the transfer of the responsibility for action from writer to reader. The reader must walk the writer's pathway of words, exercising his own muscles. The action imagined by the writer, or latent in the words of the text, can be set in motion only by the imaginative activity of the reader. The words then begin to release their stored energy, often in unpredictable ways. The way the word "transaction" is used in business in some sense applies to literature: readers pay for what they get from a literary transaction with the coin of their attention. And when they pay more, or exercise harder, they get more in return.

Certain signs on the reader's path will be more legible for the experienced and trained reader than for the novice. Any reader may lack the specific piece of knowledge required to understand an allusion to something outside the text, such as another work of literature. But the more we read, the more likely it is that we will have the relevant knowledge already, or at least recognize when we have to go "outside" for help. Even where additional knowledge is not required to understand what is going on in a story, the experienced and trained reader has a clear advantage: it is easier, for example, to see and also to interpret a pattern of bird imagery when we are experienced in thinking about how imagery works.

But much depends on the energy that the reader brings to the task, the willingness to focus the full force of one's attention on the experience at hand. Reading too quickly is the great danger. The brain must have time to take in— to register—and to respond even to small details. In this way, the imagined world of the story (what the reader sees from the path) becomes more vivid, more real to the mind's eye; and the reader is able, as well, to see something of how the path has been made.

The path metaphor leads to a curious paradox. By looking down at his feet, at the path itself, the reader is better able to take in the views that surround him. Beginning readers often don't believe this. They say that such analysis, or pausing too long over the words, destroys the pleasure of illusion; it keeps them from really "getting into" the story. Being forced by English teachers to keep looking down at their feet, they can not enjoy the view. But the words make the story—the "view" is utterly dependent on them—and if we take in only ten percent of what the words are doing, that view will be a weak and unimpressive one.

We might think of this matter in terms of resolution in printing: a crisp or precise image is made up of many more dots than is a blurred image. The writer, we might say, has given the reader enough dots (the words) for high resolution. But the reader who skips over too many of these, not giving them time to register or develop, has only a very generalized or blurry experience of the text. This printing analogy may help us to understand the importance of taking in all the data of the text: "a gnarled old man," for example, is far more vivid if we pause long enough to register the word "gnarled."

But the analogy cannot be pressed too far. Readers are not like sheets of blank paper on which the images of the text are printed. They have distinct and variable characteristics of their own, attitudes, beliefs, experiences, and expertise, which profoundly affect how the images projected by the text are received. They differ not just in how much they take in, but also in what they make of it. And readers do make, or remake, the story in their own imaginations. The reader is an active participant in the construction of meaning; in a crucial sense, she is the writer's collaborator. And the writer intends this collaboration; the words of a story are generally chosen to contain in themselves multiple possibilities, rather than to convey a single fixed image.

Put another way, the words of the story constitute a kind of energy field calculated to achieve certain effects on readers who enter the story. The reader is guided by that finite set of words, which has been engineered both to produce specific effects and to leave room for the play of the reader's imagination. The writer's control is by no means absolute. All kinds of anticipated and unanticipated effects—responses, associations—will occur or not, again depending on who the reader is. Readers may respond poorly or in wildly inappropriate ways, proposing interpretations that the words on the page exclude; they may also respond well in ways of which the writer would not approve. But writers don't want, and the kinetic or multi-valenced power of literature does not permit, an endless succession of "perfect" readers, each of whom will understand the story in exactly the same way. Fiction works by an accumulation of nuance, by suggestions which, however carefully they may have been planted by the writer, retain a certain fluidity. Thus, even writers will experience their stories differently with each re-reading.

A fictive world might be compared to virtual reality except that here the reader must continually press the switch that converts words into three-dimensional space. But the words remain words too, and the reader wanders among them, knowing that someone has put them there for a reason. Each word of the story was chosen, in preference to others: a young woman is called "handsome" rather than "pretty." The word "handsome" helps the reader to see her in a particular way, but the reader also sees the word itself—those eight letters on the page—and combines them in his mind's eye with other words: "Helen's glossy boots" or her "gallantry." The reader knows, at least on one level, that the character is made out of words rather than flesh and blood.

In seeking to understand this character, I may be inclined to ask "What do I know about Helen?" This is convenient shorthand, to speak of Helen as if she were real, and I could assess or understand her in much the same way I might try to know some flesh and blood Helen who works in my office. But in fact the process is very different. In the case of some real Helen, I might have a huge amount of unsorted data, much of which is repetitive or not particularly illuminating; also, there will be many things about Helen that I don't know. But in a story *everything* I am shown or told about Helen counts, and that is all the "data" there will ever be. Helen will always be a product of just this information—and what I do with it.

Imagine Helen now in a story that does not tell us she is a victim of sexual abuse. Nevertheless, this is what you feel. Are you right? In the writer's mind, sexual abuse might be a critical part of the history he had imagined for this character, a secret he expects the reader to uncover; it also might be simply a possibility the writer had left open. Or the writer might be surprised—and appalled or intrigued or convinced—by a reader's assertion that Helen was abused. Ultimately, the author's intention (or approval, if that could be solicited) does not matter; what matters is whether the text can support this reading.

Perhaps a reader thinks frequently about sexual abuse; certainly we live in a time when this subject is widely discussed. But the reader cannot simply invent for Helen a history of sexual abuse because that subject happens to be prominent in his consciousness, or indeed because he is looking for some deeply buried secret around which to construct an essay. It is important to be wary both of overly ingenious interpretations and of importing to the text personal preoccupations that are alien to it. Writers may reveal information in all sorts of overt and subtle ways, reflecting the ways in which we arrive at understanding in our lives; but they don't hide things just to be ornery or deep. If, however, a reader could point to certain patterns in the text that are consistent with sexual abuse, if nothing ultimately contradicts this interpretation, and if the story itself seems to grow in this new light, the interpretation might be viable. The viability of a literary interpretation is determined by whether it can "live" within the organism of the text. We might say then that the idea of sexual abuse was latent in the words, a potentiality contained within them, whether the author was aware of it or not.

The world around the writer's words is changing; textual signs that are clear in one age or culture may become obscure in another. These differences in the world that "makes" writer and reader inevitably cause some things to recede from the reader's view, and others to gain prominence. Individuals also differ from one another, and from themselves in another mood or at another time. All such change will cause the meaning and value of the story to shift, at least fractionally; it is as if the lighting were changed, so that dimensions of the text revealed in one reading may be concealed or altered in another.

The story we read and talk about is never *the* story; it is the story *we* have read, the story as we experience it at this point in time. However carefully we may have read, it is our path—our personal trajectory—through the story. Good readers often disagree, and they can also resist. They can say I don't like this, or this doesn't work, and this is why. A good reader might make something quite different out of details a, b, and c than other good readers do or than the writer who put them there presumably did. What a good reader cannot do is *ignore* a, b, and c, or how they relate to other details in the text. To that degree, we are all subject to the authority of the text.

The reader's path precedes and is broader (if less focussed) than the critic's path. In critical practice, we construct a path that is not a replica of the writer's path but a selective and analytical response to it. But before we start talking as critics, we must heed all the writer's words. The many pieces we cannot address as critics, if they have been blithely ignored on the reader's path, will still be lurking on the writer's page. And if some of these pieces are especially relevant to our chosen argument, if they disprove or weaken or cast a particularly strong light on that argument, they can be always resurrected by someone else (a teacher perhaps!) to raise questions about the merit of the critic's path.

This is a plea to *re-read*. Recall for a moment my earlier distinction between the words of the story as the writer's path and the path the writer takes to get to that finished story. Remember the difference for a writer between getting to the end of a first draft and deciding that a story is now as good as it is going to get. Our situation on the reader's path is rather like that of the writer journeying toward her finished story. A first reading is like a first draft, which may be more or less polished and more or less "right" at the first attempt. But a first reading is rarely enough, especially if we aspire to the critic's path. As the writer engages in revision (re-seeing), so we re-read in an effort to see the story whole, to get it right. We know that there is no such thing as a perfect reading of story. Still we try to hold the story in our minds, to see the whole and all its parts as fully and clearly as we can.

In the end, the writer's path is into the reader's heart and mind. But there are no certainties. Not all stories work for us, and not all readers work as hard as they might for the story. Sometimes the match between writer and reader is just not possible; and sometimes a clash of sensibilities or belief can be productive of insight. Often, the issue is one of timing. Stories that only bore or confuse us now might greatly impress us if we were to return to them at a later stage; stories that impress us now may later fail to do so. It is generally true that we become better readers as we gain experience both of the world and of how literature works. But the person you are at twenty—with the forces of belief and feeling, habits of mind, and experiences that are most potent in you at that time—can also enter some stories more effectively, with more interesting results, than would be possible at the age of forty or sixty.

So it does not matter greatly if this or that story that someone else says is wonderful does not do anything for you now, or indeed ever. The important thing is to keep on reading, and to develop your skills and confidence as a reader. If you believe that and act on it, the rewards of pleasure and understanding that lie ahead will be immense. There is so much out there, and more being made every day—so many writers' paths, some designed as if purposely to speak to you, or to the person you find yourself becoming. If you read widely and work to become a more skillful reader, it will happen. The goods—your goods—will be delivered.

PART I

STORIES

CHINUA ACHEBE

CIVIL PEACE

Chinua (Albert Chinualumogu) Achebe (b. 1930) was born in the Ibo village of Ogidi, Nigeria. Achebe learned English while attending primary school run by the Church Missionary Society, for which his father worked. As one of the first students to attend University College, Ibadan, Achebe began his studies in medicine but later turned to literary studies, a change that would prove significant in his life.

> *When I had been younger, I read these books about the good white man, you know, wandering into the jungle, and savages were after him. And I would instinctively be on the side of the white man. You see what fiction can do. ... In the university I suddenly saw that these books had to be read in a different light. Reading* Heart of Darkness, *for instance, which was a very, very highly praised book and which is still highly praised, I realized that I was one of those savages jumping up and down on the beach. Once that kind of enlightenment comes to you, you realize that someone has to write a different story.*

While following a career in Nigerian radio, Achebe wrote his first novel, Things Fall Apart *(1958), which was published to international acclaim. It has remained an international bestseller, with translations in forty languages. In 1974, as a visiting professor at the University of Massachusetts, Amherst, Achebe delivered his controversial lecture "An Image of Africa: Conrad's* Heart of Darkness." *According to Doug Killam, Achebe's writing "reflects three essential and related concerns ... first, with the legacy of colonialism at both the individual and societal level; secondly, with the fact of English as a language of national and international exchange; thirdly, with the obligations and responsibilities of the writer both to the society in which he lives and to his art." Although Achebe is not the first or the only author to write against the grain of the colonial canon, his work has been vital in generating a counter-canon for the black African experience. His reputation as a father of modern African culture has been established by his prolific and tireless work in many spheres of Nigerian life: in 1967 he became a diplomat for Biafra during the Nigerian civil war, and in 1983 he became deputy president of the People's Redemption Party. In addition to writing five novels,*

various volumes of short stories, essays, and poetry, and a number of chil-
dren's books, Achebe has edited several anthologies of African literature
for the Heinemann African Writers Series and the Nigerian literary
journal Okike, and he has directed arts councils and festivals. He has
received countless literary awards and honorary degrees. Achebe has lec-
tured at universities in the United States and Nigeria and has spoken at
numerous international events. In 1990 the University of Nigeria, where
Achebe is professor emeritus, held an international conference in his
honour which coincided with Nelson Mandela's release from prison. A
car crash later left Achebe in a wheelchair, but he continues his successful
career from his home in Annandale, New York, where he writes and
teaches at Bard College.

Jonathan Iwegbu counted himself extra-ordinarily lucky. "Happy survival!"
meant so much more to him than just a current fashion of greeting old friends
in the first hazy days of peace. It went deep to his heart. He had come out of
the war with five inestimable blessings—his head, his wife Maria's head and
the heads of three out of their four children. As a bonus he also had his old
bicycle—a miracle too but naturally not to be compared to the safety of five
human heads.

The bicycle had a little history of its own. One day at the height of the war
it was commandeered "for urgent military action." Hard as its loss would have
been to him he would still have let it go without a thought had he not had
some doubts about the genuineness of the officer. It wasn't his disreputable
rags, nor the toes peeping out of one blue and one brown canvas shoe, nor yet
the two stars of his rank done obviously in a hurry in biro, that troubled
Jonathan; many good and heroic soldiers looked the same or worse. It was
rather a certain lack of grip and firmness in his manner. So Jonathan, suspecting he might be amenable to influence, rummaged in his raffia bag and
produced the two pounds with which he had been going to buy firewood
which his wife, Maria, retailed to camp officials for extra stock-fish and corn
meal and got his bicycle back. That night he buried it in the little clearing in
the bush where the dead of the camp, including his own youngest son, were
buried. When he dug it up again a year later after the surrender all it needed
was a little palm-oil greasing. "Nothing puzzles God," he said in wonder.

He put it to immediate use as a taxi and accumulated a small pile of
Biafran money ferrying camp officials and their families across the four-mile
stretch to the nearest tarred road. His standard charge per trip was six pounds

and those who had the money were only glad to be rid of it in some way. At the end of a fortnight he had made a small fortune of one hundred and fifteen pounds. Then he made the journey to Enugu and found another miracle waiting for him. It was unbelievable. He rubbed his eyes and looked again and it was still standing there before him. But, needless to say, even that monumental blessing must be accounted also totally inferior to the five heads in the family. This newest miracle was his little house in Ogui Overside. Indeed nothing puzzles God! Only two houses away a huge concrete edifice some wealthy contractor had put up just before the war was a mountain of rubble. And here was Jonathan's little zinc house of no regrets built with mud blocks quite intact! Of course the doors and windows were missing and five sheets off the roof. But what was that? And anyhow he had returned to Enugu early enough to pick up bits of old zinc and wood and soggy sheets of cardboard lying around the neighbourhood before thousands more came out of their forest holes looking for the same things. He got a destitute carpenter with one old hammer, a blunt plane and a few bent and rusty nails in his tool bag to turn this assortment of wood, paper and metal into door and window shutters for five Nigerian shillings or fifty Biafran pounds. He paid the pounds, and moved in with his overjoyed family carrying five heads on their shoulders.

His children picked mangoes near the military cemetery and sold them to soldiers' wives for a few pennies—real pennies this time—and his wife started making breakfast akara balls for neighbours in a hurry to start life again. With his family earnings he took his bicycle to the villages around and bought fresh palm-wine which he mixed generously in his rooms with the water which had recently started running again in the public tap down the road, and opened up a bar for soldiers and other lucky people with good money.

At first he went daily, then every other day and finally once a week, to the offices of the Coal Corporation where he used to be a miner, to find out what was what. The only thing he did find out in the end was that that little house of his was even a greater blessing than he had thought. Some of his fellow ex-miners who had nowhere to return at the end of the day's waiting just slept outside the doors of the offices and cooked what meal they could scrounge together in Bournvita tins. As the weeks lengthened and still nobody could say what was what Jonathan discontinued his weekly visits altogether and faced his palm-wine bar.

But nothing puzzles God. Came the day of the windfall when after five days of endless scuffles in queues and counter-queues in the sun outside the Treasury he had twenty pounds counted into his palms as ex-gratia award for the rebel money he had turned in. It was like Christmas for him and for many others like him when the payments began. They called it (since few could manage its proper official name) *egg-rasher*.

As soon as the pound notes were placed in his palm Jonathan simply closed it tight over them and buried fist and money inside his trouser pocket. He had to be extra careful because he had seen a man a couple of days earlier collapse into near-madness in an instant before that oceanic crowd because no sooner had he got his twenty pounds than some heartless ruffian picked it off him. Though it was not right that a man in such an extremity of agony should be blamed yet many in the queues that day were able to remark quietly on the victim's carelessness, especially after he pulled out the innards of his pocket and revealed a hole in it big enough to pass a thief's head. But of course he had insisted that the money had been in the other pocket, pulling it out too to show its comparative wholeness. So one had to be careful.

Jonathan soon transferred the money to his left hand and pocket so as to leave his right free for shaking hands should the need arise, though by fixing his gaze at such an elevation as to miss all approaching human faces he made sure that the need did not arise, until he got home.

He was normally a heavy sleeper but that night he heard all the neighbourhood noises die down one after another. Even the night watchman who knocked the hour on some metal somewhere in the distance had fallen silent after knocking one o'clock. That must have been the last thought in Jonathan's mind before he was finally carried away himself. He couldn't have been gone for long, though, when he was violently awakened again.

"Who is knocking?" whispered his wife lying beside him on the floor.

"I don't know," he whispered back breathlessly.

The second time the knocking came it was so loud and imperious that the rickety old door could have fallen down.

"Who is knocking?" he asked then, his voice parched and trembling.

"Na tief-man and him people," came the cool reply. "Make you hopen de door." This was followed by the heaviest knocking of all.

Maria was the first to raise the alarm, then he followed and all their children.

"Police-o! Thieves-o! Neighbours-o! Police-o! We are lost! We are dead! Neighbours, are you asleep? Wake up! Police-o!"

This went on for a long time and then stopped suddenly. Perhaps they had scared the thief away. There was total silence. But only for a short while.

"You done finish?" asked the voice outside. "Make we help you small. Oya, everybody!"

"Police-o! Tief-man-o! Neighbours-o! we done loss-o! Police-o! ..."

There were at least five other voices besides the leader's.

Jonathan and his family were now completely paralyzed by terror. Maria and the children sobbed inaudibly like lost souls. Jonathan groaned continuously.

The silence that followed the thieves' alarm vibrated horribly. Jonathan all but begged their leader to speak again and be done with it.

"My frien," said he at long last, "we don try our best for call dem but I tink say dem au done sleep-o ... So wetin we go do now? Sometaim you wan call soja? Or you wan make we call dem for you? Soja better pass police. No be so?"

"Na so!" replied his men. Jonathan thought he heard even more voices now than before and groaned heavily. His legs were sagging under him and his throat felt like sand-paper.

"My frien, why you no de talk again. I de ask you say you wan make we call soja?"

"No."

"Awrighto. Now make we talk business. We no be bad tief. We no like for make trouble. Trouble done finish. War done finish and all the katakata wey de for inside. No Civil War again. This time na Civil Peace. No be so?"

"Na so!" answered the horrible chorus.

"What do you want from me? I am a poor man. Everything I had went with this war. Why do you come to me? You know people who have money. We ..."

"Awright! We know say you no get plenty money. But we sef no get even anini. So derefore make you open dis window and give us one hundred pound and we go commot. Orderwise we de come for inside now to show you guitar-boy like dis ..."

A volley of automatic fire rang through the sky. Maria and the children began to weep aloud again.

"Ah, missisi de cry again. No need for dat. We done talk say we na good tief. We just take our small money and go nwayorly. No molest. Abi we de molest?"

"At all!" sang the chorus.

"My friends," began Jonathan hoarsely. "I hear what you say and I thank you. If I had one hundred pounds ..."

"Look is my frien, no be play we come play for your house. If we make mistake and step for inside you no go like am-o. So derefore ..."

"To God who made me; if you come inside and find one hundred pounds, take it and shoot me and shoot my wife and children. I swear to God. The only money I have in this life is this twenty-pounds *egg-rasher* they gave me today ..."

"OK. Time de go. Make you open dis window and bring the twenty pound. We go manage am like dat."

There were now loud murmurs of dissent among the chorus: "Na lie de man de lie; e get plenty money ... Make we go inside and search properly well ... Wetin be twenty pound? ..."

"Shurrup!" rang the leader's voice like a lone shot in the sky and silenced the murmuring at once. "Are you dere? Bring the money quick!"

"I am coming," said Jonathan fumbling in the darkness with the key of the small wooden box he kept by his side on the mat.

At the first sign of light as neighbours and others assembled to commiserate with him he was already strapping his five-gallon demijohn to his bicycle carrier and his wife, sweating in the open fire, was turning over akara balls in a wide clay bowl of boiling oil. In the corner his eldest son was rinsing out dregs of yesterday's palm wine from old beer bottles.

"I count it as nothing," he told his sympathizers, his eyes on the rope he was tying. "What is *egg-rasher*? Did I depend on it last week? Or is it greater than other things that went with the war? I say, let *egg-rasher* perish in the flames! Let it go where everything else has gone. Nothing puzzles God."

ISABEL ALLENDE

Two Words

Translated by Margaret Sayers Peden

Isabel Allende (b. 1942) belongs to a generation of Latin American writers she describes as "torn limb from limb by dictatorship, violence, death, exile." Her writing comes out of that experience as a Latin American woman severed from her roots, her family, her home, and her job. For Allende, writing has been a way to deal with her past, "to open a vein and let all the demons out and call all the angels." Her stories contain strong female characters whose wisdom has been handed down through generations of mothers and daughters—women who are obsessed by the oppositions of violence and love, and whose insight, spirit, secrets, and rebellions have overcome societal subjugation. Fantastic things happen in her stories: spirits hover and magic permeates the worlds she creates. "Maybe the most important reason for writing," she has said, "is to prevent the erosion of time, so that memories will not be blown away by the wind ... to register history and name each thing. Write what should not be forgotten."

Allende was born in Lima, Peru, and raised in Chile, Bolivia, Europe, and the Middle East. She worked as a journalist in Chile until the 1973 coup that resulted in the overthrow and assassination of her uncle, Salvador Allende, the Chilean President. She settled in Venezuela with her husband, son, and daughter, where she began the writing career that enthralled the literary world with the publication of her first novel, The House of the Spirits *(1985). She followed that success with three novels,* Of Love and Shadows *(1986),* Eva Luna *(1988), and* The Infinite Plan *(1994), and with a collection of short stories,* The Stories of Eva Luna *(1991). Most recently, she has published a memoir dedicated to her daughter,* Paula *(1994). Two of her novels,* The House of the Spirits *and* Of Love and Shadows, *have been made into feature films. She has lived in the United States since 1987 and currently resides in the San Francisco Bay area with her second husband, William Gorden.*

"Two Words" recounts the tale of a young peasant woman who overwhelms a tyrant with magical words. This first story in the collection The Stories of Eva Luna *steps directly off the last pages of her novel* Eva

26

Luna. *The novel relates the exploits of a wide-eyed South American revolutionary writer and storyteller. As the novel closes, Eva's lover, Rolf Carle, asks her to tell him a story she's never told before, and Eva recounts the story of a woman whose lifework was telling stories.* The Stories of Eva Luna *begins with Rolf's memory of Eva wrapped in a silk shawl, dark hair falling delicately, in the moments after they have made love, and his repeated request: "Tell me a story ... Tell me a story you have never told anyone before. Make it up for me."*

She went by the name of Belisa Crepusculario, not because she had been baptized with that name or given it by her mother, but because she herself had searched until she found the poetry of "beauty" and "twilight" and cloaked herself in it. She made her living selling words. She journeyed through the country from the high cold mountains to the burning coasts, stopping at fairs and in markets where she set up four poles covered by a canvas awning under which she took refuge from the sun and rain to minister to her customers. She did not have to peddle her merchandise because from having wandered far and near, everyone knew who she was. Some people waited for her from one year to the next, and when she appeared in the village with her bundle beneath her arm, they would form a line in front of her stall. Her prices were fair. For five centavos she delivered verses from memory; for seven she improved the quality of dreams; for nine she wrote love letters; for twelve she invented insults for irreconcilable enemies. She also sold stories, not fantasies but long, true stories she recited at one telling, never skipping a word. This is how she carried news from one town to another. People paid her to add a line or two: our son was born; so-and-so died; our children got married; the crops burned in the field. Wherever she went a small crowd gathered around to listen as she began to speak, and that was how they learned about each others' doings, about distant relatives, about what was going on in the civil war. To anyone who paid her fifty centavos in trade, she gave the gift of a secret word to drive away melancholy. It was not the same word for everyone, naturally, because that would have been collective deceit. Each person received his or her own word, with the assurance that no one else would use it that way in this universe or the Beyond.

Belisa Crepusculario had been born into a family so poor they did not even have names to give their children. She came into the world and grew up in an inhospitable land where some years the rains became avalanches of water that bore everything away before them and others when not a drop fell from the sky and the sun swelled to fill the horizon and the world became a desert.

Until she was twelve, Belisa had no occupation or virtue other than having withstood hunger and the exhaustion of centuries. During one interminable drought, it fell to her to bury four younger brothers and sisters; when she realized that her turn was next, she decided to set out across the plains in the direction of the sea, in hopes that she might trick death along the way. The land was eroded, split with deep cracks, strewn with rocks, fossils of trees and thorny bushes, and skeletons of animals bleached by the sun. From time to time she ran into families who, like her, were heading south, following the mirage of water. Some had begun the march carrying their belongings on their back or in small carts, but they could barely move their own bones, and after a while they had to abandon their possessions. They dragged themselves along painfully, their skin turned to lizard hide and their eyes burned by the reverberating glare. Belisa greeted them with a wave as she passed, but she did not stop, because she had no strength to waste in acts of compassion. Many people fell by the wayside, but she was so stubborn that she survived to cross through that hell and at long last reach the first trickles of water, fine, almost invisible threads that fed spindly vegetation and farther down widened into small streams and marshes.

Belisa Crepusculario saved her life and in the process accidentally discovered writing. In a village near the coast, the wind blew a page of newspaper at her feet. She picked up the brittle yellow paper and stood a long while looking at it, unable to determine its purpose, until curiosity overcame her shyness. She walked over to a man who was washing his horse in the muddy pool where she had quenched her thirst.

"What is this?" she asked.

"The sports page of the newspaper," the man replied, concealing his surprise at her ignorance.

The answer astounded the girl, but she did not want to seem rude, so she merely inquired about the significance of the fly tracks scattered across the page.

"Those are words, child. Here it says that Fulgencio Barba knocked out El Negro Tiznao in the third round."

That was the day Belisa Crepusculario found out that words make their way in the world without a master, and that anyone with a little cleverness can appropriate them and do business with them. She made a quick assessment of her situation and concluded that aside from becoming a prostitute or working as a servant in the kitchens of the rich there were few occupations she was qualified for. It seemed to her that selling words would be an honorable alternative. From that moment on, she worked at that profession, and was never tempted by any other. At the beginning, she offered her merchandise unaware that words could be written outside of newspapers. When she learned otherwise, she calculated the infinite possibilities of her trade and with her savings paid a priest twenty pesos to teach her to read and write; with her three remaining coins she bought a dictionary. She poured over it from *A* to *Z* and then threw it into the sea, because it was not her intention to defraud her customers with packaged words.

One August morning several years later, Belisa Crepusculario was sitting in her tent in the middle of a plaza, surrounded by the uproar of market day, selling legal arguments to an old man who had been trying for sixteen years to get his pension. Suddenly she heard yelling and thudding hoofbeats. She looked up from her writing and saw, first, a cloud of dust, and then a band of horsemen come galloping into the plaza. They were the Colonel's men, sent under orders of El Mulato, a giant known throughout the land for the speed of his knife and his loyalty to his chief. Both the Colonel and El Mulato had spent their lives fighting in the civil war, and their names were ineradicably linked to devastation and calamity. The rebels swept into town like a stampeding herd, wrapped in noise, bathed in sweat, and leaving a hurricane of fear in their trail. Chickens took wing, dogs ran for their lives, women and children scurried out of sight, until the only living soul left in the market was Belisa Crepusculario. She had never seen El Mulato and was surprised to see him walking toward her.

"I'm looking for you," he shouted, pointing his coiled whip at her; even before the words were out, two men rushed her—knocking over her canopy and shattering her inkwell—bound her hand and foot, and threw her like a sea bag across the rump of El Mulato's mount. Then they thundered off toward the hills.

Hours later, just as Belisa Crepusculario was near death, her heart ground to sand by the pounding of the horse, they stopped, and four strong hands set her down. She tried to stand on her feet and hold her head high, but her strength failed her and she slumped to the ground, sinking into a confused dream. She awakened several hours later to the murmur of night in the camp, but before she had time to sort out the sounds, she opened her eyes and found herself staring into the impatient glare of El Mulato, kneeling beside her.

"Well, women, at last you've come to," he said. To speed her to her senses, he tipped his canteen and offered her a sip of liquor laced with gunpowder.

She demanded to know the reason for such rough treatment, and El Mulato explained that the Colonel needed her services. He allowed her to splash water on her face, and then led her to the far end of the camp where the most feared man in all the land was lazing in a hammock strung between two trees. She could not see his face, because he lay in the deceptive shadow of the leaves and the indelible shadow of all his years as a bandit, but she imagined from the way his gigantic aide addressed him with such humility that he must have a very menacing expression. She was surprised by the Colonel's voice, as soft and well-modulated as a professor's.

"Are you the woman who sells words?" he asked.

"At your service," she stammered, peering into the dark and trying to see him better.

The Colonel stood up, and turned straight toward her. She saw dark skin and the eyes of a ferocious puma, and she knew immediately that she was standing before the loneliest man in the world.

"I want to be President," he announced.

The Colonel was weary of riding across that godforsaken land, waging useless wars and suffering defeats that no subterfuge could transform into victories. For years he had been sleeping in the open air, bitten by mosquitoes, eating iguanas and snake soup, but those minor inconveniences were not why he wanted to change his destiny. What truly troubled him was the terror he saw in people's eyes. He longed to ride into a town beneath a triumphal arch with bright flags and flowers everywhere; he wanted to be cheered, and be given newly laid eggs and freshly baked bread. Men fled at the sight of him, children trembled, and women miscarried from fright; he had had enough, and so he had decided to become President. El Mulato had suggested that they ride to the capital, gallop up to the Palace, and take over the government, the way they had taken so many other things without anyone's permission. The Colonel, however, did not want to be just another tyrant; there had been enough of those before him and, besides, if he did that, he would never win people's hearts. It was his aspiration to win the popular vote in the December elections.

"To do that, I have to talk like a candidate. Can you sell me the words for a speech?" the Colonel asked Belisa Crepusculario.

She had accepted many assignments, but none like this. She did not dare refuse, fearing that El Mulato would shoot her between the eyes, or worse still, that the Colonel would burst into tears. There was more to it than that, however; she felt the urge to help him because she felt a throbbing warmth beneath her skin, a powerful desire to touch that man, to fondle him, to clasp him in her arms.

All night and a good part of the following day, Belisa Crepusculario searched her repertory for words adequate for a presidential speech, closely watched by El Mulato, who could not take his eyes from her firm wanderer's legs and virginal breasts. She discarded harsh, cold words, words that were too flowery, words worn from abuse, words that offered improbable promises, untruthful and confusing words, until all she had left were words sure to touch the minds of men and women's intuition. Calling upon the knowledge she had purchased from the priest for twenty pesos, she wrote the speech on a sheet of paper and then signaled El Mulato to untie the rope that bound her ankles to a tree. He led her once more to the Colonel, and again she felt the throbbing anxiety that had seized her when she first saw him. She handed him the paper and waited while he looked at it, holding it gingerly between thumbs and fingertips.

"What the shit does this say?" he asked finally.

"Don't you know how to read?"

"War's what I know," he replied.

She read the speech aloud. She read it three times, so her client could engrave it on his memory. When she finished, she saw the emotion in the faces of the soldiers who had gathered round to listen, and saw that the Colonel's eyes glittered with enthusiasm, convinced that with those words the presidential chair would be his.

"If after they've heard it three times, the boys are still standing there with their mouths hanging open, it must mean the thing's damn good, Colonel" was El Mulato's approval.

"All right, woman. How much do I owe you?" the leader asked.

"One peso, Colonel."

"That's not much," he said, opening the pouch he wore at his belt, heavy with proceeds from the last foray.

"The peso entitles you to a bonus. I'm going to give you two secret words," said Belisa Crepusculario.

"What for?"

She explained that for every fifty centavos a client paid, she gave him the gift of a word for his exclusive use. The Colonel shrugged. He had no interest at all in her offer, but he did not want to be impolite to someone who had served him so well. She walked slowly to the leather stool where he was sitting, and bent down to give him her gift. The man smelled the scent of a mountain cat issuing from the woman, a fiery heat radiating from her hips, he heard the terrible whisper of her hair, and a breath of sweetmint murmured into his ear the two secret words that were his alone.

"They are yours, Colonel," she said as she stepped back. "You may use them as much as you please."

El Mulato accompanied Belisa to the roadside, his eyes as entreating as a stray dog's, but when he reached out to touch her, he was stopped by an avalanche of words he had never heard before; believing them to be an irrevocable curse, the flame of his desire was extinguished.

During the months of September, October, and November the Colonel delivered his speech so many times that had it not been crafted from glowing and durable words it would have turned to ash as he spoke. He traveled up and down and across the country, riding into cities with a triumphal air, stopping in even the most forgotten villages where only the dump heap betrayed a human presence, to convince his fellow citizens to vote for him. While he spoke from a platform erected in the middle of the plaza, El Mulato and his men handed out sweets and painted his name on all the walls in gold frost. No one paid the least attention to those advertising ploys; they were dazzled by the clarity of the Colonel's proposals and the poetic lucidity of his arguments, infected by his powerful wish to right the wrongs of history, happy for the first time in their lives. When the Candidate had finished his speech, his soldiers would fire their pistols into the air and set off firecrackers, and when finally they rode off, they left behind a wake of hope that lingered for days on the air, like the splendid memory of a comet's tail. Soon the Colonel was the favorite. No one had ever witnessed such a phenomenon: a man who surfaced from the civil war, covered with scars and speaking like a professor, a man whose fame spread to every corner of the land and captured the nation's heart. The press focused their attention on him. Newspapermen came from far away to interview him and repeat his phrases, and the number of his followers and enemies continued to grow.

"We're doing great, Colonel," said El Mulato, after twelve successful weeks of campaigning.

But the Candidate did not hear. He was repeating his secret words, as he did more and more obsessively. He said them when he was mellow with nostalgia; he murmured them in his sleep; he carried them with him on horseback; he thought them before delivering his famous speech; and he caught himself savoring them in his leisure time. And every time he thought of those two words, he thought of Belisa Crepusculario, and his senses were inflamed with the memory of her feral scent, her fiery heat, the whisper of her hair, and her sweetmint breath in his ear, until he began to go around like a sleepwalker, and his men realized that he might die before he ever sat in the presidential chair.

"What's got hold of you, Colonel," El Mulato asked so often that finally one day his chief broke down and told him the source of his befuddlement: those two words that were buried like two daggers in his gut.

"Tell me what they are and maybe they'll lose their magic," his faithful aide suggested.

"I can't tell them, they're for me alone," the Colonel replied.

Saddened by watching his chief decline like a man with a death sentence on his head, El Mulato slung his rifle over his shoulder and set out to find Belisa Crepusculario. He followed her trail through all that vast country, until he found her in a village in the far south, sitting under her tent reciting her rosary of news. He planted himself, spread-legged, before her, weapon in hand.

"You! You're coming with me," he ordered.

She had been waiting. She picked up her inkwell, folded the canvas of her small stall, arranged her shawl around her shoulders, and without a word took her place behind El Mulato's saddle. They did not exchange so much as a word in all the trip; El Mulato's desire for her had turned into rage, and only his fear of her tongue prevented his cutting her to shreds with his whip. Nor was he inclined to tell her that the Colonel was in a fog, and that a spell whispered into his ear had done what years of battle had not been able to do. Three days later they arrived at the encampment, and immediately, in view of all the troops, El Mulato led his prisoner before the Candidate.

"I brought this witch here so you can give her back her words, Colonel," El Mulato said, pointing the barrel of his rifle at the woman's head. "And then she can give you back your manhood."

The Colonel and Belisa Crepusculario stared at each other, measuring one another from a distance. The men knew then that their leader would never undo the witchcraft of those accursed words, because the whole world could see the voracious-puma eyes soften as the woman walked to him and took his hand in hers.

MARGARET ATWOOD

THE PAGE

Margaret Atwood (b. 1939), born in Ottawa, Ontario, is among the best-known contemporary writers. She is intellectual, blatantly and unapologetically political, often experimental, and impressively varied in her writing. Atwood moves effortlessly across genres, being equally gifted at fiction and poetry; she is also an influential literary critic. Her voice is direct and intimate, drawing the reader and subject matter together in a conversation she frequently interrupts to underline a point. Atwood believes that fiction is "the guardian of the moral and ethical sense of [a] community," for "fiction is one of the few forms left through which we may examine our society not in its particular but in its typical aspects; through which we can see ourselves and the ways in which we behave towards each other, through which we can see others and judge them and ourselves." Margaret Atwood tirelessly supports PEN, an international organization of writers concerned with the plight of writers in prison, and is a staunch supporter of human rights and freedom of speech.

At the age of five, Atwood began writing "poems, 'novels,' comic books, and plays," though she did not decide to become a professional writer until she was in her mid teens. She attended the University of Toronto, where she studied under Northrop Frye, and graduated in 1961. Having won a Woodrow Wilson Fellowship, she then studied Victorian literature at Harvard. In 1966 she published The Circle Game *and was awarded the Governor General's Award for Poetry. She published her first novel,* The Edible Woman, *in 1969, her first collection of short stories,* Dancing Girls, *in 1977, and her first book of nonfiction,* Survival, *in 1972. Each work is a landmark in the development of a distinctive Canadian literature. For her contributions to Canadian writing, Atwood has earned many awards and literary honours.*

As a vocal feminist and critic of imperial power and the "colonial mentality" of colonized people, Atwood has often been controversial, yet she remains hugely popular. The three short prose pieces included here are selections from Murder in the Dark *(1983). In this collection of short fiction and prose, Atwood experiments with her craft and ponders the art of writing. Margaret Atwood lives in Toronto with novelist Graeme Gibson and their daughter. Her most recent novel is* Alias Grace *(1996), which won the Giller Prize and was shortlisted for the Booker Prize.*

---

1. The page waits, pretending to be blank. Is that its appeal, its blankness? What else is this smooth and white, this terrifyingly innocent? A snowfall, a glacier? It's a desert, totally arid, without life. But people venture into such places. Why? To see how much they can endure, how much dry light?

2. I've said the page is white, and it is: white as wedding dresses, rare whales, seagulls, angels, ice and death. Some say that like sunlight it contains all colours; others, that it's white because it's hot, it will burn out your optic nerves; that those who stare at the page too long go blind.

3. The page itself has no dimensions and no directions. There's no up or down except what you yourself mark, there's no thickness and weight but those you put there, north and south do not exist unless you're certain of them. The page is without vistas and without sounds, without centres or edges. Because of this you can become lost in it forever. Have you never seen the look of gratitude, the look of joy, on the faces of those who have managed to return from the page? Despite their faintness, their loss of blood, they fall on their knees, they push their hands into the earth, they clasp the bodies of those they love, or, in a pinch, any bodies they can get, with an urgency unknown to those who have never experienced the full horror of a journey into the page.

4. If you decide to enter the page, take a knife and some matches, and something that will float. Take something you can hold onto, and a prism to split the light and a talisman that works, which should be hung on a chain around your neck: that's for getting back. It doesn't matter what kind of shoes, but your hands should be bare. You should never go into the page with gloves on. Such decisions, needless to say, should not be made lightly.

   There are those, of course, who enter the page without deciding, without meaning to. Some of these have charmed lives and no difficulty, but most never make it out at all. For them the page appears as a well, a lovely pool in which they catch sight of a face, their own but better. These unfortunates do not jump: rather they fall, and the page closes over their heads without a sound, without a seam, and is immediately as whole and empty, as glassy, as enticing as before.

5. The question about the page is: what is beneath it? It seems to have only
two dimensions, you can pick it up and turn it over and the back is the
same as the front. Nothing, you say, disappointed.

But you were looking in the wrong place, you were looking *on the
back* instead of *beneath*. *Beneath the page* is another story. Beneath the
page is a story. Beneath the page is everything that has ever happened,
most of which you would rather not hear about.

The page is not a pool but a skin, a skin is there to hold in and it can
feel you touching it. Did you really think it would just lie there and do
nothing?

Touch the page at your peril: it is you who are blank and innocent,
not the page. Nevertheless you want to know, nothing will stop you. You
touch the page, it's as if you've drawn a knife across it, the page has been
hurt now, a sinuous wound opens, a thin incision. Darkness wells
through.

MARGARET ATWOOD

Hand

Your body lies on the floor, with or without you. Your eyes are closed. No good to say you are your body, though this also is true, because at the moment you are not; you are only a fist tightening somewhere at the back of the neck. It's this fist that holds you clenched and pushes you forward with short jabs of pain, it's this fist that drives you through time, along those windowless corridors we know so well, where the yellowish-white light sucks the blood from the surface of your face and your feet in their narrowing shoes hit cement, a thud and then another, clockwork. This fist is what I must open: to let you in.

I begin with the back of the neck, lightly, feeling the involved knot of muscle, in its own grip, a puzzle. A false start, to press too hard here would bruise you. I move to the feet and begin again.

The feet must be taught to see in the dark, because the dark is where they walk. The feet learn quietly; they are wiser than the eyes, they are hard to fool, like stones they are heavy and grave, they desire nothing for themselves, once they have seen they remember. I move my thumbs down between the tendons, push on the deaf white soles of the imprisoned feet.

This is your body I hold between both of my hands, its eyes closed. Now your body has become a hand that is opening, your body is the hand of a blind man, reaching out into a darkness which may in fact be light; for all you know. Behind your closed eyes the filaments of a tree unwind, take shape, red and purple, blue, a slow glow. This is not a lovers' scenario. This is the journey of the body, its hesitant footsteps as it walks back into its own flesh. I close my own eyes so I can see better where we are going. My hands move forward by knowledge and guess; my hands move you forward. Your eyes are closed but the third eye, the eye of the body, is opening. It floats before you like a ring of blue fire. Now you see into it and through it.

37

MARGARET ATWOOD

INSTRUCTIONS FOR THE THIRD EYE

The eye is the organ of vision, and the third eye is no exception to that. Open it and it sees, close it and it doesn't.

Most people have a third eye but they don't trust it. That wasn't really F., standing on the corner, hands in his overcoat pockets, waiting for the light to change: F. died two months ago. It's a trick my eyes played on me, they say. A trick of the light.

I've got nothing against telepathy, said Jane; but the telephone is so much more dependable.

What's the difference between vision and a vision? The former relates to something it's assumed you've seen, the latter to something it's assumed you haven't. Language is not always dependable either.

If you want to use the third eye you must close the other two. Then breathe evenly; then wait. This sometimes works; on the other hand, sometimes you merely go to sleep. That sometimes works also.

When you've had enough practice you don't have to bother with these preliminary steps. You find too that what you see depends partly on what you want to look at and partly on how. As I said, the third eye is only an eye.

There are some who resent the third eye. They would have it removed, if they could. They feel it as a parasite, squatting in the centre of the forehead, feeding on the brain.

To them the third eye shows only the worst scenery: the gassed and scorched corpses at the cave-mouth, the gutted babies, the spoor left by generals, and, closer to home, the hearts gone bubonic with jealousy and greed, glinting through the vests and sweaters of anyone at all. Torment, they say and see. The third eye can be merciless, especially when wounded.

38

But someone has to see these things. They exist. Try not to resist the third eye: it knows what it's doing. Leave it alone and it will show you that this truth is not the only truth. One day you will wake up and everything, the stones by the driveway, the brick houses, each brick, each leaf of each tree, your own body, will be glowing from within, lit up, so bright you can hardly look. You will reach out in any direction and you will touch the light itself.

After that there are no more instructions because there is no more choice. You see. You see.

RUSSELL BANKS

SARAH COLE:
A TYPE OF LOVE STORY

Russell Banks (b. 1940) was born in Newton, Massachusetts, the child of working-class parents. His father was an abusive alcoholic who left his wife and four children when Banks was twelve years old. Banks' working-class background and his perception of male violence as endemic in our society have both greatly influenced his fiction. After abandoning a full scholarship to Colgate University in 1958 and failing in his attempt to join Fidel Castro's army in Cuba, Russell Banks married and became the father of four daughters. He studied literature at the University of North Carolina at Chapel Hill and, with poet William Matthews, ran a small press and a literary magazine called Lillibullero. *Banks has been married four times; he presently teaches at Princeton University and is married to poet Chase Twichell.*

Russell Banks writes about American working-class people who live their lives "one step up from the lowest rung on the socioeconomic ladder ... doing battle every day with the despair that comes from violence, alcohol, and self-destructive relationships." He is a prolific writer, whose best-known novels include Continental Drift *(1985),* Affliction *(1989),* The Sweet Hereafter *(1991), now a prize-winning Atom Egoyan film, and* Rule of the Bone *(1995). His story collections include* Trailer Park *(1982) and* Success Stories *(1986), from which "Sarah Cole: A Type of Love Story" is taken. This story, told by a first-person narrator, will be an uncomfortable one for many readers. What are we to make of this good-looking man who sets out to have an affair with an ugly woman, precisely because of her looks? And where does the writer stand?*

I

To begin, then, here is a scene in which I am the man and my friend Sarah Cole is the woman. I don't mind describing it now, because I'm a decade older and don't look the same now as I did then, and Sarah Cole is dead. That is to say, on hearing this story you might think me vain if I looked the same now as I did then, because I must tell you that I was extremely handsome then. And if Sarah were not dead, you'd think I was cruel, for I must tell you that Sarah was very homely. In fact, she was the homeliest woman I have ever known. Personally, I mean. I've *seen* a few women who were more unattractive than Sarah, but they were clearly freaks of nature or had been badly injured or had been victimized by some grotesque, disfiguring disease. Sarah, however, was quite normal, and I knew her well, because for three and a half months we were lovers.

Here is the scene. You can put it in the present, even though it took place ten years ago, because nothing that matters to the story depends on when it took place, and you can put it in Concord, New Hampshire, even though that is indeed where it took place, because it doesn't matter where it took place, so it might as well be Concord, New Hampshire, a place I happen to know well and can therefore describe with sufficient detail to make the story believable. Around six o'clock on a Wednesday evening in late May, a man enters a bar. The bar, a cocktail lounge at street level, with a restaurant upstairs, is decorated with hanging plants and unfinished wood paneling, butcher-block tables and captain's chairs, with a half-dozen darkened, thickly upholstered booths along one wall. Three or four men between the ages of twenty-five and thirty-five are drinking at the bar and, like the man who has just entered, wear three-piece suits and loosened neckties. They are probably lawyers, young, unmarried lawyers gossiping with their brethren over martinis so as to postpone arriving home alone at their whitewashed town-house apartments, where they will fix their evening meals in radar ranges and afterwards, while their TVs chuckle quietly in front of them, sit on their couches and do a little extra work for tomorrow. They are, for the most part, honorable, educated, hard-working, shallow and moderately unhappy young men.

Our man, call him Ronald, Ron, in most ways is like these men, except that he is unusually good-looking, and that makes him a little less unhappy than they. Ron is effortlessly attractive, a genetic wonder, tall, slender, symmetrical and clean. His flaws—a small mole on the left corner of his square, not-too-prominent chin, a slight excess of blond hair on the tops of his tanned hands, and somewhat underdeveloped buttocks—insofar as they keep him from resembling too closely a men's store mannequin, only contribute to his beauty, for he is beautiful, the way we usually think of a woman as being beautiful. And he is nice too, the consequence, perhaps, of his seeming not to know how beautiful he is, to men as well as women, to young people (even children) as well as old, to attractive people (who realize immediately that he is so much more attractive than they as not to be competitive with them) as well as unattractive people.

Ron takes a seat at the bar, unfolds the evening paper in front of him, and before he can start reading, the bartender asks to help him, calling him "Sir," even though Ron has come into this bar numerous times at this time of day, especially since his divorce last fall. Ron got divorced because, after three years of marriage, his wife chose to pursue the career that his had interrupted, that of a fashion designer, which meant that she had to live in New York City while he had to continue to live in New Hampshire, where his career got its start. They agreed to live apart until he could continue his career near New York City, but after a few months, between conjugal visits, he started sleeping with other women and she started sleeping with other men, and that was that. "No big deal," he explained to friends, who liked both Ron and his wife, even though he was slightly more beautiful than she. "We really were too young when we got married, college sweethearts. But we're still best friends," he assured them. They understood. Most of Ron's friends were divorced by then too.

Ron orders a Scotch and soda with a twist and goes back to reading his paper. When his drink comes, before he takes a sip of it, he first carefully finishes reading an article about the recent reappearance of coyotes in northern New Hampshire and Vermont. He lights a cigarette. He goes on reading. He takes a second sip of his drink. Everyone in the room—the three or four men scattered along the bar, the tall, thin bartender and several people in the booths at the back—watches him do these ordinary things.

He has got to the classified section, is perhaps searching for someone willing to come in once a week and clean his apartment, when the woman who will turn out to be Sarah Cole leaves a booth in the back and approaches him. She comes up from the side and sits next to him. She's wearing heavy tan cowboy boots and a dark brown suede cowboy hat, lumpy jeans and a yellow T-shirt that clings to her arms, breasts and round belly like the skin of a sausage. Though he will later learn that she is thirty-eight years old, she looks older by about ten years, which makes her look about twenty years older than he actually is. (It's difficult to guess accurately how old Ron is; he looks anywhere from a mature twenty-five to a youthful forty, so his actual age doesn't seem to matter.)

"It's not bad here at the bar," she says, looking around. "More light, anyhow. Whatcha readin'?" she asks brightly, planting both elbows on the bar.

Ron looks up from his paper with a slight smile on his lips, sees the face of a woman homelier than any he has ever seen or imagined before, and goes on smiling lightly. He feels himself falling into her tiny, slightly crossed, dark brown eyes, pulls himself back, and studies for a few seconds her mottled, pocked complexion, bulbous nose, loose mouth, twisted and gapped teeth and heavy but receding chin. He casts a glance over her thatch of dun-colored hair and along her neck and throat, where acne burns against gray skin, and returns to her eyes and again feels himself falling into her.

"What did you say?" he asks.

She knocks a mentholated cigarette from her pack, and Ron swiftly lights it. Blowing smoke from her large, wing-shaped nostrils, she speaks again. Her voice is thick and nasal, a chocolate-colored voice. "I asked you whatcha readin', but I can see now." She belts out a single, loud laugh. "The paper!"

Ron laughs too. "The paper! The *Concord Monitor!*" He is not hallucinating, he clearly sees what is before him and admits—no, he asserts—to himself that he is speaking to the most unattractive woman he has ever seen, a fact that fascinates him, as if instead he were speaking to the most beautiful woman he has ever seen or perhaps ever will see, so he treasures the moment, attempts to hold it as if it were a golden ball, a disproportionately heavy object which— if he does not hold it lightly, with precision and firmness—will slip from his hand and roll across the lawn to the lip of the well and down, down to the bottom of the well, lost to him forever. It will be a memory, that's all, something to speak of wistfully and with wonder as over the years the image fades and comes in the end to exist only in the telling. His mind and body waken from their sleepy self-absorption, and all his attention focuses on the woman, Sarah Cole, her ugly face, like a warthog's, her thick, rapid speech, her dumpy, off-center wreck of a body. To keep this moment here before him, he begins to ask questions of her, he buys her a drink, he smiles, until soon it seems, even to him, that he is taking her and her life, its vicissitudes and woe, quite seriously.

He learns her name, of course, and she volunteers the information that she spoke to him on a dare from one of the two women still sitting in the booth behind her. She turns on her stool and smiles brazenly, triumphantly, at her friends, two women, also homely (though nowhere as homely as she), and dressed, like her, in cowboy boots, hats and jeans. One of the women, a blond with an underslung jaw and wearing heavy eye makeup, flips a little wave at her, and as if embarrassed, she and the other woman at the booth turn back to their drinks and sip fiercely at straws.

Sarah returns to Ron and goes on telling him what he wants to know, about her job at Rumford Press, about her divorced husband, who was a bastard and stupid and "sick," she says, as if filling suddenly with sympathy for the man. She tells Ron about her three children, the youngest, a girl, in junior high school and boy-crazy, the other two, boys, in high school and almost never at home anymore. She speaks of her children with genuine tenderness and concern and Ron is touched. He can see with what pleasure and pain she speaks of her children; he watches her tiny eyes light up and water over when he asks their names.

"You're a nice woman," he informs her.

She smiles, looks at her empty glass. "No. No, I'm not. But you're a nice man, to tell me that."

Ron, with a gesture, asks the bartender to refill Sarah's glass. She is drinking white Russians. Perhaps she has been drinking them for an hour or two, for she seems very relaxed, more relaxed than women usually do when they come up and without introduction or invitation speak to Ron.

She asks him about himself, his job, his divorce, how long he has lived in Concord, but he finds that he is not at all interested in telling her about himself. He wants to know about her, even though what she has to tell him about herself is predictable and ordinary and the way she tells it unadorned and clichéd. He wonders about her husband. What kind of man would fall in love with Sarah Cole?

II

That scene, at Osgood's Lounge in Concord, ended with Ron's departure, alone, after having bought Sarah a second drink, and Sarah's return to her friends in the booth. I don't know what she told them, but it's not hard to imagine. The three women were not close friends, merely fellow workers at Rumford Press, where they stood at the end of a long conveyor belt day after day packing *TV Guides* into cartons. They all hated their jobs, and frequently after work, when they worked the day shift, they would put on their cowboy hats and boots, which they kept all day in their lockers, and stop for a drink or two on their way home. This had been their first visit to Osgood's, however, a place that, prior to this, they had avoided out of a sneering belief that no one went there but lawyers and insurance men. It had been Sarah who had asked the others why that should keep them away, and when they had no answer for her, the three had decided to stop at Osgood's. Ron was right, they had been there over an hour when he came in, and Sarah was a little drunk. "We'll hafta come in here again," she said to her friends, her voice rising slightly.

Which they did, that Friday, and once again Ron appeared with his evening newspaper. He put his briefcase down next to his stool and ordered a drink and proceeded to read the front page, slowly, deliberately, clearly a weary, unhurried, solitary man. He did not notice the three women in cowboy hats and boots in the booth in back, but they saw him, and after a few minutes Sarah was once again at his side.

"Hi."

He turned, saw her, and instantly regained the moment he had lost when, two nights ago, once outside the bar and on his way home, he had forgotten about the ugliest woman he had ever seen. She seemed even more grotesque to him now than before, which made the moment all the more precious to him, and so once again he held the moment as if in his hands and began to speak with her, to ask questions, to offer his opinions and solicit hers.

I said earlier that I am the man in this story and my friend Sarah Cole, now dead, is the woman. I think back to that night, the second time I had seen Sarah, and I tremble, not with fear but in shame. My concern then, when I was first becoming involved with Sarah, was merely with the moment, holding on to it, grasping it wholly, as if its beginning did not grow out of some other prior moment in her life and my life separately and at the same time did not lead into future moments in our separate lives. She talked more easily than she had the night before, and I listened as eagerly and carefully as I had before, again with the same motives, to keep her in front of me, to draw her forward from the context of her life and place her, as if she were an object, into the context of mine. I did not know how cruel this was. When you have never done a thing before and that thing is not simply and clearly right or wrong, you frequently do not know if it is a cruel thing, you just go ahead and do it and maybe later you'll be able to determine whether you acted cruelly. That way you'll know if it was right or wrong of you to have done it in the first place; too late, of course, but at least you'll know.

While we drank, Sarah told me that she hated her ex-husband because of the way he treated the children. "It's not so much the money," she said, nervously wagging her booted feet from her perch on the high barstool. "I mean, I get by, barely, but I get them fed and clothed on my own okay. It's because he won't even write them a letter or anything. He won't call them on the phone, all he calls for is to bitch at me because I'm trying to get the state to take him to court so I can get some of the money he's s'posed to be paying for child support. And he won't even think to talk to the kids when he calls. Won't even ask about them."

"He sounds like a sonofabitch."

"He is, he is!" she said. "I don't know why I married him. Or stayed married. Fourteen years, for Christ's sake. He put a spell over me or something. I don't know," she said, with a note of wistfulness in her voice. "He wasn't what you'd call good-looking."

After her second drink, she decided she had to leave. Her children were at home, it was Friday night and she liked to make sure she ate supper with them and knew where they were going and who they were with when they went out on their dates. "No dates on school nights," she said to me. "I mean, you gotta have rules, you know."

I agreed, and we left together, everyone in the place following us with his or her gaze. I was aware of that, I knew what they were thinking, and I didn't care, because I was simply walking her to her car.

It was a cool evening, dusk settling onto the lot like a gray blanket. Her car, a huge, dark green Buick sedan at least ten years old, was battered almost beyond use. She reached for the door handle on the driver's side and yanked. Nothing. The door wouldn't open. She tried again. Then I tried. Still nothing.

Then I saw it, a V-shaped dent in the left front fender, binding the metal of the door against the metal of the fender in a large crimp that held the door fast. "Someone must've backed into you while you were inside," I said to her.

She came forward and studied the crimp for a few seconds, and when she looked back at me, she was weeping. "Jesus, Jesus, Jesus!" she wailed, her large, froglike mouth wide open and wet with spit, her red tongue flopping loosely over gapped teeth. "I can't pay for this! I *can't!*" Her face was red, and even in the dusky light I could see it puff out with weeping, her tiny eyes seeming almost to disappear behind wet cheeks. Her shoulders slumped, and her hands fell limply to her sides.

Placing my briefcase on the ground, I reached out to her and put my arms around her body and held her close to me, while she cried wetly into my shoulder. After a few seconds, she started pulling herself back together and her weeping got reduced to snuffling. Her cowboy hat had been pushed back and now clung to her head at a precarious, absurdly jaunty angle. She took a step away from me and said, "I'll get in the other side."

"Okay," I said, almost in a whisper. "That's fine."

Slowly, she walked around the front of the huge, ugly vehicle and opened the door on the passenger's side and slid awkwardly across the seat until she had positioned herself behind the steering wheel. Then she started the motor, which came to life with a roar. The muffler was shot. Without saying another word to me or even waving, she dropped the car into reverse gear and backed it loudly out of the parking space and headed out of the lot to the street.

I turned and started for my car, when I happened to glance toward the door of the bar, and there, staring after me, were the bartender, the two women who had come in with Sarah, and two of the men who had been sitting at the bar. They were lawyers, and I knew them slightly. They were grinning at me. I grinned back and got into my car, and then, without looking at them again, I left the place and drove straight to my apartment.

III

One night several weeks later, Ron meets Sarah at Osgood's, and after buying her three white Russians and drinking three Scotches himself, he takes her back to his apartment in his car—a Datsun fastback coupe that she says she admires—for the sole purpose of making love to her.

I'm still the man in this story, and Sarah is still the woman, but I'm telling it this way because what I have to tell you now confuses me, embarrasses me and makes me sad, and consequently I'm likely to tell it falsely. I'm likely to cover the truth by making Sarah a better woman than she actually was, while making me appear worse than I actually was or am; or else I'll do the opposite, make Sarah worse than she was and me better. The truth is, I was pretty, extremely so, and she was not, extremely so, and I knew it and she knew it. She walked out the door of Osgood's determined to make love to a man much prettier than any she had seen up close before, and I walked out determined to make love to a woman much homelier than any I had made love to before. We were, in a sense, equals.

No, that's not exactly true. (You see? This is why I have to tell the story the way I'm telling it.) I'm not at all sure she feels as Ron does. That is to say, perhaps she genuinely likes the man, in spite of his being the most physically attractive man she has ever known. Perhaps she is more aware of her homeliness than of his beauty, for Ron, despite what I may have implied, does not think of himself as especially beautiful. He merely knows that other people think of him that way. As I said before, he is a nice man.

Ron unlocks the door to his apartment, walks in ahead of her and flicks on the lamp beside the couch. It's a small, single-bedroom, modern apartment, one of thirty identical apartments in a large brick building on the Heights just east of downtown Concord. Sarah stands nervously at the door, peering in.

"Come in, come in," Ron says.

She steps timidly in and closes the door behind her. She removes her cowboy hat, then quickly puts it back on, crosses the living room and plops down in a blond easy chair, seeming to shrink in its hug out of sight to safety. Behind her, Ron, at the entry to the kitchen, places one hand on her shoulder, and she stiffens. He removes his hand.

"Would you like a drink?"

"No ... I guess not," she says, staring straight ahead at the wall opposite, where a large framed photograph of a bicyclist advertises in French the Tour de France. Around a corner, in an alcove off the living room, a silver-gray ten-speed bicycle leans casually against the wall, glistening and poised, slender as a thoroughbred racehorse.

"I don't know," she says. Ron is in the kitchen now, making himself a drink. "I don't know ... I don't know."

"What? Change your mind? I can make a white Russian for you. Vodka, cream, Kahlua and ice, right?"

Sarah tries to cross her legs, but she is sitting too low in the chair and her legs are too thick at the thigh, so she ends, after a struggle, with one leg in the air and the other twisted on its side. She looks as if she has fallen from a great height.

Ron steps out from the kitchen, peers over the back of the chair, and watches her untangle herself, then ducks back into the kitchen. After a few seconds, he returns. "Seriously. Want me to fix you a white Russian?"

"No."

Ron, again from behind and above her, places one hand on Sarah's shoulder, and this time she does not stiffen, though she does not exactly relax, either. She sits there, a block of wood, staring straight ahead.

"Are you scared?" he asks gently. Then he adds, "*I* am."

"Well, no. I'm not scared." She remains silent for a moment. "You're scared? Of what?" She turns to face him but avoids his blue eyes.

"Well ... I don't do this all the time, you know. Bring home a woman I ... ," he trails off.

"Picked up in a bar."

"No. I mean, I like you, Sarah. I really do. And I didn't just pick you up in a bar, you know that. We've gotten to be friends, you and me."

"You want to sleep with me?" she asks, still not meeting his steady gaze.

"Yes." He seems to mean it. He does not take a gulp or even a sip from his drink. He just says, "Yes," straight out, and cleanly, not too quickly, either, and not after a hesitant delay. A simple statement of a simple fact. The man wants to make love to the woman. She asked him, and he told her. What could be simpler?

"Do you want to sleep with *me*?" he asks.

She turns around in the chair, faces the wall again, and says in a low voice, "Sure I do, but ... it's hard to explain."

"What? But what?" Placing his glass down on the table between the chair and the sofa, he puts both hands on her shoulders and lightly kneads them. He knows he can be discouraged from pursuing this, but he is not sure how easily. Having got this far without bumping against obstacles (except the ones he has placed in his way himself), he is not sure what it will take to turn him back. He does not know, therefore, how assertive or how seductive he should be with her. He suspects that he can be stopped very easily, so he is reluctant to give her a chance to try. He goes on kneading her doughy shoulders.

"You and me ... we're real different." She glances at the bicycle in the corner.

"A man ... and a woman," he says.

"No, not that. I mean, different. That's all. Real different. More than you ... You're nice, but you don't know what I mean, and that's one of the things that makes you so nice. But we're different. Listen," she says, "I gotta go. I gotta leave now."

The man removes his hands and retrieves his glass, takes a sip and watches her over the rim of the glass, as, not without difficulty, the woman rises from the chair and moves swiftly toward the door. She stops at the door, squares her hat on her head, and glances back at him.

"We can be friends, okay?"

"Okay. Friends."

"I'll see you again down at Osgood's, right?"

"Oh, yeah, sure."

"Good. See you," she says, opening the door.

The door closes. The man walks around the sofa, snaps on the television set, and sits down in front of it. He picks up a *TV Guide* from the coffee table and flips through it, stops, runs a finger down the listings, stops, puts down the magazine and changes the channel. He does not once connect the magazine in his hand to the woman who has just left his apartment, even though he knows she spends her days packing *TV Guide*s into cartons that get shipped to warehouses in distant parts of New England. He'll think of the connection some other night, but by then the connection will be merely sentimental. It'll be too late for him to understand what she meant by "different."

IV

But that's not the point of my story. Certainly, it's an aspect of the story, the political aspect, if you want, but it's not the reason I'm trying to tell the story in the first place. I'm trying to tell the story so that I can understand what happened between me and Sarah Cole that summer and early autumn ten years ago. To say we were lovers says very little about what happened; to say we were friends says even less. No, if I'm to understand the whole thing, I'll have to say the whole thing, for, in the end, what I need to know is whether what happened between me and Sarah Cole was right or wrong. Character is fate, which suggests that if a man can know and then to some degree control his character, he can know and to that same degree control his fate.

But let me go on with my story. The next time Sarah and I were together we were at her apartment in the south end of Concord, a second-floor flat in a tenement building on Perley Street. I had stayed away from Osgood's for several weeks, deliberately trying to avoid running into Sarah there, though I never quite put it that way to myself. I found excuses and generated interest in and reasons for going elsewhere after work. Yet I was obsessed with Sarah by then, obsessed with the idea of making love to her, which, because it was not an actual *desire* to make love to her, was an unusually complex obsession. Passion without desire, if it gets expressed, may in fact be a kind of rape, and perhaps I sensed the danger that lay behind my obsession and for that reason went out of my way to avoid meeting Sarah again.

Yet I did meet her, inadvertently, of course. After picking up shirts at the cleaner's on South Main and Perley streets, I'd gone down Perley on my way to South State and the post office. It was a Saturday morning, and this trip on my bicycle was part of my regular Saturday routine. I did not remember that Sarah lived on Perley Street, although she had told me several times in a complaining

way—it's a rough neighborhood, packed-dirt yards, shabby apartment buildings, the carcasses of old, half-stripped cars on cinder blocks in the driveways,
broken red and yellow plastic tricycles on the cracked sidewalks—but as soon
as I saw her, I remembered. It was too late to avoid meeting her. I was riding
my bike, wearing shorts and T-shirt, the package containing my folded and
starched shirts hooked to the carrier behind me, and she was walking toward
me along the sidewalk, lugging two large bags of groceries. She saw me, and I
stopped. We talked, and I offered to carry her groceries for her. I took the bags
while she led the bike, handling it carefully, as if she were afraid she might
break it.

At the stoop we came to a halt. The wooden steps were cluttered with
half-opened garbage bags spilling eggshells, coffee grounds and old food wrap-
pers to the walkway. "I can't get the people downstairs to take care of their
garbage," she explained. She leaned the bike against the banister and reached
for her groceries.

"I'll carry them up for you," I said. I directed her to loop the chain lock
from the bike to the banister rail and snap it shut and told her to bring my
shirts up with her.

"Maybe you'd like a beer?" she said as she opened the door to the darkened hallway. Narrow stairs disappeared in front of me into heavy, damp darkness, and the air smelled like old newspapers.

"Sure," I said, and followed her up.

"Sorry there's no light. I can't get them to fix it."

"No matter. I can see you and follow along," I said, and even in the dim
light of the hall I could see the large, dark blue veins that cascaded thickly
down the backs of her legs. She wore tight, white-duck Bermuda shorts, rubber
shower sandals and a pink sleeveless sweater. I pictured her in the cashier's line
at the supermarket. I would have been behind her, a stranger, and on seeing
her, I would have turned away and studied the covers of the magazines, *TV
Guide, People,* the *National Enquirer,* for there was nothing of interest in her
appearance that in the hard light of day would not have slightly embarrassed
me. Yet here I was inviting myself into her home, eagerly staring at the backs
of her ravaged legs, her sad, tasteless clothing, her poverty. I was not detached,
however, was not staring at her with scientific curiosity, and because of my
passion, did not feel or believe that what I was doing was perverse. I felt
warmed by her presence and was flirtatious and bold, a little pushy, even.

Picture this. The man, tanned, limber, wearing red jogging shorts, Italian
leather sandals, a clinging net T-shirt of Scandinavian design and manufacture,
enters the apartment behind the woman, whose dough-colored skin, thick,
short body and homely, uncomfortable face all try, but fail, to hide themselves.

She waves him toward the table in the kitchen, where he sets down the bags and looks good-naturedly around the room. "What about the beer you bribed me with?" he asks.

The apartment is dark and cluttered with old, oversized furniture, yard sale and secondhand stuff bought originally for a large house in the country or a spacious apartment on a boulevard forty or fifty years ago, passed down from antique dealer to used-furniture store to yard sale to thrift shop, where it finally gets purchased by Sarah Cole and gets hauled over to Perley Street and shoved up the narrow stairs, she and her children grunting and sweating in the darkness of the hallway—overstuffed armchairs and couch, huge, ungainly dressers, upholstered rocking chairs, and in the kitchen, an old flat-topped maple desk for a table, a half-dozen heavy oak dining room chairs, a high, glass-fronted cabinet, all peeling, stained, chipped and squatting heavily on a dark green linoleum floor.

The place is neat and arranged in a more or less orderly way, however, and the man seems comfortable there. He strolls from the kitchen to the living room and peeks into the three small bedrooms that branch off a hallway behind the living room. "Nice place!" he calls to the woman. He is studying the framed pictures of her three children arranged as if on an altar atop the buffet. "Nice-looking kids!" he calls out. They are. Blond, round-faced, clean and utterly ordinary-looking, their pleasant faces glance, as instructed, slightly off camera and down to the right, as if they are trying to remember the name of the capital of Montana.

When he returns to the kitchen, the woman is putting away her groceries, her back to him. "Where's that beer you bribed me with?" he asks again. He takes a position against the doorframe, his weight on one hip, like a dancer resting. "You sure are quiet today, Sarah," he says in a low voice. "Everything okay?"

Silently, she turns away from the grocery bags, crosses the room to the man, reaches up to him, and holding him by the head, kisses his mouth, rolls her torso against his, drops her hands to his hips and yanks him tightly to her and goes on kissing him, eyes closed, working her face furiously against his. The man places his hands on her shoulders and pulls away, and they face each other, wide-eyed, as if amazed and frightened. The man drops his hands, and the woman lets go of his hips. Then, after a few seconds, the man silently turns, goes to the door, and leaves. The last thing he sees as he closes the door behind him is the woman standing in the kitchen doorframe, her face looking down and slightly to one side, wearing the same pleasant expression on her face as her children in their photographs, trying to remember the capital of Montana.

V

Sarah appeared at my apartment door the following morning, a Sunday, cool and rainy. She had brought me the package of freshly laundered shirts I'd left in her kitchen, and when I opened the door to her, she simply held the package out to me, as if it were a penitent's gift. She wore a yellow rain slicker and cap and looked more like a disconsolate schoolgirl facing an angry teacher than a grown woman dropping a package off at a friend's apartment. After all, she had nothing to be ashamed of.

I invited her inside, and she accepted my invitation. I had been reading the Sunday *New York Times* on the couch and drinking coffee, lounging through the gray morning in bathrobe and pajamas. I told her to take off her wet raincoat and hat and hang them in the closet by the door and started for the kitchen to get her a cup of coffee, when I stopped, turned and looked at her. She closed the closet door on her yellow raincoat and hat, turned around and faced me.

What else can I do? I must describe it. I remember that moment of ten years ago as if it occurred ten minutes ago, the package of shirts on the table behind her, the newspapers scattered over the couch and floor, the sound of windblown rain washing the side of the building outside and the silence of the room, as we stood across from one another and watched, while we each simultaneously removed our own clothing, my robe, her blouse and skirt, my pajama top, her slip and bra, my pajama bottom, her underpants, until we were both standing naked in the harsh gray light, two naked members of the same species, a male and a female, the male somewhat younger and less scarred than the female, the female somewhat less delicately constructed than the male, both individuals pale-skinned, with dark thatches of hair in the area of their genitals, both individuals standing slackly, as if a great, protracted tension between them had at last been released.

VI

We made love that morning in my bed for long hours that drifted easily into afternoon. And we talked, as people usually do when they spend half a day or half a night in bed together. I told her of my past, named and described the people whom I had loved and had loved me, my ex-wife in New York, my brother in the air force, my mother in San Diego, and I told her of my ambitions and dreams and even confessed some of my fears. She listened patiently and intelligently throughout and talked much less than I. She had already told me many of these things about herself, and perhaps whatever she had to say to me now lay on the next inner circle of intimacy or else could not be spoken of at all.

During the next few weeks, we met and made love often, and always at my apartment. On arriving home from work, I would phone her, or if not, she would phone me, and after a few feints and dodges, one would suggest to the other that we get together tonight, and a half hour later she'd be at my door. Our lovemaking was passionate, skillful, kindly and deeply satisfying. We didn't often speak of it to one another or brag about it, the way some couples do when they are surprised by the ease with which they have become contented lovers. We did occasionally joke and tease each other, however, playfully acknowledging that the only thing we did together was make love but that we did it so frequently there was no time for anything else.

Then one hot night, a Saturday in August, we were lying in bed atop the tangled sheets, smoking cigarettes and chatting idly, and Sarah suggested that we go out for a drink.

"Out? Now?"

"Sure. It's early. What time is it?"

I scanned the digital clock next to the bed. "Nine forty-nine."

"There. See?"

"That's not so early. You usually go home by eleven, you know. It's almost ten."

"No, it's only a little after nine. Depends on how you look at things. Besides, Ron, it's Saturday night. Don't you want to go out and dance or something? Or is this the only thing you know how to do?" she said, and poked me in the ribs. "You know how to dance? You like to dance?"

"Yeah, sure ... sure, but not tonight. It's too hot. And I'm tired."

But she persisted, happily pointing out that an air-conditioned bar would be as cool as my apartment, and we didn't have to go to a dance bar, we could go to Osgood's. "As a compromise," she said.

I suggested a place called the El Rancho, a restaurant with a large, dark cocktail lounge and dance bar located several miles from town on the old Portsmouth highway. Around nine the restaurant closed and the bar became something of a roadhouse, with a small country-and-western band and a clientele drawn from the four or five villages that adjoined Concord on the north and east. I had eaten at the restaurant once but had never gone to the bar, and I didn't know anyone who had.

Sarah was silent for a moment. Then she lighted a cigarette and drew the sheet over her naked body. "You don't want anybody to know about us, do you? Do you?"

"That's not it.... I just don't like gossip, and I work with a lot of people who show up sometimes at Osgood's. On a Saturday night especially."

"No," she said firmly. "You're ashamed of being seen with me. You'll sleep with me, all right, but you won't go out in public with me."

"That's not true, Sarah."

She was silent again. Relieved, I reached across her to the bed table and got my cigarettes and lighter.

"You owe me, Ron," she said suddenly, as I passed over her. "You owe me."

"What?" I lay back, lighted a cigarette, and covered my body with the sheet.

"I said, 'You owe me.'"

"I don't know what you're talking about, Sarah. I just don't like a lot of gossip going around, that's all. I like keeping my private life private, that's all. I don't *owe* you anything."

"Friendship you owe me. And respect. Friendship and respect. A person can't do what you've done with me without owing them friendship and respect."

"Sarah, I really don't know what you're talking about," I said. "I am your friend, you know that. And I respect you. I do."

"You really think so, don't you?"

"Yes. Of course."

She said nothing for several long moments. Then she sighed and in a low, almost inaudible voice said, "Then you'll have to go out in public with me. I don't care about Osgood's or the people you work with, we don't have to go there or see any of them," she said. "But you're gonna have to go to places like the El Rancho with me, and a few other places I know, too, where there's people *I* know, people *I* work with, and maybe we'll even go to a couple of parties, because *I* get invited to parties sometimes, you know. I have friends, and I have some family, too, and you're gonna have to meet my family. My kids think I'm just going around barhopping when I'm over here with you, and I don't like that, so you're gonna have to meet them so I can tell them where I am when I'm not at home nights. And sometimes you're gonna come over and spend the evening at my place!" Her voice had risen as she heard her demands and felt their rightness, until now she was almost shouting at me. "You *owe* that to me. Or else you're a bad man. It's that simple, Ron."

It was.

VII

The handsome man is overdressed. He is wearing a navy blue blazer, taupe shirt open at the throat, white slacks, white loafers. Everyone else, including the homely woman with the handsome man, is dressed appropriately—that is, like everyone else—jeans and cowboy boots, blouses or cowboy shirts or T-shirts with catchy sayings or the names of country-and-western singers printed across the front, and many of the women are wearing cowboy hats pushed back and tied under their chins.

The man doesn't know anyone at the bar or, if they're at a party, in the room, but the woman knows most of the people there, and she gladly introduces him. The men grin and shake his hand, slap him on his jacketed shoulder, ask him where he works, what's his line, after which they lapse into silence. The women flirt briefly with their faces, but they lapse into silence even before the men do. The woman with the man in the blazer does most of the talking for everyone. She talks for the man in the blazer, for the men standing around the refrigerator, or if they're at a bar, for the other men at the table, and for the other women too. She chats and rambles aimlessly through loud monologues, laughs uproariously at trivial jokes and drinks too much, until soon she is drunk, thick-tongued, clumsy, and the man has to say her goodbyes and ease her out the door to his car and drive her home to her apartment on Perley Street.

This happens twice in one week and then three times the next—at the El Rancho, at the Ox Bow in Northwood, at Rita and Jimmy's apartment on Thorndike Street, out in Warner at Betsy Beeler's new house and, the last time, at a cottage on Lake Sunapee rented by some kids in shipping at Rumford Press. Ron no longer calls Sarah when he gets home from work; he waits for her call, and sometimes, when he knows it's she, he doesn't answer the phone. Usually, he lets it ring five or six times, and then he reaches down and picks up the receiver. He has taken his jacket and vest off and loosened his tie and is about to put his supper, frozen manicotti, into the radar range.

"Hello?"

"Hi."

"How're you doing?"

"Okay, I guess. A little tired."

"Still hung over?"

"Naw. Not really. Just tired. I hate Mondays."

"You have fun last night?"

"Well, yeah, sorta. It's nice out there, at the lake. Listen," she says, brightening. "Whyn't you come over here tonight? The kids're all going out later, but if you come over before eight, you can meet them. They really want to meet you."

"You told them about me?"

"Sure. Long time ago. I'm not supposed to tell my own kids?"

Ron is silent.

She says, "You don't want to come over here tonight. You don't want to meet my kids. No, you don't want my kids to meet *you*, that's it."

"No, no, it's just ... I've got a lot of work to do...."

"We should talk," she announces in a flat voice.

"Yes," he says. "We should talk."

They agree that she will meet him at his apartment, and they'll talk, and they say goodbye and hang up.

While Ron is heating his supper and then eating it alone at his kitchen table and Sarah is feeding her children, perhaps I should admit, since we are nearing the end of my story, that I don't actually know that Sarah Cole is dead. A few years ago I happened to run into one of her friends from the press, a blond woman with an underslung jaw. Her name, she reminded me, was Glenda; she had seen me at Osgood's a couple of times and we had met at the El Rancho once when I had gone there with Sarah. I was amazed that she could remember me and a little embarrassed that I did not recognize her at all, and she laughed at that and said, "You haven't changed much, mister!" I pretended to recognize her then, but I think she knew she was a stranger to me. We were standing outside the Sears store on South Main Street, where I had gone to buy paint. I had recently remarried, and my wife and I were redecorating my apartment.

"Whatever happened to Sarah?" I asked Glenda. "Is she still down at the press?"

"Jeez, no! She left a long time ago. Way back. I heard she went back with her ex-husband. I can't remember his name, something Cole. Eddie Cole, maybe."

I asked her if she was sure of that, and she said no, she had only heard it around the bars and down at the press, but she had assumed it was true. People said Sarah had moved back with her ex-husband and was living for a while with him and the kids in a trailer in a park near Hooksett, and then when the kids, or at least the boys, got out of school, the rest of them moved down to Florida or someplace because he was out of work. He was a carpenter, she thought.

"He was mean to her," I said. "I thought he used to beat her up and everything. I thought she hated him."

"Oh, well, yeah, he was a bastard, all right. I met him a couple times, and I didn't like him. Short, ugly and mean when he got drunk. But you know what they say."

"What do they say?"

"Oh, you know, about water seeking its own level and all."

"Sarah wasn't mean when she was drunk."

The woman laughed. "Naw, but she sure was short and ugly!"

I said nothing.

"Hey, don't get me wrong," Glenda said. "I liked Sarah. But you and her ... well, you sure made a funny-looking couple. She probably didn't feel so self-conscious and all with her husband," she said somberly. "I mean, with you, all tall and blond, and poor old Sarah ... I mean, the way them kids in the press room used to kid her about her looks, it was embarrassing just to have to hear it."

"Well ... I loved her," I said.

The woman raised her plucked eyebrow in disbelief. She smiled. "Sure, you did, honey," she said, and she patted me on the arm. "Sure, you did." Then she let the smile drift off her face, turned and walked away from me.

When someone you have loved dies, you accept the fact of his or her death, but then the person goes on living in your memory, dreams and reveries. You have imaginary conversations with him or her, you see something striking and remind yourself to tell your loved one about it and then get brought up short by the knowledge of the fact of his or her death, and at night, in your sleep, the dead person visits you. With Sarah, none of that happened. When she was gone from my life, she was gone absolutely, as if she had never existed in the first place. It was only later, when I could think of her as dead and could come out and say it, my friend Sarah Cole is dead, that I was able to tell this story, for that is when she began to enter my memories, my dreams and my reveries. In that way, I learned that I truly did love her, and now I have begun to grieve over her death, to wish her alive again, so that I can say to her the things I could not know or say when she was alive, when I did not know that I loved her.

VIII

The woman arrives at Ron's apartment around eight. He hears her car, because of the broken muffler, blat and rumble into the parking lot below, and he crosses quickly from the kitchen and peers out the living room window and, as if through a telescope, watches her shove herself across the seat to the passenger's side to get out of the car, then walk slowly in the dusky light toward the apartment building. It's a warm evening, and she's wearing her white Bermuda shorts, pink sleeveless sweater and shower sandals. Ron hates those clothes. He hates the way the shorts cut into her flesh at the crotch and thigh, hates the large, dark caves below her arms that get exposed by the sweater, hates the sucking noise made by the sandals.

Shortly, there is a soft knock at his door. He opens it, turns away and crosses to the kitchen, where he turns back, lights a cigarette and watches her. She closes the door. He offers her a drink, which she declines, and somewhat formally, he invites her to sit down. She sits carefully on the sofa, in the middle, with her feet close together on the floor, as if she were being interviewed for a job. Then he comes around and sits in the easy chair, relaxed, one leg slung over the other at the knee, as if he were interviewing her for the job.

"Well," he says, "you wanted to talk."

"Yes. But now you're mad at me. I can see that. I didn't do anything, Ron."

"I'm not mad at you."

They are silent for a moment. Ron goes on smoking his cigarette.

Finally, she sighs and says, "You don't want to see me anymore, do you?"

He waits a few seconds and answers, "Yes. That's right." Getting up from the chair, he walks to the silver-gray bicycle and stands before it, running a fingertip along the slender crossbar from the saddle to the chrome-plated handlebars.

"You're a sonofabitch," she says in a low voice. "You're worse than my ex-husband." Then she smiles meanly, almost sneers, and soon he realizes that she is telling him that she won't leave. He's stuck with her, she informs him with cold precision. "You think I'm just so much meat, and all you got to do is call up the butcher shop and cancel your order. Well, now you're going to find out different. You *can't* cancel your order. I'm not meat, I'm not one of your pretty little girlfriends who come running when you want them and go away when you get tired of them. I'm *different!* I got nothing to lose, Ron. Nothing. So you're stuck with me, Ron."

He continues stroking his bicycle. "No, I'm not."

She sits back in the couch and crosses her legs at the ankles. "I think I *will* have that drink you offered."

"Look, Sarah, it would be better if you go now."

"No," she says flatly. "You offered me a drink when I came in. Nothing's changed since I've been here. Not for me and not for you. I'd like that drink you offered," she says haughtily.

Ron turns away from the bicycle and takes a step toward her. His face has stiffened into a mask. "Enough is enough," he says through clenched teeth. "I've given you enough."

"Fix me a drink, will you, honey?" she says with a phony smile.

Ron orders her to leave.

She refuses.

He grabs her by the arm and yanks her to her feet.

She starts crying lightly. She stands there and looks up into his face and weeps, but she does not move toward the door, so he pushes her. She regains her balance and goes on weeping.

He stands back and places his fists on his hips and looks at her. "Go on, go on and leave, you ugly bitch," he says to her, and as he says the words, as one by one they leave his mouth, she's transformed into the most beautiful woman he has ever seen. He says the words again, almost tenderly. "Leave, you ugly bitch." Her hair is golden, her brown eyes deep and sad, her mouth full and affectionate, her tears the tears of love and loss, and her pleading, outstretched arms, her entire body, the arms and body of a devoted woman's cruelly rejected love. A third time he says the words. "Leave me now, you disgusting, ugly bitch." She is wrapped in an envelope of golden light, a warm, dense haze that she seems to have stepped into, as into a carriage. And then she is gone, and he is alone again.

He looks around the room, as if searching for her. Sitting down in the easy chair, he places his face in his hands. It's not as if she has died; it's as if he has killed her.

DONALD BARTHELME

THE EMERALD

Donald Barthelme (1931–1989) was born in Philadelphia and raised in
Houston. His work for high-school news and literary magazines led him
from an early age into a lifelong writing career. After serving two years
with U.S. military news staff in Japan and Korea, Barthelme returned to
Houston to continue working in news and journal editing, until the publication of his story "Me and Miss Mandible" launched his career as a writer
of comedic and defiantly nonsensical short stories. In 1962 he moved to
New York to edit a short-lived art and literature review. The next year his
work was discovered by The New Yorker. For two decades the magazine
carried Barthelme's stories and commentaries, which he variously submitted signed, anonymously, or under a pen name. In 1972 he took over
John Barth's visiting professorship at the State University of New York,
and this supplementary academic career eventually landed him in Boston,
New York City, and Houston. Barthelme died of cancer in 1989.

   Sixty Stories (1981), from which "The Emerald" is taken, received
the PEN/Faulkner Award for Fiction and was nominated for the National
Book Critics Circle Award. As the theories and practices of postmodernism gained academic currency, critical interest in Barthelme resurged.
The mildness that Barthelme's characters show in navigating chaotic envi-
ronments of cultural excess and surreal worlds has provoked a confused
range of academic and popular response, but prominent among the
responses is delight.

Hey buddy what's your name?
My name is Tope. What's your name?
My name is Sallywag. You after the emerald?
Yeah I'm after the emerald you after the emerald too?
I am. What are you going to do with it if you get it?
Cut it up into little emeralds. What are you going to do with it?
I was thinking of solid emerald armchairs. For the rich.
That's an idea. What's your name, you?

Wide Boy.

You after the emerald?

Sure as shootin'.

How you going to get in?

Blast.

That's going to make a lot of noise isn't it?

You think it's a bad idea?

Well ... What's your name, you there?

Taptoe.

You after the emerald?

Right as rain. What's more, I got a plan.

Can we see it?

No it's my plan I can't be showing it to every—

Okay okay. What's that guy's name behind you?

My name is Sometimes.

You here about the emerald, Sometimes?

I surely am.

Have you got an approach?

Tunneling. I've took some test borings. Looks like a stone cinch.

If this is the right place.

You think this may not be the right place?

The last three places haven't been the right place.

You tryin' to bring me down?

Why would I want to do that? What's that guy's name, the one with the shades?

My name is Brother. Who are all these people?

Businessmen. What do you think of the general situation, Brother?

I think it's crowded. This is my pal, Wednesday.

What say, Wednesday. After the emerald, I presume?

Thought we'd have a go.

Two heads better than one, that the idea?

Yep.

What are you going to do with the emerald, if you get it?

Facet. Facet and facet and facet.

Moll talking to a member of the news media.

Tell me, as a member of the news media, what do you do?

Well we sort of figure out what the news is, then we go out and talk to people, the newsmakers, those who have made the news—

These having been identified by certain people very high up in your organization.

The editors. The editors are the ones who say this is news, this is not news, maybe this is news, damned if I know whether this is news or not—

And then you go out and talk to people and they tell you everything.

They tell you a surprising number of things, if you are a member of the news media. Even if they have something to hide, questionable behavior or one thing and another, or having killed their wife, that sort of thing, still they tell you the most amazing things. Generally.

About themselves. The newsworthy.

Yes. Then we have our experts in the various fields. They are experts in who is a smart cookie and who is a dumb cookie. They write pieces saying which kind of cookie these various cookies are, so that the reader can make informed choices. About things.

Fascinating work I should think.

Your basic glamour job.

I suppose you would have to be very well-educated to get that kind of job.

Extremely well-educated. Typing, everything.

Admirable.

Yes. Well, back to the pregnancy. You say it was a seven-year pregnancy.

Yes. When the agency was made clear to me—

The agency was, you contend, extraterrestrial.

It's a fact. Some people can't handle it.

The father was—

He sat in that chair you're sitting in. The red chair. Naked and wearing a morion.

That's all?

Yes he sat naked in the chair wearing only a morion, and engaged me in conversation.

The burden of which was—

Passion.

What was your reaction?

I was surprised. My reaction was surprise.

Did you declare your unworthiness?

Several times. He was unmoved.

Well I don't know, all this sounds a little unreal, like I mean unreal, if you know what I mean.

Oui, je sais.

What role were you playing?

Well obviously I was playing myself. Mad Moll.

What's a morion?

Steel helmet with a crest.

You considered his offer.

More in the nature of a command.

Then, the impregnation. He approached your white or pink as yet undistended belly with his hideously engorged member—

It was more fun than that.

I find it hard to believe, if you'll forgive me, that you, although quite beautiful in your own way, quite lush of figure and fair of face, still the beard on your chin and that black mark like a furry caterpillar crawling in the middle of your forehead—

It's only a small beard after all.

That's true.

And he seemed to like the black mark on my forehead. He caressed it.

So you did in fact enjoy the … event. You understand I wouldn't ask these questions, some of which I admit verge on the personal, were I not a duly credentialed member of the press. Custodian as it were of the public's right to know. Everything. Every last little slippy-dippy thing.

Well okay yes I guess that's true strictly speaking. I suppose that's true. Strictly speaking. I could I suppose tell you to buzz off but I respect the public's right to know. I think. An informed public is, I suppose, one of the basic bulwarks of—

Yes I agree but of course I would wouldn't I, being I mean in my professional capacity my professional role—

Yes I see what you mean.

But of course I exist aside from that role, as a person I mean, as a woman like you—

You're not like me.

Well no in the sense that I'm not a witch.

You must forgive me if I insist on this point. You're not like me.

Well, yes, I don't disagree, I'm not arguing, I have not after all produced after a pregnancy of seven years a gigantic emerald weighing seven thousand and thirty-five carats— Can I, could I, by the way, see the emerald?

No not right now it's sleeping.

The emerald is sleeping?

Yes it's sleeping right now. It sleeps.

It sleeps?

Yes didn't you hear me it's sleeping right now it sleeps just like any other—

What do you mean the emerald is sleeping?

Just what I said. It's asleep.

Do you talk to it?

Of course, sure I talk to it, it's mine, I mean I *gave birth* to it, I cuddle it and polish it and talk to it, what's so strange about that?

Does it talk to you?

Well I mean it's only one month old. How could it talk?

Hello?

Yes?

Is this Mad Moll?

Yes this is Mad Moll who are you?

You the one who advertised for somebody to stand outside the door and knock down anybody tries to come in?

Yes that's me are you applying for the position?

Yes I think so what does it pay?

Two hundred a week and found.

Well that sounds pretty good but tell me lady who is it I have to knock down for example?

Various parties. Some of them not yet known to me. I mean I have an inkling but no more than that. Are you big?

Six eight.

How many pounds?

Two forty-nine.

IQ?

One forty-six.

What's your best move?

I got a pretty good shove. A not-bad bust in the mouth. I can trip. I can fall on 'em. I can gouge. I have a good sense of where the ears are. I know thumbs and kneecaps.

Where did you get your training?

Just around. High school, mostly.

What's your name?

Soapbox.

That's not a very tough name if you'll forgive me.

You want me to change it? I've been called different things in different places.

No I don't want you to change it. It's all right. It'll do.

Okay do you want to see me or do I have the job?

You sound okay to me Soapbox. You can start tomorrow.

What time?

Dawn?

Understand, ye sons of the wise, what this exceedingly precious Stone crieth out to you! Seven years, close to tears. Slept for the first two, dreaming under four blankets, black, blue, brown, brown. Slept and pissed, when I wasn't dreaming I was pissing, I was a fountain. After the first year I knew something irregular was in progress, but not what. I thought, moonstrous! Salivated like a mad dog, four quarts or more a day, when I wasn't pissing I was spitting.

Chawed moose steak, moose steak and morels, and fluttered with new men—the butcher, baker, candlestick maker, especially the butcher, one Shatterhand, he was neat. Gobbled a lot of iron, liver and rust from the bottoms of boats, I had serial nosebleeds every day of the seventeenth trimester. Mood swings of course, heigh-de-ho, instances of false labor in years six and seven, palpating the abdominal wall I felt edges and thought, edges? Then on a cold February night the denouement, at six sixty-six in the evening, or a bit past seven, they sent a Miss Leek to do the delivery, one of us but not the famous one, she gave me scopolamine and a little swan-sweat, that helped, she turned not a hair when the emerald presented itself but placed it in my arms with a kiss or two and a pat or two and drove away, in a coach pulled by a golden pig.

Vandermaster has the Foot.

Yes.

The Foot is very threatening to you.

Indeed.

He is a mage and goes around accompanied by a black bloodhound.

Yes. Tarbut. Said to have been raised on human milk.

Could you give me a little more about the Foot. Who owns it?

Monks. Some monks in a monastery in Merano or outside of Merano. That's in Italy. It's their Foot.

How did Vandermaster get it?

Stole it.

Do you by any chance know what order that is?

Let me see if I can remember—Carthusian.

Can you spell that for me?

C-a-r-t-h-u-s-i-a-n. I think.

Thank you. How did Vandermaster get into the monastery?

They hold retreats, you know, for pious laymen or people who just want to come to the monastery and think about their sins or be edified, for a week or a few days ...

Can you describe the Foot? Physically?

The Foot proper is encased in silver. It's about the size of a foot, maybe slightly larger. It's cut off just above the ankle. The toe part is rather flat, it's as if people in those days had very flat toes. The whole is quite graceful. The Foot proper sits on top of this rather elaborate base, three levels, gold, little claw feet ...

And you are convinced that this, uh, reliquary contains the true Foot of Mary Magdalene.

Mary Magdalene's Foot. Yes.

He's threatening you with it.

It has a history of being used against witches, throughout history, to kill them or mar them—

He wants the emerald.

My emerald. Yes.

You won't reveal its parentage. Who the father was.

Oh well hell. It was the man in the moon. Deus Lunus.

The man in the moon ha-ha.

No I mean it, it was the man in the moon. Deus Lunus as he's called, the moon god. Deus Lunus. Him.

You mean you want me to believe—

Look woman I don't give dandelions what you believe you asked me who the father was. I told you. I don't give a zipper whether you believe me or don't believe me.

You're actually asking me to—

Sat in that chair, that chair right there. The red chair.

Oh for heaven's sake all right that's it I'm going to blow this pop stand I know I'm just a dumb ignorant media person but if you think for one minute that … I respect your uh conviction but this has got to be a delusionary belief. The man in the moon. A delusionary belief.

Well I agree it sounds funny but there it is. Where else would I get an emerald that big, seven thousand and thirty-five carats? A poor woman like me?

Maybe it's not a real emerald?

If it's not a real emerald why is Vandermaster after me?

You going to the hog wrassle?

No I'm after the emerald.

What's your name?

My name is Cold Cuts. What's that machine?

That's an emerald cutter.

How's it work?

Laser beam. You after the emerald too?

Yes I am.

What's your name?

My name is Pro Tem.

That a dowsing rod you got there?

No it's a giant wishbone.

Looks like a dowsing rod.

Well it dowses like a dowsing rod but you also get the wish.

Oh. What's his name?

His name is Plug.

Can't he speak for himself?

He's deaf and dumb.

After the emerald?

Yes. He has special skills.

What are they?

He knows how to diddle certain systems.

Playing it close to the vest is that it?

That's it.

Who's that guy there?

I don't know, all I know about him is he's from Antwerp.

The Emerald Exchange?

That's what I think.

What are all those little envelopes he's holding?

Sealed bids?

Look here, Soapbox, look here.

What's your name, man?

My name is Dietrich von Dietersdorf.

I don't believe it.

You don't believe my name is my name?

Pretty fancy name for such a pissant-looking fellow as you.

I will not be balked. Look here.

What you got?

Silver thalers, my friend, thalers big as onion rings.

That's money, right?

Right.

What do I have to do?

Fall asleep.

Fall asleep at my post here in front of the door?

Right. Will you do it?

I could. But should I?

Where does this "should" come from?

My mind. I have a mind, stewing and sizzling.

Well deal with it, man, deal with it. Will you do it?

Will I? Will I? *I don't know!*

Where is my daddy? asked the emerald. My da?

Moll dropped a glass, which shattered.

Your father.

Yes, said the emerald, amn't I supposed to have one?

He's not here.

Noticed that, said the emerald.

I'm never sure what you know and what you don't know.

I ask in true perplexity.

He was Deus Lunus. The moon god. Sometimes thought of as the man in the moon.

Bosh! said the emerald. I don't believe it.

Do you believe I'm your mother?

I do.

Do you believe you're an emerald?

I am an emerald.

Used to be, said Moll, women wouldn't drink from a glass into which the moon had shone. For fear of getting knocked up.

Surely this is superstition?

Hoo, hoo, said Moll. I like superstition.

I thought the moon was female.

Don't be culture-bound. It's been female in some cultures at some times, and in others, not.

What did it feel like? The experience.

Not a proper subject for discussion with a child.

The emerald sulking. Green looks here and there.

Well it wasn't the worst. Wasn't the worst. I had an orgasm that lasted for three hours. I judge that not the worst.

What's an orgasm?

Feeling that shoots through one's electrical system giving you little jolts, *spam spam,* many little jolts, *spam spam spam spam* ...

Teach me something. Teach me something, mother of mine, about this gray world of yours.

What have I to teach? The odd pitiful spell. Most of them won't even put a shine on a pair of shoes.

Teach me one.

"To achieve your heart's desire, burn in water, wash in fire."

What does that do?

French-fries. Anything you want French-fried.

That's all?

Well.

I have buggered up your tranquillity.

No no no no no.

I'm valuable, said the emerald. I am a thing of value. Over and above my personhood, if I may use the term.

You are a thing of value. A value extrinsic to what I value.

How much?

Equivalent I would say to a third of a sea.

Is that much?

Not inconsiderable.

People want to cut me up and put little chips of me into rings and bangles.

Yes. I'm sorry to say.

Vandermaster is not of this ilk.

Vandermaster is an ilk unto himself.

The more threatening for so being.

Yes.

What are you going to do?

Make me some money. Whatever else is afoot, this delight is constant.

Now the Molljourney the Molltrip into the ferocious Out with a wire shopping cart what's that sucker there doing? tips his hat bends his middle shuffles his feet why he's doing courtly not seen courtly for many a month he does a quite decent courtly I'll smile, briefly, out of my way there citizen sirens shrieking on this swarm summer's day here an idiot there an idiot that one's eyeing me eyed me on the corner and eyed me round the corner as the Mad Moll song has it and that one standing with his cheek crushed against the warehouse wall and that one browsing in a trash basket and that one picking that one's pocket and that one with the gotch eye and his hands on his I'll twoad 'ee bastard I'll—

Hey there woman come and stand beside me.

Buzz off buster I'm on the King's business and have no time to trifle.

You don't even want to stop a moment and look at this thing I have here?

What sort of thing is it?

Oh it's a rare thing, a beautiful thing, a jim-dandy of a thing, a thing any woman would give her eyeteeth to look upon.

Well yes okay but what is it?

Well I can't tell you. I have to show you. Come stand over here in the entrance to this dark alley.

Naw man I'm not gonna go into no alley with you what do you think I am a nitwit?

I think you're a beautiful woman even if you do have that bit of beard there on your chin like a piece of burnt toast or something, most becoming. And that mark like a dead insect on your forehead gives you a certain—

Cut the crap daddy and show me what you got. Standing right here. Else I'm on my way.

No it's too rich and strange for the full light of day we have to have some shadow, it's too—

If this turns out to be an ordinary—

No no no nothing like that. You mean you think I might be a what-do-you-call-'em, one of those guys who—

Your discourse sir strongly suggests it.

And your name?

Moll. Mad Moll. Sometimes Moll the Poor Girl.

Beautiful name. Your mother's name or the name of some favorite auntie?

Moll totals him with a bang in the balls.

Jesus Christ these creeps what can you do?

She stops at a store and buys a can of gem polish.

Polish my emerald so bloody bright it will bloody blind you.

Sitting on the street with a basket of dirty faces for sale. The dirty faces are all colors, white black yellow tan rosy-red.

Buy a dirty face! Slap it on your wife! Buy a dirty face! Complicate your life!

But no one buys.

A boy appears pushing a busted bicycle.

Hey lady what are those things there they look like faces.

That's what they are, faces.

Lady, Halloween is not until—

Okay kid move along you don't want to buy a face move along.

But those are actual faces lady Christ I mean they're *actual faces*—

Fourteen ninety-five kid you got any money on you?

I don't even want to *touch* one, look like they came off dead people.

Would you feel better if I said they were plastic?

Well I hope to God they're not—

Okay they're plastic. What's the matter with your bike?

Chain's shot.

Give it here.

The boy hands over the bicycle chain.

Moll puts the broken ends in her mouth and chews for a moment.

Okay here you go.

The boy takes it in his hands and yanks on it. It's fixed.

Shit how'd you do that, lady?

Moll spits and wipes her mouth on her sleeve.

Run along now kid beat it I'm tired of you.

Are you magic, lady?

Not enough.

Moll at home playing her oboe.

I love the oboe. The sound of the oboe.

The noble, noble oboe!

Of course it's not to every taste. Not everyone swings with the oboe.

Whoops! Goddamn oboe let me take that again.

Not perhaps the premier instrument of the present age. What would that be? The bullhorn, no doubt.

Why did he interfere with me? Why?

Maybe has to do with the loneliness of the gods. Oh thou great one whom I adore beyond measure, oh thou bastard and fatherer of bastards—

Tucked-away gods whom nobody speaks to anymore. Once so lively.

Polish my emerald so bloody bright it will bloody blind you.

Good God what's that?

Vandermaster used the Foot!

Oh my God look at that hole!

It's awful and tremendous!

What in the name of God?

Vandermaster used the Foot!

The Foot did that? I don't believe it!

You don't believe it? What's your name?

My name is Coddle. I don't believe the Foot could have done that. I one hundred percent don't believe it.

Well it's right there in front of your eyes. Do you think Moll and the emerald are safe?

The house seems structurally sound. Smoke-blackened, but sound.

What happened to Soapbox?

You mean Soapbox who was standing in front of the house poised to bop any mother's son who—

Good Lord Soapbox is nowhere to be seen!

He's not in the hole!

Let me see there. What's your name?

My name is Mixer. No, he's not in the hole. Not a shred of him in the hole.

Good, true Soapbox!

You think Moll is still inside? How do we know this is the right place after all?

Heard it on the radio. What's your name by the way?

My name is Ho Ho. Look at the ground smoking!

The whole thing is tremendous, demonstrating the awful power of the Foot!

I am shaking with awe right now! Poor Soapbox!

Noble, noble Soapbox!

Mr. Vandermaster.

Madam.

You may be seated.

I thank you.

The red chair.

Thank you very much.

May I offer you some refreshment?

Yes I will have a splash of something thank you.

It's Scotch I believe.

Yes Scotch.

And I will join you I think, as the week has been a most fatiguing one.

Care and cleaning I take it.

Yes, care and cleaning and in addition there was a media person here.

How tiresome.

Yes it was tiresome in the extreme her persistence in her peculiar vocation is quite remarkable.

Wanted to know about the emerald I expect.

She was most curious about the emerald.

Disbelieving.

Yes disbelieving but perhaps that is an attribute of the profession?

So they say. Did she see it?

No it was sleeping and I did not wish to—

Of course. How did this person discover that you had as it were made yourself an object of interest to the larger public?

Indiscretion on the part of the midwitch I suppose, some people cannot maintain even minimal discretion.

Yes that's the damned thing about some people. Their discretion is out to lunch.

Blabbing things about would be an example.

Popping off to all and sundry about matters.

Ah well.

Ah well. Could we, do you think, proceed?

If we must.

I have the Foot.

Right.

You have the emerald.

Correct.

The Foot has certain properties of special interest to witches.

So I have been told.

There is a distaste, a bad taste in the brain, when one is forced to put the boots to someone.

Must be terrible for you, terrible. Where is my man Soapbox by the way?

That thug you had in front of the door?

Yes, Soapbox.

He is probably reintegrating himself with the basic matter of the universe, right now. Fascinating experience I should think.

Good to know.

I intend only the best for the emerald, however.

What is the best?

There are as you are aware others not so scrupulous in the field. Chislers, in every sense.

And you? What do you intend for it?

I have been thinking of emerald dust. Emerald dust with soda, emerald dust with tomato juice, emerald dust with a dash of bitters, emerald dust with Ovaltine.

I beg your pardon?

I want to live twice.

Twice?

In addition to my present life, I wish another, future life.

A second life. Incremental to the one you are presently enjoying.

As a boy, I was very poor. Poor as pine.

And you have discovered a formula.

Yes.

Plucked from the arcanum.

Yes. Requires a certain amount of emerald. Powdered emerald.

Ugh!

Carat's weight a day for seven thousand thirty-five days.

Coincidence.

Not at all. Only *this* emerald will do. A moon's emerald born of human witch.

No.

I have been thinking about bouillon. Emerald dust and bouillon with a little Tabasco.

No.

No?

No.

My mother is eighty-one, said Vandermaster. I went to my mother and said, Mother, I want to be in love.

And she replied?

She said, me too.

Lily the media person standing in the hall.

I came back to see if you were ready to confess. The hoax.

It's talking now. It talks.

It what?

Lovely complete sentences. Maxims and truisms.

I don't want to hear this. I absolutely—

Look kid this is going to cost you. Sixty dollars.

Sixty dollars for what?

For the interview.

That's checkbook journalism!

Sho' nuff.

It's against the highest traditions of the profession!

You get paid, your boss gets paid, the stockholders get their slice, why not us members of the raw material? Why shouldn't the raw material get paid?

It talks?

Most assuredly it talks.

Will you take a check?

If I must.

You're really a witch.

How many times do I have to tell you?

You do tricks or anything?

Consulting, you might say.

You have clients? People who come to see you regularly on a regular basis?

People with problems, yes.

What kind of problems, for instance?

Some of them very simple, really, things that just need a specific, bit of womandrake for example—

What's womandrake?

Black bryony. Called the herb of beaten wives. Takes away black-and-blue marks.

You get beaten wives?

Stick a little of that number into the old man's pork and beans, he retches. For seven days and seven nights. It near to kills him.

I have a problem.

What's the problem?

The editor, or editor-king, as he's called around the shop.

What about him?

He takes my stuff and throws it on the floor. When he doesn't like it.

On the floor?

I know it's nothing to you but it *hurts me*. I cry. I know I shouldn't cry but I cry. When I see my stuff on the floor. Pages and pages of it, so carefully typed, *every word spelled right*—

Don't you kids have a union?

Yes but he won't speak to it.

That's this man Lather, right?

Mr. Lather. Editor-imperator.

Okay I'll look into it that'll be another sixty you want to pay now or you want to be billed?

I'll give you another check. *Can* Vandermaster live twice?

There are two theories, the General Theory and the Special Theory. I take it he is relying on the latter. Requires ingestion of a certain amount of emerald. Powdered emerald.

Can you defend yourself?

I have a few things in mind. A few little things.

Can I see the emerald now?

You may. Come this way.

Thank you. Thank you at last. My that's impressive what's that?

That's the thumb of a thief. Enlarged thirty times. Bronze. I use it in my work.

Impressive if one believed in that sort of thing ha-ha I don't mean to—

What care I? What care I? In here. Little emerald, this is Lily. Lily, this is the emerald.

Enchanté, said the emerald. What a pretty young woman you are!

This emerald is young, said Lily. Young, but good. I do not believe what I am seeing with my very eyes!

But perhaps that is a sepsis of the profession? said the emerald.

Vandermaster wants to live twice!

Oh, most foul, most foul!

He was very poor, as a boy! Poor as pine!

Hideous presumption! Cheeky hubris!

He wants to be in love! In love! Presumably with another person!

Unthinkable insouciance!

We'll have his buttons for dinner!

We'll clean the gutters with his hair!

What's your name, buddy?

My name is Tree and I'm smokin' mad!

My name is Bump and I'm just about ready to bust!

I think we should break out the naked-bladed pikes!

I think we should lay hand to torches and tar!

To live again! From the beginning! *Ahb ovo!* This concept riles the very marrow of our minds!

We'll flake the white meat from his bones!

And that goes for his damned dog, too!

Hello is this Mad Moll?

Yes who is this?

My name is Lather.

The editor?

Editor-king, actually.

Yes Mr. Lather what is the name of your publication I don't know that Lily ever—

World. I put it together. When *World* is various and beautiful, it's because I am various and beautiful. When *World* is sad and dreary, it's because I am sad and dreary. When *World* is not thy friend, it's because *I* am not thy friend. And if I am not thy friend, baby—

I get the drift.

Listen, Moll, I am not satisfied with what Lily's been giving me. She's not giving me potato chips. I have decided that I am going to handle this story personally, from now on.

She's been insufficiently insightful and comprehensive?

Gore, that's what we need, actual or psychological gore, and this twitter she's been filing—anyhow, I have sent her to Detroit.

Not Detroit!

She's going to be second night-relief paper clipper in the Detroit bureau. She's standing here right now with her bags packed and ashes in her hair and her ticket in her mouth.

Why in her mouth?

Because she needs her hands to rend garments with.

All right Mr. Lather send her back around. There is new bad news. Bad, bad, new bad news.

That's wonderful!

Moll hangs up the phone and weeps every tear she's capable of weeping, one, two, three.

Takes up a lump of clay, beats it flat with a Bible.

Let me see what do I have here?

I have Ya Ya Oil, that might do it.

I have Anger Oil, Lost & Away Oil, Confusion Oil, Weed of Misfortune, and War Water.

I have graveyard chips, salt, and coriander—enough coriander to freight a ship. Tasty coriander. Magical, magical coriander!

I'll eye-bite the son of a bitch. Have him in worm's hall by teatime.

Understand, ye sons of the wise, what this exceedingly precious Stone crieth out to you!

I'll fold that sucker's tent for him. If my stuff works. One never knows for sure, dammit. And where is Papa?

Throw in a little dwale now, a little orris ...

Moll shapes the clay into the figure of a man.

So mote it be!

What happened was that they backed a big van up to the back door.

Yes.

There were four of them or eight of them.

Yes.

It was two in the morning or three in the morning or four in the morning—I'm not sure.

Yes.

They were great big hairy men with cudgels and ropes and pads like movers have and a dolly and come-alongs made of barbed wire—that's a loop of barbed wire big enough to slip over somebody's head, with a handle—

Yes.

They wrapped the emerald in the pads and placed it on the dolly and tied ropes around it and got it down the stairs through the door and into the van.

Did they use the Foot?

No they didn't use the Foot they had four witches with them.

Which witches?

The witches Aldrin, Endrin, Lindane, and Dieldrin. Bad-ass witches.

You knew them.

Only by repute. And Vandermaster was standing there with clouds of 1, 1, 2, 2-tetrachloroethylene seething from his nostrils.

That's toxic.

Extremely. I was staggering around bumping into things, tried to hold on to the walls but the walls fell away from me and I fell after them trying to hold on.

These other witches, they do anything to you?

Kicked me in the ribs when I was on the floor. With their pointed shoes. I woke up emeraldless.

Right. Well I guess we'd better get the vast resources of our organization behind this. *World.* From sea to shining sea to shining sea. I'll alert all the bureaus in every direction.

What good will that do?

It will harry them. When a free press is on the case, you can't get away with anything really terrible.

But look at this.

What is it?

A solid silver louse. They left it.

What's it mean?

Means that the devil himself has taken an interest.
A free press, madam, is not afraid of the devil himself.

Who cares what's in a witch's head? Pretty pins for sticking pishtoshio
redthread for sewing names to shrouds gallant clankers I'll twoad 'ee and the
gollywobbles to give away and the trinkum-trankums to give away with a generous hand pricksticks for the eye damned if I do and damned if I don't what's
that upon her forehead? said my father it's a mark said my mother black mark
like a furry caterpillar I'll scrub it away with the Ajax and what's that upon her
chin? said my father it's a bit of a beard said my mother I'll pluck it away with
the tweezers and what's that upon her mouth? said my father it must be a
smirk said my mother I'll wipe it away with the heel of my hand she's got hair
down there already said my father is that natural? I'll shave it said my mother
no one will ever know and those said my father pointing *those*? just what they
look like said my mother I'll make a bandeau with this nice clean dish towel
she'll be flat as a jack of diamonds in no time and where's the belly button?
said my father flipping me about I don't see one anywhere must be coming
along later said my mother I'll just pencil one in here with the Magic Marker
this child is a bit of a mutt said my father recall to me if you will the circumstances of her conception it was a dark and stormy night said my mother ...
But who cares what's in a witch's head caskets of cankers shelves of twoads for
twoading paxwax scalpel polish people with scares sticking to their faces
memories of God who held me up and sustained me until I fell from His hands
into the world ...
      Twice? Twice? Twice? Twice?

      Hey Moll.
      Who's that?
      It's me.
      Me who?
      Soapbox.
      Soapbox!
      I got it!
      Got what?
      The Foot! I got it right here!
      I thought you were blown up!
      Naw I pretended to be bought so I was out of the way. Went with them
back to their headquarters, or den. Then when they put the Foot back in the
refrigerator I grabbed it and beat it back here.
      They kept it in the refrigerator?
      It needs a constant temperature or else it gets restless. It's hot-tempered.
They said.

It's elegant. Weighs a ton though.

Be careful you might—

Soapbox, I am not totally without—it's warm to the hand.

Yes it is warm I noticed that, look what else I got.

What are those?

Thalers. Thalers big as onion rings. Forty-two grand worth.

What are you going to do with them?

Conglomerate!

It is wrong to want to live twice, said the emerald. If I may venture an opinion.

I was very poor, as a boy, said Vandermaster. Nothing to eat but gruel. It was gruel, gruel, gruel. I was fifteen before I ever saw an onion.

These are matters upon which I hesitate to pronounce, being a new thing in the world, said the emerald. A latecomer to the welter. But it seems to me that, having weltered, the wish to *re*-welter might be thought greedy.

Gruel today, gruel yesterday, gruel tomorrow. Sometimes gruel substitutes. I burn to recoup.

Something was said I believe about love.

The ghostfish of love has eluded me these forty-five years.

That Lily person is a pleasant person I think. And pretty too. Very pretty. Good-looking.

Yes she is.

I particularly like the way she is dedicated. She's extremely dedicated. Very dedicated. To her work.

Yes I do not disagree. Admirable. A free press is, I believe, an essential component of—

She is true-blue. Probably it would be great fun to talk to her and get to know her and kiss her and sleep with her and everything of that nature.

What are you suggesting?

Well, there's then, said the emerald, that is to say, your splendid second life.

Yes?

And then there's now. Now is sooner than then.

You have a wonderfully clear head, said Vandermaster, for a rock.

Okay, said Lily. I want you to tap once for yes and twice for no. Do you understand that?

Tap.

You are the true Foot of Mary Magdalene?

Tap.

Vandermaster stole you from a monastery in Italy?

Tap.

A Carthusian monastery in Merano or outside Merano?

Tap.

Are you uncomfortable in that reliquary?

Tap tap.

Have you killed any witches lately? In the last year or so?

Tap tap.

Are you morally neutral or do you have opinions?

Tap.

You have opinions?

Tap.

In the conflict we are now witnessing between Moll and Vandermaster, which of the parties seems to you to have right and justice on her side?

Tap tap tap tap.

That mean Moll? One tap for each letter?

Tap.

Is it warm in there?

Tap.

Too warm?

Tap tap.

So you have been, in a sense, an unwilling partner in Vandermaster's machinations.

Tap.

And you would not be averse probably to using your considerable powers on Moll's behalf.

Tap.

Do you know where Vandermaster is right now?

Tap tap.

Have you any idea what his next move will be?

Tap tap.

What is your opinion of the women's movement?

Tap tap tap tap tap tap tap tap tap tap tap tap tap tap.

I'm sorry I didn't get that. Do you have a favorite color what do you think of cosmetic surgery should children be allowed to watch television after ten P.M. how do you feel about aging is nuclear energy in your opinion a viable alternative to fossil fuels how do you deal with stress are you afraid to fly and do you have a chili recipe you'd care to share with the folks?

Tap tap.

The first interview in the world with the true Foot of Mary Magdalene and no chili recipe!

Mrs. Vandermaster.

Yes.

Please be seated.

Thank you.

The red chair.

You're most kind.

Can I get you something, some iced tea or a little hit of Sanka?

A Ghost Dance is what I wouldn't mind if you can do it.

What's a Ghost Dance.

That's one part vodka to one part tequila with half an onion. Half a regular onion.

Wow wow wow wow wow.

Well when you're eighty-one, you know, there's not so much. Couple of Ghost Dances, I begin to take an interest.

I believe I can accommodate you.

Couple of Ghost Dances, I begin to look up and take notice.

Mrs. Vandermaster, you are aware are you not that your vile son has, with the aid of various parties, abducted my emerald? My own true emerald?

I mighta heard about it.

Well have you or haven't you?

'Course I don't pay much attention to that boy myself. He's bent.

Bent?

Him and his dog. He goes off in a corner and talks to the dog. Looking over his shoulder to see if I'm listening. As if I'd care.

The dog doesn't—

Just listens. *Intently.*

That's Tarbut.

Now I don't mind somebody who just addresses an occasional remark to the dog, like "Attaboy, dog," or something like that, or "Get the ball, dog," or something like that, but he *confides* in the dog. Bent.

You know what Vandermaster's profession is.

Yes, he's a mage. Think that's a little bent.

Is there anything you can do, or would do, to help me get my child back? My sweet emerald?

Well I don't have much say-so.

You don't.

I don't know too much about what-all he's up to. He comes and goes.

I see.

The thing is, he's bent.

You told me.

Wants to live twice.

I know.

I think it's a sin and a shame.

You do.

And your poor little child.
Yes.
A damned scandal.
Yes.
I'd witch his eyes out if I were you.
The thought's appealing.
His eyes like onions ...

A black bloodhound who looks as if he might have been fed on human milk.
Bloodhounding down the center of the street, nose to the ground.
You think this will work?
Soapbox, do you have a better idea?
Where did you find him?
I found him on the doorstep. Sitting there. In the moonlight.
In the moonlight?
Aureoled all around with moonglow.
You think that's significant?
Well I don't think it's happenstance.
What's his name?
Tarbut.
There's something I have to tell you.
What?
I went to the refrigerator for a beer?
Yes?
The Foot's walked.

Dead! Kicked in the heart by the Foot!
That's incredible!
Deep footprint right over the breastbone!
That's ghastly and awful!
After Lily turned him down he went after the emerald with a sledge!
Was the emerald hurt?
Chipped! The Foot got there in the nick!
And Moll?
She's gluing the chips back with grume!
What's grume?
Clotted blood!
And was the corpse claimed?
Three devils showed up! Lily's interviewing them right now!
A free press is not afraid of a thousand devils!
There are only three!

What do they look like?

Like Lather, the editor!

And the Foot?

Soapbox is taking it back to Italy! He's starting a security-guard business! Hired Sallywag, Wide Boy, Taptoe, and Sometimes!

What's your name by the way?

My name is Knucks. What's your name?

I'm Pebble. And the dog?

The dog's going to work for Soapbox too!

Curious, the dog showing up on Moll's doorstep that way!

Deus Lunus works in mysterious ways!

Deus Lunus never lets down a pal!

Well how 'bout a drink!

Don't mind if I do! What'll we drink to?

We'll drink to living once!

Hurrah for the here and now!

Tell me, said the emerald, what are diamonds like?

I know little of diamonds, said Moll.

Is a diamond better than an emerald?

Apples and oranges I would say.

Would you have *preferred* a diamond?

Nope.

Diamond-hard, said the emerald, that's an expression I've encountered.

Diamonds are a little ordinary. Decent, yes. Quiet, yes. But *gray*. Give me step-cut zircons, square-cut spodumenes, jasper, sardonyx, bloodstones, Baltic amber, cursed opals, peridots of your own hue, the padparadscha sapphire, yellow chrysoberyls, the shifty tourmaline, cabochons … But best of all, an emerald.

But what is the *meaning* of the emerald? asked Lily. I mean overall? If you can say.

I have some notions, said Moll. You may credit them or not.

Try me.

It means, one, that the gods are not yet done with us.

Gods not yet done with us.

The gods are still trafficking with us and making interventions of this kind and that kind and are not dormant or dead as has often been proclaimed by dummies.

Still trafficking. Not dead.

Just as in former times a demon might enter a nun on a piece of lettuce she was eating so even in these times a simple Mailgram might be the thin edge of the wedge.

Thin edge of the wedge.

Two, the world may congratulate itself that desire can still be raised in the dulled hearts of the citizens by the rumor of an emerald.

Desire or cupidity?

I do not distinguish qualitatively among the desires, we have referees for that, but he who covets not at all is a lump and I do not wish to have him to dinner.

Positive attitude toward desire.

Yes. Three, I do not know what this Stone portends, whether it portends for the better or portends for the worse or merely portends a bubbling of the in-between but you are in any case rescued from the sickliness of same and a small offering in the hat on the hall table would not be ill regarded.

And what now? said the emerald. What now, beautiful mother?

We resume the scrabble for existence, said Moll. We resume the scrabble for existence, in the sweet of the here and now.

JORGE LUIS BORGES

BORGES AND I

Translated by James E. Irby

Jorge Luis Borges (1899–1986) was born in Buenos Aires. His father was a lawyer and teacher, his mother an English translator. These influences, along with a childhood spent in Switzerland and Spain, helped to forge Borges's early facility and love for languages. Returning to Argentina in 1921, Borges quickly gained a reputation for literary experimentation, moving from avant-garde poetry to essays and stories that frequently plundered one another's conventions. Following a brush with death in late 1938, Borges turned his writing solely to short fiction. He also coauthored stories, edited anthologies, and translated classic English texts such as Blake's The Marriage of Heaven and Hell. *Although his career as a writer and librarian was compromised during the decade of General Perón's rule, the publication of* Ficciones *in 1944 launched Borges to international fame. Gallimard's 1951 French translation was widely read in Europe, and in 1961 the International Congress of Publishers jointly awarded Borges and Samuel Beckett the Prix Fomentor. After Perón's fall, Borges resumed his appointment as director of the National Library, which ironically coincided with the almost complete deterioration of his eyesight. Depicting Borges in his 1967* Paris Review *interview, Ronald Christ wrote:*

> *Borges arrives at the library where it is now his custom to dictate letters and poems which Miss Quinteros types and reads back to him. Following his revisions, she makes two or three, sometimes four copies of each poem before Borges is satisfied. Some afternoons she reads to him, and he carefully corrects her English pronunciation. But he is not always serious, Miss Quinteros stressed: "Always there are jokes, little practical jokes."*
>
> *His voice is unemphatic, almost a drone, seeming, possibly because of the unfocused expression of his eyes, to come from another person behind the face, and his gestures and expressions are lethargic. But when he laughs—and he laughs often—his features wrinkle into a wry question mark. Most of his statements take the form of rhetorical questions. His accent defies easy classification: a cosmopolitan diction, influenced by American movies. Retiring, even self-obliterating, he avoids personal*

*statement as much as possible and obliquely answers questions
about himself by talking of other writers, using their words and
even their books as emblems of his own thought.*

*After a hiatus from story writing, Borges revisited the genre in 1966. He
continued to write, independently, collaboratively, and under a variety of
pseudonyms, until his death from liver cancer in Geneva, Switzerland.*

*The impact of what André Maurois called Borges's "wonderful intel-
ligence, wealth of invention, and tight, almost mathematical style" has
been felt in the legacies of both South American and international literature. James E. Irby, who translated "Everything and Nothing" and
"Borges and I" for Labyrinths (1962), writes that "Borges once claimed
that the basic devices of all fantastic literature are only four in number:
the work within the work, the contamination of reality by dream, the
voyage in time, and the double."*

The other one, the one called Borges, is the one things happen to. I walk
through the streets of Buenos Aires and stop for a moment, perhaps mechanically now, to look at the arch of an entrance hall and the grillwork on the gate;
I know of Borges from the mail and see his name on a list of professors or in a
biographical dictionary. I like hourglasses, maps, eighteenth-century typogra-
phy, the taste of coffee and the prose of Stevenson; he shares these preferences, but in a vain way that turns them into the attributes of an actor. It
would be an exaggeration to say that ours is a hostile relationship; I live, let
myself go on living, so that Borges may contrive his literature, and this literature justifies me. It is no effort for me to confess that he has achieved some
valid pages, but those pages cannot save me, perhaps because what is good
belongs to no one, not even to him, but rather to the language and to tradition.
Besides, I am destined to perish, definitively, and only some instant of myself
can survive in him. Little by little, I am giving over everything to him, though I
am quite aware of his perverse custom of falsifying and magnifying things.
Spinoza knew that all things long to persist in their being; the stone eternally
wants to be a stone and the tiger a tiger. I shall remain in Borges, not in myself
(if it is true that I am someone), but I recognize myself less in his books than in
many others or in the laborious strumming of a guitar. Years ago I tried to free
myself from him and went from the mythologies of the suburbs to the games
with time and infinity, but those games belong to Borges now and I shall have
to imagine other things. Thus my life is a flight and I lose everything and everything belongs to oblivion, or to him.

I do not know which of us has written this page.

JORGE LUIS BORGES

Everything and Nothing

Translated by James E. Irby

There was no one in him; behind his face (which even through the bad paintings of those times resembles no other) and his words, which were copious, fantastic and stormy, there was only a bit of coldness, a dream dreamt by no one. At first he thought that all people were like him, but the astonishment of a friend to whom he had begun to speak of this emptiness showed him his error and made him feel always that an individual should not differ in outward appearance. Once he thought that in books he would find a cure for his ill and thus he learned the small Latin and less Greek a contemporary would speak of; later he considered that what he sought might well be found in an elemental rite of humanity, and let himself be initiated by Anne Hathaway one long June afternoon. At the age of twenty-odd years he went to London. Instinctively he had already become proficient in the habit of simulating that he was someone, so that others would not discover his condition as no one; in London he found the profession to which he was predestined, that of the actor, who on a stage plays at being another before a gathering of people who play at taking him for that other person. His histrionic tasks brought him a singular satisfaction, perhaps the first he had ever known; but once the last verse had been acclaimed and the last dead man withdrawn from the stage, the hated flavor of unreality returned to him. He ceased to be Ferrex or Tamerlane[1] and became no one again. Thus hounded, he took to imagining other heroes and other tragic fables. And so, while his flesh fulfilled its destiny as flesh in the taverns and brothels of London, the soul that inhabited him was Caesar, who disregards the augur's admonition, and Juliet, who abhors the lark, and Macbeth, who converses on the plain with the witches who are also Fates. No one has ever been so many men as this man, who like the Egyptian Proteus could exhaust all the guises of reality. At times he would leave a confession hidden away in some corner of his work, certain that it would not be deciphered; Richard affirms that in his person he plays the part of many and Iago claims with curious words "I am not what I am." The fundamental identity of existing, dreaming and acting inspired famous passages of his.

For twenty years he persisted in that controlled hallucination, but one morning he was suddenly gripped by the tedium and the terror of being so many kings who die by the sword and so many suffering lovers who converge, diverge and melodiously expire. That very day he arranged to sell his theater. Within a week he had returned to his native village, where he recovered the trees and rivers of his childhood and did not relate them to the others his muse had celebrated, illustrious with mythological allusions and Latin terms. He had to be someone; he was a retired impresario who had made his fortune and concerned himself with loans, lawsuits and petty usury. It was in this character that he dictated the arid will and testament known to us, from which he deliberately excluded all traces of pathos or literature. His friends from London would visit his retreat and for them he would take up again his role as poet.

History adds that before or after dying he found himself in the presence of God and told Him: "I who have been so many men in vain want to be one and myself." The voice of the Lord answered from a whirlwind: "Neither am I anyone; I have dreamt the world as you dreamt your work, my Shakespeare, and among the forms in my dream are you, who like myself are many and no one."

NOTE

1. *Ferrex and Porrex*, an English tragedy written c. 1570, and *Tamerlane*, a play written by Christopher Marlowe in 1590.

JANE BOWLES

CAMP CATARACT

Jane Bowles (1917–1973) was born in New York City and was educated there and in Switzerland. In 1938 she married the writer Paul Bowles, and together they shared tenancy in a Brooklyn boarding house with a community of writers, including W.H. Auden and Carson McCullers. The Bowles marriage was in many ways an unconventional affair; for example, both Jane and Paul pursued other, homosexual relationships. Bowles's own writing career was consolidated in 1943 with the publication of her novel Two Serious Ladies. *An extensive traveller, Bowles lived in Paris and Ceylon and settled with her husband in Tangier, Morocco, where she lived until her death.*

Bowles's stories typically involve eccentric characters who set out on journeys into the world. Her gifts lie in a remarkable control of voice and in an ability to navigate the psychic terrain between conformity and jeopardy which such strange personalities must tread. The alternately realistic and elliptical story "Camp Cataract" aptly demonstrates Bowles's power in depicting the tragicomic gallantry of her unusual characters. Truman Capote praises "Camp Cataract" as "a rending sample of controlled compassion: a comic tale of doom that has at its heart, and as its heart, the subtlest comprehension of eccentricity and human apartness."

Beryl knocked on Harriet's cabin door and was given permission to enter. She found her friend seated near the window, an open letter in her hand.

"Good evening, Beryl," said Harriet. "I was just reading a letter from my sister." Her fragile, spinsterish face wore a canny yet slightly hysterical expression.

Beryl, a stocky blond waitress with stubborn eyes, had developed a dogged attachment to Harriet and sat in her cabin whenever she had a moment to spare. She rarely spoke in Harriet's presence, nor was she an attentive listener.

"I'll read you what she says; have a seat." Harriet indicated a straight chair and Beryl dragged it into a dark corner where she sat down. It creaked dangerously under the weight of her husky body.

89

"Hope I don't bust the chair," said Beryl, and she blushed furiously, digging her hands deep into the pockets of the checked plus-fours she habitually wore when she was not on duty.

"'Dear Sister,'" Harriet read. "'You are still at Camp Cataract visiting the falls and enjoying them. I always want you to have a good time. This is your fifth week away. I suppose you go on standing behind the falls with much enjoyment like you told me all the guests did. I think you said only the people who don't stay overnight have to pay to stand behind the waterfall ... you stay ten weeks ... have a nice time, dear. Here everything is exactly the same as when you left. The apartment doesn't change. I have something I want to tell you, but first let me say that if you get nervous, why don't you come home instead of waiting until you are no good for the train trip? Such a thing could happen. I wonder of course how you feel about the apartment once you are by the waterfall. Also, I want to put this to you. Knowing that you have an apartment and a loving family must make Camp Cataract quite a different place than it would be if it were all the home and loving you had. There must be wretches like that up there. If you see them, be sure to give them loving because they are the lost souls of the earth. I fear nomads. I am afraid of them and afraid for them too. I don't know what I would do if any of my dear ones were seized with the wanderlust. We are meant to cherish those who through God's will are given into our hands. First of all come the members of the family, and for this it is better to live as close as possible. Maybe you would say, "Sadie is old-fashioned; she doesn't want people to live on their own." I am not old-fashioned, but I don't want any of us to turn into nomads. You don't grow rich in spirit by widening your circle but by tending your own. When you are gone, I get afraid about you. I think that you might be seized with the wanderlust and that you are not remembering the apartment very much. Particularly this trip ... but then I know this cannot be true and that only my nerves make me think such things. It's so hot out. This is a record-breaking summer. Remember, the apartment is not just a row of rooms. It is the material proof that our spirits are so wedded that we have but one blessed roof over our heads. There are only three of us in the apartment related by blood, but Bert Hoffer has joined the three through the normal channels of marriage, also sacred. I know that you feel this way too about it and that just nerves makes me think Camp Cataract can change anything. May I remind you also that if this family is a garland, you are the middle flower; for me you are anyway. Maybe Evy's love is now flowing more to Bert Hoffer because he's her husband, which is natural. I wish they didn't think you needed to go to Camp Cataract because of your spells. Haven't I always tended you when you had them? Bert's always taken Evy to the Hoffers and we've stayed together, just the two of us, with the door safely locked so you wouldn't in your excitement run to a neighbor's house at all hours of the morning. Evy liked going to the Hoffers because they always gave her chicken with dumplings or else goose with red cabbage. I hope you haven't got it in your head that just because you are an old maid you have to go somewhere and be by yourself. Remember, I am also an old maid. I must close now, but I am not satisfied with my letter because I have so much more to say. I know you love the apartment and feel the way I feel. You are simply getting a tourist's thrill out of being there in a cabin like all of us do. I count the days until your sweet return. Your loving sister, Sadie.'"

Harriet folded the letter. "Sister Sadie," she said to Beryl, "is a great lover of security."

"She sounds swell," said Beryl, as if Harriet were mentioning her for the first time, which was certainly not the case.

"I have no regard for it whatsoever," Harriet announced in a positive voice. "*None*. In fact, I am a great admirer of the nomad, vagabonds, gypsies, seafaring men. I tip my hat to them; the old prophets roamed the world for that matter too, and most of the visionaries." She folded her hands in her lap with an air of satisfaction. Then, clearing her throat as if for a public address, she continued. "I don't give a tinker's damn about feeling part of a community, I can assure you.... That's not why I stay on at the apartment ... not for a minute, but it's a good reason why she does ... I mean Sadie; she loves a community spirit and she loves us all to be in the apartment because the apartment is in the community. She can get an actual thrill out of knowing that. But of course I can't ... I never could, never in a thousand years."

She tilted her head back and half-closed her eyes. In the true style of a person given to interminable monologues, she was barely conscious of her audience. "Now," she said, "we can come to whether I, on the other hand, get a thrill out of Camp Cataract." She paused for a moment as if to consider this. "Actually, I don't," she pronounced sententiously, "but if you like, I will clarify my statement by calling Camp Cataract my *tree house*. You remember tree houses from your younger days.... You climb into them when you're a child and plan to run away from home once you are safely hidden among the leaves. They're popular with children. Suppose I tell you point-blank that I'm an extremely original woman, but also a very shallow one ... in a sense, a *very* shallow one. I am afraid of scandal." Harriet assumed a more erect position. "I despise anything that smacks of a bohemian dash for freedom; I know that this has nothing to do with the more serious things in life ... I'm sure there are hundreds of serious people who kick over their traces and jump into the gutter; but I'm too shallow for anything like that ... I know it and I enjoy knowing it. Sadie on the other hand cooks and cleans all day long and yet takes her life as seriously as she would a religion ... myself and the apartment and the Hoffers. By the Hoffers, I mean my sister Evy and her big pig of a husband Bert." She made a wry face. "I'm the only one with taste in the family but I've never even suggested a lamp for the apartment. I wouldn't lower myself by becoming involved. I do however refuse to make an unseemly dash for freedom. I refuse to be known as 'Sadie's wild sister Harriet.' There is something intensively repulsive to me about unmarried women setting out on their own ... also a very shallow attitude. You may wonder how a woman can be shallow and know it at the same time, but then, this is precisely the tragedy of any person, if he allows himself to be griped." She paused for a moment and looked into the darkness with a fierce light in her eyes. "Now let's get back to Camp Cataract," she said with renewed vigor. "The pine groves, the canoes, the sparkling purity of the brook water and cascade ... the cabins ... the marshmallows, the respectable clientele."

"Did you ever think of working in a garage?" Beryl suddenly blurted out, and then she blushed again at the sound of her own voice.

"No," Harriet answered sharply. "Why should I?"

Beryl shifted her position in her chair. "Well," she said, "I think I'd like that kind of work better than waiting on tables. Especially if I could be boss and own my garage. It's hard, though, for a woman."

Harriet stared at her in silence. "Do you think Camp Cataract smacks of the gutter?" she asked a minute later.

"No, sir...." Beryl shook her head with a woeful air.

"Well then, there you have it. It is, of course, the farthest point from the gutter that one could reach. Any blockhead can see that. My plan is extremely complicated and from my point of view rather brilliant. First I will come here for several years ... I don't know yet exactly how many, but long enough to imitate roots ... I mean to imitate the natural family roots of childhood ... long enough so that I myself will feel: 'Camp Cataract is *habit,* Camp Cataract is life, Camp Cataract is not escape.' Escape is unladylike, habit isn't. As I remove myself gradually from within my family circle and establish myself more and more solidly into Camp Cataract, then from here at some later date I can start making my sallies into the outside world almost unnoticed. None of it will seem to the onlooker like an ugly impetuous escape. I intend to rent the same cabin every year and to stay a little longer each time. Meanwhile I'm learning a great deal about trees and flowers and bushes ... I am interested in nature." She was quiet for a moment. "It's rather lucky too," she added, "that the doctor has approved of my separating from the family for several months out of every year. He's a blockhead and doesn't remotely suspect the extent of my scheme nor how perfectly he fits into it ... in fact, he has even sanctioned my request that no one visit me here at the camp. I'm afraid if Sadie did, and she's the only one who would dream of it, I wouldn't be able to avoid a wrangle and then I might have a fit. The fits are unpleasant; I get much more nervous than I usually am and there's a blank moment or two." Harriet glanced sideways at Beryl to see how she was reacting to this last bit of information, but Beryl's face was impassive.

"So you see my plan," she went on, in a relaxed, offhand manner, "complicated, a bit dotty and completely original ... but then, I *am* original ... not like my sisters ... oddly enough I don't even seem to belong socially to the same class as my sisters do. I am somehow"—she hesitated for a second—"more fashionable."

Harriet glanced out ofthe window. Night had fallen during the course of her monologue and she could see a light burning in the next cabin. "Do you think I'm a coward?" she asked Beryl.

The waitress was startled out of her torpor. Fortunately her brain registered Harriet's question as well. "No, sir," she answered. "If you were, you wouldn't go out paddling canoes solo, with all the scary shoots you run into up and down these rivers...."

Harriet twisted her body impatiently. She had a sudden and uncontrollable desire to be alone. "Good-bye," she said rudely. "I'm not coming to supper."

Beryl rose from her chair. "I'll save something for you in case you get hungry after the dining room's closed. I'll be hanging around the lodge like I always am till bedtime." Harriet nodded and the waitress stepped out of the cabin, shutting the door carefully behind her so that it would not make any noise.

Harriet's sister Sadie was a dark woman with loose features and sad eyes. She was turning slightly to fat in her middle years, and did not in any way resemble Harriet, who was only a few years her senior. Ever since she had written her last letter to Harriet about Camp Cataract and the nomads Sadie had suffered from a feeling of steadily mounting suspense—the suspense itself a curious mingling of apprehension and thrilling anticipation. Her appetite grew smaller each day and it was becoming increasingly difficult for her to accomplish her domestic tasks.

She was standing in the parlor gazing with blank eyes at her new furniture set—two enormous easy chairs with bulging arms and a sofa in the same style—when she said aloud: "I can talk to her better than I can put it in a letter." Her voice had been automatic and when she heard her own words a rush of unbounded joy flooded her heart. Thus she realized that she was going on a little journey to Camp Cataract. She often made important decisions this way, as if some prearranged plot were being suddenly revealed to her, a plot which had immediately to be concealed from the eyes of others, because for Sadie, if there was any problem implicit in making a decision, it lay, not in the difficulty of choosing, but in the concealment of her choice. To her, secrecy was the real absolution from guilt, so automatically she protected all of her deepest feelings and compulsions from the eyes of Evy, Bert Hoffer and the other members of the family, although she had no interest in understanding or examining these herself.

The floor shook; recognizing Bert Hoffer's footsteps, she made a violent effort to control the flux of her blood so that the power of her emotion would not be reflected in her cheeks. A moment later her brother-in-law walked across the room and settled in one of the easy chairs. He sat frowning at her for quite a little while without uttering a word in greeting, but Sadie had long ago grown accustomed to his unfriendly manner; even in the beginning it had not upset her too much because she was such an obsessive that she was not very concerned with outside details.

"God-damned velours," he said finally. "It's the hottest stuff I ever sat on."

"Next summer we'll get covers," Sadie reassured him, "with a flower pattern if you like. What's your favorite flower?" she asked, just to make conversation and to distract him from looking at her face.

Bert Hoffer stared at her as if she'd quite taken leave of her senses. He was a fat man with a red face and wavy hair. Instead of answering this question, which he considered idiotic, he mopped his brow with his handkerchief.

"I'll fix you a canned pineapple salad for supper," she said to him with glowing eyes. "It will taste better than heavy meat on a night like this."

"If you're going to dish up pineapple salad for supper," Bert Hoffer answered with a dark scowl, "you can telephone some other guy to come and eat it. You'll find me over at Martie's Tavern eating meat and potatoes, if there's any messages to deliver."

"I thought because you were hot," said Sadie.

"I was talking about the velvet, wasn't I? I didn't say anything about the meat."

He was a very trying man indeed, particularly in a small apartment, but Sadie never dwelled upon this fact at all. She was delighted to cook and clean for him and for her sister Evelyn so long as they consented to live under the same roof with her and Harriet.

Just then Evelyn walked briskly into the parlor. Like Sadie she was dark, but here the resemblance ceased, for she had a small and wiry build, with a flat chest, and her hair was as straight as an Indian's. She stared at her husband's shirt sleeves and at Sadie's apron with distaste. She was wearing a crisp summer dress with a very low neckline, an unfortunate selection for one as bony and fierce-looking as she.

"You both look ready for the dump heap, not for the dining room," she said to them. "Why do we bother to have a dining room ... is it just a farce?"

"How was the office today?" Sadie asked her sister.

Evelyn looked at Sadie and narrowed her eyes in closer scrutiny. The muscles in her face tightened. There was a moment of dead silence, and Bert Hoffer, cocking a wary eye in his wife's direction, recognized the dangerous flush on her cheeks. Secretly he was pleased. He loved to look on when Evelyn blew up at Sadie, but he tried to conceal his enjoyment because he did not consider it a very masculine one.

"What's the matter with you?" Evelyn asked finally, drawing closer to Sadie. "There's something wrong besides your dirty apron."

Sadie colored slightly but said nothing.

"You look crazy," Evelyn yelled. "What's the matter with you? You look so crazy I'd be almost afraid to ask you to go to the store for something. Tell me what's happened!" Evelyn was very excitable; nonetheless hers was a strong and sane nature.

"I'm not crazy," Sadie mumbled. "I'll go get the dinner." She pushed slowly past Evelyn and with her heavy step she left the parlor.

The mahogany dining table was much too wide for the small oblong-shaped room, clearing the walls comfortably only at the two ends. When many guests were present some were seated first on one side of the room and were then obliged to draw the table toward themselves, until its edge pressed painfully into their diaphragms, before the remaining guests could slide into their seats on the opposite side.

Sadie served the food, but only Bert Hoffer ate with any appetite. Evelyn jabbed at her meat once or twice, tasted it, and dropped her fork, which fell with a clatter on to her plate.

Had the food been more savory she might not have pursued her attack on Sadie until later, or very likely she would have forgotten it altogether. Unfortunately, however, Sadie, although she insisted on fulfilling the role of housewife, and never allowed the others to acquit themselves of even the smallest domestic task, was a poor cook and a careless cleaner as well. Her lumpy gravies were tasteless, and she had once or twice boiled a good cut of steak out of indifference. She was lavish, too, in spite of being indifferent, and kept her cupboards so loaded with food that a certain quantity spoiled each week and there was often an unpleasant odor about the house. Harriet, in fact, was totally unaware of Sadie's true nature and had fallen into the trap her sister had instinctively prepared for her, because beyond wearing an apron and simulating the airs of other housewives, Sadie did not possess a community spirit at all, as Harriet had stated to Beryl the waitress. Sadie certainly yearned to live in the grown-up world that her parents had established for them when they were children, but in spite of the fact that she had wanted to live in that world with Harriet, and because of Harriet, she did not understand it properly. It remained mysterious to her even though she did all the housekeeping and managed the apartment entirely alone. She couldn't ever admit to herself that she lived in constant fear that Harriet would go away, but she brooded a great deal on outside dangers, and had she tried, she could not have remembered a time when this fear had not been her strongest emotion.

Sometimes an ecstatic and voracious look would come into her eyes, as if she would devour her very existence because she loved it so much. Such passionate moments of appreciation were perhaps her only reward for living a life which she knew in her heart was one of perpetual narrow escape. Although Sadie was neither sly nor tricky, but on the contrary profoundly sincere and ingenuous, she schemed unconsciously to keep the Hoffers in the apartment with them, because she did not want to reveal the true singleness of her interest either to Harriet or to herself. She sensed as well that Harriet would find it more difficult to break away from all three of them (because as a group they suggested a little society, which impressed her sister) than she would to escape from her alone. In spite of her mortal dread that Harriet might strike out on her own, she had never brooded on the possibility of her sister's marrying. Here, too, her instinct was correct: she knew that she was safe and referred often to the "normal channels of marriage," conscious all the while that such an intimate relationship with a man would be as uninteresting to Harriet as it would to herself.

From a financial point of view this communal living worked out more than satisfactorily. Each sister had inherited some real estate which yielded her a small monthly stipend; these stipends, combined with the extra money that the Hoffers contributed out of their salaries, covered their common living expenses. In return for the extra sum the Hoffers gave toward the household expenses, Sadie contributed her work, thus saving them the money they would have spent hiring a servant, had they lived alone. A fourth sister, whose marriage had proved financially more successful than Evy's, contributed generously toward Harriet's support at Camp Cataract, since Harriet's stipend certainly did not yield enough to cover her share of their living expenses at the apartment and pay for a long vacation as well.

Neither Sadie nor Bert Hoffer had looked up when Evy's fork clattered onto her plate. Sadie was truly absorbed in her own thoughts, whereas Bert Hoffer was merely pretending to be, while secretly he rejoiced at the unmistakable signal that his wife was about to blow up.

"When I find out why Sadie looks like that if she isn't going to be crazy, then I'll eat," Evelyn announced flatly, and she folded her arms across her chest.

"I'm not crazy," Sadie said indistinctly, glancing toward Bert Hoffer, not in order to enlist his sympathies, but to avoid her younger sister's sharp scrutiny.

"There's a big danger of your going crazy because of Grandma and Harriet," said Evelyn crossly. "That's why I get so nervous the minute you look a little out of the way, like you do tonight. It's not that you get Harriet's expression ... but then you might be getting a different kind of craziness ... maybe worse. She's all right if she can go away and there's not too much excitement ... it's only in spells anyway. But you—you might get a worse kind. Maybe it would be steadier."

"I'm not going to be crazy," Sadie murmured apologetically.

Evelyn glowered in silence and picked up her fork, but then immediately she let it fall again and turned on her sister with renewed exasperation. "Why don't you ask me why *I'm* not going to be crazy?" she demanded. "Harriet's my sister and Grandma's my grandma just as much as she is yours, isn't she?"

Sadie's eyes had a faraway look.

"If you were normal," Evelyn pursued, "you'd give me an intelligent argument instead of not paying any attention. Do you agree, Hoffer?"

"Yes, I do," he answered soberly.

Evelyn stiffened her back. "I'm too much like everybody else to be crazy," she announced with pride. "At a picture show, I feel like the norm."

The technical difficulty of disappearing without announcing her plan to Evelyn suddenly occurred to Sadie, who glanced up quite by accident at her sister. She knew, of course, that Harriet was supposed to avoid contact with her family during these vacation months at the doctor's request and even at Harriet's own; but like some herd animal, who though threatened with the stick continues grazing, Sadie pursued her thoughts imperturbably. She did not really believe in Harriet's craziness nor in the necessity of her visits to Camp Cataract, but she was never in conscious opposition to the opinions of her sisters. Her attitude was rather like that of a child who is bored by the tedium of grown-up problems and listens to them with a vacant ear. As usual she was passionately concerned only with successfully dissimulating what she really felt, and had she been forced to admit openly that there existed such a remarkable split between her own opinions and those of her sisters, she would have suffered unbelievable torment. She was able to live among them, listening to their conferences with her dead outside ear (the more affluent sister was also present at these sessions, and her husband as well), and even to contribute a pittance toward Harriet's support at the camp, without questioning the validity either of their decisions or of her own totally divergent attitude. By a self-imposed taboo, awareness of this split was denied her, and she had never reflected upon it.

Harriet had gone to Camp Cataract for the first time a year ago, after a bad attack of nerves combined with a return of her pleurisy. It had been suggested by the doctor himself that she go with his own wife and child instead of traveling with one of her sisters. Harriet had been delighted with the suggestion and Sadie had accepted it without a murmur. It was never her habit to argue, and in fact she had thought nothing of Harriet's leaving at the time. It was only gradually that she had begun writing the letters to Harriet about Camp Cataract, the nomads and the wanderlust—for she had written others similar to her latest one, but never so eloquent or full of conviction. Previous letters had contained a hint or two here and there, but had been for the main part factual reports about her summer life in the apartment. Since writing this last letter she had not been able to forget her own wonderful and solemn words (for she was rarely eloquent), and even now at the dinner table they rose continually in her throat so that she was thrilled over and over again and could not bother her head about announcing her departure to Evelyn. "It will be easier to write a note," she said to herself. "I'll pack my valise and walk out tomorrow afternoon, while they're at business. They can get their own dinners for a few days. Maybe I'll leave a great big meat loaf." Her eyes were shining like stars.

"Take my plate and put it in the warmer, Hoffer," Evelyn was saying. "I won't eat another mouthful until Sadie tells us what we can expect. If she feels she's going off, she can at least warn us about it. I deserve to know how she feels ... I tell every single thing I feel to her and Harriet ... I don't sneak around the house like a thief. In the first place I don't have any time for sneaking, I'm at the office all day! Is this the latest vogue, this sneaking around and hiding everything you can from your sister? Is it?" She stared at Bert Hoffer, widening her eyes in fake astonishment. He shrugged his shoulders.

"I'm no sneak or hypocrite and neither are you, Hoffer, you're no hypocrite. You're just sore at the world, but you don't pretend you love the world, do you?"

Sadie was lightheaded with embarrassment. She had blanched at Evy's allusion to her going, which she mistook naturally for a reference to her intention of leaving for Camp Cataract.

"Only for a few days ... " she mumbled in confusion, "and then I'll be right back here at the table."

Evelyn looked at her in consternation. "What do you mean by announcing calmly how many days it's going to be?" she shouted at her sister. "That's really sacrilegious! Did you ever hear of such a crusty sacrilegious remark in your life before?" She turned to Bert Hoffer, with a horror-stricken expression on her face. "How can I go to the office and look neat and clean and happy when this is what I hear at home ... when my sister sits here and says she'll only go crazy for a few days? How *can* I go to the office after that? How can I look right?"

"I'm not going to be crazy," Sadie assured her again in a sorrowful tone, because although she felt relieved that Evelyn had not, after all, guessed the truth, hers was not a nature to indulge itself in trivial glee at having put someone off her track.

"You just said you were going to be crazy," Evelyn exclaimed heatedly. "Didn't she, Bert?"

"Yes," he answered, "she did say something like that...."

The tendons of Evelyn's neck were stretched tight as she darted her eyes from her sister's face to her husband's. "Now, tell me this much," she demanded, "do I go to the office every day looking neat and clean or do I go looking like a bum?"

"You look O.K.," Bert said.

"Then why do my sisters spit in my eye? Why do they hide everything from me if I'm so decent? I'm wide open, I'm frank, there's nothing on my mind besides what I say. Why can't they be like other sisters all over the world? One of them is so crazy that she must live in a cabin for her nerves at *my* expense, and the other one is planning to go crazy deliberately and behind my back." She commenced to struggle out of her chair, which as usual proved to be a slow and laborious task. Exasperated, she shoved the table vehemently away from her toward the opposite wall. "Why don't we leave a space all on one side when there's no company?" she screamed at both of them, for she was now annoyed with Bert Hoffer as well as with Sadie. Fortunately they were seated at either end of the table and so did not suffer as a result of her violent gesture, but the table jammed into four chairs ranged on the opposite side, pinning three of them backward against the wall and knocking the fourth onto the floor.

"Leave it there," Evelyn shouted dramatically above the racket. "Leave it there till doomsday," and she rushed headlong out of the room.

They listened to her gallop down the hall.

"What about the dessert?" Bert Hoffer asked Sadie with a frown. He was displeased because Evelyn had spoken to him sharply.

"Leftover bread pudding without raisins." She had just gotten up to fetch the pudding when Evelyn summoned them from the parlor.

"Come in here, both of you," she hollered. "I have something to say."

They found Evelyn seated on the couch, her head tilted way back on a cushion, staring fixedly at the ceiling. They settled into easy chairs opposite her.

"I could be normal and light in any other family," she said, "I'm normally a gay light girl ... not a morose one. I like all the material things."

"What do you want to do tonight?" Bert Hoffer interrupted, speaking with authority. "Do you want to be excited or do you want to go to the movies?" He was always bored by these self-appraising monologues which succeeded her explosions.

Evy looked as though she had not heard him, but after a moment or two of sitting with her eyes shut she got up and walked briskly out of the room; her husband followed her.

Neither of them had said good-bye to Sadie, who went over to the window as soon as they'd gone and looked down on the huge unsightly square below her. It was crisscrossed by trolley tracks going in every possible direction. Five pharmacies and seven cigar stores were visible from where she stood. She knew that modern industrial cities were considered ugly, but she liked them. "I'm glad Evy and Bert have gone to a picture show," Sadie remarked to herself after a while. "Evy gets high-strung from being at the office all day."

A little later she turned her back on the window and went to the dining room.

"Looks like the train went through here," she murmured, gazing quietly at the chairs tilted back against the wall and the table's unsightly angle; but the tumult in her breast had not subsided, even though she knew she was leaving for Camp Cataract. Beyond the first rush of joy she had experienced when her plan had revealed itself to her earlier, in the parlor, the feeling of suspense remained identical, a curious admixture of anxiety and anticipation, difficult to bear. Concerning the mechanics of the trip itself she was neither nervous nor foolishly excited. "I'll call up tomorrow," she said to herself, "and find out when the buses go, or maybe I'll take the train. In the morning I'll buy three different meats for the loaf, if I don't forget. It won't go rotten for a few days, and even if it does they can eat at Martie's or else Evy will make bologna and eggs ... she knows how, and so does Bert." She was not really concentrating on these latter projects any more than she usually did on domestic details.

The lamp over the table was suspended on a heavy iron chain. She reached for the beaded string to extinguish the light. When she released it the massive lamp swung from side to side in the darkness.

"Would you like it so much by the waterfall if you didn't know the apartment was here?" she whispered into the dark, and she was thrilled again by the beauty of her own words. "How much more I'll be able to say when I'm sitting right next to her," she murmured almost with reverence. "... And then we'll come back here," she added simply, not in the least startled to discover that the idea of returning with Harriet had been at the root of her plan all along.

Without bothering to clear the plates from the table, she went into the kitchen and extinguished the light there. She was suddenly overcome with fatigue.

When Sadie arrived at Camp Cataract it was raining hard.

"This shingled building is the main lodge," the hack driver said to her. "The ceiling in there is three times higher than average, if you like that style. Go up on the porch and just walk in. You'll get a kick out of it."

Sadie reached into her pocketbook for some money.

"My wife and I come here to drink beer when we're in the mood," he continued, getting out his change. "If there's nobody much inside, don't get panicky; the whole camp goes to the movies on Thursday nights. The wagon takes them and brings them back. They'll be along soon."

After thanking him she got out of the cab and climbed the wooden steps on to the porch. Without hesitating she opened the door. The driver had not exaggerated; the room was indeed so enormous that it suggested a gymnasium. Wicker chairs and settees were scattered from one end of the floor to the other and numberless sawed-off tree stumps had been set down to serve as little tables.

Sadie glanced around her and then headed automatically for a giant fireplace, difficult to reach because of the accumulation of chairs and settees that surrounded it. She threaded her way between these and stepped across the hearth into the cold vault of the chimney, high enough to shelter a person of average stature. The andirons, which reached to her waist, had been wrought in the shape of witches. She fingered their pointed iron hats. "Novelties," she murmured to herself without enthusiasm. "They must have been especially made." Then, peering out of the fireplace, she noticed for the first time that she was not alone. Some fifty feet away a fat woman sat reading by the light of an electric bulb.

"She doesn't even know I'm in the fireplace," she said to herself. "Because the rain's so loud, she probably didn't hear me come in." She waited patiently for a while and then, suspecting that the woman might remain oblivious to her presence indefinitely, she called over to her. "Do you have anything to do with managing Camp Cataract?" she asked, speaking loudly so that she could be heard above the rain.

The woman ceased reading and switched her big light off at once, since the strong glare prevented her seeing beyond the radius of the bulb.

"No, I don't," she answered in a booming voice. "Why?"

Sadie, finding no answer to this question, remained silent.

"Do you think I look like a manager?" the woman pursued, and since Sadie had obviously no intention of answering, she continued the conversation by herself.

"I suppose you might think I was manager here, because I'm stout, and stout people have that look; also I'm about the right age for it. But I'm not the manager ... I don't manage anything, anywhere. I have a domineering cranium all right, but I'm more the French type. I'd rather enjoy myself than give orders."

"French ..." Sadie repeated hesitantly.

"Not French," the woman corrected her. "French *type,* with a little of the actual blood." Her voice was cold and severe.

For a while neither of them spoke, and Sadie hoped the conversation had drawn to a definite close.

"Individuality is my god," the woman announced abruptly, much to Sadie's disappointment. "That's partly why I didn't go to the picture show tonight. I don't like doing what the groups do, and I've seen the film." She dragged her chair forward so as to be heard more clearly. "The steadies here—we call the ones who stay more than a fortnight steadies—are all crazy to get into birds-of-a-feather-flock-together arrangements. If you look around, you can see for yourself how clubby the furniture is fixed. Well, they can go in for it, if they want, but I won't. I keep my chair out in the open here, and when I feel like it I take myself over to one circle or another ... there's about ten or twelve circles. Don't you object to the confinement of a group?"

"We haven't got a group back home," Sadie answered briefly.

"I don't go in for group worship either," the woman continued, "any more than I do for the heavy social mixing. I don't even go in for individual worship, for that matter. Most likely I was born to such a vigorous happy nature I don't feel the need to worry about what's up there over my head. I get the full flavor out of all my days whether anyone's up there or not. The groups don't allow for that kind of zip ... never. You know what rotten apples in a barrel can do to the healthy ones."

Sadie, who had never before met an agnostic, was profoundly shocked by the woman's blasphemous attitude. "I'll bet she slept with a lot of men she wasn't married to when she was younger," she said to herself.

"Most of the humanity you bump into is unhealthy and nervous," the woman concluded, looking at Sadie with a cold eye, and then without further remarks she struggled out of her chair and began to walk toward a side door at the other end of the room. Just as she approached it the door was flung open from the other side by Beryl, whom the woman immediately warned of the new arrival. Beryl, without ceasing to spoon some beans out of a can she was holding, walked over to Sadie and offered to be of some assistance. "I can show you rooms," she suggested. "Unless you'd rather wait till the manager comes back from the movies."

When she realized, however, after a short conversation with Sadie, that she was speaking to Harriet's sister, a malevolent scowl darkened her countenance, and she spooned her beans more slowly.

"Harriet didn't tell me you were coming," she said at length; her tone was unmistakably disagreeable.

Sadie's heart commenced to beat very fast as she in turn realized that this woman in plus-fours was the waitress, Beryl, of whom Harriet had often spoken in her letters and at home.

"It's a surprise," Sadie told her. "I meant to come here before. I've been promising Harriet I'd visit her in camp for a long time now, but I couldn't come until I got a neighbor in to cook for Evy and Bert. They're a husband and wife ... my sister Evy and her husband Bert."

"I know about those two," Beryl remarked sullenly. "Harriet's told me all about them."

"Will you please take me to my sister's cabin?" Sadie asked, picking up her valise and stepping forward.

Beryl continued to stir her beans around without moving.

"I thought you folks had some kind of arrangement," she said. She had recorded in her mind entire passages of Harriet's monologues out of love for her friend, although she felt no curiosity concerning the material she had gathered. "I thought you folks were supposed to stay in the apartment while she was away at camp."

"Bert Hoffer and Evy have never visited Camp Cataract," Sadie answered in a tone that was innocent of any subterfuge.

"You bet they haven't," Beryl pronounced triumphantly. "That's part of the arrangement. They're supposed to stay in the apartment while she's here at camp; the doctor said so."

"They're not coming up," Sadie repeated, and she still wore, not the foxy look that Beryl expected would betray itself at any moment, but the look of a person who is attentive though being addressed in a foreign language. The waitress sensed that all her attempts at starting a scrap had been successfully blocked for the present and she whistled carefully, dragging some chairs into line with a rough hand. "I'll tell you what," she said, ceasing her activities as suddenly as she had begun them. "Instead of taking you down there to the Pine Cones— that's the name of the grove where her cabin is—I'll go myself and tell her to come up here to the lodge. She's got some nifty rain equipment so she won't get wet coming through the groves like you would ... lots of pine trees out there."

Sadie nodded in silence and walked over to a fantasy chair, where she sat down.

"They get a lot of fun out of that chair. When they're drunk," said Beryl pointing to its back, made of a giant straw disc. "Well ... so long...." She strode away. "Dear Valley ..." Sadie heard her sing as she went out the door.

Sadie lifted the top off the chair's left arm and pulled two books out of its woven hamper. The larger volume was entitled *The Growth and Development of the Texas Oil Companies,* and the smaller, *Stories from Other Climes.* Hastily she replaced them and closed the lid.

Harriet opened the door for Beryl and quickly shut it again, but even in that instant the wooden flooring of the threshold was thoroughly soaked with rain. She was wearing a lavender kimono with a deep ruffle at the neckline; above it her face shone pale with dismay at Beryl's late and unexpected visit. She feared that perhaps the waitress was drunk. "I'm certainly not hacking out a free place for myself in this world just in order to cope with drunks," she said to herself with bitter verve. Her loose hair was hanging to her shoulders and Beryl looked at it for a moment in mute admiration before making her announcement.

"Your sister Sadie's up at the lodge," she said, recovering herself; then, feeling embarrassed, she shuffled over to her usual seat in the darkest corner of the room.

"What are you saying?" Harriet questioned her sharply.

"Your sister Sadie's up at the lodge," she repeated, not daring to look at her. "Your sister Sadie who wrote you the letter about the apartment."

"But she can't be!" Harriet screeched. "She can't be! It was all arranged that no one was to visit me here."

"That's what I told her," Beryl put in.

Harriet began pacing up and down the floor. Her pupils were dilated and she looked as if she were about to lose all control of herself. Abruptly she flopped down on the edge of the bed and began gulping in great draughts of air. She was actually practicing a system which she believed had often saved her from complete hysteria, but Beryl, who knew nothing about her method, was horrified and utterly bewildered. "Take it easy," she implored Harriet. "Take it easy!"

"Dash some water in my face," said Harriet in a strange voice, but horror and astonishment anchored Beryl securely to her chair, so that Harriet was forced to stagger over to the basin and manage by herself. After five minutes of steady dousing she wiped her face and chest with a towel and resumed her pacing. At each instant the expression on her face was more indignant and a trifle less distraught. "It's the boorishness of it that I find so appalling," she complained, a suggestion of theatricality in her tone which a moment before had not been present. "If she's determined to wreck my schemes, why doesn't she do it with some style, a little slight bit of cunning? I can't picture anything more boorish than hauling oneself onto a train and simply chugging straight up here. She has no sense of scheming, of intrigue in the grand manner ... none whatever. Anyone meeting only Sadie would think the family raised potatoes for a living. Evy doesn't make a much better impression, I must say. If they met her they'd decide we were all clerks! But at least she goes to business.... She doesn't sit around thinking about how to mess my life up all day. She thinks about Bert Hoffer. Ugh!" She made a wry face.

"When did you and Sadie start fighting?" Beryl asked her.

"I don't fight with Sadie," Harriet answered, lifting her head proudly. "I wouldn't dream of fighting like a common fishwife. Everything that goes on between us goes on undercover. It's always been that way. I've always hidden everything from her ever since I was a little girl. She's perfectly aware that I know she's trying to hold me a prisoner in the apartment out of plain jealousy and she knows too that I'm afraid of being considered a bum, and that makes matters simpler for her. She pretends to be worried that I might forget myself if I left the apartment and commit a folly with some man I wasn't married to, but actually she knows perfectly well that I'm as cold as ice. I haven't the slightest interest in men ... nor in women either for that matter; still if I stormed out of the apartment dramatically the way some do, they might think I was a bum on my way to a man ... and I won't give Sadie that satisfaction, ever. As for marriage, of course I admit I'm peculiar and there's a bit wrong with me, but even so I shouldn't want to marry: I think the whole system of going through life with a partner is repulsive in every way." She paused, but only for a second. "Don't you imagine, however," she added severely, looking directly at Beryl, "don't you imagine that just because I'm a bit peculiar and different from the others, that I'm not fussy about my life. I *am* fussy about it, and I *hate* a scandal."

"To hell with sisters!" Beryl exclaimed happily. "Give 'em all a good swift kick in the pants." She had regained her own composure watching the color return to Harriet's cheeks and she was just beginning to think with pleasure that perhaps Sadie's arrival would serve to strengthen the bond of intimacy between herself and Harriet, when this latter buried her head in her lap and burst into tears. Beryl's face fell and she blushed at her own frivolousness.

"I can't any more," Harriet sobbed in anguished tones. "I can't ... I'm old ... I'm much too old." Here she collapsed and sobbed so pitifully that Beryl, wringing her hands in grief, sprang to her side, for she was a most tenderhearted person toward those whom she loved. "You are not old ... you are beautiful," she said, blushing again, and in her heart she was thankful that Providence had granted her the occasion to console her friend in a grief-stricken moment, and to compliment her at the same time.

After a bit, Harriet's sobbing subsided, and jumping up from the bed, she grabbed the waitress. "Beryl," she gasped, "you must run back to the lodge right away." There was a beam of cunning in her tear-filled eyes.

"Sure will," Beryl answered.

"Go back to the lodge and see if there's a room left up there, and if there is, take her grip into it so that there will be no question of her staying in my cabin. I can't have her staying in my cabin. It's the only place I have in the whole wide world." The beam of cunning disappeared again and she looked at Beryl with wide, frightened eyes. "... And if there's no room?" she asked.

"Then I'll put her in my place," Beryl reassured her. "I've got a neat little cabin all to myself that she can have and I'll go bunk in with some dopey waitress."

"Well, then," said Harriet, "go, and hurry! Take her grip to a room in the upper lodge annex or to your own cabin before she has a chance to say anything, and then come straight back here for me. I can't get through these pine groves alone ... now ... I know I can't." It did not occur to her to thank Beryl for the kind offer she had made.

"All right," said the waitress, "I'll be back in a jiffy and don't you worry about a thing." A second later she was lumbering through the drenched pine groves with shining eyes.

When Beryl came into the lodge and snatched Sadie's grip up without a word of explanation, Sadie did not protest. Opposite her there was an open staircase which led to a narrow gallery hanging halfway between the ceiling and the floor. She watched the waitress climbing the stairs, but once she had passed the landing Sadie did not trouble to look up and follow her progress around the wooden balcony overhead.

A deep chill had settled into her bones, and she was like a person benumbed. Exactly when this present state had succeeded the earlier one Sadie could not tell, nor did she think to ask herself such a question, but a feeling of dread now lay like a stone in her breast where before there had been stirring such powerful sensations of excitement and suspense. "I'm so low," she said to herself. "I feel like I was sitting at my own funeral." She did not say this in the spirit of hyperbolic gloom which some people nurture to work themselves out of a bad mood, but in all seriousness and with her customary attitude of passivity; in fact, she wore the humble look so often visible on the faces of sufferers who are being treated in a free clinic. It did not occur to her that a connection might exist between her present dismal state and the mission she had come to fulfill at Camp Cataract, nor did she take any notice of the fact that the words which were to enchant Harriet and accomplish her return were no longer welling up in her throat as they had done all the past week. She feared that something dreadful might happen, but whatever it was, this disaster was as remotely connected with her possible train wreck. "I hope nothing bad happens ..." she thought, but she didn't have much hope in her.

Harriet slammed the front door and Sadie looked up. For the first second or two she did not recognize the woman who stood on the threshold in her dripping rubber coat and hood. Beryl was beside her; puddles were forming around the feet of the two women. Harriet had rouged her cheeks rather more highly than usual in order to hide all traces of her crying spell. Her eyes were bright and she wore a smile that was fixed and hard.

"Not a night fit for man or beast," she shouted across to Sadie, using a voice that she thought sounded hearty and yet fashionable at the same time; she did this, not in order to impress her sister, but to keep her at a safe distance.

Sadie, instead of rushing to the door, stared at her with an air of perplexity. To her Harriet appeared more robust and coarse-featured than she had five weeks ago at the apartment, and yet she knew that such a rapid change of physiognomy was scarcely possible. Recovering, she rose and went to embrace her sister. The embrace failed to reassure her because of Harriet's wet rubber coat, and her feeling of estrangement became more defined. She backed away.

Upon hearing her own voice ring out in such hearty and fashionable tones, Harriet had felt crazily confident that she might, by continuing to affect this manner, hold her sister at bay for the duration of her visit. To increase her chances of success she had determined right then not to ask Sadie why she had come, but to treat the visit in the most casual and natural way possible.

"Have you put on fat?" Sadie asked, at a loss for anything else to say.

"I'll never be fat," Harriet replied quickly. "I'm a fruit lover, not a lover of starches."

"Yes, you love fruit," Sadie said nervously. "Do you want some? I have an apple left from my lunch."

Harriet looked aghast. "Now!" she exclaimed. "Beryl can tell you that I never eat at night; in fact I never come up to the lodge at night, *never*. I stay in my cabin. I've written you all about how early I get up ... I don't know any-thing about the lodge at night," she added almost angrily, as though her sister had accused her of being festive.

"You don't?" Sadie looked at her stupidly.

"No, I don't. Are you hungry, by the way?"

"If she's hungry," put in Beryl, "we can go into the Grotto Room and I'll bring her the food there. The tables in the main dining room are all set up for tomorrow morning's breakfast."

"I despise the Grotto," said Harriet with surprising bitterness. Her voice was getting quite an edge to it, and although it still sounded fashionable it was no longer hearty.

"I'm not hungry," Sadie assured them both. "I'm sleepy."

"Well, then," Harriet replied quickly, jumping at the opportunity, "we'll sit here for a few minutes and then you must go to bed."

The three of them settled in wicker chairs close to the cold hearth. Sadie was seated opposite the other two, who both remained in their rubber coats.

"I really do despise the Grotto," Harriet went on. "Actually I don't hang around the lodge at all. This is not the part of Camp Cataract that interests me. I'm interested in the pine groves, my cabin, the rocks, the streams, the bridge, and all the surrounding natural beauty ... the sky also."

Although the rain still continued its drumming on the roof above them, to Sadie, Harriet's voice sounded intolerably loud, and she could not rid herself of the impression that her sister's face had grown fatter. "Now," she heard Harriet saying in her loud voice, "tell me about the apartment.... What's new, how are the dinners coming along, how are Evy and Bert?"

Fortunately, while Sadie was struggling to answer these questions, which unaccountably she found it difficult to do, the stout agnostic reappeared, and Harriet was immediately distracted.

"Rover," she called gaily across the room, "come and sit with us. My sister Sadie's here."

The woman joined them, seating herself beside Beryl, so that Sadie was now facing all three.

"It's a surprise to see you up at the lodge at night, Hermit," she remarked to Harriet without a spark of mischief in her voice.

"You see!" Harriet nodded at Sadie with immense satisfaction. "I was not fibbing, was I? How are Evy and Bert?" she asked again, her face twitching a bit. "Is the apartment hot?"

Sadie nodded.

"I don't know how long you plan to stay," Harriet rattled on, feeling increasingly powerful and therefore reckless, "but I'm going on a canoe trip the day after tomorrow for five days. We're going up the river to Pocahontas Falls.... I leave at four in the morning, too, which rather ruins tomorrow as well. I've been looking forward to this trip ever since last spring when I applied for my seat, back at the apartment. The canoes are limited, and the guides.... I'm devoted to canoe trips, as you know, and can fancy myself a redskin all the way to the Falls and back, easily."

Sadie did not answer.

"There's nothing weird about it," Harriet argued. "It's in keeping with my hatred of industrialization. In any case, you can see what a chopped-up day tomorrow's going to be. I have to make my pack in the morning and I must be in bed by eight-thirty at night, the latest, so that I can get up at four. I'll have only one real meal, at two in the afternoon. I suggest we meet at two behind the souvenir booth; you'll notice it tomorrow." Harriet waited expectantly for Sadie to answer in agreement to this suggestion, but her sister remained silent.

"Speaking of the booth," said Rover, "I'm not taking home a single souvenir this year. They're expensive and they don't last."

"You can buy salt-water taffy at Gerald's Store in town," Beryl told her. "I saw some there last week. It's a little stale but very cheap."

"Why would they sell salt-water taffy in the mountains?" Rover asked irritably.

Sadie was half listening to the conversation; as she sat watching them, all three women were suddenly unrecognizable; it was as if she had flung open the door to some dentist's office and seen three strangers seated there. She sprang to her feet in terror.

Harriet was horrified. "What is it?" she yelled at her sister. "Why do you look like that? Are you mad?"

Sadie was pale and beads of sweat were forming under her felt hat, but the women opposite her had already regained their correct relation to herself and the present moment. Her face relaxed, and although her legs were trembling as a result of her brief but shocking experience, she felt immensely relieved that it was all over.

"Why did you jump up?" Harriet screeched at her. "Is it because you are at Camp Cataract and not at the apartment?"

"It must have been the long train trip and no food ..." Sadie told herself, "only one sandwich."

"Is it because you are at Camp Cataract and not at the apartment?" Harriet insisted. She was really very frightened and wished to establish Sadie's fit as a purposeful one and not as an involuntary seizure similar to one of hers.

"It was a long and dirty train trip," Sadie said in a weary voice. "I had only one sandwich all day long, with no mustard or butter ... just the processed meat. I didn't even eat my fruit."

"Beryl offered to serve you food in the Grotto!" Harriet ranted. "Do you want some now or not? For heaven's sake, speak up!"

"No ... no." Sadie shook her head sorrowfully. "I think I'd best go to bed. Take me to your cabin ... I've got my slippers and my kimono and my night-gown in my satchel," she added, looking around her vaguely, for the fact that Beryl had carried her grip off had never really impressed itself upon her con-sciousness.

Harriet glanced at Beryl with an air of complicity and managed to give her a quick pinch. "Beryl's got you fixed up in one of the upper lodge annex rooms," she told Sadie in a false, chatterbox voice. "You'll be much more com-fortable up here than you would be down in my cabin. We all use oil lamps in the grove and you know how dependent you are on electricity."

Sadie didn't know whether she was dependent on electricity or not since she had never really lived without it, but she was so tired that she said nothing.

"I get up terribly early and my cabin's drafty, besides," Harriet went on. "You'll be much more comfortable here. You'd hate the Boulder Dam wig-wams as well. Anyway, the wigwams are really for boys and they're always full. There's a covered bridge leading from this building to the annex on the upper floor, so that's an advantage."

"O.K., folks," Beryl cut in, judging that she could best help Harriet by spurring them on to action. "Let's get going."

"Yes," Harriet agreed, "if we don't get out of the lodge soon the crowd will come back from the movies and we certainly want to avoid them."

They bade good night to Rover and started up the stairs.

"This balustrade is made of young birch limbs," Harriet told Sadie as they walked along the narrow gallery overhead. "I think it's very much in keeping with the lodge, don't you?"

"Yes, I do," Sadie answered.

Beryl opened the door leading from the balcony onto a covered bridge and stepped through it, motioning to the others. "Here we go onto the bridge," she said, looking over her shoulder. "You've never visited the annex, have you?" she asked Harriet.

"I've never had any reason to," Harriet answered in a huffy tone. "You know how I feel about my cabin."

They walked along the imperfectly fitted boards in the darkness. Gusts of wind blew about their ankles and they were constantly spattered with rain in spite of the wooden roofing. They reached the door at the other end very quickly, however, where they descended two steps leading into a short, brightly lit hall. Beryl closed the door to the bridge behind them. The smell of fresh plaster and cement thickened the damp air.

"This is the annex," said Beryl. "We put old ladies here mostly, because they can get back and forth to the dining room without going outdoors ... and they've got the toilet right here, too." She flung open the door and showed it to them. "Then also," she added, "we don't like the old ladies dealing with oil lamps and here they've got electricity." She led them into a little room just at their left and switched on the light. "Pretty smart, isn't it?" she remarked, looking around her with evident satisfaction, as if she herself had designed the room; then, sauntering over to a modernistic wardrobe-bureau combination, she polished a corner of it with her pocket handkerchief. This piece was made of shiny brown wood and fitted with a rimless circular mirror. "Strong and good-looking," Beryl said, rapping on the wood with her knuckles. "Every room's got one."

Sadie sank down on the edge of the bed without removing her outer garments. Here, too, the smell of plaster and cement permeated the air, and the wind still blew about their ankles, this time from under the badly constructed doorsill.

"The cabins are much draftier than this," Harriet assured Sadie once again. "You'll be more comfortable here in the annex." She felt confident that establishing her sister in the annex would facilitate her plan, which was still to prevent her from saying whatever she had come to say.

Sadie was terribly tired. Her hat, dampened by the rain, pressed uncomfortably against her temples, but she did not attempt to remove it. "I think I've got to go to sleep," she muttered. "I can't stay awake any more."

"All right," said Harriet, "but don't forget tomorrow at two by the souvenir booth ... you can't miss it. I don't want to see anyone in the morning because I can make my canoe pack better by myself ... it's frightfully complicated.... But if I hurried I could meet you at one-thirty; would you prefer that?"

Sadie nodded.

"Then I'll do my best.... You see, in the morning I always practice imagination for an hour or two. It does me lots of good, but tomorrow I'll cut it short." She kissed Sadie lightly on the crown of her felt hat. "Good night," she said. "Is there anything I forgot to ask you about the apartment?"

"No," Sadie assured her. "You asked everything."

"Well, good night," said Harriet once again, and followed by Beryl, she left the room.

When Sadie awakened the next morning a feeling of dread still rested like a leaden weight on her chest. No sooner had she left the room than panic, like a small wing, started to beat under her heart. She was inordinately fearful that if she strayed any distance from the main lodge she would lose her way and so arrive late for her meeting with Harriet. This fear drove her to stand next to the souvenir booth fully an hour ahead of time. Fortunately the booth, situated on a small knoll, commanded an excellent view of the cataract, which spilled down from some high rock ledges above a deep chasm. A fancy bridge spanned this chasm only a few feet below her, so that she was able to watch the people crossing it as they walked back and forth between the camp site and the waterfall. An Indian chief in full war regalia was seated at the bridge entrance on a kitchen chair. His magnificent feather headdress curved gracefully in the breeze as he busied himself collecting the small toll that all the tourists paid on returning from the waterfall; he supplied them with change from a nickel-plated conductor's belt which he wore over his deer-hide jacket, embroidered with minute beads. He was an Irishman employed by the management, which supplied his costume. Lately he had grown careless, and often neglected to stain his freckled hands the deep brick color of his face. He divided his time between the bridge and the souvenir booth, clambering up the knoll whenever he sighted a customer.

A series of wooden arches, Gothic in conception, succeeded each other all the way across the bridge; bright banners fluttered from their rims, each one stamped with the initials of the camp, and some of them edged with a glossy fringe. Only a few feet away lay the dining terrace, a huge flagstone pavilion whose entire length skirted the chasm's edge.

Unfortunately, neither the holiday crowds, nor the festooned bridge, nor even the white waters of the cataract across the way could distract Sadie from her misery. She constantly glanced behind her at the dark pine groves wherein Harriet's cabin was concealed. She dreaded to see Harriet's shape define itself between the trees, but at the same time she feared that if her sister did not arrive shortly some terrible catastrophe would befall them both before she'd had a chance to speak. In truth all desire to convince her sister that she should leave Camp Cataract and return to the apartment had miraculously shriveled away, and with the desire, the words to express it had vanished too. This did not in any way alter her intention of accomplishing her mission; on the contrary, it seemed to her all the more desperately important now that she was almost certain, in her innermost heart, that her trip was already a failure. Her attitude was not an astonishing one, since like many others she conceived of her life as separate from herself; the road was laid out always a little ahead of her by sacred hands, and she walked down it without a question. This road, which was her life, would go on existing after her death, even as her death existed now while she still lived.

There were close to a hundred people dining on the terrace, and the water's roar so falsified the clamor of voices that one minute the guests seemed to be speaking from a great distance and the next right at her elbow. Every now and then she thought she heard someone pronounce her name in a dismal tone, and however much she told herself that this was merely the waterfall playing its tricks on her ears she shuddered each time at the sound of her name. Her very position next to the booth began to embarrass her. She tucked her hands into her coat sleeves so that they would not show, and tried to keep her eyes fixed on the foaming waters across the way, but she had noticed a disapproving look in the eyes of the diners nearest her, and she could not resist glancing back at the terrace every few minutes in the hope that she had been mistaken. Each time, however, she was more convinced that she had read their expressions correctly, and that these people believed, not only that she was standing there for no good reason, but that she was a genuine vagrant who could not afford the price of a dinner. She was therefore immensely relieved when she caught sight of Harriet advancing between the tables from the far end of the dining pavilion. As she drew nearer, Sadie noticed that she was wearing her black winter coat trimmed with red fur, and that her marceled hair remained neatly arranged in spite of the strong wind. Much to her relief Harriet had omitted to rouge her cheeks and her face therefore had regained its natural proportions. She saw Harriet wave at the sight of her and quicken her step. Sadie was pleased that the diners were to witness the impending meeting. "When they see us together," she thought, "they'll realize that I'm no vagrant, but a decent woman visiting her sister." She herself started down the knoll to hasten the meeting. "I thought you'd come out of the pine grove," she called out, as soon as they were within a few feet of one another. "I kept looking that way."

"I would have ordinarily," Harriet answered, reaching her side and kissing her lightly on the cheek, "but I went to the other end of the terrace first, to reserve a table for us from the waiter in charge there. That end is quieter, so it will be more suitable for a long talk."

"Good," thought Sadie as they climbed up the knoll together. "Her night's sleep has done her a world of good." She studied Harriet's face anxiously as they paused next to the souvenir booth, and discovered a sweet light reflected in her eyes. All at once she remembered their childhood together and the great tenderness Harriet had often shown towards her then.

"They have Turkish pilaff on the menu," said Harriet, "so I told the waiter to save some for you. It's such a favorite that it usually runs out at the very beginning. I know how much you love it."

Sadie, realizing that Harriet was actually eager for this dinner, the only one they would eat together at Camp Cataract, to be a success, felt the terrible leaden weight lifted from her heart; it disappeared so suddenly that for a moment or two she was like a balloon without its ballast; she could barely refrain from dancing about in delight. Harriet tugged on her arm.

"I think we'd better go now," she urged Sadie, "then after lunch we can come back here if you want to buy some souvenirs for Evy and Bert ... and maybe for Flo and Carl and Bobby too...."

Sadie bent down to adjust her cotton stockings, which were wrinkling badly at the ankles, and when she straightened up again her eyes lighted on three men dining very near the edge of the terrace; she had not noticed them before. They were all eating corn on the cob and big round hamburger sandwiches in absolute silence. To protect their clothing from spattering kernels, they had converted their napkins into bibs.

"Bert Hoffer's careful of his clothes too," Sadie reflected, and then she turned to her sister. "Don't you think men look different sitting all by themselves without women?" she asked her. She felt an extraordinary urge to chat—an urge which she could not remember ever having experienced before.

"I think," Harriet replied, as though she had not heard Sadie's comment, "that we'd better go to our table before the waiter gives it to someone else."

"I don't like men," Sadie announced without venom, and she was about to follow Harriet when her attention was arrested by the eyes of the man nearest her. Slowly lowering his corn cob to his plate, he stared across at her, his mouth twisted into a bitter smile. She stood as if rooted to the ground, and under his steady gaze all her newborn joy rapidly drained away. With desperation she realized that Harriet, darting in and out between the crowded tables, would soon be out of sight. After making what seemed to her a superhuman effort she tore herself away from the spot where she stood and lunged after Harriet shouting her name.

Harriet was at her side again almost instantly, looking up at her with a startled expression. Together they returned to the souvenir booth, where Sadie stopped and assumed a slightly bent position as if she were suffering from an abdominal pain.

"What's the trouble?" she heard Harriet asking with concern. "Are you feeling ill?"

Instead of answering Sadie laid her hand heavily on her sister's arm and stared at her with a hunted expression in her eyes.

"Please try not to look so much like a gorilla," said Harriet in a kind voice, but Sadie, although she recognized the accuracy of this observation (for she could feel very well that she was looking like a gorilla), was powerless to change her expression, at least for a moment or two. "Come with me," she said finally, grabbing Harriet's hand and pulling her along with almost brutal force. "I've got something to tell you."

She headed down a narrow path leading into a thickly planted section of the grove, where she thought they were less likely to be disturbed. Harriet followed with such a quick, light step that Sadie felt no pull behind her at all and her sister's hand, folded in her own thick palm, seemed as delicate as the body of a bird. Finally they entered a small clearing where they stopped. Harriet untied a handkerchief from around her neck and mopped her brow. "Gracious!" she said. "It's frightfully hot in here." She offered the kerchief to Sadie. "I suppose it's because we walked so fast and because the pine trees shut out all the wind.... First I'll sit down and then you must tell me what's wrong." She stepped over to a felled tree whose length blocked the clearing. Its torn roots were shockingly exposed, whereas the upper trunk and branches lay hidden in the surrounding grove. Harriet sat down; Sadie was about to sit next to her when she noticed a dense swarm of flies near the roots. Automatically she stepped toward them. "Why are they here?" she asked herself—then immediately she spotted the cause, an open can of beans some careless person had deposited inside a small hollow at the base of the trunk. She turned away in disgust and looked at Harriet. Her sister was seated on the fallen tree, her back gracefully erect and her head tilted in a listening attitude. The filtered light imparted to her face an incredibly fragile and youthful look, and Sadie gazed at her with tenderness and wonder. No sound reached them in the clearing, and she realized with a pounding heart that she could no longer postpone telling Harriet why she had come. She could not have wished for a moment more favorable to the accomplishment of her purpose. The stillness in the air, their isolation, the expectant and gentle light in Harriet's eye, all these elements should have combined to give her back her faith—faith in her own powers to persuade Harriet to come home with her and live among them once again, winter and summer alike, as she had always done before. She opened her mouth to speak and doubled over, clutching at her stomach as though an animal were devouring her. Sweat beaded her forehead and she planted her feet wide apart on the ground as if this animal would be born. Though her vision was barred with pain, she saw Harriet's tear-filled eyes searching hers.

"Let's not go back to the apartment," Sadie said, hearing her own words as if they issued not from her mouth but from a pit in the ground. "Let's not go back there ... let's you and me go out in the world ... just the two of us." A second before covering her face to hide her shame Sadie glimpsed Harriet's eyes, impossibly close to her own, their pupils pointed with a hatred such as she had never seen before.

It seemed to Sadie that it was taking an eternity for her sister to leave. "Go away ... go away ... or I'll suffocate." She was moaning the words over and over again, her face buried deep in her hands. "Go away ... please go away ... I'll suffocate...." She could not tell, however, whether she was thinking these words or speaking them aloud.

At last she heard Harriet's footstep on the dry branches, as she started out of the clearing. Sadie listened, but although one step followed another, the cracking sound of the dry branches did not grow any fainter as Harriet penetrated farther into the grove. Sadie knew then that this agony she was suffering was itself the dreaded voyage into the world—the very voyage she had always feared Harriet would make. That she herself was making it instead of Harriet did not affect her certainty that this was it.

Sadie stood at the souvenir booth looking at some birchbark canoes. The wind was blowing colder and stronger than it had a while ago, or perhaps it only seemed this way to her, so recently returned from the airless clearing. She did not recall her trip back through the grove; she was conscious only of her haste to buy some souvenirs and to leave. Some chains of paper tacked to the side of the booth as decoration kept flying into her face. The Indian chief was smiling at her from behind the counter of souvenirs.

"What can I do for you?" he asked.

"I'm leaving," said Sadie, "so I want souvenirs...."

"Take your choice; you've got birchbark canoes with or without mailing cards attached, Mexican sombrero ashtrays, exhilarating therapeutic pine cushions filled with the regional needles ... and banners for a boy's room."

"There's no boy home," Sadie said, having caught only these last words.

"How about cushions ... or canoes?"

She nodded.

"Which do you want?"

"Both," she answered quickly.

"How many?"

Sadie closed her eyes. Try as she would she could not count up the members of the family. She could not even reach an approximate figure. "Eleven," she blurted out finally, in desperation.

"Eleven of each?" he asked raising his eyebrows.

"Yes ... yes," she answered quickly, batting the paper chains out of her face, "eleven of each."

"You sure don't forget the old folks at home, do you?" he said, beginning to collect the canoes. He made an individual package of each souvenir and then wrapped them all together in coarse brown paper which he bound with thick twine.

Sadie had given him a note and he was punching his money belt for the correct change when her eyes fell on his light, freckled hand. Startled, she shifted her glance from his hand punching the nickel belt to his brick-colored face streaked with purple and vermilion paint. For the first time she noticed his Irish blue eyes. Slowly the hot flush of shame crept along the nape of her neck. It was the same unbearable mortification that she had experienced in the clearing; it spread upward from her neck to the roots of her hair, coloring her face a dark red. That she was ashamed for the Indian this time, and not of her own words, failed to lessen the intensity of her suffering; the boundaries of her pride had never been firmly fixed inside herself. She stared intently at his Irish blue eyes, so oddly light in his brick-colored face. What was it? She was tormented by the sight of an incongruity she couldn't name. All at once she remembered the pavilion and the people dining there; her heart started to pound. "They'll see it," she said to herself in a panic. "They'll see it and they'll know that I've seen it too." Somehow this latter possibility was the most perilous of all.

"They must never know I've seen it," she said, grinding her teeth, and she leaned over the counter, crushing some canoes under her chest. "Quickly," she whispered. "Go out your little door and meet me back of the booth...."

A second later she found him there. "Listen!" She clutched his hand. "We must hurry ... I didn't mean to see you ... I'm sorry ... I've been trying not to look at you for years ... for years and years and years...." She gaped at him in horror. "Why are you standing there? We've got to hurry.... They haven't caught me looking at you yet, but we've got to hurry." She headed for the bridge, leading the Indian behind her. He followed quickly without saying a word.

The water's roar increased in volume as they approached the opposite bank of the chasm, and Sadie found relief in the sound. Once off the bridge she ran as fast as she could along the path leading to the waterfall. The Indian followed close on her heels, his hand resting lightly in her own, as Harriet's had earlier when they'd sped together through the grove. Reaching the waterfall, she edged along the wall of rock until she stood directly behind the water's cascade. With a cry of delight she leaned back in the curve of the wall, insensible to its icy dampness, which penetrated even through the thickness of her woollen coat. She listened to the cataract's deafening roar and her heart almost burst for joy, because she had hidden the Indian safely behind the cascade where he could be neither seen nor heard. She turned around and smiled at him kindly. He too smiled, and she no longer saw in his face any trace of the incongruity that had shocked her so before.

The foaming waters were so beautiful to see. Sadie stepped forward, holding her hand out to the Indian.

When Harriet awakened that morning all traces of her earlier victorious mood had vanished. She felt certain that disaster would overtake her before she could start out for Pocahontas Falls. Heavyhearted and with fumbling hands, she set about making her pack. Luncheon with Sadie was an impossible cliff which she did not have the necessary strength to scale. When she came to three round cushions that had to be snapped into their rainproof casings she gave up with a groan and rushed headlong out of her cabin in search of Beryl.

Fortunately Beryl waited table on the second shift and so she found her reading a magazine, with one leg flung over the arm of her chair.

"I can't make my pack," Harriet said hysterically, bursting into Beryl's cabin without even knocking on the door.

Beryl swung her leg around and got out of her chair, "I'll make your pack," she said in a calm voice, knocking some tobacco out of her pipe. "I would have come around this morning, but you said last night you wanted to make it alone."

"It's Sadie," Harriet complained. "It's that cursed lunch with Sadie. I can't go through with it. I know I can't. I shouldn't have to in the first place. She's not even supposed to be here.... I'm an ass...."

"To hell with sisters," said Beryl. "Give 'em all a good swift kick in the pants."

"She's going to stop me from going on my canoe trip ... I know she is...." Harriet had adopted the whining tone of a little girl.

"No, she isn't," said Beryl, speaking with authority.

"Why not?" Harriet asked. She looked at Beryl almost wistfully.

"She'd better not try anything ..." said Beryl. "Ever hear of jujitsu?" She grunted with satisfaction. "Come on, we'll go make your pack." She was so pleased with Harriet's new state of dependency that she was rapidly overcoming her original shyness. An hour later she had completed the pack, and Harriet was dressed and ready.

"Will you go with me to the souvenir booth?" she begged the waitress. "I don't want to meet her alone." She was in a worse state of nerves than ever.

"I'll go with you," said Beryl, "but let's stop at my cabin on the way so I can change into my uniform. I'm on duty soon."

They were nearly twenty minutes late arriving at the booth, and Harriet was therefore rather surprised not to see Sadie standing there. "Perhaps she's been here and gone back to the lodge for a minute," she said to Beryl. "I'll find out." She walked up to the souvenir counter and questioned the Indian, with whom she was slightly familiar. "Was there a woman waiting here a while ago, Timothy?" she asked.

"A dark middle-aged woman?"

"That's right."

"She was here for an hour or more," he said, "never budged from this stall until about fifteen minutes ago."

"She couldn't have been here an hour!" Harriet argued. "Not my sister.... I told her one-thirty and it's not yet two."

"Then it wasn't your sister. The woman who was here stayed more than an hour, without moving. I noticed her because it was such a queer-looking thing. I noticed her first from my chair at the bridge and then when I came up here she was still standing by the booth. She must have stood here over an hour."

"Then it was a different middle-aged woman."

"That may be," he agreed, "but anyway, this one left about fifteen minutes ago. After standing all that time she turned around all of a sudden and bought a whole bunch of souvenirs from me ... then just when I was punching my belt for the change she said something I couldn't understand—it sounded like Polish—and then she lit out for the bridge before I could give her a penny. That woman's got impulses," he added with a broad grin. "If she's your sister, I'll give you her change, in case she don't stop here on her way back.... But she sounded to me like a Polak."

"Beryl," said Harriet, "run across the bridge and see if Sadie's behind the waterfall. I'm sure this Polish woman wasn't Sadie, but they might both be back there.... If she's not there, we'll look in the lodge."

When Beryl returned her face was dead white; she stared at Harriet in silence, and even when Harriet finally grabbed hold of her shoulders and shook her hard, she would not say anything.

DIONNE BRAND

PHOTOGRAPH

Dionne Brand (b. 1953) was born in Trinidad and has lived for close to thirty years in Canada. She studied English and philosophy as an under-graduate at the University of Toronto, and later received her M.A. in philosophy of education. A dedicated community activist, Brand was involved in the People's Revolutionary Government of Grenada; she returned to Canada upon the U.S. invasion of Grenada in 1983. In Canada, Brand has openly deployed her personal politics as black, lesbian, feminist, and socialist in a variety of professions. She has held positions as university instructor, writer in residence, poet, storyteller, columnist, historian, and documentary film director. Sisters in the Struggle *(1991) is only one of Brand's several National Film Board productions. Her collections such as* No Language Is Neutral *(1990) and* Land to Light On *(1997), which won the Governor General's award for poetry, have established Brand's fame as a poet. Her poems and stories have been widely anthologized and performed at public readings, and in 1996 she published her first novel,* In Another Place, Not Here.

On the cutting edge of Canada's literary scene, Brand's writing is uncompromisingly vivid and close to the bone. Her writing assumes a kind of guerrilla stance, making the reader painfully aware of the colonial and patriarchal prejudices inherent in language and then turning that language upon itself in precise, explosive articulations. For Brand, the revolutionary potential of literature lies in its "perfect way of speaking, of communicating between people." Brand's recent film Listening for Something *(1996) presents a dialogue between Brand and the U.S. feminist poet Adrienne Rich, who calls Brand's novel "concrete and visionary as a dream ... a great work of beauty and moral imagination."*

My grandmother has left no trace, no sign of her self. There is no photograph, except one which she took with much trouble for her identity card. I remember the day that she had to take it. It was for voting, when we got Independence; and my grandmother, with fear in her eyes, woke up that morning, got dressed, put on her hat and left. It was the small beige hat with the lace piece for the face. There was apprehension in the house. My grandmother, on these occasions, the rare ones when she left the house, patted her temples with limacol. Her smelling salts were placed in her purse. The little bottle with the green crystals and liquid had a pungent odour and a powerful aura for me until I was much older. She never let us touch it. She kept it in her purse, now held tightly in one hand, the same hand which held her one embroidered handkerchief.

That morning we all woke up and were put to work getting my grandmother ready to go to the identity card place.

One of us put the water to boil for my grandmother's bath; my big sister combed her hair and the rest of us were dispatched to get shoes, petticoat, or stockings. My grandmother's mouth moved nervously as these events took place and her fingers hardened over ours each time our clumsy efforts crinkled a pleat or spilled scent.

We were an ever-growing bunch of cousins, sisters and brothers. My grandmother's grandchildren. Children of my grandmother's daughters. We were seven in all, from time to time more, given to my grandmother for safe-keeping. Eula, Kat, Ava and I were sisters. Eula was the oldest. Genevieve, Wil and Dri were sister and brothers and our cousins. Our mothers were away. Away-away or in the country-away. That's all we knew of them except for their photographs which we used tauntingly in our battles about whose mother was prettier.

Like the bottle of smelling salts, all my grandmother's things had that same aura. We would wait until she was out of sight, which only meant that she was in the kitchen since she never left the house, and then we would try on her dresses or her hat, or open the bottom drawer of the wardrobe where she kept sheets, pillow-cases and underwear, candles and candlesticks, boxes of matches, pieces of cloth for headties and dresses and curtains, black cake and wafers, rice and sweet bread, in pillow-cases, just in case of an emergency. We would unpack my grandmother's things down to the bottom of the drawer, where she kept camphor balls, and touch them over and over again. We would wrap ourselves in pieces of cloth, pretending we were African queens; we would put on my grandmother's gold chain, pretending we were rich. We would pinch her black cakes until they were down to nothing and then we would swear that we never touched them and never saw who did. Often, she caught us and beat us, but we were always on the lookout for the next chance to interfere in my grandmother's sacred things. There was always something new there. Once, just before Christmas, we found a black doll. It caused commotion and rare dissension among us. All of us wanted it so, of course, my grandmother discovered us. None of us, my grandmother said, deserved it and on top of that she threatened that there would be no Santa Claus for us. She kept the doll at the head of her bed until she relented and gave it to Kat, who was the littlest.

We never knew how anything got into the drawer, because we never saw things enter the house. Everything in the drawer was pressed and ironed and smelled of starch and ironing and newness and oldness. My grandmother guarded them often more like burden than treasure. Their depletion would make her anxious; their addition would pose problems of space in our tiny house.

As she rarely left the house, my grandmother felt that everyone on the street where we lived would be looking at her, going to take her picture for her identity card. We felt the same too and worried as she left, stepping heavily, yet shakily down the short hill that led to the savannah, at the far end of which was the community centre. My big sister held her hand. We could see the curtains moving discreetly in the houses next to ours, as my grandmother walked, head up, face hidden behind her veil. We prayed that she would not fall. She had warned us not to hang out of the windows looking at her. We, nevertheless, hung out of the windows gawking at her, along with the woman who lived across the street, whom my grandmother thought lived a scandalous life and had scandalous children and a scandalous laugh which could be heard all the way up the street when the woman sat out blagging with her friends on her veranda. We now hung out of the windows keeping company with "Tante", as she was called, standing with her hands on her massive hips looking and praying for my grandmother. She did not stop, nor did she turn back to give us her look; but we knew that the minute she returned our ears would be burning, because we had joined Tante in disgracing my grandmother.

The photograph from that outing is the only one we have of my grandmother and it is all wrinkled and chewed up, even after my grandmother hid it from us and warned us not to touch it. Someone retrieved it when my grandmother was taken to the hospital. The laminate was now dull and my grandmother's picture was grey and creased and distant.

As my grandmother turned the corner with my sister, the rest of us turned to lawlessness, eating sugar from the kitchen and opening the new refrigerator as often as we wanted and rummaging through my grandmother's things. Dressed up in my grandmother's clothes and splashing each other with her limacol, we paraded outside the house where she had distinctly told us not to go. We waved at Tante, mincing along in my grandmother's shoes. After a while, we grew tired and querulous; assessing the damage we had done to the kitchen, the sugar bowl and my grandmother's wardrobe, we began assigning blame. We all decided to tell on each other. Who had more sugar than whom and who was the first to open the cabinet drawer where my grandmother kept our birth certificates.

We liked to smell our birth certificates, their musty smell and yellowing water-marked coarse paper was proof that my grandmother owned us. She had made such a fuss to get them from our mothers.

A glum silence descended when we realized that it was useless quarrelling. We were all implicated and my grandmother always beat everyone, no matter who committed the crime.

When my grandmother returned we were too chastened to protest her beating. We began to cry as soon as we saw her coming around the corner with my sister. By the time she hit the doorstep we were weeping buckets and the noise we made sounded like a wake, groaning in unison and holding on to each other. My grandmother, too tired from her ordeal at the identity card place, looked at us scornfully and sat down. There was a weakness in her eyes which we recognized. It meant that our beating would be postponed for hours, maybe days, until she could regain her strength. She had been what seemed like hours at the identity card place. My grandmother had to wait, leaning on my sister and having people stare at her, she said. All that indignity and the pain which always appeared in her back at these moments, had made her barely able to walk back to the house. We, too, had been so distraught that we did not even stand outside the house jumping up and down and shouting that she was coming. So at least she was spared that embarrassment. For the rest of the day we quietly went about our chores, without being told to do them and walked lightly past my grandmother's room, where she lay resting in a mound, under the pink chenille.

We had always lived with my grandmother. None of us could recollect our mothers, except as letters from England or occasional visits from women who came on weekends and made plans to take us, eventually, to live with them. The letters from England came every two weeks and at Christmas with a brown box full of foreign-smelling clothes. The clothes smelled of a good life in a country where white people lived and where bad-behaved children like us would not be tolerated. All this my grandmother said. There, children had manners and didn't play in mud and didn't dirty everything and didn't cry if there wasn't any food and didn't run under the mango trees, grabbing mangoes when the wind blew them down and walked and did not run through the house like warrahoons and did not act like little old niggers. Eula, my big sister, would read the letters to my grandmother who, from time to time, would let us listen. Then my grandmother would urge us to grow up and go away too and live well. When she came to the part about going away, we would feel half-proud and half-nervous. The occasional visits made us feel as precarious as the letters. When we misbehaved, my grandmother often threatened to send us away-away, where white men ate black children, or to quite-too-quite in the country.

Passing by my grandmother's room, bunched up under the spread, with her face tight and hollow-cheeked, her mouth set against us, the spectre of quite-to-quite and white cannibals loomed brightly. It was useless trying to "dog back" to her she said, when one of my cousins sat close to her bed, inquiring if she would like us to pick her grey hairs out. That was how serious this incident was. Because my grandmother loved us to pick her grey hairs from her head. She would promise us a penny for every ten which we could get by the root. If we broke a hair, that would not count, she said. And, if we threw the little balls of her hair out into the yard for the wind, my grandmother became quite upset since that meant that birds would fly off with her hair and send her mad, send her mind to the four corners of the earth, or they would build a nest with her hair and steal her brain. We never threw hair in the yard for the wind, at least not my grandmother's hair and we took on her indignant look when we chastised each other for doing it with our own hair. My cousin Genevieve didn't mind though. She chewed her long front plait when she sucked on her thumb and saved balls of hair to throw to the birds. Genevieve made mudpies under the house, which we bought with leaf money. You could get yellow mudpies or brown mudpies or red mudpies, this depended on the depth of the hole under the house and the wash water which my grandmother threw there on Saturdays. We took my grandmother's word that having to search the four corners of the earth for your mind was not an easy task, but Genevieve wondered what it would be like.

There's a photograph of Genevieve and me and two of my sisters someplace. We took it to send to England. My grandmother dressed us up, put my big sister in charge of us, giving her 50 cents tied up in a handkerchief and pinned to the waistband of her dress, and warned us not to give her any trouble. We marched to Wong's Studio on the Coffee, the main road in out town, and fidgeted as Mr. Wong fixed us in front of a promenade scene to take our picture. My little sister cried through it all and sucked her fingers. Nobody knows that it's me in the photograph, but my sisters and Genevieve look like themselves.

Banishment from my grandmother's room was torture. It was her room, even though three of us slept beside her each night. It was a small room with two windows kept shut most of the time, except every afternoon when my grandmother would look out of the front window, her head resting on her big arms, waiting for us to return from school. There was a bed in the room with a headboard where she kept the Bible, a bureau with a round mirror and a washstand with a jug and basin. She spent much of her time here. We too, sitting on the polished floor under the front window talking to her or against the foot of the bed, if we were trying to get back into her favour or beg her for money. We knew the smell of the brown varnished wood of her bed intimately.

My grandmother's room was rescue from pursuit. Anyone trying to catch anyone would pull up straight and get quiet, if you ducked into her room. We read under my grandmother's bed and, playing catch, we hid from each other behind the bulk of her body.

We never received that licking for the photograph day, but my grandmother could keep a silence that was punishment enough. The photograph now does not look like her. It is grey and pained. In real, she was round and comfortable. When we knew her she had a full lap and beautiful arms, her cocoa brown skin smelled of wood smoke and familiar.

My grandmother never thought that people should sleep on Saturday. She woke us up "peepee au jour" as she called it, which meant before it was light outside, and set us to work. My grandmother said that she couldn't stand a lazy house, full of lazy children. The washing had to be done and dried before three o'clock on Saturday when the baking would begin and continue until the evening. My big sister and my grandmother did the washing, leaning over the scrubbing board and the tub and when we others grew older we scrubbed the clothes out, under the eyes of my grandmother. We had to lay the soap-scrubbed clothes out on the square pile of stones so that the sun would bleach them clean, then pick them up and rinse and hang them to dry. We all learned to bake from the time that our chins could reach the table and we washed dishes standing on the bench in front of the sink. In the rainy season, the washing was done on the sunniest days. A sudden shower of rain and my grandmother would send us flying to collect the washing off the lines. We would sit for hours watching the rain gush through the drains which we had dug, in anticipation, around the flower garden in front of the house. The yellow brown water lumbered unsteadily through the drains rebuilding the mud and forming a lake at the place where our efforts were frustrated by a large stone.

In the rainy season, my big sister planted corn and pigeon peas on the right side of the house. Just at the tail end of the season, we planted the flower garden. Zinnias and jump-up-and-kiss-me, which grew easily and xora and roses which we could never get to grow. Only the soil on one side of the front yard was good for growing flowers or food. On the other side a sour-sop tree and an almond tree sucked the soil of everything, leaving the ground sandy and thin, and pushed up their roots, ridging the yard, into a hill. The almond tree, under the front window, fed a nest of ants which lived in one pillar of our house. A line of small red ants could be seen making their way from pillar to almond tree carrying bits of leaves and bark.

One Saturday evening, I tried to stay outside playing longer than allowed by my grandmother, leaning on the almond tree and ignoring her calls. "Laugh and cry live in the same house," my grandmother warned, threatening to beat me when I finally came inside. At first I only felt the bite of one ant on my leg but, no sooner, my whole body was invaded by thousands of little red ants biting my skin blue crimson. My sisters and cousins laughed, my grandmother, looking at me pitiably, sent me to the shower; but the itching did not stop and the pains did not subside until the next day.

I often polished the floor on Saturdays. At first, I hated the brown polish-dried rag with which I had to rub the floors, creeping on my hands and knees. I hated the corners of the room which collected fluff and dust. If we tried to polish the floor without first scrubbing it, my grandmother would make us start all over again. My grandmother supervised all these activities when she was ill, sitting on the bed. She saw my distaste for the rag and therefore insisted that I polish over and over again some spot which I was sure that I had gone over. I learned to look at the rag, to notice its layers of brown polish, its waxy shines in some places, its wetness when my grandmother made me mix the polish with kerosene to stretch its use. It became a rich object, all full of continuous ribbing and working, which my grandmother insisted that I do with my hands and no shortcuts of standing and doing it with the heel of my foot. We poor people had to get used to work, my grandmother said. After polishing, we would shine the floor with more rags. Up and down, until my grandmother was satisfied. Then the morris chairs, whose slats fell off every once in a while with our jumping, had to be polished and shined, and the cabinet, and all put back in their place.

She wasted nothing. Everything turned into something else when it was too old to be everything. Dresses turned into skirts and then into underwear. Shoes turned into slippers. Corn, too hard for eating, turned into meal. My grandmother herself never wore anything new, except when she went out. She had two dresses and a petticoat hanging in the wardrobe for those times. At home, she dressed in layers of old clothing, half-slip over dress, old socks, because her feet were always cold, and slippers, cut out of old shoes. A safety pin or two, anchored to the front of her dress or the hem of her skirt, to pin up our falling underwear or ruined zippers.

My grandmother didn't like it when we changed the furniture around. She said that changing the furniture around was a sign to people that we didn't have any money. Only people with no money changed their furniture around and around all the time. My grandmother had various lectures on money, to protect us from the knowledge that we had little or none. At night, we could not drop pennies on the floor, for thieves may be passing and think that we did have money and come rob us.

My grandmother always said that money ran through your hands like water, especially when you had so many mouths to feed. Every two or three weeks money would run out of my grandmother's hands. These times were as routine as our chores or going to school or the games which we played. My

grandmother had stretched it over stewed chicken, rice, provisions and macaroni pie on Sundays, split peas soup on Mondays, fish and bake on Tuesdays,
corn meal dumplings and salt cod on Wednesdays, okra and rice on
Thursdays, split peas, salt cod and rice on Fridays and pelau on Saturdays. By
the time the third week of the month came around my grandmother's
stretching would become apparent. She carried a worried look on her face and
was more silent than usual. We understood this to be a sign of lean times and
times when we could not bother my grandmother or else we would get one of
her painful explanations across our ears. Besides it really hurt my grandmother
not to give us what we needed, as we all settled with her into a depressive
hungry silence.

At times we couldn't help but look accusingly at her. Who else could we
blame for the gnawing pain in our stomachs and the dry corners of our
mouths. We stared at my grandmother hungrily, while she avoided our eyes.
We would all gather around her as she lay in bed, leaning against her or sitting
on the floor beside the bed, all in silence. We devoted these silences to hope—
hope that something would appear to deliver us, perhaps my grandfather, with
provisions from the country—and to wild imagination that we would be rich
some day and be able to buy pounds of sugar and milk. But sweet water, a thin
mixture of water and sugar, was all the balm for our hunger. When even that
did not show itself in abundance, our silences were even deeper. We drank
water, until our stomachs became distended and nautical.

My little sister, who came along a few years after we had grown accustomed to the routine of hunger and silence, could never grasp the importance of
these moments. We made her swear not to cry for food when there wasn't any
and, to give her credit, she did mean it when she promised. But the moment the
hungry silence set in, she began to cry, begging my grandmother for sweet
water. She probably cried out of fear that we would never eat again, and admittedly our silences were somewhat awesome, mixtures of despair and grief, made
potent by the weakness which the heavy hot sun brought on in our bodies.

We resented my little sister for these indiscretions. She reminded us that
we were hungry, a thought we had been transcending in our growing asceti-
cism, and we felt sorry for my grandmother having to answer her cries.
Because it was only then that my grandmother relented and sent one of us to
borrow a cup of sugar from the woman across the street, Tante. One of us suffered the indignity of crossing the road and repeating haltingly whatever words
my grandmother had told her to say.

My grandmother always sent us to Tante, never to Mrs. Sommard who
was a religious woman and our next-door neighbour, nor to Mrs. Benjamin
who had money and was our other next-door neighbour. Mrs. Sommard only
had prayers to give and Mrs. Benjamin, scorn. But Tante, with nothing, like us,

would give whatever she could manage. Mrs. Sommard was a Seventh Day Adventist and the only time my grandmother sent one of us to beg a cup of something, Mrs. Sommard sent back a message to pray. My grandmother took it quietly and never sent us there again and told us to have respect for Mrs. Sommard because she was a religious woman and believed that God would provide.

Mrs. Sommard's husband, Mr. Sommard, took two years to die. For the two years that he took to die the house was always brightly lit. Mr. Sommard was so afraid of dying that he could not sleep and didn't like it when darkness fell. He stayed awake all night and all day for two years and kept his wife and daughter awake too. My grandmother said he pinched them if they fell asleep and told them that if he couldn't sleep, they shouldn't sleep either. How this ordeal squared with Mrs. Sommard's religiousness, my grandmother was of two minds about. Either the Lord was trying Mrs. Sommard's faith or Mrs. Sommard had done some wickedness that the Lord was punishing her for.

The Benjamins, on the other side, we didn't know where they got their money from, but they seemed to have a lot of it. For Mrs. Benjamin sometimes told our friend Patsy not to play with us. Patsy lived with Mrs. Benjamin, her grandmother, Miss Lena, her aunt and her grandfather, Mr. Benjamin. We could always smell chicken that Miss Lena was cooking from their pot, even when our house fell into silence.

The Benjamins were the reason that my grandmother didn't like us running down into the backyard to pick up mangoes when the wind blew them down. She felt ashamed that we would show such hunger in the eyes of people who had plenty. The next thing was that the Benjamins' rose mango tree was so huge, it spread half its body over their fence into our yard. We felt that this meant that any mangoes that dropped on our side belonged to us and Patsy Benjamin and her family thought that it belonged to them. My grandmother took their side, not because she thought that they were right, but she thought that if they were such greedy people, they should have the mangoes. Let them kill themselves on it, she said. So she made us call to Mrs. Benjamin and give them all the rose mangoes that fell in our yard. Mrs. Benjamin thought that we were doing this out of respect for their status and so she would often tell us with superiority to keep the mangoes, but my grandmother would decline. We, grudgingly, had to do the same and, as my grandmother warned us, without a sad look on our faces. From time to time, we undermined my grandmother's pride, by pretending not to find any rose mangoes on the ground, and hid them in a stash under the house or deep in the backyard under leaves. Since my grandmother never ventured from the cover and secrecy of the walls of the house, or that area in the yard hidden by walls, she was never likely to discover our lie.

Deep in the backyard, over the drain which we called the canal, we were out of range of my grandmother's voice, since she refused to shout, and the palms of her hands, but not her eyes. We were out of reach of her broomstick which she flung at our fleeing backs or up into one of the mango trees where one of us was perched, escaping her beatings.

Deep in the back of the yard, we smoked sponge wood and danced in risqué fashion and uttered the few cuss words that we knew and made up calypsos. There, we pretended to be big people with children. We put our hands on our hips and shook our heads, as we had seen big people do, and complained about having so much children, children, children to feed.

My grandmother showed us how to kill a chicken, holding its body in the tub and placing the scrubbing board over it leaving the neck exposed, then with a sharp knife quickly cut the neck, leaving the scrubbing board over the tub. Few of us became expert at killing a chicken. The beating of the dying fowl would frighten us and the scrubbing board would slip whereupon the headless bird would escape, its warm blood still gushing, propelling its body around and around the house. My grandmother would order us to go get the chicken, which was impossible since the direction that the chicken took and the speed with which it ran were indeterminate. She didn't like us making our faces up in distaste at anything that had to do with eating or cleaning or washing. So, whoever let the chicken escape or whoever refused to go get it would have to stand holding it for five minutes until my grandmother made a few turns in the house, then they would have to pluck it and gut it and wrap the feathers and innards in newspaper, throwing it in the garbage. That person may well have to take the garbage out for a week. If you can eat, my grandmother would say, you can clean and you shouldn't scorn life.

One day we found a huge balloon down in the backyard. It was the biggest balloon we'd ever had and it wasn't even around Christmas time. Patsy Benjamin, who played through her fence with us, hidden by the rose mango tree from her aunt Lena, forgot herself and started shouting that it was hers. She began crying and ran complaining to her aunt that we had stolen her balloon. Her aunt dragged her inside and we ran around our house fighting and pulling at each other swearing that the balloon belonged to this one or that one. My grandmother grabbed one of us on the fourth or fifth round and snatched the balloon away. We never understood the cause of this, since it was such a find and never quite understood my grandmother muttering something about Tante's son leaving his "nastiness" everywhere. Tante herself had been trying to get our attention, as we raced round and round the house. This was our first brush with what was called "doing rudeness." Later, when my big sister began to menstruate and stopped hanging around with us, we heard from our classmates that men menstruated too and so we put two and two together and figured that Tante's son's nastiness must have to do with his menstruation.

On our way home from school one day, a rumour blazed its way through all the children just let out from school that there was a male sanitary napkin at the side of the road near the pharmacy on Royal Road. It was someone from the Catholic girls' school who started it and troupe after troupe of school children hurried to the scene, to see it. The rumour spread back and forth, along the Coffee, with school children corroborating and testifying that they had actually seen it. By the time we got there, we only saw an empty brown box which we skirted, a little frightened at first, then pressed in for a better view. There really wasn't very much more to see and we figured that someone must have removed it before we got there. Nevertheless, we swore that we had seen it and continued to spread the rumour along the way, until we got home, picking up the chant which was building as all the girls whipped their fingers at the boys on the street singing, "Boys have periods TOOOOOO!" We couldn't ask my grandmother if men had periods, but it was the source of weeks of arguing back and forth.

When my period came, it was my big sister who told me what to do. My grandmother was not there. By then, my mother had returned from England and an unease had fallen over us. Anyway, when I showed my big sister, she shoved a sanitary napkin and two pins at me and told me not to play with boys anymore and that I couldn't climb the mango tree anymore and that I shouldn't fly around the yard anymore either. I swore everyone not to tell my mother when she got home from work but they all did anyway and my mother with her air, which I could never determine since I never looked her in the face, said nothing.

My mother had returned. We had anticipated her arrival with a mixture of pride and fear. These added to an uncomfortable sense that things would not be the same, because in the weeks preceding her arrival my grandmother revved up the old warning about us not being able to be rude or disobey anymore, that we would have to be on our best behaviour to be deserving of this woman who had been to England, where children were not like us. She was my grandmother's favourite daughter too, so my grandmother was quite proud of her. When she arrived, some of us hung back behind my grandmother's skirt, embarrassing her before my mother who, my grandmother said, was expecting to meet well brought up children who weren't afraid of people.

To tell the truth, we were expecting a white woman to come through the door, the way my grandmother had described my mother and the way the whole street that we lived on treated the news of my mother's return, as if we were about to ascend in their respect. The more my grandmother pushed us forward to say hello to my mother, the more we clung to her skirts until she finally had to order us to say hello. In the succeeding months, my grandmother tried to push us toward my mother. She looked at us with reproach in her eyes that we did not acknowledge my mother's presence and her power. My mother brought us wieners and fried eggs and mashed potatoes, which we had never had before, and said that she longed for kippers, which we did not know. We enjoyed her strangeness but we were uncomfortable under her eyes. Her suitcase smelled strange and foreign and for weeks despite our halting welcome of her, we showed off in the neighbourhood that we had someone from away.

Then she began ordering us about and the wars began.

Those winters in England, when she must have bicycled to Hampstead General Hospital from which we once received a letter and a postcard with her smiling to us astride a bicycle, must have hardened the smile which my grandmother said that she had and which was dimly recognizable from the photograph. These winters, which she wrote about and which we envied as my sister read them to us, she must have hated. And the thought of four ungrateful children who deprived her of a new dress or stockings to travel London, made my mother unmerciful on her return.

We would run to my grandmother, hiding behind her skirt, or dive for the sanctuary of my grandmother's room. She would enter, accusing my grandmother of interfering in how she chose to discipline "her" children. We were shocked. Where my mother acquired this authority we could not imagine. At first our grandmother let her hit us, but finally she could not help but intervene and ask my mother if she thought she was beating animals. Then my mother would reply that my grandmother had brought us up as animals. This insult would galvanize us all against my mother. A back answer would fly from the child in question who would, in turn, receive a slap from my grandmother, whereupon my grandmother would turn on my mother with the length of her tongue. When my grandmother gave someone the length of her tongue, it was given in a low, intense and damning tone, punctuated by a chest beating and the biblical, "I have nurtured a viper in my bosom."

My mother often became hysterical and left the house, crying what my grandmother said were crocodile tears. We had never seen an adult cry in a rage before. The sound in her throat was a gagging yet raging sound, which frightened us, but it was the sight of her tall threatening figure which cowed us. Later, she lost hope that we would ever come around to her and she began to think and accuse my grandmother of setting her children against her. I recall her shoes mostly, white and thick, striding across the tiny house.

These accusations increased and my grandmother began to talk of dying and leaving us. Once or twice, my mother tried to intervene on behalf of one or the other of us in a dispute with my grandmother. There would be silence from both my grandmother and us, as to the strangeness of this intervention. It would immediately bring us on side to my grandmother's point of view and my mother would find herself in the company of an old woman and some children who had a life of their own—who understood their plays, their dances, gestures and signals, who were already intent on one another. My mother would find herself standing outside these gestures into which her inroads were abrupt and incautious. Each foray made our dances more secretive, our gestures subterranean.

Our life stopped when she entered the door of the house, conversations closed in mid-sentence and elegant gestures with each other turned to sharp asexual movements.

My mother sensed these closures since, at first, we could not hide these scenes fast enough to escape her jealous glance. In the end, we closed our scenes ostentatiously in her presence. My grandmother's tongue lapping over a new story or embellishing an old one would become brusque in, "Tell your mother good evening." We, telling my grandmother a story or receiving her assurance that when we get rich we would buy a this or a that, while picking out her grey hairs, would fall silent. We longed for when my mother stayed away. Most of all, we longed for when she worked nights. Then we could sit all evening in the grand darkness of my grandmother's stories.

When the electricity went out and my grandmother sat in the rocking chair, the wicker seat bursting from the weight of her hips, the stories she spun, no matter how often we heard them, languished over the darkness whose thickness we felt, rolling in and out of the veranda. Some nights the darkness billowing about us would be suffused by the perfume of lady-of-the-night, a white, velvet, yellow, orchid-like flower which grew up the street in a neighbour's yard. My grandmother's voice, brown and melodic, about how my grandfather, "Yuh Papa, one dark night, was walking from Ortoire to Guayaguayare ..."

The road was dark and my grandfather walked alone with his torchlight pointed toward his feet. He came to a spot in the road, which suddenly chilled him. Then, a few yards later, he came to a hot spot in the road, which made him feel for a shower of rain. Then, up ahead, he saw a figure and behind him he heard its footsteps. He kept walking, the footsteps pursuing him dragging a chain, its figure ahead of him. If he had stopped, the figure, which my grandfather knew to be a legahoo, would take his soul; so my grandfather walked steadily, shining his torchlight at his feet and repeating psalm twenty-three, until he passed the bridge by the sea wall and passed the savannah, until he arrived at St. Mary's, where he lived with my grandmother.

It was in the darkness of the veranda, in the honey chuckle back of my grandmother's throat, that we learned how to catch a soucouyant and a lajabless and not to answer to the "hoop! hoop! hoop!" of the duennes, the souls of dead children who were not baptized, come to call living children to play with them. To catch a soucouyant, you had to either find the barrel of rain water where she had left her skin and throw pepper in it or sprinkle salt or rice on your doorstep so that when she tried to enter the house to take your blood, she would have to count every grain of salt or rice before entering. If she dropped just one grain or miscounted, she would have to start all over again her impossible task and in the morning she would be discovered, distraught and without her skin on the doorstep.

When we lived in the country before moving to the street, my grandmother had shown us, walking along the beach in back of the house, how to identify a duenne foot. She made it with her heel in the sand and then, without laying the ball of her foot down, imprinted her toes in the front of the heel print.

Back in the country, my grandmother walked outside and up and down the beach and cut coconut with a cutlass and dug, chip-chip, on the beach and slammed the kitchen window one night just as a madman leapt to it to try to get in the house. My grandmother said that, as a child in the country, my mother had fallen and hit her head, ever since which she had been pampered and given the best food to eat and so up to this day she was very moody and could go off her head at the slightest. My mother took this liberty whenever she returned home, skewing the order of our routines in my grandmother.

It seemed that my grandmother had raised more mad children than usual, for my uncle was also mad and one time he held up a gas station which was only the second time that my grandmother had to leave the house, again on the arm of my big sister. We readied my grandmother then and she and my big sister and I went to the courthouse on the Promenade to hear my uncle's case. They didn't allow children in, but they allowed my big sister as my grandmother had to lean on her. My uncle's case was not heard that morning, so we left the court and walked up to the Promenade. We had only gone a few steps when my grandmother felt faint. My sister held the smelling salts at her nostrils, as we slowly made our way as inconspicuously as we could to a bench near the bandstand. My grandmother cried, mopping her eyes with her handkerchief and talked about the trouble her children had caused her. We, all three, sat on the bench on the Promenade near the bandstand, feeling stiff and uncomfortable. My grandmother said my uncle had allowed the public to wash their mouth in our family business. She was tired by then and she prayed that my mother would return and take care of us, so that she would be able to die in peace.

Soon after, someone must have written my mother to come home, for we received a letter saying that she was finally coming.

We had debated what to call my mother over and over again and came to no conclusions. Some of the words sounded insincere and disloyal, since they really belonged to my grandmother, although we never called her by those names. But when we tried them out for my mother, they hung so cold in the throat that we were discouraged immediately. Calling my mother by her given name was too presumptuous, even though we had always called all our aunts and uncles by theirs. Unable to come to a decision we abandoned each other to individual choices. In the end, after our vain attempts to form some word, we never called my mother by any name. If we needed to address her we stood about until she noticed that we were there and then we spoke. Finally, we never called my mother.

All of the words which we knew belonged to my grandmother. All of them, a voluptuous body of endearment, dependence, comfort, and infinite knowing. We were all full of my grandmother, she had left us full and empty of her. We dreamed in my grandmother and we woke up in her, bleary-eyed and gesturing for her arm, her elbows, her smell. We jockeyed with each other, lied to each other, quarrelled with each other and with her for the boon of lying close to her, sculpting ourselves around the roundness of her back. Braiding her hair and oiling her feet. We dreamed in my grandmother and we woke up in her, bleary-eyed and gesturing for her lap, her arms, her elbows, her smell, the fat flesh of her arms. We fought, tricked each other for the crook between her thighs and calves. We anticipated where she would sit and got there before her. We brought her achar and paradise plums.

My mother had walked the streets of London, as the legend went, with one dress on her back for years, in order to send those brown envelopes, the stamps from which I saved in an old album. But her years of estrangement had left her angry and us cold to her sacrifice. She settled into fits of fury. Rage which raised welts on our backs, faces and thin legs. When my grandmother had turned away laughing from us, saying there was no place to beat, my mother found room.

Our silences which once warded off hunger now warded off her blows. She took this to mean impudence and her rages whipped around our silences more furiously than before. I, the most ascetic of all, sustained the most terrible moments of her rage. The more enraged she grew, the more silent I became, the harder she hit, the more wooden, I. I refined this silence into a jewel of the most sacred sandalwood, finely grained, perfumed, mournful yet stoic. I became the only inhabitant of a cloistered place carrying my jewel of fullness and emptiness, voluptuousness and scarcity. But she altered the silences profoundly.

Before, with my grandmother, the silences had company, were peopled by our hope. Now, they were desolate.

She had left us full and empty of her. When someone took the time to check, there was no photograph of my grandmother, no figure of my grandmother in layers of clothing and odd-sided socks, no finger stroking the air in reprimand, no arm under her chin at the front window or crossed over her breasts waiting for us.

My grandmother had never been away from home for more than a couple of hours and only three times that I could remember. So her absence was lonely. We visited her in the hospital every evening. They had put her in a room with eleven other people. The room was bare. You could see underneath all the beds from the doorway and the floors were always scrubbed with that hospital smelling antiseptic which reeked its own sickliness and which I detested for years after. My grandmother lay in one of the beds nearest the door and I remember my big sister remarking to my grandmother that she should have a better room, but my grandmother hushed her saying that it was all right and anyway she wouldn't be there for long and the nurses were nice to her. From the chair beside my grandmother's bed in the hospital you could see the parking lot on Chancery Lane. I would sit with my grandmother, looking out the window and describing the scene to her. You could also see part of the wharf and the gulf of Paria which was murky where it held to the wharf. And St. Paul's Church, where I was confirmed, even though I did not know the catechism and only mumbled when Canon Farquar drilled us in it.

Through our talks at the window my grandmother made me swear that I would behave for my mother. We planned, when I grew up and went away, that I would send for my grandmother and that I would grow up to be something good, that she and I and Eula and Ava and Kat and Genevieve would go to Guayaguayare and live there forever. I made her promise that she would not leave me with my mother.

It was a Sunday afternoon, the last time that I spoke with my grandmother. I was describing a bicycle rider in the parking lot and my grandmother promised to buy one for me when she got out of hospital.

My big sister cried and curled herself up beneath the radio when my grandmother died. Genevieve's face was wet with tears, her front braid pulled over her nose, she, sucking her thumb.

When they brought my grandmother home, it was after weeks in the white twelve-storey hospital. We took the curtains down, leaving all the windows and doors bare, in respect for the dead. The ornaments, doilies, and plastic flowers were removed and the mirrors and furniture covered with white sheets. We stayed inside the house and did not go out to play. We kept the house clean and we fell into our routine of silence when faced with hunger. We felt alone. We did not believe. We thought that it was untrue. In disbelief, we said of my grandmother, "Mama can't be serious!"

The night of the wake, the house was full of strangers. My grandmother would never allow this. Strangers, sitting and talking everywhere, even in my grandmother's room. Someone, a great-aunt, a sister of my grandmother, whom we had never seen before, turned to me sitting on the sewing machine and ordered me in a stern voice to get down. I left the room, slinking away, feeling abandoned by my grandmother to strangers.

I never cried in public for my grandmother. I locked myself in the bathroom or hid deep in the backyard and wept. I had learned as my grandmother had taught me, never to show people your private business.

When they brought my grandmother home the next day, we all made a line to kiss her goodbye. My littlest sister was afraid; the others smiled for my grandmother. I kissed my grandmother's face hoping that it was warm.

RICHARD BRAUTIGAN

1/3, 1/3, 1/3

Richard Brautigan (1930–1984) was born in Spokane or Tacoma, Washington—no one seems quite sure which. His writing appeared first in small presses, but in the mid 1960s it attracted a cult following in underground youth movements on the U.S. West Coast. He was poet in residence at California Institute of Technology in 1967, the year his second novel, Trout Fishing in America, *was published. Of his eclectic oeuvre of poetry and prose,* Trout Fishing *is often considered Brautigan's best work. It gained widespread currency among communists and other countercultural revolutionaries before Kurt Vonnegut brought it and several other of Brautigan's works to Delacorte Press—and to the acclaim of the mainstream literary establishment—in 1969. Brautigan is often described as a kind of postmodern Thoreau. As "1/3, 1/3, 1/3" demonstrates, Brautigan's work is pervaded by ecological decay and modern disenfranchisement, against which a pastoral view of nature becomes redemptive. Brautigan committed suicide in 1984.*

It was all to be done in thirds. I was to get 1/3 for doing the typing, and she was to get 1/3 for doing the editing, and he was to get 1/3 for writing the novel.

We were going to divide the royalties three ways. We all shook hands on the deal, each knowing what we were supposed to do, the path before us, the gate at the end.

I was made a 1/3 partner because I had the typewriter.

I lived in a cardboard-lined shack of my own building across the street from the run-down old house the Welfare rented for her and her nine-year-old son Freddy.

The novelist lived in a trailer a mile away beside a sawmill pond where he was the watchman for the mill.

I was about seventeen and made lonely and strange by that Pacific Northwest of so many years ago, that dark, rainy land of 1952. I'm thirty-one now and I still can't figure out what I meant by living the way I did in those days.

She was one of those eternally fragile women in their late thirties and once very pretty and the object of much attention in the roadhouses and beer parlors, who are now on Welfare and their entire lives rotate around that one day a month when they get their Welfare checks.

The word "check" is the one religious word in their lives, so they always manage to use it at least three or four times in every conversation. It doesn't matter what you are talking about.

The novelist was in his late forties, tall, reddish, and looked as if life had given him an endless stream or two-timing girlfriends, five-day drunks and cars with bad transmissions.

He was writing the novel because he wanted to tell a story that had happened to him years before when he was working in the woods.

He also wanted to make some money: 1/3.

My entrance into the thing came about this way: One day I was standing in front of my shack, eating an apple and staring at a black ragged toothache sky that was about to rain.

What I was doing was like an occupation for me. I was that involved in looking at the sky and eating the apple. You would have thought that I had been hired to do it with a good salary and a pension if I stared at the sky long enough.

"HEY, YOU!" I heard somebody yell.

I looked across the mud puddle and it was the woman. She was wearing a kind of green Mackinaw that she wore all the time except when she had to visit the Welfare people downtown. Then she put on a shapeless duck-grey coat.

We lived in a poor part of town where the streets weren't paved. The street was nothing more than a big mud puddle that you had to walk around. The street was of no use to cars any more. They travelled on a different frequency where asphalt and gravel were more sympathetic.

She was wearing a pair of white rubber boots that she always had on in the winter, a pair of boots that gave her a kind of child-like appearance. She was so fragile and firmly indebted to the Welfare Department that she often looked like a child twelve years old.

"What do you want?" I said.

"You have a typewriter, don't you?" she said. "I've walked by your shack and heard you typing. You type a lot at night."

"Yeah, I have a typewriter," I said.

"You a good typist?" she said.

"I'm all right."

"We don't have a typewriter. How would you like to go in with us?" she yelled across the mud puddle. She looked a perfect twelve years old, standing there in her white boots, the sweetheart and darling of all mud puddles.

"What's 'go in' mean?"

"Well, he's writing a novel," she said. "He's good. I'm editing it. I've read a lot of pocketbooks and the *Reader's Digest*. We need somebody who has a typewriter to type it up. You'll get 1/3. How does that sound?"

"I'd like to see the novel," I said. I didn't know what was happening. I knew she had three or four boyfriends that were always visiting her.

"Sure!" she yelled. "You have to see it to type it. Come on around. Let's go out to his place right now and you can meet him and have a look at the novel. He's a good guy. It's a wonderful book."

"OK," I said, and walked around the mud puddle to where she was standing in front of her evil dentist house, twelve years old, and approximately two miles from the Welfare office.

"Let's go," she said.

We walked over to the highway and down the highway past mud puddles and sawmill ponds and fields flooded with rain until we came to a road that went across the railroad tracks and turned down past half a dozen small sawmill ponds that were filled with black winter logs.

We talked very little and that was only about her check that was two days late and she had called the Welfare and they said they mailed the check and it should be there tomorrow, but call again tomorrow if it's not there and we'll prepare an emergency money order for you.

"Well, I hope it's there tomorrow," I said.

"So do I or I'll have to go downtown," she said.

Next to the last sawmill pond was a yellow old trailer up on blocks of wood. One look at that trailer showed that it was never going anywhere again, that the highway was in distant heaven, only to be prayed to. It was really sad with a cemetery-like chimney swirling jagged dead smoke in the air above it.

A kind of half-dog, half-cat creature was sitting on a rough plank porch that was in front of the door. The creature half-barked and half-meowed at us, "Arfeow!" and darted under the trailer, looking out at us from behind a block.

"This is it," the woman said.

The door to the trailer opened and a man stepped out onto the porch. There was a pile of firewood stacked on the porch and it was covered with a black tarp.

The man held his hand above his eyes, shielding his eyes from a bright imaginary sun, though everything had turned dark in anticipation of the rain.

"Hello, there," he said.

"Hi," I said.

"Hello, honey," she said.

He shook my hand and welcomed me to his trailer, then he gave her a little kiss on the mouth before we all went inside.

The place was small and muddy and smelled like stale rain and had a large unmade bed that looked as if it had been a partner to some of the saddest love-making this side of The Cross.

There was a green bushy half-table with a couple of insect-like chairs and a little sink and a small stove that was used for cooking and heating.

There were some dirty dishes in the little sink. The dishes looked as if they had always been dirty: born dirty to last forever.

I could hear a radio playing Western music someplace in the trailer, but I couldn't find it. I looked all over but it was nowhere in sight. It was probably under a shirt or something.

"He's the kid with the typewriter," she said. "He'll get 1/3 for typing it."

"That sounds fair," he said. "We need somebody to type it. I've never done anything like this before."

"Why don't you show it to him?" she said. "He'd like to take a look at it."

"OK. But it isn't too carefully written," he said to me. "I only went to the fourth grade, so she's going to edit it, straighten out the grammar and commas and stuff."

There was a notebook lying on the table, next to an ashtray that probably had 600 cigarette butts in it. The notebook had a color photograph of Hopalong Cassidy on the cover.

Hopalong looked tired as if he had spent the previous night chasing star-lets all over Hollywood and barely had enough strength to get back in the saddle.

There were about twenty-five or thirty pages of writing in the notebook. It was written in a large grammar school sprawl: an unhappy marriage between printing and longhand.

"It's not finished yet," he said.

"You'll type it. I'll edit it. He'll write it," she said.

It was a story about a young logger falling in love with a waitress. The novel began in 1935 in a cafe in North Bend, Oregon.

The young logger was sitting at a table and the waitress was taking his order. She was very pretty with blond hair and rosy cheeks. The young logger was ordering veal cutlets with mashed potatoes and country gravy.

"Yeah, I'll do the editing. You can type it, can't you? It's not too bad, is it?" she said in a twelve-year-old voice with the Welfare peeking over her shoulder.

"No," I said. "It will be easy."

Suddenly the rain started to come down hard outside, without any warning, just suddenly great drops of rain that almost shook the trailer.

You sur lik veel cutlets dont you Maybell said she was holding holding her pensil up her mowth that was preti and red like an apl!

Onli wen you tak my oder Carl said he was a kind of bassful loger but big and strong lik his dead who ownd the starmill!

Ill mak sur you get plenti of gravi!

Just ten the caf door opend and in cam Rins Adams he was hansom and meen, everi bodi in thos parts was afrad of him but not Carl and his *dead* dad they wasnt afrad of him no sur!

Maybell shifard wen she saw him standing ther in his blac, macinaw he smild at her and Carl felt his blod run hot lik scallding cofee and fiting mad!

Howdi ther Rins said Maybell blushed like a *flower* flouar while we were all sitting there in that rainy trailer, pounding at the gates of American literature.

DINO BUZZATI

SEVEN FLOORS

Translated by Judith Landry

Dino Buzzati (1906–1972) was born in Belluno, Italy. He graduated from the University of Milan with a law degree but found a career in journalism, working as an editor and a correspondent for the Corriere della Sera. *The 1933 publication of his novella* Barnabo of the Mountains *inaugurated his career as a literary writer. But it was not until his novel* The Tartar Steppe *(1940) won the Italian Academy Award that Buzzati attracted the attention of the European literary mainstream. "Every writer and artist," Buzzati wrote in one of his many notebooks, "however long he may live, says only one thing. Otherwise they would not be sincere. Besides, does not the style by which a writer's personality is distinguished perhaps imply a certain uniformity or, better yet, a certain identity of meaning?" Widely translated, Buzzati's novels and stories offer surreal scenarios whose mad logic aligns them with the work of his compatriots Italo Calvino and Tomasso Landolfi. In fact, we may discern in this group the emergence of a definitive movement in Italian literature, one that resembles the tradition of the fantastic in Latin American fiction.*

One morning in March, after a night's train journey, Giovanni Corte arrived in the town where the famous nursing home was. He was a little feverish, but he was still determined to walk from the station to the hospital, carrying his small bag.

Although his was an extremely slight case, in the very earliest stages, Giovanni Corte had been advised to go to the well-known sanatorium, which existed solely for the care of the particular illness from which he was suffering. This meant that the doctors were particularly competent and the equipment particularly pertinent and efficient.

Catching sight of it from a distance—he recognised it from having seen photos in some brochure—Giovanni Corte was most favourably impressed.

The building was white, seven storeys high; its mass was broken up by a series of recesses which gave it a vague resemblance to a hotel. It was surrounded by tall trees.

After a brief visit from the doctor, prior to a more thorough one later on, Giovanni Corte was taken to a cheerful room on the seventh and top floor. The furniture was light and elegant, as was the wallpaper, there were wooden armchairs and brightly coloured cushions. The view was over one of the loveliest parts of the town. Everything was peaceful, welcoming and reassuring.

Giovanni Corte went to bed immediately, turned on the reading-lamp at his bedside and began to read a book he had brought with him. After a few moments a nurse came in to see whether he needed anything.

He didn't, but was delighted to chat with the young woman and ask her questions about the nursing home. That was how he came to know its one extremely odd characteristic: the patients were housed on each floor according to the gravity of their state. The seventh, or top floor, was for extremely mild cases. The sixth was still for mild cases, but ones needing a certain amount of attention. On the fifth floor were quite serious cases and so on, floor by floor. The second floor was for the very seriously ill. On the first floor were the hopeless cases.

This extraordinary system, apart from facilitating the general services considerably, meant that a patient only mildly affected would not be troubled by a dying co-sufferer next door and ensured a uniformity of atmosphere on each floor. Treatment, of course, would thus vary from floor to floor.

This meant that the patients were divided into seven successive castes. Each floor was a world apart, with its own particular rules and traditions. And as each floor was in the charge of a different doctor, slight but definite differences in the methods of treatment had grown up, although initially the director had given the institution a single basic bent.

As soon as the nurse had left the room Giovanni Corte, no longer feeling feverish, went to the window and looked out, not because he wanted to see the view of the town (although he was not familiar with it) but in the hopes of catching a glimpse, through the windows, of the patients on the lower floors. The structure of the building, with its large recesses, made this possible. Giovanni Corte concentrated particularly on the first floor windows, which looked a very long way away, and which he could see only obliquely. But he could see nothing interesting. Most of the windows were completely hidden by grey venetian blinds.

But Corte did see someone, a man, standing at a window right next to his own. The two looked at each other with a growing feeling of sympathy but did not know how to break the silence. At last Giovanni Corte plucked up courage and said: "Have you just arrived too?"

"Oh no," said his neighbour, "I've been here two months." He was silent for a few moments and then, apparently not sure how to continue the conversation, added: "I was watching my brother down there."

"Your brother?"

"Yes. We both came here at the same time, oddly enough, but he got worse—he's on the fourth now."

"Fourth what?"

"Fourth floor," explained the man, pronouncing the two words with such pity and horror that Giovanni Corte was vaguely alarmed.

"But in that case"—Corte proceeded with his questioning with the lightheartedness one might adopt when speaking of tragic matters which don't concern one—"if things are already so serious on the fourth floor, whom do they put on the first?"

"Oh, the dying. There's nothing for the doctors to do down there. Only the priests. And of course ..."

"But there aren't many people down there," interrupted Giovanni Corte as if seeking confirmation, "almost all the blinds are down."

"There aren't many now, but there were this morning," replied the other with a slight smile. "The rooms with the blinds down are those where someone has died recently. As you can see, on the other floors the shutters are all open. Will you excuse me," he continued, moving slowly back in, "it seems to be getting rather cold. I'm going back to bed. May I wish you all the best ..."

The man vanished from the window sill and shut the window firmly; a light was lit inside the room. Giovanni Corte remained standing at the window, his eyes fixed on the lowered blinds of the first floor. He stared at them with morbid intensity, trying to visualise the ghastly secrets of that terrible first floor where patients were taken to die; he felt relieved that he was so far away. Meanwhile, the shadows of evening crept over the city. One by one the thousand windows of the sanatorium lit up, from the distance it looked a great house lit up for a ball. Only on the first floor, at the foot of the precipice, did dozens of windows remain blank and empty.

Giovanni Corte was considerably reassured by the doctor's visit. A natural pessimist, he was already secretly prepared for an unfavourable verdict and wouldn't have been surprised if the doctor had sent him down to the next floor.

His temperature however showed no signs of going down, even though his condition was otherwise satisfactory. But the doctor was pleasant and encouraging. Certainly he was affected—the doctor said—but only very slightly; in two or three weeks he would probably be cured. "So I'm to stay on the seventh floor?" enquired Giovanni Corte anxiously at this point.

"Well of course!" replied the doctor, clapping a friendly hand on his shoulder. "Where did you think you were going? Down to the fourth perhaps?" He spoke jokingly, as though it were the most absurd thought in the world.

"I'm glad about that," said Giovanni Corte. "You know how it is, when one's ill one always imagines the worst." In fact he stayed in the room which he had originally been given. On the rare afternoons when he was allowed up he made the acquaintance of some of his fellow-patients. He followed the treatment scrupulously, concentrated his whole attention on making a rapid recovery, yet his condition seemed to remain unchanged.

About ten days later, the head nurse of the seventh floor came to see Giovanni Corte. He wanted to ask an entirely personal favour: the following day a woman with two children was coming to the hospital: there were two free rooms right next to his, but a third was needed; would Signor Corte mind very much moving into another, equally comfortable room?

Naturally, Giovanni Corte made no objection; he didn't mind what room he was in; indeed, he might have a new and prettier nurse.

"Thank you so much," said the head nurse with a slight bow; "though, mark you, such a courteous act doesn't surprise me coming from a person such as yourself. We'll start moving your things in about an hour, if you don't mind. By the way, it's one floor down" he added in a quieter tone, as though it were a negligible detail. "Unfortunately there are no free rooms on this floor. Of course it's a purely temporary arrangement," he hastened to add, seeing that Corte had sat up suddenly and was about to protest, "a purely temporary arrangement. You'll be coming up again as soon as there's a free room, which should be in two or three days."

"I must confess," said Giovanni Corte smiling, to show that he had no childish fears, "I must confess that this particular sort of change of room doesn't appeal to me in the least."

"But it has no medical basis; I quite understand what you mean, but in this case it's simply to do a favour for this woman who doesn't want to be sep-arated from her children.... Now please" he added, laughing openly, "please don't get it into your head that there are other reasons!"

"Very well," said Giovanni Corte, "but it seems to me to bode ill."

So Giovanni Corte went down to the sixth floor, and though he was con-vinced that this move did not correspond to any worsening in his own condi-tion, he felt unhappy at the thought that there was now a definite barrier between himself and the everyday world of healthy people. The seventh floor was an embarkation point, with a certain degree of contact with society; it could be regarded as a sort of annexe to the ordinary world. But the sixth was already part of the real hospital; the attitudes of the doctors, nurses, of the patients themselves were just slightly different. It was admitted openly that the patients on that floor were really sick, even if not seriously so. From his initial conversa-tion with his neighbours, staff and doctors, Giovanni Corte gathered that here the seventh floor was regarded as a joke, reserved for amateurs, all affectation and caprice; it was only on the sixth floor that things began in earnest.

One thing Giovanni Corte did realise, however, was that he would certainly have some difficulty in getting back up to the floor where, medically speaking, he really belonged; to get back to the seventh floor he would have to set the whole complex organism of the place in motion, even for such a small move; it was quite plain that, were he not to insist, no one would ever have thought of putting him back on the top floor, with the "almost-well."

So Giovanni Corte decided not to forfeit anything that was his by right and not to yield to the temptations of habit. He was much concerned to impress upon his companions that he was with them only for a few days, that it was he who had agreed to go down a floor simply to oblige a lady, that he'd be going up again as soon as there was a free room. The others listened without interest and nodded, unconvinced.

Giovanni Corte's convictions, however, were confirmed by the judgement of the new doctor. He agreed that Giovanni Corte could most certainly be on the seventh floor; the form the disease had taken was ab-so-lute-ly negligible—he stressed each syllable so as to emphasize the importance of his diagnosis—but after all it might well be that Giovanni Corte would be better taken care of on the sixth floor.

"I don't want all that nonsense all over again," Giovanni Corte interrupted firmly at this point, "you say I should be on the seventh floor, and that's where I want to be."

"No one denies that," retorted the doctor. "I was advising you not as a doc-tor, but as a re-al friend. As I say, you're very slightly affected, it wouldn't even be an exaggeration to say that you're not ill at all, but in my opinion what makes your case different from other similarly mild ones is its greater extension: the intensity of the disease is minimal, but it is fairly widespread; the destructive process of the cells"—it was the first time Giovanni Corte had heard the sinister expression—"the destructive process of the cells is absolutely in the initial stage, it may not even have begun yet, but it is tending, I say tending, to affect large expanses of the organism. This is the only reason, in my opinion, why you might be better off down here on the sixth floor, where the methods of treatment are more highly specialised and more intensive."

One day he was informed that the Director of the nursing home, after lengthy consultation with his colleagues, had decided to make a change in the subdivision of the patients. Each person's grade—so to speak—was to be lowered by half a point. From now on the patients on each floor were to be divided into two categories according to the seriousness of their condition (indeed the respective doctors had already made this subdivision, though exclusively for their own personal use) and the lower of these two halves was to be officially moved one floor down. For example, half the patients on the sixth floor, those who were slightly more seriously affected, were to go down to the fifth; the less slightly affected of the seventh floor would go down to the sixth. Giovanni

Corte was pleased to hear this, because his return to the seventh floor would certainly be much easier amid this highly complicated series of removals.

However, when he mentioned this hope to the nurse he was bitterly disappointed. He learned that he was indeed to be moved, not up to the seventh but down to the floor below. For reasons that the nurse was unable to explain, he had been classed among the more "serious" patients on the sixth floor and so had to go down to the fifth.

Once he had recovered from his initial surprise, Giovanni Corte completely lost his temper; he shouted that they were cheating him, that he refused to hear of moving downwards, that he would go back home, that rights were rights and that the hospital administration could not afford to ignore the doctors' diagnosis so brazenly.

He was still shouting when the doctor arrived to explain matters more fully. He advised Corte to calm down unless he wanted his temperature to rise and explained that there had been a misunderstanding, at least in a sense. He agreed once again that Giovanni Corte would have been equally suitably placed on the seventh floor, but added that he had a slightly different, though entirely personal, view of the case. Basically, in a certain sense, his condition could be considered as needing treatment on the sixth floor, because the symptoms were so widespread. But he himself failed to understand why Corte had been listed among the more serious cases of the sixth floor. In all probability the secretary, who had phoned him that very morning to ask about Giovanni Corte's exact medical position, had made a mistake in copying out his report. Or more likely still the administrative staff had purposely depreciated his own judgement, since he was considered an expert doctor but over optimistic. Finally, the doctor advised Corte not to worry, to accept the move without protest; what counted was the disease, not the floor on which the patient was placed.

As far as the treatment was concerned—added the doctor—Giovanni Corte would certainly not have cause for complaint: the doctor on the floor below was undoubtedly far more experienced; it was almost part of the system that the doctors became more experienced, at least in the eyes of the administration, the further down you went. The rooms were equally comfortable and elegant. The view was equally good; it was only from the third floor that it was cut off by the surrounding trees.

It was evening, and Giovanni Corte's temperature had risen accordingly; he listened to this meticulous ratiocination with an increasing feeling of exhaustion. Finally he realised that he had neither the strength nor the desire to resist this unfair removal any further. Unprotesting, he allowed himself to be taken one floor down.

Giovanni Corte's one meagre consolation on the fifth floor was the knowledge that, in the opinion of doctors, nurses and patients alike, he was the least seriously ill of anyone on the whole floor. In short, he could consider himself much the most fortunate person in that section. On the other hand he was haunted by the thought that there were now two serious barriers between himself and the world of ordinary people.

As spring progressed the weather became milder, but Giovanni Corte no longer liked to stand at the window as he used to do; although it was stupid to feel afraid, he felt a strange movement of terror at the sight of the first floor windows, always mostly closed and now so much nearer.

His own state seemed unchanged; though after three days on the fifth floor a patch of eczema appeared on his right leg and showed no signs of clearing up during the following days. The doctor assured him that this was something absolutely independent of the main disease; it could have happened to the most healthy person in the world. Intensive treatment with digamma rays would clear it up in a few days.

"And can't one have that here?" asked Giovanni Corte.

"Certainly," replied the doctor delighted; "we have everything here. There's only one slight inconvenience ..."

"What?" asked Giovanni Corte with vague foreboding.

"Inconvenience in a manner of speaking," the doctor corrected himself. "The fourth floor is the only one with the relevant apparatus and I wouldn't advise you to go up and down three times a day."

"So it's out of the question?"

"It would really be better if you would be good enough to go down to the fourth floor until the eczema has cleared up."

"That's enough," shrieked Giovanni Corte exasperated. "I've had enough of going down! I'd rather die than go down to the fourth floor!"

"As you wish," said the doctor soothingly, so as not to annoy him, "but as the doctor responsible, I must point out that I forbid you to go up and down three times a day."

The unfortunate thing was that the eczema, rather than clearing up, began to spread gradually. Giovanni Corte couldn't rest, he tossed and turned in bed. His anger held out for three days but finally he gave in. Of his own accord, he asked the doctor to arrange for the ray treatment to be carried out, and to move to the floor below.

Here Corte noticed, with private delight, that he really was an exception. The other patients on the floor were certainly much more seriously affected and unable to move from their beds at all. He, on the other hand, could afford the luxury of walking from his bedroom to the room where the rays were, amid the compliments and amazement of the nurses themselves.

He made a point of stressing the extremely special nature of his position to the new doctor. A patient who, basically, should have been on the seventh floor was in fact on the fourth. As soon as his eczema was better, he would be going up again. This time there could be absolutely no excuse. He, who could still legitimately have been on the seventh floor!

"On the seventh?" exclaimed the doctor who had just finished examining him, with a smile. "You sick people do exaggerate so! I'd be the first to agree that you should be pleased with your condition; from what I see from your medical chart, it hasn't changed much for the worse. But—forgive my rather brutal honesty—there's quite a difference between that and the seventh floor. You're one of the least worrying cases, I quite agree, but you're definitely ill."

"Well then," said Giovanni Corte, scarlet in the face, "what floor would you personally put me on?"

"Well really, it's not easy to say, I've only examined you briefly, for any final judgement I'd have to observe you for at least a week."

"All right," insisted Corte, "but you must have some idea."

To calm him, the doctor pretended to concentrate on the matter for a moment and then, nodding to himself, said slowly: "Oh dear! Look, to please you, I think after all one might say the sixth. Yes," he added as if to persuade himself of the rightness of what he was saying, "The sixth would probably be all right."

The doctor thought that this would please his patient. But an expression of terror spread over Giovanni Corte's face: he realised that the doctors of the upper floors had deceived him; here was this new doctor, plainly more expert and honest, who in his heart of hearts—it was quite obvious—would place him not on the seventh but on the sixth floor, possibly even the lower fifth! The unexpected disappointment prostrated Corte. That evening his temperature rose appreciably.

His stay on the fourth floor was the most peaceful period he had had since coming to the hospital. The doctor was a delightful person, attentive and pleasant; he often stayed for whole hours to talk about all kinds of things. Giovanni Corte too was delighted to have an opportunity to talk, and drew the conversation around to his normal past life as a lawyer and man of the world. He tried to convince himself that he still belonged to the society of healthy men, that he was still connected with the world of business, that he was really still interested in matters of public import. He tried, but unsuccessfully. The conversation invariably came round, in the end, to the subject of his illness.

The desire for any sign of improvement had become an obsession. Unfortunately the digamma rays had succeeded in preventing the spread of the eczema but they had not cured it altogether. Giovanni Corte talked about this at length with the doctor every day and tried to appear philosophical, even ironic about it, without ever succeeding.

"Tell me, doctor," he said one day, "how is the destructive process of the cells coming along?"

"What a frightful expression," said the doctor reprovingly. "Wherever did you come across that? That's not at all right, particularly for a patient. I never want to hear anything like that again."

"All right," objected Corte, "but you still haven't answered."

"I'll answer right away," replied the doctor pleasantly. "The destructive process of your cells, to use your own horrible expression is, in your very minor case, absolutely negligible. But obstinate, I must say."

"Obstinate, you mean chronic?"

"Now don't credit me with things I haven't said. I only said obstinate. Anyhow that's how it is in minor cases. Even the mildest infections often need long and intensive treatment."

"But tell me, doctor, when can I expect to see some improvement?"

"When? It's difficult to say in these cases.... But listen," he added after pausing for thought, "I can see that you're positively obsessed with the idea of recovery ... if I weren't afraid of angering you, do you know what I'd suggest?"

"Please do say ..."

"Well, I'll put the situation very clearly. If I had this disease even slightly and were to come to this sanatorium, which is probably the best there is, I would arrange of my own accord, and from the first day—I repeat from the first day—to go down to one of the lower floors. In fact I'd even go to the ..."

"To the first?" suggested Corte with a forced smile.

"Oh dear no!" replied the doctor with a deprecating smile, "Oh dear no! But to the third or even the second. On the lower floors the treatment is far better, you know, the equipment is more complete, more powerful, the staff are more expert. And then you know who is the real soul of this hospital?"

"Isn't it Professor Dati?"

"Exactly. It was he who invented the treatment carried out here, he really planned the whole place. Well, Dati, the master-mind, operates, so to speak, between the first and second floors. His driving force radiates from there. But I assure you that it never goes beyond the third floor: further up than that the details of his orders are glossed over, interpreted more slackly; the heart of the hospital is on the lowest floors, and that's where you must be to have the best treatment."

"So in short," said Giovanni Corte, his voice shaking, "so you would advise me...."

"And there's something else," continued the doctor unperturbed, "and that is that in your case there's also the eczema to be considered. I agree that it's quite unimportant, but it is rather irritating, and in the long run it might lower your morale; and you know how important peace of mind is for your recovery. The rays have been only half successful. Now why? It might have been pure chance, but it might also have been that they weren't sufficiently intense. Well, on the third floor the apparatus is far more powerful. The chances of curing your eczema would be much greater. And the point is that once the cure is under way, the hardest part is over. Once you really feel better, there's absolutely no reason why you shouldn't come up here again, or indeed higher still, according to your 'deserts,' to the fifth, the sixth, possibly even the seventh ..."

"But do you think this will hasten my recovery?"

"I've not the slightest doubt it will. I've already said what I'd do if I were in your place."

The doctor talked like this to Giovanni Corte every day. And at last, tired of the inconveniences of the eczema, despite his instinctive reluctance to go down a floor, he decided to take the doctor's advice and move to the floor below.

He noticed immediately that the third floor was possessed of a special gaiety affecting both doctors and nurses, even though the cases treated on that floor were very serious. He noticed too that this gaiety increased daily; consumed with curiosity, as soon as he got to know the nurse, he asked why on earth they were all so cheerful.

"Oh, didn't you know?" she replied, "in three days time we're all going on holiday."

"On holiday?"

"That's right. The whole floor closes for a fortnight and the staff go off and enjoy themselves. Each floor takes it in turn to have a holiday."

"And what about the patients?"

"There are relatively few of them, so two floors are converted into one."

"You mean you put the patients of the third and fourth floors together?"

"No no," the nurse corrected him, "of the third and second. The patients on this floor will have to go down."

"Down to the second?" asked Giovanni Corte, suddenly pale as death. "You mean I'll have to go down to the second?"

"Well, yes. What's so odd about that? When we come back, in a fortnight, you'll come back here, in this same room. I can't see anything so terrifying about it."

But Giovanni Corte—as if forewarned by some strange instinct—was horribly afraid. However, since he could hardly prevent the staff from going on their holidays, and convinced that the new treatment with the stronger rays would do him good—the eczema had almost cleared up—he didn't dare offer any formal opposition to this new move. But he did insist, despite nurses' banter, that the label on the door of his new room should read "Giovanni Corte, third floor, temporary." Such a thing had never been done before in the whole history of the sanatorium, but the doctors didn't object, fearing that the prohibition of even such a minor matter might cause a serious shock to a patient as highly strung as Giovanni Corte.

After all, it was simply a question of waiting for fourteen days, neither more nor less. Giovanni Corte began to count them with stubborn eagerness, lying motionless on his bed for hours on end, staring at the furniture, which wasn't as pleasant and modern here as on the higher floors, but more cumbersome, gloomy and severe. Every now and again he would listen intently, thinking he heard sounds from the floor below, the floor of the dying, the "condemned"—vague sounds of death in action.

Naturally he found all this very dispiriting. His agitation seemed to nourish the disease, his temperature began to rise, the state of continued weakness began to affect him vitally. From the window—which was almost always open, since it was now mid-summer—he could no longer see the roofs nor even the houses, but only the green wall of the surrounding trees.

A week later, one afternoon about two o'clock, his room was suddenly invaded by the head nurse and three nurses, with a trolley. "All ready for the move, then?" asked the head nurse jovially.

"What move?" asked Giovanni Corte weakly, "what's all this? The third floor staff haven't come back after a week have they?"

"Third floor?" repeated the head nurse uncomprehendingly, "my orders are to take you down to the first floor," and he produced a printed form for removal to the first floor signed by none other than Professor Dati himself.

Giovanni Corte gave vent to his terror, his diabolical rage in long angry shrieks, which resounded throughout the whole floor. "Less noise, please," begged the nurses, "there are some patients here who are not at all well." But it would have taken more than that to calm him.

At last the second floor doctor appeared—a most attentive person. After being given the relevant information he looked at the form and listened to Giovanni Corte's side of the story. He then turned angrily to the head nurse and told him there had been a mistake, he himself had had no such orders, for some time now the place had been an impossible muddle, he himself knew nothing about what was going on ... at last, when he had had his say with his inferior, he turned politely to his patient, highly apologetic.

"Unfortunately, however," he added, "unfortunately Professor Dati left the hospital about an hour ago—he'll be away for a couple of days. I'm most awfully sorry, but his orders can't be overlooked. He would be the first to regret it, I assure you ... an absurd mistake! I fail to understand how it could have happened!"

Giovanni Corte had begun to tremble piteously. He was now completely unable to control himself, overcome with fear like a small child. His slow desperate sobbing echoed throughout the room.

It was as a result of this execrable mistake, then, that he was removed to his last resting place: he who basically, according to the most stringent medical opinion, was fit for the sixth, if not the seventh floor as far as his illness was concerned! The situation was so grotesque that from time to time Giovanni Corte felt inclined simply to roar with laughter.

Stretched out on his bed, while the afternoon warmth flowed calmly over the city, he would stare at the green of the trees through the window and feel that he had come to a completely unreal world, walled in with sterilised tiles, full of deathly arctic passages and soulless white figures. It even occurred to him that the trees he thought he saw through the window were not real; finally, when he noticed that the leaves never moved, he was certain of it.

Corte was so upset by this idea that he called the nurse and asked for his spectacles, which he didn't use in bed, being short-sighted; only then was he a little reassured: the lenses proved that they were real leaves and that they were shaken, though very slightly, by the wind.

When the nurse had gone out, he spent half an hour in complete silence. Six floors, six solid barriers, even if only because of a bureaucratic mistake, weighed implacably above Giovanni Corte. How many years (for obviously it was now a question of years) would it be before he could climb back to the top of that precipice?

But why was the room suddenly going so dark? It was still mid-afternoon. With a supreme effort, for he felt himself paralysed by a strange lethargy, Giovanni Corte turned to look at his watch on the locker by his bed. Three-thirty. He turned his head the other way and saw that the venetian blinds, in obedience to some mysterious command, were dropping slowly, shutting out the light.

ITALO CALVINO

THE SPIRAL

Translated by William Weaver

Italo Calvino (1923–1985) was born in Cuba and grew up in San Remo, Italy. The son of two botanists, Calvino went on to study agriculture at the University of Turin. But "attracted by another kind of vegetation," as he would later reflect, "that of the written word," Calvino left his scientific training to pursue journalism and writing. His participation in the Resistance against Fascism in wartime Italy galvanized his literary career, resulting in a novel, The Path to the Nest of Spiders *(1947), and a collection of short stories,* Adam, One Afternoon *(1949). Calvino also worked as an editor, living for fifteen years in Paris, where he married and raised a family. Calvino won several European literary prizes, including Italy's prestigious Premio Feltrinelli award in 1973 for* Invisible Cities. *His formidable oeuvre includes* Italian Folktales *(1956),* If On a Winter's Night a Traveler *(1979), and the essay collection* The Literature Machine *(1980). Calvino died of a cerebral hemorrhage in 1985.*

Because it weaves together realistic and fantastic elements, Calvino's work is often compared to that of Gabriel García Márquez and Jorge Luis Borges; however, such comparisons tend to obscure critical differences between writers. Calvino's stories occupy the border zones between science and myth and between theory and history, exploring the ways in which we make reality familiar. Qfwfq, the enigmatic narrator of "The Spiral," appears in several stories in Cosmicomics *(1965) and* T Zero *(1967), shifting both shape and voice to take the reader through strange and comical investigations into the conventions of time and space, the nature of life and its origins, and the mysteries of love and death. "It is entirely possible," writes Salman Rushdie, "that Calvino is not a human being at all, but a planet ... seeing into the deepest recesses of human minds and then bringing their dreams to life."*

For the majority of mollusks, the visible organic form has little importance in the life of the members of a species, since they cannot see one another and

*have, at most, only a vague perception of other individuals and of their sur-
roundings. This does not prevent brightly colored striping and forms which
seem very beautiful to our eyes (as in many gastropod shells) from existing
independently of any relationship to visibility.*

I

Like me, when I was clinging to that rock, you mean?—*Qfwfq asked,*—With
the waves rising and falling, and me there, still, flat, sucking what there was to
suck and thinking about it all the time? If that's the time you want to know
about, there isn't much I can tell you. Form? I didn't have any; that is, I didn't
know I had one, or rather I didn't know you *could* have one. I grew more or
less on all sides, at random; if this is what you call radial symmetry, I suppose I
had radial symmetry, but to tell you the truth I never paid any attention to it.
Why should I have grown more on one side than on the other? I had no eyes,
no head, no part of the body that was different from any other part; now I try
to persuade myself that the two holes I had were a mouth and an anus, and
that I therefore already had my bilateral symmetry, just like the trilobites and
the rest of you, but in my memory I really can't tell those holes apart, I passed
stuff from whatever side I felt like, inside or outside was the same, differences
and repugnances came along much later. Every now and then I was seized by
fantasies, that's true; for example, the notion of scratching my armpit, or
crossing my legs, or once even of growing a mustache. I use these words here
with you, to make myself clear; then there were many details I couldn't foresee:
I had some cells, one more or less the same as another, and they all did more or
less the same job. But since I had no form I could feel all possible forms in
myself, and all actions and expressions and possibilities of making noises, even
rude ones. In short, there were no limitations to my thoughts, which weren't
thoughts, after all, because I had no brain to think them; every cell on its own
thought every thinkable thing all at once, not through images, since we had no
images of any kind at our disposal, but simply in that indeterminate way of
feeling oneself there, which did not prevent us from feeling ourselves equally
there in some other way.

It was a rich and free and contented condition, my condition at that time,
quite the contrary of what you might think. I was a bachelor (our system of
reproduction in those days didn't require even temporary couplings), healthy,
without too many ambitions. When you're young, all evolution lies before
you, every road is open to you, and at the same time you can enjoy the fact of
being there on the rock, flat mollusk-pulp, damp and happy. If you compare
yourself with the limitations that came afterwards, if you think of how having
one form excludes other forms, of the monotonous routine where you finally
feel trapped, well, I don't mind saying life was beautiful in those days.

To be sure, I lived a bit withdrawn into myself, that's true, no comparison with our interrelated life nowadays; and I'll also admit that—partly because of my age and partly under the influence of my surroundings—I was what they call a narcissist to a slight extent; I mean I stayed there observing myself all the time, I saw all my good points and all my defects, and I liked myself for the former and for the latter; I had no terms of comparison, you must remember that, too.

But I wasn't so backward that I didn't know something else existed beyond me: the rock where I clung, obviously, and also the water that reached me with every wave, but other stuff, too, farther on: that is, the world. The water was a source of information, reliable and precise: it brought me edible substances which I absorbed through all my surface, and other inedible ones which still helped me form an idea of what there was around. The system worked like this: a wave would come, and I, still sticking to the rock, would raise myself up a little bit, imperceptibly—all I had to do was loosen the pressure slightly—and, splat, the water passed beneath me, full of substances and sensations and stimuli. You never knew how those stimuli were going to turn out, sometimes a tickling that made you die laughing, other times a shudder, a burning, an itch; so it was a constant seesaw of amusement and emotion. But you mustn't think I just lay there passively, dumbly accepting everything that came: after a while I had acquired some experience and I was quick to analyze what sort of stuff was arriving and to decide how I should behave, to make the best use of it or to avoid the more unpleasant consequences. It was all a kind of game of contractions, with each of the cells I had, or of relaxing at the right moment: and I could make my choices, reject, attract, even spit.

And so I learned that there were *the others,* the element surrounding me was filled with traces of them, *others* hostile and different from me or else disgustingly similar. No, now I'm giving you a disagreeable idea of my character, which is all wrong. Naturally, each of us went about on his own business, but the presence of the *others* reassured me, created an inhabited zone around me, freed me from the fear of being an alarming exception, which I would have been if the fact of existing had been my fate alone, a kind of exile.

So I knew that some of the *others* were female. The water transmitted a special vibration, a kind of brrrum brrrum brrrum, I remember when I became aware of it the first time, or rather, not the first, I remember when I became aware of being aware of it as a thing I had always known. At the discovery of these vibrations' existence, I was seized with a great curiosity, not so much to see them, or to be seen by them either—since, first, we hadn't any sight, and secondly, the sexes weren't yet differentiated, each individual was identical with every other individual and at looking at one or another I would have felt no more pleasure than in looking at myself—but a curiosity to know whether something would happen between me and them. A desperation filled me, a desire not to do anything special, which would have been out of place, knowing that there was nothing special to do, or nonspecial either, but to respond in some way to that vibration with a corresponding vibration, or rather, with a personal vibration of my own, because, sure enough, there was something there that wasn't exactly the same as the other, I mean now you might say it came from hormones, but for me it was very beautiful.

So then, one of them, shlup shlup shlup, emitted her eggs, and I , shlup shlup shlup, fertilized them: all down inside the sea, mingling in the water tepid from the sun; oh, I forgot to tell you, I could feel the sun, which warmed the sea and heated the rock.

One of them, I said. Because, among all those female messages that the sea slammed against me like an indistinct soup at first where everything was all right with me and I grubbed about paying no attention to what one was like or another, suddenly I understood what corresponded best to my tastes, tastes which I hadn't known before that moment, of course. In other words, I had fallen in love. What I mean is: I had begun to recognize, to isolate the signs of one of those from the others, in fact I waited for these signs I had begun to recognize, I sought them, responded to those signs I awaited with other signs I made myself, or rather it was I who aroused them, these signs from her, which I answered with other signs of my own, I mean I was in love with her and she with me, so what more could I want from life?

Now habits have changed, and it already seems inconceivable to you that one could love a female like that, without having spent any time with her. And yet, through that unmistakable part of her still in solution in the sea water, which the waves placed at my disposal, I received a quantity of information about her, more than you can imagine: not the superficial, generic information you get now, seeing and smelling and touching and hearing a voice, but essential information, which I could then develop at length in my imagination. I could think of her with minute precision, thinking not so much of how she was made, which would have been a banal and vulgar way of thinking of her, but of how from her present formlessness she would be transformed into one of the infinite possible forms, still remaining herself, however. I didn't imagine the forms that she might assume, but I imagined the special quality that, in taking them, she would give to those forms.

I knew her well, in other words. And I wasn't sure of her. Every now and then I was overcome with suspicion, anxiety, rage. I didn't let anything show, you know my character, but beneath that impassive mask passed suppositions I can't bring myself to confess even now. More than once I suspected she was unfaithful to me, that she sent messages not only to me but also to others; more than once I thought I had intercepted one, or that I had discovered a tone of insincerity in a message addressed to me. I was jealous, I can admit it now, not so much out of distrust of her as out of unsureness of myself: who could assure me that she had really understood who I was? Or that she had understood the fact that I was? This relationship achieved between us thanks to the sea water—a full, complete relationship, what more could I ask for?—was for me something absolutely personal, between two unique and distinct individualities; but for her? Who could assure me that what she might find in me she hadn't also found in another, or in another two or three or ten or a hundred like me? Who could assure me that her abandon in our shared relations wasn't an indiscriminate abandon, slapdash, a kind of—who's next?—collective ecstasy?

The fact that these suspicions did not correspond to the truth was confirmed, for me, by the subtle, soft, private vibration, at times still trembling with modesty, in our correspondences; but what if, precisely out of shyness and inexperience, she didn't pay enough attention to my characteristics and others took advantage of this innocence to worm their way in? And what if she, a novice, believed it was still I and couldn't distinguish one from the other, and so our most intimate play was extended to a circle of strangers ... ?

It was then that I began to secrete calcareous matter. I wanted to make something to mark my presence in an unmistakable fashion, something that would defend this individual presence of mine from the indiscriminate instability of all the rest. Now it's no use my piling up words, trying to explain the novelty of this intention I had; the first word I said is more than enough: *make,* I wanted to *make,* and considering the fact that I had never made anything or thought you could make anything, this in itself was a big event. So I began to make the first thing that occurred to me, and it was a shell. From the margin of that fleshy cloak on my body, using certain glands, I began to give off secretions which took on a curving shape all around, until I was covered with a hard and variegated shield, rough on the outside and smooth and shiny inside. Naturally, I had no way of controlling the form of what I was making: I just stayed there all huddled up, silent and sluggish, and I secreted. I went on even after the shell covered my whole body; I began another turn; in short, I was getting one of those shells all twisted into a spiral, which you, when you see them, think are so hard to make, but all you have to do is keep working and giving off the same matter without stopping, and they grow like that, one turn after the other.

Once it existed, this shell was also a necessary and indispensable place to stay inside of, a defense for my survival; it was a lucky thing I had made it, but while I was making it I had no idea of making it because I needed it; on the contrary, it was like when somebody lets out an exclamation he could perfectly well not make, and yet he makes it, like "Ha" or "hmph!," that's how I made the shell: simply to express myself. And in this self-expression I put all the thoughts I had about her, I released the anger she made me feel, my amorous way of thinking about her, my determination to exist for her, the desire for me to be me, and for her to be her, and the love for myself that I put in my love for her— all the things that could be said only in that conch shell wound into a spiral.

At regular intervals the calcareous matter I was secreting came out colored, so a number of lovely stripes were formed running straight through the spirals, and this shell was a thing different from me but also the truest part of me, the explanation of who I was, my portrait translated into a rhythmic system of volumes and stripes and colors and hard matter, and it was the portrait of her as she was, because at the same time she was making herself a shell identical to mine and without knowing it I was copying what she was doing and she without knowing it was copying what I was doing, and all the others were copying all the others, so we would be back where we had been before except for the fact that in saying these shells were the same I was a bit hasty, because when you looked closer you discovered all sorts of little differences that later on might become enormous.

So I can say that my shell made itself, without my taking any special pains to have it come out one way rather than another, but this doesn't mean that I was absent-minded during that time; I applied myself, instead, to that act of secreting, without allowing myself a moment's distraction, never thinking of anything else, or rather: thinking always of something else, since I didn't know how to think of the shell, just as, for that matter, I didn't know how to think of anything else either, but I accompanied the effort of making the shell with the effort of thinking I was making something, that is anything: that is, I thought of all the things it would be possible to make. So it wasn't even a monotonous task, because the effort of thinking which accompanied it spread toward countless types of thoughts which spread, each one, toward countless types of actions that might each serve to make countless things, and making each of these things was implicit in making the shell grow, turn after turn ...

II

*(And so now, after five hundred million years have gone by, I look around and, above the rock, I see the railway embankment and the train passing along it with a party of Dutch girls looking out of the window and, in the last compartment, a solitary traveler reading Herodotus in a bilingual edition, and the train vanishes into the tunnel under the highway, where there is a sign with the pyramids and the words "*VISIT EGYPT,*" and a little ice-cream wagon tries to pass a big truck laden with installments of* Rh-Stijl, *a periodical encyclopedia that comes out in paperback, but then it puts its brakes on because its visibility*

is blocked by a cloud of bees which crosses the road coming from a row of hives in a field from which surely a queen bee is flying away, drawing behind her a swarm in the direction opposite to the smoke of the train, which has reappeared at the other end of the tunnel, so you can see hardly anything thanks to the cloudy stream of bees and coal smoke, except a few yards farther up there is a peasant breaking the ground with his mattock and, unaware, he brings to light and reburies a fragment of a Neolithic mattock similar to his own, in a garden that surrounds an astronomical observatory with its telescopes aimed at the sky and on whose threshold the keeper's daughter sits reading the horoscopes in a weekly whose cover displays the face of the star of Cleopatra: I see all this and I feel no amazement because making the shell implied also making the honey in the wax comb and the coal and the telescopes and the reign of Cleopatra and the films about Cleopatra and the pyramids and the design of the zodiac of the Chaldean astrologers and the wars and empires Herodotus speaks of and the words written by Herodotus and the works written in all languages including those of Spinoza in Dutch and the fourteenth-line summary of Spinoza's life and works in the installment of the encyclopedia in the truck passed by the ice-cream wagon, and so I feel as if, in making the shell, I had also made the rest.

I look around, and whom am I looking for? She is still the one I seek; I've been in love for five hundred million years, and if I see a Dutch girl on the sand with a beachboy wearing a gold chain around his neck and showing her the swarm of bees to frighten her, there she is: I recognize her from her inimitable way of raising one shoulder until it almost touches her cheek, I'm almost sure, or rather I'd say absolutely sure if it weren't for a certain resemblance that I find also in the daughter of the keeper of the observatory, and in the photograph of the actress made up as Cleopatra, or perhaps in Cleopatra as she really was in person, for what part of the true Cleopatra they say every representation of Cleopatra contains, or in the queen bee flying at the head of the swarm with that forward impetuousness, or in the paper woman cut out and pasted on the plastic windshield of the little ice-cream wagon, wearing a bathing suit like the Dutch girl on the beach now listening over a little transistor radio to the voice of a woman singing, the same voice that the encyclopedia truck driver hears over his radio, and the same one I'm now sure I've heard for five million years, it is surely she I hear singing and whose image I look for all around, seeing only gulls volplaning on the surface of the sea where a school of anchovies glistens and for a moment I am certain I recognize her in a female gull and a moment later I suspect that instead she's an anchovy, though she might just as well be any queen or slave-girl named by Herodotus or only hinted at in the pages of the volume left to mark the seat of the reader who has stepped into the corridor of the train to strike up a conversation with

*the party of Dutch tourists; I might say I am in love with each of those girls
and at the same time I am sure of being in love always with her alone.*

*And the more I torment myself with love for each of them, the less I can
bring myself to say to them: "Here I am!," afraid of being mistaken and even
more afraid that she is mistaken, taking me for somebody else, for somebody
who, for all she knows of me, might easily take my place, for example the
beachboy with the gold chain, or the director of the observatory, or a gull, or a
male anchovy, or the reader of Herodotus, or Herodotus himself, or the
vendor of ice cream, who has come down to the beach along a dusty road
among the prickly pears and is now surrounded by the Dutch girls in their
bathing suits, or Spinoza, or the truck driver who is transporting the life and
works of Spinoza summarized and repeated two thousand times, or one of the
drones dying at the bottom of the hive after having fulfilled his role in the continuation of the species.)*

III

... Which doesn't mean that the shell wasn't, first and foremost, a shell, with its
particular form, which couldn't be any different because it was the very form I
had given it, the only one I could or would give it. Since the shell had a form,
the form of the world was also changed, in the sense that now it included the
form of the world as it had been without a shell plus the form of the shell.

And that had great consequences: because the waving vibrations of light,
striking bodies, produce particular effects from them, color first of all, namely,
that matter I used to make stripes with which vibrated in a different way from
the rest; but there was also the fact that a volume enters into a special relationship of volumes with other volumes, all phenomena I couldn't be aware of,
though they existed.

The shell in this way was able to create visual images of shells, which are
things very similar—as far as we know—to the shell itself, except that the shell
is here, whereas the images of it are formed elsewhere, possibly on a retina. An
image therefore presupposes a retina, which in turn presupposes a complex
system stemming from an encephalon. So, in producing the shell, I also produced its image—not one, of course, but many, because with one shell you can
make as many shell-images as you want—but only potential images because to
form an image you need all the requisites I mentioned before: an encephalon
with its optic ganglia, and an optic nerve to carry the vibrations from outside
to inside, and this optic nerve, at the other extremity, ends in something made
purposely to see what there is outside, namely the eye. Now it's ridiculous to
think that, having an encephalon, one would simply drop a nerve like a fishing
line cast into the darkness; until the eyes crop up, one can't know whether

there is something to be seen outside or not. For myself, I had none of this equipment, so I was the least authorized to speak of it; however, I had conceived an idea of my own, namely that the important thing was to form some visual images, and the eyes would come later in consequence. So I concentrated on making the part of me that was outside (and even the interior part of me that conditioned the exterior) give rise to an image, or rather to what would later be called a lovely image (when compared to other images considered less lovely, or rather ugly, or simply revoltingly hideous).

When a body succeeds in emitting or in reflecting luminous vibrations in a distinct and recognizable order—I thought—what does it do with these vibrations? Put them in its pocket? No, it releases them on the first passer-by. And how will the latter behave in the face of vibrations he can't utilize and which, taken in this way, might even be annoying? Hide his head in a hole? No, he'll thrust it out in that direction until the point most exposed to the optic vibrations becomes sensitized and develops the mechanism for exploiting them in the form of images. In short, I conceived of the eye-encephalon link as a kind of tunnel dug from the outside by the force of what was ready to become image, rather than from within by the intention of picking up any old image.

And I wasn't mistaken: even today I'm sure that the project—in its over-all aspect—was right. But my error lay in thinking that sight would also come to us, that is to me and to her. I elaborated a harmonious, colored image of myself to enter her visual receptivity, to occupy its center, to settle there, so that she could utilize me constantly, in dreaming and in memory, with thought as well as with sight. And I felt at the same time she was radiating an image of herself so perfect that it would impose itself on my foggy, backward senses, developing in me an interior visual field where it would blaze forth definitely.

So our efforts led us to become those perfect objects of a sense whose nature nobody quite knew yet, and which later became perfect precisely through the perfection of its object, which was, in fact, us. I'm talking about sight, the eyes; only I had failed to foresee one thing: the eyes that finally opened to see us didn't belong to us but to others.

Shapeless, colorless beings, sacks of guts stuck together carelessly, peopled the world all around us, without giving the slightest thought to what they should make of themselves, to how to express themselves and identify themselves in a stable, complete form, such as to enrich the visual possibilities of whoever saw them. They came and went, sank a while, then emerged, in that space between air and water and rock, wandering about absently; and we in the meanwhile, she and I and all those intent on squeezing out a form of ourselves, were there slaving away at our dark task. Thanks to us, that badly defined space became a visual field; and who reaped the benefit? These intruders, who had never before given a thought to the possibility of eyesight (ugly as they were, they wouldn't have gained a thing by seeing one another), these creatures who had always turned a deaf ear to the vocation of form. While we were bent over, doing the hardest part of the job, that is, creating something to be seen, they were quietly taking on the easiest part: adapting their lazy, embryonic receptive organs to what there was to receive; our images. And they needn't try telling me now that their job was toilsome too: from that gluey mess that filled their heads anything could have come out, and a photosensitive mechanism doesn't take all that much trouble to put together. But when it comes to perfecting it, that's another story! How can you, if you don't have visible objects to see, gaudy ones even, the kind that impose themselves on the eyesight? To sum it up in a few words: they developed eyes at our expense.

So sight, *our* sight, which we were obscurely waiting for, was the sight that the others had of us. In one way or another, the great revolution had taken place: all of a sudden, around us, eyes were opening, and corneas and irises and pupils: the swollen, colorless eye of polyps and cuttlefish, the dazed and gelatinous eyes of bream and mullet, the protruding and peduncled eyes of crayfish and lobsters, the bulging and faceted eyes of flies and ants. A seal now comes forward, black and shiny, winking little eyes like pinheads. A snail extends ball-like eyes at the end of long antennae. The inexpressive eyes of the gull examine the surface of the water. Beyond a glass mask the frowning eyes of an underwater fisherman explore the depths. Through the lens of a spyglass a sea captain's eyes and the eyes of a woman bathing converge on my shell, then look at each other, forgetting me. Framed by far-sighted lenses I feel on me the far-sighted eyes of a zoologist, trying to frame me in the eye of a Rolleiflex. At that moment a school of tiny anchovies, barely born, passes before me, so tiny that in each little white fish it seems there is room only for the eye's black dot, and it is a kind of eye-dust that crosses the sea.

All these eyes were mine. I had made them possible; I had had the active part; I furnished them the raw material, the image. With eyes had come all the rest, so everything that the others, having eyes, had become, their every form and function, and the quantity of things that, thanks to eyes, they had managed to do, in their every form and function, came from what I had done. Of course, they were not just casually implicit in my being there, in my having relations with others, male and female, et cetera, in my setting out to make a shell, et cetera. In other words, I had foreseen absolutely everything.

And at the bottom of each of those eyes I lived, or rather another me lived, one of the images of me, and it encountered the image of her, the most faithful image of her, in that beyond which opens, past the semiliquid sphere of the irises, in the darkness of the pupils, the mirrored hall of the retinas, in our true element which extends without shores, without boundaries.

ALBERT CAMUS

THE GUEST

Translated by Justin O'Brien

Albert Camus (1913–1960) was born and educated in Algeria and worked as a teacher in that country from 1940 to 1942. Rejected from active service because of his poor health, Camus spent the later years of World War II as a member of the French Underground. After the war he was a journalist, playwright, and novelist in Paris, and he achieved immediate recognition in 1942 with the publication of his first novel, The Stranger, *and his long essay on the absurd,* The Myth of Sysiphus. *A member of the Communist party during his twenties, Camus became increasingly apolitical as he grew older. Almost against his will, he became the leading moral voice of his generation, exploring ideas of moral neutrality and responsibility, and advocating nature and moderation rather than historicism and violence. With Jean-Paul Sartre, Albert Camus was a leading figure in French existentialism—one of the most important philosophical movements of the twentieth century. In 1957 he won the Nobel Prize in literature. In 1960, at the height of his fame, Camus was killed in an auto accident near Sens, France.*

"The Guest" is from Camus's only collection of short stories, Exile and the Kingdom *(1957). He wrote these stories after the outbreak of the Franco-Algerian war in 1954. Camus tries to "mediate the situation in Algeria by dramatizing the differences between the two countries" because, in his view, "the aim of art, the aim of a life can only be to increase the sum of freedom and responsibility to be found in every man and in the world." He believed in "differences not in uniformity." He saw such differences as the "roots without which the tree of liberty, the sap of creation and of civilization, dries up." This collection of short stories was the last major work completed before his death. His other publications include several plays, two more novels,* The Plague *(1947) and* The Fall *(1956), and the essay* The Rebel: An Essay on Man in Revolt *(1951).*

The schoolmaster was watching the two men climb toward him. One was on horseback, the other on foot. They had not yet tackled the abrupt rise leading to the schoolhouse built on the hillside. They were toiling onward, making slow progress in the snow, among the stones, on the vast expanse of the high, deserted plateau. From time to time the horse stumbled. He could not be heard yet but the breath issuing from his nostrils could be seen. The schoolmaster calculated that it would take them a half hour to get onto the hill. It was cold; he went back into the school to get a sweater.

He crossed the empty, frigid classroom. On the blackboard the four rivers of France, drawn with four different colored chalks, had been flowing toward their estuaries for the past three days. Snow had suddenly fallen in mid-October after eight months of drought without the transition of rain, and the twenty pupils, more or less, who lived in the villages scattered over the plateau had stopped coming. With fair weather they would return. Daru now heated only the single room that was his lodging, adjoining the classroom. One of the windows faced, like the classroom windows, the south. On that side the school was a few kilometers from the point where the plateau began to slope toward the south. In clear weather the purple mass of the mountain range where the gap opened onto the desert could be seen.

Somewhat warmed, Daru returned to the window from which he had first noticed the two men. They were no longer visible. Hence they must have tackled the rise. The sky was not so dark, for the snow had stopped falling during the night. The morning had dawned with a dirty light which had scarcely become brighter as the ceiling of clouds lifted. At two in the afternoon it seemed as if the day were merely beginning. But still this was better than those three days when the thick snow was falling amidst unbroken darkness with little gusts of wind that rattled the double door of the classroom. Then Daru had spent long hours in his room, leaving it only to go to the shed and feed the chickens or get some coal. Fortunately the delivery truck from Tadjid, the nearest village to the north, had brought his supplies two days before the blizzard. It would return in forty-eight hours.

Besides, he had enough to resist a siege, for the little room was cluttered with bags of wheat that the administration had left as a supply to distribute to those of his pupils whose families had suffered from the drought. Actually they had all been victims because they were all poor. Every day Daru would distribute a ration to the children. They had missed it, he knew, during these bad days. Possibly one of the fathers or big brothers would come this afternoon and he could supply them with grain. It was just a matter of carrying them over to the next harvest. Now shiploads of wheat were arriving from France and the worst was over. But it would be hard to forget that poverty, that army of ragged ghosts wandering in the sunlight, the plateaus burned to a cinder month after month, the earth shriveled up little by little, literally scorched, every stone bursting into dust under one's foot. The sheep had died then by thousands, and even a few men, here and there, sometimes without anyone's knowing.

In contrast with such poverty, he who lived almost like a monk, in his remote schoolhouse, had felt like a lord with his whitewashed walls, his narrow couch, his unpainted shelves, his well, and his weekly provisioning with water and food. And suddenly this snow, without warning, without the foretaste of rain. This is the way the region was, cruel to live in, even without men, who didn't help matters either. But Daru had been born here. Everywhere else, he felt exiled.

He went out and stepped forward on the terrace in front of the schoolhouse. The two men were now halfway up the slope. He recognized the horseman to be Balducci, the old gendarme he had known for a long time. Balducci was holding at the end of a rope an Arab walking behind him with hands bound and head lowered. The gendarme waved a greeting to which Daru did not reply, lost as he was in contemplation of the Arab dressed in a faded blue *jellaba,* his feet in sandals but covered with socks of heavy raw wool, his head crowned with a narrow, short *chèche.* Balducci was holding back his horse in order not to hurt the Arab, and the group was advancing slowly.

Within earshot, Balducci shouted, "One hour to do the three kilometers from El Ameur!" Daru did not answer. Short and square in his thick sweater, he watched them climb. Not once had the Arab raised his head. "Hello," said Daru when they got up onto the terrace. "Come in and warm up." Balducci painfully got down from his horse without letting go of the rope. He smiled at the schoolmaster from under his bristling mustache. His little dark eyes, deepset under a tanned forehead, and his mouth surrounded with wrinkles made him look attentive and studious. Daru took the bridle, led the horse to the shed, and came back to the two men who were now waiting for him in the school. He led them into his room. "I am going to heat up the classroom," he said. "We'll be more comfortable there."

When he entered the room again, Balducci was on the couch. He had undone the rope tying him to the Arab, who had squatted near the stove. His hands still bound, the *chèche* pushed back on his head, the Arab was looking toward the window. At first Daru noticed only his huge lips, fat, smooth, almost Negroid; yet his nose was straight, his eyes dark and full of fever. The *chèche* uncovered an obstinate forehead and, under the weathered skin now rather discolored by the cold, the whole face had a restless and rebellious look. "Go into the other room," said the schoolmaster, "and I'll make you some mint tea." "Thanks," Balducci said. "What a chore! How I long for retirement." And addressing his prisoner in Arabic, he said, "Come on, you." The Arab got up and, slowly, holding his bound wrists in front of him, went into the classroom.

With the tea, Daru brought a chair. But Balducci was already sitting in state at the nearest pupil's desk, and the Arab had squatted against the teacher's platform facing the stove, which stood between the desk and the window. When he held out the glass of tea to the prisoner, Daru hesitated at the sight of his bound hands. "He might perhaps be untied." "Sure," said Balducci. "That was for the trip." He started to get to his feet. But Daru, setting the glass on the floor, had knelt beside the Arab. Without saying anything, the Arab watched him with his feverish eyes. Once his hands were free, he rubbed his swollen wrists against each other, took the glass of tea and sucked up the burning liquid in swift little sips.

"Good," said Daru. "And where are you headed?"

Balducci withdrew his mustache from the tea. "Here, son."

"Odd pupils! And you're spending the night?"

"No. I'm going back to El Ameur. And you will deliver this fellow to Tinguit. He is expected at police headquarters."

Balducci was looking at Daru with a friendly little smile.

"What's this story?" asked the schoolmaster. "Are you pulling my leg?"

"No, son. Those are the orders."

"The orders? I'm not ..." Daru hesitated, not wanting to hurt the old Corsican. "I mean, that's not my job."

"What! What's the meaning of that? In wartime people do all kinds of jobs."

"Then I'll wait for the declaration of war!"

Balducci nodded. "O.K. But the orders exist and they concern you too. Things are bubbling, it appears. There is talk of forthcoming revolt. We are mobilized, in a way."

Daru still had his obstinate look.

"Listen, son," Balducci said. "I like you and you've got to understand. There's only a dozen of us at El Ameur to patrol the whole territory of a small department and I must be back in a hurry. He couldn't be kept there. His village was beginning to stir; they wanted to take him back. You must take him to Tinguit tomorrow before the day is over. Twenty kilometers shouldn't faze a husky fellow like you. After that, all will be over. You'll come back to your pupils and your comfortable life."

Behind the wall the horse could be heard snorting and pawing the earth. Daru was looking out the window. Decidedly the weather was clearing and the light was increasing over the snowy plateau. When all the snow was melted, the sun would take over again and once more would burn the fields of stone. For days still, the unchanging sky would shed its dry light on the solitary expanse where nothing had any connection with man.

"After all," he said, turning around toward Balducci, "what did he do?" And, before the gendarme had opened his mouth, he asked, "Does he speak French?"

"No, not a word. We had been looking for him for a month, but they were hiding him. He killed his cousin."

"Is he against us?"

"I don't think so. But you can never be sure."

"Why did he kill?"

"A family squabble, I think. One owed grain to the other, it seems. It's not at all clear. In short, he killed his cousin with a billhook. You know, like a sheep, *kreezk!*"

Balducci made the gesture of drawing a blade across his throat, and the Arab, his attention attracted, watched him with a sort of anxiety. Daru felt a sudden wrath against the man, against all men with their rotten spite, their tireless hates, their blood lust.

But the kettle was singing on the stove. He served Balducci more tea, hesitated, then served the Arab again, who drank avidly a second time. His raised arms made the *jellaba* fall open, and the schoolmaster saw his thin, muscular chest.

"Thanks, son," Balducci said. "And now I'm off."

He got up and went toward the Arab, taking a small rope from his pocket.

"What are you doing?" Daru asked dryly.

Balducci, disconcerted, showed him the rope.

"Don't bother."

The old gendarme hesitated. "It's up to you. Of course, you are armed?"

"I have my shotgun."

"Where?"

"In the trunk."

"You ought to have it near your bed."

"Why? I have nothing to fear."

"You're crazy, son. If there's an uprising, no one is safe; we're all in the same boat."

"I'll defend myself. I'll have time to see them coming."

Balducci began to laugh, then suddenly the mustache covered the white teeth. "You'll have time? O.K. That's just what I was saying. You always have been a little cracked. That's why I like you; my son was like that."

At the same time he took out his revolver and put it on the desk. "Keep it; I don't need two weapons from here to El Ameur."

The revolver shone against the black paint of the table. When the gendarme turned toward him, the schoolmaster caught his smell of leather and horseflesh.

"Listen, Balducci," Daru said suddenly, "all this disgusts me, beginning with your fellow here. But I won't hand him over. Fight, yes, if I have to. But not that."

The old gendarme stood in front of him and looked at him severely.

"You're being a fool," he said slowly. "I don't like it either. You don't get used to putting a rope on a man even after years of it, and you're even ashamed—yes, ashamed. But you can't let them have their way."

"I won't hand him over," Daru said again.

"It's an order, son, and I repeat it."

"That's right. Repeat to them what I've said to you: I won't hand him over."

Balducci made a visible effort to reflect. He looked at the Arab and at Daru. At last he decided.

"No, I won't tell them anything. If you want to drop us, go ahead; I'll not denounce you. I have an order to deliver the prisoner and I'm doing so. And now you'll just sign this paper for me."

"There's no need. I'll not deny that you left him with me."

"Don't be mean with me. I know you'll tell the truth. You're from around these parts and you are a man. But you must sign; that's the rule."

Daru opened his drawer, took out a little square bottle of purple ink, the red wooden penholder with the "sergeant-major" pen he used for models of handwriting, and signed. The gendarme carefully folded the paper and put it into his wallet. Then he moved toward the door.

"I'll see you off," Daru said.

"No," said Balducci. "There's no use being polite. You insulted me."

He looked at the Arab, motionless in the same spot, sniffed peevishly, and turned away toward the door. "Good-by, son," he said. The door slammed behind him. His footsteps were muffled by the snow. The horse stirred on the other side of the wall and several chickens fluttered in fright. A moment later Balducci reappeared outside the window leading the horse by the bridle. He walked toward the little rise without turning around and disappeared from sight with the horse following him.

Daru walked back toward the prisoner, who, without stirring, never took his eyes off him. "Wait," the schoolmaster said in Arabic and went toward the bedroom. As he was going through the door, he had a second thought, went to the desk, took the revolver, and stuck it in his pocket. Then, without looking back, he went into his room.

For some time he lay on his couch watching the sky gradually close over, listening to the silence. It was this silence that had seemed painful to him during the first days here, after the war. He had requested a post in the little town at the base of the foothills separating the upper plateaus from the desert. There rocky walls, green and black to the north, pink and lavender to the south, marked the frontier of eternal summer. He had been named to a post farther north, on the plateau itself. In the beginning, the solitude and the silence had been hard for him on these wastelands peopled only by stones. Occasionally, furrows suggested cultivation, but they had been dug to uncover a certain kind of stone good for building. The only plowing here was to harvest rocks. Elsewhere a thin layer of soil accumulated in the hollows would be scraped out to enrich paltry village gardens. This is the way it was: bare rock covered three quarters of the region. Towns sprang up, flourished, then disappeared; men came by, loved one another or fought bitterly, then died. No one in this desert, neither he nor his guest, mattered. And yet, outside this desert neither of them, Daru knew, could have really lived.

When he got up, no noise came from the classroom. He was amazed at the unmixed joy he derived from the mere thought that the Arab might have fled and that he would be alone with no decision to make. But the prisoner was there. He had merely stretched out between the stove and the desk and he was staring at the ceiling. In that position, his thick lips were particularly notice- able, giving him a pouting look. "Come," said Daru. The Arab got up and fol- lowed him. In the bedroom the schoolmaster pointed to a chair near the table under the window. The Arab sat down without ceasing to watch Daru.

"Are you hungry?"

"Yes," the prisoner said.

Daru set the table for two. He took flour and oil, shaped a cake in a frying pan, and lighted the little stove that functioned on bottled gas. While the cake was cooking, he went out to the shed to get cheese, eggs, dates, and condensed milk. When the cake was done he set it on the window sill to cool, heated some condensed milk diluted with water, and beat up the eggs into an omelette. In one of his motions he bumped into the revolver stuck in his right pocket. He set the bowl down, went into the classroom, and put the revolver in his desk drawer. When he came back to the room, night was falling. He put on the light and served the Arab. "Eat," he said. The Arab took a piece of the cake, lifted it eagerly to his mouth, and stopped short.

"And you?" he asked.

"After you. I'll eat too."

The thick lips opened slightly. The Arab hesitated, then bit into the cake determinedly.

The meal over, the Arab looked at the schoolmaster. "Are you the judge?"

"No, I'm simply keeping you until tomorrow."

"Why do you eat with me?"

"I'm hungry."

The Arab fell silent. Daru got up and went out. He brought back a camp cot from the shed and set it up between the table and the stove, at right angles to his own bed. From a large suitcase which, upright in a corner, served as a shelf for papers, he took two blankets and arranged them on the cot. Then he stopped, felt useless, and sat down on his bed. There was nothing more to do or to get ready. He had to look at this man. He looked at him therefore, trying to imagine his face bursting with rage. He couldn't do so. He could see nothing but the dark yet shining eyes and the animal mouth.

"Why did you kill him?" he asked in a voice whose hostile tone surprised him.

The Arab looked away. "He ran away. I ran after him."

He raised his eyes to Daru again and they were full of a sort of woeful interrogation. "Now what will they do to me?"

"Are you afraid?"

The Arab stiffened, turning his eyes away.

"Are you sorry?"

The Arab stared at him openmouthed. Obviously he did not understand. Daru's annoyance was growing. At the same time he felt awkward and self-conscious with his big body wedged between the two beds.

"Lie down there," he said impatiently. "That's your bed."

The Arab didn't move. He cried out. "Tell me!"

The schoolmaster looked at him.

"Is the gendarme coming back tomorrow?"

"I don't know."

"Are you coming with us?"

"I don't know. Why?"

The prisoner got up and stretched out on top of the blankets, his feet toward the window. The light from the electric bulb shone straight into his eyes and he closed them at once.

"Why?" Daru repeated, standing beside the bed.

The Arab opened his eyes under the blinding light and looked at him, trying not to blink. "Come with us," he said.

In the middle of the night, Daru was still not asleep. He had gone to bed after undressing completely; he generally slept naked. But when he suddenly realized that he had nothing on, he wondered. He felt vulnerable and the temptation came to him to put his clothes back on. Then he shrugged his shoulders; after all, he wasn't a child and, if it came to that, he could break his adversary in two. From his bed, he could observe him lying on his back, still motionless, his eyes closed under the harsh light. When Daru turned out the light, the darkness seemed to congeal all of a sudden. Little by little, the night came back to life in the window where the starless sky was stirring gently. The school-master soon made out the body lying at his feet. The Arab was still motionless but his eyes seemed open. A faint wind was prowling about the schoolhouse. Perhaps it would drive away the clouds and the sun would reappear.

During the night the wind increased. The hens fluttered a little and then were silent. The Arab turned over on his side with his back to Daru, who thought he heard him moan. Then he listened for his guest's breathing, which had become heavier and more regular. He listened to that breathing so close to him and mused without being able to go to sleep. In the room where he had been sleeping alone for a year, this presence bothered him. But it bothered him also because it imposed on him a sort of brotherhood he refused to accept in the present circumstances; yet he was familiar with it. Men who share the same rooms, soldiers or prisoners, develop a strange alliance as if, having cast off their armor with their clothing, they fraternized every evening, over and above their differences, in the ancient community of dream and fatigue. But Daru shook himself; he didn't like such musings, and it was essential for him to sleep.

A little later, however, when the Arab stirred slightly, the schoolmaster was still not asleep. When the prisoner made a second move, he stiffened, on the alert. The Arab was lifting himself slowly on his arms with almost the motion of a sleepwalker. Seated upright in bed, he waited motionless without turning his head toward Daru, as if he were listening attentively. Daru did not stir; it had just occurred to him that the revolver was still in the drawer of his desk. It was better to act at once. Yet he continued to observe the prisoner, who, with the same slithery motion, put his feet on the ground, waited again, then stood up slowly. Daru was about to call out to him when the Arab began to walk, in a quite natural but extraordinarily silent way. He was heading toward the door at the end of the room that opened into the shed. He lifted the latch with pre-caution and went out, pushing the door behind him but without shutting it.

Daru had not stirred. "He is running away," he merely thought. "Good riddance!" Yet he listened attentively. The hens were not fluttering; the guest must be on the plateau. A faint sound of water reached him, and he didn't know what it was until the Arab again stood framed in the doorway, closed the door carefully, and came back to bed without a sound. Then Daru turned his back on him and fell asleep. Still later he seemed, from the depths of his sleep, to hear furtive steps around the schoolhouse. "I'm dreaming! I'm dreaming!" he repeated to himself. And he went on sleeping.

When he awoke, the sky was clear; the loose window let in a cold, pure air. The Arab was asleep, hunched up under the blankets now, his mouth open, utterly relaxed. But when Daru shook him he started dreadfully, staring at Daru with wild eyes as if he had never seen him and with such a frightened expression that the schoolmaster stepped back. "Don't be afraid. It is I. You must eat." The Arab nodded his head and said yes. Calm had returned to his face, but his expression was vacant and listless.

The coffee was ready. They drank it seated together on the cot as they munched their pieces of the cake. Then Daru let the Arab under the shed and showed him the faucet where he washed. He went back into the room, folded the blankets on the cot, made his own bed, and put the room in order. Then he went through the classroom and out onto the terrace. The sun was already rising in the blue sky; a soft, bright light enveloped the deserted plateau. On the ridge the snow was melting in spots. The stones were about to reappear. Crouched on the edge of the plateau, the schoolmaster looked at the deserted expanse. He thought of Balducci. He had hurt him, for he had sent him off as though he didn't want to be associated with him. He could still hear the gendarme's farewell and, without knowing why, he felt strangely empty and vulnerable.

At that moment, from the other side of the schoolhouse, the prisoner coughed. Daru listened to him almost despite himself and then, furious, threw a pebble that whistled through the air before sinking into the snow. That man's stupid crime revolted him, but to hand him over was contrary to honor; just thinking of it made him boil with humiliation. He simultaneously cursed his own people who had sent him this Arab and the Arab who had dared to kill and not managed to get away. Daru got up, walked in a circle on the terrace, waited motionless, and then went back into the schoolhouse.

The Arab, leaning over the cement floor of the shed, was washing his teeth with two fingers. Daru looked at him and said, "Come." He went back into the room ahead of the prisoner. He slipped a hunting jacket on over his sweater and put on walking shoes. Standing, he waited until the Arab had put on his *chèche* and sandals. They went into the classroom, and the schoolmaster pointed to the exit saying, "Go ahead." The fellow didn't budge. "I'm coming," said Daru. The Arab went out. Daru went back into the room and made a package with pieces of rusk, dates, and sugar in it. In the classroom, before going out, he hesitated a second in front of his desk, then crossed the threshold and locked the door. "That's the way," he said. He started toward the east, followed by the prisoner. But a short distance from the schoolhouse he thought he heard a slight sound behind him. He retraced his steps and examined the surroundings of the house; there was no one there. The Arab watched him without seeming to understand. "Come on," said Daru.

They walked for an hour and rested beside a sharp needle of limestone. The snow was melting faster and faster and the sun was drinking up the puddles just as quickly, rapidly cleaning the plateau, which gradually dried and vibrated like the air itself. When they resumed walking, the ground rang under their feet. From time to time a bird rent the space in front of them with a joyful cry. Daru felt a sort of rapture before the vast familiar expanse, now almost entirely yellow under its dome of blue sky. They walked an hour more, descending toward the south. They reached a sort of flattened elevation made up of crumbly rocks. From there on, the plateau sloped down—eastward toward a low plain on which could be made out a few spindly trees, and to the south toward outcroppings of rock that gave the landscape a chaotic look.

Daru surveyed the two directions. Not a man could be seen. He turned toward the Arab, who was looking at him blankly. Daru offered the package to him. "Take it," he said. "There are dates, bread, and sugar. You can hold out for two days. Here are a thousand francs too."

The Arab took the package and the money but kept his full hands at chest level as if he didn't know what to do with what was being given him.

"Now look," the schoolmaster said as he pointed in the direction of the east, "there's the way to Tinguit. You have a two-hour walk. At Tinguit are the administration and the police. They are expecting you."

The Arab looked toward the east, still holding the package and the money against his chest. Daru took his elbow and turned him rather roughly toward the south. At the foot of the elevation on which they stood could be seen a faint path. "That's the trail across the plateau. In a day's walk from here you'll find pasturelands and the first nomads. They'll take you in and shelter you according to their law."

The Arab had now turned toward Daru, and a sort of panic was visible in his expression. "Listen," he said.

Daru shook his head. "No, be quiet. Now I'm leaving you." He turned his back on him, took two long steps in the direction of the school, looked hesitantly at the motionless Arab, and started off again. For a few minutes he heard nothing but his own step resounding on the cold ground, and he did not turn his head. A moment later, however, he turned around. The Arab was still there on the edge of the hill, his arms hanging now, and he was looking at the schoolmaster. Daru felt something rise in his throat. But he swore with impatience, waved vaguely, and started off again. He had already gone a distance when he again stopped and looked. There was no longer anyone on the hill.

Daru hesitated. The sun was now rather high in the sky and beginning to beat down on his head. The schoolmaster retraced his steps, at first somewhat uncertainly, then with decision. When he reached the little hill, he was bathed in sweat. He climbed it as fast as he could and stopped, out of breath, on the top. The rock fields to the south stood out sharply against the blue sky, but on the plain to the east a steamy heat was rising. And in that light haze, Daru, with heavy heart, made out the Arab walking slowly on the road to prison.

A little later, standing before the window of the classroom, the schoolmaster was watching the clear light bathing the whole surface of the plateau.

Behind him on the blackboard, among the winding French rivers, sprawled the clumsily chalked up words he had just read: "You handed over our brother. You will pay for this." Daru looked at the sky, the plateau, and, beyond, the invisible lands stretching all the way to the sea. In this vast landscape he had loved so much, he was alone.

RAYMOND CARVER

CATHEDRAL

Raymond Carver (1938–1988) was born in Clatskanie, Oregon, and grew up among the working class of the Pacific Northwest. Married with children before he was twenty, Carver held down a series of "crap jobs" to feed his family. He took a creative-writing course with John Gardner at Chico State College in 1958, but it wasn't until 1963 that Carver earned his B.A. from Humboldt State College. In the 1960s he and his family moved between Iowa and California as various jobs demanded. Carver's early stories and poems met with limited and sporadic success. In 1971 Carver came to the attention of his future editor at Knopf, Gordon Lish, and began a series of academic appointments.

Alcoholism and domestic problems forced the Carvers into bankruptcy in 1974 and into separation in 1978. In 1976 Lish became Carver's editor and mentor in the ruthless art of revision, publishing Carver's first major short-story collection, Will You Please Be Quiet, Please? The book was nominated for the 1997 National Book Award. Carver stopped drinking, and he met the poet Tess Gallagher, who would become not only his life partner, but also a close creative collaborator. Carver's evolving mastery of the short story earned him great success in the early 1980s. The collection What We Talk About When We Talk About Love appeared in 1981, and Cathedral was published in 1984. "His work with the short story," writes Gallagher, "has revived the form and given it a currency whose reverberations are now being felt around the world." Editing and contributing to a variety of journals and anthologies, Carver enjoyed an immense popularity during his lifetime. In 1987 he was diagnosed with lung cancer, and in the summer of 1988, having married Gallagher just months before, Carver died in Port Angeles, Washington.

Introducing the book Cathedral, from which the title story is taken, Lish writes:

> A new vision, a new method, a new tonality are the components of the program that has elevated Carver to international prominence. What is promptly recognizable in his work is the queer effect that issues from its surface simplicity. Carver's world is the world of the homely and the unexceptional, colorless people going about the business of their colorless lives. How

*Carver makes of their uninflected histories a primer on moral
terror speaks to the magic of his force as a literary artist. The
stories in this book constitute a kind of grammar of that feathery
language only the heart ever hears, and only at four o'clock in
the morning.*

*Of "Cathedral" in particular, Lish remarks that "Carver has passed a
wand over words on paper, and thus made of this story a version of the
thing itself, the charmed interior of that edifice, the cathedral—a spa-
ciousness that is hushed, severe, transporting."*

This blind man, an old friend of my wife's, he was on his way to spend the
night. His wife had died. So he was visiting the dead wife's relatives in
Connecticut. He called my wife from his in-laws'. Arrangements were made.
He would come by train, a five-hour trip, and my wife would meet him at the
station. She hadn't seen him since she worked for him one summer in Seattle
ten years ago. But she and the blind man had kept in touch. They made tapes
and mailed them back and forth. I wasn't enthusiastic about his visit. He was
no one I knew. And his being blind bothered me. My idea of blindness came
from the movies. In the movies, the blind moved slowly and never laughed.
Sometimes they were led by seeing-eye dogs. A blind man in my house was not
something I looked forward to.

That summer in Seattle she had needed a job. She didn't have any money.
The man she was going to marry at the end of the summer was in officers'
training school. He didn't have any money, either. But she was in love with the
guy, and he was in love with her, etc. She'd seen something in the paper: HELP
WANTED—*Reading to Blind Man,* and a telephone number. She phoned and
went over, was hired on the spot. She'd worked with this blind man all
summer. She read stuff to him, case studies, reports, that sort of thing. She
helped him organize his little office in the county social-service department.
They'd become good friends, my wife and the blind man. How do I know these
things? She told me. And she told me something else. On her last day in the
office, the blind man asked if he could touch her face. She agreed to this. She
told me he touched his fingers to every part of her face, her nose—even her
neck! She never forgot it. She even tried to write a poem about it. She was
always trying to write a poem. She wrote a poem or two every year, usually
after something really important had happened to her.

When we first started going out together, she showed me the poem. In the
poem, she recalled his fingers and the way they had moved around over her

face. In the poem, she talked about what she had felt at the time, about what went through her mind when the blind man touched her nose and lips. I can remember I didn't think much of the poem. Of course, I didn't tell her that. Maybe I just don't understand poetry. I admit it's not the first thing I reach for when I pick up something to read.

Anyway, this man who'd first enjoyed her favors, the officer-to-be, he'd been her childhood sweetheart. So okay. I'm saying that at the end of the summer she let the blind man run his hands over her face, said goodbye to him, married her childhood etc., who was now a commissioned officer, and she moved away from Seattle. But they'd kept in touch, she and the blind man. She made the first contact after a year or so. She called him up one night from an Air Force base in Alabama. She wanted to talk. They talked. He asked her to send him a tape and tell him about her life. She did this. She sent the tape. On the tape, she told the blind man about her husband and about their life together in the military. She told the blind man she loved her husband but she didn't like it where they lived and she didn't like it that he was a part of the military-industrial thing. She told the blind man she'd written a poem and he was in it. She told him that she was writing a poem about what it was like to be an Air Force officer's wife. The poem wasn't finished yet. She was still writing it. The blind man made a tape. He sent her the tape. She made a tape. This went on for years. My wife's officer was posted to one base and then another. She sent tapes from Moody AFB, McGuire, McConnell, and finally Travis, near Sacramento, where one night she got to feeling lonely and cut off from people she kept losing in that moving-around life. She got to feeling she couldn't go it another step. She went in and swallowed all the pills and capsules in the medicine chest and washed them down with a bottle of gin. Then she got into a hot bath and passed out.

But instead of dying, she got sick. She threw up. Her officer—why should he have a name? he was the childhood sweetheart, and what more does he want?—came home from somewhere, found her, and called the ambulance. In time, she put it all on a tape and sent the tape to the blind man. Over the years, she put all kinds of stuff on tapes and sent the tapes off lickety-split. Next to writing a poem every year, I think it was her chief means of recreation. On one tape, she told the blind man she'd decided to live away from her officer for a time. On another tape, she told him about her divorce. She and I began going out, and of course she told her blind man about it. She told him everything, or so it seemed to me. Once she asked me if I'd like to hear the latest tape from the blind man. This was a year ago. I was on the tape, she said. So I said okay, I'd listen to it. I got us drinks and we settled down in the living room. We made ready to listen. First she inserted the tape into the player and adjusted a couple of dials. Then she pushed a lever. The tape squeaked and someone began to talk in this loud voice. She lowered the volume. After a few minutes of harmless chitchat, I heard my own name in the mouth of this stranger, this blind man I didn't even know! And then this: "From all you've said about him, I can only conclude——" But we were interrupted, a knock at the door, something, and we didn't ever get back to the tape. Maybe it was just as well. I'd heard all I wanted to.

Now this same blind man was coming to sleep in my house.

"Maybe I could take him bowling," I said to my wife. She was at the draining board doing scalloped potatoes. She put down the knife she was using and turned around.

"If you love me," she said, "you can do this for me. If you don't love me, okay. But if you had a friend, any friend, and the friend came to visit, I'd make him feel comfortable." She wiped her hands with the dish towel.

"I don't have any blind friends," I said.

"You don't have *any* friends," she said. "Period. Besides," she said, "goddamn it, his wife's just died! Don't you understand that? The man's lost his wife!"

I didn't answer. She'd told me a little about the blind man's wife. Her name was Beulah. Beulah! That's a name for a colored woman.

"Was his wife a Negro?" I asked.

"Are you crazy?" my wife said. "Have you just flipped or something?" She picked up a potato. I saw it hit the floor, then roll under the stove. "What's wrong with you?" she said. "Are you drunk?"

"I'm just asking," I said.

Right then my wife filled me in with more detail that I cared to know. I made a drink and sat at the kitchen table to listen. Pieces of the story began to fall into place.

Beulah had gone to work for the blind man the summer after my wife had stopped working. Pretty soon Beulah and the blind man had themselves a church wedding. It was a little wedding—who'd want to go to such a wedding in the first place?—just the two of them, plus the minister and the minister's wife. But it was a church wedding just the same. It was what Beulah had wanted, he'd said. But even then Beulah must have been carrying the cancer in her glands. After they had been inseparable for eight years—my wife's word, *inseparable*—Beulah's health went into a rapid decline. She died in a Seattle hospital room, the blind man sitting beside the bed and holding on to her hand. They'd married, lived and worked together, slept together—had sex, sure—and then the blind man had to bury her. All this without his having ever seen what the goddamned woman looked like. It was beyond my understanding. Hearing this, I felt sorry for the blind man for a little bit. And then I found myself thinking what a pitiful life this woman must have led. Imagine a woman who could never see herself as she was seen in the eyes of her loved one. A woman who could go on day after day and never receive the smallest compliment from her beloved. A woman whose husband could never read the expression on her face, be it misery or something better. Someone who could wear makeup or not—what difference to him? She could, if she wanted, wear green eyeshadow around one eye, a straight pin in her nostril, yellow slacks and purple shoes, no matter. And then to slip off into death, the blind man's hand on her hand, his blind eyes streaming tears—I'm imagining now—her last thought maybe this: that he never even knew what she looked like, and she on an express to the grave. Robert was left with a small insurance policy and half of a twenty-peso Mexican coin. The other half of the coin went into the box with her. Pathetic.

So when the time rolled around, my wife went to the depot to pick him up. With nothing to do but wait—sure, I blamed him for that—I was having a drink and watching the TV when I heard the car pull into the drive. I got up from the sofa with my drink and went to the window to have a look.

I saw my wife laughing as she parked the car. I saw her get out of the car and shut the door. She was still wearing a smile. Just amazing. She went around to the other side of the car to where the blind man was already starting to get out. This blind man, feature this, he was wearing a full beard! A beard on a blind man! Too much, I say. The blind man reached into the back seat and dragged out a suitcase. My wife took his arm, shut the car door, and, talking all the way, moved him down the drive and then up the steps to the front porch. I turned off the TV. I finished my drink, rinsed the glass, dried my hands. Then I went to the door.

My wife said, "I want you to meet Robert. Robert, this is my husband. I've told you all about him." She was beaming. She had this blind man by his coat sleeve.

The blind man let go of his suitcase and up came his hand.

I took it. He squeezed hard, held my hand, and then he let it go.

"I feel like we've already met," he boomed.

"Likewise," I said. I didn't know what else to say. Then I said, "Welcome. I've heard a lot about you." We began to move then, a little group, from the porch into the living room, my wife guiding him by the arm. The blind man was carrying his suitcase in his other hand. My wife said things like, "To your left here, Robert. That's right. Now watch it, there's a chair. That's it. Sit down right here. This is the sofa. We just bought this sofa two weeks ago."

I started to say something about the old sofa. I'd liked that old sofa. But I didn't say anything. Then I wanted to say something else, small-talk, about the scenic ride along the Hudson. How going *to* New York, you should sit on the right-hand side of the train, and coming *from* New York, the left-hand side.

"Did you have a good train ride?" I said. "Which side of the train did you sit on, by the way?"

"What a question, which side!" my wife said. "What's it matter which side?" she said.

"I just asked," I said.

"Right side," the blind man said. "I hadn't been on a train in nearly forty years. Not since I was a kid. With my folks. That's been a long time. I'd nearly forgotten the sensation. I have winter in my beard now," he said. "So I've been told, anyway. Do I look distinguished, my dear?" the blind man said to my wife.

"You look distinguished, Robert," she said. "Robert," she said. "Robert, it's just so good to see you."

My wife finally took her eyes off the blind man and looked at me. I had the feeling she didn't like what she saw. I shrugged.

I've never met, or personally known, anyone who was blind. This blind man was late forties, a heavy-set, balding man with stooped shoulders, as if he carried a great weight there. He wore brown slacks, brown shoes, a light-brown shirt, a tie, a sports coat. Spiffy. He also had this full beard. But he didn't use a cane and he didn't wear dark glasses. I'd always thought dark glasses were a must for the blind. Fact was, I wished he had a pair. At first glance, his eyes looked like anyone else's eyes. But if you looked close, there was something different about them. Too much white in the iris, for one thing, and the pupils seemed to move around in the sockets without his knowing it or being able to stop it. Creepy. As I stared as his face, I saw the left pupil turn in toward his nose while the other made an effort to keep in one place. But it was only an effort, for that eye was on the roam without his knowing it or wanting it to be.

I said, "Let me get you a drink. What's your pleasure? We have a little of everything. It's one of our pastimes."

"Bub, I'm a Scotch man myself," he said fast enough in this big voice.

"Right," I said. Bub! "Sure you are. I knew it."

He let his fingers touch his suitcase, which was sitting alongside the sofa. He was taking his bearings. I didn't blame him for that.

"I'll move that up to your room," my wife said.

"No, that's fine," the blind man said loudly. "It can go up when I go up."

"A little water with the Scotch?" I said.

"Very little," he said.

"I knew it," I said.

He said, "Just a tad. The Irish actor, Barry Fitzgerald? I'm like that fellow. When I drink water, Fitzgerald said, I drink water. When I drink whiskey, I drink whiskey." My wife laughed. The blind man brought his hand up under his beard. He lifted his beard slowly and let it drop.

I did the drinks, three big glasses of Scotch with a splash of water in each. Then we made ourselves comfortable and talked about Robert's travels. First the long flight from the West Coast to Connecticut, we covered that. Then from Connecticut up here by train. We had another drink concerning that leg of the trip.

I remembered having read somewhere that the blind didn't smoke because, as speculation had it, they couldn't see the smoke they exhaled. I thought I knew that much and that much only about blind people. But this blind man smoked his cigarette down to the nubbin and then lit another one. This blind man filled his ashtray and my wife emptied it.

When we sat down at the table for dinner, we had another drink. My wife heaped Robert's plate with cube steak, scalloped potatoes, green beans. I buttered him up two slices of bread. I said, "Here's bread and butter for you." I swallowed some of my drink. "Now let us pray," I said, and the blind man lowered his head. My wife looked at me, her mouth agape. "Pray the phone won't ring and the food doesn't get cold," I said.

We dug in. We ate everything there was to eat on the table. We ate like there was no tomorrow. We didn't talk. We ate. We scarfed. We grazed that table. We were into serious eating. The blind man had right away located his foods, he knew just where everything was on his plate. I watched with admiration as he used his knife and fork on the meat. He'd cut two pieces of meat, fork the meat into his mouth, and then go all out for the scalloped potatoes, the beans next, and then he'd tear off a hunk of buttered bread and eat that. He'd follow this up with a big drink of milk. It didn't seem to bother him to use his fingers once in a while, either.

We finished everything, including half a strawberry pie. For a few moments, we sat as if stunned. Sweat beaded on our faces. Finally, we got up from the table and left the dirty plates. We didn't look back. We took ourselves into the living room and sank into our places again. Robert and my wife sat on the sofa. I took the big chair. We had us two or three more drinks while they talked about the major things that had come to pass for them in the past ten years. For the most part, I just listened. Now and then I joined in. I didn't want him to think I'd left the room, and I didn't want her to think I was feeling left out. They talked of things that had happened to them—to them!—these past ten years. I waited in vain to hear my name on my wife's sweet lips: "And then my dear husband came into my life"—something like that. But I heard nothing of the sort. More talk of Robert. Robert had done a little of everything, it seemed, a regular blind jack-of-all-trades. But most recently he and his wife had had an Amway distributorship, from which, I gathered, they'd earned their living, such as it was. The blind man was also a ham radio operator. He talked in his loud voice about conversations he'd had with fellow operators in

Guam, in the Philippines, in Alaska, and even in Tahiti. He said he'd have a lot of friends there if he ever wanted to go visit those places. From time to time, he'd turn his blind face toward me, put his hand under his beard, ask me something. How long had I been in my present position? (Three years.) Did I like my work? (I didn't.) Was I going to stay with it? (What were the options?) Finally, when I thought he was beginning to run down, I got up and turned on the TV.

My wife looked at me with irritation. She was heading toward a boil. Then she looked at the blind man and said, "Robert, do you have a TV?"

The blind man said, "My dear, I have two TVs. I have a color set and a black-and-white thing, an old relic. It's funny, but if I turn the TV on, and I'm always turning it on, I turn on the color set. It's funny, don't you think?"

I didn't know what to say to that. I had absolutely nothing to say to that. No opinion. So I watched the news program and tried to listen to what the announcer was saying.

"This is a color TV," the blind man said. "Don't ask me how, but I can tell."

"We traded up a while ago," I said.

The blind man had another taste of his drink. He lifted his beard, sniffed it, and let it fall. He leaned forward on the sofa. He positioned his ashtray on the coffee table, then put the lighter to his cigarette. He leaned back on the sofa and crossed his legs at the ankles.

My wife covered her mouth, and then she yawned. She stretched. She said, "I think I'll go upstairs and put on my robe. I think I'll change into something else. Robert, you make yourself comfortable," she said.

"I'm comfortable," the blind man said.

"I want you to feel comfortable in this house," she said.

"I am comfortable," the blind man said.

After she'd left the room, he and I listened to the weather report and then to the sports roundup. By that time, she'd been gone so long I didn't know if she was going to come back. I thought she might have gone to bed. I wished she'd come back downstairs. I didn't want to be left alone with a blind man. I asked him if he wanted another drink, and he said sure. Then I asked if he wanted to smoke some dope with me. I said I'd just rolled a number. I hadn't, but I planned to do so in about two shakes.

"I'll try some with you," he said.

"Damn right," I said. "That's the stuff."

I got our drinks and sat down on the sofa with him. Then I rolled us two fat numbers. I lit one and passed it. I brought it to his fingers. He took it and inhaled.

"Hold it as long as you can," I said. I could tell he didn't know the first thing.

My wife came back downstairs wearing her pink robe and her pink slippers.

"What do I smell?" she said.

"We thought we'd have us some cannabis," I said.

My wife gave me a savage look. Then she looked at the blind man and said, "Robert, I didn't know you smoked."

He said, "I do now, my dear. There's a first time for everything. But I don't feel anything yet."

"This stuff is pretty mellow," I said. "This stuff is mild. It's dope you can reason with," I said. "It doesn't mess you up."

"Not much it doesn't, bub," he said, and laughed.

My wife sat on the sofa between the blind man and me. I passed her the number. She took it and toked and then passed it back to me. "Which way is this going?" she said. Then she said, "I shouldn't be smoking this. I can hardly keep my eyes open as it is. That dinner did me in. I shouldn't have eaten so much."

"It was the strawberry pie," the blind man said. "That's what did it," he said, and he laughed his big laugh. Then he shook his head.

"There's more strawberry pie," I said.

"Do you want some more, Robert?" my wife said.

"Maybe in a little while," he said.

We gave our attention to the TV. My wife yawned again. She said, "Your bed is made up when you feel like going to bed, Robert. I know you must have had a long day. When you're ready to go to bed, say so." She pulled his arm. "Robert?"

He came to and said, "I've had a real nice time. This beats tapes, doesn't it?"

I said, "Coming at you," and I put the number between his fingers. He inhaled, held the smoke, and then let it go. It was like he'd been doing it since he was nine years old.

"Thanks, bub," he said. "But I think this is all for me. I think I'm beginning to feel it," he said. He held the burning roach out for my wife.

"Same here," she said. "Ditto. Me, too." She took the roach and passed it to me. "I may just sit here for a while between you two guys with my eyes closed. But don't let me bother you, okay? Either one of you. If it bothers you, say so. Otherwise, I may just sit here with my eyes closed until you're ready to go to bed," she said. "Your bed's made up, Robert, when you're ready. You wake me up now, you guys, if I fall asleep." She said that and then she closed her eyes and went to sleep.

The news program ended. I got up and changed the channel. I sat back down on the sofa. I wished my wife hadn't pooped out. Her head lay across the back of the sofa, her mouth open. She'd turned so that her robe had slipped away from her legs, exposing a juicy thigh. I reached to draw her robe back over her, and it was then that I glanced at the blind man. What the hell! I flipped the robe open again.

"You say when you want some strawberry pie," I said.

"I will," he said.

I said, "Are you tired? Do you want me to take you up to your bed? Are you ready to hit the hay?"

"Not yet," he said. "No, I'll stay up with you, bub. If that's all right. I'll stay up until you're ready to turn in. We haven't had a chance to talk. Know what I mean? I feel like me and her monopolized the evening." He lifted his beard and he let it fall. He picked up his cigarettes and his lighter.

"That's all right," I said. Then I said, "I'm glad for the company."

And I guess I was. Every night I smoked dope and stayed up as long as I could before I fell asleep. My wife and I hardly ever went to bed at the same time. When I did go to sleep, I had these dreams. Sometimes I'd wake up from one of them, my heart going crazy.

Something about the church and the Middle Ages was on the TV. Not your run-of-the-mill TV fare. I wanted to watch something else. I turned to the other channels. But there was nothing on them, either. So I turned back to the first channel and apologized.

"Bub, it's all right," the blind man said. "It's fine with me. Whatever you want to watch is okay. I'm always learning something. Learning never ends. It won't hurt me to learn something tonight. I got ears," he said.

We didn't say anything for a time. He was leaning forward with his head turned at me, his right ear aimed in the direction of the set. Very disconcerting. Now and then his eyelids drooped and then they snapped open again. Now and then he put his fingers into his beard and tugged, like he was thinking about something he was hearing on the television.

On the screen, a group of men wearing cowls was being set upon and tormented by men dressed in skeleton costumes and men dressed as devils. The men dressed as devils wore devil masks, horns, and long tails. This pageant was part of a procession. The Englishman who was narrating the thing said it took place in Spain once a year. I tried to explain to the blind man what was happening.

"Skeletons," he said. "I know about skeletons," he said, and he nodded.

The TV showed this one cathedral. Then there was a long, slow look at another one. Finally, the picture switched to the famous one in Paris, with its flying buttresses and its spires reaching up to the clouds. The camera pulled away to show the whole of the cathedral rising above the skyline.

There were times when the Englishman who was telling the thing would shut up, would simply let the camera move around over the cathedrals. Or else the camera would tour the countryside, men in fields walking behind oxen. I waited as long as I could. Then I felt I had to say something. I said, "They're showing the outside of this cathedral now. Gargoyles. Little statues carved to look like monsters. Now I guess they're in Italy. Yeah, they're in Italy. There's paintings on the walls of this one church."

"Are those fresco paintings, bub?" he asked, and sipped from his drink.

I reached for my glass. But it was empty. I tried to remember what I could remember. "You're asking me are those frescoes?" I said. "That's a good question. I don't know."

The camera moved to a cathedral outside Lisbon. The differences in the Portuguese cathedral compared with the French and Italian were not that great. But they were there. Mostly the interior stuff. Then something occurred to me, and I said, "Something has occurred to me. Do you have any idea what a cathedral is? What they look like, that is? Do you follow me? If somebody says cathedral to you, do you have any notion what they're talking about? Do you know the difference between that and a Baptist church, say?"

He let the smoke dribble from his mouth. "I know they took hundreds of workers fifty or a hundred years to build," he said. "I just heard the man say that, of course. I know generations of the same families worked on a cathedral. I heard him say that, too. The men who began their life's work on them, they never lived to see the completion of their work. In that wise, bub, they're no different from the rest of us, right?" He laughed. Then his eyelids drooped again. His head nodded. He seemed to be snoozing. Maybe he was imagining himself in Portugal. The TV was showing another cathedral now. This one was in Germany. The Englishman's voice droned on. "Cathedrals," the blind man said. He sat up and rolled his head back and forth. "If you want the truth, bub, that's about all I know. What I just said. What I heard him say. But maybe you could describe one to me? I wish you'd do it. I'd like that. If you want to know, I really don't have a good idea."

I stared hard at the shot of the cathedral on the TV. How could I even begin to describe it? But say my life depended on it. Say my life was being threatened by an insane guy who said I had to do it or else.

I stared some more at the cathedral before the picture flipped off into the countryside. There was no use. I turned to the blind man and said, "To begin with, they're very tall." I was looking around the room for clues. "They reach way up. Up and up. Toward the sky. They're so big, some of them, they have to have these supports. To help hold them up, so to speak. These supports are called buttresses. They remind me of viaducts, for some reason. But maybe you don't know viaducts, either? Sometimes the cathedrals have devils and such carved into the front. Sometimes lords and ladies. Don't ask me why this is," I said.

He was nodding. The whole upper part of his body seemed to be moving back and forth.

"I'm not doing so good, am I?" I said.

He stopped nodding and leaned forward on the edge of the sofa. As he listened to me, he was running his fingers through his beard. I wasn't getting through to him, I could see that. But he waited for me to go on just the same. He nodded, like he was trying to encourage me. I tried to think what else to say. "They're really big," I said. "They're massive. They're built of stone. Marble, too, sometimes. In those olden days, when they built cathedrals, men wanted to be close to God. In those olden days, God was an important part of everyone's life. You could tell this from their cathedral-building. I'm sorry," I said, "but it looks like that's the best I can do for you. I'm just no good at it."

"That's all right, bub," the blind man said. "Hey, listen. I hope you don't mind my asking you. Can I ask you something? Let me ask you a simple question, yes or no. I'm just curious and there's no offense. You're my host. But let me ask if you are in any way religious? You don't mind my asking?"

I shook my head. He couldn't see that, though. A wink is the same as a nod to a blind man. "I guess I don't believe in it. In anything. Sometimes it's hard. You know what I'm saying?"

"Sure, I do," he said.

"Right," I said.

The Englishman was still holding forth. My wife sighed in her sleep. She drew a long breath and went on with her sleeping.

"You'll have to forgive me," I said. "But I can't tell you what a cathedral looks like. It just isn't in me to do it. I can't do any more than I've done."

The blind man sat very still, his head down, as he listened to me.

I said, "The truth is, cathedrals don't mean anything special to me. Nothing. Cathedrals. They're something to look at on late-night TV. That's all they are."

It was then that the blind man cleared his throat. He brought something up. He took a handkerchief from his back pocket. Then he said, "I get it, bub. It's okay. It happens. Don't worry about it," he said. "Hey, listen to me. Will you do me a favor? I got an idea. Why don't you find us some heavy paper? And a pen. We'll do something. We'll draw one together. Get us a pen and some heavy paper. Go on, bub, get the stuff," he said.

So I went upstairs. My legs felt like they didn't have any strength in them. They felt like they did after I'd done some running. In my wife's room, I looked around. I found some ballpoints in a little basket on her table. And then I tried to think where to look for the kind of paper he was talking about.

Downstairs, in the kitchen, I found a shopping bag with onion skins in the bottom of the bag. I emptied the bag and shook it. I brought it into the living room and sat down with it near his legs. I moved some things, smoothed the wrinkles from the bag, spread it out on the coffee table.

The blind man got down from the sofa and sat next to me on the carpet.

He ran his fingers over the paper. He went up and down the sides of the paper. The edges, even the edges. He fingered the corners.

"All right," he said. "All right, let's do her."

He found my hand, the hand with the pen. He closed his hand over my hand. "Go ahead, bub, draw," he said. "Draw. You'll see. I'll follow along with you. It'll be okay. Just begin now like I'm telling you. You'll see. Draw," the blind man said.

So I began. First I drew a box that looked like a house. It could have been the house I lived in. Then I put a roof on it. At either end of the roof, I drew spires. Crazy.

"Swell," he said. "Terrific. You're doing fine," he said. "Never thought anything like this could happen in your lifetime, did you, bub? Well, it's a strange life, we all know that. Go on now. Keep it up."

I put in windows with arches. I drew flying buttresses. I hung great doors. I couldn't stop. The TV station went off the air. I put down the pen and closed and opened my fingers. The blind man felt around over the paper. He moved the tips of his fingers over the paper, all over what I had drawn, and he nodded.

"Doing fine," the blind man said.

I took up the pen again, and he found my hand. I kept at it. I'm no artist. But I kept drawing just the same.

My wife opened up her eyes and gazed at us. She sat up on the sofa, her robe hanging open. She said, "What are you doing? Tell me, I want to know."

I didn't answer her.

The blind man said, "We're drawing a cathedral. Me and him are working on it. Press hard," he said to me. "That's right. That's good," he said. "Sure. You got it, bub. I can tell. You didn't think you could. But you can, can't you? You're cooking with gas now. You know what I'm saying? We're going to really have us something here in a minute. How's the old arm?" he said. "Put some people in there now. What's a cathedral without people?"

My wife said, "What's going on? Robert, what are you doing? What's going on?"

"It's all right," he said to her. "Close your eyes now," the blind man said to me.

I did it. I closed them just like he said.

"Are they closed?" he said. "Don't fudge."

"They're closed," I said.

"Keep them that way," he said. He said, "Don't stop now. Draw."

So we kept on with it. His fingers rode my fingers as my hand went over the paper. It was like nothing else in my life up to now.

Then he said, "I think that's it. I think you got it," he said. "Take a look. What do you think?"

But I had my eyes closed. I thought I'd keep them that way for a little longer. I thought it was something I ought to do.

"Well?" he said. "Are you looking?"

My eyes were still closed. I was in my house. I knew that. But I didn't feel like I was inside anything.

"It's really something," I said.

WILLA CATHER

PAUL'S CASE

Willa Cather (1873–1947) was born in rural Virginia, the oldest of seven children. She and her family moved to the frontier Nebraska town of Red Cloud when she was nine years old. Initially drawn to medicine, Cather graduated from the University of Nebraska with a degree in literary studies. She began a career in journalism, which took her from Nebraska to Pittsburgh, where she also taught English and Latin. During her time as a teacher, Cather's poems and stories were published: the former in April Twilights *(1902), and the latter in* The Troll Garden *(1905), in which "Paul's Case" first appeared. The promise of a literary career led Cather in 1906 to New York, where she accepted a position as editor of* McClure's *magazine. In 1911 Sarah Orne Jewett, Cather's friend and chief literary influence, encouraged Cather to resign from McClure's in order to devote her time to honing her literary craft. A visit to Red Cloud in 1912 inspired Cather to transmute the malaise that had plagued her childhood there into a devotion that yielded her most famous novels,* O Pioneers! *(1913),* The Song of the Lark *(1915), and* My Ántonia *(1918). Keeping in touch with her Red Cloud friends and relations, Cather remained in New York and produced eight more novels and three more volumes of short stories before her death in 1947.*

Eve Kosofsky Sedgwick reads "Paul's Case," Cather's favourite of all her own stories, in the context of Cather's strangely condemnatory columns in 1895 on the homosexuality trials of Oscar Wilde. "Paul is to be hounded to exhaustion or death for a crime that hovers indeterminately between sex/gender irregularity and spoilt sensibility or bad art." Sedgwick reads words such as art, nature, and the gaze as having distinctly gendered meanings, which are transformed in Cather's work. In this way, she considers that "Paul's Case" represents "the mannish lesbian author's coming together with the effeminate boy" in an exploration of Cather's sense of gender and identity.

It was Paul's afternoon to appear before the faculty of the Pittsburgh High School to account for his various misdemeanors. He had been suspended a week ago, and his father had called at the Principal's office and confessed his perplexity about his son. Paul entered the faculty room suave and smiling. His clothes were a trifle outgrown and the tan velvet on the collar of his open over-coat was frayed and worn; but for all that there was something of the dandy about him, and he wore an opal pin in his neatly knotted black four-in-hand, and a red carnation in his buttonhole. This latter adornment the faculty somehow felt was not properly significant of the contrite spirit befitting a boy under the ban of suspension.

Paul was tall for his age and very thin, with high, cramped shoulders and a narrow chest. His eyes were remarkable for a certain hysterical brilliancy and he continually used them in a conscious, theatrical sort of way, peculiarly offensive in a boy. The pupils were abnormally large, as though he were addicted to belladonna, but there was a glassy glitter about them which that drug does not produce.

When questioned by the Principal as to why he was there, Paul stated, politely enough, that he wanted to come back to school. This was a lie, but Paul was quite accustomed to lying; found it, indeed, indispensable for over-coming friction. His teachers were asked to state their respective charges against him, which they did with such a rancor and aggrievedness as evinced that this was not a usual case. Disorder and impertinence were among the offenses named, yet each of his instructors felt that it was scarcely possible to put into words the real cause of the trouble, which lay in a sort of hysterically defiant manner of the boy's; in the contempt which they all knew he felt for them, and which he seemingly made not the least effort to conceal. Once, when he had been making a synopsis of a paragraph at the blackboard, his English teacher had stepped to his side and attempted to guide his hand. Paul had started back with a shudder and thrust his hands violently behind him. The astonished woman could scarcely have been more hurt and embarrassed had he struck at her. The insult was so involuntary and definitely personal as to be unforgettable. In one way and another, he had made all his teachers, men and women alike, conscious of the same feeling of physical aversion. In one class he habitually sat with his hand shading his eyes; in another he always looked out of the window during the recitation; in another he made a running commentary on the lecture, with humorous intention.

His teachers felt this afternoon that his whole attitude was symbolized by his shrug and his flippantly red carnation flower, and they fell upon him without mercy, his English teacher leading the pack. He stood through it smiling, his pale lips parted over his white teeth. (His lips were continually twitching, and he had a habit of raising his eyebrows that was contemptuous and irritating to the last degree.) Older boys than Paul had broken down and shed tears under that baptism of fire, but his set smile did not once desert him, and his only sign of discomfort was the nervous trembling of the fingers that toyed with the buttons of his overcoat, and an occasional jerking of the other hand that held his hat. Paul was always smiling, always glancing about him, seeming to feel that people might be watching him and trying to detect something. This conscious expression, since it was as far as possible from boyish mirthfulness, was usually attributed to insolence or "smartness."

As the inquisition proceeded, one of his instructors repeated an impertinent remark of the boy's, and the Principal asked him whether he thought that a courteous speech to make to a woman. Paul shrugged his shoulders slightly and his eyebrows twitched.

"I don't know," he replied. "I didn't mean to be polite or impolite, either. I guess it's a sort of way I have of saying things regardless."

The Principal, who was a sympathetic man, asked him whether he didn't think that a way it would be well to get rid of. Paul grinned and said he guessed so. When he was told that he could go, he bowed gracefully and went out. His bow was but a repetition of the scandalous red carnation.

His teachers were in despair, and his drawing master voiced the feeling of them all when he declared there was something about the boy which none of them understood. He added: "I don't really believe that smile of his comes altogether from insolence; there's something sort of haunted about it. The boy is not strong, for one thing. I happen to know that he was born in Colorado, only a few months before his mother died out there of a long illness. There is something wrong about the fellow."

The drawing master had come to realize that, in looking at Paul, one saw only his white teeth and the forced animation of his eyes. One warm afternoon the boy had gone to sleep at his drawing-board, and his master had noted with amazement what a white, blue-veined face it was; drawn and wrinkled like an old man's about the eyes, the lips twitching even in his sleep, and stiff with a nervous tension that drew them back from his teeth.

His teachers left the building dissatisfied and unhappy; humiliated to have felt so vindictive toward a mere boy, to have uttered this feeling in cutting terms, and to have set each other on, as it were, in the gruesome game of intemperate reproach. Some of them remembered having seen a miserable street cat set at bay by a ring of tormentors.

As for Paul, he ran down the hill whistling the Soldiers' Chorus from *Faust*, looking wildly behind him now and then to see whether some of his teachers were not there to writhe under this light-heartedness. As it was now late in the afternoon and Paul was on duty that evening as usher at Carnegie Hall, he decided that he would not go home to supper. When he reached the concert hall the doors were not yet open and, as it was chilly outside, he decided to go up into the picture gallery—always deserted at this hour—where there were some of Raffelli's gay studies of Paris streets and an airy blue Venetian scene or two that always exhilarated him. He was delighted to find no one in the gallery but the old guard, who sat in one corner, a newspaper on his knee, a black patch over one eye and the other closed. Paul possessed himself of the place and walked confidently up and down, whistling under his breath. After a while he sat down before a blue Rico and lost himself. When he bethought him to look at his watch, it was after seven o'clock, and he rose with a start and ran downstairs, making a face at Augustus, peering out from the cast-room, and an evil gesture at the Venus of Milo as he passed her on the stairway.

When Paul reached the ushers' dressing-room half-a-dozen boys were there already, and he began excitedly to tumble into his uniform. It was one of the few that at all approached fitting, and Paul thought it very becoming— though he knew that the tight, straight coat accentuated his narrow chest, about which he was exceedingly sensitive. He was always considerably excited while he dressed, twanging all over to the tuning of the strings and the preliminary flourishes of the horns in the music-room; but tonight he seemed quite beside himself, and he teased and plagued the boys until, telling him that he was crazy, they put him down on the floor and sat on him.

Somewhat calmed by his suppression, Paul dashed out to the front of the house to seat the early comers. He was a model usher; gracious and smiling he ran up and down the aisles; nothing was too much trouble for him; he carried messages and brought programmes as though it were his greatest pleasure in life, and all the people in his section thought him a charming boy, feeling that he remembered and admired them. As the house filled, he grew more and more vivacious and animated, and the color came to his cheeks and lips. It was very much as though this were a great reception and Paul were the host. Just as the musicians came out to take their places, his English teacher arrived with checks for the seats which a prominent manufacturer had taken for the season. She betrayed some embarrassment when she handed Paul the tickets, and a *hauteur* which subsequently made her feel very foolish. Paul was startled for a moment, and had the feeling of wanting to put her out; what business had she here among all these fine people and gay colors? He looked her over and decided that she was not appropriately dressed and must be a fool to sit downstairs in such togs. The tickets had probably been sent her out of kindness, he reflected as he put down a seat for her, and she had about as much right to sit there as he had.

When the symphony began Paul sank into one of the rear seats with a long sigh of relief, and lost himself as he had done before the Rico. It was not that symphonies, as such, meant anything in particular to Paul, but the first sigh of the instruments seemed to free some hilarious and potent spirit within him; something that struggled there like the Genius in the bottle found by the Arab fisherman. He felt a sudden zest of life; the lights danced before his eyes and the concert hall blazed into unimaginable splendor. When the soprano soloist came on, Paul forgot even the nastiness of his teacher's being there and gave himself up to the peculiar stimulus such personages always had for him. The soloist chanced to be a German woman, by no means in her first youth, and the mother of many children; but she wore an elaborate gown and a tiara, and above all she had that indefinable air of achievement, that world-shine upon her, which, in Paul's eyes, made her a veritable queen of Romance.

After a concert was over Paul was always irritable and wretched until he got to sleep, and tonight he was even more than usually restless. He had the feeling of not being able to let down, of its being impossible to give up this delicious excitement which was the only thing that could be called living at all. During the last number he withdrew and, after hastily changing his clothes in the dressing-room, slipped out to the side door where the soprano's carriage stood. Here he began pacing rapidly up and down the walk, waiting to see her come out.

Over yonder the Schenley, in its vacant stretch, loomed big and square through the fine rain, the windows of its twelve stories glowing like those of a lighted cardboard house under a Christmas tree. All the actors and singers of the better class stayed there when they were in the city, and a number of the big manufacturers of the place lived there in the winter. Paul had often hung about the hotel, watching the people go in and out, longing to enter and leave school-masters and dull care behind him forever.

At last the singer came out, accompanied by the conductor, who helped her into her carriage and closed the door with a cordial *auf wiedersehen* which set Paul to wondering whether she were not an old sweetheart of his. Paul followed the carriage over to the hotel, walking so rapidly as not to be far from the entrance when the singer alighted and disappeared behind the swinging glass doors that were opened by a negro in a tall hat and a long coat. In the moment that the door was ajar it seemed to Paul that he, too, entered. He seemed to feel himself go after her up the steps, into the warm, lighted building, into an exotic, a tropical world of shiny, glistening surfaces and basking ease. He reflected upon the mysterious dishes that were brought into the dining-room, the green bottles in buckets of ice, as he had seen them in the supper party pictures of the *Sunday World* supplement. A quick gust of wind brought the rain down with sudden vehemence, and Paul was startled to find that he was still outside in the slush of the gravel driveway; that his boots were letting in the water and his scanty overcoat was clinging wet about him; that the lights in front of the concert hall were out, and that the rain was driving in sheets between him and the orange glow of the windows above him. There it was, what he wanted—tangibly before him, like the fairy world of a Christmas pantomime, but mocking spirits stood guard at the doors, and, as the rain beat in his face, Paul wondered whether he were destined always to shiver in the black night outside, looking up at it.

He turned and walked reluctantly toward the car tracks. The end had to come sometime; his father in his night-clothes at the top of the stairs, explanations that did not explain, hastily improvised fictions that were forever tripping him up, his upstairs room and its horrible yellow wall-paper, the creaking bureau with the greasy plush collar-box, and over his painted wooden bed the pictures of George Washington and John Calvin, and the framed motto, "Feed my Lambs," which had been worked in red worsted by his mother.

Half an hour later, Paul alighted from his car and went slowly down one of the side streets off the main thoroughfare. It was a highly respectable street, where all the houses were exactly alike, and where businessmen of moderate means begot and reared large families of children, all of whom went to Sabbath-school and learned the shorter catechism, and were interested in arithmetic; all of whom were as exactly alike as their homes, and of a piece of the monotony in which they lived. Paul never went up Cordelia Street without a shudder of loathing. His home was next to the house of the Cumberland minister. He approached it tonight with the nerveless sense of defeat, the hopeless feeling of sinking back forever into ugliness and commonness that he had always had when he came home. The moment he turned into Cordelia Street he felt the waters close above his head. After each of these orgies of living, he experienced all the physical depression which follows a debauch; the loathing of respectable beds, of common food, of a house penetrated by kitchen odors; a shuddering repulsion for the flavorless, colorless mass of every-day existence; a morbid desire for cool things and soft lights and fresh flowers.

The nearer he approached the house, the more absolutely unequal Paul felt to the sight of it all; his ugly sleeping chamber; the cold bathroom with the grimy zinc tub, the cracked mirror, the dripping spiggots; his father, at the top of the stairs, his hairy legs sticking out from his night-shirt, his feet thrust into carpet slippers. He was so much later than usual that there would certainly be inquiries and reproaches. Paul stopped short before the door. He felt that he could not be accosted by his father tonight; that he could not toss again on that miserable bed. He would not go in. He would tell his father that he had no car fare, and it was raining so hard he had gone home with one of the boys and stayed all night.

Meanwhile, he was wet and cold. He went around to the back of the house and tried one of the basement windows, found it open, raised it cautiously, and scrambled down the cellar wall to the floor. There he stood, holding his breath, terrified by the noise he had made, but the floor above him was silent, and there was no creak on the stairs. He found a soap-box, and carried it over to the soft ring of light that streamed from the furnace door, and sat down. He was horribly afraid of rats, so he did not try to sleep, but sat looking distrustfully at the dark, still terrified lest he might have awakened his father. In such reactions, after one of the experiences which made days and nights out of the dreary blanks of the calendar, when his senses were deadened, Paul's head was always singularly clear. Suppose his father had heard him getting in at the window and had come down and shot him for a burglar? Then, again, suppose his father had come down, pistol in hand, and he had cried out in time to save himself, and his father had been horrified to think how nearly he had killed him? Then, again, suppose a day should come when his father would remember that night, and wish there had been no warning cry to stay his hand? With this last supposition Paul entertained himself until daybreak.

The following Sunday was fine; the sodden November chill was broken by the last flash of autumnal summer. In the morning Paul had to go to church and Sabbath-school, as always. On seasonable Sunday afternoons the burghers of Cordelia Street always sat out on their front "stoops," and talked to their neighbors on the next stoop, or called to those across the street in neighborly fashion. The men usually sat on gay cushions placed upon the steps that led down to the sidewalk, while the women, in their Sunday "waists," sat in rockers on the cramped porches, pretending to be greatly at their ease. The children played in the streets; there were so many of them that the place resembled the recreation grounds of a kindergarten. The men on the steps—all in their shirt sleeves, their vests unbuttoned—sat with their legs well apart, their stomachs comfortably protruding, and talked of the prices of things, or told anecdotes of the sagacity of their various chiefs and overlords. They occasionally looked over the multitude of squabbling children, listened affectionately to their high-pitched, nasal voices, smiling to see their own proclivities reproduced in their offspring, and interspersed their legends of the iron kings with remarks about their sons' progress at school, their grades in arithmetic, and the amounts they had saved in their toy banks.

On this last Sunday of November, Paul sat all the afternoon on the lowest step of his "stoop," staring into the street, while his sisters, in their rockers, were talking to the minister's daughters next door about how many shirt-waists they had made in the last week, and how many waffles some one had eaten at the last church supper. When the weather was warm, and his father was in a particularly jovial frame of mind, the girls made lemonade, which was always brought out in a red-glass pitcher, ornamented with forget-me-nots in blue enamel. This the girls thought very fine, and the neighbors always joked about the suspicious color of the pitcher.

Today Paul's father sat on the top step, talking to a young man who shifted a restless baby from knee to knee. He happened to be the young man who was daily held up to Paul as a model, and after whom it was his father's dearest hope that he would pattern. This young man was of a ruddy complexion, with a compressed, red mouth, and faded, near-sighted eyes, over which he wore thick spectacles, with gold bows that curved about his ears. He was clerk to one of the magnates of a great steel corporation, and was looked upon in Cordelia Street as a young man with a future. There was a story that, some five years ago—he was now barely twenty-six—he had been a trifle dissipated but in order to curb his appetites and save the loss of time and strength that a sowing of wild oats might have entailed, he had taken his chief's advice, oft reiterated to his employees, and at twenty-one had married the first woman whom he could persuade to share his fortunes. She happened to be an angular school-mistress, much older than he, who also wore thick glasses, and who had now borne him four children, all near-sighted, like herself.

The young man was relating how his chief, now cruising in the Mediterranean, kept in touch with all the details of the business, arranging his office hours on his yacht just as though he were at home, and "knocking off work enough to keep two stenographers busy." His father told, in turn, the plan his corporation was considering, of putting in an electric railway plant at Cairo. Paul snapped his teeth; he had an awful apprehension that they might spoil it all before he got there. Yet he rather liked to hear these legends of the iron kings, that were told and retold on Sundays and holidays; these stories of palaces in Venice, yachts on the Mediterranean, and high play at Monte Carlo appealed to his fancy, and he was interested in the triumphs of these cash boys who had become famous, though he had no mind for the cash-boy stage.

After supper was over, and he had helped to dry the dishes, Paul nervously asked his father whether he could go to George's to get some help in his geometry, and still more nervously asked for car fare. This latter request he had to repeat, as his father, on principle, did not like to hear requests for money, whether much or little. He asked Paul whether he could not go to some boy who lived nearer, and told him that he ought not to leave his school work until Sunday; but he gave him the dime. He was not a poor man, but he had a worthy ambition to come up in the world. His only reason for allowing Paul to usher was that he thought a boy ought to be earning a little.

Paul bounded upstairs, scrubbed the greasy odor of the dish-water from his hands with the ill-smelling soap he hated, and then shook over his fingers a few drops of violet water from the bottle he kept hidden in his drawer. He left the house with his geometry conspicuously under his arm, and the moment he got out of Cordelia Street and boarded a downtown car, he shook off the lethargy of two deadening days, and began to live again.

The leading juvenile of the permanent stock company which played at one of the downtown theatres was an acquaintance of Paul's, and the boy had been invited to drop in at the Sunday-night rehearsals whenever he could. For more than a year Paul had spent every available moment loitering about Charley Edward's dressing-room. He had won a place among Edward's following not only because the young actor, who could not afford to employ a dresser, often found him useful, but because he recognized in Paul something akin to what churchmen term "vocation."

It was at the theatre and at Carnegie Hall that Paul really lived; the rest was but a sleep and a forgetting. This was Paul's fairy tale, and it had for him all the allurement of a secret love. The moment he inhaled the gassy, painty, dusty odor behind the scenes, he breathed like a prisoner set free, and felt within him the possibility of doing or saying splendid, brilliant, poetic things. The moment the cracked orchestra beat out the overture from *Martha*, or jerked at the serenade from *Rigoletto*, all stupid and ugly things slid from him, and his senses were deliciously, yet delicately fired.

Perhaps it was because, in Paul's world, the natural nearly always wore the guise of ugliness, that a certain element of artificiality seemed to him necessary in beauty. Perhaps it was because his experience of life elsewhere was so full of Sabbath-school picnics, petty economies, wholesome advice as to how to succeed in life, and the unescapable odors of cooking, that he found this existence so alluring, these smartly-clad men and women so attractive, that he was so moved by these starry apple orchards that bloomed perennially under the lime-light.

It would be difficult to put it strongly enough how convincingly the stage entrance of that theatre was for Paul the actual portal of Romance. Certainly none of the company ever suspected it, least of all Charley Edwards. It was very like the old stories that used to float about London of fabulously rich Jews, who had subterranean halls there, with palms, and fountains, and soft lamps and richly apparelled women who never saw the disenchanting light of London day. So, in the midst of that smoke-palled city, enamored of figures and grimy toil, Paul had his secret temple, his wishing carpet, his bit of blue-and-white Mediterranean shore bathed in perpetual sunshine.

Several of Paul's teachers had a theory that his imagination had been perverted by garish fiction, but the truth was that he scarcely ever read at all. The books at home were not such as would either tempt or corrupt a youthful mind, and as for reading the novels that some of his friends urged upon him— well, he got what he wanted much more quickly from music; any sort of music, from an orchestra to a barrel organ. He needed only the spark, the indescribable thrill that made his imagination master of his senses, and he could make plots and pictures enough of his own. It was equally true that he was not stage struck—not, at any rate, in the usual acceptation of that expression. He had no desire to become an actor, any more than he had to become a musician. He felt no necessity to do any of these things; what he wanted was to see, to be in the atmosphere, float on the wave of it, to be carried out, blue league after blue league, away from everything.

After a night behind the scenes, Paul found the school-room more than ever repulsive; the bare floors and naked walls; the prosy men who never wore frock coats, or violets in their buttonholes; the women with their dull gowns, shrill voices, and pitiful seriousness about prepositions that govern the dative. He could not bear to have the other pupils think, for a moment, that he took these people seriously; he must convey to them that he considered it all trivial, and was there only by way of a jest, anyway. He had autographed pictures of all the members of the stock company which he showed his classmates, telling them the most incredible stories of his familiarity with these people, of his acquaintance with the soloists who came to Carnegie Hall, his suppers with them and the flowers he sent them. When these stories lost their effect, and his audience grew listless, he became desperate and would bid all the boys good-bye, announcing that he was going to travel for a while; going to Naples, to Venice, to Egypt. Then, next Monday, he would slip back, conscious and nervously smiling; his sister was ill, and he should have to defer his voyage until spring.

Matters went steadily worse with Paul at school. In the itch to let his instructors know how heartily he despised them and their homilies, and how thoroughly he was appreciated elsewhere, he mentioned once or twice that he had no time to fool with theorems; adding—with a twitch of the eyebrows and a touch of that nervous bravado which so perplexed them—that he was helping the people down at the stock company; they were old friends of his.

The upshot of the matter was that the Principal went to Paul's father, and Paul was taken out of school and put to work. The manager at Carnegie Hall was told to get another usher in his stead; the door-keeper at the theatre was warned not to admit him to the house; and Charley Edwards remorsefully promised the boy's father not to see him again.

The members of the stock company were vastly amused when some of Paul's stories reached them—especially the women. They were hard-working women, most of them supporting indigent husbands or brothers, and they laughed rather bitterly at having stirred the boy to such fervid and florid inventions. They agreed with the faculty and with his father that Paul's was a bad case.

The east-bound train was ploughing through a January snow-storm; the dull dawn was beginning to show grey when the engine whistled a mile out of Newark. Paul started up from the seat where he had lain curled in uneasy slumber, rubbed the breath-misted window glass with his hand, and peered out. The snow was whirling in curling eddies above the white bottom lands, and the drifts lay already deep in the fields and along the fences, while here and there the long dead grass and dried weed stalks protruded black above it. Lights shone from the scattered houses, and a gang of laborers who stood beside the track waved their lanterns.

Paul had slept very little, and he felt grimy and uncomfortable. He had made the all-night journey in a day coach, partly because he was ashamed, dressed as he was, to go into a Pullman, and partly because he was afraid of being seen there by some Pittsburgh businessman, who might have noticed him in Denny & Carson's office. When the whistle awoke him, he clutched quickly at his breast pocket, glancing about him with an uncertain smile. But the little, clay-bespattered Italians were still sleeping, the slatternly women across the aisle were in open-mouthed oblivion, and even the crumby, crying babies were for the nonce stilled. Paul settled back to struggle with his impatience as best he could.

When he arrived at the Jersey City station, he hurried through his breakfast, manifestly ill at ease and keeping a sharp eye about him. After he reached the Twenty-third Street station, he consulted a cabman, and had himself driven to a men's furnishing establishment that was just opening for the day. He spent upward of two hours there, buying with endless reconsidering and great care. His new street suit he put on in the fitting-room; the frock coat and dress clothes he had bundled into the cab with his linen. Then he drove to a hatter's and a shoe house. His next errand was at Tiffany's, where he selected his silver and a new scarf-pin. He would not wait to have his silver marked, he said. Lastly, he stopped at a trunk shop on Broadway, and had his purchases packed into various travelling bags.

It was a little after one o'clock when he drove up to the Waldorf, and after settling with the cabman, went into the office. He registered from Washington; said his mother and father had been abroad, and that he had come down to await the arrival of their steamer. He told his story plausibly and had no trouble, since he volunteered to pay for them in advance, in engaging his rooms; a sleeping-room, sitting-room, and bath.

Not once, but a hundred times Paul had planned this entry into New York. He had gone over every detail of it with Charley Edwards, and in his scrap book at home there were pages of description about New York hotels, cut from the Sunday papers. When he was shown to his sitting-room on the eighth floor, he saw at a glance that everything was as it should be; there was but one detail in his mental picture that the place did not realize, so he rang for the bell boy and sent him down for flowers. He moved about nervously until the boy returned, putting away his new linen and fingering it delightedly as he did so. When the flowers came, he put them hastily into water, and then tumbled into a hot bath. Presently he came out of his white bath-room, resplendent in his new silk underwear, and playing with the tassels of his red robe. The snow was whirling so fiercely outside his windows that he could scarcely see across the street, but within the air was deliciously soft and fragrant. He put the violets and jonquils on the taboret beside the couch, and threw himself down, with a long sigh, covering himself with a Roman blanket. He was thoroughly tired; he had been in such haste, he had stood up to such a strain, covered so much ground in the last twenty-four hours, that he wanted to think how it had all come about. Lulled by the sound of the wind, the warm air, and the cool fragrance of the flowers, he sank into deep, drowsy retrospection.

It had been wonderfully simple; when they had shut him out of the theatre and concert hall, when they had taken away his bone, the whole thing was virtually determined. The rest was a mere matter of opportunity. The only thing that at all surprised him was his own courage—for he realized well enough that he had always been tormented by fear, a sort of apprehensive dread that, of late years, as the meshes of the lies he had told closed about him, had been pulling the muscles of his body tighter and tighter. Until now, he could not remember the time when he had not been dreading something. Even when he was a little boy, it was always there—behind him, or before, or on either side. There had always been the shadowed corner, the dark place into which he dared not look, but from which something seemed always to be watching him—and Paul had done things that were not pretty to watch, he knew.

But now he had a curious sense of relief, as though he had at last thrown down the gauntlet to the thing in the corner.

Yet it was but a day since he had been sulking in the traces; but yesterday afternoon that he had been sent to the bank with Denny & Carson's deposit, as usual—but this time he was instructed to leave the book to be balanced. There was above two thousand dollars in checks, and nearly a thousand in the bank notes which he had taken from the book and quietly transferred to his pocket. At the bank he had made out a new deposit slip. His nerves had been steady enough to permit of his returning to the office, where he had finished his work and asked for a full day's holiday tomorrow, Saturday, giving a perfectly reasonable pretext. The bank book, he knew, would not be returned before Monday or Tuesday, and his father would be out of town for the next week. From the time he slipped the bank notes into his pocket until he boarded the night train for New York, he had not known a moment's hesitation. It was not the first time Paul had steered through treacherous waters.

How astonishingly easy it had all been; here he was, the thing done; and this time there would be no awakening, no figure at the top of the stairs. He watched the snow flakes whirling by his window until he fell asleep.

When he awoke, it was three o'clock in the afternoon. He bounded up with a start; half of one of his precious days gone already! He spent more than an hour in dressing, watching every stage of his toilet carefully in the mirror.

Everything was quite perfect; he was exactly the kind of boy he had always wanted to be.

When he went downstairs, Paul took a carriage and drove up Fifth Avenue toward the Park. The snow had somewhat abated; carriages and tradesmen's wagons were hurrying soundlessly to and fro in the winter twilight; boys in woollen mufflers were shovelling off the doorsteps; the avenue stages made fine spots of color against the white street. Here and there on the corners were stands, with whole flower gardens blooming under glass cases, against the sides of which the snow flakes stuck and melted; violets, roses, carnations, lilies of the valley—somewhat vastly more lovely and alluring that they blossomed thus unnaturally in the snow. The Park itself was a wonderful stage winterpiece.

When he returned, the pause of the twilight had ceased, and the tune of the streets had changed. The snow was falling faster, lights streamed from the hotels that reared their dozen stories fearlessly up into the storm, defying the raging Atlantic winds. A long, black stream of carriages poured down the avenue, intersected here and there by other streams, tending horizontally. There were a score of cabs about the entrance of his hotel, and his driver had to wait. Boys in livery were running in and out of the awning stretched across the sidewalk, up and down the red velvet carpet laid from the door to the street. Above, about, within it all was the rumble and roar, the hurry and toss of thousands of human beings as hot for pleasure as himself, and on every side of him towered the glaring affirmation of the omnipotence of wealth.

The boy set his teeth and drew his shoulders together in a spasm of realization: the plot of all dramas, the text of all romances, the nerve-stuff of all sensations was whirling about him like the snow flakes. He burnt like a faggot in a tempest.

When Paul went down to dinner, the music of the orchestra came floating up the elevator shaft to greet him. His head whirled as he stepped into the thronged corridor, and he sank back into one of the chairs against the wall to get his breath. The lights, the chatter, the perfumes, the bewildering medley of color—he had, for a moment, the feeling of not being able to stand it. But only for a moment; these were his own people, he told himself. He went slowly about the corridors, through the writing-rooms, smoking-rooms, reception-rooms, as though he were exploring the chambers of an enchanted palace, built and peopled for him alone.

When he reached the dining-room he sat down at a table near a window. The flowers, the white linen, the many-colored wine glasses, the gay toilettes of the women, the low popping of corks, the undulating repetitions of the *Blue Danube* from the orchestra, all flooded Paul's dream with bewildering radiance. When the roseate tinge of his champagne was added—that cold, precious, bubbling stuff that creamed and foamed in his glass—Paul wondered that there were honest men in the world at all. This was what all the world was fighting for, he reflected; this was what all the struggle was about. He doubted the reality of his past. Had he ever known a place called Cordelia Street, a place where fagged-looking businessmen got on the early car; mere rivets in a machine they seemed to Paul—sickening men, with combings of children's hair always hanging to their coats, and the smell of cooking in their clothes. Cordelia Street—Ah! that belonged to another time and country; had he not always been thus, had he not sat here night after night, from as far back as he could remember, looking pensively over just such shimmering textures, and slowly twirling the stem of a glass like this one between his thumb and middle finger? He rather thought he had.

He was not in the least abashed or lonely. He had no especial desire to meet or to know any of these people; all he demanded was the right to look on and conjecture, to watch the pageant. The mere stage properties were all he contended for. Nor was he lonely later in the evening, in his loge at the Metropolitan. He was now entirely rid of his nervous misgivings, of his forced aggressiveness, of the imperative desire to show himself different from his surroundings. He felt now that his surroundings explained him. Nobody questioned the purple; he had only to wear it passively. He had only to glance down at his attire to reassure himself that here it would be impossible for anyone to humiliate him.

He found it hard to leave his beautiful sitting-room to go to bed that night, and sat long watching the raging storm from his turret window. When he went to sleep it was with the lights turned on in his bedroom; partly because of his old timidity, and partly so that, if he should wake in the night, there would be no wretched moment of doubt, no horrible suspicion of yellow wall-paper, or of Washington or Calvin above his bed.

Sunday morning the city was practically snow-bound. Paul breakfasted late, and in the afternoon he fell in with a wild San Francisco boy, a freshman at Yale, who said he had run down for a "little flyer" over Sunday. The young man offered to show Paul the night side of the town, and the two boys went out together after dinner, not returning to the hotel until seven o'clock the next morning. They had started out in the confiding warmth of a champagne friendship, but their parting in the elevator was singularly cool. The freshman pulled himself together to make his train, and Paul went to bed. He awoke at two o'clock in the afternoon, very thirsty and dizzy, and rang for ice-water, coffee, and the Pittsburgh papers.

On the part of the hotel management, Paul excited no suspicion. There was this to be said for him, that he wore his spoils with dignity and in no way made himself conspicuous. Even under the glow of his wine he was never boisterous, though he found the stuff like a magician's wand for wonder-building. His chief greediness lay in his ears and eyes, and his excesses were not offensive ones. His dearest pleasures were the grey winter twilights in his sitting-room; his quiet enjoyment of his flowers, his clothes, his wide divan, his cigarette, and his sense of power. He could not remember a time when he had felt so at peace with himself. The mere release from the necessity of petty lying, lying every day and every day, restored his self-respect. He had never lied for pleasure, even at school; but to be noticed and admired, to assert his difference from other Cordelia Street boys; and he felt a good deal more manly, more honest, even, now that he had no need for boastful pretensions, now that he could, as his actor friends used to say, "dress the part." It was characteristic that remorse did not occur to him. His golden days went by without a shadow, and he made each as perfect as he could.

On the eighth day after his arrival in New York, he found the whole affair exploited in the Pittsburgh papers, exploited with a wealth of detail which indicated that local news of a sensational nature was at a low ebb. The firm of Denny & Carson announced that the boy's father had refunded the full amount of the theft, and that they had no intention of prosecuting. The Cumberland minister had been interviewed, and expressed his hope of yet reclaiming the motherless lad, and his Sabbath-school teacher declared that she would spare no effort to that end. The rumor had reached Pittsburgh that the boy had been seen in a New York hotel, and his father had gone East to find him and bring him home.

Paul had just come in to dress for dinner; he sank into a chair, weak to the knees, and clasped his head in his hands. It was to be worse than jail, even; the tepid waters of Cordelia Street were to close over him finally and forever. The grey monotony stretched before him in hopeless, unrelieved years; Sabbath-school, Young People's Meeting, the yellow-papered room, the damp dish-towels; it all rushed back upon him with a sickening vividness. He had the old feeling that the orchestra had suddenly stopped, the sinking sensation that the play was over. The sweat broke out on his face, and he sprang to his feet, looked about him with his white, conscious smile, and winked at himself in the mirror. With something of the old childish belief in miracles with which he had so often gone to class, all his lessons unlearned, Paul dressed and dashed whistling down the corridor to the elevator.

He had no sooner entered the dining-room and caught the measure of the music than his remembrance was lightened by his old elastic power of claiming the moment, mounting with it, and finding it all sufficient. The glare and glitter about him, the mere scenic accessories had again, and for the last time, their old potency. He would show himself that he was game, he would finish the thing splendidly. He doubted, more than ever, the existence of Cordelia

Street, and for the first time he drank his wine recklessly. Was he not, after all, one of those fortunate beings born to the purple, was he not still himself and in his own place? He drummed a nervous accompaniment to the Pagliacci music and looked about him, telling himself over and over that it had paid.

He reflected drowsily, to the swell of the music and the chill sweetness of his wine, that he might have done it more wisely. He might have caught an outboard steamer and been well out of their clutches before now. But the other side of the world had seemed too far away and too uncertain then; he could not have waited for it; his need had been too sharp. If he had to choose over again, he would do the same thing tomorrow. He looked affectionately about the dining-room, now gilded with a soft mist. Ah, it had paid indeed!

Paul was awakened next morning by a painful throbbing in his head and feet. He had thrown himself across the bed without undressing, and had slept with his shoes on. His limbs and hands were lead heavy, and his tongue and throat were parched and burnt. There came upon him one of those fateful attacks of clear-headedness that never occurred except when he was physically exhausted and his nerves hung loose. He lay still and closed his eyes and let the tide of things wash over him.

His father was in New York; "stopping at some joint or other," he told himself. The memory of successive summers on the front stoop fell upon him like a weight of black water. He had not a hundred dollars left; and he knew now, more than ever, that money was everything, the wall that stood between all he loathed and all he wanted. The thing was winding itself up; he had thought of that on his first glorious day in New York, and had even provided a way to snap the thread. It lay on his dressing-table now; he had got it out last night when he came blindly up from dinner, but the shiny metal hurt his eyes, and he disliked the looks of it.

He rose and moved about with a painful effort, succumbing now and again to attacks of nausea. It was the old depression exaggerated; all the world had become Cordelia Street. Yet somehow he was not afraid of anything, was absolutely calm; perhaps because he had looked into the dark corner at last and knew. It was bad enough, what he saw there, but somehow not so bad as his long fear of it had been. He saw everything clearly now. He had a feeling that he had made the best of it, that he had lived the sort of life he was meant to live, and for half an hour he sat staring at the revolver. But he told himself that was not the way, so he went downstairs and took a cab to the ferry.

When Paul arrived at Newark, he got off the train and took another cab, directing the driver to follow the Pennsylvania tracks out of the town. The snow lay heavy on the roadways and had drifted deep in the open fields. Only here and there the dead grass or dried weed stalks projected, singularly black, above it. Once well into the country, Paul dismissed the carriage and walked, floundering along the tracks, his mind a medley of irrelevant things. He seemed to hold in his brain an actual picture of everything he had seen that morning. He remembered every feature of both his drivers, of the toothless old woman from whom he had bought the red flowers in his coat, the agent from whom he had got his ticket, and all of his fellow-passengers on the ferry. His mind, unable to cope with vital matters near at hand, worked feverishly and deftly at sorting and grouping these images. They made for him a part of the ugliness of the world, of the ache in his head, and the bitter burning on his tongue. He stopped and put a handful of snow into his mouth as he walked, but that, too, seemed hot. When he reached a little hillside, where the tracks ran through a cut some twenty feet below him, he stopped and sat down.

The carnations in his coat were drooping with the cold, he noticed; their red glory all over. It occurred to him that all the flowers he had seen in the glass cases that first night must have gone the same way, long before this. It was only one splendid breath they had, in spite of their brave mockery at the winter outside the glass; and it was a losing game in the end, it seemed, this revolt against the homilies by which the world is run. Paul took one of the blossoms carefully from his coat and scooped a little hole in the snow, where he covered it up. Then he dozed a while, from his weak condition, seemingly insensible to the cold.

The sound of an approaching train awoke him, and he started to his feet, remembering only his resolution, and afraid lest he should be too late. He stood watching the approaching locomotive, his teeth chattering, his lips drawn away from them in a frightened smile; once or twice he glanced nervously sidewise, as though he were being watched. When the right moment came, he jumped. As he fell, the folly of his haste occurred to him with merciless clearness, the vastness of what he had left undone. There flashed through his brain, clearer than ever before, the blue of Adriatic water, the yellow of Algerian sands.

He felt something strike his chest, and that his body was being thrown swiftly through the air, on and on, immeasurably far and fast, while his limbs were gently relaxed. Then, because the picture making mechanism was crushed, the disturbing visions flashed into black, and Paul dropped back into the immense design of things.

ANTON CHEKHOV

THE LADY WITH
THE PET DOG

Anton Chekhov (1860–1904) was a great playwright and one of the most influential and prolific short-story writers of the late nineteenth century. He was born in southwestern Russia, the son of a serf who had purchased his family's freedom. The Chekhov family was poor, and throughout much of his life Anton would provide financial support to his parents and several siblings. It was this need to earn extra money for his family which first encouraged the young Chekhov to begin composing humorous sketches, theatrical notices, and short stories. However, his chief occupation was physician, rather than writer. Medicine, he said, was his "lawful wife," but as it was neither financially nor emotionally satisfying, literature was his mistress. He moved back and forth between the two, offering free medical care to the poor and sending his stories off to magazines for whatever he could charge. He would maintain this balance until his own poor health made it necessary to stop treating patients. Then "the mistress came to supplant the wife."

Chekhov was a generous, gentle man, "humane to the tips of his fingers," according to Somerset Maugham. He enjoyed the friendship of some of Russia's most highly regarded authors, including Tolstoy and Gorky, though he never aligned himself with them politically. The closest thing he had to a credo was a belief in freedom. "My holy of holies is the human body, health, intelligence, talent, inspiration, love and absolute freedom—freedom from violence and falsehood, no matter how the last two manifest themselves." Chekhov saw as much threat to individual freedom in Russia's swelling revolutionary fervour as he did in the status quo. "For him a man's own conscience was the sole arbiter of right and wrong." His fiction shows little concern with "social questions and less with political matters." Though he was certainly aware of "social evils and had a strong sense of civic responsibility ... he felt that what counted was individual initiative, personal effort."

Chekhov became one of Russia's most popular writers. In 1886 he published his first collection of short stories, Motley Stories, and, a year later, his second collection, In the Twilight, which won him the Russian

Academy's Pushkin Prize for literary achievement. In the course of his career, he wrote over eight hundred stories. In 1897 Chekhov was diagnosed with tuberculosis and spent the last years of his life in the milder climate of Yalta, on the southern coast of the Crimea. During this period Chekhov wrote his best-known plays, none of which enjoyed much immediate success on the stage. The Cherry Orchard *was perhaps his most successful;* The Seagull *and* Uncle Vanya *have since become a mainstay of theatres around the world. Through the theatre Chekhov met his wife, the actress Olga Knipper. They married in 1901, just three years before his death at a spa in Germany.*

American writer Eudora Welty suggests that Chekhov brought about a revolution in the short story by removing the plot and allowing the story to evolve out of itself. He tried to efface his presence as a writer, to allow his characters their own shape and his readers their own interpretation. In a letter to his brother, Chekhov described his method of building a story based on objective detail: "In descriptions of Nature one ought to seize upon the little particulars, grouping them in such a way that, in reading, when you shut your eyes, you get a picture." In another letter defending himself against the claim that he was indifferent to good and evil, that he lacked ideals in drawing his characters, he said: "Let the jury judge them; it's my job simply to show what sort of people they are."

I

A new person, it was said, had appeared on the esplanade: a lady with a pet dog. Dmitry Dmitrich Gurov, who had spent a fortnight at Yalta and had got used to the place, had also begun to take an interest in new arrivals. As he sat in Vernet's confectionery shop, he saw, walking on the esplanade, a fair-haired young woman of medium height, wearing a beret; a white Pomeranian was trotting behind her.

And afterwards he met her in the public garden and in the square several times a day. She walked alone, always wearing the same beret and always with the white dog; no one knew who she was and everyone called her simply "the lady with the pet dog."

"If she is here alone without husband or friends," Gurov reflected, "it wouldn't be a bad thing to make her acquaintance."

He was under forty, but he already had a daughter twelve years old, and two sons at school. They had found a wife for him when he was very young, a student in his second year, and by now she seemed half as old again as he. She was a tall, erect woman with dark eyebrows, stately and dignified and, as she said of herself, intellectual. She read a great deal, used simplified spelling in her letters, called her husband, not Dmitry, but Dimitry, while he privately considered her of limited intelligence, narrow-minded, dowdy, was afraid of her, and did not like to be at home. He had begun being unfaithful to her long ago—had been unfaithful to her often and, probably for that reason, almost always spoke ill of women, and when they were talked of in his presence used to call them "the inferior race."

It seemed to him that he had been sufficiently tutored by bitter experience to call them what he pleased, and yet he could not have lived without "the inferior race" for two days together. In the company of men he was bored and ill at ease, he was chilly and uncommunicative with them; but when he was among women he felt free, and knew what to speak to them about and how to comport himself; and even to be silent with them was no strain on him. In his appearance, in his character, in his whole make-up there was something attractive and elusive that disposed women in his favor and allured them. He knew that, and some force seemed to draw him to them, too.

Oft-repeated and really bitter experience had taught him long ago that with decent people—particularly Moscow people—who are irresolute and slow to move, every affair which at first seems a light and charming adventure inevitably grows into a whole problem of extreme complexity, and in the end a painful situation is created. But at every new meeting with an interesting woman this lesson of experience seemed to slip from his memory, and he was eager for life, and everything seemed so simple and diverting.

One evening while he was dining in the public garden the lady in the beret walked up without haste to take the next table. Her expression, her gait, her dress, and the way she did her hair told him that she belonged to the upper class, that she was married, that she was in Yalta for the first time and alone, and that she was bored there. The stories told of the immorality in Yalta are to a great extent untrue; he despised them, and knew that such stories were made up for the most part by persons who would have been glad to sin themselves if they had had the chance; but when the lady sat down at the next table three paces from him, he recalled these stories of easy conquests, of trips to the mountains, and the tempting thought of a swift, fleeting liaison, a romance with an unknown woman of whose very name he was ignorant suddenly took hold of him.

He beckoned invitingly to the Pomeranian, and when the dog approached him, shook his finger at it. The Pomeranian growled; Gurov threatened it again.

The lady glanced at him and at once dropped her eyes.

"He doesn't bite," she said and blushed.

"May I give him a bone?" he asked; and when she nodded he inquired affably, "Have you been in Yalta long?"

"About five days."

"And I am dragging out the second week here."

There was a short silence.

"Time passes quickly, and yet it is so dull here!" she said, not looking at him.

"It's only the fashion to say it's dull here. A provincial will live in Belyov or Zhizdra and not be bored, but when he comes here it's 'Oh, the dullness! Oh, the dust!' One would think he came from Granada."

She laughed. Then both continued eating in silence, like strangers, but after dinner they walked together and there sprang up between them the light banter of people who are free and contented, to whom it does not matter where they go or what they talk about. They walked and talked of the strange light on the sea: the water was a soft, warm, lilac color, and there was a golden band of moonlight upon it. They talked of how sultry it was after a hot day. Gurov told her that he was a native of Moscow, that he had studied languages and literature at the university, but had a post in a bank; that at one time he had trained to become an opera singer but had given it up, that he owned two houses in Moscow. And he learned from her that she had grown up in Petersburg, but had lived in S—— since her marriage two years previously, that she was going to stay in Yalta for about another month, and that her husband, who needed a rest, too, might perhaps come to fetch her. She was not certain whether her husband was a member of a Government Board or served on a Zemstvo Council, and this amused her. And Gurov learned too that her name was Anna Sergeyevna.

Afterwards in his room at the hotel he thought about her—and was certain that he would meet her the next day. It was bound to happen. Getting into bed he recalled that she had been a schoolgirl only recently, doing lessons like his own daughter; he thought how much timidity and angularity there was still in her laugh and her manner of talking with a stranger. It must have been the first time in her life that she was alone in a setting in which she was followed, looked at, and spoken to for one secret purpose alone, which she could hardly fail to guess. He thought of her slim, delicate throat, her lovely gray eyes.

"There's something pathetic about her, though," he thought, and dropped off.

II

A week had passed since they had struck up an acquaintance. It was a holiday. It was close indoors, while in the street the wind whirled the dust about and blew people's hats off. One was thirsty all day, and Gurov often went into the restaurant and offered Anna Sergeyevna a soft drink or ice cream. One did not know what to do with oneself.

In the evening when the wind had abated they went out on the pier to watch the steamer come in. There were a great many people walking about the dock; they had come to welcome someone and they were carrying bunches of flowers. And two peculiarities of a festive Yalta crowd stood out: the elderly ladies were dressed like young ones and there were many generals.

Owing to the choppy sea, the steamer arrived late, after sunset, and it was a long time tacking about before it put in at the pier. Anna Sergeyevna peered at the steamer and the passengers through her lorgnette as though looking for acquaintances, and whenever she turned to Gurov her eyes were shining. She talked a great deal and asked questions jerkily, forgetting the next moment what she had asked; then she lost her lorgnette in the crush.

The festive crowd began to disperse; it was now too dark to see people's faces; there was no wind any more, but Gurov and Anna Sergeyevna still stood as though waiting to see someone else come off the steamer. Anna Sergeyevna was silent now, and sniffed her flowers without looking at Gurov.

"The weather has improved this evening," he said. "Where shall we go now? Shall we drive somewhere?"

She did not reply.

Then he looked at her intently, and suddenly embraced her and kissed her on the lips, and the moist fragrance of her flowers enveloped him; and at once he looked round him anxiously, wondering if anyone had seen them.

"Let us go to your place," he said softly. And they walked off together rapidly.

The air in her room was close and there was the smell of perfume she had bought at the Japanese shop. Looking at her, Gurov thought: "What encounters life offers!" From the past he preserved the memory of carefree, good-natured women whom love made gay and who were grateful to him for the happiness he gave them, however brief it might be; and of women like his wife who loved without sincerity, with too many words, affectedly, hysterically, with an expression that it was not love or passion that engaged them but something more significant; and of two or three others, very beautiful, frigid women, across whose faces would suddenly flit a rapacious expression—an obstinate desire to take from life more than it could give, and these were women no longer young, capricious, unreflecting, domineering, unintelligent, and when Gurov grew cold to them their beauty aroused his hatred, and the lace on their lingerie seemed to him to resemble scales.

But here there was the timidity, the angularity of inexperienced youth, a feeling of awkwardness; and there was a sense of embarrassment, as though someone had suddenly knocked at the door. Anna Sergeyevna, "the lady with the pet dog," treated what had happened in a peculiar way, very seriously, as though it were her fall—so it seemed, and this was odd and inappropriate. Her features drooped and faded, and her long hair hung down sadly on either side of her face; she grew pensive and her dejected pose was that of a Magdalene in a picture by an old master.

"It's not right," she said. "You don't respect me now, you first of all."

There was a watermelon on the table. Gurov cut himself a slice and began eating it without haste. They were silent for at least half an hour.

There was something touching about Anna Sergeyevna; she had the purity of a well-bred, naive woman who has seen little of life. The single candle burning on the table barely illumined her face, yet it was clear that she was unhappy.

"Why should I stop respecting you, darling?" asked Gurov. "You don't know what you're saying."

"God forgive me," she said, and her eyes filled with tears. "It's terrible."

"It's as though you were trying to exonerate yourself."

"How can I exonerate myself? No. I am a bad, low woman; I despise myself and I have no thought of exonerating myself. It's not my husband but myself I have deceived. And not only just now; I have been deceiving myself for a long time. My husband may be a good, honest man, but he is a flunkey! I don't know what he does, what his work is, but I know he is a flunkey! I was twenty when I married him. I was tormented by curiosity; I wanted something better. 'There must be a different sort of life,' I said to myself. I wanted to live! To live, to live! Curiosity kept eating at me—you don't understand it, but I swear to God I could no longer control myself; something was going on in me: I could not be held back. I told my husband I was ill, and came here. And here I have been walking about as though in a daze, as though I were mad; and now I have become a vulgar, vile woman whom anyone may despise."

Gurov was already bored with her; he was irritated by her naive tone, by her repentance, so unexpected and so out of place; but for the tears in her eyes he might have thought she was joking or play-acting.

"I don't understand, my dear," he said softly. "What do you want?"

She hid her face on his breast and pressed close to him.

"Believe me, believe me, I beg you," she said, "I love honesty and purity, and sin is loathsome to me; I don't know what I'm doing. Simple people say, 'The Evil One had led me astray.' And I may say of myself now that the Evil One has led me astray."

"Quiet, quiet," he murmured.

He looked into her fixed, frightened eyes, kissed her, spoke to her softly and affectionately, and by degrees she calmed down, and her gaiety returned; both began laughing.

Afterwards when they went out there was not a soul on the esplanade. The town with its cypresses looked quite dead, but the sea was still sounding as it broke upon the beach; a single launch was rocking on the waves and on it a lantern was blinking sleepily.

They found a cab and drove to Oreanda.

"I found out your surname in the hall just now: it was written on the board—von Dideritz," said Gurov. "Is your husband German?"

"No; I believe his grandfather was German, but he is Greek Orthodox himself."

At Oreanda they sat on a bench not far from the church, looked down at the sea, and were silent. Yalta was barely visible through the morning mist; white clouds rested motionlessly on the mountaintops. The leaves did not stir on the trees, cicadas twanged, and the monotonous muffled sound of the sea that rose from below spoke of the peace, the eternal sleep awaiting us. So it rumbled below when there was no Yalta, no Oreanda here; so it rumbles now, and it will rumble as indifferently and as hollowly when we are no more. And in this constancy, in this complete indifference to the life and death of each of us, there lies, perhaps, a pledge of our eternal salvation, of the unceasing advance of life upon earth, of unceasing movement towards perfection. Sitting beside a young woman who in the dawn seemed so lovely, Gurov, soothed and spellbound by these magical surroundings—the sea, the mountains, the clouds, the wide sky—thought how everything is really beautiful in this world when one reflects: everything except what we think or do ourselves when we forget the higher aims of life and our own human dignity.

A man strolled up to them—probably a guard—looked at them and walked away. And this detail, too, seemed so mysterious and beautiful. They saw a steamer arrive from Feodosia, its lights extinguished in the glow of dawn.

"There is dew on the grass," said Anna Sergeyevna, after a silence.

"Yes, it's time to go home."

They returned to the city.

Then they met every day at twelve o'clock on the esplanade, lunched and dined together, took walks, admired the sea. She complained that she slept badly, that she had palpitations, asked the same questions, troubled now by jealousy and now by the fear that he did not respect her sufficiently. And often in the square or the public garden, when there was no one near them, he suddenly drew her to him and kissed her passionately. Complete idleness, these kisses in broad daylight exchanged furtively in dread of someone's seeing them, the heat, the smell of the sea, and the continual flitting before his eyes of idle, well-dressed, well-fed people, worked a complete change in him; he kept telling Anna Sergeyevna how beautiful she was, how seductive, was urgently passionate; he would not move a step away from her, while she was often pensive and continually pressed him to confess that he did not respect her, did not love her in the least, and saw in her nothing but a common woman. Almost every evening rather late they drove somewhere out of town, to Oreanda or to the waterfall; and the excursion was always a success, the scenery invariably impressed them as beautiful and magnificent.

They were expecting her husband, but a letter came from him saying that he had eye-trouble, and begging his wife to return home as soon as possible. Anna Sergeyevna made haste to go.

"It's a good thing I am leaving," she said to Gurov. "It's the hand of Fate!"

She took a carriage to the railway station, and he went with her. They were driving the whole day. When she had taken her place in the express, and when the second bell had rung, she said, "Let me look at you once more—let me look at you again. Like this."

She was not crying but was so sad that she seemed ill, and her face was quivering.

"I shall be thinking of you—remembering you," she said. "God bless you; be happy. Don't remember evil against me. We are parting forever—it has to be, for we ought never to have met. Well, God bless you."

The train moved off rapidly, its lights soon vanished, and a minute later there was no sound of it, as though everything had conspired to end as quickly as possible that sweet trance, that madness. Left alone on the platform, and gazing into the dark distance, Gurov listened to the twang of the grasshoppers and the hum of the telegraph wires, feeling as though he had just waked up. And he reflected, musing, that there had now been another episode or adventure in his life, and it, too, was at an end, and nothing was left of it but a memory. He was moved, sad, and slightly remorseful: this young woman whom he would never meet again had not been happy with him; he had been warm and affectionate with her, but yet in his manner, his tone, and his caresses there had been a shade of light irony, the slightly coarse arrogance of a happy male who was, besides, almost twice her age. She had constantly called him kind, exceptional, high-minded; obviously he had seemed to her different from what he really was, so he had involuntarily deceived her.

Here at the station there was already a scent of autumn in the air; it was a chilly evening.

"It is time for me to go north, too," thought Gurov as he left the platform. "High time!"

III

At home in Moscow the winter routine was already established: the stoves were heated, and in the morning it was still dark when the children were having breakfast and getting ready for school, and the nurse would light the lamp for a short time. There were frosts already. When the first snow falls, on the first day the sleighs are out, it is pleasant to see the white earth, the white roofs; one draws easy, delicious breaths, and the season brings back the days of one's youth. The old limes and birches, white with hoar-frost, have a good-natured look; they are closer to one's heart than cypresses and palms, and near them one no longer wants to think of mountains and the sea.

Gurov, a native of Moscow, arrived there on a fine frosty day, and when he put on his fur coat and warm gloves and took a walk along Petrovka, and when on Saturday night he heard the bells ringing, his recent trip and the places he had visited lost all charm for him. Little by little he became immersed in Moscow life, greedily read three newspapers a day, and declared that he did not read the Moscow papers on principle. He already felt a longing for restaurants, clubs, formal dinners, anniversary celebrations, and it flattered him to entertain distinguished lawyers and actors, and to play cards with a professor at the physicians' club. He could eat a whole portion of meat stewed with pickled cabbage and served in a pan, Moscow style.

A month or so would pass and the image of Anna Sergeyevna, it seemed to him, would become misty in his memory, and only from time to time he would dream of her with her touching smile as he dreamed of others. But more than a month went by, winter came into its own, and everything was still clear in his memory as though he had parted from Anna Sergeyevna only yesterday. And his memories glowed more and more vividly. When in the evening stillness the voices of his children preparing their lessons reached his study, or when he listened to a song or to an organ playing in a restaurant, or when the storm howled in the chimney, suddenly everything would rise up in his memory: what had happened on the pier and the early morning with the mist on the mountains, and the steamer coming from Feodosia, and the kisses. He would pace about his room a long time, remembering and smiling; then his memories passed into reveries, and in his imagination the past would mingle with what was to come. He did not dream of Anna Sergeyevna, but she followed him about everywhere and watched him. When he shut his eyes he saw her before him as though she were there in the flesh, and she seemed to him lovelier, younger, tenderer than she had been, and he imagined himself a finer man than he had been in Yalta. Of evenings she peered out at him from the bookcase, from the fireplace, from the corner—he heard her breathing, the caressing rustle of her clothes. In the street he followed the women with his eyes, looking for someone who resembled her.

Already he was tormented by a strong desire to share his memories with someone. But in his home it was impossible to talk of his love, and he had no one to talk to outside; certainly he could not confide in his tenants or in anyone at the bank. And what was there to talk about? He hadn't loved her then, had he? Had there been anything beautiful, poetical, edifying, or simply interesting in his relations with Anna Sergeyevna? And he was forced to talk vaguely of love, of women, and no one guessed what he meant; only his wife would twitch her black eyebrows and say, "The part of a philanderer does not suit you at all, Dimitry."

One evening, coming out of the physicians' club with an official with whom he had been playing cards, he could not resist saying:

"If you only knew what a fascinating woman I became acquainted with at Yalta!"

The official got into his sledge and was driving away, but turned suddenly and shouted:

"Dmitry Dmitrich!"

"What is it?"

"You were right this evening: the sturgeon was a bit high."

These words, so commonplace, for some reason moved Gurov to indignation, and struck him as degrading and unclean. What savage manners, what mugs! What stupid nights, what dull, humdrum days! Frenzied gambling, gluttony, drunkenness, continual talk always about the same things! Futile pursuits and conversations always about the same topics take up the better part of one's time, the better part of one's strength, and in the end there is left a life clipped and wingless, an absurd mess, and there is no escaping or getting away from it—just as though one were in a madhouse or a prison.

Gurov, boiling with indignation, did not sleep all night. And he had a headache all the next day. And the following nights too he slept badly; he sat up in bed, thinking, or paced up and down his room. He was fed up with his children, fed up with the bank; he had no desire to go anywhere or to talk of anything.

In December during the holidays he prepared to take a trip and told his wife he was going to Petersburg to do what he could for a young friend—and he set off for S—— What for? He did not know, himself. He wanted to see Anna Sergeyevna and talk with her, to arrange a rendezvous if possible.

He arrived at S—— in the morning, and at the hotel took the best room, in which the floor was covered with gray army cloth, and on the table there was an inkstand, gray with dust and topped by a figure on horseback, its hat in its raised hand and its head broken off. The porter gave him the necessary information: von Dideritz lived in a house of his own on Staro-Goncharnaya Street, not far from the hotel: he was rich and lived well and kept his own horses; everyone in the town knew him. The porter pronounced the name: "Dridiritz."

Without haste Gurov made his way to Staro-Goncharnaya Street and found the house. Directly opposite the house stretched a long gray fence studded with nails.

"A fence like that would make one run away," thought Gurov, looking now at the fence, now at the windows of the house.

He reflected: this was a holiday, and the husband was apt to be at home. And in any case, it would be tactless to go into the house and disturb her. If he were to send her a note, it might fall into her husband's hands, and that might spoil everything. The best thing was to rely on chance. And he kept walking up and down the street and along the fence, waiting for the chance. He saw a beggar go in at the gate and heard the dogs attack him; then an hour later he heard a piano, and the sound came to him faintly and indistinctly. Probably it was Anna Sergeyevna playing. The front door opened suddenly, and an old woman came out, followed by the familiar white Pomeranian. Gurov was on the point of calling to the dog, but his heart began beating violently, and in his excitement he could not remember the Pomeranian's name.

He kept walking up and down, and hated the gray fence more and more, and by now he thought irritably that Anna Sergeyevna had forgotten him, and was perhaps already diverting herself with another man, and that that was very natural in a young woman who from morning till night had to look at that damn fence. He went back to his hotel room and sat on the couch for a long while, not knowing what to do, then he had dinner and a long nap.

"How stupid and annoying all this is!" he thought when he woke and looked at the dark windows: it was already evening. "Here I've had a good sleep for some reason. What am I going to do at night?"

He sat on the bed, which was covered with a cheap gray blanket of the kind seen in hospitals, and he twitted himself in his vexation:

"So there's your lady with the pet dog. There's your adventure. A nice place to cool your heels in."

That morning at the station a playbill in large letters had caught his eye. *The Geisha* was to be given for the first time. He thought of this and drove to the theater.

"It's quite possible that she goes to first nights," he thought.

The theater was full. As in all provincial theaters, there was a haze above the chandelier, the gallery was noisy and restless; in the front row, before the beginning of the performance the local dandies were standing with their hands clasped behind their backs; in the Governor's box the Governor's daughter, wearing a boa, occupied the front seat, while the Governor himself hid modestly behind the portiere and only his hands were visible; the curtain swayed; the orchestra was a long time tuning up. While the audience were coming in and taking their seats, Gurov scanned the faces eagerly.

Anna Sergeyevna, too, came in. She sat down in the third row, and when Gurov looked at her his heart contracted, and he understood clearly that in the whole world there was no human being so near, so precious, and so important to him; she, this little, undistinguished woman, lost in a provincial crowd, with a vulgar lorgnette in her hand, filled his whole life now, was his sorrow and his joy, the only happiness that he now desired for himself, and to the sounds of the bad orchestra, of the miserable local violins, he thought how lovely she was. He thought and dreamed.

A young man with small side-whiskers, very tall and stooped, came in with Anna Sergeyevna and sat down beside her; he nodded his head at every step and seemed to be bowing continually. Probably this was the husband whom at Yalta, in an access of bitter feeling, she had called a flunkey. And there really was in his lanky figure, his side-whiskers, his small bald patch, something of a flunkey's retiring manner; his smile was mawkish, and in his buttonhole there was an academic badge like a waiter's number.

During the first intermission the husband went out to have a smoke; she remained in her seat. Gurov, who was also sitting in the orchestra, went up to her and said in a shaky voice, with a forced smile:

"Good evening!"

She glanced at him and turned pale, then looked at him again in horror, unable to believe her eyes, and gripped the fan and the lorgnette tightly together in her hands, evidently trying to keep herself from fainting. Both were silent. She was sitting, he was standing, frightened by her distress and not daring to take a seat beside her. The violins and the flute that were being tuned up sang out. He suddenly felt frightened: it seemed as if all the people in the boxes were looking at them. She got up and went hurriedly to the exit; he followed her, and both of them walked blindly along the corridors and up and down stairs, and figures in the uniforms prescribed for magistrates, teachers, and officials of the Department of Crown Lands, all wearing badges, flitted before their eyes, as did also ladies, and fur coats on hangers; they were conscious of drafts and the smell of stale tobacco. And Gurov, whose heart was beating violently, thought:

"Oh, Lord! Why are these people here and this orchestra!"

And at that instant he suddenly recalled how when he had seen Anna Sergeyevna off at the station he had said to himself that all was over between them and that they would never meet again. But how distant the end still was!

On the narrow, gloomy staircase over which it said "To the Amphitheatre," she stopped.

"How you frightened me!" she said, breathing hard, still pale and stunned. "Oh, how you frightened me! I am barely alive. Why did you come? Why?"

"But do understand, Anna, do understand—" he said hurriedly, under his breath. "I implore you, do understand—"

She looked at him with fear, with entreaty, with love; she looked at him intently, to keep his features more distinctly in her memory.

"I suffer so," she went on, not listening to him. "All this time I have been thinking of nothing but you; I live only by the thought of you. And I wanted to forget, to forget; but why, oh, why have you come?"

On the landing above them two high school boys were looking down and smoking, but it was all the same to Gurov; he drew Anna Sergeyevna to him and began kissing her face and her hands.

"What are you doing, what are you doing!" she was saying in horror, pushing him away. "We have lost our senses. Go away today; go away at once— I conjure you by all that is sacred, I implore you— People are coming this way!"

Someone was walking up the stairs.

"You must leave," Anna Sergeyevna went on in a whisper. "Do you hear, Dmitry Dmitrich? I will come and see you in Moscow. I have never been happy; I am unhappy now, and I never, never shall be happy, never! So don't make me suffer still more! I swear I'll come to Moscow. But now let us part. My dear, good, precious one, let us part!"

She pressed his hand and walked rapidly downstairs, turning to look round at him, and from her eyes he could see that she really was unhappy. Gurov stood for a while, listening, then when all grew quiet, he found his coat and left the theater.

IV

And Anna Sergeyevna began coming to see him in Moscow. Once every two or three months she left S——, telling her husband that she was going to consult a doctor about a woman's ailment from which she was suffering—and her husband did and did not believe her. When she arrived in Moscow she would stop at the Slavyansky Bazar Hotel, and at once send a man in a red cap to Gurov. Gurov came to see her, and no one in Moscow knew of it.

Once he was going to see her in this way on a winter morning (the messenger had come the evening before and not found him in). With him walked his daughter, whom he wanted to take to school: it was on the way. Snow was coming down in big wet flakes.

"It's three degrees above zero, and yet it's snowing," Gurov was saying to his daughter. "But this temperature prevails only on the surface of the earth; in the upper layers of the atmosphere there is quite a different temperature."

"And why doesn't it thunder in winter, papa?"

He explained that, too. He talked, thinking all the while that he was on his way to a rendezvous, and no living soul knew of it, and probably no one would ever know. He had two lives: an open one, seen and known by all who needed to know it, full of conventional truth and conventional falsehood, exactly like the lives of his friends and acquaintances; and another life that went on in secret. And through some strange, perhaps accidental, combination of circumstances, everything that was of interest and importance to him, everything that was essential to him, everything about which he felt sincerely and did not deceive himself, everything that constituted the core of his life, was going on concealed from others; while all that was false, the shell in which he hid to cover the truth—his work at the bank, for instance, his discussions at the club, his references to the "inferior race," his appearances at anniversary celebrations with his wife—all that went on in the open. Judging others by himself, he did not believe what he saw, and always fancied that every man led his real, most interesting life under cover of secrecy as under cover of night. The personal life of every individual is based on secrecy, and perhaps it is partly for that reason that civilized man is so nervously anxious that personal privacy should be respected.

Having taken his daughter to school, Gurov went on to the Slavyansky Bazar Hotel. He took off his fur coat in the lobby, went upstairs, and knocked gently at the door. Anna Sergeyevna, wearing his favorite gray dress, exhausted by the journey and by waiting, had been expecting him since the previous evening. She was pale, and looked at him without a smile, and he had hardly entered when she flung herself on his breast. Their kiss was a long, lingering one, as though they had not seen one another for two years.

"Well, darling, how are you getting on there?" he asked. "What news?"

"Wait; I'll tell you in a moment— I can't speak."

She could not speak; she was crying. She turned away from him, and pressed her handkerchief to her eyes.

"Let her have her cry; meanwhile I'll sit down," he thought, and he seated himself in an armchair.

Then he rang and ordered tea, and while he was having his tea she remained standing at the window with her back to him. She was crying out of sheer agitation, in the sorrowful consciousness that their life was so sad; that they could only see each other in secret and had to hide from people like thieves! Was it not a broken life?

"Come, stop now, dear!" he said.

It was plain to him that this love of theirs would not be over soon, that the end of it was not in sight. Anna Sergeyevna was growing more and more attached to him. She adored him, and it was unthinkable to tell her that their love was bound to come to an end some day; besides, she would not have believed it!

He went up to her and took her by the shoulders, to fondle her and say something diverting, and at that moment he caught sight of himself in the mirror.

His hair was already beginning to turn gray. And it seemed odd to him that he had grown so much older in the last few years, and lost his looks. The shoulders on which his hands rested were warm and heaving. He felt compassion for this life, still so warm and lovely, but probably already about to begin to fade and wither like his own. Why did she love him so much? He always seemed to women different from what he was, and they loved in him not himself, but the man whom their imagination created and whom they had been eagerly seeking all their lives; and afterwards, when they saw their mistake, they loved him nevertheless. And not one of them had been happy with him. In the past he had met women, come together with them, parted from them, but he had never once loved; it was anything you please, but not love. And only now when his head was gray he had fallen in love, really, truly—for the first time in his life.

Anna Sergeyevna and he loved each other as people do who are very close and intimate, like man and wife, like tender friends; it seemed to them that Fate itself had meant them for one another, and they could not understand why he had a wife and she a husband; and it was as though they were a pair of migratory birds, male and female, caught and forced to live in different cages. They forgave each other what they were ashamed of in their past, they forgave everything in the present, and felt that this love of theirs had altered them both.

Formerly in moments of sadness he had soothed himself with whatever logical arguments came into his head, but now he no longer cared for logic; he felt profound compassion, he wanted to be sincere and tender.

"Give it up now, my darling," he said. "You've had your cry; that's enough. Let us have a talk now, we'll think up something."

Then they spent a long time taking counsel together, they talked of how to avoid the necessity for secrecy, for deception, for living in different cities, and not seeing one another for long stretches of time. How could they free themselves from these intolerable fetters?

"How? How?" he asked, clutching his head. "How?"

And it seemed as though in a little while the solution would be found, and then a new and glorious life would begin; and it was clear to both of them that the end was still far off, and that what was to be most complicated and difficult for them was only just beginning.

ALFRED CHESTER

CRADLE SONG

*Alfred Chester (1928–1971) produced edgy, difficult works that, during
his lifetime, appealed to only a narrow group of readers who enjoyed his
distinct style. Over the last ten years, however, his work has been redis-
covered; as Edward Field suggests, its popularity is due in part to the
"accompanying legend of a doomed, self-destructive, but larger-than-life,
mad genius." In the middle of the century, Alfred Chester was a social
outlaw—a homosexual with a quirky intellect, a Brooklyn Jew, and a
man who suffered the childhood trauma of losing all his hair—and his fiction grew out of his sense of being different and isolated.*

*In 1950 Chester dropped out of New York University, where Cynthia
Ozick, a constant champion of Chester's work, had been his classmate.
Like many Americans interested in literature at that time, he then sailed
for France. He became well known on the Paris scene and remained there
almost a decade, meeting many of the great literary figures of his generation and publishing in small literary magazines throughout Europe.
Although his early fiction showed the influence of the Southern-Gothic
school of Truman Capote and Carson McCullers, his style eventually took
on a surrealist quality. By the end of the fifties, Chester had been discovered in America. Because it dealt unapologetically with homosexual
themes, his fiction was always controversial.*

*In 1959 Chester returned to the United States. He continued to pub-
lish in small literary magazines and supplemented his income by writing
critical articles for prestigious journals. Though he was much in demand
for his biting columns, which critically examined the work of many of his
contemporaries, he saw this employment as a diversion from writing fiction. In 1963 he moved to Morocco to escape the New York literary
scene. He lived in Morocco until his antisocial behaviour, a result of
increasing madness, caused his expulsion in 1965. His last years were a
torment of wandering, and little remains of his writing from this period.
His books include* Jamie Is My Heart's Desire *(1956),* Behold Goliath
(1964), Head of a Sad Angel, *edited by Edward Field, and* Looking for
Genet: Literary Essays and Reviews, *edited and with a foreword by Field.*

O Love Larry I never so much as kissed a boy except my cousin Bob twice under a misiltoe at fifteen years of age. If there was ever another I hope God tears Calvin from my bosom like He took you away. But He won't for I was pure as snow tho its hard to believe in consideration of my behavior the very first night we met and not an hour after you walked in on that party. How is it possible that your good self opened the door of Lilah Krinsky's house and let in every devil of hell to grab hold of me. But thats how it was the minute I laid eyes on you with those big bullsholders and thick arms, and those long black lashes that I could see at ten yards away.

He's a railroad engineer, Lilah whispered when she saw my face but you were more to me like a steam engine. Come on she says, I'll introduce you but watch yourself Dolly. He's fast really fast and I dont mean maybe.

Larry I could hardly stand on my legs in front of you but just the same I said yes when you asked me would I care to dance. So we did tho it didn't seem like dancing more like passing away in a dead faint every other second while those black lashes went brushing into the soul of me.

Presently you says Would you care for a highball?

And before I can say No thanks, I never touch the stuff, you says You look like a girl who can hold a shot or two. Personally I can't stand women who won't take a drink with a man.

No your not a bit to blame Larry and did I ever say you are? Even if I was cold sober I'd of gone just as fast out to Lilah's backyard with you that night. How could you guess I was a Virgin as I didn't once say no or try to stop you a bit from dancing me out to the garden. Its true I laid my own dizzy self down in those lilies and my body was a pair of lips that drank all the stars from the sky.

O when I think of the lilies the pansies the daisies the dandelions that tore and crushed under our pleasures that year! For after that first night I was wild and let you through the whole of spring and into summer so nowadays I can hardly go across a field a grassy space in town without feeling it shake under me like it remembers. Maybe if I'd listened back then I'd of heard all those broken flowers and the soiled earth shouting up about my sins. But how was I supposed to hear with a regular Niagra of blood falling down in my ears? O did I love you Larry so madly and said and said and said and said and you said Sure you love me to but men didn't make such a fuss about it as women did. To talk of men and women, we nineteen.

Love was I happy til near the end of July when I felt a coolness growing on you, just not the same craziness in your carress and gone even those few very manly love words. It made me sad alright maybe you noticed tho I did what I could to hold in my grief while you were more and more solemn or badtempered or restless and sometimes so unusually brutal. Tho not over the flowers.

There you never were abandoned anymore until the very end. *But then!!!* O it began to be so awful at the very end the way you drove at me like an enemy so I'd feel like I was waking up in the middle of the night with someone sticking a dagger in my heart. Til finally one August night when we lay in Nahano Park on the bank beside the gully you stopped amidst and sat back and cried wailed sobbed and I joined in with you I dont know why the way one infant bawls on account of another or one dog howls on account of another, all smeared out upon a selfsame agony so I didnt know where I ended or began. Then you jumped up suddenly and buttoned up and without a further word left me alone wailing in the grass there.

You did not call on me for two weeks, sixteen days to be exact.

I didn't think you were sick tho once just in case I phoned up your house maybe your mother told you. When she answered I says Is Larry there?

No she says, He's at work. Whose this?

But I hung up as I didn't want her to think I was chasing after you. So that was how I knew you weren't sick and I thought you were merely tired of me. It was all over I thought. And I will not tell you how I suffered those long and many days. But then on the seventeenth evening I walked out and there you were in front of the drugstore where I worked waiting to walk home with me.

How pale you looked and retched sick, saying not a word, only lifting your cap and taking my arm to lead me in the direction of home. It was so long before you spoke a word with me uncapable of saying boo or good to see you again.

Halfways over you tell me Dolly what we have done is wrong.

The fires of rebuke suddenly like that out of your mouth! Did you remind me of it? Didn't I even know, having been as pure as Mary til some weeks before and having let my flower fly without a care or thought? Well my heart repented alright you can be sure even if til then it didnt occur to me nothing did only this busting. Only felt my abdomin and pelvic parts swollen swollen til they was stuffed with all the blooms we laid on and could destroy me. How where was there room for remembering everything was wrong? til you said so. As you will recall I nodded too sick to speak. Then we had no other talk til we sat down on the damp bench near my house on the esplanade.

You looked faraway in the distance and says Dolly I love you. That is why what we have done is wrong.

My repenting heart sprang to be sure larry, it was so different from anyway you ever said it before, like a sermon. And at the same time, at that very exact moment I knew I was bearing a fruit of our love.

You continued But marriage is naturally out of the question. We ought not even to see each other in consideration of our wrong, you says. We will have to do this grajually. It was too much to fight against these passed two weeks.

I could cry now thinking how my heart broke then. But it all turned out alright at least that part did'nt it? So why am I sitting here bawling now like I was at the pictures? Look!!! A tear stain on this paper.

I says Yes Larry I understand so well how what you say is right.

Then up we get from the bench and arm in arm walk toward the stoop of my house, tho I am swinging gayly my heavy broken heart is eaten up. Then all at once you just got so angry out of nowhere and scared me I can tell you my god gracious. You yell Why O why O why did you go out with me to the garden, Lilah's garden, that first night?

To which I replied Didn't you want me to? I thought you did. O Larry because I loved you already then and there from the instant you walked in a regular man tho young and bully as a boy and I wouldn't of cared if you danced me over to a bed of nails let alone lilies, I fairly yelled.

You says meanly with your sweet mouth that was to sensitive to be mean you says Did you love a lot of others?

I knew perfectly well what you meant to say thou you knew I was pure before and then again after until the day we wed, you yourself remarked upon the blood. I says NO NO never another.

You says Sure but you would of gone on nails or spikes or hot coals if you just so happened to.

I replied and do and will always will NO! NO! there couldnt of been another other than you.

And after that we were cast out of our gardens of paradise and instead went on dates to movies or dances or parties like two every other young couple. And when you saw me home you kissed me with your lips closed except on Saturday nights and Sunday afternoons with your tongue tasting of lemon drops and your hands so nervous on my twin hearts but only on the outside of my dress so I gave up wearing a brassiere the weekends which was'nt noticable except when you squeezed as my cupcakes were swelling. For by the end of September I had to admit to myself that the fruit of our love was ripening apace and I knew soon I would have to make plans on account of living with my folks. But I didn't plan right away. I only ate very little and prayed.

O the unusual frost that came that year early and hard killing all the harvests but not mine, then went quick as it came with summer following again. So then when I thought it would be the end of us soon after I thought anyways we had a squeezed year together and all the seasons. That day as you will well remember when summer came back, on the night of, we went to Nahano instead of the pictures the air being a treat and in Nahano the grass was grey.

I says as we sat near the bridge over the gully where the ancient Indian river is now a dry little black thing I says The summer is a big giant that got old and they thought he was dead so they buried him and now here is his grey head pushing out of the ground because he was'nt dead at all.

That is very lovely Dolly, you says and kissed me with your tongue althou it was a Wednesday. Then I almost died of fright when you put youre hand on my abdomin for I thought you'd feel The Child!!! But you said When we're married Dolly you will say lovely things all the time.

To imagine such a thing—I didnt expect it for a minute. Or maybe a little I did but not much. And I hoped then youd feel The Child but you didn't so I thought I would tell you then but decided Later on, not just then. How did it happen we went so wild all at once as in the beginning and I cried out My heavens I feel your birdie fluttering against my thigh.

You tell me with a load of pretty suffering in your lovely face you says He wants to be free.

And we freed him for a moment only but not to fly away but to set quietly in my palm its heart beating to beat the band. You will recall no doubt that this innocent thing brought all the evil into me again and I hollered aloud Put him put the birdie in his nest!

Instead you jerked away from me saying No we must not. We must wait until we are married.

But O there I had forgotten again all right and wrong and fought of you pleading It doesnt matter.

You shouted Yes Yes it does matter like anything for I want a Virgin in my wedding bed.

Not understanding I was without so much as a word and you said I will not have an impure woman for my wife not even if it was myself what violated her.

How I felt all chilled and frightened what did you mean I wondered.

I said But Larry.

You said to me whispering but angry so deturmined I could tell you says No buts. We must do things the right way. Hard as it is we must wait and you must remain a Virgin. We cannot sin before we are wed and believe me I'm thinking more of you than of myself. We must be married clean before the eyes of God.

What is there in the minds of men? A woman I can sometimes understand but not a man never a man not you Larry from first to last. There surely is a darkness in mens' minds connected out to things that aren't everyday, coming back into the world to say all the most very strange things. Sometimes frinstince on the radio the news announcers voice comes out, the six pm ones, such a nice young man's voice like he just finished eating a peach in January. How happy I sit and listen at first about this and that war and flood coming so peachy off his tongue. Then all at once I can hear something in the back of his voice some news he isnt going to talk about.

I hear it.

If he says it I know I'll die for sure. My heart comes bouncing up in my throat while I listen tight up to him.

Then I hear him say This morning the pryminister of Suchasuch and my ears stop up. O I'm going to croak. He might say something plain frinstance and I think he is going to say my name, he is going to say, say, DOLORES to millions of listeners, no more than only Dolores and it wont be just my name but will be all connected up with that dark part of his mind that is connected out and out and out among the smashing shooting stars!! Like it would be suddenly the voice of Our Lord hollering my name to everyone threwout the world. And floods and wars and all of it will be for real for very real come pouring great catastropheas THE WORLD WILL CROAK and I will croak out there upon the stars the peachy voice til I turn off the radio and try to quieten my ears my heart.

So after you proposed Larry the seasons became right again and my fruit ripened through that cold dry autumn, hung up shut in my mind as it was in my uterus. I didn't tell you anything but only feared you might hear the creature grow. Feel it you wouldnt. See it you couldn't for I not only starved myself but wrapped my belly in scarves and later choked up my middle with laced up corsets. And I knew the child would be born dead. So through the fall we loved deeply and purely and I knew that when you had the devil you went driving it out in another. How? I knew. A woman knows. For you didn't want to soil me with so few months to wait and the wedding to be in May.

I had the infant in Febuary, sooner than I expected. That morning at the drugstore the pains began and I told the boss I was gravely sick would he excuse me for the day? Thou I didn't have a plan in my head my prayers were answered truly and without a premeditated thought I bought a secondhand valise and a pile of old newspapers. Then I walked across town and rented a room with a bath at the Riviera Palace which now is down but was then the most elegant.

The child was a long time coming.

I sat in the tub until after nightfall all naked with a towel between my teeth to break the pain on for it hurt. At last he came My God and was attached! I never knew before they were attached. My horror Larry like a Siammeese twin I thought and to go my life with him connected to me. Lord God it was the fittest punishment He could hope to inflinge upon my flaming soul. So first I tugged O I turn and shudder now remembering then I raised myself a little and took the drinking glass from the sink. I smashed it on the outside of the tub quickly like a jiffy cut him away from me. I must of fainted right away then as next I saw all over vomit and mud and blood and the child was making funny machiney noises. He was alive.

He was miserable being not altogether passed over so I ended his poor suffering by putting the towel on his face. Then he was still. He was a he I saw. I picked him up and put him to my breast. How wellmade he was I mean so perfect with all the little veins and the tiny fingers and that little cutie birdie. My God to make something so perfect like that and it being a waste. Imagine an automobile or a washing machine being all shaped up with all the little tiny cutie details so perfect and then all to waste. It couldnt be. And I thought What is he?

Here in this bathroom with me and my big milky tit in the face and the tub and the walls and the towel and all, for a minute before he died it was all alive in him, warm in him like it was in me. I was warm in him. Larry I felt my stomach unhinge. Me and that whole bathroom we werent alive anymore we were the cold outside. O didnt that thought hurt me. It had all been inside him and now was not. Is it that all to be dead Larry? That the outside isnt alive anymore?

When I laid him down again and crawled out the tub I cut my feet to pieces on the pieces of glass but did'nt mind only wrapped the child in newspapers and put him in the suitcase with the pieces of glass. How weak as I was I washed out the tub and myself and the towel and the floor where I tracked blood from my feet.

I thought Now I'll go home.

I thought My folks must be worried sick.

But you will understand I was so weak otherwise I would not of worried you as it turned out I did. For I lay down on the bed just to catch back my strength a minute and fell fast asleep only to wake in the midst of the night. The baby was crying from the suitcase!!! O never never did I hear such a terrible sound in my entire life except one other and of that to you dont know.

I said over and over to myself That I am too young to hear such a sound too young, for I was twenty only some weeks before. I am too young.

I stopped up my ears with my fingers but heard it still til I put the pillows over my head and cried my own sweet self so that my own noises were louder and more important. I fell asleep again that way and when next I woke we were both still and it was still night. As I pulled myself out of the bed I felt like all hades had dropped right out of me, and thought O if you knew what I done while you believed me pure as snow tho really I was. I dressed and then shook the suitcase but no sound came so left the room and checked out of the hotel saying I have to catch a bus.

Will you forgive and pity me if I tell you I walked weak as I was back across town and went down the bank into the gully at Nahano in the pitch dark under the footbridge and pulled dragged scratched the pebbles stones, and rocks til it was 2 foot deep. Then put the suitcase in and thought noone will ever trouble about it thinking it a dog or cat for many poor beasts lay there in the gully just near the little black creek-trickle. Still I covered it all up well almost dead myself and my fingers feet and internalls aching and bruised. O at last then I got myself across the gully and up the other bank and dragged myself home to see the light on from outside and in you sitting worried with my folks.

Just then it flashed through my head to say I'd been raped but I knew such a thing would kill you the very idea so evil. There's no end to my sins and you wanting everything to be perfect as it should so goodminded never suspecting anything awful of me.

After you all tell me Why Dolly you look retched sick what is wrong where have you been?

I says to you That I got sick at work.

Yes says Mama, Larry went to see your boss.

So I tell her It was on account of him, the boss I mean, that it happened. I had a little headache at the store and he gave me a powder but got the powders mixed up. I saw afterwards that he made a mistake and gave me a mild poison! Then I ran to the hospital and they cleaned me out and let me go in the evening but on the way home I fainted in Nahano. In the freezing cold noone passed or saw me but now I'm fine alright all better and you better not call the doctor for youll only get my boss in trouble. I had a hard time lying to them at the hospital so they wouldn't know.

Mama said Alright no doctor.

And Papa said Larry you better call the police again and say she was out with a girlfriend. The cops were looking for you all night Dolly.

But then after everything was fine and how sweet you were to stay and care for me the whole next two days while I was in bed, not going to work yourself, and how I made you touch my soft belly just once, just like you used to tho it was still somewhat swollen.

May came. My God there in the photo how happy I look looking so little in those tons of white chiffon and lace like an actress sitting in a bubble bath. You look happy too Larry and you were werent you? and it was true you took a Virgin to your weding bed. Only what happened I don't know. Maybe a woman who isnt a man's wife is more interesting like I was before. Maybe they smell different. I dont know but I knew already then before the first year of our marraig was over that you were carrying on first with one then with another. How? I just knew thats all in your carress maybe which seemed as ever loving and not the same maybe like the spurt of a man that would'nt poureth forth seed. Did I ever blame you? And don't think I'm bitter because it was my just punishment for even if I didn't do wrong I did too.

O let me say it quick!

She came. *There!*

She came and said Are you Dolores, Larry's Dolores?

There that's put down at long last. Then it was we'd been married a year and a half and settled into a quiet way not yet being able to afford children but everything going a normal fashion with my knowing secretly of the other. Then in the morning while you were away at work came the knock at the front door and I saw this middleage distinguished lady standing there.

You don't know who I am, she says But I know Larry.

I smiled very kindly being twenty years younger than her at the least and anyways liking her right off I says Yes maybe I do know who you are. Wont you step inside?

In she comes and sits down in the parlor. Then to make things plain I opened the box of chocolates and looking down says You are the woman that Larry.

Good heavens, she says shaking her head, No no you are mixing me up with my sister.

O it is your sister, I says sitting down I says Could I ask you why you are calling on me?

She says My sister has had a child.

Well I got so dizzy then I tell you expecting God knows what out of her mouth.

She says It is Larry's child.

I believed it alright without a doubt, she was plain to see an honest woman and I expected the same was true for her sister. Well what could I do Larry if they had our child instead of us? But so as she wouldn't think I wasnt loyal to you I argued a little saying It was impossible.

Yes my dear, Miss Portingal said, I expected you to doubt. I haven't come to you for blackmail purposes but only to tell you that my beloved sister is dying. Larry has not seen her in months and does'nt know of the child. By profession I am a school teacher and can'nt possibly care for him and there is noone else but a married brother who could not possibly.

I saw what she wanted and I thought of that poor child and I interrupted her No please let me have him. How old is he?

She says That he was only born two days before.

So I combed my hair and put on my coat for it was cool though only October and went with Miss Portingal. And behold there was Calvin red as Russia in a basket in the kitchen for as you well know there was only the other room and in that one lay Myrtle. But thou red as he was how lovely he looked, a strong little rose and broke my heart he was so much like the other.

I said Could I see your sister?

Miss Portingal seemed surprised She is unconschious.

Just I says to take a peek.

So she opened the kitchen door and I looked through. O Larry how bad off she was! She was'nt beautiful maybe she was before the child tho you werent ever much for a face only but she looked tempting alright even thin and dark as a black olive gone grey as she was. Tempting and furtile.

Miss Portingal says I am old enough to be my Myrtle's mother.

To be polite I shook my head You wouldn't think so at all.

But she gave me such an angry look You would if youd seen her before this tragedy. Maybe I raised her in a bad way. She was always a wild girl and her love for Larry brought her here at last to Calvary. She is only twenty years old.

So that is where he comes from Larry and that's why I wanted to call him Calvin after Calvary for Myrtles sake may you and her rest in the peaceful arms of the Lord. Amen!!

She closed the kitchen door saying What about adoption formalities.

I says No I'll just take him, it's better Larry doesn't know.

But she says My dear how will you explain to him and to the authorities?

I told her Never mind That I'll find the right words at the right time.

Before I left I says Did you tell me that Larry doesn't see Myrtle anymore?

She says Yes he hasn't seen her for months she says. They fought I don't know what about. Maybe she tried to make him jealous. That is her way.

As I took up the basket Miss Portingal gave me the formulas and diapers then kissed Calvin and my own self and says with wet eyes God bless you both, all three, goodbye.

Tho I saw her again four days later and from her mouth came the worst thing I ever heard in my life except the baby crying out of the valise. Well then after I left the Portingals I rode in a taxi to Nahano Park then stepped out and paid and walked over the Park then down into the gully tho it was bright noon. But noone to be seen. I went over to that very spot under the bridge where the other child lay and I put Calvin, the basket of with him in it, on the gravel and stones, then put a few little stones near his face and heart. I prayed may God Omighty give me back the soul of the other. I took the stones out of the basket and went on home.

Weren't you surprised thou when you got back from work? I never saw such a face on you before or after.

You says Where the hell does this come from?

I says From the good Lord.

Then I told you how I went walking in the fresh air over the footbridge and there saw underneath a woman leaving a basket there. When I called her What are you doing there? She looked up at me in fright and says What can I do? I have no family and am going to die very soon.

So I went down to her and indeed she was frail and delicate, dried up like an old olive tho so young.

I says But just the same you cant do that leave him here like that.

She says If you make me take him away I'll put him somewhere else. God isn't there someone who will raise and love this child? When I die what will become of him anyways?

O did I ever believe you could be in such a rage Larry my heavens!

What the damn hell you think we're running an orphan asylum? You shouted Raise another man's bastard? Some idea.

Larry Larry no, I says He's not a bastard, she wore a ring on her finger and was all in black and told me her husband had passed away.

Well til I calmed you down as you will recall was no easy work. But then you fed him a bottle and learned to love him a little and so that was that, our child returned and we kept him. Calvin.

But Miss Portingal came a second time bearing ill tidings. It made me nervous I can tell you to see her for I hoped she wouldnt become a regular caller and drop in while you were home one day. But she was in mourning so I knew that Myrtle had gone.

I says Can I get you anything to drink a cup of tea maybe or excuse me something stronger. Because I could see her sorrow was deep.

No she says, Listen to me Dolores. Myrtle was buried today. For all her wildness she was based on a good girl. And I am an honest woman.

O dont I know that Miss Portingal I says in tears for her and poor Myrtle.

Please don't interrupt me my dear. My story is a difficult one to tell. The day you took the child Myrtle came to herself for a while before the end and she asked me where was the baby and who would look after him when she was gone.

I told her Do'nt be afraid my precious he will be well cared for. I've given him to Larrys' wife.

Myrtle wept like an infant for a long time and before the end came she says Alice, Alice I have lied to you. It is not Larry's child.

I needn't tell you of my shock Dolores. She said no more and didn't give an explanation. She merely repeated it several times He is not Larry's child.

O love Larry if I didn't see plain black and not from Miss Portingal's dress.

She continued Who is the father Dolores I have no idea. For three days now I have been in conflicts with myself as to what I must do. But in all right-iousness I felt bound in duty to tell you what I heard with my own ears. Naturally if you want to return the child you will be justified in doing so. What I will do with him I cant myself think. God knows.

So she talked on like that and I did'nt know what to wonder except no I could never whoever made him part with Calvin.

Miss Portingal says You dont of course have to decide right away.

I told her No No Miss Portingal he is my child. And I cried like a baby. He is mine. He is ours.

Now that you know the facts, Miss Portingal says My heart and mind are clear. It is your decision.

Then she asked to see Calvin one last time and kissed him again but didn't kiss me now. She left saying You are a good woman. Larry is a most fortunate man. It is a lucky child that has you for its mother.

JULIO CORTÁZAR

THE LINES OF THE HAND

Translated by Paul Blackburn

Julio Cortázar (1914–1984) was born in Brussels and grew up in a suburb of Buenos Aires. Earning degrees in teaching, languages, and law, Cortázar taught at public schools and at the University of Cuyo, where he led courses in French literature until 1945, when he was arrested for participating in the university's anti-Perón protest. Cortázar left Argentina in 1951 to settle in Paris as a freelance translator. This move coincided with the publication of his first collection of short stories, Bestiario (Bestiary). The experimental writings of the early Surrealists and of his mentor, Jorge Luis Borges, influenced Cortázar's writing. Although his literary life was slow to unfold, he was swiftly marked, along with Borges and Gabriel García Márquez, as a vital member of the boom in Latin American literature. Cortázar's expatriate status and seemingly apolitical writings drew intense criticism from his fellow Argentinians. Yet he defended his Argentine identity on the grounds that his readership so identified him. In justifying his style, Cortázar stated in 1968 that "one of the most urgent of Latin American problems is that we need more than ever the Ché Guevara's of language, revolutionaries of literature rather than literati of revolution."*

Until his death in Paris, Cortázar avidly supported the socialist revolutionary struggles in Latin America, and he increasingly melded political activism with his literary endeavours. In 1971 he and several other Latin American intellectuals provoked a debate with Castro over the imprisonment of the "counterrevolutionary" poet Herberto Padilla. On several occasions, with titles such as Fantomas Against the Multinational Vampires *(1975), Cortázar contributed his royalties to socialist and humanitarian causes.*

Cortázar argued that a certain "osmosis" of "the fantastic and the ordinary" generates a kind of fiction that transcends these categories. "There are people who at a certain time cease to be themselves and their circumstances, there is a moment when you want to be both yourself and something unexpected, yourself and the moment when the door, which

before and after opens onto the hallway, opens slowly to show us the field
where the unicorn sings."

———————

From a letter thrown on the top of a table, a line comes which runs across the
pine board and descends by one leg. Enough to see it clearly, to describe how
the line continues along the parquet floor, climbs back up the wall, marches
into a print reproducing a painting of Boucher's, delineates the back of a
woman reclining on a divan, escaping the room at last by the roof from which
it descends by the chain of the lightning rod to the street. There, it is difficult to
follow it on account of the traffic, but with some attention it is seen to mount
the wheel of a bus stopped at the corner and proceed to the door. There it goes
on down via the seam of a shiny nylon stocking belonging to the blondest passenger, works its way into the hostile territory of the customs officers, slopes,
wriggles and zigzags up to the main pier and there (but it is difficult to see it,
only the rats follow it climbing aboard) boards the boat whose turbines give
off an agreeable sound, races across the planks of the first-class deck, negoti-
ates the main hatchway with difficulty, and, in a cabin where an unhappy man
is drinking cognac and listening to the hooting of the stack signifying departure, climbs the seam of his trousers, past the knitted vest, slips back as far as
the elbow, and with a final burst of energy, take refuge in the palm of his right
hand just at that moment when it begins to close around the handle of a
revolver.

LOUISE ERDRICH

FLEUR

Louise Erdrich (b. 1954) is, like many of the characters in her fiction, of mixed Native American descent. Her mother was born on the Turtle Mountain Chippewa Reservation, where Erdrich's grandfather had been tribal chairman. Her father was a German American who taught at the nearby Bureau of Indian Affairs boarding school, where her mother was also a teacher. The small North Dakota town in which she was raised and her close family and community ties provide much of the everyday life that influences Erdrich's writing. Storytelling was a way of life, a rich tradition passed on by community and family members, especially her grandfather. In Erdrich's stories, different speakers narrate events that span a century, reflecting "a traditional Chippewa motif in storytelling, which is a cycle of stories having to do with a central mythological figure, a culture hero. One tells a story ... that leads to another in the life of this particular figure. Night after night, or day after day, it's a storytelling cycle."

Although her stories are not autobiographical, they do draw heavily upon Erdrich's own experience. During her early years as a writer and student, she held a variety of minimum-wage jobs, many of which have found their way into her fiction. Stories are also set in places she knew well, such as the elder care centre where Erdrich worked, or the harsh landscapes of the Great Plains where she lived much of her life. She has said that she feels at home writing out of her own experience, as she needs this familiar visual backdrop for her stories and needs to understand the landscape, the people, and the everyday events of the worlds she creates. "I didn't leave home until I was 18, so I really grew up with one set of people in a small town, still know those people, what's happened to them. I keep in very close contact with them."

"Fleur," first published as a short story, then as a chapter in Erdrich's third novel, Tracks *(1988), is the story of a Chippewa woman who beats a group of drunken men in a card game and their fury over losing. Michael Dorris, Erdrich's husband and collaborator, describes the story as "alternately hilarious and terribly sad, a building swirl of impressions that [cling] to the imagination with incredible power." As a poet, short-story writer, novelist, children's author, and travel writer, Louise Erdrich has become one of the best known of Native American writers. Erdrich's*

widely celebrated works include Tales of Burning Love *(1996),* The Bingo Palace *(1994),* Love Medicine *(1984),* Baptism of Desire *(1991), and* The Beet Queen *(1986).*

The first time she drowned in the cold and glassy waters of Lake Turcot, Fleur Pillager was only a girl. Two men saw the boat tip, saw her struggle in the waves. They rowed over to the place she went down, and jumped in. When they dragged her over the gunwales, she was cold to the touch and stiff, so they slapped her face, shook her by the heels, worked her arms back and forth, and pounded her back until she coughed up lake water. She shivered all over like a dog, then took a breath. But it wasn't long afterward that those two men disappeared. The first wandered off, and the other, Jean Hat, got himself run over by a cart.

It went to show, my grandma said. It figured to her, all right. By saving Fleur Pillager, those two men had lost themselves.

The next time she fell in the lake, Fleur Pillager was twenty years old and no one touched her. She washed onshore, her skin a dull dead gray, but when George Many Women bent to look closer, he saw her chest move. Then her eyes spun open, sharp black riprock, and she looked at him. "You'll take my place," she hissed. Everybody scattered and left her there, so no one knows how she dragged herself home. Soon after that we noticed Many Women changed, grew afraid, wouldn't leave his house, and would not be forced to go near water. For his caution, he lived until the day that his sons brought him a new tin bathtub. Then the first time he used the tub he slipped, got knocked out, and breathed water while his wife stood in the other room frying breakfast.

Men stayed clear of Fleur Pillager after the second drowning. Even though she was good-looking, nobody dared to court her because it was clear that Misshepeshu, the waterman, the monster, wanted her for himself. He's a devil, that one, love-hungry with desire and maddened for the touch of young girls, the strong and daring especially, the ones like Fleur.

Our mothers warn us that we'll think he's handsome, for he appears with green eyes, copper skin, a mouth tender as a child's. But if you fall into his arms, he sprouts horns, fangs, claws, fins. His feet are joined as one and his skin, brass scales, rings to the touch. You're fascinated, cannot move. He casts a shell necklace at your feet, weeps gleaming chips that harden into mica on your breasts. He holds you under. Then he takes the body of a lion or a fat brown worm. He's made of gold. He's made of beach moss. He's a thing of dry foam, a thing of death by drowning, the death a Chippewa cannot survive.

Unless you are Fleur Pillager. We all knew she couldn't swim. After the first time, we thought she'd never go back to Lake Turcot. We thought she'd keep to herself, live quiet, stop killing men off by drowning in the lake. After the first time, we thought she'd keep the good ways. But then, after the second drowning, we knew that we were dealing with something much more serious. She was haywire, out of control. She messed with evil, laughed at the old women's advice, and dressed like a man. She got herself into some half-for-gotten medicine, studied ways we shouldn't talk about. Some say she kept the finger of a child in her pocket and a powder of unborn rabbits in a leather thong around her neck. She laid the heart of an owl on her tongue so she could see at night, and went out, hunting, not even in her own body. We know for sure because the next morning, in the snow or dust, we followed the tracks of her bare feet and saw where they changed, where the claws sprang out, the pad broadened and pressed into the dirt. By night we heard her chuffing cough, the bear cough. By day her silence and the wide grin she threw to bring down our guard made us frightened. Some thought that Fleur Pillager should be driven off the reservation, but not a single person who spoke like this had the nerve. And finally, when people were just about to get together and throw her out, she left on her own and didn't come back all summer. That's what this story is about.

During that summer, when she lived a few miles south in Argus, things happened. She almost destroyed that town.

When she got down to Argus in the year of 1920, it was just a small grid of six streets on either side of the railroad depot. There were two elevators, one central, the other a few miles west. Two stores competed for the trade of the three hundred citizens, and three churches quarreled with one another for their souls. There was a frame building for Lutherans, a heavy brick one for Episcopalians, and a long narrow shingled Catholic church. This last had a tall slender steeple, twice as high as any building or tree.

No doubt, across the low, flat wheat, watching from the road as she came near Argus on foot, Fleur saw that steeple rise, a shadow thin as a needle. Maybe in that raw space it drew her the way a lone tree draws lightning. Maybe, in the end, the Catholics are to blame. For if she hadn't seen that sign of pride, that slim prayer, that marker, maybe she would have kept walking.

But Fleur Pillager turned, and the first place she went once she came into town was to the back door of the priest's residence attached to the landmark church. She didn't go there for a handout, although she got that, but to ask for work. She got that too, or the town got her. It's hard to tell which came out worse, her or the men or the town, although the upshot of it all was that Fleur lived.

The four men who worked at the butcher's had carved up about a thousand carcasses between them, maybe half of that steers and the other half pigs, sheep, and game animals like deer, elk, and bear. That's not even mentioning the chickens, which were beyond counting. Pete Kozka owned the place, and employed Lily Veddar, Tor Grunewald, and my stepfather, Dutch James, who had brought my mother down from the reservation the year before she disappointed him by dying. Dutch took me out of school to take her place. I kept house half the time and worked the other in the butcher shop, sweeping floors, putting sawdust down, running a hambone across the street to a customer's bean pot or a package of sausage to the corner. I was a good one to have around because until they needed me, I was invisible. I blended into the stained brown walls, a skinny, big-nosed girl with staring eyes. Because I could fade into a corner or squeeze beneath a shelf, I knew everything, what the men said when no one was around, and what they did to Fleur.

Kozka's Meats served farmers for a fifty-mile area, both to slaughter, for it had a stock pen and chute, and to cure the meat by smoking it or spicing it in sausage. The storage locker was a marvel, made of many thicknesses of brick, earth insulation, and Minnesota timber, lined inside with sawdust and vast blocks of ice cut from Lake Turcot, hauled down from home each winter by horse and sledge.

A ramshackle board building, part slaughterhouse, part store, was fixed to the low, thick square of the lockers. That's where Fleur worked. Kozka hired her for her strength. She could lift a haunch or carry a pole of sausages without stumbling, and she soon learned cutting from Pete's wife, a string-thin blonde who chain-smoked and handled the razor-sharp knives with nerveless precision, slicing close to her stained fingers. Fleur and Fritzie Kozka worked afternoons, wrapping their cuts in paper, and Fleur hauled the packages to the lockers. The meat was left outside the heavy oak doors that were only opened at 5:00 each afternoon, before the men ate supper.

Sometimes Dutch, Tor, and Lily ate at the lockers, and when they did I stayed too, cleaned floors, restoked the fires in the front smokehouses, while the men sat around the squat cast-iron stove spearing slats of herring onto hardtack bread. They played long games of poker or cribbage on a board made from the planed end of a salt crate. They talked and I listened, although there wasn't much to hear since almost nothing ever happened in Argus. Tor was married, Dutch had lost my mother, and Lily read circulars. They mainly discussed about the auctions to come, equipment, or women.

Every so often, Pete Kozka came out front to make a whist, leaving Fritzie to smoke cigarettes and fry raised doughnuts in the back room. He sat and played a few rounds but kept his thoughts to himself. Fritzie did not tolerate him talking behind her back, and the one book he read was the New

Testament. If he said something, it concerned weather or a surplus of sheep stomachs, a ham that smoked green or the markets for corn and wheat. He had a good-luck talisman, the opal-white lens of a cow's eye. Playing cards, he rubbed it between his fingers. That soft sound and the slap of cards was about the only conversation.

Fleur finally gave them a subject.

Her cheeks were wide and flat, her hands large, chapped, muscular. Fleur's shoulders were broad as beams, her hips fishlike, slippery, narrow. An old green dress clung to her waist, worn thin where she sat. Her braids were thick like the tails of animals, and swung against her when she moved, deliberately, slowly in her work, held in and half-tamed, but only half. I could tell, but the others never saw. They never looked into her sly brown eyes or noticed her teeth, strong and curved and very white. Her legs were bare, and since she padded around in beadwork moccasins they never saw that her fifth toes were missing. They never knew she'd drowned. They were blinded, they were stupid, they only saw her in the flesh.

And yet it wasn't just that she was a Chippewa, or even that she was a woman, it wasn't that she was good-looking or even that she was alone that made their brains hum. It was how she played cards.

Women didn't usually play with men, so the evening that Fleur drew a chair up to the men's table without being so much as asked, there was a shock of surprise.

"What's this," said Lily. He was fat, with a snake's cold pale eyes and precious skin, smooth and lily-white, which is how he got his name. Lily had a dog, a stumpy mean little bull of a thing with a belly drum-tight from eating pork rinds. The dog liked to play cards just like Lily, and straddled his barrel thighs through games of stud, rum poker, vingt-un. The dog snapped at Fleur's arm that first night, but cringed back, its snarl frozen, when she took her place.

"I thought," she said, her voice soft and stroking, "you might deal me in."

There was a space between the heavy bin of spiced flour and the wall where I just fit. I hunkered down there, kept my eyes open, saw her black hair swing over the chair, her feet solid on the wood floor. I couldn't see up on the table where the cards slapped down, so after they were deep in their game I raised myself up in the shadows, and crouched on a sill of wood.

I watched Fleur's hands stack and ruffle, divide the cards, spill them to each player in a blur, rake them up and shuffle again. Tor, short and scrappy, shut one eye and squinted the other at Fleur. Dutch screwed his lips around a wet cigar.

"Gotta see a man," he mumbled, getting up to go out back to the privy. The others broke, put their cards down, and Fleur sat alone in the lamplight that glowed in a sheen across the push of her breasts. I watched her closely, then she paid me a beam of notice for the first time. She turned, looked straight at me, and grinned the white wolf grin a Pillager turns on its victims, except that she wasn't after me.

"Pauline there," she said, "how much money you got?"

We'd all been paid for the week that day. Eight cents was in my pocket.

"Stake me," she said, holding out her long fingers. I put the coins in her palm and then I melted back to nothing, part of the walls and tables. It was a long time before I understood that the men would not have seen me no matter what I did, how I moved. I wasn't anything like Fleur. My dress hung loose and my back was already curved, an old woman's. Work had roughened me, reading made my eyes sore, caring for my mother before she died had hardened my face. I was not much to look at, so they never saw me.

When the men came back and sat around the table, they had drawn together. They shot each other small glances, stuck their tongues in their cheeks, burst out laughing at odd moments, to rattle Fleur. But she never minded. They played their vingt-un, staying even as Fleur slowly gained. Those pennies I had given her drew nickels and attracted dimes until there was a small pile in front of her.

Then she hooked them with five-card draw, nothing wild. She dealt, discarded, drew, and then she sighed and her cards gave a little shiver. Tor's eye gleamed, and Dutch straightened in his seat.

"I'll pay to see that hand," said Lily Veddar.

Fleur showed, and she had nothing there, nothing at all.

Tor's thin smile cracked open, and he threw his hand in too.

"Well, we know one thing," he said, leaning back in his chair, "the squaw can't bluff."

With that I lowered myself into a mound of swept sawdust and slept. I woke up during the night, but none of them had moved yet, so I couldn't either. Still later, the men must have gone out again, or Fritzie come out to break the game, because I was lifted, soothed, cradled in a woman's arms and rocked so quiet that I kept my eyes shut while Fleur rolled me into a closet of grimy ledgers, oiled paper, balls of string, and thick files that fit beneath me like a mattress.

The game went on after work the next evening. I got my eight cents back five times over, and Fleur kept the rest of the dollar she'd won for a stake. This time they didn't play so late, but they played regular, and then kept going at it night after night. They played poker now, or variations, for one week straight, and each time Fleur won exactly one dollar, no more and no less, too consistent for luck.

By this time, Lily and the other men were so lit with suspense that they got Pete to join the game with them. They concentrated, the fat dog sitting tense in

Lily Veddar's lap, Tor suspicious, Dutch stroking his huge square brow, Pete steady. It wasn't that Fleur won that hooked them in so, because she lost hands too. It was rather that she never had a freak hand or even anything above a straight. She only took on her low cards, which didn't sit right. By chance, Fleur should have gotten a full or flush by now. The irritating thing was she beat with pairs and never bluffed, because she couldn't, and still she ended up each night with exactly one dollar. Lily couldn't believe, first of all, that a woman could be smart enough to play cards, but even if she was, that she would then be stupid enough to cheat for a dollar a night. By day I watched him turn the problem over, his hard white face dull, small fingers probing at his knuckles, until he finally thought he had Fleur figured out as a bit-time player, caution her game. Raising the stakes would throw her.

More than anything now, he wanted Fleur to come away with something but a dollar. Two bits less or ten more, the sum didn't matter, just so he broke her streak.

Night after night she played, won her dollar, and left to stay in a place that just Fritzie and I knew about. Fleur bathed in the slaughtering tub, then slept in the unused brick smokehouse behind the lockers, a windowless place tarred on the inside with scorched fats. When I brushed against her skin I noticed that she smelled of the walls, rich and woody, slightly burnt. Since that night she put me in the closet I was no longer afraid of her, but followed her close, stayed with her, became her moving shadow that the men never noticed, the shadow that could have saved her.

August, the month that bears fruit, closed around the shop, and Pete and Fritzie left for Minnesota to escape the heat. Night by night, running, Fleur had won thirty dollars, and only Pete's presence had kept Lily at bay. But Pete was gone now, and one payday, with the heat so bad no one could move but Fleur, the men sat and played and waited while she finished work. The cards sweat, limp in their fingers, the table was slick with grease, and even the walls were warm to the touch. The air was motionless. Fleur was in the next room boiling heads.

Her green dress, drenched, wrapped her like a transparent sheet. A skin of lakeweed. Black snarls of veining clung to her arms. Her braids were loose, half-unraveled, tied behind her neck in a thick loop. She stood in steam, turning skulls through a vat with a wooden paddle. When scraps boiled to the surface, she bent with a round tin sieve and scooped them out. She'd filled two dishpans.

"Ain't that enough now?" called Lily. "We're waiting." The stump of a dog trembled in his lap, alive with rage. It never smelled me or noticed me above Fleur's smoky skin. The air was heavy in my corner, and pressed me down. Fleur sat with them.

"Now what do you say?" Lily asked the dog. It barked. That was the signal for the real game to start.

"Let's up the ante," said Lily, who had been stalking this night all month. He had a roll of money in his pocket. Fleur had five bills in her dress. The men had each saved their full pay.

"Ante a dollar then," said Fleur, and pitched hers in. She lost, but they let her scrape along, cent by cent. And then she won some. She played unevenly, as if chance was all she had. She reeled them in. The game went on. The dog was stiff now, poised on Lily's knees, a ball of vicious muscle with its yellow eyes slit in concentration. It gave advice, seemed to sniff the lay of Fleur's cards, twitched and nudged. Fleur was up, then down, saved by a scratch. Tor dealt seven cards, three down. The pot grew, round by round, until it held all the money. Nobody folded. Then it all rode on one last card and they went silent. Fleur picked hers up and blew a long breath. The heat lowered like a bell. Her card shook, but she stayed in.

Lily smiled and took the dog's head tenderly between his palms.

"Say, Fatso," he said, crooning the words, "you reckon that girl's bluffing?"

The dog whined and Lily laughed. "Me too," he said, "let's show." He swept his bills and coins into the pot and then they turned their cards over.

Lily looked once, looked again, then he squeezed the dog up like a fist of dough and slammed it on the table.

Fleur threw her arms out and drew the money over, grinning that same wolf grin that she'd used on me, the grin that had them. She jammed the bills in her dress, scooped the coins up in waxed white paper that she tied with string.

"Let's go another round," said Lily, his voice choked with burrs. But Fleur opened her mouth and yawned, then walked out back to gather slops for the one big hog that was waiting in the stock pen to be killed.

The men sat still as rocks, their hands spread on the oiled wood table. Dutch had chewed his cigar to damp shreds, Tor's eye was dull. Lily's gaze was the only one to follow Fleur. I didn't move. I felt them gathering, saw my stepfather's veins, the ones in his forehead that stood out in anger. The dog had rolled off the table and curled in a knot below the counter, where none of the men could touch it.

Lily rose and stepped out back to the closet of ledgers where Pete kept his private stock. He brought back a bottle, uncorked and tipped it between his fingers. The lump in his throat moved, then he passed it on. They drank, quickly felt the whiskey's fire, and planned with their eyes things they couldn't say out loud.

When they left, I followed. I hid out back in the clutter of broken boards and chicken crates beside the stock pen, where they waited. Fleur could not be seen at first, and then the moon broke and showed her, slipping cautiously along the rough board chute with a bucket in her hand. Her hair fell, wild and coarse, to her waist, and her dress was a floating patch in the dark. She made a pig-calling sound, rang the tin pail lightly against the wood, froze suspiciously. But too late. In the sound of the ring Lily moved, fat and nimble, stepped right behind Fleur and put out his creamy hands. At his first touch, she whirled and doused him with the bucket of sour slops. He pushed her against the big fence and the package of coins split, went clinking and jumping, winked against the wood. Fleur rolled over once and vanished in the yard.

The moon fell behind a curtain of ragged clouds, and Lily followed into the dark muck. But he tripped, pitched over the huge flank of the pig, who lay mired to the snout, heavily snoring. I sprang out of the weeds and climbed the side of the pen, stuck like glue. I saw the sow rise to her neat, knobby knees, gain her balance, and sway, curious, as Lily stumbled forward. Fleur had backed into the angle of rough wood just beyond, and when Lily tried to jostle past, the sow tipped up on her hind legs and struck, quick and hard as a snake. She plunged her head into Lily's thick side and snatched a mouthful of his shirt. She lunged again, caught him lower, so that he grunted in pained surprise. He seemed to ponder, breathing deep. Then he launched his huge body in a swimmer's dive.

The sow screamed as his body smacked over hers. She rolled, striking out with her knife-sharp hooves, and Lily gathered himself upon her, took her foot-long face by the ears and scraped her snout and cheeks against the trestles of the pen. He hurled the sow's tight skull against an iron post, but instead of knocking her dead, he merely woke her from her dream.

She reared, shrieked, drew him with her so that they posed standing upright. They bowed jerkily to each other, as if to begin. Then his arms swung and flailed. She sank her black fangs into his shoulder, clasping him, dancing him forward and backward through the pen. Their steps picked up pace, went wild. The two dipped as one, box-stepped, tripped each other. She ran her split foot through his hair. He grabbed her kinked tail. They went down and came up, the same shape and then the same color, until the men couldn't tell one from the other in that light and Fleur was able to launch herself over the gates, swing down, hit gravel.

The men saw, yelled, and chased her at a dead run to the smokehouse. And Lily too, once the sow gave up in disgust and freed him. That is where I should have gone to Fleur, saved her, thrown myself on Dutch. But I went stiff with fear and couldn't unlatch myself from the trestles or move at all. I closed my eyes and put my head in my arms, tried to hide, so there is nothing to describe but what I couldn't block out. Fleur's hoarse breath, so loud it filled me, her cry in the old language, and my name repeated over and over among the words.

The heat was still dense the next morning when I came back to work. Fleur was gone but the men were there, slack-faced, hung over. Lily was paler and softer than ever, as if his flesh had steamed on his bones. They smoked, took pulls off a bottle. It wasn't noon yet. I worked awhile, waiting shop and sharpening steel. But I was sick, I was smothered, I was sweating so hard that my hands slipped on the knives, and I wiped my fingers clean of the greasy touch of the customers' coins. Lily opened his mouth and roared once, not in anger. There was no meaning to the sound. His boxer dog, sprawled limp beside his foot, never lifted its head. Nor did the other men.

They didn't notice when I stepped outside, hoping for a clear breath. And then I forgot them because I knew that we were all balanced, ready to tip, to fly, to be crushed as soon as the weather broke. The sky was so low that I felt the weight of it like a yoke. Clouds hung down, witch teats, a tornado's green-brown cones, and as I watched one flicked out and became a delicate probing thumb. Even as I picked up my heels and ran back inside, the wind blew suddenly, cold, and then came rain.

Inside, the men had disappeared already and the whole place was trembling as if a huge hand was pinched at the rafters, shaking it. I ran straight through, screaming for Dutch or for any of them, and then I stopped at the heavy doors of the lockers, where they had surely taken shelter. I stood there a moment. Everything went still. Then I heard a cry building in the wind, faint at first, a whistle and then a shrill scream that tore through the walls and gathered around me, spoke plain so I understood that I should move, put my arms out, and slam down the great iron bar that fit across the hasp and lock.

Outside, the wind was stronger, like a hand held against me. I struggled forward. The bushes tossed, the awnings flapped off storefronts, the rails of porches rattled. The odd cloud became a fat snout that nosed along the earth and sniffled, jabbed, picked at things, sucked them up, blew them apart, rooted around as if it was following a certain scent, then stopped behind me at the butcher shop and bored down like a drill.

I went flying, landed somewhere in a ball. When I opened my eyes and looked, stranger things were happening.

A herd of cattle flew through the air like giant birds, dropping dung, their mouths opened in stunned bellows. A candle, still lighted, blew past, and tables, napkins, garden tools, a whole school of drifting eyeglasses, jackets on hangers, hams, a checkerboard, a lampshade, and at last the sow from behind the lockers, on the run, her hooves a blur, set free, swooping, diving, screaming as everything in Argus fell apart and got turned upside down, smashed, and thoroughly wrecked.

Days passed before the town went looking for the men. They were bachelors, after all, except for Tor, whose wife had suffered a blow to the head that made her forgetful. Everyone was occupied with digging out, in high relief because even though the Catholic steeple had been torn off like a peaked cap and sent across five fields, those huddled in the cellar were unhurt. Walls had fallen, windows were demolished, but the stores were intact and so were the bankers and shop owners who had taken refuge in their safes or beneath their cash registers. It was a fair-minded disaster, no one could be said to have suffered much more than the next, at least not until Fritzie and Pete came home.

Of all the businesses in Argus, Kozka's Meats had suffered worst. The boards of the front building had been split to kindling, piled in a huge pyramid, and the shop equipment was blasted far and wide. Pete paced off the distance the iron bathtub had been flung—a hundred feet. The glass candy case went fifty, and landed without so much as a cracked pane. There were other surprises as well, for the back rooms where Fritzie and Pete lived were undisturbed. Fritzie said the dust still coated her china figures, and upon her kitchen table, in the ashtray, perched the last cigarette she'd put out in haste. She lit it up and finished it, looking through the window. From there, she could see that the old smokehouse Fleur had slept in was crushed to a reddish sand and the stockpens were completely torn apart, the rails stacked helter-skelter. Fritzie asked for Fleur. People shrugged. Then she asked about the others and, suddenly, the town understood that three men were missing.

There was a rally of help, a gathering of shovels and volunteers. We passed boards from hand to hand, stacked them, uncovered what lay beneath the pile of jagged splinters. The lockers, full of the meat that was Pete and Fritzie's investment, slowly came into sight, still intact. When enough room was made for a man to stand on the roof, there were calls, a general urge to hack through and see what lay below. But Fritzie shouted that she wouldn't allow it because the meat would spoil. And so the work continued, board by board, until at last the heavy oak doors of the freezer were revealed and people pressed to the entry. Everyone wanted to be the first, but since it was my stepfather lost, I was let go in when Pete and Fritzie wedged through into the sudden icy air.

Pete scraped a match on his boot, lit the lamp Fritzie held, and then the three of us stood still in its circle. Light glared off the skinned and hanging carcasses, the crates of wrapped sausages, the bright and cloudy blocks of lake ice, pure as winter. The cold bit into us, pleasant at first, then numbing. We must have stood there a couple of minutes before we saw the men, or more rightly, the humps of fur, the iced and shaggy hides they wore, the bearskins they had taken down and wrapped around themselves. We stepped closer and tilted the lantern beneath the flaps of fur into their faces. The dog was there, perched among them, heavy as a doorstop. The three had hunched around a barrel where the game was still laid out, and a dead lantern and an empty bottle, too. But they had thrown down their last hands and hunkered tight, clutching one another, knuckles raw from beating at the door they had also attacked with hooks. Frost stars gleamed off their eyelashes and the stubble of their beards. Their faces were set in concentration, mouths open as if to speak some careful thought, some agreement they'd come to in each other's arms.

Power travels in the bloodlines, handed out before birth. It comes down through the hands, which in the Pillagers were strong and knotted, big, spidery, and rough, with sensitive fingertips good at dealing cards. It comes through the eyes, too, belligerent, darkest brown, the eyes of those in the bear clan, impolite as they gaze directly at a person.

In my dreams, I look straight back at Fleur, at the men. I am no longer the watcher on the dark sill, the skinny girl.

The blood draws us back, as if it runs through a vein of earth. I've come home and, except for talking to my cousins, live a quiet life. Fleur lives quiet too, down on Lake Turcot with her boat. Some say she's married to the waterman, Misshepeshu, or that she's living in shame with white men or windigos, or that she's killed them all. I'm about the only one here who ever goes to visit her. Last winter, I went to help out in her cabin when she bore the child, whose green eyes and skin the color of an old penny made more talk, as no one could decide if the child was mixed blood or what, fathered in a smokehouse, or by a man with brass scales, or by the lake. The girl is bold, smiling in her sleep, as if she knows what people wonder, as if she hears the old men talk, turning the story over. It comes up different every time and has no ending, no beginning. They get the middle wrong too. They only know that they don't know anything.

WILLIAM FAULKNER

BARN BURNING

William Faulkner (1897–1962), one of the most important writers of the twentieth century, was born in Mississippi and spent most of his life in the small North Mississippi town of Oxford. When he was a young man, Faulkner was considered something of a wastrel. He dropped out of school early, as he was "more interested in hunting, girls, and football," though he was not particularly successful in any of these pursuits. In 1918 he got a job clerking at a munitions factory. Then, late in the war, Faulkner joined the Royal Air Force of Canada to train as a cadet pilot. Although he never actually went overseas to fight, he made much of his battle exploits back in Oxford, "swaggering around the Square in his uniform, telling spurious tales about his combat in France." In 1928 he married Estelle Franklin, a divorcee to whom he had once been engaged. Their marriage was generally unhappy, "marred by recriminations and alcoholism." They had one child, a daughter born in 1933.

In 1925 he moved to New Orleans, where he met Sherwood Anderson, the great American short-story writer, who was instrumental in having Faulkner's first novel published (Soldier's Pay). Anderson advised the young writer to concentrate on what Faulkner came to call his "little postage-stamp of soil" in Mississippi. From 1929 to 1942, Faulkner wrote the most important novels of his career, including The Sound and the Fury *(1929),* As I Lay Dying *(1930),* Absolom, Absolom! *(1936), and a book of interrelated stories called* Go Down Moses *(1942). He set all this fiction in or around the imaginary town of Jefferson, in the fictional county of Yoknapatawpha, a setting inspired by his home town of Oxford. Faulkner often had to scramble for money, and he spent several unhappy periods in Hollywood as a scriptwriter.*

The 1946 Malcolm Cowley collection, The Portable Faulkner, *marked a turning point in Faulkner's career. It spawned a reassessment of Faulkner's writing, which resulted in his being awarded the 1950 Nobel Prize in literature. In accepting his prize, Faulkner delivered a short but powerful acceptance speech, which caused a sensation; he predicted that "man will not only endure; he will prevail." William Faulkner defined his subject matter as "the human heart in conflict with itself, which alone can make good writing because only that is worth writing about." His work is steeped in an intimate understanding of the American South—its history, its traditions, and its social and spiritual turmoil—that does not flinch from dark places.*

The store in which the Justice of the Peace's court was sitting smelled of cheese. The boy, crouched on his nail keg at the back of the crowded room, knew he smelled cheese, and more: from where he sat he could see the ranked shelves close-packed with the solid, squat, dynamic shapes of tin cans whose labels his stomach read, not from the lettering which meant nothing to his mind but from the scarlet devils and the silver curve of fish—this, the cheese which he knew he smelled and the hermetic meat which his intestines believed he smelled coming in intermittent gusts momentary and brief between the other constant one, the smell and sense just a little of fear because mostly of despair and grief, the old fierce pull of blood. He could not see the table where the Justice sat and before which his father and his father's enemy (*our enemy* he thought in that despair; *ourn! mine and hisn both! He's my father!*) stood, but he could hear them, the two of them that is, because his father had said no word yet:

"But what proof have you, Mr. Harris?"

"I told you. The hog got into my corn. I caught it up and sent it back to him. He had no fence that would hold it. I told him so, warned him. The next time I put the hog in my pen. When he came to get it I gave him enough wire to patch up his pen. The next time I put the hog up and kept it. I rode down to his house and saw the wire I gave him still rolled on to the spool in his yard. I told him he could have the hog when he paid me a dollar pound fee. That evening a nigger came with the dollar and got the hog. He was a strange nigger. He said, 'He say to tell you wood and hay kin burn.' I said, 'What?' 'That whut he say to tell you,' the nigger said. 'Wood and hay kin burn.' That night my barn burned. I got the stock out but I lost the barn."

"Where is the nigger? Have you got him?"

"He was a strange nigger, I tell you. I don't know what became of him."

"But that's not proof. Don't you see that's not proof?"

"Get that boy up here. He knows." For a moment the boy thought too that the man meant his older brother until Harris said, "Not him. The little one. The boy," and, crouching, small for his age, small and wiry like his father, in patched and faded jeans even too small for him, with straight, uncombed, brown hair and eyes gray and wild as storm scud, he saw the men between himself and the table part and become a lane of grim faces, at the end of which he saw the Justice, a shabby, collarless, graying man in spectacles, beckoning him. He felt no floor under his bare feet; he seemed to walk beneath the palpable weight of the grim turning faces. His father, stiff in his black Sunday coat donned not for the trial but for the moving, did not even look at him. *He aims for me to lie,* he thought, again with that frantic grief and despair. *And I will have to do hit.*

"What's your name, boy?" the Justice said.

"Colonel Sartoris Snopes," the boy whispered.

"Hey?" the Justice said. "Talk louder. Colonel Sartoris? I reckon anybody named for Colonel Sartoris in this country can't help but tell the truth, can they?" The boy said nothing. *Enemy! Enemy!* he thought; for a moment he could not even see, could not see that the Justice's face was kindly nor discern that his voice was troubled when he spoke to the man named Harris: "Do you want me to question this boy?" But he could hear, and during those subsequent long seconds while there was absolutely no sound in the crowded little room save that of quiet and intent breathing it was as if he had swung outward at the end of a grape vine, over a ravine, and at the top of the swing had been caught in a prolonged instant of mesmerized gravity, weightless in time.

"No!" Harris said violently, explosively. "Damnation! Send him out of here!" Now time, the fluid world, rushed beneath him again, the voices coming to him again through the smell of cheese and sealed meat, the fear and despair and the old grief of blood:

"This case is closed. I can't find against you, Snopes, but I can give you advice. Leave this country and don't come back to it."

His father spoke for the first time, his voice cold and harsh, level, without emphasis: "I aim to. I don't figure to stay in a country among people who ..." he said something unprintable and vile, addressed to no one.

"That'll do," the Justice said. "Take your wagon and get out of this country before dark. Case dismissed."

His father turned, and he followed the stiff black coat, the wiry figure walking a little stiffly from where a Confederate provost's man's musket ball had taken him in the heel on a stolen horse thirty years ago, followed the two backs now, since his older brother had appeared from somewhere in the crowd, no taller than the father but thicker, chewing tobacco steadily, between the two lines of grim-faced men and out of the store and across the worn gallery and down the sagging steps and among the dogs and half-grown boys in the mild May dust, where as he passed a voice hissed:

"Barn burner!"

Again he could not see, whirling; there was a face in a red haze, moonlike, bigger than the full moon, the owner of it half again his size, he leaping in the red haze toward the face, feeling no blow, feeling no shock when his head struck the earth, scrabbling up and leaping again, feeling no blow this time either and tasting no blood, scrabbling up to see the other boy in full flight and himself already leaping into pursuit as his father's hand jerked him back, the harsh, cold voice speaking above him: "Go get in the wagon."

It stood in a grove of locusts and mulberries across the road. His two hulking sisters in their Sunday dresses and his mother and her sister in calico and sunbonnets were already in it, sitting on and among the sorry residue of the dozen and more movings which even the boy could remember—the battered stove, the broken beds and chairs, the clock inlaid with mother-of-pearl, which would not run, stopped at some fourteen minutes past two o'clock of a dead and forgotten day and time, which had been his mother's dowry. She was crying, though when she saw him she drew her sleeve across her face and began to descend from the wagon. "Get back," the father said.

"He's hurt. I got to get some water and wash his ..."

"Get back in the wagon," his father said. He got in too, over the tail-gate. His father mounted to the seat where the older brother already sat and struck the gaunt mules two savage blows with the peeled willow, but without heat. It was not even sadistic; it was exactly that same quality which in later years would cause his descendants to over-run the engine before putting a motor car into motion, striking and reining back in the same movement. The wagon went on, the store with its quiet crowd of grimly watching men dropped behind; a curve in the road hid it. *Forever* he thought. *Maybe he's done satisfied now, now that he has ...* stopping himself, not to say it aloud even to himself. His mother's hand touched his shoulder.

"Does hit hurt?" she said.

"Naw," he said. "Hit don't hurt. Lemme be."

"Can't you wipe some of the blood off before hit dries?"

"I'll wash to-night," he said. "Lemme be, I tell you."

The wagon went on. He did not know where they were going. None of them ever did or ever asked, because it was always somewhere, always a house of sorts waiting for them a day or two days or even three days away. Likely his father had already arranged to make a crop on another farm before he ... Again he had to stop himself. He (the father) always did. There was something about his wolflike independence and even courage when the advantage was at least neutral which impressed strangers, as if they got from his latent ravening ferocity not so much a sense of dependability as a feeling that his ferocious conviction in the rightness of his own actions would be of advantage to all whose interest lay with his.

That night they camped, in a grove of oaks and beeches where a spring ran. The nights were still cool and they had a fire against it, of a rail lifted from a nearby fence and cut into lengths—a small fire, neat, niggard almost, a shrewd fire; such fires were his father's habit and custom always, even in freezing weather. Older, the boy might have remarked this and wondered why not a big one; why should not a man who had not only seen the waste and extravagance of war, but who had in his blood an inherent voracious prodigality with material not his own, have burned everything in sight? Then he might have gone a step farther and thought that that was the reason: that niggard blaze was the living fruit of nights passed during those four years in the woods hiding from all men, blue or gray, with his strings of horses (captured horses, he called them). And older still, he might have divined the true reason: that the element of fire spoke to some deep mainspring of his father's being, as the element of steel or of powder spoke to other men, as the one weapon for the preservation of integrity, else breath were not worth the breathing, and hence to be regarded with respect and used with discretion.

But he did not think this now and he had seen those same niggard blazes all his life. He merely ate his supper beside it and was already half asleep over his iron plate when his father called him, and once more he followed the stiff back, the stiff and ruthless limp, up the slope and on to the starlit road where, turning, he could see his father against the stars but without face or depth—a shape black, flat, and bloodless as though cut from tin in the iron folds of the frockcoat which had not been made for him, the voice harsh like tin and without heat like tin:

"You were fixing to tell them. You would have told him." He didn't answer. His father struck him with the flat of his hand on the side of the head, hard but without heat, exactly as he had struck the two mules at the store, exactly as he would strike either of them with any stick in order to kill a horse fly, his voice still without heat or anger: "You're getting to be a man. You got to learn. You got to learn to stick to your own blood or you ain't going to have any blood to stick to you. Do you think either of them, any man there this morning, would? Don't you know all they wanted was a chance to get at me because they knew I had them beat? Eh?" Later, twenty years later, he was to tell himself, "If I had said they wanted only truth, justice, he would have hit me again." But now he said nothing. He was not crying. He just stood there. "Answer me," his father said.

"Yes," he whispered. His father turned.

"Get on to bed. We'll be there to-morrow."

To-morrow they were there. In the early afternoon the wagon stopped before a paintless two-room house identical almost with the dozen others it had stopped before even in the boy's ten years, and again, as on the other dozen occasions, his mother and aunt got down and began to unload the wagon, although his two sisters and his father and brother had not moved.

"Likely hit ain't fitten for hawgs," one of the sisters said.

"Nevertheless, fit it will and you'll hog it and like it," his father said. "Get out of them chairs and help your Ma unload."

The two sisters got down, big, bovine, in a flutter of cheap ribbons; one of them drew from the jumbled wagon bed a battered lantern, the other a worn broom. His father handed the reins to the older son and began to climb stiffly over the wheel. "When they get unloaded, take the team to the barn and feed them." Then he said, and at first the boy thought he was still speaking to his brother: "Come with me."

"Me?" he said.

"Yes," his father said. "You."

"Abner," his mother said. His father paused and looked back—the harsh level stare beneath the shaggy, graying, irascible brows.

"I reckon I'll have a word with the man that aims to begin to-morrow owning me body and soul for the next eight months."

They went back up the road. A week ago—or before last night, that is—he would have asked where they were going, but not now. His father had struck him before last night but never before had he paused afterward to explain why; it was as if the blow and the following calm, outrageous voice still rang, repercussed, divulging nothing to him to save the terrible handicap of being young, the light weight of his few years, just heavy enough to prevent his soaring free of the world as it seemed to be ordered but not heavy enough to keep him footed solid in it, to resist it and try to change the course of its events.

Presently he could see the grove of oaks and cedars and the other flowering trees and shrubs where the house would be, though not the house yet. They walked beside a fence massed with honeysuckle and Cherokee roses and came to a gate swinging open between two brick pillars, and now, beyond a sweep of drive, he saw the house for the first time and at that instant he forgot his father and the terror and despair both, and even when he remembered his father again (who had not stopped) the terror and despair did not return. Because, for all the twelve movings, they had sojourned until now in a poor country, a land of small farms and fields and houses, and he had never seen a house like this before. *Hit's big as a courthouse* he thought quietly, with a surge of peace and joy whose reason he could not have thought into words, being too young for that: *They are safe from him. People whose lives are a part of this peace and dignity are beyond his touch, he no more to them than a buzzing wasp: capable of stinging for a little moment but that's all; the spell of this peace and dignity rendering even the barns and stable and cribs which belong to it impervious to the puny flames he might contrive ...* this, the peace and joy, ebbing for an instant as he looked again at the stiff black back, the stiff and implacable limp of the figure which was not dwarfed by the house, for the reason that it had never looked big anywhere and which now, against the

serene columned backdrop, had more than ever that impervious quality of
something cut ruthlessly from tin, depthless, as though, sidewise to the sun, it
would cast no shadow. Watching him, the boy remarked the absolutely undevi-
ating course which his father held and saw the stiff foot come squarely down
in a pile of fresh droppings where a horse had stood in the drive and which his
father could have avoided by a simple change of stride. But it ebbed only for a
moment, though he could not have thought this into words either, walking on
in the spell of the house, which he could ever want but without envy, without
sorrow, certainly never with that ravening and jealous rage which unknown to
him walked in the ironlike black coat before him: *Maybe he will feel it too.*
Maybe it will even change him now from what maybe he couldn't help but be.

They crossed the portico. Now he could hear his father's stiff foot as it
came down on the boards with clocklike finality, a sound out of all proportion
to the displacement of the body it bore and which was not dwarfed either by
the white door before it, as though it had attained to a sort of vicious and
ravening minimum not to be dwarfed by anything—the flat, wide, black hat,
the formal coat of broadcloth which had once been black but which had now
that friction-glazed greenish cast of the bodies of old house flies, the lifted
sleeve which was too large, the lifted hand like a curled claw. The door opened
so promptly that the boy knew the Negro must have been watching them all
the time, an old man with neat grizzled hair, in a linen jacket, who stood bar-
ring the door with his body, saying, "Wipe yo foots, white man, fo you come in
here. Major ain't home nohow."

"Get out of my way, nigger," his father said, without heat too, flinging the
door back and the Negro also and entering, his hat still on his head. And now
the boy saw the prints of the stiff foot on the doorjamb and saw them appear
on the pale rug behind the machinelike deliberation of the foot which seemed
to bear (or transmit) twice the weight which the body compassed. The Negro
was shouting "Miss Lula! Miss Lula!" somewhere behind them, then the boy,
deluged as though by a warm wave by a suave turn of carpeted stair and a pen-
dant glitter of chandeliers and a mute gleam of gold frames, heard the swift
feet and saw her too, a lady—perhaps he had never seen her like before
either—in a gray, smooth gown with lace at the throat and an apron tied at the
waist and the sleeves turned back, wiping cake or biscuit dough from her
hands with a towel as she came up the hall, looking not at his father at all but
at the tracks on the blond rug with an expression of incredulous amazement.

"I tried," the Negro cried. "I tole him to ..."

"Will you please go away?" she said in a shaking voice. "Major de Spain
is not at home. Will you please go away?"

His father had not spoken again. He did not speak again. He did not even
look at her. He just stood stiff in the center of the rug, in his hat, the shaggy

iron-gray brows twitching slightly above the pebble-colored eyes as he appeared to examine the house with brief deliberation. Then with the same deliberation he turned; the boy watched him pivot on the good leg and saw the stiff foot drag round the arc of the turning, leaving a final long and fading smear. His father never looked at it, he never once looked down at the rug. The Negro held the door. It closed behind them, upon the hysteric and indistinguishable woman-wail. His father stopped at the top of the steps and scraped his boot clean on the edge of it. At the gate he stopped again. He stood for a moment, planted stiffly on the stiff foot, looking back at the house. "Pretty and white, ain't it?" he said. "That's sweat. Nigger sweat. Maybe it ain't white enough yet to suit him. Maybe he wants to mix some white sweat with it."

Two hours later the boy was chopping wood behind the house within which his mother and aunt and the two sisters (the mother and aunt, not the two girls, he knew that; even at this distance and muffled by walls the flat loud voices of the two girls emanated an incorrigible idle inertia) were setting up the stove to prepare a meal, when he heard the hooves and saw the linen-clad man on a fine sorrel mare, whom he recognized even before he saw the rolled rug in front of the Negro youth following on a fat bay carriage horse—a suffused, angry face vanishing, still at full gallop, beyond the corner of the house where his father and brother were sitting in the two tilted chairs; and a moment later, almost before he could have put the axe down, he heard the hooves again and watched the sorrel mare go back out of the yard, already galloping again. Then his father began to shout one of the sisters' names, who presently emerged backward from the kitchen door dragging the rolled rug along the ground by one end while the other sister walked behind it.

"If you ain't going to tote, go on and set up the wash pot," the first said.

"You, Sarty!" the second shouted. "Set up the wash pot!" His father appeared at the door, framed against that shabbiness, as he had been against that other bland perfection, impervious to either, the mother's anxious face at his shoulder.

"Go on," the father said. "Pick it up." The two sisters stooped, broad, lethargic; stooping, they presented an incredible expanse of pale cloth and a flutter of tawdry ribbons.

"If I thought enough of a rug to have to git hit all the way from France I wouldn't keep hit where folks coming in would have to tromp on hit," the first said. They raised the rug.

"Abner," the mother said. "Let me do it."

"You go back and git dinner," his father said. "I'll tend to this."

From the woodpile through the rest of the afternoon the boy watched them, the rug spread flat in the dust beside the bubbling wash-pot, the two sisters stooping over it with that profound and lethargic reluctance, while the father stood over them in turn, implacable and grim, driving them though never raising his voice again. He could smell the harsh homemade lye they were using; he saw his mother come to the door once and look toward them with an expression not anxious now but very like despair; he saw his father turn, and he fell to with the axe and saw from the corner of his eye his father raise from the ground a flattish fragment of field stone and examine it and return to the pot, and this time his mother actually spoke: "Abner. Abner. Please don't. Please, Abner."

Then he was done too. It was dusk; the whippoorwills had already begun. He could smell coffee from the room where they would presently eat the cold food remaining from the mid-afternoon meal, though when he entered the house he realized they were having coffee again probably because there was a fire on the hearth, before which the rug now lay spread over the backs of the two chairs. The tracks of his father's foot were gone. Where they had been were now long, water-cloudy scoriations resembling the sporadic course of a lilliputian mowing machine.

It still hung there while they ate the cold food and then went to bed, scattered without order or claim up and down the two rooms, his mother in one bed, where his father would later lie, the older brother in the other, himself, the aunt, and the two sisters on pallets on the floor. But his father was not in bed yet. The last thing the boy remembered was the depthless, harsh silhouette of the hat and coat bending over the rug and it seemed to him that he had not even closed his eyes when the silhouette was standing over him, the fire almost dead behind it, the stiff foot prodding him awake. "Catch up the mule," his father said.

When he returned with the mule his father was standing in the black door, the rolled rug over his shoulder. "Ain't you going to ride?" he said.

"No. Give me your foot."

He bent his knee into his father's hand, the wiry, surprising power flowed smoothly, rising, he rising with it, on to the mule's bare back (they had owned a saddle once; the boy could remember it though not when or where) and with the same effortlessness his father swung the rug up in front of him. Now in the starlight they retraced the afternoon's path, up the dusty road rife with honey-suckle, through the gate and up the black tunnel of the drive to the lightless house, where he sat on the mule and felt the rough warp of the rug drag across his thighs and vanish.

"Don't you want me to help?" he whispered. His father did not answer and now he heard again that stiff foot striking the hollow portico with that wooden and clocklike deliberation, that outrageous overstatement of the weight it carried. The rug, hunched, not flung (the boy could tell that even in the darkness) from his father's shoulder struck the angle of wall and floor with a sound unbelievably loud, thunderous, then the foot again, unhurried and enormous; a light came on in the house and the boy sat, tense, breathing steadily and quietly and just a little fast, though the foot itself did not increase its beat at all, descending the steps now; now the boy could see him.

"Don't you want to ride now?" he whispered. "We kin both ride now," the light within the house altering now, flaring up and sinking. *He's coming down the stairs now,* he thought. He had already ridden the mule up beside the horse block; presently his father was up behind him and he doubled the reins over and slashed the mule across the neck, but before the animal could begin to trot the hard, thin arm came round him, the hard, knotted hand jerking the mule back to a walk.

In the first red rays of the sun they were in the lot, putting plow gear on the mules. This time the sorrel mare was in the lot before he heard it at all, the rider collarless and even bareheaded, trembling, speaking in a shaking voice as the woman in the house had done, his father merely looking up once before stooping again to the hame he was buckling, so that the man on the mare spoke to his stooping back:

"You must realize you have ruined that rug. Wasn't there anybody here, any of your women ..." he ceased, shaking, the boy watching him, the older brother leaning now in the stable door, chewing, blinking slowly and steadily at nothing apparently. "It cost a hundred dollars. But you never had a hundred dollars. You never will. So I'm going to charge you twenty bushels of corn against your crop. I'll add it in your contract and when you come to the commissary you can sign it. That won't keep Mrs. de Spain quiet but maybe it will teach you to wipe your feet off before you enter her house again."

Then he was gone. The boy looked at his father, who still had not spoken or even looked up again, who was now adjusting the logger-head in the hame.

"Pap," he said. His father looked at him—the inscrutable face, the shaggy brows beneath which the gray eyes glinted coldly. Suddenly the boy went toward him, fast, stopping as suddenly. "You done the best you could!" he cried. "If he wanted hit done different why didn't he wait and tell you how? He won't git no twenty bushels! He won't git none! We'll gether hit and hide hit! I kin watch ..."

"Did you put the cutter back in that straight stock like I told you?"

"No, sir," he said.

"Then go do it."

That was Wednesday. During the rest of that week he worked steadily, at what was within his scope and some which was beyond it, with an industry that did not need to be driven nor even commanded twice; he had this from his mother, with the difference that some at least of what he did he liked to do, such as splitting wood with the half-size axe which his mother and aunt had earned; or saved money somehow, to present him with at Christmas. In company with the two older women (and on one afternoon, even one of the sisters), he built pens for the shoat and the cow which were a part of his father's contract with the landlord, and one afternoon, his father being absent, gone somewhere on one of the mules, he went to the field.

They were running a middle buster now, his brother holding the plow straight while he handled the reins, and walking beside the straining mule, the rich black soil shearing cool and damp against his bare ankles, he thought *Maybe this is the end of it. Maybe even that twenty bushels that seems hard to have to pay for just a rug will be a cheap price for him to stop forever and always from being what he used to be;* thinking, dreaming now, so that his brother had to speak sharply to him to mind the mule: *Maybe he even won't collect the twenty bushels. Maybe it will all add up and balance and vanish— corn, rug, fire; the terror and grief, the being pulled two ways like between two teams of horses—gone, done with for ever and ever.*

Then it was Saturday; he looked up from beneath the mule he was harnessing and saw his father in the black coat and hat. "Not that," his father said. "The wagon gear." And then, two hours later, sitting in the wagon bed behind his father and brother on the seat, the wagon accomplished a final curve, and he saw the weathered paintless store with its tattered tobacco- and patent-medicine posters and the tethered wagons and saddle animals below the gallery. He mounted the gnawed steps behind his father and brother, and there again was the lane of quiet, watching faces for the three of them to walk through. He saw the man in spectacles sitting at the plank table and he did not need to be told this was a Justice of the Peace; he sent one glare of fierce, exultant, partisan defiance at the man in collar and cravat now, whom he had seen but twice before in his life, and that on a galloping horse, who now wore on his face an expression not of rage but of amazed unbelief which the boy could not have known was at the incredible circumstance of being sued by one of his own tenants, and came and stood against his father and cried at the Justice: "He ain't done it! He ain't burnt ..."

"Go back to the wagon," his father said.

"Burnt?" the Justice said. "Do I understand this rug was burned too?"

"Does anybody here claim it was?" his father said. "Go back to the wagon." But he did not, he merely retreated to the rear of the room, crowded as that other had been, but not to sit down this time, instead, to stand pressing among the motionless bodies, listening to the voices:

"And you claim twenty bushels of corn is too high for the damage you did to the rug?"

"He brought the rug to me and said he wanted the tracks washed out of it. I washed the tracks out and took the rug back to him."

"But you didn't carry the rug back to him in the same condition it was in before you made the tracks on it."

His father did not answer, and now for perhaps half a minute there was no sound at all save that of breathing, the faint, steady suspiration of complete and intent listening.

"You decline to answer that, Mr. Snopes?" Again his father did not answer. "I'm going to find against you, Mr. Snopes. I'm going to find that you were responsible for the injury to Major de Spain's rug and hold you liable for it. But twenty bushels of corn seems a little high for a man in your circumstances to have to pay. Major de Spain claims it cost a hundred dollars. October corn will be worth about fifty cents. I figure that if Major de Spain can stand a ninety-five dollar loss on something he paid cash for, you can stand a five-dollar loss you haven't earned yet. I hold you in damages to Major de Spain to the amount of ten bushels of corn over and above your contract with him, to be paid to him out of your crop at gathering time. Court adjourned."

It had taken no time hardly, the morning was but half begun. He thought they would return home and perhaps back to the field, since they were late, far behind all other farmers. But instead his father passed on behind the wagon, merely indicating with his hand for the older brother to follow with it, and crossed the road toward the blacksmith shop opposite, pressing on after his father, overtaking him, speaking, whispering up at the harsh, calm face beneath the weathered hat: "He won't git no ten bushels neither. He won't git one. We'll ..." until his father glanced for an instant down at him, the face absolutely calm, the grizzled eyebrows tangled above the cold eyes, the voice almost pleasant, almost gentle:

"You think so? Well, we'll wait till October anyway."

The matter of the wagon—the setting of a spoke or two and the tightening of the tires—did not take long either, the business of the tires accomplished by driving the wagon into the spring branch behind the shop and letting it stand there, the mules nuzzling into the water from time to time, and the boy on the seat with the idle reins, looking up the slope and through the sooty tunnel of the shed where the slow hammer rang and where his father sat on an upended cypress bolt, easily, either talking or listening, still sitting there when the boy brought the dripping wagon up to the branch and halted it before the door.

"Take them on to the shade and hitch," his father said. He did so and returned. His father and the smith and a third man squatting on his heels inside the door were talking, about crops and animals; the boy, squatting too in the ammoniac dust and hoof-parings and scales of rust, heard his father tell a long and unhurried story out of the time before the birth of the older brother even when he had been a professional horsetrader. And then his father came up beside him where he stood before a tattered last year's circus poster on the other side of the store, gazing rapt and quiet at the scarlet horses, the incredible poisings and convolutions of tulle and tights and the painted leers of comedians, and said, "It's time to eat."

But not at home. Squatting beside his brother against the front wall, he watched his father emerge from the store and produce from a paper sack a segment of cheese and divide it carefully and deliberately into three with his pocket knife and produce crackers from the same sack. They all three squatted on the gallery and ate, slowly, without talking; then in the store again, they drank from a tin dipper tepid water smelling of the cedar bucket and of living beech trees. And still they did not go home. It was a horse lot this time, a tall rail fence upon and along which men stood and sat and out of which one by one horses were led, to be walked and trotted and then cantered back and forth along the road while the slow swapping and buying went on and the sun began to slant westward, they—the three of them—watching and listening, the older brother with his muddy eyes and his steady, inevitable tobacco, the father commenting now and then on certain of the animals, to no one in particular.

It was after sundown when they reached home. They ate supper by lamplight, then, sitting on the doorstep, the boy watched the night fully accomplish, listening to the whippoorwills and the frogs, when he heard his mother's voice: "Abner! No! No! Oh, God. Oh, God. Abner!" and he rose, whirled, and saw the altered light through the door where a candle stub now burned in a bottle neck on the table and his father, still in the hat and coat, at once formal and burlesque as though dressed carefully for some shabby and ceremonial violence, emptying the reservoir of the lamp back into the five-gallon kerosene can from which it had been filled, while the mother tugged at his arm until he shifted the lamp to the other hand and flung her back, not savagely or viciously, just hard, into the wall, her hands flung out against the wall for balance, her mouth open and in her face the same quality of hopeless despair as had been in her voice. Then his father saw him standing in the door. "Go to the barn and get that can of oil we were oiling the wagon with," he said. The boy did not move. Then he could speak.

"What ..." he cried. "What are you ..."

"Go get that oil," his father said. "Go."

Then he was moving, running, outside the house, toward the stable: this the old habit, the old blood which he had not been permitted to choose for himself, which had been bequeathed him willy nilly and which had run for so long (and who knew where, battening on what of outrage and savagery and lust) before it came to him. *I could keep on,* he thought. *I could run on and on and never look back, never need to see his face again. Only I can't. I can't,* the rusted can in his hand now, the liquid sploshing in it as he ran back to the house and into it, into the sound of his mother's weeping in the next room, and handed the can to his father.

"Ain't you going to even send a nigger?" he cried. "At least you sent a nigger before!"

This time his father didn't strike him. The hand came even faster than the blow had, the same hand which had set the can on the table with almost excruciating care flashing from the can toward him too quick for him to follow it, gripping him by the back of his shirt and on to tiptoe before he had seen it quit the can, the face stooping at him in breathless and frozen ferocity, the cold, dead voice speaking over him to the older brother who leaned against the table, chewing with that steady, curious, sidewise motion of cows:

"Empty the can into the big one and go on. I'll catch up with you."

"Better tie him up to the bedpost," the brother said.

"Do like I told you," the father said. Then the boy was moving, his bunched shirt and the hard, bony hand between his shoulder-blades, his toes just touching the floor, across the room and into the other one, past the sisters sitting with spread heavy thighs in the two chairs over the cold hearth, and to where his mother and aunt sat side by side on the bed, the aunt's arms about his mother's shoulders.

"Hold him," the father said. The aunt made a startled movement. "Not you," the father said. "Lennie. Take hold of him. I want to see you do it." His mother took him by the wrist. "You'll hold him better than that. If he gets loose don't you know what he is going to do? He will go up yonder." He jerked his head toward the road. "Maybe I'd better tie him."

"I'll hold him," his mother whispered.

"See you do then." Then his father was gone, the stiff foot heavy and measured upon the boards, ceasing at last.

Then he began to struggle. His mother caught him in both arms, he jerking and wrenching at them. He would be stronger in the end, he knew that. But he had no time to wait for it. "Lemme go! he cried. "I don't want to have to hit you!"

"Let him go!" the aunt said. "If he don't go, before God, I am going up there myself!"

"Don't you see I can't?" his mother cried. "Sarty! Sarty! No! No! Help me, Lizzie!"

Then he was free. His aunt grasped at him but it was too late. He whirled, running, his mother stumbled forward on to her knees behind him, crying to the nearer sister: "Catch him, Net! Catch him!" But that was too late too, the sister (the sisters were twins, born at the same time, yet either of them now gave the impression of being, encompassing as much living meat and volume and weight as any other two of the family) not yet having begun to rise from the chair, her head, face, alone merely turned, presenting to him in the flying instant an astonishing expanse of young female features untroubled by any surprise even, wearing only an expression of bovine interest. Then he was out of the room, out of the house, in the mild dust of the starlit road and the heavy rifeness of honeysickle, the pale ribbon unspooling with terrific slowness under his running feet, reaching the gate at last and turning in, running, his heart and lungs drumming, on up the drive toward the lighted house, the lighted door. He did not knock, he burst in, sobbing for breath, incapable for the moment of speech; he saw the astonished face of the Negro in the linen jacket without knowing when the Negro had appeared.

"De Spain!" he cried, panted. "Where's ..." then he saw the white man too emerging from a white door down the hall. "Barn!" he cried. "Barn!"

"What?" the white man said. "Barn?"

"Yes!" the boy cried. "Barn!"

"Catch him!" the white man shouted.

But it was too late this time too. The Negro grasped his shirt, but the entire sleeve, rotten with washing, carried away, and he was out that door too and in the drive again, and had actually never ceased to run even while he was screaming into the white man's face.

Behind him the white man was shouting, "My horse! Fetch my horse!" and he thought for an instant of cutting across the park and climbing the fence into the road, but he did not know the park nor how high the vine-massed fence might be and he dared not risk it. So he ran on down the drive, blood and breath roaring; presently he was in the road again though he could not see it. He could not hear either: the galloping mare was almost upon him before he heard her, and even then he held his course, as if the very urgency of his wild grief and need must in a moment more find him wings, waiting until the ultimate instant to hurl himself aside and into the weed-choked roadside ditch as the horse thundered past and on, for an instant in furious silhouette against the stars, the tranquil early summer night sky which, even before the shape of the horse and rider vanished, stained abruptly and violently upward: a long, swirling roar incredible and soundless, blotting the stars, and he springing up and into the road again, running again, knowing it was too late yet still running even after he heard the shot and, an instant later, two shots, pausing now without knowing he had ceased to run, crying "Pap! Pap!," running again before he knew he had begun to run, stumbling, tripping over something and scrabbling up again without ceasing to run, looking backward over his shoulder at the glare as he got up, running on among the invisible trees, panting, sobbing, "Father! Father!"

At midnight he was sitting on the crest of a hill. He did not know it was midnight and he did not know how far he had come. But there was no glare behind him now and he sat now, his back toward what he had called home for four days anyhow, his face toward the dark woods which he would enter when breath was strong again, small, shaking steadily in the chill darkness, hugging himself into the remainder of his thin, rotten shirt, the grief and despair now no longer terror and fear but just grief and despair. *Father. My father*, he thought. "He was brave!" he cried suddenly, aloud but not loud, no more than a whisper: "He was! He was in the war! He was in Colonel Sartoris' cav'ry!" not knowing that his father had gone to that war a private in the fine old European sense, wearing no uniform, admitting the authority of and giving fidelity to no man or army or flag, going to war as Malbrouck himself did: for booty—it meant nothing and less than nothing to him if it were enemy booty or his own.

The slow constellations wheeled on. It would be dawn and then sun-up after a while and he would be hungry. But that would be to-morrow and now he was only cold, and walking would cure that. His breathing was easier now and he decided to get up and go on, and then he found that he had been asleep because he knew it was almost dawn, the night almost over. He could tell that from the whippoorwills. They were everywhere now among the dark trees below him, constant and inflectioned and ceaseless, so that, as the instant for giving over to the day birds drew nearer and nearer, there was no interval at all between them. He got up. He was a little stiff, but walking would cure that too as it would the cold, and soon there would be the sun. He went on down the hill, toward the dark woods within which the liquid silver voices of the birds called unceasing—the rapid and urgent beating of the urgent and quiring heart of the late spring night. He did not look back.

JACQUES FERRON

MÉLIE AND THE BULL

Jacques Ferron (1921–1985), born in Louiseville, Quebec, was a physician, social activist, and writer. He wrote plays, fiction, and essays, and, during the last twenty-five years of his life, "emerged among the Quebecois working class and intelligentsia as one of the most charismatic figures not just of his period but of the whole literary history of Quebec." He grew up in a stimulating home environment, where politics and literature often were discussed. During his years at the Jesuit College Jean-de-Brebeuf in Montreal, where he was a contemporary of Pierre Elliott Trudeau, Ferron came to appreciate Quebec's cultural heritage, but he also experienced for the first time the intracultural class prejudice that would eventually direct his political views toward socialist causes.

After graduating from medical school, Ferron joined the Canadian army and served as a doctor at camps in Quebec and New Brunswick. In 1946 he went into private practice on the Gaspé Peninsula, and in 1948 he established a practice in Montreal, in the working-class suburb of Ville Jacques-Cartier (Longueuil). Ferron's work as a doctor also served him as a "literary and political apprenticeship" by introducing him to the men and women he would champion as a writer and a revolutionary. His political celebrity began during the fifties, when he became involved with the postwar peace movement, and reached its climax in his association with the Quebec separatist movement. During the 1970 October Crisis, Ferron was called on to act as a government mediator with the FLQ (Front de Liberation du Québec), and in the 1980 Quebec referendum he worked actively to promote a "yes" vote.

Ferron began his literary career in 1949 with the publication of L'Ogre, a satirical play, but it was in his fiction that Ferron's ideology and imagination found their finest expression. In 1963 he won the Governor General's Literary Award for his collection of short stories, Contes du pays incertain, *which established him as a writer of consequence in Canada. He has since produced many collections of short stories, including* The Selected Tales of Jacques Ferron *(1984), in which "Mélie and the Bull" appears. Paul Matthew St. Pierre describes Ferron's stories as "mixtures of fantasy and realism, sentimentality and satire, simplicity and obfuscation, humour and hostility, spontaneity and contrivance, allegory and absurdity ... fiction*

and fact." Ferron also published a number of novels, including Cotnoir
(1962), translated as Dr. Cotnoir; Le Ciel de Québec *(1969), translated as*
The Penniless; *and* L'Amélanchier *(1970), or* The Juneberry Tree.

Mélie Caron had only thirteen children. She expected to have more, one a year
until she died; but after the thirteenth, Jean-Baptiste Caron, her husband, said
to her, "Stop, Mélie!"

So the poor woman stopped, not yet fifty years old. She remained unsatisfied, deprived of her due, all warm and trembling like an animal checked in full
career. However her trouble was not without remedy: did she not have her
thirteen children? Thirteen children is not much; but it is a family. Alas! The
consolation was shortlived. One by one her children left her. She had fed them
too well: full of ardour were the boys, ripe and tender the girls; once fully
grown there was no holding them back. In the end Mélie lost them all. She
remained alone with her old man.

He, like a prisoner whose sentence is served, now found his freedom. He
was no longer to be found at home, but spent most of his time with the other
freedmen of the village, old eccentrics of the same breed as himself, parleying
and laying down the law, drinking whenever the opportunity arose, and then
pissing, drop by drop, the burning fire of his repentance. Mélie would take
advantage of this to offer herself: "Let me help you, old man."

The suggestion was enough to make the waters flow again. Forty years of
married life had taught the old man much; he knew that at the slightest sign of
weakness his wife would get him into her clutches and not let go till she had
mollycoddled him into senility. He remained on his guard.

"Thank you, Mélie. I'm all right now."

Now it came to pass that the old lady, deprived of children and husband,
her corpulence notwithstanding, began to feel confined, loath to be restricted
to her own company. Humours began to rise to her brain. At first this made
her head swim, then she felt unsteady. It was the end of August. Alone in her
kitchen, with her fly-swatter in her hand, she listened: not a fly in the house.
This silence astounded her. In the absence of flies she was prepared for much
worse: for the appearance of snakes, of preposterous frogs, of demons armed
with scapularies, against which her fly-swatter would have been useless; prepared for an attack of raving madness. She was on the point of screaming
when she heard a moo which saved her. Fleeing her monsters, she rushed out.

Outside, giving shade to the door, there rose a cherry tree, with flashes of
sunlight and the redness of cherries moving among its leaves: beyond that there

stretched a garden, then, as far as the river, a field. Mélie crossed the garden. The calf in the field saw her; with his tail in the air he came up towards her with faltering little leaps. The fence which separated the field from the garden brought them both to a stop. The old lady leant down; the calf raised a round, wet muzzle: they looked at each other. And suddenly Mélie Caron was moved by a feeling worthy of her heart. This muzzle, this trust had overwhelmed her; tears came to her eyes; had she been able to cry tears of milk she would have wept buckets to satisfy the appetite of the poor animal.

That evening when Jean-Baptiste Caron came home, she announced to him: "In future I shall look after the calf."

The soup was steaming on the table.

"Fine," said the old man, sitting down. Discussions have never been known to keep soup hot. Better polish it off now and talk later. When he had eaten his fill: "Why look after the calf, Mélie?" he asked.

She replied: "Because I want to."

"Have I by any chance not taken good care of him?"

"Good or bad, you'll not take care of him any more."

"Fine," said the old man, who in actual fact was not particularly concerned about the calf.

He was nevertheless surprised a few days later to see his old lady in the field, sitting under a huge, black umbrella, which protected her from the sun and whose light shade, far from hiding her from view, made her most conspicuous.

"What are you doing there, Mélie?"

"Knitting."

And so she was.

"Perhaps you'd be more comfortable knitting in the house."

"No, old man, I'm more comfortable here." And she added: "Besides, I can't leave him now."

He asked anxiously: "Leave who?"

"Come now, old man, the calf, of course!"

The animal was lying at Mélie's feet. The picture was not lacking in charm. But to Jean-Baptiste it gave not the slightest pleasure.

"Shall I tell you something, Mélie? Shall I?"

She made no objection.

"Well," he said, "you look like an escaped lunatic, and that's a fact."

"Old fool, yourself," she replied.

You cannot reason with a woman when she is in full possession of her faculties, much less when she loses them. Reason attacks front on; such bluntness is a draw-back; with the weaker sex you have to use some stratagem, or simply take them from behind.

"If Mélie were twenty years younger," the old man said to himself, "a few little pats on the behind would bring her to her senses."

In fact he could have done with shedding a few years himself: he had long since lost the art of those little pats. So how was he to bring about a recovery? What could he do to stop the old lady's madness becoming the talk of the village?

"It'll be quite simple," thought Jean-Baptiste Caron. "Since she's mad over the calf, I'll sell the calf."

In this way he hoped to cure her. The remedy was simple indeed. He went off at once and made the necessary arrangements with the butcher. The next morning at daybreak along came his man, paunch bulging beneath a white apron. He had donned for the occasion a bowler hat. He took away the calf. Soon afterwards old Mélie, still heavy with sleep, came out of the house suspecting nothing. The cherry tree, branches held high, for it had not yet lowered its panoply, revealed a strangely slender trunk. The sun was coming up. Dazzled, the old lady stopped a moment to blink her eyes, and then set off along the garden path, calling: "Littl'un! Littl'un!"

She reached the fence; there was still no sign of the calf. Again she called him, but with no better luck. Then she made a thorough search: she searched high and she searched low, but, from the garden to the river, the field was empty.

"Ah, mercy me!" she cried.

And back she rushed, the sight of the water having convinced her that the animal had drowned. Is it Christian to put rivers at the bottom of fields? This arrangement of Nature's filled her with indignation. In her haste she bumped into the cherry tree, who, pre-occupied himself, had not seen her coming, absorbed as he was in the foliage, distributing his fruit to the birds. The birds flew away, cherries fell to the ground, and the wicked servant was caught in the act at his very roots. Much to his surprise the old lady continued on her way. So he signalled to the birds to come back.

Mélie Caron went back into the house.

"Old man, old man, the most terrible thing has happened."

This most terrible thing roused no interest.

"Can you hear me, old man?"

He could not hear her, and for a very simple reason: he was not there. The old lady ran to his room: she searched high and she searched low, but the bed of Jean-Baptiste Caron was empty.

"Ah, mercy me!"

But at the sight of the chamber-pot she was not alarmed. No old fellow who has trouble pissing is ever swept away by the flood. Besides the pot was empty. However, this incapacity of her husband's for drowning did not altogether lessen the mystery of his disappearance. Mélie Caron remained as in a dream. At first her dream revealed nothing; on the contrary it masked her view; the veil was coloured, for she was dreaming with her eyes open. Suddenly the veil was drawn aside: she saw a knife, and behind the knife, holding it, his paunch bulging beneath a white apron, wearing for the occasion a bowler hat—the butcher.

"I'm dreaming," she said to herself.

With which statement the butcher agreed, closing the curtain. Then old Mother Mélie rushed into the wings, and off to the butcher's she trotted. On her way she passed the church.

"Mother Mélie," said the priest, "you're tripping along like a young girl."

"Yes, yes, Father, if you say so—like a young girl. But have you seen my old man?"

"I saw your old man and your calf, one joyful, the other pathetic."

"Oh, the poor dear! Oh, the ruffian! Pray for him, Father."

And the old lady continued on her way. She arrived at the butcher's. The butcher, who had not had time to remove his hat, was surprised to see her again so soon.

"Good day, butcher. Where is my calf?"

"Good day, ma'am. I don't know your calf."

"Oh, don't you now!"

She paused in the doorway just long enough to blink her eyes. The morning was behind her, radiant, making the room in front of her dark. However she was soon able to distinguish the carcasses hanging there.

"There are many calves here," said the butcher, showing her the carcasses. "Only they all look alike since we undressed them."

"I see one that seems to have kept its coat on."

"Where's that, Mistress Mélie?"

"Here."

And pointing her finger, she touched a very shame-faced Jean-Baptiste.

"That's your old man, Mistress Mélie."

"Cut me off a leg all the same."

"He's very skinny."

"Cut it off, I tell you!"

The butcher refused. The old lady took away his knife.

"Then I'll help myself to that leg."

Whereupon Jean-Baptiste Caron intervened. "Don't act so foolish, Mélie. Your calf's here."

He handed her a rope; the poor dear animal was on the end of it, his eyes startled, his muzzle round and wet.

"Littl'un!"

"We weren't going to hurt him," said Jean-Baptiste Caron: "only cut him."

"A calf develops better that way," volunteered the butcher.

"Quiet, you liars! My calf shall remain entire, as the Lord made him."

Having made sure that he still had all his vital parts, including his little phallus, the old lady set off with him. The priest, who had not yet finished his breviary, was still in front of the church.

"Well, Mother Mélie, I see you've found your calf."

"Yes, Father, but I got there just in time: they were about to cut him, the poor dear animal. I stopped their cruelty. You see, Father, he still has all his vital parts, including his little pointed phallus."

"So I see, Mother Mélie, so I see."

The old lady continued on her way, pulling her calf behind her. Soon afterwards the old man, Jean-Baptiste, appeared on the scene, looking very dejected indeed.

"It appears," said the priest, "that you're jealous of a calf. Your old lady showed me what you were planning to deprive him of."

"She showed you! Forgive her—she's not herself any more."

"Forgive her for what? I don't take offense at that. Surely you wouldn't expect her to put drawers on her calf?"

The bell for mass began to ring. The priest was obliged to leave the old man. One month later the latter called at the presbytery. He was looking even more dejected; he walked bent double. When he sat down the priest noticed his face: he thought he seemed worried.

"Worried, no. Let's just say I'm weak."

"Well now! You're getting older."

"That may be, but it's not just age; for the last month I've eaten nothing but mash and grass."

"No!"

"Yes, mash and grass."

"The same as a calf?"

"You said it, Father; the same as a calf. I like meat, beans and lean pork. This food doesn't suit me at all and Mélie won't listen to me. She says we're all one nation."

"What language do you speak at home?"

"We still speak like people, but only because we don't know how to moo."

The priest began to laugh. "It's just the same with French Canadians; they still speak like people, but only because they don't know English."

Jean-Baptiste Caron nodded his head. "It's quite possible that calf is English," said he; "he's taking my place."

"Your place! You mean you live in the stable?"

"No, Father, we don't live in the stable. But the calf is living in the house."

"You don't say," said the priest, "he must be an English calf."

"He must be: he's not at all religious."

The priest rose to his feet. "We must drive him out."

This was also the opinion of Jean-Baptiste Caron.

"But how?"

Jean-Baptiste Caron also wondered how. The priest put a finger to his forehead, and this was very effective.

"Return to your house," he said to the old man. "But first pull yourself together and look cheerful. Once home, eat your mash as though you enjoyed it and be loving to the poor dear little animal."

"I won't be able to."

"You will. After a week or two Mélie will think you share her feelings. At the same time, bring other animals into your house."

"You must be joking, Father!"

"Cats, dogs, mice, rabbits, even hens. I don't say you should bring in cows or pigs. Just domestic animals Mélie will grow attached to and so become less attached to the calf. Then it will be possible to use a stratagem."

Jean-Baptiste Caron: "A stratagem?"

The priest: "You will tell Mélie that you are worried about the calf's future."

"I'll tell her the truth: in six months he'll be a bull. It seems to me that's something to worry about."

"Exactly, this is what we must prevent. After all he's an English calf: mating isn't for him."

"All the same, we're not going to send him to school!"

"No, not to school: to a seminary."

The priest added: "A professional in the family is no disgrace."

"You're right, Father; a professional in the family is no disgrace."

At times advice is worth heeding, especially when it comes from one's priest. Jean-Baptiste Caron decided to make use of that offered him. Under the circumstances there was little else for him to do. He therefore declared himself to be in favour of calves, which won him the confidence of the old lady. Then he brought up the subject of education.

"Well now, it's no joke; a professional in the family is a worthwhile and honourable thing."

Mélie Caron knew it was no joke. But completely wrapped up in her calf, she was not particularly concerned about honour or the family; she wondered which of the two, the bull or the professional, would suit her best. Her heart inclined to the one, her reason to the other, and the animal looked at her puzzled. She too was puzzled.

"What are we going to do with you, poor little fellow?" she asked him.

"Moo, moo," replied the calf.

This reply did not help her in the slightest. Then she reflected, not unreasonably, that once educated the animal would express himself more clearly. So she opted for the professional, telling herself that if by chance he did not like this condition he could always go back to being a bull. Without further delay she went to the priest and told him of her decision.

"A good idea, Mother Mélie! And since you want him to be educated, send him to the Quebec Seminary: that is where I studied."

The old lady looked at the priest. "You don't say!"

The priest was forced to climb down a little. "We mustn't exaggerate," he said. "But all the same I do think, with his intelligence, this little fellow could become a lawyer or even a doctor."

The old lady seemed disappointed.

"A doctor, that's no joke!"

The old lady knew it was no joke. She simply said, "Pooh!"

"A lawyer then?"

She preferred the lawyer.

"Then the matter's settled, Mother Mélie; next week they'll come for your little one: a lawyer he shall be."

As had been arranged, one week later to the very day the Father Superior of the Quebec Seminary sent his representative, a great giant of a man, part beadle, part deputy, who arrived with much to-do in a carriage drawn by three horses. The carriage drew up in the courtyard of the presbytery. Immediately the postulant was brought forth.

"*Ali baba perfectus babam,*" cried the representative.

Which is to say that at first sight, without further inspection, he had judged the calf fit to become a lawyer. On hearing these words the animal moved his ears. The priest noticed this.

"Well, well, he understands Latin!"

Mélie Caron did not understand it. She said "Amen," however, with a heavy heart.

This amen had an effect she had not foreseen: the representative rose to his feet and standing up in the carriage, pointed his finger at her:

"Thou, *Mélia, repetatus.*"

"Amen," repeated the old lady.

Then the giant of a man leapt from the carriage; seized hold of the calf, and carried him off into the church barn.

"He's not as good as the Father Superior of the Quebec Seminary," said the priest, "only being his representative, but you'll see, Mother Mélie, he still knows all about giving an education."

Indeed, no sooner had he entered the barn with the calf, than he appeared, alone, holding in his hands a long object, which he gave to the old lady.

"Thou, *Mélia, repetatus.*"

"Amen," said she.

And the terrible pedagogue went back into the barn.

"But it's my Littl'un's tail!" cried Mélie Caron.

"Yes," replied the priest, "it is your Littl'un's tail. Keep it. He no longer has any use for it."

At the same moment the door of the barn opened, and who should appear but the calf, stiff, in a long black frock-coat, walking like a little man.

"Littl'un!"

He stopped and slowly turned his head toward the old lady. This head did not fit, it was shaky and too high, its features motionless. And he stared at her with vacant eyes.

"Littl'un!" the old lady called again.

He did not even twitch his ears. The old lady did not know what to think. What had they done to her little one in the church barn that he should come out looking so distant? They had cut off his tail, to be sure; they had put clothes on him, true; he was walking on his hind legs like a prime minister, so much the better! In short they had educated him, but did that mean they had to make him blind and deaf? This being the case, education did make the farewell easier.

The seminarian calf, drawing a white handkerchief from his frock-coat, waved it, but distantly, oh so distantly: the fingers holding the handkerchief were already human. Mélie Caron made no attempt to hold him back. He climbed into the carriage beside the representative of the Father Superior of the Quebec Seminary, and there sat upright on his little behind, he who had never used it before. The carriage moved off and soon disappeared from sight.

"Well?" asked the priest.

Well, what? The old lady did not know, so she made no reply.

"Well, yes," the priest began again, "he is gifted, that little fellow! He's not even at the Seminary yet, and all there is left of the calf is its head. Education is for him. A lawyer he shall be, and what a lawyer!"

"What lawyer?" asked the old lady.

"Why, Lawyer Bull! A famous lawyer. Come, come, be proud: he'll be a credit to you."

Mother Mélie was holding the calf's tail in her hands, and it hung there pitifully. Proud? with her head down and her tail, so to speak, between her legs, she did not feel in the least like being proud. "I'm very happy," she said; and very sadly she went off. To see her leave like that worried the priest. The next day after mass, without stopping to have lunch, he went to call on her, and found her in her garden, feeding the hens.

"I was afraid I might find you in bed, Mother Mélie."

"I very nearly did stay in bed, Father. When I woke up I had no desire to do anything, only to die. Surely at my age I'm entitled to a rest. Then I heard the clucking of the hens, the barking of the dog, the animals making their morning noise, and I thought of my poor rabbits twitching their noses without a sound. Who else would have looked after all these animals but me? So I got up."

The priest took off his hat while he recovered his breath. His plan had worked, the calf was out of the way, the old lady cured; what more could he ask, under the circumstances? He was satisfied; he remembered that he was hungry. Mélie Caron gave him a meal and he ate till he could eat no more. When he rose from the table she was still not satisfied: "Just one more little mouthful, Father?"

"So you're not cross with me, Mother Mélie?"

She was cross that he had eaten so little. Apart from that she had nothing against him, considering him to be a good Christian.

"But what about your calf, Mother Mélie?"

She saw no reason why she should be cross about that. Hadn't she parted with her calf so that he could become a lawyer? It had been for his own good; of what importance was the sacrifice she, poor woman, had made?

"Besides," said Mélie Caron, "I am used to these separations."

She was thinking of her thirteen children, well fed all of them, full of ardour the boys, ripe and tender the girls, who had left her one by one. And where had they gone? One to Maniwaki, another to the States, a third out West. As for the rest, she did not know. Besides, Maniwaki, Maniwaki ... she had never been outside of Sainte-Clothilde de Bellechasse: what could Maniwaki mean to her? Or the States? or Abitibi? or the Farwest? "I lost my children, Father; I can part with a calf. Besides I still have my hens, some rabbits, a dog, a cat and some mice, enough to keep me going for some time yet. My supply still hasn't run out."

"You'll die one day, all the same."

"The worms will console me."

"Come, come, Mother Mélie? And what about the good Lord?"

"After, once the worms have eaten their fill."

The priest thought of his position; there was nothing in the Scriptures to prevent Mélie Caron having her bones cleaned off by worms before going up to join the Almighty. "Very well," he said, taking his hat and preparing to leave. Whereupon Mélie Caron, still not satisfied, asked him if he thought that at the Seminary the little fellow would keep his head.

"His calf's head? Of course not."

"Then how shall I recognize him?"

The priest thought of his position and either because he had forgotten his theology or because the question had not been dealt with, he could think of nothing very Catholic to say in reply. He hesitated, feeling somewhat ill at ease in his cassock.

"Mother Mélie," he said at last, "there exists something which, as a young bull, your little fellow would have worn in all innocence, but which as a lawyer he will have to conceal; it is by that incorruptible root—for education cannot touch it—that you will recognize him."

And doubtless judging he had gone too far, without explaining himself at greater length, he went off, leaving the old lady with her curiosity, naturally, unsatisfied. So when Jean-Baptiste Caron came home she eagerly asked him for an explanation. Jean-Baptiste Caron, who was not inhibited by theology, answered without hesitation: "It's the phallus, pointed in the case of a calf which has become a young bull."

"And in the case of Littl'un?"

"Likewise, since education cannot touch it. He'll keep his root even though he's a lawyer, and in this way will be easy to recognize."

And so, reassured, Mélie went back to her daily routine, and the months passed, the winter months, then spring, and the cherry tree bloomed; then came the summer months, June, July, and the ripe hay was harvested. In August the newspapers announced the famous fair to be held at Quebec in the early fall, and which Jean-Baptiste Caron had been wanting to see for a long time.

"Old girl," said he, "we really should see the Provincial Exhibition before we die."

The old lady burst out laughing. "Have you gone crazy, old man?"

In order that she might judge for herself he handed her a page of the newspaper. On it she found this professional announcement: "Maître Bull, lawyer."

"Anyway," she said, "it's not such a bad idea."

So to Quebec they went, their hearts heavy, their eyes wide. The city, the fair, amusement and pleasure soon lifted the weight from their hearts. Fatigue came more slowly; however, after two or three days, they could hardly keep their eyes open, and were beginning to miss the peace and quiet of Sainte-Clothilde.

"But," said the old lady, "before we go back, there's someone I have to see."

Jean-Baptiste Caron was not in the least surprised.

"Someone you have to see?" he asked.

"Yes, old man! Just because we've never had any fallings out, that's no reason why we shouldn't see a lawyer before we die."

Old Mélie was right: they should see a lawyer. It was unfortunate, however, that the lawyer had to be Maître Bull. Jean-Baptiste Caron could see no good coming of the encounter. It is one thing to recognize a young bull under a gown, but quite another to get the lawyer to agree to the test. At any rate, Mélie should go alone.

I'm thirsty," said Jean-Baptiste Caron, "I'll wait for you at the Hôtel de la Traverse."

So Mélie went alone. To Maître Bull's office she came. "Come in," cried he in a beautiful deep voice. She went in and found, in a dusty little office, a young man dressed in black, handsome as an archangel, sad as an orphan, who, after the normal formalities, asked for her name, first name and place of residence: Mélie Caron of Sainte-Clothilde. And the purpose of her visit: whom did she wish to bring action against?

"No one," the old lady answered.

Surprised, he looked at her, and said, with relief: "Thank you."

It was the old lady's turn to express surprise. He explained to her that the lawyer's profession served as an alibi.

"Who are you then?"

"A poet," he replied.

"Oh," said she.

"I keep it a secret; if men knew they would look upon me as some kind of animal."

Mélie Caron lowered her eyes at this modesty.

"Your name again?" the lawyer asked her.

"Mélie Caron."

"I do not know why," he said, "but that name brings to my mind the image of a field and the sound of a river."

At these words, no longer doubting that this was her Littl'un, the poor dear animal, old Mélie pulled from her bag the pitiful object which she had kept, and let it hang beside her. Meanwhile the archangel, the orphan, the young man in black, went on in his beautiful deep voice, saying that it was not the sound of a river, but that of the wind in the grass, the wind whose waters bleach it white in the sun.

"Earth's back is dark and stains the hand, but when the wind passes she forgets her sorrow and, moved, turns over, showing her white belly, where the grass is soft as down, where each blade is a nipple gorged with milk."

"Poor dear," thought the old lady, "he badly needs to graze!"

"Do you sometimes hear a voice?" she asked him. "A voice calling you: Littl'un! Littl'un!"

"Yes, I hear it."

"It is mine," said Mélie Caron.

"I did not know," said the lawyer. "Besides I cannot answer. I am imprisoned in a cage of bone. The bird in his cage of bone is death building his nest. There was a time when I hoped to free myself by writing, but the poems I wrote then did not render my cry."

"Poor dear," thought the old lady, "he badly needs to moo."

"Are you married, Littl'un?"

The young man gave a horrified start; his archangel's wings trembled; he was deeply offended at being thought capable of something so low.

"Quite so, quite so," said the old lady, "I didn't mean to offend you. I only wanted to find out if you were free."

"I am free," he said, "subject only to the will of the ineffable."

She handed him the hairy member.

"Then take back your tail, Little'un, and follow me."

She lead him to the Hôtel de la Traverse where Jean-Baptiste Caron was waiting for them.

"Old man, it's Littl'un!"

Of this she seemed so sure that the old man lowered his eyes, embarrassed. Together they returned to Sainte-Clothilde. "Well, well!" called the priest, "it's back to the land, I see!" And back to the land it was! Though they had surpassed the prophesied return. Indeed, once he had grazed, it was not long before Maître Bull had recovered his élan. Meanwhile his gown was falling to shreds. Soon there was nothing left of the fine education he had received at the Quebec Seminary. One day, at last, he was able to utter his poet's cry, a bellow such as to drive all the cows in the county mad. Faithful to his root, he had found his destiny. From that day on, before the wondering eyes of old Mélie, he led an existence befitting his nature, and left behind him in Bellechasse, where they called him The Scholar, the memory of a famous bull.

RICHARD FORD

ROCK SPRINGS

Richard Ford (b. 1944) is a celebrated American novelist and short-story writer. He was born in Jackson, Mississippi, and he attended Michigan State, followed by the University of California, Irvine, where he earned an M.A. After graduation, Ford worked on short stories and a novel, A Piece of My Heart, which was published in 1976. The Ultimate Good Luck (1981) and The Sportswriter (1986) furthered his reputation as a novelist who "contemplates existentialist themes and conflicts. His novels feature restless and alienated male protagonists who are haunted by painful experiences that render them incapable of emotional commitment."

In 1987 Ford published a collection of short stories, Rock Springs, whose widely anthologized title story appears below. In all of these stories Ford deals with the lives of characters on the move from one way of life, or place to another. This book established Ford as a master of the short story. In 1990 he returned to the novel with Wildlife, which has variously been called "obsessional and over-tidy" and "beautifully made," criticism and praise that are as contradictory as Ford's own vision of America. In addition to fiction, Richard Ford has written essays for many leading American magazines. He also coedited The Best American Short Stories 1990, edited The Granta Book of the American Short Story in 1992, and wrote a screenplay based on his short stories "Children" and "Great Falls," entitled Bright Angel, 1992. In 1995 he won a Pulitzer Prize and the PEN/Faulkner Award for his novel Independence Day. Ford's most recent work is Women with Men (1997).

Edna and I had started down from Kalispell, heading for Tampa-St. Pete where I still had some friends from the old glory days who wouldn't turn me in to the police. I had managed to scrape with the law in Kalispell over several bad checks—which is a prison crime in Montana. And I knew Edna was already looking at her cards and thinking about a move, since it wasn't the first time I'd been in law scrapes in my life. She herself had already had her own troubles, losing her kids and keeping her ex-husband, Danny, from breaking in her house and stealing her things while she was at work, which was really why I had moved in in the first place, that and needing to give my little daughter, Cheryl, a better shake in things.

I don't know what was between Edna and me, just beached by the same tides when you got down to it. Though love has been built on frailer ground than that, as I well know. And when I came in the house that afternoon, I just asked her if she wanted to go to Florida with me, leave things where they sat, and she said, "Why not? My datebook's not that full."

Edna and I had been a pair eight months, more or less man and wife, some of which time I had been out of work, and some when I'd worked at the dog track as a lead-out and could help with the rent and talk sense to Danny when he came around. Danny was afraid of me because Edna had told him I'd been in prison in Florida for killing a man, though that wasn't true. I had once been in jail in Tallahassee for stealing tires and had gotten into a fight on the county farm where a man lost his eye. But I hadn't done the hurting, and Edna just wanted the story worse than it was so Danny wouldn't act crazy and make her have to take her kids back, since she had made a good adjustment to not having them, and I already had Cheryl with me. I'm not a violent person and would never put a man's eye out, much less kill someone. My former wife, Helen, would come all the way from Waikiki Beach to testify to that. We never had violence, and I believe in crossing the street to stay out of trouble's way. Though Danny didn't know that.

But we were half down through Wyoming, going towards I-80 and feeling good about things, when the oil light flashed on in the car I'd stolen, a sign I knew to be a bad one.

I'd gotten us a good car, a cranberry Mercedes I'd stolen out of an ophthalmologist's lot in Whitefish, Montana. I stole it because I thought it would be comfortable over a long haul, because I thought it got good mileage, which it didn't, and because I'd never had a good car in my life, just old Chevy junkers and used trucks back from when I was a kid swamping citrus with Cubans.

The car made us all high that day. I ran the windows up and down, and Edna told us some jokes and made faces. She could be lively. Her features would light up like a beacon and you could see her beauty, which wasn't ordinary. It all made me giddy, and I drove clear down to Bozeman, then straight on through the park to Jackson Hole. I rented us the bridal suite in the Quality Court in Jackson and left Cheryl and her little dog, Duke, sleeping while Edna and I drove to a rib barn and drank beer and laughed till after midnight.

It felt like a whole new beginning for us, bad memories left behind and a new horizon to build on. I got so worked up, I had a tattoo done on my arm that said FAMOUS TIMES, and Edna bought a Bailey hat with an Indian feather band and a little turquoise-and-silver bracelet for Cheryl, and we made love on the seat of the car in the Quality Court parking lot just as the sun was burning up on the Snake River, and everything seemed then like the end of the rainbow.

It was that very enthusiasm, in fact, that made me keep the car one day longer instead of driving it into the river and stealing another one, like I should've done and *had* done before.

Where the car went bad there wasn't a town in sight or even a house, just some low mountains maybe fifty miles away or maybe a hundred, a barbed-wire fence in both directions, hardpan prairie, and some hawks riding the evening air seizing insects.

I got out to look at the motor, and Edna got out with Cheryl and the dog to let them have a pee by the car. I checked the water and checked the oil stick, and both of them said perfect.

"What's that light mean, Earl?" Edna said. She had come and stood by the car with her hat on. She was just sizing things up for herself.

"We shouldn't run it," I said. "Something's not right in the oil."

She looked around at Cheryl and Little Duke, who were peeing on the hardtop side-by-side like two little dolls, then out at the mountains, which were becoming black and lost in the distance. "What're we doing?" she said. She wasn't worried yet, but she wanted to know what I was thinking about.

"Let me try it again."

"That's a good idea," she said, and we all got back in the car.

When I turned the motor over, it started right away and the red light stayed off and there weren't any noises to make you think something was wrong. I let it idle a minute, then pushed the accelerator down and watched the red bulb. But there wasn't any light on, and I started wondering if maybe I hadn't dreamed I saw it, or that it had been the sun catching an angle off the window chrome, or maybe I was scared of something and didn't know it.

"What's the matter with it, Daddy?" Cheryl said from the backseat. I looked back at her, and she had on her turquoise bracelet and Edna's hat set back on the back of her head and that little black-and-white Heinz dog on her lap. She looked like a little cowgirl in the movies.

"Nothing, honey, everything's fine now," I said.

"Little Duke tinkled where I tinkled," Cheryl said, and laughed.

"You're two of a kind," Edna said, not looking back. Edna was usually good with Cheryl, but I knew she was tired now. We hadn't had much sleep, and she had a tendency to get cranky when she didn't sleep. "We oughta ditch this damn car first chance we get," she said.

"What's the first chance we got?" I asked, because I knew she'd been at the map.

"Rock Springs, Wyoming," Edna said with conviction. "Thirty miles down this road." She pointed out ahead.

I had wanted all along to drive the car into Florida like a big success story. But I knew Edna was right about it, that we shouldn't take crazy chances. I had kept thinking of it as my car and not the ophthalmologist's, and that was how you got caught in these things.

"Then my belief is we ought to go to Rock Springs and negotiate ourselves a new car," I said. I wanted to stay upbeat, like everything was panning out right.

"That's a great idea," Edna said, and she leaned over and kissed me hard on the mouth.

"That's a great idea," Cheryl said. "Let's pull on out of here right now."

The sunset that day I remember as being the prettiest I'd ever seen. Just as it touched the rim of the horizon, it all at once fired the air into jewels and red sequins the precise likes of which I had never seen before and haven't seen since. The West has it all over everywhere for sunsets, even Florida, where it's supposedly flat but where half the time trees block your view.

"It's cocktail hour," Edna said after we'd driven a while. "We ought to have a drink and celebrate something." She felt better thinking we were going to get rid of the car. It certainly had dark troubles and was something you'd want to put behind you.

Edna had out a whiskey bottle and some plastic cups and was measuring levels on the glove-box lid. She liked drinking, and she liked drinking in the car, which was something you got used to in Montana, where it wasn't against the law, but where, strangely enough, a bad check would land you in Deer Lodge Prison for a year.

"Did I ever tell you I once had a monkey?" Edna said, setting my drink on the dashboard where I could reach it when I was ready. Her spirits were already picked up. She was like that, up one minute and down the next.

"I don't think you ever did tell me that," I said. "Where were you then?"

"Missoula," she said. She put her bare feet on the dash and rested the cup on her breasts. "I was waitressing at the AmVets. This was before I met you. Some guy came in one day with a monkey. A spider monkey. And I said, just to be joking, 'I'll roll you for that monkey.' And the guy said, 'Just one roll?' And I said, 'Sure.' He put the monkey down on the bar, picked up the cup, and rolled out boxcars. I picked it up and rolled out three fives. And I just stood there looking at the guy. He was just some guy passing through, I guess a vet. He got a strange look on his face—I'm sure not as strange as the one I had—but he looked kind of sad and surprised and satisfied all at once. I said, 'We can roll again.' But he said, 'No, I never roll twice for anything.' And he sat and drank a beer and talked about one thing and another for a while, about nuclear war and building a stronghold somewhere up in the Bitterroot, whatever it was, while I just watched the monkey, wondering what I was going to do with it when the guy left. And pretty soon he got up and said, 'Well, good-bye, Chipper'—that was this monkey's name, of course. And then he left before I could say anything. And the monkey just sat on the bar all that night. I don't know what made me think of that, Earl. Just something weird. I'm letting my mind wander."

"That's perfectly fine," I said. I took a drink of my drink. "I'd never own a monkey," I said after a minute. "They're too nasty. I'm sure Cheryl would like a monkey, though, wouldn't you, honey?" Cheryl was down on the seat playing with Little Duke. She used to talk about monkeys all the time then. "What'd you ever do with that monkey?" I said, watching the speedometer. We were having to go slower now because the red light kept fluttering on. And all I could do to keep it off was go slower. We were going maybe thirty-five and it was an hour before dark, and I was hoping Rock Springs wasn't far away.

"You really want to know?" Edna said. She gave me a quick glance, then looked back at the empty desert as if she was brooding over it.

"Sure," I said. I was still upbeat. I figured I could worry about breaking down and let other people be happy for a change.

"I kept it a week." And she seemed gloomy all of a sudden, as if she saw some aspect of the story she had never seen before. "I took it home and back and forth to the AmVets on my shifts. And it didn't cause any trouble. I fixed a chair up for it to sit on, back of the bar, and people liked it. It made a nice little clicking noise. We changed its name to Mary because the bartender figured out it was a girl. Though I was never really comfortable with it at home. I felt like it watched me too much. Then one day a guy came in, some guy who'd been in Vietnam, still wore a fatigue coat. And he said to me, 'Don't you know that a monkey'll kill you? It's got more strength in its fingers than you got in your whole body.' He said people had been killed in Vietnam by monkeys, bunches of them marauding while you were asleep, killing you and covering you with leaves. I didn't believe a word of it, except that when I got home and got undressed I started looking over across the room at Mary on her chair in the dark watching me. And I got the creeps. And after a while I got up and went out to the car, got a length of clothesline wire, and came back in and wired her to the doorknob through her little silver collar, then went back and tried to sleep. And I guess I must've slept the sleep of the dead—though I don't remember it—because when I got up I found Mary had tipped off her chair-back and hanged herself on the wire line. I'd made it too short."

Edna seemed badly affected by that story and slid low in the seat so she couldn't see over the dash. "Isn't that a shameful story, Earl, what happened to that poor little monkey?"

"I see a town! I see a town!" Cheryl started yelling from the back seat, and right up Little Duke started yapping and the whole car fell into a racket. And sure enough she had seen something I hadn't, which was Rock Springs,

Wyoming, at the bottom of a long hill, a little glowing jewel in the desert with I-80 running on the north side and the black desert spread out behind.

"That's it, honey," I said. "That's where we're going. You saw it first."

"We're hungry," Cheryl said. "Little Duke wants some fish, and I want spaghetti." She put her arms around my neck and hugged me.

"Then you'll just get it," I said. "You can have anything you want. And so can Edna and so can Little Duke." I looked over at Edna, smiling, but she was staring at me with eyes that were fierce with anger. "What's wrong?" I said.

"Don't you care anything about that awful thing that happened to me?" Her mouth was drawn tight, and her eyes kept cutting back at Cheryl and Little Duke, as if they had been tormenting her.

"Of course I do," I said. "I thought that was an awful thing." I didn't want her to be unhappy. We were almost there, and pretty soon we could sit down and have a real meal without thinking somebody might be hurting us.

"You want to know what I did with that monkey?" Edna said.

"Sure I do," I said.

"I put her in a green garbage bag, put it in the trunk of my car, drove to the dump, and threw her in the trash." She was staring at me darkly, as if the story meant something to her that was real important but that only she could see and that the rest of the world was a fool for.

"Well, that's horrible," I said. "But I don't see what else you could do. You didn't mean to kill her. You'd have done it differently if you had. And then you had to get rid of it, and I don't know what else you could have done. Throwing it away might seem unsympathetic to somebody, probably, but not to me. Sometimes that's all you can do, and you can't worry about what somebody else thinks." I tried to smile at her, but the red light was staying on if I pushed the accelerator at all, and I was trying to gauge if we could coast to Rock Springs before the car gave out completely. I looked at Edna again. "What else can I say?" I said.

"Nothing," she said, and stared back at the dark highway. "I should've known that's what you'd think. You've got a character that leaves something out, Earl. I've known that a long time."

"And yet here you are," I said. "And you're not doing so bad. Things could be a lot worse. At least we're all together here."

"Things could always be worse," Edna said. "You could go to the electric chair tomorrow."

"That's right," I said. "And somewhere somebody probably will. Only it won't be you."

"I'm hungry," said Cheryl. "When're we gonna eat? Let's find a motel. I'm tired of this. Little Duke's tired of it too."

Where the car stopped rolling was some distance from the town, though you could see the clear outline of the interstate in the dark with Rock Springs lighting up the sky behind. You could hear the big tractors hitting the spacers in the overpass, revving up for the climb to the mountains.

I shut off the lights.

"What're we going to do now?" Edna said irritably, giving me a bitter look.

"I'm figuring it," I said. "It won't be hard, whatever it is. You won't have to do anything."

"I'd hope not," she said and looked the other way.

Across the road and across a dry wash a hundred yards was what looked like a huge mobile-home town, with a factory or a refinery of some kind lit up behind it and in full swing. There were lights on in a lot of the mobile homes, and there were cars moving along an access road that ended near the freeway overpass a mile the other way. The lights in the mobile homes seemed friendly to me, and I knew right then what I should do.

"Get out," I said, opening my door.

"Are we walking?" Edna said.

"We're pushing."

"I'm not pushing." Edna reached up and locked her door.

"All right," I said. "Then you just steer."

"You're pushing us to Rock Springs, are you, Earl? It doesn't look like it's more than about three miles."

"I'll push," Cheryl said from the back.

"No, hon. Daddy'll push. You just get out with Little Duke and move out of the way."

Edna gave me a threatening look, just as if I'd tried to hit her. But when I got out she slid into my seat and took the wheel, staring angrily ahead straight into the cottonwood scrub.

"Edna can't drive that car," Cheryl said from out in the dark. "She'll run it in the ditch."

"Yes, she can, hon. Edna can drive it as good as I can. Probably better."

"No she can't," Cheryl said. "No she can't either." And I thought she was about to cry, but she didn't.

I told Edna to keep the ignition on so it wouldn't lock up and to steer into the cottonwoods with the parking lights on so she could see. And when I started, she steered it straight off into the trees, and I kept pushing until we were twenty yards into the cover and the tires sank in the soft sand and nothing at all could be seen from the road.

"Now where are we?" she said, sitting at the wheel. Her voice was tired and hard, and I knew she could have put a good meal to use. She had a sweet nature, and I recognized that this wasn't her fault but mine. Only I wished she could be more hopeful.

"You stay right here, and I'll go over to that trailer park and call us a cab," I said.

"What cab?" Edna said, her mouth wrinkled as if she'd never heard anything like that in her life.

"There'll be cabs," I said, and tried to smile at her. "There's cabs everywhere."

"What're you going to tell him when he gets here? Our stolen car broke down and we need a ride to where we can steal another one? That'll be a big hit, Earl."

"I'll talk," I said. "You just listen to the radio for ten minutes and then walk on out to the shoulder like nothing was suspicious. And you and Cheryl act nice. She doesn't need to know about this car."

"Like we're not suspicious enough already, right?" Edna looked up at me out of the lighted car. "You don't think right, did you know that, Earl? You think the world's stupid and you're smart. But that's not how it is. I feel sorry for you. You might've *been* something, but things just went crazy someplace."

I had a thought about poor Danny. He was a vet and crazy as a shit-house mouse, and I was glad he wasn't in for all this. "Just get the baby in the car," I said, trying to be patient. "I'm hungry like you are."

"I'm tired of this," Edna said. "I wish I'd stayed in Montana."

"Then you can go back in the morning," I said. "I'll buy the ticket and put you on the bus. But not till then."

"Just get on with it, Earl." She slumped down in the seat, turning off the parking lights with one foot and the radio on with the other.

The mobile-home community was as big as any I'd ever seen. It was attached in some way to the plant that was lighted up behind it, because I could see a car once in a while leave one of the trailer streets, turn in the direction of the plant, then go slowly into it. Everything in the plant was white, and you could see that all the trailers were painted and looked exactly alike. A deep hum came out of the plant, and I thought as I got closer that it wouldn't be a location I'd ever want to work in.

I went right to the first trailer where there was a light, and knocked on the metal door. Kids' toys were lying in the gravel around the little wood steps, and I could hear talking on TV that suddenly went off. I heard a woman's voice talking, and then the door opened wide.

A large Negro woman with a wide, friendly face stood in the doorway. She smiled at me and moved forward as if she was going to come out, but she stopped at the top step. There was a little Negro boy behind her peeping out from behind her legs, watching me with his eyes half closed. The trailer had that feeling that no one else was inside, which was a feeling I knew something about.

"I'm sorry to intrude," I said. "But I've run up on a little bad luck tonight. My name's Earl Middleton."

The woman looked at me, then out into the night toward the freeway as if what I had said was something she was going to be able to see. "What kind of bad luck?" she said, looking down at me again.

"My car broke down out on the highway," I said. "I can't fix it myself, and I wondered if I could use your phone to call for help."

The woman smiled down at me knowingly. "We can't live without cars, can we?"

"That's the honest truth," I said.

"They're like our hearts," she said, her face shining in the little bulb light that burned beside the door. "Where's your car situated?"

I turned and looked over into the dark, but I couldn't see anything because of where we'd put it. "It's over there," I said. "You can't see it in the dark."

"Who all's with you now?" the woman said. "Have you got your wife with you?"

"She's with my little girl and our dog in the car," I said. "My daughter's asleep or I would have brought them."

"They shouldn't be left in the dark by themselves," the woman said and frowned. "There's too much unsavouriness out there."

"The best I can do is hurry back." I tried to look sincere, since everything except Cheryl being asleep and Edna being my wife was the truth. The truth is meant to serve you if you'll let it, and I wanted it to serve me. "I'll pay for the phone call," I said. "If you'll bring the phone to the door I'll call from right here."

The woman looked at me again as if she was searching for a truth of her own, then back out into the night. She was maybe in her sixties, but I couldn't say for sure. "You're not going to rob me, are you, Mr. Middleton?" She smiled like it was a joke between us.

"Not tonight," I said, and smiled a genuine smile. "I'm not up to it tonight. Maybe another time."

"Then I guess Terrel and I can let you use our phone with Daddy not here, can't we, Terrel? This is my grandson, Terrel Junior, Mr. Middleton." She put her hand on the boy's head and looked down at him. "Terrel won't talk. Though if he did he'd tell you to use our phone. He's a sweet boy." She opened the screen for me to come in.

The trailer was a big one with a new rug and a new couch and a living room that expanded to give the space of a real house. Something good and sweet was cooking in the kitchen, and the trailer felt like it was somebody's comfortable new home instead of just temporary. I've lived in trailers, but they were just snailbacks with one room and no toilet, and they always felt cramped and unhappy—though I've thought maybe it might've been me that was unhappy in them.

There was a big Sony TV and a lot of kids' toys scattered on the floor. I recognized a Greyhound bus I'd gotten for Cheryl. The phone was beside a new leather recliner, and the Negro woman pointed for me to sit down and call and gave me the phone book. Terrel began fingering his toys and the woman sat on the couch while I called, watching me and smiling.

There were three listings for cab companies, all with one number different. I called the numbers in order and didn't get an answer until the last one, which answered with the name of the second company. I said I was on the highway beyond the interstate and that my wife and family needed to be taken to town and I would arrange for a tow later. While I was giving the location, I looked up the name of a tow service to tell the driver in case he asked.

When I hung up, the Negro woman was sitting looking at me with the same look she had been staring with into the dark, a look that seemed to want truth. She was smiling, though. Something pleased her and I reminded her of it.

"This is a very nice home," I said, resting in the recliner, which felt like the driver's seat of the Mercedes, and where I'd have been happy to stay.

"This isn't *our* house, Mr. Middleton," the Negro woman said. "The company owns these. They give them to us for nothing. We have our own home in Rockford, Illinois."

"That's wonderful," I said.

"It's never wonderful when you have to be away from home, Mr. Middleton, though we're only here three months, and it'll be easier when Terrel Junior begins his special school. You see, our son was killed in the war, and his wife ran off without Terrel Junior. Though you shouldn't worry. He can't understand us. His little feelings can't be hurt." The woman folded her hands in her lap and smiled in a satisfied way. She was an attractive woman, and had on a blue-and-pink floral dress that made her seem bigger than she could've been, just the right woman to sit on the couch she was sitting on. She was good nature's picture, and I was glad she could be, with her little brain-damaged boy, living in a place where no one in his right mind would want to live a minute. "Where do *you* live, Mr. Middleton?" she said politely, smiling in the same sympathetic way.

"My family and I are in transit," I said. "I'm an ophthalmologist, and we're moving back to Florida, where I'm from. I'm setting up practice in some little town where it's warm year-round. I haven't decided where."

"Florida's a wonderful place," the woman said. "I think Terrel would like it there."

"Could I ask you something?" I said.

"You certainly may," the woman said. Terrel had begun pushing his Greyhound across the front of the TV screen, making a scratch that no one watching the set could miss. "Stop that, Terrel Junior," the woman said quietly. But Terrel kept pushing his bus on the glass, and she smiled at me again as if we both understood something sad. Except I knew Cheryl would never damage a television set. She had respect for nice things, and I was sorry for the lady that Terrel didn't. "What did you want to ask?" the woman said.

"What goes on in that plant or whatever it is back there beyond these trailers, where all the lights are on?"

"Gold," the woman said and smiled.

"It's what?" I said.

"Gold," the Negro woman said, smiling as she had for almost all the time I'd been there. "It's a gold mine."

"They're mining gold back there?" I said, pointing.

"Every night and every day." She smiled in a pleased way.

"Does your husband work there?" I said.

"He's the assayer," she said. "He controls the quality. He works three months a year, and we live the rest of the time at home in Rockford. We've waited a long time for this. We've been happy to have our grandson, but I won't say I'll be sorry to have him go. We're ready to start our lives over." She smiled broadly at me and then at Terrel, who was giving her a spiteful look from the floor. "You said you had a daughter," the Negro woman said. "And what's her name?"

"Irma Cheryl," I said. "She's named for my mother."

"That's nice. And she's healthy, too. I can see it in your face." She looked at Terrel Junior with pity.

"I guess I'm lucky," I said.

"So far you are. But children bring you grief, the same way they bring you joy. We were unhappy for a long time before my husband got his job in the gold mine. Now, when Terrel starts to school, we'll be kids again." She stood up. "You might miss your cab, Mr. Middleton," she said, walking toward the door, though not to be forcing me out. She was too polite. "If *we* can't see your car, the cab surely won't be able to."

"That's true." I got up off the recliner, where I'd been so comfortable. "None of us have eaten yet, and your food makes me know how hungry we probably all are."

"There are fine restaurants in town, and you'll find them," the Negro woman said. "I'm sorry you didn't meet my husband. He's a wonderful man. He's everything to me."

"Tell him I appreciate the phone," I said. "You saved me."

"You weren't hard to save," the woman said. "Saving people is what we were all put on earth to do. I just passed you on to whatever's coming to you."

"Let's hope it's good," I said, stepping back into the dark.

"I'll be hoping, Mr. Middleton. Terrel and I will both be hoping."

I waved to her as I walked out into the darkness toward the car where it was hidden in the night.

The cab had already arrived when I got there. I could see its little red-and-green roof lights all the way across the dry wash, and it made me worry that Edna was already saying something to get us in trouble, something about the car or where we'd come from, something that would cast suspicion on us. I thought, then, how I never planned things well enough. There was always a gap between my plan and what happened, and I only responded to things as they came along and hoped I wouldn't get in trouble. I was an offender in the law's eyes. But I always *thought* differently, as if I weren't an offender and had no intention of being one, which was the truth. But as I read on a napkin once, between the idea and the act a whole kingdom lies. And I had a hard time with my acts, which were oftentimes offender's acts, and my ideas, which were as good as the gold they mined there where the bright lights were blazing.

"We're waiting for you, Daddy," Cheryl said when I crossed the road. "The taxicab's already here."

"I see, hon," I said, and gave Cheryl a big hug. The cabdriver was sitting in the driver's seat having a smoke with the lights on inside. Edna was leaning against the back of the cab between the taillights, wearing her Bailey hat. "What'd you tell him?" I said when I got close.

"Nothing," she said. "What's there to tell?"

"Did he see the car?"

She glanced over in the direction of the trees where we had hid the Mercedes. Nothing was visible in the darkness, though I could hear Little Duke combing around in the underbrush tracking something, his little collar tinkling. "Where're we going?" she said. "I'm so hungry I could pass out."

"Edna's in a terrible mood," Cheryl said. "She already snapped at me."

"We're tired, honey," I said. "So try to be nicer."

"She's never nice," Cheryl said.

"Run go get Little Duke," I said. "And hurry back."

"I guess *my* questions come last here, right?" Edna said.

I put my arm around her. "That's not true."

"Did you find somebody over there in the trailers you'd rather stay with? You were gone long enough."

"That's not a thing to say," I said. "I was just trying to make things look right, so we don't get put in jail."

"So *you* don't, you mean." Edna laughed a little laugh I didn't like hearing.

"That's right. So I don't," I said. "I'd be the one in Dutch." I stared out at the big, lighted assemblage of white buildings and white lights beyond the

trailer community, plumes of white smoke escaping up into the heartless
Wyoming sky, the whole company of buildings looking like some unbelievable
castle, humming away in a distorted dream. "You know what all those buildings are there?" I said to Edna, who hadn't moved and who didn't really seem
to care if she ever moved anymore ever.

"No. But I can't say it matters, because it isn't a motel and it isn't a restaurant."

"It's a gold mine," I said, staring at the gold mine, which, I knew now, was
a greater distance from us than it seemed, though it seemed huge and near, up
against the cold sky. I thought there should've been a wall around it with
guards instead of just the lights and no fence. It seemed as if anyone could go
in and take what they wanted, just the way I had gone up to that woman's
trailer and used the telephone, though that obviously wasn't true.

Edna began to laugh then. Not the mean laugh I didn't like, but a laugh
that had something caring behind it, a full laugh that enjoyed a joke, a laugh
she was laughing the first time I laid eyes on her, in Missoula in the East Gate
Bar in 1979, a laugh we used to laugh together when Cheryl was still with her
mother and I was working steady at the track and not stealing cars or passing
bogus checks to merchants. A better time all around. And for some reason it
made me laugh just hearing her, and we both stood there behind the cab in the
dark, laughing at the gold mine in the desert, me with my arm around her and
Cheryl out rustling up Little Duke and the cabdriver smoking in the cab and
our stolen Mercedes-Benz, which I'd had such hopes for in Florida, stuck up to
its axle in sand, where I'd never get to see it again.

"I always wondered what a gold mine would look like when I saw it,'
Edna said, still laughing, wiping a tear from her eye.

"Me too," I said. "I was always curious about it."

"We're a couple of fools, aren't we, Earl?" she said, unable to quit
laughing completely. "We're two of a kind."

"It might be a good sign, though," I said.

"How could it be? It's not our gold mine. There aren't any drive-up windows." She was still laughing.

"We've seen it," I said, pointing. "That's it right there. It may mean we're
getting closer. Some people never see it at all."

"In a pig's eye, Earl," she said. "You and me see it in a pig's eye."

And she turned and got in the cab to go.

The cabdriver didn't ask anything about our car or where it was, to mean he'd
noticed something queer. All of which made me feel like we had made a clean
break from the car and couldn't be concerned with it until it was too late, if
ever. The driver told us a lot about Rock Springs while he drove, that because

of the gold mine a lot of people had moved there in just six months, people from all over, including New York, and that most of them lived out in the trailers. Prostitutes from New York City, who he called "B-girls," had come into town, he said, on the prosperity tide, and Cadillacs with New York plates cruised the little streets every night, full of Negroes with big hats who ran the women. He told us that everybody who got in his cab now wanted to know where the women were, and when he got our call he almost didn't come because some of the trailers were brothels operated by the mine for engineers and computer people away from home. He said he got tired of running back and forth out there just for vile business. He said that *60 Minutes* had even done a program about Rock Springs and that a blow-up had resulted in Cheyenne, though nothing could be done unless the boom left town. "It's prosperity's fruit," the driver said. "I'd rather be poor, which is lucky for me."

He said all the motels were sky-high, but since we were a family he could show us a nice one that was affordable. But I told him we wanted a first-rate place where they took animals, and the money didn't matter because we had had a hard day and wanted to finish on a high note. I also knew that it was in the little nowhere places that the police would look for you and find you. People I'd known were always being arrested in cheap hotels and tourist courts with names you'd never heard of before. Never in Holiday Inns or TraveLodges.

I asked him to drive us to the middle of town and back out again so Cheryl could see the train station, and while we were there I saw a pink Cadillac with New York plates and a TV aerial being driven slowly by a Negro in a big hat down a narrow street where there were just bars and a Chinese restaurant. It was an odd sight, nothing you could ever expect.

"There's your pure criminal element," the cabdriver said and seemed sad. "I'm sorry for people like you to see a thing like that. We've got a nice town here, but there's some that want to ruin it for everybody. There used to be a way to deal with trash and criminals, but those days are gone forever."

"You said it," Edna said.

"You shouldn't let it get *you* down," I said to him. "There's more of you than them. And there always will be. You're the best advertisement this town has. I know Cheryl will remember you and not *that* man, won't you, honey?" But Cheryl was asleep by then, holding Little Duke in her arms on the taxi seat.

The driver took us to the Ramada Inn on the interstate, not far from where we'd broken down. I had a small pain of regret as we drove under the Ramada awning that we hadn't driven up in a cranberry-coloured Mercedes but instead in a beat-up old Chrysler taxi driven by an old man full of complaints. Though I knew it was for the best. We were better off without the car; better, really, in any other car but that one, where the signs had turned bad.

I registered under another name and paid for the room in cash so there wouldn't be any questions. On the line where it said "Representing" I wrote "Ophthalmologist" and put "M.D." after the name. It had a nice look to it, even though it wasn't my name.

When we got to the room, which was in the back where I'd asked for it, I put Cheryl on one of the beds and Little Duke beside her so they'd sleep. She'd missed dinner, but it only meant she'd be hungry in the morning, when she could have anything she wanted. A few missed meals don't make a kid bad. I'd missed a lot of them myself and haven't turned out completely bad.

"Let's have some fried chicken," I said to Edna when she came out of the bathroom. "They have good fried chicken at Ramadas, and I noticed the buffet was still up. Cheryl can stay right here, where it's safe, till we're back."

"I guess I'm not hungry anymore," Edna said. She stood at the window staring out into the dark. I could see out the window past her some yellowish foggy glow in the sky. For a moment I thought it was the gold mine out in the distance lighting the night, though it was only the interstate.

"We could order up," I said. "Whatever you want. There's a menu on the phone book. You could just have a salad."

"You go ahead," she said. "I've lost my hungry spirit." She sat on the bed beside Cheryl and Little Duke and looked at them in a sweet way and put her hand on Cheryl's cheek just as if she'd had a fever. "Sweet little girl," she said. "Everybody loves you."

"What do you want to do?" I said. "I'd like to eat. Maybe *I'll* order up some chicken."

"Why don't you do that?" She said. "It's your favourite." And she smiled at me from the bed.

I sat on the other bed and dialed room service. I asked for chicken, garden salad, potato and a roll, plus a piece of hot apple pie and iced tea. I realized I hadn't eaten all day. When I put down the phone I saw that Edna was watching me, not in a hateful way or a loving way, just in a way that seemed to say she didn't understand something and was going to ask me about it.

"When did watching me get so entertaining?" I said and smiled at her. I was trying to be friendly. I knew how tired she must be. It was after nine o'clock.

"I was just thinking how much I hated being in a motel without a car that was mine to drive. Isn't that funny? I started feeling like that last night when that purple car wasn't mine. That purple car just gave me the willies, I guess, Earl."

"One of those cars *outside* is yours," I said. "Just stand right there and pick it out."

"I know," she said. "But that's different, isn't it?" She reached and got her blue Bailey hat, put it on her head, and set it way back like Dale Evans. She looked sweet. "I used to like to go to motels, you know," she said. "There's something secret about them and free—I was never paying, of course. But you felt safe from everything and free to do what you wanted because you'd made the decision to be there and paid that price, and all the rest was the good part. Fucking and everything, you know." She smiled at me in a good-natured way.

"Isn't that the way this is?" I was sitting on the bed, watching her, not knowing what to expect her to say next.

"I don't guess it is, Earl," she said and stared out the window. "I'm thirty-two and I'm going to have to give up on motels. I can't keep that fantasy going anymore."

"Don't you like this place?" I said and looked around at the room. I appreciated the modern paintings and the lowboy bureau and the big TV. It seemed like a plenty nice enough place to me, considering where we'd been.

"No, I don't," Edna said with real conviction. "There's no use in my getting mad at you about it. It isn't your fault. You do the best you can for everybody. But every trip teaches you something. And I've learned I need to give up on motels before some bad thing happens to me. I'm sorry."

"What does that mean?" I said, because I really didn't know what she had in mind to do, though I should've guessed.

"I guess I'll take that ticket you mentioned," she said, and got up and faced the window. "Tomorrow's soon enough. We haven't got a car to take me anyhow."

"Well, that's a fine thing," I said, sitting on the bed, feeling like I was in shock. I wanted to say something to her, to argue with her, but I couldn't think what to say that seemed right. I didn't want to be mad at her, but it made me mad.

"You've got a right to be mad at me, Earl," she said, "but I don't think you can really blame me." She turned around and faced me and sat on the windowsill, her hands on her knees. Someone knocked on the door, and I just yelled for them to set the tray down and put it on the bill.

"I guess I *do* blame you," I said, and I was angry. I thought about how I could've disappeared into that trailer community and hadn't, had come back to keep things going, had tried to take control of things for everybody when they looked bad.

"Don't. I wish you wouldn't," Edna said and smiled at me like she wanted me to hug her. "Anybody ought to have their choice in things if they can. Don't you believe that, Earl? Here I am out here in the desert where I don't know anything, in a stolen car, in a motel room under an assumed name, with no money of my own, a kid that's not mine, and the law after me. And I have a choice to get out of all of it by getting on a bus. What would you do? I know exactly what you'd do."

"You think you do," I said. But I didn't want to get into an argument about it and tell her all I could've done and didn't do. Because it wouldn't have done any good. When you get to the point of arguing, you're past the point of changing anybody's mind, even though it's supposed to be the other way, and maybe for some classes of people it is, just never mine.

Edna smiled at me and came across the room and put her arms around me where I was sitting on the bed. Cheryl rolled over and looked at us and smiled, then closed her eyes, and the room was quiet. I was beginning to think of Rock Springs in a way I knew I would always think of it, a lowdown city full of crimes and whores and disappointments, a place where a woman left me, instead of a place where I got things on the straight track once and for all, a place I saw a gold mine.

"Eat your chicken, Earl," Edna said. "Then we can go to bed. I'm tired, but I'd like to make love to you anyway. None of this is a matter of not loving you, you know that."

Sometime late in the night, after Edna was asleep, I got up and walked outside into the parking lot. It could've been anytime because there was still the light from the interstate frosting the low sky and the big red Ramada sign humming motionlessly in the night and no light at all in the east to indicate it might be morning. The lot was full of cars all nosed in, a couple of them with suitcases strapped to their roofs and their trunks weighed down with belongings the people were taking someplace, to a new home or a vacation resort in the mountains. I had laid in bed a long time after Edna was asleep, watching the Atlanta Braves on television, trying to get my mind off how I'd feel when I saw that bus pull away the next day, and how I'd feel when I turned around and there stood Cheryl and Little Duke and no one to see about them but me alone, and that the first thing I had to do was get hold of some automobile and get the plates switched, then get them some breakfast and get us all on the road to Florida, all in the space of probably two hours, since that Mercedes would certainly look less hid in the daytime than the night, and word travels fast. I've always taken care of Cheryl myself as long as I've had her with me. None of the women ever did. Most of them didn't even seem to like her, though they took care of me in a way so that I could take care of her. And I knew that once Edna left, all that was going to get harder. Though what I wanted most to do was not think about it just for a while, try to let my mind go limp so it could be strong for the rest of what there was. I thought that the difference between a successful life and an unsuccessful one, between me at that moment and all the people who owned the cars that were nosed into their proper places in the lot, maybe between me and that woman out in the trailers by the gold mine, was how well you were able to put things like this out of your mind and not be bothered by them, and maybe, too, by how many troubles like this one you had to face in a lifetime. Through luck or design they had all faced fewer troubles, and by their own characters, they forgot them faster. And that's what I wanted for me. Fewer troubles, fewer memories of trouble.

I walked over to a car, a Pontiac with Ohio tags, one of the ones with bundles and suitcases strapped to the top and a lot more in the trunk, by the way it was riding. I looked inside the driver's window. There were maps and paperback books and sunglasses and the little plastic holders for cans that hang on the window wells. And in the back there were kid's toys and some pillows and a cat box with a cat sitting in it staring up at me like I was the face of the moon. It all looked familiar to me, the very same things I would have in my car if I had a car. Nothing seemed surprising, nothing different. Though I had a funny sensation at that moment and turned and looked up at the windows along the back of the motel. All were dark except two. Mine and another one. And I wondered, because it seemed funny, what would you think a man was doing if you saw him in the middle of the night looking in the windows of cars in the parking lot of the Ramada Inn? Would you think he was trying to get his head cleared? Would you think he was trying to get ready for a day when trouble would come down on him? Would you think his girlfriend was leaving him? Would you think he had a daughter? Would you think he was anybody like you?

MAVIS GALLANT

MY HEART IS BROKEN

Mavis Gallant (b. 1922) was born in Montreal and attended seventeen schools there and in New York before starting a career in journalism during World War II. In 1944, Gallant worked as a reporter for the Montreal Standard, *and she began to publish literary work as well. In 1950 she moved to Europe, settling permanently in Paris. Gallant's move was prompted by her need "to see if I could live on writing," a desire realized when* The New Yorker *published her story "Madeleine's Birthday" in 1951 and two more stories the next year. Gallant's status as an expatriate Canadian has somewhat dampened the domestic reception of her work, a difficulty mitigated by* Home Truths: Selected Canadian Stories *(1981). Often confronted with questions of identity and allegiance, Gallant maintains that there can be no question about these things: "I am a Canadian and a writer and a woman."*

Gallant established her literary reputation almost exclusively through her mastery of the short story. She has published eight volumes of stories; she has written two novels, Green Water, Green Sky *(1960) and* A Fairly Good Time *(1970), and a nonfiction collection,* Paris Notebooks *(1986), whose title work is a compassionate eyewitness account of the Paris revolt of May 1968. Gallant's oeuvre also includes a play,* What Is to Be Done? *(1984), and a long unfinished work on the historical French anti-Semitic case, the Dreyfus affair. Her* Collected Stories *appeared in 1996. Gallant tells her stories with an understated finesse, a vivid attention to memory, and a dispassionate voice, whose pervasive sense of irony permits her to explore a wide range of characters and situations and often prevents easy sympathy with such characters. George Woodcock argues that Gallant's art of fiction, conceived in the fallout of World War II, has become an "archaeology of war." The devastations of both international war and the invisible war waged on women are linked to Gallant's interest in memory by writer Janice Kulyk Keefer in her critical book* Reading Mavis Gallant *(1989): "The fictive worlds Gallant creates can be mapped between the poles of progress—historical time, with its blind, violent forward drive—and the project of memory—the desire to stop and make whole what has been smashed: to make sense out of the shambles."*

"When that Jean Harlow died," Mrs. Thompson said to Jeannie, "I was on the 83 streetcar with a big, heavy paper parcel in my arms. I hadn't been married for very long, and when I used to visit my mother she'd give me a lot of canned stuff and preserves. I was standing up in the streetcar because nobody'd given me a seat. All the men were unemployed in those days, and they just sat down wherever they happened to be. You wouldn't remember what Montreal was like then. *You* weren't even on earth. To resume what I was saying to you, one of these men sitting down had an American paper—the *Daily News*, I guess it was—and I was sort of leaning over him, and I saw in big print 'JEAN HARLOW DEAD.' You can believe me or not, just as you want to, but that was the most terrible shock I ever had in my life. I never got over it."

Jeannie had nothing to say to that. She lay flat on her back across the bed, with her head toward Mrs. Thompson and her heels just touching the crate that did as a bedside table. Balanced on her flat stomach was an open bottle of coral-pink Cutex nail polish. She held her hands up over her head and with some difficulty applied the brush to the nails of her right hand. Her legs were brown and thin. She wore nothing but shorts and one of her husband's shirts. Her feet were bare.

Mrs. Thompson was the wife of the paymaster in a road-construction camp in northern Quebec. Jeannie's husband was an engineer working on the same project. The road was being pushed through country where nothing had existed until now except rocks and lakes and muskeg. The camp was established between a wild lake and the line of raw dirt that was the road. There were no towns between the camp and the railway spur, sixty miles distant.

Mrs. Thompson, a good deal older than Jeannie, had become her best friend. She was a nice, plain, fat, consoling sort of person, with varicosed legs, shoes unlaced and slit for comfort, blue flannel dressing gown worn at all hours, pudding-bowl haircut, and coarse gray hair. She might have been Jeannie's own mother, or her Auntie Pearl. She rocked her fat self in the rocking chair and went on with what she had to say: "What I was starting off to tell you is you remind me of her, of Jean Harlow. You've got the same teeny mouth, Jeannie, and I think your hair was a whole lot prettier before you started fooling around with it. That peroxide's no good. It splits the ends. I know you're going to tell me it isn't peroxide but something more modern, but the result is the same."

Vern's shirt was spotted with coral-pink that had dropped off the brush. Vern wouldn't mind; at least, he wouldn't say that he minded. If he hadn't objected to anything Jeannie did until now, he wouldn't start off by complaining about a shirt. The campsite outside the uncurtained window was silent and dark. The waning moon would not appear until dawn. A passage of thought made Mrs. Thompson say, "Winter soon."

Jeannie moved sharply and caught the bottle of polish before it spilled. Mrs. Thompson was crazy; it wasn't even September.

"Pretty soon," Mrs. Thompson admitted. "Pretty soon. That's a long season up here, but I'm one person doesn't complain. I've been up here or around here every winter of my married life, except for that one winter Pops was occupying Germany."

"I've been up here seventy-two days," said Jeannie, in her soft voice. "Tomorrow makes seventy-three."

"Is that right?" said Mrs. Thompson, jerking the rocker forward, suddenly snappish. "Is that a fact? Well, who asked you to come up here? Who asked you to come and start counting days like you was in some kind of jail? When you got married to Vern, you must of known where he'd be taking you. He told you, didn't he, that he liked road jobs, construction jobs, and that? Did he tell you, or didn't he?"

"Oh, he told me," said Jeannie.

"You know what, Jeannie?" said Mrs. Thompson. "If you'd of just listened to me, none of this would have happened. I told you that first day, the day you arrived here in your high-heeled shoes, I said, 'I know this cabin doesn't look much, but all the married men have the same sort of place.' You remember I said that? I said, 'You just get some curtains up and some carpets down and it'll be home.' I took you over and showed you my place, and you said you'd never seen anything so lovely."

"I meant it," said Jeannie. "Your cabin is just lovely. I don't know why, but I never managed to make this place look like yours."

Mrs. Thompson said, "That's plain enough." She looked at the cold grease spattered behind the stove, and the rag of towel over by the sink. "It's partly the experience," she said kindly. She and her husband knew exactly what to take with them when they went on a job, they had been doing it for so many years. They brought boxes for artificial flowers, a brass door knocker, a portable bar decorated with sea shells, a cardboard fireplace that looked real, and an electric fire that sent waves of light rippling over the ceiling and walls. A concealed gramophone played the records they loved and cherished—the good old tunes. They had comic records that dated back to the year I, and sad soprano records about shipwrecks and broken promises and babies' graves. The first time Jeannie heard one of the funny records, she was scared to death.

She was paying a formal call, sitting straight in her chair, with her skirt pulled around her knees. Vern and Pops Thompson were talking about the Army.

"I wish to God I was back," said old Pops.

"Don't I?" said Vern. He was fifteen years older than Jeannie and had been through a lot.

At first there were only scratching and whispering noises, and then a mosquito orchestra started to play, and a dwarf's voice came into the room. "Little Johnnie Green, little Sallie Brown," squealed the dwarf, higher and faster than any human ever could. "Spooning in the park with the grass all around."

"Where is he?" Jeannie cried, while the Thompsons screamed with laughter and Vern smiled. The dwarf sang on: "And each little bird in the treetop high/Sang 'Oh you kid!' and winked his eye."

It was a record that had belonged to Pops Thompson's mother. He had been laughing at it all his life. The Thompsons loved living up north and didn't miss cities or company. Their cabin smelled of cocoa and toast. Over their beds were oval photographs of each other as children, and they had some Teddy bears and about a dozen dolls.

Jeannie capped the bottle of polish, taking care not to press it against her wet nails. She sat up with a single movement and set the bottle down on the bedside crate. Then she turned to face Mrs. Thompson. She sat cross-legged, with her hands outspread before her. Her face was serene.

"Not an ounce of fat on you," said Mrs. Thompson. "You know something? I'm sorry you're going. I really am. Tomorrow you'll be gone. You know that, don't you? You've been counting days, but you won't have to any more. I guess Vern'll take you back to Montreal. What do you think?"

Jeannie dropped her gaze, and began smoothing wrinkles on the bedspread. She muttered something Mrs. Thompson could not understand.

"Tomorrow you'll be gone," Mrs. Thompson continued. "I know it for a fact. Vern is at this moment getting his pay, and borrowing a jeep from Mr. Sherman, and a Polack driver to take you to the train. He sure is loyal to *you*. You know what I heard Mr. Sherman say? He said to Vern, 'If you want to send her off, Vern, you can always stay,' and Vern said, 'I can't very well do that, Mr. Sherman.' And Mr. Sherman said, 'This is the second time you've had to leave a job on account of her, isn't it?' and then Mr. Sherman said, 'In my opinion, no man by his own self can rape a girl, so there were either two men or else she's invented the whole story.' Then he said, 'Vern, you're either a saint or a damn fool.' That was all I heard. I came straight over here, Jeannie, because I thought you might be needing me." Mrs. Thompson waited to hear she was needed. She stopped rocking and sat with her feet flat and wide apart. She struck her knees with her open palms and cried, "I *told* you to keep away from the men. I told you it would make trouble, all that being cute and dancing around. I said to you, I remember saying it, I said nothing makes trouble faster in a place like this than a grown woman behaving like a little girl. Don't you remember?"

"I only went out for a walk," said Jeannie. "Nobody'll believe me, but that's all. I went down the road for a walk."

"In high heels?" said Mrs. Thompson. "With a purse on your arm, and a hat on your head? You don't go taking a walk in the bush that way. There's no place to walk *to*. Where'd you think you were going? I could smell Evening in Paris a quarter mile away."

"There's no place to go," said Jeannie, "but what else is there to do? I just felt like dressing up and going out."

"You could have cleaned up your home a bit," said Mrs. Thompson. "There was always that to do. Just look at that sink. That basket of ironing's been under the bed since July. I know it gets boring around here, but you had the best of it. You had the summer. In winter it gets dark around three o'clock. Then the wives have a right to go crazy. I knew one used to sleep the clock around. When her Nembutal ran out, she took about a hundred aspirin. I knew another learned to distill her own liquor, just to kill time. Sometimes the men get so's they don't like the life, and that's death for the wives. But here you had a nice summer, and Vern liked the life."

"He likes it better than anything," said Jeannie. "He liked the Army, but this was his favorite life after that."

"There," said Mrs. Thompson. "You had every reason to be happy. What'd you do if he sent you off alone, now, like Mr. Sherman advised? You'd be alone and you'd have to work. Women don't know when they're well off. Here you've got a good, sensible husband working for you and you don't appreciate it. You have to go and do a terrible thing."

"I only went for a walk," said Jeannie. "That's all I did."

"It's possible," said Mrs. Thompson, "but it's a terrible thing. It's about the worst thing that's ever happened around here. I don't know why you let it happen. A woman can always defend what's precious, even if she's attacked ... I hope you remembered to think about bacteria."

"What d'you mean?"

"I mean Javel, or something."

Jeannie looked uncomprehending and then shook her head.

"I wonder what it must be like," said Mrs. Thompson after a time, looking at the dark window. "I mean, think of Berlin and them Russians and all. Think of some disgusting fellow you don't know. Never said hello to, even. Some girls ask for it, though. You can't always blame the man. The man loses his job, his wife if he's got one, everything, all because of a silly girl."

Jeannie frowned, absently. She pressed her nails together, testing the polish. She licked her lips and said, "I was more beaten up, Mrs. Thompson. It wasn't exactly what you think. It was only afterwards I thought to myself, Why, I was raped and everything."

Mrs. Thompson gasped, hearing the word from Jeannie. She said, "Have you got any marks?"

"On my arms. That's why I'm wearing this shirt. The first thing I did was change my clothes."

Mrs. Thompson thought this over, and went on to another thing: "Do you ever think about your mother?"

"Sure."

"Do you pray? If this goes on at nineteen—"

"I'm twenty."

"—what'll you be by the time you're thirty? You've already got a terrible, terrible memory to haunt you all your life."

"I already can't remember it," said Jeannie. "Afterwards I started walking back to camp, but I was walking the wrong way. I met Mr. Sherman. The back of his car was full of coffee, flour, all that. I guess he'd been picking up supplies. He said, 'Well, get in.' He didn't ask any questions at first. I couldn't talk anyway."

"Shock," said Mrs. Thompson wisely.

"You know, I'd have to see it happening to know what happened. All I remember is that first we were only talking ..."

"You and Mr. Sherman?"

"No, no, before. When I was taking my walk."

"Don't say who it was," said Mrs. Thompson. "We don't any of us need to know."

"We were just talking, and he got sore all of a sudden and grabbed my arm."

"Don't say the name!" Mrs. Thompson cried.

"Like when I was little, there was this Lana Turner movie. She had two twins. She was just there and then a nurse brought her in the two twins. I hadn't been married or anything, and I didn't know anything, and I used to think if I just kept on seeing the movie I'd know how she got the two twins, you know, and I went, oh, I must have seen it six times, the movie, but in the end I never knew any more. They just brought her the two twins."

Mrs. Thompson sat quite still, trying to make sense of this. "Taking advantage of a woman is a criminal offense," she observed. "I heard Mr. Sherman say another thing, Jeannie. He said, 'If your wife wants to press a charge and talk to some lawyer, let me tell you,' he said, 'you'll never work again anywhere,' he said. Vern said, 'I know that, Mr. Sherman.' And Mr.

Sherman said, 'Let me tell you, if any reporters or any investigators start coming around here, they'll get their ... they'll never ...' Oh, he was mad. And Vern said, 'I came over to tell you I was quitting, Mr. Sherman.'" Mrs. Thompson had been acting this with spirit, using a quiet voice when she spoke for Vern and a blustering tone for Mr. Sherman. In her own voice, she said, "If you're wondering how I came to hear all this, I was strolling by Mr. Sherman's office window—his bungalow, that is. I had Maureen out in her pram." Maureen was the Thompsons' youngest doll.

Jeannie might not have been listening: She started to tell something else: "You know, where we were before, on Vern's last job, we weren't in a camp. He was away a lot, and he left me in Amos, in a hotel. I liked it. Amos isn't all that big, but it's better than here. There was this German in the hotel. He was selling cars. He'd drive me around if I wanted to go to a movie or anything. Vern didn't like him, so we left. It wasn't anybody's fault."

"So he's given up two jobs," said Mrs. Thompson. "One because he couldn't leave you alone, and now this one. Two jobs, and you haven't been married five months. Why should another man be thrown out of work? We don't need to know a thing. I'll be sorry if it was Jimmy Quinn," she went on, slowly. "I like that boy. Don't say the name, dear. There's Evans. Susini. Palmer. But it might have been anybody, because you had them all on the boil. So it might have been Jimmy Quinn—let's say—and it could have been anyone else, too. Well, now let's hope they can get their minds back on the job."

"I thought they all liked me," said Jeannie sadly. "I get along with people. Vern never fights with me."

"Vern never fights with anyone. But he ought to have thrashed *you*."

"If he ... you know. I won't say the name. If he'd liked me, I wouldn't have minded. If he'd been friendly. I really mean that. I wouldn't have gone wandering up the road, making all this fuss."

"Jeannie," said Mrs. Thompson, "you don't even know what you're saying."

"He could at least have liked me," said Jeannie. "He wasn't even friendly. It's the first time in my life somebody hasn't liked me. My heart is broken, Mrs. Thompson. My heart is just broken."

She has to cry, Mrs. Thompson thought. She has to have it out. She rocked slowly, tapping her foot, trying to remember how she'd felt about things when she was twenty, wondering if her heart had ever been broken, too.

MAVIS GALLANT

IRINA

One of Irina's grandsons, nicknamed Riri, was sent to her at Christmas. His mother was going into hospital, but nobody told him that. The real cause of his visit was that since Irina had become a widow her children worried about her being alone. The children, as Irina would call them forever, were married and in their thirties and forties. They did not think they were like other people, because their father had been a powerful old man. He was a Swiss writer, Richard Notte. They carried his reputation and the memory of his puritan equity like an immense jar filled with water of which they had been told not to spill a drop. They loved their mother, but they had never needed to think about her until now. They had never fretted about which way her shadow might fall, and whether to stay in the shade or get out by being eccentric and bold. There were two sons and three daughters, with fourteen children among them. Only Riri was an only child. The girls had married an industrial designer, a Lutheran minister (perhaps an insolent move, after all, for the daughter of a militant atheist), and an art historian in Paris. One boy had become a banker and the other a lecturer on Germanic musical tradition. These were the crushed sons and loyal daughters to whom Irina had been faithful, whose pictures had travelled with her and lived beside her bed.

Few of Notte's obituaries had even mentioned a family. Some of his literary acquaintances were surprised to learn there had been any children at all, though everyone paid homage to the soft, quiet wife to whom he had dedicated his books, the subject of his first rapturous poems. These poems, conventional verse for the most part, seldom translated out of German except by unpoetical research scholars, were thought to be the work of his youth. Actually, Notte was forty when he finally married, and Irina barely nineteen. The obituaries called Notte the last of a breed, the end of a Tolstoyan line of moral lightning rods—an extinction which was probably hard on those writers who came after him, and still harder on his children. However, even to his family the old man had appeared to be the very archetype of a respected European novelist—prophet, dissuader, despairingly opposed to evil, cracked-voiced after having made so many pronouncements. Otherwise, he was not all that typical as a Swiss or as a Western, liberal, Protestant European, for he neither saved, nor invested, nor hid, nor disguised his material returns.

"What good is money, except to give away?" he often said. He had a wife, five children, and an old secretary who had turned into a dependent. It was

300

true that he claimed next to nothing for himself. He rented shabby, ramshackle houses impossible to heat or even to clean. Owning was against his convictions, and he did not want to be tied to a gate called home. His room was furnished with a cot, a lamp, a desk, two chairs, a map of the world, a small bookshelf—no more, not even carpets or curtains. Like his family, he wore thick sweaters indoors as out, and crouched over inadequate electric fires. He seldom ate meat—though he did not deprive his children—and drank water with his meals. He had married once—once and for all. He could on occasion enjoy wine and praise restaurants and good-looking women, but these festive outbreaks were on the rim of his real life, as remote from his children—as strange and as distorted to them—as some other country's colonial wars. He grew old early, as if he expected old age to suit him. By sixty, his eyes were sunk in pockets of lizard skin. His hair became bleached and lustrous, like the scrap of wedding dress Irina kept in a jeweller's box. He was photographed wearing a dark suit and a woman's plaid shawl—he was always cold by then, even in summer—and with a rakish felt hat shading half his face. His wife still let a few photographers in, at the end—but not many. Her murmured "He is working" had for decades been a double lock. He was as strong as Rasputin, his enemies said; he went on writing and talking and travelling until he positively could not focus his eyes or be helped aboard a train. Nearly to the last, he and Irina swung off on their seasonal cycle of journeys to Venice, to Rome, to cities where their married children lived, to Liège and Oxford for awards and honors. His place in a hotel dining room was recognizable from the door because of the pills, drops, and powders lined up to the width of a dinner plate. Notte's hypochondria had been known and gently caricatured for years. His sons, between them, had now bought up most of the original drawings: Notte, in infant's clothing, downing his medicine like a man (he had missed the Nobel); Notte quarrelling with Aragon and throwing up Surrealism; a grim female figure called "Existentialism" taking his pulse; Notte catching Asian flu on a cultural trip to Peking. During the final months of his life his children noticed that their mother had begun acquiring medicines of her own, as if hoping by means of mirror-magic to draw his ailments to herself.

If illness became him, it was only because he was fond of ritual, the children thought—even the hideous ceremonial of pain. But Irina had not been intended for sickness and suffering; she was meant to be burned dry and consumed by the ritual of him. The children believed that the end of his life would surely be the death of their mother. They did not really expect Irina to turn her face to the wall and die, but an exclusive, even a selfish, alliance with Notte had seemed her reason for being. As their father grew old, then truly old, then old in mind, and querulous, and unjust, they observed the patient tenderness with which she heeded his sulks and caprices, his almost insane commands. They supposed this ardent submission of hers had to do with love, but it was not a sort of love they had ever experienced or tried to provoke. One of his sons saw Notte crying because Irina had buttered toast for him when he wanted it dry. She stroked the old man's silky hair, smiling. The son hated this. Irina was diminishing a strong, proud man, making a senile child of him, just as Notte was enslaving and debasing her. At the same time the son felt a secret between the two, a mystery. He wondered then, but at no other time, if the secret might not be Irina's invention and property.

Notte left a careful will for such an unworldly person. His wife was to be secure in her lifetime. Upon her death the residue of income from his work would be shared among the sons and daughters. There were no gifts or bequests. The will was accompanied by a testament which the children had photocopied for the beauty of the handwriting and the charm of the text. Irina, it began, belonged to a generation of women shielded from decisions, allowed to grow in the sun and shade of male protection. This flower, his flower, he wrote, was to be cherished now as if she were her children's child.

"In plain words," said Irina, at the first reading, in a Zurich lawyer's office, "I am the heir." She was wearing dark glasses because her eyes were tired, and a tight hat. She looked tense and foreign.

Well, yes, that was it, although Notte had put it more gracefully. His favorite daughter was his literary executor, entrusted with the unfinished manuscripts and the journals he had kept for sixty-five years. But it soon became evident that Irina had no intention of giving these up. The children adored their mother, but even without love as a factor would not have made a case of it; Notte's lawyer had already told them about disputes ending in mazelike litigation, families sundered; contents of a desk sequestered, diaries rotting in bank vaults while the inheritors thrashed it out. Besides, editing Notte's papers would keep Irina busy and an occupation was essential now. In loving and unloving families alike, the same problem arises after a death: What to do about the widow?

Irina settled some of it by purchasing an apartment in a small Alpine town. She chose a tall, glassy, urban-looking building of the kind that made conservationist groups send round-robin letters, accompanied by incriminating photographs, to newspapers in Lausanne. The apartment had a hall, an up-to-date kitchen, a bedroom for Irina, a spare room with a narrow bed in it, one bathroom, and a living room containing a couch. There was a glassed-in cube of a balcony where in a pinch an extra cot might have fitted, but Irina used the space for a table and chairs. She ordered red lampshades and thick curtains and the pale furniture that is usually sold to young couples. She seemed to come into her own in that tight, neutral flat, the children thought. They read some of the interviews she gave, and approved: she said, in English and Italian, in German and French, that she would not be a literary widow, detested by critics, resented by Notte's readers. Her firm diffidence made the children smile, and they were proud to read about her dignified beauty. But as for her intelligence—well, they supposed that the interviewers had confused fluency with wit. Irina's views and her way of expressing them were all camouflage, simply part of a ladylike undereducation, long on languages and bearing, short on history and arithmetic. Her origins were Russian and Swiss and probably pious; the children had not been drawn to that side of the family. Their father's legendary peasant childhood, his isolated valley-village had filled their imaginations and their collective past. There was a sudden April lightness in her letters now that relieved and yet troubled them. They knew it was a sham happiness, Nature's way of protecting the survivor from immediate grief. The crisis would come later, when her most secret instincts had built a seawall. They took turns invading her at Easter and in the summer, one couple at a time, bringing a child apiece—there was no room for more. Winter was a problem, however, for the skiing was not good just there, and none of them liked to break up their families at Christmastime. Not only was Irina's apartment lacking in beds but there was absolutely no space for a tree. Finally, she offered to visit them, in regular order. That was how they settled it. She went to Bern, to Munich, to Zurich, and then came the inevitable Christmas when it was not that no one wanted her but just that they were all doing different things.

She had written in November of that year that a friend, whom she described, with some quaintness, as "a person," had come for a long stay. They liked that. A visit meant winter company, lamps on at four, China tea, conversation, the peppery smell of carnations (her favorite flower) in a warm room. For a week or two of the visit her letters were blithe, but presently they noticed that "the person" seemed to be having a depressing effect on their mother. She wrote that she had been working on Notte's journals for three years now. Who would want to read them except old men and women? His moral and political patterns were fossils of liberalism. He had seen the cracks in the Weimar Republic. He had understood from the beginning what Hitler meant. If at first he had been wrong about Mussolini, he had changed his mind even before Croce changed his, and had been safely back on the side of democracy in time to denounce Pirandello. He had given all he could, short of his life, to the Spanish Republicans. His measure of Stalin had been so wise and unshakably just that he had never been put on the Communist index—something rare for a Western Socialist. No one could say, ever, that Notte had hedged or retreated or kept silent when a voice was needed. Well, said Irina, what of it? He had written, pledged, warned, signed, declared. And what had he changed, diverted, or stopped? She suddenly sent the same letter to all five children: "This Christmas I don't want to go anywhere. I intend to stay here, in my own home."

They knew this was the crisis and that they must not leave her to face it alone, but that was the very winter when all their plans ran down, when one daughter was going into hospital, another moving to a different city, the third probably divorcing. The elder son was committed to a Christmas with his wife's parents, the younger lecturing in South Africa—a country where Irina, as Notte's constant reflection, would certainly not wish to set foot. They wrote and called and cabled one another: What shall we do? Can you? Will you? I can't.

Irina had no favorites among her children, except possibly one son who had been ill with rheumatic fever as a child and required long nursing. To him she now confided that she longed for her own childhood sometimes, in order to avoid having to judge herself. She was homesick for a time when nothing had crystallized and mistakes were allowed. Now, in old age, she had no excuse for errors. Every thought had a long meaning; every motive had angles and corners, and could be measured. And yet whatever she saw and thought and attempted was still fluid and vague. The shape of a table against afternoon light still held a mystery, awaited a final explanation. You looked for clarity, she wrote, and the answer you had was paleness, the flat white cast that a snowy sky throws across a room.

Part of this son knew about death and dying, but the rest of him was a banker and thoroughly active. He believed that, given an ideal situation, one should be able to walk through a table, which would save time and round-about decisions. However, like all of Notte's children he had been raised with every awareness of solid matter too. His mother's youthful, yearning, and probably religious letter made him feel bland and old. He told his wife what he thought it contained, and she told a sister-in-law what she thought he had said. Irina was tired. Her eyesight was poor, perhaps as a result of prolonged work on those diaries. Irina did not need adult company, which might lead to morbid conversation; what she craved now was a symbol of innocent, continuing life. An animal might do it. Better still, a child.

Riri did not know that his mother would be in hospital the minute his back was turned. Balanced against a tame Christmas with a grandmother was a midterm holiday, later, of high-altitude skiing with his father. There was also some further blackmail involving his holiday homework, and then the vague state of behavior called "being reasonable"—that was all anyone asked. They celebrated a token Christmas on the twenty-third, and the next day he packed his presents (a watch and a tape recorder) and was put on a plane at Orly West. He flew from Paris to Geneva, where he spent the real Christmas Eve in a strange, bare apartment into which an aunt and a large family of cousins had just moved. In the morning he was wakened when it was dark and taken to a six-o'clock train. He said goodbye to his aunt at the station, and added, "If you ask the conductor or anyone to look after me, I'll—" Whatever threat was in his mind he seemed ready to carry out. He wore an R.A.F. badge on his jacket and carried a Waffen-S.S. emblem in his pocket. He knew better than to keep it in sight. At home they had already taken one away but he had acquired another at school. He had Astérix comic books for reading, chocolate-covered hazelnuts for support, and his personal belongings in a fairly large knapsack. He made a second train on his own and got down at the right station.

He had been told that he knew this place, but his memory, if it was a memory, had to do with fields and a picnic. No one met him. He shared a taxi through soft snow with two women, and paid his share—actually more than his share, which annoyed the women; they could not give less than a child in the way of a tip. The taxi let him off at a dark, shiny tower on stilts with granite steps. In the lobby a marble panel, looking like the list of names of war dead in his school, gave him his grandmother on the eighth floor. The lift, like the façade of the building, was made of dark mirrors into which he gazed seriously. A dense, thoughtful person looked back. He took off his glasses and the blurred face became even more remarkable. His grandmother had both a bell and a knocker at her door. He tried both. For quite a long time nothing happened. He knocked and rang again. It was not nervousness that he felt but a new sensation that had to do with a shut, foreign door.

His grandmother opened the door a crack. She had short white hair and a pale face and blue eyes. She held a dressing gown gripped at the collar. She flung the door back and cried, "Darling Richard, I thought you were arriving much later. Oh," she said, "I must look dreadful to you. Imagine finding me like this, in my dressing gown!" She tipped her head away and talked between her fingers, as he had been told never to do, because only liars cover their mouths. He saw a dark hall and a bright kitchen that was in some disorder, and a large dark, curtained room opposite the kitchen. This room smelled stuffy, of old cigarettes and of adults. But then his grandmother pushed the draperies apart and wound up the slatted shutters, and what had been dark, mound-like objects turned into a couch and a bamboo screen and a round table and a number of chairs. On a bookshelf stood a painting of three tulips that must have fallen out of their vase. Behind them was a sky that was all black except for a rainbow. He unpacked a portion of the things in his knapsack—wrapped presents for his grandmother, his new tape recorder, two school textbooks, a notebook, a Bic pen. The start of this Christmas lay hours behind him and his breakfast had died long ago.

"Are you hungry?" said his grandmother. He heard a telephone ringing as she brought him a cup of hot milk with a little coffee in it and two fresh croissants on a plate. She was obviously someone who never rushed to answer any bell. "My friend, who is an early riser, even on Christmas Day, went out and got these croissants. Very bravely, I thought." He ate his new breakfast, dipping the croissants in the milk, and heard his grandmother saying, "Well, I must have misunderstood. But he managed…. He didn't bring his skis. Why not? … I see." By the time she came back he had a book open. She watched him for a second and said, "Do you read at meals at home?"

"Sometimes."

"That's not the way I brought up your mother."

He put his nose nearer the page without replying. He read aloud from the page in a soft schoolroom plainchant: "'Go, went, gone. Stand, stood, stood. Take, took, taken.'"

"Richard," said his grandmother. When he did not look up at once, she said, "I know what they call you at home, but what are you called at school?"

"Riri."

"I have three Richard grandsons," she said, "and not one is called Richard exactly."

"I have an Uncle Richard," he said.

"Yes, well, he happens to be a son of mine. I never allowed nicknames. Have you finished your breakfast?"

"Yes."

"Yes who? Yes what? What is your best language, by the way?"

"I am French," he said, with a sharp, sudden, hard hostility, the first tense bud of it, that made her murmur, "So soon?" She was about to tell him that he was not French—at least, not really—when an old man came into the room. He was thin and walked with a cane.

"Alec, this is my grandson," she said. "Riri, say how do you do to Mr. Aiken, who was kind enough to go out in this morning's snow to buy croissants for us all."

"I knew he would be here early," said the old man, in a stiff French that sounded extremely comical to the boy. "Irina has an odd ear for times and trains." He sat down next to Riri and clasped his hands on his cane; his hands at once began to tremble violently. "What does that interesting-looking book tell you?" he asked.

"'The swallow flew away,'" answered Irina, reading over the child's head. "'The swallow flew away with my hopes.'"

"Good God, let me look at that!" said the old man in his funny French. Sure enough, those were the words, and there was a swallow of a very strange blue, or at least a sapphire-and-turquoise creature with a swallow's tail. Riri's grandmother took her spectacles out of her dressing-gown pocket and brought the book up close and said in a loud, solemn way, "'The swallows will have flown away.'" Then she picked up the tape recorder, which was the size of a glasses case, and after snapping the wrong button on and off, causing agonizing confusion and wastage, she said with her mouth against it, "'When shall the swallows have flown away?'"

"No," said Riri, reaching, snatching almost. As if she had always given in to men, even to male children, she put the book down and the recorder too, saying "Mr. Aiken can help you with your English. He has the best possible accent. When he says 'the girl' you will think he is saying 'de Gaulle.'"

"Irina has an odd ear for English," said the old man calmly. He got up slowly and went to the kitchen, and she did too, and Riri could hear them whispering and laughing at something. Mr. Aiken came back alone carrying a small glass of clear liquid. "The morning heart-starter," he said. "Try it." Riri took a sip. It lay in his stomach like a warm stone. "No more effect on you than a gulp of milk," said the old man, marvelling, sitting down close to Riri again. "You could probably do with pints of this stuff. I can tell by looking at you you'll be a drinking man." His hands on the walking stick began to tremble anew. "I'm not the man I was," he said. "Not by any means." Because he did not speak English with a French or any foreign accent, Riri could not really understand him. He went on, "Fell down the staircase at the Trouville casino. Trouville, or that other place. Shock gave me amnesia. Hole in the stair carpet—must have been. I went there for years." he said. "Never saw a damned hole in anything. Now my hands shake."

"When you lift your glass to drink they don't shake," called Riri's grandmother from the kitchen. She repeated this in French, for good measure.

"She's got an ear like a radar unit," said Mr. Aiken.

Riri took up his tape recorder. In a measured chant, as if demonstrating to his grandmother how these things should be done, he said, "'The swallows would not fly away if the season is fine.'"

"Do you know what any of it means?" said Mr. Aiken.

"He doesn't need to know what it means," Riri's grandmother answered for him. "He just needs to know it by heart."

They were glassed in on the balcony. The only sound they could hear was of their own voices. The sun on them was so hot that Riri wanted to take off his sweater. Looking down, he saw a chalet crushed in the shadows of two white blocks, not so tall as their own. A large, spared spruce tree suddenly seemed to retract its branches and allow a great weight of snow to slip off. Cars went by, dogs barked, children called—all in total silence. His grandmother talked English to the old man. Riri, when he was not actually eating, read "Astérix in Brittany" without attracting her disapproval.

"If people can be given numbers, like marks in school," she said, "Then children are zero." She was enveloped in a fur cloak, out of which her hands and arms emerged as if the fur had dissolved in certain places. She was pink with wine and sun. The old man's blue eyes were paler than hers. "Zero." She held up her thumb and forefinger in an O. "I was there with my five darling zeros while he ... You are probably wondering if I was *ever* happy. At the beginning, in the first days, when I thought he would give me interesting books to read, books that would change all my life. Riri," she said, shading her eyes, "the cake and the ice cream were, I am afraid, the end of things for the moment. Could I ask you to clear the table for me?"

"I don't at home." Nevertheless he made a wobbly pile of dishes and took them away and did not come back. They heard him, indoors, starting all over: "'Go, went, gone.'"

"I have only half a memory for dates," she said. "I forget my children's birthdays until the last minute and have to send them telegrams. But I know *that* day...."

"The twenty-sixth of May," he said. "What I forget is the year."

"I know that I felt young."

"You were. You *are* young," he said.

"Except that I was forty if a day." She glanced at the hands and wrists emerging from her cloak as if pleased at their whiteness. "The river was so sluggish, I remember. And the willows trailed in the river."

"Actually, there was a swift current after the spring rains."

"But no wind. The clouds were heavy."

"It was late in the afternoon," he said. "We sat on the grass."

"On a raincoat. You had thought in the morning those clouds meant rain."

"A young man drowned," he said. "Fell out of a boat. Funny, he didn't try to swim. So people kept saying."

"We saw three firemen in gleaming metal helmets. They fished for him so languidly—the whole day was like that. They had a grappling hook. None of them knew what to do with it. They kept pulling it up and taking the rope from each other."

"They might have been after water lilies, from the look of them."

"One of them bailed out the boat with a blue saucepan. I remember that. They'd got that saucepan from the restaurant."

"Where we had lunch," he said. "Trout, and a coffee cream pudding. You left yours."

"It was soggy cake. But the trout was perfection. So was the wine. The bridge over the river filled up slowly with holiday people. The three firemen rowed to shore."

"Yes, and one of them went off on a shaky bicycle and came back with a coil of frayed rope on his shoulder."

"The railway station was just behind us. All those people on the bridge were waiting for a train. When the firemen's boat slipped off down the river, they moved without speaking from one side of the bridge to the other, just to watch the boat. The silence of it."

"Like the silence here."

"This is planned silence," she said.

Riri played back his own voice. A tinny, squeaky Riri said, "'Go, went, gone. Eat, ate, eaten. See, saw, sen.'"

"'Seen!'" called his grandmother from the balcony. "'Seen, not 'sen.' His mother made exactly that mistake," she said to the old man. "Oh, stop that," she said. He was crying. "Please, please, stop that. How could I have left five children?"

"Three were grown," he gasped, wiping his eyes.

"But they didn't know it. They didn't know they were grown. They still don't know it. And it made six children, counting him."

"The secretary mothered him," he said. "All he needed."

"I know, but you see she wasn't his wife, and he liked saying to strangers 'my wife,' 'my wife this,' 'my wife that.' What is it, Riri? Have you come to finish doing the thing I asked?"

He moved close to the table. His round glasses made him look desperate and stern. He said, "Which room is mine!" Darkness had gathered round him in spite of the sparkling sky and a row of icicles gleaming and melting in the most dazzling possible light. Outrage, a feeling that consideration had been wanting—that was how homesickness had overtaken him. She held his hand (he did not resist—another sign of his misery) and together they explored the apartment. He saw it all—every picture and cupboard and doorway—and in the end it was he who decided that Mr. Aiken must keep the spare room and he, Riri, would be happy on the living-room couch.

The old man passed them in the hall; he was obviously about to rest on the very bed he had just been within an inch of losing. He carried a plastic bottle of Evian. "Do you like the bland taste of water?" he said.

Riri looked boldly at his grandmother and said, "Yes," bursting into unexplained and endless-seeming laughter. He seemed to feel a relief at this substitute for impertinence. The old man laughed too, but broke off, coughing.

At half past four, when the windows were as black as the sky in the painting of tulips and began to reflect the lamps in a disturbing sort of way, they drew the curtains and had tea around the table. They pushed Riri's books and belongings to one side and spread a cross-stitched tablecloth. Riri had hot chocolate, a croissant left from breakfast and warmed in the oven, which made it deliciously greasy and soft, a slice of lemon sponge cake, and a banana. This time he helped clear away and even remained in the kitchen, talking, while his grandmother rinsed the cups and plates and stacked them in the machine.

The old man sat on a chair in the hall struggling with snow boots. He was going out alone in the dark to post some letters and to buy a newspaper and to bring back whatever provisions he thought were required for the evening meal.

"Riri, do you want to go with Mr. Aiken? Perhaps you should have a walk."

"At home I don't have to."

His grandmother looked cross; no, she looked worried. She was biting something back. The old man had finished the contention with his boots and now he put on a scarf, a fur-lined coat, a fur hat with earflaps, woollen gloves, and he took a list and a shopping bag and a different walking stick, which looked something like a ski pole. His grandmother stood still, as if dreaming, and then (addressing Riri) decided to wash all her amber necklaces. She fetched a wicker basket from her bedroom. It was lined with orange silk and filled with strings of beads. Riri followed her to the bathroom and sat on the end of the tub. She rolled up her soft sleeves and scrubbed the amber with laundry soap and a stiff brush. She scrubbed and rinsed and began all over again.

"I am good at things like this," she said. "Now, unless you hate to discuss it, tell me something about your school."

At first he had nothing to say, but then he told her how stupid the younger boys were and what they were allowed to get away with.

"The younger boys would be seven, eight?" Yes, about that. "A hopeless generation?"

He wasn't sure; he knew that his class had been better.

She reached down and fetched a bottle of something from behind the bathtub and they went back to the sitting room together. They put a lamp between them, and Irina began to polish the amber with cotton soaked in turpentine. After a time the amber began to shine. The smell made him homesick, but not unpleasantly. He carefully selected a necklace when she told him he might take one for his mother, and he rubbed it with a soft cloth. She showed him how to make the beads magnetic by rolling them in his palms.

"You can do that even with plastic," he said.

"Can you? How very sad. It is dead matter."

"Amber is too," he said politely.

"What do you want to be later on? A scientist?"

"A ski instructor." He looked all round the room, at the shelves and curtains and at the bamboo folding screen, and said, "If you didn't live here, who would?"

She replied, "If you see anything that pleases you, you may keep it. I want you to choose your own present. If you don't see anything, we'll go out tomorrow and look in the shops. Does that suit you?" He did not reply. She held the necklace he had picked and said, "Your mother will remember seeing this as I bent down to kiss her good night. Do you like old coins? One of my sons was a collector." In the wicker basket was a lacquered box that contained his uncle's coin collection. He took a coin but it meant nothing to him; he let it fall. It clinked, and he said, "We have a dog now." The dog wore a metal tag that rang when the dog drank out of a china bowl. Through a sudden rainy

blur of new homesickness he saw that she had something else, another lacquered box, full of old cancelled stamps. She showed him a stamp with Hitler
and one with an Italian king. "I've kept funny things," she said. "Like this
beautiful Russian box. It belonged to my grandmother, but after I have died I
expect it will be thrown out. I gave whatever jewelry I had left to my daughters. We never had furniture, so I became attached to strange little baskets and
boxes of useless things. My poor daughters—I had precious little to give. But
they won't be able to wear rings any more than I could. We all come into our
inherited arthritis, these knotted-up hands. Our true heritage. When I was
your age, about, my mother was dying of ... I wasn't told. She took a ring from
under her pillow and folded my hand on it. She said that I could always sell it
if I had to, and no one need know. You see, in those days women had nothing
of their own. They were like brown paper parcels tied with string. They were
handed like parcels from their fathers to their husbands. To make the parcel
look attractive it was decked with curls and piano lessons, and rings and gold
coins and banknotes and shares. After appraising all the decoration, the new
owner would undo the knots."

"Where is that ring?" he said. The blur of tears was forgotten.

"I tried to sell it when I needed money. The decoration on the brown
paper parcel was disposed of by then. Everything thrown, given away. Not by
me. My pearl necklace was sold for Spanish refugees. Victims, flotsam, the
injured, the weak—they were important. I wasn't. The children weren't. I had
my ring. I took it to a municipal pawnshop. It is a place where you take things
and they give you money. I wore dark glasses and turned up my coat collar, like
a spy." He looked as though he understood that. "The man behind the counter
said that I was a married woman and I needed my husband's written consent. I
said the ring was mine. He said nothing could be mine, or something to that
effect. Then he said he might have given me something for the gold in the band
of the ring but the stones were worthless. He said this happened in the finest of
families. Someone had pried the real stones out of their setting."

"Who did that?"

"A husband. Who else would? Someone's husband—mine, or my mother's,
or my mother's mother's, when it comes to that."

"With a knife?" said Riri. He said, "The man might have been pretending.
Maybe he took out the stones and put in glass."

"There wasn't time. And they were perfect imitations—the right shapes
and sizes."

"He might have had glass stones all different sizes."

"The women in the family never wondered if men were lying," she said.
"They never questioned being dispossessed. They were taught to think that lies
were a joke on the liar. That was why they lost out. He gave me the price of the
gold in the band, as a favour, and I left the ring there. I never went back."

He put the lid on the box of stamps, and it fitted; he removed it, put it back, and said, "What time do you turn on your TV?"

"Sometimes never. Why?"

"At home I have it from six o'clock."

The old man came in with a pink-and-white face, bearing about him a smell of cold and of snow. He put down his shopping bag and took things out—chocolate and bottles and newspapers. He said, "I had to go all the way to the station for the papers. There is only one shop open, and even then I had to go round to the back door."

"I warned you that today was Christmas," Irina said.

Mr. Aiken said to Riri, "When I was still a drinking man this was the best hour of the day. If I had a glass now, I could put ice in it. Then I might add water. Then if I had water I could add whiskey. I know it is all the wrong way around, but at least I've started with a glass."

"You had wine with your lunch and gin instead of tea and I believe you had straight gin before lunch," she said, gathering up the beads and coins and the turpentine and making the table Riri's domain again.

"Riri drank that," he said. It was so obviously a joke that she turned her head and put the basket down and covered her laugh with her fingers, as she had when she'd opened the door to him—oh, a long time ago now.

"I haven't a drop of anything left in the house," she said. That didn't matter, the old man said, for he had found what he needed. Riri watched and saw that when he lifted his glass his hand did not tremble at all. What his grandmother had said about that was true.

They had early supper and then Riri, after a courageous try at keeping awake, gave up even on television and let her make his bed of scented sheets, deep pillows, a feather quilt. The two others sat for a long time at the table, with just one lamp, talking in low voices. She had a pile of notebooks from which she read aloud and sometimes she showed Mr. Aiken things. He could see them through the chinks in the bamboo screen. He watched the lamp shadows for a while and then it was as if the lamp had gone out and he slept deeply.

The room was full of mound shapes, as it had been that morning when he arrived. He had not heard them leave the room. His Christmas watch had hands that glowed in the dark. He put on his glasses. It was half past ten. His grandmother was being just a bit loud at the telephone; that was what had woken him up. He rose, put on his slippers, and stumbled out to the bathroom.

"Just answer yes or no," she was saying. "No, he can't. He has been asleep for an hour, two hours, at least.... Don't lie to me—I am bound to find the truth out. Was it a tumor? An extrauterine pregnancy? ... Well, look.... Was she or was she not pregnant? What can you mean by 'not exactly'? If you don't know, who will?" She happened to turn her head, and saw him and said without a change of tone, "Your son is here, in his pajamas; he wants to say good night to you."

She gave up the telephone and immediately went away so that the child could talk privately. She heard him say, "I drank some kind of alcohol."

So that was the important part of the day: not the journey, not the necklace, not even the strange old guest with the comic accent. She could tell from the sound of the child's voice that he was smiling. She picked up his bathrobe, went back to the hall, and put it over his shoulders. He scarcely saw her: he was concentrated on the distant voice. He said, in a matter-of-fact way, "All right, goodbye," and hung up.

"What a lot of things you have pulled out of that knapsack," she said.

"It's a large one. My father had it for military service."

Now, why should that make him suddenly homesick when his father's voice had not? "You are good at looking after yourself," she said. "Independent. No one has to tell you what to do. Of course, your mother had sound training. Once when I was looking for a nurse for your mother and her sisters, a great peasant woman came to see me, wearing a black apron and black buttoned boots. I said, 'What can you teach children?' And she said, 'To be clean and polite.' Your grandfather said, 'Hire her,' and stamped out of the room."

His mother interested, his grandfather bored him. He had the Christian name of a dead old man.

"You will sleep well," his grandmother promised, pulling the feather quilt over him. "You will dream short dreams at first, and by morning they will be longer and longer. The last one of all just before you wake up will be like a film. You will wake up wondering where you are, and then you will hear Mr. Aiken. First he will go round shutting all the windows, then you will hear his bath. He will start the coffee in an electric machine that makes a noise like a door rattling. He will pull on his snow boots with a lot of cursing and swearing and go out to fetch our croissants and the morning papers. Do you know what day it will be? The day after Christmas." He was almost asleep. Next to his watch and his glasses on a table close to the couch was an Astérix book and Irina's Russian box with old stamps in it. "Have you decided you want the stamps?"

"The box. Not the stamps."

He had taken, by instinct, the only object she wanted to keep. "For a special reason?" she said. "Of course, the box is yours. I am only wondering."

"The cover fits," he said.

She knew that the next morning he would have been here forever and that at parting time, four days later, she would have to remind him that leaving was the other half of arriving. She smiled, knowing how sorry he would be to go and how soon he would leave her behind. "This time yesterday ..." he might say, but no more than once. He was asleep. His mouth opened slightly and the hair on his forehead became dark and damp. A doubled-up arm looked uncomfortable but Irina did not interfere; his sunken mind, his unconscious movements, had to be independent, of her or anyone, particularly of her. She did not love him more or less than any of her grandchildren. You see, it all worked out, she was telling him. You, and your mother, and the children being so worried, and my old friend. Anything can be settled for a few days at a time, though not for longer. She put out the light, for which his body was grateful. His mind, at that moment, in a sunny icicle brightness, was not only skiing but flying.

GABRIEL GARCÍA MÁRQUEZ

A Very Old Man with
Enormous Wings

Translated by Gregory Rabassa

Gabriel García Márquez (b. 1928) was born in the Colombian port of Aracataca. Raised in his grandparents' home, he was influenced from an early age by his grandmother's storytelling. He studied law at the National University of Colombia, Bogotá, and during this time published his first stories. In 1948 García Márquez moved to Cartagena, eventually forsaking law for a career in journalism. His first book, Leaf Storm and Other Stories, *in which "A Very Old Man with Enormous Wings" appears, was published in 1955. The next year saw García Márquez living in Paris and travelling to several socialist countries across Europe. Following the Cuban revolution, he worked for Cuba's Prensa Latina. In 1967 García Márquez's goal to achieve international success was realized with the publication of his novel* One Hundred Years of Solitude, *which Pablo Neruda called "the greatest revelation in the Spanish language since* Don Quixote." *Though he wrote several more novels and stories through the 1970s, it was* One Hundred Years of Solitude *that was largely responsible for the Nobel Prize in literature that García Márquez received in 1982. García Márquez currently lives in Mexico City and Barcelona.*

In his essay "The Master's Voice," Robert Coover identifies in García Márquez's storytelling voice an "easy self-assurance and exuberant zest for tale-spinning" that draws heavily on invention and exaggeration. The stories of García Márquez, Borges, and Cortázar have engendered the term "magic realism" in current criticism. M.H. Abrams defines magic realism as prose that interweaves, "in an ever-shifting pattern, a sharply etched realism with fantastic and dreamlike elements" which "violate standard novelistic expectations by ... fusions of the everyday, the fantastic, the mythical, and the nightmarish." The English critic Raymond Williams has interpreted "A Very Old Man with Enormous Wings" as "a parody of the interpretive process.... The reader fictionalized in this story appreciates invention in itself and learns to accept its privileged function." Yet despite the praise that critics have lavished on his fabulous inventiveness, in his 1982 Nobel acceptance lecture, "The Solitude of Latin America," García Márquez articulates a passionate resistance to the magic-realist label:

It is [Latin America's] outsized reality, and not just its literary expression, that has deserved the attention of the Swedish Academy of Letters.... Poets and beggars, musicians and prophets, warriors and scoundrels, all creatures of that unbridled reality, we have had to ask but little of imagination, for our crucial problem has been a lack of conventional means to render our lives believable.... And if these difficulties, whose essence we share, hinder us, it is understandable that the rational talents on this [European] side of the world, exalted in the contemplation of their own cultures, should have found themselves without a valid means to interpret us.... The interpretation of our reality through patterns not our own serves only to make us ever more unknown, ever less free, ever more solitary.

On the third day of rain they had killed so many crabs inside the house that Pelayo had to cross his drenched courtyard and throw them into the sea, because the newborn child had a temperature all night and they thought it was due to the stench. The world had been sad since Tuesday. Sea and sky were a single ash-gray thing and the sands of the beach, which on March nights glimmered like powdered light, had become a stew of mud and rotten shellfish. The light was so weak at noon that when Pelayo was coming back to the house after throwing away the crabs, it was hard for him to see what it was that was moving and groaning in the rear of the courtyard. He had to go very close to see that it was an old man, a very old man, lying face down in the mud, who, in spite of his tremendous efforts, couldn't get up, impeded by his enormous wings.

Frightened by that nightmare, Pelayo ran to get Elisenda, his wife, who was putting compresses on the sick child, and he took her to the rear of the courtyard. They both looked at the fallen body with mute stupor. He was dressed like a ragpicker. There were only a few faded hairs left on his bald skull and very few teeth in his mouth, and his pitiful condition of a drenched great-grandfather had taken away any sense of grandeur he might have had. His huge buzzard wings, dirty and half-plucked, were forever entangled in the mud. They looked at him so long and so closely that Pelayo and Elisenda very soon overcame their surprise and in the end found him familiar. Then they dared speak to him, and he answered in an incomprehensible dialect with a strong sailor's voice. That was how they skipped over the inconvenience of the wings and quite intelligently concluded that he was a lonely castaway from some foreign ship wrecked by the storm. And yet, they called in a neighbor woman who knew everything about life and death to see him, and all she needed was one look to show them their mistake.

"He's an angel," she told them. "He must have been coming for the child, but the poor fellow is so old that the rain knocked him down."

On the following day everyone knew that a flesh-and-blood angel was held captive in Pelayo's house. Against the judgment of the wise neighbor woman, for whom angels in those times were the fugitive survivors of a celestial conspiracy, they did not have the heart to club him to death. Pelayo watched over him all afternoon from the kitchen, armed with his bailiff's club, and before going to bed he dragged him out of the mud and locked him up with the hens in the wire chicken coop. In the middle of the night, when the rain stopped, Pelayo and Elisenda were still killing crabs. A short time afterward the child woke up without a fever and with a desire to eat. Then they felt magnanimous and decided to put the angel on a raft with fresh water and provisions for three days and leave him to his fate on the high seas. But when they went out into the courtyard with the first light of dawn, they found the whole neighborhood in front of the chicken coop having fun with the angel, without the slightest reverence, tossing him things to eat through the openings in the wire as if he weren't a supernatural creature but a circus animal.

Father Gonzaga arrived before seven o'clock, alarmed at the strange news. By that time onlookers less frivolous than those at dawn had already arrived and they were making all kinds of conjectures concerning the captive's future. The simplest among them thought that he should be named mayor of the world. Others of sterner mind felt that he should be promoted to the rank of five-star general in order to win all wars. Some visionaries hoped that he could be put to stud in order to implant on earth a race of winged wise men who could take charge of the universe. But Father Gonzaga, before becoming a priest, had been a robust woodcutter. Standing by the wire, he reviewed his catechism in an instant and asked them to open the door so that he could take a close look at that pitiful man who looked more like a huge decrepit hen among the fascinated chickens. He was lying in a corner drying his open wings in the sunlight among the fruit peels and breakfast leftovers that the early risers had thrown him. Alien to the impertinences of the world, he only lifted his antiquarian eyes and murmured something in his dialect when Father Gonzaga went into the chicken coop and said good morning to him in Latin. The parish priest had his first suspicion of an imposter when he saw that he did not understand the language of God or how to greet His ministers. Then he noticed that seen up close he was much too human: he had an unbearable smell of the outdoors, the back side of his wings was strewn with parasites and his main feathers has been mistreated by terrestrial winds, and nothing about him measured up to the proud dignity of angels. Then he came out of the chicken coop and in a brief sermon warned the curious against the risks of being ingenuous. He reminded them that the devil had the bad habit of making use of carnival tricks in order to confuse the unwary. He argued that if wings were not the essential element in determining the difference between a hawk and an airplane, they were even less so in the recognition of angels. Nevertheless, he promised to write a letter to his bishop so that the latter would write to his primate so that the latter would write to the Supreme Pontiff in order to get the final verdict from the highest courts.

His prudence fell on sterile hearts. The news of the captive angel spread with such rapidity that after a few hours the courtyard had the bustle of a marketplace and they had to call in troops with fixed bayonets to disperse the mob that was about to knock the house down. Elisenda, her spine all twisted from sweeping up so much marketplace trash, then got the idea of fencing in the yard and charging five cents admission to see the angel.

The curious came from far away. A traveling carnival arrived with a flying acrobat who buzzed over the crowd several times, but no one paid any attention to him because his wings were not those of an angel but, rather, those of a sidereal bat. The most unfortunate invalids on earth came in search of health: a poor woman who since childhood had been counting her heartbeats and had run out of numbers; a Portuguese man who couldn't sleep because the noise of the stars disturbed him; a sleep-walker who got up at night to undo the things he had done while awake; and many others with less serious ailments. In the midst of that shipwreck disorder that made the earth tremble, Pelayo and Elisenda were happy with fatigue, for in less than a week they had crammed their rooms with money and the line of pilgrims waiting their turn to enter still reached beyond the horizon.

The angel was the only one who took no part in his own act. He spent his time trying to get comfortable in his borrowed nest, befuddled by the hellish heat of the oil lamps and sacramental candles that had been placed along the wire. At first they tried to make him eat some mothballs, which, according to the wisdom of the wise neighbor woman, were the food prescribed for angels. But he turned them down, just as he turned down the papal lunches that the penitents brought him, and they never found out whether it was because he was an angel or because he was an old man that in the end he ate nothing but eggplant mush. His only supernatural virtue seemed to be patience. Especially during the first days, when the hens pecked at him, searching for the stellar parasites that proliferated in his wings, and the crippled pulled out feathers to touch their defective parts with, and even the most merciful threw stones at him, trying to get him to rise so they could see him standing. The only time they succeeded in arousing him was when they burned his side with an iron for branding steers, for he had been motionless for so many hours that they thought he was dead. He awoke with a start, ranting in his hermetic language and with tears in his eyes, and he flapped his wings a couple of times, which brought on a whirlwind of chicken dung and lunar dust and a gale of panic that did not seem to be of this world. Although many thought that his reaction had been one not of rage but of pain, from then on they were careful not to annoy him, because the majority understood that his passivity was not that of a hero taking his ease but that of a cataclysm in repose.

Father Gonzaga held back the crowd's frivolity with formulas of maidservant inspiration while awaiting the arrival of a final judgment on the nature of the captive. But the mail from Rome showed no sense of urgency. They spent their time finding out if the prisoner had a navel, if his dialect had any connection with Aramaic, how many times he could fit on the head of a pin, or whether he wasn't just a Norwegian with wings. Those meager letters might have come and gone until the end of time if a providential event had not put an end to the priest's tribulations.

It so happened that during those days, among so many other carnival attractions, there arrived in town the traveling show of the woman who had been changed into a spider for having disobeyed her parents. The admission to see her was not only less than the admission to see the angel, but people were permitted to ask her all manner of questions about her absurd state and to examine her up and down so that no one would ever doubt the truth of her horror. She was a frightful tarantula the size of a ram and with the head of a sad maiden. What was most heart-rending, however, was not her outlandish shape but the sincere affliction with which she recounted the details of her misfortune. While still practically a child she had sneaked out of her parents' house to go to a dance, and while she was coming back through the woods after having danced all night without permission, a fearful thunderclap rent the sky in two and through the crack came the lightning bolt of brimstone that changed her into a spider. Her only nourishment came from the meatballs that charitable souls chose to toss into her mouth. A spectacle like that, full of so much human truth and with such a fearful lesson, was bound to defeat without even trying that of a haughty angel who scarcely deigned to look at mortals. Besides, the few miracles attributed to the angel showed a certain mental disorder, like the blind man recover his sight but grew three new teeth, or the paralytic who didn't get to walk but almost won the lottery, and the leper whose sores sprouted sunflowers. Those consolation miracles, which were more like mocking fun, had already ruined the angel's reputation when the woman who had been changed into a spider finally crushed him completely. That was how Father Gonzaga was cured forever of his insomnia and Pelayo's courtyard went back to being as empty as during the time it had rained for three days and crabs walked through the bedrooms.

The owners of the house had no reason to lament. With the money they saved they built a two-story mansion with balconies and gardens and high netting so that crabs wouldn't get in during the winter, and with iron bars on the windows so that angels wouldn't get in. Pelayo also set up a rabbit warren close to town and gave up his job as bailiff for good, and Elisenda bought some satin pumps with high heels and many dresses of iridescent silk, the kind worn on Sunday by the most desirable women in those times. The chicken coop was the only thing that didn't receive any attention. If they washed it down with creolin and burned tears of myrrh inside it every so often, it was not in homage to the angel but to drive away the dungheap stench that still hung everywhere like a ghost and was turning the new house into an old one. At first, when the child learned to walk, they were careful that he not get too close to the chicken coop. But then they began to lose their fears and got used to the smell, and before the child got his second teeth he'd gone inside the chicken coop to play, where the wires were falling apart. The angel was no less standoffish with him than with other mortals, but he tolerated the most ingenious infamies with the patience of a dog who had no illusions. They both came down with chicken pox at the same time. The doctor who took care of the child couldn't resist the temptation to listen to the angel's heart, and he found so much whistling in the heart and so many sounds in his kidneys that it seemed impossible for him to be alive. What surprised him most, however, was the logic of his wings. They seemed so natural on the completely human organism that he couldn't understand why other men didn't have them too.

When the child began school it had been some time since the sun and rain had caused the collapse of the chicken coop. The angel went dragging himself about here and there like a stray dying man. They would drive him out of the bedroom with a broom and a moment later find him in the kitchen. He seemed to be in so many places at the same time that they grew to think that he'd been duplicated, that he was reproducing himself all through the house, and the exasperated and unhinged Elisenda shouted that it was awful living in that hell full of angels. He could scarcely eat and his antiquarian eyes had also become so foggy that he went about bumping into posts. All he had left were the bare cannulae of his last feathers. Pelayo threw a blanket over him and extended him the charity of letting him sleep in the shed, and only then did they notice that he had a temperature at night, and was delirious with the tongue twisters of an old Norwegian. That was one of the few times they became alarmed, for they thought he was going to die and not even the wise neighbor woman had been able to tell them what to do with dead angels.

And yet he not only survived his worst winter, but seemed improved with the first sunny days. He remained motionless for several days in the farthest corner of the courtyard, where no one would see him, and at the beginning of December some large, stiff feathers began to grow on his wings, the feathers of a scarecrow, which looked more like another misfortune of decrepitude. But he must have known the reason for those changes, for he was quite careful that no one should notice them, that no one should hear the sea chanteys that he sometimes sang under the stars. One morning Elisenda was cutting some bunches of onions for lunch when a wind that seemed to come from the high seas blew into the kitchen. Then she went to the window and caught the angel in his first attempts at flight. They were so clumsy that his fingernails opened a furrow in the vegetable patch and he was on the point of knocking the shed down with the ungainly flapping that slipped on the light and couldn't get a grip on the air. But he did manage to gain altitude. Elisenda let out a sigh of relief, for herself and for him, when she saw him pass over the last houses, holding himself up in some way with the risky flapping of a senile vulture. She kept watching him even when she was through cutting the onions and she kept on watching until it was no longer possible for her to see him, because then he was no longer an annoyance in her life but an imaginary dot on the horizon of the sea.

CONNIE GAULT

INSPECTION OF A
SMALL VILLAGE

*Connie Gault (b. 1949), born in rural Saskatchewan, is both a playwright
and writer of fiction. Relatively new on the Canadian literary scene, hers
is a fresh, clear voice from a generation of writers who are not bound by
the usual conventions of storytelling. Her subject is the human imagination. As she moves from the past to the present and from rural settings in
Saskatchewan to the capitals of Europe, her characters imagine their
worlds into being, and they dream their fellow characters into existence.
"Inspection of a Small Village" comes from a collection of short stories by
the same name, published in 1996, which won the Saskatchewan Best
Fiction Award; the story itself won the* Prairie Schooner *Reader's Choice
Award from the University of Nebraska in 1994. The story tells of a
young woman who sits in the library of the village in which she was born,
imagining her own coming into being and reinventing herself.*

*Currently living in Regina, Connie Gault is married and the mother
of two grown sons. Other published works include a previous collection
of short stories,* Some of Eve's Daughters, *and two plays,* Sky *and* The
Soft Eclipse.

In a room defined by tables and windows the adulteress sits at her task. She
has set herself the task to occupy her mind. The room is at the provincial
archives; the adulteress is waiting for a folder of information on the town in
which she was born. She has decided to stop treating herself like someone who
may break with any breath she takes, but she holds herself delicately without
realizing what she is doing and she sits very straight, with her hands in her lap
and her head just so on her neck.

A slight young man slides the folder across the table toward her. He turns
and disappears behind a swinging door without a word. This is a quiet room.
Any words that are spoken by the half-dozen people distributed among the
tables (with maximum space between them) are quiet words.

The folder contains the archives' local histories clippings file for the town in which she was born. Of the four items in the file, only one interests her enough that she picks it up and reads it. She holds the few pages of the badly typed report up to the fluorescent light that blankets the room, that cancels the light from the windows. She reads the words over and over and wills them to replace her thoughts. This is her task, this expulsion of her thoughts. It's a task appropriate to her dilemma, which is not so much that of being an adulteress as that of being sorry she is herself. She is young and has come against the fact of herself, a person born here, now. She thinks if she were a person born there, then, everything would be different. Given a choice, she'd be born French. Even better, she'd be born in a French movie. Those people really don't give a damn.

Report on a Systematic Inspection of the Village of Kerrody
July 8, 1958

Kerrody is a small thriving Village, busy by virtue of its central location in the southwest sector of Health Region No. 2. With an estimated population of 310, there are 119 houses standing and 5 new buildings under construction. Most of the single dwellings are small and well-maintained. This pleasant Village has no slum area to speak of, no corrupting influences. The outhouses are in good repair.

The report was written by the doctor who was the Regional Medical Health Officer at the time. Likely he had no resemblance to the man the adulteress pictures; she sees a man with his elbows on the table at the Kerrody hotel and his head in his hands. A conscientious man. It is Dr. Tolley she sees with his head in his hands. The adulteress has given her medical health officer the name Tolley because that is the name of the man who has made her heart sing. She doesn't really see him sitting at the table with his head in his hands so much as she feels the presence of his body, and "heart sing" isn't the euphemism she first thought. She can't quite erase it.

Dr. Tolley is sitting in the Kerrody hotel eating a chicken sandwich. He's not sitting with his head in his hands. Not yet. He has a report to write. A report that looks like seersucker from the sweat on his hands. No, he's not anxious yet. It's hot. It's a very hot day but his hands don't sweat.

Dr. Tolley eats his sandwich and begins his report. He is new at his job but already he is determined to work as he goes while in the field and to spend as much time as possible with his wife when he's home. If Dr. Tolley is ever inclined to be smug it is on two accounts, his efficiency and his great good fortune in marriage. He is humble enough to realize that neither have come to him through his own efforts to attain them. Rather, they have been by-products of his attempts to overcome his one real weakness, his fear that he isn't good enough. He fears not being good enough in his work and with women, and for the same reason: he harbours a slight but seemingly irremediable aversion to the human body. He became a physician to conquer the body and, like others equally pretentious, he has failed. The body, in all the thousands of manifestations that have passed before his eyes and under his hands, in spite of passing before his eyes and under his hands, has gone on being corrupted and insulted by disease and injury and abuse. The body in its most pristine forms displays its ugly potential. His wife has sensed his dilemma and protects him. She never dresses or undresses in front of him and always slips between their sheets in attire no one would remark on if the house caught fire and she had to stand on the lawn with their neighbours in the middle of the night watching it burn.

The adulteress tries to focus again on the words in the report, where no one's wife is mentioned. But the man named Tolley lingers. How has he made her heart sing? Only by wanting her body and by being unable to keep her from knowing. That's all it takes to make her heart sing, to set her mind ticking, timed for any moment, just say the word, look the look. Or say nothing, look nothing: think and she'll know.

Her doctor's head is in his hands. No, not yet. He is sitting with his pen poised, going over his thoughts. And his thoughts are all of the town in which the adulteress was born. That morning Dr. Tolley walked up and down the back alleys of Kerrody. He spent more than an hour of a hot morning stepping in and out of outhouses, making notes on the night soil levels and swatting flies away from his face so that, forty years later, she will read his meticulous thoughts.

She almost believes this. She doesn't understand it—why in the world she's doing this, imagining him this way, but she almost believes it. She smiles to think of him holding his breath, stepping into yet another biffy in a time just before she was born, all for her, somehow.

Sewage and Slop

Except for seven houses in which modern sewage removal systems have been installed, and appear to be pumping satisfactorily, all the private dwellings in the Village continue to employ pit privies. My one concern with these privies, during a routine inspection, is in regard to night soil levels. When they reach approximately 4 feet from the surface, these nearly full pits become a dangerous source of fly breeding.

Dr. Tolley is taking his lunch late. Yes, he's there, at the table, with his chicken sandwich and his crumpled report. He is the only person eating in the hotel, having just inspected the kitchen. The hotel owners knew he'd be coming sometime during the month as did the owners of the other premises he plans to inspect. He wanted to start by being strict but fair. He believes it's in the interest of everyone to provoke higher standards before he arrives rather than to make surprise visits and uncover poor conditions. He thinks about things like this even though he's only begun this job.

He underlines the word Hotel for his next heading and looks over his shoulder to be sure what he writes can't be seen by another. He is inclined to rate the hotel more highly than it deserves because he has become acquainted with the man and his wife who run it, but he can't know exactly what he will say until he writes it. He's learned that in writing, one thing can lead to another and that he might surprise himself, leaping from toilets to sinks to refrigerators, with an opinion he doesn't know he holds. In this way writing is like diagnosis. He was becoming a good diagnostician when he quit his medical practice; he was finding that by emptying his mind and letting his senses and intuition carry him, one thing invariably led to another. Unfortunately the end result was only briefly satisfying. What he won by successful diagnosis he often lost for lack of a cure.

She likes him so much, the young adulteress. Isn't that worth something?

Hotel
There is one hotel in the Village. Its sixteen rooms are of such small proportions (8'x10') that they are not suitable for double occupancy. I am assured that they are usually required by single guests. The bedrooms are adequately furnished and appear to be regularly cleaned. I am of the opinion that the comfort of guests could be increased by the installation of louvred ventilation above each door.

Dr. Tolley is of the private opinion that more than louvred ventilation will be required if he is going to get to sleep tonight. The upstairs rooms have already reached a temperature close to a hundred degrees. However, it's not the hotel's fault he's arrived in a heat wave. Dr. Tolley takes his handkerchief out of his breast pocket and wipes his face. Sweat is unbecoming to a member of the medical profession and this poses a problem because he feels he must wear a suit in the field and should remove his jacket only in his own room, whatever the consequences to his personal comfort.

The cook, who is co-owner of the hotel with her husband, comes out of the kitchen to clear his table. He slides his elbow across his report and declines her offer of lemonade. He says he might drop in later for a cold drink.

The cook is a tall woman with a slouch that gives her more of a stomach than she should have for her weight. She stands close to him with her hands clasped over her protruding apron. He notices that her hands are red and rough and very clean and commends her on them.

"I just made pastry," she says. "It's always good for cleaning your finger-nails."

He can't tell if she's teasing him. Her face is deadpan. He slips the pages of his report into his briefcase and excuses himself.

When he is outside walking down the one cement sidewalk, with the sun high overhead and no more than inches of shade anywhere, the heat sizzles on his skin. It feels hot enough to scorch the fabric of his suit. A wash of sweat cascades from his back and chest and collects at his waistband. Within seconds his waistband is soaked and his belt slides up and down, chafing his middle. He ducks into the Red and White store. The difference in light blinds him momentarily. He sighs as the impression of coolness almost like a breeze floats over him.

"Everybody does that when they come in today," the store owner says. He is just like everybody else, Dr. Tolley, just like any man doing his job the best he can. This morning, after the outhouses, he went with the mayor to visit the well, the village rest rooms, the nuisance ground and the cemetery. On his list for the afternoon are the two general stores, the restaurant, the meat market, the hairdresser's, the hospital, and the dairy, then he must meet with the local medical practitioner. Up and down Main Street he will walk on the shady side, once it develops, and he will smile into the heat, his only obstacle. He mops his face good-naturedly now, in the Red and White store, and grins. He is just like everybody else.

At the end of the afternoon, he hasn't quite accomplished all he set out to do. He decides to put off the dairy for the morning on his way out of town. This makes him a little early for his meeting with the town's only doctor, but he thinks that's preferable to being late. As he stands in the vestibule before the doctor's office, he mops his face for the hundredth time. His grin is weary, not much more than practice. He does not like Bob Berriman. Nevertheless, he's accepted his invitation to take supper with him.

People tend to accept Dr. Berriman's invitations. The adulteress, sitting in the quiet room full of tables and windows, remembers this without knowing how she remembers.

They had planned to meet later, at the Chinese restaurant, but Dr. Tolley is dropping in to see if his colleague will join him for a drink first at the hotel. He thinks a few ounces of whiskey will make supper bearable.

The vestibule is tiny and panelled with dark wood. Stairs to the second floor face the outside entrance. To Dr. Tolley's right is the office door, closed because office hours are over. A square of wavy glass in the top of the door lets a faint shadowy light pass either way but doesn't allow him to see inside. He opens the door.

Directly in front of him a young woman is scrubbing the board floor on her hands and knees. She is wearing short shorts and a white cotton brassiere.

He sees her from the side. He sees the tan and white wings of her breasts folded into the brassiere, and her raised, startled face. She has stopped her scrubbing and looked up, but not at Dr. Tolley. She has raised her eyes to Dr. Berriman, who leans against the receptionist's desk with his feet stretched before him, watching her. This tableau lasts only a second or two, then Bob Berriman, his face angry and red, crosses the room with his hand outstretched. He stands in front of the kneeling woman and shakes Dr. Tolley's hand. His footprints remain on the wet floorboards.

"Ready early, are we?" he says. He scoops his jacket off a hook, takes Dr. Tolley's elbow, and steers him out of the office. Dr. Tolley has no opportunity for a second look. A second look isn't necessary.

Bob Berriman asks questions on the way to the hotel, questions about Dr. Tolley's day which Dr. Tolley answers. But not exactly as if nothing has happened. They drink their doubles at the hotel bar in silence. In the Chinese restaurant, where the service is quick, they discuss mutual acquaintances and Dr. Tolley's wife (briefly, Dr. Tolley doesn't like her name on Berriman's lips), and then the possibility of the townspeople adopting septic tanks in place of outhouses. They stretch the meal out with coffee until just after eight when their unexpressed mutual dislike overcomes the conversation and they part. With a long, bright evening before him and his hotel room unbearably hot, Dr. Tolley takes his briefcase to the bar and makes himself busy.

He begins to write about the meat market. He writes that the chopping block was sweet and clean, that the display cases looked as if they had been scoured, that the standard of storage for both implements and meat was high. His pen skims the paper, describing the seemly and professional methods of the butcher in the operation of his shop.

He reports that conditions at the hairdresser in the village were found to be unsatisfactory.

> ... but it is to be hoped that what I discovered did not represent the usual custom. Neither formalin nor dettol were utilized for sterilizing scissors or combs and one must protest the practice of draping the same rather grimy cape over each unwary client.

Next Dr. Tolley reports on the horrors of the pool hall toilet and the potentially risky practice of discarding hospital garbage in flimsy, insecure containers. And when he has finished that, he caps his pen and puts it down. It comes to him that maybe he has been putting too black an interpretation on the tableau he witnessed in Dr. Berriman's office. Maybe the young woman removed her top in order to be cooler while she worked, not realizing that Berriman was still in the inner office, and Berriman came out and surprised her. Maybe she got up to put her top back on and Berriman said not to bother, she was as decently covered as she would have been at the beach and after all he was a doctor. Maybe she was a casual young woman and agreed. Maybe the fear he thought he felt in the room was his own fear.

Dr. Tolley packs up his papers and takes himself to his room, away from the eyes of two old men who have been drinking coffee in the corner all evening, who have just switched to beer. His room is stifling; it is not possible to remain there.

The thermometer nailed to the hotel wall by the front door says eighty. He contemplated going out in his shirt sleeves, yet he is still dressed in his suit. Even though it's nearly midnight. He could meet someone. It's not for himself he wants to look respectable but for the office.

He strolls up and down the streets and alleys of the village, the same streets and alleys he travelled this morning. They look different in the dark but he hardly notices them; he might be anywhere.

The entire town can be walked in half an hour. In half an hour he turns up Main Street and heads for the hotel. An unexpected sound causes him to notice his surroundings. The sound is of a door opening. He is outside Berriman's office building. He watches as the door swings slowly back against the stucco and a figure steps out into the darkness. It is the young office cleaner. She is completely naked. He thinks that: completely naked. While he watches her walk toward him, he understands: it is a state that can be complete.

She is sleepwalking. Her eyes are open but unseeing. He backs out of her way. She passes close to him (smells of warm bedclothes) and turns to walk down the sidewalk. He follows her.

Now he sees everything in sharp focus, as in a dream. He sees the pock marks in the cement sidewalk and the pebbles in front of her feet, where her feet will land. He hears the soft pad of her bare soles on the cement. On the soles of his own feet, through his shoes, he believes he can feel the coolness and graininess of the cement surface, just as she feels it on her skin.

She passes under the street lamp on the corner. Her dark hair is for a second back lit then the light falls on her shoulders, on the curve of her buttocks and down her calves. She wears a paleness on her torso, like a transparent bathing suit. She walks easily and he walks behind her and the false fronts and cluttered signs and dusty windows of Kerrody roll past them and fall away.

There's only the gleam of the gravel road and the similar faint gleam of her skin. She walks. He follows. A beautiful quiet prevails. He's never been out in the night before, like this. He exhales; it's possible he's been holding his breath since leaving the town. With his breathing resumed, he starts to hear his brogues crunching down, scattering small stones, and the chirping of frogs, loud and exuberant as birds' singing. A splash. So they are near the slough, about a mile from town.

She stops, then turns and walks into the ditch.

Dr. Tolley thinks: she will walk into the slough and drown herself. Then the absurdity of the situation strikes him. He has been following her as if part of her dream, as if a spectator in her dream, with no volition of his own—or as if the dream were his own, as if he had dreamed her and could only watch to see how his dream would end—while in fact he is a responsible medical doctor, a respectable married man, following a naked woman down a country road. Why hasn't he woken her gently, covered her decently and taken her home?

At the edge of the slough is a large rock where that morning, driving into the town, he saw two children fishing. She has climbed up onto that rock. He can just see her pale skin, the slip of water, dark shapes and the sky which, he suddenly notices, is crammed with stars. He has never seen so many stars, near and far, layers and layers of them from the brilliant to the distant almost unseeable. Just for a second he forgets who he is. Then is embarrassed for himself. How easily an atmosphere can fool a man into thinking nothing matters.

She is awake now, she has stepped down from the rock. She is climbing to the road from the ditch and hasn't yet seen him, and then sees him. The sound she makes is a whimper. His body responds with something like pity—a similar fear. Then he remembers who he is.

"I'm Dr. Tolley, the Regional Health Inspector," he says. They look into one another's faces. They both laugh. They laugh harder. It is so absurd, who he is. He takes off his suit jacket and hands it to her. They walk back to town silently. Dr. Tolley allows himself to think of her breasts and belly and buttocks inside his suit jacket.

The door opens as they walk up the path to Berriman's office building. The young woman's husband stands in the vestibule watching them. Before they reach him, he turns and walks up the stairs, which are lit by a bare bulb above the landing. The young woman follows her husband and Dr. Tolley follows her up into a suite of rooms.

"Excuse us," the young man says politely to Dr. Tolley. He leads his wife into their bedroom, closing the door behind them. A few seconds later he emerges with Dr. Tolley's suit jacket.

"Thank you," he says as he hands the jacket to Dr. Tolley. Dr. Tolley drapes it over his arm. The young man stands marooned in the centre of the room. Dr. Tolley could introduce himself, which might be reassuring. He could talk in a clinical way about sleepwalking. He could explain how he'd happened on her. But it all seems superfluous. Without a word he walks out of the room and leaves the young couple behind.

In the morning he drinks a pot of coffee. He sits at his table in the hotel with his head in his hands. The couple who run the hotel speculate, in the kitchen, about what kind of night he had and how long he'll last in this job. He knows they'll be talking about him and doesn't care. All night he lay semi-conscious in a heat-drugged fugue.

He skips the dairy. No, he's much too conscientious to do that. He drives out and drags himself around the milk house, sniffing at the cans, bottles, filters, cooler, and milker, and then he drags himself around the stable and the yard. He is so grateful for the dairy's cleanliness and the remarkable absence of flies that he will give it his most glowing commendation.

Before he turns onto the highway to head home, Dr. Tolley stops to remove his suit jacket. Another hot day is predicted and he can be forgiven, he thinks, for driving in his shirt sleeves in the privacy of his own car. He stops the car at the intersection and steps out to take his jacket off. Just for a second he appreciates the benevolent sky, his solitude. As is his usual practice, he folds the jacket with the lining facing outwards. When he gets into the car, he places the jacket on the passenger seat beside him and starts in third and stalls. That is the last time he will betray himself.

In the room of many tables and windows, the adulteress tries to remember the real story of the town in which she was born. She was very young when they moved away and has little memory of the 119 houses and the small businesses mentioned in the medical health officer's report. Her only vivid memory isn't even her own, it comes from a time before she was born, the memory of a story she heard many times of a short spell in her mother's life when her mother sleepwalked. The high point of the story is the time her mother escaped naked into the night. In the story, the adulteress's father discovered her mother was missing and hauled himself out of bed, pulled on his pants and a shirt, and followed her down Main Street. It was the adulteress's father who brought her mother home. Order was restored and anyone who was told the story laughed to think her mother—her shy young mother of all people—had walked naked through the dark streets where anyone might have seen her.

There is another memory that didn't get made into a story, a more shadowy memory that had to do with the doctor who owned the building they lived in, who had his office on the ground floor. The adulteress's mother cleaned the office for him in exchange for some money off the rent. But that was in a different time and place and the memory is too shadowy to get hold of.

She slips the report into its folder. She is thinking about her mother opening the door, stepping out. She thinks: I've inherited my mother's body. Forgetting where she is, she lifts her arms and stretches—her body is tired from sitting so long perusing those few pages. Across the room, a man looks up.

CHARLOTTE PERKINS GILMAN

THE YELLOW WALLPAPER

Charlotte Perkins Gilman (1860–1935) is best known today for "The Yellow Wallpaper" (1892), a story embraced by contemporary critics as a classic of nineteenth-century literature and as an emblem of feminist rebellion. This story is based loosely on the author's experience as the patient of Dr. S. Weir Mitchell, a prominent physician who specialized in the treatment of women with "nervous prostration." For Gilman, writing "The Yellow Wallpaper" was an act of defiance and of self-recovery in the face of medical advice that admonished her to "live as domestic a life as far as possible," to "have but two hours' intellectual life a day," and "never to touch pen, brush, or pencil again" as long as she lived. Having rejected this regime when she recognized that it was driving her mad, Gilman sent a copy of her story to Dr. Mitchell. He never acknowledged its receipt, Gilman said, but "many years later I was told that the great specialist had admitted to friends of his that he had altered his treatment of neurasthenia since reading 'The Yellow Wallpaper.'"

Gilman was born in Hartford, Connecticut. Her father abandoned his family shortly after Gilman's birth, and her early years were spent in relative poverty, a circumstance that accounts for her concern with social injustice, for her strong moral and social commitment to work, and for her determination to be independent and self-supporting. She studied art and earned her living through teaching and commercial design. In 1884 she married fellow artist Charles Stetson, but their marriage did not survive Gilman's extreme depression following the birth of their daughter. She left her husband in 1888 and later married George Houghton Gilman.

Gilman was widely known as a lecturer, a writer of feminist tracts, and the author of such sociological studies as Women and Economics *(1898),* Concerning Children *(1900),* The Home *(1904),* Human Work *(1904), and* The Man-Made World *(1911). She believed that women should be educated and financially independent and that they should fully contribute to the shaping of society. Suffering from cancer, Gilman brought about her death in 1935 with typical self-determination by chloroforming herself.*

It is very seldom that mere ordinary people like John and myself secure ancestral halls for the summer.

A colonial mansion, a hereditary estate, I would say a haunted house and reach the height of romantic felicity—but that would be asking too much of fate!

Still I will proudly declare that there is something queer about it.

Else, why should it be let so cheaply? And why have stood so long untenanted?

John laughs at me, of course, but one expects that.

John is practical in the extreme. He has no patience with faith, an intense horror of superstition, and he scoffs openly at any talk of things not to be felt and seen and put down in figures.

John is a physician, and *perhaps*—(I would not say it to a living soul, of course, but this is dead paper and a great relief to my mind)—*perhaps* that is one reason I do not get well faster.

You see, he does not believe I am sick! And what can one do?

If a physician of high standing, and one's own husband, assures friends and relatives that there is really nothing the matter with one but temporary nervous depression—a slight hysterical tendency—what is one to do?

My brother is also a physician, and also of high standing, and he says the same thing.

So I take phosphates or phosphites—whichever it is—and tonics, and air and exercise, and journeys, and am absolutely forbidden to "work" until I am well again.

Personally, I disagree with their ideas.

Personally, I believe that congenial work, with excitement and change, would do me good.

But what is one to do?

I did write for a while in spite of them; but it *does* exhaust me a good deal—having to be so sly about it, or else meet with heavy opposition.

I sometimes fancy that in my condition, if I had less opposition and more society and stimulus—but John says the very worst thing I can do is to think about my condition, and I confess it always makes me feel bad.

So I will let it alone and talk about the house.

The most beautiful place! It is quite alone, standing well back from the road, quite three miles from the village. It makes me think of English places that you read about, for there are hedges and walls and gates that lock, and lots of separate little houses for the gardeners and people.

There is a *delicious* garden! I never saw such a garden—large and shady, full of box-bordered paths, and lined with long grape-covered arbors with seats under them.

There were greenhouses, but they are all broken now.

There was some legal trouble, I believe, something about the heirs and co-heirs; anyhow, the place has been empty for years.

That spoils my ghostliness, I am afraid, but I don't care—there is something strange about the house—I can feel it.

I even said so to John one moonlight evening, but he said what I felt was a draught, and shut the window.

I get unreasonably angry with John sometimes. I'm sure I never used to be so sensitive. I think it is due to this nervous condition.

But John says if I feel so I shall neglect proper self-control; so I take pains to control myself—before him, at least, and that makes me very tired.

I don't like our room a bit. I wanted one downstairs that opened onto the piazza and had roses all over the window, and such pretty old-fashioned chintz hangings! But John would not hear of it.

He said there was only one window and not room for two beds, and no near room for him if he took another.

He is very careful and loving, and hardly lets me stir without special direction.

I have a schedule prescription for each hour in the day; he takes all care from me, and so I feel basely ungrateful not to value it more.

He said he came here solely on my account, that I was to have perfect rest and all the air I could get. "Your exercise depends on your strength, my dear," said he, "and your food somewhat on your appetite; but air you can absorb all the time." So we took the nursery at the top of the house.

It is a big, airy room, the whole floor nearly, with windows that look all ways, and air and sunshine galore. It was nursery first, and then playroom and gymnasium, I should judge, for the windows are barred for little children, and there are rings and things in the walls.

The paint and paper look as if a boys' school had used it. It is stripped off—the paper—in great patches all around the head of my bed, about as far as I can reach, and in a great place on the other side of the room low down. I never saw a worse paper in my life. One of those sprawling, flamboyant patterns committing every artistic sin.

It is dull enough to confuse the eye in following, pronounced enough constantly to irritate and provoke study, and when you follow the lame uncertain curves for a little distance they suddenly commit suicide—plunge off at outrageous angles, destroy themselves in unheard-of contradictions.

The color is repellent, almost revolting: a smouldering unclean yellow, strangely faded by the slow-turning sunlight. It is a dull yet lurid orange in some places, a sickly sulphur tint in others.

No wonder the children hated it! I should hate it myself if I had to live in this room long.

There comes John, and I must put this away—he hates to have me write a word.

We have been here two weeks, and I haven't felt like writing before, since that first day.

I am sitting by the window now, up in this atrocious nursery, and there is nothing to hinder my writing as much as I please, save lack of strength.

John is away all day, and even some nights when his cases are serious.

I am glad my case is not serious!

But these nervous troubles are dreadfully depressing.

John does not know how much I really suffer. He knows there is no reason to suffer, and that satisfies him.

Of course it is only nervousness. It does weigh on me so not to do my duty in any way!

I meant to be such a help to John, such a real rest and comfort, and here I am a comparative burden already!

Nobody would believe what an effort it is to do what little I am able—to dress and entertain, and order things.

It is fortunate Mary is so good with the baby. Such a dear baby!

And yet I *cannot* be with him, it makes me so nervous.

I suppose John never was nervous in his life. He laughs at me so about this wallpaper!

At first he meant to repaper the room, but afterward he said that I was letting it get the better of me, and that nothing was worse for a nervous patient that to give way to such fancies.

He said that after the wallpaper was changed it would be the heavy bedstead, and then the barred windows, and then that gate at the head of the stairs, and so on.

"You know the place is doing you good," he said, "and really, dear, I don't care to renovate the house just for a three months' rental."

"Then do let us go downstairs," I said. "There are such pretty rooms there."

Then he took me in his arms and called me a blessed little goose, and said he would go down cellar, if I wished, and have it whitewashed into the bargain.

But he is right enough about the beds and windows and things.

It is as airy and comfortable a room as anyone need wish, and, of course, I would not be so silly as to make him uncomfortable just for a whim.

I'm really getting quite fond of the big room, all but that horrid paper.

Out of one window I can see the garden—those mysterious deep-shaded arbors, the riotous old-fashioned flowers, and bushes and gnarly trees.

Out of another I get a lovely view of the bay and a little private wharf belonging to the estate. There is a beautiful shaded lane that runs down there from the house. I always fancy I see people walking in these numerous paths and arbors, but John has cautioned me not to give way to fancy in the least. He says that with my imaginative power and habit of story-making, a nervous weakness like mine is sure to lead to all manner of excited fancies, and that I ought to use my will and good sense to check the tendency. So I try.

I think sometimes that if I were only well enough to write a little it would relieve the press of ideas and rest me.

But I find I get pretty tired when I try.

It is so discouraging not to have any advice and companionship about my work. When I get really well, John says we will ask Cousin Henry and Julia down for a long visit; but he says he would as soon put fireworks in my pillow-case as to let me have those stimulating people about now.

I wish I could get well faster.

But I must not think about that. This paper looks to me as if it *knew* what a vicious influence it had!

There is a recurrent spot where the pattern lolls like a broken neck and two bulbous eyes stare at you upside down.

I get positively angry with the impertinence of it and the everlastingness. Up and down and sideways they crawl, and those absurd unblinking eyes are everywhere. There is one place where two breadths didn't match, and the eyes go all up and down the line, one a little higher than the other.

I never saw so much expression in an inanimate thing before, and we all know how much expression they have! I used to lie awake as a child and get more entertainment and terror out of blank walls and plain furniture than most children could find in a toy-store.

I remember what a kindly wink the knobs of our big old bureau used to have, and there was one chair that always seemed like a strong friend.

I used to feel that if any of the other things looked too fierce I could always hop into that chair and be safe.

The furniture in this room is no worse than inharmonious, however, for we had to bring it all from downstairs. I suppose when this was used as a play-room they had to take the nursery things out, and no wonder! I never saw such ravages as the children have made here.

The wallpaper, as I said before, is torn off in spots, and it sticketh closer than a brother—they must have had perseverance as well as hatred.

Then the floor is scratched and gouged and splintered, the plaster itself is dug out here and there, and this great heavy bed, which is all we found in the room, looks as if it had been through the wars.

But I don't mind a bit—only the paper.

There comes John's sister. Such a dear girl as she is, and so careful of me! I must not let her find me writing.

She is a perfect and enthusiastic housekeeper, and hopes for no better profession. I verily believe she thinks it is the writing which made me sick!

But I can write when she is out, and see her a long way off from these windows.

There is one that commands the road, a lovely shaded winding road, and one that just looks off over the country. A lovely country, too, full of great elms and velvet meadows.

This wallpaper has a kind of subpattern in a different shade, a particularly irritating one, for you can only see it in certain lights, and not clearly then.

But in the places where it isn't faded and where the sun is just so—I can see a strange, provoking, formless sort of figure that seems to skulk about behind that silly and conspicuous front design.

There's sister on the stairs!

Well, the Fourth of July is over! The people are all gone, and I am tired out. John thought it might do me good to see a little company, so we just had Mother and Nellie and the children down for a week.

Of course I didn't do a thing. Jennie sees to everything now.

But it tired me all the same.

John says if I don't pick up faster he shall send me to Weir Mitchell in the fall.

But I don't want to go there at all. I had a friend who was in his hands once, and she says he is just like John and my brother, only more so!

Besides, it is such an undertaking to go so far.

I don't feel as if it was worthwhile to turn my hand over for anything, and I'm getting dreadfully fretful and querulous.

I cry at nothing, and cry most of the time.

Of course I don't when John is here, or anybody else, but when I am alone.

And I am alone a good deal just now. John is kept in town very often by serious cases, and Jennie is good and lets me alone when I want her to.

So I walk a little in the garden or down that lovely lane, sit on the porch under the roses, and lie down up here a good deal.

I'm getting really fond of the room in spite of the wallpaper. Perhaps *because* of the wallpaper.

It dwells in my mind so!

I lie here on this great immovable bed—it is nailed down, I believe—and follow that pattern about by the hour. It is as good as gymnastics, I assure you. I start, we'll say, at the bottom, down in the corner over there where it has not been touched, and I determine for the thousandth time that I *will* follow that pointless pattern to some sort of a conclusion.

I know a little of the principle of design, and I know this thing was not arranged on any laws of radiation, or alternation, or repetition, or symmetry, or anything else that I ever heard of.

It is repeated, of course, by the breadths, but not otherwise.

Looked at in one way, each breadth stands alone; the bloated curves and flourishes—a kind of "debased Romanesque" with delirium tremens go waddling up and down in isolated columns of fatuity.

But, on the other hand, they connect diagonally, and the sprawling outlines run off in great slanting waves of optic horror, like a lot of wallowing seaweeds in full chase.

The whole thing goes horizontally, too, at least it seems so, and I exhaust myself trying to distinguish the order of its going in that direction.

They have used a horizontal breadth for a frieze, and that adds wonderfully to the confusion.

There is one end of the room where it is almost intact, and there, when the crosslights fade and the low sun shines directly upon it, I can almost fancy radiation after all—the interminable grotesque seems to form around a common center and rush off in headlong plunges of equal distraction.

It makes me tired to follow it. I will take a nap, I guess.

I don't know why I should write this.

I don't want to.

I don't feel able.

And I know John would think it absurd. But I *must* say what I feel and think in some way—it is such a relief!

But the effort is getting to be greater than the relief.

Half the time now I am awfully lazy, and lie down ever so much. John says I mustn't lose my strength, and has me take cod liver oil and lots of tonics and things, to say nothing of ale and wines and rare meat.

Dear John! He loves me very dearly, and hates to have me sick. I tried to have a real earnest reasonable talk with him the other day, and tell him how I wish he would let me go and make a visit to Cousin Henry and Julia.

But he said I wasn't able to go, nor able to stand it after I got there; and I did not make out a very good case for myself, for I was crying before I had finished.

It is getting to be a great effort for me to think straight. Just this nervous weakness, I suppose.

And dear John gathered me up in his arms, and just carried me upstairs and laid me on the bed, and sat by me and read to me till it tired my head.

He said I was his darling and his comfort and all he had, and that I must take care of myself for his sake, and keep well.

He says no one but myself can help me out of it, that I must use my will and self-control and not let any silly fancies run away with me.

There's one comfort—the baby is well and happy, and does not have to occupy this nursery with the horrid wallpaper.

If we had not used it, that blessed child would have! What a fortunate escape! Why, I wouldn't have a child of mine, an impressionable little thing, live in such a room for worlds.

I never thought of it before, but it is lucky that John kept me here after all; I can stand it so much easier than a baby, you see.

Of course I never mention it to them any more—I am too wise—but I keep watch for it all the same.

There are things in the wallpaper that nobody knows about but me, or ever will.

Behind that outside pattern the dim shapes get clearer every day.

It is always the same shape, only very numerous.

And it is like a woman stooping down and creeping about behind that pattern. I don't like it a bit. I wonder—I begin to think—I wish John would take me away from here!

It is so hard to talk with John about my case, because he is so wise, and because he loves me so.

But I tried it last night.

It was moonlight. The moon shines in all around just as the sun does.

I hate to see it sometimes, it creeps so slowly, and always comes in by one window or another.

John was asleep and I hated to waken him, so I kept still and watched the moonlight on that undulating wallpaper till I felt creepy.

The faint figure behind seemed to shake the pattern, just as if she wanted to get out.

I got up softly and went to feel and see if the paper *did* move, and when I came back John was awake.

"What is it, little girl?" he said. "Don't go walking about like that—you'll get cold."

I thought it was a good time to talk, so I told him that I really was not gaining here, and that I wished he would take me away.

"Why, darling!" he said. "Our lease will be up in three weeks, and I can't see how to leave before.

"The repairs are not done at home, and I cannot possibly leave town just now. Of course, if you were in any danger, I could and would, but you really are better, dear, whether you can see it or not. I am a doctor, dear, and I know. You are gaining flesh and color, your appetite is better, I feel really much easier about you."

"I don't weigh a bit more," said I, "nor as much; and my appetite may be better in the evening when you are here but it is worse in the morning when you are away!"

"Bless her little heart!" said he with a big hug. "She shall be as sick as she pleases! But now let's improve the shining hours by going to sleep, and talk about it in the morning!"

"And you won't go away?" I asked gloomily.

"Why, how can I, dear? It is only three weeks more and then we will take a nice little trip for a few days while Jennie is getting the house ready. Really, dear, you are better!"

"Better in body perhaps—" I began, and stopped short, for he sat up straight and looked at me with such a stern, reproachful look that I could not say another word.

"My darling," said he, "I beg you, for my sake and for our child's sake, as well as for your own, that you will never for one instant let that idea enter your mind! There is nothing so dangerous, so fascinating, to a temperament like yours. It is a false and foolish fancy. Can you trust me as a physician when I tell you so?"

So of course I said no more on that score, and we went to sleep before long. He thought I was asleep first, but I wasn't, and lay there for hours trying to decide whether that front pattern and the back pattern really did move together or separately.

On a pattern like this, by daylight, there is a lack of sequence, a defiance of law, that is a constant irritant to a normal mind.

The color is hideous enough, and unreliable enough, and infuriating enough, but the pattern is torturing.

You think you have mastered it, but just as you get well under way in following, it turns a back-somersault and there you are. It slaps you in the face, knocks you down, and tramples upon you. It is like a bad dream.

The outside pattern is a florid arabesque, reminding one of a fungus. If you can imagine a toadstool in joints, an interminable string of toadstools, budding and sprouting in endless convolutions—why, that is something like it.

That is, sometimes!

There is one marked peculiarity about this paper, a thing nobody seems to notice but myself, and that is that it changes as the light changes.

When the sun shoots in through the east window—I always watch for that first long, straight ray—it changes so quickly that I never can quite believe it.

That is why I watch it always.

By moonlight—the moon shines in all night when there is a moon—I wouldn't know it was the same paper.

At night in any kind of light, in twilight, candlelight, lamplight, and worst of all by moonlight, it becomes bars! The outside pattern, I mean, and the woman behind it is as plain as can be.

I didn't realize for a long time what the thing was that showed behind, that dim subpattern, but now I am quite sure it is a woman.

By daylight she is subdued, quiet. I fancy it is the pattern that keeps her so still. It is so puzzling. It keeps me quiet by the hour.

I lie down ever so much now. John says it is good for me, and to sleep all I can.

Indeed he started the habit by making me lie down for an hour after each meal.

It is a very bad habit, I am convinced, for you see, I don't sleep.

And that cultivates deceit, for I don't tell them I'm awake—oh, no!

The fact is I am getting a little afraid of John.

He seems very queer sometimes, and even Jennie has an inexplicable look.

It strikes me occasionally, just as a scientific hypothesis, that perhaps it is the paper!

I have watched John when he did not know I was looking, and come into the room suddenly on the most innocent excuses, and I've caught him several times *looking at the paper!* And Jennie too. I caught Jennie with her hand on it once.

She didn't know I was in the room, and when I asked her in a quiet, a very quiet voice, with the most restrained manner possible, what she was doing with the paper, she turned around as if she had been caught stealing, and looked quite angry—asked me why I should frighten her so!

Then she said that the paper stained everything it touched, that she had found yellow smooches on all my clothes and John's and she wished we would be more careful!

Did that not sound innocent? But I know she was studying that pattern, and I am determined that nobody shall find it out but myself!

Life is very much more exciting now than it used to be. You see, I have something more to expect, to look forward to, to watch. I really do eat better, and am more quiet than I was.

John is so pleased to see me improve! He laughed a little the other day, and said I seemed to be flourishing in spite of my wallpaper.

I turned it off with a laugh. I had no intention of telling him it was *because* of the wallpaper—he would make fun of me. He might even want to take me away.

I don't want to leave now until I have found it out. There is a week more, and I think that will be enough.

I'm feeling so much better!

I don't sleep much at night, for it is so interesting to watch developments; but I sleep a good deal during the daytime.

In the daytime it is tiresome and perplexing.

There are always new shoots on the fungus, and new shades of yellow all over it. I cannot keep count of them, though I have tried conscientiously.

It is the strangest yellow, that wallpaper! It makes me think of all the yellow things I ever saw—not beautiful ones like buttercups, but old, foul, bad yellow things.

But there is something else about that paper—the smell! I noticed it the moment we came into the room, but with so much air and sun it was not bad. Now we have had a week of fog and rain, and whether the windows are open or not, the smell is here.

It creeps all over the house.

I find it hovering in the dining-room, skulking in the parlor, hiding in the hall, lying in wait for me on the stairs.

It gets into my hair.

Even when I go to ride, if I turn my head suddenly and surprise it—there is that smell!

Such a peculiar odor, too! I have spent hours in trying to analyze it, to find what it smelled like.

It is not bad—at first—and very gentle, but quite the subtlest, most enduring odor I ever met.

In this damp weather it is awful. I wake up in the night and find it hanging over me.

It used to disturb me at first. I thought seriously of burning the house—to reach the smell.

But now I am used to it. The only thing I can think of that it is like is the *color* of the paper! A yellow smell.

There is a very funny mark on this wall, low down, near the mopboard. A streak that runs round the room. It goes behind every piece of furniture, except the bed, a long, straight, even *smooch*, as if it had been rubbed over and over.

I wonder how it was done and who did it, and what they did it for. Round and round and round—round and round and round—it makes me dizzy!

I really have discovered something at last.

Through watching so much at night, when it changes so, I have finally found out.

The front pattern *does* move—and no wonder! The woman behind shakes it!

Sometimes I think there are a great many women behind, and sometimes only one, and she crawls around fast, and her crawling shakes it all over.

Then in the very bright spots she keeps still, and in the very shady spots she just takes hold of the bars and shakes them hard.

And she is all the time trying to climb through. But nobody could climb through that pattern—it strangles so; I think that is why it has so many heads.

They get through and then the pattern strangles them off and turns them upside down, and makes their eyes white!

If those heads were covered or taken off it would not be half so bad.

I think that woman gets out in the daytime!

And I'll tell you why—privately—I've seen her!

I can see her out of every one of my windows!

It is the same woman, I know, for she is always creeping, and most women do not creep by daylight.

I see her in that long shaded lane, creeping up and down. I see her in those dark grape arbors, creeping all round the garden.

I see her on that long road under the trees, creeping along, and when a carriage comes she hides under the blackberry vines.

I don't blame her a bit. It must be very humiliating to be caught creeping by daylight!

I always lock the door when I creep by daylight. I can't do it at night, for I know John would suspect something at once.

And John is so queer now that I don't want to irritate him. I wish he would take another room! Besides, I don't want anybody to get that woman out at night but myself.

I often wonder if I could see her out of all the windows at once.

But, turn as fast as I can, I can only see out of one at one time.

And though I always see her, she *may* be able to creep faster than I can turn! I have watched her sometimes away off in the open country, creeping as fast as a cloud shadow in a wind.

If only that top pattern could be gotten off from the under one! I mean to try it, little by little.

I have found out another funny thing, but I shan't tell it this time! It does not do to trust people too much.

There are only two more days to get this paper off, and I believe John is beginning to notice. I don't like the look in his eyes.

And I heard him ask Jennie a lot of professional questions about me. She had a very good report to give.

She said I slept a good deal in the daytime.

John knows I don't sleep very well at night, for all I'm so quiet!

He asked me all sorts of questions too, and pretended to be very loving and kind.

As if I couldn't see through him!

Still, I don't wonder he acts so, sleeping under this paper for three months.

It only interests me, but I feel sure John and Jennie are affected by it.

Hurrah! This is the last day, but it is enough. John is to stay in town over night, and won't be out until this evening.

Jennie wanted to sleep with me—the sly thing; but I told her I should undoubtedly rest better for a night all alone.

That was clever, for really I wasn't alone a bit! As soon as it was moonlight and that poor thing began to crawl and shake the pattern, I got up and ran to help her.

I pulled and she shook. I shook and she pulled, and before morning we had peeled off yards of that paper.

A strip about as high as my head and half around the room.

And then when the sun came and that awful pattern began to laugh at me, I declared I would finish it today!

We go away tomorrow, and they are moving all my furniture down again to leave things as they were before.

Jennie looked at the wall in amazement, but I told her merrily that I did it out of pure spite at the vicious thing.

She laughed and said she wouldn't mind doing it herself, but I must not get tired.

How she betrayed herself that time!

But *I* am here, and no person touches this paper but Me—not *alive!*

She tried to get me out of the room—it was too patent! But I said it was so quiet and empty and clean now that I believed I would lie down again and sleep all I could, and not to wake me even for dinner—I would call when I woke.

So now she is gone, and the servants are gone, and the things are gone, and there is nothing left but that great bedstead nailed down, with the canvas mattress we found on it.

We shall sleep downstairs tonight, and take the boat home tomorrow.

I quite enjoy the room, now it is bare again.

How those children did tear about here!

This bedstead is fairly gnawed!

But I must get to work.

I have locked the door and thrown the key down into the front path.

I don't want to go out, and I don't want to have anybody come in, till John comes.

I want to astonish him.

I've got a rope up here that even Jennie did not find. If that woman does get out, and tries to get away, I can tie her!

But I forgot I could not reach far without anything to stand on!

This bed will *not* move!

I tried to lift and push it until I was lame, and then I got so angry I bit off a little piece at one corner—but it hurt my teeth.

Then I peeled off all the paper I could reach standing on the floor. It sticks horribly and the pattern just enjoys it! All those strangled heads and bulbous eyes and waddling fungus growths just shriek with derision!

I am getting angry enough to do something desperate. To jump out of the window would be admirable exercise, but the bars are too strong even to try.

Besides I wouldn't do it. Of course not. I know well enough that a step like that is improper and might be misconstrued.

I don't like to *look* out of the windows even—there are so many of those creeping women, and they creep so fast.

I wonder if they all come out of that wallpaper as I did!

But I am securely fastened now by my well-hidden rope—you don't get *me* out in the road there!

I suppose I shall have to get back behind the pattern when it comes night, and that is hard!

It is so pleasant to be out in this great room and creep around as I please!

I don't want to go outside. I won't, even if Jennie asks me to.

For outside you have to creep on the ground, and everything is green instead of yellow.

But here I can creep smoothly on the floor, and my shoulder just fits in that long smooch around the wall, so I cannot lose my way.

Why, there's John at the door!

It is no use, young man, you can't open it!

How he does call and pound!

Now he's crying to Jennie for an axe.

It would be a shame to break down that beautiful door!

"John, dear!" said I in the gentlest voice. "The key is down by the front steps, under a plantain leaf!"

That silenced him for a few moments.

Then he said, very quietly indeed, "Open the door, my darling!"

"I can't," said I. "The key is down by the front door under a plantain leaf!" And then I said it again, several times, very gently and slowly, and said it so often that he had to go and see, and he got it of course, and came in. He stopped short by the door.

"What is the matter?" he cried. "For God's sake, what are you doing!"

I kept on creeping just the same, but I looked at him over my shoulder.

"I've got out at last," said I, "in spite of you and Jane. And I've pulled off most of the paper, so you can't put me back!"

Now why should that man have fainted? But he did, and right across my path by the wall, so that I had to creep over him every time!

GITHA HARIHARAN

THE REMAINS OF THE FEAST

Githa Hariharan (b. 1954) is one of those Indian writers born since the 1950s who write primarily in English for an Indian audience; these post-colonial voices have been inspired in large part by the success of Salmon Rushdie's Midnight's Children. English-language publishing in India is fraught with political and practical problems, not the least of which is "rendering experience in a language in which it does not occur." Writers in English have been accused of exoticizing India, ignoring the country's social unrest, and wallowing in middle-class values. But Indo-English writing is no brash newcomer, as Hariharan explains. "It is a very young literature, which is progressing step by step. There is no need for us to do right away all that literature can do!"

Hariharan grew up in Bombay and Manila. She later studied in the United States and worked in public television, but she returned to India in 1979 to work in publishing in Bombay, Madras, and New Delhi. The Thousand Faces of Night, published in 1992, won the Commonwealth Prize for the best first novel. Her other writing includes The Ghosts of Vasu Master (1994), A Southern Harvest (1993), and The Art of Dying (1993), the collection of short stories from which "The Remains of the Feast" is taken.

The room still smells of her. Not as she did when she was dying, an overripe smell that clung to everything that had touched her, sheets, saris, hands. She had been in the nursing home for only ten days but a bedsore grew like an angry red welt on her back. Her neck was a big hump, and she lay in bed like a moody camel that would snap or bite at unpredictable intervals. The goitred lump, the familiar swelling I had seen on her neck all my life, that I had stroked and teasingly pinched as a child, was now a cancer that spread like a fire down the old body, licking clean everything in its way.

The room now smells like a pressed, faded rose. A dry, elusive smell. Burnt, a candle put out.

We were not exactly room-mates, but we shared two rooms, one corner of the old ancestral house, all my twenty-year-old life.

She was Rukmini, my great-grandmother. She was ninety when she died last month, outliving by ten years her only son and daughter-in-law. I don't know how she felt when they died, but later she seemed to find something slightly hilarious about it all. That she, an ignorant village-bred woman, who signed the papers my father brought her with a thumb-print, should survive; while they, city-bred, ambitious, should collapse of weak hearts and arthritic knees at the first sign of old age.

Her sense of humour was always quaint. It could also be embarrassing. She would sit in her corner, her round, plump face reddening, giggling like a little girl. I knew better than ask her why, I was a teenager by then. But some uninitiated friend would be unable to resist, and would go up to my great-grandmother and ask her why she was laughing. This, I knew, would send her into uncontrollable peals. The tears would flow down her cheeks, and finally, catching her breath, still weak with laughter, she would confess. She could fart exactly like a train whistling its way out of the station, and this achievement gave her as much joy as a child might get when she saw or heard a train.

So perhaps it is not all that surprising that she could be so flippant about her only child's death, especially since ten years had passed.

"Yes, Ratna, you study hard and become a big doctor-madam," she would chuckle, when I kept the lights on all night and paced up and down the room, reading to myself.

"The last time I saw a doctor, I was thirty years old."

"Your grandfather was in the hospital for three months. He would faint every time he saw his own blood."

And as if that summed up the progress made between two generations, she would pull her blanket over her head and begin snoring almost immediately.

I have two rooms, the entire downstairs to myself now, since my great-grandmother died. I begin my course at medical college next month, and I am afraid to be here alone at night.

I have to live up to the gold medal I won last year. I keep late hours, reading my anatomy textbook before the course begins. The body is a solid, reliable thing. It is a wonderful, resilient machine. I hold on to the thick, hard-bound book and flip through the new-smelling pages greedily. I stop every time I find an illustration, and look at it closely. It reduces us to pink, blue and white, colour-coded, labelled parts. Muscles, veins, tendons. Everything has a name. Everything is linked, one with the other, all parts of a functioning whole.

It is poor consolation for the nights I have spent in her warm bed, surrounded by that safe, familiar, musty smell.

She was cheerful and never sick. But she was also undeniably old, and so it was no great surprise to us when she took to lying in bed all day a few weeks before her ninetieth birthday.

She had been lying in bed for close to two months, ignoring concern, advice, scolding, and then she suddenly gave up. She agreed to see a doctor.

The young doctor came out of her room, his face puzzled and angry. My father begged him to sit down and drink a tumbler of hot coffee.

"She will need all kinds of tests," the doctor said. "How long has she had that lump on her neck? Have you had it checked?"

My father shifted uneasily in his cane chair. He is a cadaverous looking man, prone to nervousness and sweating. He keeps a big jar of antacids on his office desk. He has a nine to five accountant's job in a government-owned company, the kind that never fires its employees.

My father pulled out the small towel he uses in place of a handkerchief. Wiping his forehead, he mumbled, "You know how these old women are. Impossible to argue with them."

"The neck," the doctor said more gently. I could see he pitied my father.

"I think it was examined once, long ago. My father was alive then. There was supposed to have been an operation, I think. But you know what they thought in those days. An operation meant an unnatural death. All the relatives came over to scare her, advise her with horror stories. So she said no. You know how it is. And she was already a widow then, my father was the head of the household. How could he, a fourteen-year-old, take the responsibility?"

"Hm," said the doctor. He shrugged his shoulders. "Let me know when you want to admit her in my nursing home. But I suppose it's best to let her die at home."

When the doctor left, we looked at each other, the three of us, like shifty accomplices. My mother, practical as always, broke the silence and said, "Let's not tell her anything. Why worry her? And then we'll have all kinds of difficult old aunts and cousins visiting, it will be such a nuisance. How will Ratna study in the middle of all that chaos?"

But when I went to our room that night, my great-grandmother had a sly look on her face. "Come here, Ratna," she said. "Come here, my darling little gem."

I went, my heart quaking at the thought of telling her. She held my hand and kissed each finger, her half-closed eyes almost flirtatious.

"Tell me something, Ratna," she began in a wheedling voice.

"I don't know, I don't know anything about it," I said quickly.

"Of course you do!" She was surprised, a little annoyed. "Those small cakes you got from the Christian shop that day. Do they have eggs in them?"

I was speechless with relief.

"Do they?" she persisted. "Will you," and her eyes narrowed with cunning, "will you get one for me?"

So we began a strange partnership, my great-grandmother and I. I smuggled cakes and ice cream, biscuits and samosas, made by non-Brahmin hands, into a vegetarian invalid's room. To the deathbed of a Brahmin widow who had never eaten anything but pure, home-cooked food for almost a century.

She would grab it from my hand, late at night after my parents had gone to sleep. She would hold the pastry in her fingers, turn it round and round, as if on the verge of an earthshaking discovery.

"And does it really have egg in it?" she would ask again, as if she needed the password for her to bite into it with her gums.

"Yes, yes," I would say, a little tired of midnight feasts by then. The pastries were a cheap yellow colour, topped by white frosting with hard, grey pearls.

"Lots and lots of eggs," I would say, wanting her to hurry up and put it in her mouth. "And the bakery is owned by a Christian. I think he hires Muslim cooks too."

"Ooooh," she would sigh. Her little pink tongue darted out and licked the frosting. Her toothless mouth worked its way steadily, munching, making happy sucking noises.

Our secret was safe for about a week. Then she became bold. She was bored with the cakes, she said. They gave her heartburn.

She became a little more adventurous every day. Her cravings were varied and unpredictable. Laughable and always urgent.

"I'm thirsty," she moaned, when my mother asked her if she wanted anything. "No, no, I don't want water, I don't want juice." She stopped the moaning and looked at my mother's patient, exasperated face. "I'll tell you what I want," she whined. "Get me a glass of that brown drink Ratna bought in the bottle. The kind that bubbles and makes a popping sound when you open the bottle. The one with the fizzy noise when you pour it out."

"A Coca-Cola?" said my mother, shocked. "Don't be silly, it will make you sick."

"I don't care what it is called," my great-grandmother said and started moaning again. "I want it."

So she got it and my mother poured out a small glassful, tight-lipped, and gave it to her without a word. She was always a dutiful grand-daughter-in-law.

"Ah," sighed my great-grandmother, propped up against her pillows, the steel tumbler lifted high over her lips. The lump on her neck moved in little gurgles as she drank. Then she burped a loud, contented burp, and asked, as if she had just thought of it, "Do you think there is something in it? You know, alcohol?"

A month later, we had got used to her unexpected, inappropriate demands. She had tasted, by now, lemon tarts, garlic, three types of aerated drinks, fruit cake laced with brandy, bhel-puri from the fly-infested bazaar nearby.

"There's going to be trouble," my mother kept muttering under her breath. "She's losing her mind, she is going to be a lot of trouble."

And she was right, of course. My great-grandmother could no longer swallow very well. She would pour the coke into her mouth and half of it would trickle out of her nostrils, thick, brown, nauseating.

"It burns, it burns," she would yell then, but she pursed her lips tightly together when my mother spooned a thin gruel into her mouth. "No, no," she screamed deliriously. "Get me something from the bazaar. Raw onions. Fried bread. Chickens and goats."

Then we knew she was lost to us. She was dying.

She was in the nursing home for ten whole days. My mother and I took turns sitting by her, sleeping on the floor by the hospital cot.

She lay there quietly, the pendulous neck almost as big as her face. But she would not let the nurses near her bed. She would squirm and wriggle like a big fish that refused to be caught. The sheets smelled, and the young doctor shook his head. "Not much to be done now," he said. "The cancer has left nothing intact."

The day she died, she kept searching the room with her eyes. Her arms were held down by the tubes and needles, criss-cross, in, out. The glucose dripped into her veins but her nose still ran, the clear, thin liquid trickling down like dribble on to her chin. Her hands clenched and unclenched with the effort and she whispered, like a miracle, "Ratna."

My mother and I rushed to her bedside. Tears streaming down her face, my mother bent her head before her and pleaded, "Give me your blessings, Paati. Bless me before you go."

My great-grandmother looked at her for a minute, her lips working furiously, noiselessly. For the first time in my life I saw a fine veil of perspiration on her face. The muscles on her face twitched in mad, frenzied jerks. Then she pulled one arm free of the tubes, in a sudden, crazy spurt of strength, and the I.V. pole crashed to the floor.

"Bring me a red sari," she screamed. "A red one with a big wide border of gold. And," her voice cracked, "bring me peanuts with chilli powder from the corner shop. Onion and green chilli bondas deep-fried in oil."

Then the voice gurgled and gurgled, her face and neck swayed, rocked like a boat lost in a stormy sea. She retched, and as the vomit flew out of her mouth and her nose, thick like the milkshakes she had drunk, brown like the alcoholic coke, her head slumped forward, her rounded chin buried in the cancerous neck.

When we brought the body home—I am not yet a doctor and already I can call her that—I helped my mother to wipe her clean with a wet, soft cloth. We wiped away the smells, the smell of the hospital bed, the smell of an old woman's juices drying. Her skin was dry and papery. The stubble on her head—she had refused to shave her head once she got sick—had grown, like the soft, white bristles of a hairbrush.

She had had only one child though she had lived so long. But the skin on her stomach was crumpled, frayed velvet, the creases running to and fro in fine, silvery rivulets.

"Bring her sari," my mother whispered, as if my great-grandmother could still hear her.

I looked at the stiff, cold body that I was seeing naked for the first time. She was asleep at last, quiet at last. I had learnt, in the last month or two, to expect the unexpected from her. I waited, in case she changed her mind and sat up, remembering one more taboo to be tasted.

"Bring me your eyebrow tweezers," I heard her say. "Bring me that hair-removing cream. I have a moustache and I don't want to be an ugly old woman."

But she lay still, the wads of cotton in her nostrils and ears shutting us out. Shutting out her belated ardour.

I ran to my cupboard and brought her the brightest, reddest sari I could find: last year's Diwali sari, my first silk.

I unfolded it, ignoring my mother's eyes which were turning aghast. I covered her naked body lovingly. The red silk glittered like her childish laughter.

"Have you gone mad," my mother whispered furiously. "She was a sick old woman, she didn't know what she was saying."

She rolled up the sari and flung it aside, as if it had been polluted. She wiped the body again to free it from foolish, trivial desires.

They burnt her in a pale-brown sari, her widow's weeds. The prayer beads I had never seen her touch encircled the bulging, obscene neck.

I am still a novice at anatomy. I hover just over the body, I am just beneath the skin. I have yet to look at the insides, the entrails of memories she told me nothing about, the pain congealing into a cancer.

She has left me behind with nothing but a smell, a legacy that grows fainter every day. For a while I haunt the dirtiest bakeries and tea-stalls I can find. I search for her, my sweet great-grandmother, in plate after plate of stale confections, in needle-sharp green chillies, deep-fried in rancid oil. I plot her revenge for her, I give myself diarrhoea for a week.

Then I open all the windows and her cupboard and air the rooms. I tear her dirty, grey saris to shreds. I line the shelves of her empty cupboard with my thick, newly-bought, glossy-jacketed texts, one next to the other. They stand straight and solid, row after row of armed soldiers. They fill up the small cupboard quickly.

ERNEST HEMINGWAY

A Clean, Well-Lighted Place

Ernest Hemingway (1899–1961) was born in Oak Park, Illinois. His father, a doctor, played a strong role in shaping Hemingway's love of outdoor sport and camping. Ernest Hemingway began writing as a reporter for his high-school newspaper and after graduation became a reporter for the Kansas City Star. In World War I he volunteered as a Red Cross ambulance driver and served in the infantry; wounded in action, he was decorated and discharged. He resided briefly in Toronto, writing for the Toronto Star, then settled in Paris. There, he joined a circle of U.S. expatriate writers which included Gertrude Stein and F. Scott Fitzgerald, who greatly influenced his career as a fiction writer. While in Paris, Hemingway published his first poems and stories; his first short-story collection, In Our Time, *was published in the United States in 1925. The Sun Also Rises (1926), Hemingway's first and favourite novel, distinguished him as the voice of Stein's celebrated "lost generation" and made famous his ruthlessly honed style, which he based on the "iceberg" dictum: "There is seven-eighths of it under water for every part that shows. Anything you know you can eliminate and it only strengthens your iceberg. It is the part that doesn't show."*

After the Depression, Hemingway lived in Florida and Cuba. He travelled extensively to Europe and Africa, writing nonfiction accounts of the torero *(Death in the Afternoon, 1932) and of big-game hunting in Africa (The Green Hills of Africa, 1935). "About morals, I know only that what is moral is what you feel good after and what is immoral is what you feel bad after and judged by these moral standards, which I do not defend, the bullfight is very moral to me because I feel very fine while it is going on and have a feeling of life and death and mortality and immortality and after it is over I feel very sad but very fine."*

Hemingway reported on the Spanish Civil War, an experience that inspired For Whom the Bell Tolls *(1939). His European coverage of World War II was followed by a long withdrawal from writing. His most popular work,* The Old Man and the Sea, *emerged in 1952 as an instant classic, winning the 1953 Pulitzer Prize and ensuring Hemingway's 1954*

*receipt of the Nobel Prize in literature "for his powerful, style-forming
mastery of the art of narration." In 1961, at his home in Ketchum, Idaho,
Hemingway committed suicide with a handgun.*

———————

It was late and every one had left the café except an old man who sat in the
shadow the leaves of the tree made against the electric light. In the day time the
street was dusty, but at night the dew settled the dust and the old man liked to
sit late because he was deaf and now at night it was quiet and he felt the difference. The two waiters inside the café knew that the old man was a little drunk,
and while he was a good client they knew that if he became too drunk he
would leave without paying, so they kept watch on him.

"Last week he tried to commit suicide," one waiter said.

"Why?"

"He was in despair."

"What about?"

"Nothing."

"How do you know it was nothing?"

"He has plenty of money."

They sat together at a table that was close against the wall near the door
of the café and looked at the terrace where the tables were all empty except
where the old man sat in the shadow of the leaves of the tree that moved
slightly in the wind. A girl and a soldier went by in the street. The street light
shone on the brass number on his collar. The girl wore no head covering and
hurried beside him.

"The guard will pick him up," one waiter said.

"What does it matter if he gets what he's after?"

"He had better get off the street now. The guard will get him. They went
by five minutes ago."

The old man sitting in the shadow rapped on his saucer with his glass. The
younger waiter went over to him.

"What do you want?"

The old man looked at him. "Another brandy," he said.

"You'll be drunk," the waiter said. The old man looked at him. The waiter
went away.

"He'll stay all night," he said to his colleague. "I'm sleepy now. I never get
into bed before three o'clock. He should have killed himself last week."

The waiter took the brandy bottle and another saucer from the counter
inside the café and marched out to the old man's table. He put down the saucer
and poured the glass full of brandy.

"You should have killed yourself last week," he said to the deaf man. The old man motioned with his finger. "A little more," he said. The waiter poured on into the glass so that the brandy slopped over and ran down the stem into the top saucer of the pile. "Thank you," the old man said. The waiter took the bottle back inside the café. He sat down at the table with his colleague again.

"He's drunk now," he said.

"He's drunk every night."

"What did he want to kill himself for?"

"How should I know."

"How did he do it?"

"He hung himself with a rope."

"Who cut him down?"

"His niece."

"Why did they do it?"

"Fear for his soul."

"How much money has he got?"

"He's got plenty."

"He must be eighty years old."

"Anyway I should say he was eighty."

"I wish he would go home. I never get to bed before three o'clock. What kind of hour is that to go to bed?"

"He stays up because he likes it."

"He's lonely. I'm not lonely. I have a wife waiting in bed for me."

"He had a wife once too."

"A wife would be no good to him now."

"You can't tell. He might be better with a wife."

"His niece looks after him. You said she cut him down."

"I know."

"I wouldn't want to be that old man. An old man is a nasty thing."

"Not always. This old man is clean. He drinks without spilling. Even now, drunk. Look at him."

"I don't want to look at him. I wish he would go home. He has no regard for those who must work."

The old man looked from his glass across the square, then over at the waiters.

"Another brandy," he said, pointing to his glass. The waiter who was in a hurry came over.

"Finished," he said, speaking with that omission of syntax stupid people employ when talking to drunken people or foreigners. "No more tonight. Close now."

"Another," said the old man.

"No. Finished." The waiter wiped the edge of the table with a towel and shook his head.

The old man stood up, slowly counted the saucers, took a leather coin purse from his pocket, and paid for the drinks, leaving half a peseta tip.

The waiter watched him go down the street, a very old man walking unsteadily but with dignity.

"Why didn't you let him stay and drink?" the unhurried waiter asked. They were putting up the shutters. "It is not half-past two."

"I want to go home to bed."

"What is an hour?"

"More to me than to him."

"An hour is the same."

"You talk like an old man yourself. He can buy a bottle and drink at home."

"It's not the same."

"No, it is not," agreed the waiter with a wife. He did not wish to be unjust. He was only in a hurry.

"And you? You have no fear of going home before your usual hour?"

"Are you trying to insult me?"

"No, hombre, only to make a joke."

"No," the waiter who was in a hurry said, rising from pulling down the metal shutters. "I have confidence. I am all confidence."

"You have youth, confidence, and a job," the older waiter said, "You have everything."

"And what do you lack?"

"Everything but work."

"You have everything I have."

"No. I have never had confidence and I am not young."

"Come on. Stop talking nonsense and lock up."

"I am of those who like to stay late at the café," the older waiter said. "With all those who do not want to go to bed. With all those who need a light for the night."

"I want to go home and into bed."

"We are of two different kinds," the older waiter said. He was now dressed to go home. "It is not only a question of youth and confidence although those things are very beautiful. Each night I am reluctant to close up because there may be someone who needs the café."

"Hombre, there are bodegas open all night long."

"You do not understand. This is a clean and pleasant café. It is well lighted. The light is very good and also, now, there are shadows of the leaves."

"Good night," said the younger waiter.

"Good night," the other said. Turning off the electric light he continued the conversation with himself. It is the light of course but it is necessary that the place be clean and pleasant. You do not want music. Certainly you do not want music. Nor can you stand before a bar with dignity although that is all that is provided for these hours. What did he fear? It was not fear or dread. It was a nothing that he knew too well. It was all a nothing and a man was nothing too. It was only that and light was all it needed and a certain cleanness and order. Some lived in it and never felt it but he knew it all was nada y pues nada y nada y pues nada.[1] Our nada who art in nada, nada be the name thy kingdom nada thy will be nada in nada as it is in nada. Give us this nada our daily nada and nada us our nada as we nada our nadas and nada us not into nada but deliver us from nada; pues nada. Hail nothing full of nothing, nothing is with thee. He smiled and stood before a bar with a shining steam pressure coffee machine.

"What's yours?" asked the barman.

"Nada."

"Otro loco más," said the barman and turned away.

"A little cup," said the waiter.

The barman poured it for him.

"The light is very bright and pleasant but the bar is unpolished," the waiter said.

The barman looked at him but did not answer. It was too late at night for conversation.

"You want another copita?" the barman asked.

"No, thank you," said the waiter and went out. He disliked bars and bodegas. A clean, well-lighted café was a very different thing. Now, without thinking further, he would go home to his room. He would lie in the bed and finally, with daylight, he would go to sleep. After all, he said to himself, it is probably only insomnia. Many must have it.

NOTE

1. *nada y pues nada*: Spanish for "nothing, and then nothing."

BASIL JOHNSTON

Cowboys and Indians

Basil Johnston (b. 1929) was born on the Ojibway reserve at Parry Island, Ontario. He graduated from Loyola College in Montreal in 1954 and later attended the Ontario College of Education, where he earned a secondary school teaching certificate. He taught history in high school until 1969, when he became involved with the Royal Ontario Museum, where he was a member of the Department of Ethnography from 1972 until his recent retirement. A specialist in Ojibway culture and language, Johnston explores tribal culture and history, Ojibway language instruction, and short fiction in his writing. In 1976 he received the Samuel Fels Literary Award for "Zhowmin and Mandamin." His titles include Moose Meat and Wild Rice *(1978),* Tales Our Elders Told *(1981), and* Indian School Days *(1988).*

Johnston is deeply troubled by the threats faced by Native peoples in sustaining their heritage through Native languages, which he warns are "one generation from extinction." "There remain but three aboriginal languages out of the original fifty-three found in Canada that may survive several more generations." For Johnston, the teaching of Native literature and languages are inseparable. His storytelling takes as its goal the empowerment of Native peoples.

> *In order to write truly about the Native insights, you have to know the language.... If you can't articulate those things, you can't live by those principles.... The words work on several levels, anyway. There is the surface, where everybody understands. Then there are two or three meanings, take for example, "man-itou." It has many meanings, depending on the context of the conversation. The context will tell you the precise sense in which that is to be applied. "Medicine-strength," "Earth-strength." Then you think about that. How is its application? There is the person debilitated by disease. To be restored to strength, he has got to get the strength of the Earth passed to him through this medicine.... You have to know the language in order to be able to understand that.*

Hollywood grew fast and big. By the 1930s there were many studios employing many actors in the production of many motion pictures. Within the same few years as the studios got bigger, techniques improved; as techniques improved so did the quality of acting; and as acting got better, so did the range and variety of themes enlarge. And of course viewers' tastes became more refined and discriminating, requiring of Hollywood and the studios more authenticity and less artificiality in their productions.

And the studios were willing to oblige.

It was decided by the producer and director of a major studio planning a western picture with either Hoot Gibson, Tom Mix, or Ken Maynard as the principal star, to hire real Indians to take part in the production. With real Indians the advantages were obvious. Besides lending authenticity to the motion picture, Indians represented a substantial saving. Their natural pigmentation would reduce expenses in cosmetics and make-up artists; their natural horsemanship would save time and expenses usually incurred in training greenhorns to ride; their possession of herds of ponies would save time and outlay in the rental and feeding of horses; and their natural talent for art would obviate the need for anthropologists to act as consultants in authenticating Indian art and design. The only expense to be incurred was the fee of $2.00 per day for the movie extras.

Management calculated that 500 Indians along with 500 horses were needed for no more than two days to shoot an attack upon a wagon-train. The producer and the director also decided that there would be substantial savings by establishing the location of the filming near an Indian reservation somewhere in the west.

Inquiries, preliminary and cursory, made of historians and the Bureau of Indian Affairs in Washington indicated that the Crow Indians of Montana, having retained their traditions and still owning large herds of horses, would be best suited for a motion picture of the kind planned by the studio. Besides, the terrain in the area was genuine honest-to-goodness Indian country, excellent for camera work.

Negotiations with the Bureau of Indian Affairs for permission to treat with the Crows for their services as actors and for the provision of horses began at once. Permission was granted by Washington; and the Crows were more than willing to take part.

Crew and cast arrived by train in Billings, Montana. Anxious to get started and to finish shooting the siege of a wagon-train in as short a time as possible, the producer and director sent a limousine to the reservation to fetch the chief.

Over a meal with the chief and his retinue of councillors and hangers-on, the producer, portly and bald, beneath a cloud of smoke produced by a fat cigar, informed the chief that it was a great privilege to work with the Crows and that it was an honour and a distinction for his studio to set precedent in the entire industry by being the first to use real, live honest-to-goodness Indians in a motion picture. For the Crows, it would mean fame and national recognition ... and money ... $2.00 a day for those taking part; $1.00 per day for those providing horses; and $1.00 per day for those providing art work and the loan of teepees.

An interpreter translated for the chief.

The producer smiled and blew a cloud of smoke out of the side of his mouth. The Crow responded "How! How! How!"

"It shouldn't take long chief, three or four days ... no more. A day to get ready and two or three to film the scene. We don't want to interfere too much in your affairs, you've probably got a lot to do and ... we are working under a pretty tight schedule."

The interpreter relayed this information to the chief.

"Now chief. We want 500 warriors; 500 horses; bows and arrows and ... maybe fifty or so rifles ... feathers, head-dresses, buckskin jackets, and ... buckskin leggings ... and four or five people who can paint designs on horses and put make-up on warriors." The producer continued, "The scene itself will be easy. The warriors will attack the wagon-train at day-break. It shouldn't take more than half an hour. Very easy, really don't need any rehearsals. My colleague will tell you what to do. Probably the easiest two bucks you'll ever make ... cash, as soon as the scene's shot. Can you get all this stuff by tomorrow night, chief?" And the producer flicked the ashes from his fat cigar.

The interpreter prattling in Crow to his chief and councillors pounded the table, slashed the air, shrugged his shoulders to emphasize his message to his listeners, who looked dumbfounded. Nevertheless they injected a "How! How!" frequently enough into the discourse to intimate some understanding.

The chief said something.

"How many horses?"

"500, the producer might even settle for 450."

The interpreter addressed his chief who shook his head grunting "How!"

"Ain't got 500 horses," the interpreter said sadly.

"450?"

"Ain't dat many on de reservation."

"300?"

"No, not dat many; not like long time ago."

"Well! How many have you got?" the producer asked, his face pinching into worried lines and his voice losing its cheer and vitality.

"Maybe 10 ... 20 ... an' not very good dem."

"Keeee ... rice ...!" And the producer bit a chunk of cigar, crushing the other end in the ashtray. "Are there any horses around here?"

"Yeah. Ranchers and farmers got dem."

To his assistant, the producer instructed "Get 500 horses by tomorrow evening. We have to shoot that scene next morning with the Indians charging down the slope."

The interpreter whispered to his chief who shook his head.

"Say, mister," the interpreter addressed the producer, "how about saddles?"

"Saddles!" the word erupted.

"Yeah, saddles."

There was a moment of cosmic silence. "Saddles!" the producer repeated mouthing the word in disbelief. "What do you mean ... saddles! You're all going to ride bare-back. This film is going to be authentic ... who ever heard of Indians riding on saddles ... supposed to be the finest horsemen in the world!"

The interpreter stiffened in fright at the thought that he might be one of the warriors to ride bare-back, and he hung his head.

"Don't know how to ride ... us. Forgot how ... long time ago ... Need saddles ... might fall off an' git hurt ... us."

"This is incredible! ... unbelievable! ... no horses! ... can't ride! ..." the producer gasped as he sank into the chair. "Keeeeee-rice."

Hope waning from his brow and voice, the producer tried, "You still got bows an' arrows?"

The interpreter slouched even lower. "No! Got none of dem t'ings, us."

"Buckskin outfits?"

"No," another shameful shrug.

"Moccasins?"

"Some," a little brighter.

"Head-dresses?"

"Maybe two, three—very old dem."

"Teepees?"

"No more—live in houses us."

"Anyone know Indian designs ... you know—war paint for warriors ... and horses?"

"Don't t'ink so ... everybody forgot."

The producer groaned. "This is astounding ... I can't believe it ... No horses ... can't ride ... no teepees ... no buckskin ... no ... no moccasins ... no ... no head-dresses ... and ... probably not even loin-cloths ..." and he was quivering. "It boggles the mind."

"What do we do?" the director asked.

For several moments the producer assessed the circumstances, and possessing an analytical mind he stated what needed to be done.

"With all our crew and cast here, with our wagon-train and canon and horses, we can't very well go back now. We'll have to train these Indians to ride. Now ... Adams," the producer's assistant, "I want you to get on the line right away. Get a guy who knows something about Indians, from the Bureau of Indian Affairs. I want you to get maybe a dozen chiefs' outfits; and 500 loin-cloths, bows an' arrows for everyone, about a dozen head-dresses and moccasins ... everything we need to make these Indians ... *Indians*. Is that clear? And get those horses by tomorrow night."

"Yes sir!"

"In the meantime, I'll call the studio office for more money. Let's get movin'."

The assistant went out.

"How long we gotta stay in this miserable God-forsaken cow-town?" Ken Maynard inquired.

"Couplea weeks ... maybe."

Ken Maynard groaned.

"Now!" directing his cigar at the interpreter and his remarks to the chief, the producer said, "Tell the chief to get 500 young men to learn to ride bare-back; an' to learn fast."

The interpreter apprised his chief of the message. The chief responded.

"He say $2.00 a day!"

"Keeee-rice! Tell him, okay!"

Two mornings later, 500 horses borrowed and rented from the local ranchers were delivered to the Indian reservation. 500 Crows began practising the art of horsemanship at once, and in earnest. And while it is true that many Crows shied away from the horses, just as many horses shied away from the Crows, so that there was much anxious circling of horses around Indians and Indians around horses, pulling and jerking midst the clamour of pleas "Whoa! Whoa! Steady there Nellie! Easy there!" all in Crow; and the horses perhaps because they were unfamiliar with Crow refusing to "whoa." Eventually, horses and Crows overcame their mutual distrust and suspicions and animosities to enable the Indians to mount their beasts.

There were of course some casualties, a few broken legs, sprained ankles, cracked ribs, and bruised behinds suffered by the novices on the first day. But by the third day most of the young men, while not accomplished equestrians, were able to ride passably well; that is, they fell off their mounts less often.

With the arrival of the equipment, bows and arrows, head-dresses, moccasins, loin-cloths, shipped by express from Washington, one day was set aside for the Crow warriors to practise shooting arrows from bows, first from a standing position and then from horseback. There were a few more casualties but nothing serious.

Along with the equipment came twelve make-up artists accompanied by an anthropologist to advise the artists in war-paint designs and to instruct the Crow in war-hooping. Twelve immense pavilions were erected, outside of each bill boards bearing symbols and markings representative of warrior war-paint and horse-paint designs. Each Indian having selected the design that best suited his taste and his horse entered a pavilion where he and his steed were painted, emerging at the other end of the massive tent looking very fierce and ready for war.

The movie moguls decided that they would film the siege of the wagon-train at 5 a.m. regardless of the readiness of the Indians. "So what if a few Red-skins fall off their horses ... be more realistic."

As planned and according to the script ten Crows, dressed in white buck-skin heavily beaded and wearing war-bonnets to represent leadership, along with 450 warriors wearing only loin-cloths and armed with bows and arrows were assembled in a shallow depression unseen from the wagon-train. The horses pawed the ground and snorted and whinnied, while the director, pro-ducer, assorted assistants, and camera-men waited for the sun to cast its beams upon the wagon-train. When that critical moment occurred, signalled by an assistant with a wave of an arm, the director shouted "Action! Cameras roll!"

450 Indians on 450 horses erupted over the lip of the valley a 'hoopin' an' a hollerin', their savage war-cries splitting the air while 1800 hooves thundered down the slope, shaking the earth. Wagon-train passengers spilled out of the covered-wagons, splashed up from blankets, seized rifles, yelling "Injuns! Injuns!" and hurled themselves behind boxes and crates and barrels and began firing. At one end of the valley, Ken Maynard on his white charger waited for his cue; at the other end fifty cavalrymen waited to charge to the rescue. Bang! Bang! Bang! The Crows, a 'hoopin' an' a hollerin' were riding round and round the wagon-train, firing their arrows into the covered wagon and into boxes and crates and barrels. Bang! Bang! Bang! Round and round rode the Crows.

"Cut! Cut! Cut!" everyone was shouting. "Cut! Cut! Cut!" everyone was waving his arms. Cut! Cut! Cut! 450 Crows, yelling whoa! whoa! whoa! brought their steeds to a halt.

The director, also on a horse, was livid with rage. He almost choked "Somebody's gotta die; when you're shot, you fall off your horse and die. Don't you understand?"

The Indians nodded and grunted "How! How!"

The director in disgust rode off leaving the cast and crew to repair 3000 to 4000 punctures and perforations inflicted by arrows on the canvas of the cov-ered wagons. Six members of the cast suffering injuries from stray arrows needed medical attention. The Indians, with the arrows they had recovered, retired to the reservation to mend their weapons.

Just before sun-up the next day there was a final admonition. "Get it done right this time!" The warriors responded "How! How!"

At the hand signal, "Action! Cameras roll!" were uttered.

450 Indians on 450 horses boiled over the lip of the valley a 'hoopin' an' a hollerin', their savage war cries rending the peace, while 1800 hooves pounded down the slope convulsing the ground. Wagon-train patrons scurried out of covered wagons, sprang from blankets, seized their rifles, yelling "Injuns! Injuns!" and dove behind boxes and crates and barrels and began firing Bang! Bang! Bang!

Seventy-five of the Crows, a 'hoopin' an' a hollerin' fell off their horses. Bang! Bang! Bang! 200 more Crows, a 'hoopin' an' a hollerin' spun off their mounts. Bang! Bang! Bang! The rest pitched off their steeds who fled in all directions.

"Cut! Cut! Cut!" everyone was shouting. 450 Crows suspended their moanin' an' a groanin' an' a rollin' on the ground, even though many had sustained real injuries, to listen and to watch the director.

There was a torrent of curses, sulphuric glares, which eventually subsided into mutterings, the gist of which was relayed by the interpreter to the chiefs and warriors "that not everyone should have fallen off his horse." To this the chief replied $2.00.

The scene was re-enacted the next day without incident. After the shooting there were hand-shakes all around; and expressions of admiration tendered by Ken Maynard to the Crows for the speed with which they had developed horsemanship, remarking that "it must be inbred."

Crew and cast were celebrating over wine and whiskey, cheese and crackers, when the film editor summoned the director. "Come here and look at these," he said, thrusting a magnifying glass to his superior. The director held the film strip against the light; he applied the magnifying glass to the stills.

"Sun-glasses! Keeee-rice ... sun-glasses ... those damned Indians. Keeee-rice ... what next ..."

When told, the producer kicked a chair after hurling a bottle into a corner; for close to ten minutes he cursed Indians. But it was useless, the scene had to be shot again.

Horses and Indians had to be recalled and reassembled for retakes for which the good chief demanded $2.00 for his people. It took another week before the wagon-train siege was filmed to the satisfaction of the producer and his director. In the interim there were two days of rain, one filming aborted by several Crows wearing watches, an extra filming of a prairie fire ignited by Ken Maynard that miscarried because several Crow warriors, supposedly dead, moved to avoid getting burned during a critical segment of the filming. When the first real epic of "Cowboys and Indians" was finally done, the

Crows were jubilant, indebted to their chief for the prosperity and lasting renown that he exacted during difficult times. The producer and director, cast and crew, departed in disquiet over having exceeded their budget.

But whatever doubts the producer and the director might have entertained were more than vindicated by reviews of the film in which the horsemanship of the Crow was acclaimed and the genius of the producer for his vision and for his foresight in using Indians in motion pictures.

JAMES JOYCE

COUNTERPARTS

James Joyce (1882–1941) was born in Dublin, Ireland, a place on which he would base all his major writings but from which he would leave at twenty in self-imposed exile. In 1888 he was sent to Clongowes Wood College, a Jesuit boarding school, but was forced to withdraw owing to his family's dwindling finances. In 1898 he entered the Faculty of Arts in University College, Dublin, graduating in 1902 with a degree in modern languages—and with a firm, rebellious agnosticism. In 1902 he left Dublin for Paris, purportedly to study medicine, but he returned the next year when his mother became terminally ill.

Joyce again left Ireland for Europe in 1904, seeking a more tolerant cultural climate wherein he could live unmarried with his partner Nora Barnacle (whom he would marry in 1931). Settling first in Trieste, Joyce worked on his fiction and taught English to support his family. Dubliners, his signature collection of short stories, was accepted for publication in 1906; however, an editorial conflict over potentially libellous passages delayed its publication until 1914, the same year that the poet Ezra Pound took an interest in Joyce's autobiographical novel A Portrait of the Artist as a Young Man (published serially from 1914 to 1915). Pound sponsored Joyce and introduced him to literary circles in Paris, where, after weathering the war in Zurich, Joyce's family settled for some twenty years.

In Paris, Joyce soon became the centre of his own circle of friends and fellow intellectuals, and he lived largely on the gifts of such patrons as Harriet Weaver. Joyce's revolutionary novel Ulysses was published in 1922 by Sylvia Beach, an American who owned a bookshop in Paris (the book was banned in America until 1934). Joyce devoted the rest of his life to writing and revising Ulysses's nocturnal complement, the formidably experimental Finnegan's Wake (1939). The onset of World War II forced him and his family to return to Zurich, where he fell ill and died in 1941.

Joyce's intention in Dubliners was to write "in a style of scrupulous meanness" a moral portrait of his homeland's capital. "I always write about Dublin," Joyce said, "because if I can get to the heart of Dublin I can get to the heart of all the cities in the world. In the particular is contained the universal." One of Joyce's most critical contributions to the short story was, as Northrop Frye puts it, his "nontheological use of the *theological term*" epiphany: "*a sudden spiritual manifestation, whether in the vulgarity of speech or of gesture or in a memorable expression of the mind itself.*"

———————

The bell rang furiously and, when Miss Parker went to the tube, a furious voice called out in a piercing North of Ireland accent:

—Send Farrington here!

Miss Parker returned to her machine, saying to a man who was writing at a desk:

—Mr. Alleyne wants you upstairs.

The man muttered *Blast him!* under his breath and pushed back his chair to stand up. When he stood up he was tall and of great bulk. He had a hanging face, dark wine-coloured, with fair eyebrows and moustache: his eyes bulged forward slightly and the whites of them were dirty. He lifted up the counter and, passing by the clients, went out of the office with a heavy step.

He went heavily upstairs until he came to the second landing, where a door bore a brass plate with the inscription *Mr. Alleyne*. Here he halted, puffing with labour and vexation, and knocked. The shrill voice cried:

—Come in!

The man entered Mr. Alleyne's room. Simultaneously Mr. Alleyne, a little man wearing gold-rimmed glasses on a cleanshaven face, shot his head up over a pile of documents. The head itself was so pink and hairless that it seemed like a large egg reposing on the papers. Mr. Alleyne did not lose a moment:

—Farrington? What is the meaning of this? Why have I always to complain of you? May I ask you why you haven't made a copy of that contract between Bodley and Kirwan? I told you it must be ready by four o'clock.

—But Mr. Shelley said, sir—

—*Mr. Shelley said, sir....* Kindly attend to what I say and not to what *Mr. Shelley says, sir*. You have always some excuse or another for shirking work. Let me tell you that if the contract is not copied before this evening I'll lay the matter before Mr. Crosbie.... Do you hear me now?

—Yes, sir.

—Do you hear me now? ... Ay and another little matter! I might as well be talking to the wall as talking to you. Understand once for all that you get a half an hour for your lunch and not an hour and a half. How many courses do you want, I'd like know.... Do you mind me, now?

—Yes, sir.

Mr. Alleyne bent his head again upon his pile of papers. The man stared fixedly at the polished skull which directed the affairs of Crosbie & Alleyne, gauging its fragility. A spasm of rage gripped his throat for a few moments and then passed, leaving after it a sharp sensation of thirst. The man recognised the sensation and felt that he must have a good night's drinking. The middle of the month was passed and, if he could get the copy done in time, Mr. Alleyne might give him an order on the cashier. He stood still, gazing fixedly at the head upon the pile of papers. Suddenly Mr. Alleyne began to upset all the papers, searching for something. Then, as if he had been unaware of the man's presence till that moment, he shot up his head again, saying:

—Eh? Are you going to stand there all day? Upon my word, Farrington, you take things easy!

—I was waiting to see ...

—Very good, you needn't wait to see. Go downstairs and do your work.

The man walked heavily towards the door and, as he went out of the room, he heard Mr. Alleyne cry after him that if the contract was not copied by evening Mr. Crosbie would hear of the matter.

He returned to his desk in the lower office and counted the sheets which remained to be copied. He took up his pen and dipped it in the ink but he continued to stare stupidly at the last words he had written: *In no case shall the said Bernard Bodley be* ... The evening was falling and in a few minutes they would be lighting the gas: then he could write. He felt that he must slake the thirst in his throat. He stood up from his desk and, lifting the counter as before, passed out of the office. As he was passing out the chief clerk looked at him inquiringly.

—It's all right, Mr. Shelley, said the man, pointing with his finger to indicate the objective of his journey.

The chief clerk glanced at the hat-rack but, seeing the row complete, offered no remark. As soon as he was on the landing the man pulled a shepherd's plaid cap out of his pocket, put it on his head and ran quickly down the rickety stairs. From the street door he walked on furtively on the inner side of the path towards the corner and all at once dived into a doorway. He was now safe in the dark snug of O'Neill's shop, and, filling up the little window that looked into the bar with his inflamed face, the colour of dark wine or dark meat, he called out:

—Here, Pat, give us a g.p., like a good fellow.

The curate brought him a glass of plain porter. The man drank it at a gulp and asked for a caraway seed. He put his penny on the counter and, leaving the curate to grope for it in the gloom, retreated out of the snug as furtively as he had entered it.

Darkness, accompanied by a thick fog, was gaining upon the dusk of February and the lamps in Eustace Street had been lit. The man went up by the houses until he reached the door of the office, wondering whether he could finish his copy in time. On the stairs a moist pungent odour of perfumes saluted his nose: evidently Miss Delacour had come while he was out in O'Neill's. He crammed his cap back again into his pocket and re-entered the office, assuming an air of absent-mindedness.

—Mr. Alleyne has been calling for you, said the chief clerk severely. Where were you?

The man glanced at the two clients who were standing at the counter as if to intimate that their presence prevented him from answering. As the clients were both male the chief clerk allowed himself a laugh.

—I know that game, he said. Five times in one day is a little bit.... Well, you better look sharp and get a copy of our correspondence in the Delacour case for Mr. Alleyne.

This address in the presence of the public, his run upstairs and the porter he had gulped down so hastily confused the man and, as he sat down at his desk to get what was required, he realised how hopeless was the task of finishing his copy of the contract before half past five. The dark damp night was coming and he longed to spend it in the bars, drinking with his friends amid the glare of gas and the clatter of glasses. He got out the Delacour correspondence and passed out of the office. He hoped Mr. Alleyne would not discover that the last two letters were missing.

The moist pungent perfume lay all the way up to Mr. Alleyne's room. Miss Delacour was a middle-aged woman of Jewish appearance. Mr. Alleyne was said to be sweet on her or on her money. She came to the office often and stayed a long time when she came. She was sitting beside his desk now in an aroma of perfumes, smoothing the handle of her umbrella and nodding the great black feather in her hat. Mr. Alleyne had swivelled his chair round to face her and thrown his right foot jauntily upon his left knee. The man put the correspondence on the desk and bowed respectfully but neither Mr. Alleyne nor Miss Delacour took any notice of his bow. Mr. Alleyne tapped a finger on the correspondence and then flicked it towards him as if to say: *That's all right: you can go.*

The man returned to the lower office and sat down again at his desk. He stared intently at the incomplete phrase: *In no case shall the said Bernard Bodley be ...* and thought how strange it was that the last three words began with the same letter. The chief clerk began to hurry Miss Parker, saying she would never have the letters typed in time for post. The man listened to the clicking of the machine for a few minutes and then set to work to finish his copy. But his head was not clear and his mind wandered away to the glare and rattle of the public-house. It was a night for hot punches. He struggled on with his copy, but when the clock struck five he had still fourteen pages to write. Blast it! He couldn't finish it in time. He longed to execrate aloud, to bring his fist down on something violently. He was so enraged that he wrote *Bernard Bernard* instead of *Bernard Bodley* and had to begin again on a clean sheet.

He felt strong enough to clear out the whole office singlehanded. His body ached to do something, to rush out and revel in violence. All the indignities of his life enraged him.... Could he ask the cashier privately for an advance? No, the cashier was no good, no damn good: he wouldn't give an advance.... He knew where he would meet the boys: Leonard and O'Halloran and Nosey Flynn. The barometer of his emotional nature was set for a spell of riot.

His imagination had so abstracted him that his name was called twice before he answered. Mr. Alleyne and Miss Delacour were standing outside the counter and all the clerks had turned round in anticipation of something. The man got up from his desk. Mr. Alleyne began a tirade of abuse, saying that two letters were missing. The man answered that he knew nothing about them, that he had made a faithful copy. The tirade continued: it was so bitter and violent that the man could hardly restrain his fist from descending upon the head of the manikin before him.

—I know nothing about any other two letters, he said stupidly.

—*You—know—nothing.* Of course you know nothing, said Mr. Alleyne. Tell me, he added, glancing first for approval to the lady beside him, do you take me for a fool? Do you think me an utter fool?

The man glanced from the lady's face to the little egg-shaped head and back again; and, almost before he was aware of it, his tongue had found a felicitous moment:

—I don't think, sir, he said, that that's a fair question to put to me.

There was a pause in the very breathing of the clerks. Everyone was astounded (the author of the witticism no less than his neighbours) and Miss Delacour, who was a stout amiable person, began to smile broadly. Mr. Alleyne flushed to the hue of a wild rose and his mouth twitched with a dwarf's passion. He shook his fist in the man's face till it seemed to vibrate like the knob of some electric machine:

—You impertinent ruffian! You impertinent ruffian! I'll make short work of you! Wait till you see! You'll apologise to me for your impertinence or you'll quit the office instanter! You'll quit this, I'm telling you, or you'll apologise to me!

He stood in a doorway opposite the office watching to see if the cashier would come out alone. All the clerks passed out and finally the cashier came out with the chief clerk. It was no use trying to say word to him when he was with the chief clerk. The man felt that his position was bad enough. He had been obliged to offer an abject apology to Mr. Alleyne for his impertinence but he knew what a hornet's nest the office would be for him. He could remember the way in which Mr. Alleyne had hounded little Peake out of the office in order to make room for his own nephew. He felt savage and thirsty and revengeful, annoyed with himself and with everyone else. Mr. Alleyne would never give him an hour's rest; his life would be a hell to him. He had made a proper fool of himself this time. Could he not keep his tongue in his cheek? But they had never pulled together from the first, he and Mr. Alleyne, ever since the day Mr. Alleyne had overheard him mimicking his North of Ireland accent to amuse Higgins and Miss Parker: that had been the beginning of it. He might have tried Higgins for the money, but sure Higgins never had anything for himself. A man with two establishments to keep up, of course he couldn't....

He felt his great body again aching for the comfort of the public-house. The fog had begun to chill him and he wondered could he touch Pat in O'Neill's. He could not touch him for more than a bob—and a bob was no use. Yet he must get money somewhere or other: he had spent his last penny for the g.p. and soon it would be too late for getting money anywhere. Suddenly, as he was fingering his watch-chain, he thought of Terry Kelly's pawn-office in Fleet Street. That was the dart! Why didn't he think of it sooner?

He went through the narrow alley of Temple Bar quickly, muttering to himself that they could all go to hell because he was going to have a good night of it. The clerk in Terry Kelly's said *A crown!* but the consignor held out for six shillings; and in the end the six shillings was allowed him literally. He came out of the pawn-office joyfully, making a little cylinder of the coins between his thumb and fingers. In Westmoreland Street the footpaths were crowded with young men and women returning from business and ragged urchins ran here and there yelling out the names of the evening editions. The man passed through the crowd, looking on the spectacle generally with proud satisfaction and staring masterfully at the office-girls. His head was full of the noises of tram-gongs and swishing trolleys and his nose already sniffed the curling fumes of punch. As he walked on he preconsidered the terms in which he would narrate the incident to the boys:

—So, I just looked at him—coolly, you know, and looked at her. Then I looked back at him again—taking my time, you know. *I don't think that that's a fair question to put to me*, says I.

Nosey Flynn was sitting up in his usual corner of Davy Byrne's and, when he heard the story, he stood Farrington a half-one, saying it was as smart a thing as ever he heard. Farrington stood a drink in his turn. After a while O'Halloran and Paddy Leonard came in and the story was repeated to them. O'Halloran stood tailors of malt, hot, all round and told the story of the retort he had made to the chief clerk when he was in Callan's of Fownes's Street; but, as the retort was after the manner of the liberal shepherds in the eclogues, he had to admit that it was not so clever as Farrington's retort. At this Farrington told the boys to polish off that and have another.

Just as they were naming their poisons who should come in but Higgins! Of course he had to join in with the others. The men asked him to give his version of it, and he did so with great vivacity for the sight of five small hot whiskies was very exhilarating. Everyone roared laughing when he showed the way in which Mr. Alleyne shook his fist in Farrington's face. Then he imitated Farrington, saying, *And here was my nabs, as cool as you please*, while Farrington looked at the company out of his heavy dirty eyes, smiling and at times drawing forth stray drops of liquor from his moustache with the aid of his lower lip.

When that round was over there was a pause. O'Halloran had money but neither of the other two seemed to have any; so the whole party left the shop somewhat regretfully. At the corner of Duke Street Higgins and Nosey Flynn bevelled off to the left while the other three turned back towards the city. Rain was drizzling down on the cold streets and, when they reached the Ballast Office, Farrington suggested the Scotch House. The bar was full of men and loud with the noise of tongues and glasses. The three men pushed past the whining match-sellers at the door and formed a little party at the corner of the counter. They began to exchange stories. Leonard introduced them to a young fellow named Weathers who was performing at the Tivoli as an acrobat and knockabout *artiste*. Farrington stood a drink all round. Weathers said he would take a small Irish and Apollinaris. Farrington, who had definite notions of what was what, asked the boys would they have an Apollinaris too; but the boys told Tim to make theirs hot. The talk became theatrical. O'Halloran stood a round and then Farrington stood another round, Weathers protesting that the hospitality was too Irish. He promised to get them in behind the scenes and introduce them to some nice girls. O'Halloran said that he and Leonard would go but that Farrington wouldn't go because he was a married man; and Farrington's heavy dirty eyes leered at the company in token that he understood he was being chaffed. Weathers made them all have just one little tincture at his expense and promised to meet them later on at Mulligan's in Poolbeg Street.

When the Scotch House closed they went round to Mulligan's. They went into the parlour at the back and O'Halloran ordered small hot specials all round. They were all beginning to feel mellow. Farrington was just standing another round when Weathers came back. Much to Farrington's relief he drank a glass of bitter this time. Funds were running low but they had enough to keep them going. Presently two young women with big hats and a young man in a check suit came in and sat at a table close by. Weathers saluted them and told the company that they were out of the Tivoli. Farrington's eyes wandered at every moment in the direction of one of the young women. There was something striking in her appearance. An immense scarf of peacock-blue muslin was wound round her hat and knotted in a great bow under her chin;

and she wore bright yellow gloves, reaching to the elbow. Farrington gazed admiringly at the plump arm which she moved very often and with much grace; and when, after a little time, she answered his gaze he admired still more her large dark brown eyes. The oblique staring expression in them fascinated him. She glanced at him once or twice and, when the party was leaving the room, she brushed against his chair and said *O, pardon!* in a London accent. He watched her leave the room in the hope that she would look back at him, but he was disappointed. He cursed his want of money and cursed all the rounds he had stood, particularly all the whiskies and Apollinaris which he had stood to Weathers. If there was one thing that he hated it was a sponge. He was so angry that he lost count of the conversation of his friends.

When Paddy Leonard called him he found that they were talking about feats of strength. Weathers was showing his biceps muscle to the company and boasting so much that the other two had called on Farrington to uphold the national honour. Farrington pulled up his sleeve accordingly and showed his biceps muscle to the company. The two arms were examined and compared and finally it was agreed to have a trial of strength. The table was cleared and the two men rested their elbows on it, clasping hands. When Paddy Leonard said *Go!* each was to try to bring down the other's hand on to the table. Farrington looked very serious and determined.

The trial began. After about thirty seconds Weathers brought his opponent's hand slowly down on to the table. Farrington's dark wine-coloured face flushed darker still with anger and humiliation at having been defeated by such a stripling.

—You're not to put the weight of your body behind it. Play fair, he said.

—Who's not playing fair? said the other.

—Come on again. The two best out of three.

The trial began again. The veins stood out on Farrington's forehead, and the pallor of Weathers' complexion changed to peony. Their hands and arms trembled under the stress. After a long struggle Weathers again brought his opponent's hand slowly on to the table. There was a murmur of applause from the spectators. The curate, who was standing beside the table, nodded his red head toward the victor and said with loutish familiarity:

—Ah! that's the knack!

—What the hell do you know about it? said Farrington fiercely, turning on the man. What do you put in your gab for?

—Sh, sh! said O'Halloran, observing the violent expression of Farrington's face. Pony up, boys. We'll have just one little smahan more and then we'll be off.

A very sullen-faced man stood at the corner of O'Connell Bridge waiting for the little Sandymount tram to take him home. He was full of smouldering anger and revengefulness. He felt humiliated and discontented; he did not even feel drunk; and he had only twopence in his pocket. He cursed everything. He had done for himself in the office, pawned his watch, spent all his money; and he had not even got drunk. He began to feel thirsty again and he longed to be back again in the hot reeking public-house. He had lost his reputation as a strong man, having been defeated twice by a mere boy. His heart swelled with fury and, when he thought of the woman in the big hat who had brushed against him and said *Pardon!* his fury nearly choked him.

His tram let him down at Shelbourne Road and he steered his great body along in the shadow of the wall of the barracks. He loathed returning to his home. When he went in by the side-door he found the kitchen empty and the kitchen fire nearly out. He bawled upstairs:

—Ada! Ada!

His wife was a little sharp-faced woman who bullied her husband when he was sober and was bullied by him when he was drunk. They had five children. A little boy came running down the stairs.

—Who is that? said the man, peering through the darkness.

—Me, pa.

—Who are you? Charlie?

—No, pa. Tom.

—Where's your mother?

—She's out at the chapel.

—That's right.... Did she think of leaving any dinner for me?

—Yes, pa. I—

—Light the lamp. What do you mean by having the place in darkness? Are the other children in bed?

The man sat down heavily on one of the chairs while the little boy lit the lamp. He began to mimic his son's flat accent, saying half to himself: *At the chapel. At the chapel, if you please!* When the lamp was lit he banged his fist on the table and shouted:

—What's for my dinner?

—I'm going ... to cook it, pa, said the little boy.

The man jumped up furiously and pointed to the fire.

—On that fire! You let the fire out! By God, I'll teach you to do that again!

He took a step to the door and seized the walking-stick which was standing behind it.

—I'll teach you to let the fire out! he said, rolling up his sleeve in order to give his arm free play.

The little boy cried *O, pa!* and ran whimpering round the table, but the man followed him and caught him by the coat. The little boy looked about him wildly but, seeing no way of escape fell upon his knees.

—Now, you'll let the fire out the next time! said the man, striking at him viciously with the stick. Take that, you little whelp!

The boy uttered a squeal of pain as the stick cut his thigh. He clasped his hands together in the air and his voice shook with fright.

—O, pa! he cried. Don't beat me, pa! And I'll ... I'll say a *Hail Mary* for you.... I'll say a *Hail Mary* for you, pa, if you don't beat me.... I'll say a *Hail Mary*....

FRANZ KAFKA

THE METAMORPHOSIS

Translated by Willa and Edwin Muir

Franz Kafka (1883–1924) was born in Prague, Czechoslovakia, to Jewish parents with whom he lived for most of his life. His complicated relationship with his family, particularly his father, psychologically shaped his fiction. Kafka was so afraid of his authoritarian father that he stuttered in his presence. He attended German schools and in 1906 received his doctorate in jurisprudence. For many years thereafter he worked as a civil-service lawyer, investigating claims at the state Worker's Accident Insurance Institute while writing fiction late into the night. During his lifetime he published only a few slim volumes, including The Metamorphosis *(1915),* In the Penal Colony *(1919), and* A Country Doctor *(1920).*

"The Metamorphosis," Kafka's best-known story, is a kind of waking nightmare about a young man who opens his eyes one morning to find himself transformed into a gigantic insect. This story (or novella) projects a peculiarly modern view of the human condition. American writer John Updike says that "Kafka epitomizes one aspect of [the] modern mind-set: a sensation of anxiety and shame whose center cannot be located and therefore cannot be placated." In his essay "Kafka and Modern History," Czech novelist Milan Kundera speculates on how this "solitary, introverted man immersed in his own life and his art" has come to be recognized as a prophet of modern history. How is it that Kafka was the first to grasp the modern state's progressive concentration of power, its tendency toward depersonalization and bureaucracy? Kundera's conclusion is that the "psychological mechanisms that function in great (apparently incredible and inhuman) historical events are the same as those that regulate private (quite ordinary and very human) situations." After his death from tuberculosis, Kafka's great novels Amerika, The Castle, *and* The Trial *were published, despite his instructions to his literary executor that they be destroyed.*

I

As Gregor Samsa awoke one morning from uneasy dreams he found himself transformed in his bed into a gigantic insect. He was lying on his hard, as it were armour-plated, back and when he lifted his head a little he could see his dome-like brown belly divided into stiff arched segments on top of which the bed quilt could hardly keep in position and was about to slide off completely. His numerous legs, which were pitifully thin compared to the rest of his bulk, waved helplessly before his eyes.

What has happened to me? he thought. It was no dream. His room, a regular human bedroom, only rather too small, lay quiet between the four familiar walls. Above the table on which a collection of cloth samples was unpacked and spread out—Samsa was a commercial traveller—hung the picture which he had recently cut out of an illustrated magazine and put into a pretty gilt frame. It showed a lady, with a fur cap on and a fur stole, sitting upright and holding out to the spectator a huge fur muff into which the whole of her forearm had vanished!

Gregor's eyes turned next to the window, and the overcast sky—one could hear rain drops beating on the window gutter—made him quite melancholy. What about sleeping a little longer and forgetting all this nonsense, he thought, but it could not be done, for he was accustomed to sleep on his right side and in his present condition he could not turn himself over. However violently he forced himself towards his right side he always rolled on to his back again. He tried it at least a hundred times, shutting his eyes to keep from seeing his struggling legs, and only desisted when he began to feel in his side a faint dull ache he had never experienced before.

Oh God, he thought, what an exhausting job I've picked on! Traveling about day in, day out. It's much more irritating work than doing the actual business in the office, and on top of that there's the trouble of constant travelling, of worrying about train connections, the bad and irregular meals, casual acquaintances that are always new and never become intimate friends. The devil take it all! He felt a slight itching up on his belly; slowly pushed himself on his back nearer to the top of the bed so that he could lift his head more easily; identified the itching place which was surrounded by many small white spots the nature of which he could not understand and made to touch it with a leg, but drew the leg back immediately, for the contact made a cold shiver run through him.

He slid down again into his former position. This getting up early, he thought, makes one quite stupid. A man needs his sleep. Other commercials live like harem women. For instance, when I come back to the hotel of a morning to write up the orders I've got, these others are only sitting down to breakfast. Let me just try that with my chief; I'd be sacked on the spot. Anyhow, that might be quite a good thing for me, who can tell? If I didn't have to hold my hand because of my parents I'd have given notice long ago, I'd have gone to the chief and told him exactly what I think of him. That would knock him endways from his desk! It's a queer way of doing, too, this sitting on high at a desk and talking down to employees, especially when they have to come quite near because the chief is hard of hearing. Well, there's still hope; once I've saved enough money to pay back my parents' debts to him—that should take another five or six years—I'll do it without fail. I'll cut myself completely loose then. For the moment, though, I'd better get up, since my train goes at five.

He looked at the alarm clock ticking on the chest. Heavenly Father! he thought. It was half-past six o'clock and the hands were quietly moving on, it was even past the half-hour, it was getting on toward a quarter to seven. Had the alarm clock not gone off? From the bed one could see that it had been properly set for four o'clock; of course it must have gone off. Yes, but was it possible to sleep quietly through that ear-splitting noise? Well, he had not slept quietly, yet apparently all the more soundly for that. But what was he to do now? The next train went at seven o'clock; to catch that he would need to hurry like mad and his samples weren't even packed up, and he himself wasn't feeling particularly fresh and active. And even if he did catch the train he wouldn't avoid a row with the chief, since the firm's porter would have been waiting for the five o'clock train and would have long since reported his failure to turn up. The porter was a creature of the chief's, spineless and stupid. Well, supposing he were to say he was sick? But that would be most unpleasant and would look suspicious, since during his five years' employment he had not been ill once. The chief himself would be sure to come with the sick-insurance doctor, would reproach his parents with their son's laziness and would cut all excuses short by referring to the insurance doctor, who of course regarded all mankind as perfectly healthy malingerers. And would he be so far wrong on this occasion? Gregor really felt quite well, apart from a drowsiness that was utterly superfluous after such a long sleep, and he was even unusually hungry.

As all this was running through his mind at top speed without his being able to decide to leave his bed—the alarm clock had just struck a quarter to seven—there came a cautious tap at the door behind the head of his bed. "Gregor," said a voice—it was his mother's—"it's a quarter to seven. Hadn't you a train to catch?" That gentle voice! Gregor had a shock as he heard his own voice answering hers, unmistakably his own voice, it was true, but with a persistent horrible twittering squeak behind it like an undertone, that left the words in their clear shape only for the first moment and then rose up reverberating round them to destroy their sense, so that one could not be sure one had heard them rightly. Gregor wanted to answer at length and explain everything, but in the circumstances he confined himself to saying: "Yes, yes, thank you, Mother, I'm getting up now." The wooden door between them must have kept the change in his voice from being noticeable outside, for his mother contented herself with this statement and shuffled away. Yet this brief exchange of words had made the other members of the family aware that Gregor was still in the house, as they had not expected, and at one of the side doors his father was already knocking, gently, yet with his fist. "Gregor, Gregor," he called, "what's the matter with you?" And after a little while he called again in a deeper voice: "Gregor! Gregor!" At the other side door his sister was saying in a low, plaintive tone: "Gregor! Aren't you well? Are you needing anything?" He answered them both at once: "I'm just ready," and did his best to make his voice sound as normal as possible by enunciating the words very clearly and leaving long pauses between them. So his father went back to his breakfast, but his sister whispered: "Gregor, open the door, do." However, he was not thinking of opening the door, and felt thankful for the prudent habit he had acquired in travelling of locking all doors during the night, even at home.

His immediate intention was to get up quietly without being disturbed, to put on his clothes and above all eat his breakfast, and only then to consider what else was to be done, since in bed, he was well aware, his meditations would come to no sensible conclusion. He remembered that often enough in bed he had felt small aches and pains, probably caused by awkward postures, which had proved purely imaginary once he got up, and he looked forward eagerly to seeing this morning's delusions gradually fall away. That the change in his voice was nothing but the precursor of a severe chill, a standing ailment of commercial travellers, he had not the least possible doubt.

To get rid of the quilt was quite easy; he had only to inflate himself a little and it fell off by itself. But the next move was difficult, especially because he was so uncommonly broad. He would have needed arms and hands to hoist himself up; instead he had only the numerous little legs which never stopped waving in all directions and which he could not control in the least. When he tried to bend one of them it was the first to stretch itself straight; and did he succeed at last in making it do what he wanted, all the other legs meanwhile waved the more wildly in a high degree of unpleasant agitation. "But what's the use of lying idle in bed," said Gregor to himself.

He thought that he might get out of bed with the lower part of his body first, but this lower part, which he had not yet seen and of which he could form no clear conception, proved too difficult to move; it shifted so slowly; and when finally, almost wild with annoyance, he gathered his forces together and thrust out recklessly, he had miscalculated the direction and bumped heavily against the lower end of the bed, and the stinging pain he felt informed him that precisely this lower part of his body was at the moment probably the most sensitive.

So he tried to get the top part of himself out first, and cautiously moved his head towards the edge of the bed. That proved easy enough, and despite its breadth and mass the bulk of his body at last slowly followed the movement of his head. Still, when he finally got his head free over the edge of the bed he felt too scared to go on advancing, for after all if he let himself fall in this way it would take a miracle to keep his head from being injured. And at all costs he must not lose consciousness now, precisely now; he would rather stay in bed.

But when after a repetition of the same efforts he lay in his former position again, sighing, and watched his little legs struggling against each other more wildly than ever, if that were possible, and saw no way of bringing any order into this arbitrary confusion, he told himself again that it was impossible to stay in bed and that the most sensible course was to risk everything for the smallest hope of getting away from it. At the same time he did not forget meanwhile to remind himself that cool reflection, the coolest possible, was much better than desperate resolves. In such moments he focused his eyes as sharply as possible on the window, but, unfortunately, the prospect of the morning fog, which muffled even the other side of the narrow street, brought him little encouragement and comfort. "Seven o'clock already," he said to himself when the alarm clock chimed again, "seven o'clock already and still such a thick fog." And for a little while he lay quiet, breathing lightly, as if perhaps expecting such complete repose to restore all things to their real and normal condition.

But then he said to himself: "Before it strikes a quarter past seven I must be quite out of this bed, without fail. Anyhow, by that time someone will have come from the office to ask for me, since it opens before seven." And he set himself to rocking his whole body at once in a regular rhythm, with the idea of swinging it out of the bed. If he tipped himself out in that way he could keep his head from injury by lifting it at an acute angle when he fell. His back seemed to be hard and was not likely to suffer from a fall on the carpet. His biggest worry was the loud crash he would not be able to help making, which would probably cause anxiety, if not terror, behind all the doors. Still, he must take the risk.

When he was already half out of the bed—the new method was more a game than an effort, for he needed only to hitch himself across by rocking to and fro—it struck him how simple it would be if he could get help. Two strong people—he thought of his father and the servant girl—would be amply sufficient; they would only have to thrust their arms under his convex back, lever him out of the bed, bend down with their burden and then be patient enough to let him turn himself right over on to the floor, where it was to be hoped his legs would then find their proper function. Well, ignoring the fact that the doors were all locked, ought he really to call for help? In spite of his misery he could not suppress a smile at the very idea of it.

He had got so far that he could barely keep his equilibrium when he rocked himself strongly, and he would have to nerve himself very soon for the final decision since in five minutes' time it would be a quarter past seven—when the front door bell rang. "That's someone from the office," he said to himself, and grew almost rigid, while his little legs only jigged about all the faster. For a moment everything stayed quiet. "They're not going to open the door," said Gregor to himself, catching at some kind of irrational hope. But then of course the servant girl went as usual to the door with her heavy tread and opened it. Gregor needed only to hear the first good morning of the visitor to know immediately who it was—the chief clerk himself. What a fate, to be condemned to work for a firm where the smallest omission at once gave rise to the gravest suspicion! Were all employees in a body nothing but scoundrels, was there not among them one single loyal devoted man who, had he wasted only an hour or so of the firm's time in a morning, was so tormented by con-science as to be driven out of his mind and actually incapable of leaving his bed? Wouldn't it really have been sufficient to send an apprentice to inquire—if any inquiry were necessary at all—did the chief clerk himself have to come and thus indicate to the entire family, an innocent family, that this suspicious circumstance could be investigated by no one less versed in affairs than him-self? And more through the agitation caused by these reflections than through any act of will Gregor swung himself out of bed with all his strength. There was a loud thump, but it was not really a crash. His fall was broken to some extent by the carpet, his back, too, was less stiff than he thought, and so there was merely a dull thud, not so very startling. Only he had not lifted his head carefully enough and had hit it; he turned it and rubbed it on the carpet in pain and irritation.

"That was something falling down in there," said the chief clerk in the next room to the left. Gregor tried to suppose to himself that something like what had happened to him today might some day happen to the chief clerk; one really could not deny that it was possible. But as if in brusque reply to this supposition the chief clerk took a couple of firm steps in the next-door room and his patent leather boots creaked. From the right-hand room his sister was whispering to inform him of the situation: "Gregor, the chief clerk's here." "I know," muttered Gregor to himself; but he didn't dare to make his voice loud enough for his sister to hear it.

"Gregor," said his father now from the left-hand room, "the chief clerk has come and wants to know why you didn't catch the early train. We don't know what to say to him. Besides, he wants to talk to you in person. So open the door, please. He will be good enough to excuse the untidiness of your room." "Good morning, Mr. Samsa," the chief clerk was calling amiably meanwhile. "He's not well," said his mother to the visitor, while his father was still speaking through the door, "he's not well, sir, believe me. What else would make him miss a train! The boy thinks about nothing but his work. It makes me almost cross the way he never goes out in the evenings; he's been here the last eight days and has stayed at home every single evening. He just sits there quietly at the table reading a newspaper or looking through railway timetables. The only amusement he gets is doing fretwork. For instance, he spent two or three evenings cutting out a little picture frame; you would be surprised to see how pretty it is; it's hanging in his room; you'll see it in a minute when Gregor opens the door. I must say I'm glad you've come, sir; we should never have got him to unlock the door by ourselves; he's so obstinate; and I'm sure he's unwell, though he wouldn't have it to be so this morning." "I'm just coming," said Gregor slowly and carefully, not moving an inch for fear of losing one word of the conversation. "I can't think of any other explanation, madam," said the chief clerk, "I hope it's nothing serious. Although on the other hand I must say that we men of business—fortunately or unfortunately—very often simply have to ignore any slight indisposition, since business must be attended to." "Well, can the chief clerk come in now?" asked Gregor's father impatiently, again knocking on the door. "No," said Gregor. In the left-hand room a painful silence followed this refusal, in the right-hand room his sister began to sob.

Why didn't his sister join the others? She was probably newly out of bed and hadn't even begun to put on her clothes yet. Well, why was she crying? Because he wouldn't get up and let the chief clerk in, because he was in danger of losing his job, and because the chief would begin dunning his parents again for the old debts? Surely these were things one didn't need to worry about for the present. Gregor was still at home and not in the least thinking of deserting the family. At the moment, true, he was lying on the carpet and no one who knew the condition he was in could seriously expect him to admit the chief clerk. But for such a small discourtesy, which could plausibly be explained away somehow later on, Gregor could hardly be dismissed on the spot. And it seemed to Gregor that it would be much more sensible to leave him in peace for the present that to trouble him with tears and entreaties. Still, of course, their uncertainty bewildered them all and excused their behaviour.

"Mr. Samsa," the chief clerk called now in a louder voice, "what's the matter with you? Here you are, barricading yourself in your room, giving only 'yes' and 'no' for answers, causing your parents a lot of unnecessary trouble and neglecting—I mention this only in passing—neglecting your business duties in an incredible fashion. I am speaking here in the name of your parents and of your chief, and I beg you quite seriously to give me an immediate and precise explanation. You amaze me, you amaze me. I thought you were a quiet, dependable person, and now all at once you seem bent on making a disgraceful exhibition of yourself. The chief did hint to me early this morning a possible explanation for your disappearance with reference to the cash payments that were entrusted to you recently—but I almost pledged my solemn word of honour that this could not be so. But now that I see how incredibly obstinate you are, I no longer have the slightest desire to take your part at all. And your position in the firm is not so unassailable. I came with the intention of telling you all this in private, but since you are wasting my time so needlessly I don't see why your parents shouldn't hear it too. For some time past your work has been most unsatisfactory; this is not the season of the year for a business boom, of course, we admit that, but a season of the year for doing no business at all, that does not exist, Mr. Samsa, must not exist."

"But, sir," cried Gregor, beside himself and in his agitation forgetting everything else. "I'm just going to open the door this very minute. A light illness, an attack of giddiness, has kept me from getting up. I'm still lying in bed. But I feel all right again. I'm getting out of bed now. Just give me a moment or two longer! I'm not quite so well as I thought. But I'm all right, really. How a thing like that can suddenly strike one down! Only last night I was quite well, my parents can tell you, or rather I did have a slight presentiment. I must have showed some sign of it. Why didn't I report it at the office! But one always thinks that an indisposition can be got over without staying in the house. Oh sir, do spare my parents! All that you're reproaching me with now has no foundation; no one has ever said a word to me about it. Perhaps you haven't looked at the last orders I sent in. Anyhow, I can still catch the eight o'clock train, I'm much the better for my few hours' rest. Don't let me detain you here, sir; I'll be attending to business very soon, and do be good enough to tell the chief so and to make my excuses to him!"

And while all this was tumbling out pell-mell and Gregor hardly knew what he was saying, he had reached the chest quite easily, perhaps because of the practice he had had in bed, and was now trying to lever himself upright by means of it. He meant actually to open the door, actually to show himself and speak to the chief clerk; he was eager to find out what the others, after all their insistence, would say at the sight of him. If they were horrified then the responsibility was no longer his and he could stay quiet. But if they took it calmly, then he had no reason either to be upset, and could really get to the station for the eight o'clock train if he hurried. At first he slipped down a few times from the polished surface of the chest, but at length with a last heave he stood upright; he paid no more attention to the pains in the lower part of his body, however they smarted. Then he let himself fall against the back of a near-by chair, and clung with his little legs to the edges of it. That brought him into control of himself again and he stopped speaking, for now he could listen to what the chief clerk was saying.

"Did you understand a word of it?" the chief clerk was asking; "surely he can't be trying to make fools of us?" "Oh dear," cried his mother, in tears, "perhaps he's terribly ill and we're tormenting him. Grete! Grete!" she called out then. "Yes Mother?" called his sister from the other side. They were calling to each other across Gregor's room. "You must go this minute for the doctor. Gregor is ill. Go for the doctor, quick. Did you hear how he was speaking?" "That was no human voice," said the chief clerk in a voice noticeably low beside the shrillness of the mother's. "Anna! Anna!" his father was calling through the hall to the kitchen, clapping his hands, "get a locksmith at once!" And the two girls were already running through the hall with a swish of skirts—how could his sister have got dressed so quickly?—and were tearing the front door open. There was no sound of its closing again; they had evidently left it open, as one does in houses where some great misfortune has happened.

But Gregor was now much calmer. The words he uttered were no longer understandable, apparently, although they seemed clear enough to him, even clearer than before, perhaps because his ear had grown accustomed to the sound of them. Yet at any rate people now believed that something was wrong with him, and were ready to help him. The positive certainty with which these first measures had been taken comforted him. He felt himself drawn once more into the human circle and hoped for great and remarkable results from both the doctor and the locksmith, without really distinguishing precisely between them. To make his voice as clear as possible for the decisive conversation that was now imminent he coughed a little, as quietly as he could, of course, since this noise too might not sound like a human cough for all he was able to judge. In the next room meanwhile there was complete silence. Perhaps his parents were sitting at the table with the chief clerk, whispering, perhaps they were all leaning against the door and listening.

Slowly Gregor pushed the chair towards the door, then let go of it, caught hold of the door for support—the soles at the end of his little legs were somewhat sticky—and rested against it for a moment after his efforts. Then he set himself to turning the key in the lock with his mouth. It seemed, unhappily, that he hadn't really any teeth—what could he grip the key with?—but on the other hand his jaws were certainly very strong; with their help he did manage to set the key in motion, heedless of the fact that he was undoubtedly damaging them somewhere, since a brown fluid issued from his mouth, flowed over the key and dripped on the floor. "Just listen to that," said the chief clerk next door; "he's turning the key." That was a great encouragement to Gregor; but they should all have shouted encouragement to him, his father and mother too: "Go on Gregor," they should have called out, "keep going, hold on to that key!" And in the belief that they were all following his efforts intently, he clenched his jaws recklessly on the key with all the force at his command. As the turning of the key progressed he circled round the lock, holding on now only with his mouth, pushing on the key, as required, or pulling it down again with all the weight of his body. The louder click of the finally yielding lock literally quickened Gregor. With a deep breath of relief he said to himself: "So I didn't need the locksmith," and laid his head on the handle to open the door wide.

Since he had to pull the door towards him, he was still invisible when it was really wide open. He had to edge himself slowly round the near half of the double door, and to do it very carefully if he was not to fall plump upon his back just on the threshold. He was still carrying out this difficult manoeuvre, with no time to observe anything else, when he heard the chief clerk utter a loud "Oh!"—it sounded like a gust of wind—and now he could see the man, standing as he was nearest to the door, clapping one hand before his open mouth and slowly backing away as if driven by some invisible steady pressure. His mother—in spite of the chief clerk's being there her hair was still undone and sticking up in all directions—first clasped her hands and looked at his father, then took two steps towards Gregor and fell on the floor among her outspread skirts, her face quite hidden on her breast. His father knotted his fist with a fierce expression on his face as if he meant to knock Gregor back into his room, covered his eyes with his hands and wept till his great chest heaved.

Gregor did not go now into the living room, but leaned against the inside of the firmly shut wing of the door, so that only half his body was visible and his head above it bending sideways to look at the others. The light had meanwhile strengthened; on the other side of the street one could see clearly a section of the endlessly long, dark grey building opposite—it was a hospital—abruptly punctuated by its row of regular windows; the rain was still falling, but only in large singly discernible and literally singly splashing drops. The breakfast dishes were set out on the table lavishly, for breakfast was the most important meal of the day to Gregor's father, who lingered it out for hours over various newspapers. Right opposite Gregor on the wall hung a photograph of himself on military service, as a lieutenant, hand on sword, a carefree smile on his face, inviting one to respect his uniform and military bearing. The door leading to the hall was open, and one could see that the front door stood open too, showing the landing beyond and the beginning of the stairs going down.

"Well," said Gregor, knowing perfectly that he was the only one who had retained any composure, "I'll put my clothes on at once, pack up my samples and start off. Will you only let me go? You see, sir, I'm not obstinate, and I'm willing to work; travelling is hard life, but I couldn't live without it. Where are you going, sir? To the office? Yes? Will you give a true account of all this? One can be temporarily incapacitated, but that's just the moment for remembering former services and bearing in mind that later on, when the incapacity has been got over, one will certainly work with all the more industry and concentration. I'm loyally bound to serve the chief, you know that very well. Besides, I have to provide for my parents and my sister. I'm in great difficulties, but I'll get out of them again. Don't make things any worse for me than they are. Stand up for me in the firm. Travelers are not popular there, I know. People think they earn sacks of money and just have a good time. A prejudice there's no particular reason for revising. But you, sir, have a more comprehensive view of affairs than the rest of the staff, yes, let me tell you in confidence, a more comprehensive view than the chief himself, who, being the owner, lets his judgement easily be swayed against one of his employees. And you know very well that the traveller, who is never seen in the office almost the whole year round, can so easily fall a victim to gossip and ill luck and unfounded complaints, which he mostly knows nothing about, except when he comes back exhausted from his rounds, and only then suffers in person from their evil consequences, which he can no longer trace back to the original causes. Sir, sir, don't go away without a word to me to show that you think me in the right at least to some extent!"

But at Gregor's very first words the chief clerk had already backed away and only stared at him with parted lips over one twitching shoulder. And while Gregor was speaking he did not stand still one moment but stole away towards the door, without taking his eyes off Gregor, yet only an inch at a time, as if obeying some secret injunction to leave the room. He was already at the hall, and the suddenness with which he took his last step out of the living room would have made one believe he had burned the sole of his foot. Once in the hall he stretched his right arm before him towards the staircase, as if some supernatural power were waiting there to deliver him.

Gregor perceived that the chief clerk must on no account be allowed to go away in this frame of mind if his position in the firm were not to be endangered to the utmost. His parents did not understand this so well; they had convinced themselves in the course of years that Gregor was settled for life in this firm, and besides they were so preoccupied with their immediate troubles that all foresight had forsaken them. Yet Gregor had this foresight. The chief clerk must be detained, soothed, and persuaded and finally won over; the whole future of Gregor and his family depended on it! If only his sister had been there! She was intelligent; she had begun to cry while Gregor was still lying quietly on his back. And no doubt the chief clerk, so partial to ladies, would have been guided by her; she would have shut the door of the flat and in the hall talked him out of his horror. But she was not there, and Gregor would have to handle the situation himself. And without remembering that he was still unaware what powers of movement he possessed, without even remembering that his words in all possibility, indeed in all likelihood, would again be unintelligible, he let go the wing of the door, pushed himself through the opening, started to walk towards the chief clerk, who was already ridiculously clinging with both hands to the railing on the landing; but immediately, as he was feeling for a support, he fell down with a little cry upon all his numerous legs. Hardly was he down when he experienced for the first time this morning a sense of physical comfort; his legs had firm ground under them; they were completely obedient, as he noted with joy; they even strove to carry him forward in whatever direction he chose; and he was inclined to believe that a final relief from all his sufferings was at hand. But in the same moment as he found himself on the floor, rocking with suppressed eagerness to move, not far from his mother, indeed just in front of her, she, who had seemed so completely crushed, sprang all at once to her feet, her arms and fingers outspread, cried: "Help, for God's sake, help!" bent her head down as if to see Gregor better, yet on the contrary kept backing senselessly away; had quite forgotten that the laden table stood behind her; sat upon it hastily, as if in absence of mind, when she bumped into it; and seemed altogether unaware that the big coffee pot beside her was upset and pouring coffee in a flood over the carpet.

"Mother, Mother," said Gregor in a low voice, and looked up at her. The chief clerk, for the moment, had quite slipped from his mind; instead, he could not resist snapping his jaws together at the sight of the streaming coffee. That made his mother scream again, she fled from the table and fell into the arms of his father, who hastened to catch her. But Gregor had now no time to spare for his parents; the chief clerk was already on the stairs; with his chin on the banisters he was taking one last backward look. Gregor made a spring, to be as sure as possible of overtaking him; the chief clerk must have divined his intention, for he leaped down several steps and vanished; he was still yelling "Ugh!" and it echoed through the whole staircase.

Unfortunately, the flight of the chief clerk seemed completely to upset Gregor's father, who had remained relatively calm until now, for instead of running after the man himself, or at least not hindering Gregor in his pursuit, he seized in his right hand the walking stick which the chief clerk had left behind on a chair, together with a hat and greatcoat, snatched in his left hand a large newspaper from the table and began stamping his feet and flourishing the stick and the newspaper to drive Gregor back into his room. No entreaty of Gregor's availed, indeed no entreaty was even understood, however humbly he bent his head his father only stamped on the floor more loudly. Behind his father his mother had torn open a window, despite the cold weather, and was leaning far out of it with her face in her hands. A strong draught set in from the street to the staircase, the window curtains blew in, the newspapers on the table fluttered, stray pages whisked over the floor. Pitilessly Gregor's father drove him back, hissing and crying "Shoo!" like a savage. But Gregor was quite unpractised in walking backwards, it really was a slow business. If he only had a chance to turn round he could get back to his room at once, but he was afraid of exasperating his father by the slowness of such a rotation and at any moment the stick in his father's hand might hit him a fatal blow on the back or on the head. In the end, however, nothing else was left for him to do since to his horror he observed that in moving backwards he could not even control the direction he took; and so, keeping an anxious eye on his father all the time over his shoulder, he began to turn round as quickly as he could, which was in reality very slowly. Perhaps his father noted his good intentions, for he did not interfere except every now and then to help him in the manoeuvre from a distance with the point of the stick. If only he would have stopped making that unbearable hissing noise! It made Gregor lose his head. He had turned almost completely round when the hissing noise so distracted him that he even turned a little the wrong way again. But when at last his head was fortunately right in front of the doorway, it appeared that his body was too broad simply to get through the opening. His father, of course, in his present mood was far from thinking of such a thing as opening the other half of the door, to let Gregor have enough space. He had merely the fixed idea of driving Gregor back into his room as quickly as possible. He would never have suffered Gregor to make the circumstantial preparations for standing up on end and perhaps slipping his way through the door. Maybe he was now making more noise than ever to urge Gregor forward, as if no obstacle impeded him; to Gregor, anyhow, the noise in his rear sounded no longer like the voice of one single father; this was really no joke, and Gregor thrust himself—come what might—into the doorway. One side of his body rose up, he was tilted at an angle in the doorway; his flank was quite bruised, horrid blotches stained the white door, soon he was stuck fast and, left to himself, could not have moved at all, his legs on one side fluttered trembling in the air, those on the other were crushed painfully to the floor—when from behind his father gave him a strong push which was literally a deliverance and he flew far into the room, bleeding freely. The door was slammed behind him with the stick, and then at last there was silence.

II

Not until it was twilight did Gregor awake out of a deep sleep, more like a swoon than a sleep. He would certainly have waked up of his own accord not much later, for he felt himself sufficiently rested and well-slept, but it seemed to him as if a fleeting step and a cautious shutting of the door leading into the hall had aroused him. The electric lights in the street cast a pale sheen here and there on the ceiling and the upper surfaces of the furniture, but down below, where he lay, it was dark. Slowly, awkwardly trying out his feelers, which he now first learned to appreciate, he pushed his way to the door to see what had been happening there. His left side felt like one single long, unpleasantly tense scar, and he had actually to limp on his two rows of legs. One little leg, more-over, had been severely damaged in the course of that morning's events—it was almost a miracle that only one had been damaged—and trailed uselessly behind him.

He had reached the door before he discovered what had really drawn him to it: the smell of food. For there stood a basin filled with fresh milk in which floated little sops of white bread. He could almost have laughed with joy, since he was not still hungrier than in the morning, and he dipped his head almost over the eyes straight into the milk. But soon in disappointment he withdrew it again; not only did he find it difficult to feed because of his tender left side—and he could only feed with the palpitating collaboration of his whole body—he did not like the milk either, although milk had been his favourite drink and that was certainly why his sister had set it there for him, indeed it was almost with repulsion that he turned away from the basin and crawled back to the middle of the room.

He could see through the crack of the door that the gas was turned on in the living room, but while usually at this time his father made a habit of reading the afternoon newspaper in a loud voice to his mother and occasion-ally his sister as well, not a sound was now to be heard. Well, perhaps his father had recently given up this habit of reading aloud, which his sister had mentioned so often in conversation and in her letters. But there was the same silence all around, although the flat was certainly not empty of occupants. "What a quiet life our family has been leading," said Gregor to himself, and as he sat there motionless staring into the darkness he felt great pride in the fact that he had been able to provide such a life for his parents and sister in such a fine flat. But what if all the quiet, the comfort, the contentment were now to end in horror? To keep himself from being lost in such thoughts Gregor took refuge in movement and crawled up and down in the room.

Once during the long evening one of the side doors was opened a little and quickly shut again, later the other side door too; someone had apparently wanted to come in and then thought better of it. Gregor now stationed himself immediately before the living room door, determined to persuade any hesi-tating visitor to come in or at least to discover who it might be; but the door was not opened again and he waited in vain. In the early morning, when the doors were locked, they had all wanted to come in, now that he had opened the door and the other had apparently been opened during the day, no one came in and even the keys were on the other side of the doors.

It was late at night before the gas went out in the living room, and Gregor could easily tell that his parents and his sister had all stayed awake until then, for he could clearly hear the three of them stealing away on tiptoe. No one was likely to visit him, not until the morning, that was certain; so he had plenty of time to meditate at his leisure on how he was to arrange his life afresh. But the lofty, empty room in which he had to lie flat on the floor filled him with an apprehension he could not account for, since it had been his very own room for the past five years—and with a half-unconscious action, not without a slight feeling of shame, he scuttled under the sofa, where he felt comfortable at once, although his back was a little cramped and he could not lift his head up, and his only regret was that his body was too broad to get the whole of it under the sofa.

He stayed there all night, spending the time partly in a light slumber, from which his hunger kept waking him up with a start, and partly worrying and sketching vague hopes, which all led to the same conclusion, that he must lie low for the present and, by exercising patience and the utmost consideration, help the family to bear the inconvenience he was bound to cause them in his present condition.

Very early in the morning, it was still almost night, Gregor had the chance to test the strength of his new resolutions, for his sister, nearly fully dressed, opened the door from the hall and peered. She did not see him at once, yet when she caught sight of him under the sofa—well, he had to be somewhere, he couldn't have flown away, could he?—she was so startled that without being able to help it she slammed the door shut again. But as if regretting her behaviour she opened the door again immediately and came in on tiptoe, as if she were visiting an invalid or even a stranger. Gregor had pushed his head forward to the very edge of the sofa and watched her. Would she notice that he had left the milk standing, and not for lack of hunger, and would she bring in some other kind of food more to his taste? If she did not do it of her own accord, he would rather starve than draw her attention to the fact, although he felt a wild impulse to dart out from under the sofa, throw himself at her feet and beg her for something to eat. But his sister at once noticed, with surprise, that the basin was still full, except for a little milk that had been spilt all around it, she lifted it immediately, not with her bare hands, true, but with a cloth and carried it away. Gregor was wildly curious to know what she would bring instead, and made various speculations about it. Yet what she actually did next, in the goodness of her heart, he could never have guessed at. To find out what he liked she brought him a whole selection of food, all set out on an old newspaper. There were old, half-decayed vegetables, bones from last night's supper covered with a white sauce that had thickened; some raisins and almonds; a piece of cheese that Gregor would have called uneatable two days ago; a dry roll of bread, a buttered roll, and a roll both buttered and salted. Besides all that, she set down again the same basin, into which she had poured some water, and which was apparently to be reserved for his exclusive use. And with fine tact, knowing that Gregor would not eat in her presence, she withdrew quickly and even turned the key, to let him understand that he could take his ease as much as he liked. Gregor's legs all whizzed towards the food. His wounds must have healed completely, moreover, for he felt no disability, which amazed him and made him reflect how more than a month ago he had cut one finger a little with a knife and had still suffered pain from the wound only the day before yesterday. Am I less sensitive now? he thought, and sucked greedily at the cheese, which above all the other edibles attracted him at once and strongly. One after another and with tears of satisfaction in his eyes he quickly devoured the cheese, the vegetables and the sauce; the fresh food, on the other hand, had no charms for him, he could not even stand the smell of it and actually dragged away to some little distance the things he could eat. He had long finished his meal and was only lying lazily on the same spot when his sister turned the key slowly as a sign for him to retreat. That roused him at once, although he was nearly asleep, and he hurried under the sofa again. But it took considerable self-control for him to stay under the sofa, even for the short time his sister was in the room, since the large meal had swollen his body somewhat and he was so cramped he could hardly breathe. Slight attacks of breathlessness afflicted him and his eyes were starting a little out of his head as he watched his unsuspecting sister sweeping together with a broom not only the remains of what he had eaten but even the things he had not touched, as if these were now of no use to anyone, and hastily shovelling it all into a bucket, which she covered with a wooden lid and carried away. Hardly had she turned her back when Gregor came out from under the sofa and stretched and puffed himself out.

In this manner Gregor was fed, once in the early morning while his parents and the servant girl were still asleep, and a second time after they had all had their midday dinner, for then his parents took a short nap and the servant give could be sent on some errand or other by his sister. Not that they would have wanted him to starve, of course, but perhaps they could not have borne to know more about his feeding than from hearsay, perhaps too his sister wanted to spare them such little anxieties wherever possible, since they had quite enough to bear as it was.

Under what pretext the doctor and the locksmith had been got rid of on the first morning Gregor could not discover, for since what he said was not understood by the others it never struck any of them, not even his sister, that he could understand what they said, and so whenever his sister came into his room he had to content himself with hearing her utter only a sigh now and then and an occasional appeal to the saints. Later on, when she had got a little used to the situation—of course she could never get completely used to it—she sometimes threw out a remark which was kindly meant or could be so interpreted. "Well, he liked his dinner today," she would say when Gregor had made a good clearance of his food; and when he had not eaten, which gradually happened more and more often, she would say almost sadly: "Everything's been left standing again."

But although Gregor could get no news directly, he overheard a lot from the neighbouring rooms, and as soon as voices were audible, he would run to the door of the room concerned and press his whole body against it. In the first few days especially there was no conversation that did not refer to him somehow, even if only indirectly. For two whole days there were family consultations at every mealtime about what should be done; but also between meals the same subject was discussed, for there were always at least two members of the family at home, since no one wanted to be alone in the flat and to leave it quite empty was unthinkable. And on the very first of these days the household cook—it was not quite clear what and how much she knew of the situation—went down on her knees to his mother and begged leave to go, and when she departed, a quarter of an hour later, gave thanks for her dismissal with tears in her eyes as if for the greatest benefit that could have been conferred on her, and without any prompting swore a solemn oath that she would never say a single word to anyone about what had happened.

Now Gregor's sister had to cook too, helping her mother; true, the cooking did not amount to much, for they ate scarcely anything. Gregor was always hearing one of the family vainly urging another to eat and getting no answer but: "Thanks, I've had all I want," or something similar. Perhaps they drank nothing either. Time and again his sister kept asking his father if he wouldn't like some beer and offered kindly to go and fetch it herself, and when he made no answer suggested that she could ask the concierge to fetch it, so that he need feel no sense of obligation, but then a round "No" came from his father and no more was said about it.

In the course of that very first day Gregor's father explained the family's financial position and prospects to both his mother and sister. Now and then he rose from the table to get some voucher or memorandum out of the small safe he had rescued from the collapse of his business five years earlier. One could hear him opening the complicated lock and rustling papers out and shutting it again. This statement made by his father was the first cheerful information Gregor had heard since his imprisonment. He had been of the opinion that nothing at all was left over from his father's business, at least his father had never said anything to the contrary, and of course he had not asked him directly. At that time Gregor's sole desire was to do his utmost to help the family to forget as soon as possible the catastrophe which had overwhelmed the business and thrown them all into a state of complete despair. And so he had set to work with unusual ardour and almost overnight had become a commercial traveller instead of a little clerk, with of course much greater chances of earning money, and his success was immediately translated into good round coin which he could lay on the table for his amazed and happy family. These had been fine times, and they had never recurred, at least not with the same sense of glory, although later on Gregor had earned so much money that he was able to meet the expenses of the whole household and did so. They had simply got used to it, both the family and Gregor; the money was gratefully accepted and gladly given, but there was no special uprush of warm feeling. With his sister alone had he remained intimate, and it was a secret plan of his that she, who loved music, unlike himself, and could play movingly on the violin, should be sent next year to study at the Conservatorium, despite the great expense that would entail, which must be made up in some other way. During his brief visits home the Conservatorium was often mentioned in the talks he had with his sister, but always merely as a beautiful dream which could never come true, and his parents discouraged even these innocent references to it; yet Gregor had made up his mind firmly about it and meant to announce the fact with due solemnity on Christmas Day.

Such were the thoughts, completely futile in his present condition, that went through his head as he stood clinging upright to the door and listening. Sometimes out of sheer weariness he had to give up listening and let his head fall negligently against the door, but he always had to pull himself together again at once, for even the slight sound his head made was audible next door and brought all conversation to a stop. "What can he be doing now?" his father would say after a while, obviously turning towards the door, and only then would the interrupted conversation gradually be set going again.

Gregor was now informed as amply as he could wish—for his father tended to repeat himself in his explanations, partly because it was a long time since he had handled such matters and partly because his mother could not always grasp things at once—that a certain amount of investments, a very small amount it was true, had survived the wreck of their fortunes and had even increased a little because the dividends had not been touched meanwhile. And besides that, the money Gregor brought home every month—he had kept only a few dollars for himself—had never been quite used up and now amounted to a small capital sum. Behind the door Gregor nodded his head eagerly, rejoiced at this evidence of unexpected thrift and foresight. True, he could really have paid off some more of his father's debts to the chief with this extra money, and so brought much nearer the day on which he could quit his job, but doubtless it was better the way his father had managed it.

Yet this capital was by no means sufficient to let the family live on the interest of it; for one year, perhaps, or at the most two, they could live on the principal, that was all. It was simply a sum that ought not to be touched and should be kept for a rainy day; money for living expenses would have to be earned. Now his father was still hale enough but an old man, and he had done no work for the past five years and could not be expected to do much; during these five years, the first years of leisure in his laborious though unsuccessful life, he had grown rather fat and become sluggish. And Gregor's old mother, how was she to earn a living with her asthma, which troubled her even when she walked through the flat and kept her lying on a sofa every other day panting for breath beside an open window? And was his sister to earn her bread, she who was still a child of seventeen and whose life hitherto had been so pleasant, consisting as it did in dressing herself nicely, sleeping long, helping in the housekeeping, going out to a few modest entertainments and above all playing the violin? At first whenever the need for earning money was mentioned Gregor let go his hold on the door and threw himself down on the cool leather sofa beside it, he felt so hot with shame and grief.

Often he just lay there the long nights through without sleeping at all, scrabbling for hours on the leather. Or he nerved himself to the great effort of pushing an armchair to the window, then crawled up over the window sill and, braced against the chair, leaned against the window panes, obviously in some recollection of the sense of freedom that looking out of a window always used to give him. For in reality day by day things that were even a little way off were growing dimmer to his sight; the hospital across the street, which he used to execrate for being all too often before his eyes, was now quite beyond his range of vision, and if he had not known that he lived in Charlotte Street, a quiet street but still a city street, he might have believed that his window gave on a desert waste where grey sky and grey land blended indistinguishably into each other. His quick-witted sister only needed to observe twice that the armchair stood by the window; after that whenever she tidied the room she always pushed the chair back to the same place at the window and even left the inner casements open.

If he could have spoken to her and thanked her for all she had to do for him, he could have borne her ministrations better; as it was, they oppressed him. She certainly tried to make as light as possible of whatever was disagreeable in her task, and as time went on she succeeded, of course, more and more, but time brought more enlightenment to Gregor too. The very way she came in distressed him. Hardly was she in the room when she rushed to the window, without even taking time to shut the door, careful as she was usually to shield the sight of Gregor's room from the others, and as if she were almost suffocating tore the casements open with hasty fingers, standing then in the open draught for a while even in the bitterest cold and drawing deep breaths. This noisy scurry of hers upset Gregor twice a day; he would crouch trembling under the sofa all the time, knowing quite well that she would certainly have spared him such a disturbance had she found it at all possible to stay in his presence without opening the window.

On one occasion, about a month after Gregor's metamorphosis, when there was surely no reason for her to be still startled at his appearance, she came a little earlier than usual and found him gazing out of the window, quite motionless, and thus well placed to look like a bogey. Gregor would not have been surprised had she not come in at all, for she could not immediately open the window while he was there, but not only did she retreat, she jumped back as if in alarm and banged the door shut; a stranger might well have thought that he had been lying in wait for her there meaning to bite her. Of course he hid himself under the sofa at once, but he had to wait until midday before she came again, and she seemed more ill at ease than usual. This made him realize how repulsive the sight of him still was to her, and that it was bound to go on being repulsive, and what an effort it must cost her not to run away even from the sight of the small portion of his body that stuck out from under the sofa. In order to spare her that, therefore, one day he carried a sheet on his back to the sofa—it cost him four hours' labour—and arranged it there in such a way as to hide him completely, so that even if she were to bend down she could not see him. Had she considered the sheet unnecessary, she would certainly have stripped it off the sofa again, for it was clear enough that this curtaining and confining of himself was not likely to conduce to Gregor's comfort, but she left it where it was, and Gregor even fancied that he caught a thankful glance from her eye when he lifted the sheet carefully a very little with his head to see how she was taking the new arrangement.

For the first fortnight his parents could not bring themselves to the point of entering his room, and he often heard them expressing their appreciation of his sister's activities, whereas formerly they had frequently scolded her for being as they thought a somewhat useless daughter. But now, both of them often waited outside the door, his father and his mother, while his sister tidied his room, and as soon as she came out she had to tell exactly how things were in the room, what Gregor had eaten, how he had conducted himself this time and whether there was not perhaps some slight improvement in his condition. His mother, moreover, began relatively soon to want to visit him, but his father and sister dissuaded her at first with arguments which Gregor listened to very attentively and altogether approved. Later, however, she had to be held back by main force, and when she cried out: "Do let me in to Gregor, he is my unfortunate son! Can't you understand that I must go to him?" Gregor thought that it might be well to have her come in, not every day, of course, but perhaps once a week; she understood things, after all, much better than his sister, who was only a child despite the efforts she was making and had perhaps taken on so difficult a task merely out of childish thoughtlessness.

Gregor's desire to see his mother was soon fulfilled. During the daytime he did not want to show himself at the window, out of consideration for his parents, but he could not crawl very far around the few square yards of floor space he had, nor could he bear lying quietly at rest all during the night, while he was fast losing any interest he had ever taken in food, so that for mere recreation he had formed the habit of crawling crisscross over the walls and ceiling. He especially enjoyed hanging suspended from the ceiling; it was much better than lying on the floor; one could breathe more freely; one's body swung and rocked lightly; and in the almost blissful absorption induced by this suspension it could happen to his own surprise that he let go and fell plump on the floor. Yet he now had his body much better under control than formerly, and even such a big fall did him no harm. His sister at once remarked the new distraction Gregor had found for himself—he left traces behind him of the sticky stuff on his soles wherever he crawled—and she got the idea in her head of giving him as wide a field as possible to crawl in and of removing pieces of furniture that hindered him, above all the chest of drawers and the writing desk. But that was more than she could manage all by herself; she did not dare ask her father to help her; and as for the servant girl, a young creature of sixteen who had had the courage to stay on after the cook's departure, she could not be asked to help, for she had begged as an especial favour that she might keep the kitchen door locked and open it only on a definite summons; so there was nothing left but to apply to her mother at an hour when her father was out. And the old lady did come, with exclamations of joyful eagerness, which, however, died away at the door of Gregor's room. Gregor's sister, of course, went in first, to see that everything was in order before letting his mother enter. In great haste Gregor pulled the sheet lower and rucked it more in folds so that it really looked as if it had been thrown accidentally over the sofa. And this time he did not peer out from under it; he renounced the pleasure of seeing his mother on this occasion and was only glad that she had come at all. "Come in, he's out of sight," said his sister, obviously leading her mother in by the hand. Gregor could now hear the two women struggling to shift the heavy old chest from its place, and his sister claiming the greater part of the labour for herself, without listening to the admonitions of her mother who feared she might overstrain herself. It took a long time. After at least a quarter of an hour's tugging his mother objected that the chest had better be left where it was, for in the first place it was too heavy and could never be got out before his father came home, and standing in the middle of the room like that it would only hamper Gregor's movements, while in the second place it was not at all certain that removing the furniture would be doing a service to Gregor. She was inclined to think to the contrary; the sight of the naked walls made her own heart heavy, and why shouldn't Gregor have the same feeling, considering that he had been used to his furniture for so long and might feel forlorn without it. "And doesn't it look," she concluded in a low voice—in fact she had been almost whispering all the time as if to avoid letting Gregor, whose exact whereabouts she did not know, hear even the tones of her voice, for she was convinced that he could not understand her words—"doesn't it look as if we were showing him, by taking away his furniture, that we have given up hope of his ever getting better and are just leaving him coldly to himself? I think it would be best to keep his room exactly as it has always been, so that when he comes back to us he will find everything unchanged and be able all the more easily to forget what has happened in between."

On hearing these words from his mother Gregor realized that the lack of all direct human speech for the past two months together with the monotony of family life must have confused his mind, otherwise he could not account for the fact that he had quite earnestly looked forward to having his room emptied of furnishing. Did he really want his warm room, so comfortably fitted with old family furniture, to be turned into a naked den in which he would certainly be able to crawl unhampered in all directions but at the price of shedding simultaneously all recollection of his human background? He had indeed been so near the brink of forgetfulness that only the voice of his mother, which he had not heard for so long, had drawn him back from it. Nothing should be taken out of his room; everything must stay as it was; he could not dispense with the good influence of the furniture on his state of mind; and even if the furniture did hamper him in his senseless crawling round and round, that was no drawback but a great advantage.

Unfortunately his sister was of the contrary opinion; she had grown accustomed, and not without reason, to consider herself an expert in Gregor's affairs as against her parents, and so her mother's advice was now enough to make her determined on the removal not only of the chest and the writing desk, which had been her first intention, but of all the furniture except the indispensable sofa. This determination was not, of course, merely the outcome of childish recalcitrance and of the self-confidence she had recently developed so unexpectedly and at such cost; she had in fact perceived that Gregor needed a lot of space to crawl about in, while on the other hand he never used the furniture at all, so far as could be seen. Another factor might have been also the enthusiastic temperament of an adolescent girl, which seeks to indulge itself on every opportunity and which now tempted Grete to exaggerate the horror of her brother's circumstances in order that she might do all the more for him. In a room where Gregor lorded it all alone over empty walls no one save herself was likely ever to set foot.

And so she was not to be moved from her resolve by her mother, who seemed moreover to be ill at ease in Gregor's room and therefore unsure of herself, was soon reduced to silence and helped her daughter as best she could to push the chest outside. Now, Gregor could do without the chest, if need be, but the writing desk he must retain. As soon as the two women had got the chest out of his room, groaning as they pushed it, Gregor stuck his head out from under the sofa to see how he might intervene as kindly and cautiously as possible. But as bad luck would have it, his mother was the first to return, leaving Grete clasping the chest in the room next door where she was trying to shift it all by herself, without of course moving it from the spot. His mother however was not accustomed to the sight of him, it might sicken her and so in alarm Gregor backed quickly to the other end of the sofa, yet could not prevent the sheet from swaying a little in front. That was enough to put her on the alert. She paused, stood still for a moment and then went back to Grete.

Although Gregor kept reassuring himself that nothing out of the way was happening, but only a few bits of furniture were being changed round, he soon had to admit that all this trotting to and fro of the two women, their little ejaculations and the scraping of furniture along the floor affected him like a vast disturbance coming from all sides at once, and however much he tucked in his head and legs and cowered to the very floor he was bound to confess that he would not be able to stand it for long. They were clearing his room out; taking away everything he loved; the chest in which he kept his fret saw and other tools was already dragged off; they were now loosening the writing desk which had almost sunk into the floor, the desk at which he had done all his homework when he was at the commercial academy, at the grammar school before that, and, yes, even at the primary school—he had no more time to waste in weighing the good intentions of the two women, whose existence he had by now almost forgotten, for they were so exhausted that they were labouring in silence and nothing could be heard but the heavy scuffling of their feet.

And so he rushed out—the women were just leaning against the writing desk in the next room to give themselves a breather—and four times changed his direction, since he really did not know what to rescue first, then on the wall opposite, which was already otherwise cleared, he was struck by the picture of the lady muffled in so much fur and quickly crawled up to it and pressed himself to the glass, which was a good surface to hold on to and comforted his hot belly. This picture at least, which was entirely hidden beneath him, was going to be removed by nobody. He turned his head towards the door of the living room so as to observe the women when they came back.

They had not allowed themselves much of a rest and were already coming; Grete had twined her arm round her mother and was almost supporting her. "Well, what shall we take now?" said Grete, looking round. Her eyes met

Gregor's from the wall. She kept her composure, presumably because of her mother, bent her head down to her mother, to keep her from looking up, and said, although in a fluttering, unpremeditated voice: "Come, hadn't we better go back to the living room for a moment?" Her intentions were clear enough to Gregor, she wanted to bestow her mother in safety and then chase him down from the wall. Well, just let her try it! He clung to his picture and would not give it up. He would rather fly in Grete's face.

But Grete's words had succeeded in disquieting her mother, who took a step to one side, caught sight of the huge brown mass on the flowered wall-paper, and before she was really conscious that what she saw was Gregor screamed in a loud, hoarse voice: "Oh God, oh God!" fell with outspread arms over the sofa as if giving up and did not move. "Gregor!" cried his sister, shaking her fist and glaring at him. This was the first time she had directly addressed him since his metamorphosis. She ran into the next room for some aromatic essence with which to rouse her mother from her fainting fit. Gregor wanted to help too—there was still time to rescue the picture—but he was stuck fast to the glass and had to tear himself loose; he then ran after his sister into the next room as if he could advise her, as he used to do; but then had to stand helplessly behind her; she meanwhile searched among various small bot-tles and when she turned round started in alarm at the sight of him; one bottle fell on the floor and broke; a splinter of glass cut Gregor's face and some kind of corrosive medicine splashed him; without pausing a moment longer Grete gathered up all the bottles she could carry and ran to her mother with them; she banged the door shut with her foot. Gregor was now cut off from his mother, who was perhaps nearly dying because of him; he dared not open the door for fear of frightening away his sister, who had to stay with her mother; there was nothing he could do but wait; and harassed by self-reproach and worry he began now to crawl to and fro, over everything, walls, furniture and ceiling, and finally, in his despair, when the whole room seemed to be reeling round him, fell down on to the middle of the big table.

A little while elapsed, Gregor was still lying there feebly and all around was quiet, perhaps that was a good omen. Then the doorbell rang. The servant girl was of course locked in her kitchen, and Grete would have to open the door. It was his father. "What's been happening?" were his first words; Grete's face must have told him everything. Grete answered in a muffled voice, appar-ently hiding her head on his breast: "Mother has been fainting, but she's better now. Gregor's broken loose." "Just what I expected," said his father, "just what I've been telling you, but you women would never listen." It was clear to Gregor that his father had taken the worst interpretation of Grete's all too brief statement and was assuming that Gregor had been guilty of some violent act. Therefore Gregor must now try to propitiate his father, since he had neither time nor means for an explanation. And so he fled to the door of his own room and crouched against it, to let his father see as soon as he came in from the hall that his son had the good intention of getting back into his room immediately and that it was not necessary to drive him there, but that if only the door were opened he would disappear at once.

Yet his father was not in the mood to perceive such fine distinctions. "Ah!" he cried as soon as he appeared, in a tone which sounded at once angry and exultant. Gregor drew his head back from the door and lifted it to look at his father. Truly, this was not the father he had imagined to himself; admittedly he had been too absorbed of late in his new recreation of crawling over the ceiling to take the same interest as before in what was happening elsewhere in the flat, and he ought really to be prepared for some changes. And yet, and yet, could that be his father? The man who used to lie wearily sunk in bed whenever Gregor set out on a business journey; who welcomed him back of an evening lying in a long chair in a dressing gown; who could not really rise to his feet but only lifted his arms in greeting, and on the rare occasions when he did go out with his family, on one or two Sundays a year and on high holidays, walked between Gregor and his mother, who were slow walkers anyhow, even more slowly than they did, muffled in his old greatcoat, shuffling laboriously forward with the help of his crook-handled stick which he set down most cautiously at every step and, whenever he wanted to say anything, nearly always came to a full stop and gathered his escort around him? Now he was standing there in fine shape; dressed in a smart blue uniform with gold buttons, such as bank messengers wear; his strong double chin bulged over the stiff high collar of his jacket; from under his bushy eyebrows his black eyes darted fresh and penetrating glances; his onetime tangled white hair had been combed flat on either side of a shining and carefully exact parting. He pitched his cap, which bore a gold monogram, probably the badge of some bank, in a wide sweep across the whole room on to a sofa and with the tailends of his jacket thrown back, his hands in his trouser pockets, advanced with a grim visage towards Gregor. Likely enough he did not himself know what he meant to do; at any rate he lifted his feet uncommonly high, and Gregor was dumbfounded at the enormous size of his shoe soles. But Gregor could not risk standing up to him, aware as he had been from the very first day of his new life that his father believed only the severest measures suitable for dealing with him. And so he ran before his father, stopping when he stopped and scuttling forward again when his father made any kind of move. In this way they circled the room several times without anything decisive happening, indeed the whole operation did not even look like a pursuit because it was carried out so slowly. And so Gregor did not leave the floor, for he feared that his father might take as a piece of peculiar wickedness any excursion of his over the walls or the ceiling.

All the same, he could not stay this course much longer, for while his father took one step he had to carry out a whole series of movements. He was already beginning to feel breathless, just as in his former life his lungs had not been very dependable. As he was staggering along, trying to concentrate his energy on running, hardly keeping his eyes open; in his dazed state never even thinking of any other escape than simply going forward; and having almost forgotten that the walls were free to him, which in this room were well provided with finely carved pieces of furniture full of knobs and crevices—suddenly something lightly flung landed close behind him and rolled before him. It was an apple; a second apple followed immediately; Gregor came to a stop in alarm; there was no point in running on, for his father was determined to bombard him. He had filled his pockets with fruit from the dish on the sideboard and was now shying apple after apple, without taking particularly good aim for the moment. The small red apples rolled about the floor as if magnetized and cannoned into each other. An apple thrown without much force grazed Gregor's back and glanced off harmlessly. But another following immediately landed right on his back and sank in; Gregor wanted to drag himself forward, as if this startling, incredible pain could be left behind him; but he felt as if nailed to the spot and flattened himself out in a complete derangement of all his senses. With his last conscious look he saw the door of his room being torn open and his mother rushing out ahead of his screaming sister, in her underbodice, for her daughter had loosened her clothing to let her breathe more freely and recover from her swoon, he saw his mother rushing towards his father, leaving one after another behind her on the floor her loosened petticoats, stumbling over her petticoats straight to his father and embracing him, in complete union with him—but here Gregor's sight began to fail—with her hands clasped round his father's neck as she begged for her son's life.

III

The serious injury done to Gregor, which disabled him for more than a month—the apple went on sticking in his body as a visible reminder, since no one ventured to remove it—seemed to have made even his father recollect that Gregor was a member of the family, despite his present unfortunate and repulsive shape, and ought not to be treated as an enemy, that, on the contrary, family duty required the suppression of disgust and the exercise of patience, nothing put patience.

And although his injury had impaired, probably for ever, his powers of movement, and for the time being it took him long, long minutes to creep across his room like an old invalid—there was no question now of crawling up the wall—yet in his own opinion he was sufficiently compensated for this worsening of his condition by the fact that towards evening the living-room door, which he used to watch intently for an hour or two beforehand, was always thrown open, so that lying in the darkness of his room invisible to the family, he could see them all at the lamp-lit table and listen to their talk, by general consent as it were, very different from his earlier eavesdropping.

True, their intercourse lacked the lively character of former times, which he had always called to mind with a certain wistfulness in the small hotel bedrooms where he had been wont to throw himself down, tired out, on damp bedding. They were now mostly very silent. Soon after supper his father would fall asleep in his armchair; his mother and sister would admonish each other to be silent; his mother, bending low over the lamp, stitched at fine sewing for an underwear firm; his sister, who had taken a job as a salesgirl, was learning shorthand and French in the evenings on the chance of bettering herself. Sometimes his father woke up, and as if quite unaware that he had been sleeping said to his mother: "What a lot of sewing you're doing today!" and at once fell asleep again, while the two women exchanged a tired smile.

With a kind of mulishness his father persisted in keeping his uniform on even in the house; his dressing gown hung uselessly on its peg and he slept fully dressed where he sat, as if he were ready for service at any moment and even here only at the beck and call of his superior. As a result, his uniform, which was not brand-new to start with, began to look dirty, despite all the loving care of the mother and sister to keep it clean, and Gregor often spent whole evenings gazing at the many greasy spots on the garment, gleaming with gold buttons always in a high state of polish, in which the old man sat sleeping in extreme discomfort and yet quite peacefully.

As soon as the clock struck ten his mother tried to rouse his father with gentle words and to persuade him after that to get into bed for sitting there he could not have a proper sleep and that was what he needed most, since he had to go on duty at six. But with the mulishness that had obsessed him since he became a bank messenger he always insisted on staying longer at the table, although he regularly fell asleep again and in the end only with the greatest trouble could be got out of his armchair and into his bed. However insistently Gregor's mother and sister kept urging him with gentle reminders, he would go on slowly shaking his head for a quarter of an hour, keeping his eyes shut, and refuse to get to his feet. The mother plucked at his sleeve, whispering endearments in his ear, the sister left her lessons to come to her mother's help, but Gregor's father was not to be caught. Not until the two women hoisted him up by the armpits did he open his eyes and look at them both, one after the other, usually with the remark: "This is a life. This is the peace and quiet of my old age." And leaning on the two of them he would heave himself up, with difficulty, as if he were a great burden to himself, suffer them to lead him as far as the door and then wave them off and go on alone, while the mother abandoned her needlework and the sister her pen in order to run after him and help him farther.

Who could find time, in this overworked and tired-out family, to bother about Gregor more than was absolutely needful? The household was reduced more and more; the servant girl was turned off; a gigantic bony charwoman with white hair flying round her head came in morning and evening to do the rough work; everything else was done by Gregor's mother, as well as great piles of sewing. Even various family ornaments, which his mother and sister used to wear with pride at parties and celebrations, had to be sold, as Gregor discovered of an evening from hearing them all discuss the prices obtained. But what they lamented most was the fact that they could not leave the flat which was much too big for their present circumstances, because they could not think of any way to shift Gregor. Yet Gregor saw well enough that consideration for him was not the main difficulty preventing the removal, for they could have easily shifted him in some suitable box with a few air holes in it; what really kept them from moving into another flat was rather their own complete hopelessness and the belief that they had been singled out for a misfortune such as had never happened to any of their relations or acquaintances. They fulfilled to the utmost all that the world demands of poor people, the father fetched breakfast for the small clerks in the bank, the mother devoted her energy to making underwear for strangers, the sister trotted to and fro behind the counter at the behest of customers, but more than this they had not the strength to do. And the wound in Gregor's back began to nag at him afresh when his mother and sister, after getting his father into bed, came back again, left their work lying, drew close to each other and sat cheek by cheek; when his mother, pointing towards his room, said: "Shut that door now, Grete," and he was left again in darkness, while next door the women mingled their tears or perhaps sat dry-eyed staring at the table.

Gregor hardly slept at all by night or by day. He was often haunted by the idea that next time the door opened he would take the family's affairs in hand again just as he used to do; once more, after this long interval, there appeared in his thoughts the figures of the chief and the chief clerk, the commercial travellers and the apprentices, the porter who was so dull-witted, two or three friends in other firms, a chambermaid in one of the rural hotels, a sweet and fleeting memory, a cashier in a milliner's shop, whom he had wooed earnestly but too slowly—they all appeared, together with strangers or people he had quite forgotten, but instead of helping him and his family they were one and all unapproachable and he was glad when they vanished. At other times he would not be in the mood to bother about his family, he was only filled with rage at the way they were neglecting him, and although he had no clear idea of what he might care to eat he would make plans for getting into the larder to take the food that was after all his due, even if he were not hungry. His sister no longer took thought to bring him what might especially please him, but in the morning and at noon before she went to business hurriedly pushed into his room with her foot any food that was available, and in the evening cleared it out again with one sweep of the broom, heedless of whether it had been merely tasted, or—as most frequently happened—left untouched. The cleaning of his room, which she now did always in the evenings, could not have been more hastily done. Streaks of dirt stretched along the walls, here and there lay balls of dust and filth. At first Gregor used to station himself in some particularly filthy corner when his sister arrived, in order to reproach her with it, so to speak. But he could have sat there for weeks without getting her to make any improvement; she could see the dirt as well as he did, but she had simply made up her mind to leave it alone. And yet, with a touchiness that was new to her, which seemed anyhow to have infected the whole family, she jealously guarded her claim to be the sole caretaker of Gregor's room. His mother once subjected his room to a thorough cleaning, which was achieved only by means of several buckets of water—all this dampness of course upset Gregor too and he lay widespread, sulky and motionless on the sofa—but she was well punished for it. Hardly had his sister noticed the changed aspect of his room that evening than she rushed in high dudgeon into the living room and, despite the imploringly raised hands of her mother, burst into a storm of weeping, while her parents—her father had of course been startled out of his chair—looked on at first in helpless amazement; then they too began to go into action; the father reproached the mother on his right for not having left the cleaning of Gregor's room to his sister; shrieked at the sister on his left that never again was she to be allowed to clean Gregor's room; while the mother tried to pull the father into his bedroom, since he was beyond himself with agitation, the sister, shaken with sobs, then beat upon the table with her small fists; and Gregor hissed loudly with rage because not one of them thought of shutting the door to spare him such a spectacle and so much noise.

Still, even if the sister, exhausted by her daily work, had grown tired of looking after Gregor as she did formerly, there was no need for his mother's intervention or for Gregor's being neglected at all. The charwoman was there. This old widow, whose strong bony frame had enabled her to survive the worst a long life could offer, by no means recoiled from Gregor. Without being in the least curious she had once by chance opened the door of his room and at the sight of Gregor, who, taken by surprise, began to rush to and fro although no one was chasing him, merely stood there with her arms folded. From that time she never failed to open his door a little for a moment, morning and evening, to have a look at him. At first she even used to call him to her, with words which apparently she took to be friendly, such as "Come along, then, you old dung beetle!" or "Look at the old dung beetle, then!" To such allocutions Gregor made no answer, but stayed motionless where he was, as if the door had never been opened. Instead of being allowed to disturb him so senselessly whenever the whim took her, she should rather have been ordered to clean out his room daily, that charwoman! Once, early in the morning—heavy rain was lashing on the windowpanes, perhaps a sign that spring was on the way— Gregor was so exasperated when she began addressing him again that he ran at her, as if to attack her, although slowly and feebly enough. But the charwoman instead of showing fright merely lifted high a chair that happened to be beside the door, and as she stood there with her mouth wide open it was clear that she meant to shut it only when she brought the chair down on Gregor's back. "So you're not coming any nearer?" she asked, as Gregor turned away again, and quietly put the chair back into the corner.

Gregor was now eating hardly anything. Only when he happened to pass the food laid out for him did he take a bit of something in his mouth as a pastime, kept it there for an hour at a time and usually spat it out again. At first he thought it was chagrin over the state of his room that prevented him from eating, yet he soon got used to the various changes in his room. It had become a habit in the family to push into his room things there was no room for elsewhere, and there were plenty of these now, since one of the rooms had been let to three lodgers. These serious gentlemen—all three of them with full beards, as Gregor once observed through a crack in the door—had a passion for order, not only in their own room but, since they were now members of the household, in all its arrangements, especially in the kitchen. Superfluous, not to say dirty, objects they could not bear. Besides, they had brought with them most of the furnishings they needed. For this reason many things could be dispensed with that it was no use trying to sell but that should not be thrown away either. All of them found their way into Gregor's room. The ash can likewise and the kitchen garbage can. Anything that was not needed for the moment was simply flung into Gregor's room by the charwoman, who did everything in a hurry; fortunately Gregor usually saw only the object, whatever it was, and the hand that held it. Perhaps she intended to take the things away again as time and opportunity offered, or to collect them until she could throw them all out in a heap, but in fact they just lay wherever she happened to throw them, except when Gregor pushed his way through the junk heap and shifted it somewhat, at first out of necessity, because he had not room enough to crawl, but later with increasing enjoyment, although after such excursions, being sad and weary to death, he would lie motionless for hours. And since the lodgers often ate their supper at home in the common living room, the living-room door stayed shut many an evening, yet Gregor reconciled himself quite easily to the shutting of the door, for often enough on evenings when it was opened he had disregarded it entirely and lain in the darkest corner of his room, quite unnoticed by the family. But on one occasion the charwoman left the door open a little and it stayed ajar even when the lodgers came in for supper and the lamp was lit. They set themselves at the top end of the table where formerly Gregor and his father and mother had eaten their meals, unfolded their napkins and took knife and fork in hand. At once his mother appeared in the other doorway with a dish of meat and close behind her his sister with a dish of potatoes piled high. The food steamed with a thick vapour. The lodgers bent over the food set before them as if to scrutinize it before eating, in fact the man in the middle, who seemed to pass for an authority with the other two, cut a piece of meat as it lay on the dish, obviously to discover if it were tender or should be sent back to the kitchen. He showed satisfaction, and Gregor's mother and sister, who had been watching anxiously, breathed freely and began to smile.

The family itself took its meals in the kitchen. None the less, Gregor's father came into the living room before going into the kitchen and with one prolonged bow, cap in hand, made a round of the table. The lodgers all stood up and murmured something in their beards. When they were alone again they ate their food in almost complete silence. It seemed remarkable to Gregor that among the various noises coming from the table he could always distinguish the sound of their masticating teeth, as if this were a sign to Gregor that one needed teeth in order to eat, and that with toothless jaws even of the finest make one could do nothing. "I'm hungry enough," said Gregor sadly to himself, "but not for that kind of food. How these lodgers are stuffing themselves, and here am I dying of starvation!"

On that very evening—during the whole of his time there Gregor could not remember ever having heard the violin—the sound of violin-playing came from the kitchen. The lodgers had already finished their supper, the one in the middle had brought out a newspaper and given the other two a page apiece, and now they were leaning back at ease reading and smoking. When the violin began to play they pricked up their ears, got to their feet, and went on tiptoe to the hall door where they stood huddled together. Their movements must have been heard in the kitchen, for Gregor's father called out: "Is the violin-playing disturbing you, gentlemen? It can be stopped at once." "On the contrary," said the middle lodger, "could not Fraulein Samsa come and play in this room, beside us, where it is much more convenient and comfortable?" "Oh certainly," cried Gregor's father, as if he were the violin-player. The lodgers came back into the living room and waited. Presently Gregor's father arrived with the music stand, his mother carrying the music and his sister with the violin. His sister quietly made everything ready to start playing; his parents, who had never let rooms before and so had an exaggerated idea of the courtesy due to lodgers, did not venture to sit down on their own chairs; his father leaned against the door, the right hand thrust between two buttons of his livery coat, which was formally buttoned up; but his mother was offered a chair by one of the lodgers and, since she left the chair just where he had happened to put it, sat down in a corner to one side.

Gregor's sister began to play; the father and mother, from either side, intently watched the movements of her hands. Gregor, attracted by the playing, ventured to move forward a little until his head was actually inside the living room. He felt hardly any surprise at his growing lack of consideration for the others; there had been a time when he prided himself on being considerate. And yet just on this occasion he had more reason than ever to hide himself, since owing to the amount of dust which lay thick in his room and rose into the air at the slightest movement, he too was covered with dust; fluff and hair and remnants of food trailed with him, caught on his back and along his sides; his indifference to everything was much too great for him to turn on his back and scrape himself clean on the carpet, as once he had done several times a day. And in spite of his condition, no shame deterred him from advancing a little over the spotless floor of the living room.

To be sure, no one was aware of him. The family was entirely absorbed in the violin-playing; the lodgers, however, who first of all had stationed themselves, hands in pockets, much too close behind the music stand so that they could all have read the music, which must have bothered his sister, had soon retreated to the window, half-whispering with downbent heads, and stayed there while his father turned an anxious eye on them. Indeed, they were making it more than obvious that they had been disappointed in their expectation of hearing good or enjoyable violin-playing, that they had had more than enough of the performance and only out of courtesy suffered a continued disturbance of their peace. From the way they all kept blowing the smoke of their cigars high in the air through nose and mouth one could divine their irritation. And yet Gregor's sister was playing so beautifully. Her face leaned sideways, intently and sadly her eyes followed the notes of the music. Gregor crawled a little farther forward and lowered his head to the ground so that it might be possible for his eyes to meet hers. Was he an animal, that music had such an effect upon him? He felt as if the way were opening before him to the unknown nourishment he craved. He was determined to push forward till he reached his sister, to pull at her skirt and so let her know that she was to come into his room with her violin, for no one here appreciated her playing as he would appreciate it. He would never let her out of his room, at least, not so long as he lived; his frightful appearance would become, for the first time, useful to him; he would watch all the doors of his room at once and spit at intruders; but his sister should need no constraint, she should stay with him of her own free will; she should sit beside him on the sofa, bend down her ear to him and hear him confide that he had had the firm intention of sending her to the Conservatorium, and that, but for his mishap, last Christmas—surely Christmas was long past?—he would have announced it to everybody without allowing a single objection. After this confession his sister would be so touched that she would burst into tears, and Gregor would then raise himself to her shoulder and kiss her on the neck, which, now that she went to business, she kept free of any ribbon or collar.

"Mr. Samsa!" cried the middle lodger, to Gregor's father, and pointed, without wasting any more words, at Gregor, now working himself slowly forwards. The violin fell silent, the middle lodger first smiled to his friends with a shake of the head and then looked at Gregor again. Instead of driving Gregor out, his father seemed to think it more needful to begin by soothing down the lodgers, although they were not at all agitated and apparently found Gregor more entertaining than the violin-playing. He hurried towards them and, spreading out his arms, tried to urge them back into their own room and at the same time to block their view of Gregor. They now began to be really a little angry, one could not tell whether because of the old man's behaviour or because it had just dawned on them that all unwittingly they had such a neighbour as Gregor next door. They demanded explanations of his father, they waved their arms like him, tugged uneasily at their beards, and only with reluctance backed towards their room. Meanwhile Gregor's sister, who stood there as if lost when her playing was so abruptly broken off, came to life again, pulled herself together all at once after standing for a while holding violin and bow in nervelessly hanging hands and staring at her music, pushed her violin into the lap of her mother, who was still sitting in her chair fighting asthmatically for breath, and ran into the lodgers' room to which they were now being shepherded by her father rather more quickly than before. One could see the pillows and blankets on the beds flying under her accustomed fingers and being laid in order. Before the lodgers had actually reached their room she had finished making the beds and slipped out.

The old man seemed once more to be so possessed by his mulish self-assertiveness that he was forgetting all the respect he should show to his lodgers. He kept driving them on and driving them on until in the very door of the bedroom the middle lodger stamped his foot loudly on the floor and so brought him to a halt. "I beg to announce," said the lodger, lifting one hand and looking also at Gregor's mother and sister, "that because of the disgusting conditions prevailing in this household and family"—here he spat on the floor with emphatic brevity—"I give you notice on the spot. Naturally I won't pay you a penny for the days I have lived here, on the contrary I shall consider bringing an action for damages against you, based on claims—believe me—

that will be easily susceptible of proof." He ceased and stared straight in front of him, as if he expected something. In fact his two friends at once rushed into the breach with these words: "And we too give notice on the spot." On that he seized the door-handle and shut the door with a slam.

Gregor's father, groping with his hands, staggered forward and fell into his chair; it looked as if he were stretching himself there for his ordinary evening nap, but the marked jerkings of his head, which was as if uncontrollable, showed that he was far from asleep. Gregor had simply stayed quietly all the time on the spot where the lodgers had espied him. Disappointment at the failure of his plan, perhaps also the weakness arising from extreme hunger, made it impossible for him to move. He feared, with a fair degree of certainty, that at any moment the general tension would discharge itself in a combined attack upon him, and he lay waiting. He did not react even to the noise made by the violin as it fell off his mother's lap from under her trembling fingers and gave out a resonant note.

"My dear parents," said his sister, slapping her hand on the table by way of introduction, "things can't go on like this. Perhaps you don't realize that, but I do. I won't utter my brother's name in the presence of this creature, and so all I say is: we must try to get rid of it. We've tried to look after it and to put up with it as far as is humanly possible, and I don't think anyone could reproach us in the slightest."

"She is more than right," said Gregor's father to himself. His mother, who was still choking for lack of breath, began to cough hollowly into her hand with a wild look in her eyes.

His sister rushed over to her and held her forehead. His father's thoughts seemed to have lost their vagueness at Grete's words, he sat more upright, fingering his service cap that lay among the plates still lying on the table from the lodgers' supper, and from time to time looked at the still form of Gregor.

"We must try to get rid of it," his sister now said explicitly to her father, since her mother was coughing too much to hear a word, "it will be the death of both of you, I can see that coming. When one has to work as hard as we do, all of us, one can't stand this continual torment at home on top of it. At least I can't stand it any longer." And she burst into such a passion of sobbing that her tears dropped on her mother's face, where she wiped them off mechanically.

"My dear," said the old man sympathetically, and with evident understanding, "but what can we do?"

Gregor's sister merely shrugged her shoulders to indicate the feeling of helplessness that had now overmastered her during her weeping fit, in contrast to her former confidence.

"If he could understand us," said her father, half questioningly; Grete, still sobbing, vehemently waved a hand to show how unthinkable that was.

"If he could understand us," repeated the old man, shutting his eyes to consider his daughter's conviction that understanding was impossible, "then perhaps we might come to some agreement with him. But as it is—"

"He must go," cried Gregor's sister, "that's the only solution, Father. You must just try to get rid of the idea that this is Gregor. The fact that we've believed it for so long is the root of all our trouble. But how can it be Gregor? If this were Gregor, he would have realized long ago that human beings can't live with such a creature, and he'd have gone away on his own accord. Then we wouldn't have any brother, but we'd be able to go on living and keep his memory in honour. As it is, this creature persecutes us, drives away our lodgers, obviously wants the whole apartment to himself and would have us all sleep in the gutter. Just look, Father," she shrieked all at once, "he's at it again!" And in an access of panic that was quite incomprehensible to Gregor she even quitted her mother, literally thrusting the chair from her as if she would rather sacrifice her mother than stay so near to Gregor, and rushed behind her father, who also rose up, being simply upset by her agitation, and half-spread his arms out as if to protect her.

Yet Gregor had not the slightest intention of frightening anyone, far less his sister. He had only begun to turn round in order to crawl back to his room, but it was certainly a startling operation to watch, since because of his disabled condition he could not execute the difficult turning movements except by lifting his head and then bracing it against the floor over and over again. He paused and looked round. His good intentions seemed to have been recognized; the alarm had only been momentary. Now they were all watching him in melancholy silence. His mother lay in her chair, her legs stiffly outstretched and pressed together, her eyes almost closing for sheer weariness; his father and his sister were sitting beside each other, his sister's arm around the old man's neck.

Perhaps I can go on turning round now, thought Gregor, and began his labours again. He could not stop himself from panting with the effort, and had to pause now and then to take breath. Nor did anyone harass him, he was left entirely to himself. When he had completed the turn-round he began at once to crawl straight back. He was amazed at the distance separating him from his room and could not understand how in his weak state he had managed to accomplish the same journey so recently, almost without remarking it. Intent on crawling as fast as possible, he barely noticed that not a single word, not an ejaculation from his family, interfered with his progress. Only when he was already in the doorway did he turn his head round, not completely, for his neck muscles were getting stiff, but enough to see that nothing had changed behind him except that his sister had risen to her feet. His last glance fell on his mother, who was not quite overcome by sleep.

Hardly was he well inside his room when the door was hastily pushed shut, bolted and locked. The sudden noise in his rear startled him so much that his little legs gave beneath him. It was his sister who had shown such haste. She had been standing ready waiting and had made a light spring forward, Gregor had not even heard her coming, and she cried "At last!" to her parents as she turned the key in the lock.

"And what now?" said Gregor to himself, looking round in the darkness. Soon he made the discovery that he was now unable to stir a limb. This did not surprise him, rather it seemed unnatural that he should ever actually have been able to move on these feeble little legs. Otherwise he felt relatively comfortable. True, his whole body was aching, but it seemed that the pain was gradually growing less and would finally pass away. The rotting apple in his back and the inflamed area around it, all covered with soft dust, already hardly troubled him. He thought of his family with tenderness and love. The decision that he must disappear was one that he held to even more strongly than his sister, if that were possible. In this state of vacant and peaceful meditation he remained until the tower clock struck three in the morning. The first broadening of light in the world outside the window entered his consciousness once more. Then his head sank to the floor of its own accord and from his nostrils came the last faint flicker of his breath.

When the charwoman arrived early in the morning—what between her strength and her impatience she slammed all the doors so loudly, never mind how often she had been begged not to do so, that no one in the whole apartment could enjoy any quiet sleep after her arrival—she noticed nothing unusual as she took her customary peep into Gregor's room. She thought he was lying motionless on purpose, pretending to be in the sulks; she credited him with every kind of intelligence. Since she happened to have the long-handled broom in her hand she tried to tickle him up with it from the doorway. When that too produced no reaction she felt provoked and poked at him a little harder, and only when she had pushed him along the floor without meeting any resistance was her attention aroused. It did not take her long to establish the truth of the matter, and her eyes widened, she let out a whistle, yet did not waste much time over it but tore open the door of the Samsas' bedroom and yelled into the darkness at the top of her voice: "Just look at this, it's dead; it's lying here dead and done for!"

Mr. and Mrs. Samsa started up in their double bed and before they realized the nature of the charwoman's announcement had some difficulty in overcoming the shock of it. But then they got out of bed quickly, one on either side, Mr. Samsa throwing a blanket over his shoulders, Mrs. Samsa in nothing but her nightgown; in this array they entered Gregor's room. Meanwhile the door of the living room opened, too, where Grete had been sleeping since the advent of the lodgers; she was completely dressed as if she had not been to bed, which seemed to be confirmed also by the paleness of her face. "Dead?" said Mrs. Samsa, looking questioningly at the charwoman, although she could have investigated for herself, and the fact was obvious enough without investigation. "I should say so," said the charwoman, proving her words by pushing Gregor's corpse a long way to one side with her broomstick. Mrs. Samsa made a movement as if to stop her, but checked it. "Well," said Mr. Samsa, "now thanks be to God." He crossed himself, and the three women followed his example. Grete, whose eyes never left the corpse, said: "Just see how thin he was. It's such a long time since he's eaten anything. The food came out again just as it went in." Indeed, Gregor's body was completely flat and dry, as could only now be seen when it was no longer supported by the legs and nothing prevented one from looking closely at it.

"Come in beside us, Grete, for a little while," said Mrs. Samsa with a tremulous smile, and Grete, not without looking back at the corpse, followed her parents into their bedroom. The charwoman shut the door and opened the window wide. Although it was so early in the morning a certain softness was perceptible in the fresh air. After all, it was already the end of March.

The three lodgers emerged from their room and were surprised to see no breakfast; they had been forgotten. "Where's our breakfast?" said the middle lodger peevishly to the charwoman. But she put her finger to her lips and hastily, without a word, indicated by gestures that they should go into Gregor's room. They did so and stood, their hands in the pockets of their somewhat shabby coats, around Gregor's corpse in the room where it was now fully light.

At that the door of the Samsas' bedroom opened and Mr. Samsa appeared in his uniform, his wife on one arm, his daughter on the other. They all looked a little as if they had been crying; from time to time Grete hid her face on her father's arm.

"Leave my house at once!" said Mr. Samsa, and pointed to the door without disengaging himself from the women. "What do you mean by that?" said the middle lodger, taken somewhat aback, with a feeble smile. The two others put their hands behind them and kept rubbing them together, as if in gleeful expectation of a fine set-to in which they were bound to come off the winners. "I mean just what I say," answered Mr. Samsa, and advanced in a straight line with his two companions towards the lodger. He stood his ground at first quietly, looking at the floor as if his thoughts were taking a new pattern in his head. "Then let us go, by all means," he said, and looked up at Mr. Samsa as if in a sudden access of humility he were expecting some renewed sanction for this decision. Mr. Samsa merely nodded briefly once or twice with meaning eyes. Upon that the lodger really did go with long strides into the hall, his two friends had been listening and had quite stopped rubbing their hands for some moments and now went scuttling after him as if afraid that Mr. Samsa might get into the hall before them and cut them off from their leader. In the hall they all three took their hats from the rack, their sticks from the umbrella stand, bowed in silence and quitted the apartment. With a suspiciousness which proved quite unfounded Mr. Samsa and the two women followed them out to the landing; leaning over the banister they watched the three figures slowly but surely going down the long stairs, vanishing from sight at a certain turn of the staircase on every floor and coming into view again after a moment or so; the more they dwindled, the more the Samsa family's interest in them dwindled, and when a butcher's boy met them and passed them on the stairs coming up proudly with a tray on his head, Mr. Samsa and the two women soon left the landing and as if a burden had been lifted from them went back into their apartment.

They decided to spend this day in resting and going for a stroll; they had not only deserved such a respite from work, but absolutely needed it. And so they sat down at the table and wrote three notes of excuse, Mr. Samsa to his board of management, Mrs. Samsa to her employer and Grete to the head of her firm. While they were writing, the charwoman came in to say that she was going now, since her morning's work was finished. At first they only nodded without looking up, but as she kept hovering there they eyed her irritably. "Well?" said Mr. Samsa. The charwoman stood grinning in the doorway as if she had good news to impart to the family but meant not to say a word unless properly questioned. The small ostrich feather standing upright on her hat, which had annoyed Mr. Samsa ever since she was engaged, was waving gaily in all directions. "Well, what is it then?" asked Mrs. Samsa, who obtained more respect from the charwoman than the others. "Oh," said the charwoman, giggling so amiably that she could not at once continue, "just this, you don't need to bother about how to get rid of the thing next door. It's been seen to already." Mrs. Samsa and Grete bent over their letters again, as if preoccupied; Mr. Samsa, who perceived that she was eager to begin describing it all in detail, stopped her with a decisive hand. But since she was not allowed to tell her story, she remembered the great hurry she was in, being obviously deeply huffed: "Bye, everybody," she said, whirling off violently, and departed with a frightful slamming of doors.

"She'll be given notice tonight," said Mr. Samsa, but neither from his wife nor his daughter did he get any answer, for the charwoman seemed to have shattered again the composure they had barely achieved. They rose, went to the window and stayed there, clasping each other tight. Mr. Samsa turned in his chair to look at them and quietly observed them for a little. Then he called out: "Come along, now, do. Let bygones be bygones. And you might have some consideration for me." The two of them complied at once, hastened to him, caressed him and quickly finished their letters.

Then they all three left the apartment together, which was more than they had done for months, and went by tram into the open country outside the

town. The tram, in which they were the only passengers, was filled with warm
sunshine. Leaning comfortably back in their seats they canvassed their
prospects for the future, and it appeared on closer inspection that these were
not at all bad, for the jobs they had got, which so far they had never really discussed with each other, were all three admirable and likely to lead to better
things later on. The greatest immediate improvement in their condition would
of course arise from moving to another house; they wanted to take a smaller
and cheaper but also better situated and more easily run apartment than the
one they had, which Gregor had selected. While they were thus conversing, it
struck both Mr. and Mrs. Samsa, almost at the same moment, as they became
aware of their daughter's increasing vivacity, that in spite of all the sorrow of
recent times, which had made her cheeks pale, she had bloomed into a pretty
girl with a good figure. They grew quieter and half unconsciously exchanged
glances of complete agreement, having come to the conclusion that it would
soon be time to find a good husband for her. And it was like a confirmation of
their new dreams and excellent intentions that at the end of their journey their
daughter sprang to her feet first and stretched her young body.

THOMAS KING

THE ONE ABOUT
COYOTE GOING WEST

Thomas King (b. 1943) is a Native Canadian writer whose Cherokee and Greco-German heritage have instilled in him a strong and iconoclastic sense of kinship. "I think of myself as a Native writer and a Canadian writer," says King. "I'm not from one of the tribes up here. But all of my short stories were published here in Canada." King studied at California State University and at the University of Utah, and has pursued an academic career while working in a variety of creative media. Novels, short fiction, and radio and screen writing complement King's distinguished roles of lecturer, critic, and anthologist. He spent ten years as a professor of Native studies at the University of Lethbridge, Alberta, and several more as chair of the American Indian studies department at the University of Minnesota, Minneapolis, and currently is on the English faculty at the University of Guelph.

King's work in various media—as an anthologist, a photographer, a screenwriter, and a fiction writer—is characterized by an idiosyncratic brand of humour, which Margaret Atwood has likened to "a double-bladed knife ... a subversive weapon for people who find themselves in a fairly tight spot without other, more physical weapons." King deploys comedy to confront the European oppression, exploitation, and appropriation that has framed the Native experience in North America. "The One About Coyote Going West," from his collection One Good Story, That One *(1994), draws on Native oral storytelling traditions and plays with conventions of children's literature. King portrays the universal "web of kinship," through which we "accept the responsibilities by living our lives in a harmonious and moral manner," providing a testament to "a certain cultural tenacity that keeps us going."*

This one is about Coyote. She was going west. Visiting her relations. That's what she said. You got to watch that one. Tricky one. Full of bad business. No, no, no, no, that one says. I'm just visiting.

Going to see Raven.

Boy, I says. That's another tricky one.

Coyote comes by my place. She wag her tail. Make them happy noises. Sit on my porch. Look around. With them teeth. With that smile. Coyote put her nose in my tea. My good tea. Get that nose out of my tea, I says.

I'm going to see my friends, she says. Tell those stories. Fix this world. Straighten it up.

Oh boy, pretty scary that, Coyote fix the world, again.

Sit down, I says. Eat some food. Hard work that fix up the world. Maybe you have a song. Maybe you have a good joke.

Sure, says Coyote. That one wink her ears. Lick her whiskers.

I tuck my feet under that chair. Got to hide my toes. Sometimes that tricky one leave her skin sit in that chair. Coyote skin. No Coyote. Sneak around. Bite them toes. Make you jump.

I been reading those books, she says.

You must be one smart Coyote, I says.

You bet, she says.

Maybe you got a good story for me, I says.

I been reading about that history, says Coyote. She tricks that nose back in my tea. All about who found us Indians.

Ho, I says. I like those old ones. Them ones are the best. You tell me your story, I says. Maybe some biscuits will visit us. Maybe some moose-meat stew come along, listen to your story.

Okay, she says and she sings her story song.

> Snow's on the ground the snakes are asleep.
> Snow's on the ground my voice is strong.
> Snow's on the ground the snakes are asleep.
> Snow's on the ground my voice is strong.

She sings like that. With that tail, wagging. With that smile. Sitting there.

Maybe I tell you the one about Eric the Lucky and the Vikings play hockey for the Old-timers, find us Indians in Newfoundland, she says.

Maybe I tell you the one about Christopher Cartier looking for something good to eat. Find us Indians in a restaurant in Montreal.

Maybe I tell you the one about Jacques Columbus come along that river, Indians waiting for him. We all wave and say, here we are, here we are.

Everyone knows those stories, I says. White man stories. Baby stories you got in your mouth.

No, no, no, no, says the Coyote. I read these ones in that old book.

Ho, I says. You are trying to bite my toes. Everyone knows who found us Indians. Eric the Lucky and that Christopher Cartier and that Jacques Columbus come along later. Those ones get lost. Float about. Walk around.

Get mixed up. Ho, ho, ho, ho, those ones cry, we are lost. So we got to find them. Help them out. Feed them. Show them around.

Boy, I says. Bad mistake that one.

You are very wise, grandmother, says Coyote, bring her eyes down. Like she is sleepy. Maybe you know who discovered Indians.

Sure, I says. Everyone knows that. It was Coyote. She was the one.

Oh, grandfather, that Coyote says. Tell me that story. I love those stories about that sneaky one. I don't think I know that story, she says.

All right, I says. Pay attention.

Coyote was heading west. That's how I always start this story. There was nothing else in the world. Just Coyote. She could see all the way, too. No mountains then. No rivers. No forests then. Pretty flat then. So she starts to make things. So she starts to fix this world.

This is exciting, says Coyote, and she takes her nose out of my tea.

Yes, I says. Just the beginning, too. Coyote got a lot of things to make.

Tell me, grandmother, says Coyote. What does the clever one make first?

Well, I says. Maybe she makes that tree grows by the river. Maybe she makes that buffalo. Maybe she makes that mountain. Maybe she makes them clouds.

Maybe she makes that beautiful rainbow, says Coyote.

No, I says. She don't make that thing. Mink makes that.

Maybe she makes that beautiful moon, says Coyote.

No, I says. She don't do that either. Otter finds that moon in a pond later on.

Maybe she makes the oceans with that blue water, says Coyote.

No, I says. Oceans are already here. She don't do any of that. The first thing Coyote makes, I tell Coyote, is a mistake.

Boy, Coyote sit up straight. Them eyes pop open. That tail stop wagging. That one swallow that smile.

Big one, too, I says. Coyote is going west thinking of things to make. That one is trying to think of everything to make at once. So she don't see that hole. So she falls in that hole. Then those thoughts bump around. They run into each other. Those ones fall out of Coyote's ears. In that hole. Ho, that Coyote cries. I have fallen into a hole. I must have made a mistake. And she did.

So, there is that hole. And there is that Coyote in that hole. And there is that big mistake in that hole with Coyote. Ho, says that mistake. You must be Coyote.

That mistake is real big and that hole is small. Not much room. I don't want to tell you what that mistake looks like. First mistake in the world. Pretty scary. Boy, I can't look. I got to close my eyes. You better close your eyes, too, I tell Coyote.

Okay, I'll do that, she says, and she puts her hands over her eyes. But she don't fool me. I can see she's peeking.

Don't peek, I says.

Okay, she says. I won't do that.

Well, you know, that Coyote thinks about the hole. And she thinks about how she's going to get out of that hole. She thinks how she's going to get that big mistake back in her head.

Say, says that mistake. What is that you're thinking about?

I'm thinking of a song, says Coyote. I'm thinking of a song to make this hole bigger.

That's a good idea, says that mistake. Let me hear your hole song.

But that's not what Coyote sings. She sings a song to make the mistake smaller. But that mistake hears her. And that mistake grabs Coyote's nose. And that one pulls off her mouth so she can't sing. And that one jumps up and down on Coyote until she is flat. Then that one leaps out of that hole, wanders around looking for things to do.

Well, Coyote is feeling pretty bad, all flat her nice fur coat full of stomp holes. So she thinks hard, and she think about a healing song. And she tries to sing a healing song, but her mouth is in other places. So she thinks harder and tries to sing that song through her nose. But that nose don't make any sound, just drip a lot. She tries to sing that song out her ears, but those ears don't hear anything.

So, that silly one thinks real hard and tries to sing out her butt-hole. Pssst! Pssst! That is what that butt-hole says, and right away things don't smell so good in that hole. Pssst.

Boy, Coyote thinks. Something smells.

That Coyote lies there flat and practise and practise. Pretty soon, maybe two days, maybe one year, she teach that butt-hole to sing. That song. That healing song. So that butt-hole sings that song. And Coyote begins to feel better. And Coyote don't feel so flat anymore. Pssst! Pssst! Things still smell pretty bad, but Coyote is okay.

That one look around in that hole. Find her mouth. Put that mouth back. So, she says to that butt-hole. Okay, you can stop singing now. You can stop making them smells now. But, you know, that butt-hole is liking all that singing, and so that butt-hole keeps on singing.

Stop that, says Coyote. You going to stink up the whole world. But it don't. So Coyote jumps out of that hole and runs across the prairies real fast. But that butt-hole follows her. Pssst. Pssst. Coyote jumps into a lake, but that butt-hole don't drown. It just keeps on singing.

Hey, who is doing all that singing, someone says.

Yes, and who is making that bad smell, says another voice.

It must be Coyote, says a third voice.

Yes, says a fourth voice. I believe it is Coyote.

That Coyote sit in my chair, put her nose in my tea, say, I know who that voice is. It is that big mistake playing a trick. Nothing else is made yet.

No, I says. That mistake is doing other things.

Then those voices are spirits, says Coyote.

No, I says. Them voices belong to them ducks.

Coyote stand up on my chair. Hey, she says, where did them ducks come from?

Calm down, I says. This story is going to be okay. This story is doing just fine. This story knows where it is going. Sit down. Keep your skin on.

So.

Coyote look around, and she see them four ducks. In that lake. Ho, she says. Where did you ducks come from? I didn't make you yet.

Yes, says them ducks. We were waiting around, but you didn't come. So we got tired of waiting. So we did it ourselves.

I was in a hole, says Coyote.

Pssst. Pssst.

What's that noise, says them ducks. What's that bad smell?

Never mind, says Coyote. Maybe you've seen something go by. Maybe you can help me find something I lost. Maybe you can help me get it back.

Those duck swim around and talk to themselves. Was it something awful to look at? Yes, says Coyote, it certainly was. Was it something with ugly fur? Yes, says Coyote, I think it had that, too. Was it something that made a lot of noise? ask them ducks. Yes, it was pretty noisy, says Coyote. Did it smell bad, them ducks want to know. Yes, says Coyote. I guess you ducks have seen my something.

Yes, says them ducks. It is right there behind you.

So that Coyote turn around, and there is nothing there.

It's still behind you, says those ducks.

So Coyote turn around again but she don't see anything.

Pssst! Pssst!

Boy, says those ducks. What a noise! What a smell! They say that, too. What an ugly thing with all that fur!

Never mind, says that Coyote, again. That is not what I'm looking for. I'm looking for something else.

Maybe you're looking for Indians, says those ducks.

Well, that Coyote is real surprised because she hasn't created Indians, either. Boy, says that one, mischief is everywhere. This world is getting bent.

All right.

So Coyote and those ducks are talking, and pretty soon they hear a noise. And pretty soon there is something coming. And those ducks says, oh, oh, oh, oh. They say that like they see trouble, but it is not trouble. What comes along is a river.

Hello, says that river. Nice day. Maybe you want to take a swim. But Coyote don't want to swim, and she looks at that river and she looks at that river again. Something's not right here, she says. Where are those rocks? Where are those rapids? What did you do with them waterfalls? How come you're so straight?

And Coyote is right. That river is nice and straight and smooth without any bumps or twists. It runs both ways, too, not like a modern river.

We got to fix this, says Coyote, and she does. She puts some rocks in that river, and she fixes it so it only runs one way. She puts a couple of waterfalls in and makes a bunch of rapids where things get shallow fast.

Coyote is tired with all this work, and those ducks are tired just watching. So that Coyote sits down. So she closes her eyes. So she puts her nose in her tail. So those ducks shout, wake up, wake up! Something big is heading this way! And they are right.

Mountain comes sliding along, whistling. Real happy mountain. Nice and round. This mountain is full of grapes and other good things to eat. Apples, peaches, cherries. Howdy-do, says the polite mountain, nice day for whistling.

Coyote looks at that mountain, and that one shakes her head. Oh, no, she says, this mountain is all wrong. How come you're so nice and round? Where are those craggy peaks? Where are all them cliffs? What happened to all that snow? Boy, we got to fix this thing, too. So she does.

Grandfather, grandfather, says that Coyote, sit in my chair, put her nose in my tea. Why is that Coyote changing all those good things?

That is a real sly one, ask me that question. I look at those eyes. Grab them ears. Squeeze that nose. Hey, let go my nose, that Coyote says.

Okay, I says. Coyote still in Coyote skin. I bet you know why Coyote change that happy river. Why she change that mountain sliding along whistling.

No, says that Coyote, look around my house, lick her lips, make them baby noises.

Maybe it's because she is mean, I says.

Oh, no, says Coyote. That one is sweet and kind.

Maybe it's because that one is not too smart.

Oh, no, says Coyote. That Coyote is very wise.

Maybe it's because she made a mistake.

Oh, no, says Coyote. She made one of those already.

All right, I says. Then Coyote must be doing the right thing. She must be fixing up the world so it is perfect.

Yes, says Coyote. That must be it. What does that brilliant one do next?

Everyone knows what Coyote does next, I says. Little babies know what Coyote does next.

Oh no, says Coyote. I have never heard this story. You are a wonderful storyteller. You tell me your good Coyote story.

Boy, you got to watch that one all the time. Hide them toes.

Well, I says. Coyote thinks about that river. And she thinks about that mountain. And she thinks somebody is fooling around. So she goes looking around. She goes looking for that one who is messing up the world.

She goes to the north, and there is nothing. She goes to the south, and there is nothing there, either. She goes to the east, and there is still nothing there. She goes to the west, and there is a pile of snow tires.

And there is some televisions. And there is some vacuum cleaners. And there is a bunch of pastel sheets. And there is an air humidifier. And there is a big mistake sitting on a portable gas barbecue reading a book. Big book. Department store catalogue.

Hello, says that mistake. Maybe you want a hydraulic jack.

No, says that Coyote. I don't want one of them. But she don't tell that mistake what she want because she don't want to miss her mouth again. But when she thinks about being flat and full of stomp holes, that butt-hole wakes up and begins to sing. Pssst. Pssst.

What's that noise? says that big mistake.

I'm looking for Indians, says that Coyote, real quick. Have you seen any? What's that bad smell?

Never mind, says Coyote. Maybe you have some Indians around here.

I got some toaster ovens, says that mistake.

We don't need that stuff, says Coyote. You got to stop making all those things. You're going to fill up this world.

Maybe you want a computer with a colour monitor. That mistake keeps looking through that book and those things keep landing in piles all around Coyote.

Stop, stop, cries Coyote. Golf cart lands on her foot. Golf balls bounce off her head. You got to give me that book before the world gets lopsided.

These are good things, says that mistake. We need these things to make up the world. Indians are going to need this stuff.

We don't have any Indians, says Coyote.

And that mistake can see that that's right. Maybe we better make some Indians, says that mistake. So that one looks in that catalogue, but it don't have any Indians. And Coyote don't know how to do that, either. She has already made four things.

I've made four things already, she says. I got to have help.

We can help, says some voices and it is those ducks come swimming along.
We can help you make Indians, says the white duck. Yes, we can do that, says
the green duck. We have been thinking about this, says that blue duck. We
have a plan, says the red duck.

Well, that Coyote don't know what to do. So she tells them ducks to go
ahead because this story is pretty long and it's getting late and everyone wants
to go home.

You still awake, I says to Coyote. You still here?

Oh yes, grandmother, says Coyote. What do those clever ducks do?

So I tell Coyote that those ducks lay some eggs. Ducks do that, you know.
That white duck lay an egg, and it is blue. That red duck lay an egg, and it is
green. That blue duck lay an egg, and it is red. That green duck lay an egg, and
it is white.

Come on, says those ducks. We got to sing a song. We got to do a dance.
So they do. Coyote and that big mistake and those four ducks dance around
the eggs. So they dance and sing for a long time, and pretty soon Coyote gets
hungry.

I know this dance, she says, but you got to close your eyes when you do it
or nothing will happen. You got to close your eyes tight. Okay, says those
ducks. We can do that. And they do. And that big mistake closes its eyes, too.

But Coyote, she don't close her eyes, and all of them start dancing again,
and Coyote dances up close to that white duck, and she grabs that white duck
by her neck.

When Coyote grabs that duck, that duck flaps her wings, and that big mistake hears the noise and opens them eyes. Say, says that big mistake, that's not
the way the dance goes.

By golly, you're right, says Coyote, and she lets that duck go. I am getting
it mixed up with another dance.

So they start to dance again. And Coyote is very hungry, and she grabs
that blue duck, and she grabs his wings, too. But Coyote's stomach starts to
make hungry noises, and that mistake opens them eyes and sees Coyote with
the blue duck. Hey, says that mistake, you got yourself mixed up again.

That's right, says Coyote, and she drops that duck and straightens out that
neck. It sure is good you're around to help me with this dance.

They all start that dance again, and, this time, Coyote grabs the green
duck real quick and tries to stuff it down that greedy throat, and there is
nothing hanging out but them yellow duck feet. But those feet are flapping in
Coyote's eyes, and she can't see where she is going, and she bumps into the big
mistake and the mistake turns around to see what has happened.

Ho, says that big mistake, you can't see where you're going with them
yellow duck feet flapping in your eyes, and that mistake pulls that green duck
out of Coyote's throat. You could hurt yourself dancing like that.

You are one good friend, look after me like that, says Coyote.

Those ducks start to dance again, and Coyote dances with them, but that red duck says, we better dance with one eye open, so we can help Coyote with this dance. So they dance some more, and, then, those eggs begin to move around, and those eggs crack open. And if you look hard, you can see something inside those eggs.

I know, I know, says that Coyote, jump up and down on my chair, shake up my good tea. Indians come out of those eggs. I remember this story, now. Inside those eggs are the Indians Coyote's been looking for.

No, I says. You are one crazy Coyote. What comes out of those duck eggs are baby ducks. You better sit down, I says. You may fall and hurt yourself. You may spill my tea. You may fall on top of this story and make it flat.

Where are the Indians? says that Coyote. This story was about how Coyote found the Indians. Maybe the Indians are in the eggs with the baby ducks.

No, I says, nothing in those eggs but little ducks. Indians will be along in a while. Don't lose your skin.

So.

When those ducks see what has come out of the eggs, they says, boy, we didn't get that quite right. We better try that again. So they do. They lay them eggs. They dance that dance. They sing that song. Those eggs crack open and out comes some more baby ducks. They do this seven times and each time, they get more ducks.

By golly, says those four ducks. We got more ducks than we need. I guess we got to be the Indians. And so they do that. Before Coyote or that big mistake can mess things up, those four ducks turn into Indians, two women and two men. Good-looking Indians, too. They don't look at all like ducks any more.

But those duck-Indians aren't happy. They look at each other and they begin to cry. This is pretty disgusting, they says. All this ugly skin. All these bumpy bones. All this awful black hair. Where are our nice soft feathers? Where are our beautiful feet? What happened to our wonderful wings? It's probably all that Coyote's fault because she didn't do the dance right, and those four duck-Indians come over and stomp all over Coyote until she is flat like before. Then they leave. That big mistake leave, too. And that Coyote, she starts to think about a healing song.

Pssst. Pssst.

That's it, I says. It is done.

But what happens to Coyote, says Coyote. That wonderful one is still flat.

Some of these stories are flat, I says. That's what happens when you try to fix this world. This world is pretty good all by itself. Best to leave it alone. Stop messing around with it.

I better get going, says Coyote. I will tell Raven your good story. We going to fix this world for sure. We know how to do it now. We know to do it right.

So, Coyote drinks my tea and that one leave. And I can't talk any more because I got to watch the sky. Got to watch out for falling things that land in piles. When that Coyote's wandering around looking to fix things, nobody in this world is safe.

IVAN KLIMA

THE SMUGGLER'S STORY

Translated by Paul Wilson

Ivan Klima (b. 1931) was born in Prague. His work has been published internationally, despite the political constraints under which he has lived for much of his life. He writes plays, stories, novels, and essays. Part Jewish, he spent three years during World War II in the Terezin concentration camp, where he began writing. After the war he completed his secondary education at Charles University in Prague, where he studied Czech and literature. He has lived in Czechoslovakia for five decades, enduring the political turmoil of Stalin's repressive regimes of the 1950s, the celebrations and hope of the Prague Spring, the despair of the 1968 Soviet invasion, and the recent resurgence of democracy in Czech Republic. His writing is motivated by a need to document his country's turbulent history with honesty and with hope. Klima's work includes My Merry Mornings, My First Loves *(1989),* A Summer Affair *(1990),* Love and Garbage *(1991),* My Golden Trades *(1993), from which* The Smuggler's Story *is taken, and* The Spirit of Prague *(1994).*

I heard a familiar voice coming over the phone. "Santa Claus here. Got an hour this afternoon?"

I had.

"Sensational," said the voice on the other end, in an inimitable accent that could only belong to someone with a Mexican father and an Indian mother. Then he hung up. He obviously believed that the briefer our conversation was, the less suspicion it would arouse in anyone listening in. Whenever he announced himself as Santa Claus, it meant that he'd returned from one of his frequent business trips abroad and was bringing me books.

It was eleven-thirty and snowing heavily. My wife had taken the car earlier that morning, and it would be noon before I could reach her. I'm not very fond of driving, but I had no idea how many bags of contraband St. Nicholas had purchased and brought in. He was hard to fathom. There could well be more than I could carry.

I had met Nicholas by accident. The water-pump on my ancient Renault had given up and, after the car had been immobile in the garage for three months, someone gave me Nicholas's name and address, saying that he often travelled out of the country and would certainly bring me a new pump.

Why should he do that, when he didn't even know me?

He would do it because I was a writer. He loved literature or, to be more precise, he worshipped his wife, who loved literature.

And how would I pay him?

I wasn't to worry about that: for a rich businessman a spare part was no more than a kilo of apples would be for me. Give him a signed copy of one of your books. Or invite him to lunch.

I hesitated for almost a month, but when the water pump for my car was still unavailable, I rang the stranger's doorbell.

In a week I not only had my pump, I had a package of books as well.

He smiled. He was tall, greying, and had a dark complexion. He said it was a pleasure to be able to help me. He held art in the highest esteem, he said, and he understood what a difficult situation I was in.

I gave one of my books to him, with a dedication, and I invited him and his wife to dinner.

Having grown up in an era of paranoia, I was guarded during their visit and did not reveal the secrets of my writing—the only secrets I could have betrayed. But Nicholas did not pry. For a while, he spoke about the world of business, something that for me was exotic and far away. After that his wife, Angela, did most of the talking. She was at least twenty years younger than he was and looked liked the angel in her name. We talked about Borges, Márquez and most of all about Cortázar's *Rayuela*, which both of us admired though we disagreed somewhat over the scene in which the heroine crawls across some rickety boards stretched between two windows four storeys above the ground merely to satisfy the whims of two strange and indolent men, bringing them a package of *mate* and a handful of nails across the abyss in the punishing heat. Angela saw in that scene an image of the slavish position of women in her country, while I argued that the scene was meant to represent the heroine's inability to choose between the two men. At the same time, I suggested, the author was paying tribute to women for their courage: women are generally capable of taking risks; men can only admire them for it.

Angela conversed and listened with an intensity that had inspired me to talk about writing, which I normally avoid doing. The conversation seemed to make her happy, and her husband looked content as well.

A month later he unexpectedly called and brought me a package of books, most of which were in Czech. He even brought two or three copies of the same books. He knew, he said, that some of my colleagues were in the same position as I was, and he was sure the books would interest us.

Certainly, but what gave him the idea to bring them to us?

Angela claimed that this was the only way we'd ever get to see such books. I allowed that this was so, thanked him, and distributed the books among my friends.

Some time later he brought me two parcels, not only books this time but also a few magazines, which were even harder to come by. I was delighted, but at the same time I began to feel slightly afraid.

I remembered how, 247 years ago, Jiřík Vostrý, a Protestant missionary, had been caught trying to smuggle forbidden books from Saxony into Bohemia. They threw him straight into prison but, of course, what interested them most was who the books were for. The jailer pretended to be a friend and told the young, inexperienced smuggler that he would take a letter out for him. That letter, which I recently read in a collection of documents in Litomyšl, spoke to me in a language I knew well:

> Kladivo,
> I am writing to you from my prison cell with a plea. Should there be
> any books still in your possession I pray you hide them safely away.
> And make this known to those you know. I, a prisoner in the name
> of the Lord, pray you to this in His name. I assure you I have
> betrayed no one, so look that you comport yourself likewise. Read
> this letter, and then give it to him who is faithful ...

My wife wasn't at work; she had just gone to pick up the washing from the laundry. Another delay.

I was anxious because Nicholas had asked me to come in the afternoon, when he wasn't usually at home. He was probably worried that if he left it till the evening, when he came home from work, he could be followed. It occasionally happened to him, as it did to every foreigner—and to everyone else in the country. His tail would stick with him right up to the building where he lived and then stay there, watching, or at the most retreat to the tennis-courts at the top of the street. From there, it was easy to keep an eye not only on the matches but also on the entrance to Nicholas's building. There they would stay until they were relieved or called off. I would certainly not want to appear in their sight, let alone be caught carrying off a bag of books.

I don't know if I can speak for Nicholas, but personally I had never imagined that one day I would take up smuggling. By the rules that apply in most of the world, smugglers are devious people, with a close knowledge of their territory and their pursuers; men and women with nerves of steel and contempt for the law, both the kind that is written in the statute book and the kind that, although it is not written down anywhere, we sense stands above our every action. I have contempt for neither kind of law, but in our situation, where they contradicted each other, I had to choose between them. Thus, despite my natural disinclination, I have more than once found myself prepared to receive smuggled goods. I find consolation in the fact that, in the conditions prevailing here, it is rare for someone to be doing what he was trained to do, or what he is suited for.

Not long ago Nicholas brought me enough books to fill two bags. Dragging them on to the tram, I looked so suspicious, so desperate even, that people began staring at me, which didn't add to my peace of mind. To make matters worse a man I'd noticed earlier got into the same car as I did. I put one of the bags on my lap and put the other one under the seat so I wouldn't look so burdened. At the same time, I racked my brains trying to think what I'd do and say if the man really was who I feared he was. What if he wanted to search my bags? As it turned out, he didn't, but when I got out of the car I was so pre-occupied that I forgot about the bag under the seat. I was already on my way out when a kind woman called me back. Is there any way I can thank her enough? In the bag I was apparently determined to leave behind on the tram were all my identification papers. I don't know how I'd have explained the contents of the bag to those who consider all books that have not passed through a censor's hands to be contraband.

The thing I'd almost done startled and frightened me. I began thinking I should ask Nicholas not to bring me any more books, but I was ashamed to refuse gifts offered to me with such magnanimity just because of my fear. Beyond that, the books seemed to me the last bridge to a part of the world that was fading every more rapidly from view.

As more items are prohibited, more amateurs take up smuggling. I learned this in the ghetto during the war, where almost everything became unobtain-able—rice, cocoa, cigarette-lighters, writing-paper, coffee and candles, not to mention jewellery, cigarettes or money. Even the most decent, law-abiding souls decided to ignore such perverted regulations. Where the law goes berserk, all of us become felons. My father, a scholar led by the very essence of his work to be a man of anxious propriety, brought within the ghetto walls a roll of thousand-crown notes and for the first time in his life was confronted with the basic problem every smuggler faces: where to hide his stash.

In the room we were forced to live in at the time, there was only a single piece of furniture—an old sideboard with many battered drawers. When the drawer on the extreme left was pulled out, a small depression could be felt on the side wall, a flaw left by the cabinet-maker. It proved an ideal hiding place for our treasure. The opening for the drawer was so narrow that only a child's arm could reach in, so I was given the task of placing the roll of money into the depression. I wasn't to breathe a word of what I had done to anyone, nor was I allowed to get fat, or the hiding place would have become inaccessible. I carried out my task faithfully, and thus at the age of ten found myself a member of the criminal fraternity.

I entered that company in the firm conviction that I had done good work.

It was two-thirty when I finally reached Nicholas's house. It was still snowing heavily. Here, on the outskirts of the city, the snow did not melt, but settled thickly on tree branches and the roof-tops. The chain-link fence surrounding the tennis-courts stretched like a swag of lace between iron poles. In the middle of the road, cars had made deep ruts in the snow. I knew this end of the city well. My first love had lived not far from here and we had often wandered the neighbouring streets looking for dark corners where we could embrace. Right now I wasn't thinking about that. Right now the world had become an alien and hostile place, and everyone in it was a potential threat.

You should always mentally rehearse how you would behave and what you would say if you were arrested. It wasn't hard to guess what they would ask.

"What books have you brought with you?" the investigator asked the twenty-seven-year-old smuggler of subversive books, Jiřík Vostrý, on 19 April, 1732.

"I have brought three. One: *The New Testament*; Two: *On True Christianity*, Three: *Two Countrymen Converse on the Subject of Faith*."

"Where are those books now and for whom were they intended?"

"*On True Christianity* was received by Litochlev; he gave me one score and ten groschen for it. *Two Countrymen Converse*, that went to Kaliban, a miller from Kamenné Sedliště. And the third remained in my pocket; it was confiscated when I was taken."

"At first you claimed you traded only with Litochleb in Morašice and Kladivo in Lubný. Now you tell me you also called upon the miller in Sedliště?"

"I did. I had forgotten."

"And how did you come by the knowledge that the miller of Sedliště also cleaved to your cause?"

"I was told he had knowledge of our faith. Litochlev told me."

"What did you do when you were with this miller, this Kaliban? What was your talk about?"

"Our talk was of God. He told me his people were in sore need of help, for they were weak in the faith. I assured him the Lord God would give them strength."

"And what else?"

"I don't remember."

"Who else did you speak with? Who were you going to see? What others have knowledge of your faith?"

"I know none."

That was two and a half centuries ago. It's exactly the same now, right down to the inaccuracies in the report. How well I know it! They are incapable of setting down names correctly.

I took a careful look around the tennis-courts. Two mothers were pushing prams alongside the lace fence. No one else was in sight. But there was a delivery van parked at the top of the street. The spies could easily be secreted inside with their cameras. I studied the vehicle. Though I couldn't see inside, it appeared cold and empty.

The street I now entered was a dead end—a perfect trap. I had to walk past three small villas before I got to the building where Nicholas lived. I looked around once more. A snow-covered Saab was parked by the kerb opposite his house—but that belonged here. A short distance down the street, however, I saw a caravan that hadn't been here two months ago.

That frightened me.

I don't feel a great affinity for those who smuggled books into this country before the Edict of Toleration of 1781, subversive books which the authorities of that time thought should have been burned. Or at least—unlike those book smugglers of old—I don't hold printed paper in such high regard. The things we write are no longer prompted by God and therefore they are as we ourselves are: good and evil, sometimes wise, and often foolish. Censorship may add to a book's appeal, but it can add nothing to its wisdom.

I walked over to the caravan. The snow around it was untouched, and the boarded window on the windward side was completely covered with sticky snow; there was no opening through which a hidden camera might peer. I went up to the main entrance to Nicholas's building. I was just reaching out to ring the bell when I realized I'd forgotten to take a final look around. I withdrew my hand, stared a moment longer at the column of name-plates by the gate, even though I normally pay no attention to them. Then I turned around slowly. The windows of the building across the street were dark, the curtains drawn. If anyone were hiding behind them, I had no hope of seeing. An elderly lady leading a reddish boxer was walking in my direction from the tiny park. The dog stopped and plunged his muzzle into the snow; the lady bent over him. I could still pretend that I hadn't found the name I was looking for and stroll over to the main entrance of the next apartment building, but I suddenly felt disgusted at the comedy I'd been playing to this innocent old woman. I pressed the doorbell.

Ten years ago my wife and I went on a cruise to Israel, our first visit to that part of the world. The trip had been my wife's idea and she had triumphed over the customary reluctance of officials to permit such journeys to happen. She had moved about the ship in a state of rapture. She was delighted to discover that there were several Israeli citizens on board and she immediately set about to make friends. Her favourite was a black-haired, dark-skinned Levantine woman, who reminded me of the gypsies that ran carnival merry-go-rounds. She taught my wife Israeli songs and won her heart. It turned out that the woman's gesture was not entirely altruistic. As we neared Haifa, she came forward with a request. She was taking her mother a small rug from Greece. Nothing special, but customs officials tend to be more difficult with their own citizens than with foreigners. Could my wife take the carpet through customs for her? The Levantine thrust at my wife a roll of something that weighed more than all our baggage put together. It was carefully wrapped in dark brown paper.

I asked my wife if she was aware that the parcel might well contain a disassembled machine-gun or cocaine or a stolen Leonardo or gold bars, but she was positive the parcel contained nothing but a carpet. Why should her new friend lie to her? I tried to explain that she could be the victim of a professional smuggler and that it would be prudent either to return the parcel or at least to unwrap it and see what was really inside.

My wife said that she would never stoop to open someone else's parcel.

Meanwhile the boat had docked and the owner of the parcel had vanished into the crowd of passengers. We could leave the parcel on the boat, throw it overboard or carry it through customs. My wife was never particularly strong, but she refused to let me carry the parcel because I didn't trust its contents. She heaved it on to her shoulder and, bending under its weight, walked down the gangplank.

We entered an enormous hall where there was a crowd of people, some in uniform and some not. It became clear that the most thorough customs inspection I had ever witnessed was taking place. We approached a long counter where, under the customs officers' gaze, people were being asked to empty their suitcases, hand luggage and purses. I watched with astonishment the transformation this wrought in my wife. She straightened up so that the heavy roll on her shoulders seemed almost to float, and then with an expression of confidence and certainty that only the utter absence of guilt can produce, she stepped up to the counter. When she was asked what was in the parcel on her shoulder, she replied that it was a carpet for an acquaintance.

They waved us through the barrier.

We will never know what it was we were actually carrying, but I understood then what sort of face a good smuggler should put on. I also knew that given my anxieties, I would never make the grade.

Angela came to the gate, greeted the woman with the dog and held her mouth up to be kissed.

On a bench in the hall inside their flat were three bags, crammed full. "These are for you," she said. "Would you like tea?"

It would have been impolite to pick up the bags and scoot out of the door with them, as I had hoped to do. I could see Angela wanted me to sit and talk with her for a while. She must have been bored, spending all those hours alone in a strange flat on the edge of a strange city in the middle of a strange land and among people whose language she did not understand. I peered into one of the bags and saw the flash of shiny covers, but I overcame the desire to kneel down beside the bag and begin rummaging inside. This time I had been bold enough to give Nicholas a list of some books I particularly wanted to read. Had he managed to get them? I pulled the zip shut and went to wait for the tea.

Angela came in with a silver tray holding a teapot. She poured me a cup of *mate*.

Angela is Argentinian, and whenever I find myself near her, I'm always subliminally aware of the distance she has travelled to appear before me. Between us lay jungles and wide rivers, the pampas; a landscape I will almost certainly never behold.

She sat down opposite me, poured herself a glass of wine, tossed back her long black hair so that it fell over her left shoulder down to her waist, removed her glasses and looked at me intently. The colour and shape of her eyes revealed some of her ancestors to be Indians. Angela should have married a poet, not a businessman. Had she done so, either she would have been happy or she would have discovered that poets are people just as businessmen are, and that you can be as happy or as miserable with them as you can with anyone else.

I knew that her journey away from her country—and thus to Nicholas—had not been easy.

Borders, or rather their guardians, present barriers not only to smugglers and fleeing criminals. Of course, the more ruthless the guardians, the more inventive and daring those who feel themselves imprisoned by the border guards become. They dig tunnels under the walls or barbed wire, they sew together hot-air balloons from bed-sheets, they construct trolleys to run along high-tension wires, and they fling themselves against the barbed wire, knowing that they will most likely be shot. They undergo all this in order to carry themselves across the invisible borderline, over the prison wall. For a moment, a man transforms himself into a thing, turns himself into a piece of contraband, in the hope that he may never again be an object of arbitrary power.

Angela said that her escape from her country had been less dramatic. Her friends got her a false passport. But she still occasionally dreamed about a moment when an armed guard at the border takes her passport, looks at the photograph, then at her face, and nods to someone invisible. From a concealed place, some monster with foam dripping from his fangs comes roaring out, grabs her and drags her off. Sometimes she is taken to the very border, which runs along a narrow path on a ridge of mountain peaks. On each side an abyss drops away, and she knows that they will fling her down on one side or the other.

She poured me more tea, more wine for herself, and began to talk about her life before she left her country.

Her father was a colonel in the army. Their household had servants, but it was loveless. Her father behaved in a military fashion: he was courtly and self-less to others, but arrogant and unyielding towards his own. He expected Angela's mother to ensure that everything was done to his satisfaction. When she became seriously ill, he took it as a personal affront. He ignored his wife's suffering, refused to change his ways or even to give up drinking with his companions. He was drunk when she died. After she was gone, he began to miss her, or at least to miss the care she took of him. He drank more, hung around the casinos, and eventually squandered his house and his reputation. He moved into a tiny, ramshackle structure on the fringes of Rosario. They let the maid go. Angela was only twelve at the time, but she devoted herself to her father, making sure he always found everything in order, that he always had his evening meal. She wanted to recreate a feeling of home—but he scarcely took any notice. Except once, when he came back from the casino in a particularly elated mood. He pulled a fistful of banknotes from his pocket, probably money he had won at baccarat or poker, and forced her to accept them, saying she deserved it. He didn't understand her at all.

I had no idea why Angela was telling this to me today, but I listened to her attentively, and would have listened with more compassion had my mental clock not reminded me of the danger of staying too long. A professional smuggler, I felt, wouldn't linger knowing his mortal enemies could be approaching.

The poverty they found themselves in, Angela continued, had a profound effect on her brother. He studied law, but then left school and began to work in the unions. Several times she went to see him address meetings. He captivated his audience like the lead actor in a drama. But this wasn't theatre. One day her brother didn't come home. She never heard from him again. For a long time, she consoled herself with the thought that he was in hiding somewhere, but then one by one his companions began to disappear, most of them without a trace. They only ever found one of them. His mutilated body was washed up by the Paraná River. The corpse had its eyes poked out and there were patches of burned skin on its chest. From that day on, waking or sleeping, Angela could not get out of her mind an image of her brother with his arms and legs bound together, and strange men beating and torturing him. She saw the iron rod being driven into his eyes.

I could see her pain and suffering. And instead of taking advantage of the falling darkness and creeping away with the bags of books, I reached out my hand to stroke her long hair, forgetting that in ancient myths, long hair was a harbinger of danger.

It seems to me that there is a raging demon, a monstrous cloud of our own creation, wandering the earth. Its shadow falls on different parts of the world, sometimes darkening whole continents. The cloud had been suspended above Angela's country. God knows where it would stop next.

"I had to run away," she whispered, as though she were apologizing. "They wipe out entire families, and even burn down their houses." At first it was not easy, then she met Nicholas. Nicholas is an exceptional person; perhaps he shouldn't be a businessman at all, because he has a need to help others. Did I know that his mother knew Gandhi personally, and took part in most of his non-violent actions?

Eventually, what had to happen did happen—outside I heard the sound of an approaching car.

Angela ran to the window. "Nicholas," she announced. "It looks like he's being followed. And I kept you here so long!"

It no longer made any sense to hurry. I sat talking to Nicholas for a while, then arranged to stop by for the bags in three days so I wouldn't be showing up here too often. I thanked Nicholas for everything he was doing for me. He smiled. "They're only books," he said, and we parted.

The men who had tailed Nicholas were waiting in a car by the tennis-courts. When I walked out through the gate, they turned their headlights on, perhaps to let me know they were there, or perhaps just to get a better look at me.

Through the windows of the neighbouring houses the blue light of television screens glowed. "Why do people watch television?" Nicholas had once asked me in amazement. "They must know they're being lied to."

I suddenly realized why he smuggled in all those books. Though a foreigner, he divined that those books—mostly written by Czechs, and banned by our overlords—belonged to us. Like his mother, he believed in non-violent resistance.

During the war the rooms in which we were imprisoned were patrolled by three especially well-trained spies. Accompanied by an armed man, these Three Fates, or Three Sowbugs, as they were called, would usually sweep in early in the morning, before the men had gone to work, and search our rooms for contraband. They emptied suitcases, burrowed into sheets, slit open straw mattresses and eiderdowns, felt coatsleeves, poured sugar, ersatz coffee or other luxuries on to the floor, and even prised up floorboards. They rarely discovered anything. But anyone found guilty was sent away to a place where only gas chambers awaited them.

One morning they came bursting in on us. I was still asleep and when I saw them in that first moment of awakening, anxiety gripped me by the throat.

I had to get up, dress, all the time looking on while they worked. I knew all too well where the contraband was hidden—the roll of banknotes burned a hole in the wood and fell to my feet like ash—but I also knew that I must not look in that direction. So I stared at the wall in front of me, and occasionally stole a glance at those three women absorbed in their unwomanly work. Sidelong, I saw them only as strange, moving monster with fuzzy outlines.

Until they approached the sideboard that is; then I suddenly saw them sharply: three fat ugly old women, one of whom was just opening the fateful drawer. I remember noticing clearly her chubby hands and realizing at that moment that not one of the women could have reached into our hiding place. I felt the joyous laughter of relief rising within me. I was able to suppress it, but it rang inside me all the time those women were rummaging among our things. It was a laughter which, on that occasion at least, ushered death from our door.

I walked casually back to my car. I might have left it there, walked past the tennis-court and run down some of the steep lanes on the hillside, but if they were determined to follow me there was little I could do to escape. Moreover, I didn't have a single illegal item on me. I wasn't carrying rice or cocoa or writing-paper. But the definition of contraband changes with the wandering of that monstrous cloud. The current definition took greatest exception to ideas, that is, to anything that could disseminate them. Instead of being entrusted three fat women, the search for contraband was now conducted by entire special departments provided with expensive but effective technology. Everything was done to ensure that not a single impulse of the spirit nor the sound of pure speech could ever occur in the territory they controlled.

Normally, I don't even notice the activities of these departments, or at least I try not to let them get to me. I don't want them to smother my world. Occasionally, however, they make an appearance. I open my eyes in the morning and see them slitting open my books, dusting white powder on my floor, reading my letters. Or I hear about the flames they leave behind in their footsteps. Or they emerge from the darkness and shine their lights on me, reminders of death with whom they are allied. At such moments, I am possessed by a will to resist; I must do something quickly—to show myself that I am still alive, that the world in which I move is still human. I am prepared to weave in and out of the lights that pursue me, to seek out a secret hiding place, and when it seems at last that I have deceived their vigilance, I hear inside me the laughter of relief.

I knocked the snow off my boots, swung my arms back and forth to let them know that my hands were empty. I unlocked the car and got in. I had to drive past them; there was no other way out. They started off behind me.

I shouldn't have cared. There was nothing in the car but a basket of damp laundry my wife had picked up. They could have noted down my registration number before I drove off.

So why were they following me? Did they know something about those occasional bags full of books? Or did they not know, but suspect something else? Or was it that they didn't know, and suspected nothing in particular, but were merely running a routine check on Nicholas to see who he associated with? Who did Nicholas associate with? I had no idea.

They were keeping close. They had a better, newer car than I did, and it was equipped with a two-way radio they could use to call for help, or to send instructions ahead to stop me at the first major intersection. Nevertheless, I longed to escape them.

I drove slowly through the fresh drifts of snow. At the first junction I braked, and my followers came to a halt behind me. The street I was intending to take climbed steeply up to the top of a hill. Several cars were descending towards the junction, and I waited until they were very close, then I moved out, stepped on the accelerator, and roared up the hill. Halfway up, I looked around. They hadn't managed to get away; they were still waiting until the cars descending the slippery hill had cleared the junction. I managed to reach the next corner before I saw them in the distance.

For a while I wound through some narrow back streets, constantly turning corners until, yes, there was a building I knew, with a wide gate leading to a large inner courtyard. As far as I could remember there was, or had been, a small park inside. There was even a bench hidden under the trees where my first love and I had necked. I drove through the gate. The trees had grown and there were more cars than I remembered, but I managed to find an empty space and parked in it. I walked back to the gate, and watched the street outside. There was no sign of them.

I got into my car again and, on a sudden whim, drove directly to the place where they would least expect to find me.

I stopped in front of Nicholas's house.

"What an idea," said Angela, surprised to see me. "You'd have probably tried to walk across those planks, too," she added, referring to our conversation about Cortázar. Nicholas took one of the bags and carried it out for me.

I threw the bags on the floor between the front and back seats, then got in and drove off, taking the route I had followed a while before, except that instead of turning up the hill, I drove down it towards my home. The only problem was that to get there I had to drive right across the city. If they wanted to, they could certainly find me somewhere along the way. Returning for the bags probably hadn't been a very wise thing to do. I could still hear Angela's excited voice evoking images of bloody faces, tortured bodies and burning homes.

Night was falling and the snow was beginning to freeze. As I drove around a corner the car went into a dangerous skid. All it needed was a car coming in the other direction: a collision would have brought out the very people I wanted to avoid. It was better not to think about it. A pair of headlights glared in my rear-view mirror. Was it them? What should I do now that I was really carrying smuggled goods? I drove on, watching the mirror. I tried, without success, to determine how many people were in the car, and what kind of people they were. Not looking where I was driving, I hit a large pothole in the middle of the road; the suspension complained and the basket of laundry slid forward and bumped into the back my seat. I slowed down. I was in danger of becoming paranoid. I turned on to a main street that would take me to the river. There were several cars behind me now, as well as in front. It made no sense to try to keep track of them.

Last spring, outside the house where I live, two workmen were repairing a fence. They were a product of our era. They drank beer, stood by the fence and enjoyed the spring sun, delighted that they'd been sent to work in such a pretty and remote part of town. They managed to spread work that should have taken two days over the whole week. Occasionally they would ring my doorbell and offer to drink coffee with me, or something stronger. One day, when the bell rang just before noon, I assumed it was them again and toyed with the idea of pretending I hadn't heard them.

Outside the door stood a short, pale man. Even before I spoke, I could see he was a foreigner. He wanted to be reassured that he wasn't putting me in any danger by coming in. Once inside the door, he asked me if I was always so closely watched. He'd been trying to visit me for three days.

He was a young priest and he'd smuggled in several books for me that were as innocent as he was. When he saw the two men lounging about, never actually working but never going far from my gate, he assumed they were secret policemen. He'd buried the books under some leaves in a nearby wood.

On the way to the wood I explained his mistake to him.

He laughed and, as if to apologize, remarked that when a man enters the kingdom of Satan, he expects to see devils at every turn.

Paranoia is something that diseased spirits succumb to, but if we live in a diseased world it requires ever greater efforts to banish sinister expectations.

I saw them from a distance. The yellow car was parked by the edge of the road, and one of the uniformed officers was signalling to me in the regulation manner with a luminous baton.

Of course. Why should they chase me when they could simply lie in wait? The road was like a mountain pass—the only route a smuggler can take, and where he is most frequently apprehended.

I stopped.

"Road check. Could I see your documents, please?"

I turned off the engine and got out of the car. The road was covered in slush; the salt truck must already have gone by. The man in the uniform leafed through my I.D.

The advantage that Jiřík Vostrý—arrested two and a half centuries ago with three books—had over me is that I had three bags of books. My only advantage might have been that I was older and therefore more experienced. I knew that I should speak as little as possible, mention no names, never get into an argument or try to persuade them of anything, even if they looked as though they were listening with interest or sympathy. What a person says in good confidence is bound to be turned against him or, what is worse, against those close to him.

"Who were you with in Pardubice, and why did you go there?" they asked Jiřík Vostrý.

"I went there to do trade in textiles," was the excuse he came up with.

I was coming from the laundry, but this would not explain anything if I was caught with the evidence.

About a month ago, they sent a young woman to jail for a year for typing copies of several books like the ones now in my possession. Her books would not have quarter-filled one of my bags. She had two small children; usually the court took such factors into account and handed down a suspended sentence. On this occasion her crime had obviously been of such a serious and dangerous nature that it warranted more.

"You were with someone, and also brought some books with you," they said to Jiřík Vostrý.

"I was with no one, nor did I bring any books with me. I was searched at the customs house."

"Who brought you here to the jail?"

"Some four men."

"What did you say to them on the way?"

"I said that in our country we do not bow to the cross, for that is idolatry."

In his zeal he had said more than he should have and they—for it is part of their nature—reported everything. The smuggler of long ago had a difficult time; he had also entrusted his jailer with the secret letter.

"Is it true that from the magistrate's jail you sent a letter alerting someone to danger?"

"My message was that if they had books they ought to put them away."

"And whom did you so advise?"

"Litochleb and Kladivo and also Kaliban, the miller from Sedliště."

"Is this message?" *[Exhibitae eidem schedulae, quae in allegatis lit. A et B videntur.]*

"It is."

"Through whose offices did you write and send this letter?"

"The jailer led me to believe he would deliver it."

"You must have been here bearing books before; and you must also know of people who cleave to your faith."

"I know nothing; nor of anyone."

The worst crime of all was to circulate forbidden books. Three young men from the place where Jiřík Vostrý was apprehended 247 years ago were recently given a total of six and a half years in prison for the same activity.

"Aren't you employed anywhere?" asked the officer leafing through my I.D. He seemed surprised. He was rather heavily built. There was a small moustache under his nose.

"I'm free-lance."

He looked at me suspiciously, as if this was the first time he had heard the expression. Perhaps he simply did not like the word "free." Could I prove that? he asked.

I handed him a piece of paper confirming that I was covered by social insurance.

He pretended to examine the paper, then folded it and handed it back to me. He kept my other documents. "Have you had anything to drink, sir?"

I hadn't. I had no intention of tempting fate any more than necessary.

He put on an expression that suggested he did not entirely believe me. Then he asked me to turn on the headlights.

They were working properly.

Could he see my first-aid kit?

I would have to open the back door. I saw with relief that the laundry basket almost completely covered the bags containing the books. But in my excitement I could not remember where I kept my first-aid kit. I groped haphazardly under the seat, trying to shield the books with my body.

The uniformed men watched with interest. "Do you know what they call the first-aid kit, sir?" the one who had not previously spoken asked. "I'll tell you. They call it 'handy.' And do you know why?"

I was forced to listen to the etymology of the word "handy."

"Why aren't you carrying your laundry in the boot?" said the first officer, suddenly bringing the conversation to its point.

About five years ago, my theatrical agent from the United States came to see me. She was an older woman who had been born in Europe and had experienced all that continent's cultural benefits, including a concentration camp. In other words she was well equipped to understand the course of events that had determined my life. I needed to send a letter to a friend in Switzerland. The content of the letter was harmless even with regard to our vigilant laws, but the notion that a third party might read it disturbed me. I asked my American friend if she would take the letter across the border for me. At the airport, however, she was subjected to a thorough search. When she was forced to take the letter from her pocket, she tore open the envelope and, before they were able to snatch the letter from her hand, she put it into her mouth and, before the customs officers' eyes, chewed and swallowed it.

Could I eat three bags of books?

My only consolation was the knowledge that the worst cloud had already passed over our country: they wouldn't put out my eyes.

I finally found the first-aid kit and handed it to the officer with the moustache. "My spare tyre is in the boot." I said, by way of explanation.

"Could you show us?"

The first-aid kit under a pile of rags; bags on the floor; a basket full of laundry on the seat; the spare tyre in the boot. Sir, there's something about you we don't like. Put the spare where it belongs. Put the first-aid kit in the glove-compartment. And take those bags and put them in the boot. Here, we'll help you. My goodness, sir, these bags weigh a ton. What on earth do you have in them?

Both officers leaned into the boot and tested the depth of the tread on my spare tyre. "I'm not surprised you keep this hidden, sir. When was the last time you put any air in it?"

"A few days ago." I could not understand why they were putting off the moment when they would display interest in what they were really after.

"A few days ago. Would you mind checking the pressure for us?"

I had a gauge in a compartment next to the steering-wheel. Regardless of the pressure it always gave a reading of two atmospheres.

"You're in luck," one of them said, looking sceptically at the needle, which was pointing reliably to the two.

"You may close the boot," said the other one.

"Get back in to the car," said the first.

Suddenly I understood the mystery of this pointless and rather protracted game. Their orders were to stop me and detain me. The officers who were really interested in me and my contraband had, for some reason, been held up. When they arrived and saw my bags, they would be delighted: Surely you don't mean to tell me someone put these bags in your car without your knowledge, sir?

Indeed, such a claim would not sound credible. Where, then, had I got the bags from? It's odd that although we've had 247 years to work on it, we have not yet come up with even a slightly probable reply to a highly probable question.

What alibi could I come up with on the spur of the moment? I had brought them from home, where a stranger had left them. But why would I have them in my car now? In a rush, I weighed various unconvincing explanations in my mind. I just put them there and then forgot about them? I wanted to store them at a relative's flat, then changed my mind? I was on my way to hand them in to the authorities?

He opens one of them. I realize I've made another irretrievable mistake. I'd spent the whole afternoon with Angela and without so much as glancing into the three bags. Unlike Jiřík Vostrý, I didn't know what books I had on my hands. I might have had magazines in the bags; they tend to get very upset about magazines.

So you're bringing them from home. Well, what about this one? And with great distaste, he spells out the name of the author and the title. Is this your book?

It's my book.

Who did you get it from?

I was given it. That's not against the law.

And did you read it?

I have a lot of books I haven't managed to read yet.

You might at least have unwrapped it, he says, looking at me disapprovingly. You've left it all wrapped up like a piece of cheese. Not only that, you've got two copies of it. He rummages around in the bag some more and corrects himself: Three! Where were you taking these bags?

For years now I've had a running debate with those who liken books to explosives or drugs. During that time, I've prepared a lengthy speech in which I defend freedom of creation, which is part of a dignified and truthful life. But I have never had the occasion to deliver the speech. The temptation to do it now is powerful. But I mustn't succumb. To entrust my own convictions to these men in uniform would be just as silly now as it was two and a half centuries ago.

The two of them were talking something over; perhaps they were radioing in a query. It seemed undignified to watch.

When the others, whom they are clearly waiting for, come, I should at least pose them a question: Why, by what authority, do you of all people, who are so convinced that the life of a man is limited to this insignificant little patch of time when he dwells upon the earth, transform our lives into a suffocating mixture of lies, filth and repression?

No one else comes, but the two uniformed officers return to my car.

"Sir, are you aware of which traffic regulation you've broken?" They wait for a moment, and then the one with the moustache tries to help out: "When you stopped, did you turn out your lights?"

"Was I driving without my headlights on?" It was not my negligence that astonished me, but the fact that they had spent so long in coming up with something so trivial.

"That's right, sir. And in this weather. Do you know that this could have cost you your license?" The two of them watched me, and when I didn't protest, the one with the moustache asked: "Are you willing to pay us a hundred crown fine on the spot?"

I took out a big, green banknote and then, with dismay, I realized that I was handing it over far too willingly.

They gave me the requisite ticket from their booklet, and wished me a good trip. From their expressions I could tell that this had made them feel good; they'd done some useful work.

My wife was waiting impatiently, afraid that something bad had happened. We carried the bags into the room, and I unwrapped the books, which smelled of newness. The titles promised the intellectual consolation of pure, original language.

I opened one of the volumes, but I was unable to concentrate on the contents.

Nicholas had indeed bought two, or even three copies of some of the books. That meant that the next day, I would be a messenger and go to Morašice, to Lubný, and then to see Kaliban in Kamenné Sedlištĕ.

What was Jiřík Vostrý's fate? They let him go, of course. The eighteenth century wasn't the middle ages, after all. The archives have preserved a later report of him. The incorrigible smuggler—now thirty years old—was apprehended again. From the interrogation it is clear that in the intervening years Vostrý had not been idle. At one time he had been imprisoned at Lytomyšl where he "remained for three years less eight weeks." (We will never know how often, during the rest of those years, he had successfully evaded capture.) He was released for good behaviour, and he rushed home to his wife and children.

No record has been preserved of how he fared in his last trial, but everything suggests that this time he didn't get off so easily. The Edict of Toleration, which made book smuggling pointless for the next two hundred years, was soon to be law. If only Vostrý had been twenty years younger.

But such is the deceitful game of history. People sacrifice their time, put their freedom and even their lives at risk just to cross, or eliminate, borders they know are absurd. And then—often soon afterwards—in a single instant, as a consequence of a single decree, the border disappears without a trace.

In revealing their transience, these borders also seem to expose the futility of all former sacrifices. But perhaps it is really the other way around: if it weren't for those who, in their battle against borders, risked everything, the borders would not disappear, but would become a net and all of us trapped insects inside.

Suddenly my wife thought of something: "Did you bring in the laundry basket?"

The basket was still in the car.

It was no longer snowing outside, and stars were shining through ragged, fast flying clouds. The snow sparkled in the light of the streetlamps. In the distance, I could hear a police siren.

I unlocked the garage and pulled the laundry basket out of the car. It seemed unusually heavy and, when I walked up the stairs, something inside it clinked metallically.

I felt like lifting up the laundry to see what was hidden underneath it, but I managed to control my curiosity. I set the basket down on the dining-room table as carefully as possible and went away to read.

D.H. LAWRENCE

THE ROCKING-HORSE WINNER

D.H. Lawrence (1885–1930) was born in Nottinghamshire, England, the son of a former schoolteacher and a coal miner. As a sickly child, Lawrence developed a close relationship with his mother, who was determined that her youngest son would have the benefit of an education so that he might escape the hardships of a coal miner's life. He won a scholarship to attend Nottingham High School, and he later studied at Nottingham University College. After college he left his home town to become a teacher, although by this time he was disenchanted with education. In 1910 his mother died of cancer, just prior to the publication of his first novel, The White Peacock, *and in 1911 his own ill health persuaded him to leave his teaching career. Shortly afterwards, a lonely, aimless Lawrence met the woman with whom he would spend the rest of his turbulent life.*

Freida Weekly was the German wife of one of his Nottingham professors and the mother of two grown children. She had already engaged in many secret sexual liaisons both in England and in Europe, combining her belief in free love with the notion that women should use their strength to nurture male genius. Her influence on Lawrence was tremendous. Their attraction was immediate, and together they left England to travel in Europe while Lawrence worked on Sons and Lovers *(1913), a novel that established his reputation as a major literary figure. Lawrence followed this novel with two celebrated works of fiction,* The Rainbow *(1915) and* Women in Love *(1916). Both novels were suppressed on the grounds of obscenity, and neither was published uncut during Lawrence's lifetime. The obscenity trial surrounding the publication of another novel,* Lady Chatterly's Lover *(1928), has become a classic case in the history of censorship. Although Lawrence and Frieda did eventually return to England, ill health, public hostility toward the couple, which was exacerbated during the war years by Frieda's German background, and the continued censorship of Lawrence's work caused them to leave England for good in 1919.*

For the balance of his life, Lawrence wandered from Italy to Ceylon, New Mexico, Australia, and eventually southern France in search of "a more fulfilling mode of life than industrial Western civilization could offer." His health steadily declined, though he remained a prolific writer, producing novels, stories, poetry, plays, essays, travel books, translations, and lively correspondence. He died of tuberculosis at the age of forty-four. His views on sexuality and women, as well as his often bitter diatribes against social convention, made Lawrence a controversial figure in his lifetime, a legacy that endures as his work continues to provoke debate. Critics see "The Rocking-Horse Winner," a nightmarish story written late in his career, as portraying Lawrence's psychological makeup, through its suggestion of mothers devouring sons.

There was a woman who was beautiful, who started with all the advantages, yet she had no luck. She married for love, and the love turned to dust. She had bonny children, yet she felt they had been thrust upon her, and she could not love them. They looked at her coldly, as if they were finding fault with her. And hurriedly she felt she must cover up some fault in herself. Yet what it was that she must cover up she never knew. Nevertheless, when her children were present, she always felt the center of her heart go hard. This troubled her, and in her manner she was all the more gentle and anxious for her children, as if she loved them very much. Only she herself knew that at the center of her heart was a hard little place that could not feel love, no, not for anybody. Everybody else said of her: "She is such a good mother. She adores her children." Only she herself, and her children themselves, knew it was not so. They read it in each other's eyes.

There were a boy and two little girls. They lived in a pleasant house, with a garden, and they had discreet servants, and felt themselves superior to anyone in the neighbourhood.

Although they lived in style, they felt always an anxiety in the house. There was never enough money. The mother had a small income, and the father had a small income, but not nearly enough for the social position which they had to keep up. The father went into town to some office. But though he had good prospects, these prospects never materialized. There was always the grinding sense of the shortage of money, though the style was always kept up.

At last the mother said: "I will see if *I* can't make something." But she did not know where to begin. She racked her brains, and tried this thing and the other, but could not find anything successful. The failure made deep lines come into her face. Her children were growing up, they would have to go to school. There must be more money, there must be more money. The father, who was always very handsome and expensive in his tastes, seemed as if he never *would* be able to do anything worth doing. And the mother, who had a great belief in herself, did not succeed any better, and her tastes were just as expensive.

And so the house came to be haunted by the unspoken phrase: *There must be more money! There must be more money!* The children could hear it all the time though nobody said it aloud. They heard it at Christmas, when the expensive and splendid toys filled the nursery. Behind the shining modern rocking horse, behind the smart doll's house, a voice would start whispering: "There *must* be more money! There *must* be more money!" And the children would stop playing, to listen for a moment. They would look into each other's eyes, to see if they had all heard. And each one saw in the eyes of the other two that they too had heard. "There *must* be more money! There *must* be more money!"

It came whispering from the springs of the still-swaying rocking horse, and even the horse, bending his wooden, champing head, heard it. The big doll, sitting so pink and smirking in her new pram, could hear it quite plainly, and seemed to be smirking all the more self-consciously because of it. The foolish puppy, too, that took the place of the teddy bear, he was looking so extraordinarily foolish for no other reason but that he heard the secret whisper all over the house: "There *must* be more money!"

Yet nobody ever said it aloud. The whisper was everywhere, and therefore no one spoke of it. Just as no one ever says: "We are breathing!" in spite of the fact that breath is coming and going all the time.

"Mother," said the boy Paul one day, "why don't we keep a car of our own? Why do we always use Uncle's, or else a taxi?"

"Because we're the poor members of the family," said the mother.

"But why *are* we, Mother?"

"Well—I suppose," she said slowly and bitterly, "it's because your father has no luck."

The boy was silent for some time.

"Is luck money, Mother?" he asked rather timidly.

"No, Paul. Not quite. It's what causes you to have money."

"Oh!" said Paul vaguely. "I thought when Uncle Oscar said *filthy lucker,* it meant money."

"*Filthy lucre* does mean money," said the mother. "But it's lucre, not luck."

"Oh!" said the boy. "Then what *is* luck, Mother?"

"It's what causes you to have money. If you're lucky you have money. That's why it's better to be born lucky than rich. If you're rich, you may lose your money. But if you're lucky, you will always get more money."

"Oh! Will you? And is Father not lucky?"

"Very unlucky, I should say," she said bitterly.

The boy watched her with unsure eyes.

"Why?" he asked.

"I don't know. Nobody ever knows why one person is lucky and another unlucky."

"Don't they? Nobody at all? Does *nobody* know?"

"Perhaps God. But He never tells."

"He ought to, then. And aren't you lucky either, Mother?"

"I can't be, if I married an unlucky husband."

"But by yourself, aren't you?"

"I used to think I was, before I married. Now I think I am very unlucky indeed."

"Why?"

"Well—never mind! Perhaps I'm not really," she said.

The child looked at her, to see if she meant it. But he saw, by the lines of her mouth, that she was only trying to hide something from him.

"Well, anyhow," he said stoutly, "I'm a lucky person."

"Why?" said his mother, with a sudden laugh.

He stared at her. He didn't even know why he had said it.

"God told me," he asserted, brazening it out.

"I hope He did, dear!" she said, again with a laugh, but rather bitter.

"He did, Mother!"

"Excellent!" said the mother.

The boy saw she did not believe him; or, rather, that she paid no attention to his assertion. This angered him somewhat, and made him want to compel her attention.

He went off by himself, vaguely, in a childish way, seeking for the clue to "luck." Absorbed, taking no heed for other people, he went about with a sort of stealth, seeking inwardly for luck. He wanted luck, he wanted it, he wanted it. When the two girls were playing dolls in the nursery, he would sit on his big rocking horse, charging madly into space, with a frenzy that made the little girls peer at him uneasily. Wildly the horse careered, the waving dark hair of the boy tossed, his eyes had a strange glare in them. The little girls dared not speak to him.

When he had ridden to the end of his mad little journey, he climbed down and stood in front of his rocking horse, staring fixedly into its lowered face. Its red mouth was slightly open, its big eye was wide and glassy-bright.

Now! he could silently command the snorting steed. Now, take me to where there is luck! Now take me!

And he would slash the horse on the neck with the little whip he had asked Uncle Oscar for. He *knew* the horse could take him to where there was luck, if only he forced it. So he would mount again, and start on his furious ride, hoping at last to get there. He knew he could get there.

"You'll break your horse, Paul!" said the nurse.

"He's always riding like that! I wish he'd leave off!" said his elder sister Joan.

But he only glared down on them in silence. Nurse gave him up. She could make nothing of him. Anyhow he was growing beyond her.

One day his mother and his uncle Oscar came in when he was on one of his furious rides. He did not speak to them.

"Hallo, you young jockey! Riding a winner?" said his uncle.

"Aren't you growing too big for a rocking horse? You're not a very little boy any longer, you know," said his mother.

But Paul only gave a blue glare from his big, rather close-set eyes. He would speak to nobody when he was in full tilt. His mother watched him with an anxious expression on her face.

At last he suddenly stopped forcing his horse into the mechanical gallop, and slid down.

"Well, I got there!" he announced fiercely, his blue eyes still flaring, and his sturdy long legs straddling apart.

"Where did you get to?" asked his mother.

"Where I wanted to go," he flared back at her.

"That's right, son!" said Uncle Oscar. "Don't you stop till you get there. What's the horse's name?"

"He doesn't have a name," said the boy.

"Gets on without all right?" asked the uncle.

"Well, he has different names. He was called Sansovino last week."

"Sansovino, eh? Won the Ascot. How did you know his name?"

"He always talks about horse races with Bassett," said Joan.

The uncle was delighted to find that his small nephew was posted with all the racing news. Bassett, the young gardener, who had been wounded in the left foot in the war and had got his present job through Oscar Cresswell, whose batman he had been, was a perfect blade of the "turf." He lived in the racing events, and the small boy lived with him.

Oscar Cresswell got it all from Bassett.

"Master Paul comes and asks me, so I can't do more than tell him, sir," said Bassett, his face terribly serious, as if he were speaking of religious matters.

"And does he ever put anything on a horse he fancies?"

"Well—I don't want to give him away—he's a young sport, a fine sport, sir. Would you mind asking him himself? He sort of takes a pleasure in it, and perhaps he'd feel I was giving him away, sir, if you don't mind."

Bassett was serious as a church.

The uncle went back to his nephew and took him off for a ride in the car.

"Say, Paul, old man, do you ever put anything on a horse?" the uncle asked.

The boy watched the handsome man closely.

"Why, do you think I oughtn't to?" he parried.

"Not a bit of it! I thought perhaps you might give me a tip for the Lincoln."

The car sped on into the country, going down to Uncle Oscar's place in Hampshire.

"Honor bright?" said the nephew.

"Honor bright, son!" said the uncle.

"Well, then, Daffodil."

"Daffodil! I doubt it, sonny. What about Mirza?"

"I only know the winner," said the boy. "That's Daffodil."

"Daffodil, eh?"

There was a pause. Daffodil was an obscure horse comparatively.

"Uncle!"

"Yes, son?"

"You won't let it go any further, will you? I promised Bassett."

"Basset be damned, old man! What's he got to do with it?"

"We're partners. We've been partners from the first. Uncle, he lent me my first five shillings, which I lost. I promised him, honor bright, it was only between me and him; only you gave me that ten-shilling note I started winning with, so I thought you were lucky. You won't let it go any further, will you?"

The boy gazed at his uncle from those big, hot, blue eyes, set rather close together. The uncle stirred and laughed uneasily.

"Right you are, son! I'll keep your tip private. Daffodil, eh? How much are you putting on him?"

"All except twenty pounds," said the boy. "I keep that in reserve."

The uncle thought it a good joke.

"You keep twenty pounds in reserve, do you, you young romancer? What are you betting, then?"

"I'm betting three hundred," said the boy gravely. "But it's between you and me, Uncle Oscar! Honor bright?"

The uncle burst into a roar of laughter.

"It's between you and me all right, you young Nat Gould,"[1] he said, laughing. "But where's your three hundred?"

"Bassett keeps it for me. We're partners."

"You are, are you! And what is Bassett putting on Daffodil?"

"He won't go quite as high as I do, I expect. Perhaps he'll go a hundred and fifty."

"What, pennies?" laughed the uncle.

"Pounds," said the child, with a surprised look at his uncle. "Bassett keeps a bigger reserve than I do."

Between wonder and amusement Uncle Oscar was silent. He pursued the matter no further, but he determined to take his nephew with him to the Lincoln races.

"Now, son," he said, "I'm putting twenty on Mirza, and I'll put five for you on any horse you fancy. What's your pick?"

"Daffodil, Uncle."

"No, not the fiver on Daffodil!"

"I should if it was my own fiver," said the child.

"Good! Good! Right you are! A fiver for me and a fiver for you on Daffodil."

The child had never been to a race meeting before, and his eyes were blue fire. He pursed his mouth tight, and watched. A Frenchman just in front had put his money on Lancelot. Wild with excitement, he flailed his arms up and down, yelling "*Lancelot! Lancelot!*" in his French accent.

Daffodil came in first, Lancelot second, Mirza third. The child, flushed and with eyes blazing, was curiously serene. His uncle brought him four five-pound notes, four to one.

"What am I to do with these?" he cried, waving them before the boy's eyes.

"I suppose we'll talk to Bassett," said the boy. "I expect I have fifteen hundred now; and twenty in reserve; and this twenty."

His uncle studied him for some moments.

"Look here, son!" he said. "You're not serious about Bassett and that fifteen hundred, are you?"

"Yes, I am. But it's between you and me, Uncle. Honor bright!"

"Honor bright all right, son! But I must talk to Bassett."

"If you'd like to be a partner, Uncle, with Bassett and me, we could all be partners. Only, you'd have to promise, honor bright, Uncle, not to let it go beyond us three. Bassett and I are lucky, and you must be lucky, because it was your ten shillings I started winning with...."

Uncle Oscar took both Bassett and Paul into Richmond Park for an afternoon, and there they talked.

"It's like this, you see, sir," Bassett said. "Master Paul would get me talking about racing events, spinning yarns, you know, sir. And he was always keen on knowing if I'd made or if I'd lost. It's about a year since, now, that I put five shillings on Blush of Dawn for him—and we lost. Then the luck turned, with that ten shillings he had from you, that we put on Singhalese. And since then, it's been pretty steady, all things considering. What do you say, Master Paul?"

"We're all right when we're sure," said Paul. "It's when we're not quite sure that we go down."

"Oh, but we're careful then," said Bassett.

"But when are you *sure?*" Uncle Oscar smiled.

"It's Master Paul, sir" said Bassett, in a secret, religious voice. "It's as if he had it from heaven. Like Daffodil, now, for the Lincoln. That was as sure as eggs."

"Did you put anything on Daffodil?" asked Oscar Cresswell.

"Yes, sir. I made my bit."

"And my nephew?"

Bassett was obstinately silent, looking at Paul.

"I made twelve hundred, didn't I, Bassett? I told Uncle I was putting three hundred on Daffodil."

"That's right," said Bassett, nodding.

"But where's the money?" asked the uncle.

"I keep it safe locked up, sir. Master Paul he can have it any minute he likes to ask for it."

"What, fifteen hundred pounds?"

"And twenty! And *forty*, that is, with the twenty he made on the course."

"It's amazing!" said the uncle.

"If Master Paul offers you to be partners, sir, I would, if I were you; if you'll excuse me," said Bassett.

Oscar Cresswell thought about it.

"I'll see the money," he said.

They drove home again, and sure enough, Bassett came round to the garden house with fifteen hundred pounds in notes. The twenty pounds reserve was left with Joe Glee, in the Turf Commission deposit.

"You see, it's all right, Uncle, when I'm *sure!* Then we go strong, for all we're worth. Don't we, Bassett?"

"We do that, Master Paul."

"And when are you sure?" said the uncle, laughing.

"Oh, well, sometimes I'm *absolutely* sure, like about Daffodil," said the boy; "and sometimes I have an idea; and sometimes I haven't even an idea, have I, Bassett? Then we're careful, because we mostly go down."

"You do, do you! And when you're sure, like about Daffodil, what makes you sure, sonny?"

"Oh, well, I don't know," said the boy uneasily. "I'm sure, you know, Uncle; that's all."

"It's as if he had it from heaven, sir," Bassett reiterated.

"I should say so!" said the uncle.

But he became a partner. And when the Leger was coming on, Paul was "sure" about Lively Spark, which was a quite inconsiderable horse. The boy insisted on putting a thousand on the horse, Bassett went for five hundred, and Oscar Cresswell two hundred. Lively Spark came in first, and the betting had been ten to one against him. Paul had made ten thousand.

"You see," he said, "I was absolutely sure of him."

Even Oscar Cresswell had cleared two thousand.

"Look here, son," he said, "this sort of thing makes me nervous."

"It needn't, Uncle! Perhaps I shan't be sure again for a long time."

"But what are you going to do with your money?" asked the uncle.

"Of course," said the boy. "I started it for Mother. She said she had no luck, because Father is unlucky, so I thought if *I* was lucky, it might stop whispering."

"What might stop whispering?"

"Our house. I *hate* our house for whispering."

"What does it whisper?"

"Why—why"—the boy fidgeted— "why, I don't know. But it's always short of money, you know, Uncle."

"I know it, son, I know it."

"You know people send Mother writs, don't you, Uncle?"

"I'm afraid I do," said the uncle.

"And then the house whispers, like people laughing at you behind your back. It's awful, that is! I thought if I was lucky...."

"You might stop it," added the uncle.

The boy watched him with big blue eyes, that had an uncanny cold fire in them, and he said never a word.

"Well, then!" said the uncle. "What are we doing?"

"I shouldn't like Mother to know I was lucky," said the boy.

"Why not, son?"

"She'd stop me."

"I don't think she would."

"Oh!"—and the boy writhed in an odd way—"I *don't* want her to know, Uncle."

"All right, son! We'll manage it without her knowing."

They managed it very easily. Paul, at the other's suggestion, handed over five thousand pounds to his uncle, who deposited it with the family lawyer, who was then to inform Paul's mother that a relative had put five thousand pounds in his hands, which sum was to be paid out a thousand pounds at a time, on the mother's birthday, for the next five years.

"So she'll have a birthday present of a thousand pounds for five successive years," said Uncle Oscar. "I hope it won't make it all the harder for her later."

Paul's mother had her birthday in November. The house had been "whispering" worse than ever lately, and, even in spite of his luck, Paul could not bear up against it. He was very anxious to see the effect of the birthday letter, telling his mother about the thousand pounds.

When there were no visitors, Paul now took his meals with his parents, as he was beyond the nursery control. His mother went into town nearly every day. She had discovered that she had an odd knack of sketching furs and dress materials, so she worked secretly in the studio of a friend who was the chief artist for the leading drapers. She drew the figures of ladies in furs and ladies in silk and sequins for the newspaper advertisements. This young woman artist earned several thousand pounds a year, but Paul's mother only made several hundreds, and she was again dissatisfied. She so wanted to be first in something, and she did not succeed, even in making sketches for drapery advertisements.

She was down to breakfast on the morning of her birthday. Paul watched her face as she read her letters. He knew the lawyer's letter. As his mother read it, her face hardened and became more expressionless. Then a cold, determined look came on her mouth. She hid the letter under the pile of others, and said not a word about it.

"Didn't you have anything nice in the post for your birthday, Mother?" said Paul.

"Quite moderately nice," she said, her voice cold and absent.

She went away to town without saying more.

But in the afternoon Uncle Oscar appeared. He said Paul's mother had had a long interview with the lawyer, asking if the whole five thousand could not be advanced at once, as she was in debt.

"What do you think, Uncle?" said the boy.

"I leave it to you, son."

"Oh, let her have it, then! We can get some more with the other," said the boy.

"A bird in the hand is worth two in the bush, laddie!" said Uncle Oscar.

"But I'm sure to *know* for the Grand National; or the Lincolnshire; or else the Derby. I'm sure to know for *one* of them," said Paul.

So Uncle Oscar signed the agreement, and Paul's mother touched the whole five thousand. Then something very curious happened. The voices in the house suddenly went mad, like a chorus of frogs on a spring evening. There were certain new furnishings, and Paul had a tutor. He was *really* going to Eton, his father's school, in the following autumn. There were flowers in the winter, and a blossoming of the luxury Paul's mother had been used to. And yet the voices in the house, behind the sprays of mimosa and almond blossom, and from under the piles of iridescent cushions, simply trilled and screamed in a sort of ecstasy: "There *must* be more money! Oh-h-h; there *must* be more money. Oh, now, now-w! Now-w-w—there *must* be more money!—more than ever! More than ever!"

D.H. Lawrence

It frightened Paul terribly. He studied away at his Latin and Greek. But his intense hours were spent with Bassett. The Grand National had gone by; he had not "known," and had lost a hundred pounds. Summer was at hand. He was in agony for the Lincoln. But even for the Lincoln he didn't "know," and he lost fifty pounds. He became wild-eyed and strange, as if something were going to explode in him.

"Let it alone, son! Don't you bother about it!" urged Uncle Oscar. But it was as if the boy couldn't really hear what his uncle was saying.

"I've got to know for the Derby! I've got to know for the Derby!" the child reiterated, his big blue eyes blazing with a sort of madness.

His mother noticed how overwrought he was.

"You'd better go to the seaside. Wouldn't you like to go now to the seaside, instead of waiting? I think you'd better," she said, looking down at him anxiously, her heart curiously heavy because of him.

But the child lifted his uncanny blue eyes. "I couldn't possibly go before the Derby, Mother!" he said. "I couldn't possibly!"

"Why not?" she said, her voice becoming heavy when she was opposed. "Why not? You can still go from the seaside to see the Derby with your uncle Oscar, if that's what you wish. No need for you to wait here. Besides, I think you care too much about these races. It's a bad sign. My family has been a gambling family, and you won't know till you grow up how much damage it has done. But it has done damage. I shall have to send Bassett away, and ask Uncle Oscar not to talk racing to you, unless you promise to be reasonable about it; go away to the seaside and forget it. You're all nerves!"

"I'll do what you like, Mother, so long as you don't send me away till after the Derby," the boy said.

"Send you away from where? Just from this house?"

"Yes," he said, gazing at her.

"Why, you curious child, what makes you care about this house so much, suddenly? I never knew you loved it."

He gazed at her without speaking. He had a secret within a secret, something he had not divulged, even to Bassett or to his uncle Oscar.

But his mother, after standing undecided and a little bit sullen for some moments, said:

"Very well, then! Don't go to the seaside till after the Derby, if you don't wish it. But promise me you won't let your nerves go to pieces. Promise you won't think so much about horse racing and *events*, as you call them!"

"Oh, no," said the boy casually. "I won't think much about them, Mother. You needn't worry. I wouldn't worry, Mother, if I were you."

"If you were me and I were you," said his mother, "I wonder what we *should* do!"

"But you know you needn't worry, Mother, don't you?" the boy repeated.

"I should be awfully glad to know it," she said wearily.

"Oh, well you *can*, you know. I mean, you *ought* to know you needn't worry," he insisted.

"Ought I? Then I'll see about it," she said.

Paul's secret of secrets was his wooden horse, that which had no name. Since he was emancipated from a nurse and a nursery governess, he had had his rocking horse removed to his own bedroom at the top of the house.

"Surely, you're too big for a rocking horse!" his mother had remonstrated.

"Well, you see, Mother, till I can have a *real* horse, I like to have *some* sort of animal about," had been his quaint answer.

"Do you feel he keeps you company?" She laughed.

"Oh, yes! He's very good, he always keeps me company, when I'm there," said Paul.

So the horse, rather shabby, stood in an arrested prance in the boy's bedroom.

The Derby was drawing near, and the boy grew more and more tense. He hardly heard what was spoken to him, he was very frail, and his eyes were really uncanny. His mother had sudden strange seizures of uneasiness about him. Sometimes, for half an hour, she would feel a sudden anxiety about him that was almost anguish. She wanted to rush to him at once, and know he was safe.

Two nights before the Derby, she was at a big party in town, when one of her rushes of anxiety about her boy, her firstborn, gripped her heart till she could hardly speak. She fought with the feeling, might and main, for she believed in common sense. But it was too strong. She had to leave the dance and go downstairs to telephone to the country. The children's nursery governess was terribly surprised and startled at being rung up in the night.

"Are the children all right, Miss Wilmot?"

"Oh, yes, they are quite all right."

"Master Paul? Is he all right?"

"He went to bed as right as a trivet. Shall I run up and look at him?"

"No," said Paul's mother reluctantly. "No! Don't trouble. It's all right. Don't sit up. We shall be home fairly soon." She did not want her son's privacy intruded upon.

"Very good," said the governess.

It was about one o'clock when Paul's mother and father drove up to their house. All was still. Paul's mother went to her room and slipped off her white fur cloak. She had told her maid not to wait up for her. She heard her husband downstairs, mixing a whisky and soda.

And then, because of the strange anxiety at her heart, she stole upstairs to her son's room. Noiselessly she went along the upper corridor. Was there a faint noise? What was it?

She stood, with arrested muscles, outside his door, listening. There was a strange, heavy, and yet not loud noise. Her heart stood still. It was a soundless noise, yet rushing and powerful. Something huge, in violent, hushed motion. What was it? What in God's name was it? She ought to know. She felt that she knew the noise. She knew what it was.

Yet she could not place it. She couldn't say what it was. And on and on it went, like a madness.

Softly, frozen with anxiety and fear, she turned the door handle.

The room was dark. Yet in the space near the window, she heard and saw something plunging to and fro. She gazed in fear and amazement.

Then suddenly she switched on the light, and saw her son, in his green pajamas, madly surging on the rocking horse. The blaze of light suddenly lit him up, as he urged the wooden horse, and lit her up, as she stood, blonde, in her dress of pale green and crystal, in the doorway.

"Paul!" she cried. "Whatever are you doing?"

"It's Malabar!" he screamed, in a powerful, strange voice. "It's Malabar!"

His eyes blazed at her for one strange and senseless second, as he ceased urging his wooden horse. Then he fell with a crash to the ground, and she, all her tormented motherhood flooding upon her, rushed to gather him up.

But he was unconscious, and unconscious he remained, with some brain fever. He talked and tossed, and his mother sat stonily by his side.

"Malabar! It's Malabar! Bassett, Bassett, I *know!* It's Malabar!"

So the child cried, trying to get up and urge the rocking horse that gave him his inspiration.

"What does he mean by Malabar?" asked the heart-frozen mother.

"I don't know," said the father stonily.

"What does he mean by Malabar?" she asked her brother Oscar.

"It's one of the horses running for the Derby," was the answer.

And, in spite of himself, Oscar Cresswell spoke to Bassett, and himself put a thousand on Malabar: at fourteen to one.

The third day of the illness was critical: they were waiting for a change. The boy, with his rather long, curly hair, was tossing ceaselessly on the pillow. He never slept nor regained consciousness, and his eyes were like blue stones. His mother sat, feeling her heart had gone, turned actually into a stone.

In the evening, Oscar Cresswell did not come, but Bassett sent a message, saying could he come up for one moment, just one moment? Paul's mother was very angry at the intrusion, but on second thought she agreed. The boy was the same. Perhaps Bassett might bring him to consciousness.

The gardener, a shortish fellow with a little brown mustache, and sharp little brown eyes, tiptoed into the room, touched his imaginary cap to Paul's mother, and stole to the bedside, staring with glittering, smallish eyes at the tossing, dying child.

"Master Paul!" he whispered. "Master Paul! Malabar came in first all right, a clean win. I did as you told me. You've made over seventy thousand pounds, you have; you've got over eighty thousand. Malabar came in all right, Master Paul."

"Malabar! Malabar! Did I say Malabar, Mother? Did I say Malabar? Do you think I'm lucky, Mother? I knew Malabar, didn't I? Over eighty thousand pounds! I call that lucky, don't you, Mother? Over eighty thousand pounds! I knew, didn't I know I knew? Malabar came in all right. If I ride my horse till I'm sure, then I tell you, Bassett, you can go as high as you like. Did you go for all you were worth, Bassett?"

"I went a thousand on it, Master Paul."

"I never told you, Mother, that if I can ride my horse, and *get there*, then I'm absolutely sure—oh, absolutely! Mother, did I ever tell you? I *am* lucky!"

"No, you never did," said the mother.

But the boy died in the night.

And even as he lay dead, his mother heard her brother's voice saying to her: "My God, Hester, you're eighty-odd thousand to the good, and a poor devil of a son to the bad. But, poor devil, poor devil, he's best gone out of a life where he rides his rocking horse to find a winner."

NOTE

1. Nathaniel Gould (1857–1919), a popular British writer who wrote novels about horse racing.

HENRY LAWSON

THE DROVER'S WIFE

Henry Lawson (1867–1922) was born in New South Wales, Australia. He wrote fiction and poetry and also worked as a journalist. His family had been poor, and Lawson had great sympathy for Australia's growing Socialist movement. Writing with compassion and respect about people living and working under harsh conditions in the Australian bush, Lawson was also constructing a potent Australian myth. His vivid pictures of life in the bush—in particular, his depiction of the "macho" Australian male—have enormously influenced Australia's sense of itself. "The Drover's Wife," from While the Billy Boils *(1896), is his most famous story. It tells of a bushwoman who for one night "lays down her work and watches, and listens, and thinks" of things in her own life, revealing great strength of character under dreary and lonely conditions. Her forbearance and perfect loyalty to her mate became a model of conduct for Australian women, one against which contemporary readers have often rebelled. Lawson's story inspired a famous 1945 painting by Russell Drysdale, also called "The Drover's Wife," and two stories by the same name: a parody of the original story written by Murray Bail in 1975 and a tongue-in-cheek fictional piece written in 1980 by Frank Moorhouse, the "urban answer to Henry Lawson," which analyzes its predecessors from a cultural and literary perspective. For contemporary Australian writers of the short story, Henry Lawson has become a launching point for many directions. "So legend follows legend."*

The two-roomed house is built of round timber, slabs, and stringybark, and floored with split slabs. A big bark kitchen standing at one end is larger than the house itself, veranda included.

Bush all round—bush with no horizon, for the country is flat. No ranges in the distance. The bush consists of stunted, rotten native apple-trees. No undergrowth. Nothing to relieve the eye save the darker green of a few she-oaks which are sighing above the narrow, almost waterless creek. Nineteen miles to the nearest sign of civilization—a shanty on the main road.

The drover, an ex-squatter, is away with sheep. His wife and children are left here alone.

Four ragged, dried-up-looking children are playing about the house. Suddenly one of them yells: "Snake! Mother, here's a snake!"

The gaunt, sun-browned bushwoman dashes from the kitchen, snatches her baby from the ground, holds it on her left hip, and reaches for a stick.

"Where is it?"

"Here! gone into the woodheap!" yells the eldest boy—a sharp-faced urchin of eleven. "Stop there, mother! I'll have him. Stand back! I'll have the beggar!"

"Tommy, come here, or you'll be bit. Come here at once when I tell you, you little wretch!"

The youngster comes reluctantly, carrying a stick bigger than himself. Then he yells, triumphantly:

"There it goes—under the house!" and darts away with club uplifted. At the same time the big, black, yellow-eyed dog-of-all-breeds, who has shown the wildest interest in the proceedings, breaks his chain and rushes after that snake. He is a moment late, however, and his nose reaches the crack in the slabs just as the end of its tail disappears. Almost at the same moment the boy's club comes down and skins the aforesaid nose. Alligator takes small notice of this, and proceeds to undermine the building; but he is subdued after a struggle and chained up. They cannot afford to lose him.

The drover's wife makes the children stand together near the dog-house while she watches for the snake. She gets two small dishes of milk and sets them down near the wall to tempt it to come out; but an hour goes by and it does not show itself.

It is near sunset, and a thunderstorm is coming. The children must be brought inside. She will not take them into the house, for she knows the snake is there, and may at any moment come up through a crack in the rough slab floor: so she carries several armfuls of firewood into the kitchen, and then takes the children there. The kitchen has no floor—or, rather, an earthen one—called a "ground floor" in this part of the bush. There is a large, roughly-made table in the centre of the place. She brings the children in, and makes them get on this table. They are two boys and two girls—mere babies. She gives them some supper, and then, before it gets dark, she goes into the house, and snatches up some pillows and bedclothes—expecting to see or lay her hand on the snake any minute. She makes a bed on the kitchen table for the children, and sits down beside it to watch all night.

She has an eye on the corner, and a green sapling club laid in readiness on the dresser by her side; also her sewing basket and a copy of the *Young Ladies' Journal*. She has brought the dog into the room.

Tommy turns in, under protest, but says he'll be awake all night and smash that blinded snake.

His mother asks him how many times she has told him not to swear.

He has his club with him under the bedclothes, and Jacky protests: "Mummy! Tommy's skinnin' me alive wif his club. Make him take it out."

Tommy: "Shet up, you little——! D'yer want to be bit with the snake?"

Jacky shuts up.

"If yer bit," says Tommy, after a pause, "you'll swell up, an' smell, an' turn red an' green an' blue all over till yer bust. Won't he, mother?"

"Now then, don't frighten the child. Go to sleep," she says.

The two younger children go to sleep, and now and then Jacky complains of being "skeezed." More room is made for him. Presently Tommy says:

"Mother! listen to them (adjective) little possums. I'd like to screw their blanky necks."

And Jacky protests drowsily.

"But they don't hurt us, the little blanks!"

Mother: "There, I told you you'd teach Jacky to swear." But the remark makes her smile. Jacky goes to sleep.

Presently Tommy asks:

"Mother! Do you think they'll ever extricate the (adjective) kangaroo?"

"Lord! How am I to know, child? Go to sleep."

"Will you wake me if the snake comes out?"

"Yes. Go to sleep."

Near midnight. The children are all asleep and she sits there still, sewing and reading by turns. From time to time she glances round the floor and wall-plate, and whenever she hears a noise she reaches for the stick. The thunder-storm comes on, and the wind, rushing through the cracks in the slab wall, threatens to blow out her candle. She places it on a sheltered part of the dresser and fixes up a newspaper to protect it. At every flash of lightning the cracks between the slabs gleam like polished silver. The thunder rolls, and the rain comes down in torrents.

Alligator lies at full length on the floor, with his eyes turned towards the partition. She knows by this that the snake is there. There are large cracks in that wall opening under the floor of the dwelling-house.

She is not a coward, but recent events have shaken her nerves. A little son of her brother-in-law was lately bitten by a snake, and died. Besides, she has not heard from her husband for six months, and is anxious about him.

He was a drover, and started squatting here when they were married. The drought of 18— ruined him. He had to sacrifice the remnant of his flock and go droving again. He intends to move his family into the nearest town when he comes back, and, in the meantime, his brother, who keeps a shanty on the main road, comes over about once a month with provisions. The wife has still a couple of cows, one horse, and a few sheep. The brother-in-law kills one of the latter occasionally, gives her what she needs of it, and takes the rest in return for other provisions.

She is used to being left alone. She once lived like this for eighteen months. As a girl she built the usual castles in the air; but all her girlish hopes and aspirations have long been dead. She finds all the excitement and recreation she needs in the *Young Ladies' Journal*, and—Heaven help her!—takes a pleasure in the fashion-plates.

Her husband is an Australian, and so is she. He is careless, but a good enough husband. If he had the means he would take her to the city and keep her there like a princess. They are used to being apart, or at least she is. "No use fretting," she says. He may forget sometimes that he is married; but if he has a good cheque when he comes back he will give most of it to her. When he had money he took her to the city several times—hired a railway sleeping compartment, and put up at the best hotels. He also bought her a buggy, but they had to sacrifice that along with the rest.

The last two children were born in the bush—one while her husband was bringing a drunken doctor, by force, to attend to her. She was alone on this occasion, and very weak. She had been ill with a fever. She prayed to God to send her assistance. God sent Black Mary—the "whitest" gin in all the land. Or, at least, God sent King Jimmy first, and he sent Black Mary. He put his black face round the door-post, took in the situation at a glance, and said cheerfully: "All right, missus—I bring my old woman, she down along a creek."

One of the children died while she was here alone. She rode nineteen miles for assistance, carrying the dead child.

It must be near one or two o'clock. The fire is burning low. Alligator lies with his head resting on his paws, and watches the wall. He is not a very beautiful dog, and the light shows numerous old wounds where the hair will not grow. He is afraid of nothing on the face of the earth or under it. He will tackle a bullock as readily as he will tackle a flea. He hates all other dogs—except kangaroo-dogs—and has a marked dislike to friends or relations of the family. They seldom call, however. He sometimes makes friends with strangers. He hates snakes and has killed many, but he will be bitten some day and die; most snake-dogs end that way.

Now and then the bushwoman lays down her work and watches, and listens, and thinks. She thinks of things in her own life, for there is little else to think about.

The rain will make the grass grow, and this reminds her how she fought a bushfire once while her husband was away. The grass was long, and very dry, and the fire threatened to burn her out. She put on an old pair of her husband's trousers and beat out the flames with a green bough, till great drops of sooty perspiration stood out on her forehead and ran in streaks down her blackened arms. The sight of his mother in trousers greatly amused Tommy, who worked like a little hero by her side, but the terrified baby howled lustily for his "mummy." The fire would have mastered her but for four excited bushmen who arrived in the nick of time. It was a mixed-up affair all round; when she went to take up the baby he screamed and struggled convulsively, thinking it was a "blackman"; and Alligator, trusting more to the child's sense than his own instinct, charged furiously, and (being old and slightly deaf) did not in his excitement at first recognize his mistress's voice, but continued to hang on to the moleskins until choked off by Tommy with a saddle-strap. The dog's sorrow for his blunder, and his anxiety to let it be known that it was all a mistake, was as evident as his ragged tail and twelve-inch grin could make it. It was a glorious time for the boys; a day to look back to, and talk about, and laugh over for many years.

She thinks how she fought a flood during her husband's absence. She stood for hours in the drenching downpour, and dug an overflow gutter to save the dam across the creek. But she could not save it. There are things that a bushwoman cannot do. Next morning the dam was broken, and her heart was nearly broken too, for she thought how her husband would feel when he came home and saw the result of years of labour swept away. She cried then.

She also fought the pleuro-pneumonia—dosed and bled the few remaining cattle, and wept again when her two best cows died.

Again, she fought a mad bullock that besieged the house for a day. She made bullets and fired at him through cracks in the slabs with an old shot-gun. He was dead in the morning. She skinned him and got seventeen-and-sixpence for the hide.

She also fights the crows and eagles that have designs on her chickens. Her plan of campaign is very original. The children cry "Crows, mother!" and she rushes out and aims a broomstick at the birds as though it were a gun, and says "Bung!" The crows leave in a hurry; they are cunning, but a woman's cunning is greater.

Occasionally a bushman in the horrors, or a villainous-looking sundowner, comes and nearly scares the life out of her. She generally tells the suspicious-looking stranger that her husband and two sons are at work below the dam, or over at the yard, for he always cunningly inquires for the boss.

Only last week a gallows-faced swagman—having satisfied himself that there were no men on the place—threw his swag down on the veranda, and demanded tucker. She gave him something to eat; then he expressed his intention of staying for the night. It was sundown then. She got a batten from the sofa, loosened the dog, and confronted the stranger, holding the batten in one hand and the dog's collar with the other. "Now you go!" she said. He looked at her and at the dog, said "All right, mum," in a cringing tone, and left. She was a determined-looking woman, and Alligator's yellow eyes glared unpleasantly—besides, the dog's chawing-up apparatus greatly resembled that of the reptile he was named after.

She has few pleasures to think of as she sits here alone by the fire, on guard against a snake. All days are much the same to her; but on Sunday afternoon she dresses herself, tidies the children, smartens up baby, and goes for a lonely walk along the bush-track, pushing an old perambulator in front of her. She does this every Sunday. She takes as much care to make herself and the children look smart as she would if she were going to do the block in the city. There is nothing to see, however, and not a soul to meet. You might walk twenty miles along this track without being able to fix a point in your mind, unless you are a bushman. This is because of the everlasting, maddening sameness of the stunted trees—that monotony which makes a man long to break away and travel as far as trains can go, and sail as far as ship can sail—and further.

But this bushwoman is used to the loneliness of it. As a girl-wife she hated it, and now she would feel strange away from it.

She is glad when her husband returns, but she does not gush or make a fuss about it. She gets him something good to eat, and tidies up the children.

She seems contented with her lot. She loves her children, but has no time to show it. She seems harsh to them. Her surroundings are not favourable to the development of the "womanly" or sentimental side of nature.

It must be near morning now; but the clock is in the dwelling-house. Her candle is nearly done; she forgot that she was out of candles. Some more wood must be got to keep the fire up, and so she shuts the dog inside and hurries round to the woodheap. The rain has cleared off. She seizes a stick, pulls it out, and—crash! the whole pile collapses.

Yesterday she bargained with a stray blackfellow to bring her some wood, and while he was at work she went in search of a missing cow. She was absent an hour or so, and the native black made good use of his time. On her return she was so astonished to see a good heap of wood by the chimney that she gave him an extra fig of tobacco, and praised him for not being lazy. He thanked her, and left with head erect and chest well out. He was the last of his tribe and a King; but he had built that woodheap hollow.

She is hurt now, and tears spring to her eyes as she sits down again by the table. She takes up a handkerchief to wipe the tears away, but pokes her eyes with her bare fingers instead. The handkerchief is full of holes, and she finds that she has put her thumb through one, and her forefinger through another.

This makes her laugh, to the surprise of the dog. She has a keen, very keen, sense of the ridiculous; and some time or other she will amuse bushmen with the story.

She had been amused before like that. One day she sat down "to have a good cry," as she said—and the old cat rubbed against her dress and "cried too." Then she had to laugh.

It must be near daylight now. The room is very close and hot because of the fire. Alligator still watches the wall from time to time. Suddenly he becomes greatly interested; he draws himself a few inches nearer the partition, and a thrill runs through his body. The hair on the back of his neck begins to bristle, and the battle-light is in his yellow eyes. She knows what this means, and lays her hand on the stick. The lower end of one of the partition slabs has a large crack on both sides. An evil pair of small bright bead-like eyes glisten at one of these holes. The snake—a black one—comes slowly out, about a foot, and moves its head up and down. The dog lies still, and the woman sits as one fascinated. The snake comes out a foot further. She lifts her stick, and the reptile, as though suddenly aware of danger, sticks his head in through the crack on the other side of the slab, and hurries to get his tail round after him. Alligator springs, and his jaws come together with a snap. He misses, for his nose is large, and the snake's body is close down in the angle formed by the slabs and the floor. He snaps again as the tail comes round. He has the snake now, and tugs it out eighteen inches. Thud, thud, comes the woman's club on the ground. Alligator pulls again. Thud, thud. Alligator gives another pull and he has the snake out—a black brute, five feet long. The head rises to dart about, but the dog has the enemy close to the neck. He is a big, heavy dog, but quick as a terrier. He shakes the snake as though he felt the original curse in common with mankind. The eldest boy wakes up, seizes his stick, and tries to get out of bed, but his mother forces him back with a grip of iron. Thud, thud—the snake's back is broken in several places. Thud, thud—its head is crushed, and Alligator's nose skinned again.

She lifts the mangled reptile on the point of her stick, carries it to the fire, and throws it in; then piles on the wood and watches the snake burn. The boy and dog watch too. She lays her hand on the dog's head, and all the fierce, angry light dies out of his yellow eyes. The younger children are quieted, and presently go to sleep. The dirty-legged boy stands for a moment in his shirt, watching the fire. Presently he looks up at her, sees the tears in her eyes, and, throwing his arms round her neck, exclaims:

"Mother, I won't never go drovin'; blast me if I do!"

And she hugs him to her worn-out breast and kisses him; and they sit thus together while the sickly daylight breaks over the bush.

THE BONES

SKY Lee (b. 1952), a feminist Chinese Canadian writer and artist, was born in Port Alberni, British Columbia. She received her B.F.A. from the University of British Columbia and also holds a diploma in nursing from Douglas College. She has one son. SKY Lee is best known for the novel Disappearing Moon Cafe *(1990), which was shortlisted for the Governor General's Literary Award for fiction; "The Bones" is a self-contained excerpt from the beginning of this novel. Her short stories have appeared in numerous magazines, and she has illustrated a children's book,* Teach Me How to Fly, Skyfighter *(1983). A second novel appeared in 1997.*

*According to Audre Lord, "*Disappearing Moon Cafe *is an immense and touching story, the stuff of human tragedy and survival where the true villains, hatred and exploitation, are never named." The title of the novel refers to a restaurant owned by the Wong family in Vancouver's Chinatown, and the novel covers four generations, beginning with Wong Gwei Chen in 1982 and focusing to a large extent on the remarkable women of the Wong family.* Disappearing Moon Cafe *is concerned with a clash of cultures and with how differently the Chinese Canadian identity is experienced by succeeding generations. Moving back and forth with consummate skill between these generations and between China and Canada, SKY Lee creates a complex work of fiction on the foundations of too often ignored or suppressed historical fact. The language of this novel, with its extraordinary mix of voices, is a particularly stunning achievement. In "The Bones," we meet the young Wong Gwei Chen, as well as the half-Chinese, half-Native woman he will marry, and observe Gwei Chen's efforts to bring the bones of his "uncles" home.*

Gwei Chang remembered that, one evening, after a meal of rice, fresh salmon and unfamiliar mushrooms, Old Chen said, "I've been waiting for someone like you to come along for many years—so many years that I even forgot I was waiting." He always looked at Gwei Chang as though he was going to burst into laughter at any time. He said that he knew of many burial sites and had heard of many people who knew of many more, though the bones must be dust by now.

"But the Benevolent Associations have already sent many on the same mission," Gwei Chang replied.

"Yes, but they have not thought to come up here to ask chinaman Chen, have they?"

"Well, it is a little out of the way!" Gwei Chang felt obliged to say, glancing at Kelora whose eyes looked remote and made him want to follow. Already, he was forgetting that there was a whole other world with its own determined way of life out there, somewhere, and that he was from there.

"What are your plans, boy?" There was no edge to Chen's question, merely a sense of duty that had to be recalled.

Gwei Chang turned to face him squarely. "I'm not sure, Uncle." He shrugged his shoulders. Of course, he thought he was just being modest. He had maps, with sections of the railroad numbered. He pointed out the gravesites, haphazardly described at the end of each section. He'd been told that there would be markers, or cairns, or something. How hard could it be ...

"Hah! You're a dunce!" Chen's expletive clipped him on the chin. "Come with me! Bring your so-called maps!"

"Now? It's black out there."

"Light, dark, what difference does it make," Chen's voice boomed, "when we've got brothers to send home." Since Kelora didn't even blink an eye, Gwei Chang could only imagine that this kind of gesture was not at all out of the ordinary, so he followed Chen out into the moonlit forest.

After a two-hour trek, mostly along the train tracks made silver now and then by an isolated moonbeam, Chen led Gwei Chang to the first of many left-over work camp gangs. This one, an independent group of gold dredgers, dour and suspicious, was camped out on the edge of a clearing beside a stream. That late at night, there were no words wasted. The only remark was from a watchman, that Old Man Chen had come. Gwei Chang was thrown a rag to sleep under, and he wandered about until he found some rotten barrels that would support a plank of sorts, and a sluice box. That was his bed for several nights.

In the morning, Gwei Chang shared their cold rice while they scrutinized his maps and criticized his information. Then he was given a shovel. They talked while they worked. That's how Gwei Chang found out a few things. He found out that old overseas chinese never wasted anything—not their time, not their leisure. They worked unceasingly, as if they would fall apart if they ever stopped. They also sat up all night, gossiping and swearing and laughing. They were strange men, maybe because of the shadow of loneliness and isolation that hovered over them. In their midst, Chen seemed less peculiar to Gwei Chang. In fact, Chen was well liked and a regular visitor. Because Gwei Chang came with Chen, he was immediately a friend. When Chen told them what Gwei Chang was doing, he was taken seriously at once.

News of Gwei Chang and his work went ahead of him. Eventually, he could stroll into any bull gang or small Chinatown, onto any farm or campsite, and they would have been expecting him, ready to share food and whatever else he needed. Over and over again, he watched groups shed their surliness at his approach and spread in front of him all that they had from their pitiful little hovels.

At first, he didn't value their reverence for him. Thinking back, he knew how unthinking he had been then, grabbing opportunities for fun—sitting up all night, gossiping, selfishly filling his pockets with goods and information to make his work easier. He saw the loneliness in the brothers, toiling, poor—left behind to rot because the CPR had reneged on its contract to pay the chinese railway workers' passage home. But he felt only a little disdain for them. He was fresh off the boat from China. When they hankered for news from their villages, he thought he was doing them a real big favour by telling them stories. He was too young, and he didn't understand.

Not until he touched the bones. When he finally did, he was awed by them. At first, he actually dreaded the macabre work. What were a few dried bones to him, except disgusting? But the spirits in the mountains were strong and persuasive. The bones gathered themselves into the human shapes of young men, each dashing and bold. They followed him about wherever he roamed, whispered to him, until he knew each one to be a hero, with yearnings from the same secret places in his own heart.

How could he not be touched by the spirit of these wilderness uncles who had trekked on an incredible journey and pitted their lives against mountain rocks and human cruelty? In the perfect silence of a hot afternoon, he used to stop here and there to run his hands along the sheer rock face of a mountain, the surface still biting hot from a dynamite blast. He imagined the mountain shuddering, roaring out in pain, demanding human sacrifice for this profanity. And the real culprits held out blood-splattered chinamen in front of them like a protective talisman.

By then, he understood. By then, in the utter peace of the forests, he had met them all—uncles who had climbed mountain heights then fallen from them, uncles who had drowned in deep surging waters, uncles who had clawed to their deaths in the dirt of caved-in mines. By then, he wasn't afraid and they weren't alien any more. Like them, he would piece himself together again from scattered, shattered bone and then endure.

The next time Gwei Chang walked into a work camp, he was ready to share with them instead of taking from them. He took on their surliness and learned to talk tough and blunt, a chiselled edge to his words to express the backbreaking task of survival that all of them shared day after day. They talked like comrades-in-arms after the battle, still grateful to feel the ache of so many work-worn years, to fill their lungs with mountain mist, to see their shadows walk ahead of them, homesick.

When Kelora took him into the forests of "the hidden place," another world opened up. She had a way of murmuring as they walked. Gwei Chang remembered chinese women doing the very same.

"We go into the forest," she might say. "It's old. Look at how big the trees are." He watched her as she smiled up at the canopy of wind-swept boughs against a glorious sky. Her braids fell away from her ears, exposing an earlobe that looked inviting, as if it would taste sweet.

"It is hot outside, but in here, it is always cool and wet," she said. When he tore his eyes away from her, he looked up, and wished she could have shot him like an arrow, straight up into the endless blue.

"Look, a yellow cedar tree! If I need to gather cedar, then I have to say a few words to the tree, to thank the tree for giving part of itself up to me. I take only a small part too, but not today. Look, the path is worn and smooth. Many women have come here to gather what they need. When we walk in the forest, we say 'we walk with our grandmothers.' She wore a cotton shift, faded gingham against her deep brown skin. Her baskets, mats and hat hung by a thong behind her left shoulder.

"Look at that swampy place!" Kelora tugged on his arm, and Gwei Chang beamed down on her. "See there! We call those rushes 'the geese eat it' plant. The women say to boil it for medicine when some old men can't urinate." This reduced them to giggles. She gave him a playful push that landed him in a garden of ferns. And he lunged at her, but she took off like a little bird.

Kelora and Gwei Chang wandered high and low in the summers, like deer foraging through new pastures, like children. Summertime gathering was women's work, and Kelora would have to go and gather her berries, dawn until dusk sometimes. And Gwei Chang would have to go and find his bones. Yet they found many ways to flow together, like wind brushing against leaves. Like lake and lakeshore, a slow meandering dance of lovers.

He would help her pound her berries, and she would help him scrape bones and carefully stack them into neat bundles. She wasn't afraid and seemed to understand the rituals that had to be performed around them. More amazing, she had a peculiar intuition for locating gravesites whose markers had long ago deteriorated. More than once, she wandered ahead of him; by the time Gwei Chang caught up, she would be pointing at the site where he was to dig. These occasions made his skin crawl. She laughed at him, tittering behind a cupped hand.

When he asked her how she knew, she said, "Chinaman, first listen to yourself sing! Every soul has its own voice."

Chinamen are a superstitious bunch. Gwei Chang got to wondering what she heard. Before he became a human being himself, he mistook her meaning. Kelora was a strange one, with her own private language—neither chinese nor indian, but from deep within the wildness of her soul. Fascinated, he began to press his ear against the ground too. He followed her everywhere, even as she went about her woman's work. She taught him to love the same mother earth and to see her sloping curves in the mountains. He forgot that he had once thought of them as barriers. He learned how to cling onto her against a raging river, or bury into her away from the pelting rain. Or he could be somewhere, anywhere, cold and bone-tired, but he would stare at the consummate beauty of a bare branch trembling in the breeze. He would watch red buds bloom into freshly peeled blossoms. Clouds tinted pink-gold, slanting over the mirror of an alpine lake; this beautiful mother filled his heart and soul.

Old Chen came at Gwei Chang with two questions at the same time. He asked, "How are you going to transport those bones down to the coast?"

He also asked, "Do you have anything you can give me as a gift? If you don't have anything, then I'll give you something to give back to me."

Gwei Chang played dumb. "Huh?"

"It's the custom," Chen said, "to give a gift when you take a wife. Even nowadays." Kelora's maternal aunt shuffled in and out of the cabin, excitedly shouting at the young boys who had followed her up the bluff, carrying fifty-pound bags of flour in their arms.

"I have a gold watch," Gwei Chang replied without hesitation, "and a bowie knife I bought off a drunk demon in Spuzzum. Oh yes, those farmers gave me six Hudson's Bay Company blankets in exchange for a few days' work—used but not worn out."

Chen looked relieved. Gwei Chang didn't let on that he had been preparing all along. By then, he was well aware of what caught Kelora's eyes and what didn't.

"Not bad," Chen said, "not bad at all for a boy who was starving, eating 'chinook' wind just a while back! Go with Kelora and give them all to her people. Politely! You and me, of course, we can forego the usual ceremony. They're just to keep the women happy anyway."

The other question was not so easily answered. Gwei Chang knew it would provoke some controversy because he had already tried it on some elders in the Chinatown at North Bend. He figured Chen must have surely heard about his idea by now. He could well imagine the indignant sputters Chen would have had to face.

"You know what that crazy Wong boy was thinking about? Him and that hothead, Lee Chong. Did they get that stupid idea from you? People have been saying that that crazy old Chen had a hand in it. Who else!"

Gwei Chang had a wonderful idea! Lee Chong thought it was a good idea too. Kelora said it was worth a try. When you're young and stupidly proud, everything is worth a try. Lee Chong was a small, wiry fellow—face like a rat in those days. He had quit his laundry job in a huff, and when Gwei Chang met up with him, he was on his way back to Victoria. Lee Chong came up to Gwei Chang and asked if he would give him a job.

"Yeah," Gwei Chang said, "I need someone to take the bones all the way back down to Victoria." Lee Chong looked enthusiastic, which was a relief to him. It wasn't easy trying to find someone who didn't mind hauling a load of skeletons back down the old Cariboo Road, through hostile territory ridden with whites, and camping out alone with ghosts in the mountains, in the dark.

Gwei Chang asked if Lee Chong had a horse and wagon. "Nope," he said, "don't you?"

Lee Chong and Gwei Chang hit it off right away. It was the height of summer then, and Lee Chong didn't have much trouble finding odd jobs here and there, picking fruit, hand to mouth, so to speak, while he waited around for Gwei Chang to make up his mind. Lee Chong wasn't in any hurry. By then, Gwei Chang had been very successful at his bone-searching expedition and thought much of himself.

The Benevolent Associations hadn't given Gwei Chang any specific instructions on how to get the bones to Victoria. The assumption had been that the first bone searchers would find their own way, with the minimum of expense and manpower. All the monies for their transport had been donated, and there were so many bones left still. This was in 1892, the beginning of the retrieval of bones, which lasted well into the 1930s.

Gwei Chang had travelled up and down the Fraser Canyon and watched many an indian canoe skimming down the white rapids, the travellers whooping and hollering, their hair plastered straight back behind their heads. He thought it an exhilarating way to travel! Those raging waters mesmerized him. They didn't seem like dangerous obstacles. Then, one day, he saw white men, on axe-hewn rafts, come dancing around the bend, men and boxes securely tied down with a strong network of ropes. That decided him. What could be easier?

"Look," he said to Lee Chong, "I don't have a wagon, but I've got something better, faster. More challenging."

Lee Chong and Gwei Chang started to build their craft. They asked around to find out how. They traded with indians for hand-woven cedar ropes, and the indians told them which trees were the most buoyant; the hardwood for sternposts; tough flexibility for poles and hand-hewn rudders.

The other chinamen fumed, "If you capsize and spill your cracked brains, that's O.K. by us, but if you lose any bones, you're condemning human spirits to ten thousand years of aimless wandering."

Lee Chong and Gwei Chang saw things differently. They told each other, "Old women, every one of them! Got no gall! We just want to give the spirits of those mountain heroes one last thrilling ride." Lee Chong and Gwei Chang figured the spirits would laugh at peril. After all, they had died for adventure and daring. Why should they object now?

When they finished lashing their craft together, Lee Chong and Gwei Chang figured it could fall down hundreds of feet of a waterfall without splintering. They were ready to bet their lives on it, but were the dead ones prepared to risk their souls on another long shot?

Well, in order to avoid the wrong people answering that question, early at dawn the next morning, with cedar boxes full of bones lashed down in the centre of the raft, Lee Chong and Gwei Chang pushed off. Once out of Chen's protective cul-de-sac, the eddies of the big river grabbed the craft and threw them along the most dizzying, joyful ride of their lives.

The sun shone through the fine mist spray which lifted out of the river and doused them with fancy. They just let the river take them. Sometimes the river was calm and giving; sometimes it knocked their senses askew. The world encircling them was raw and beautiful. The life that blew into them was inspiring and intoxicating. They careened along, hemmed in by the steep rise of gorges and canyon cliffs. Sometimes the river was fretful, contorting back on itself, treacherous. Other times, the river sprawled and meandered through pastures and rich flatlands; they glided along its shimmering reflections. The pair felt like they had ridden the river dragon, and it had lifted their souls skyward. At the end of their journey, they walked away transformed, feeling a little closer to immortality.

Gwei Chang parted ways with the bones at the bone-house in Victoria and with Lee Chong on Tang People's Street, and began his trek back home to Kelora.

DORIS LESSING

OUT OF THE FOUNTAIN

Doris Lessing (b. 1919) was born in what was then Persia and is now Iran, but in 1924 she moved with her family to Southern Rhodesia, now called Zimbabwe, where her father hoped to make his fortune in farming. Most of Lessing's young life was spent in Africa, where she attended a Roman Catholic school. At fourteen she left home to become a nurse-maid, and later married Frank Wisdom, with whom she had two children. She became deeply involved in the political struggles of Rhodesia, a country troubled by colonial racism, and left Wisdom to marry Gottfried Lessing, a Marxist immigrant with whom she had another child. This marriage also ended, and in 1949 Lessing left Rhodesia with her young son and moved to London, where she still lives and writes.

Africa, however, remained large in her memory, and her earliest books came directly out of her experience there. Like a great deal of Lessing's work, a later collection, African Stories *(1964), is important not only as fiction, but also as political and social commentary; it includes stories that "confirm in precise and painful detail, like stitches in a wound, the abuse of the native population of Southern Rhodesia by the white settlers of British descent." Lessing's writing is often autobiographical; she draws heavily on childhood memories, relationships with men, and her own serious engagement with politics and social concerns. Martha Quest, for example, Lessing's heroine in her* Children of Violence *series of novels, moves through the same time and space as her creator. The Golden Notebook (1962), perhaps her most influential novel, explores the "destructive relationships between men and women that mirror the lack of coherence and order in our fragmented, materialistic century."*

Doris Lessing has played an important role in the feminist literary tradition, with novels such as The Summer Before the Dark *(1973) and* Memoirs of a Survivor *(1975). She also attracts readers who share her interest in Sufism, a quasi-mystical philosophical tradition with roots in ancient Persia, and who look to Lessing as a great teacher. Besides being one of the great short story writers of our age, she has also written a remarkable series of science-fiction novels, the* Canopus in Argos: Archives *series. Lessing believes that a writer must accept responsibility as the "architect of the soul," that writing is one of the few art forms left where "the artist speaks directly, in clear words, to the audience." In an increasingly depersonalized world, she considers this direct communication particularly important. "Out of the Fountain," from* The Story of a Non-Marrying Man and Other Stories *(1972), is a mysterious piece that bears the imprint of Lessing's interest in the Sufi "teaching story." Lessing's recent works include the first two volumes of her autobiography and the novel* Love Again.

I could begin, There was once a man called Ephraim who lived in ... but for me this story begins with a fog. Fog in Paris delayed a flight to London by a couple of hours, and so a group of travellers sat around a table drinking coffee and entertaining each other.

A woman from Texas joked that a week before she had thrown coins into the fountain in Rome for luck—and had been dogged by minor ill-fortune ever since. A Canadian said he had spent far too much money on a holiday and at the same fountain three days ago had been tempted to lift coins out with a magnet when no one was looking. Someone said that in a Berlin theatre last night there had been a scene where a girl flung money all about the stage in a magnificently scornful gesture. Which led us on to where money is trampled on, burned, flung about or otherwise ritually scorned; which is odd, since such gestures never take place in life. Not at all, said a matron from New York—she had seen with her own eyes some Flower Children burning money on a sidewalk to show their contempt for it; but for her part what it showed was that they must have rich parents. (This dates the story, or at least the fog.)

All the same, considering the role money plays in all our lives, it *is* odd how often authors cause characters to insult dollar bills, roubles, pound notes. Which enables audience, readers, to go home, or to shut the book, feeling cleansed of the stuff? Above it?

Whereas we are told that in less surly days sultans on feast days flung gold coins into crowds happy to scramble for it; that kings caused showers of gold to descend on loved ministers; and that if jewels fell in showers from the sky no one would dream of asking suspicious questions.

The nearest any one of us could remember to this kingly stuff was a certain newspaper mogul in London who would reward a promising young journalist for an article which he (the mogul) liked, with an envelope stuffed full of five pound notes sent around by special messenger—but this kind of thing is only too open to unkind interpretation; and the amount of ill-feeling aroused in the bosoms of fellow journalists, and the terror in that of the recipient for fear the thing might be talked about, is probably why we stage such scenes as it were in reverse, and why, on the edge of a magic fountain, we slide in a single coin, like a love letter into an envelope during an affair which one's better sense entirely deplores. Sympathetic magic—but a small magic, a mini-magic, a most furtive summoning of the Gods of Gold. And, if a hand rose from the fountain to throw us coins and jewels, it is more than likely that, schooled as we are by recent literature, we'd sneer and throw them back in its teeth—so to speak.

And now a man who had not spoken at all said that he knew of a case where jewels had been flung into the dust of a public square in Italy. No one had thrown them back. He took from his pocket a wallet, and from the wallet a fold of paper such as jewellers use, and on the paper lay a single spark or gleam of light. It was a slice of milk-and-rainbow opal. Yes, he said, he had been there. He had picked up the fragment and kept it. It wasn't valuable, of course. He would tell us the story if he thought there was time, but for some reason it was a tale so precious to him that he didn't want to bungle it through having to hurry. Here there was another swirl of silkily gleaming fog beyond the glass of the restaurant wall, and another announcement of unavoidable delay.

So he told the story. One day someone will introduce me to a young man called Nikki (perhaps, or what you will) who was born during the Second World War in Italy. His father was a hero, and his mother now the wife of the Ambassador to ... Or perhaps in a bus, or at a dinner party, there will be a girl who has a pearl hanging around her neck on a chain, and when asked about it she will say: Imagine, my mother was given this pearl by a man who was practically a stranger, and when she gave it to me she said ... Something like that will happen: and then this story will have a different beginning, not a fog at all ...

There was a man called Ephraim who lived in Johannesburg. His father was to do with diamonds, as had been his father. The family were immigrants. This is still true of all people from Johannesburg, a city a century old. Ephraim was a middle son, not brilliant or stupid, not good or bad. He was nothing in particular. His brothers became diamond merchants, but Ephraim was not cut out for anything immediately obvious, and so at last he was apprenticed to an uncle to learn the trade of diamond-cutting.

To cut a diamond perfectly is an act like a samurai's sword thrust, or a master archer's centred arrow. When an important diamond is shaped a man may spend a week, or even weeks, studying it, accumulating powers of attention, memory, intuition, till he has reached that moment when he finally knows that a tap, no more, at just *that* point of tension in the stone will split it exactly *so*.

While Ephraim learned to do this, he lived at home in a Johannesburg suburb; and his brothers and sisters married and had families. He was the son who took his time about getting married, and about whom the family first joked, saying that he was choosy; and then they remained silent when others talked of him with that edge on their voices, irritated, a little malicious, even frightened, which is caused by those men and women who refuse to fulfil the ordinary purposes of nature. The kind ones said he was a good son, working nicely under his uncle Ben, and living respectably at home, and on Sunday nights playing poker with bachelor friends. He was twenty-five, then thirty, thirty-five, forty. His parents became old and died, and he lived alone in the family house. People stopped noticing him. Nothing was expected of him.

Than a senior person became ill, and Ephraim was asked to fly in his stead to Alexandria for a special job. A certain rich merchant of Alexandria had purchased an uncut diamond as a present for his daughter, who was to be married shortly. He wished only the best for the diamond. Ephraim, revealed by this happening as one of the world's master diamond-cutters, flew to Egypt, spent some days in communion with the stone in a quiet room in the merchant's house, and then caused it to fall apart into three lovely pieces. These were for a ring and earrings.

Now he should have flown home again; but the merchant asked him to dinner. An odd chance that—unusual. Not many people got inside that rich closed world. But perhaps the merchant had become infected by the week of rising tension while Ephraim became one with the diamond in a quiet room.

At dinner Ephraim met the girl for whom the jewels were destined.

And now—but what can be said about the fortnight that followed? Certainly not that Ephraim, the little artisan from Johannesburg, fell in love with Mihrène, daughter of a modern merchant prince. Nothing so simple. And that the affair had about it a quality out of the ordinary was shown by the reaction of the merchant himself, Mihrène's conventional papa.

Conventional, commonplace, banal—these are the words for the members of the set, or class, to which Mihrène Kantannis belonged. In all the cities about the Mediterranean they lived in a scattered community, very rich, but tastefully so, following international fashions, approving Paris when they should and London when they should, making trips to New York or Rome, summering on whichever shore they have chosen, by a kind of group instinct, to be the right one for the year, and sharing comfortably tolerant opinions. They were people, are people, with nothing remarkable about them but their wealth, and the enchanting Mihrène, whom Ephraim first saw in the mist of white embroidered muslin standing by a fountain, was a girl neither more pretty nor more gifted than, let's say, a dozen that evening in Alexandria, a thousand or so in Egypt, hundreds of thousands in the countries round about, all of which produce so plentifully her particular type—her beautiful type: small-boned, black-haired, black-eyed, apricot-skinned, lithe.

She had lived for twenty years in this atmosphere of well-chosen luxury; loved and bickered with her mother and her sisters; respected her papa; and was intending to marry Paulo, a young man from South America with whom she would continue to live exactly the same kind of life, only in Buenos Aires.

For her it was an ordinary evening, a family dinner at which a friend of Papa's was present. She did not know about the diamonds: they were to be a surprise. She was wearing last year's dress and a choker of false pearls: that season it was smart to wear "costume" pearls, and to leave one's real pearls in a box on one's dressing-table.

Ephraim, son of jewellers, saw the false pearls around that neck and suffered.

Why, though? Johannesburg is full of pretty girls. But he had not travelled much, and Johannesburg, rough, built on gold, as it were breathing by the power of gold, a city waxing and waning with the fortunes of gold (as befits this story), may be exciting, violent, vibrant, but it has no mystery, nothing for the imagination, no invisible dimensions. Whereas Alexandria ... This house, for instance, with its discreetly blank outer walls that might conceal anything, crime, or the hidden court of an exiled king, held inner gardens and fountains, and Mihrène, dressed appropriately in moonwhite and who ... well, perhaps she wasn't entirely at her best that evening. There were those who said she had an ugly laugh. Sometimes the family joked that it was lucky she would never have to earn a living. At one point during dinner, perhaps feeling that she ought to contribute to the entertainment, she told a rather flat and slightly bitchy story about a friend. She was certainly bored, yawned once or twice, and did not try too hard to hide the yawns. The diamond-cutter from Johannesburg gazed at her, forgot to eat, and asked twice why she wore false pearls in a voice rough with complaint. He was gauche, she decided—and forgot him.

He did not return home, but wired for money. He had never spent any, and so had a great deal available for the single perfect pearl which he spent days looking for, and which he found at last in a back room in Cairo, where he sat bargaining over coffee cups for some days with an old Persian dealer who knew as much about gems as he did, and who would not trade in anything but the best.

With the jewel he arrived at the house of Mihrène's father, and when he was seated in a room opening on to an inner court where jasmine clothed a wall, and lily pads a pool, he asked permission to give the pearl to the young girl.

It had been strange that Papa had invited this tradesman to dinner. It was strange that now Papa did not get angry. He was shrewd: it was his life to be shrewd. There was no nuance of commercial implication in a glance, a tone of voice, a turn of phrase, that he was not certain to assess rightly. Opposite this fabulously rich man into whose house only the rich came as guests, sat a little diamond-cutter who proposed to give his daughter a small fortune in the shape of a pearl, and who wanted nothing in return for it.

They drank coffee, and then they drank whisky, and they talked of the world's jewels and of the forthcoming wedding, until for the second time Ephraim was asked to dinner.

At dinner Mihrène sat opposite the elderly gentleman (he was forty-five or so) who was Papa's business friend, and was ordinarily polite: then slightly more polite because of a look from Papa. The party was Mihrène, her father, her fiancé Paulo, and Ephraim. The mother and sisters were visiting elsewhere. Nothing happened during the meal. The young couple were rather inattentive to the older pair. At the end, Ephraim took a screw of paper from his pocket, and emptied from it a single perfect pearl that had a gleam like the flesh of a rose, or of a twenty-year-old girl. This pearl he offered to Mihrène, with the remark that she oughtn't to wear false pearls. Again it was harshly inflected; a complaint, or a reproach for imperfect perfection.

The pearl lay on white damask in candlelight. Into the light above the pearl was thrust the face of Ephraim, whose features she could reconstruct from the last time she had seen him a couple of weeks before only with the greatest of difficulty.

It was, of course, an extraordinary moment. But not dramatic—no, it lacked that high apex of decisiveness as when Ephraim tapped a diamond, or an archer lets loose his bow. Mihrène looked at her father for an explanation. So, of course, did her fiancé. Her father did not look confused, or embarrassed, so much as that he wore the air of somebody standing on one side because here is a situation which he has never professed himself competent to judge. And Mihrène had probably never before in her life been left free to make a decision.

She picked up the pearl from the damask, and let it lie in her palm. She, her fiancé, and her father, looked at the pearl whose value they were all well equipped to assess, and Ephraim looked sternly at the girl. Then she lifted long, feathery black lashes and looked at him—in inquiry? An appeal to be let off? His eyes were judging, disappointed; they said what his words had said: Why are you content with the second-rate?

Preposterous ...

Impossible ...

Finally Mihrène gave the slightest shrug of shoulders, tonight covered in pink organza, and said to Ephraim, "Thank you, thank you very much."

They rose from the table. The four drank coffee on the terrace over which rose a wildly evocative Alexandrian moon, two nights away from the full, a moon quite unlike any that might shine over strident Johannesburg. Mihrène let the pearl lie on her palm and reflect moonrays, while from time to time her black eyes engaged with Ephraim's—but what colour his were had never been, would never be, of interest to anyone—and, there was no doubt of it, he was like someone warning, or reminding, or even threatening.

Next day he went back to Johannesburg, and on Mihrène's dressing-table lay a small silver box in which was a single perfect pearl.

She was to marry in three weeks.

Immediately the incident became in the family: "That crazy little Jew who fell for Mihrène ..." Her acceptance of the pearl was talked of as an act of delicacy on her part, of kindness. "Mihrène was so kind to the poor old thing ..." Thus they smoothed over what had happened, made acceptable an incident which could have no place in their life, their thinking. But they knew, of course, and most particularly did Mihrène know, that something else had happened.

When she refused to marry Paulo, quite prettily and nicely, Papa and Mamma Kantannis made ritual remarks about her folly, her ingratitude, and so forth, but in engagements like these no hearts are expected to be broken, for the marriages are like the arranged marriages of dynasties. If she did not marry Paulo, she would marry someone like him—and she was very young.

They remarked that she had not been herself since the affair of the pearl. Papa said to himself that he would see to it no more fly-by-nights arrived at his dinner-table. They arranged for Mihrène to visit cousins in Istanbul.

Meanwhile in Johannesburg a diamond-cutter worked at his trade, cutting diamonds for engagement rings, dress rings, tie pins, necklaces, bracelets. He imagined a flat bowl of crystal, which glittered like diamonds, in which were massed roses. But the roses were all white, shades of white. He saw roses which were cold marble white, white verging on coffee colour, greenish white, like the wings of certain butterflies, white that blushed, a creamy white, white that was nearly beige, white that was almost yellow. He imagined a hundred shades of white in rose shapes. These he pressed together, filled a crystal dish with them and gave them to—Mihrène? It is possible that already he scarcely thought of her. He imagined how he would collect stones in shades of white, and create a perfect jewel, bracelet, necklet, or crescent for the hair, and present this jewel to—Mihrène? Does it matter whom it was for? He bought opals, like mist held behind glass on which lights moved and faded, like milk where fire lay buried, like the congealed breath of a girl on a frosty night. He bought pearls, each one separately, each one perfect. He bought fragments of mother-of-pearl. He bought moonstones like clouded diamonds. He even bought lumps of glass that someone had shaped to reflect light perfectly. He bought white jade and crystals and collected chips of diamond to make the suppressed fires in pearl and opal flash out in reply to their glittering frost. These jewels he had in folded flat paper, and they were kept first in a small cigarette box, and then were transferred to a larger box that had been for throat lozenges, and then to an even larger box that had held cigars. He played with these gems, dreamed over them, arranged them in his mind in a thousand ways. Sometimes he remembered an exquisite girl dressed in moonmist: the memory was becoming more and more like a sentimental postcard or an old-fashioned calendar.

In Istanbul Mihrène married, without her family's approval, a young Italian engineer whom normally she would never have met. Her uncle was engaged in reconstructing a certain yacht; the engineer was in the uncle's office to discuss the reconstruction when Mihrène came in. It was she who made the first move: it would have to be. He was twenty-seven, with nothing but his salary, and no particular prospects. His name was Carlos. He was political. That is, precisely, he was revolutionary, a conspirator. Politics did not enter the world of Mihrène. Or rather, it could be said that such families *are* politics, politics in their aspect of wealth, but this becomes evident only when deals are made that are so vast that they have international cachet, and repute, like the alliances or rifts between countries.

Carlos called Mihrène "a white goose" when she tried to impress him with her seriousness. He called her "a little rich bitch." He made a favour of taking her to meetings where desperately serious young men and women discussed the forthcoming war—the year was 1939. It was an affair absolutely within the traditions of such romances: her family were bound to think she was throwing herself away; he and his friends on the whole considered that it was he who was conferring the benefits.

To give herself courage in her determination to be worthy of this young hero, she would open a tiny silver box where a pearl lay on silk, and say to herself: *He* thought I was worth something ...

She married her Carlos in the week Paulo married a girl from a French dynasty. Mihrène went to Rome and lived in a small villa without servants, and with nothing to fall back on but the memory of a nondescript elderly man who had sat opposite her throughout two long, dull dinners and who had given her a pearl as if he were giving her a lesson. She thought that in all her life no one else had ever demanded anything of her, ever asked anything, ever taken her seriously.

The war began. In Buenos Aires the bride who had taken her place lived in luxury. Mihrène, a poor housewife, saw her husband who was a conspirator against the fascist Mussolini become a conscript in Mussolini's armies, then saw him go away to fight, while she waited for the birth of her first child.

The war swallowed her. When she was heard of again, her hero was dead, and her first child was dead, and her second, conceived on Carlos's final leave, was due to be born in a couple of months. She was in a small town in the centre of Italy with no resources at all but her pride: she had sworn she would not earn the approval of her parents on any terms but her own. The family she had married into had suffered badly: she had a room in the house of an aunt.

The Germans were retreating through Italy: after them chased the victorious armies of the Allies ... but that sounds like an official war history.

To try again: over a peninsula that was shattered, ruinous, starved by war, two armies of men foreign to the natives of the place were in movement; one in retreat up towards the body of Europe, the other following it. There were places where these opposing bodies were geographically so intermingled that only uniforms distinguished them. Both armies were warm, well clothed, well fed, supplied with alcohol and cigarettes. The native inhabitants had no heat, no warm clothes, little food, no cigarettes. They had, however, a great deal of alcohol.

In one army was a man called Ephraim who, being elderly, was not a combatant, but part of the machinery which supplied it with food and goods. He was a sergeant, and as unremarkable in the army as he was in civilian life. For the four years he had been a soldier, for the most part in North Africa, he had pursued a private interest, or obsession, which was, when he arrived anywhere at all, to seek out the people and places that could add yet another fragment of iridescent or gleaming substance to the mass which he carried around in a flat tin in his pack.

The men he served with found him and his preoccupation mildly humorous. He was not disliked or liked enough to make a target for that concentration of unease caused by people who alarm others. They did not laugh at him, or call him madman. Perhaps he was more like that dog who is a regiment's pet. Once he mislaid his tin of loot and a couple of men went into a moderate danger to get it back: sometimes a comrade would bring him a bit of something or other picked up in a bazaar—amber, an amulet, a jade. He advised them how to make bargains; he went on expeditions with them to buy stones for wives and girls back home.

He was in Italy that week when—*everything disintegrated*. Anyone who has been in, or near, war (which means, by now, everyone, or at least everyone in Europe and Asia) knows that time—a week, days, sometimes hours—when everything falls apart, when all forms of order dissolve, including those which mark the difference between enemy and enemy.

During this time old scores of all kinds are settled. It is when unpopular officers get killed by "accident." It is when a man who has an antipathy for another will kill him, or beat him up. A man who wants a woman will rape her, if she is around, or rape another in her stead if she is not. Women get raped; and those who want to be will make sure they are where the raping is. A woman who hates another will harm her. In short, it is a time of anarchy, of looting, of arson and destruction for destruction's sake. There are those who believe that this time out of ordinary order is the reason for war, its hidden justification, its purpose and law, another pattern behind the one we see. Afterwards there are no records of what has happened. There is no one to keep records: everyone is engaged in participating, or in protecting himself.

Ephraim was in a small town near Florence when his war reached that phase. There was a certain corporal, also from Johannesburg, who always had a glitter in his look when they talked of Ephraim's tin full of jewels. On an evening when every human being in the place was hunter or hunted, manoeuvred for advantage, or followed scents of gain, this man, in civilian life a storekeeper, looked across a room at Ephraim and grinned. Ephraim knew what to expect. Everyone knew what to expect—at such moments much older knowledges come to the surface together with old instincts. Ephraim quietly left a schoolroom for that week converted into a mess, and went out into the early dark of streets emptied by fear, where walls still shook and dust fell in clouds because of near gunfire. But it was also very quiet. Terror's cold nausea silences, places invisible hands across mouths ... The occasional person hurrying through those streets kept his eyes in front, and his mouth tight. Two such people meeting did not look at each other except for a moment when their eyes violently encountered in a hard clash of inquiry. Behind every shutter or pane or door people stood, or sat or crouched, waiting for the time out of order to end, and guns and sharp instruments stood near their hands.

Through these streets went Ephraim. The Corporal had not seen him go, but by now would certainly have found the scent. At any moment he would catch up with Ephraim who carried in his hand a flat tin, and who as he walked looked into holes in walls and in pavements, peered into a church half-filled with rubble, investigated torn earth where bomb fragments had fallen and even looked up into the branches of trees as he passed and at the plants growing at doorways. Finally, as he passed a fountain clogged with debris, he knelt for a moment and slid his tin down into the mud. He walked away, fast, not looking back to see if he had been seen, and around the corner of the church he met Corporal Van der Merwe. As Ephraim came up to his enemy he held out empty hands and stood still. The Corporal was a big man and twenty years younger. Van der Merwe gave him a frowning look, indicative of his powers of shrewd assessment, rather like Mihrène's father's look when he heard how this little nonentity proposed to give his daughter a valuable pearl for no reason at all, and when Ephraim saw it, he at once raised his hands above his head like a prisoner surrendering, while Van der Merwe frisked him. There was a moment when Ephraim might very well have been killed: it hung in the balance. But down the street a rabble of soldiers were looting pictures and valuables from another church, and Van der Merwe, his attention caught by them, simply watched Ephraim walk away, and then ran off himself to join the looters.

By the time that season of anarchy had finished, Ephraim was a couple of hundred miles north. Six months later, in a town ten miles from the one where he had nearly been murdered by a man once again his military subordinate (but that incident had disappeared, had become buried in the foreign texture of another time, or dimension), Ephraim asked for an evening's leave and travelled as he could to V——, where he imagined, perhaps, that he would walk through deserted streets to a rubble-filled fountain and beside the fountain would kneel, and slide his hand into dirty water to retrieve his treasure.

But the square was full of people, and though this was not a time when a café served more than a cup of bad coffee or water flavoured with chemicals, the two cafés had people in them who were half starved but already inhabiting the forms of ordinary life. They served, of course, unlimited quantities of cheap wine. Everyone was drunken, or tipsy. In a wine country, when there is no food, wine becomes a kind of food, craved like food. Ephraim walked past the fountain and saw that the water was filthy, too dirty to let anyone see what was in it, or whether it had been cleared of rubble, and, with the rubble, his treasure.

He sat on the pavement under a torn awning, by a cracked wood table, and ordered coffee. He was the only soldier there; or at least, the only uniform. The main tide of soldiery was washing back and forth to one side of this little town. Uniforms meant barter, meant food, clothing, cigarettes. In a moment half a dozen little boys were at his elbow offering him girls. Women of all ages were sauntering past or making themselves visible, or trying to catch his eye, since the female population of the town were for the most part in that condition for which in our debased time we have the shorthand term: being prepared to sell themselves for a cigarette. Old women, old men, cripples, all kinds of person, stretched in front of him hands displaying various more or less useless objects—lighters, watches, old buckles or bottles or brooches— hoping to get chocolate or food in return. Ephraim sat on, sad with himself because he had not brought eggs or tinned stuffs or chocolate. He had not thought of it. He sat while hungry people with sharp faces that glittered with a winy fever pressed about him and the bodies of a dozen or so women arranged themselves in this or that pose for his inspection. He felt sick. He was almost ready to go away and forget his tin full of gems. Then a tired-looking woman in a much-washed print dress lifted high in front because of pregnancy came to sit at his table. He thought she was there to sell herself, and hardly looked at her, unable to bear it that a pregnant woman was brought to such a pass.

She said: "Don't you remember me?"

And now he searched her face, and she searched his. He looked for Mihrène; and she tried to see in him what it was that changed her life, to find what it was that that pearl embodied which she carried with her in a bit of cloth sewn into her slip.

They sat trying to exchange news; but these two people had so little in common they could not even say: And how is so and so? What has happened to him, or to her?

The hungry inhabitants of the town withdrew a little way, because this soldier had become a person, a man who was a friend of Mihrène, who was their friend.

The two were there for a couple of hours. They were on the whole more embarrassed than anything. It was clear to both by now that whatever events had taken place between them, momentous or not (they were not equipped to say), these events were in some realm or on a level where their daylight selves were strangers. It was certainly not the point that she, the unforgettable girl of Alexandria, had become a rather drab young woman waiting to give birth in a war-shattered town; not the point that for her he had carried with him for four years of war a treasury of gems, some precious, some mildly valuable, some worthless, bits of substance with one thing in common: their value related to some other good which had had, arbitrarily and for a short time the name *Mihrène*.

It had become intolerable to sit there, over coffee made of burned grain, while all round great hungry eyes focused on him, the soldier, who had come so cruelly to their starving town with empty hands. He had soon to leave. He had reached this town on the back boards of a peasant's cart, there being no other transport; and if he did not get another lift of the same kind, he would have to walk ten miles before midnight.

Over the square was rising a famished watery moon, unlike the moons of his own city, unlike the wild moons of Egypt. At last he simply got up and walked to the edge of the evil-smelling fountain. He kneeled down on its edge, plunged in his hand, encountered all sorts of slimy things, probably dead rats or cats or even bits of dead people, and after some groping, felt the familiar shape of his tin. He pulled it out, wiped it dry on some old newspaper that had blown there, went back to the table, sat down, opened the tin. Pearls are fed on light and air. Opals don't like being shut away from light which makes their depths come alive. But no water had got in, and he emptied the glittering, gleaming heap on to the cracked wood of the table top.

All round pressed the hungry people who looked at the gems and thought of food.

She took from her breast a bit of cloth and untwisted her pearl. She held it out to him.

"I never sold it," she said.

And now he looked at her—sternly, as he had done before.

She said, in the pretty English of those who have learned it from governesses: "I have sometimes needed food, I've been hungry, you know! I've had no servants ..."

He looked at her. Oh, how she knew that look, how she had studied it in her memory! Irritation, annoyance, grief. All these, but above all disappointment. And more than these, a warning, or reminder. It said, she felt: Silly white goose! Rich little bitch! Poor little nothing! Why do you always get it wrong? Why are you stupid? What is a pearl compared with what it stands for? If you are hungry and need money, sell it, of course!

She sat in that sudden stillness that says a person is fighting not to weep. Her beautiful eyes brimmed. Then she said stubbornly: "I'll never sell it. Never!"

As for him he was muttering: I should have brought food. I was a dummkopf. What's the use of these things ...

But in the hungry eyes around him he read that they were thinking how even in times of famine there are always men and women who have food hidden away to be bought by gold or jewels.

"Take them," he said to the children, to the women, to the old people.

They did not understand him, did not believe him.

He said again: "Go on. Take them!"

No one moved. Then he stood up and began flinging into the air pearls, opals, moonstones, gems of all kinds, to fall as they would. For a few moments there was a mad scene of people bobbing and scrambling, and the square emptied as people raced back to the corners they lived in with what they had picked up out of the dust. It was not yet time for the myth to start, the story of how a soldier had walked into the town, and inexplicably pulled treasure out of the fountain which he flung into the air like a king or a sultan—treasure that was ambiguous and fertile like a king's, since one man might pick up the glitter of a diamond that later turned out to be worthless glass, and another be left with a smallish pearl that had nevertheless been so carefully chosen it was worth months of food, or even a house or small farm.

"I must go," said Ephraim to his companion.

She inclined her head in farewell, as to an acquaintance re-encountered. She watched a greying, dumpy little man walk away past a fountain, past a church, then out of sight.

Later that night she took out the pearl and held it in her hand. If she sold it, she would remain comfortably independent of her own family. Here, in the circle of the family of her dead husband, she would marry again, another engineer or civil servant: she would be worth marrying, even as a widow with a child. Of course if she returned to her own family, she would also remarry, as a rich young widow with a small child from that dreadful war, luckily now over.

Such thoughts went through her head: at last she thought that it didn't make any difference what she did. Whatever function Ephraim's intervention had performed in her life was over when she refused to marry Paulo, had married Carlos, had come to Italy and given birth to two children, one dead from an unimportant children's disease that had been fatal only because of the quality of war-food, war-warmth. She had been wrenched out of her pattern, had been stamped, or claimed, by the pearl—by something else. Nothing she could do now would put her back where she had been. It did not matter whether she stayed in Italy or returned to the circles she had been born in.

As for Ephraim, he went back to Johannesburg when the war finished, and continued to cut diamonds and to play poker on Sunday nights.

This story ended more or less with the calling of the flight number. As we went to the tarmac where illuminated wisps of fog still lingered, the lady from Texas asked the man who had told the story if perhaps he was Ephraim?

"No," said Dr. Rosen, a man of sixty or so from Johannesburg, a brisk, well-dressed man with nothing much to notice about him—like most of the world's citizens.

No, he was most emphatically not Ephraim.

Then how did he know all this? Perhaps he was there?

Yes, he was there. But if he was to tell us how he came to be a hundred miles from where he should have been, in that chaotic, horrible week—it was horrible, horrible!—and in civvies, then that story would be even longer than the one he had already told us.

Couldn't he tell us *why* he was there?

Perhaps he was after that tin of Ephraim's too! We could think so if we liked. It would be excusable of us to think so. There was a fortune in that tin, and everyone in the regiment knew it.

He was a friend of Ephraim's then? He knew Ephraim?

Yes, he could say that. He had known Ephraim for, let's see, nearly fifty years. Yes, he thought he could say he was Ephraim's friend.

In the aircraft Dr. Rosen sat reading, with nothing more to tell us.

But one day I'll meet a young man called Nikki, or Raffele; or a girl wearing a single pearl around her neck on a gold chain; or perhaps a middle-aged woman who says she thinks pearls are unlucky, she would never touch them herself: a man once gave her younger sister a pearl and it ruined her entire life. Something like that will happen, and this story will have a different shape.

ALISTAIR MacLEOD

THE BOAT

Alistair MacLeod (b. 1936) was born in North Battleford, Saskatchewan, to parents who had left Cape Breton during the Depression. After a decade in the Prairies, the MacLeods moved back to Nova Scotia. In 1956 MacLeod earned a teaching certificate, and in 1960 he received a B.A. from St. Francis Xavier University. MacLeod devoted most of the 1960s to his academic career, completing his doctoral studies at the University of Notre Dame, Indiana, and teaching English at both Canadian and U.S. universities. In 1969 he joined the department of English at the University of Windsor in Ontario, where he continues to teach and to edit fiction for the University of Windsor Review.

MacLeod is one of the most important figures in Maritime literature. His stories are collected in two volumes: The Lost Salt Gift of Blood *(1976) and* As Birds Bring Forth the Sun *(1986). "The Boat," taken from the former collection, earned a place in 1969's* The Best American Short Stories, *and is one of the three MacLeod stories that have been adapted to stage or screen. In a 1985 essay on MacLeod's short fiction in* Canadian Literature, *Colin Nicholson writes that "it is in the sculpting of the emotional infrastructure of any given situation that MacLeod's talent shines."*

There are times even now, when I awake at four o'clock in the morning with the terrible fear that I have overslept; when I imagine that my father is waiting for me in the room below the darkened stairs or that the shorebound men are tossing pebbles against my window while blowing their hands and stomping their feet impatiently on the frozen steadfast earth. There are times when I am half out of bed and fumbling for socks and mumbling for words before I realize that I am foolishly alone, that no one waits at the base of the stairs and no boat rides restlessly in the waters by the pier.

At such times only the grey corpses on the overflowing ashtray beside my bed bear witness to the extinction of the latest spark and silently await the crushing out of the most recent of their fellows. And then because I am afraid to be alone with death, I dress rapidly, make a great to-do about clearing my throat, turn on both faucets in the sink and proceed to make loud splashing ineffectual noises. Later I go out and walk the mile to the all-night restaurant.

In the winter it is a very cold walk and there are often tears in my eyes when I arrive. The waitress usually gives a sympathetic shiver and says, "Boy, it must be really cold out there; you got tears in your eyes."

"Yes," I say, "it sure is; it really is."

And then the three or four of us who are always in such places at such times make uninteresting little protective chit-chat until the dawn reluctantly arrives. Then I swallow the coffee which is always bitter and leave with a great busy rush because by that time I have to worry about being late and whether I have a clean shirt and whether my car will start and about all the other countless things one must worry about when he teaches at a great Midwestern university. And I know then that that day will go by as have all the days of the past ten years, for the call and the voices and the shapes and the boat were not really there in the early morning's darkness and I have all kinds of comforting reality to prove it. They are only shadows and echoes, the animals a child's hands make on the wall by lamplight, and the voices from the rain barrel; the cuttings from an old movie made in the black and white of long ago.

I first became conscious of the boat in the same way and at almost the same time that I became aware of the people it supported. My earliest recollection of my father is a view from the floor of gigantic rubber boots and then of being suddenly elevated and having my face pressed against the stubble of his cheek, and of how it tasted of salt and of how he smelled of salt from his red-soled rubber boots to the shaggy whiteness of his hair.

When I was very small, he took me for my first ride in the boat. I rode the half-mile from our house to the wharf on his shoulders and I remember the sound of his rubber boots galumphing along the gravel beach, the tune of the indecent little song he used to sing, and the odour of the salt.

The floor of the boat was permeated with the same odour and in its constancy I was not aware of change. In the harbour we made our little circle and returned. He tied the boat by its painter, fastened the stern to its permanent anchor and lifted me high over his head to the solidity of the wharf. Then he climbed up the little iron ladder that led to the wharf's cap, placed me once more upon his shoulders, and galumphed off again.

When we returned to the house everyone made a great fuss over my precocious excursion and asked, "How did you like the boat?" "Were you afraid in the boat?" "Did you cry in the boat?" They repeated "the boat" at the end of all their questions and I knew it must be very important to everyone.

My earliest recollection of my mother is of being alone with her in the mornings while my father was away in the boat. She seemed to be always repairing clothes that were "torn by the boat," preparing food "to be eaten in the boat" or looking for "the boat" through our kitchen window which faced upon the sea. When my father returned about noon, she would ask, "Well, how did things go in the boat today?" It was the first question I remember asking. "Well, how did things go in the boat today?" "Well, how did things go in the boat today?"

The boat in our lives was registered at Port Hawkesbury. She was what Nova Scotians called a Cape Island boat and was designed for the small inshore fishermen who sought the lobsters of the spring and the mackerel of the summer and later the cod and haddock and hake. She was thirty-two feet long and nine wide, and was powered by an engine from a Chevrolet truck. She had a marine clutch and a high-speed reverse gear and was painted light green with the name *Jenny Lynn* stencilled in black letters on her bow and painted on an oblong plate across her stern. Jenny Lynn had been my mother's maiden name and the boat was called after her as another link in the chain of tradition. Most of the boats that berthed at the wharf bore the names of some female member of their owner's household.

I say this now as if I knew it all then. All at once, all about boat dimensions and engines, and as if on the day of my first childish voyage I noticed the difference between a stencilled name and a painted name. But of course it was not that way at all, for I learned it all very slowly and there was not time enough.

I learned first about our house which was one of about fifty which marched around the horseshoe of our harbour and the wharf which was its heart. Some of them were so close to the water that during a storm the sea spray splashed against their windows while others were built farther along the beach as was the case with ours. The houses and their people, like those of the neighbouring towns and villages, were the result of Ireland's discontent and Scotland's Highland Clearances and America's War of Independence. Impulsive emotional Catholic Celts who could not bear to live with England and shrewd determined Protestant Puritans who, in the years after 1776, could not bear to live without.

The most important room in our house was one of those oblong old-fashioned kitchens heated by a wood- and coal-burning stove. Behind the stove was a box of kindlings and beside it a coal scuttle. A heavy wooden table with leaves that expanded or reduced its dimensions stood in the middle of the floor. There were five wooden homemade chairs which had been chipped and hacked by a variety of knives. Against the east wall, opposite the stove, there was a couch which sagged in the middle and had a cushion for a pillow, and above it a shelf which contained matches, tobacco, pencils, odd fish hooks, bits of twine, and a tin can filled with bills and receipts. The south wall was dominated by a window which faced the sea and on the north there was a five-foot board which bore a variety of clothes hooks and the burdens of each. Beneath the board there was a jumble of odd footwear, mostly of rubber. There was also, on this wall, a barometer, a map of the marine area, and a shelf which held a tiny radio. The kitchen was shared by all of us and was a buffer zone between the immaculate order of ten other rooms and the disruptive chaos of the single room that was my father's.

My mother ran her house as her brothers ran their boats. Everything was clean and spotless and in order. She was tall and dark and powerfully energetic. In later years she reminded me of the women of Thomas Hardy, particularly Eustacia Vye, in a physical way. She fed and clothed a family of seven children, making all of the meals and most of the clothes. She grew miraculous gardens and magnificent flowers and raised broods of hens and ducks. She would walk miles on berry-picking expeditions and hoist her skirts to dig for clams when the tide was low. She was fourteen years younger than my father, whom she had married when she was twenty-six, and had been a local beauty for a period of ten years. My mother was of the sea as were all of her people, and her horizons were the very literal one she scanned with her dark and fearless eyes.

Between the kitchen clothes rack and barometer a door opened into my father's bedroom. It was a room of disorder and disarray. It was as if the wind which so often clamoured about the house succeeded in entering this single room and after whipping it into turmoil stole quietly away to renew its knowing laughter from without.

My father's bed was against the south wall. It always looked rumpled and unmade because he lay on top of it more than he slept within any folds it might have had. Beside it, there was a little brown table. An archaic goose-necked reading light, a battered table radio, a mound of wooden matches, one or two packages of tobacco, a deck of cigarette papers, and an overflowing ashtray cluttered its surface. The brown larvae of tobacco shreds and the grey flecks of ash covered both the table and the floor beneath it. The once-varnished surface of the table was disfigured by numerous black scars and gashes inflicted by the neglected burning cigarettes of many years. They had tumbled from the ashtray unnoticed and branded their statements permanently and quietly into the wood until the odour of their burning caused the snuffing-out of their lives. At the bed's foot there was a single window which looked upon the sea.

Against the adjacent wall there was a battered bureau and beside it there was a closet which held his single ill-fitting serge suit, the two or three white shirts that strangled him and the square black shoes that pinched. When he took off his more friendly clothes, the heavy woollen sweaters, mitts, and socks which my mother knitted for him and the woollen and doeskin shirts, he dumped them unceremoniously on a single chair. If a visitor entered the room while he was lying on the bed, he would be told to throw the clothes on the floor and take their place upon the chair.

Magazines and books covered the bureau and competed with the clothes for domination of the chair. They further overburdened the heroic little table and lay on top of the radio. They filled a baffling and unknowable cave beneath the bed, and in the corner by the bureau they spilled from the walls and grew up from the floor.

The magazines were the most conventional: *Time, Newsweek, Life, Maclean's, The Family Herald, The Reader's Digest.* They were the result of various cut-rate subscriptions or of the gift subscriptions associated with Christmas, "the two whole years for only $3.50."

The books were more varied. There were a few hard-cover magnificents and bygone Book of the Month wonders and some were Christmas or birthday gifts. The majority of them, however, were used paperbacks which came from those second-hand bookstores which advertise in the backs of magazines: "Miscellaneous Used Paperbacks 10¢ Each." At first he sent for them himself, although my mother resented the expense, but in later years they came more and more often from my sisters who had moved to the cities. Especially at first they were very weird and varied. Mickey Spillane and Ernest Haycox vied with Dostoyevsky and Faulkner, and the Penguin Poets edition of Gerard Manley Hopkins arrived in the same box as a little book on sex technique called *Getting the Most Out of Love.* The former had been assiduously annotated by a very fine hand using a very blue-inked fountain pen, while the latter had been studied by someone with very large thumbs, the prints of which were still visible in the margins. At the slightest provocation it would open almost automatically to particularly graphic and well-smudged pages.

When he was not in the boat, my father spent most of his time lying on the bed in his socks, the top two buttons of his trousers undone, his discarded shirt on the everready chair and the sleeves of the woollen Stanfield underwear, which he wore both summer and winter, drawn halfway up to his elbows. The pillows propped up the whiteness of his head and the goose-necked lamp illuminated the pages in his hands. The cigarettes smoked and smouldered on the ashtray and on the table and the radio played constantly, sometimes low and sometimes loud. At midnight and at one, two, three and four, one could sometimes hear the radio, his occasional cough, the rustling thud of a completed book being tossed to the corner heap, or the movement necessitated by his sitting on the edge of the bed to roll the thousandth cigarette. He seemed never to sleep, only to doze, and the light shone constantly from his window to the sea.

My mother despised the room and all it stood for and she had stopped sleeping in it after I was born. She despised disorder in rooms and in houses and in hours and in lives, and she had not read a book since high school. There she had read *Ivanhoe* and considered it a colossal waste of time. Still the room remained, like a solid rock of opposition in the sparkling waters of a clear deep harbour, opening off the kitchen where we really lived our lives, with its door always open and its contents visible to all.

The daughters of the room and of the house were very beautiful. They were tall and willowy like my mother and had her fine facial features set off by the reddish copper-coloured hair that had apparently once been my father's before it turned to white. All of them were very clever in school and helped my mother a great deal about the house. When they were young they sang and were very happy and very nice to me because I was the youngest and the family's only boy.

My father never approved of their playing about the wharf like the other children, and they went there only when my mother sent them on an errand. At such times they almost always overstayed, playing screaming games of tag or hide-and-seek in and about the fishing shanties, the piled traps and tubs of trawl, shouting down to the perch that swam languidly about the wharf's algae-covered piles, or jumping in and out of the boats that tugged gently at their lines. My mother was never uneasy about them at such times, and when her husband criticized her she would say, "Nothing will happen to them there," or "They could be doing worse things in worse places."

By about the ninth or tenth grade my sisters one by one discovered my father's bedroom and then the change would begin. Each would go into the room one morning when he was out. She would go with the ideal hope of imposing order or with the more practical objective of emptying the ashtray, and later she would be found spellbound by the volume in her hand. My mother's reaction was always abrupt, bordering on the angry. "Take your nose out of that trash and come and do your work," she would say, and once I saw her slap my youngest sister so hard that the print of her hand was scarletly emblazoned upon her daughter's cheek while the broken-spined paperback fluttered uselessly to the floor.

Thereafter my mother would launch a campaign against what she had discovered but could not understand. At times, although she was not overly religious, she would bring God to bolster her arguments saying, "In the next world God will see to those who waste their lives reading useless books when they should be about their work." Or without theological aid, "I would like to know how books help anyone to live a life." If my father were in, she would repeat the remarks louder than necessary, and her voice would carry into his room where he lay upon his bed. His usual reaction was to turn up the volume of the radio, although that action in itself betrayed the success of the initial thrust.

Shortly after my sisters began to read the books, they grew restless and lost interest in darning socks and baking bread, and all of them eventually went to work as summer waitresses in the Sea Food Restaurant. The restaurant was run by a big American concern from Boston and catered to the tourists that flooded the area during July and August. My mother despised the whole operation. She said the restaurant was not run by "our people," and "our people" did not eat there, and that it was run by outsiders for outsiders.

"Who are these people anyway?" she would ask, tossing back her dark hair, "and what do they, though they go about with their cameras for a hundred years, know about the way it is here, and what do they care about me and mine, and why should I care about them?"

She was angry that my sisters should even conceive of working in such a place and more angry when my father made no move to prevent it, and she was worried about herself and about her family and about her life. Sometimes she would say softly to her sisters, "I don't know what's the matter with my girls. It seems none of them are interested in any of the right things." And sometimes there would be bitter savage arguments. One afternoon I was coming in with three mackerel I'd been given at the wharf when I heard her say, "Well I hope you'll be satisfied when they come home knocked up and you'll have had your way."

It was the most savage thing I'd ever heard my mother say. Not just the words but the way she said them, and I stood there in the porch afraid to breathe for what seemed like the years from ten to fifteen, feeling the damp moist mackerel with their silver glassy eyes growing clammy against my leg.

Through the angle in the screen door I saw my father, who had been walking into his room, wheel around on one of his rubber-booted heels and look at her with his blue eyes flashing like clearest ice beneath the snow that was his hair. His usually ruddy face was drawn and grey, reflecting the exhaustion of a man of sixty-five who had been working in those rubber boots for eleven hours on an August day, and for a fleeting moment I wondered what I would do if he killed my mother while I stood there in the porch with those three foolish mackerel in my hand. Then he turned and went into his room and the radio blared forth the next day's weather forecast and I retreated under the noise and returned again, stamping my feet and slamming the door too loudly to signal my approach. My mother was busy at the stove when I came in, and did not raise her head when I threw the mackerel in a pan. As I looked into my father's room, I said, "Well, how did things go in the boat today?" and he replied, "Oh, not too badly, all things considered." He was lying on his back and lighting the first cigarette and the radio was talking about the Virginia coast.

All of my sisters made good money on tips. They bought my father an electric razor which he tried to use for a while, and they took out even more magazine subscriptions. They bought my mother a great many clothes of the type she was very fond of, the wide-brimmed hats and the brocaded dresses, but she locked them all in trunks and refused to wear any of them.

On one August day my sisters prevailed upon my father to take some of their restaurant customers for an afternoon ride in the boat. The tourists with their expensive clothes and cameras and sun glasses awkwardly backed down the iron ladder at the wharf's side to where my father waited below, holding the rocking *Jenny Lynn* in snug against the wharf with one hand on the iron ladder and steadying his descending passengers with the other. They tried to look both prim and wind-blown like the girls in the Pepsi-Cola ads and did the best they could, sitting on the thwarts where the newspapers were spread to cover the splattered blood and fish entrails, crowding to one side so that they were in danger of capsizing the boat, taking the inevitable pictures or merely trailing their fingers through the water of their dreams.

All of them liked my father very much and, after he'd brought them back from their circles in the harbour, they invited him to their rented cabins which were located high on a hill overlooking the village to which they were so alien. He proceeded to get very drunk up there with the beautiful view and the strange company and the abundant liquor, and late in the afternoon he began to sing.

I was just approaching the wharf to deliver my mother's summons when he began, and the familiar yet unfamiliar voice that rolled down from the cabins made me feel as I never felt before in my young life or perhaps as I had always felt without really knowing it, and I was ashamed yet proud, young yet old and saved yet forever lost, and there was nothing I could do to control my legs which trembled nor my eyes which wept for what they could not tell.

The tourists were equipped with tape recorders and my father sang for more than three hours. His voice boomed down the hill and bounced off the surface of the harbour, which was an unearthly blue on that hot August day, and was then reflected to the wharf and the fishing shanties where it was absorbed amidst the men who were baiting their lines for the next day's haul.

He sang all the old sea chanties which had come across from the old world and by which men like him had pulled ropes for generations, and he sang the East Coast sea songs which celebrated the sealing vessels of Northumberland Strait and the long liners of the Grand Banks, and of Anticosti, Sable Island, Grand Manan, Boston Harbor, Nantucket, and Block Island. Gradually he shifted to the seemingly unending Gaelic drinking songs with their twenty or more verses and inevitable refrains, and the men in the shanties smiled at the coarseness of some of the verses and at the thought that the singer's immediate audience did not know what they were applauding nor recording to take back to staid old Boston. Later as the sun was setting he switched to the laments and the wild and haunting Gaelic war songs of those spattered Highland ancestors he had never seen, and when his voice ceased, the savage melancholy of three hundred years seemed to hang over the peaceful harbour and the quiet boats and the men leaning in the doorways of their shanties with their cigarettes glowing in the dusk and the women looking to the sea from their open windows with their children in their arms.

When he came home he threw the money he had earned on the kitchen table as he did with all his earnings but my mother refused to touch it and the next day he went with the rest of the men to bait his trawl in the shanties. The tourists came to the door that evening and my mother met them there and told them that her husband was not in although he was lying on the bed only a few feet away with the radio playing and the cigarette upon his lips. She stood in the doorway until they reluctantly went away.

In the winter they sent him a picture which had been taken on the day of the singing. On the back it said, "To Our Ernest Hemingway" and the "Our" was underlined. There was also an accompanying letter telling how much they had enjoyed themselves, how popular the tape was proving, and explaining who Ernest Hemingway was. In a way it almost did look like one of those unshaven, taken in Cuba pictures of Hemingway. He looked both massive and incongruous in the setting. His bulky fisherman's clothes were too big for the green and white lawn chair in which he sat, and his rubber boots seemed to take up all of the well-clipped grass square. The beach umbrella jarred with his sunburned face and because he had already been singing for some time, his lips which chapped in the winds of spring and burned in the water glare of summer had already cracked in several places producing tiny flecks of blood at their corners and on the whiteness of his teeth. The bracelets of brass chain which he wore to protect his wrists from chafing seemed abnormally large and his broad leather belt had been slackened and his heavy shirt and underwear were open at the throat revealing an uncultivated wilderness of white chest hair bordering on the semi-controlled stubble of his neck and chin. His blue eyes had looked directly into the camera and his hair was whiter than the two tiny clouds which hung over his left shoulder. The sea was behind him and its immense blue flatness stretched out to touch the arching blueness of the sky. It seemed very far away from him or else he was so much in the foreground that he seemed too big for it.

Each year another of my sisters would read the books and work in the restaurant. Sometimes they would stay out quite late on the hot summer nights and when they came up the stairs my mother would ask them many long and involved questions which they resented and tried to avoid. Before ascending the stairs they would go into my father's room and those of us who waited above could hear them throwing his clothes off the chair before sitting on it or the squeak of the bed as they sat on its edge. Sometimes they would talk to him a long time, the murmur of their voices blending with the music of the radio into a mysterious vapour-like sound which floated softly up the stairs.

I say this again as if it all happened at once and as if all of my sisters were of identical ages and like so many lemmings going into another sea and, again, it was of course not that way at all. Yet go they did, to Boston, to Montreal, to New York with the young men they met during the summers and later married in those far away cities. The young men were very articulate and handsome and wore fine clothes and drove expensive cars and my sisters, as I said, were very tall and beautiful with their copper-coloured hair and were tired of darning socks and baking bread.

One by one they went. My mother had each of her daughters for fifteen years, then lost them for two and finally forever. None married a fisherman. My mother never accepted any of the young men, for in her eyes they seemed always a combination of the lazy, the effeminate, the dishonest, and the unknown. They never seemed to do any physical work and she could not comprehend their luxurious vacations and she did not know from whence they came nor who they were. And in the end she did not really care, for they were not of her people and they were not of her sea.

I say this now with a sense of wonder at my own stupidity in thinking I was somehow free and would go on doing well in school and playing and helping in the boat and passing into my early teens while streaks of grey began to appear in my mother's dark hair and my father's rubber boots dragged sometimes on the pebbles of the beach as he trudged home from the wharf. And there were but three of us in the house that had at one time been so loud.

Then during the winter that I was fifteen he seemed to grow old and ill at once. Most of January he lay upon the bed, smoking and reading and listening to the radio while the wind howled about the house and the needlelike snow blistered off the ice-covered harbour and the doors flew out of people's hands if they did not cling to them like death.

In February when the men began overhauling their lobster traps he still did not move, and my mother and I began to knit lobster trap headings in the evenings. The twine was as always very sharp and harsh, and blisters formed upon our thumbs and little paths of blood snaked quietly down between our fingers while the seals that had drifted down from distant Labrador wept and moaned like human children on the ice floes of the Gulf.

In the daytime my mother's brother, who had been my father's partner as long as I could remember, also came to work upon the gear. He was a year older than my mother and was tall and dark and the father of twelve children.

By March we were very far behind and although I began to work very hard in the evenings I knew it was not hard enough and that there were but eight weeks left before the opening of the season on May first. And I knew that my mother worried and my uncle was uneasy and that all of our very lives depended on the boat being ready with her gear and two men, by the date of May the first. And I knew then that *David Copperfield* and *The Tempest* and all of those friends I had dearly come to love must really go forever. So I bade them all good-bye.

The night after my first full day at home and after my mother had gone upstairs he called me into his room where I sat upon the chair beside his bed. "You will go back tomorrow," he said simply.

I refused then, saying I had made my decision and was satisfied.

"That is no way to make a decision," he said, "and if you are satisfied I am not. It is best that you go back." I was almost angry then and told him as all children do that I wished he would leave me alone and stop telling me what to do.

He looked at me a long time then, lying there on the same bed on which he had fathered me those sixteen years before, fathered me his only son, out of who knew what emotions, when he was already fifty-six and his hair had turned to snow. Then he swung his legs over the edge of the squeaking bed and sat facing me and looked into my own dark eyes with his of crystal blue and placed his hand upon my knee. "I am not telling you to do anything," he said softly, "only asking you."

The next morning I returned to school. As I left, my mother followed me to the porch and said, "I never thought a son of mine would choose useless books over the parents that gave him life."

In the weeks that followed he got up rather miraculously and the gear was ready and the *Jenny Lynn* was freshly painted by the last two weeks of April when the ice began to break up and the lonely screaming gulls returned to haunt the silver herring as they flashed within the sea.

On the first day of May the boats raced out as they had always done, laden down almost to the gunwales with their heavy cargoes of traps. They were almost like living things as they plunged through the waters of the spring and manoeuvred between the still floating icebergs of crystal-white and emerald green on their way to the traditional grounds that they sought out every May. And those of us who sat that day in the High School on the hill, discussing the water imagery of Tennyson, watched them as they passed back and forth beneath us until by afternoon the piles of traps which had been stacked upon the wharf were no longer visible but were spread about the bottoms of the sea. And the *Jenny Lynn* went too, all day, with my uncle, tall and dark, like a latter-day Tashtego standing at the tiller with his legs wide apart and guiding her deftly between the floating pans of ice and my father in the stern standing in the same way with his hand upon the ropes that lashed the cargo to the deck. And at night my mother asked, "Well, how did things go in the boat today?"

And the spring wore on and the summer came and school ended in the third week of June and the lobster season on July first and I wished that the two things I loved so dearly did not exclude each other in a manner that was so blunt and too clear.

At the conclusion of the lobster season my uncle said he had been offered a berth on a deep sea dragger and had decided to accept. We all knew that he was leaving the *Jenny Lynn* forever and that before the next lobster season he would buy a boat of his own. He was expecting another child and would be supporting fifteen people by the next spring and could not chance my father against the family that he loved.

I joined my father then for the trawling season, and he made no protest and my mother was quite happy. Through the summer we baited the tubs of trawl in the afternoon and set them at sunset and revisited them in the darkness of the early morning. The men would come tramping by our house at 4:00 a.m. and we would join them and walk with them to the wharf and be on our way before the sun rose out of the ocean where it seemed to spend the night. If I was not up they would toss pebbles to my window and I would be very embarrassed and tumble downstairs to where my father lay fully clothed atop his bed, reading his book and listening to his radio and smoking his cigarette. When I appeared he would swing off his bed and put on his boots and be instantly ready and then we would take the lunches my mother had prepared the night before and walk off towards the sea. He would make no attempt to wake me himself.

It was in many ways a good summer. There were few storms and we were out almost every day and we lost a minimum of gear and seemed to land a maximum of fish and I tanned dark and brown after the manner of my uncles.

My father did not tan—he never tanned—because of his reddish complexion, and the salt water irritated his skin as it had for sixty years. He burned and reburned over and over again and his lips still cracked so that they bled when he smiled, and his arms, especially the left, still broke out into the oozing salt-water boils as they had ever since as a child I had first watched him soaking and bathing them in a variety of ineffectual solutions. The chafe-preventing bracelets of brass linked chain that all the men wore about their wrists in early spring were his the full season, and he shaved but painfully and only once a week.

And I saw then, that summer, many things that I had seen all my life as if for the first time and I thought that perhaps my father had never been intended for a fisherman either physically or mentally. At least not in the manner of my uncles; he had never really loved it. And I remembered that, one evening in his room when we were talking about *David Copperfield*, he had said that he had always wanted to go to the university and I had dismissed it then in the way one dismisses his father's saying he would like to be a tight-rope walker, and we had gone on to talk about the Peggotys and how they loved the sea.

And I thought then to myself that there were many things wrong with all of us and all our lives and I wondered why my father, who was himself an only son, had not married before he was forty and then I wondered why he had. I even thought that perhaps he had had to marry my mother and checked the dates on the flyleaf of the Bible where I learned that my oldest sister had been born a prosaic eleven months after the marriage, and I felt myself then very dirty and debased for my lack of faith and for what I had thought and done.

And then there came into my heart a very great love for my father and I thought it was very much braver to spend a life doing what you really do not want rather than selfishly following forever your own dreams and inclinations. And I knew then that I could never leave him alone to suffer the iron-tipped harpoons which my mother would forever hurl into his soul because he was a failure as a husband and a father who had retained none of his own. And I felt that I had been very small in a little secret place within me and that even the completion of high school was for me a silly shallow selfish dream.

So I told him one night very resolutely and very powerfully that I would remain with him as long as he lived and we would fish the sea together. And he made no protest but only smiled through the cigarette smoke that wreathed his bed and replied, "I hope you will remember what you've said."

The room was now so filled with books as to be almost Dickensian, but he would not allow my mother to move or change them and he continued to read them, sometimes two or three a night. They came with great regularity now, and there were more hard covers, sent by my sisters who had gone so long ago and now seemed so distant and so prosperous, and sent also pictures of small red-haired grandchildren with baseball bats and dolls which he placed upon his bureau and which my mother gazed at wistfully when she thought no one would see. Red-haired grandchildren with baseball bats and dolls who would never know the sea in hatred or in love.

And so we fished through the heat of August and into the cooler days of September when the water was so clear we could almost see the bottom and the white mists rose like delicate ghosts in the early morning dawn. And one day my mother said to me, "You have given added years to his life."

And we fished on into October when it began to roughen and we could no longer risk night sets but took our gear out each morning and returned at the first sign of the squalls; and on into November when we lost three tubs of trawl and the clear blue water turned to a sullen grey and the trochoidal waves rolled rough and high and washed across our bows and decks as we ran within their troughs. We wore heavy sweaters now and the awkward rubber slickers and the heavy woollen mitts which soaked and froze into masses of ice that hung from our wrists like the limbs of gigantic monsters until we thawed them against the exhaust pipe's heat. And almost every day we would leave for home before noon, driven by the blasts of the northwest wind, coating our eyebrows with ice and freezing our eyelids closed as we leaned into a visibility that was hardly there, charting our course from the compass and the sea, running with the waves and between them but never confronting their towering might.

And I stood at the tiller now, on these homeward lunges, stood in the place and in the manner of my uncle, turning to look at my father, and to shout over the roar of the engine and the slop of the sea to where he stood in the stern, drenched and dripping with the snow and the salt and the spray and his bushy eyebrows caked in ice. But on November twenty-first, when it seemed we might be making the final run of the season, I turned and he was not there and I knew even in that instant that he would never be again.

On November twenty-first the waves of the grey Atlantic are very very high and the waters are very cold and there are no signposts on the surface of the sea. You cannot tell where you have been five minutes before and in the squalls of snow you cannot see. And it takes longer than you would believe to check a boat that has been running before a gale and turn her ever so carefully in a wide and stupid circle, with timbers creaking and straining, back into the face of the storm. And you know that it is useless and that your voice does not carry the length of the boat and that even if you knew the original spot, the relentless waves would carry such a burden perhaps a mile or so by the time you could return. And you know also, the final irony, that your father, like your uncles and all the men that form your past, cannot swim a stroke.

The lobster beds off the Cape Breton coast are still very rich and now, from May to July, their offerings are packed in crates of ice, and thundered by the gigantic transport trucks, day and night, through New Glasgow, Amherst, Saint John and Bangor and Portland and into Boston where they are tossed still living into boiling pots of water, their final home.

And though the prices are higher and the competition tighter, the grounds to which the *Jenny Lynn* once went remain untouched and unfished as they have for the last ten years. For if there are no signposts on the sea in storm there are certain ones in calm and the lobster bottoms were distributed in calm before any of us can remember and the grounds my father fished were those his father fished before him and there were others before and before and before. Twice the big boats have come from forty and fifty miles, lured by the promise of the grounds, and strewn the bottom with their traps, and twice they have returned to find their buoys cut adrift and their gear lost and destroyed. Twice the Fisheries Office and the Mounted Police have come and asked many long and involved questions and twice they have received no answers from the men leaning in the doors of their shanties and the women standing at their windows with their children in their arms. Twice they have gone away saying: "There are no legal boundaries in the Marine area"; "No one can own the sea"; "Those grounds don't wait for anyone."

But the men and the women, with my mother dark among them, do not care for what they say, for to them the grounds are sacred and they think they wait for me.

It is not an easy thing to know that your mother lives alone on an inadequate insurance policy and that she is too proud to accept any other aid. And that she looks through her lonely window onto the ice of winter and the hot flat calm of summer and the rolling waves of fall. And that she lies awake in the early morning's darkness when the rubber boots of the men scrunch upon the gravel as they pass beside her house on their way down to the wharf. And she knows that the footsteps never stop, because no man goes from her house, and she alone of all the Lynns has neither son nor son-in-law that walks toward the boat that will take him to the sea. And it is not an easy thing to know that your mother looks upon the sea with love and on you with bitterness because the one has been so constant and the other so untrue.

But neither is it easy to know that your father was found on November twenty-eighth, ten miles to the north and wedged between two boulders at the base of the rock-strewn cliffs where he had been hurled and slammed so many many times. His hands were shredded ribbons as were his feet which had lost their boots to the suction of the sea, and his shoulders came apart in our hands when we tried to move him from the rocks. And the fish had eaten his testicles and the gulls had pecked out his eyes and the white-green stubble of his whiskers had continued to grow in death, like the grass on graves, upon the purple, bloated mass that was his face. There was not much left of my father, physically, as he lay there with the brass chains on his wrists and the seaweed in his hair.

KATHERINE MANSFIELD

THE FLY

Katherine Mansfield (1888–1923) was born in Wellington, New Zealand, the "third, difficult, least loved daughter" of a wealthy banker. From an early age she was rebellious and inquisitive, and she demanded much more from life than was thought appropriate for a proper young Victorian lady. She lived on a daring level of "extravagant lies" and intense passion, and she died early and tragically. Her life is the stuff of literary legend. By the time she was twenty-one, she had fallen in love with at least one woman, become pregnant, had an abortion, and married a much older man, only to leave him on their wedding night. Her friends were the giants of modernist literature, as were her enemies. She exists now in faded photographs and in the biographies, critical essays, letters, diaries, fiction, and drama of others. She was this century's "New Woman," and along with Joyce, Lawrence, and Conrad, she transformed the modern English-language short story.

In 1903 Mansfield travelled to London from New Zealand to study music. She returned home in 1906, but London "was set like a stage for a young woman of independent mind and talent," and in 1908 she persuaded her father to let her return, with an allowance. She gave up music in favour of writing, and her first book of short stories, In a German Pension, *was published in 1911. In the same year, she met John Middleton Murray, the celebrated literary figure with whom she would live for years. He eventually became her husband and, after her death from tuberculosis at the age of thirty-four, her literary executor. With the publication of* Bliss and Other Stories, *in 1920, Mansfield's reputation as an important writer was established;* The Garden-Party, *published two years later, confirmed it.*

A great stylist, Mansfield developed a narrative technique that made psychological drama from the most casual of incidents. Willa Cather wrote: "Katherine Mansfield's peculiar gift lay in her interpretation of [the] secret accords and antipathies which lie hidden under our everyday behaviour, and which more than any outward events make our lives happy or unhappy." On the surface, "The Fly" is about a boss who shuts himself up in his office to mourn the wartime death of his only son, lording it over a former employee who pays him a visit and systematically tormenting a fly who has had the misfortune to appear at his desk. This juxtaposition of apparently unrelated incidents takes on a different cast when considered against "the interplay between the conscious and the unconscious mind." "The Fly" is particularly interesting in the way it explores the Freudian idea of the unconscious as a layer of the mind in which feelings we cannot acknowledge often lurk. Mansfield's stories more typically focus on female experience.

––––––––––––––

"Y'are very snug in here," piped old Mr. Woodifield, and he peered out of the great, green leather armchair by his friend the boss's desk as a baby peers out of its pram. His talk was over; it was time for him to be off. But he did not want to go. Since he had retired, since his ... stroke, the wife and the girls kept him boxed up in the house every day of the week except Tuesday. On Tuesday he was dressed up and brushed and allowed to cut back to the City for the day. Though what he did there the wife and girls couldn't imagine. Made a nuisance of himself to his friends, they supposed.... Well, perhaps so. All the same, we cling to our last pleasures as the tree clings to its last leaves. So there sat old Woodifield, smoking a cigar and staring almost greedily at the boss, who rolled in his office chair, stout, rosy, five years older than he, and still going strong, still at the helm. It did one good to see him.

Wistfully, admiringly, the old voice added, "It's snug in here, upon my word!"

"Yes, it's comfortable enough," agreed the boss, and he flipped the *Financial Times* with a paper-knife. As a matter of fact he was proud of his room; he liked to have it admired, especially by old Woodifield. It gave him a feeling of deep, solid satisfaction to be planted there in the midst of it in full view of that frail old figure in the muffler.

"I've had it done up lately," he explained, as he had explained for the past—how many?—weeks. "New carpet," and he pointed to the bright red carpet with a pattern of large white rings. "New furniture," and he nodded towards the massive bookcase and the table with legs like twisted treacle. "Electric heating!" He waved almost exultantly towards the five transparent, pearly sausages glowing so softly in the tilted copper pan.

But he did not draw old Woodifield's attention to the photograph over the table of a grave-looking boy in uniform standing in one of those spectral photographers' parks with photographers' storm-clouds behind him. It was not new. It had been there for over six years.

"There was something I wanted to tell you," said old Woodifield, and his eyes grew dim remembering. "Now what was it? I had it in my mind when I started out this morning." His hands began to tremble, and patches of red showed above his beard.

Poor old chap, he's on his last pins, thought the boss. And, feeling kindly, he winked at the old man, and said jokingly, "I tell you what. I've got a little drop of something here that'll do you good before you go out into the cold again. It's beautiful stuff. It wouldn't hurt a child." He took a key off his watch-chain, unlocked a cupboard below his desk, and drew forth a dark, squat bottle. "That's the medicine," said he. "And the man from whom I got it told me on the strict Q.T. it came from the cellars of Windsor Cassel."

Old Woodifield's mouth fell open at the sight. He couldn't have looked more surprised if the boss had produced a rabbit.

"It's whisky, ain't it?" he piped, feebly.

The boss turned the bottle and lovingly showed him the label. Whisky it was.

"D'you know," said he, peering up at the boss wonderingly, "they won't let me touch it at home." And he looked as though he was going to cry.

"Ah, that's where we know a bit more than the ladies," cried the boss, swooping across for two tumblers that stood on the table with the water-bottle, and pouring a generous finger into each. "Drink it down. It'll do you good. And don't put any water with it. It's sacrilege to tamper with stuff like this. Ah!" He tossed off his, pulled out his handkerchief, hastily wiped his moustaches, and cocked an eye at old Woodifield, who was rolling his in his chaps.

The old man swallowed, was silent a moment, and then said faintly, "It's nutty!"

But it warmed him; it crept into his chill old brain—he remembered.

"That was it," he said, heaving himself out of his chair. "I thought you'd like to know. The girls were in Belgium last week having a look at poor Reggie's grave, and they happened to come across your boy's. They're quite near each other, it seems."

Old Woodifield paused, but the boss made no reply. Only a quiver in his eyelids showed that he heard.

"The girls were delighted with the way the place is kept," piped the old voice. "Beautifully looked after. Couldn't be better if they were at home. You've not been across, have yer?"

"No, no!" For various reasons the boss had not been across.

"There's miles of it," quavered old Woodifield, "and it's all as neat as a garden. Flowers growing on all the graves. Nice broad paths." It was plain from his voice how much he liked a nice broad path.

The pause came again. Then the old man brightened wonderfully.

"D'you know what the hotel made the girls pay for a pot of jam?" he piped. "Ten francs! Robbery, I call it. It was a little pot, so Gertrude says, no bigger than a half-crown. And she hadn't taken more than a spoonful when they charged her ten francs. Gertrude brought the pot away with her to teach 'em a lesson. Quite right, too; it's trading on our feelings. They think because we're over there having a look around we're ready to pay anything. That's what it is." And he turned towards the door.

"Quite right, quite right!" cried the boss, though what was quite right he hadn't the least idea. He came round by his desk, followed the shuffling foot-steps to the door, and saw the old fellow out. Woodifield was gone.

For a long moment the boss stayed, staring at nothing, while the grey-haired office messenger, watching him, dodged in and out of his cubby-hole like a dog that expects to be taken for a run. Then: "I'll see nobody for half an hour, Macey," said the boss. "Understand? Nobody at all."

"Very good, sir."

The door shut, the firm heavy steps recrossed the bright carpet, the fat body plumped down in the spring chair, and leaning forward, the boss covered his face with his hands. He wanted, he intended, he had arranged to weep....

It had been a terrible shock to him when old Woodifield sprang that remark upon him about the boy's grave. It was exactly as though the earth had opened and he had seen the boy lying there with Woodifield's girls staring down at him. For it was strange. Although over six years had passed away, the boss never thought of the boy except as lying unchanged, unblemished in his uniform, asleep for ever. "My son!" groaned the boss. But no tears came yet. In the past, in the first months and even years after the boy's death, he had only to say those words to be overcome by such grief that nothing short of a violent fit of weeping could relieve him. Time, he had declared then, he had told every-body, could make no difference. Other men perhaps might recover, might live their loss down, but not he. How was it possible? His boy was an only son. Ever since his birth the boss had worked at building up this business for him; it had no other meaning if it was not for the boy. Life itself had come to have no other meaning. How on earth could he have slaved, denied himself, kept going all those years without the promise for ever before him of the boy's stepping into his shoes and carrying on where he left off?

And that promise had been so near being fulfilled. The boy had been in the office learning the ropes for a year before the war. Every morning they had started off together; they had come back by the same train. And what congrat-ulations he had received as the boy's father! No wonder; he had taken to it marvelously. As to his popularity with the staff, every man jack of them down to old Macey couldn't make enough of the boy. And he wasn't in the least spoilt. No, he was just his bright, natural self, with the right word for every-body, with that boyish look and his habit of saying, "Simply splendid!"

But all that was over and done with as though it never had been. The day had come when Macey had handed him the telegram that brought the whole place crashing about his head. "Deeply regret to inform you ..." And he had left the office a broken man, with his life in ruins.

Six years ago, six years ... How quickly time passed! It might have happened yesterday. The boss took his hands from his face; he was puzzled. Something seemed to be wrong with him. He wasn't feeling as he wanted to feel. He decided to get up and have a look at the boy's photograph. But it wasn't a favorite photograph of his; the expression was unnatural. It was cold, even stern-looking. The boy had never looked like that.

At that moment the boss noticed that a fly had fallen into his broad inkpot, and was trying feebly but desperately to clamber out again. Help! help! said those struggling legs. But the sides of the inkpot were wet and slippery; it fell back again and began to swim. The boss took up a pen, picked the fly out of the ink, and shook it on to a piece of blotting-paper. For a fraction of a second it lay still on the dark patch that oozed round it. Then the front legs waved, took hold, and, pulling its small sodden body up it began the immense task of cleaning the ink from its wings. Over and under, over and under, went a leg along a wing, as the stone goes over and under the scythe. Then there was a pause, while the fly, seeming to stand on the tips of its toes, tried to expand first one wing and then the other. It succeeded at last, and, sitting down, it began, like a minute cat, to clean its face. Now one could imagine that the little front legs rubbed against each other lightly, joyfully. The horrible danger was over; it had escaped; it was ready for life again.

But just then the boss had an idea. He plunged his pen back into the ink, leaned his thick wrist on the blotting paper, and as the fly tried its wings down came a great heavy blot. What would it make of that? What indeed! The little beggar seemed absolutely cowed, stunned, and afraid to move because of what would happen next. But then, as if painfully, it dragged itself forward. The front legs waved, caught hold, and, more slowly this time, the task began from the beginning.

He's a plucky little devil, thought the boss, and he felt a real admiration for the fly's courage. That was the way to tackle things; that was the right spirit. Never say die; it was only a question of ... But the fly had again finished its laborious task, and the boss had just time to refill his pen, to shake fair and square on the new-cleaned body yet another dark drop. What about it this time? A painful moment of suspense followed. But behold, the front legs were again waving; the boss felt a rush of relief. He leaned over the fly and said to it tenderly, "You artful little b ..." And he actually had the brilliant notion of breathing on it to help the drying process. All the same, there was something timid and weak about its efforts now, and the boss decided that this time should be the last, as he dipped the pen into the inkpot.

It was. The last blot on the soaked blotting-paper, and the draggled fly lay in it and did not stir. The back legs were stuck to the body; the front legs were not to be seen.

"Come on," said the boss. "Look sharp!" And he stirred it with his pen—in vain. Nothing happened or was likely to happen. The fly was dead.

The boss lifted the corpse on the end of the paper-knife and flung it into the waste-paper basket. But such a grinding feeling of wretchedness seized him that he felt positively frightened. He started forward and pressed the bell for Macey.

"Bring me some fresh blotting-paper," he said, sternly, "and look sharp about it." And while the old dog padded away he fell to wondering what it was he had been thinking about before. What was it? It was ... He took out his handkerchief and passed it inside his collar. For the life of him he could not remember.

HERMAN MELVILLE

Bartleby, The Scrivener: A Story of Wall-Street

Herman Melville (1819–1891) was born in New York City. He attended the New York Male High School until his father's importing business failed, forcing the poverty-stricken family to move upstate to Albany. His father died in 1832, and Melville worked at a variety of clerical, manual, and teaching jobs before joining the crew of the St. Lawrence *for the summer of 1839. Two years later he joined the crew of the Pacific-bound whaler* Acushnet. *Eighteen months in the whaling industry under a tyrannical captain provoked Melville to desert the ship in French Polynesia, where began a series of adventures in the South Seas which eventually led him to join the U.S. Navy in 1843. Discharged in Boston a year later, Melville was inspired to write of his voyages. His first books,* Typee *(1846) and its sequel* Omoo *(1847), proved so popular that Melville determined to make a career in writing. The ambitious* Moby-Dick *(1851) marked the apex of Melville's novel-writing career and consolidated his reputation as a giant of nineteenth-century literature, but unfortunately his next novel,* Pierre *(1852), was a critical failure, prompting his switch to short-story writing. The* Piazza Tales *(1856), a collection of stories and sketches that had appeared in* Harper's *and other magazines, contained "Bartleby, the Scrivener" and represented an important step toward realism for the short story. Like Gogol's "The Overcoat," "Bartleby" signals a democratizing shift of literary attention to "the little man." Melville's later writings failed to reclaim his previous popularity, and he moved from the Berkshires farm where he had spent the greater part of his writing career to settle permanently in New York City. From 1866 to 1885 he worked as a customs inspector, and he continued to write poetry and the posthumously published novella,* Billy Budd, *until his death.*

I am a rather elderly man. The nature of my avocations, for the last thirty years, has brought me into more than ordinary contact with what would seem an interesting and somewhat singular set of men, of whom, as yet, nothing, that I know of, has ever been written—I mean, the law-copyists, or scriveners. I have known very many of them professionally and privately, and, if I pleased, could relate divers histories, at which good-natured gentlemen might smile, and sentimental souls might weep. But I waive the biographies of all other scriveners, for a few passages in the life of Bartleby, who was a scrivener, the strangest I ever saw, or heard of. While, of other law-copyists, I might write the complete life, of Bartleby nothing of that sort can be done. I believe that no materials exist, for a full and satisfactory biography of this man. It is an irreparable loss to literature. Bartleby was one of those beings of whom nothing is ascertainable, except from the original sources, and, in his case, those are very small. What my own astonished eyes saw of Bartleby, that is all I know of him, except, indeed, one vague report, which will appear in the sequel.

Ere introducing the scrivener, as he first appeared to me, it is fit I make some mention of myself, my *employés,* my business, my chambers, and general surroundings; because some such description is indispensable to an adequate understanding of the chief character about to be presented. Imprimis: I am a man who, from his youth upwards, has been filled with a profound conviction that the easiest way of life is the best. Hence, though I belong to a profession proverbially energetic and nervous, even to turbulence, at times, yet nothing of that sort have I ever suffered to invade my peace. I am one of those unambitious lawyers who never address a jury, or in any way draw down public applause; but, in the cool tranquillity of a snug retreat, do a snug business among rich men's bonds, and mortgages, and title-deeds. All who know me, consider me an eminently *safe* man. The late John Jacob Astor, a personage little given to poetic enthusiasm, had no hesitation in pronouncing my first grand point to be prudence; my next, method. I do not speak it in vanity, but simply record the fact, that I was not unemployed in my profession by the late John Jacob Astor; a name which, I admit, I love to repeat; for it hath a rounded and orbicular sound to it, and rings like unto bullion. I will freely add, that I was not insensible to the late John Jacob Astor's good opinion.

Some time prior to the period at which this little history begins, my avocations had been largely increased. The good old office, now extinct in the State of New York, of a Master in Chancery, had been conferred upon me. It was not a very arduous office, but very pleasantly remunerative. I seldom lose my temper; much more seldom indulge in dangerous indignation at wrongs and outrages; but I must be permitted to be rash here and declare, that I consider the sudden and violent abrogation of the office of Master in Chancery, by the new Constitution, as a—premature act; inasmuch as I had counted upon a life-lease of the profits, whereas I only received those of a few short years. But this is by the way.

My chambers were up stairs, at No.— Wall Street. At one end, they looked upon the white wall of the interior of a spacious skylight shaft, penetrating the building from top to bottom.

This view might have been considered rather tame than otherwise, deficient in what landscape painters call "life." But, if so, the view from the other end of my chambers offered, at least, a contrast, if nothing more. In that direction, my windows commanded an unobstructed view of a lofty brick wall, black by age and everlasting shade; which wall required no spy-glass to bring out its lurking beauties, but, for the benefit of all near-sighted spectators, was pushed up to within ten feet of my window-panes. Owing to the great height of the surrounding buildings, and my chambers being on the second floor, the interval between this wall and mine not a little resembled a huge square cistern.

At the period just preceding the advent of Bartleby, I had two persons as copyists in my employment, and a promising lad as an office-boy. First, Turkey; second, Nippers; third, Ginger Nut. These may seem names, the like of which are not usually found in the Directory. In truth, they were nicknames, mutually conferred upon each other by my three clerks, and were deemed expressive of their respective persons or characters. Turkey was a short, pursy Englishman, of about my own age—that is, somewhere not far from sixty. In the morning, one might say, his face was of a fine florid hue, but after twelve o'clock, meridian—his dinner hour—it blazed like a grate full of Christmas coals; and continued blazing—but, as it were, with a gradual wane—till six o'clock, P.M., or there-abouts; after which, I saw no more of the proprietor of the face, which, gaining its meridian with the sun, seemed to set with it, to rise, culminate, and decline the following day, with the like regularity and undiminished glory. There are many singular coincidences I have known in the course of my life, not the least among which was the fact, that, exactly when Turkey displayed his fullest beams from his red and radiant countenance, just then, too, at that critical moment, began the daily period when I considered his business capacities as seriously disturbed for the remainder of the twenty-four hours. Not that he was absolutely idle, or averse to business then; far from it. The difficulty was, he was apt to be altogether too energetic. There was a strange, inflamed, flurried, flighty recklessness of activity about him. He would be incautious in dipping his pen into his inkstand. All his blots upon my documents were dropped there after twelve o'clock, meridian. Indeed, not only would he be reckless, and sadly given to making blots in the afternoon, but, some days, he went further, and was rather noisy. At such times, too, his face flamed with augmented blazonry, as if cannel coal had been heaped on anthracite. He made an unpleasant racket with his chair; spilled his sand-box; in mending his pens, impatiently split them all to pieces, and threw them on the floor in a sudden passion; stood up, and leaned over his table, boxing his papers about in a most indecorous manner, very sad to behold in an elderly man like him. Nevertheless, as he was in many ways a most valuable person to me, and all the time before twelve o'clock, meridian, was the quickest, steadiest creature, too, accomplishing a great deal of work in a style not easily to be matched—for these reasons, I was willing to overlook his eccentricities, though, indeed, occasionally, I remonstrated with him. I did this very gently, however, because, though the civilest, nay, the blandest and most reverential of men in the morning, yet, in the afternoon, he was disposed, upon provocation, to be slightly rash with his tongue—in fact, insolent. Now, valuing his morning services as I did, and resolved not to lose them—yet, at the same time, made uncomfortable by his inflamed ways after twelve o'clock—and being a man of peace, unwilling by my admonitions to call forth unseemly retorts from him, I took upon me, one Saturday noon (he was always worse on Saturdays) to hint to him, very kindly, that, perhaps, now that he was growing old, it might be well to abridge his labours; in short, he need not come to my chambers after twelve o'clock, but, dinner over, had best go home to his lodgings, and rest himself till tea-time. But no; he insisted upon his afternoon devotions. His countenance became intolerably fervid, as he oratorically assured me—gesticulating with a long ruler at the other end of the room—that if his services in the morning were useful, how indispensable, then, in the afternoon?

"With submission, sir," said Turkey, on this occasion, "I consider myself your right-hand man. In the morning I but marshal and deploy my columns; but in the afternoon I put myself at their head, and gallantly charge the foe, thus"—and he made a violent thrust with the ruler.

"But the blots, Turkey," intimated I.

"True; but, with submission, sir, behold these hairs! I am getting old. Surely, sir, a blot or two of a warm afternoon is not to be severely urged against grey hairs. Old age—even if it blot the page—is honourable. With submission, sir, we *both* are getting old."

This appeal to my fellow-feeling was hardly to be resisted. At all events, I saw that go he would not. So, I made up my mind to let him stay, resolving, nevertheless, to see to it that, during the afternoon, he had to do with my less important papers.

Nippers, the second on my list, was a whiskered, sallow, and, upon the whole, rather piratical-looking young man, of about five-and-twenty. I always deemed him the victim of two evil powers—ambition and indigestion. The ambition was evinced by a certain impatience of the duties of a mere copyist, an unwarrantable usurpation of strictly professional affairs, such as the original drawing up of legal documents. The indigestion seemed betokened in an occasional nervous testiness and grinning irritability, causing the teeth to audibly grind together over mistakes committed in copying; unnecessary male-dictions, hissed, rather than spoken, in the heat of business; and especially by a continual discontent with the height of the table where he worked. Though of a very ingenious mechanical turn, Nippers could never get this table to suit him. He put chips under it, blocks of various sorts, bits of pasteboard, and at last went so far as to attempt an exquisite adjustment, by final pieces of folded blotting paper. But no invention would answer. If, for the sake of easing his back, he brought the table-lid at a sharp angle well up towards his chin, and wrote there like a man using the steep roof of a Dutch house for his desk, then he declared that it stopped the circulation in his arms. If now he lowered the table to his waistbands, and stooped over it in writing, then there was a sore aching in his back. In short, the truth of the matter was, Nippers knew not what he wanted. Or, if he wanted anything, it was to be rid of a scrivener's table altogether. Among the manifestations of his diseased ambition was a fondness he had for receiving visits from certain ambiguous-looking fellows in seedy coats, whom he called his clients. Indeed, I was aware that not only was he, at times, considerable of a ward-politician, but he occasionally did a little business at the Justices' courts, and was not unknown on the steps of the Tombs. I have good reason to believe, however, that one individual who called upon him at my chambers, and who, with a grand air, he insisted was his client, was no other than a dun, and the alleged title-deed, a bill. But, with all his failings, and the annoyances he caused me, Nippers, like his compatriot Turkey, was a very useful man to me; wrote a neat, swift hand; and, when he chose, was not deficient in a gentlemanly sort of deportment. Added to this, he always dressed in a gentlemanly sort of way; and so, incidentally, reflected credit upon my chambers. Whereas, with respect to Turkey, I had much ado to keep him from being a reproach to me. His clothes were apt to look oily, and smell of eating house. He wore his pantaloons very loose and baggy in summer. His coats were execrable; his hat not to be handled. But while the hat was a thing of indifference to me, inasmuch as his natural civility and deference, as a dependent Englishman, always led him to doff it the moment he entered the room, yet his coat was another matter. Concerning his coats, I reasoned with him; but with no effect. The truth was, I suppose, that a man with so small an income could not afford to sport such a lustrous face and a lustrous coat at one and the same time. As Nippers once observed, Turkey's money went chiefly for red ink. One winter day, I presented Turkey with a highly respectable looking coat of my own—a padded grey coat, of a most comfortable warmth, and which buttoned straight up from the knee to the neck. I thought Turkey would appreciate the favour, and abate his rashness and obstreperousness of after-noons. But no; I verily believe that buttoning himself up in so downy and blanket-like a coat had a pernicious effect upon him—upon the same principle that too much oats are bad for horses. In fact, precisely as a rash, restive horse is said to feel his oats, so Turkey felt his coat. It made him insolent. He was a man whom prosperity harmed.

Though, concerning the self-indulgent habits of Turkey, I had my own private surmises, yet, touching Nippers, I was well persuaded that, whatever might be his faults in other respects, he was, at least, a temperate young man. But, indeed, nature herself seemed to have been his vintner, and, at his birth, charged him so thoroughly with an irritable, brandy-like disposition, that all subsequent potations were needless. When I consider how, amid the stillness of my chambers, Nippers would sometimes impatiently rise from his seat, and stopping over his table, spread his arms wide apart, seize the whole desk, and move it, and jerk it, with a grim, grinding motion on the floor, as if the table were a perverse voluntary agent, intent on thwarting and vexing him, I plainly perceive that, for Nippers, brandy-and-water were altogether superfluous.

It was fortunate for me that, owing to its peculiar cause—indigestion—the irritability and consequent nervousness of Nippers were mainly observable in the morning, while in the afternoon he was comparatively mild. So that, Turkey's paroxysms only coming on about twelve o'clock, I never had to do with their eccentricities at one time. Their fits relieved each other, like guards. When Nipper's was on, Turkey's was off; and *vice versa*. This was a good natural arrangement under the circumstances.

Ginger Nut, the third on my list, was a lad, some twelve years old. His father was a carman, ambitious of seeing his son on the bench instead of a cart, before he died. So he sent him to my office, as student at law, errand-boy, cleaner and sweeper, at the rate of one dollar a week. He had a little desk to himself, but he did not use it much. Upon inspection, the drawer exhibited a great array of the shells of various sorts of nuts. Indeed, to this quick-witted youth, the whole noble science of the law was contained in a nut-shell. Not the least among the employments of Ginger Nut, as well as one which he discharged with the most alacrity, was his duty as cake and apple purveyor for Turkey and Nippers. Copying law-papers being proverbially a dry, husky sort of business, my two scriveners were fain to moisten their mouths very often with Spitzenbergs, to be had at the numerous stalls nigh the Custom House and Post Office. Also, they sent Ginger Nut very frequently for that peculiar cake—small, flat, round, and very spicy—after which he had been named by them. Of a cold morning, when business was but dull, Turkey would gobble up scores of these cakes, as if they were mere wafers—indeed, they sell them at the rate of six or eight for a penny—the scrape of his pen blending with the crunching of the crisp particles in his mouth. Of all the fiery afternoon blunders and flurried rashnesses of Turkey, was his once moistening a ginger cake between his lips, and clapping it on to a mortgage, for a seal. I came within an ace of dismissing him then. But he mollified me by making an oriental bow, and saying—

"With submission, sir, it was generous of me to find you in stationery on my account."

Now my original business—that of a conveyancer and title hunter, and drawer-up of recondite documents of all sorts—was considerably increased by receiving the Master's office. There was now great work for scriveners. Not only must I push the clerks already with me, but I must have additional help.

In answer to my advertisement, a motionless young man one morning stood upon my office threshold, the door being open, for it was summer. I can see that figure now—pallidly neat, pitiably respectable, incurably forlorn! It was Bartleby.

After a few words touching his qualifications, I engaged him, glad to have among my corps of copyists a man of so singularly sedate an aspect, which I thought might operate beneficially upon the flighty temper of Turkey, and the fiery one of Nippers.

I should have stated before that ground-glass folding-doors divided my premises into two parts, one of which was occupied by my scriveners, the other by myself. According to my humour, I threw open these doors, or closed them. I resolved to assign Bartleby a corner by the folding-doors, but on my side of them, so as to have this quiet man within easy call, in case any trifling thing was to be done. I placed his desk close up to a small side-window in that part of the room, a window which originally had afforded a lateral view of certain grimy back-yards and bricks, but which, owing to subsequent erections, commanded at present no view at all, though it gave some light. Within three feet of the panes was a wall, and the light came down from far above, between two lofty buildings, as from a very small opening in a dome. Still further to a satisfactory arrangement, I procured a high green folding screen, which might entirely isolate Bartleby from my sight, though not remove him from my voice. And thus, in a manner, privacy and society were conjoined.

At first, Bartleby did an extraordinary quantity of writing. As if long famishing for something to copy, he seemed to gorge himself on my documents. There was no pause for digestion. He ran a day and night line copying by sunlight and by candle-light. I should have been quite delighted with his application, had he been cheerfully industrious. But he wrote on silently, palely, mechanically.

It is, of course, an indispensable part of a scrivener's business to verify the accuracy of his copy, word by word. Where there are two or more scriveners in an office, they assist each other in this examination, one reading from the copy, the other holding the original. It is a very dull, wearisome, and lethargic affair. I can readily imagine that, to some sanguine temperaments, it would be altogether intolerable. For example, I cannot credit that the mettlesome poet, Byron, would have contentedly sat down with Bartleby to examine a law document of, say five hundred pages, closely written in a crimpy hand.

Now and then, in the haste of business, it has been my habit to assist in comparing some brief document myself, calling Turkey or Nippers for this purpose. One object I had, in placing Bartleby so handy to me behind the screen, was, to avail myself of his services on such trivial occasions. It was on the third day, I think, of his being with me, and before any necessity had arisen for having his own writing examined, that, being much hurried to complete a small affair I had in hand, I abruptly called to Bartleby. In my haste and natural expectancy of instant compliance, I sat with my head bent over the original on my desk, and my right hand sideways, and somewhat nervously extended with the copy, so that, immediately upon emerging from his retreat, Bartleby might snatch it and proceed to business without the least delay.

In this very attitude did I sit when I called to him, rapidly stating what it was I wanted him to do—namely, to examine a small paper with me. Imagine my surprise, nay, my consternation, when, without moving from his privacy, Bartleby, in a singularly mild, firm voice, replied, "I would prefer not to."

I saw awhile in perfect silence, rallying my stunned faculties. Immediately it occurred to me that my ears had deceived me, or Bartleby had entirely misunderstood my meaning. I repeated my request in the clearest tone I could assume; but in quite as clear a one came the previous reply, "I would prefer not to."

"Prefer not to," echoed I, rising in high excitement, and crossing the room with a stride. "What do you mean? Are you moon-struck? I want you to help me compare this sheet here—take it," and I thrust it towards him.

"I would prefer not to," said he.

I looked at him steadfastly. His face was leanly composed; his grey eye dimly calm. Not a wrinkle of agitation rippled him. Had there been the least uneasiness, anger, impatience or impertinence in his manner; in other words, had there been anything ordinarily human about him, doubtless I should have violently dismissed him from the premises. But as it was, I should have as soon thought of turning my pale plaster-of-paris bust of Cicero out of doors. I stood gazing at him awhile, as he went on with his own writing, and then reseated myself at my desk. This is very strange, thought I. What had one best do? But my business hurried me. I concluded to forget the matter for the present, reserving it for my future leisure. So, calling Nippers from the other room, the paper was speedily examined.

A few days after this, Bartleby concluded four lengthy documents, being quadruplicates of a week's testimony taken before me in my High Court of Chancery. It became necessary to examine them. It was an important suit, and great accuracy was imperative. Having all things arranged, I called Turkey,

Nippers and Ginger Nut, from the next room, meaning to place the four copies in the hands of my four clerks, while I should read from the original. Accordingly, Turkey, Nippers and Ginger Nut had taken their seats in a row, each with his document in his hand, when I called to Bartleby to join this interesting group.

"Bartleby! quick, I am waiting."

I heard a slow scrape of his chair legs on the uncarpeted floor, and soon he appeared standing at the entrance of his hermitage.

"What is wanted?" said he, mildly.

"The copies, the copies," said I, hurriedly. "We are going to examine them. There"—and I held towards him the fourth quadruplicate.

"I would prefer not to," said he, and gently disappeared behind the screen.

For a few moments I was turned into a pillar of salt, standing at the head of my seated column of clerks. Recovering myself, I advanced towards the screen, and demanded the reason for such extraordinary conduct.

"*Why* do you refuse?"

"I would prefer not to."

With any other man I should have flown outright into a dreadful passion, scorned all further words, and thrust him ignominiously from my presence. But there was something about Bartleby that not only strangely disarmed me, but, in a wonderful manner, touched and disconcerted me. I began to reason with him.

"These are your own copies we are about to examine. It is labour saving to you, because one examination will answer for your four papers. It is common usage. Every copyist is bound to help examine his copy. Is it not so? Will you not speak? Answer!"

"I prefer not to," he replied in a flute-like tone. It seemed to me that, while I had been addressing him, he carefully revolved every statement that I made; fully comprehended the meaning; could not gainsay the irresistible conclusion; but, at the same time, some paramount consideration prevailed with him to reply as he did.

"You are decided, then, not to comply with my request—a request made according to common usage and common sense?"

He briefly gave me to understand, that on that point my judgment was sound. Yes: his decision was irreversible.

It is not seldom the case that, when a man is browbeaten in some unprecedented and violently unreasonable way, he begins to stagger in his own plainest faith. He begins, as it were, vaguely to surmise that, wonderful as it may be, all the justice and all the reason is on the other side. Accordingly, if any disinterested persons are present, he turns to them for some reinforcement for his own faltering mind.

"Turkey," said I, "what do you think of this? Am I not right?"

"With submission, sir," said Turkey, in his blandest tone, "I think you are."

"Nippers," said I, "what do *you* think of it?" "I think I should kick him out of the office."

(The reader of nice perceptions will here perceive that, it being morning Turkey's answer is couched in polite and tranquil terms, but Nippers replies in ill-tempered ones. Or, to repeat a previous sentence, Nipper's ugly mood was on duty, and Turkey's off.)

"Ginger Nut," said I, willing to enlist the smallest suffrage in my behalf, "what do you think of it?"

"I think, sir, he's a little *luny*," replied Ginger Nut, with a grin. "You hear what they say," said I, turning towards the screen, "come forth and do your duty."

But he vouchsafed no reply. I pondered a moment in sore perplexity. But once more business hurried me. I determined again to postpone the consideration of this dilemma to my future leisure. With a little trouble we made out to examine the papers without Bartleby, though at every page or two Turkey deferentially dropped his opinion, that this proceeding was quite out of the common; while Nippers, twitching in his chair with a dyspeptic nervousness, ground out, between his set teeth, occasional hissing maledictions against the stubborn oaf behind the screen. And for his (Nipper's) part, this was the first and the last time he would do another man's business without pay.

Meanwhile Bartleby sat in his hermitage, oblivious to everything but his own peculiar business there.

Some days passed, the scrivener being employed upon another lengthy work. His late remarkable conduct led me to regard his ways narrowly. I observed that he never went to dinner; indeed, that he never went anywhere. As yet I had never, of my personal knowledge, known him to be outside of my office. He was a perpetual sentry in the corner. At about eleven o'clock though, in the morning, I noticed that Ginger Nut would advance toward the opening in Bartleby's screen, as if silently beckoned thither by a gesture invisible to me where I sat. The boy would then leave the office, jingling a few pence, and reappear with a handful of ginger nuts, which he delivered in the hermitage, receiving two of the cakes for his trouble.

He lives, then, on ginger-nuts, thought I; never eats a dinner, properly speaking; he must be a vegetarian, then, but no; he never eats even vegetables, he eats nothing but ginger-nuts. My mind then ran on in reveries concerning the probable effects upon the human constitution of living entirely on ginger-nuts. Ginger-nuts are so called, because they contain ginger as one of their peculiar constituents and the final flavouring one. Now, what was ginger? A hot, spicy thing. Was Bartleby hot and spicy? Not at all. Ginger, then, had no effect upon Bartleby. Probably he preferred it should have none.

Nothing so aggravates an earnest person as a passive resistance. If the individual so resisted by of a not inhumane temper, and the resisting one perfectly harmless in his passivity, then, in the better moods of the former, he will endeavour charitably to construe to his imagination what proves impossible to be solved by his judgment. Even so, for the most part, I regarded Bartleby and his ways. Poor fellow! thought I, he means no mischief, it is plain he intends no insolence; his aspect sufficiently evinces that his eccentricities are involuntary. He is useful to me. I can get along with him. If I turn him away, the chances are he will fall in with some less indulgent employer, and then he will be rudely treated, and perhaps driven forth miserably to starve. Yes. Here I can cheaply purchase a delicious self-approval. To befriend Bartleby; to humour him in his strange willfulness, will cost me little or nothing, while I lay up in my soul what will eventually prove a sweet morsel for my conscience. But this mood was not invariable with me. The passiveness of Bartleby sometimes irritated me. I felt strangely goaded on to encounter him in a new opposition—to elicit some angry spark from him answerable to my own. But, indeed, I might as well have essayed to strike fire with my knuckles against a bit of Windsor soap. But one afternoon the evil impulse in me mastered me, and the following little scene ensued:

"Bartleby," said I, "when those papers are all copied, I will compare them with you."

"I would prefer not to."

"How? Surely you do not mean to persist in that mulish vagary?"

No answer.

I threw open the folding-doors near by, and, turning upon Turkey and Nippers, exclaimed:

"Bartleby a second time says, he won't examine his papers. What do you think of it, Turkey?"

It was afternoon, be it remembered. Turkey sat glowing like a brass boiler; his bald head steaming; his hands reeling among his blotted papers.

"Think of it?" roared Turkey. "I think I'll just step behind his screen, and black his eyes for him!"

So saying, Turkey rose to his feet and threw his arms into a pugilistic position. He was hurrying away to make good his promise, when I detained him, alarmed at the effect of incautiously rousing Turkey's combativeness after dinner.

"Sit down, Turkey," said I, "and hear what Nippers has to say. What do you think of it, Nippers? Would I not be justified in immediately dismissing Bartleby?"

"Excuse me, that is for you to decide, sir. I think his conduct quite unusual, and, indeed, unjust, as regards Turkey and myself. But it may only be a passing whim."

"Ah," exclaimed I, "you have strangely changed your mind, then—you speak very gently of him now."

"All beer," cried Turkey; "gentleness is effects of beer—Nippers and I dined together to-day. You see how gentle I am, sir. Shall I go and black his eyes?"

"You refer to Bartleby, I suppose. No, not to-day, Turkey," I replied; "pray, put up your fists."

I closed the doors, and again advanced towards Bartleby. I felt additional incentives tempting me to my fate. I burned to be rebelled against again. I remembered that Bartleby never left the office.

"Bartleby," said I, "Ginger Nut is away; just step around to the Post Office, won't you?" (it was but a three minutes' walk) "and see if there is anything for me."

"I would prefer not to."

"You *will* not?"

"I *prefer* not."

I staggered to my desk, and sat there in a deep study. My blind inveteracy returned. Was there any other thing in which I could procure myself to be ignominiously repulsed by this lean, penniless wight?—my hired clerk? What added thing is there, perfectly reasonable, that he will be sure to refuse to do?

"Bartleby!"

No answer.

"Bartleby," in a louder tone.

No answer.

"Bartleby," I roared.

Like a very ghost, agreeably to the laws of magical invocation, at the third summons, he appeared at the entrance of his hermitage.

"Go to the next room, and tell Nippers to come to me."

"I prefer not to," he respectfully and slowly said, and mildly disappeared.

"Very good, Bartleby," said I, in a quiet sort of serenely-severe self-possessed tone, intimating the unalterable purpose of some terrible retribution very close at hand. At the moment I half intended something of the kind. But upon the whole, as it was drawing towards my dinner-hour, I thought it best to put on my hat and walk home for the day, suffering much from perplexity and distress of mind.

Shall I acknowledge it? The conclusion of this whole business was, that it soon became a fixed fact of my chambers, that a pale young scrivener, by the name of Bartleby, had a desk there; that he copied for me at the usual rate of four cents a folio (one hundred words); but he was permanently exempt from examining the work done by him, that duty being transferred to Turkey and Nippers, out of compliment, doubtless, to their superior acuteness; moreover, said Bartleby was never, on any account, to be dispatched on the most trivial errand of any sort; and that even if entreated to take upon him such a matter, it was generally understood that he would "prefer not to"—in other words, that he would refuse point-blank.

As days passed on, I became considerably reconciled to Bartleby. His steadiness, his freedom from all dissipation, his incessant industry (except when he chose to throw himself into a standing revery behind his screen), his great stillness, his unalterableness of demeanour under all circumstances, made him a valuable acquisition. One prime thing was this—*he was always there*—first in the morning, continually through the day, and the last at night. I had a singular confidence in his honesty. I felt my most precious papers perfectly safe in his hands. Sometimes, to be sure, I could not, for the very soul of me, avoid falling into sudden spasmodic passions with him. For it was exceeding difficult to bear in mind all the time those strange peculiarities, privileges, and unheard-of exemptions, forming the tacit stipulations on Bartleby's part under which he remained in my office. Now and then, in the eagerness of dispatching pressing business, I would inadvertently summon Bartleby, in a short, rapid tone, to put his finger, say, on the incipient tie of a bit of red tape with which I was about compressing some papers. Of course, from behind the screen the usual answer, "I prefer not to," was sure to come; and then, how could a human creature, with the common infirmities of our nature, refrain from bitterly exclaiming upon such perverseness—such unreasonableness? However, every added repulse of this sort which I received only tended to lessen the probability of my repeating the inadvertence.

Here it must be said, that, according to the custom of most legal gentlemen occupying chambers in densely-populated law buildings, there were several keys to my door. One was kept by a woman residing in the attic, which person weekly scrubbed and daily swept and dusted my apartments. Another was kept by Turkey for convenience sake. The third I sometimes carried in my own pocket. The fourth I knew not who had.

Now, one Sunday morning I happened to go to Trinity Church, to hear a celebrated preacher, and finding myself rather early on the ground I thought I would walk round to my chambers for a while. Luckily I had my key with me; but upon applying it to the lock, I found it resisted by something inserted from the inside. Quite surprised, I called out; when to my consternation a key was turned from within; and thrusting his lead visage at me, and holding the door ajar, the apparition of Bartleby appeared, in his shirt-sleeves, and otherwise in a strangely tattered deshabille, saying quietly that he was sorry, but he was deeply engaged just then, and—preferred not admitting me at present. In a brief word or two, he moreover added, that perhaps I had better walk round the block two or three times, and by that time he would probably have concluded his affairs.

Now, the utterly unsurmised appearance of Bartleby, tenanting my law-chambers of a Sunday morning, with his cadaverously gentlemanly *nonchalance*, yet withal firm and self-possessed, has such a strange effect upon me, that incontinently I slunk away from my own door, and did as desired. But not without sundry twinges of impotent rebellion against the mild effrontery of this unaccountable scrivener. Indeed, it was his wonderful mildness chiefly, which not only disarmed me, but unmanned me, as it were. For I consider that one, for the time, is a sort of unmanned when he tranquilly permits his hired clerk to dictate to him, and order him away from his own premises. Furthermore, I was full of uneasiness as to what Bartleby could possibly be doing in my office in his shirt-sleeves, and in an otherwise dismantled condition of a Sunday morning. Was anything amiss going on? Nay, that was out of the question. It was not to be thought of for a moment that Bartleby was an immoral person. But what could he be doing there—copying? Nay again, whatever might be his eccentricities, Bartleby was an eminently decorous person. He would be the last man to sit down to his desk in any state approaching to nudity. Besides, it was Sunday; and there was something about Bartleby that forbade the supposition that he would by any secular occupation violate the proprieties of the day.

Nevertheless, my mind was not pacified; and full of a restless curiosity, at last I returned to the door. Without hindrance I inserted my key, opened it, and entered. Bartleby was not to be seen. I looked round anxiously, peeped behind his screen; but it was very plain that he was gone. Upon more closely examining the place, I surmised that for an indefinite period Bartleby must have ate, dressed, and slept in my office, and that too without plate, mirror, or bed. The cushioned seat of a rickety old sofa in one corner bore the faint impress of a lean, reclining form. Rolled away under his desk, I found a blanket; under the empty grate, a blacking box and brush; on a chair, a tin basin, with soap and a ragged towel; in a newspaper a few crumbs of ginger-nuts and a morsel of cheese. Yes, thought I, it is evident enough that Bartleby had been making his home here, keeping bachelor's hall all by himself. Immediately then the thought came sweeping across me, what miserable friendlessness and loneliness are here revealed! His poverty is great; but his solitude, how horrible! Think of it. Of a Sunday, Wall Street is deserted as Petra; and every night of every day it is an emptiness. This building, too, which of week-days hums with industry and life, at nightfall echoes with sheer vacancy, and all through Sunday is forlorn. And here Bartleby makes his home; sole spectator of a solitude which he has seen all populous—a sort of innocent and transformed Marius brooding among the ruins of Carthage!

For the first time in my life a feeling of overpowering stinging melancholy seized me. Before, I had never experienced aught but a not unpleasing sadness. The bond of a common humanity now drew me irresistibly to gloom. A fraternal melancholy! For both I and Bartleby were sons of Adam. I remembered the bright silks and sparkling faces I had seen that day, in gala trim, swan-like sailing down the Mississippi of Broadway; and I contrasted them with the pallid copyist, and thought to myself, Ah, happiness courts the light, so we deem the world is gay; but misery hides aloof, so we deem that misery there is none. These sad fancyings—chimeras, doubtless of a sick and silly brain—led on to other and more special thoughts, concerning the eccentricities of Bartleby. Presentiments of strange discoveries hovered round me. The scrivener's pale form appeared to me laid out, among uncaring strangers, in its shivering winding-sheet.

Suddenly I was attracted by Bartleby's closed desk, the key in open sight left in the lock.

I mean no mischief, seek the gratification of no heartless curiosity, thought I; besides, the desk is mine, and its contents, too, so I will make bold to look within. Everything was methodically arranged, the papers smoothly placed. The pigeon-holes were deep, and removing the files of documents, I groped into their recesses. Presently I felt something there, and dragged it out. It was an old bandanna handkerchief, heavy and knotted. I opened it, and saw it was a savings' bank.

I now recalled all the quiet mysteries which I had noted in the man. I remembered that he never spoke but to answer; that, though at intervals he had considerable time to himself, yet I had never seen him reading—no, not even a newspaper; that for long periods he would stand looking out, at his pale window behind the screen, upon the dead brick wall; I was quite sure he never visited any refectory or eating-house; while his pale face clearly indicated that he never drank beer like Turkey, or tea and coffee even, like other men; that he never went anywhere in particular that I could learn; never went out for a walk, unless, indeed, that was the case at present; that he had declined telling who he was or whence he came, or whether he had any relatives in the world; that though so thin and pale, he never complained of ill-health. And more than all, I remembered a certain unconscious air of pallid—how shall I call it?—of pallid haughtiness, say, or rather an austere reserve about him which had positively awed me into my tame compliance with his eccentricities, when I had feared to ask him to do the slightest incidental thing for me, even though I might know, from his long continued motionlessness, that behind his screen he must be standing in one of those dead-wall reveries of his.

Revolving all these things, and coupling them with the recently discovered fact, that he made my office his constant abiding place and home, and not forgetful of his morbid moodiness; revolving all these things, a prudential feeling began to steal over me. My first emotions had been those of pure melancholy and sincerest pity; but just in proportion as the forlornness of Bartleby grew and grew to my imagination, did that same melancholy merge into fear, that pity into repulsion. So true it is, and so terrible, too, that up to a certain point the thought or sight of misery enlists our best affections; but, in certain special cases, beyond that point it does not. They err who would assert that invariably this is owing to the inherent selfishness of the human heart. It rather proceeds from a certain hopelessness of remedying excessive and organic ill. To a sensitive being, pity is not seldom pain. And when at last it is perceived that such pity cannot lead to effectual succor, common sense bids the soul be rid of it. What I saw that morning persuaded me that the scrivener was the victim of innate and incurable disorder. I might give alms to his body; but his body did not pain him; it was his soul that suffered, and his soul I could not reach.

I did not accomplish the purpose of going to Trinity Church that morning. Somehow, the things I had seen disqualified me for the time from church-going. I walked homeward, thinking what I would do with Bartleby. Finally, I resolved upon this—I would put certain calm questions to him the next morning, touching his history, etc., and if he declined to answer them openly and unreservedly (and I supposed he would prefer not), then to give him a twenty dollar bill over and above whatever I might owe him, and tell him his services were no longer required; but that if in any other way I could assist him, I would be happy to do so, especially if he desired to return to his native place, wherever that might be, I would willingly help to defray the expenses. Moreover, if, after reaching home, he found himself at any time in want of aid, a letter from him would be sure of reply.

The next morning came.

"Bartleby," said I, gently calling to him behind his screen.

No reply.

"Bartleby," said I, in a still gentler tone, "come here; I am not going to ask you to do anything you would prefer not to do—I simply wish to speak to you."

Upon this he noiselessly slid into view.

"Will you tell me, Bartleby, where you were born?"

"I would prefer not to."

"Will you tell me *anything* about yourself?"

"I would prefer not to."

"But what reasonable objection can you have to speak to me? I feel friendly towards you."

He did not look at me while I spoke, but kept his glance fixed upon my bust of Cicero, which, as I then sat, was directly behind me, some six inches above my head.

"What is your answer, Bartleby?" said I, after waiting a considerable time for a reply, during which his countenance remained immovable, only there was the faintest conceivable tremor of the white attenuated mouth.

"At present I prefer to give no answer," he said, and retired into his hermitage.

It was rather weak of me, I confess, but his manner, on this occasion, nettled me. Not only did there seem to lurk in it a certain calm disdain, but his perverseness seemed ungrateful, considering the undeniable good usage and indulgence he had received from me.

Again I sat ruminating what I should do. Mortified as I was at his behaviour, and resolved as I had been to dismiss him when I entered my office, nevertheless I strangely felt something superstitious knocking at my heart, and forbidding me to carry out my purpose, and denouncing me for a villain if I dared to breathe one bitter word against this forlornest of mankind. At last, familiarly drawing my chair behind his screen, I sat down and said: "Bartleby, never mind, then, about revealing your history; but let me entreat you, as a friend, to comply as far as may be with the usages of this office. Say now, you will help to examine papers to-morrow or next day: in short, say now, that in a day or two you will begin to be a little reasonable:—say so, Bartleby."

"At present I would prefer not to be a little reasonable," was his mildly cadaverous reply.

Just then the folding-doors opened, and Nippers approached. He seemed suffering from an unusually bad night's rest, induced by severer indigestion than common. He overheard those final words of Bartleby.

"*Prefer not*, eh?" gritted Nippers—"I'd *prefer* him, if I were you, sir," addressing me—"I'd *prefer* him; I'd give him preferences, the stubborn mule! What is it, sir, pray, that he *prefers* not to do now?"

Bartleby moved not a limb.

"Mr. Nippers," said I, "I'd prefer that you would withdraw for the present."

Somehow, of late, I had got into the way of involuntarily using this word "prefer" upon all sorts of not exactly suitable occasions. And I trembled to think that my contact with the scrivener had already and seriously affected me in a mental way. And what further and deeper aberration might it not yet produce? This apprehension had not been without efficacy in determining me to summary measures.

As Nippers, looking very sour and sulky, was departing, Turkey blandly and deferentially approached.

"With submission, sir," said he, "yesterday I was thinking about Bartleby here, and I think that if he would but prefer to take a quart of good ale every day it would do much towards mending him, and enabling him to assist in examining his papers."

"So you have got the word, too," said I, slightly excited.

"With submission, what word, sir?" asked Turkey, respectfully crowding himself into the contracted space behind the screen, and by so doing making me jostle the scrivener. "What word, sir?"

"I would prefer to be left alone here," said Bartleby, as if offended at being mobbed in his privacy.

"*That's* the word, Turkey," said I—"*that's* it."

"Oh, *prefer*? oh yes—queer word. I never use it myself. But, sir, as I was saying, if he would but prefer—"

"Turkey," interrupted I, "you will please withdraw."

"Oh certainly, sir, if you prefer that I should."

As he opened the folding-door to retire, Nippers at his desk caught a glimpse of me, and asked whether I would prefer to have a certain paper copied on blue paper or white. He did not in the least roguishly accent the word "prefer." It was plain that it involuntarily rolled from his tongue. I thought to myself, surely I must get rid of a demented man, who already has in some degree turned the tongues, if not the heads of myself and clerks. But I thought it prudent not to break the dismission at once.

The next day I noticed that Bartleby did nothing but stand at his window in his dead-wall revery. Upon asking him why he did not write, he said that he had decided upon doing no more writing.

"Why, how now? what next?" exclaimed I, "do no more writing?"

"No more."

"And what is the reason?"

"Do you not see the reason for yourself?" he indifferently replied.

I looked steadfastly at him, and perceived that his eyes looked dull and glazed. Instantly it occurred to me, that his unexampled diligence in copying by his dim window for the first few weeks of his stay with me might have temporarily impaired his vision.

I was touched. I said something in condolence with him. I hinted that of course he did wisely in abstaining from writing for a while; and urged him to embrace that opportunity of taking wholesome exercise in the open air. This, however, he did not do. A few days after this, my other clerks being absent, and being in a great hurry to dispatch certain letters by the mail, I thought that, having nothing else earthly to do, Bartleby would surely be less inflexible than usual, and carry these letters to the post-office. But he blankly declined. So, much to my inconvenience, I went myself.

Still added days went by. Whether Bartleby's eyes improved or not, I could not say. To all appearance, I thought they did. But when I asked him if they did, he vouchsafed no answer. At all events, he would do no copying. At last, in reply to my urgings, he informed me that he had permanently given up copying.

"What!" exclaimed I; "suppose your eyes should get entirely well—better than ever before—would you not copy then?"

"I have given up copying," he answered, and slid aside.

He remained as ever, a fixture in my chamber. Nay—if that were possible—he became still more of a fixture than before. What was to be done? He would do nothing in the office; why should he stay there? In plain fact, he had now become a millstone to me, not only useless as a necklace, but afflictive to bear. Yet I was sorry for him. I speak less than truth when I say that, on his own account, he occasioned me uneasiness. If he would but have named a single relative or friend, I would instantly have written, and urged their taking the poor fellow away to some convenient retreat. But he seemed alone, absolutely alone in the universe. A bit of wreck in the mid-Atlantic. At length, necessities connected with my business tyrannized over all other considerations. Decently as I could, I told Bartleby that in six days' time he must unconditionally leave the office. I warned him to take measures, in the interval, for procuring some other abode. I offered to assist him in this endeavour, if he himself would but take the first step towards a removal. "And when you finally quit me, Bartleby," added I, "I shall see that you go not away entirely unprovided. Six days from this hour, remember."

At the expiration of that period, I peeped behind the screen, and lo! Bartleby was there.

I buttoned up my coat, balanced myself; advanced slowly towards him, touched his shoulder, and said, "The time has come; you must quit this place; I am sorry for you; here is money; but you must go."

"I would prefer not," he replied, with his back still towards me. "You *must*."

He remained silent.

Now I had an unbounded confidence in this man's common honesty. He had frequently restored to me sixpences and shillings carelessly dropped upon the floor, for I am apt to be very reckless in such shirt-button affairs. The proceeding, then, which followed will not be deemed extraordinary.

"Bartleby," said I, "I owe you twelve dollars on account; here are thirty-two, the odd twenty are yours—Will you take it?" and I handed the bills towards him.

But he made no motion.

"I will leave them here, then," putting them under a weight on the table. Then taking my hat and cane and going to the door, I tranquilly turned and added—"After you have removed your things from these offices, Bartleby, you will of course lock the door—since every one is now gone for the day but you—and if you please, slip your key underneath the mat, so that I may have it in the morning. I shall not see you again; so good-bye to you. If, hereafter, in your new place of abode, I can be of any service to you, do not fail to advise me by letter. Good-bye, Bartleby, and fare you well."

But he answered not a word; like the last column of some ruined temple, he remained standing mute and solitary in the middle of the otherwise deserted room.

As I walked home in a pensive mood, my vanity got the better of my pity. I could not but highly plume myself on my masterly management in getting rid of Bartleby. Masterly I call it, and such it must appear to any dispassionate thinker. The beauty of my procedure seemed to consist in its perfect quietness. There was no vulgar bullying, no bravado of any sort, no choleric hectoring, and striding to and fro across the apartment, jerking out vehement commands for Bartleby to bundle himself off with his beggarly traps. Nothing of the kind. Without loudly bidding Bartleby depart—as an inferior genius might have done—I *assumed* the ground that depart he must; and upon that assumption built all I had to say. The more I thought over my procedure, the more I was charmed with it. Nevertheless, next morning, upon awakening, I had my doubts—I had somehow slept off the fumes of vanity. One of the coolest and wisest hours a man has, is just after he awakes in the morning. My procedure seemed as sagacious as ever—but only in theory. How it would prove in prac-tice—there was the rub. It was truly a beautiful thought to have assumed Bartleby's departure; but, after all, that assumption was simply my own, and none of Bartleby's. The great point was, not whether I had assumed that he would quit me, but whether he would prefer so to do. He was more a man of preferences than assumptions.

After breakfast, I walked down town, arguing the probabilities *pro* and *con*. One moment I thought it would prove a miserable failure, and Bartleby would be found all alive at my office as usual; the next moment it seemed cer-tain that I should find his chair empty. And so I kept veering about. At the corner of Broadway and Canal Street, I saw quite an excited group of people standing in earnest conversation.

"I'll take odds he doesn't," said a voice as I passed.

"Doesn't go?—done!" said I, "put up your money."

I was instinctively putting my hand in my pocket to produce my own, when I remembered that this was an election day. The words I had overheard bore no reference to Bartleby, but to the success or non-success of some candi-date for the mayoralty. In my intent frame of mind, I had, as it were, imagined that all Broadway shared in my excitement, and were debating the same ques-tion with me. I passed on, very thankful that the uproar of the street screened my momentary absent-mindedness.

As I had intended, I was earlier than usual at my office door. I stood lis-tening for a moment. All was still. He must be gone. I tried the knob. The door was locked. Yes, my procedure had worked to a charm; he indeed must be vanished. Yet a certain melancholy mixed with this: I was almost sorry for my brilliant success. I was fumbling under the door mat for the key which Bartleby was to have left there for me, when accidentally my knee knocked against a panel, producing a summoning sound, and in response a voice came to me from within—"Not yet, I am occupied."

It was Bartleby.

I was thunderstruck. For an instant I stood like the man who, pipe in mouth, was killed one cloudless afternoon long ago in Virginia, by summer lightning; at his own warm open window he was killed, and remained leaning out there upon the dreamy afternoon, till some one touched him, when he fell.

"Not gone!" I murmured at last. But again obeying that wondrous ascendancy which the inscrutable scrivener had over me, and from which ascendancy, for all my chafing, I could not completely escape, I slowly went down stairs and out into the street, and while walking round the block, considered what I should next do in this unheard-of perplexity. Turn the man out by an actual thrusting I could not; to drive him away by calling him hard names would not do; calling in the police was an unpleasant idea; and yet, permit him to enjoy his cadaverous triumph over me—this, too, I could not think of. What was to be done? or, if nothing could be done, was there anything further that I could *assume* in the matter? Yes, as before I had prospectively assumed that Bartleby would depart, so now I might retrospectively assume that departed he was. In the legitimate carrying out of this assumption, I might enter my office in a great hurry, and pretending not to see Bartleby at all, walk straight against him as if he were air. Such a proceeding would in a singular degree have the appearance of a home-thrust. It was hardly possible that Bartleby could withstand such an application of the doctrine of assumptions. But upon second thoughts the success of the plan seemed rather dubious. I resolved to argue the matter over with him again.

"Bartleby," said I, entering the office, with a quietly severe expression, "I am seriously displeased. I am pained, Bartleby. I had thought better of you. I had imagined you of such a gentlemanly organization, that in any delicate dilemma a slight hint would suffice—in short, an assumption. But it appears I am deceived. Why," I added, unaffectedly starting, "you have not even touched that money yet," pointing to it, just where I had left it the evening previous.

He answered nothing.

"Will you, or will you not, quit me?" I now demanded in a sudden passion, advancing close to him.

"I would prefer *not* to quit you," he replied, gently emphasizing the *not*.

"What earthly right have you to stay here? Do you pay any rent? Do you pay my taxes? Or is this property yours?"

He answered nothing.

"Are you ready to go on and write now? Are your eyes recovered? Could you copy a small paper for me this morning? or help examine a few lines? or step round to the post-office? In a word, will you do anything at all, to give a colouring to your refusal to depart the premises?"

He silently retired into his hermitage.

I was now in such a state of nervous resentment that I thought it but prudent to check myself at present from further demonstrations. Bartleby and I were alone. I remembered the tragedy of the unfortunate Adams and the still more unfortunate Colt in the solitary office of the latter; and how poor Colt, being dreadfully incensed by Adams, and imprudently permitting himself to get wildly excited, was at unawares hurried into his fatal act—an act which certainly no man could possibly deplore more than the actor himself. Often it had occurred to me in my ponderings upon the subject that had that altercation taken place in the public street, or at a private residence, it would not have terminated as it did. It was the circumstance of being alone in a solitary office, up stairs, or a building entirely unhallowed by humanizing domestic associations—an uncarpeted office, doubtless, of a dusty, haggard sort of appearance—this it must have been, which greatly helped to enhance the irritable desperation of the hapless Colt.

But when this old Adam of resentment rose in me and tempted me concerning Bartleby, I grappled him and threw him. How? Why, simply by recalling the divine injunction: "A new commandment give I unto you, that ye love one another." Yes, this it was that saved me. Aside from higher considerations, charity often operates as a vastly wise and prudent principle—a great safeguard to its possessor. Men have committed murder for jealousy's sake, and anger's sake, and hatred's sake, and selfishness' sake, and spiritual pride's sake; but no man, that ever I heard of, ever committed a diabolical murder for sweet charity's sake. Mere self-interest, then, if no better motive can be enlisted, should, especially with high tempered men, prompt all beings to charity and philanthropy. At any rate, upon the occasion in question, I strove to drown my exasperated feelings towards the scrivener by benevolently construing his conduct. Poor fellow, poor fellow! thought I, he don't mean anything; and besides, he has seen hard times, and ought to be indulged.

I endeavoured, also, immediately to occupy myself, and at the same time to comfort my despondency. I tried to fancy, that in the course of the morning, at such time as might prove agreeable to him, Bartleby, of his own free accord, would emerge from his hermitage and take up some decided line of march in the direction of the door. But no. Half-past twelve o'clock came; Turkey began to glow in the face, overturn his inkstand, and become generally obstreperous; Nippers abated down into quietude and courtesy; Ginger Nut munched his

noon apple; and Bartleby remained standing at his window in one of his pro-
foundest dead-wall reveries. Will it be credited? Ought I to acknowledge it?
That afternoon I left the office without saying one further word to him.

Some days now passed, during which, at leisure intervals I looked a little
into "Edwards on the Will," and "Priestly on Necessity." Under the circumstances, those books induced a salutary feeling. Gradually I slid into the persuasion that these troubles of mine, touching the scrivener, had been all
predestinated from eternity, and Bartleby was billeted upon me for some mysterious purpose of an all-wise Providence, which it was not for a mere mortal
like me to fathom. Yes, Bartleby, stay there behind your screen, thought I; I
shall persecute you no more; you are harmless and noiseless as any of these old
chairs; in short, I never feel so private as when I know you are here. At last I
see it, I feel it; I penetrate to the predestinated purpose of my life. I am content.
Others may have loftier parts to enact; but my mission in this world, Bartleby,
is to furnish you with office-room for such period as you may see fit to remain.

I believe that this wise and blessed frame of mind would have continued
with me, had it not been for the unsolicited and uncharitable remarks obtruded
upon me by my professional friends who visited the rooms. But thus it often is,
that the constant friction of illiberal minds wears out at last the best resolves of
the more generous. Though to be sure, when I reflected upon it, it was not
strange that people entering my office should be struck by the peculiar aspect
of the unaccountable Bartleby, and so be tempted to throw out some sinister
observations concerning him. Sometimes an attorney, having business with me,
and calling at my office, and finding no one but the scrivener there, would
undertake to obtain some sort of precise information from him touching my
whereabouts; but without heeding his idle talk, Bartleby would remain
standing immovable in the middle of the room. So after contemplating him in
that position for a time, the attorney would depart, no wiser than he came.

Also, when a reference was going on, and the room full of lawyers and
witnesses, and business driving fast, some deeply-occupied legal gentleman
present, seeing Bartleby wholly unemployed, would request him to run round
to his (the legal gentleman's) office and fetch some papers for him. Thereupon,
Bartleby would tranquilly decline, and yet remain idle as before. Then the
lawyer would give a great stare, and turn to me. And what could I say? At last
I was made aware that all through the circle of my professional acquaintance,
a whisper of wonder was running round, having reference to the strange creature I kept at my office. This worried me very much. And as the idea came
upon me of his possibly turning out a long-lived man, and keep occupying my
chambers, and denying my authority; and perplexing my visitors; and scandal-
izing my professional reputation; and casting a general gloom over the
premises; keeping soul and body together to the last upon his savings (for

doubtless he spent but half a dime a day), and in the end perhaps outlive me, and claim possession of my office by right of his perpetual occupancy: as all these dark anticipations crowded upon me more and more, and my friends continually intruded their relentless remarks upon the apparition in my room, a great change was wrought in me. I resolved to gather all my faculties together, and forever rid me of this intolerable incubus.

Ere revolving any complicated project, however, adapted to this end, I first simply suggested to Bartleby the propriety of his permanent departure. In a calm and serious tone, I commended the idea to his careful and mature consideration. But, having taken three days to meditate upon it, he apprised me, that his original determination remained the same; in short, that he still preferred to abide with me.

What shall I do? I now said to myself, buttoning up my coat to the last button. What shall I do? what ought I to do? What does conscience say I *should* do with this man, or, rather, ghost. Rid myself of him, I must; go, he shall. But how? You will not thrust him, the poor, pale, passive mortal—you will not thrust such a helpless creature out of your door? you will not dishonour yourself by such cruelty? No, I will not, I cannot do that. Rather would I let him live and die here, and then mason up his remains in the wall. What, then, will you do? For all your coaxing, he will not budge. Bribes he leaves under your own paper-weight on your table; in short, it is quite plain that he prefers to cling to you.

Then something severe, something unusual must be done. What! surely you will not have him collared by a constable, and commit his innocent pallor to the common jail? And upon what ground could you procure such a thing to be done?—a vagrant, is he? What! he a vagrant, a wanderer, who refuses to budge? It is because he will *not* be a vagrant, then, that you seek to count him *as* a vagrant. That is too absurd. No visible means of support: there I have him. Wrong again: for indubitably he *does* support himself, and that is the only unanswerable proof that any man can show of his possessing the means so to do. No more then. Since he will not quit me, I must quit him. I will change my offices; I will move elsewhere, and give him fair notice, that if I find him on my new premises I will then proceed against him as a common trespasser.

Acting accordingly, next day I thus addressed him: "I find these chambers too far from the City Hall; the air is unwholesome. In a word, I propose to remove my offices next week, and shall no longer require your services. I tell you this now, in order that you may seek another place."

He made no reply, and nothing more was said.

On the appointed day I engaged carts and men, proceeded to my chambers, and, having but little furniture, everything was removed in a few hours. Throughout, the scrivener remained standing behind the screen, which I directed to be removed the last thing. It was withdrawn; and, being folded up like a huge folio, left him the motionless occupant of a naked room. I stood in the entry watching him a moment, while something from within me upbraided me.

I re-entered, with my hand in my pocket—and—and my heart in my mouth.

"Good-bye, Bartleby; I am going—good-bye, and God some way bless you; and take that," slipping something in his hand. But it dropped upon the floor, and then—strange to say—I tore myself from him whom I had so longed to be rid of.

Established in my new quarters, for a day or two I kept the door locked, and started at every footfall in the passages. When I returned to my rooms, after any little absence, I would pause at the threshold for an instant, and attentively listen, ere applying my key. But these fears were needless. Bartleby never came nigh me.

I thought all was going well, when a perturbed-looking stranger visited me, inquiring whether I was the person who had recently occupied rooms at No.— Wall Street.

Full of forebodings, I replied that I was.

"Then, sir," said the stranger, who proved a lawyer, "you are responsible for the man you left there. He refuses to do any copying; he refuses to do any-thing; he says he prefers not to; and he refuses to quit the premises."

"I am very sorry, sir," said I, with assumed tranquillity, but an inward tremor, "but, really, the man you allude to is nothing to me—he is no relation or apprentice of mine, that you should hold me responsible for him."

"In mercy's name, who is he?"

"I certainly cannot inform you. I know nothing about him. Formerly I employed him as a copyist; but he has done nothing for me now for some time past."

"I shall settle him, then—good morning, sir."

Several days passed, and I heard nothing more; and, though I often felt a charitable prompting to call at the place and see poor Bartleby, yet a certain squeamishness, of I know not what, withheld me.

All is over with him, by this time, thought I, at last, when, through another week, no further intelligence reached me. But, coming to my room the day after, I found several persons waiting at my door in a high state of nervous excitement.

"That's the man—here he comes," cried the foremost one, whom I recog-nized as the lawyer who had previously called upon me alone.

"You must take him away, sir, at once," cried a portly person among them, advancing upon me, and whom I knew to be the landlord of No.— Wall

Street. "These gentlemen, my tenants, cannot stand it any longer; Mr.B——,"
pointing to the lawyer, "has turned him out of his room, and he now persists in
haunting the building generally, sitting upon the banisters of the stairs by day,
and sleeping in the entry by night. Everybody is concerned; clients are leaving
the offices; some fears are entertained of a mob; something you must do, and
that without delay."

Aghast at this torrent, I fell back before it, and would fain have locked
myself in my new quarters. In vain I persisted that Bartleby was nothing to
me—no more than to any one else. In vain—I was the last person known to
have anything to do with him, and they held me to the terrible account.
Fearful, then, of being exposed in the papers (as one person present obscurely
threatened), I considered the matter, and, at length, said, that if the lawyer
would give me a confidential interview with the scrivener, in his (the lawyer's)
own room, I would, that afternoon, strive my best to rid them of the nuisance
they complained of.

Going up stairs to my old haunt, there was Bartleby silently sitting upon
the banister at the landing.

"What are you doing here, Bartleby?" said I.

"Sitting upon the banister," he mildly replied.

I motioned him into the lawyer's room, who then left us.

"Bartleby," said I, "are you aware that you are the cause of great tribula-
tion to me, by persisting in occupying the entry after being dismissed from the
office?"

No answer.

"Now one of two things must take place. Either you must do something,
or something must be done to you. Now what sort of business would you like
to engage in? Would you like to re-engage in copying for some one?"

"No, I would prefer not to make any change."

"Would you like a clerkship in a dry-goods store?"

"There is too much confinement about that. No, I would not like a clerkship; but I am not particular."

"Too much confinement," I cried, "why, you keep yourself confined all
the time!"

"I would prefer not to take a clerkship," he rejoined, as if to settle that
little item at once.

"How would a bar-tender's business suit you? There is no trying of the
eye-sight in that."

"I would not like it at all; though, as said before, I am not particular."

His unwonted wordiness inspired me. I returned to the charge.

"Well, then, would you like to travel through the country collecting bills
for the merchants? That would improve your health."

"No, I would prefer to be doing something else."

"How, then, would going as a companion to Europe, to entertain some young gentleman with your conversation—how would that suit you?"

"Not at all. It does not strike me that there is anything definite about that. I like to be stationary. But I am not particular."

"Stationary you shall be, then," I cried, now losing all patience, and, for the first time in all my exasperating connection with him, fairly flying into a passion. "If you do not go away from these premises before night, I shall feel bound—indeed, I *am* bound—to—to—to quit the premises myself!" I rather absurdly concluded, knowing not with what possible threat to try to frighten his immobility into compliance. Despairing of all further efforts, I was precipitately leaving him, when a final thought occurred to me—one which had not been wholly unindulged before.

"Bartleby," said I, in the kindest tone I could assume under such exciting circumstances, "will you go home with me now—not to my office,—but my dwelling—and remain there till we can conclude upon some convenient arrangement for you at our leisure? Come, let us start now, right away."

"No: at present I would prefer not to make any change at all."

I answered nothing; but, effectually dodging every one by the suddenness and rapidity of my flight, rushed from the building, ran up Wall Street towards Broadway, and, jumping into the first omnibus, was soon removed from pursuit. As soon as tranquillity returned, I distinctly perceived that I had now done all that I possibly could, both in respect to the demands of the landlord and his tenants, and with regard to my own desire and sense of duty, to benefit Bartleby, and shield him from rude persecution. I now strove to be entirely care-free and quiescent; and my conscience justified me in the attempt; though, indeed, it was not so successful as I could have wished. So fearful was I of being again hunted out by the incensed landlord and his exasperated tenants, that, surrendering my business to Nippers, for a few days, I drove about the upper part of the town and through the suburbs, in my rockaway; crossed over to Jersey City and Hoboken, and paid fugitive visits to Manhattanville and Astoria. In fact, I almost lived in my rockaway for the time.

When again I entered my office, lo, a note from the landlord lay upon the desk. I opened it with trembling hands. It informed me that the writer had sent to the police, and had Bartleby removed to the Tombs as a vagrant. Moreover, since I knew more about him than anyone else, he wished me to appear at that place, and make a suitable statement of the facts. These tidings had a conflicting effect upon me. At first I was indignant; but, at last, almost approved. The landlord's energetic, summary disposition, had led him to adopt a procedure which I do not think I would have decided upon myself; and yet, as a last resort, under such peculiar circumstances, it seemed the only plan.

As I afterwards learned, the poor scrivener, when told that he must be conducted to the Tombs, offered not the slightest obstacle, but, in his pale,
unmoving way, silently acquiesced.

Some of the compassionate and curious by-standers joined the party; and
headed by one of the constables arm-in-arm with Bartleby, the silent procession filed its way through all the noise, and heat, and joy of the roaring thor-
oughfares at noon.

The same day I received the note, I went to the Tombs; or, to speak more
properly, the Halls of Justice. Seeking the right officer, I stated the purpose of
my call, and was informed that the individual I described was, indeed, within. I
then assured the functionary that Bartleby was a perfectly honest man, and
greatly to be compassionated, however unaccountably eccentric. I narrated all
I knew, and closed by suggesting the idea of letting him remain in as indulgent
confinement as possible, till something less harsh might be done though,
indeed, I hardly knew what. At all events, if nothing else could be decided
upon, the alms-house must receive him. I then begged to have an interview.

Being under no disgraceful charge, and quite serene and harmless in all his
ways, they had permitted him freely to wander about the prison, and, especially, in the inclosed grass-platted yards thereof. And so I found him there,
standing all alone in the quietest of the yards, his face towards a high wall,
while all around, from the narrow slits of the jail windows, I thought I saw
peering out upon him the eyes of murderers and thieves.

"Bartleby!"

"I know you," he said, without looking round—"and I want nothing to
say to you."

"It was not I that brought you here, Bartleby," said I, keenly pained at his
implied suspicion, "and to you, this should not be so vile a place. Nothing
reproachful attaches to you by being here. And see, it is not so sad a place as
one might think. Look, there is the sky, and here is the grass."

"I know where I am," he replied, but would say nothing more, and so I
left him.

As I entered the corridor again, a broad meat-like man in an apron
accosted me, and, jerking his thumb over his shoulder, said—"Is that your
friend?"

"Yes."

"Does he want to starve? If he does, let him live on the prison fare, that's
all."

"Who are you?" asked I, not knowing what to make of such an unoffi-
cially speaking person in such a place.

"I am the grub-man. Such gentlemen as have friends here, hire me to provide them with something good to eat."

"Is this so?" said I, turning to the turnkey. He said it was.

"Well, then," said I, slipping some silver into the grubman's hands (for so they called him), "I want you to give particular attention to my friend there; let him have the best dinner you can get. And you must be as polite to him as possible."

"Introduce me, will you?" said the grub-man, looking at me with an expression which seemed to say he was all impatience for an opportunity to give a specimen of his breeding.

Thinking it would prove of benefit to the scrivener, I acquiesced; and, asking the grub-man his name, went up with him to Bartleby.

"Bartleby, this is a friend; you will find him very useful to you."

"Your servant, sir, your servant," said the grub-man, making a low salutation behind his apron. "Hope you find it pleasant here, sir; nice ground—cool apartment—hope you'll stay with us some time—try to make it agreeable. What will you have for dinner to-day?"

"I prefer not to dine to-day," said Bartleby, turning away. "It would disagree with me; I am unused to dinners." So saying, he slowly moved to the other side of the inclosure, and took up a position fronting the dead-wall.

"How's this?" said the grub-man, addressing me with a stare of astonishment. "He's odd, ain't he?"

"I think he is a little deranged," said I, sadly.

"Deranged? deranged is it? Well, now, upon my word, I thought that friend of yourn was a gentleman forger; they are always pale and genteel-like, them forgers. I can't help pity 'em—can't help it, sir. Did you know Monroe Edwards?" he added, touchingly, and paused. Then, laying his hand piteously on my shoulder, sighed, "He died of consumption at Sing-Sing. So you weren't acquainted with Monroe?"

"No, I was never socially acquainted with any forgers. But I cannot stop longer. Look to my friend yonder. You will not lose by it. I will see you again."

Some few days after this, I again obtained admission to the Tombs, and went through the corridors in quest of Bartleby; but without finding him.

"I saw him coming from his cell not long ago," said a turnkey, "maybe he's gone to loiter in the yards."

So I went in that direction.

"Are you looking for the silent man?" said another turnkey, passing me. "Yonder he lies—sleeping in the yard there. 'Tis not twenty minutes since I saw him lie down."

The yard was entirely quiet. It was not accessible to the common prisoners. The surrounding walls, of amazing thickness, kept off all sounds behind them. The Egyptian character of the masonry weighed upon me with its gloom. But a soft imprisoned turf grew under foot. The heart of the eternal pyramids, it seemed, wherein, by some strange magic, through the clefts, grass-seed, dropped by birds, had sprung.

Strangely huddled at the base of the wall, his knees drawn up, and lying on his side, his head touching the cold stones, I saw the wasted Bartleby. But nothing stirred. I paused; then went close up to him; stooped over, and saw that his dim eyes were open; otherwise he seemed profoundly sleeping. Something prompted me to touch him. I felt his hand, when a tingling shiver ran up my arm and down my spine to my feet.

The round face of the grub-man peered upon me now. "His dinner is ready. Won't he dine to-day, either? Or does he live without dining?"

"Lives without dining," said I, and closed the eyes.

"Eh!—He's asleep, ain't he?"

"With kings and counselors," murmured I.

There would seem little need for proceeding further in this history. Imagination will readily supply the meagre recital of poor Bartleby's internment. But, ere parting with the reader, let me say, that if this little narrative has sufficiently interested him, to awaken curiosity as to who Bartleby was, and what manner of life he led prior to the present narrator's making his acquaintance, I can only reply, that in such curiosity I fully share, but am wholly unable to gratify it. Yet here I hardly know whether I should divulge one little item of rumour, which came to my ear a few months after the scrivener's decease. Upon what basis it rested, I could never ascertain; and hence, how true it is I cannot now tell. But, inasmuch as this vague report has not been without a certain suggestive interest to me, however sad, it may prove the same with some others, and so I will briefly mention it. The report was this: that Bartleby had been a subordinate clerk in the Dead Letter Office at Washington, from which he had been suddenly removed by a change in the administration. When I think over this rumour, hardly can I express the emotions which seize me. Dead letters! Does it not sound like dead men? Conceive a man by nature and misfortune prone to a pallid hopelessness: can any business seem more fitted to heighten it than that of continually handling these dead letters, and assorting them for the flames? For by the cart-load they are annually burned. Sometimes from out the folded paper the pale clerk takes a ring—the finger it was meant for, perhaps, moulders in the grave; a bank-note sent in swiftest charity—he whom it would relieve, nor eats nor hungers any more; pardon for those who died despairing; hope for those who died unhoping; good tidings for those who died stifled by unrelieved calamities. On errands of life, these letters speed to death.

Ah, Bartleby! Ah, humanity!

ROHINTON MISTRY

AUSPICIOUS OCCASION

Rohinton Mistry (b. 1952) is a relatively new Canadian author who has enjoyed tremendous early success, not only in Canada but also internationally. He was born in Bombay and immigrated to Canada in 1975, where he began working in a Toronto bank. While attending the University of Toronto in 1983, Mistry started writing stories and winning campus prizes. Tales from Firozsha Baag (1987), in which "Auspicious Occasion" appeared, was itself a remarkably auspicious first book; it was shortlisted for the Governor General's Literary Award and won international attention. In these stories, Mistry brings his "sharp eye and gentle wit" to bear upon "the secret eroticism of a puritan culture ... treat[ing] his characters with warmth and compassion, expressing their world in language that conveys the true flavour of their lives." Mistry followed this collection with a brilliant first novel, Such a Long Journey, which won the Governor General's Literary Award in 1991 and was shortlisted for the Booker Prize. His most recent novel, A Fine Balance, is astonishingly painful, comic, tender, and inventive; it is set during the political unrest of the 1970s, when Indira Gandhi was prime minister of India, and it treats the lives of the four desperately impoverished central figures with a leisurely amplitude and a fullness of detail that is reminiscent of nineteenth-century fiction. A Fine Balance won the 1995 Giller Prize and the 1996 Commonwealth Writer's Prize and was shortlisted for the 1996 Booker Prize. Mistry is married, writes full time, and lives in Brampton, Ontario.

With a bellow Rustomji emerged from the WC. He clutched his undone pyjama drawstring, an extreme rage distorting his yet unshaven features. He could barely keep the yellow-stained pyjamas from falling.

"Mehroo! *Arré* Mehroo! Where are you?" he screamed. "I am telling you, this is more than I can take! Today, of all days, on *Behram roje*. Mehroo! Are you listening?"

Mehroo came, her slipper flopping in time—ploof ploof—one two. She was considerably younger than her husband, having been married off to a thirty-six-year-old man when she was a mere girl of sixteen, before completing her final high-school year. Rustomji, a successful Bombay lawyer, had been considered a fine catch by Mehroo's parents—no one had anticipated that he would be wearing dentures by the time he was fifty. Who, while trapped in the fervor of matchmaking at the height of the wedding season, could imagine a toothless gummy mouth, morning after morning, greeting a woman in her absolute prime? No one. Certainly not Mehroo. She came from an orthodox Parsi family which observed all important days on the Parsi calendar, had the appropriate prayers and ceremonies performed at the fire-temple, and even set aside a room with an iron-frame bed and an iron stool for the women during their unclean time of the month.

Mehroo had welcomed her destiny and had carried to her new home all the orthodoxy of her parents. Except for the separate "unclean" room which Rustomji would not hear of, she was permitted everything. In fact, Rustomji secretly enjoyed most of the age-old traditions while pretending indifference. He loved going to the fire-temple dressed up in his sparkling white *dugli*, starched white trousers, the carefully brushed *pheytoe* on his head—he had a fine head of hair, not yet gone the way of his teeth.

To Rustomji's present yelling Mehroo responded good-humoredly. She tried to remain calm on this morning which was to culminate in prayers at the fire-temple; nothing would mar the perfection of *Behram roje* if she could help it. This day on the Parsi calendar was particularly dear to her; on *Behram roje* her mother had given birth to her at the Awabai Petit Parsi Lying-In Hospital; it was also the day her *navjote* had been performed at the age of seven, when she was confirmed a Zoroastrian by the family priest, *Dustoor* Dhunjisha; and finally, Rustomji had married her on *Behram roje* fourteen years ago, with feasting and celebration continuing into the wee hours of the morning—it was said that not one beggar had gone hungry, such were the quantities of food dumped in the garbage cans of Cama Garden that Day.

Indeed, *Behram roje* meant a lot to Mehroo. Which is why with a lilt in her voice she sang out: "Com—ing! Com—ing!"

Rustomji growled back, "You are deaf or what? Must I scream till my lungs burst?"

"Coming, coming! Two hands, so much to do, the *gunga* is late and the house is unswept—"

"*Arré* forget your *gunga-bunga!*" howled Rustomji. "That stinking lavatory upstairs is leaking again! God only knows what they do to make it leak. There I was, squatting—barely started—when someone pulled the flush. Then on my head I felt—pchuk—all wet! On my head!"

"On your head? Chhee chhee chhee! How horrible! How inauspicious! How ..." and words failed her as she cringed and recoiled from the befouling event. Gingerly she peeked into the WC, fearing a deluge of ordure and filth. What she did see, however, was a steady leak—drip drip drip drip—rhythmical and regular, straight into the toilet bowl, so that using it was out of the question. Rustomji, still clutching his pyjama drawstring, a wild unraveled look about him, fumed behind her as she concluded her inspection.

"Why not call a good plumber ourselves this time instead of complaining to the Baag trustees?" Mehroo ventured. "They will once again do shoddy work."

"I will not spend one paisa of my hard-earned earnings! Those scoundrels sitting with piles of trust money hidden under their arses should pay for it!" stormed Rustomji, making sweeping gestures with the hand that was free of the pyjama string. "I will crap at their office, I will go to crap at their houses, I will crap on their doorsteps if necessary!"

"Hush, Rustomji, don't say such things on *Behram roje*," Mehroo chided. "If you still have to go, I will see if Hirabai next door does not mind."

"With her stupid husband there? A thousand times I've told you I will not step inside in Nariman's presence. Anyway, it is gone now. Vanished," said Rustomji with finality. "Now my whole day will be spoilt. And who knows," he added darkly with perverse satisfaction, "this may even lead to constipation."

"Nariman must have left for the library. I will ask Hirabai, you might have to go later. I am going there now to telephone the office, and when I come back I will make you a nice hot cup of tea. Drink that quickly, *gudh-gudh*, the urge will return," soothed Mehroo, and left. Rustomji decided to boil the water for his bath. He felt unclean all over.

The copper vessel was already filled with water. But someone had forgotten to cover it, and plaster from the ceiling had dripped into it. It floated on the surface, little motes of white. Like the little motes that danced before Rustomji's eyes when he was very tired, after a long day in the hot, dusty courthouse, or when he was very angry, after shouting at the boys of Firozsha Baag for making a nuisance with their cricket in the compound.

Plaster had been dripping for some years now in his A Block flat, as it had been in most of the flats in Firozsha Baag. There had been a respite when Dr. Mody, gadfly to the trustees (bless his soul), had pressed for improvement with the Baag management. But that period ended, and the trustees adopted a new policy to stop all maintenance work not essential to keep the buildings from being condemned.

Following a period of resistance, most of the tenants had taken to looking after their own flats, getting them re-plastered and painted. But to this day Rustomji stubbornly held out, calling his neighbors fools for making things easy for the trustees instead of suffering the discomfort of peeling walls till the scoundrels capitulated.

When the neighbors, under the leadership of Nariman Hansotia, had decided to pool some money and hire a contractor to paint the exterior of A Block, Rustomji, on principle, refused to hand over his share. The building had acquired an appalling patina of yellow and gray griminess. But even the like-able and retired Nariman, who drove every day except Sunday in his 1932 Mercedes-Benz to the Cawasji Framji Memorial Library to read the daily papers from around the world, could not persuade Rustomji to participate.

Totally frustrated, Nariman had returned to Hirabai: "That curmudgeon won't listen to reason, he has sawdust in his head. But if I don't make him the laughing-stock, my name isn't Nariman." Out of the exchange had grown an appended name: Rustomji-the-curmudgeon, and it had spread through Firozsha Baag, enjoying long life and considerable success.

And Nariman Hansotia had then convinced the neighbors to go ahead with the work, advising the contractor to leave untouched the exterior of Rustomji's flat. It would make Rustomji ashamed of himself, he thought, when the painting was finished and the sparkling façade of the building sported one begrimed square. But Rustomji was delighted. He triumphantly told everyone he met, "Mr. Hansotia bought a new suit, and it has a patch on one knee!"

Rustomji chuckled now as he remembered the incident. He filled the copper vessel with fresh water and hoisted it onto the gas stove. The burner hesitated before it caught. He suspected the gas cylinder was about to run out; over a week ago he had telephoned the blasted gas company to deliver a new one. He wondered if there was going to be another shortage, like last year, when they had to burn coals in a *sigri*—the weekly quota of kerosene had been barely enough to make the morning tea.

Tea, thank God for tea, he thought, anticipating with pleasure the second cup Mehroo had promised. He would drink it in copious draughts, piping hot, one continuous flow from cup to saucer to mouth. It just might induce his offended bowels to move and salvage something of this ill-omened morning. Of course, there was the WC of Hirabai Hansotia's that he would have to con-tend with—his bowels were recalcitrant in strange surroundings. It was a matter of waiting and seeing which would prevail: Mehroo's laxative tea or Hirabai's sphincter-tightening lavatory.

He picked up the *Times of India* and settled in his easy chair, waiting for the bath water to boil. Something would have to be done about the peeling paint and plaster; in some places the erosion was so bad, red brick lay exposed. The story went that these flats had been erected in an incredibly short time and with very little money. Cheap materials had been used, and sand carted from nearby Chaupatty beach had been mixed in abundance with substandard cement. Now during the monsoon season beads of moisture trickled down the walls, like sweat down a coolie's back, which considerably hastened the crumbling paint and plaster.

From time to time, Mehroo pointed out the worsening problem, and Rustomji took refuge in railing at the trustees. But today he did not need to worry. She would never mention it on a day like *Behram roje*. There was not any time for argument. Her morning had started early: she had got the children ready for school and packed their lunch; cooked *dhandar-paalyo* and *sali-boti* for dinner; starched and ironed his white shirt, trousers, and *dugli,* all washed the night before, and her white blouse, petticoat and sari; and now those infernal people upstairs had made the WC leak. If Gajra, their *gunga*, did not arrive soon, Mehroo would also have to sweep and mop before she could decorate the entrance with colored chalk designs, hand up the *tohrun* (waiting since the flowerwalla's six a.m. delivery) and spread the fragrance of *loban* through the flat—it was considered unlucky to omit or change the prescribed sequence of these things.

But celebrating in this manner was Mehroo's own choice. As far as Rustomji was concerned, these customs were dead and meaningless. Besides, he had repeatedly explained to her what he called the psychology of *gungas*: "If a particular day is important, never let the *gunga* know, pretend everything is normal. And never, never ask her to come earlier than usual, for she will deliberately come late." But Mehroo did not learn; she trusted, confided, and continued to suffer.

Gajra was the latest in a long line of *gungas* to toil at the house. Before her it had been Tanoo.

For two years, Tanoo came every morning to their flat to sweep and mop, do the dishes, and wash their clothes. A woman in her early seventies, tall and skinny, she was bow-legged and half blind, with an astonishing quantity of wrinkles on her face and limbs. Where her skin was not wrinkled, it was scaly and rough. She had large ears that stuck out under wisps of stringy, coconut-oiled gray hair, and wore spectacles (one lens of which was missing) balanced precariously on a thin pointed nose.

The trouble with Tanoo was that she was always breaking a dish or a cup or saucer. Mehroo was prepared to overlook the inferior sweeping and mopping; the breakage, however, was a tangible loss which Rustomji said would one day ruin them if a stop was not put to it.

Tanoo was periodically threatened with pay cuts and other grimmer forms of retribution. But despite her good intentions and avowals and resolutions there was never any improvement. Her dim eyes were further handicapped by hands which shook and fumbled because of old age and the long unhappiness of a life out of which her husband had fled after bringing into it two sons she single-handedly had to raise, and who were now drunkards, lazy good-for-nothings, and the sorrow of her old age.

"Poor, poor Tanoo," Mehroo would say, helpless to do anything. "Very sad," Rustomji would agree, but would not do more.

So plates and saucers continued to slip out of Tanoo's old, weary hands, continued to crash and shatter, causing Rustomji fiscal grief and Mehroo sorrow—sorrow because she knew that Tanoo would have to go. Rustomji too would have liked to feel sorrow and compassion. But he was afraid. He had decided long ago that this was no country for sorrow or compassion or pity— these were worthless and, at best, inappropriate.

There was a time during his college days, as a volunteer with the Social Service League, when he had thought differently (foolishly, he now felt). Sometimes, he still remembered the SSL camps fondly, the long train rides full of singing and merriment to remote villages lacking the most basic of necessities, where they dug roads and wells, built schoolhouses, and taught the villagers. Hard work, all of it, and yet so much fun, what a wonderful gang they had been, like Dara the Daredevil, the way he jumped in and out of moving trains, he called himself the Tom Mix of the locomotive; and Bajun the Banana Champion—at one camp he had eaten twenty-one of them, not small *ailchee* ones either, regular long green ones; everyone had been a real character.

But Rustomji was not one to allow nostalgia to taint the color of things as he saw them now. He was glad he had put it all behind him.

The way it ended for Tanoo, however, eased the blow a little for Mehroo. Tanoo arranged to leave Bombay and return to the village she had left so long ago, to end her days with her sister's family there. Mehroo was happy for her. Rustomji heaved a great sigh of relief. He had no objections when Mehroo gave her generous gifts at the time of parting. He even suggested getting her a new pair of spectacles. But Tanoo declined the offer, saying she would not have much use for them in the village, with no china plates and saucers to wash.

And so, Tanoo departed and Gajra arrived: young and luscious, and notorious for tardiness.

Coconut hair oil was the only thing Gajra had in common with Tanoo. She was, despite her plumpness, quite pretty; she was, Rustomji secretly thought, voluptuous. And he did not tire of going into the kitchen while Gajra was washing dishes, crouched on her haunches within the parapet of the *mori*. When still a young boy, Rustomji had heard that most *gungas* had no use for underwear—neither brassiere nor knickers. He had confirmed this several times through observation as a lad in his father's house. Gajra provided further proof, proof which popped out from beneath her short blouse during the exertion of sweeping or washing. With a deft movement she would tuck back the ample bosom into her *choli*, unabashed, but not before Rustomji had gazed his fill. Like two prime Ratnagiri mangoes they were, he felt, juicy and golden smooth.

"Her cups runneth over," he would gleefully think, remembering time and time again the little joke from his beloved school days at St. Xavier's. Though not given to proselytizing, the school had a custom of acquainting all its students, Catholic or otherwise, with the Lord's Prayer and the more popular Psalms.

Rustomji's one fervent wish was that some day Gajra's breasts should slip out far enough from under her *choli* to reveal her nipples. "*Dada Ormuzd*, just once let me see them, only once," he would yearn in his depths, trying to picture the nipples: now dark brown and the size of a gram but with the hidden power to swell; now uncontrollably aroused and black, large and pointed.

While waiting for his wish to come true, Rustomji enjoyed watching Gajra modify her sari each morning before she started work: she hauled it up between her thighs and tucked it in around the waist so it would not get wet in the *mori*. When altered like this, the layers produced a very large, very masculine lump over the crotch. But her movements while she, steatopygic, completed her daily transformation—bending her knees, thighs apart, patting her behind to smooth down the fabric—were extremely erotic for Rustomji.

Mehroo was usually present when this went on, so he would have to pretend to read the *Times of India*, looking surreptitiously from behind or over or under and taking his chances. Sometimes, he remembered a little Marathi rhyme he had picked up as a boy. It formed part of a song which was sung at every boisterous, rollicking party his father used to give for his Parsi colleagues from Central Bank. At that time, little Rustom had not understood the meaning, but it went:

> *Sakubai la zaoli*
> *Dadra chi khalti ...*

After many years and many parties, as Rustom grew up, he was allowed to sit with the guests instead of being sent out to play in the compound. The day came when he was allowed his first sip of Scotch and soda from his father's glass. Mother had protested that he was too young, but father had said, "What is there in one sip, you think he will become a drunkard?" Rustom had enjoyed that first sip and had wanted more, to the delight of the guests. "Takes after his father, really likes his peg!" they had guffawed.

It was also around this time that Rustom started to understand the meaning of the rhyme and the song: it was about the encounter of a Parsi gentleman with a *gunga* he caught napping under a dark stairwell—he seduces her quite easily, then goes his merry way. Later, Rustom had sung it to his friends in St. Xavier's, the song which he remembered today, on *Behram roje*, in his easy chair with the *Times of India*. He hoped Gajra would arrive before Mehroo finished using Hirabai's telephone. He could then ogle brazenly, unhindered.

But even as Rustomji thought his impure thoughts and relished them all, Mehroo returned; the office had promised to send the plumber right away. "I told him, '*Bawa*, you are a Parsi too, you know how very important *Behram roje* is' and he said he understands, he will have the WC repaired today."

"The bloody swine understands? Ha! Now he knows it, he will purposely delay; to make you miserable. Go, be frank with the whole world; go, be unhappy." And Mehroo went, to make his tea.

The doorbell rang. Rustomji knew it must be Gajra. But even as he hurried to answer it, he sensed he was walking toward another zone of frustration, that his concupiscence would be thwarted as rudely as his bowels.

His instinct proved accurate. Mehroo rushed out from the kitchen as fast as her flopping slippers would allow, scolding and shooing Gajra away to do only the sweeping—the rest could wait till tomorrow—and leave. Sulking, Rustomji returned to the *Times of India*.

Mehroo then hurriedly made chalk designs at the entrance, not half as elaborate or colorful as planned. Time was running out; she had to get to the fire-temple by eleven. Dreading the inauspiciousness of a delay, she hung a *tohrun* over each doorway (the flowers, languishing since six a.m., luckily retained a spark of life) and went to dress.

When she was ready to leave, Rustomji was still coaxing his bowels with tea. Disgruntled over Gajra's abrupt departure, he nursed his loss silently, blaming Mehroo. "You go ahead," he said, "I will meet you at the fire-temple."

Mehroo took the H route bus. She looked radiant in her white sari, worn the Parsi way, across the right shoulder and over the forehead. The H route bus meandered through narrow streets of squalor once it left the Firozsha Baag neighborhood. It went via Bhindi Bazaar, through Lohar Chawl and Crawford Market, crawling painfully amidst the traffic of cars and people, handcarts and trucks.

Usually, during a bus ride to the fire-temple, Mehroo attentively watched the scene unfolding as the bus made its creeping way, wondering at the resilient ingenuity with which life was made liveable inside dingy little holes and inhospitable, frightful structures. Now, however, Mehroo sat oblivious to the bustle and meanness of lives on these narrow streets. None of it pierced the serenity with which she anticipated the perfect peace and calm she would soon be a part of inside the fire-temple.

She looked with pleasure at the white sari draping her person, and adjusted the border over her forehead. When she returned home, the sari would be full of the fragrance of sandalwood, absorbed from the smoke of the sacred fire. She would hang it up beside her bed instead of washing it, to savor the fragrance as long as it lasted. She remembered how, as a child, she would wait for her mother to return from the fire-temple so she could bury her face in her lap and breathe in the sandalwood smell. Her father's *dugli* gave off the same perfume, but her mother's white sari was better, it felt so soft. Then there was the ritual of *chasni*: all the brothers and sisters wearing their prayer caps would eagerly sit around the dining-table to partake of the fruit and sweets blessed during the day's prayer ceremonies.

Mehroo was a little saddened when she thought of her own children, who did not give a second thought to these things; she had to coax them to finish the *chasni* or it would sit for days, unnoticed and untouched.

Even as a child, Mehroo had adored going to the fire-temple. She loved its smells, its tranquility, its priests in white performing their elegant, mystical rituals. Best of all she loved the inner sanctuary, the sanctum sanctorum, dark and mysterious, with marble floor and marble walls, which only the officiating priest could enter, to tend to the sacred fire burning in the huge, shining silver *afargaan* on its marble pedestal. She felt she could sit for hours outside the sanctuary, watching the flames in their dance of life, seeing the sparks fly up the enormous dark dome resembling the sky. It was her own private key to the universe, somehow making less frightening the notions of eternity and infinity.

In high school she would visit the fire-temple before exam week. Her offering of a sandalwood stick would be deposited in the silver tray at the door of the inner sanctuary, and she would reverently smear her forehead and throat with the gray ash left in the tray for this purpose. *Dustoor* Dhunjisha, in his flowing white robe, would always be there to greet her with a hug, always addressing her as his dear daughter. The smell of his robe would remind her of mother's sari fragrant with sandalwood. Serene and fortified, she would go to write her exam.

Dustoor Dhunjisha was now almost seventy-five, and was not always around when Mehroo went to the fire-temple. Some days, when he did not feel well, he stayed in his room and let a younger priest look after the business of prayer and worship. But today she hoped he would be present; she wanted to see that gentle face from her childhood, the long white beard, the reassuring paunch.

After marrying Rustomji and moving into Firozsha Baag, Mehroo had continued to go to *Dustoor* Dhunjisha for all ceremonies. In this, she risked the ire of the *dustoorji* who lived in their own block on the second floor. The latter believed that he had first claim to the business of Firozsha Baag tenants, that they should all patronize his nearby *agyaari* as long as he could accommodate them. But Mehroo persisted in her loyalty to Dhunjisha. She paid no attention to the high dudgeon the A Block priest directed at her, or to Rustomji's charges.

Under the priestly garb of Dhunjisha, protested Rustomji, lurked a salacious old man taking advantage of his venerable image: "Loves to touch and feel women, the old goat—the younger and fleshier, the more fun he has hugging and squeezing them." Mehroo did not believe it for a moment. She was always pleading with him not to say nasty things about such a holy figure.

But this was not all. Rustomji swore that Dhunjisha and his ilk had been known to exchange lewd remarks between lines of prayer, to slip them in amidst scripture recitals, especially on days of ceremony when sleek nubile women in their colorful finery attended in large numbers. The oft-repeated *Ashem Vahoo* was his favorite example:

> *Ashem Vahoo*
> See the tits on that chickie-boo ...

This version was a popular joke among the less religious, and Mehroo dismissed it as more of Rustomji's irreverence. He assured her they did it very skilfully and thus went undetected. Besides, the white kerchief all *dustoors* were required to wear over the nose and mouth, like masked bandits, to keep their breath from polluting the sacred fire, made it difficult to hear their muttering in the first place. Rustomji claimed it took a trained ear to sift through their mumbles and separate the prayers from the obscenities.

The H route bus stopped at Marine Lines. Mehroo alighted and walked down Princess Street, wondering about the heavy traffic. Cars and buses were backed up all the way on the flyover from Princess Street to Marine Drive.

She neared the fire-temple and saw parked outside its locked gates two police cars and a police van. Her step quickened. The last time the gates had been closed, as far as she knew, was during Hindu-Muslim riots following partition; she was afraid to think what calamity had now come to pass. Parsis and non-Parsis were craning and peering through the bars of the gates; the same human curiosity had touched them all. A policeman was trying to persuade them to disperse.

Mehroo lingered on the periphery of the crowd, irresolute, then plunged into it. She saw *Dustoor* Kotwal leave the temple building and walk purposefully towards the gate. Jostling her way through the milling people, she attempted to get his attention. He was, like *Dustoor* Dhunjisha, a resident temple priest, and knew her well.

Dustoor Kotwal had an announcement for the Parsis: "All prayers and ceremonies scheduled for today have been cancelled, except the prayer for the dead." He was gone before Mehroo could reach the gate.

She now began to pick up alarming words in the crowd: "... murdered last night ... stabbed in the back ... police and CID." Her spirits faltered. All this on *Behram roje* which she had done everything to make perfect? Why were things being so cruelly wrenched out of her control? She made up her mind to stay till she could speak to someone who knew what had happened.

Rustomji finished his cup of tea as Mehroo left. He decided to wait awhile before his bath, to give his obdurate bowels one more chance.

But after another ten minutes of the *Times of India* and not a murmur from his depths, he gave up. Getting things ready for the bath, he arched his back till his bottom stuck out, then raised one foot slightly and tensed. Nothing happened. Not even a little fart. He inspected his *dugli* and trousers: the starch was just right—not too limp, not too stiff. He rubbed his stomach and hoped he would not have to go later at the fire-temple; the WC there was horrid, with urine usually spattered outside the toilet bowl or excrement not flushed away. To look at it, it was not Parsis who used the WC, he felt, but uneducated, filthy, ignorant barbarians.

Rustomji performed his ablutions, trying to forget the disgusting leak from above while he had squatted below. Fortunately, with every mugful of hot water he scooped from the bucket and poured down his back, splashed on his face, and felt trickle down his crotch and thighs, that foul leak was reduced to a memory growing dimmer by the moment; the cleansing water which flowed down the drain swept away what remained of that memory to a distant remove; and once he had dried himself, it was blotted out completely. Rustomji was whole again.

Now all that lingered was the fresh refreshing scent, as the advertisement proclaimed, of lifegiving Lifebuoy Soap. Lifebuoy Soap and Johnnie Walker Scotch were the only two items which endured in the sumptuary laws passed down to Rustomji through three generations, and he relished them both. The one change wrought by the passing years was that Johnnie Walker Scotch, freely available under the British, could now be obtained only on the black market, and was responsible for Rustomji's continuing grief over the British departure.

Emerging from the bathroom, he was pleased to discover his bowels no longer bothered him. The desultoriness plaguing his morning hours had fled, and a new alacrity took charge of his actions. The bows on the *dugli* gave him some trouble as he dressed—usually it was Mehroo who tied these. But in his present mood he was more than a match for them. With a last brush to his brilliantined hair he perched the *pheytoe* on it, gave a final tug of encouragement to the bows and surveyed himself in the mirror. Pleased with what he saw, he was ready for the fire-temple.

The H route bus stop was his destination as he stepped out buoyantly. The compound was deserted, the boys were all at school. In the evening, their noisy games would fill it with rowdiness and nuisance that he would have to combat if he was to enjoy peace and quiet. Confident of his control over them, he decided to pass the H route bus stop and walk further, to the A-1 Express, past Tar Gully and its menacing mouth. His starchy whiteness aroused in him feelings of resplendence and invincibility, and he had no objection to the viewing of his progress by the street.

There was a long queue at the A-1 bus stop. Rustomji disregarded the entire twisting, curving length and stationed himself at the head. He stared benignly into space, deaf to the protests of the queue's serpentine windings, and pondered the options of upper deck and lower deck. He decided on the lower—it might prove difficult to negotiate the steep flight of steps to the upper with as much poise as befitted his attire.

The bus arrived and the conductor was yelling out, even before it came to a standstill, "Upper deck upper deck! Everybody upper deck!" Rustomji, of course, had already settled the question. Ignoring the conductor, he grasped the overhead railing and stood jauntily on the lower deck. The usually belligerent conductor said nothing.

The bus approached Marine Lines, and Rustomji moved towards the door to prepare for his descent. He managed quite well despite the rough and bumpy passage of the bus. Without bruising his mien or his attire, he reached the door and waited.

But unbeknownst to Rustomji, on the upper deck sat fate in the form of a mouth chewing tobacco and betel nut, a mouth with a surfeit of juice and aching jaws crying for relief. And when the bus halted at Marine Lines, fate leaned out the window to release a generous quantity of sticky, viscous, dark red stuff.

Dugli gleaming in the midday sun, Rustomji emerged and stepped to the pavement. The squirt of tobacco juice caught him between the shoulder blades: blood red on sparkling white.

Rustomji felt it and whirled around. Looking up, he saw a face with crimson lips trickling juice, mouth chewing contentedly, and in an instant knew what had happened. He roared in agony, helpless, screaming as painfully as though it was a knife in the back, while the bus slowly pulled away.

"*Saala gandoo* Filthy son of a whore! Shameless animal—spitting *paan* from the bus! Smash your face I will, you pimp ..."

A small crowd gathered around Rustomji. Some were curious, a few sympathetic; but most were enjoying themselves.

"What happened? Who hurt the ..."

"Tch tch, someone spat *paan* on his *dugli* ..."

"Heh heh heh! *Bawaji* got *paan pichkari* right on his white *dugli* ..."

"*Bawaji bawaji, dugli* looks very nice now, red and white, just like in technicolor ..."

The taunting and teasing added to the outrage of tobacco juice made Rustomji do something dangerously foolish. He diverted his anger from the harmlessly receding bus to the crowd, overlooking the fact that unlike the bus, it was close enough to answer his vituperation with fury of its own.

"*Arré* you sisterfucking *ghatis*, what are you laughing for? Have you no shame? *Sasla chootia* spat *paan* on my *dugli* and you think that is fun?"

A ripple of tension went through the crowd. It diplaced the former light-hearted teasing they were indulging in at the spectacle of the *paan*-drenched *bawaji*.

"*Arré* who does he think he is, abusing us, giving such bad-bad *ghali?*" Someone pushed Rustomji from behind.

"*Bawaji*, we'll break all your bones. *Maaro saala bawajiko!* Beat up the bloody *bawaji*."

"*Arré* your arse we'll tear to shreds!" People were jostling him from every side. The *phytoe* was plucked from his head, and they tugged at the bows of the *dugli*.

All anger forgotten, Rustomji feared for his person. He knew he was in serious trouble. Not one friendly face in this group which was now looking for fun of a different sort. In panic he tried to undo the hostility: "*Arré* please *yaar*, why harass an old man? *Jaané dé, yaar*. Let me go, friends."

Then his desperate search for a way out was rewarded—a sudden inspiration which just might work. He reached his fingers into his mouth, dislodged the dentures, and spat them out onto his palm. Two filaments of saliva, sparkling in the midday sun, momentarily connected the dentures to his gums. They finally broke and dribbled down his chin. With much effort and spittle, he sputtered: "Look, such an old man, no teeth even," and held out his hand for viewing.

The collapsed mouth and flapping lips appeased everyone. A general tittering spread through the assembly. Rustomji the clown was triumphant. He has restored to himself the harmlessness of the original entertaining spectacle, *pheytoe* back on head, teeth back in mouth.

Then, under the amused gaze of the crowd, Rustomji undid the bows of the *dugli* and removed it. Going to the fire-temple was out of the question. Tears of shame and rage welled in his eyes, and through the mist he saw the blood-red blotch. With the *dugli* off he still felt a little damp on the back—the juice had penetrated his shirt and *sudnra* as well. For the second time that day he had been soiled in a most repulsive way.

Someone handed him a newspaper to wrap the *dugli* in; another picked up the packet of sandalwood he had dropped. At that moment, when Rustomji looked most helpless, a bus arrived and the crowd departed.

He was left alone, holding the newspapered *dugli* and the sandalwood in brown paper. The angle of his *pheytoe* had shifted, and he no longer looked or felt unassailable. Feebly, he hailed a taxi. It was a small Morris, and he had to stoop low to get in, to keep the *pheytoe* from being knocked off his head.

The horror of what Mehroo had found out at the fire-temple abated on the way home. Her thoughts turned to Rustomji; surely he should have finished his bath and arrived at the fire-temple, she had waited there for over two hours, first outside the gates then inside. Maybe Rustomji has already found out, she hoped, maybe he knows the prayers were canceled.

She turned the latchkey and entered the flat. Rustomji lay sprawled on the easy chair. Thrown on the teapoy beside him was his *dugli*, the blood-red *paan* stain prominent.

He was surprised to see her back so soon, looking so distressed. Mehroo always came from the fire-temple with something resembling beatitude shining on her face. Today she looked as though she had seen *sataan* himself inside the fire-temple, thought Rustomji.

She moved closer to the teapoy, and the light caught the *dugli*. She shrieked in terror: "*Dustoor* Dhunjisha's *dugli!* But ... but ... how did you—?"

"What rubbish are you talking again? Some swine spat *paan* on my *dugli*." He decided not to mention his narrow escape. "Why would I have that fat rascal Dhunjisha's *dugli?*"

Mehroo sat down weakly. "God forgive you your words, you do not know *Dustoor* Dhunjisha's was murdered!"

"What! In the fire-temple? But who would—?"

"I will tell you everything if you wait for one minute. First I need a drink of water, I feel so tired."

Rustomji's stolidity was pierced through. He hurried to the kitchen for a glass of water. Mehroo then told how Dhunjisha had been stabbed by a *chasniwalla* employed at the fire-temple. The *chasniwalla* had confessed. He was trying to steal some silver trays from the fire-temple when Dhunjisha had unwittingly wandered into the room; the *chasniwalla* panicked and killed him. Then, to be rid of the corpse, he threw it in the sacred fire-temple well.

"They found the body this morning," continued Mehroo. "I was let inside later on, and the police were examining the body, nothing had been removed, he was still wearing his *dugli*, it looked exactly like ..." She motioned towards Rustomji's on the teapoy, shuddered, and fell silent.

She began to busy herself. She carried her glass back to the kitchen along with Rustomji's teacup from earlier that morning, and lit the stove to get lunch ready. She came back, examined the blot of *paan* on his *dugli* and wondered aloud about the best way to remove the stain, then was silent again.

Rustomji heaved a sigh. "What is happening in the world I don't know. Parsi killing Parsi ... *chasniwalla* and *dustoor* ..."

He, too, fell silent, slowly shaking his head. He gazed pensively at the walls and ceiling, where bits of paint and plaster were waiting to peel, waiting to fall into their pots and pans, their vessels of water, their lives. Tomorrow, Gajra would come and sweep away the flakes of white from the floor; she would clean out the pots and pans, and fill fresh water into the vessels. The *Times of India* would arrive, he would read it as he sipped his tea, and see

Nariman Hansotia drive past in his 1932 Mercedes-Benz to the Cawasji Framji Memorial Library to read the daily papers from around the world. Mehroo would wipe away with water the colored chalk designs at the front entrance and take down the *tohrun* from over the doorways—the flowers would be dry shrunken scraps by morning.

Mehroo looked at Rustomji musing on the easy chair, and felt inside herself the melancholy of his troubled, distant gaze. This rare glimpse of the softness underneath his tough exterior touched her. She slipped away quietly to the bedroom, to change her sari.

The unraveled yards of crumpled fabric, unredeemed by sandalwood fragrance, were deposited on the bed. There was no point in folding and hanging up the sari beside the bed, it could go straight for washing. She regarded it with something close to despair and noticed, on the wall beside the bed, marks left by trickling water from last year's rains.

This year's monsoons were due soon; they would wash clean the narrow streets she had passed through that morning on her way to the fire-temple. And in the flat the rain would send new beads of moisture, to replace last year's marks with new imprints.

The aroma of *dhandar-paatyo*, wafting from the kitchen, gently penetrated her meditation. It reminded her that *Behram roje* was not over yet. But she returned to the kitchen and put off the stove—it would still be a while to lunch, she knew. Instead, she prepared two cups of tea. Between ten a.m. and four p.m. she never drank tea, it was one of her strictest rules. Today, for Rustomji's sake, she would make an exception.

She went back to him, asked if he was ready for lunch and, receiving the anticipated refusal, smiled to herself with a tender satisfaction—how well she knew her Rustomji. She felt very close to him at this moment. He shook his head slowly from side to side, gazing pensively into the distance. "Stomach is still heavy. Must be constipated."

"And the wc?"

"Still leaking."

She re-emerged with the two cups she had left ready in the kitchen: "Another cup of tea then?"

Rustomji nodded gratefully.

ALICE MUNRO

ROYAL BEATINGS

Alice Munro (b. 1931) was raised in Wingham, Ontario, the kind of small town that features so prominently in her most famous stories. Munro has sometimes, quite wrongly, been thought of as a regional writer; in fact, the eccentricities and the rich texture of her working-class childhood in rural southwestern Ontario provided fertile ground for Munro's fiction. Flannery O'Connor, the brilliant short story writer of the American South, used regional material in much the same way. Munro is often compared to O'Connor whom Munro cites as an early and lasting enthusiasm. Like O'Connor and fellow Canadian Mavis Gallant, Munro is now recognized internationally as one of the finest short-story writers. The settings of Munro's fiction, however, now range widely over the map of Canada and beyond, as Munro continues to use her autobiographical material and acute powers of observation. Munro's work, unlike O'Connor's, has also been read as a major force in the contemporary articulation of female experience.

Munro studied at the University of Western Ontario, married, and moved to Vancouver and Victoria. At this stage of her life, when she had the competing claims of husband, house, and young daughters to attend to, Munro turned seriously to fiction. During the 1950s and 1960s Munro sent her stories off to various periodicals, and then in 1968 published her first collection, Dance of the Happy Shades. *This book won the Governor General's Literary Award for fiction, launching the author's remarkable career. She followed this book with* Lives of Girls and Women *(1972), a book of linked stories that is sometimes called a novel and that Munro describes as "the classic childhood, adolescence, break-through into maturity book."*

Her marriage to Victoria bookseller Jim Munro having ended, Alice Munro moved back to Ontario in 1972. Subsequent collections of stories include Something I've Been Meaning to Tell You *(1974);* Who Do You Think You Are? *(1978), which was another book of linked stories of which "Royal Beatings" is the first;* The Moons of Jupiter *(1982);* The Progress of Love *(1986);* Friend of My Youth *(1991); and* Open Secrets *(1994), from which "The Jack Randa Hotel" is taken. Munro has also published* Selected Stories *(1996), which includes twenty-eight of the stories from her seven collections.*

Munro is the recipient of three Governor General's Literary Awards, the Commonwealth Writer's Prize, the Canada-Australia Literary Award, and the 1990 Molson Prize for her "outstanding lifetime contribution to the cultural and intellectual life of Canada." "I never intended to be a short story writer," Munro has said. "I started writing them because I didn't have time to write anything else ... And then I got used to writing stories, so I saw my material that way, and now I don't think I'll ever write a novel."

Royal Beating. That was Flo's promise. You are going to get one Royal Beating.

The word Royal lolled on Flo's tongue, took on trappings. Rose had a need to picture things, to pursue absurdities, that was stronger than the need to stay out of trouble, and instead of taking this threat to heart she pondered: how is a beating royal? She came up with a tree-lined avenue, a crowd of formal spectators, some white horses and black slaves. Someone knelt, and the blood came leaping out like banners. An occasion both savage and splendid. In real life they didn't approach such dignity, and it was only Flo who tried to supply the event with some high air of necessity and regret. Rose and her father soon got beyond anything presentable.

Her father was king of the royal beatings. Those Flo gave never amounted to much; they were quick cuffs and slaps dashed off while her attention remained elsewhere. You get out of my road, she would say. You mind your own business. You take that look off your face.

They lived behind a store in Hanratty, Ontario. There were four of them: Rose, her father, Flo, Rose's young half brother Brian. The store was really a house, bought by Rose's father and mother when they married and set up here in the furniture and upholstery repair business. Her mother could do upholstery. From both parents Rose should have inherited clever hands, a quick sympathy with materials, an eye for the nicest turns of mending, but she hadn't. She was clumsy, and when something broke she couldn't wait to sweep it up and throw it away.

Her mother had died. She said to Rose's father during the afternoon, "I have a feeling that is so hard to describe. It's like a boiled egg in my chest, with the shell left on." She died before night, she had a blood clot on her lung. Rose was a baby in a basket at the time, so of course could not remember any of this. She heard it from Flo, who must have heard it from her father. Flo came along soon afterwards, to take over Rose in the basket, marry her father, open up the front room to make a grocery store. Rose, who had known the house only as a store, who had known only Flo for a mother, looked back on the sixteen or so months her parents spent here as an orderly, far gentler and more ceremonious time, with little touches of affluence. She had nothing to go on but some egg cups her mother had bought, with a pattern of vines and birds on them, delicately drawn as if with red ink; the pattern was beginning to wear away. No books or clothes or pictures of her mother remained. Her father must have got rid of them, or else Flo would. Flo's only story about her mother, the one about her death, was oddly grudging. Flo liked the details of a death: the things people said, the way they protested or tried to get out of bed or swore or laughed (some did those things), but when she said that Rose's mother mentioned a hard-boiled egg in her chest she made the comparison sound slightly foolish, as if her mother really was the kind of person who might think you could swallow an egg whole.

Her father had a shed out behind the store, where he worked at his furniture repairing and restoring. He caned chair seats and backs, mended wickerwork, filled cracks, put legs back on, all most admirably and skillfully and cheaply. That was his pride: to startle people with such fine work, such moderate, even ridiculous charges. During the Depression people could not afford to pay more, perhaps, but he continued the practice through the war, through the years of prosperity after the war, until he died. He never discussed with Flo what he charged or what was owing. After he died she had to go out and unlock the shed and take all sorts of scraps of paper and torn envelopes from the big wicked-looking hooks that were his files. Many of these she found were not accounts or receipts at all but records of the weather, bits of information about the garden, things he had been moved to write down.

> *Ate new potatoes 25th June. Record.*
> *Dark Day, 1880's, nothing supernatural.*
> *Clouds of ash from forest fires.*
> *Aug 16, 1938. Giant thunderstorm in evng.*
> *Lightning str. Pres. Church,*
> *Turberry Twp. Will of God?*
> *Scald strawberries to remove acid.*
> *All things are alive. Spinoza.*

Flo thought Spinoza must be some new vegetable he planned to grow, like broccoli or eggplant. He would often try some new thing. She showed the scrap of paper to Rose and asked, did she know what Spinoza was? Rose did know, or had an idea—she was in her teens by that time—but she replied that she did not. She had reached an age where she thought she could not stand to know any more, about her father, or about Flo; she pushed any discovery aside with embarrassment and dread.

There was a stove in the shed, and many rough shelves covered with cans of paint and varnish, shellac and turpentine, jars of soaking brushes and also some dark sticky bottles of cough medicine. Why should a man who coughed constantly, whose lungs took in a whiff of gas in the War (called, in Rose's earliest childhood, not the First, but the Last, War) spend all his days breathing fumes of paint and turpentine? At the time, such questions were not asked as often as they are now. On the bench outside Flo's store several old men from the neighborhood sat gossiping, drowsing, in the warm weather, and some of these old men coughed all the time too. The fact is they were dying, slowly and discreetly, of what was called, without any particular sense of grievance, "the foundry disease." They had worked all their lives at the foundry in town, and now they sat still, with their wasted yellow faces, coughing, chuckling, drifting into aimless obscenity on the subject of women walking by, or any young girl on a bicycle.

From the shed came not only coughing, but speech, a continual muttering, reproachful or encouraging, usually just below the level at which separate words could be made out. Slowing down when her father was at a tricky piece of work, taking on a cheerful speed when he was doing something less demanding, sandpapering or painting. Now and then some words would break through and hang clear and nonsensical on the air. When he realized they were out, there would be a quick bit of cover-up coughing, a swallowing, an alert, unusual silence.

"Macaroni, pepperoni, Botticelli, beans—"

What could that mean? Rose used to repeat such things to herself. She could never ask him. The person who spoke these words and the person who spoke to her as her father were not the same, though they seemed to occupy the same space. It would be the worst sort of taste to acknowledge the person who was not supposed to be there; it would not be forgiven. Just the same, she loitered and listened.

The cloud-capped towers, she heard him say once.

"The cloud-capped towers, the gorgeous palaces."

That was like a hand clapped against Rose's chest, not to hurt, but astonish her, to take her breath away. She had to run then, she had to get away. She knew that was enough to hear, and besides, what if he caught her? It would be terrible.

This was something the same as bathroom noises. Flo had saved up, and had a bathroom put in, but there was no place to put it except in a corner of the kitchen. The door did not fit, the walls were only beaverboard. The result was that even the tearing of a piece of toilet paper, the shifting of a haunch, was audible to those working or talking or eating in the kitchen. They were all familiar with each other's nether voices, not only in their more explosive moments but in their intimate sighs and growls and pleas and statements. And they were all most prudish people. So no one ever seemed to hear, or be listening, and no reference was made. The person creating the noise in the bathroom was not connected with the person who walked out.

They lived in a poor part of town. There was Hanratty and West Hanratty, with the river flowing between them. This was West Hanratty. In Hanratty the social structure ran from doctors and dentists and lawyers down to foundry workers and factory workers and draymen; in West Hanratty it ran from factory workers and foundry workers down to large improvident families of casual bootleggers and prostitutes and unsuccessful thieves. Rose thought of her own family as straddling the river, belonging nowhere, but that was not true. West Hanratty was where the store was and they were, on the straggling tail end of the main street. Across the road from them was a blacksmith shop, boarded up about the time the war started, and a house that had been another store at one time. The Salada Tea sign had never been taken out of the front window; it remained as a proud and interesting decoration though there was no Salada Tea for sale inside. There was just a bit of sidewalk, too cracked and tilted for roller-skating, though Rose longed for roller skates and often pictured herself whizzing along in a plaid skirt, agile and fashionable. There was one street light, a tin flower; then the amenities gave up and there were dirt roads and boggy places, front-yard dumps and strange-looking houses. What made the houses strange-looking were the attempts to keep them from going completely to ruin. With some the attempt had never been made. These were gray and rotted and leaning over, falling into a landscape of scrub hollows, frog ponds, cattails and nettles. Most houses, however, had been patched up with tarpaper, a few fresh shingles, sheets of tin, hammered-out stovepipes, even cardboard. This was, of course, in the days before the war, days of what would later be legendary poverty, from which Rose would remember mostly low-down things—serious-looking anthills and wooden steps, and a cloudy, interesting, problematical light on the world.

There was a long truce between Flo and Rose in the beginning. Rose's nature was growing like a prickly pineapple, but slowly, and secretly, hard pride and skepticism overlapping, to make something surprising even to herself. Before she was old enough to go to school, and while Brian was still in the baby carriage, Rose stayed in the store with both of them—Flo sitting on the high stool behind the counter, Brian asleep by the window; Rose knelt or lay on the wide creaky floorboards working with crayons on pieces of brown paper too torn or irregular to be used for wrapping.

People who came to the store were mostly from the houses around. Some country people came too, on their way home from town, and a few people from Hanratty, who walked across the bridge. Some people were always on the main street, in and out of stores, as if it was their duty to be always on display and their right to be welcomed. For instance, Becky Tyde.

Becky Tyde climbed up on Flo's counter, made room for herself beside an open tin of crumbly jam-filled cookies.

"Are these any good?" she said to Flo, and boldly began to eat one.

"When are you going to give us a job, Flo?"

"You could go and work in the butcher shop," said Flo innocently. "You could go and work for your brother."

"Roberta?" said Becky with a stagey sort of contempt. "You think I'd work for him?" Her brother who ran the butcher shop was named Robert but was often called Roberta, because of his meek and nervous ways. Becky Tyde laughed. Her laugh was loud and noisy like an engine bearing down on you.

She was a big-headed loud-voiced dwarf, with a mascot's sexless swagger, a red velvet tam, a twisted neck that forced her to hold her head on one side, always looking up and sideways. She wore little polished high-heeled shoes, real lady's shoes. Rose watched her shoes, being scared of the rest of her, of her laugh and her neck. She knew from Flo that Becky Tyde had been sick with polio as a child, that was why her neck was twisted and why she had not grown any taller. It was hard to believe that she started out differently, that she had ever been normal. Flo said she was not cracked, she had as much brains as anybody, but she knew she could get away with anything.

"You know I used to live out here?" Becky said, noticing Rose. "Hey! What's-your-name! Didn't I used to live out here, Flo?"

"If you did it was before my time," said Flo, as if she didn't know anything.

"That was before the neighborhood got so downhill. Excuse me saying so. My father built his house out here and he built his slaughter-house and we had half an acre of orchard."

"Is that so?" said Flo, using her humoring voice, full of false geniality, humility even. "Then why did you ever move away?"

"I told you, it got to be such a downhill neighborhood," said Becky. She would put a whole cookie in her mouth if she felt like it, let her cheeks puff out like a frog's. She never told any more.

Flo knew anyway, as who didn't. Everyone knew the house, red brick with the veranda pulled off and the orchard, what was left of it, full of the usual outflow—car seats and washing machines and bedsprings and junk. The house would never look sinister, in spite of what had happened in it, because there was so much wreckage and confusion all around.

Becky's old father was a different kind of butcher from her brother according to Flo. A bad-tempered Englishman. And different from Becky in the matter of mouthiness. His was never open. A skinflint, a family tyrant.

After Becky had polio he wouldn't let her go back to school. She was seldom seen outside the house, never outside the yard. He didn't want people gloating. That was what Becky said, at the trial. Her mother was dead by that time and her sisters married. Just Becky and Robert at home. People would stop Robert on the road and ask him, "How about your sister, Robert? Is she altogether better now?"

"Yes."

"Does she do the housework? Does she get your supper?"

"Yes."

"And is your father good to her, Robert?"

The story being that the father beat them, had beaten all his children and beaten his wife as well, beat Becky more now because of her deformity, which some people believed he had caused (they did not understand about polio). The stories persisted and got added to. The reason that Becky was kept out of sight was now supposed to be her pregnancy, and the father of the child was supposed to be her own father. Then people said it had been born, and disposed of.

"What?"

"Disposed of," Flo said. "They used to say go and get your lamb chops at Tyde's, get them nice and tender! It was all lies in all probability," she said regretfully.

Rose could be drawn back—from watching the wind shiver along the old torn awning, catch in the tear—by this tone of regret, caution, in Flo's voice. Flo telling a story—and this was not the only one, or even the most lurid one, she knew—would incline her head and let her face go soft and thoughtful, tantalizing, warning.

"I shouldn't even be telling you this stuff."

More was to follow.

Three useless young men, who hung around the livery stable, got together—or were got together, by more influential and respectful men in town—and prepared to give old man Tyde a horsewhipping, in the interests of public morality. They blacked their faces. They were provided with whips and a quart of whiskey apiece, for courage. They were: Jelly Smith, a horse-racer and a drinker; Bob Temple, a ballplayer and strongman; and Hat Nettleton, who worked on the town dray, and had his nickname from a bowler hat he wore, out of vanity as much as for the comic effect. (He still worked on the dray, in fact; he had kept the name if not the hat, and could often be seen in public—almost as often as Becky Tyde—delivering sacks of coal, which blackened his face and arms. That should have brought to mind his story, but didn't. Present time and past, the shady melodramatic past of Flo's stories, were quite separate, at least for Rose. Present people could not be fitted into the past. Becky herself, town oddity and public pet, harmless and malicious, could never match the butcher's prisoner, the cripple daughter, a white streak at the window: mute, beaten, impregnated. As with the house, only a formal connection could be made.)

The young men primed to do the horsewhipping showed up late, outside Tyde's house, after everybody had gone to bed. They had a gun, but they used up their ammunition firing it off in the yard. They yelled for the butcher and beat on the door; finally they broke it down. Tyde concluded they were after his money, so he put some bills in a handkerchief and sent Becky down with them, maybe thinking those men would be touched or scared by the sight of a little wry-necked girl, a dwarf. But that didn't content them. They came upstairs and dragged the butcher out from under his bed, in his nightgown. They dragged him outside and stood him in the snow. The temperature was four below zero, a fact noted later in court. They meant to hold a mock trial but they could not remember how it was done. So they began to beat him and kept beating until he fell. They yelled at him, *Butcher's meat!* and continued beating him while his nightgown and the snow he was lying in turned red. His son Robert said in court that he had not watched the beating. Becky said that Robert had watched at first but had run away and hid. She herself had watched all the way through. She watched the men leave at last and her father make his delayed bloody progress through the snow and up the steps of the veranda. She did not go out to help him, or open the door until he got to it. Why not? she was asked in court, and she said she did not go out because she just had her nightgown on, and she did not open the door because she did not want to let the cold into the house.

Old man Tyde then appeared to have recovered his strength. He sent Robert to harness the horse, and made Becky heat water so that he could wash. He dressed and took all the money and with no explanation to his children got into the cutter and drove to Belgrave where he left the horse tied in the cold and took the early morning train to Toronto. On the train he behaved oddly, groaning and cursing as if he was drunk. He was picked up on the streets of Toronto a day later, out of his mind with fever, and was taken to a hospital, where he died. He still had all the money. The cause of death was given as pneumonia.

But the authorities got wind, Flo said. The case came to trial. The three men who did it all received long prison sentences. A farce, said Flo. Within a year they were all free, had all been pardoned and had jobs waiting for them. And why was that? It was because too many higher-ups were in on it. And it seemed as if Becky and Robert had no interest in seeing justice done. They were left well-off. They bought a house in Hanratty. Robert went into the store. Becky after her long seclusion started on a career of public sociability and display.

That was all. Flo put the lid down on the story as if she was sick of it. It reflected no good on anybody.

"Imagine," Flo said.

Flo at this time must have been in her early thirties. A young woman. She wore exactly the same clothes that a woman of fifty, or sixty, or seventy, might wear: print housedresses loose at the neck and sleeves as well as the waist; bib aprons, also of print, which took off when she came from the kitchen into the store. This was a common costume at the time, for a poor though not absolutely poverty-stricken woman; it was also, in a way, a scornful deliberate choice. Flo scorned slacks, she scorned the outfits of people trying to be in style, she scorned lipstick and permanents. She wore her own black hair cut straight across, just long enough to push behind her ears. She was tall but fine-boned, with narrow wrists and shoulders, a small head, a pale, freckled, mobile, monkeyish face. If she had thought it worthwhile, and had the resources, she might have had a black-and-pale, fragile, nurtured sort of pretti-ness; Rose realized that later. But she would have to have been a different person altogether; she would have to have learned to resist making faces, at herself and others.

Rose's earliest memories of Flo were of extraordinary softness and hard-ness. The soft hair, the long, soft, pale cheeks, soft almost invisible fuzz in front of her knees, hardness of her lap, flatness of her front.

When Flo sang:

> Oh the buzzin' of the bees in the cigarette trees
> And the soda-water fountain ...

Rose thought of Flo's old life before she married her father, when she worked as a waitress in the coffee shop in Union Station, and went with her girl friends Mavis and Irene to Centre Island, and was followed by men on dark streets and knew how payphones and elevators worked. Rose heard in her voice the reckless dangerous life of cities, the gum-chewing sharp answers.

And when she sang:

> Then slowly, slowly, she got up
> And slowly she came nigh him
> And all she said, that she ever did say,
> Was young man I think, you're dyin'!

Rose thought of a life Flo seemed to have had beyond that, earlier than that, crowded and legendary, with Barbara Allen and Becky Tyde's father and all kinds of old outrages and sorrows jumbled up together in it.

The royal beatings. What got them started?

Suppose a Saturday, in spring. Leaves not out yet but the doors open to the sunlight. Crows. Ditches full of running water. Hopeful weather. Often on

Saturdays Flo left Rose in charge of the store—it's a few years now, these are the years when Rose was nine, ten, eleven, twelve—while she herself went across the bridge to Hanratty (going uptown they called it) to shop and see people, and listen to them. Among the people she listened to were Mrs. Lawyer Davies, Mrs. Anglican Rector Henley-Smith, and Mrs. Horse-Doctor McKay. She came home and imitated them at supper: their high-flown remarks, their flibberty voices. Monsters, she made them seem; of foolishness, and showiness, and self-approbation.

When she finished shopping she went into the coffee shop of the Queen's Hotel and had a sundae. What kind? Rose and Brian wanted to know when she got home, and they would be disappointed if it was only pineapple or butterscotch, pleased if it was a Tin Roof, or Black and White. Then she smoked a cigarette. She had some ready-rolled, that she carried with her, so that she wouldn't have to roll one in public. Smoking was the one thing she did that she would have called showing off in anybody else. It was a habit left over from her working days, from Toronto. She knew it was asking for trouble. Once the Catholic priest came over to her right in the Queen's Hotel, and flashed his lighter at her before she could get matches out. She thanked him but did not enter into conversation, lest he should try to convert her.

Another time, on the way home, she saw at the town end of the bridge a boy in a blue jacket, apparently looking at the water. Eighteen, nineteen years old. Nobody she knew. Skinny, weakly looking, something the matter with him, she saw at once. Was he thinking of jumping? Just as she came up even with him, what does he do but turn and display, holding his jacket open, also his pants. What he must have suffered from the cold, on a day that had Flo holding her coat collar tight around her throat.

When she first saw what he had in his hand, Flo said, all she could think of was, what is he doing out here with a baloney sausage?

She could say that. It was offered as truth; no joke. She maintained that she despised dirty talk. She would go out and yell at the old men sitting in front of her store.

"If you want to stay where you are you better clean your mouths out!"

Saturday, then. For some reason Flo is not going uptown, has decided to stay home and scrub the kitchen floor. Perhaps this has put her in a bad mood. Perhaps she was in a bad mood anyway, due to people not paying their bills, or the stirring-up of feelings in spring. The wrangle with Rose has already commenced, has been going on forever, like a dream that goes back and back into other dreams, over hills and through doorways, maddeningly dim and populous and familiar and elusive. They are carting all the chairs out of the kitchen preparatory to the scrubbing, and they have also got to move some extra provisions for the store, some cartons of canned goods, tins of maple syrup, coal-oil cans, jars of vinegar. They take these things out to the woodshed. Brian who is five or six by this time is helping drag the tins.

"Yes," says Flo, carrying on from our lost starting-point. "Yes, and that filth you taught to Brian."

"What filth?"

"And he doesn't know any better."

There is one step down from the kitchen to the woodshed, a bit of carpet on it so worn Rose can't ever remember seeing the pattern. Brian loosens it, dragging a tin.

"Two Vancouvers," she says softly.

Flo is back in the kitchen. Brian looks from Flo to Rose and Rose says again in a slightly louder voice, an encouraging sing-song, "Two Vancouvers—"

"Fried in snot!" finishes Brian, not able to control himself any longer.

"Two pickled arseholes—"

"—tied in a knot!"

There it is. The filth.

> *Two Vancouvers fried in snot!*
> *Two pickled arseholes tied in a knot!*

Rose has known that for years, learned it when she first went to school. She came home and asked Flo, what is a Vancouver?

"It's a city. It's a long ways away."

"What else besides a city?"

Flo said, what did she mean, what else? How could it be fried, Rose said, approaching the dangerous moment, the delightful moment, when she would have to come out with the whole thing.

"Two Vancouvers fried in snot!/Two pickled arseholes tied in a knot!"

"You're going to get it!" cried Flo in a predictable rage. "Say that again and you'll get a good clout!"

Rose couldn't stop herself. She hummed it tenderly, tried saying the innocent words aloud, humming through the others. It was not just the words snot and arsehole that gave her pleasure, though of course they did. It was the pickling and tying and the unimaginable Vancouvers. She saw them in her mind shaped rather like octopuses, twitching in the pan. The tumble of reason; the spark and spit of craziness.

Lately she has remembered it again and taught it to Brian, to see if it has the same effect on him, and of course it has.

"Oh, I heard you!" says Flo. "I heard that! And I'm warning you!"

So she is. Brian takes the warning. He runs away, out the woodshed door, to do as he likes. Being a boy, free to help or not, involve himself or not. Not committed to the household struggle. They don't need him anyway, except to use against each other, they hardly notice his going. They continue, can't help continuing, can't leave each other alone. When they seem to have given up they were really just waiting and building up steam.

Flo gets out the scrub pail and the brush and the rag and the pad for her knees, a dirty red rubber pad. She starts to work on the floor. Rose sits on the kitchen table, the only place left to sit, swinging her legs. She can feel the cool oilcloth, because she is wearing shorts, last summer's tight faded shorts dug out of the summer-clothes bag. The smell a bit moldy from winter storage.

Flo crawls around underneath, scrubbing with the brush, wiping with the rag. Her legs are long, white and muscular, marked all over with blue veins as if somebody had been drawing rivers on them with an indelible pencil. An abnormal energy, a violent disgust, is expressed in the chewing of the brush at the linoleum, the swish of the rag.

What do they have to say to each other? It doesn't really matter. Flo speaks of Rose's smart-aleck behavior, rudeness and sloppiness and conceit. Her willingness to make work for others, her lack of gratitude. She mentions Brian's innocence, Rose's corruption. Oh, don't you think you're somebody, says Flo, and a moment later, Who do you think you are? Rose contradicts and objects with such poisonous reasonableness and mildness, displays theatrical unconcern. Flo goes beyond her ordinary scorn and self-possession and becomes amazingly theatrical herself, saying it was for Rose that she sacrificed her life. She saw her father saddled with a baby daughter and she thought, what is that man going to do? So she married him, and here she is, on her knees.

At that moment the bell rings, to announce a customer in the store. Because the fight is on, Rose is not permitted to go into the store and wait on whoever it is. Flo gets up and throws off her apron, groaning—but not communicatively, it is not a groan whose exasperation Rose is allowed to share—and goes in and serves. Rose hears her using her normal voice.

"About time! Sure is!"

She comes back and ties on her apron and is ready to resume.

"You never have a thought for anybody but your ownself! You never have a thought for what I'm doing."

"I never asked you to do anything. I wished you never had. I would have been a lot better off."

Rose says this smiling directly at Flo, who has not yet gone down on her knees. Flo sees the smile, grabs the scrub rag that is hanging on the side of the pail, and throws it at her. It may be meant to hit her in the face but instead it falls against Rose's leg and she raises her foot and catches it, swinging it negligently against her ankle.

"All right," says Flo. "You've done it this time. All right."

Rose watches her go to the woodshed door, hears her tramp through the woodshed, pause in the doorway, where the screen door hasn't yet been hung, and the storm door is standing open, propped with a brick. She calls Rose's father. She calls him in a warning, summoning voice, as if against her will preparing him for bad news. He will know what this is about.

The kitchen floor has five or six different patterns of linoleum on it. Ends, which Flo got for nothing and ingeniously trimmed and fitted together, bordering them with tin strips and tacks. While Rose sits on the table waiting, she looks at the floor, at this satisfying arrangement of rectangles, triangles, some other shape whose name she is trying to remember. She hears Flo coming back through the woodshed, on the creaky plank walk laid over the dirt floor. She is loitering, waiting, too. She and Rose can carry this no further, by themselves.

Rose hears her father come in. She stiffens, a tremor runs through her legs, she feels them shiver on the oilcloth. Called away from some peaceful absorbing task, away from the words running in his head, called out of himself, her father has to say something. He says, "Well? What's wrong?"

Now comes another voice of Flo's. Enriched, hurt, apologetic, it seems to have been manufactured on the spot. She is sorry to have called him from his work. Would never have done it, if Rose was not driving her to distraction. How to distraction? With her back-talk and impudence and her terrible tongue. The things Rose has said to Flo are such that, if Flo had said them to her mother, she knows her father would have thrashed her into the ground.

Rose tries to butt in, to say this isn't true.

What isn't true?

Her father raises a hand, doesn't look at her, says "Be quiet."

When she says it isn't true, Rose means that she herself didn't start this, only responded, that she was goaded by Flo, who is now, she believes, telling the grossest sort of lies, twisting everything to suit herself. Rose puts aside her other knowledge that whatever Flo has said or done, whatever she herself has said or done, does not really matter at all. It is the struggle itself that counts, and that can't be stopped, can never be stopped, short of where it has got to, now.

Flo's knees are dirty, in spite of the pad. The scrub rag is still hanging over Rose's foot.

Her father wipes his hands, listening to Flo. He takes his time. He is slow at getting into the spirit of things, tired in advance, maybe, on the verge of rejecting the role he has to play. He won't look at Rose, but at any sound or stirring from Rose, he holds up his hand.

"Well we don't need the public in on this, that's for sure," Flo says, and she goes to lock the door of the store, putting in the store window the sign that says "Back Soon," a sign Rose made for her with a great deal of fancy curving and shading of letters in black and red crayon. When she comes back she shuts the door to the store, then the door to the stairs, then the door to the woodshed.

Her shoes have left marks on the clean wet part of the floor.

"Oh, I don't know," she says now, in a voice worn down from its emotional peak. "I don't know what to do about her." She looks down and sees her dirty knees (following Rose's eyes) and rubs at them viciously with her bare hands, smearing the dirt around.

"She humiliates me," she says, straightening up. There it is, the explanation. "She humiliates me," she repeats with satisfaction. "She has no respect."

"I do not!"

"Quiet, you!" says her father.

"If I hadn't called your father you'd still be sitting there with that grin on your face! What other way is there to manage you?"

Rose detects in her father some objections to Flo's rhetoric, some embarrassment and reluctance. She is wrong, and ought to know she is wrong, in thinking that she can count on this. The fact that she knows about it, and he knows she knows, will not make things any better. He is beginning to warm up. He gives her a look. This look is at first cold and challenging. It informs her of his judgment, of the hopelessness of her position. Then it clears, it begins to fill up with something else, the way a spring fills up when you clear the leaves away. It fills with hatred and pleasure. Rose sees that and knows it. Is that just a description of anger, should she see his eyes filling up with anger? No. Hatred is right. Pleasure is right. His face loosens and changes and grows younger, and he holds up his hand this time to silence Flo.

"All right," he says, meaning that's enough, more than enough, this part is over, things can proceed. He starts to loosen his belt.

Flo has stopped anyway. She has the same difficulty Rose does, a difficulty in believing that what you know must happen really will happen, that there comes a time when you can't draw back.

"Oh, I don't know, don't be too hard on her." She is moving around nervously as if she has thoughts of opening some escape route. "Oh, you don't have to use the belt on her. Do you have to use the belt?"

He doesn't answer. The belt is coming off, not hastily. It is being grasped at the necessary point. *All right you.* He is coming over to Rose. He pushes her off the table. His face, like his voice, is quite out of character. He is like a bad actor, who turns a part grotesque. As if he must savor and insist on just what is shameful and terrible about this. That is not to say he is pretending, that he is acting, and does not mean it. He is acting, and he means it. Rose knows that, she knows everything about him.

She has since wondered about murders, and murderers. Does the thing have to be carried through, in the end, partly for the effect, to prove to the audience of one—who won't be able to report, only register, the lesson—that such a thing can happen, that there is nothing that can't happen, that the most dreadful antic is justified, feelings can be found to match it?

She tries again looking at the kitchen floor, that clever and comforting geometrical arrangement, instead of looking at him or his belt. How can this go on in front of such daily witnesses—the linoleum, the calendar with the mill and creek and autumn trees, the old accommodating pots and pans?

Hold out your hand!

Those things aren't going to help her, none of them can rescue her. They turn bland and useless, even unfriendly. Pots can show malice, the patterns of linoleum can leer up at you, treachery is the other side of dailiness.

At the first, or maybe the second, crack of pain, she draws back. She will not accept it. She runs around the room, she tries to get to the doors. Her father blocks her off. Not an ounce of courage or of stoicism in her, it would seem. She runs, she screams, she implores. Her father is after her, cracking the belt at her when he can, then abandoning it and using his hands. Bang over the ear, then bang over the other ear. Back and forth, her head ringing. Bang in the face. Up against the wall and bang in the face again. He shakes her and hits her against the wall, he kicks her legs. She is incoherent, insane, shrieking. *Forgive me! Oh please, forgive me!*

Flo is shrieking too. *Stop, stop!*

Not yet. He throws Rose down. Or perhaps she throws herself down. He kicks her legs again. She has given up on words but is letting out a noise, the sort of noise that makes Flo cry, *Oh, what if people can hear her?* The very last-ditch willing sound of humiliation and defeat it is, for it seems Rose must play her part in this with the same grossness, the same exaggeration, that her father displays, playing his. She plays his victim with a self-indulgence that arouses, and maybe hopes to arouse, his final, sickened contempt.

They will give this anything that is necessary, it seems, they will go to any lengths.

Not quite. He has never managed to really injure her, though there are times, of course, when she prays that he will. He hits her with an open hand, there is some restraint in his kicks.

Now he stops, he is out of breath. He allows Flo to move in, he grabs Rose up and gives her a push in Flo's direction, making a sound of disgust. Flo retrieves her, opens the stair door, shoves her up the stairs.

"Go on up to your room now! Hurry!"

Rose goes up the stairs, stumbling, letting herself stumble, letting herself fall against the steps. She doesn't bang her door because a gesture like that could still bring him after her, and anyway, she is weak. She lies on the bed. She can hear through the stovepipe hole Flo snuffling and remonstrating, her father saying angrily that Flo should have kept quiet then, if she did not want

Rose punished she should not have recommended it. Flo says she never recommended a hiding like that.

They argue back and forth on this. Flo's frightened voice is growing stronger, getting its confidence back. By stages, by arguing, they are being drawn back into themselves. Soon it's only Flo talking; he will not talk any more. Rose has had to fight down her noisy sobbing, so as to listen to them, and when she loses interest in listening, and wants to sob some more, she finds she can't work herself up to it. She has passed into a state of calm, in which outrage is perceived as complete and final. In this state events and possibilities take on a lovely simplicity. Choices are mercifully clear. The words that come to mind are not the quibbling, seldom the conditional. Never is a word to which the right is suddenly established. She will never speak to them, she will never look at them with anything but loathing, she will never forgive them. She will punish them; she will finish them. Encased in these finalities, and in her bodily pain, she floats in curious comfort, beyond herself, beyond responsibility.

Suppose she dies now? Suppose she commits suicide? Suppose she runs away? Any of these things would be appropriate. It is only a matter of choosing, of figuring out the way. She floats in her pure superior state as if kindly drugged.

And just as there is a moment, when you are drugged, in which you feel perfectly safe, sure, unreachable, and then without warning and right next to it a moment in which you know the whole protection has fatally cracked, though it is still pretending to hold soundly together, so there is a moment now—the moment, in fact, when Rose hears Flo step on the stairs—that contains for her both present peace and freedom and a sure knowledge of the whole down-spiraling course of events from now on.

Flo comes into the room without knocking, but with a hesitation that shows it might have occurred to her. She brings a jar of cold cream. Rose is hanging on to advantage as long as she can, lying face down on the bed, refusing to acknowledge or answer.

"Oh come on," Flo says uneasily. "You aren't so bad off, are you? You put some of this on and you'll feel better."

She is bluffing. She doesn't know for sure what damage has been done. She has the lid off the cold cream. Rose can smell it. The intimate, babyish, humiliating smell. She won't allow it near her. But in order to avoid it, the big ready clot of it in Flo's hand, she has to move. She scuffles, resists, loses dignity, and lets Flo see there is not really much the matter.

"All right," Flo says. "You win. I'll leave it here and you can put it on when you like."

Later still a tray will appear. Flo will put it down without a word and go away. A large glass of chocolate milk on it, made with Vita-Malt from the store. Some rich streaks of Vita-Malt around the bottom of the glass. Little sandwiches, neat and appetizing. Canned salmon of the first quality and reddest color, plenty of mayonnaise. A couple of butter tarts from a bakery package, chocolate biscuits with a peppermint filling. Rose's favorites, in the sandwich, tart and cookie line. She will turn away, refuse to look, but left alone with these eatables will be miserably tempted, roused and troubled and drawn back from thoughts of suicide or flight by the smell of salmon, the anticipation of crisp chocolate, she will reach out a finger, just to run it around the edge of one of the sandwiches (crusts cut off!) to get the overflow, get a taste. Then she will decide to eat one, for strength to refuse the rest. One will not be noticed. Soon, in helpless corruption, she will eat them all. She will drink the chocolate milk, eat the tarts, eat the cookies. She will get the malty syrup out of the bottom of the glass with her finger, though she sniffles with shame. Too late.

Flo will come up and get the tray. She may say, "I see you got your appetite still," or, "Did you like the chocolate milk, was it enough syrup in it?" depending on how chastened she is feeling, herself. At any rate, all advantage will be lost. Rose will understand that life has started up again, that they will all sit around the table eating again, listening to the radio news. Tomorrow morning, maybe even tonight. Unseemly and unlikely as that may be. They will be embarrassed, but rather less than you might expect considering how they have behaved. They will feel a queer lassitude, a convalescent indolence, not far off satisfaction.

One night after a scene like this they were all in the kitchen. It must have been summer, or at least warm weather, because her father spoke of the old men who sat on the bench in front of the store.

"Do you know what they're talking about now?" he said, and nodded his head towards the store to show who he meant, though of course they were not there now, they went home at dark.

"Those old coots," said Flo. "What?"

There was about them both a geniality not exactly false but a bit more emphatic than was normal, without company.

Rose's father told them then that the old men had picked up the idea somewhere that what looked like a star in the western sky, the first star that came out after sunset, the evening star, was in reality an airship hovering over Bay City, Michigan, on the other side of Lake Huron. An American invention, sent up to rival the heavenly bodies. They were all in agreement about this, the idea was congenial to them. They believed it to be lit by ten thousand electric light bulbs. Her father had ruthlessly disagreed with them, pointing out that it was the planet Venus they saw, which had appeared in the sky long before the invention of an electric light bulb. They had never heard of the planet Venus.

"Ignoramuses," said Flo. At which Rose knew, and knew her father knew, that Flo had never heard of the planet Venus either. To distract them from this, or even apologize for it, Flo put down her teacup, stretched out with her head resting on the chair she had been sitting on and her feet on another chair (somehow she managed to tuck her dress modestly between her legs at the same time), and lay stiff as a board, so that Brian cried out in delight, "Do that! Do that!"

Flo was double-jointed and very strong. In moments of celebration or emergency she would do tricks.

They were silent while she turned herself around, not using her arms at all but just her strong legs and feet. Then they all cried out in triumph, though they had seen it before.

Just as Flo turned herself Rose got a picture in her mind of that airship, an elongated transparent bubble, with its strings of diamond lights, floating in the miraculous American sky.

"The planet Venus!" her father said, applauding Flo. "Ten thousand electric lights!"

There was a feeling of permission, relaxation, even a current of happiness, in the room.

Years later, many years later, on a Sunday morning, Rose turned on the radio. This was when she was living by herself in Toronto.

Well sir.

It was a different kind of a place in our day. Yes it was.

It was all horses then. Horses and buggies. Buggy races up and down the main street on the Saturday nights.

"Just like the chariot races," says the announcer's, or interviewer's, smooth encouraging voice.

I never seen a one of them.

"No sir, that was the old Roman chariot races I was referring to. That was before your time."

Musta been before my time. I'm a hunerd and two years old.

"That's a wonderful age, sir."

It is so.

She left it on, as she went around the apartment kitchen, making coffee for herself. It seemed to her that this must be a staged interview, a scene from some play, and she wanted to find out what it was. The old man's voice was so vain and belligerent, the interviewer's quite hopeless and alarmed, under its practiced gentleness and ease. You were surely meant to see him holding the microphone up to some toothless, reckless, preening centenarian, wondering what in God's name he was doing here, and what would he say next?

"They must have been fairly dangerous."

What was dangerous?

"Those buggy races."

They was. Dangerous. Used to be the runaway horses. Used to be a-plenty of accidents. Fellows was dragged along the gravel and cut their face open. Wouldna matter so much if they was dead. Heh.

Some of them horses was the high-steppers. Some, they had to have the mustard under their tail. Some wouldn step out for nothin. That's the thing it is with the horses. Some'll work and pull till drop down dead and some wouldn pull your cock out of a pail of lard. Hehe.

It must be a real interview after all. Otherwise they wouldn't have put that in, wouldn't have risked it. It's all right if the old man says it. Local color. Anything rendered harmless and delighted by his hundred years.

Accidents all the time then. In the mill. Foundry. Wasn't the precautions.

"You didn't have so many strikes then, I don't suppose? You didn't have so many unions?"

Everybody taking it easy nowadays. We worked and we was glad to get it. Worked and was glad to get it.

"You didn't have television."

Didn't have no T.V. Didn't have no radio. No picture show.

"You made your own entertainment."

That's the way we did.

"You had a lot of experiences young men growing up today will never have."

Experiences.

"Can you recall any of them for us?"

I eaten groundhog meat one time. One winter. You wouldna cared for it. Heh.

There was a pause, of appreciation, it would seem, then the announcer's voice saying that the foregoing had been an interview with Mr. Wilfred Nettleton of Hanratty, Ontario, made on his hundred and second birthday, two weeks before his death, last spring. A living link with our past. Mr. Nettleton had been interviewed in the Wawanash County Home for the Aged.

Hat Nettleton.

Horsewhipper into centenarian. Photographed on his birthday, fussed over by nurses, kissed no doubt by a girl reporter. Flash bulbs popping at him. Tape recorder drinking in the sound of his voice. Oldest resident. Oldest horsewhipper. Living link with our past.

Looking out from her kitchen window at the cold lake, Rose was longing to tell somebody. It was Flo who would enjoy hearing. She thought of her saying *Imagine!* in a way that meant she was having her worst suspicions gorgeously confirmed. But Flo was in the same place Hat Nettleton had died in, and there wasn't any way Rose could reach her. She had been there even when that interview was recorded, though she would not have heard it, would not have known about it. After Rose put her in the Home, a couple of years earlier, she had stopped talking. She had removed herself, and spent more of her time sitting in a corner of her crib, looking crafty and disagreeable, not answering anybody, though she occasionally showed her feelings by biting a nurse.

ALICE MUNRO

The Jack Randa Hotel

On the runway, in Honolulu, the plane loses speed, loses heart, falters and veers onto the grass, and bumps to a stop. A few yards it seems from the ocean. Inside, everybody laughs. First a hush, then the laugh. Gail laughed herself. Then there was a flurry of introductions all around. Beside Gail are Larry and Phyllis, from Spokane.

Larry and Phyllis are going to a tournament of Left-handed Golfers, in Fiji, as are many other couples on this plane. It is Larry who is the left-handed golfer—Phyllis is the wife going along to watch and cheer and have fun.

They sit on the plane—Gail and the Left-handed Golfers—and lunch is served in picnic boxes. No drinks. Dreadful heat. Jokey and confusing announcements are made from the cockpit. *Sorry about the problem. Nothing serious but it looks like it will keep us stewing here a while longer.* Phyllis has a terrible headache, which Larry tries to cure by applying finger-pressure to points on her wrist and palm.

"It's not working," Phyllis says. "I could have been in New Orleans by now with Suzy."

Larry says, "Poor lamb."

Gail catches the fierce glitter of diamond rings as Phyllis pulls her hand away. Wives have diamond rings and headaches, Gail thinks. They still do. The truly successful ones do. They have chubby husbands, left-handed golfers, bent on a lifelong course of appeasement.

Eventually the passengers who are not going to Fiji, but on to Sydney, are taken off the plane. They are led into the terminal and there deserted by their airline guide they wander about, retrieving their baggage and going through customs, trying to locate the airline that is supposed to honor their tickets. At one point, they are accosted by a welcoming committee from one of the Island's hotels, who will not stop singing Hawaiian songs and flinging garlands around their necks. But they find themselves on another plane at last. They eat and drink and sleep and the lines to the toilets lengthen and the aisles fill up with debris and the flight attendants hide in their cubbyholes chatting about children and boyfriends. Then comes the unsettling bright morning and the yellow-sanded coast of Australia far below, and the wrong time of day, and even the best-dressed, best-looking passengers are haggard and unwilling, torpid, as from a long trip in steerage. And before they can leave the plane

570

there is one more assault. Hairy men in shorts swarm aboard and spray everything with insecticide.

"So maybe this is the way it will be getting into Heaven," Gail images herself saying to Will. "People will fling flowers on you that you don't want, and everybody will have headaches and be constipated and then you will have to be sprayed for Earth germs."

Her old habit, trying to think up clever and lighthearted things to say to Will.

After Will went away, it seemed to Gail that her shop was filling up with women. Not necessarily buying clothes. She didn't mind this. It was like the long-ago days, before Will. Women were sitting around in ancient armchairs beside Gail's ironing board and cutting table, behind the faded batik curtains, drinking coffee. Gail started grinding the coffee beans herself, as she used to do. The dressmaker's dummy was soon draped with beads and had a scattering of scandalous graffiti. Stories were told about men, usually about men who had left. Lies and injustices and confrontations. Betrayal so horrific—yet so trite—that you could only rock with laughter when you heard them. Men made fatuous speeches (*I am sorry, but I no longer feel committed to this marriage.*) They offered to sell back to the wives cars and furniture that the wives themselves had paid for. They capered about in self-satisfaction because they had managed to impregnate some dewy dollop of womanhood younger than their own children. They were fiendish and childish. What could you do but give up on them? In all honor, in pride, and for your own protection?

Gail's enjoyment of all this palled rather quickly. Too much coffee could make your skin look livery. An underground quarrel developed among the women when it turned out that one of them had placed an ad in the Personal Column. Gail shifted from coffee with friends to drinks with Cleata, Will's mother. As she did this, oddly enough her spirits grew more sober. Some giddiness still showed in the notes she pinned to her door so that she could get away early on summer afternoons. (Her clerk, Donalda, was on her holidays, and it was too much trouble to hire anybody else.)

> Gone to the Opera.
> Gone to the Funny Farm.
> Gone to stock up on the Sackcloth and Ashes.

Actually these were not her own inventions, but things Will used to write out and tape on her door in the early days when they wanted to go upstairs. She heard that such flippancy was not appreciated by people who had driven some distance to buy a dress for a wedding, or girls on an expedition to buy clothes for college. She did not care.

On Cleata's veranda Gail was soothed, she became vaguely hopeful. Like most serious drinkers, Cleata stuck to one drink—hers was Scotch—and seemed amused by variations. But she would make Gail a gin and tonic, a white rum and soda. She introduced her to tequila. "This is Heaven," Gail sometimes said, meaning not just the drink but the screened veranda and hedged back yard, the old house behind them with its shuttered windows, varnished floors, inconveniently high kitchen cupboards, and out-of-date flowered curtains. (Cleata despised decorating.) This was the house where Will, and Cleata too, had been born, and when Will first brought Gail into it, she had thought, This is how really civilized people live. The carelessness and propriety combined, the respect for old books and old dishes. The absurd things that Will and Cleata thought it natural to talk about. And the things she and Cleata didn't talk about—Will's present defection, the illness that has made Cleata's arms and legs look like varnished twigs within their deep tan, and has hollowed the cheeks framed by her looped-back white hair. She and Will have the same slightly monkeyish face, with dreamy, mocking dark eyes.

Instead, Cleata talked about the book she was reading, *The Anglo-Saxon Chronicle*. She said that the reason the Dark Ages were dark was not that we couldn't learn anything about them but that we could not remember anything we did learn, and that was because of the names.

"Caedwalla," she said. "Egfrith. These are just not names on the tip of your tongue anymore."

Gail was trying to remember which ages, or centuries, were dark. But her ignorance didn't embarrass her. Cleata was making fun of all that, anyway.

"Aelfflaed," said Cleata, and spelled it out. "What kind of a heroine is Aelfflaed?"

When Cleata wrote to Will, she probably wrote about Aelfflaed and Egfrith. Not about Gail. Not *Gail was here looking very pretty in some kind of silky gray summer-pajamas outfit. She was in good form, made various witty remarks* ... No more than she would say to Gail, "I have my doubts about the lovebirds. Reading between the lines, I can't help wondering if disillusionment isn't setting in...."

When she met Will and Cleata, Gail thought they were like characters in a book. A son living with his mother, apparently contentedly, into middle age. Gail saw a life that was ceremonious and absurd and enviable, with at least the appearance of celibate grace and safety. She still sees some of that, though the truth is Will has not always lived at home, and he is neither celibate nor discreetly homosexual. He had been gone for years, into his own life—working for the National Film Board and the Canadian Broadcasting Corporation—and had given that up only recently, to come back to Walley and be a teacher. What made him give it up? This and that, he said. Machiavellis here and there. Empire-building. Exhaustion.

Gail came to Walley one summer in the seventies. The boyfriend she was with then was a boatbuilder, and she sold clothes that she made—capes with appliqués, shirts with billowing sleeves, long bright skirts. She got space in the back of the craft shop, when winter came on. She learned about importing ponchos and thick socks from Bolivia and Guatemala. She found local women to knit sweaters. One day Will stopped her on the street and asked her to help him with the costumes for the play he was putting on—*The Skin of Our Teeth*. Her boyfriend moved to Vancouver.

She told Will some things about herself early on, in case he should think that with her capable build and pink skin and wide gentle forehead she was exactly the kind of a woman to start a family on. She told him that she had had a baby, and that when she and her boyfriend were moving some furniture in a borrowed van, from Thunder Bay to Toronto, carbon-monoxide fumes had leaked in, just enough to make them sick but enough to kill the baby, who was seven weeks old. After that Gail was sick—she had a pelvic inflammation. She decided she did not want to have another child and it would have been difficult anyway, so she had a hysterectomy.

Will admired her. He said so. He did not feel obliged to say, What a tragedy! He did not even obliquely suggest that the death was the result of choices Gail had made. He was entranced with her then. He thought her brave and generous and resourceful and gifted. The costumes she designed and made for him were perfect, miraculous. Gail thought that his view of her, of her life, showed a touching innocence. It seemed to her that far from being a free and generous spirit, she had often been anxious and desperate and had spent a long time doing laundry and worrying about money and feeling she owed so much to any man who took up with her. She did not think she was in love with Will then, but she liked his looks—his energetic body, so upright it seemed taller than it was, his flung-back head, shiny high forehead, springy ruff of graying hair. She liked to watch him at rehearsals, or just talking to his students. How skilled and intrepid he seemed as a director, how potent a personality as he walked the high-school halls or the streets of Walley. And then the slightly quaint, admiring feelings he had for her, his courtesy as a lover, the foreign pleasantness of his house and his life with Cleata—all this made Gail feel like somebody getting a unique welcome in a place where perhaps she did not truly have a right to be. That did not matter then—she had the upper hand.

So when did she stop having it? When he got used to sleeping with her when they moved in together, when they did so much work on the cottage by the river and it turned out that she was better at that kind of work than he was?

Was she a person who believed that somebody had to have the upper hand?

There came a time when just the tone of his voice, saying "Your shoelace is undone" as she went ahead of him on a walk—just that—could fill her with despair, warning her that they had crossed over into a bleak country where his disappointment in her was boundless, his contempt impossible to challenge. She would stumble eventually, break out in a rage—they would have days and nights of fierce hopelessness. Then the breakthrough, the sweet reunion, the jokes, and bewildered relief. So it went on in their life—she couldn't really understand it or tell if it was like anybody else's. But the peaceful periods seemed to be getting longer, the dangers retreating, and she had no inkling that he was waiting to meet somebody like this new person, Sandy, who would seem to him as alien and delightful as Gail herself had once been.

Will probably had no inkling of that, either.

He had never had much to say about Sandy—Sandra—who had come to Walley last year on an exchange program to see how drama was being taught in Canadian schools. He had said she was a young Turk. Then he said she mightn't even have heard that expression. Very soon, there had developed some sort of electricity, or danger, around her name. Gail got some information from other sources. She heard that Sandy had challenged Will in front of his class. Sandy had said that the plays he wanted to do were "not relevant." Or maybe it was "not revolutionary."

"But he likes her," one of his students said. "Oh, yeah, he *really likes* her."

Sandy didn't stay around long. She went on to observe the teaching of drama in the other schools. But she wrote to Will, and presumably he wrote back. For it turned out that they had fallen in love. Will and Sandy had fallen seriously in love, and at the end of the school year Will followed her to Australia.

Seriously in love. When Will told her that, Gail was smoking dope. She had taken it up again, because being around Will was making her so nervous.

"You mean it's not me?" Gail said. "You mean I'm not the trouble?"

She was giddy with relief. She got into a bold and boisterous mood and bewildered Will into going to bed with her.

In the morning they tried to avoid being in the same room together. They agreed not to correspond. Perhaps later, Will said. Gail said, "Suit yourself."

But one day at Cleata's house Gail saw his writing on an envelope that had surely been left where she could see it. Cleata had left it—Cleata who never spoke one word about the fugitives. Gail wrote down the return address: 16 Eyre Rd., Toowong, Brisbane, Queensland, Australia.

It was when she saw Will's writing that she understood how useless everything had become to her. This bar-fronted pre-Victorian house in Walley, and the veranda, and the drinks, and the catalpa tree that she was always looking at, in Cleata's back yard. All the trees and streets in Walley, all the liberating views of the lake and the comfort of the shop. Useless cutouts, fakes and props. The real scene was hidden from her, in Australia.

That was why she found herself sitting on the plane beside the woman with the diamond rings. Her own hands have no rings on them, no polish on the nails—the skin is dry from all the work she does with cloth. She used to call the clothes she made "handcrafted," until Will made her embarrassed about that description. She still doesn't quite see what was wrong.

She sold the shop—she sold it to Donalda, who had wanted to buy it for a long time. She took the money, and she got herself onto a flight to Australia and did not tell anyone where she was going. She lied, talking about a long holiday that would start off in England. Then somewhere in Greece for the winter, then who knows?

The night before she left, she did a transformation on herself. She cut off her heavy reddish-gray hair and put a dark-brown rinse on what was left of it. The color that resulted was strange—a deep maroon, obviously artificial but rather too sombre for any attempt at glamour. She picked out from her shop—even though the contents no longer belonged to her—a dress of a kind she would never usually wear, a jacket-dress of dark-blue linen-look polyester with lightning stripes of red and yellow. She is tall, and broad in the hips, and she usually wears things that are loose and graceful. This outfit gives her chunky shoulders, and cuts her leg at an unflattering spot above the knees. What sort of woman did she think she was making herself into? The sort that a woman like Phyllis would play bridge with? If so, she has got it wrong. She has come out looking like somebody who has spent most of her life in uniform, at some worthy, poorly paid job (perhaps in a hospital cafeteria?), and now has spent too much money for a dashing dress that will turn out to be inappropriate and uncomfortable, on the holiday of her life.

That doesn't matter. It is a disguise.

In the airport washroom, on a new continent, she sees that the dark hair coloring, insufficiently rinsed out the night before, has mixed with her sweat and is trickling down her neck.

Gail has landed in Brisbane, still not used to what time of day it is and persecuted by so hot a sun. She is still wearing her horrid dress, but she has washed her hair so that the color no longer runs.

She has taken a taxi. Tired as she is, she cannot settle, cannot rest until she has seen where they live. She has already bought a map and found Eyre Road. A short, curving street. She asks to be let out at the corner, where there is a little grocery store. This is the place where they buy their milk, most likely, or other things that they may have run out of. Detergent, aspirin, tampons.

The fact that Gail never met Sandy was of course an ominous thing. It must have meant that Will knew something very quickly. Later attempts to ferret out a description did not yield much. Tall rather than short. Thin rather than fat. Fair rather than dark. Gail had a mental picture of one of those long-legged, short-haired, energetic, and boyishly attractive girls. *Women*. But she wouldn't know Sandy if she ran into her.

Would anybody know Gail? With her dark glasses and her unlikely hair, she feels so altered as to be invisible. It's also the fact of being in a strange country that has transformed her. She's not tuned into it yet. Once she gets tuned in, she may not be able to do the bold things she can do now. She has to walk this street, look at the house, right away, or she may not be able to do it at all.

The road that the taxi climbed was steep, up from the brown river. Eyre Road runs along a ridge. There is no sidewalk, just a dusty path. No one walking, no cars passing, no shade. Fences of boards or a kind of basket-weaving—wattles?—or in some cases high hedges covered with flowers. No, the flowers are really leaves of a purplish-pink or crimson color. Trees unfamiliar to Gail are showing over the fences. They have tough-looking dusty foliage, scaly or stringy bark, a shabby ornamental air. An indifference or vague ill will about them, which she associated with the tropics. Walking on the path ahead of her are a pair of guinea hens, stately and preposterous.

The house where Will and Sandy live is hidden by a board fence, painted a pale green. Gail's heart shrinks—her heart is in a cruel clutch, to see that fence, that green.

The road is a dead end so she has to turn around. She walks past the house again. In the fence there are gates to let a car in and out. There is also a mail slot. She noticed one of these before in a fence in front of another house, and the reason she noticed it was that there was a magazine sticking out. So the mailbox is not very deep, and a hand, slipping in, might be able to find an envelope resting on its end. If the mail has not been taken out yet by a person in the house. And Gail does slip a hand in. She can't stop herself. She finds a letter there, just as she had thought it might be. She puts it into her purse.

She calls a taxi from the shop at the corner of the street. "What part of the States are you from?" the man in the shop asks her.

"Texas," she says. She has an idea that they would like you to be from Texas, and indeed the man lifts his eyebrows, whistles.

"I thought so," he says.

It is Will's own writing on the envelope. Not a letter to Will, then, but a letter from him. A letter he had sent to Ms. Catherine Thornaby, 491 Hawtre Street. Also in Brisbane. Another hand has scrawled across it "Return to Sender, Died Sept. 13." For a moment, in her disordered state of mind, Gail thinks that this means that Will has died.

She has go to calm down, collect herself, stay out of the sun for a bit.

Nevertheless, as soon as she has read the letter in her hotel room, and tidied herself up, she takes another taxi, this time to Hawtre Street, and finds, as she expected, a sign in the window: "Flat to Let."

But what is in the letter that Will has written Ms. Catherine Thornaby, on Hawtre Street?

> *Dear Ms. Thornaby,*
>
> *You do not know me, but I hope that once I have explained myself, we may meet and talk. I believe that I may be a Canadian cousin of yours, my grandfather having come to Canada from Northumberland sometime in the 1870s about the same time as a brother of his went to Australia. My grandfather's name was William, like my own, his brother's name was Thomas. Of course I have no proof that you are descended from this Thomas. I simply looked in the Brisbane phone book and was delighted to find there a Thornaby spelled in the same way. I used to think this family-tracing busies was the silliest, most boring thing imaginable but now that I find myself doing it, I discover there is a strange excitement about it. Perhaps it is my age—I am 56—that urges me to find connections. And I have more time on my hands than I am used to. My wife is working with a theatre here which keeps her busy till all hours. She is a very bright and energetic young woman. (She scolds me if I refer to any female over 18 as a girl and she is all of 28!) I taught drama in a Canadian high school but I have not yet found any work in Australia.*

Wife. He is trying to be respectable in the eyes of the possible cousin.

> *Dear Mr. Thornaby,*
>
> *The name we share may be a more common one than you suppose, though I am at present its only representative in the Brisbane phone book. You may not know that the name comes from Thorn Abbey, the ruins of which are still to be seen in Northumberland. The spelling varies—Thornaby, Thornby, Thornabbey, Thornabby. In the middle Ages the name of the Lord of the Manor would be taken as a surname by all the people working on the estate, including laborers, blacksmiths, carpenters, etc. As a result there are many people scattered around the world bearing a name that in the strict sense they have no right to. Only those who can trace their descent from the family in the twelfth century are the true, armigerous Thornabys. That is, they have the right to display the family coat of arms. I am one of these Thornabys and since you do not mention anything about the coat of arms and do not trace your ancestry back beyond this William I assume that you are not. My grandfather's name was Jonathan.*

Gail writes this on an old portable typewriter that she has bought form the secondhand shop down the street. By this time she is living at 491 Hawtre Street, in an apartment building called the Miramar. It is a two-story building covered with dingy cream stucco, with twisted pillars on either side of a grilled entryway. It has a perfunctory Moorish or Spanish or Californian air, like that of an old movie theatre. The manager told her that the flat was very modern.

"An elderly lady had it, but she had to go to the hospital. Then somebody came when she died and got her effects out, but it still has the basic furniture that goes with the flat. What part of the States are you from?"

Oklahoma, Gail said. Mrs. Massie, from Oklahoma.

The manager looks to be about seventy years old. He wears glasses that magnify his eyes, and he walks quickly, but rather unsteadily, tilting forward. He speaks of difficulties—the increase of the foreign element in the population, which makes it hard to find good repairmen, the carelessness of certain tenants, the malicious acts of passersby who continually litter the grass. Gail asks if he had put in a notice yet to the Post Office. He says he has been intending to, but the lady did not receive hardly any mail. Except one letter came. It was a strange thing that it came right the day after she died. He sent it back.

"I'll do it," Gail said. "I'll tell the Post Office."

"I'll have to sign it, though. Get me one of those forms they have and I'll sign it and you can give it in. I'd be obliged."

The walls of the apartment are painted white—this must be what is modern about it. It has bamboo blinds, a tiny kitchen, a green sofa bed, a table, a dresser, and two chairs. On the wall one picture, which might have been a painting or a tinted photograph. A yellowish-green desert landscape, with rocks and bunches of sage and dim distant mountains. Gail is sure that she has seen this before.

She paid the rent in cash. She had to be busy for a while, buying sheets and towels and groceries, a few pots and dishes, the typewriter. She had to open a bank account, become a person living in the country, not a traveller. There are shops hardly a block away. A grocery store, a secondhand store, a drugstore, a tea shop. They are all humble establishments with strips of colored paper hanging in the doorways, wooden awnings over the sidewalk in front. Their offering are limited. The tea shop has only two tables, the secondhand store contains scarcely more than the tumbled-out accumulation of one ordinary house. The cereal boxes in the grocery store, the bottles of cough syrup and packets of pills in the drugstore are set out singly on the shelves, as if they were of special value or significance.

But she has found what she needs. In the secondhand store she found some loose flowered cotton dresses, a straw bag for her groceries. Now she looks like the other women she sees on the street. Housewives, middle-aged, with bare but pale arms and legs, shopping in the early morning or late afternoon. She bought a floppy straw hat too, to shade her face as the women do. Dim, soft, freckly, blinking faces.

Night comes suddenly around six o'clock and she must find occupation for the evenings. There is no television in the apartment. But a little beyond the shops there is a lending library, run by an old woman out of the front room of her house. This woman wears a hairnet and gray lisle stockings in spite of the heat. (Where, nowadays, can you find gray lisle stockings?) She has an undernourished body and colorless, tight, unsmiling lips. She is the person Gail calls to mind when she writes the letter from Catherine Thornaby. She thinks of this library woman by that name whenever she sees her, which is almost every day, because you are only allowed one book at a time, and Gail usually reads a book a night. She thinks, There is Catherine Thornaby, dead and moved into a new existence a few blocks away.

All the business about armigerous and non-armigerous Thornabys came out of a book. Not one of the books that Gail is reading now but one she read in her youth. The hero was the non-armigerous but deserving heir to a great property. She cannot remember the title. She lived with people then who were always reading *Steppenwolf*, or *Dune*, or something by Krishnamurti, and she read historical romances apologetically. She did not think Will would have read such a book or picked up this sort of information. And she is sure that he will have to reply, to tell Catherine off.

She waits, and reads the books from the lending library, which seem to come from an even earlier time than those romances she read twenty years ago. Some of them she took out of the public library in Winnipeg before she left home, and they seemed old-fashioned even then. *The Girl of the Limberlost*. *The Blue Castle*. *Maria Chapdelaine*. Such books remind her, naturally, of her life before Will. There was such a life and she could still salvage something from it, if she wanted to. She has a sister living in Winnipeg. She has an aunt there, in a nursing home, who still reads books in Russian. Gail's grandparents came from Russia, her parents could still speak Russian, her real name is not Gail, but Galya. She cut herself off from her family—or they cut her off—when she left home at eighteen to wander about the country, as you did in those days. First with friends, then with a boyfriend, then with another boyfriend. She strung beads and tie-dyed scarves and sold them on the street.

> Dear Ms. Thornaby,
>
> I must thank you for enlightening me as to the important distinction between the armigerous and the non-armigerous Thornabys. I gather that you have a strong suspicion that I may turn out to be one of the latter. I beg your pardon—I had no intention of treading

*on such sacred ground or of wearing the Thornaby coat of arms on
my T-shirt. We do not take much account of such things in my
country and I did not think you did so in Australia, but I see that I
am mistaken. Perhaps you are too far on in years to have noticed the
change in values. It is quite different with me, since I have been in
the teaching profession and am constantly brought up, as well,
against the energetic arguments of a young wife.*

*My innocent intention was simply to get in touch with somebody
in this country outside the theatrical-academic circle that my wife
and I seem to be absorbed in. I have a mother in Canada, whom I
miss. In fact your letter reminded me of her a little. She would be
capable of writing such a letter for a joke but I doubt whether you
are joking. It sounds like a case of Exalted Ancestry to me.*

When he is offended and disturbed in a certain way—a way that is hard to
predict and hard for most people to recognize—Will becomes heavily sarcastic.
Irony deserts him. He flails about, and the effect is to make people embarrassed not for themselves, as he intends, but for him. This happens seldom,
and usually when it happens it means that he feels deeply unappreciated. It
means that he has even stopped appreciating himself.

So that is what happened. Gail thinks so. Sandy and her young friends
with their stormy confidence, their crude righteousness might be making him
miserable. His wit not taken notice of, his enthusiasms out-of-date. No way of
making himself felt amongst them. His pride in being attached to Sandy going
gradually sour.

She thinks so. He is shaky and unhappy and casting about to know somebody else. He has thought of family ties, here in this country of non-stop
blooming and impudent bird life and searing days and suddenly clamped-
down nights.

Dear Mr. Thornaby,

*Did you really expect me, just because I have the same surname
as you, to fling open my door and put out the "welcome mat"—as I
think you say in America and that inevitably includes Canada? You
may be looking for another mother here, but that hardly obliges me
to be one. By the way you are quite wrong about my age—I am
younger than you by several years, so do not picture me as an elderly
spinster in a hairnet with gray lisle stockings. I know the world
probably as well as you do. I travel a good deal, being a fashion
buyer for a large store. So my ideas are not so out-of-date as you
suppose.*

You do not say whether your busy energetic young wife was to be
a part of this familial friendship. I am surprised you feel the need for
other contacts. It seems I am always reading or hearing on the media
about these "May–December" relationships and how invigorating
they are and how happily the men are settling down to domesticity
and parenthood. (No mention of the "trial runs" with women closer
to their own age or mention of how those women are settling down
to their lives of loneliness!) So perhaps you need to become a papa
to give you a "sense of family"!

Gail is surprised at how fluently she writes. She has always found it hard to write letters, and the results have been dull and sketchy, with many dashes and incomplete sentences and pleas of insufficient time. Where has she got this fine nasty style—out of some book, like the armigerous nonsense? She goes out in the dark to post her letter feeling bold and satisfied. But she wakes up early the next morning thinking that she has certainly gone too far. He will never answer that, she will never hear from him again.

She gets up and leaves the building, goes for a morning walk. The shops are still shut up, the broken venetian blinds are closed, as well as they can be, in the windows of the front-room library. She walks as far as the river, where there is a strip of park beside a hotel. Later in the day, she could not walk or sit there because the verandas of the hotel were always crowded with uproarious beer-drinkers, and the park was within their verbal or even bottle-throwing range. Now the verandas are empty, the doors are closed, and she walks in under the trees. The brown water of the river spreads sluggishly among the mangrove stumps. Birds are flying over the water, lighting on the hotel roof. They are not sea gulls, as she thought at first. They are smaller than gulls, and their bright white wings and breasts are touched with pink.

In the park two men are sitting—one on a bench, one in a wheelchair beside the bench. She recognizes them—they live in her building, and go for walks every day. Once, she held the grille open for them to pass through. She has seen them at the shops, and sitting at the table in the tearoom window. The man in the wheelchair looks quite old and ill. His face is puckered like old blistered paint. He wears dark glasses and a coal-black toupee and a black beret over that. He is all wrapped up in a blanket. Even later in the day, when the sun is hot—every time she has seen them—he has been wrapped in this plaid blanket. The man who pushes the wheelchair and who now sits on the bench is young enough to look like an overgrown boy. He is tall and large-limbed but not manly. A young giant, bewildered by his own extent. Strong but not athletic, with a stiffness, maybe of timidity, in his thick arms and legs and neck. Red hair not just on his head but on his bare arms and above the button of his shirt.

Gail halts in her walk past them, she says good morning. The young man answers almost inaudibly. It seems to be his habit to look out at the world with majestic indifference, but she thinks her greeting has given him a twitch of embarrassment or apprehension. Nevertheless she speaks again, she says, "What are those birds I see everywhere?"

"Galah birds," the young man says, making it sound something like her childhood name. She is going to ask him to repeat it, when the old man bursts out in what seems like a string of curses. The words are knotted and incomprehensible to her, because of the Australian accent on top of some European accent, but the concentrated viciousness is beyond any doubt. And these words are meant for her—he is leaning forward, in fact struggling to free himself from the straps that hold him in. He wants to leap at her. Lunge at her, chase her out of sight. The young man makes no apology and does not take any notice of Gail but leans towards the old man and gently pushes him back, saying things to him which she cannot hear. She sees that there will be no explanation. She walks away.

For ten days, no letter. No word. She cannot think what to do. She walks every day—that is mostly what she does. The Miramar is only about a mile or so away from Will's street. She never walks in that street again or goes into the shop where she told the man that she was from Texas. She cannot imagine how she could have been so bold, the first day. She does walk in the streets nearby. Those street all go along ridges. In between the ridges, which the houses cling to, there are steep-sided gullies full of birds and trees. Even as the sun grows hot, those birds are not quiet. Magpies keep up their disquieting conversation and sometimes emerge to make menacing flights at her light-colored hat. The birds with the name like her own cry out foolishly as they rise and whirl about and subside into the leaves. She walks till she is dazed and sweaty and afraid of sunstroke. She shivers in the heat—most fearful, most desirous, of seeing Will's utterly familiar figure, that one rather small and jaunty, free-striding package, of all that could pain or appease her, in the world.

> *Dear Mr. Thornaby,*
> *This is just a short note to beg your pardon if I was impolite and*
> *hasty in my replies to you, as I am sure I was. I have been under*
> *some stress lately, and have taken a leave of absence to recuperate.*
> *Under these circumstances one does not always behave as well as*
> *would hope or see things as rationally....*

One day she walks past the hotel and the park. The verandas are clamorous with the afternoon drinking. All the trees in the park have come out in bloom. The flowers are a color that she has seen and could not have imagined on trees before—a shade of silvery blue, or silvery purple, so delicate and beautiful that you would think it would shock everything into quietness, into contemplation, but apparently it has not.

When she gets back to the Miramar, she finds the young man with the red hair standing in the downstairs hall, outside the door of the apartment where he lives with the old man. From behind the closed apartment door come the sounds of a tirade.

The young man smiles at her, this time. She stops and they stand together, listening.

Gail says, "If you would ever like a place to sit down while you're waiting, you know you're welcome to come upstairs."

He shakes his head, still smiling as if this was a joke between them. She thinks she should say something else before she leave him there, so she asks him about the trees in the park. "Those trees beside the hotel," she says. "Where I saw you the other morning? They are all out in bloom now. What are they called.?"

He says a word she cannot catch. She asks him to repeat it. "Jack Randa," he says. "That's the Jack Randa Hotel."

Dear Ms. Thornaby,

I have been away and when I came back I found both your letters waiting for me. I opened them in the wrong order, though that really doesn't matter.

My mother has died. I have been "home" to Canada for her funeral. It is cold there, autumn. Many things have changed. Why I should want to tell you this I simply do not know. We have certainly got off on the wrong track with each other. Even if I had not got your note of explanation after the first letter you wrote, I think I would have been glad in a peculiar way to get the first letter. I wrote you a very snippy and unpleasant letter and you wrote me back one of the same. The snippiness and unpleasantness and readiness to take offense seems somehow familiar to me. Ought I to risk your armigerous wrath by suggesting that we may be related after all?

I feel adrift here. I admire my wife and her theatre friends, with their zeal and directness and commitment, their hope of using their talents to create a better world. (I must say though that it often seems to me that the hope and zeal exceed the talents.) I cannot be one of them. I must say they saw this before I did. It must be because I am woozy with jet lag after that horrendous flight that I can face up to this fact and that I write it down in a letter to someone like you who has her own troubles and quite correctly has

indicated that she doesn't want to be bothered with mine. I had
better close, in fact, before I burden you with further claptrap from
my psyche. I wouldn't blame you if you had stopped reading before
you got this far....

Gail lies on the sofa pressing this letter with both hands against her stomach. Many things are changed. He has been in Walley, then—he has been told how she sold the shop and started out on her great world trip. But wouldn't he have heard that anyway, from Cleata? Maybe not, Cleata was close-mouthed. And when she went into the hospital, just before Gail left, she said, "I don't want to see or hear from anybody for a while or bother with letters. These treatments are bound to be a bit melodramatic."

Cleata is dead.

Gail knew that Cleata would die, but somehow thought that everything would hold still, nothing could really happen there while she, Gail, remained here. Cleata is dead and Will is alone except for Sandy, and Sandy perhaps has stopped being of much use to him.

There is a knock on the door. Gail jumps up in a great disturbance, looking for a scarf to cover her hair. It is the manger, calling her false name.

"I just wanted to tell you I had somebody here asking questions. He asked me about Miss Thornaby and I said, Oh, she's dead. She's been dead for some time now. He said, Oh, has she? I said, Yes, she has, and he said, Well, that's strange."

"Did he say why?" Gail says, "Did he say why it was strange?"

"No. I said, She died in the hospital and I've got an American lady in the flat now. I forgot where you told me you came from. He sounded like an American himself, so it might've meant something to him. I said, There was a letter come for Miss Thornaby after she was dead, did you write that letter? I told him I sent it back. Yes, he said, I wrote it, but I never got it back. There must be some kind of mistake, he said."

Gail says there must be. "Like a mistaken identity," she says.

"Yes. Like that."

Dear Ms. Thornaby,

It has come to my attention that you are dead. I know that life is strange, but I have never found it quite this strange before. Who are you and what is going on? It seems this rigamarole about the Thornabys must have been just that—a rigamarole. You must certainly be a person with time on your hands and a fantasizing turn of mind. I resent being taken in but I suppose I understand the temptation. I do think you owe me an explanation now as to whether or

> *not my explanation is true and this is some joke. Or am I dealing*
> *with some "fashion buyer" from beyond the grave? (Where did you*
> *get that touch or is it the truth?)*

When Gail goes out to buy food, she uses the back door of the building, she takes a roundabout route to the shops. On her return by the same back-door route, she comes upon the young red-haired man standing between the dustbins. If he had not been so tall, you might have said that he was hidden there. She speaks to him but he doesn't answer. He looks at her through tears, as if the tears were nothing but a wavy glass, something usual.

"Is your father sick?" Gail says to him. She has decided that this must be the relationship, though the age gap seem greater than usual between father and son, and the two of them are quite unalike in looks, and the young man's patience and fidelity are so far beyond—nowadays they seem even contrary to—anything a son customarily shows. But they go beyond anything a hired attendant might show, as well.

"No," the young man says, and though his expression stays calm, a drowning flush spreads over his face, under the delicate redhead's skin.

Lovers, Gail thinks. She is suddenly sure of it. She feels a shiver of sympathy, an odd gratification.

Lovers.

She goes down to her mailbox after dark and finds there another letter.

> *I might have thought that you were out of town on one of your*
> *fashion-buying jaunts but the manager tells me you have not been*
> *away since taking the flat, so I must suppose your "leave of*
> *absence" continues. He tells me also that you are a brunette. I sup-*
> *pose we might exchange descriptions—and then, with trepidation,*
> *photographs—in the brutal manner of people meeting through*
> *newspaper ads. It seems that in my attempt to get to know you I am*
> *willing to make a quite a fool of myself. Nothing new of course in*
> *that....*

Gail does not leave the apartment for two days. She does without milk, drinks her coffee black. What will she do when she runs out of coffee? She eats odd meals—tuna fish spread on crackers when she has no bread to make a sandwich, a dry end of cheese, a couple of mangos. She goes out into the upstairs hall of the Miramar—first opening the door a crack, testing the air for an occupant—and walks to the arched window that overlooks the street. And from long ago a feeling comes back to her—the feeling of watching a street, the visible bit of a street, where a car is expected to appear, or may appear or may not appear. She even remembers now the cars themselves—a blue Austin mini, a maroon Chevrolet, a family station wagon. Cars in which she travelled short distances, illicitly and in a bold daze of consent. Long before Will.

She doesn't know what clothes Will will be wearing, or how his hair is cut, or if he will have some change in his walk or expression, some change appropriate to his life here. He cannot have changed more than she has. She has no mirror in the apartment except the little one on the bathroom cupboard, but even that can tell her how much thinner she has got and how the skin of her face has toughened. Instead of fading and wrinkling as fair skin often does in this climate, hers has got a look of dull canvas. It could be fixed up—she sees that. With the right kind of makeup a look of exotic sullenness could be managed. Her hair is more of a problem—the red shows at the roots, with shiny strands of gray. Nearly all the time she keeps it hidden by a scarf.

When the manager knocks on her door again, she has only a second or two of crazy expectation. He begins to call her name. "Mrs. Massie, Mrs. Massie! Oh I hoped you'd be in. I wondered if you could just come down and help me. It's the old bloke downstairs, he's fallen off the bed."

He goes ahead of her down the stairs, holding to the railing and dropping each foot shakily, precipitately, onto the step below.

"His friend isn't there. I wondered. I didn't see him yesterday. I try and keep track of people but I don't like to interfere. I thought he probably would've come back in the night. I was sweeping out the foyer and I heard a thump and I went back in there—I wondered what was going on. Old bloke all by himself, on the floor."

The apartment is no larger than Gail's, and laid out in the same way. It has curtains down over the bamboo blinds, which make it very dark. It smells of cigarettes and old cooking and some kind of pine-scented air freshener. The sofa bed has been pulled out, and made into a double bed, and the old man is lying on the floor beside it, having dragged some of the bedclothes with him. His head without the toupee is smooth, like a dirty piece of soap. His eyes are half shut and a noise is coming from deep inside him like the noise of an engine hopelessly trying to turn over.

"Have you phoned the ambulance?" Gail says.

"If you could just pick up the one end of him," the manager says. "I have a bad back and I dread putting it out again."

"Where is the phone?" says Gail. "He may have had a stroke. He may have broken his hip. He'll have to go to the hospital."

"Do you think so? His friend could lift him back and forth so easy. He had the strength. And now he's disappeared."

Gail says, "I'll phone."

"Oh, no. Oh, no. I have the number written down over the phone in my office. I don't let any other person go in there."

Left alone with the old man, who probably cannot hear her, Gail says, "It's all right. It's all right. We're getting help for you." Her voice sounds foolishly sociable. She leans down to pull the blanket up over his shoulder, and to her great surprise a hand flutters out, searches for and grabs her own. His hand is slight and bony, but warm enough, and dreadfully strong. "I'm here, I'm here," she says, and wonders if she is impersonating the red-haired young man, or some other young man, or a woman, or even his mother.

The ambulance comes quickly, with its harrowing pulsing cry, and the ambulance men with the stretcher cart are soon in the room, the manager stumping after them, saying, "... couldn't be moved. Here is Mrs. Massie came down to help in the emergency."

While they are getting the old man onto the stretcher, Gail has to pull her hand away, and he begins to complain, or she thinks he does—that steady involuntary-sounding noise he is making acquires an extra *ah-unh-anh*. So she takes his hand again as soon as she can, and trots beside him as he is wheeled out. He has such a grip on her that she feels as if he is pulling her along.

"He was the owner of the Jacaranda Hotel," the manager says. "Years ago. He was."

A few people are in the street, but nobody stops, nobody wants to be caught gawking. They want to see, they don't want to see.

"Shall I ride with him?" Gail says. "He doesn't seem to want to let go of me."

"It's up to you," one of the ambulance men says, and she climbs in. (She is dragged in, really, by that clutching hand.) The ambulance man puts down a little seat for her, the doors are closed, the siren starts as they pull away.

Through the window in the back door then she sees Will. He is about a block away from the Miramar and walking towards it. He is wearing a light-colored short-sleeved jacket and matching pants—probably a safari suit—and his hair has grown whiter or been bleached by the sun, but she knows him at once, she will always know him, and will always have to call out to him when she sees him, as she does now, even trying to jump up from the seat, trying to pull her hand out of the old man's grasp.

"It's Will," she says to the ambulance man. "Oh, I'm sorry. It's my husband."

"Well, he better not see you jumping out of a speeding ambulance," the man says. Then he says, "Oh-oh. What's happened here?" For the next minute or so he pays professional attention to the old man. Soon he straightens up and says, "Gone."

"He's still holding on to me," says Gail. But she realizes as she says this that it isn't true. A moment ago he was holding on—with great force, it seemed, enough force to hold her back, when she would have sprung towards Will. Now it is she who is hanging on to him. His fingers are still warm.

When she gets back from the hospital, she finds the note that she is expecting.

> *Gail. I know it's you.*

Hurry. Hurry. Her rent is paid. She must leave a note for the manager. She must take the money out of the bank, get herself to the airport, find a flight. Her clothes can stay behind—her humble pale-print dresses, her floppy hat. The last library book can remain on the table under the sagebrush picture. It can remain there, accumulating fines.

Otherwise, what will happen?

What she has surely wanted. What she is suddenly, as surely, driven to escape.

> *Gail, I know you're in there! I know you're there on the other side of the door.*
> *Gail! Galya!*
> *Talk to me, Gail. Answer me. I know you're there.*
> *I can hear you. I can hear your heart beating through the keyhole and your stomach rumbling and your brain jumping up and down.*
> *I can smell you through the keyhole. You. Gail.*

Words most wished for can change. Something can happen to them, while you are waiting. *Love—need—forgive. Love—need—forever.* The sound of such words can become a din, a battering, a sound of hammers in the street. And all you can do is run away, so as not to honor them out of habit.

In the airport shop she sees a number of little boxes, made by Australian aborigines. They are round, and light as pennies. She picks out one that has a pattern of yellow dots, irregularly spaced on a dark-red ground. Against this is a swollen black figure—turtle, maybe, with short splayed legs. Helpless on its back.

Gail is thinking, A present for Cleata. As if her whole time here had been a dream, something she could discard, going back to a chosen point, a beginning.

Not for Cleata. A present for Will?

A present for Will, then. Send it now? No, take it back to Canada, all the way back, send it from there.

The yellow dots flung out in that way remind Gail of something she saw last fall. She and Will saw it. They went for a walk on a sunny afternoon. They walked from their house by the river up the wooded bank, and there they came on a display that they had heard about but never sees before.

Hundreds, maybe thousands, of butterflies were hanging in the trees, resting before their long flight down the shore of Lake Huron and across Lake

Erie, then on south to Mexico. They hung there like metal leaves, beaten gold—like flakes of gold tossed up and caught in the branches.

"Like the shower of gold in the Bible," Gail said.

Will told her that she was confusing Jove and Jehovah.

On that day, Cleata had already begun to die and Will had already met Sandy. This dream had already begun—Gail's journey and her deceits, then the words she imagined—believed—that she heard shouted through the door.

> *Love—forgive*
> *Love—forget*
> *Love—forever*

Hammers in the street.

What could you put in a box like that before you wrapped it up and sent it far away? A bead, a feather, a potent pill? Or a note, folded up tight, to about the size of a spitball.

> *Now it's up to you to follow me.*

ADOLPH MUSCHIG

THE SCYTHE HAND,
OR THE HOMESTEAD

Translated by Michael Hamburger

Adolf Muschig (b. 1934) is a playwright, novelist, biographer, literary critic, and short-story writer. He was born near Lake Zurich in Switzerland and began his writing career at the age of thirty-one. He writes in German and is one of the few Swiss writers to have had a major influence on German literature. Muschig's reputation was established early with his widely acclaimed first novel, Im Sommer des Hasen *(The Summer of the Hare, 1965). His work began to appear in English translation in 1975 with Michael Hamburger's translation of "The Scythe Hand or The Homestead," which was later reprinted in* The Blue Man and Other Stories *(1983). According to Marlix Zeller Cambon, Muschig is "above all a German-speaking European and shares in the themes of twentieth-century Europe: existential anxiety, metaphysical skepticism, distrust in human institutions, a strong psychological interest in the motivating forces of our conscious and unconscious selves, and of course the dilemma of language between renewal and limits of communication."*

"The Scythe Hand or The Homestead" is a disturbing story told in the halting voice of a mountain peasant who, in the words of one critic, "pleads for a court's understanding of his life's circumstances. His language accentuates the gulf between the moral codes of a respectable society and the creature needs of a humanity on the fringe." Muschig does not explain or interpret, and he does not judge his protagonist. The reader must debate the merits of the narrator's plea.

Perhaps the Court of Enquiry is not aware that with my late wife Elisabeth I farmed for fifteen years at Frogs' Well and was of good repute there, had enough to live on, too, till the same burned to the ground for dubious reasons in the year 1951 with our son Christian, aged two at that time, and I also lost all our livestock, as well as vehicles, because the fire spread too fast and the fire brigade did not arrive in time. Frogs' Well had been in the family for more than a century, and my grandfather farmed it to everyone's satisfaction in his time. Consequently my father, deceased, was even elected to the School Board, and I take the liberty of mentioning that I was able to attend the Secondary School at Krummbach, because my mother, deceased, skimped no sacrifice. Water could have been drawn from the hydrant by the well, but the fire chief insisted on his view that this was frozen over, which was quite correct, but all that was needed was to break the thin ice. So more than one hour passed before the hose was laid across from Hasenrain, and the main building too could not be saved. The death of Christian gave rise to many ugly rumors, although he was quite small and we had always looked after him well. That was a great blow to us at the time. Since the indemnity was never adequate and at first we were housed at Shady Bank, that too gave rise to sharp friction, and my dear wife survived it only for one year, because she had caught cold during the conflagration, which turned out to be cancer. That also is a cause of great distress to us, when everyone knew that we used to manage well and had been punished enough as it was, and had paid our ground-rent regularly. But the indemnity was reduced out of malice, and the operation cost 5000 francs, which I could hardly raise, and it became too much for the farmeress at Shady Bank, because of my daughters, although Lina was already 22 and gave a hand everywhere, as I did in the field, while they said that I scared the cows and therefore must not milk them. It wasn't Barbara's fault that she was only three years old, though she did cause a lot of work in which as a man I could not assist enough, and the farmeress at Shady Bank was herself expecting. So we had to move out and take out a lease for Torgel Alp from the municipality, for which I had reason to be grateful too, because the previous tenant had caught his death there after running down the farm and hanging himself. The place was too lonely for him as well.

So up on Torgel Alp nothing had been done for years, but Lina and I got the homestead back into working order, and we succeeded, too, in bringing up Barbara satisfactorily, so that she kept her health. Only her way to school was so long that in winter she could not always manage it, so that she fell behind and lost much joy, even though I cleared the track each morning and this wasn't even laid down in the contract.

I cleared the road as far as the dairy farm, but didn't hang about there, nor in the village, because of the people, not even to collect money owing for milk. If that gave rise to new rumors, that's typical, but the real trouble was the great remoteness of the homestead, which often set in as early as mid-October because of snow.

Also, I had to go over completely to dairy farming, which I should not have dreamed of doing at Frogs' Well, but carried out in the teeth of all sorts of obstacles.

Also, the ground-rent was so high that with the best will in the world we had to borrow again. At first I had the good luck to be able to graze 15–20 bullocks, privately, but then for no evident reason the number decreased, although I only asked for my due, the bullocks returned to the valley in good condition, too, but I never stayed there long enough to forestall the rumors. Furthermore, my older daughter Lina was often sick, which did not affect the running of the farm, since I kept her at work and exertions all the same, and our younger one had had to learn early on to help her sister, even though this kept her away from school. I must add that Lina was a strong support for me without words and despite the pain she had in her belly, and would be still if she hadn't been taken into care now, for which she is not to blame, and I only hope that now she is receiving medical attention, because she has earned it. It was a blow to us when the municipality would send no more bullocks for grazing because of irregularities that were completely unfounded, or what were due only to all the special circumstances there, and because I didn't spend all my time defending myself, so that I was thrown back on my meager resources.

Sheer slander it was, their saying that I was out of my mind, only because I could no longer control a twitching in my cheek, and I'm sure that caused no inconvenience to anyone, but never allowed a bad word to cross my lips, as the Vicar can testify, as long as he came to see us, that is, for he stopped, as everyone knows, until it was too late. When people wouldn't look at me because of the twitch, I sent Barbara out with the milk, which would have done her no harm, I'm sure, and she only bought the most necessary things at the shop, because we couldn't afford more in any case, and if she sometimes stayed for a while it was only because she had to wait and other people can afford more than they could in my time.

And if they say my milk wasn't 100%, no one has proved that and none of those gentlemen saw how I looked after my cattle, they always got fed before we did, and as for sick cows, I had to telephone to report such a case if it occurred, so that the vet could get there in time, even though a jeep was put in his disposal by the municipality.

I too am a member of the municipality, but that doesn't mean that my daughters can simply be taken into care, only because they aren't to blame for anything. It is always being said, too, that I ceased to go to church or to confession, but there I should like you to consider that I should have gone when the trouble started, but it was too far away, and so we had to cope with the trouble on our own. If that is sin, my daughters couldn't help it, and you gentlemen of the Court should admit it, because of their youth for one thing, because of their poverty for another, and you should take into account that, given all those things, Barbara may have been a bit backward. Nevertheless, when it had happened, no sort of deterioration took place in the household, no, it improved if anything, since at last we lived together in peace and could raise the ground-rent for once, which was like a miracle, and I thanked God for it, until the Vicar arrived and, after him, the Justice of the Peace, all because of the slander. For it is my opinion that if you leave a family alone for so long you must allow them to solve their problems in their own way. But since she has been taken into care now, I don't want to stand in the way of my daughter's happiness, only hope that this is what's in question, not somebody's profit because my daughter has learned how to work, and I also request that there shall be no recriminations, because I did not corrupt her, although, as you know, unlawful acts did take place. These were only for the sake of her peace, as Barbara can confirm if she likes, and I forgive her in my heart, she must not fret because she got me into prison, for that was our fate, it seems, and that's all there is to it. So I will thank God that she came down from Torgel Alp, and beg the honorable Court only for some attention to her, so that she survives. I was fond of her, there's no getting away from it, and consequently could not do otherwise, and wouldn't know today what to do. And even my late wife would have had no objection. I know that, when I had the privilege to know her kind heart for twenty-four years, and she was glad, too, to be blessed with late children, first Barbara, then Christian who stayed behind in the fire. That is why, too, she departed this life and left the family to their own devices, that was a bit much all at once, when on top of it you are penalized and have to move to Torgel Alp. If my older daughter Lina hadn't taken after her late mother, hadn't been the split image of her, I don't know what would have become of us up there.

One should not forget, though, that a girl has other thoughts in her head beyond housekeeping, even an older girl.

In any case Lina was no longer ill when you separated us, that may not have suited the Rev. Vicar, because his mind boggled, but then he was clerical and past the age when a person is tormented.

But should Lina now be ailing once more, then it's those people who did that to her, for my daughter has a strong constitution and recovers every time she is needed. I myself couldn't know—could I?—that at 57 I should be tormented again, and it was a cold morning too. I was about to go out and feed the cows, and I noticed that she hadn't lit the fire, but the kitchen was empty, and your breath froze in front of your nose. I was startled, dear Court of Enquiry, for I can only say that nothing like that had happened in ten years, even when she did have a bellyache she'd drag herself downstairs and put the coffee on the stove. All the windows were covered in frost, and the place quiet as a churchyard, that's where she ought to have appeared to me, for it hadn't been as quiet as that since the death of my wife. But this didn't occur to me at that instant, I can promise you, didn't come over me till later.

Went upstairs to the bedroom, the little one was asleep for we'd always let her sleep when it was too cold, and there was only a little boxroom for her, but a warm bed, there she was coziest, why take her anywhere else. My only thought was that there could be one fewer of us again, and that made me shake with fear, I never so much as knocked on Lina's door but tore it open. I only write this much so that you will know the circumstances, not so that you'll come to dirty conclusions again. For there in the cold bedroom my wife sat in her shift, her bare shift, honorable Court of Enquiry, never turned her head but went on as before, leaning forward a little, so as to see herself in the mirror, only a small one it was, and passed the brush over her hair. But she did that so slowly that this slowness, together with the mere shift and the breath clouding the mirror, so that she had to wipe it clear with her free hand, all this cut into my heart and made me feel quite faint, I can't describe it, when my wife had been dead all those years. What are you doing, I asked, why don't you stop, or you'll catch cold. She said, without turning round: Why not, she said, quite calm and funny. Later she said she had dreamed of her mother, and only then, I promise you, I remembered that I too had dreamed of her mother, but by then it was too late.

As long as I stood there, by the door, I saw only that she didn't so much as turn round and, in consequence, that her hair had already turned gray in places. You should bear in mind that Lina was not quite 37, which is normal, save that as her father I had never paid attention to it, also the cold, and that the shock had left me in an abnormal state of mind. That is why everything happened so fast that I can't recall how it came about, I didn't lie about that, even though you want to know the exact details, but what's the use of them now. On my honor and salvation, all I know is that suddenly I felt relieved and Lina's face, with a rosy and languid look she hadn't had since her childhood, lay beside me on the pillow, and the two of us breathed. I am sorry I cannot tell you more, save that it happened, and that was all, and you are grown-up people after all, nor was I aware of the illegality of the act at that moment, but it wasn't my age, on the contrary, 57 doesn't amount to old age, I wish it did. Next item, I went to feed the animals, and when I returned Lina was at the stove as usual, humming a tune, and the coffee was already made. That's how it went till the evening, save that I couldn't get to sleep and was cruelly tormented. I drank several glasses of brandy, fill yourself up, I said to myself, and you won't feel so sore about it. But this was not the case, the whole mood of the place was changed, too, like at Christmas, for which reason I retired for self-abuse, as in all the previous years, when tormented. The mood would not leave me, though, but you must not think that this happened often, I'd been tormented daily only in the four or five years after my wife's death, then once a month perhaps, and then it stopped completely and I lived like a decent widower. I said to myself, what's up, then, you have no right to any Christmas any more, have you, you aren't even sleepy, and so I took a walk over to the cattle, which nearly always helped.

Although by then I had only two cows of my own and six goats, and your breath froze on your nose, I got into a sweat as soon as I so much as looked at them, though I'd seen the same thing a thousand times if I'd seen it once, and they turned their heads to look at me, too, as though they wanted to do something to me, as though bewitched, so that I went out again and on and on through the snow, as far as the place where I took it into my head to lie down, thinking that will make you feel better. But then in the cold it struck me that my daughters wouldn't be able to raise the money for my funeral, but would be exposed to mockery, though behind hands held to the face as usual, I didn't want them to suffer that, couldn't get my daughters out of my mind at all, but not in the way you think, and I got up again. So I suddenly found myself back at the homestead, must have walked in a semi-circle, that happens in the snow. It wasn't my own homestead either, I'd always known that, but when you're tired and the above has occurred, you see things as though for the first time. So I stood like a stranger in front of this homestead and no longer knew what was what, was afraid to go in. I thought, something will happen of itself if you stand here long enough, sooner or later the music will stop, for I had heard music all that night, and the stars were out, it was getting colder fast, near dawn. But because the snow itself made everything bright I saw that a window upstairs was open, please, my God, don't, I said to that, but nothing helped, so I called out, shut it, then, shut it, you pig, yes, that's what I called out, but don't know whether she heard me, my voice was feeble too, and all remained as it was.

If I turned my head a bit could see it more clearly, but still, couldn't tell for certain, what, if I looked at it straight it was there at one moment, gone the next, but it was something white all the time.

A man wants to know, gentlemen, whether someone his own is standing so long at an open window in such a frost and catching her death of it, so I went inside and upstairs, but it wasn't the torment, when I couldn't even feel my own feet. In Lina's bedroom everything was open, and the window too, but no one was standing there, and I began to fear what she might have done to herself. Stretched out my hand, I did, to where it was darkest, for that's where the bed was, till I felt something warm, something alive, that was there. Said, Thank God for that, without her being able to hear me, because she was under the cover and I wanted to comfort her. But she held on to my hand and said, come on, then, you idiot, you chicken, and said it quite clearly, and I responded to it, because I suddenly lost all consciousness of myself, and it must have happened for the second time, for suddenly there was peace again and no music any more. You must not hold that chicken against my daughter, it was clearly meant to be a sort of joke. I had called out pig, too, and hadn't meant it. You can call that sin, but there was this cold all the time, and I'm no chicken I'm sorry to say, so I stayed till it was warm. No one thanks you, anyway, for suffering the cold, and the need is too great to be forgiven us, as the Vicar said, whether we live as husband and wife now or not.

After that Lina was cured of her bellyache, we were kinder to each other, too, and took good care of each other, and that year I could pay off my ground-rent in time, because a blessing had been put on it. Was able to buy two more cows and have all four served, and they produced cow calves and got a prize a year later, which was made possible because the judges at Krummbach didn't know so much about my situation, and it became evident that without prejudice I could manage well, received a loan from the Small Farmers' Assistance too, which enabled me to have the roof re-thatched and to build a long-needed reservoir, but created more bad blood in the village. For, High Court of Justice, it is true, on my oath, that one can stand on one's head, bad blood can't be made any better, especially if the village is small.

It was also true that I could have a new dress bought for each of my daughters, which nowadays is no luxury even in remote places, and I waited till the sales for that and certainly did not live in splendor and affluence. When we only had just enough for us to get used to our state of affairs.

As for me, I can only add that since the death of my lamented wife I had never lived in a family, but this was now the case more than ever. My younger daughter caught me singing, too, as I whitewashed the cowshed. That was more than I deserved, I'm sure, and I give all the credit for it to my dear daughters.

After finishing her school years Barbara did not want to take any employment, since she'd had enough teasing, the spasms in her face grew more violent too, which she must have inherited, though in myself I was not always aware of them. The vet couldn't find a good reason for them either, save that they were nervous, though I should have paid him to the last penny for his pills. So it came about that Barbara stayed with us, nor expressed any desire for an apprenticeship, which I should certainly have let her have, never wanting to deprive my daughters of anything, since I am fond of them both, though not in the way you think. Nor did I know that in the shed she was subject to regular molestation by the scythe hand, that Füllemann who is well known to you, who took advantage of her extremity, because she never said anything about it in public, perhaps thinking we had enough trouble already. It would have been better if she had, though, for in that case I should have bashed in the scythe hand's skull without qualms. What I am charged with, though, because the scythe hand got it out of her, that was quite different from the gossip it gave rise to, the reason why I am now in prison. Because I was fond of my daughter, and concerned about her health, about which I knew no better when even a vet wouldn't take the trouble, I couldn't resist, but I never implanted any pride in her on that score, so that she would go and boast to the scythe hand about something that certainly happened as an emergency measure and under the stress of too much molestation, when she was still half a child, as she is to this day.

For, High Court of Justice, you wouldn't have done any different either if your daughter had begged for it so urgently and you couldn't bear to see her suffer, only because the girl doesn't know the facts of life, but was physically mature and plagued by it, again because of the remoteness of the homestead, which could happen only up on Torgel Alp. Our Frogs' Well was burnt down, as you know, my wife departed and I alone with the girls, of whom one was now 37, the other 21, a great gap, but not with regard to the female body, that makes it hard to show no love when Lina is better all at once, but the younger one sleeps just behind the thin partition and is tormented in her fashion.

Since she slept lightly I wanted to relieve her of that, there was no other motive, and the longer it went on the less anyone thought anything of it, if the scythe hand hadn't got it out of her, I bet he had his reasons. And if it is said that she burst into tears, I'd like to have seen you if as half a child still you'd got under the scythe hand, and that wasn't till seven months later, the tears too came because of the Vicar, who got there late enough, it had never happened with me.

Rather the facts of the case were as follows, my younger daughter came to me in the spring, complaining that I didn't esteem her, because Lina was privileged, and she was only her sister. At first I dismissed that, till my younger girl went to bed ill and wouldn't get up again, the twitches in her face got so bad, too, that mine broke out again and I feared for her sanity, and she sang so loud when I was with Lina that I thought a sow was being struck, but she never dared come in, because she was a decent girl. In March, though, she developed such a bellyache that I thought, Oh, hell, maybe it would be better for you to give her peace, talked about it with Lina, who'd turned into a real housewife. But it isn't true that she advised me to do it, she only knew, what must be, must be. So, when Lina had gone to the road house with the milk, I took Barbara a jug of milk warm from the cow to her bedroom, since I had to take everything up to her, which became troublesome, and it was March 23rd. She grabbed hold of my hand at once so that I could feel if there wasn't a swelling there, and when I felt her she started that cruel screaming again, as well as spasms which ran visibly across her whole body, and I felt so sorry for her that I couldn't help myself but allowed what followed to occur. Then she got up quite amiable and smiled like a rogue, but I was too fond of my daughter to bear her any grudge, only begged her sincerely never to let it happen again. Whereupon she quite easily drank the milk which she had pushed far away from her before, and went quite sensibly to the kitchen, and prepared an evening meal, which she hadn't done for a long time, indeed started cooking and frying so much that I got alarmed and we fed well that evening, in great obliviousness even drank brandy till it gave rise to new acts, and I was even the instigator, which I would beg to have taken into account today in my daughters' favor. That was March 23rd. For I must add that because of constant physical labor I am still full of sap, quite unexpectedly, nor knew any remedy for it till Lina took the matter into her hand, but this occurred with good will on both sides, like the relations with my younger daughter, which I did not need any more, as you will understand.

But let the respected Court tell me of a way to help a poor person like Barbara out of her predicament, when the partition is thin and there's no prospect of her finding a suitable man, when already at school she couldn't keep up, but only because of Torgel Alp, where one couldn't make a secret of our situation, as other people do. For, dear Court, poverty had come first, I must say that quite plainly, and poverty brings many troubles in its train, of which one can relieve only the most pressing, if no one else offers any help.

It would have been the first time I preferred one daughter to the other, that is why I had to take her on in turn, not because I was tormented. After that all went smoothly in our house, you can ask anyone, and if it was a sin and no one wants to have anything to do with us now, I do beseech you not to make too great an issue of our intercourse, for neither did we, but peace was the main thing, and we did not disturb anyone, but were never bedded on roses. And I assure you that the abomination was no unmitigated pleasure, a thing that is quite unknown on Torgel Alp, but only a kind of comfort.

Earlier on we did have a conscience about it, but that ceased because my daughters no longer suffered from a bellyache, and this was better than a deal of worrying about it and even made us quite merry at times in the winter. There are always people who talk about their conscience but don't tell a man all the same what's to be done against the cold or against pains, at least nobody told us. When the Vicar arrived at last we no longer expected him and didn't really know what to do about it, and nor did he. For he walked up quite slowly, Lina saw him from a long way off, and she said, O my God. So, when he could think of nothing to say but only asked, don't you want to confess, I could not back him up and answered quite legitimately, I wouldn't know what to confess, and he replied, he thought I did know, and he couldn't even look me straight in the eyes. For years he could have observed how Barbara's face twitched, and my daughter Lina's bellyache, but all that had been nothing to him, not so now that all was going well, though without his blessing. I told him what I thought about that. He said that he never listened to gossip but was answerable for preventing the spreading of the bacillus, which would make half the community sick at the very mention of us, and that I could bear even less to be answerable for it, either toward God or toward my daughters. I said I could bear to be answerable for many things as long as a man needs help and the ways are not always clear to him, in short I refused point-blank to make a confession of it, when he still couldn't look me in the face, but only stroked his hip with one hand.

I then offered him a glass of schnapps, whereupon he did not come in, but said: if you will not avail yourself of the secrecy of confession I must ask you as a fellow citizen to give yourself up, because otherwise you will be in trouble, you will make the village unhappy with your state of affairs, or would you prefer to have your roof set on fire one night? High Court of Justice, that gave me a fright, to hear him talk of a fire, when I had lost one child in a fire before, and there too the cause had remained obscure, although I had never given offense to anyone. Whereupon my daughter Barbara rushed into the room and made our distress very great by screaming that the Vicar was a dirty old man and ought to wipe his nose after sticking it into everyone's pots, when it wasn't his business, and did the scythe hand confess too what he had done to her? So the cat was out of the bag, as far as the scythe hand was concerned, and it then came out that the same had repeatedly lain in wait for her when she was help-less because of the heavy pails she was carrying, and had grabbed hold of her in spite of her protests. Finally, at the end of June, he had gone so far as to bash her head against a stone near the milking-shed, so that she couldn't struggle, and used her, because there was no help for her nearby, and on top of that had said to her mockingly, how well the meadow had been mown already, and hadn't he hurt her? Whereupon my daughter had screamed in her half-con-scious state, with his miserable stub he couldn't do anyone any harm, let alone any good. Whereupon the same had merely buttoned up his trousers, saying, all right, all the more power to our buck, who had all the nanny-goats to him-self, now that the farmer had come to an agreement with his daughters, and she was to give his regards to the whole happy household, put on his hat and left. That was a sad speech, since it is well known that lonely men have to make do with animals, when for years they cannot find a single human being, something I did not do even in my worst plight, but only deviated from the straight and narrow path to give my daughters peace, of which certainly the younger one ought not to have bragged, nor did I ever implant such arrogance in her heart.

Nevertheless, High Court of Justice, you should take into account that she was used by the scythe hand, and this without any understanding between them.

I have always believed that in such things there must be an agreement, and that two are needed for that, even with poor folk, and a little joy, which even beasts do not fail to feel in their fashion. But between my daughters and me this was so, because we did it for the sake of warmth and it was not the most important thing, but so that the family would be kept together, nor was violence ever used. But the scythe hand confessed his crime to the Vicar and got rid of his sin by bringing down justice upon our homestead, and we all had to pay dearly for Barbara's little lapse into pride. Now you want to know more than I can offer you, when the real shock and perdition came only after everyone took such a lively interest in the affair.

The scythe hand got off lightly because he is young and daft as a duck, but older flesh is never forgiven when it's tormented, and yet its trials are harder than those of any loud-mouthed young ruffian. But if my daughter Lina had been younger, and without my fears, I should never have violated her, but it was because I saw her gray hairs and pity took hold of me like a rage that this daughter of mine was not to be taken for what she was, but must drag her bellyache around in silence all her life, which to this day seems more bestial to me than everything else. And this too was not because of the flesh, but because the flesh is tormented by a soul and has nothing left to hope for if it finds no warmth, something I could not bear to watch any longer. Everything else, as I have set it down, followed logically from that, because I could not slight Barbara, and never pursued those relations for their own sake, but only so that the girls should have some kindness in their lives.

And I raise no objection now if the whole responsibility falls on me, because men should always know better. I did not know better, only did what I could in those criminal acts to find the right course.

By taking my daughters into care and appointing a guardian doubtless you know better, and I only ask that my daughters, because they are girls, will be spared as much of the disgrace as possible, perhaps in another valley, where they are not known. For we have never in our lives received as much attention as after the Vicar's visit, in which connection I will name only the Justice of the Peace, then Lina's old teacher, twice the constable, and then a regular police action even with dogs, as though we had ever thought of running away, when we couldn't even have known where to. All the nets are so tightly meshed everywhere. I have never seen my daughters again since then, and enough of cross-examinations, if I may say so, don't know whether they had to undergo them too and if that was of any use, they will hardly have understood your words, but surely taken them to heart. So let me apologize at this point on their behalf. Nor do I want or receive a letter ever again from my daughters, if that could do them harm, would only like to know whether they are well cared for as far as the circumstances permit, and should be much gratified to obtain an assurance to that effect from you. I also beg for instructions as to how, once and for all, I am to express myself under interrogation, since I can see very well that I was far from satisfying the gentlemen with my way of speaking, but may well have made matters even worse, though I spoke the truth.

About the abnormality in my face which I got rid of but which has now returned, I beg of you not to be disturbed, nor to be put off by it, if that is possible. I shall manage all right.

Details of the criminal act, I am sorry to say, embarrass me, since the process is familiar enough to grown-up people, and I should only like to observe that most of those can go through the same in more favorable circumstances, nor do I believe that more is to be learned about it from my daughters than what every real man or woman knows.

Make an end of it, at last, honorable Court, because you are better off, or I could begin to say things I should be sorry about, all right, I will admit to having led my daughters into misdemeanor, if you insist on it and I can lessen the plight of those girls by saying so.

Perhaps it is possible, too, to choose a guardian for my daughters who is not a clergyman. These, I regret to say, often fall into false assumptions which their wards then have to swallow, but can't always, which leads to tragedies.

Every man and woman is tormented in their way, and I have learned that those who are stronger will then oppress others because of it, by which I don't mean to deny their good will, and please don't hold those words against me.

I have written to you only because my spoken words are not adequate for your satisfaction and because perhaps you will take the opportunity, nonetheless, to convey a greeting to my daughters, which I set down herewith, but this too not for my sake, but because in those years my daughters grew accustomed again to a little warmth.

May it please you to tell them that they are on my mind by day and by night, but not in the way the High Court of Justice thinks.

FLANNERY O'CONNOR

REVELATION

*Flannery O'Connor (1925–1964) was born and raised in Savannah,
Georgia. The family moved first to Atlanta and then to Milledgeville,
where O'Connor's father, who had been diagnosed with the hereditary
disease lupus, died in 1941. O'Connor enrolled at Georgia State College
for Women, where she edited the literary journal. During this time she
also began publishing her own short stories, which drew such attention
that in 1946, shortly after O'Connor's first publication in a national magazine, the GSCW library began a Flannery O'Connor collection. She
earned her M.F.A. at the celebrated University of Iowa Writers Workshop
in 1947. On discovering that she too had contracted lupus, O'Connor
retreated to her family's Milledgeville farm, where she wrote and raised
peacocks. Her first novel,* Wise Blood, *appeared in 1952 and her first collection of stories,* A Good Man is Hard to Find, *in 1955. She published a
second novel,* The Violent Bear It Away, *and collected her last stories for*
Everything That Rises Must Converge *(1965), in which "Revelation"
appears. The early, painful death of Flannery O'Connor in 1964 was recognized as an incalculable loss to the literary world.*

*O'Connor was a devout Roman Catholic; in Milledgeville she
attended the Sacred Heart Catholic Church, the land for which had been
donated by her great-grandparents. She was frank about the religious
motivation for her art, a position that some critics found strange, given
the degree to which her stories are punctuated by scenes of grotesque violence.* Time *magazine called her writing "highly unladylike," possessing
"a brutal irony, a slam-bang humour, and a style of writing as balefully
direct as a death sentence." In her essay collection* Mystery and Manners
*(1969), O'Connor explained the connection between violence and
Catholic redemption:*

> *In my own stories I have found that violence is strangely capable
> of returning my characters to reality and preparing them to
> accept their moment of grace. Their heads are so hard that
> almost nothing else will do the work. This idea, that reality is
> something to which we must be returned at considerable cost, is*

*one which is seldom understood by the casual reader, but it is
one which is implicit in the Christian view of the world.*

The doctor's waiting room, which was very small, was almost full when the Turpins entered and Mrs. Turpin, who was very large, made it look even smaller by her presence. She stood looming at the head of the magazine table set in the center of it, a living demonstration that the room was inadequate and ridiculous. Her little bright black eyes took in all the patients as she sized up the seating situation. There was one vacant chair and a place on the sofa occupied by a blond child in a dirty blue romper who should have been told to move over and make room for the lady. He was five or six, but Mrs. Turpin saw at once that no one was going to tell him to move over. He was slumped down in the sear, his arms idle at his sides and his eyes idle in his head; his nose ran unchecked.

Mrs. Turpin put a firm hand on Claud's shoulder and said in a voice that included anyone who wanted to listen, "Claud, you sit in that chair there," and gave him a push down into the vacant one. Claud was florid and bald and sturdy, somewhat shorter than Mrs. Turpin, but he sat down as if he were accustomed to doing what she told him to.

Mrs. Turpin remained standing. The only man in the room besides Claud was a lean stringy old fellow with a rusty hand spread out on each knee, whose eyes were closed as if he were asleep or dead or pretending to be so as not to get up and offer her his seat. Her gaze settled agreeably on a well-dressed gray-haired lady whose eyes met hers and whose expression said: if that child belonged to me, he would have some manners and move over—there's plenty of room there for you and him too.

Claud looked up with a sigh and made as if to rise.

"Sit down," Mrs. Turpin said. "You know you're not supposed to stand on that leg. He has an ulcer on his leg," she explained.

Claud lifted his foot onto the magazine table and rolled his trouser leg up to reveal a purple swelling on a plump marble-white calf.

"My!" the pleasant lady said. "How did you do that?"

"A cow kicked him," Mrs. Turpin said.

"Goodness!" said the lady.

Claud rolled his trouser leg down.

"Maybe the little boy would move over," the lady suggested, but the child did not stir.

"Somebody will be leaving in a minute," Mrs. Turpin said. She could not understand why a doctor—with as much money as they made charging five dollars a day to just stick their head in the hospital door and look at you— couldn't afford a decent-sized waiting room. This one was hardly bigger than a garage. The table was cluttered with limp-looking magazines and at one end of it there was a big green glass ash tray full of cigarette butts and cotton wads with little blood spots on them. If she had had anything to do with the running of the place, that would have been emptied every so often. There were no chairs against the wall at the head of the room. It had a rectangular-shaped panel in it that permitted a view of the office where the nurse came and went and the secretary listened to the radio. A plastic fern in a gold pot sat in the opening and trailed its fronds down almost to the floor. The radio was softly playing gospel music.

Just then the inner door opened and a nurse with the highest stack of yellow hair Mrs. Turpin had ever seen put her face in the crack and called for the next patient. The woman sitting beside Claud grasped the two arms of her chair and hoisted herself up; she pulled her dress free from her legs and lumbered through the door where the nurse had disappeared.

Mrs. Turpin eased into the vacant chair, which held her tight as a corset. "I wish I could reduce," she said, and rolled her eyes and gave a comic sigh.

"Oh, *you* aren't fat," the stylish lady said.

"Ooooo I am too," Mrs. Turpin said. "Claud he eats all he wants to and never weighs over one hundred and seventy-five pounds, but me I just look at something good to eat and I gain some weight," and her stomach and shoulders shook with laughter. "You can eat all you want to, can't you, Claud?" she asked, turning to him.

Claud only grinned.

"Well, as long as you have such a good disposition," the stylish lady said, "I don't think it makes a bit of difference what size you are. You just can't beat a good disposition."

Next to her was a fat girl of eighteen or nineteen, scowling into a thick blue book which Mrs. Turpin saw was entitled *Human Development*. The girl raised her head and directed her scowl at Mrs. Turpin as if she did not like her looks. She appeared annoyed that anyone should speak while she tried to read. The poor girl's face was blue with acne and Mrs. Turpin thought how pitiful it was to have a face like that at that age. She gave the girl a friendly smile but the girl only scowled the harder. Mrs. Turpin herself was fat but she had always had good skin, and, though she was forty-seven years old, there was not a wrinkle in her face except around her eyes from laughing too much.

Next to the ugly girl was the child, still in exactly the same position, and next to him was a thin leathery old woman in a cotton print dress. She and

Claud had three sacks of chicken feed in their pump house that was in the same print. She had seen from the first that the child belonged with the old woman. She could tell by the way they sat—kind of vacant and white-trashy, as if they would sit there until Doomsday if nobody called and told them to get up. And at right angles but next to the well-dressed pleasant lady was a lank-faced woman who was certainly the child's mother. She had on a yellow sweat shirt and wine-colored slacks, both gritty-looking, and the rims of her lips were stained with snuff. Her dirty yellow hair was tied behind with a little piece of red paper ribbon. Worse than niggers any day, Mrs. Turpin thought.

The gospel hymn playing was, "When I looked up and He looked down," and Mrs. Turpin, who knew it, supplied the last line mentally, "And wona these days I know I'll we-eara crown."

Without appearing to, Mrs. Turpin always noticed people's feet. The well-dressed lady had on red and gray suede shoes to match her dress. Mrs. Turpin had on her good black patent leather pumps. The ugly girl had on Girl Scout shoes and heavy socks. The old woman had on tennis shoes and the white-trashy mother had on what appeared to be bedroom slippers, black straw with gold braid threaded through them—exactly what you would have expected her to have on.

Sometimes at night when she couldn't go to sleep, Mrs. Turpin would occupy herself with the question of who she would have chosen to be if she couldn't have been herself. If Jesus had said to her before he made her, "There's only two places available for you. You can either be a nigger or white-trash," what would she have said? "Please, Jesus, please," she would have said, "just let me wait until there's another place available," and he would have said, "No, you have to go right now and I have only those two places so make up your mind." She would have wiggled and squirmed and begged and pleaded but it would have been no use and finally she would have said, "All right, make me a nigger then—but that don't mean a trashy one." And he would have made her a neat clean respectable Negro woman, herself but black.

Next to the child's mother was a red-headed youngish woman, reading one of the magazines and working a piece of chewing gum, hell for leather, as Claud would say. Mrs. Turpin could not see the woman's feet. She was not white-trash, just common. Sometimes Mrs. Turpin occupied herself at night naming the classes of people. On the bottom of the heap were most colored people, not the kind she would have been if she had been one, but most of them; then next to them—not above, just away from—were the white-trash; then above them were the home-owners, and above them them the home-and-land owners, to which she and Claud belonged. Above she and Claud were people with a lot of money and much bigger houses and much more land. But here the complexity of it would begin to bear in on her, for some of the people with a lot of money were common and ought to be below she and Claud and some of the people who had good blood had lost their money and had to rent and then there were colored people who owned their homes and land as well. There was a colored dentist in town who had two red Lincolns and a swimming pool and a farm with registered white-face cattle on it. Usually by the time she had fallen asleep all the classes of people were moiling and roiling around in her head, and she would dream they were all crammed in together in a box car, being ridden off to be put in a gas oven.

"That's a beautiful clock," she said and nodded to her right. It was a big wall clock, the face encased in a brass sunburst.

"Yes, it's very pretty," the stylish lady said agreeably. "And right on the dot too," she added, glancing at her watch.

The ugly girl beside her cast an eye upward at the clock, smirked, then looked directly at Mrs. Turpin and smirked again. Then she returned her eyes to her book. She was obviously the lady's daughter because, although they didn't look anything alike as to disposition, they both had the same shape of face and the same blue eyes. On the lady they sparkled pleasantly but in the girl's seared face they appeared alternately to smolder and to blaze.

What if Jesus had said, "All right, you can be white-trash or a nigger or ugly"!

Mrs. Turpin felt an awful pity for the girl, though she thought it was one thing to be ugly and another to act ugly.

The woman with the snuff-stained lips turned around in her chair and looked up at the clock. Then she turned back and appeared to look a little to the side of Mrs. Turpin. There was a cast in one of her eyes. "You want to know wher you can get you one of themther clocks?" she asked in a loud voice.

"No, I already have a nice clock," Mrs. Turpin said. Once somebody like her got a leg in the conversation, she would be all over it.

"You can get you one with green stamps," the woman said. "That's most likely wher he got hisn. Save you up enough, you can get you most anythang. I got me some joo'ry."

Ought to have got you a wash rag and some soap, Mrs. Turpin thought.

"I get contour sheets with mine," the pleasant lady said.

The daughter slammed her book shut. She looked straight in front of her, directly through Mrs. Turpin and on through the yellow curtain and the plate glass window which made the wall behind her. The girl's eyes seemed lit all of a sudden with a peculiar light, an unnatural light like night road signs give. Mrs. Turpin turned her head to see if there was anything going on outside that she should see, but she could not see anything. Figures passing cast only a pale shadow through the curtain. There was no reason the girl should single her out for her ugly looks.

"Miss Finley," the nurse said, cracking the door. The gum-chewing woman got up and passed in front of her and Claud and went into the office. She had on red high-heeled shoes.

Directly across the table, the ugly girl's eyes were fixed on Mrs. Turpin as if she had some very special reason for disliking her.

"This is wonderful weather, isn't it?" the girl's mother said.

"It's good weather for cotton if you can get the niggers to pick it," Mrs. Turpin said, "but niggers don't want to pick cotton any more. You can't get the white folks to pick it and now you can't get the niggers—because they got to be right up there with the white folks."

"They gonna *try* anyways," the white-trash woman said, leaning forward.

"Do you have one of the cotton-picking machines?" the pleasant lady asked.

"No," Mrs. Turpin said, "they leave half the cotton in the field. We don't have much cotton anyway. If you want to make it farming now, you have to have a little of everything. We got a couple of acres of cotton and a few hogs and chickens and just enough white-face that Claud can look after them himself."

"One thang I don't want," the white-trash woman said, wiping her mouth with the back of her hand. "Hogs. Nasty stinking things, a-gruntin and a-rootin all over the place."

Mrs. Turpin gave her the merest edge of her attention. "Our hogs are not dirty and they don't stink," she said. "They're cleaner than some children I've seen. Their feet never touch the ground. We have a pig-parlor—that's where you raise them on concrete," she explained to the pleasant lady, "and Claud scoots them down with the hose every afternoon and washes off the floor." Cleaner by far than that child right there, she thought. Poor nasty little thing. He had not moved except to put the thumb of his dirty hand into his mouth.

The woman turned her face away from Mrs. Turpin. "I know I wouldn't scoot down no hog with no hose," she said to the wall.

You wouldn't have no hog to scoot down, Mrs. Turpin said to herself.

"A-gruntin and a-rootin and a-groanin," the woman muttered.

"We got a little of everything," Mrs. Turpin said to the pleasant lady. "It's no use in having more than you can handle yourself with help like it is. We found enough niggers to pick our cotton this year but Claud he has to go after them and take them home again in the evening. They can't walk that half a mile. No they can't. I tell you," she said and laughed merrily, "I sure am tired of buttering up niggers, but you got to love em if you want em to work for you. When they come in the morning, I run out and I say, 'Hi yawl this morning?' and when Claud drives them off to the field I just wave to beat the band and they just wave back." And she waved her hand rapidly to illustrate.

"Like you read out of the same book," the lady said, showing she understood perfectly.

"Child, yes," Mrs. Turpin said. "And when they come in from the field, I run out with a bucket of icewater. That's the way it's going to be from now on," she said. "You may as well face it."

"One thang I know," the white-trash woman said. "Two thangs I ain't going to do: love no niggers or scoot down no hog with no hose." And she let out a bark of contempt.

The look that Mrs. Turpin and the pleasant lady exchanged indicated they both understood that you had to *have* certain things before you could *know* certain things. But every time Mrs. Turpin exchanged a look with the lady, she was aware that the ugly girl's peculiar eyes were still on her, and she had trouble bringing her attention back to the conversation.

"When you got something," she said, "you got to look after it." And when you ain't got a thing but breath and britches, she added to herself, you can afford to come to town every morning and just sit on the Court House coping and spit.

A grotesque revolving shadow passed across the curtain behind her and was thrown palely on the opposite wall. Then a bicycle clattered down against the outside of the building. The door opened and a colored boy glided in with a tray from the drugstore. It had two large red and white paper cups on it with tops on them. He was a tall, very black boy in discolored white pants and a green nylon shirt. He was chewing gum slowly, as if to music. He set the tray down in the office opening next to the fern and stuck his head through to look for the secretary. She was not in there. He rested his arms on the ledge and waited, his narrow bottom stuck out, swaying to the left and right. He raised a hand over his head and scratched the base of his skull.

"You see that button there, boy?" Mrs. Turpin said. "You can punch that and she'll come. She's probably in the back somewhere."

"Is that right?" the boy said agreeably, as if he had never seen the button before. He leaned to the right and put his finger on it. "She sometime out," he said and twisted around to face his audience, his elbows behind him on the counter. The nurse appeared and he twisted back again. She handed him a dollar and he rooted in his pocket and made the change and counted it out to her. She gave him fifteen cents for a tip and he want out with the empty tray. The heavy door swung to slowly and closed at length with the sound of suction. For a moment no one spoke.

"They ought to send all them niggers back to Africa," the white-trash woman said. "That's wher they come from in the first place."

"Oh, I couldn't do without my good colored friends," the pleasant lady said.

"There's a heap of things worse than a nigger," Mrs. Turpin agreed. "It's all kinds of them just like it's all kinds of us."

"Yes, and it takes all kinds to make the world go round," the lady said in her musical voice.

As she said it, the raw-complexioned girl snapped her teeth together. Her lower lip turned downwards and inside out, revealing the pale pink inside of her mouth. After a second it rolled back up. It was the ugliest face Mrs. Turpin had ever seen anyone make and for a moment she was certain that the girl had made it at her. She was looking at her as if she had known and disliked her all her life—all of Mrs. Turpin's life, it seemed too, not just all the girl's life. Why, girl, I don't even know you, Mrs. Turpin said silently.

She forced her attention back to the discussion. "It wouldn't be practical to send them back to Africa," she said. "They wouldn't want to go. They got it too good here."

"Wouldn't be what they wanted—if I had anythang to do with it," the woman said.

"It wouldn't be a way in the world you could get all the niggers back over there," Mrs. Turpin said. "They'd be hiding out and lying down and turning sick on you and wailing and hollering and raring and pitching. It wouldn't be a way in the world to get them over there."

"They got over here," the trashy woman said. "Get back like they got over."

"It wasn't so many of them then," Mrs. Turpin explained.

The woman looked at Mrs. Turpin as if here was an idiot indeed but Mrs. Turpin was not bothered by the look, considering where it came from.

"Nooo," she said, "they're going to stay here where they can go to New York and marry white folks and improve their color. That's what they all want to do, every one of them, improve their color."

"You know what comes of that, don't you?" Claud asked.

"No, Claud, what?" Mrs. Turpin said.

Claud's eyes twinkled. "White-faced niggers," he said with never a smile.

Everybody in the office laughed except the white-trash and the ugly girl. The girl gripped the book in her lap with white fingers. The trashy woman looked around her from face to face as if she thought they were all idiots. The old woman in the feed sack dress continued to gaze expressionless across the floor at the high-top shoes of the man opposite her, the one who had been pretending to be asleep when the Turpins came in. He was laughing heartily, his hands still spread out on his knees. The child had fallen to the side and was lying now almost face down in the old woman's lap.

While they recovered from their laughter, the nasal chorus on the radio kept the room from silence.

"You go to blank blank
And I'll go to mine
But we'll all blank along
To-geth-ther,
And all along the blank
We'll hep eachother out
Smile-ling in any kind of
Weath-ther!"

Mrs. Turpin didn't catch every word but she caught enough to agree with the spirit of the song and it turned her thoughts sober. To help anybody out that needed it was her philosophy of life. She never spared herself when she found somebody in need, whether they were white or black, trash or decent. And of all she had to be thankful for, she was most thankful that this was so. If Jesus had said, "You can be high society and have all the money you want and be thin and svelte-like, but you can't be a good woman with it," she would have had to say, "Well don't make me that then. Make me a good woman and it don't matter what else, how fat or ugly or how poor!" Her heart rose. He had not made her a nigger or white-trash or ugly! He had made her herself and given her a little of everything. Jesus, thank you! she said. Thank you thank you thank you! Whenever she counted her blessings she felt as buoyant as if she weighed one hundred and twenty-five pounds instead of one hundred and eighty.

"What's wrong with your little boy?" the pleasant lady asked the white-trashy woman.

"He has a ulcer," the woman said proudly. "He ain't give me a minute's peace since he was born. Him and her are just alike," she said, nodding at the old woman, who was running her leathery fingers through the child's pale hair. "Look like I can't get nothing down them two but Co' Cola and candy."

That's all you try to get down em, Mrs. Turpin said to herself. Too lazy to light the fire. There was nothing you could tell her about people like them that she didn't know already. And it was not just that they didn't have anything. Because if you gave them everything, in two weeks it would all be broken or filthy or they would have chopped it up for lightwood. She knew all this from her own experience. Help them you must, but help them you couldn't.

All at once the ugly girl turned her lips inside out again. Her eyes fixed like two drills on Mrs. Turpin. This time there was no mistaking that there was something urgent behind them.

Girl, Mrs. Turpin exclaimed silently, I haven't done a thing to you! The girl might be confusing her with somebody else. There was no need to sit by and let herself be intimidated. "You must be in college," she said boldly, looking directly at the girl. "I see you reading a book there."

The girl continued to stare and pointedly did not answer.

Her mother blushed at this rudeness. "The lady asked you a question, Mary Grace," she said under her breath.

"I have ears," Mary Grace said.

The poor mother blushed again. "Mary Grace goes to Wellesley College," she explained. She twisted one of the buttons on her dress. "In Massachusetts," she added with a grimace. "And in the summer she just keeps right on studying. Just reads all the time, a real book worm. She's done real well at Wellesley; she's taking English and Math and History and Psychology and Social Studies," she rattled on, "and I think it's too much. I think she ought to get out and have fun."

The girl looked as if she would like to hurl them all through the plate glass window.

"Way up north," Mrs. Turpin murmured and thought, well, it hasn't done much for her manners.

"I'd almost rather to have him sick," the white-trash woman said, wrenching the attention back to herself. "He's so mean when he ain't. Look like some children just take natural to meanness. It's some gets bad when they get sick but he was the opposite. Took sick and turned good. He don't give me no trouble now. It's me waitin to see the doctor," she said.

If I was going to send anybody back to Africa, Mrs. Turpin thought, it would be your kind, woman. "Yes, indeed," she said aloud, but looking up at the ceiling, "it's a heap of things worse than a nigger." And dirtier than a hog, she added to herself.

"I think people with bad dispositions are more to be pitied than anyone on earth," the pleasant lady said in a voice that was decidedly thin.

"I thank the Lord he has blessed me with a good one," Mrs. Turpin said. "The day has never dawned that I couldn't find something to laugh at."

"Not since she married me anyways," Claud said with a comical straight face.

Everybody laughed except the girl and the white-trash.

Mrs. Turpin's stomach shook. "He's such a caution," she said, "that I can't help but laugh at him."

The girl made a loud ugly noise through her teeth.

Her mother's mouth grew thin and tight. "I think the worst thing in the world," she said, "is an ungrateful person. To have everything and not appreciate it. I know a girl," she said, "who has parents who would give her anything, a little brother who loves her dearly, who is getting a good education, who wears the best clothes, but who can never say a kind word to anyone, who never smiles, who just criticizes and complains all day long."

"Is she too old to paddle?" Claud asked.

"Yes," the lady said, "I'm afraid there's nothing to do but leave her to her folly. Some day she'll wake up and it'll be too late."

"It never hurt anyone to smile," Mrs. Turpin said. "It just makes you feel better all over."

"Of course," the lady said sadly, "but there are just some people you can't tell anything to. They can't take criticism."

"If it's one thing I am," Mrs. Turpin said with feeling, "it's grateful. When I think who all I could have been besides myself and what all I got, a little of everything, and a good disposition besides, I just feel like shouting, 'Thank you, Jesus, for making everything the way it is!' It could have been different!" For one thing, somebody else could have got Claud. At the thought of this, she was flooded with gratitude and a terrible pang of joy ran through her. "Oh thank you, Jesus, Jesus, thank you!" she cried aloud.

The book struck her directly over her left eye. It struck almost at the same instant that she realized the girl was about to hurl it. Before she could utter a sound, the raw face came crashing across the table toward her, howling. The girl's fingers sank like clamps into the soft flesh of her neck. She heard the mother cry out and Claud shout, "Whoa!" There was an instant when she was certain that she was about to be in an earthquake.

All at once her vision narrowed and she saw everything as if it were happening in a small room far away, or as if she were looking at it through the wrong end of a telescope. Claud's face crumpled and fell out of sight. The nurse ran in, then out, then in again. Then the gangling figure of the doctor rushed out of the inner door. Magazines flew this way and that as the table turned over. The girl fell with a thud and Mrs. Turpin's vision suddenly reversed itself and she saw everything large instead of small. The eyes of the white-trashy woman were staring hugely at the floor. There the girl, held down on one side by the nurse and on the other by her mother, was wrenching and turning in their grasp. The doctor was kneeling astride her, trying to hold her arm down. He managed after a second to sink a long needle into it.

Mrs. Turpin felt entirely hollow except for her heart which swung from side to side as if it were agitated in a great empty drum of flesh.

"Somebody that's not busy call for the ambulance," the doctor said in the off-hand voice young doctors adopt for terrible occasions.

Mrs. Turpin could not have moved a finger. The old man who had been sitting next to her skipped nimbly into the office and made the call, for the secretary still seemed to be gone.

"Claud!" Mrs. Turpin called.

He was not in his chair. She knew she must jump up and find him but she felt like some one trying to catch a train in a dream, when everything moves in slow motion and the faster you try to run the slower you go.

"Here I am," a suffocated voice, very unlike Claud's, said.

He was doubled up in the corner on the floor, pale as paper, holding his leg. She wanted to get up and go to him but she could not move. Instead, her gaze was drawn slowly downward to the churning face on the floor, which she could see over the doctor's shoulder.

The girl's eyes stopped rolling and focused on her. They seemed a much lighter blue than before, as if a door that had been tightly closed behind them was now open to admit light and air.

Mrs. Turpin's head cleared and her power of motion returned. She leaned forward until she was looking directly into the fierce brilliant eyes. There was no doubt in her mind that the girl did know her, knew her in some intense and personal way, beyond time and place and condition. "What you got to say to me?" she asked hoarsely and held her breath, waiting, as for a revelation.

The girl raised her head. Her gaze locked with Mrs. Turpin's. "Go back to hell where you came from, you old wart hog," she whispered. Her voice was low but clear. Her eyes burned for a moment as if she saw with pleasure that her message had struck its target.

Mrs. Turpin sank back in her chair.

After a moment the girl's eyes closed and she turned her head wearily to the side.

The doctor rose and handed the nurse the empty syringe. He leaned over and put both hands for a moment on the mother's shoulders, which were shaking. She was sitting on the floor, her lips pressed together, holding Mary Grace's hand in her lap. The girl's fingers were gripped like a baby's around her thumb. "Go on to the hospital," he said. "I'll call and make the arrangements."

"Now let's see that neck," he said in a jovial voice to Mrs. Turpin. He began to inspect her neck with his first two fingers. Two little moon-shaped lines like pink fish bones were indented over her windpipe. There was the beginning of an angry red swelling above her eye. His fingers passed over this also.

"Lea' me be," she said thickly and shook him off. "See about Claud. She kicked him."

"I'll see about him in a minute," he said and felt her pulse. He was a thin gray-haired man, given to pleasantries. "Go home and have yourself a vacation the rest of the day," he said and patted her on the shoulder.

Quit your pattin me, Mrs. Turpin growled to herself.

"And put an ice pack over that eye," he said. Then he went and squatted down beside Claud and looked at his leg. After a moment he pulled him up and Claud limped after him into the office.

Until the ambulance came, the only sounds in the room were the tremulous moans of the girl's mother, who continued to sit on the floor. The white-trash woman did not take her eyes off the girl. Mrs. Turpin looked straight ahead at nothing. Presently the ambulance drew up, a long dark shadow, behind the curtain. The attendants came in and set the stretcher down beside the girl and lifted her expertly onto it and carried her out. The nurse helped the mother gather up her things. The shadow of the ambulance moved silently away and the nurse came back in the office.

"That ther girl is going to be a lunatic, ain't she?" the white-trash woman asked the nurse, but the nurse kept on to the back and never answered her.

"Yes, she's going to be a lunatic," the white-trash woman said to the rest of them.

"Po' critter," the old woman murmured. The child's face was still in her lap. His eyes looked idly out over her knees. He had not moved during the disturbance except to draw one leg up under him.

"I thank Gawd," the white-trash woman said fervently, "I ain't a lunatic."

Claud came limping out and the Turpins went home.

As their pick-up truck turned into their own dirt road and made the crest of the hill, Mrs. Turpin gripped the window ledge and looked out suspiciously. The land sloped gracefully down through a field dotted with lavender weeds and at the start of the rise their small yellow frame house, with its little flower beds spread out around it like a fancy apron, sat primly in its accustomed place between two giant hickory trees. She would not have been startled to see a burnt wound between two blackened chimneys.

Neither of them felt like eating so they put on their house clothes and lowered the shade in the bedroom and lay down, Claud with his leg on a pillow and herself with a damp washcloth over her eye. The instant she was flat on her back, the image of a razor-backed hog with warts on its face and horns coming out behind its ears snorted into her head. She moaned, a low quiet moan.

"I am not," she said tearfully, "a wart hog. From hell." But the denial had no force. The girl's eyes and her words, even the tone of her voice, low but clear, directed only to her, brooked no repudiation. She had been singled out for the message, though there was trash in the room to whom it might justly have been applied. The full force of this fact struck her only now. There was a woman there who was neglecting her own child but she had been overlooked. The message had been given to Ruby Turpin, a respectable, hard-working, church-going woman. The tears dried. Her eyes began to burn instead with wrath.

She rose on her elbow and the washcloth fell into her hand. Claud was lying on his back, snoring. She wanted to tell him what the girl had said. At the same time, she did not wish to put the image of herself as a wart hog from hell into his mind.

"Hey, Claud," she muttered and pushed his shoulder.

Claud opened one pale baby blue eye.

She looked into it warily. He did not think about anything. He just went his way.

"Wha, whasit?" he said and closed the eye again.

"Nothing," she said. "Does your leg pain you?"

"Hurts like hell," Claud said.

"It'll quit terreckly," she said and lay back down. In a moment Claud was snoring again. For the rest of the afternoon they lay there. Claud slept. She scowled at the ceiling. Occasionally she raised her fist and made a small stabbing motion over her chest as if she was defending her innocence to invisible guests who were like the comforters of Job, reasonable-seeming but wrong.

About five-thirty Claud stirred. "Got to go after those niggers," he sighed, not moving.

She was looking straight up as if there were unintelligible handwriting on the ceiling. The protuberance over her eye had turned a greenish-blue. "Listen here," she said.

"What?"

"Kiss me."

Claud leaned over and kissed her loudly on the mouth. He pinched her side and their hands interlocked. Her expression of ferocious concentration did not change. Claud got up, groaning and growling, and limped off. She continued to study the ceiling.

She did not get up until she heard the pick-up truck coming back with the Negroes. Then she rose and thrust her feet in her brown oxfords, which she did not bother to lace, and stumped out onto the back porch and got her red plastic bucket. She emptied a tray of ice cubes into it and filled it half full of water and went out into the back yard. Every afternoon after Claud brought the hands in, one of the boys helped him put out hay and the rest waited in the back of the truck until he was ready to take them home. The truck was parked in the shade under one of the hickory trees.

"Hi yawl this evening?" Mrs. Turpin asked grimly, appearing with the bucket and the dipper. There were three women and a boy in the truck.

"Us doing nicely," the oldest woman said. "Hi you doin?" and her gaze stuck immediately on the dark lump on Mrs. Turpin's forehead. "You done fell down, ain't you?" she asked in a solicitous voice. The old woman was dark and almost toothless. She had on an old felt hat of Claud's set back on her head. The other two women were younger and lighter and they both had new bright green sunhats. One of them had hers on her head; the other had taken hers off and the boy was grinning beneath it.

Mrs. Turpin set the bucket down on the floor of the truck. "Yawl hep yourselves," she said. She looked around to make sure Claud had gone. "No, I didn't fall down," she said, folding her arms. "It was something worse than that."

"Ain't nothing bad happen to you!" the old woman said. She said it as if they all knew that Mrs. Turpin was protected in some special way by Divine Providence. "You just had you a little fall."

"We were in town at the doctor's office for where the cow kicked Mr. Turpin," Mrs. Turpin said in a flat tone that indicated they could leave off their foolishness. "And there was this girl there. A big fat girl with her face all broke out. I could look at that girl and tell she was peculiar but I couldn't tell how. And me and her mama was just talking and going along and all of a sudden WHAM! She throws this big book she was reading at me and ..."

"Naw!" the old woman cried out.

"And then she jumps over the table and commences to choke me."

"Naw!" they all exclaimed, "naw!"

"Hi come she do that?" the old woman asked. "What ail her?"

Mrs. Turpin only glared in front of her.

"Somethin ail her," the old woman said.

"They carried her off in an ambulance," Mrs. Turpin continued, "but before she went she was rolling on the floor and they were trying to hold her down to give her a shot and she said something to me." She paused. "You know what she said to me?"

"What she say?" they asked.

"She said," Mrs. Turpin began, and stopped, her face very dark and heavy. The sun was getting whiter and whiter, blanching the sky overhead so that the leaves of the hickory tree were black in the face of it. She could not bring forth the words. "Something real ugly," she muttered.

"She sho shouldn't said nothin ugly to you," the old woman said. "You so sweet. You the sweetest lady I know."

"She pretty too," the one with the hat on said.

"And stout," the other one said. "I never knowed no sweeter white lady."

"That's the truth befo' Jesus," the old woman said. "Amen! You des as sweet and pretty as you can be."

Mrs. Turpin knew exactly how much Negro flattery was worth and it added to her rage. "She said," she began again and finished this time with a fierce rush of breath, "that I was an old wart hog from hell."

There was an astounded silence.

"Where she at?" the youngest woman cried in a piercing voice.

"Lemme see her. I'll kill her!"

"I'll kill her with you!" the other one cried.

"She b'long in the sylum," the old woman said emphatically. "You the sweetest white lady I know."

"She pretty too," the other two said. "Stout as she can be and sweet. Jesus satisfied with her!"

"Deed he is," the old woman declared.

Idiots! Mrs. Turpin growled to herself. You could never say anything intelligent to a nigger. You could talk at them but not with them. "Yawl ain't drunk your water," she said shortly. "Leave the bucket in the truck when you're finished with it. I got more to do than just stand around and pass the time of day," and she moved off and into the house.

She stood for a moment in the middle of the kitchen. The dark protuberance over her eye looked like a miniature tornado cloud which might any moment sweep across the horizon of her brow. Her lower lip protruded dangerously. She squared her massive shoulders. Then she marched into the front of the house and out the side door and started down the road to the pig parlor. She had the look of a woman going single-handed, weaponless, into battle.

The sun was a deep yellow now like a harvest moon and was riding westward very fast over the far tree line as if it meant to reach the hogs before she did. The road was rutted and she kicked several good-sized stones out of her path as she strode along. The pig parlor was on a little knoll at the end of a lane that ran off from the side of the barn. It was a square of concrete as large as a small room, with a board fence about four feet high around it. The concrete floor sloped slightly so that the hog wash could drain off into a trench where it was carried to the field for fertilizer. Claud was standing on the outside, on the edge of the concrete, hanging onto the top board, hosing down the floor inside. The hose was connected to the faucet of a water trough nearby.

Mrs. Turpin climbed up beside him and glowered down at the hogs inside. There was seven long-snouted bristly shoats in it—tan with liver-colored spots—and an old sow a few weeks off from farrowing. She was lying on her side grunting. The shoats were running about shaking themselves like idiot children, their little slit pig eyes searching the floor for anything left. She had read that pigs were the most intelligent animal. She doubted it. They were supposed to be smarter than dogs. There had even been a pig astronaut. He had performed his assignment perfectly but died of a heart attack afterwards because they left him in his electric suit, sitting upright throughout his examination when naturally a hog should be on all fours.

A-gruntin and a-rootin and a-groanin.

"Gimme that hose," she said, yanking it away from Claud. "Go on and carry them niggers home and then get off that leg."

"You look like you might have swallowed a mad dog," Claud observed, but he got down and limped off. He paid no attention to her humors.

Until he was out of earshot, Mrs. Turpin stood on the side of the pen, holding the hose and pointing the stream of water at the hind quarters of any shoat that looked as if it might try to lie down. When he had had time to get over the hill, she turned her head slightly and her wrathful eyes scanned the path. He was nowhere in sight. She turned back again and seemed to gather herself up. Her shoulders rose and she drew in her breath.

"What do you send me a message like that for?" she said in a low fierce voice, barely above a whisper but with the force of a shout in its concentrated fury. "How am I a hog and me both? How am I saved and from hell too?" Her free fist was knotted and with the other she gripped the hose, blindly pointing the stream of water in and out of the eye of the old sow whose outraged squeal she did not hear.

The pig parlor commanded a view of the back pasture where their twenty beef cows were gathered around the hay-bales Claud and the boy had put out. The freshly cut pasture sloped down to the highway. Across it was their cotton field and beyond that a dark green dusty wood which they owned as well. The sun was behind the wood, very red, looking over the paling of trees like a farmer inspecting his own hogs.

"Why me?" she rumbled. "It's no trash around here, black or white, that I haven't given to. And break my back to the bone every day working. And do for the church."

She appeared to be the right size woman to command the arena before her. "How am I a hog?" she demanded. "Exactly how am I like them?" and she jabbed the stream of water at the shoats. "There was plenty of trash there. It didn't have to be me.

"If you like trash better, go get yourself some trash then," she railed. "You could have made me trash. Or a nigger. If trash is what you wanted why didn't you make me trash?" She shook her fist with the hose in it and a watery snake appeared momentarily in the air. "I could quit working and take it easy and be filthy," she growled. "Lounge about the sidewalks all day drinking root beer. Dip snuff and spit in every puddle and have it all over my face. I could be nasty.

"Or you could have made me a nigger. It's too late for me to be a nigger," she said with deep sarcasm, "but I could act like one. Lay down in the middle of the road and stop traffic. Roll on the ground."

In the deepening light everything was taking on a mysterious hue. The pasture was growing a peculiar glassy green and the streak of highway had turned lavender. She graced herself for a final assault and this time her voice rolled out over the pasture. "Go on," she yelled, "call me a hog! Call me a hog again. From hell. Call me a wart hog from hell. Put that bottom rail on top. There'll still be a top and bottom!"

A garbled echo returned to her.

A final surge of fury shook her and she roared, "Who do you think you are?

The color of everything, field and crimson sky, burned for a moment with a transparent intensity. The question carried over the pasture and across the highway and the cotton field and returned to her clearly like an answer from beyond the wood.

She opened her mouth but no sound came out of it.

A tiny truck, Claud's, appeared on the highway, heading rapidly out of sight. Its gears scraped thinly. It looked like a child's toy. At any moment a bigger truck might smash into it and scatter Claud's and the niggers' brains all over the road.

Mrs. Turpin stood there, her gaze fixed on the highway, all her muscles rigid, until in five or six minutes the truck reappeared, returning. She waited until it had had time to turn into their own road. Then like a monumental statue coming to life, she bent her head slowly and gazed, as if through the very heart of mystery, down into the pig parlor at the hogs. They had settled all in one corner around the old sow who was grunting softly. A red glow suffused them. They appeared to pant with a secret life.

Until the sun slipped finally behind the tree line, Mrs. Turpin remained there with her gaze bent to them as if she was absorbing some abysmal life-giving knowledge. At last she lifted her head. There was only a purple streak in the sky, cutting through a field of crimson and leading, like an extension of the highway, into the descending dusk. She raised her hands from the side of the pen in a gesture hieratic and profound. A visionary light settled in her eyes. She saw the streak as a vast swinging bridge extending upward from the earth through a field of living fire. Upon it a vast horde of souls were rumbling toward heaven. There were whole companies of white-trash, clean for the first time in their lives, and bands of black niggers in white robes, and battalions of freaks and lunatics shouting and clapping and leaping like frogs. And bringing up the end of the procession was a tribe of people whom she recognized at once as those who, like herself and Claud, had always had a little of everything and the God-given wit to use it right. She leaned forward to observe them closer. They were marching behind the others with great dignity, accountable as they had always been for good order and common sense and respectable behavior. They alone were on key. Yet she could see by their shocked and altered faces that even their virtues were being burned away. She lowered her hands and gripped the rail of the hog pen, her eyes small but fixed unblinkingly on what lay ahead. In a moment the vision faded but she remained where she was, immobile.

At length she got down and turned off the faucet and made her slow way on the darkening path to the house. In the woods around her the invisible cricket choruses had struck up, but what she heard were the voices of the souls climbing upward into the starry field and shouting hallelujah.

TILLIE OLSEN

TELL ME A RIDDLE

Tillie Olsen (b. 1913) was born Tillie Lerner in Omaha, Nebraska, the daughter of Russian revolutionaries who chose exile in the United States over repression at home. Her high-school education was cut short during the Depression. As a young woman, Olsen took an active role in workers' movements, and throughout her work she has been passionately committed to the socialism that was her parents' legacy. In 1932 she began writing her novel Yonnondio, *which remained unfinished and unpublished until 1974. She abandoned the novel in 1937 to cope with the demands posed by her new family with husband Jack Olsen and by her political work. She held down a number of service and industrial jobs over the next decade and in 1953 resumed her writing career by taking a creative-writing course at San Francisco State College. Olsen's landmark volume of short fiction,* Tell Me a Riddle, *appeared in 1961 and established her reputation both as a powerful storyteller and as a leading advocate of radical feminism. Following this publication, there was another long silence.*

Since the late 1960s, Tillie Olsen has taught or served as writer in residence at numerous universities, including MIT, Norway, and UCLA. Olsen has received many fellowships and awards. In 1978 she published an influential collection of essays, Silences (1978), *in which she explored obstacles to women's writing.*

"Tell Me a Riddle" has been described as "the most sensitive and artistically rendered of American short stories. 'People read it for the twentieth time and they weep.'" When asked to name her favourite stories, those that she would include in an ideal anthology, Alice Munro named "Tell Me a Riddle" the one indispensable entry.

The story originally appeared in New World Writing *(No. 16, 1960), where this anthology's editors first were introduced to it. "Tell Me a Riddle" was reissued in hardcover in 1978, with considerable revisions in punctuation and spelling; it is the version reprinted here.*

"These Things Shall Be"

1

For forty-seven years they had been married. How deep back the stubborn, gnarled roots of the quarrel reached, no one could say—but only now, when tending to the needs of others no longer shackled them together, the roots swelled up visible, split the earth between them, and the tearing shook even to the children, long since grown.

Why now, why now? wailed Hannah.

As if when we grew up weren't enough, said Paul.

Poor Ma. Poor Dad. It hurts so for both of them, said Vivi. They never had very much; at least in old age they should be happy.

Knock their heads together, insisted Sammy; tell 'em: you're too old for this kind of thing; no reason not to get along now.

Lennie wrote to Clara: They've lived over so much together; what could possibly tear them apart?

Something tangible enough.

Arthritic hands, and such work as he got, occasional. Poverty all his life, and there was little breath left for running. He could not, could not turn away from this desire: to have the troubling of responsibility, the fretting with money, over and done with; to be free, to be *care*free where success was not measured by accumulation, and there was use for the vitality still in him.

There was a way. They could sell the house, and with the money join his lodge's Haven, cooperative for the aged. Happy communal life, and was he not already an official; had he not helped organize it, raise funds, served as a trustee?

But she—would not consider it.

"What do we need all this for?" he would ask loudly, for her hearing aid was turned down and the vacuum was shrilling. "Five rooms" (pushing the sofa so she could get into the corner) "furniture" (smoothing down the rug) "floors and surfaces to make work. Tell me, why do we need it?" And he was glad he could ask in a scream.

"Because I'm use't."

"Because you're use't. This is a reason, Mrs. Word Miser? Used to can get unused!"

"Enough unused I have to get used to already.... Not enough words?" turning off the vacuum a moment to hear herself answer. "Because soon enough we'll need only a little closet, no windows, no furniture, nothing to make work, but for worms. Because now I want room.... Screech and blow like you're doing, you'll need that closet even sooner.... Ha, again!" for the vacuum bag wailed, puffed half up, hung stubbornly limp. "This time fix it so it stays; quick before the phone rings and you get too important-busy."

But while he struggled with the motor, it seethed in him. Why fix it? Why have to bother? And if it can't be fixed, have to wring the mind with how to pay the repair? At the Haven they come in with their own machines to clean your room or your cottage; you fish, or play cards, or make jokes in the sun, not with knotty fingers fight to mend vacuums.

Over the dishes, coaxingly: "For once in your life, to be free, to have everything done for you, like a queen."

"I never liked queens."

"No dishes, no garbage, no towel to sop, no worry what to buy, what to eat."

"And what else would I do with my empty hands? Better to eat at my own table when I want, and to cook and eat how I want."

"In the cottages they buy what you ask, and cook it how you like. *You* are the one who always used to say: better mankind born without mouths and stomachs than always to worry for money to buy, to shop, to fix, to cook, to wash, to clean."

"How cleverly you hid that you heard. I said it then because eighteen hours a day I ran. And you never scraped a carrot or knew a dish towel sops. Now—for you and me—who cares? A herring out of a jar is enough. But when *I* want, and nobody to bother." And she turned off her ear button, so she would not have to hear.

But as *he* had no peace, juggling and rejuggling the money to figure: how will I pay for this now?; prying out the storm windows (there they take care of this); jolting in the streetcar on errands (there I would not have to ride to take care of this or that); fending the patronizing relatives just back from Florida (at the Haven it matters what one is, not what one can afford), he gave *her* no peace.

"Look! In their bulletin. A reading circle. Twice a week it meets."

"Haumm," her answer of not listening.

"A reading circle. Chekhov they read that you like, and Peretz. Cultured people at the Haven that you would enjoy."

"Enjoy!" She tasted the word. "Now, when it pleases you, you find a reading circle for me. And forty years ago when the children were morsels and there was a Circle, did you stay home with them once so I could go? Even once? You trained me well. I do not need others to enjoy. Others!" Her voice trembled. "Because *you* want to be there with others. Already it makes me sick to think of you always around others. Clown, grimacer, floormat, yesman, entertainer, whatever they want of you."

And now it was he who turned on the television loud so he need not hear.

Old scar tissue ruptured and the wounds festered anew. Chekhov indeed. She thought without softness of that young wife, who in the deep night hours while she nursed the current baby, and perhaps held another in her lap, would try to stay awake for the only time there was to read. She would feel again the weather of the outside on his cheek when, coming late from a meeting, he would find her so, and stimulated and ardent, sniffing her skin, coax: "I'll put the baby to bed, and you—put the book away, don't read, don't read."

That had been the most beguiling of all the "don't read, put your book away" her life had been. Chekhov indeed!

"Money?" She shrugged him off. "Could we get poorer than once we were? And in America, who starves?"

But as still he pressed:

"Let me alone about money. Was there ever enough? Seven little ones—for every penny I had to ask—and sometimes, remember, there was nothing. But always *I* had to manage. Now *you* manage. Rub your nose in it good."

But from those years she had had to manage, old humiliations and terrors rose up, lived again, and forced her to relive them. The children's needings; that grocer's face or this merchant's wife she had had to beg credit from when credit was a disgrace; the scenery of the long blocks walked around when she could not pay; school coming, and the desperate going over the old to see what could yet be remade; the soups of meat bones begged "for-the-dog" one winter....

Enough. Now they had no children. Let *him* wrack his head for how they would live. She would not exchange her solitude for anything. *Never again to be forced to move to the rhythms of others.*

For in this solitude she had won to a reconciled peace.

Tranquillity from having the empty house no longer an enemy, for it stayed clean—not as in the days when it was her family, the life in it, that had seemed the enemy: tracking, smudging, littering, dirtying, engaging her in endless defeating battle—and on whom her endless defeat had been spewed.

The few old books, memorized from rereading; the pictures to ponder (the magnifying glass superimposed on her heavy eye-glasses). Or if she wishes, when he is gone, the phonograph, that if she turns up very loud and strains, she can hear: the ordered sounds and the struggling.

Out in the garden, growing things to nurture. Birds to be kept out of the pear tree, and when the pears are heavy and ripe, the old fury of work, for all must be canned, nothing wasted.

And her one social duty (for she will not go to luncheons or meetings) the boxes of old clothes left with her, as with a life-practised eye for finding what is still wearable within the worn (again the magnifying glass superimposed on the heavy glasses) she scans and sorts—this for rag or rummage, that for mending and cleaning, and this for sending away.

Being able at last to live within, and not move to the rhythms of others, as life had forced her to: denying; removing; isolating; taking the children one by one; then deafening, half-blinding—and at last, presenting her solitude.

And in it she had won to a reconciled peace.

Now he was violating it with his constant campaigning: *Sell the house and move to the Haven.* (You sit, you sit—there too you could sit like a stone.) He was making of her a battleground where old grievances tore. (Turn on your ear button—I am talking.) And stubbornly she resisted—so that from wheedling, reasoning, manipulation, it was bitterness he now started with.

And it came to where every happening lashed up a quarrel.

"I will sell the house anyway," he flung at her one night. "I am putting it up for sale. There will be a way to make you sign."

The television blared, as always it did on the evenings he stayed home, and as always it reached her only as noise. She did not know if the tumult was in her or outside. Snap! she turned the sound off. "Shadows," she whispered to him, pointing to the screen, "look, it is only shadows." And in a scream: "Did you say that you will sell the house? Look at me, not at that. I am no shadow. You cannot sell without me."

"Leave on the television. I am watching."

"Like Paulie, like Jenny, a four-year-old. Staring at shadows. *You cannot sell the house.*"

"I will. We are going to the Haven. There you would not hear the television when you do not want it. I could sit in the social room and watch. You could lock yourself up to smell your unpleasantness in a room by yourself—for who would want to come near you?

"No, no selling." A whisper now.

"The television is shadows. Mrs. Enlightened! Mrs. Cultured! A world comes into your house—and it is shadows. People you would never meet in a thousand lifetimes. Wonders. When you were four years old, yes, like Paulie, like Jenny, did you know of Indian dances, alligators, how they use bamboo in Malaya? No, you scratched in your dirt with the chickens and thought Olshana was the world. Yes, Mrs. Unpleasant, I will sell the house, for there better can we be rid of each other than here."

She did not know if the tumult was outside, or in her. Always a ravening inside, a pull to the bed, to lie down, to succumb.

"Have you thought maybe Ma should let a doctor have a look at her?" asked their son Paul after Sunday dinner, regarding his mother crumpled on the couch, instead of, as was her custom, busying herself in Nancy's kitchen.

"Why not the President too?"

"Seriously, Dad. This is the third Sunday she's lain down like that after dinner. Is she that way at home?"

"A regular love affair with the bed. Every time I start to talk to her."

Good protective reaction, observed Nancy to herself. The workings of hos-til-ity.

"Nancy could take her. I just don't like how she looks. Let's have Nancy arrange an appointment."

"You think she'll go?" regarding his wife gloomily. "All right, we have to have doctor bills, we have to have doctor bills." Loudly: "Something hurts you?"

She startled, looked to his lips. He repeated: "Mrs. Take It Easy, something hurts?"

"Nothing.... Only you."

"A woman of honey. That's why you're lying down?"

"Soon I'll get up to do the dishes, Nancy."

"Leave them, Mother, I like it better this way."

"Mrs. Take It Easy, Paul says you should start ballet. You should go to see a doctor and ask: how soon can you start ballet?"

"A doctor?" she begged. "Ballet?"

"We were talking, ma," explained Paul, "you don't seem any too well. It would be a good idea for you to see a doctor for a checkup."

"I get up now to do the kitchen. Doctors are bills and foolishness, my son. I need no doctors."

"At the Haven," he could not resist pointing out, "a doctor is *not* bills. He lives beside you. You start to sneeze, he is there before you open up a Kleenex. You can be sick there for free, all you want."

"Diarrhea of the mouth, is there a doctor to make you dumb?"

"Ma. Promise me you'll go. Nancy will arrange it."

"It's all of a piece when you think of it," said Nancy, "the way she attacks my kitchen, scrubbing under every cup hook, doing the inside of the oven so I can't enjoy Sunday dinner, knowing that half-blind or not, she's going to find every speck of dirt...."

"Don't, Nancy, I've told you—it's the only way she knows to be useful. What did the *doctor* say?"

"A real fatherly lecture. Sixty-nine is young these days. Go out, enjoy life, find interests. Get a new hearing aid, this one is antiquated. Old age is sickness only if one makes it so. Geriatrics, Inc."

"So there was nothing physical."

"Of course there was. How can you live to yourself like she does without there being? Evidence of a kidney disorder, and her blood count is low. He gave her a diet, and she's to come back for follow-up and lab work.... But he was clear enough: Number One prescription—start living like a human being.... When I think of your dad, who could really play the invalid with that arthritis of his, as active as a teenager, and twice as much fun...."

"You didn't tell me the doctor says your sickness is in you, how you live." He pushed his advantage. "Life and enjoyments you need better than medicine. And this diet, how can you keep it? To weigh each morsel and scrape away each bit of fat, to make this soup, that pudding. There, at the Haven, they have a dietician, they would do it for you."

She is silent.

"You would feel better there, I know it," he says gently. "There there is life and enjoyments all around."

"What is the matter, Mr. Importantbusy, you have no card game or meeting you can go to?"—turning her face to the pillow.

For a while he cut his meetings and going out, fussed over her diet, tried to wheedle her into leaving the house, brought in visitors:

"I should come to a fashion tea. I should sit and look at pretty babies in clothes I cannot buy. This is pleasure?"

"Always you are better than everyone else. The doctor said you should go out. Mrs. Brem comes to you with goodness and you turn her away."

"Because *you* asked her to, she asked me."

"They won't come back. People you need, the doctor said. Your own cousins I asked; they were willing to come and make peace as if nothing had happened...."

"No more crushers of people, pushers, hypocrites, around me. No more in *my* house. You go to them if you like."

"Kind he is to visit. And you, like ice."

"A babbler. All my life around babblers. Enough!"

"She's even worse, Dad? Then let her stew a while," advised Nancy. "You can't let it destroy you; it's a psychological thing, maybe too far gone for any of us to help."

So he let her stew. More and more she lay silent in bed, and sometimes did not even get up to make the meals. No longer was the tongue-lashing inevitable if he left the coffee cup where it did not belong, or forgot to take out the garbage or mislaid the broom. The birds grew bold that summer and for once pocked the pears, undisturbed.

A bellyful of bitterness and every day the same quarrel in a new way and a different old grievance the quarrel forced her to enter and relive. And the new torment: I am not really sick, the doctor said it, then why do I feel so sick?

One night she asked him: "You have a meeting tonight? Do not go. Stay ... with me."

He had planned to watch "This Is Your Life," but half sick himself from the heavy heat, and sickening therefore the more after the brooks and woods of the Haven, with satisfaction he grated:

"Hah, Mrs. Live Alone And Like It wants company all of a sudden. It doesn't seem so good the time of solitary when she was a girl exile in Siberia. 'Do not go. Stay with me.' A new song for Mrs. Free As A Bird. Yes, I am going out, and while I am gone chew this aloneness good, and think how you keep us both from where if you want people, you do not need to be alone."

"Go, go. All your life you have gone without me."

After him she sobbed curses he had not heard in years, old-country curses from their childhood: Grow, oh shall you grow like an onion, with your head in the ground. Like the hide of a drum shall you be, beaten in life, beaten in death. Oh shall you be like a chandelier, to hang, and to burn....

She was not in their bed when he came back. She lay on the cot on the sun porch. All week she did not speak or come near him; nor did he try to make peace or care for her.

He slept badly, so used to her next to him. After all the years, old harmonies and dependencies deep in their bodies; she curled to him, or he coiled to her, each warmed, warming, turning as the other turned, the nights a long embrace.

It was not the empty bed or the storm that woke him, but a faint singing. *She* was singing. Shaking off the drops of rain, the lightning riving her lifted face, he saw her so; the cot covers on the floor.

"This is a private concert?" he asked. "Come in, you are wet."

"I can breathe now," she answered; "my lungs are rich." Though indeed the sound was hardly a breath.

"Come in, come in." Loosing the bamboo shades. "Look how wet you are." Half helping, half carrying her, still faint-breathing her song.

A Russian love song of fifty years ago.

He had found a buyer, but before he told her, he called together those children who were close enough to come. Paul, of course, Sammy from New Jersey, Hannah from Connecticut, Vivi from Ohio.

With a kindling of energy for her beloved visitors, she arrayed the house, cooked and baked. She was not prepared for the solemn after-dinner conclave, they too probing in and tearing. Her frightened eyes watched from mouth to mouth as each spoke.

His stories were eloquent and funny of her refusal to go back to the doctor; of the scorned invitations; of her stubborn silence or the bile "like a

Niagara"; of her contrariness: "If I clean it's no good how I cleaned; if I don't clean, I'm still a master who thinks he has a slave."

(Vinegar he poured on me all his life; I am well marinated; how can I be honey now?)

Deftly he marched in the rightness for moving to the Haven; their money from social security free for visiting the children, not sucked into daily needs and into the house; the activities in the Haven for him; but mostly the Haven for *her*: her health, her need of care, distraction, amusement, friends who shared her interests.

"This does offer an outlet for Dad," said Paul; "he's always been an active person. And economic peace of mind isn't to be sneezed at, either. I could use a little of that myself."

But when they asked: "And you, Ma, how do you feel about it?" could only whisper:

"For him it is good. It is not for me. I can no longer live between people."

"You lived all your life *for* people," Vivi cried.

"Not with." Suffering doubly for the unhappiness on her children's faces.

"You have to find some compromise," Sammy insisted. "Maybe sell the house and buy a trailer. After forty-seven years there's surely some way you can find to live in peace."

"There is no help, my children. Different things we need."

"Then live alone!" He could control himself no longer. "I have a buyer for the house. Half the money for you, half for me. Either alone or with me to the Haven. You think I can live any longer as we are doing now?"

"Ma doesn't have to make a decision this minute, however you feel, Dad," Paul said quickly, "and you wouldn't want her to. Let's let it lay a few months, and then talk some more."

"I think I can work it out to take Mother home with me for a while," Hannah said. "You both look terrible, but especially you, Mother. I'm gong to ask Phil to have a look at you."

"Sure," cracked Sammy. "What's the use of a doctor husband if you can't get free service out of him once in a while for the family? And absence might make the heart ... you know."

"There was something after all," Paul told Nancy in a colorless voice. "That was Hannah's Phil calling. Her gall bladder.... Surgery."

"Her *gall* bladder. If that isn't classic. 'Bitter as gall'—talk of psychosom——"

He stepped closer, put his hand over her mouth, and said in the same colorless, plodding voice. "We have to get Dad. They operated at once. The cancer was everywhere, surrounding the liver, everywhere. They did what they could ... at best she has a year. Dad ... we have to tell him."

2

Honest in his weakness when they told him, and that she was not to know. "I'm not an actor. She'll know right away by how I am. Oh that poor woman. I am old too, it will break me into pieces. Oh that poor woman. She will spit on me: 'So my sickness was how I live.' Oh Paulie, how she will be, that poor woman. Only she should not suffer.... I can't stand sickness, Paulie, I can't go with you."

But went. And play-acted.

"A grand opening and you did not even wait for me.... A good thing Hannah took you with her."

"Fashion teas I needed. They cut out what tore in me; just in my throat something hurts yet.... Look! So many flowers, like a funeral. Vivi called, did Hannah tell you? And Lennie from San Francisco, and Clara; and Sammy is coming." Her gnome's face pressed happily into the flowers.

It is impossible to predict in these cases, but once over the immediate effects of the operation, she should have several months of comparative well-being.

The money, where will come the money?

Travel with her, Dad. Don't take her home to the old associations. The other children will want to see her.

The money, where will I wring the money?

Whatever happens, she is not to know. No, you can't ask her to sign papers to sell the house; nothing to upset her. Borrow instead, then after....

I had wanted to leave you each a few dollars to make life easier, as other fathers do. There will be nothing left now. (Failure! you and your "business is exploitation." Why didn't you make it when it could be made?—Is that what you're thinking of me, Sammy?)

Sure she's unreasonable, Dad—but you have to stay with her; if there's to be any happiness in what's left of her life, it depends on you.

Prop me up, children, think of me, too. Shuffled, chained with her, bitter woman. No Haven, and the little money going.... How happy she looks, poor creature.

The look of excitement. The straining to hear everything (the new hearing aid turned full). Why are you so happy, dying woman?

How the petals are, fold on fold, and the gladioli color. The autumn air.

Stranger grandsons, tall above the little gnome grandmother, the little spry grandfather. Paul in a frenzy of picture-taking before going.

She, wandering the great house. Feeling the books; laughing at the maple shoemaker's bench of a hundred years ago used as a table. The ear turned to music.

"Let us go home. See how good I walk now." "One step from the hospital," he answers, "and she wants to fly. Wait till Doctor Phil says."

"Look—the birds too are flying home. Very good Phil is and will not show it, but he is sick of sickness by the time he comes home."

"Mrs. Telepathy, to read minds," he answers; "read mine what it says: when the trunks of medicines become a suitcase, then we will go."

The grandboys, they do not know what to say to us.... Hannah, she runs around here, there, when is there time for herself?

Let us go home. Let us go home.

Musing; gentleness—but for the incidents of the rabbi in the hospital, and of the candles of benediction.

Of the rabbi in the hospital:
> Now tell me what happened, Mother.
> From the sleep I awoke, Hannah's Phil, and he stands there like a devil in a dream and calls me by name. I cannot hear. I think he prays. Go away, please, I tell him, I am not a believer. Still he stands, while my heart knocks with fright.
> You scared *him*, Mother. He thought you were delirious.
> Who sent him? Why did he come to me?
> It is a custom. The men of God come to visit those of their religion they might help. The hospital makes up the list for them—race, religion—and you are on the Jewish list.
> Not for rabbis. At once go and make them change. Tell them to write: Born, human; Religion, none.

And of the candles of benediction:
> Look how you have upset yourself, Mrs. Excited Over Nothing. Pleasant memories you should leave.
> Go in, go back to Hannah and the lights. Two weeks I saw the candles and said nothing. But she asked me.
> So what was so terrible? She forgets you never did, she asks you to light the Friday candles and say the benediction like Phil's mother when she visits. If the candles give her pleasure, why shouldn't she have the pleasure?

Not for pleasure she does it. For emptiness. Because his family does. Because all around her do.

That is not a good reason too? But you did not hear her. For heritage, she told you. For the boys, from the past they should have tradition.

Superstition! From the savages, savages, afraid of the dark, of themselves: mumbo words and magic lights to scare away ghosts.

She told you: how it started does not take away the goodness. For centuries, peace in the house it means.

Swindler! Does she look back on the dark centuries? Candles bought instead of bread and stuck into a potato for a candlestick? Religion that stifled and said: in Paradise, woman, you will be the footstool of your husband, and in life—poor chosen Jew—ground under, despised, trembling in cellars. And cremated. And cremated.

This religion's fault? You think you are still an orator of the 1905 revolution? Where are the pills for quieting? Which are they?

Heritage. How have we come from the savages, how no longer to be savages—this to teach. To look back and learn what humanizes—this to teach. To smash all ghettos that divide us—not to go back, not to go back—this to teach. Learned books in the house, will humankind live or die, and she gives to her boys—superstition.

Hannah that is so good to you. Take your pill, Mrs. Excited For Nothing, swallow.

Heritage! But when did I have time to teach? Of Hannah I asked only hands to help.

Swallow.

Otherwise—musing; gentleness.

Not to travel. To go home.

The children want to see you. We have to show them you are as thorny a flower as ever.

Not to travel.

Vivi wants you should see her new baby. She sent the tickets—airplane tickets—a Mrs. Roosevelt she wants to make of you. To Vivi's we have to go.

A new baby. How many warm, seductive babies. She holds him stiffly, *away* from her, so that he wails. And a long shudder begins, and the sweat beads on her forehead.

"Hush, shush," croons the grandfather, lifting him back. "You should forgive your grandmamma, little prince, she has never held a baby before, only seen them in glass cases. Hush, shush."

"You're tired, Ma," says Vivi. "The travel and the noisy dinner. I'll take you to lie down."

(*A long travel from, to, what the feel of a baby evokes.*)

In the airplane, cunningly designed to encase from motion (no wind, no feel of flight), she had sat severely and still, her face turned to the sky through which they cleaved and left no scar.

So this was how it looked, the determining, the crucial sky, and this was how man moved through it, remote above the dwindled earth, the concealed human life. Vulnerable life, that could scar.

There was a steerage ship of memory that shook across a great, circular sea: clustered, ill human beings; and through the thick-stained air, tiny fretting waters in a window round like the airplane's—sun round, moon round. (The round thatched roofs of Olshana.) Eye round—like the smaller window that framed distance the solitary year of exile when only her eyes could travel, and no voice spoke. And the polar winds hurled themselves across snows trackless and endless and white—like the clouds which had closed together below and hidden the earth.

Now they put a baby in her lap. Do not ask me, she would have liked to beg. Enough the worn face of Vivi, the remembered grandchildren. I cannot, cannot....

Cannot what? Unnatural grandmother, not able to make herself embrace a baby.

She lay there in the bed of the two little girls, her new hearing aid turned full, listening to the sound of the children going to sleep, the baby's fretful crying and hushing, the clatter of dishes being washed and put away. They thought she slept. Still she rode on.

It was not that she had not loved her babies, her children. The love—the passion of tending—had risen with the need like a torrent; and like a torrent drowned and immolated all else. But when the need was done—oh the power that was lost in the painful damming back and drying up of what still surged, but had nowhere to go. Only the thin pulsing left that could not quiet, suffering over lives one felt, but could no longer hold nor help.

On that torrent she had borne them to their own lives, and the riverbed was desert long years now. Not there would she dwell, a memoried wraith. Surely that was not all, surely there was more. Still the springs, the springs were in her seeking. Somewhere an older power that beat for life. Somewhere coherence, transport, meaning. If they would but leave her in the air now stilled of clamor, in the reconciled solitude, to journey on.

And they put a baby in her lap. Immediacy to embrace, and the breath of *that* past: warm flesh like this that had claims and nuzzled away all else and with lovely mouths devoured; hot-living like an animal—intensely and now; the turning maze; the long drunkenness; the drowning into needing and being needed. Severely she looked back—and the shudder seized her again, and the sweat. Not that way. Not there, not now could she, not yet....

And all that visit, she could not touch the baby.

"Daddy, is it the ... sickness she's like that?" asked Vivi. "I was so glad to be having the baby—for her. I told Tim, it'll give her more happiness than anything, being around a baby again. And she hasn't played with him once."

He was not listening, "Aahh little seed of life, little charmer," he crooned, "Hollywood should see you. A heart of ice you would melt. Kick, kick. The future you'll have for a ball. In 2050 still kick. Kick for your grandaddy then."

Attentive with the older children; sat through their performances (command performance; we command you to be the audience); helped Ann sort autumn leaves to find the best for a school program; listened gravely to Richard tell about his rock collection, while her lips mutely formed the words to remember: *igneous, sedimentary, metamorphic;* looked for missing socks, books, and bus tickets; watched the children whoop after their grandfather who knew how to tickle, chuck, lift, toss, do tricks, tell secrets, make jokes, match riddle for riddle. (Tell me a riddle, Grammy. I know no riddles, child.) Scrubbed sills and woodwork and furniture in every room; folded the laundry; straightened drawers; emptied the heaped baskets waiting for ironing (while he or Vivi or Tim nagged: You're supposed to rest here, you've been sick) but to none tended or gave food—and could not touch the baby.

After a week she said: "Let us go home. Today call about the tickets."

"You have important business, Mrs. Inahurry? The President waits to consult with you?" He shouted, for the fear of the future raced in him. "The clothes are still warm from the suitcase, your children cannot show enough how glad they are to see you, and you want home. There is plenty of time for home. We cannot be with the children at home."

"Blind to around you as always: the little ones sleep four in a room because we take their bed. We are two more people in a house with a new baby, and no help."

"Vivi is happy so. The children should have their grandparents a while, she told to me. I should have my mommy and daddy...."

"Babbler and blind. Do you look at her so tired? How she starts to talk and she cries? I am not strong enough yet to help. Let us go home."

(To reconciled solitude.)

For it seemed to her the crowded noisy house was listening to her, listening for her. She could feel it like a great ear pressed under her heart. And everything knocked: quick constant raps: let me in, let me in.

How was it that soft reaching tendrils also became blows that knocked?

C'mon, Grandma, I want to show you....

Tell me a riddle, Grandma. (*I know no riddles.*)

Look, Grammy, he's so dumb he can't even find his hands. (Dody and the baby on a blanket over the fermenting autumn mound.)

I made them—for you (Ann) (Flat paper dolls with aprons that lifted on scalloped skirts that lifted on flowered pants; hair of yarn and great ringed questioning eyes.)

Watch me, Grandma. (Richard snaking up the tree, hanging exultant, free, with one hand at the top. Below Dody hunching over in pretend-cooking.) (*Climb too, Dody, climb and look.*)

Be my nap bed, Grammy. (The "No!" too late.) Morty's abandoned heaviness, while his fingers ladder up and down her hearing-aid cord to his drowsy chant: eentsiebeentsiespider. (*Children trust.*)

It's to start off your own rock collection, Grandma. "That's a trilobite fossil, 200 millions years old (millions of years on a boy's mouth) and that one's obsidian, black glass.

Knocked and knocked.

Mother, I *told* you the teacher said we had to bring it back all filled out this morning. Didn't you even ask Daddy? Then tell *me* which plan and I'll check it: evacuate or stay in the city or wait for you to come and take me away. (Seeing the look of straining to hear.) It's for Disaster, Grandma. (*Children trust.*)

Vivi in the maze of the long, the lovely drunkenness. The old old noises: baby sounds; screaming of a mother flayed to exasperation; children quarreling; children playing; singing; laughter.

And Vivi's tears and memories, spilling so fast, half the words not understood.

She had started remembering out loud deliberately, so her mother would know the past cherished, still lived in her.

Nursing the baby: My friends marvel, and I tell them, oh it's easy to be such a cow. I remember how beautiful my mother seemed nursing my brother, and the milk just flows.... Was that Davy? It must have been Davy....

Lowering a hem: How did you ever ... when I think how you made everything we wore ... Tim, just think, seven kids and Mommy sewed everything ... do I remember you sang while you sewed? That white dress with the red apples on the skirt you fixed over for me, was it Hannah's or Clara's before it was mine?

Washing sweaters: Ma, I'll never forget, one of those days so nice you washed clothes outside; one of the first spring days it must have been. The bubbles just danced while you scrubbed, and we chased after, and you stopped to show us how to blow our own bubbles with green onion stalks ... you always....

"Strong onion, to still make you cry after so many years," her father said, to turn the tears into laughter.

While Richard bent over his homework: Where is it now, do we still have it, the Book of The Martyrs? It always seemed so, well—exalted, when you'd put it on the round table and we'd all look at it together, there was even a halo from the lamp. The lamp with the beaded fringe you could move up and down; they're in style again, pulley lamps like that, but without the fringe. You know the book I'm talking about, Daddy, the book of the Martyrs, the first picture was a bust of Socrates? I wish there was something like that for the children, Mommy, to give them what you.... (And the tears splashed again.)

(What I intended and did not? Stop it, daughter, stop it, leave that time. And he, the hypocrite, sitting there with tears in his eyes—it was nothing to you then, nothing.)

... The time you came to school and I almost died of shame because of your accent and because I knew you knew I was ashamed; how could I? ... Sammy's harmonica and you danced to it once, yes you did, you and Davy squealing in your arms.... That time you bundled us up and walked us down to the railway station to stay the night 'cause it was heated and we didn't have any coal, that winter of the strike, you didn't think I remembered that, did you, Mommy? ... How you'd call us out to see the sunsets....

Day after day, the spilling memories. Worse now, questions, too. Even the grandchildren: Grandma, in the olden days, when you were little....

It was the afternoon that saved.

While they thought she napped, she would leave the mosaic on the wall (of children's drawings, maps, calendars, pictures, Ann's cardboard dolls with their great ringed questioning eyes) and hunch in the girls' cupboard, on the low shelf where the shoes stood, and the girls' dresses covered.

For that while she would painfully sheathe against the listening house, the tendrils and noises that knocked, and Vivi's spilling memories. Sometimes it helped to braid and unbraid the sashes that dangled, or to trace the pattern on the hoop slips.

Today she had jacks and children under jet trails to forget. Last night, Ann and Dody silhouetted in the window against a sunset of flaming man-made clouds of jet trail, their jacks ball accenting the peaceful noise of dinner being made. Had she told them, yes she had told them of how they played jacks in her village though there was no ball, no jacks. Six stones, round and flat, toss them out, the seventh on the back of the hand, toss, catch and swoop up as many as possible, toss again....

Of stones (repeating Richard) there are three kinds: earth's fire jetting; rock of layered centuries; crucibled new out of the old (*igneous, sedimentary, metamorphic*). But there was that other—frozen to black glass, never to transform or hold the fossil memory ... (let not my seed fall on stone). There was an ancient man who fought to heights a great rock that crashed back down eternally—eternal labor, freedom, labor ... (stone will perish, but the word remain). And you, David, who with a stone slew, screaming: Lord, take my heart of stone and give me flesh.

Who was screaming? Why was she back in the common room of the prison, the sun motes dancing in the shafts of light, and the informer being brought in, a prisoner now, like themselves. And Lisa leaping, yes, Lisa, the gentle and tender, biting at the betrayer's jugular. Screaming and screaming.

No, it is the children screaming. Another of Paul and Sammy's terrible fights?

In Vivi's house. Severely: you are in Vivi's house.

Blows, screams, a call: "Grandma!" For her? Oh please not for her. Hide, hunch behind the dresses deeper. But a trembling little body hurls itself beside her—surprised, smothered laughter, arms surround her neck, tears rub dry on her cheek, and words too soft to understand whisper into her ear (Is this where you hide too, Grammy? It's my secret place, we have a secret now).

And the sweat beads, and the long shudder seizes.

It seemed the great ear pressed inside now, and the knocking. "We have to go home," she told him, "I grow ill here."

"It's your own fault, Mrs. Busybody, you do not rest, you do too much." He raged, but the fear was in his eyes. "It was a serious operation, they told you to take care.... All right, we will go to where you can rest."

But where? Not home to death, not yet. He had thought to Lennie's, to Clara's; beautiful visits with each of the children. She would have to rest first, be stronger. If they could but go to Florida—it glittered before him, the never-realized promise of Florida. California: of course. (The money, the money, dwindling!) Los Angeles first for sun and rest, then to Lennie's in San Francisco.

He told her the next day. "You saw what Nancy wrote: snow and wind back home, a terrible winter. And look at you—all bones and a swollen belly. I called Phil: he said: 'A prescription, Los Angeles sun and rest.'"

She watched the words on his lips. "You have sold the house," she cried, "that is why we do not go home. That is why you talk no more of the Haven, why there is money for travel. After the children you will drag me to the Haven."

"The Haven! Who thinks of the Haven any more? Tell her, Vivi, tell Mrs. Suspicious: a prescription, sun and rest, to make you healthy.... And how could I sell the house without *you?*"

At the place of farewells and greetings, of winds of coming and winds of going, they say their good-byes.

They look back at her with the eyes of others before them: Richard with her own blue blaze; Ann with the nordic eyes of Tim; Morty's dreaming brown of a great-grandmother he will never know; Dody with the laughing eyes of him who had been her springtide love (who stands beside her now); Vivi's, all tears.

The baby's eyes are closed in sleep.

Good-bye, my children.

3

It is to the back of the great city he brought her, to the dwelling places of the cast-off old. Bounced by two lines of amusement piers to the north and to the south, and between a long straight paving rimmed with black benches facing the sand—sands so wide the ocean is only a far fluting.

In the brief vacation season, some of the boarded stores fronting the sands open, and families, young people and children, may be seen. A little tasselled tram shuttles between the piers, and the lights of roller coasters prink and tweak over those who come to have sensation made in them.

The rest of the year it is abandoned to the old, all else boarded up and still; seemingly empty, except the occasional days and hours when the sun, like a tide, sucks them out of the low rooming houses, casts them onto the benches and sandy rim of the walk—and sweeps them into decaying enclosures once again.

A few newer apartments glint among the low bleached squares. It is in one of these Lennie's Jeannie has arranged their rooms. "Only a few miles north and south people pay hundreds of dollars a month for just this gorgeous air, Grandaddy, just this ocean closeness."

She had been ill on the plane, lay ill for days in the unfamiliar room. Several times the doctor came by—left medicine she would not take. Several times Jeannie drove in the twenty miles from work, still in her Visiting Nurse uniform, the lightness and brightness of her like a healing.

"Who can believe it is winter?" he asked one morning. "Beautiful it is outside like an ad. Come, Mrs. Invalid, come to taste it. You are well enough to sit in here, you are well enough to sit outside. The doctor said it too."

But the benches were encrusted with people, and the sands at the sidewalk's edge. Besides, she had seen the far ruffle of the sea: "there take me," and though she leaned against him, it was she who led.

Plodding and plodding, sitting often to rest, he grumbling. Patting the sand so warm. Once she scooped up a handful, cradling it close to her better eye; peered, and flung it back. And as they came almost to the brink and she could see the glistening wet, she sat down, pulled off her shoes and stockings, left him and began to run. "You'll catch cold," he screamed, but the sand in his shoes weighed him down—he who had always been the agile one—and already the white spray creamed her feet.

He pulled her back, took a handkerchief to wipe off the wet and the sand. "Oh no," she said, "the sun will dry," seized the square and smoothed it flat, dropped on it a mound of sand, knotted the kerchief corners and tied it to a bag—"to look at with the strong glass" (for the first time in years explaining an action of hers)—and lay down with the little bag against her cheek, looking toward the shore that nurtured life as it first crawled toward consciousness the millions of years ago.

He took her one Sunday in the evil-smelling bus, past flat miles of blister houses, to the home of relatives. Oh what is this? she cried as the light began to smoke and the houses to dim and recede. Smog, he said, everyone knows but you.... Outside he kept his arms about her, but she walked with hands pushing the heavy air as if to open it, whispered: who has done this? sat down suddenly to vomit at the curb and for a long while refused to rise.

One's age as seen on the altered face of those known in youth. Is this they he has come to visit? This Max and Rose, smooth and pleasant, introducing them to polite children, disinterested grandchildren, "the whole family, once a month on Sundays. And why not? We have the room, the help, the food."

Talk of cars, of houses, of success: this son that, that daughter this. And *your* children? Hastily skimped over, the intermarriages, the obscure work— "my doctor son-in-law, Phil"—all he has to offer. She silent in a corner (Carsick like a baby, he explains.) Years since he has taken her to visit anyone but the children, and old apprehensions prickle: "no incidents," he silently begs, "no incidents." He itched to tell them. "A very sick woman," significantly, indicating her with his eyes, "a very sick woman." Their restricted faces did not react. "Have you thought maybe she'd do better at Palm Springs?" Rose asked. "Or at least a nicer section of the beach, nicer people, a pool." Not to have to say "money" he said instead: "would she have sand to look at through a magnifying glass?" and went on, detail after detail, the old habit betraying of parading the queerness of her for laughter.

After dinner—the others into the living room in men-or women-clusters, or into the den to watch TV—the four of them alone. She sat close to him, and did not speak. Jokes, stories, people they had known, beginning of reminiscence, Russia fifty-sixty years ago. Strange words across the Duncan Phyfe table: *hunger; secret meetings; human rights; spies; betrayals; prison; escape*— interrupted by one of the grandchildren: "Commercial's on; any Coke left? Gee, you're missing a real hair-raiser." And then a granddaughter (Max proudly: "look at her, an American queen") drove them home on her way back to U.C.L.A. No incident—except there had been no incidents.

The first few mornings she had taken with her the magnifying glass, but he would sit only on the benches, so she rested at the foot, where slatted bench shadows fell, and unless she turned her hearing aid down, other voices invaded.

Now on the days when the sun shone and she felt well enough, he took her on the tram to where the benches ranged in oblongs, some with tables for checkers or cards. Again the blanket on the sand in the striped shadows, but she no longer brought the magnifying glass. He played cards, and she lay in the sun and looked towards the waters; or they walked—two blocks down to the scaling hotel, two blocks back—past chili-hamburger stands, open-doored bars. Next to New and Perpetual Rummage Sale stores.

Once, out of the aimless walkers, slow and shuffling like themselves, someone ran unevenly towards them, embraced, kissed, wept: "dear friends, old friends." A friend of *hers,* not his: Mrs. Mays who had lived next door to them in Denver when the children were small.

Thirty years are compressed into a dozen sentences; and the present, not even in three. All is told: the children scattered; the husband dead; she lives in a room two blocks up from the sing hall—and points to the domed auditorium jutting before the pier. The leg? phlebitis; the heavy breathing? that, one does not ask. She, too, comes to the benches each day to sit. And tomorrow, tomorrow, are they going to the community sing? Of course he would have heard of it, everybody goes—the big doings they wait for all week. They have never been? She will come to them for dinner tomorrow and they will all go together.

So it is that she sits in the wind of the singing, among the thousand various faces of age.

She had turned off her hearing aid at once they came into the auditorium—as she would have wished to turn off sight.

One by one they streamed by and imprinted on her—and though the savage zest of their singing came voicelessly soft and distant, the faces still roared—the faces densened the air—chorded into

children-chants, mother-croons, singing of the chained love serenades, Beethoven storms, mad Lucia's scream drunken joy-songs, keens for the dead, work-singing

> *while from floor to balcony to dome a bare-footed sore-covered little girl*
> *threaded the sound-thronged tumult, danced her ecstasy of grimace to*
> *flutes that scratched at a cross-roads village wedding*

Yes, faces became sound, and the sound became faces; and faces and sound became weight—pushed, pressed

"Air"—her hands claw his.

"Whenever I enjoy myself ..." Then he saw the gray sweat on her face. "Here. Up. Help me, Mrs. Mays," and they support her out to where she can gulp the air in sob after sob.

"A doctor, we should get for her a doctor."

"Tch, it's nothing," says Ellen Mays, "I get it all the time. You've missed the tram; come to my place. Fix your hearing aid, honey ... close ... tea. My view. See, she *wants* to come. Steady now, that's how." Adding mysteriously: "Remember your advice, easy to keep your head above water, empty things float. Float."

The singing a fading march for them, tall woman with a swollen leg, weaving little man, and the swollen thinness they help between.

The stench in the hall: mildew? decay? "We sit and rest then climb. My gorgeous view. We help each other and here we are."

The stench along into the slab of room. A washstand for a sink, a box with oilcloth tacked around for a cupboard, a three-burner gas plate. Artificial flowers, colorless with dust. Everywhere pictures foaming: wedding, baby, party, vacation, graduation, family pictures. From the narrow couch under a slit of window, sure enough the view: lurching rooftops and a scallop of ocean heaving, preening, twitching under the moon.

"While the water heats. Excuse me ... down the hall." Ellen Mays has gone.

"You'll live?" he asks mechanically, sat down to feel his fright; tried to pull her alongside.

She pushed him away. "For air," she said; stood clinging to the dresser. Then, in a terrible voice:

After a lifetime of room. Of many rooms.

Shhh.

You remember how she lived. Eight children. And now one room like a coffin.

She pays rent!

Shrinking the life of her into one room like a coffin Rooms and rooms like this I lie on the quilt and hear them talk

Please, Mrs. Orator-without-Breath.

Once you went for coffee I walked I saw A Balzac a Chekhov to write it Rummage Alone On scraps

Better old here than in the old country!

On scraps Yet they sang like like Wondrous! *Humankind one has to believe* So strong For what? To rot not grow?

Your poor lungs beg you. They sob between each word.

Singing. Unused the life in them. She in this poor room with her pictures Max You The children Everywhere unused the life And who has meaning? Century after century still all in us not to grow?

Coffins, rummage, plants: sick woman. Oh lay down. We will get for you the doctor.

"And when will it end. Oh, *the end*." *That* nightmare thought, and this time she writhed, crumpled against him, seized his hand (for a moment again the weight, the soft distant roaring of humanity) and on the strangled-for breath, begged: "Man ... we'll destroy ourselves?"

And looking for answer—in the helpless pity and fear for her (for *her*) that distorted his face—she understood the last months, and knew that she was dying.

4

"Let us go home," she said after several days.

"You are in training for a cross-country run? That is why you do not even walk across the room? Here, like a prescription Phil said, till you are stronger from the operation. You want to break doctor's orders?"

She saw the fiction was necessary to him, was silent; then: "At home I will get better. If the doctor here says?"

"And winter? And the visits to Lennie and to Clara? All right," for he saw the tears in her eyes, "I will write Phil, and talk to the doctor."

Days passed. He reported nothing. Jeannie came and took her out for air, past the boarded concessions, the hooded and tented amusement rides, to the end of the pier. They watched the spent waves feeding the new, the gulls in the clouded sky; even up where they sat, the wind-blown sand stung.

She did not ask to go down the crooked steps to the sea.

Back in her bed, while he was gone to the store, she said: "Jeannie, this doctor, he is not one I can ask questions. Ask him for me, can I go home?"

Jeannie looked at her, said quickly: "Of course, poor Granny. You want your own things around you, don't you? I'll call him tonight.... Look, I've something to show you," and from her purse unwrapped a large cookie, intricately shaped like a little girl. "Look at the curls—can you hear me well, Granny?—and the darling eyelashes. I just came from a house where they were baking them."

"The dimples, there in the knees," she marveled, holding it to the better light, turning, studying, "like art. Each singly they cut, or a mold?"

"Singly," said Jeannie, "and if it is a child only the mother can make them. Oh Granny, it's the likeness of a real little girl who died yesterday—Rosita. She was three years old. *Pan del Muerto*, the Bread of the Dead. It was the custom in the part of Mexico they came from."

Still she turned and inspected. "Look, the hollow in the throat, the little cross necklace.... I think for the mother it is a good thing to be busy with such bread. You know the family?"

Jeannie nodded. "On my rounds. I nursed.... Oh Granny, it is like a party; they play songs she liked to dance to. The coffin is lined with pink velvet and she wears a white dress. There are candles...."

"In the house?" Surprised, "They keep her in the house?"

"Yes," said Jeannie, "and it is against the health law. I think she is ... prepared there. The father said it will be sad to bury her in this country; in Oaxaca they have a feast night with candles each year; everyone picnics on the graves of those they loved until dawn."

"Yes, Jeannie, the living must comfort themselves." And closed her eyes.

"You want to sleep, Granny?"

"Yes, tired from the pleasure of you. I may keep the Rosita? There stand it, on the dresser, where I can see; something of my own around me."

In the kitchenette, helping her grandfather unpack the groceries, Jeannie said in her light voice:

"I'm resigning my job, Grandaddy."

"Ah, the lucky young man. Which one is he?"

"Too late. You're spoken for." She made a pyramid of cans, unstacked, and built again.

"Something is wrong with the job?"

"With me. I can't be"—she searched for the word—"What they call professional enough. I let myself feel things. And tomorrow I have to report a family...." The cans clicked again. "It's not that, either. I just don't know what I want to do, maybe go back to school, maybe go to art school. I thought if you went to San Francisco I'd come along and talk it over with Momma and Daddy. But I don't see how you can go. She wants to go home. She asked me to ask the doctor."

The doctor told her himself. "Next week you may travel, when you are a little stronger." But next week there was the fever of an infection, and by the time that was over, she could not leave the bed—a rented hospital bed that stood beside the double bed he slept in alone now.

Outwardly the days repeated themselves. Every other afternoon and evening he went out to his newfound cronies, to talk and play cards. Twice a week, Mrs. Mays came. And the rest of the time, Jeannie was there.

By the sickbed stood Jeannie's FM radio. Often into the room the shapes of music came. She would lie curled on her side, her knees drawn up, intense in listening (Jeannie sketched her so, coiled, convoluted like an ear), then thresh her hand out and abruptly snap the radio mute—still to lie in her attitude of listening, concealing tears.

Once Jeannie brought in a young Marine to visit, a friend from high-school days she had found wandering near the empty pier. Because Jeannie asked him to, gravely, without self-consciousness, he sat himself cross-legged on the floor and performed for them a dance of his native Samoa.

Long after they left, a tiny thrumming sound could be heard where, in her bed, she strove to repeat the beckon, flight, surrender of his hands, the fluttering foot-beats, and his low plaintive calls.

Hannah and Phil sent flowers. To deepen her pleasure, he placed one in her hair. "Like a girl," he said, and brought the hand mirror so she could see. She looked at the pulsing red flower, the yellow skull face; a desolate, excited laugh shuddered from her, and she pushed the mirror away—but let the flower burn.

The week Lennie and Helen came, the fever returned. With it the excited laugh, and incessant words. She, who in her life had spoken but seldom and then only when necessary (never having learned the easy, social uses of words), now in dying spoke incessantly.

In a half-whisper: "Like Lisa she is, your Jeannie. Have I told you of Lisa who taught me to read? Of the highborn she was, but noble in herself. I was sixteen; they beat me; my father beat me so I would not go to her. It was forbidden, she was a Tolstoyan. At night, past dogs that howled, terrible dogs, my son, in the snows of winter to the road, I to ride in her carriage like a lady, to books. To her, life was holy, knowledge was holy, and she taught me to read. They hung her. Everything that happens one must try to understand why. She killed one who betrayed many. Because of betrayal, betrayed all she lived and believed. In one minute she killed, before my eyes (there is so much blood in a human being, my son), in prison with me. All that happens, one must try to understand.

"The name?" Her lips would work. "The name that was their pole star; the doors of the death houses fixed to open on it; I read of it my year of penal servitude. Thuban!" very excited, "Thuban, in ancient Egypt the pole star. Can you see, look out to see it, Jeannie, if it swings around *our* pole star that seems to *us* not to move.

"Yes, Jeannie, at your age my mother and grandmother had already buried children ... yes, Jeannie, it is more than oceans between Olshana and you ... yes, Jeannie, they danced, and for all the bodies they had they might as well be chickens, and indeed, they scratched and flapped their arms and hopped.

"And Andrei Yefimitch, who for twenty years had never known of it and never wanted to know, said as if he wanted to cry: but why my dear friend this malicious laughter?" Telling to herself half-memorized phrases from her few books. "Pain I answer with tears and cries, baseness with indignation, meanness with repulsion ... for life may be hated or wearied of, but never despised."

Delirious: "Tell me, my neighbor, Mrs. Mays, the pictures never lived, but what of the flowers? Tell them who ask: no rabbis, no ministers, no priests, no speeches, no ceremonies: ah, false—let the living comfort themselves. Tell Sammy's boy, he who flies, tell him to go to Stuttgart and see where Davy has no grave. And what? ... And what? where millions have no graves—save air."

In delirium or not, wanting the radio on; not seeming to listen, the words still jetting, wanting the music on. Once, silently it abruptly as of old, she began to cry, unconcealed tears this time. "You have pain, Granny?" Jeannie asked.

"The music," she said, "still it is there and we do not hear; knocks, and our poor human ears too weak. What else, what else we do not hear?"

Once she knocked his hand aside as he gave her a pill, swept the bottles from her bedside table: "no pills, let me feel what I feel," and laughed as on his hands and knees he groped to pick them up.

Nighttimes her hand reached across the bed to hold his.

A constant retching began. Her breath was too faint for sustained speech now, but still the lips moved:

> *When no longer necessary to injure others*
> *Pick pick pick blind chicken*
> *As a human being responsibility*

"David!" imperious, "Basin!" and she would vomit, rinse her mouth, the wasted throat working to swallow, and begin the chant again.

She will be better off in the hospital now, the doctor said.

He sent the telegrams to the children, was packing her suitcase, when her hoarse voice startled. She had roused, was pulling herself to sitting.

"Where now?" she asked. "Where now do you drag me?"

"You do not even have to have a baby to go this time," he soothed, looking for the brush to pack. "Remember, after Davy you told me—worthy to have a baby for the pleasure of the ten-day rest in the hospital?"

"Where now? Not home yet?" Her voice mourned. "Where *is* my home?"

He rose to ease her back. "The doctor, the hospital," he started to explain, but deftly, like a snake, she had slithered out of bed and stood swaying, propped behind the night table.

"Coward," she hissed, "runner."

"You stand," he said senselessly.

"To take me there and run. Afraid of a little vomit."

He reached her as she fell. She struggled against him, half slipped from his arms, pulled herself up again.

"Weakling," she taunted, "to leave me there and run. Betrayer. All your life you have run."

He sobbed, telling Jeannie. "A Marilyn Monroe to run for her virtue. Fifty-nine pounds she weighs, the doctor said, and she beats me like a Dempsey. Betrayer, she cries, and I running like a dog when she calls; day and night, running to her, her vomit, the bedpan...."

"She needs you, Grandaddy," said Jeannie. "Isn't that what they call love? I'll see if she sleeps, and if she does, poor worn-out darling, we'll have a party, you and I: I brought us rum babas."

They did not move her. By her bed now stood the tall hooked pillar that held the solutions—blood and dextrose—to feed her veins. Jeannie moved down the hall to take over the sickroom, her face so radiant, her grandfather asked her once: "you are in love?" (Shameful the joy, the pure overwhelming joy from being with her grandmother; the peace, the serenity that breathed.) "My darling escape," she answered incoherently, "my darling Granny"—as if that explained.

Now one by one the children came, those that were able. Hannah, Paul, Sammy. Too late to ask: and what did you learn with your living, Mother, and what do we need to know?

Clara, the eldest, clenched:

Pay me back, Mother, pay me back for all you took from me. Those others you crowded into your heart. The hands I needed to be for you, the heaviness, the responsibility.

Is this she? Noises the dying make, the crablike hands crawling over the covers. The ethereal singing.

She hears that music, that singing from childhood; forgotten sound—not heard since, since.... And the hardness breaks like a cry: Where did we lose each other, first mother, singing mother?

Annulled: the quarrels, the gibing, the harshness between, the fall into silence and the withdrawal.

I do not know you, Mother. Mother, I never knew you.

Lennie, suffering not alone for her who was dying, but for that in her which never lived (for that which in him might never live). From him too, unspoken words: *good-bye Mother who taught me to mother myself.*

Not Vivi, who must stay with her children; not Davy, but he is already here, having to die again with *her* this time, for the living take their dead with them when they die.

Light she grew, like a bird, and, like a bird, sound bubbled in her throat while the body fluttered in agony. Night and day, asleep or awake (though indeed there was no difference now) the songs and the phrases leaping.

And he, who had once dreaded a long dying (from fear of himself, from horror of the dwindling money) now desired her quick death profoundly, for *her* sake. He no longer went out, except when Jeannie forced him to: no longer laughed, except when, in the bright kitchenette, Jeannie coaxed his laugher (and she, who seemed to hear nothing else, would laugh too, conspiratorial wisps of laughter).

Like, like a bird, the fluttering body, the little claw hands, the beaked shadow on her face; and the throat, bubbling, straining.

He tried not to listen, as he tried not to look on the face in which only the forehead remained familiar, but trapped with her the long nights in that little room, the sounds worked themselves into his consciousness, with their punctuation of death swallows, whimpers, gurglings.

Even in reality (swallow) *life's lack of it*
 Slaveships deathtrains clubs eenough
The bell summons what enables
 78,000 in one minute (whisper of a scream) *78,000 human beings we'll*
destroy ourselves?

"Aah, Mrs. Miserable," he said, as if she could hear, "all your life working, and now in bed you lie, servants to tend, you do not even need to call to be tended, and still you work. Such hard work it is to die? Such hard work?"

The body threshed, her hand clung in his. A melody, ghost-thin, hovered on her lips, and like a guilty ghost, the vision of her bent in listening to it, silencing the record instantly he was near. Now, heedless of his presence, she floated the melody on and on.

"Hid it from me," he complained, "how many times you listened to remember it so?" And tried to think when she had first played it, or first begun to silence her few records when he came near—but could reconstruct nothing. There was only this room with its tall hooked pillar and its swarm of sounds.

No man one except through others
 Strong with the not yet in the now
 Dogma dead war dead one country

"It helps, Mrs. Philosopher, words from books? It helps?" And it seemed to him that for seventy years she had hidden a tape recorder, infinitely microscopic, within her, that it had coiled infinite mile on mile, trapping every song, every melody, every word read, heard, and spoken—and that maliciously she was playing back only what said nothing of him, of the children, of their intimate life together.

"Left us indeed, Mrs. Babbler," he reproached, "you who called others babbler and cunningly saved your words. A lifetime you tended and loved, and now not a word of us, for us. Left us indeed? Left me."

And he took out his solitaire deck, shuffled the cards loudly, slapped them down.

Left high banner of reason (tatter of an orator's voice) *justice freedom*
light
 Humankind life worthy capacities
 Seeks (blur of shudder) *belong human being*

"Words, words," he accused, "and what human beings did *you* seek around you, Mrs. Live Alone, and what humankind think worthy?"

Though even as he spoke, he remembered she had not always been isolated, had not always wanted to be alone (as he knew there had been a voice before this gossamer one; before the hoarse voice that broke from silence to lash, make incidents, shame him—a girl's voice of eloquence that spoke their holiest dreams). But again he could reconstruct, image, nothing of what had been before, or when, or how, it had changed.

Ace, queen, jack. The pillar shadow fell, so, in two tracks; in the mirror depths glistened, a moonlike blob, the empty solution bottle. And it worked in him: *of reason and justice and freedom ... Dogma dead:* he remembered the full quotation, laughed bitterly. "Hah, good you do not know what you say; good Victor Hugo died and did not see it, his twentieth century."

Deuce, ten, five. Dauntlessly she began a song of their youth of belief:

> *These things shall be, a loftier race*
> *than e'er the world hath known shall rise*
> *with flame of freedom in their souls*
> *and light of knowledge in their eyes*

King, four jack. "In the twentieth century, hah!"

> *They shall be gentle, brave and strong*
> *to spill no drop of blood, but dare*
> *all ...*

> *on earth and fire and sea and air*

"To spill no drop of blood, hah! So, cadaver, and you too, cadaver Hugo, 'in the twentieth century ignorance will be dead, dogma will be dead, war will be dead, and for all mankind one country—of fulfilment?' Hah!"

> *And every life* (long strangling cough) *shall*
> *be a song*

The cards fell from his fingers. Without warning, the bereavement and betrayal he had sheltered—compounded through the years—hidden even from himself—revealed itself.

uncoiled,

released,

sprung

and with it the monstrous shapes of what had actually happened in the century.

A ravening hunger or thirst seized him. He groped into the kitchenette, switched on all three lights, piled a tray—"you have finished your night snack, Mrs. Cadaver, now I will have mine." And he was shocked at the tears that splashed on the tray.

"Salt tears. For free. I forgot to shake on salt?"

Whispered: "Lost, how much I lost."

Escaped to the grandchildren whose childhoods were childish, who had never hungered, who lived unravaged by disease in warm houses of many rooms, had all the school for which they cared, could walk on any street, stood a head taller than their grandparents, towered above—beautiful skins, straight backs, clear straightforward eyes. "Yes, you in Olshana," he said to the town of sixty years ago, "they would seem nobility to you."

And was this not the dream then, come true in ways undreamed? he asked.

And are there no other children in the world? he answered, as if in her harsh voice.

And the flame of freedom, the light of knowledge?

And the drop, to spill no drop of blood?

And he thought that at six Jeannie would get up and it would be his turn to go to her room and sleep, that he could press the buzzer and she would come now; that in the afternoon Ellen Mays was coming, and this time they would play cards and he could marvel at how rouge can stand half an inch on the cheek; that in the evening the doctor would come, and he could beg him to be merciful, to stop the feeding solutions, to let her die.

To let her die, and with their youth of belief out of which her bright, betrayed words foamed; stained words, that on her working lips came stainless.

Hours yet before Jeannie's turn. He could press the buzzer and wake her up to come now; he could take a pill, and with it sleep; he could pour more brandy into his milk glass, though what he had poured was not yet touched.

Instead he went back, checked her pulse, gently tended with his knotty fingers as Jeannie had taught.

She was whimpering; her hand crawled across the covers for his. Compassionately he enfolded it, and with his free hand gathered up the cards again. Still was there thirst or hunger ravening in him.

That world of their youth—dark, ignorant, terrible with hate and disease—how was it that living in it, in the midst of corruption, filth, treachery, degradation, they had not mistrusted man nor themselves; had believed so beautifully, so ... falsely?

"Aaah, children," he said out loud, "how we believed, how we belonged." And he yearned to package for each of the children, the grandchildren, for everyone, *that joyous certainty, that sense of mattering, of moving and being moved, of being one and indivisible with the great of the past, with all that freed, ennobled.* Package it, stand on corners, in front of stadiums and on crowded beaches, knock on doors, give it as a fabled gift.

"And why not in cereal boxes, in soap packages?" he mocked himself. "Aah. You have taken my senses, cadaver."

Words foamed, died unsounded. Her body writhed; she made kissing motions with her mouth. (Her lips moving as she read, poring over the Book of the Martyrs, the magnifying glass superimposed over the heavy eyeglasses.) *Still she believed?* "Eva!" he whispered. "Still you believed? You lived by it? These Things Shall Be?"

"One pound soup meat," she answered distinctly, "one soup bone."

"My ears heard you. Ellen Mays was witness: 'Humankind ... one has to believe.'" Imploringly: "Eva!"

"Bread, day-old." She was mumbling. "Please, in a wooden box ... for kindling. The thread, hah, the thread breaks. Cheap thread"—and a gurgling, enormously loud, began in her throat.

"I ask for stone; she gives me bread—day-old." He pulled his hand away, shouted: "Who wanted questions? Everything you have to wake?" Then dully, "Ah, let me help you turn, poor creature."

Words jumbled, cleared. In a voice of crowded terror:

Paul, Sammy, don't fight.

"Hannah, have I ten hands?"

"How can I give it, Clara, how can I give it if I don't have?"

"You lie," he said sturdily, "there was joy too." Bitterly: "Ah how cheap you speak of us at the last."

As if to rebuke him, as if her voice had no relationship with her flailing body, she sang clearly, beautifully, a school song the children had taught her when they were little; begged:

"Not look my hair where they cut...."

(The crown of braids shorn.) And instantly he left the mute old woman poring over the Book of the Martyrs; went past the mother treading at the sewing machine, singing with the children; past the girl in her wrinkled prison dress, hiding her hair with scarred hands, lifting to him her awkward, shamed, imploring eyes of love; and took her in his arms, dear, personal, fleshed, in all the heavy passion he had loved to rouse from her.

"Eva!"

Her little claw hand beat the covers. How much, how much can a man stand? He took up the cards, put them down, circled the beds, walked to the dresser, opened, shut drawers, brushed his hair, moved his hand bit by bit over the mirror to see what of the reflection he could blot out with each move, and felt that at any moment he would die of what was unendurable. Went to press the buzzer to wake Jeannie, looked down, saw on Jeannie's sketch pad the hospital bed, with *her*; the double bed alongside, with him; the tall pillar feeding into her veins, and their hands, his and hers, clasped, feeding each other. And as if he had been instructed he went to his bed, lay down, holding the sketch (as if it could shield against the monstrous shapes of loss, of betrayal, of death) and with his free hand took hers back into his.

So Jeannie found them in the morning.

The last day the agony was perpetual. Time after time it lifted her almost off the bed, so they had to fight to hold her down. He could not endure and left the room; wept as if there never would be tears enough.

Jeannie came to comfort him. In her light voice she said: Grandaddy, Grandaddy don't cry. She is not there, she promised me. On the last day, she said she would go back to when she first heard music, a little girl on the road of the village where she was born. She promised me. It is a wedding and they dance, while the flutes so joyous and vibrant tremble in the air. Leave her there, Grandaddy, it is all right. She promised me. Come back, come back and help her poor body to die.

CYNTHIA OZICK

THE SHAWL

Cynthia Ozick (b. 1928), a writer from New York City, has enjoyed a remarkable career as novelist, essayist, critic, translator, and author of short fiction. Along the way she also worked in advertising and taught English and creative writing in various universities and colleges. In 1983 she won a grant, which freed her from teaching and allowed her to concentrate on her craft. An inventive and meticulous writer, she says: "I treat each sentence with the respect I would give to a line of a poem. I will not let it go until it is as 'perfect' as I can make it." She mixes fantasy, mysticism, comedy, satire, and Judaic law and history. Robert R. Harris describes her as being "obsessed with the words she puts on paper, with what it means to imagine a story and to tell it, with what fiction is."

Her first book, Trust *(1966), was about personal and political betrayal. She followed this book with three award-winning collections of short fiction, which established her literary reputation,* The Pagan Rabbi and Other Stories *(1971),* Bloodshed and Three Novellas *(1976),* Levitation: Five Fictions *(1982) and* The Messiah of Stockholm *(1987). In 1983 Ozick published a volume of essays,* Art and Ardor: Essays, *which collected her new perspectives on writers such as Forster, James, and Wharton. More recent collections of essays include* Metaphor and Memory *(1989),* What Henry James Knew, and Other Essays on Writers *(1993), and* Fame and Folly *(1996). "The Shawl" was originally published in* The New Yorker *and later chosen for the 1981* Best American Short Stories. *This chilling story of a march to a death camp and the murder of an infant is told in the third person in repetitive, almost monosyllabic language. Lauded by critics for its "achievement of the moral imagination," it was reproduced in 1989 along with its sequel, "Rosa," in* The Shawl.

Stella, cold, cold, the coldness of hell. How they walked on the roads together, Rosa with Magda curled up between sore breasts, Magda wound up in the shawl. Sometimes Stella carried Magda. But she was jealous of Magda. A thin girl of fourteen, too small, with thin breasts of her own, Stella wanted to be wrapped in a shawl, hidden away, asleep, rocked by the march, a baby, a round infant in arms. Magda took Rosa's nipple, and Rosa never stopped walking, a walking cradle. There was not enough milk; sometimes Magda sucked air; then she screamed. Stella was ravenous. Her knees were tumors on sticks, her elbows chicken bones.

Rosa did not feel hunger; she felt light, not like someone walking but like someone in a faint, in trance, arrested in a fit, someone who is already a floating angel, alert and seeing everything, but in the air, not there, not touching the road. As if teetering on the tips of her fingernails. She looked into Magda's face through a gap in the shawl: a squirrel in a nest, safe, no one could reach her inside the little house of the shawl's windings. The face, very round, a pocket mirror of a face: but it was not Rosa's bleak complexion, dark like cholera, it was another kind of face altogether, eyes blue as air, smooth feathers of hair nearly as yellow as the Star sewn into Rosa's coat. You could think she was one of *their* babies.

Rosa, floating, dreamed of giving Magda away in one of the villages. She could leave the line for a minute and push Magda into the hands of any woman on the side of the road. But if she moved out of line they might shoot. And even if she fled the line for half a second and pushed the shawl-bundle at a stranger, would the woman take it? She might be surprised, or afraid; she might drop the shawl, and Magda would fall out and strike her head and die. The little round head. Such a good child, she gave up screaming, and sucked now only for the taste of the drying nipple itself. The neat grip of the tiny gums. One mite of a tooth tip sticking up in the bottom gum, how shining, an elfin tombstone of white marble gleaming there. Without complaining, Magda relinquished Rosa's teats, first the left, then the right; both were cracked, not a sniff of milk. The duct-crevice extinct, a dead volcano, blind eye, chill hole, so Magda took the corner of the shawl and milked it instead. She sucked and sucked, flooding the threads with wetness. The shawl's good flavor, milk of linen.

It was a magic shawl, it could nourish an infant for three days and three nights. Magda did not die, she stayed alive, although very quiet. A peculiar smell, of cinnamon and almonds, lifted out of her mouth. She held her eyes open every moment, forgetting how to blink or nap, and Rosa and sometimes Stella studied their blueness. On the road they raised one burden of a leg after another and studied Magda's face. "Aryan," Stella said, in a voice grown as thin as a string; and Rosa thought how Stella gazed at Magda like a young cannibal. And the time that Stella said "Aryan," it sounded to Rosa as if Stella had really said "Let us devour her."

But Magda lived to walk. She lived that long, but she did not walk very well, partly because she was only fifteen months old, and partly because the spindles of her legs could not hold up her fat belly. It was fat with air, full and round. Rosa gave almost all her food to Magda, Stella gave nothing; Stella was ravenous, a growing child herself, but not growing much. Stella did not menstruate. Rosa did not menstruate. Rosa was ravenous, but also not; she learned from Magda how to drink the taste of a finger in one's mouth. They were in a place without pity, all pity was annihilated in Rosa, she looked at Stella's bones without pity. She was sure that Stella was waiting for Magda to die so she could put her teeth into the little thighs.

Rosa knew Magda was going to die very soon; she should have been dead already, but she had been buried away deep inside the magic shawl, mistaken there for the shivering mound of Rosa's breasts; Rosa clung to the shawl as if it covered only herself. No one took it away from her. Magda was mute. She never cried. Rosa hid her in the barracks, under the shawl, but she knew that one day someone would inform; or one day someone, not even Stella, would steal Magda to eat her. When Magda began to walk Rosa knew that Magda was going to die very soon, something would happen. She was afraid to fall asleep; she slept with the weight of her thigh on Magda's body; she was afraid she would smother Magda under her thigh. The weight of Rosa was becoming less and less; Rosa and Stella were slowly turning into air.

Magda was quiet, but her eyes were horribly alive, like blue tigers. She watched. Sometimes she laughed—it seemed a laugh, but how could it be? Magda had never seen anyone laugh. Still, Magda laughed at her shawl when the wind blew its corners, the bad wind with pieces of black in it, that made Stella's and Rosa's eyes tear. Magda's eyes were always clear and tearless. She watched like a tiger. She guarded her shawl. No one could touch it; only Rosa could touch it. Stella was not allowed. The shawl was Magda's own baby, her pet, her little sister. She tangled herself up in it and sucked on one of the corners when she wanted to be very still.

Then Stella took the shawl away and made Magda die.

Afterward Stella said: "I was cold."

And afterward she was always cold, always. The cold went into her heart: Rosa saw that Stella's heart was cold. Magda flopped onward with her little pencil legs scribbling this way and that, in search of the shawl; the pencils faltered at the barracks opening, where the light began. Rosa saw and pursued. But already Magda was in the square outside the barracks, in the jolly light. It was the roll-call arena. Every morning Rosa had to conceal Magda under the shawl against a wall of the barracks and go out and stand in the arena with Stella and hundreds of others, sometimes for hours, and Magda, deserted, was quiet under the shawl, sucking on her corner. Every day Magda was silent, and so she did not die. Rosa saw that today Magda was going to die, and at the same time a fearful joy ran in Rosa's two palms, her fingers were on fire, she was astonished, febrile: Magda, in the sunlight, swaying on her pencil legs, was howling. Ever since the drying up of Rosa's nipples, ever since Magda's last scream on the road, Magda had been devoid of any syllable; Magda was a mute. Rosa believed that something had gone wrong with her vocal cords, with her windpipe, with the cave of her larynx; Magda was defective, without a voice; perhaps she was deaf; there might be something amiss with her intelligence; Magda was dumb. Even the laugh that came when the ash-stippled wind made a clown out of Magda's shawl was only the air-blown showing of her teeth. Even when the lice, head lice and body lice, crazed her so that she became as wild as one of the big rats that plundered the barracks at day-break looking for carrion, she rubbed and scratched and kicked and bit and rolled without a whimper. But now Magda's mouth was spilling a long viscous rope of clamor.

"Maaaa—"

It was the first noise Magda had ever sent out from her throat since the drying up of Rosa's nipples.

"Maaaa ... aaa!"

Again! Magda was wavering in the perilous sunlight of the arena, scribbling on such pitiful little bent shins. Rosa saw. She saw that Magda was grieving for the loss of her shawl, she saw that Magda was going to die. A tide of commands hammered in Rosa's nipples: Fetch, get, bring! But she did not know which to go after first, Magda or the shawl. If she jumped out into the arena to snatch Magda up, the howling would not stop, because Magda would still not have the shawl; but if she ran back into the barracks to find the shawl, and if she found it, and if she came after Magda holding it and shaking it, then she would get Magda back, Magda would put the shawl in her mouth and turn dumb again.

Rosa entered the dark. It was easy to discover the shawl. Stella was heaped under it, asleep in her thin bones. Rosa tore the shawl free and flew—she could fly, she was only air—into the arena. The sunheat murmured of another life, of butterflies in summer. The light was placid, mellow. On the other side of the steel fence, far away, there were green meadows speckled with dandelions and deep-colored violets; beyond them, even farther, innocent tiger lilies, tall, lifting their orange bonnets. In the barracks they spoke of "flowers," of "rain": excrement, thick turd-braids, and the slow stinking maroon waterfall that slunk down from the upper bunks, the stink mixed with a bitter fatty floating smoke that greased Rosa's skin. She stood for an instant at the margin of the arena. Sometimes the electricity inside the fence would seem to hum; even Stella said it was only an imagining, but Rosa heard real sounds in the wire: grainy sad voices. The farther she was from the fence, the more clearly the voices crowded at her. The lamenting voices strummed so convincingly, so passionately, it was impossible to suspect them of being phantoms. The voices told her to hold up the shawl, high; the voices told her to shake it, to whip with it, to unfurl it like a flag. Rosa lifted, shook, whipped, unfurled. Far off, very far, Magda leaned across her air-fed belly, reaching out with the rods of her arms. She was high up, elevated, riding someone's shoulder. But the shoulder that carried Magda was not coming toward Rosa and the shawl, it was drifting away, the speck of Magda was moving more and more into the smoky distance. Above the shoulder a helmet glinted. The light tapped the helmet and sparkled it into a goblet. Below the helmet a black body like a domino and a pair of black boots hurled themselves in the direction of the electrified fence. The electric voices began to chatter wildly. "Maamaa, maaa-maaa," they all hummed together. How far Magda was from Rosa now, across the whole square, past a dozen barracks, all the way on the other side! She was no bigger than a moth.

All at once Magda was swimming through the air. The whole of Magda traveled through loftiness. She looked like a butterfly touching a silver vine. And the moment Magda's feathered round head and her pencil legs and balloonish belly and zigzag arms splashed against the fence, the steel voices went mad in their growling, urging Rosa to run and run to the spot where Magda had fallen from her flight against the electrified fence; but of course Rosa did not obey them. She only stood, because if she ran they would shoot, and if she tried to pick up the sticks of Magda's body they would shoot, and if she let the wolf's screech ascending now through the ladder of her skeleton break out, they would shoot; so she took Magda's shawl and filled her own mouth with it, stuffed it in and stuffed it in, until she was swallowing up the wolf's screech and tasting the cinnamon and almond depth of Magda's saliva; and Rosa drank Magda's shawl until it dried.

GRACE PALEY

THE LONG-DISTANCE RUNNER

Grace Paley (b. 1922) was born in New York to Russian immigrants. She grew up in the Bronx, immersed both in her family's Russian-Jewish culture and in the street life of New York City. She attended Hunter College and New York University and studied poetry with W.H. Auden at the New School for Social Research. It was not until the 1950s that she began writing stories; her first collection, The Little Disturbances of Man *(1959), commanded a great deal of critical and popular attention. In the early 1960s Paley taught at Columbia and Syracuse, and she has taught literature at Sarah Lawrence College since 1966. In addition to volumes of essays and poetry, she has published two other collections of short fiction,* Enormous Changes at the Last Minute *(1975), from which "The Long-Distance Runner" is taken, and* Later the Same Day *(1985). In 1986 she received the Edith Wharton Citation of Merit, which named her the first official state author of New York. In 1994 Farrar, Strauss and Giroux published* The Collected Stories.*

Paley's remarkable stories are distinctive in their use of dialogue to suggest character. "You have two ears," Paley says. "One ear is that literary ear, and it's a good old ear." The "other ear" which completes the writer's repertoire of voices "is the ear of the language of home, and the language of your street and your own people." When asked to offer a personal literary touchstone, Paley drew upon her Jewish heritage, citing "We were strangers in Egypt," from* Exodus. *"It's the Jewish part of me. I am reminded of it in every part of our political life." Politics play a strong role not only in Paley's fiction but also in her daily life. Paley's involvement in feminist and pacifist groups is as important to her as her literary craft. "It may come from my political feelings, but I think art, literature, fiction, poetry, whatever it is, makes justice in the world."*

One day, before or after forty-two, I became a long-distance runner. Though I was stout and in many ways inadequate to this desire, I wanted to go far and fast, not as fast as bicycles and trains, not as far as Taipei, Hingwen, places like that, islands of the slant-eyed cunt, as sailors in bus stations say when speaking of travel, but round and round the county from the sea side to the bridges, along the old neighbourhood streets a couple of times, before old age and urban renewal ended them and me.

I tried the country first, Connecticut, which being wooded is always full of buds in spring. All creation is secret, isn't that true? So I trained in the wide-zoned suburban hills where I wasn't known. I ran all spring in and out of dog-wood bloom, then laurel.

People sometimes stopped and asked me why I ran, a lady in silk shorts halfway down over her fat thighs. In training, I replied and rested only to answer if closely questioned. I wore a white sleeveless undershirt as well, with excellent support, not to attract the attention of old men and prudish children.

Then summer came, my legs seemed strong. I kissed the kids goodbye. They were quite old by then. It was near the time for parting anyway. I told Mrs. Raftery to look in now and then and give them some of that rotten Celtic supper she makes.

I told them they could take off any time they wanted to. Go lead your private life, I said. Only leave me out of it.

A word to the wise ... said Richard.

You're depressed Faith, Mrs. Raftery said. Your boy friend Jack, the one you think's so hotsy-totsy, hasn't called and you're as gloomy as a tick on Sunday.

Cut the folkshit with me, Raftery, I muttered. Her eyes filled with tears because that's who she is: folkshit from bunion to topknot. That's how she got liked by me, loved, invented and endured.

When I walked out the door they were all reclining before the television set, Richard, Tonto and Mrs. Raftery, gazing at the news. Which proved with moving pictures that there *had* been a voyage to the moon and Africa and South America hid in a furious whorl of clouds.

I said, Goodbye. They said, Yeah, O.K., sure.

If that's how it is, forget it, I hollered and took the Independent subway to Brighton Beach.

At Brighton Beach I stopped at the Salty Breezes Locker Room to change my clothes. Twenty-five years ago my father invested $500 in its future. In fact he still clears about $3.50 a year, which goes directly (by law) to the Children of Judea to cover their deficit.

No one paid too much attention when I started to run, easy and light on my feet. I ran on the boardwalk first, past my mother's leafleting station—between a soft-ice-cream stand and a degenerated dune. There she had been assigned by her comrades to halt the tides of cruel American enterprise with simple socialist sense.

I wanted to stop and admire the long beach. I wanted to stop in order to think admiringly about New York. There aren't many rotting cities so tan and sandy and speckled with citizens at their salty edges. But I had already spent a lot of life lying down or standing and staring. I had decided to run.

After about a mile and a half I left the boardwalk and began to trot into the old neighborhood. I was running well. My breath was long and deep. I was thinking pridefully about my form.

Suddenly I was surrounded by about three hundred blacks.

Who you?

Who that?

Look at her! Just look! When you seen a fatter ass?

Poor thing. She ain't right. Leave her, you boys, you bad boys.

I used to live here, I said.

Oh yes, they said, in the white old days. That time too bad to last.

But we loved it here. We never went to Flatbush Avenue or Times Square. We loved our block.

Tough black titty.

I like your speech, I said. Metaphor and all.

Right on. We get that from talking.

Yes my people also had a way of speech. And don't forget the Irish. The gift of gab.

Who they? said a small boy.

Cops.

Nowadays, I suggested, there's more than Irish on the police force.

You right, said two ladies. More more, much much more. They's French Chinamen Russkies Congoleans. Oh missee, you too right.

I lived in that house, I said. That apartment house. All my life. Till I got married.

Now that *is* nice. Live in one place. My mother live that way in South Carolina. One place. Her daddy farmed. She said. They ate. No matter winter war bad times. Roosevelt. Something! Ain't that wonderful! And it weren't cold! Big trees!

That apartment. I looked up and pointed. There. The third floor.

They all looked up. So what! You blubrous devil! said a dark young man. He wore horn-rimmed glasses and had that intelligent look that City College boys used to have when I was eighteen and first looked at them.

He seemed to lead them in contempt and anger, even the littlest ones who moved toward me with dramatic stealth singing, Devil, Oh Devil. I don't think the little kids had bad feeling because they poked a finger into me, then laughed.

Still I thought it might be wise to keep my head. So I jumped right in with some facts. I said, How many flowers' names do you know? Wild flowers, I mean. My people only knew two. That's what they say now anyway. Rich or poor, they only had two flowers' names. Rose and violet.

Daisy, said one boy immediately.

Weed, said another. That *is* a flower, I thought. But everyone else got the joke.

Saxifrage, lupine, said a lady. Viper's bugloss, said a small Girl Scout in medium green with a dark green sash. She held up a *Handbook of Wild Flowers*.

How many you know, fat mama? a boy asked warmly. He wasn't against my being a mother or fat. I turned all my attention to him.

Oh sonny, I said, I'm way ahead of my people. I know in yellows alone: common cinquefoil, trout lily, yellow adder's-tongue, swamp buttercup and common buttercup, golden sorrel, yellow or hop clover, devil's-paintbrush, evening primrose, black-eyed Susan, golden aster, also the yellow pickerelweed growing down by the water if not in the water, and dandelions of course. I've seen all these myself. Seen them.

You could see China from the boardwalk, a boy said. When it's nice.

I know more flowers than countries. Mostly young people these days have traveled in many countries.

Not me. I ain't been nowhere.

Not me either, said about seventeen boys.

I'm not allowed, said a little girl. There's drunken junkies.

But *I! I!* cried out a tall black youth, very handsome and well dressed. I am an African. My father came from the high stolen plains. *I* have been everywhere. I was in Moscow six months, learning machinery. I was in France, learning French. I was in Italy, observing the peculiar Renaissance and the people's sweetness. I was in England, where I studied the common law and the urban blight. I was at the Conference of Dark Youth in Cuba to understand our passion. I am now here. Here am I to become an engineer and return to my people, around the Cape of Good Hope in a Norwegian sailing vessel. In this way I will learn the fine old art of sailing in case the engines of the new society of my old inland country should fail.

We had an extraordinary amount of silence after that. Then one old lady in a black dress and high white lace collar said to another old lady dressed exactly the same way, Glad tidings when someone got brains in the head not fish juice. Amen, said a few.

Whyn't you go up to Mrs. Luddy living in your house, you lady, huh? The Girl Scout asked this.

Why she just groove to see you, said some sarcastic snickerer.

She got palpitations. Her man, he give it to her.

That ain't all, he a natural gift-giver.

I'll take you, said the Girl Scout. My name is Cynthia. I'm in Troop 355, Brooklyn.

I'm not dressed, I said, looking at my lumpy knees.

You shouldn't wear no undershirt like that without no runnin number or no team writ on it. It look like a undershirt.

Cynthia! Don't take her up there, said an important boy. Her head strange. Don't you take her. Hear?

Lawrence, she said softly, you tell me once more what to do I'll wrap you round that lamppost.

Git! she said, powerfully addressing *me*.

In this way I was led into the hallway of the whole house of my childhood.

The first door I saw was still marked in flaky gold, 1A. That's where the janitor lived, I said. He was a Negro.

How come like that? Cynthia made an astonished face. How come the janitor was a black man?

Oh Cynthia, I said. Then I turned to the opposite door, first floor front, 1B. I remembered. Now, here, this was Mrs. Goreditsky, very very fat lady. All her children died at birth. Born, then one, two, three. Dead. Five children, then Mr. Goreditsky said, I'm bad luck on you Tessie and he went away. He sent $15 a week for seven years. Then no one heard.

I know her, poor thing, said Cynthia. The city come for her summer before last. The way they knew, it smelled. They wropped her up in a canvas. They couldn't get through the front door. It scraped off a piece of her. My uncle Ronald had to help them, but he got disgusted.

Only two years ago. She was still here! Wasn't she scared?

So we all, said Cynthia. White ain't everything.

Who lived up here, she asked, 2B. Right now, my best friend Nancy Rosalind lives here. She got two brothers, and her sister married and got a baby. She very light-skinned. Not her mother. We got all colors amongst us.

Your best friend? That's funny. Because it was *my* best friend. Right in that apartment. Joanna Rosen.

What become of her? Cynthia asked. She got a running shirt too?

Come on Cynthia, if you really want to know, I'll tell you. She married this man, Marvin Steirs.

Who's he?

I recollected his achievements. Well, he's the president of a big corporation, JoMar Plastics. This corporation owns a steel company, a radio station, a new Xerox-type machine that lets you do twenty-five different pages at once.

This corporation has a foundation, the JoMar Fund for Research in Conservation. Capitalism is like that, I added, in order to be politically useful.

How come you know? You go over their house a lot?

No. I happened to read all about them on the financial page, just last week. It made me think: a different life. That's all.

Different spokes for different folks, said Cynthia.

I sat down on the cool marble steps and remembered Joanna's cousin Ziggie. He was older than we were. He wrote a poem which told us we were lovely flowers and our legs were petals, which nature would force open no matter how many times we said no.

Then I had several other interior thoughts that I couldn't share with a child, the kind that give your face a blank or melancholy look.

Now you're not interested, said Cynthia. Now you're not gonna say a thing. Who lived here, 2A? Who? Two men lives here now. Women coming and women going. My mother says, Danger sign: Stay away, my darling, stay away.

I don't remember, Cynthia. I really don't.

You got to. What'd you come for, anyways?

Then I tried. 2A. 2A. Was it the twins? I felt a strong obligation as though remembering was in charge of the *existence* of the past. This is not so.

Cynthia, I said, I don't want to go any further. I don't even want to remember.

Come on, she said, tugging at my shorts, don't you want to see Mrs. Luddy, the one lives in your old house? That be fun, no?

No. No, I don't want to see Mrs. Luddy.

Now you shouldn't pay no attention to those boys downstairs. She will like you. I mean, she is kind. She don't like most white people, but she might like you.

No Cynthia, it's not that, but I don't want to see my father and mother's house now.

I didn't know what to say. I said, Because my mother's dead. This was a lie, because my mother lives in her own room with my father in the Children of Judea. With her hand over her socialist heart, she reads the paper every morning after breakfast. Then she says sadly to my father. Every day the same. Dying ... dying, dying from killing.

My mother's dead Cynthia. I can't go in there.

Oh ... oh, the poor thing, she said, looking into my eyes. Oh, if my mother died, I don't know what I'd do. Even if I was old as you. I could kill myself. Tears filled her eyes and started down her cheeks. If my mother died, what would I do? She is my protector, she won't let the pushers get me. She hold me tight. She gonna hide me in the cedar box if my Uncle Rudford comes try to get me back. She *can't* die, my mother.

Cynthia—honey—she won't die. She's young. I put my arm out to comfort her. You could come live with me, I said. I got two boys, they're nearly grown up. I missed it, not having a girl.

What? What you mean now, live with you and boys. She pulled away and ran for the stairs. Stay way from me, honky lady. I know them white boys. They just gonna try and jostle my black womanhood. My mother told me about that, keep you white honky devil boys to your devil self, you just leave me be you old bitch you. Somebody help me, she started to scream, you hear. Somebody help. She gonna take me away.

She flattened herself to the wall, trembling. I was too frightened by her fear of me to say, honey, I wouldn't hurt you, it's me. I heard her helpers, the voices of large boys crying. We coming, we coming, hold your head up, we coming. I ran past her fear to the stairs and up them two at a time. I came to my old own door. I knocked like the landlord, loud and terrible.

Mama not home, a child's voice said. No, no, I said. It's me! a lady! Someone's chasing me, let me in. Mama not home, I ain't allowed to open up for nobody.

It's me! I cried out in terror. Mama! Mama! let me in!

The door opened. A slim woman whose age I couldn't invent looked at me. She said, Get in and shut the door tight. She took a hard pinching hold on my upper arm. Then she bolted the door herself. Them hustlers after you. They make me pink. Hide this white lady now, Donald. Stick her under your bed, you got a high bed.

Oh that's O.K. I'm fine now, I said. I felt safe and at home.

You in my house, she said. You do as I say. For two cents, I throw you out.

I squatted under a small kid's pissy mattress. Then I heard the knock. It was tentative and respectful. My mama don't allow me to open. Donald! someone called. Donald!

Oh no, he said. Can't do it. She gonna wear me out. You know her. She already tore up my ass this morning once. Ain't *gonna* open up.

I lived there for about three weeks with Mrs. Luddy and Donald and three little baby girls nearly the same age. I told her a joke about Irish twins. Ain't Irish, she said.

Nearly every morning the babies woke us at about 6:45. We gave them all a bottle and went back to sleep till 8:00. I made coffee and she changed diapers. Then it really stank for a while. At this time I usually said, Well listen, thanks really, but I've got to go I guess. I guess I'm going. She'd usually say, Well, guess again. *I* guess you ain't. Or if she was feeling disgusted she'd say, Go on now! Get! You wanna go, I guess by now I have snorted enough white lady stink to choke a horse. Go on!

I'd get to the door and then I'd hear voices. I'm ashamed to say I'd become fearful. Despite my wide geographical love of mankind, I would be attacked by local fears.

There was a sentimental truth that lay beside all that going and not going. It *was* my house where I'd lived long ago my family life. There was a tile on the bathroom floor that I myself had broken, dropping a hammer on the toe of my brother Charles as he stood dreamily shaving, his prick halfway up his undershorts. Astonishment and knowledge first seized me right there. The kitchen was the same. The table was the enameled table common to our class, easy to clean, with wooden undercorners for indigent and old cockroaches that couldn't make it to the kitchen sink. (However, it was not the same table, because I have inherited that one, chips and all.)

The living room was something like ours, only we had less plastic. There may have been less plastic in the world at that time. Also, my mother had set beautiful cushions everywhere, on beds and chairs. It was the way she expressed herself, artistically, to embroider at night or take strips of flowered cotton and sew them across ordinary white or blue muslin in the most delicate designs, the way women have always used materials that live and die in hunks and tatters to say: This is my place.

Mrs. Luddy said, Uh huh!

Of course, I said, men don't have that outlet. That's how come they run around so much.

Till they drunk enough to lay down, she said.

Yes, I said, on a large scale you can see it in the world. First they make something, then they murder it. Then they write a book about how interesting it is.

You got something there, she said. Sometimes she said, Girl, you don't know *nothing*.

We often sat at the window looking out and down. Little tufts of breeze grew on that windowsill. The blazing afternoon was around the corner and up the block.

You say men, she said. Is that men? she asked. What you call—a Man?

Four flights below us, leaning on the stoop, were about a dozen people and around them devastation. Just a minute, I said. I had seen devastation on my way, running, gotten some of the pebbles of it in my running shoe and the dust of it in my eyes. I had thought with the indignant courtesy of a citizen, This is a disgrace to the City of New York which I love and am running through.

But now, from the commanding heights of home, I saw it clearly. The tenement in which Jack my old and present friend had come to gloomy manhood had been destroyed, first by fire, then by demolition (which is a swinging ball of steel that cracks bedrooms and kitchens). Because of this work, we could see several blocks wide and a block and a half long. Crazy Eddy's house still stood, famous 1510 gutted, with black window frames, no glass, open laths. The stubbornness of the supporting beams! Some persons or families still lived on the lowest floors. In the lots between a couple of old sofas lay on their fat faces, their springs sticking up into the air. Just as in wartime, a half-dozen ailanthus trees had already found their first quarter inch of earth and begun a living attack on the dead yards. At night I knew animals roamed the place, squalling and howling, furious New York dogs and street cats and mighty rats. You would think you were in Bear Mountain Park, the terror of venturing forth.

Someone ought to clean that up, I said.

Mrs. Luddy said, Who you got in mind? Mrs. Kennedy?—

Donald made a stern face. He said, That just what I gonna do when I get big. Gonna get the Sanitary Man in and show it to him. You see that, you big guinea you, you clean it up right now! Then he stamped his feet and fierced his eyes.

Mrs. Luddy said, Come here, you little nigger. She kissed the top of his head and gave him a whack on the backside all at one time.

Well, said Donald, encouraged, look out there now you all! Go on I say, look! Though we had already seen, to please him we looked. On the stoop men and boys lounged, leaned, hopped about, stood on one leg, then another, took their socks off, and scratched their toes, talked, sat on their haunches, heads down, dozing.

Donald said, Look at them. They ain't got self-respect. They got Afros *on* their heads, but they don't know they black *in* their heads.

I thought he ought to learn to be more sympathetic. I said, There are reasons that people are that way.

Yes, ma'am, said Donald.

Anyway, how come you never go down and play with the other kids, how come you're up here so much?

My mama don't like me do that. Some of them is bad. Bad. I might become a dope addict. I got to stay clear.

You just a dope, that's a fact, said Mrs. Luddy.

He ought to be with kids his age more, I think.

He see them in school, miss. Don't trouble your head about it if you don't mind.

Actually, Mrs. Luddy didn't go down into the street either. Donald did all the shopping. She let the welfare investigator in, the meterman came in to the kitchen to read the meter. I saw him from the back room, where I hid. She did pick up her check. She cashed it. She returned to wash the babies, change their diapers, wash clothes, iron, feed people, and then in free half hours she sat by that window. She was waiting.

I believed she was watching and waiting for a particular man. I wanted to discuss this with her, talk lovingly like sisters. But before I could freely say, Forget about that son of a bitch, he's a pig, I did have to offer a few solid facts about myself, my kids, about fathers, husbands, passers-by, evening companions, and the life of my father and mother in this room by this exact afternoon window.

I told her for instance, that in my worst times I had given myself one extremely simple physical pleasure. This was cream cheese for breakfast. In fact, I insisted on it, sometimes depriving the children of very important articles and foods.

Girl, you don't know nothing, she said.

Then for a little while she talked gently as one does to a person who is innocent and insane and incorruptible because of stupidity. She had had two such special pleasures for hard times she said. The first, men, but they turned rotten, white women had ruined the best, give them the idea their dicks made of solid gold. The second pleasure she had tried was wine. She said, I do like wine. You *has* to have something just for yourself by yourself. Then she said, But you can't raise a decent boy when you liquor-dazed every night.

White or black, I said, returning to men, they did think they were bringing a rare gift, whereas it was just sex, which is common like bread, though essential.

Oh, you can do without, she said. There's folks does without.

I told her Donald deserved the best. I loved him. If he had flaws, I hardly noticed them. It's one of my beliefs that children do not have flaws, even the worst do not.

Donald was brilliant—like my boys except that he had an easier disposition. For this reason I decided, almost the second moment of my residence in that household, to bring him up to reading level at once. I told him we would work with books and newspapers. He went immediately to his neighborhood library and brought some hard books to amuse me, *Black Folktales* by Julius Lester and *The Pushcart War*, which is about another neighborhood but relevant.

Donald always agreed with me when we talked about reading and writing. In fact, when I mentioned poetry, he told me he knew all about it, that David Henderson, a known black poet, had visited his second-grade class. So Donald was, as it turned out, well ahead of my nosy tongue. He was usually very busy shopping. He also had to spend a lot of time making faces to force the little serious baby girls into laughter. But if the subject came up, he could take *the* poem right out of the air into which language and event had just gone.

An example: That morning, his mother had said, Whew, I just got too much piss and diapers and wash. I wanna just sit down by that window and rest myself. He wrote a poem:

> *Just got too much pissy diapers*
> *and wash and wash*

just wanna sit down by that window
and look out
            ain't nothing there.

Donald, I said, you are plain brilliant. I'm never going to forget you. For God's sakes don't you forget me.

You fool with him too much, said Mrs. Luddy. He already don't even remember his grandma, you never gonna meet someone like her, a curse never come past her lips.

I do remember, Mama, I remember. She lying in bed, right there. A man standing in the door. She say, Esdras, I put a curse on you head. You worsen tomorrow. How come she said like that?

Gomorrah, I believe Gomorrah, she said. She know the Bible inside out.

Did she live with you?

No. No, she visiting. She come up to see us all, her children, how we doing. She come up to see sights. Then she lay down and died. She was old.

I remained quiet because of the death of mothers. Mrs. Luddy looked at me thoughtfully, then she said:

My mama had stories to tell, she raised me on. *Her* mama was a little thing, no sense. Stand in the door of the cabin all day, sucking her thumb. It was slave times. One day a young field boy come storming along. He knock on the door of the first cabin hollering, Sister, come out, it's freedom. She come out. She say, Yeah? When? He say, Now! It's freedom now! Then he knock at the next door and say, Sister! It's freedom! Now! From one cabin he run to the next cabin, crying out, Sister, it's freedom now!

Oh I remember that story, said Donald. Freedom now! Freedom now! He jumped up and down.

You don't remember nothing boy. Go on, get Eloise, she want to get into the good times.

Eloise was two but undersized. We got her like that, said Donald. Mrs. Luddy let me buy her ice cream and green vegetables. She was waiting for kale and chard, but it was too early. The kale liked cold. You not about to be here November, she said. No, no. I turned away, lonesomeness touching me and sang our Eloise song:

Eloise loves the bees
the bees they buzz
like Eloise does.

Then Eloise crawled all over the splintery floor, buzzing wildly.

Oh you crazy baby, said Donald, buzz buzz buzz.

Mrs. Luddy sat down by the window.

You all make a lot of noise, she said sadly. You just right on noisy.

The next morning Mrs. Luddy woke me up.

Time to go, she said.

What?

Home.

What? I said.

Well, don't you think your little spoiled boys crying for you? Where's Mama? They standing in the window. Time to go lady. This ain't Free Vacation Farm. Time we was by ourself a little.

Oh Ma, said Donald, she ain't a lot of trouble. Go on, get Eloise, she hollering. And button up your lip.

She didn't offer me coffee. She looked at me strictly all the time. I tried to look strictly back, but I failed because I loved the sight of her.

Donald was teary, but I didn't dare turn my face to him, until the parting minute at the door. Even then, I kissed the top of his head a little too forcefully and said, Well, I'll see you.

On the front stoop there were about half a dozen mid-morning family people and kids arguing about who had dumped garbage out of which window. They were very disgusted with one another.

Two young men in handsome dashikis stood in counsel and agreement at the street corner. They divided a comment. How come white womens got rotten teeth? And look so old? A young woman waiting at the light said, Hush ...

I walked past them and didn't begin my run till the road opened up somewhere along Ocean Parkway. I was a little stiff because my way of life had used only small movements, an occasional stretch to put a knife or teapot out of reach of the babies. I ran about ten, fifteen blocks. Then my second wind came, which is classical, famous among runners, it's the beginning of flying.

In the three weeks I'd been off the street, jogging had become popular. It seemed that I was only one person doing her thing, which happened like most American eccentric acts to be the most "in" thing I could have done. In fact, two young men ran alongside of me for nearly a mile. They ran silently beside me and turned off at Avenue H. A gentleman with a mustache, running poorly in the opposite direction, waved. He called out, Hi, señora.

Near home I ran through our park, where I had aired my children on weekends and late-summer afternoons. I stopped at the northeast playground, where I met a dozen young mothers intelligently handling their little ones. In order to prepare them, meaning no harm, I said, In fifteen years, you girls will be like me, wrong in everything.

At home it was Saturday morning. Jack had returned looking grim as ever, but he'd brought cash and a vacuum cleaner. While the coffee perked, he showed Richard how to use it. They were playing tick tack toe on the dusty wall.

Richard said, Well! Look who's here! Hi!

Any news, I asked.

Letter from Daddy, he said. From the lake and water country in Chile. He says it's like Minnesota.

He's never been to Minnesota, I said. Where's Anthony?

Here I am, said Tonto, appearing. But I'm leaving.

Oh yes, I said. Of course. Every Saturday he hurries through breakfast or misses it. He goes to visit his friends in institutions. These are well-known places like Bellevue, Hillside, Rockland State, Central Islip, Manhattan. These visits take him all day and sometimes half the night.

I found some chocolate-chip cookies in the pantry. Take them, Tonto, I said. I remember nearly all his friends as little boys and girls always hopping, skipping, jumping and cookie-eating. He was annoyed. He said, No! Chocolate cookies is what the commissaries are full of. How about money?

Jack dropped the vacuum cleaner. He said, No! They have parents for that.

I said, Here, five dollars for cigarettes, one dollar each.

Cigarettes! said Jack. Goddamnit! Black lungs and death! Cancer! Emphysema! He stomped out of the kitchen, breathing. He took the bike from the back room and started for Central Park, which had been closed to cars but opened to bicycle riders. When he'd been gone about ten minutes, Anthony said, It's really open only on Sundays.

Why didn't you say so? Why can't you be decent to him? I asked. It's important to me.

Oh Faith, he said, patting me on the head because he'd grown so tall, all that air. It's good for his lungs. And his muscles! He'll be back soon.

You should ride too, I said. You don't want to get mushy in your legs. You should go swimming once a week.

I'm too busy, he said. I have to see my friends.

Then Richard, who had been vacuuming under his bed, came into the kitchen. You still here, Tonto?

Going going gone, said Anthony, don't bat your eye.

Now listen, Richard said, here's a note. It's for Judy, if you get as far as Rockland. Don't forget it. Don't open it. Don't read it. I know he'll read it.

Anthony smiled and slammed the door.

Did I lose weight? I asked. Yes, said Richard. You look O.K. You never look too bad. But where were you? I got sick of Raftery's boiled potatoes. Where were you, Faith?

Well! I said. Well! I stayed a few weeks in my old apartment, where Grandpa and Grandma and me and Hope and Charlie lived, when we were little. I took you there long ago. Not so far from the ocean where Grandma made us very healthy with sun and air.

What are you talking about, said Richard. Cut the baby talk.

Anthony came home earlier than expected that evening because some people were in shock therapy and someone else had run away. He listened to me for a while. Then he said, I don't know what she's talking about either.

Neither did Jack, despite the understanding often produced by love after absence. He said, Tell me again. He was in a good mood. He said, You can even tell it to me twice.

I repeated the story. They all said, What?

Because it isn't usually so simple. Have you known it to happen much nowadays? A woman inside the steamy energy of middle age runs and runs. She finds the houses and streets where her childhood happened. She lives in them. She learns as though she was still a child what in the world is coming next.

LUIGI PIRANDELLO

IN THE ABYSS

Translated by Frederick May

Luigi Pirandello (1867–1936) was born in Sicily. He attended the University of Rome and Germany's Bonn University. He taught in Rome until his plays, fiction, essays, and poetry began to command the attention of critics, after which he devoted his energies to writing, producing, and touring plays in the grotesco *style of grotesque, psychological expressionist theatre, which he is credited with having invented. Mussolini was a patron of Pirandello's work, and in 1924 Pirandello joined Italy's Fascist Party as high commander of St. Maurice. In 1934 he won the Nobel Prize in literature. His most famous work is the play* Six Characters in Search of an Author *(1921). Pirandello died in Rome in 1936.*

"In the Abyss," which first appeared in 1913, exemplifies Pirandello's thematic concern with deep-rooted psychological trauma and with the gap between reality and illusion. Introducing this story in the translated edition of Pirandello's Short Stories, *Frederick May notes that "'In the Abyss' [is] an astonishingly early and far-ranging exploration of the subconscious.... The whole atmosphere of the story is one of hallucination, a world of contending shadows indicative of the contradictory layers of identity within the characters."*

At the Rackets Club they talked of nothing else the whole evening.

The first man to give them the news was Respi—Nicolino Respi—who was terribly grieved by it. As usual, however, despite the emotion he felt, he was quite unable to prevent his lips from curling in that nervous little smile which—even in the most serious discussions and in the most difficult moments of play—made his small, pale, jaundiced face, with its sharp features, so completely and so characteristically *his*.

His friends clustered around him in consternation.

"Has he *really* gone out of his mind?"

"Oh, no! Only for a joke."

Traldi, who was buried deep in the settee, with the entire weight of his enormous pachydermatous body driving him farther in, gave a series of heaves in an attempt to prop himself into a more upright position. The effort made his bovine bloodshot eyes open wide and pop out of their sockets. He asked, "Forgive the question, old man, but have you ... *Oooh! Oooh!* Have you—I mean, did he give *you* that look, too?"

"Did he ...? Give *me* ... that ... look? What do you mean?" asked Nicolino Respi in return, utterly astonished, and turning questioningly to his friends. "I arrived only this morning from Milan, to find this wonderful item of news waiting for me. I don't know a thing. I still can't understand how it is that Romeo Daddi—My God, Romeo Daddi of *all* people! The most even-tempered, serene, level-headed one of the lot of us ...!"

"Have they locked him up?"

"Of course they have! Didn't I say so? Three o'clock this afternoon. In the Monte Mario Asylum!"

"Poor Daddi!"

"How's Donna Bicetta taking it? But, how on——! Did *she* ...? I mean, was it Donna Bicetta who sent for them?"

"No, of course it wasn't! No, as a matter of fact, *she* wouldn't hear of it! No, her father dashed down from Florence the day before yesterday."

"Oh, so that's why ...!"

"Precisely. He made her take the decision, to—— For *his* sake as well. But tell me how it all happened. Traldi, why did you ask me whether Daddi'd given *me* that look as well?"

Carlo Traldi had blissfully buried himself again in the settee with his head thrown back, and his purple, sweaty double-chin exposed to full view. Wriggling his little slender frog's legs, which his exorbitantly huge belly forced him perpetually to keep obscenely apart, and continually and no less obscenely moistening his lips, he replied abstractedly, "Oh yes, so I did. Because I thought that *that* was why you said he'd gone mad."

"What do you mean, *that* was why?"

"Why, of course! That's how his madness revealed itself to him. He looked at everybody in a particular way, my dear fellow. Oh, don't make me talk, you chaps, *you* tell him how poor Daddi looked."

Whereupon his friends told Nicolino Respi that Daddi, after he'd got back from his holiday in the country, had appeared to all of them like someone completely dazed. It was as if he were somehow *outside* himself. He'd look at you with an empty smile on his lips, his eyes dull and glazed. He wasn't *really* looking at you, as was obvious when anyone called him. Then that astounded look had disappeared and been transformed into an acute and strange kind of staring. First of all, he'd stared at things from a distance, obliquely. Then, gradually, as if attracted by certain signs which he thought he could observe in one or other of his most intimate friends—especially in those who most assiduously frequented his house—highly *natural* signs, for everyone was thrown into a state of utter consternation by that sudden and extraordinary change. It was so completely in contrast with the usual serenity of his character. Gradually, he'd come to watch them attentively from close to, and in the last days he'd become downright unbearable. He'd suddenly plonk himself in front of now one, now another of them, place his hands on the man's shoulders, look into his eyes—deep, deep down into them he'd look.

"God Almighty, it gave you the shudders!" Traldi exclaimed at that point, dragging himself up again, in an attempt to get his body into a slightly more upright position.

"But—— Why?" asked Respi, nervously.

"Listen to what I'm going to tell you, if you want to know why!" Traldi exclaimed in reply. "Ugh! So you want to know why we all got the shudders, do you? My dear fellow, I'd like to have seen *you* getting to grips with that look of his! I suppose you change your shirt every day. You're quite sure your feet are clean, and that your socks haven't got holes in them. But are you quite sure you haven't got anything mucky inside, on your conscience, down in your subconscious?"

"Oh, my God, I'd say——"

"Bunkum! You're not being honest with yourself!"

"And you are?"

"Yes, I am! That's one thing I am sure about! And believe me, it happens to all of us. We all discover, in some lucid interval, that, to a greater or lesser degree, we're swine! Almost every night—for quite some time now—when I put out the candle, before dropping off to sleep ..."

"You're getting old, my dear chap, you're getting old!" all his friends yelled at him in chorus.

"Maybe I am getting old," admitted Traldi. "So much the worse! It's no fun foreseeing that in the end I'll be firmly fixed in such an opinion of myself. An old swine, that's what I'll be in my own eyes. Anyway, wait a minute! Now that I've told you this, let's try a little experiment shall we? Shut up, you lot! Quiet!"

And Carlo Traldi got laboriously to his feet. He placed his hands on Nicolino Respi's shoulders and shouted in his face, "Look into my eyes! Deep down into my eyes! No, don't laugh, my dear fellow! Look into my eyes! Deep down into my eyes! Wait! And you lot wait, too! Shut up!"

They all became silent. They were held in suspense, intent on that strange experiment.

Traldi, his huge oval, bloodshot eyes popping out of their sockets, stared acutely into the eyes of Nicolino Respi, and it seemed as if that malignant, shining gaze, which got gradually more and more acute and intense, was rummaging in his conscience, in his sub-conscious.... Discovering, there in the most intimate hiding-places, the most wicked and atrocious things. Little by little, Nicolino Respi began to grow pale and—although lower on his face his lips, with their usual little smile still playing upon them, seemed to be saying, "Oh rubbish! I'm only taking part in your little joke because——"; his eyes started to cloud over. He found he couldn't meet Traldi's gaze all the time, till finally, amidst the silence of his friends Traldi, in a strange voice, without lowering his staring gaze, without slackening one jot the intensity of his gaze, said victoriously, "There you are, you see? There you are!"

"Oh, rubbish!" burst out Respi, unable to stand it any longer, and shaking himself vigorously.

"The same to you, with nobs on! We understand one another all right!" shouted Traldi. "You're a worse swine than I am!" And he burst out laughing. The others laughed too, with a sense of unexpected relief. Traldi resumed, "Now this has been a joke. Only for a joke can one of us set himself to look at another of us like that. Because you and I alike still have that little machine known as civilization in good working order inside us; so we let the whole bang shoot of all our actions, all our thoughts, all our feelings sit there, hidden, at the bottom of our consciousness. But, now suppose that someone, whose little civilization machine's broken down, comes along and looks at you as I looked at you just now, no longer as a joke, but in all seriousness, and without your expecting it removes from the bottom of your consciousness all that assembly of thoughts, actions, and feelings which you've got inside you. ... Then tell me that you wouldn't get the shudders!"

Saying which, Carlo Traldi moved furiously towards the door. Then he turned back and added, "And do you know what he was murmuring under his breath ...? Poor Daddi, I mean! Go on, you lot; you tell him what he was murmuring! I must fly!"

"'What an abyss.... What an abyss....'"

"Just like that?"

"Yes, 'What an abyss.... What an abyss....'"

After Traldi left the group broke up and Nicolino Respi was left, feeling thoroughly disturbed, in the company of just two friends, who went on talking for a little while about the terrible misfortune which had overtaken poor Daddi.

About two months before he'd gone to visit him at his villa near Perugia. He'd found him as calm and serene as ever, together with his wife and a friend of hers, Gabriella Vanzi—an old school-friend, who'd recently married a naval officer, who was then on a cruise. He'd spent three days at the villa, and not once—not once—had Romeo Daddi looked at him in the way that Traldi had described.

If he *had* looked at him like that ...

A wave of dismay swept over Nicolino Respi. He felt suddenly giddy, and for support he took the arm of one of those two friends of his, making it look like a confidential gesture. His face was very pale, but the smile was still on his lips.

What had happened? What was that they were saying? Torture? What kind of torture? Oh, the torture Daddi had inflicted on his wife....

"Afterwards, eh?" the words escaped from his lips.

They both turned and looked at him. "What do you mean, afterwards?"

"Oh.... No, what I meant was afterwards—when his ... Well, when his little machine broke down."

"Oh, it must have been! It certainly couldn't have been before!"

"My God, they were a miracle of conjugal harmony and domestic bliss! It's obvious that something must have happened while they were on holiday in the country!"

"Why, yes! At the very least some sort of suspicion must have been aroused in him."

"Oh, don't be so utterly——! Concerning his wife?" burst out Nicolino Respi. "That, if anything, might have been the *result* of his madness, certainly not its cause! Only a madman——"

"Agreed! Agreed!" his friends cried, "A wife like Donna Bicetta!"

"No one could possibly suspect her! But—— Besides ...!"

Nicolino Respi could no longer bear to stand there listening to the pair of them. He felt as if he were stifling. He needed air. He needed to walk about in the open air. On his own. He made some excuse and got away.

A terrible, tormenting doubt had insinuated itself into his mind and brought turmoil with it.

No one could know better than he that Donna Bicetta was completely above suspicion. For more than a year he'd persisted in declaring his love for her, besieged her with his courtship, without ever once obtaining anything more than a very gentle and compassionate smile in recompense for all his wasted labour. With that serenity which comes from being very sure of yourself, without either feeling insulted or rebelling against his onslaught, she'd made it perfectly plain to him that any kind of persistence on his part would be quite in vain, because she was just as much in love as he was—perhaps more than he was—but with her husband. Since she was in love with her husband, if he really loved her, he'd realize that her love could never grow less. If he didn't realize that, then he didn't really love her. So ...?

Sometimes, in certain solitary bathing spots, the sea water is so limpid, so clear, and so transparent that, however great your desire to immerse yourself in it, to enjoy its delicious refreshing coolness, you feel an almost sacred restraint inhibiting you from bringing turmoil into it.

Nicolino Respi always had the same feeling of limpidity and restraint when approaching the soul of Donna Bicetta Daddi. This woman loved life, with such a tranquil, attentive, and gentle love! Only once—it was during those three days spent in her villa near Perugia—had he, overcome by his burning desire, done violence to that restraint, had he brought turmoil into that limpidity, and he had been sternly repulsed.

Now his terrible tormenting doubt was this: that perhaps the turmoil he'd caused in those three days hadn't quietened down again after he'd left. Perhaps it had grown so great that her husband had become aware of it. Certainly, on his arrival at the villa, Romeo Daddi had been perfectly calm, and within a few days of his departure he'd gone out of his mind.

Well then, was it on *his* account? Had she, then, been left profoundly disturbed, quite overcome by his amorous aggression?

Why, of course! Yes. Why doubt it?

All night long Nicolino Respi argued the question backwards and forwards in his own mind. He twisted from one frenzied extreme to the other. One moment he was torn by remorse away from a malign and impetuous sense of joy; the next he was torn by this joy away from his remorse.

The following morning, as soon as he thought he might properly do so, he rushed round to Donna Bicetta Daddi's house. He simply had to see her. He simply had to clear things up at once. Somehow resolve those doubts of his. Perhaps she wouldn't see him. But, in any case, he wanted to present himself at her house, ready to confront and submit to the consequences of that situation.

Donna Bicetta Daddi wasn't at home.

For the past hour, without in the least wishing to, without knowing she was doing it, she'd been inflicting the most cruel of martyrdoms on her friend Gabriella Vanzi, the woman who'd been her guest for three months at her villa.

She'd gone to see her, so that together they might try and work out—not the reason, alas! No, what had driven him to—what had caused that misfortune of his. Try and pinpoint the moment in three days during their stay in the country—the last days of their time there—when it had first revealed itself. And, though she'd ransacked her memory, she hadn't succeeded in discovering anything.

For the past hour she'd been stubbornly calling back those last days, reconstructing them minute by minute. "Do you remember this? Do you remember that morning he went down into the garden without taking his linen hat, and called up for it to be thrown down to him from the window? Then he came back up, laughing, with that bunch of roses. Do you remember—he wanted me to wear a couple of them? Then he went with me to the gate and helped me into the car, and told me he'd like me to bring him back those books from Perugia. Wait a moment! One was—— Oh, I don't know. Something to do with seeds—do you remember? Do you remember?"

So thoroughly upset was she by the grief the re-evocation of so many minute and valueless details was inflicting on her, that she didn't observe the steadily growing anguish and agitation of her friend.

Already she'd re-evoked without the slightest indication of being upset the three days spent in the villa by Nicolino Respi, and she hadn't for one moment paused to consider whether her husband had found provocation for his madness in the innocent courtship of that man. It wasn't even remotely possible. It had been very much a laughing matter for the three of them, that courtship of his after Respi's departure for Milan. How could she possibly imagine that——? Besides, after his departure, hadn't her husband remained quite serene, quite tranquil for ...? Well, it was more than a fortnight.

No, never! Never the remotest hint of suspicion! Never once, in seven whole years of marriage! How, where, would he ever have found cause for suspicion? And yet look, all of a sudden, there amidst the peace and quiet of the Umbrian countryside, without anything at all happening——

"Oh, Gabriella! Gabriella, my dear! I'm going out of my mind now! Believe me, I'm going mad too!"

Suddenly, as she was recovering from that crisis of desperation, Donna Bicetta Daddi, raising her weeping eyes to look at her friend's face, discovered that it had become very set and gone deathly pale. She looked just like a corpse. She was trying to get control over a paroxysm of unbearable anguish. She was panting. Her nostrils were flaring. And she was watching her with evil in her eyes. Oh, God! Almost the same look in her eyes as that with which, in those last days, her husband had stood there looking at her.

She felt her blood freezing. She felt terror crowding in upon her.

"Why—— You as well? Why?" She stammered, trembling all over. "Why are *you* looking at me like that?"

Gabriella Vanzi made a hideous effort to force the expression on her face, which she'd assumed quite unknown to herself, to dissolve into a benign smile of compassion. "Me ...? Was I looking? No, I was thinking. Yes, look—— I meant to ask you. Yes, I know—you're so sure of yourself—is there nothing that you—absolutely nothing—nothing you've got to reproach yourself with?"

Donna Bicetta was startled out of her wits. With her hands clasped to her cheeks, and her eyes wide and staring, she cried, "What? *You're* saying it to me now! His very words as well! How ...? How *can* you?"

Gabriella Vanzi's face took on a false expression and her eyes glazed over, "How can *I* ...?"

"Yes, you! Oh, my God! And now you're getting all dismayed, just like him! What does it all mean? What does it all mean?"

She felt herself gradually sinking deeper and deeper. She was still whimpering "What does it all mean?" when she found her friend in her arms, and clinging tightly to her breast.

"Bice. Bice. Do you suspect me? You came here—because you suspected me, didn't you?"

"No! No! I give you my solemn oath, Gabriella. Now, however.... Only now——"

"You do now, don't you? Yes, you do! But you're wrong, you're wrong, Bice! Because you can't understand."

"What's happened? Gabriella! Now, come on! Tell me! What's happened?"

"You can't understand. You can't understand. I know why—I know the reason why your husband's gone mad!"

"The reason why ...? *Which* reason?"

"I know the reason why he—— Because it's in me. It's in me too. This reason for going mad. Because of what happened to both of us!"

"To *both* of you?"

"Yes! Yes! To me and your husband."

"Well?"

"No! No! It's not what you're thinking! You can't possibly understand. Without any attempt at deceiving anybody—without thinking about it— without wanting it to happen.... In an instant; something *horrible*! And nobody can blame himself for it. You see how I'm talking to you about it? How I *can* talk to you about it? Because I'm not to blame! And neither is he! But just because that's how things are. Listen! *Listen!* And when you've found out everything, maybe *you'll* go mad as well, in the same way as *I'm* just about to go mad! In the same way as *he's* gone mad! Listen! You've been busy reliving that day when you went into Perugia from the villa, in the car, haven't you? The day he gave you those two roses and asked you to bring him back those books."

"Yes."

"Well. It was that morning!"

"*What* was?"

"Everything that happened. Everything and nothing.... Let me tell you, for pity's sake! It was terribly hot, do you remember? After seeing you off, he and I walked back through the garden. The sun was simply scorching and the chirping of the crickets was quite deafening. We went back into the house and sat down in the drawing-room, over by the dining-room door. The blinds were drawn, the shutters were pulled to. It was almost dark in there. There was a feeling of coolness. Everything was still. I'm giving you my impression of it now—the only one I could possibly have. The one I remember. The one I shall always remember. Maybe he had the same memory of it himself. He must have done, otherwise I'd never be able to explain anything to myself! It was that stillness, that coolness, coming after all that sunshine and the deafening noise of the crickets. In an instant—— Without thinking about it, I swear! Never, never.... Neither he nor I.... Oh yes, of that I'm positive——! As if there were some irresistible attraction implicit within that astonished emptiness, within the delicious coolness of that semi-darkness.... Bice, Bice.... It happened just like that.... I swear it! In an instant!"

With a sudden movement, Donna Bicetta Daddi leapt to her feet—impelled to do so by a sudden access of hatred, anger, and contempt.

"Oh, so that's why?" she hissed between her teeth, drawing away like a cat.

"No, that's not why!" cried Gabriella, stretching her arms towards her in a gesture of despair and supplication. "That's not why! That's not why, Bice! Your husband went mad on your account, on *your* account, not because of me"!

"He went mad on my account? What do you mean? Out of remorse?"

"No! What do you mean, remorse? There's no occasion for remorse, when you haven't willed the sin.... You can't understand! Just as I shouldn't have been able to understand things if, in thinking about what's happened to your husband, I hadn't thought about my own! Yes, yes, I can now understand your husband's madness, because I think of my own husband, who'd go mad in the same way, if what happened to your husband with me ever happened to him! Without remorse! Without remorse! And precisely because it is without remorse ...! Do you realize? This is the horrible thing about it! Oh, I don't know how to make you understand! *I* understand it, I repeat, only if I think of my own husband and see myself, like this, without remorse for a sin I had no desire to commit. You see how I can talk to you about it, without blushing? Because I don't know, Bice, I really don't know anything about your husband—physically—just as he most certainly doesn't, *can't* know anything about me. It was like an abyss. Do you understand me? Like an abyss which suddenly opened up between us. There we were, all unsuspecting, and it seized hold of us and overthrew us in an instant. Then, just as suddenly, it closed again, leaving not the slightest trace behind it! Immediately afterwards the consciousness of each one of us was once again quite limpid and undisturbed. We didn't think any more about it, about what had happened between us. Not even for an instant. Our disturbance had been purely momentary. We left the room, he through one door, I through the other. But the moment we were alone—nothing. It was just as if nothing whatever had happened. Not only when we were with you—when you returned home shortly afterwards—but even when we two were alone together. We could look into one another's eyes

and talk to one another, just as before, *exactly* as before, because no longer
was there in us—I swear it!—the slightest vestige of what, for an instant, *had
been*. Nothing. Nothing. Not even the shadow of a memory. Not even the
shadow of desire. Nothing! Everything was over and done with. It had disappeared. The secret of an instant was buried for ever. Well, this is what's driven
your husband mad—not the sin itself, which neither of us thought of committing! No, it's this: his being able to imagine what can happen—that an honest
woman who's in love with her own husband can, in an instant, without
wanting to, as a result of a sudden ambush of the sense, because of a mysterious conspiracy of time and place, fall into the arms of another man. And, a
moment later, everything's over—for ever. The abyss has closed again. The
secret's buried. There's no remorse. No turmoil. No effort's needed to lie in
front of others. To one another. He waited a day, two days, three.... He didn't
feel any further stirring there inside himself, either in your presence, or in
mine. He could see that I'd gone back to being what I was before—just what I
was before—both with you and with him. He saw, shortly afterwards—do you
remember?—my husband arrive at the villa. He saw how I welcomed him—
with what concern, with what love. And then the abyss, in which our secret
was buried deep, for ever, without leaving the slightest trace, began gradually
to exercise a fatal attraction for him. Till finally it overthrew his reason. He
thought of you. He began to wonder whether perhaps you too ...?"

"Whether I too?"

"Oh, Bice, I'm sure it's never happened to you! I can quite well believe it!
Yes, Bice, my dear! But I ... He and I, we know from experience what can
happen! And we know that, since it was possible in our case without our
wanting it, it can quite well be possible for anyone at all! He'll probably have
thought of how there've been times when, coming back home, he'll have found
you alone in the drawing-room with a friend of his. And he'll have thought of
how, in an instant, there could quite well have happened to you and to that
friend of his, what happened to me and to him. In exactly the same way. He'll
have thought of how you'd have been able to shut up inside yourself, without
there being any trace of it, to hide without lying, the same secret that *I* shut up
inside myself and hid from my husband without lying. And the moment this
thought entered his mind a subtle, acute, burning sensation would begin to
gnaw away at his brain, as he saw you, so detached, so happy, so loving, with
him. Just as I was with my husband. With my husband whom I love, I swear,
more than I love myself, more than I love anything in the world! He started
thinking, 'And yet, this woman, who's behaving like this towards her husband,
was in my arms for a moment? So, perhaps, my wife too, in a moment.... Who
knows? Who can *ever* know?' And he went out of his mind. Oh, hush, Bice!
Hush! For pity's sake!"

Gabriella Vanzi got up. She was trembling and terribly pale.

She'd heard the front door open, out there in the little hall. Her husband was coming back in.

Donna Bicetta Daddi, seeing her friend suddenly transformed like this, suddenly in control of herself again—her face had become pink, her eyes were now limpid, and there was a smile on her lips, as she went to meet her husband—was left standing there, almost annihilated.

Nothing. Yes, it was quite true what Gabriella had said.... No more turmoil, no remorse, no trace of——

And Donna Bicetta understood perfectly why her husband Romeo Daddi, had gone out of his mind.

EDGAR ALLAN POE

THE CASK OF
AMONTILLADO

*Edgar Allan Poe (1809–1849), the son of travelling actors, was an orphan
at the age of two. John and Frances Allan of Richmond, Virginia, unoffi-
cially adopted Poe, sending him to school in England and to the
University of Virginia. When Poe incurred gambling debts at university
and then engineered his own dishonourable discharge from the military
academy at West Point, the Allans disowned him. Poe turned to commercial writing to make a living, editing for newspapers in Richmond,
Philadelphia, and New York. He contributed critical and creative writings
to various papers and journals before becoming editor of the* Southern
Literary Messenger. *In 1836 Poe married his thirteen-year-old cousin,
Virginia Clemm. The following year the* Messenger *fired Poe, marking the
onset of his gradual decline into poverty and substance abuse at the same
time as the rise of his literary work to popular success. In 1845* The Raven
and Other Poems *won Poe fame both domestically and abroad. But hard
times returned for Poe in 1847 when Virginia died after a long struggle
against tuberculosis. Immersed in grief and liquor, Poe died in the
Baltimore streets in 1849, possibly of rabies, as recent medical research
suggests.*

*Poe had a foundational role in pioneering and theorizing the modern
short story. He has been credited with generating prototypes for
murder-mystery or detective fiction, science fiction, and stream-of-consciousness narratives, all from within the formal conventions outlined in
"The Importance of the Single Effect in a Prose Tale." Poe's innovations
in literary form influenced European literature via the translations of
Baudelaire, and his impression on internationally renowned writers such
as Borges and Cortázar has been central in shaping the contemporary
short story. Cortázar, for instance, has argued that "in boxing terms ... the
novel always wins on points; the short story must win by a knockout." In
the concision of its nightmarish plot, the brevity of its narrative time, and
the distinctive, passionate voice of its narrator, "The Cask of
Amontillado," first published in* Godey's Lady's Book *(November 1846),*

vividly demonstrates Poe's theories on the form and content of the genre that has ignited the twentieth century's most unusual imaginations.

The thousand injuries of Fortunato I had borne as I best could; but when he ventured upon insult, I vowed revenge. You, who so well know that nature of my soul, will not suppose, however, that I gave utterance to a threat. *At length* I would be avenged; this was a point definitely settled—but the very definitiveness with which it was resolved precluded the idea of risk. I must not only punish, but punish with impunity. A wrong is unredressed when retribution overtakes its redresser. It is equally unredressed when the avenger fails to make himself felt as such to him who has done the wrong.

It must be understood, that neither by word nor deed had I given Fortunato cause to doubt my good-will. I continued, as was my want, to smile in his face, and he did not perceive that my smile *now* was at the thought of his immolation.

He had a weak point—this Fortunato—although in other regards he was a man to be respected and even feared. He prided himself on his connoisseurship in wine. Few Italians have the true virtuoso spirit. For the most part their enthusiasm is adopted to suit the time and opportunity—to practise imposture upon the British and Austrian *millionnaires*. In painting and gemmary Fortunato, like his countrymen, was a quack—but in the matter of old wines he was sincere. In this respect I did not differ from him materially: I was skilful in the Italian vintages myself, and bought largely whenever I could.

It was about dusk, one evening during the supreme madness of the carnival season, that I encountered my friend. He accosted me with excessive warmth, for he had been drinking much. The man wore motley. He had on a tight-fitting parti-striped dress, and his head was surmounted by the conical cap and bells. I was so pleased to see him, that I thought I should never have done wringing his hand.

I sand to him: "My dear Fortunato, you are luckily met. How remarkably well you are looking to-day! But I have received a pipe[1] of what passes for Amontillado, and I have my doubts."

"How?" said he. "Amontillado? A pipe? Impossible! And in the middle of the carnival!"

"I have my doubts," I replied; "and I was silly enough to pay the full Amontillado price without consulting you in the matter. You were not to be found, and I was fearful of losing a bargain."

"Amontillado!"

"I have my doubts."

"Amontillado!"

"And I must satisfy them."

"Amontillado!"

"As you are engaged, I am on my way to Luchesi. If any one has a critical turn, it is he. He will tell me——"

"Luchesi cannot tell Amontillado from Sherry."

"And yet some fools will have it that his taste is a match for your own."

"Come, let us go."

"Whither?"

"To your vaults."

"My friend, no; I will not impose upon your good nature. I perceive you have an engagement. Luchesi——"

"I have no engagement;—come."

"My friend, no. It is not the engagement, but the severe cold with which I perceive you are afflicted. The vaults are insufferably damp. They are encrusted with nitre."

"Let us go, nevertheless. The cold is merely nothing. Amontillado! You have been imposed upon. And as for Luchesi, he cannot distinguish Sherry from Amontillado."

Thus speaking, Fortunato possessed himself of my arm. Putting on a mask of black silk, and drawing a *roquelaire*[2] closely about my person, I suffered him to hurry me to my palazzo.

There were no attendants at home; they had absconded to make merry in honor of the time. I had told them that I should not return until the morning, and had given them explicit orders not to stir from the house. These orders were sufficient, I well knew, to insure their immediate disappearance, one and all, as soon as my back was turned.

I took from their sconces two flambeaux, and giving one to Fortunato, bowed him through several suites of rooms to the archway that led into the vaults. I passed down a long and winding staircase, requesting him to be cautious as he followed. We came at length to the foot of the descent, and stood together on the damp ground of the catacombs of the Montresors.

The gait of my friend was unsteady, and the bells upon his cap jingled as he strode.

"The pipe?" said he.

"It is farther on," said I; "but observe the white web-work which gleams from these cavern walls."

He turned toward me, and looked into my eyes with two filmy orbs that distilled the rheum of intoxication.

"Nitre?" he asked, at length.

"Nitre," I replied. "How long have you had that cough?"

"Ugh! ugh! ugh!—ugh! ugh! ugh!—ugh! ugh! ugh!—ugh! ugh! ugh!—ugh! ugh! ugh!"

My poor friend found it impossible to reply for many minutes.

"It is nothing," he said, at last.

"Come," I said, with decision, "we will go back; your health is precious. You are rich, respected, admired, beloved; you are happy, as once I was. You are a man to be missed. For me it is no matter. We will go back; you will be ill, and I cannot be responsible. Besides, there is Luchesi——"

"Enough," he said; "the cough is a mere nothing; it will not kill me. I shall not die of a cough."

"True—true," I replied; "and, indeed, I had no intention of alarming you unnecessarily; but you should use all proper caution. A draught of this Medoc[3] will defend us from the damps."

Here I knocked off the neck of a bottle which I drew from a long row of its fellows that lay upon the mould.

"Drink," I said, presenting him the wine.

He raised it to his lips with a leer. He paused and nodded to me familiarly, while his bells jingled.

"I drink," he said, "to the buried that repose around us."

"And I to your long life."

He again took my arm, and we proceeded.

"These vaults," he said, "are extensive."

"The Montresors," I replied, "were a great and numerous family."

"I forgot your arms."

"A huge human foot d'or,[4] in a field azure; the foot crushes a serpent rampant[5] whose fangs are imbedded in the heel."

"And the motto?"

"*Nemo me impune lacessit.*"[6]

"Good!" he said.

The wine sparkled in his eyes and the bells jingled. My own fancy grew warm with the Medoc. We had passed through walls of piled bones, with casks and puncheons intermingling into the inmost recesses of the catacombs. I paused again, and this time I made bold to seize Fortunato by an arm above the elbow.

"The nitre!" I said; "see, it increases. It hangs like moss upon the vaults. We are below the river's bed. The drops of moisture trickle among the bones. Come, we will go back ere it is too late. Your cough——"

"It is nothing," he said; "let us go on. But first, another draught of the Medoc."

I broke and reached him a flagon of De Grâve.[7] He emptied it at a breath. His eyes flashed with a fierce light. He laughed and threw the bottle upward with a gesticulation I did not understand.

I looked at him in surprise. He repeated the movement—a grotesque one.

"You do not comprehend?" he said.

"Not, I," I replied.

"Then you are not of the brotherhood."

"How?"

"You are not of the masons."

"Yes, yes," I said; "yes, yes."

"You? Impossible! A mason?"

"A mason," I replied.

"A sign," he said.

"It is this," I answered, producing a trowel from beneath the folds of my *roquelaire*.

"You jest," he exclaimed, recoiling a few paces. "But let us proceed to the Amontillado."

"Be it so," I said, replacing the tool beneath the cloak, and again offering him my arm. He leaned upon it heavily. We continued our route in search of the Amontillado. We passed through a range of low arches, descended, passed on, and descending again, arrived at a deep crypt, in which the foulness of the air caused our flambeaux rather to glow than flame.

At the most remote end of the crypt there appeared another less spacious. Its walls had been lined with human remains, piled to the vault overhead, in the fashion of the great catacombs of Paris. Three sides of this interior crypt were still ornamented in this manner. From the fourth the bones had been thrown down, and lay promiscuously upon the earth, forming at one point a mound of some size. Within the wall thus exposed by the displacing of the bones, we perceived a still interior recess, in depth about four feet, in width three, in height six or seven. It seemed to have been constructed for no especial use within itself, but formed merely the interval between two of the colossal supports of the roof of the catacombs, and was backed by one of their circumscribing walls of solid granite.

It was in vain that Fortunato, uplifting his dull torch, endeavored to pry into the depth of the recess. Its termination the feeble light did not enable us to see.

"Proceed," I said; "herein is the Amontillado. As for Luchesi——"

"He is an ignoramus," interrupted my friend, as he stepped unsteadily forward, while I followed immediately at his heels. In an instant he had reached the extremity of the niche, and finding his progress arrested by the rock, stood stupidly bewildered. A moment more and I had fettered him to the granite. In its surface were two iron staples, distant from each other about two feet, horizontally. From one of these depended a short chain, from the other a padlock. Throwing the links about his waist, it was but the work of a few seconds to secure it. He was too much astounded to resist. Withdrawing the key I stepped back from the recess.

"Pass your hand," I said, "over the wall; you cannot help feeling the nitre. Indeed it is *very* damp. Once more let me *implore* you to return. No? Then I must positively leave you. But I must first render you all the little attentions in my power."

"The Amontillado!" ejaculated my friend, not yet recovered from his astonishment.

"True," I replied; "the Amontillado."

As I said these words I busied myself among the pile of bones of which I have before spoken. Throwing them aside, I soon uncovered a quantity of building stone and mortar. With these materials and with the aid of my trowel, I began vigorously to wall up the entrance of the niche.

I had scarcely laid the first tier of the masonry when I discovered that the intoxication of Fortunato had in a great measure worn off. The earliest indication I had of this was a low moaning cry from the depth of the recess. It was *not* the cry of a drunken man. There was then a long and obstinate silence. I laid the second tier, and the third, and the fourth; and then I heard the furious vibrations of the chain. The noise lasted for several minutes, during which, that I might hearken to it with the more satisfaction, I ceased my labors and sat down upon the bones. When at last the clanking subsided, I resumed the trowel, and finished without interruption the fifth, the sixth, and the seventh tier. The wall was now nearly upon a level with my breast. I again paused, and holding the flambeaux over the masonwork, threw feeble rays upon the figure within.

A succession of loud and shrill screams, bursting suddenly from the throat of the chained form, seemed to thrust me violently back. For a brief moment I hesitated—I trembled. Unsheathing my rapier, I began to grope with it about the recess; but the thought of an instant reassured me. I placed my hand upon the solid fabric of the catacombs, and felt satisfied. I reapproached the wall. I replied to the yells of him who clamored. I reechoed—I aided—I surpassed them in volume and in strength. I did this, and the clamorer grew still.

It was now midnight, and my task was drawing to a close. I had completed the eighth, the ninth, and the tenth tier. I had finished a portion of the last and the eleventh; there remained but a single stone to be fitted and plastered in. I struggled with its weight; I placed it partially in its destined position. But now there came from out the niche a low laugh that erected the hairs upon my head. It was succeeded by a sad voice, which I had difficulty in recognizing as that of the noble Fortunato. The voice said—

"Ha! ha! ha!—he! he!—a very good joke indeed—an excellent jest. We will have many a rich laugh about it at the palazzo—he! he! he!—over our wine—he! he! he!"

"The Amontillado!" I said.

"He! he! he!—he! he! he!—yes, the Amontillado. But is it not getting late? Will not they be awaiting us at the palazzo, the Lady Fortunato and the rest? Let us be gone."

"Yes," I said, "let us be gone."

"*For the love of God, Montresor!*"

"Yes," I said, "for the love of God!"

But to these words I hearkened in vain for a reply. I grew impatient. I called aloud:

"Fortunato!"

No answer. I called again:

"Fortunato!"

No answer still, I thrust a torch through the remaining aperture and let it fall within. There came forth in return only a jingling of the bells. My heart grew sick—on account of the dampness of the catacombs. I hastened to make an end of my labor. I forced the last stone into its position; I plastered it up. Against the new masonry I re-erected the old rampart of bones. For the half of a century no mortal has disturbed them. *In pace requiescat!*

ENDNOTES

1. A French derivative. A large cask or keg.
2. A short cloak.
3. Correctly, "Médoc," the French claret.
4. Of gold.
5. "Rampant" here means "rearing up."
6. "No one attacks (or wounds) me with impunity"; the motto of the royal arms of Scotland.
7. Correctly, "Graves," the light Bordeaux wine.

LEON ROOKE

A Bolt of White Cloth

Leon Rooke (b. 1934), novelist, short-story writer, playwright, and editor,
was born in Roanoke Rapids, North Carolina, and has lived in Canada
for most of his writing career. His fiction relies strongly on voice and
often challenges literary convention.

Rooke has published sixteen short-story collections, including The
Love Parlour *(1977),* Cry Evil *(1980),* Death Suite *(1981),* A Bolt of
White Cloth *(1984),* Who Do You Love? *(1990),* The Happiness of
Others *(1991) and* Oh! Twenty-Seven Stories *(1997). Nearly three hun-*
dred stories have been published, and his work appears in numerous
national and international anthologies, including Best Canadian Stories,
Best American Short Stories, O. Henry Prize Stories, *and* Pushcart Prize
Stories. *He has been writer in residence at more than a dozen U.S. and*
Canadian universities. In 1981 he was awarded the Canada-Australia
Literary Prize for overall body of work, and in 1983 he won the
Governor General's Literary Award for his novel Shakespeare's Dog.
Other novels include Fat Woman *and* A Good Baby. *Rooke has also*
coedited with John Metcalf six annual collections of Canadian fiction,
including Best Canadian Stories, The MacMillan Anthology, *and* Best
Canadian Short Fiction. *He lives in Eden Mills, Ontario, where he and his*
wife, Constance, began and continue to help mount the annual Eden Mills
Writers' Festival.

A man came by our road carrying an enormous bolt of white cloth on his back.
Said he was from the East. Said whoever partook of this cloth would come to
know true happiness. Innocence without heartbreak, he said, if that person
proved worthy. My wife fingered his cloth, having in mind something for new
curtains. It was good quality, she said. Beautifully woven, of a fine, light texture, and you certainly couldn't argue with the color.

"How much is it?" she asked.

"Before I tell you that," the man said, "you must tell me truthfully if
you've ever suffered."

"Oh, I've suffered," she said. "I've known suffering of some description every day of my natural life."

I was standing over by the toolshed, with a big smile. My wife is a real joker, who likes nothing better than pulling a person's leg. She's known hardships, this and that upheaval, but nothing I would call down-and-out suffering. Mind you, I don't speak for her. I wouldn't pretend to speak for another person.

This man with the bolt of cloth, however, he clearly had no sense of my wife's brand of humor. She didn't get an itch of a smile out of him. He kept the cloth neatly balanced on his shoulder, wincing a little from the weight and from however far he'd had to carry it, staring hard and straight at my wife the whole time she fooled with him, as if he hoped to peer clear through to her soul. His eyes were dark and brooding and hollowed out some. He was like no person either my wife or me had ever seen before.

"Yes," he said, "but suffering of what kind?"

"Worse than I hope forever to carry, I'll tell you that," my wife said. "But why are you asking me these questions? I like your cloth and if the price is right I mean to buy it."

"You can only buy my cloth with love," he said.

We began right then to understand that he was some kind of oddity. He was not like anybody we'd ever seen and he didn't come from around here. He'd come from a place we'd never heard of, and if that was the East, or wherever, then he was welcome to it.

"Love?" she said. "Love? There's love and there's love, mister. What kind are you talking about?" She hitched a head my way, rolling her eyes, as if to indicate that if it was passionate love he was talking about then he'd first have to do something with me. He'd have to get me off my simmer and onto full boil. That's what she was telling him, with this mischief in her eyes.

I put down my pitchfork about here, and strolled nearer. I liked seeing my wife dealing with difficult situations. I didn't want to miss anything. My life with that woman has been packed with the unusual. Unusual circumstances, she calls them. Any time she's ever gone out anywhere without me, whether for a day or an hour or for five minutes, she's come back with whopping good stories about what she's seen and heard and what's happened to her. She's come back with reports on these unusual circumstances, these little adventures in which so many people have done so many extraordinary things or behaved in such fabulous or foolish ways. So what was rare this time, I thought, was that it had come visiting. She hadn't had to go out and find it.

"Hold these," my wife told me. And she put this washtub of clothes in my hands, and went back to hanging wet pieces on the line, which is what she'd been doing when this man with the bolt of cloth ventured up into our yard.

"Love," she told him. "You tell me what kind I need, if I'm to buy that cloth. I got good ears and I'm listening."

The man watched her stick clothespins in her mouth, slap out a good wide sheet, and string it up. He watched her hang two of these, plus a mess of towels, and get her mouth full again before he spoke. He looked about the unhappiest I've ever seen any man look. He didn't have any joy in him. I wondered why he didn't put down that heavy bolt of cloth, and why he didn't step around into a spot of shade. The sun was lick-killing bright in that yard. I was worried he'd faint.

"The ordinary kind," he said. "Your ordinary kind of love will buy this cloth."

My wife flapped her wash and laughed. He was really tickling her. She was having herself a wonderful time.

"What's ordinary?" she said. "I've never known no ordinary love."

He jumped right in. He got excited just for a second.

"The kind such as might exist between the closest friends," he said. "The kind such as might exist between a man and his wife or between parents and children or for that matter the love a boy might have for his dog. That kind of love."

"I've got that," she said. "I've had all three. Last year this time I had me a fourth, but it got run over. Up on the road there, by the tall trees, by a man in a red car who didn't even stop."

"That would have been your cat," he said. "I don't know much about cats."

I put down the washtub. My wife let her arms drop. We looked at him, wondering how he knew about that cat. Then I laughed, for I figured someone down the road must have told him of my wife's mourning over that cat. She'd dug it a grave under the grapevine and said sweet words over it. She sorely missed that cat.

"What's wrong with loving cats?" she asked him. "Or beasts of the fields? I'm surprised at you."

The man shifted his burden and worked one shoe into the ground. He stared off at the horizon. He looked like he knew he'd said something he shouldn't.

She pushed me out of the way. She wanted to get nearer to him. She had something more to say.

"Now listen to me," she said. "I've loved lots of things in my life. Lots and lots. "Him!" she said (pointing at me), "it" (pointing at our house), "them!" (pointing to the flower beds), "that!" (pointing to the sky), "those" (pointing to the woods), "this" (pointing to the ground)—"practically everything! There isn't any of it I've hated, and not much I've been indifferent to. Including cats. So put that in your pipe and smoke it."

Then swooping up her arms and laughing hard, making it plain she bore no grudge but wasn't just fooling.

Funny thing was, hearing her say it, I felt the same way. It, them, that, those—they were all beautiful. I couldn't deny it was love I was feeling.

The man with the cloth had turned each way she'd pointed. He'd staggered a time or two but he'd kept up. In fact, it struck me that he'd got a little ahead of her. That he knew where her arm was next going. Some trickle of pleasure was showing in his face. And something else was happening, something I'd never seen. He had his face lifted up to this burning sun. It was big and orange, that sun, and scorching-hot, but he was staring smack into it. He wasn't blinking or squinting. His eyes were wide open.

Madness or miracle, I couldn't tell which.

He strode over to a parcel of good grass.

"I believe you mean it," he said. "How much could you use?"

He placed the bolt of white cloth down on the grass and pulled out shiny scissors from his back pocket.

"I bet he's blind," I whispered to my wife. "I bet he's got false eyes."

My wife shushed me. She wasn't listening. She had her excitement hat on; her unusual circumstances look. He was offering free cloth for love, ordinary love, and she figured she'd go along with the gag.

How much?

"Oh," she said, "maybe eight yards. Maybe ten. It depends on how many windows I end up doing, plus what hang I want, plus the pleating I'm after."

"You mean to make these curtains yourself?" he asked. He was already down on his knees, smoothing the bolt. Getting set to roll it out.

"Why, sure," she said. "I don't know who else would do it for me. I don't know who else I would ask."

He nodded soberly, not thinking about it. "That's so," he said casually. "Mend your own fences first." He was perspiring in the sun, and dishevelled, as though he'd been on the road a long time. His shoes had big holes in them and you could see the blistered soles of his feet, but he had an air of exhilaration now. His hair fell down over his eyes and he shoved the dark locks back. I got the impression that some days he went a long time between customers; that he didn't find cause to give away this cloth every day.

He got a fair bit unrolled. It certainly did look like prime goods, once you saw it spread out on the grass in that long expanse.

"It's so pretty!" my wife said. "Heaven help me, but I think it is prettier than grass!"

"It's pretty, all right," he said. "It's a wing-dinger. Just tell me when to stop," he said. "Just shout yoo-hoo."

"Hold up a minute," she said. "I don't want to get greedy. I don't want you rolling off more than we can afford."

"You can afford it," he said.

He kept unrolling. He was up past the well house by now, whipping it off fast, though the bolt didn't appear to be getting any smaller. My wife had both hands up over her mouth. Half of her wanted to run into the house and get her purse so she could pay; the other half wanted to stay and watch this man unfurl his beautiful cloth. She whipped around to me, all agitated.

"I believe he means it," she said. "He means us to have this cloth. What do I do?"

I shook my head. This was her territory. It was the kind of adventure constant to her nature and necessary to her well-being.

"Honey," I said, "you deal with it."

The sun was bright over everything. It was whipping-hot. There wasn't much wind but I could hear the clothes flapping on the line. A woodpecker had himself a tree somewhere and I could hear him pecking. The sky was wavy blue. The trees seemed to be swaying.

He was up by the front porch now, still unrolling. It surprised us both that he could move so fast.

"Yoo-hoo," my wife said. It was no more than a peep, the sound you might make if a butterfly lands on your ear.

"Wait," he said. "One thing. One question I meant to ask. All this talk of love, your it, your those and them, it slipped my mind."

"Let's hear it," my wife said. "Ask away." It seemed to me that she spoke out of a trance. That she was as dazzled as I was.

"You two got no children," he said. "Why is that? You're out here on this nice farm, and no children to your name. Why is that?"

We hadn't expected this query from him. It did something to the light in the yard and how we saw it. It was as if some giant dark bird had fluttered between us and the sun. Without knowing it, we sidled closer to each other. We fumbled for the other's hand. We stared off every which way. No one on our road had asked that question in a long, long time; they hadn't asked it in some years.

"We're not able," we said. Both of us spoke at the same time. It seemed to me that it was my wife's voice which carried; mine was some place down in my chest, and dropping, as if it meant to crawl on the ground.

"We're not able," we said. That time it came out pure, without any grief to bind it. It came out the way we long ago learned how to say it.

"Oh," he said. "I see." He mumbled something else. He kicked the ground and took a little walk back and forth. He seemed angry, though not at us. "Wouldn't you know it?" he said. "Wouldn't you know it?"

He swore a time or two. He kicked the ground. He surely didn't like it.

"We're over that now," my wife said. "We're past that caring."

"I bet you are," he said. "You're past that little misfortune."

He took to unrolling his bolt again, working with his back to the sun. Down on his knees, scrambling, smoothing the material. Sweating and huffing. He was past the front porch now, and still going, getting on toward that edge where the high weeds grew.

"About here, do you think?" he asked.

He'd rolled off about fifty yards.

My wife and I slowly shook our heads, not knowing what to think.

"Say the word," he told us. "I can give you more if more is what you want."

"I'd say you were giving us too much," my wife said. "I'd say we don't need nearly that much."

"Never mind that," he said. "I'm feeling generous today."

He nudged the cloth with his fingers and rolled off a few yards more. He would have gone on unwinding his cloth had the weeds not stopped him. He stood and looked back over the great length he had unwound.

"Looks like a long white road, don't it?" he said. "You could walk that road and your feet never get dirty."

My wife clenched my hand; it was what we'd both been thinking.

SnipSnipSnip. He began snipping. His scissors raced over the material. SnipSnipSnip. The cloth was sheared clear and clean of his bolt, yet it seemed to me the size of that bolt hadn't lessened any. My wife saw it too.

"He's got cloth for all eternity," she said. "He could unroll that cloth till doomsday."

The man laughed. We were whispering this, but way up by the weeds he heard us. "There's doom and there's doom," he said. "Which doomsday?"

I had the notion he'd gone through more than one. That he knew the picture from both sides.

"It is smart as grass," he said. "Smarter. It never needs watering." He chuckled at that, spinning both arms. Dancing a little. "You could make nighties out of this," he said. "New bedsheets. Transform your whole bedroom."

My wife made a face. She wasn't too pleased, talking nighties with another man.

Innocence without heartbreak, I thought. That's what we're coming to.

He nicely rolled up the cloth he'd sheared off and presented it to my wife. "I hope you like it," he said. "No complaints yet. Maybe you can make yourself a nice dress as well. Maybe two or three. Make him some shirts. I think you'll find there's plenty here."

"Goodness, it's light," she said.

"Not if you've been carrying it long as I have," he said. He pulled a blue bandanna from his pocket and wiped his face and neck. He ran his hand through his hair and slicked it back. He looked up at the sky. His dark eyes seemed to have cleared up some. They looked less broody now. "Gets hot," he said, "working in this sun. But a nice day. I'm glad I found you folks home."

"Oh, we're most always home," my wife said.

I had to laugh at that. My wife is forever gallivanting over the countryside, checking up on this person and that, taking them her soups and jams and breads.

"We're homebodies, us two."

She kept fingering the cloth and sighing over it. She held it up against her cheek and with her eyes closed rested herself on it. The man hoisted his own bolt back on his shoulder; he seemed ready to be going. I looked at my wife's closed lids, at the soft look she had.

I got trembly, fearful of what might happen if that cloth didn't work out.

"Now look," I said to him, "what's wrong with this cloth? Is it going to rot inside a week? Tomorrow is some other stranger going to knock on our door saying we owe him a hundred or five hundred dollars for this cloth? Mister, I don't understand you," I said.

He hadn't bothered with me before; now he looked me dead in the eye. "I can't help being a stranger," he said. "If you never set eyes on me before, I guess that's what I would have to be. Don't you like strangers? Don't you trust them?"

My wife jumped in. Her face was fiery, like she thought I had wounded him. "We like strangers just fine," she said. "We've helped out many a-one. No, I can't say our door has ever been closed to whoever it is comes by. Strangers can sit in our kitchen just the same as our friends."

He smiled at her but kept his stern look for me. "As to your questions," he said, "you're worried about the golden goose, I can see that. Fair enough. No, your cloth will not rot. It will not shred, fade, or tear. Nor will it ever need cleaning, either. This cloth requires no upkeep whatsoever. Though a sound heart helps. A sweet disposition, too. Innocence without heartbreak, as I told you. And your wife, if it's her making the curtains or making herself a dress, she will find it to be an amazingly easy cloth to work with. It will practically do the job itself. No, I don't believe you will ever find you have any reason to complain of the quality of that cloth."

My wife had it up to her face again. She had her face sunk in it.

"Goodness," she said. "it's soft! It smells so fresh. It's like someone singing a song to me."

The man laughed. "It is soft," he said. "But it can't sing a note, or has never been known to."

It was my wife singing. She had this little hum under her breath.

"This is the most wonderful cloth in the world," she said.

He nodded. "I can't argue with you on that score," he said. Then he turned again to me. "I believe your wife is satisfied," he said. "But if you have any doubts, if you're worried someone is going to knock on your door tomorrow asking you for a hundred or five hundred dollars, I suppose I could write you up a guarantee. I could give you a PAID IN FULL."

He was making me feel ashamed of myself. They both were. "No, no," I said, "if she's satisfied then I am. And I can see she's tickled pink. No, I beg your pardon. I meant no offense."

"No offense taken," he said.

But his eyes clouded a token. He gazed off at our road and up along the stand of trees and his eyes kept roaming until they snagged the sun. He kept his eyes there, unblinking, open, staring at the sun. I could see the red orbs reflected in his eyes.

"There is one thing," he said.

I caught my breath and felt my wife catch hers. The hitch? A hitch, after all? Coming so late?

We waited.

He shuffled his feet. He brought out his bandanna and wiped his face again. He stared at the ground.

"Should you ever stop loving," he said, "you shall lose this cloth and all else. You shall wake up one morning and it and all else will no longer be where you left it. It will all be gone and you will not know where you are. You will not know what to do with yourself. You will wish you had never been born."

My wife's eyes went saucer-size.

He had us in some kind of spell.

Hocus-pocus, I thought. He is telling us some kind of hocus-pocus. Yet I felt my skin shudder; I felt the goose bumps rise.

"That's it?" my wife said. "That's the only catch?"

He shrugged. "That's it," he said. "Not much, is it? Not a whisper of menace for a pair such as yourselves."

My wife's eyes were gauzed over; there was a wetness in them.

"Hold on," she said. "Don't you be leaving yet. Hold this, honey."

She put the cloth in my arms. Then she hastened over to the well, pitched the bucket down, and drew it up running over with fresh water.

"Here," she said, coming back with a good dipperful. "Here's a nice drink of cool water. You need it on a day like this."

The man drank. He held the dipper in both hands, with the tips of his fingers, and drained the dipper dry, then wiped his chin with the back of his hand.

"I did indeed," he said. "That's very tasty water. I thank you."

"That's good water," she said. "That well has been here lo a hundred years. You could stay on for supper," she said. "It's getting on toward that time and I have a fine stew on the stove, with plenty to spare."

"That's kind of you," he said back, "and I'm grateful. But I'd best pass on up your road while there's still daylight left, and see who else might have need of this cloth."

My wife is not normally a demonstrative woman, not in public. Certainly not with strangers. You could have knocked me over with a feather when she up and kissed him full on the mouth, with a nice hug to boot.

"There's payment," she said, "if our money's no good."

He blushed, trying to hide his pleasure. It seemed to me she had him wrapped around her little finger ... or the other way around.

"You kiss like a woman," he said. "Like one who knows what kissing is for, and can't hardly stop herself."

It was my wife's turn to blush.

I took hold of her hand and held her down to grass, because it seemed to me another kiss or two and she'd fly right away with him.

He walked across the yard and up by the well house, leaving by the same route he had come. Heading for the road. At the turn, he spun around and waved.

"You could try the Hopkins place!" my wife called. "There's a fat woman down that road got a sea of troubles. She could surely use some of that cloth."

He smiled and again waved. Then we saw his head and his bolt of white cloth bobbing along the weeds as he took the dips and rises in the road. Then he went on out of sight.

"There's that man with some horses down that road!" my wife called. "You be careful of him!"

It seemed we heard some sound come back, but whether it was his we couldn't say.

My wife and I stood a long time in the yard, me holding the dipper and watching her, while she held her own bolt of cloth in her arms, staring off to where he'd last been.

Then she sighed dreamily and went inside.

I went on down to the barn and looked after the animals. Getting my feeding done. I talked a spell to them. Talking to animals is soothing to me, and they like it too. They pretend to stare at the walls or the floor as they're munching their feed down, but I know they listen to me. We had us an unusual circumstances chat. "That man with the cloth," I said. "Maybe you can tell me what you make of him."

In no time at all I heard my wife excitedly calling me. She was standing out on the back doorstep, with this incredulous look.

"I've finished," she said. "I've finished the windows. Nine windows. It beats me how."

I started up to the house. Her voice was all shaky. Her face flushed, flinging her arms about. Then she got this new look on.

"Wait!" she said. "Stay there! Give me ten minutes!"

And she flung herself back inside, banging the door. I laughed. It always gave me a kick how she ordered me around.

I got the milk pail down under the cow. Before I'd touched and drained all four teats she was calling again.

"Come look, come look, oh come look!"

She was standing in the open doorway, with the kitchen to her back. Behind her, through the windows, I could see the streak of a red sunset and how it lit up the swing of trees. But I wasn't looking there. I was looking at her. Looking and swallowing hard and trying to remember how a body produced human speech. I had never thought of white as a color she could wear. White, it pales her some. It leaves her undefined and washes out what parts I like best. But she looked beautiful now. In her new dress she struck me down to my bootstraps. She made my chest break.

"Do you like it?" she said.

I went running up to her. I was up against her, hugging her and lifting her before she'd even had a chance to get set. I'd never held on so tightly or been so tightly held back.

Truth is, it was the strangest thing. Like we were both so innocent we hadn't yet shot up out of new ground.

"Come see the curtains," she whispered. "Come see the new sheets. Come see what else I've made. You'll see it all. You'll see how our home has been transformed."

I crept inside. There was something holy about it. About it and about us and about those rooms and the whole wide world. Something radiant. Like you had to put your foot down easy and hold it down or you'd float on up.

"That's it," she said. "That's how I feel too."

That night in bed, trying to figure it out, we wondered how Ella Mae down the road had done. How the people all along our road had made out.

"No worry," my wife said. "That man will have found a bonanza around here. There's heaps of decent people in this neck of the woods."

"Wonder where he is now?" we said.

"Wonder where he goes next?"

"Where he gets that cloth?"

"Who he is?"

We couldn't get to sleep, wondering about that.

SINCLAIR ROSS

THE PAINTED DOOR

Sinclair Ross (1908–1996) grew up in Saskatchewan, north of Prince Albert, and spent his early career working for the Union Bank of Canada. In 1933 he moved to Winnipeg. In 1934 he published his first story after winning third prize in a writers' competition, and during the war years, when he was in the army, he published several more short stories. His fiction is set in his own prairie time and place, a setting that is integral to the development of the story—the drought, the Depression, and the hardship and poverty of the plains during the 1930s serve as metaphors for twentieth-century loneliness, alienation, and struggle. Margaret Laurence wrote of his stories in The Lamp and Other Stories *(1968) that "the outer situation always mirrors the inner. The emptiness of the landscape, the bleakness of the land, reflect the inability of these people to touch one another with assurance and gentleness." "The Painted Door," drawn from this collection, is the story of a lonely wife who makes a tragic decision while isolated with a handsome neighbour during a blizzard. The tale is told from a woman's point of view, as are many of Ross's stories, and is a carefully crafted weave of setting, action, and character.*

In 1941 Sinclair Ross published his first novel, As For Me and My House, *which has become a classic of Canadian literature, and in 1958 published his second,* The Well. *Retiring in 1968, he moved to Athens, Greece, and then to Spain, where he remained until 1980, when he returned to Canada. By the time of his return, Ross had four novels to his credit, including* Sawbones Memorial *(1970). Another collection of stories,* The Race and Other Stories, *was published in 1982. Sinclair Ross spent the last years of his life in a hospital in Vancouver, a victim of Parkinson's Disease. He belongs to the generation of Canadian prairie writers that precedes Robert Kroetsch, Margaret Laurence, and Rudy Wiebe. Ross's characters reflect an awareness of their own insignificance in the face of "man's predicament as a finite being in a world in which he can achieve only limited understanding, and in a life over which he has only limited control."*

Straight across the hills it was five miles from John's farm to his father's. But in winter, with the roads impassable, a team had to make a wide detour and skirt the hills, so that from five the distance was more than trebled to seventeen.

"I think I'll walk," John said at breakfast to his wife. "The drifts in the hills wouldn't hold a horse, but they'll carry me all right. If I leave early I can spend a few hours helping him with his chores, and still be back by suppertime."

Moodily she went to the window, and thawing a clear place in the frost with her breath, stood looking across the snowswept farmyard to the huddle of stables and sheds. "There was a double wheel around the moon last night," she countered presently. "You said yourself we could expect a storm. It isn't right to leave me here alone. Surely I'm as important as your father."

He glanced up uneasily, then drinking off his coffee tried to reassure her. "But there's nothing to be afraid of—even if it does start to storm. You won't need to go near the stable. Everything's fed and watered now to last till night. I'll be back at the latest by seven or eight."

She went on blowing against the frosted pane, carefully elongating the clear place until it was oval-shaped and symmetrical. He watched her a moment or two longer, then more insistently repeated, "I say you won't need to go near the stable. Everything's fed and watered, and I'll see that there's plenty of wood in. That will be all right, won't it?"

"Yes—of course—I heard you—" It was a curiously cold voice now, as if the words were chilled by their contact with the frosted pane. "Plenty to eat— plenty of wood to keep me warm—what more could a woman ask for?"

"But he's an old man—living there all alone. What is it, Ann? You're not like yourself this morning."

She shook her head without turning. "Pay no attention to me. Seven years a farmer's wife—it's time I was used to staying alone."

Slowly the clear place on the glass enlarged: oval, then round, then oval again. The sun was risen above the frost mists now, so keen and hard a glitter on the snow that instead of warmth its rays seemed shedding cold. One of the two-year-old colts that had cantered away when John turned the horses out for water stood covered with rime at the stable door again, head down and body hunched, each breath a little plume of steam against the frosty air. She shivered, but did not turn. In the clear, bitter light the long white miles of prairie landscape seemed a region strangely alien to life. Even the distant farmsteads she could see served only to intensify a sense of isolation. Scattered across the face of so vast and bleak a wilderness it was difficult to conceive them as a testimony of human hardihood and endurance. Rather they seemed futile, lost. Rather they seemed to cower before the implacability of snow-swept earth and clear pale sun-chilled sky.

And when at last she turned from the window there was a brooding stillness in her face as if she had recognized this mastery of snow and cold. It troubled John. "If you're really afraid," he yielded, "I won't go today. Lately it's been so cold, that's all. I just wanted to make sure he's all right in case we do have a storm."

"I know—I'm not really afraid." She was putting in a fire now, and he could no longer see her face. "Pay no attention to me. It's ten miles there and back, so you'd better get started."

"You ought to know by now I wouldn't stay away," he tried to brighten her. "No matter how it stormed. Twice a week before we were married I never missed—and there were bad blizzards that winter too."

He was a slow, unambitious man, content with his farm and cattle, naïvely proud of Ann. He had been bewildered by it once, her caring for a dull-witted fellow like him; then assured at last of her affection he had relaxed against it gratefully, unsuspecting it might ever be less constant than his own. Even now, listening to the restless brooding in her voice, he felt only a quick, unformulated kind of pride that after seven years his absence for a day should still concern her. While she, his trust and earnestness controlling her again:

"I know. It's just that sometimes when you're away I get lonely.... There's a long cold tramp in front of you. You'll let me fix a scarf around your face."

He nodded. "And on my way I'll drop in at Steven's place. Maybe he'll come over tonight for a game of cards. You haven't seen anybody but me for the last two weeks."

She glanced up sharply, then busied herself clearing the table. "It will mean another two miles if you do. You're going to be cold and tired enough as it is. When you're gone I think I'll paint the kitchen woodwork. White this time—you remember we got the paint last fall. It's going to make the room a lot lighter. I'll be too busy to find the day long."

"I will though," he insisted, "and if a storm gets up you'll feel safer, knowing that he's coming. That's what you need, Ann—someone to talk to besides me."

She stood at the stove motionless a moment, then turned to him uneasily. "Will you shave then, John—now—before you go?"

He glanced at her questioningly, and avoiding his eyes she tried to explain, "I mean—he may be here before you're back—and you won't have a chance then."

"But it's only Steven—he's seen me like this—"

"He'll be shaved, though—that's what I mean—and I'd like you too to spend a little time on yourself."

He stood up, stroking the heavy stubble on his chin. "Maybe I should all right, but it makes the skin too tender. Especially when I've got to face the wind."

She nodded and began to help him dress, bringing heavy socks and a big woollen sweater from the bedroom, wrapping a scarf around his face and forehead. "I'll tell Steven to come early," he said, as he went out. "In time for supper. Likely there'll be chores for me to do, so if I'm not back by six don't wait."

From the bedroom window she watched him nearly a mile along the road. The fire had gone down when at last she turned away, and already through the house there was an encroaching chill. A blaze sprang up again when the drafts were opened, but as she went on clearing the table her movements were furtive and constrained. It was the silence weighing upon her—the frozen silence of the bitter fields and sun-chilled sky—lurking outside as if alive, relentlessly in wait, mile-deep between her now and John. She listened to it, suddenly tense, motionless. The fire crackled and the clock ticked. Always it was there. "I'm a fool," she whispered hoarsely, rattling the dishes in defiance, going back to the stove to put in another fire. "Warm and safe—I'm a fool. It's a good chance when he's away to paint. The day will go quickly. I won't have time to brood."

Since November now the paint had been waiting warmer weather. The frost in the walls on a day like this would crack and peel it as it dried, but she needed something to keep her hands occupied, something to stave off the gathering cold and loneliness. "First of all," she said aloud, opening the paint and mixing it with a little turpentine, "I must get the house warmer. Fill up the stove and open the oven door so that all the heat comes out. Wad something along the window sills to keep out the drafts. Then I'll feel brighter. It's the cold that depresses."

She moved briskly, performing each little task with careful and exaggerated absorption, binding her thoughts to it, making it a screen between herself and the surrounding snow and silence. But when the stove was filled and the windows sealed it was more difficult again. Above the quiet, steady swishing of her brush against the bedroom door the clock began to tick. Suddenly her movements became precise, deliberate, her posture self-conscious, as if someone had entered the room and were watching her. It was the silence again, aggressive, however. The fire spit and crackled at it. Still it was there. "I'm a fool," she repeated. "All farmers' wives have to stay alone. I mustn't give in this way. I mustn't brood. A few hours now and they'll be here."

The sound of her voice reassured her. She went on: "I'll get them a good supper—and for coffee tonight after cards bake some of the little cakes with raisins that he likes.... Just three of us, so I'll watch, and let John play. It's better with four, but at least we can talk. That's all I need—someone to talk to. John never talks. He's stronger—he doesn't understand. But he likes Steven— no matter what the neighbours say. Maybe he'll have him come again, and some other young people too. It's what we need, both of us, to help keep young ourselves.... And then before we know it we'll be into March. It's cold

still in March sometimes, but you never mind the same. At least you're beginning to think about spring."

She began to think about it now. Thoughts that outstripped her words,
that left her alone again with herself and the ever-lurking silence. Eager and
hopeful first; then clenched, rebellious, lonely. Windows open, sun and
thawing earth again, the urge of growing, living things. Then the days that
began in the morning at half-past four and lasted till ten at night; the meals at
which John gulped his food and scarcely spoke a word; the brute-tired stupid
eyes he turned on her if ever she mentioned town or visiting.

For spring was drudgery again. John never hired a man to help him. We
wanted a mortgage-free farm; then a new house and pretty clothes for her.
Sometimes, because with the best of crops it was going to take so long to pay
off anyway, she wondered whether they mightn't better let the mortgage wait a
little. Before they were worn out, before their best years were gone. It was
something of life she wanted, not just a house and furniture; something of
John, not pretty clothes when she would be too old to wear them. But John of
course couldn't understand. To him it seemed only right that she should have
the clothes—only right that he, fit for nothing else, should slave away fifteen
hours a day to give them to her. There was in his devotion a baffling, insur-
mountable humility that made him feel the need of sacrifice. And when his
muscles ached, when his feet dragged stolidly with weariness, then it seemed
that in some measure at least he was making amends for his big hulking body
and simple mind. That by his sacrifice he succeeded only in the extinction of
his personality never occurred to him. Year after year their lives went on in the
same little groove. He drove his horses in the field; she milked the cow and
hoed potatoes. By dint of his drudgery he saved a few months' wages, added a
few dollars more each fall to his payments on the mortgage; but the only real
difference that it all made was to deprive her of his companionship, to make
him a little duller, older, uglier than he might otherwise have been. He never
saw their lives objectively. To him it was not what he actually accomplished by
means of the sacrifice that mattered, but the sacrifice itself, the gesture—something done for her sake.

And she, understanding, kept her silence. In such a gesture, however futile,
there was a graciousness not to be shattered lightly.

"John" she would begin sometimes, "you're doing too much. Get a man
to help you—just for a month—" but smiling down at her he would answer
simply, "I don't mind. Look at the hands on me. They're made for work."
While in his voice there would be a stalwart ring to tell her that by her
thoughtfulness she had made him only the more resolved to serve her, to prove
his devotion and fidelity.

They were useless such thoughts. She knew. It was his very devotion that
made them useless, that forbade her to rebel. Yet over and over, sometimes

hunched still before their bleakness, sometimes her brush making swift sharp strokes to pace the chafe and rancour that they brought, she persisted in them.

This now, the winter, was their slack season. She could sleep sometimes till eight, and John till seven. They could linger over their meals a little, read, play cards, go visiting the neighbours. It was the time to relax, to indulge and enjoy themselves; but instead, fretful and impatient, they kept on waiting for the spring. They were compelled now, not by labour, but by the spirit of labour. A spirit that pervaded their lives and brought with idleness a sense of guilt. Sometimes they did sleep late, sometimes they did play cards, but always uneasily, always reproached by the thought of more important things that might be done. When John got up at five to attend to the fire he wanted to stay up and go out to the stable. When he sat down to a meal he hurried his food and pushed his chair away again, from habit, from sheer work-instinct, even though it was only to put more wood in the stove, or go down cellar to cut up beets and turnips for the cows.

And anyway, sometimes she asked herself, why sit trying to talk with a man who never talked? Why talk when there was nothing to talk about but crops and cattle, the weather and the neighbours? The neighbours, too—why go visiting them when still it was the same—crops and cattle, the weather and the other neighbours?

Why go to the dances in the schoolhouse to sit among the older women, one of them now, married seven years, or to waltz with the work-bent tired old farmers to a squeaky fiddle tune? Once she had danced with Steven six or seven times in the evening, and they had talked about it for as many months. It was easier to stay at home. John never danced or enjoyed himself. He was always uncomfortable in his good suit and shoes. He didn't like shaving in the cold weather oftener than once or twice a week. It was easier to stay at home, to stand at the window staring out across the bitter fields, to count the days and look forward to another spring.

But now, alone with herself in the winter silence, she saw the spring for what it really was. This spring—next spring—all the springs and summers still to come. While they grew old, while their bodies warped, while their minds kept shrivelling dry and empty like their lives. "I mustn't," she said aloud again. "I married him—and he's a good man. I mustn't keep on this way. It will be noon before long, and then time to think about supper.... Maybe he'll come early—and as soon as John is finished at the stable we can all play cards."

It was getting cold again, and she left her painting to put in more wood. But this time the warmth spread slowly. She pushed a mat up to the outside door, and went back to the window to pat down the woollen shirt that was wadded along the sill. Then she paced a few times round the room, then poked the fire and rattled the stove lids, then paced again. The fire crackled, the clock ticked. The silence now seemed more intense than ever, seemed to have reached a pitch where it faintly moaned. She began to pace on tiptoe, listening, her shoulders drawn together, not realizing for a while that it was the wind she heard, thin-strained and whimpering through the eaves.

Then she wheeled to the window, and with quick short breaths thawed the frost to see again. The glitter was gone. Across the drifts sped swift and snake-like little tongues of snow. She could not follow them, where they sprang from, or where they disappeared. It was as if all across the yard the snow was shivering awake—roused by the warnings of the wind to hold itself in readiness for the impending storm. The sky had become a sombre, whitish grey. It, too, as if in readiness, had shifted and lay close to earth. Before her as she watched a mane of powdery snow reared up breast-high against the darker background of the stable, tossed for a moment angrily, and then subsided again as if whipped down to obedience and restraint. But another followed, more reckless and impatient than the first. Another reeled and dashed itself against the window where she watched. Then ominously for a while there were only the angry little snakes of snow. The wind rose, creaking the troughs that were wired beneath the eaves. In the distance, sky and prairie now were merged into one another linelessly. All round her it was gathering; already in its press and whimpering there strummed a boding of eventual fury. Again she saw a mane of snow spring up, so dense and high this time that all the sheds and stables were obscured. Then others followed, whirling fiercely out of hand; and, when at last they cleared, the stables seemed in dimmer outline than before. It was the snow beginning, long lancet shafts of it, straight from the north, borne almost level by the straining wind. "He'll be there soon," she whispered, "and coming home it will be in his back. He'll leave again right away. He saw the double wheel—he knows the kind of storm there'll be."

She went back to her painting. For a while it was easier, all her thoughts half-anxious ones of John in the blizzard, struggling his way across the hills; but petulantly again she soon began, "I knew we were going to have a storm— I told him so—but it doesn't matter what I say. Big stubborn fool—he goes his own way anyway. It doesn't matter what becomes of me. In a storm like this he'll never get home. He won't even try. And while he sits keeping his father company I can look after his stable for him, go ploughing through snowdrifts up to my knees—nearly frozen—"

Not that she meant or believed her words. It was just an effort to convince herself that she did have a grievance, to justify her rebellious thoughts, to prove John responsible for her unhappiness. She was young still, eager for excitement and distractions; and John's steadfastness rebuked her vanity, made her complaints seem weak and trivial. Fretfully she went on, "If he'd listen to me sometimes and not be so stubborn we wouldn't be living still in a house like this. Seven years in two rooms—seven years and never a new stick of furniture.... There—as if another coat of paint could make it different anyway."

She cleaned her brush, filled up the stove again, and went back to the window. There was a void white moment that she thought must be frost formed on the window pane; then, like a fitful shadow through the whirling snow, she recognized the stable roof. It was incredible. The sudden, maniac raging of the storm struck from her face all its pettishness. Her eyes glazed with fear a little; her lips blanched. "If he starts for home now," she whispered silently— "But he won't—he knows I'm safe—he knows Steven's coming. Across the hills he would never dare."

She turned to the stove, holding out her hands to the warmth. Around her now there seemed a constant sway and tremor, as if the air were vibrating with the violent shudderings of the walls. She stood quite still, listening. Sometimes the wind struck with sharp, savage blows. Sometimes it bore down in a sustained, minute-long blast, silent with effort and intensity, then with a foiled shriek of threat wheeled away to gather and assault again. Always the eavestroughs creaked and sawed. She started towards the window again, then detecting the morbid trend of her thoughts, prepared fresh coffee and forced herself to drink a few mouthfuls. "He would never dare," she whispered again. "He wouldn't leave the old man anyway in such a storm. Safe in here—there's nothing for me to keep worrying about. It's after one already. I'll do my baking now, and then it will be time to get supper ready for Steven."

Soon, however, she began to doubt whether Steven would come. In such a storm even a mile was enough to make a man hesitate. Especially Steven, who, for all his attractive qualities, was hardly the one to face a blizzard for the sake of someone else's chores. He had a stable of his own to look after anyway. It would be only natural for him to think that when the storm rose John had turned again for home. Another man would have—would have put his wife first.

But she felt little dread or uneasiness at the prospect of spending the night alone. It was the first time she had been left like this on her own resources, and her reaction, now that she could face and appraise her situation calmly, was gradually to feel it a kind of adventure and responsibility. It stimulated her. Before nightfall she must go to the stable and feed everything. Wrap up in some of John's clothes—take a ball of string in her hand, one end tied to the door, so that no matter how blinding the storm she could at least find her way back to the house. She had heard of people having to do that. It appealed to her now because suddenly it made life dramatic. She had not felt the storm yet, only watched it for a minute through the window.

It took nearly an hour to find enough string, to choose the right socks and sweaters. Long before it was time to start out she tried on John's clothes, changing and rechanging, striding around the room to make sure there would be play enough for pitching hay and struggling over snowdrifts; then she took them off again, and for a while busied herself baking the little cakes with raisins that he liked.

Night came early. Just for a moment on the doorstep she shrank back, uncertain. The slow dimming of the light clutched her with an illogical sense of abandonment. It was like the covert withdrawal of an ally, leaving the alien miles unleashed and unrestrained.

Watching the hurricane of writhing snow rage past the little house she forced herself, "They'll never stand the night unless I get them fed. It's nearly dark already, and I've work to last an hour."

Timidly, unwinding a little of the string, she crept out from the shelter of the doorway. A gust of wind spun her forward a few yards, then plunged her headlong against a drift that in the dense white whirl lay invisible across her path. For nearly a minute she huddled still, breathless and dazed. The snow was in her mouth and nostrils, inside her scarf and up her sleeves. As she tried to straighten a smothering scud flung itself against her face, cutting off her breath a second time. The wind struck from all sides, blustering and furious. It was as if the storm had discovered her, as if all its forces were concentrated upon her extinction. Seized with panic suddenly she threshed out a moment with her arms, then stumbled back and sprawled her length across the drift.

But this time she regained her feet quickly, roused by the whip and batter of the storm to retaliative anger. For a moment her impulse was to face the wind and strike back blow for blow; then, as suddenly as it had come, her frantic strength gave way to limpness and exhaustion. Suddenly, a comprehension so clear and terrifying that it struck all thought of the stable from her mind, she realized in such a storm her puny insignificance. And the realization gave her new strength, stilled this time to a desperate persistence. Just for a moment the wind held her, numb and swaying in its vise; then slowly, buckled far forward, she groped her way again towards the house.

Inside, leaning against the door, she stood tense and still a while. It was almost dark now. The top of the stove glowed a deep, dull red. Heedless of the storm, self-absorbed and self-satisfied, the clock ticked on like a glib little idiot. "He shouldn't have gone," she whispered silently. "He saw the double wheel—he knew. He shouldn't have left me here alone."

For so fierce now, so insane and dominant did the blizzard seem, that she could not credit the safety of the house. The warmth and lull around her was not real yet, not to be relied upon. She was still at the mercy of the storm. Only her body pressing hard like this against the door was staving it off. She didn't dare move. She didn't dare ease the ache and strain. "He shouldn't have gone," she repeated, thinking of the stable again, reproached by her helplessness. "They'll freeze in their stalls—and I can't reach them. He'll say it's all my fault. He won't believe I tried."

Then Steven came. Quickly, startled to quietness and control, she let him in and lit the lamp. He stared at her a moment, then flinging off his cap crossed to where she stood by the table and seized her arms. "You're so white—what's wrong? Look at me—" It was like him in such little situations to be masterful. "You should have known better than to go out on a day like this. For a while I thought I wasn't going to make it here myself—"

"I was afraid you wouldn't come—John left early, and there was the stable—"

But the storm had unnerved her, and suddenly at the assurance of his touch and voice the fear that had been gripping her gave way to an hysteria of relief. Scarcely aware of herself she seized his arm and sobbed against it. He remained still a moment, unyielding, then slipped his other arm around her shoulder. It was comforting and she relaxed against it, hushed by a sudden sense of lull and safety. Her shoulders trembled with the easing of the strain, then fell limp and still. "You're shivering," —he drew her gently towards the stove. "There's nothing to be afraid of now, though. I'm going to do the chores for you."

It was a quiet, sympathetic voice, yet with an undertone of insolence, a kind of mockery even, that made her draw away quickly and busy herself putting in a fire. With his lips drawn in a little smile he watched her till she looked at him again. The smile too was insolent, but at the same time companionable; Steven's smile, and therefore difficult to reprove. It lit up his lean, still-boyish face with a peculiar kind of arrogance: features and smile that were different from John's, from other men's—wilful and derisive, yet naïvely so— as if it were less the difference itself he was conscious of, than the long-accustomed privilege that thereby fell his due. He was erect, tall, square-shouldered. His hair was dark and trim, his young lips curved soft and full. While John, she made the comparison swiftly, was thickset, heavy-jowled, and stooped. He always stood before her helpless, a kind of humility and wonderment in his attitude. And Steven now smiled on her appraisingly with the worldly-wise assurance of one for whom a woman holds neither mystery nor illusion.

"It was good of you to come, Steven," she responded, the words running into a sudden, empty laugh. "Such a storm to face—I suppose I should feel flattered."

For his presumption, his misunderstanding of what had been only a momentary weakness, instead of angering quickened her, roused from latency and long disuse all the instincts and resources of her femininity. She felt eager, challenged. Something was at hand that hitherto had always eluded her, even in the early days with John, something vital, beckoning, meaningful. She didn't understand, but she knew. The texture of the moment was satisfyingly dream-like: an incredibility perceived as such, yet acquiesced in. She was John's wife—she knew—but also she knew that Steven standing here was different from John. There was no thought or motive, no understanding of herself as the

knowledge persisted. Wary and poised round a sudden little core of blind
excitement she evaded him, "But it's nearly dark—hadn't you better hurry if
you're going to do the chores? Don't trouble—I can get them off myself—"

An hour later when he returned from the stable she was in another dress,
hair rearranged, a little flush of colour in her face. Pouring warm water for
him from the kettle into the basin she said evenly, "By the time you're washed
supper will be ready. John said we weren't to wait for him."

He looked at her a moment, "But in a storm like this you're not expecting
John?"

"Of course." As she spoke she could feel the colour deepening in her face.
"We're going to play cards. He was the one that suggested it."

He went on washing, and then as they took their places at the table,
resumed, "So John's coming. When are you expecting him?"

"He said it might be seven o'clock—or a little later." Conversation with
Steven at other times had always been brisk and natural, but now suddenly she
found it strained. "He may have work to do for his father. That's what he said
when he left. Why do you ask, Steven?"

"I was just wondering—it's a rough night."

"He always comes. There couldn't be a storm bad enough. It's easier to do
the chores in daylight, and I knew he'd be tired—that's why I started out for the
stable."

She glanced up again and he was smiling at her. The same insolence, the
same little twist of mockery and appraisal. It made her flinch suddenly, and ask
herself why she was pretending to expect John—why there should be this
instinct of defence to force her. This time, instead of poise and excitement, it
brought a reminder that she had changed her dress and rearranged her hair. It
crushed in a sudden silence, through which she heard the whistling wind again,
and the creaking saw of the eaves. Neither spoke now. There was something
strange, almost terrifying, about this Steven and his quiet, unrelenting smile; but
strangest of all was the familiarity: the Steven she had never seen or encountered, and yet had always known, always expected, always waited for. It was
less Steven himself that she felt than his inevitability. Just as she had felt the
snow, the silence and the storm. She kept her eyes lowered, on the window past
his shoulder, on the stove, but his smile now seemed to exist apart from him, to
merge and hover with the silence. She clinked a cup—listened to the whistle of
the storm—always it was there. He began to speak, but her mind missed the
meaning of his words. Swiftly she was making comparisons again; his face so
different to John's, so handsome and young and clean-shaven. Swiftly, helplessly, feeling the imperceptible and relentless ascendancy that thereby he was
gaining over her, sensing sudden menace in this new, more vital life, even as she
felt drawn towards it.

The lamp between them flickered as an onslaught of the storm sent shudderings through the room. She rose to build up the fire again and he followed her. For a long time they stood close to the stove, their arms almost touching. Once as the blizzard creaked the house she spun around sharply, fancying it was John at the door; but quietly he intercepted her. "Not tonight—you might as well make up your mind to it. Across the hills in a storm like this—it would be suicide to try."

Her lips trembled suddenly in an effort to answer, to parry the certainty in his voice, then set thin and bloodless. She was afraid now. Afraid of his face so different from John's—of his smile, of her own helplessness to rebuke it. Afraid of the storm, isolating her here alone with him in its impenetrable fastness. They tried to play cards, but she kept starting up at every creak and shiver of the walls. "It's too rough a night," he repeated. "Even for John. Just relax a few minutes—stop worrying and pay a little attention to me."

But in his tone there was a contradiction to his words. For it implied that she was not worrying—that her only concern was lest it really might be John at the door.

And the implication persisted. He filled up the stove for her, shuffled the cards—won—shuffled—still it was there. She tried to respond to his conversation, to think of the game, but helplessly into her cards instead she began to ask, Was he right? Was that why he smiled? Why he seemed to wait, expectant and assured?

The clock ticked, the fire crackled. Always it was there. Furtively for a moment she watched him as he deliberated over his hand. John, even in the days before they were married, had never looked like that. Only this morning she had asked him to shave. Because Steven was coming—because she had been afraid to see them side by side—because deep within herself she had known even then. The same knowledge, furtive and forbidden, that was flaunted now in Steven's smile. "You look cold," he said at last, dropping his cards and rising from the table. "We're not playing, anyway. Come over to the stove for a few minutes and get warm."

"But first I think we'll hang blankets over the door. When there's a blizzard like this we always do." It seemed that in sane, commonplace activity there might be release, a moment or two in which to recover herself. "John has nails in to put them on. They keep out a little of the draft."

He stood on a chair for her, and hung the blankets that she carried from the bedroom. Then for a moment they stood silent, watching the blankets sway and tremble before the blade of wind that spurted around the jamb. "I forgot," she said at last, "that I painted the bedroom door. At the top there, see—I've smeared the blankets coming through."

He glanced at her curiously, and went back to the stove. She followed him, trying to imagine the hills in such a storm, wondering whether John would come. "A man couldn't live in it," suddenly he answered her thoughts, lowering the oven door and drawing up their chairs one on each side of it. "He knows you're safe. It isn't likely that he'd leave his father, anyway."

"The wind will be in his back," she persisted. "The winter before we were married—all the blizzards that we had that year—and he never missed—"

"Blizzards like this one? Up in the hills he wouldn't be able to keep his direction for a hundred yards. Listen to it a minute and ask yourself."

His voice seemed softer, kindlier now. She met his smile a moment, its assured little twist of appraisal, then for a long time sat silent, tense, careful again to avoid his eyes.

Everything now seemed to depend on this. It was the same as a few hours ago when she braced the door against the storm. He was watching her, smiling. She dared not move, unclench her hands, or raise her eyes. The flames crackled, the clock ticked. The storm wrenched the walls as if to make them buckle in. So rigid and desperate were all her muscles set, withstanding, that the room around her seemed to swim and reel. So rigid and strained that for relief at last, despite herself, she raised her head and met his eyes again.

Intending that it should be for only an instant, just to breathe again, to ease the tension that had grown unbearable—but in his smile now, instead of the insolent appraisal that she feared, there seemed a kind of warmth and sympathy. An understanding that quickened and encouraged her—that made her wonder why but a moment ago she had been afraid. It was as if the storm had lulled, as if she had suddenly found calm and shelter.

Or perhaps, the thought seized her, perhaps instead of his smile it was she that had changed. She who, in the long, wind-creaked silence, had emerged from the increment of codes and loyalties to her real, unfettered self. She who now felt suddenly an air of appraisal as nothing more than an understanding of the unfulfilled woman that until this moment had lain within her brooding and unadmitted, reproved out of consciousness by the insistence of an outgrown, routine fidelity.

For there had always been Steven. She understood now. Seven years— almost as long as John—ever since the night they first danced together.

The lamp was burning dry, and through the dimming light, isolated in the fastness of silence and storm, they watched each other. Her face was white and struggling still. His was handsome, clean-shaven, young. Her eyes were fanatic, believing desperately, fixed upon him as if to exclude all else, as if to find justification. His were cool, bland, drooped a little with expectancy. The light kept dimming, gathering the shadows round them, hushed, conspiratorial. He was smiling still. Her hands again were clenched up white and hard.

"But he always came," she persisted. "The wildest, coldest nights—even such a night as this. There was never a storm—"

"Never a storm like this one." There was a quietness in his smile now, a kind of simplicity almost, as if to reassure her. "You were out in it yourself for a few minutes. He would have five miles, across the hills.... I'd think twice myself, on such a night, before risking even one."

Long after he was asleep she lay listening to the storm. As a check on the draft up the chimney they had left one of the stovelids partly off, and through the open bedroom door she could see the flickerings of flame and shadow on the kitchen wall. They leaped and sank fantastically. The longer she watched the more alive they seemed to be. There was one great shadow that struggled towards her threateningly, massive and black and engulfing all the room. Again and again it advanced, about to spring, but each time a little whip of light subdued it to its place among the others on the wall. Yet though it never reached her still she cowered, feeling that gathered there was all the frozen wilderness, its heart of terror and invincibility.

Then she dozed a while, and the shadow was John. Interminably he advanced. The whips of light still flicked and coiled, but now suddenly they were the swift little snakes that this afternoon she had watched twist and shiver across the snow. And they too were advancing. They writhed and vanished and came again. She lay still, paralysed. He was over her now, so close that she could have touched him. Already it seemed that a deadly tightening hand was on her throat. She tried to scream but her lips were locked. Steven beside her slept on heedlessly.

Until suddenly as she lay staring up at him a gleam of light revealed his face. And in it was not a trace of threat or anger—only calm, and stonelike hopelessness.

That was like John. He began to withdraw, and frantically she tried to call him back. "It isn't true—not really true—listen, John—" but the words clung frozen to her lips. Already there was only the shriek of wind again, the sawing eaves, the leap and twist of shadow on the wall.

She sat up, startled now and awake. And so real had he seemed there, standing close to her, so vivid the sudden age and sorrow in this face, that at first she could not make herself understand she had been only dreaming. Against the conviction of his presence in the room it was necessary to insist over and over that he must still be with his father on the other side of the hills. Watching the shadows she had fallen asleep. It was only her mind, her imagination, distorted to a nightmare by the illogical and unadmitted dread of his return. Be he wouldn't come. Steven was right. In such a storm he would never try. They were safe, alone. No one would ever know. It was only fear, morbid

712 Sinclair Ross

and irrational; only the sense of guilt that even her new-found and challenged womanhood could not entirely quell.

She knew now. She had not let herself understand or acknowledge it as guilt before, but gradually through the wind-torn silence of the night his face compelled her. The face that had watched her from the darkness with its stone-like sorrow—the face that was really John—John more than his features of mere flesh and bone could ever be.

She wept silently. The fitful gleam of light began to sink. On the ceiling and wall at last there was only a faint dull flickering glow. The little house shuddered and quailed, and a chill crept in again. Without wakening Steven she slipped out to build up the fire. It was burned to a few spent embers now, and the wood she put on seemed a long time catching light. The wind swirled through the blankets they had hung around the door, and struck her flesh like laps of molten ice. Then hollow and moaning it roared up the chimney again, as if against its will drawn back to serve still longer with the onrush of the storm.

For a long time she crouched over the stove, listening. Earlier in the evening, with the lamp lit and the fire crackling, the house had seemed a stand against the wilderness, against its frozen, blizzard-breathed implacability, a refuge of feeble walls wherein persisted the elements of human meaning and survival. Now, in the cold, creaking darkness, it was strangely extinct, looted by the storm and abandoned again. She lifted the stove lid and fanned the embers till at last a swift little tongue of flame began to lick around the wood. Then she replaced the lid, extended her hands, and as if frozen in that attitude stood waiting.

It was not long now. After a few minutes she closed the drafts, and as the flames whirled back upon each other, beating against the top of the stove and sending out flickers of light again, a warmth surged up to relax her stiffened limbs. But shivering and numb it had been easier. The bodily well-being that the warmth induced gave play again to an ever more insistent mental suffering. She remembered the shadow that was John. She saw him bent towards her, then retreating, his features pale and overcast with unaccusing grief. She re-lived their seven years together and, in retrospect, found them to be years of worth and dignity. Until crushed by it all at last, seized by a sudden need to suffer and atone, she crossed to where the draft was bitter, and for a long time stood unflinching on the icy floor.

The storm was close here. Even through the blankets she could feel a sift of snow against her face. The eaves sawed, the walls creaked. Above it all, like a wolf in howling flight, the wind shrilled lone and desolate.

And yet, suddenly she asked herself, hadn't there been other storms, other blizzards? And through the worst of them hadn't he always reached her?

Clutched by the thought she stood rooted a minute. It was hard now to understand how she could have so deceived herself—how a moment of passion could have quieted within her not only conscience, but reason and discretion too. John always came. There could never be a storm to stop him. He was strong, inured to the cold. He had crossed the hills since his boyhood, knew every creekbed and gully. It was madness to go on like this—to wait. While there was still time she must waken Steven, and hurry him away.

But in the bedroom again, standing at Steven's side, she hesitated. In his detachment from it all, in his quiet, even breathing, there was such sanity, such realism. For him nothing had happened; nothing would. If she wakened him he would only laugh and tell her to listen to the storm. Already it was long past midnight, either John had lost his way or not set out at all. And she knew that in his devotion there was nothing foolhardy. He would never risk a storm beyond his endurance, never permit himself a sacrifice likely to endanger her lot or future. They were both safe. No one would ever know. She must control herself—be sane like Steven.

For comfort she let her hand rest a while on Steven's shoulder. It would be easier were he awake now, with her, sharing her guilt; but gradually as she watched his handsome face in the glimmering light she came to understand that for him no guilt existed. Just as there had been no passion, no conflict. Nothing but the sane appraisal of their situation, nothing but the expectant little smile, and the arrogance of features that were different from John's. She winced deeply, remembering how she had fixed her eyes on those features, how she had tried to believe that so handsome and young, so different from John's, they must in themselves be her justification.

In the flickering light they were still young, still handsome. No longer her justification—she knew now—John was the man—but wistfully still, wondering sharply at their power and tyranny, she touched them a moment with her fingertips again.

She could not blame him. There had been no passion, no guilt; therefore there could be no responsibility. Suddenly looking down at him as he slept, half-smiling still, his lips relaxed in the conscienceless complacency of his achievement, she understood and thus he was revealed in his entirety—all there ever was or ever could be. John was the man. With him lay all the future. For tonight, slowly and contritely through the day and years to come, she would try to make amends.

Then she stole back to the kitchen, and without thought, impelled by overwhelming need again, returned to the door where the draft was bitter still. Gradually towards morning the storm began to spend itself. Its terror blast became a feeble, wornout moan. The leap of light and shadow sank, and a chill crept in again. Always the eaves creaked, tortured with wordless prophecy. Heedless of it all the clock ticked on in idiot content.

They found him the next day, less than a mile from home. Drifting with the storm he had run against his own pasture fence and overcome had frozen there, erect still, both hands clasping fast the wire.

"He was south of here," they said wonderingly when she told them how he had come across the hills. "Straight south—you'd wonder how he could have missed the buildings. It was the winds last night, coming every way at once. He shouldn't have tried. There was a double wheel around the moon."

She looked past them a moment, then as if to herself said simply, "If you knew him, though—John would try."

It was later, when they had left her a while to be alone with him, that she knelt and touched his hand. Her eyes dimmed, still it was such a strong and patient hand; then, transfixed, they suddenly grew wide and clear. On the palm, white even against its frozen whiteness, was a little smear of paint.

GABRIELLE ROY

A Tramp at the Door

Translated by Alan Brown

Gabrielle Roy (1914–1983) was born in Saint-Boniface, Manitoba, the youngest child of parents who had come from Quebec to live in the small prairie village that is now part of Winnipeg. Roy attended the Winnipeg Normal Institute and upon graduation began a teaching career that would last until 1937, when she left for London to study acting. While touring in England and France, Roy began writing articles on Europe and on Canada for newspapers in her home town and in Paris. She returned to Canada just before the Second World War and settled in Montreal, in the working-class district of Saint-Henri, which inspired her to begin writing Bonheur d'Occasion (The Tin Flute).

The novel was published in 1945 and, as Helen Hoy writes, was universally "welcomed for its innovative subject matter (breaking with the tradition of the soil), its manner (unflinchingly honest rather than sentimental), and its language (the vernacular of the street)." Roy won the French Prix Femina and became the first woman fellow of the Royal Society of Canada. In English translation, The Tin Flute won a Governor General's Award and the Royal Society of Canada's Lorne Pierce Medal. It eventually sold over a million copies worldwide. It is an emotional story concerned with the human condition in a cruel urban environment.

In 1947 Roy married and travelled with her husband to France, where they lived for three years. It was there, among the cathedrals and ruins of war, that she conceived her second book, La Petite Poule d'eau (published in English in 1951 as Where Nests the Water Hen); this novel is set in a dream-like place, "at the beginning of all time." Hugo McPherson has noted that an extreme shift was represented here which would continue throughout Roy's career as she moved back and forth from "the cage to the garden, [between] the world of experience and the world of innocence."

"A Tramp at the Door," from Un Jardin au bout du monde (Garden in the Wind), published in English in 1977, is a story that mixes the two impulses of Roy's work: the onset and the waning of enchantment, in this case at the hands of a vagabond who inspires an isolated Manitoba family

715

to re-embrace the idea of a forgotten home place and family. Gabrielle Roy's last book, which considers the first thirty years of her life, was appropriately entitled, La Détresse et l'enchantement (Enchantment and Sorrow: The Autobiography of Gabrielle Roy) *and was published in English in 1987.*

My mother was expecting something or other. She kept going to the door, drawing back from the windowpane the white curtain hemmed in red linen and staring long and vaguely out at the drenched countryside. Suddenly she gave a start, one hand going up to her forehead.

"Somebody's coming," she announced, and went on, her voice filled with surprise: "Coming here, it looks like!"

Rain was rattling on the roof. On either side of the house we could hear water from the spouts splashing down from the overflowing rain barrels. Evening was falling. From the ditches, filled to their banks, a white steam went up. Beyond the slope of the rye field you could see no more than a few blackened, bare treetops emerging soaked from the mist. For two days we hadn't seen a living soul pass by. "Not a cat, not even a beggar," my mother had sighed.

The man pushed the gate open. We could see him tip back his head and try to smile as he saw the two gable windows of the house and perhaps the smoke from the chimney. With every step he had to fight the wind, pulling his dark coat tight around him. The garden shrubs near him were twisted and tousled by the wind. Because of the shadow that already lay dark beneath the hedge, the man was on top of Farouche's kennel before he saw our German shepherd about to spring.

My mother stifled a cry.

Almost at once we saw Farouche wagging his tail, wiggling his body and crouching in front of this man whose strangely gentle, coaxing tone we in the house could catch between the gusts of the storm.

My mother breathed a great sigh, even more astonished than she was relieved.

"Well," she said, "that's the first time I ever saw Farouche make friends that fast!"

The man straightened up and seemed to be surveying all the ways of entering the house. Finally, overcoming his hesitation, he made a half-turn and came rapping on the back door which looked out on the farmyard.

My father, sitting by the fire, was in the grip of the unbearable boredom he suffered with each return of the wet season to our country of the plains. The whole day long he hadn't said a word. You wondered if he really felt he belonged there with the rest of us. Buried in his thoughts, he hadn't seen the stranger coming, and even the sound of our voices had most likely not come through to him.

"It's somebody who doesn't know his way around here." This was my mother again as she gestured to me to open the door.

As soon as autumn came we lived in the big room. The small lean-to that served as a kitchen in the summertime now turned into a kind of storage space where we could pile furniture and tools no longer needed. I went through this freezing space and with difficulty lifted the rusty latch. A wallop of rain took me in the face. The man's head appeared, feebly lit by a vestige of light coming from the big puddles around the pump. All in all, it was a rather nice tramp's face, the kind that isn't any particular age and asks for a bowl of soup and will go on his way right afterwards if he isn't offered an attic for the night. We didn't see those people often in our out-of-the-way parts, maybe one or two a year, if that. But this one seemed to have a certain dignity and wasn't in a hurry to beg. A short, reddish, frizzy beard, pearled with great raindrops, invaded half his cheeks; the peak of his cap threw a clean line of shadow on his forehead. His eyes, very gentle and smiling, almost tender, sparkled under the wet fringe of his lashes.

"Well! My little cousin!" he cried in a voice that was as soft and flexible and unsettling as his gaze. "You must be my little cousin Alice!" he went on, laughing.

I shook my head.

"No? Must be Agnes, then!"

"No," I said, irritated. "I'm Ghislaine."

"Of course, just what I thought! Of course you're Ghislaine. I should have known it, even if I never saw you."

As he spoke, his hands made as if they were drying each other, and he laughed behind his beard and his foot cleverly pushed at the door I was holding slightly open.

Somehow he was inside.

"This is the Rondeaus' house, I guess!" he asked, and his incredible, friendly smile swept around the interior of the damp, cold shed as if he found it welcoming and filled with people.

"No," I said, "we're the Trudeaus."

"Why, sure, just as I was going to say," he went on coolly. "Rondeau, Trudeau, names as like as peas. Right, cousin?"

He gave me a little nudge, and I saw his eyes shining with satisfaction.

"Now, little girl, you just go and tell your father there's a cousin here from the land of Quebec."

I went before him into the big room—he was right on my heels—and blurted out to my father, as if in mocking reproach: "He says he's a cousin from Quebec."

My father stood up and made an odd gesture, as if to take the stranger in his arms, but the impulse failed him. Yet his handsome, aging, peaceful face betrayed not so much a withdrawal as the vagueness of someone suddenly awakened from a dream.

"Well, now! What part of Quebec? Saint-Alphonse?"

"Saint Alphonse," said the man.

He approached the stove. His clothes were starting to steam. My mother brought the Aladdin lamp. She lifted it a little above the stranger and you could see great rips in his clothing, some held together by bits of string, others gaping to reveal glimpses of his red shirt.

But the man directed at my mother a gaze so filled with friendship that she set down the lamp and busied herself elsewhere without speaking. We could see that she was excited from the way she opened all the drawers of the sideboard without finding what she wanted.

For a moment the man stood alone in the middle of the room, trying to catch our eyes, which fled his. He drew up a chair by the stove, sat down and breathed a great sigh of well-being.

Then in the silence, two or three times, we could hear his soft, rather drawling voice: "Saint-Alphonse, yes sir. That's where I come from, Saint-Alphonse ..."

My father took out his tobacco pouch. He was about to fill his pipe when the stranger held out a hand and, unabashed, helped himself to the tobacco. Then, after lighting a short clay pipe, he settled back in his chair and murmured distinctly: "Thank you. Much obliged."

The two men smoked. My mother fussed among her pots with an unusual amount of noise. And sometimes her lips opened as if she were about to say some wounding word. The stranger looked around at us children sitting in the corners, observing one after the other, and smiled out of his beard. He made little jabs with his chin, winked at each of us, then started the rounds again. A badger that we had tamed, still highly suspicious of strangers, actually slipped under the man's chair. He took it by the scruff of the neck and laid it in his lap. The little animal, far from protesting, licked his wet beard and, its claws retracted, allowed itself to be rocked like a baby. As wild and speechless as our only friends—our animals—we were astounded to see that two of them had taken up with this stranger. Even my mother seemed impressed, and that must have aggravated her ill humour. Little by little we slid off our chairs to come nearer. The strange man gave us signs of encouragement in the manner of the magician our parents had once taken us to see at the rodeo in the next village.

My father had stood up. He was pacing to and fro in the room, his hands behind his back. Then, planting himself in front of the vagabond, he asked: "But whose boy would you be then?"

"Me?" said the man. "Why, the one that disappeared."

A glimmer of interest showed beneath my father's lowered eyelids.

"Gustave?"

"Yep. Gustave."

"But they thought he was dead!"

"He wasn't dead. He went to the States. I'm his boy."

"Oh!" said my father. "You're his boy!"

"I'm his boy," the stranger repeated in a voice that was soft and stubborn.

And he turned his smiling face to where my mother was beating her pancake batter. He seemed determined to drag from her a look, a smile, a word. But she was speeding up her supper preparations so as to stay out of the conversation. It wasn't long before the first spoonful of batter dropped into the hot frying pan. A pleasant odour filled the room. Outside, darkness spread over the desolate, naked landscape. All that could still be seen through the windowpanes was the vague glimmer of water accumulated in great pools between the patches of brush, in the hollows of the plain or running in streams. The man stretched out his legs. He took time to look around the room, low-ceilinged, large, furnished with an oak sideboard and old, modest, but solid pieces so well-polished and softened by use that they reflected a long contentment. Then, without moving, he began smiling at nothing again, to himself.

"But what put you onto our trail?" my father asked suddenly.

The stranger raised his blue eyes, which shone in the direct rays of the lamp.

"In Saint-Alphonse."

"Oh!"

My father gave a long sigh.

"It's been a might long time since I saw hide or hair of any of them from Saint-Alphonse."

It was his turn to look toward my mother, so tiny, so much younger than he. A big apron tied around her waist, she was leaning attentively above her pan and the flame at times leapt perilously close to her face.

"How long is it now, Albertine, since I was in those parts?"

And indeed it was she who was charged with refreshing his memory on events he had described to her about people she had never seen.

She took a little while to reflect, mentally juggling dates, her pretty eyebrows arched high and her mouth a little open.

"You told me you were fourteen when you left home and you hadn't set foot there since. You figure it out. About fifty years, if you were telling the truth."

She always ended up with that reservation, as if to throw back the error, if error there was, solely upon my father.

Then, sulking a little, and because the stranger's presence doubtless irritated her, she added:

"What's more, you haven't written the folks at home for fifteen years. It's a real shame!"

"Yes," said my father, ignoring his wife's last remark. "It'll be fifty years. I wouldn't even know them back there anymore."

He looked down, his face lit up by distant, melancholy memories.

My mother placed her fists on her hips. Quickly, without looking at the stranger, she said: "It's ready! Come on, children. Come and eat, Arthur."

The tramp too stood up gaily. He chose a seat by the wall, slid in, pulling his wretched jacket tight around him, and, once established, seized his fork.

"Yes," my father mused, "there's a lot of things back there I never heard a word about."

The man speared a large slice of bread with his fork. He bit the bread in the middle, then, smiling, his mouth full, he promised: "I'll tell you all about it after."

II

After supper he actually did begin to tell us about the relatives, helped along by my father who would situate things by his questions: "Marcelline, now, you must have found she'd aged? And I suppose Eustache took over the farm ..."

We knew very little about my father's people. He'd never told us at one time how many brothers and sisters he had. On occasion, and as his reveries would have it, he would let a name drop: Marcelline, Philomène, Aristide. His tone changed, too, according to his mood.

One day, for example, when the soup was too salty, he had grumbled: "Albertine, are you going to start making salty soup like Philomène?"

"Who is Philomène?" we asked.

My father seemed more disconcerted at having provoked the question than by our breathless curiosity. Philomène, he finally admitted, was his father's second wife. A sign from my mother at that moment advised us not to put our researches any further. So it was that my father managed to keep the shades of his childhood for himself alone. At times, though, he himself renewed this singular aura of mystery attached to our uncles and aunts in Quebec. He spoke of ill-defined figures and always in the past tense, as if they had ceased to exist. That's why we were surprised that evening to hear him say, "Marcelline, now, she must have aged?"

Marcelline had made her entry into our family one evening when my father, seeing my mother patching old clothes, protested: "Now don't you start going on like that penny pincher Marcelline!" The moment his sister's name had slipped out he walled himself in silence.

Others popped up, as faceless as Marcelline. They seemed incredibly far away yet, like that Marcelline, they would suddenly become attached to our lives through their penchant for patching old rags or because of a dreamy warmth that would spread at twilight through the house. And we never knew how many shadowy beings would rise up at our next question, behind Philomène or Marcelline, or if they'd be revealed thanks to some irritation of my father's or in a moment of more tender feeling. One thing we did know: you had to wait for these confidences, never push.

Well, that evening my father sat close to our strange visitor and, behold, names were flying from his lips, those associated with his ill humour as well as the ones we heard on feast days—and others we had never heard at all: Uncle France, Aunt Eléonore, Cousin Brault. You'd have thought a dike that had stood too long against the past had given under the flood of hurrying memories. The visitor gave little signs of approval. His eyes followed my father with an attentiveness that was ingratiating, sustained and encouraging, an attentiveness I have in later life observed in very few human beings. Truly, we might have imagined that it was my father who had just arrived from his travels and that the other one was there only to corroborate the facts or testify to them.

At last, when my father gave the other his turn, our visitor started in with his own stories. He spoke in a restful voice that he seldom raised. He dipped into his memories as into a heap of thick and rustling leaves, fallen at the trees' roots, in autumn.

We, the Trudeaus, were, according to him, a family out of the ordinary. The old couple, alas! had died working, on land that was richer in stones than pasture. But they had left behind them solid testimonials to their ingenuity, a thousand things well done, well carried out, if it was no more than a fence, a barn door or a delicately sculptured weathercock on the roof of that same barn. Whereas nowadays ...

Several times he stopped to make sure that my father was listening with pleasure. In fact, my father seemed to have changed, to have emerged from a kind of penumbra as he renewed touch, so to speak, with his family, divided and scattered to all corners of the country by obscure misfortunes or obstinacies. In one swift glance our visitor would seize the trace of an emotion: then, sure of his trail, he would take off again without more emphasis but as if animated by a great desire to please.

What began to strike us then about this singular creature was that from the depths of his solitude he accused no one but seemed rather to assume all faults himself.

On the subject of family, however, it can't be said that he gave us many important details that first evening. Apart from that, he described minutely Christmas parties, New Years' parties, winter-evening parties, wedding parties, and suddenly Montreal, the great city, and suddenly Joliette, the small city, where the people of Saint-Alphonse went shopping. Then he'd comment on pioneer days, only to drift unexpectedly to meals of buckwheat cakes and wild honey or memories of square dances in the kitchen; and we'd see my father tapping lightly on the floor with toe and heel.

But already, through our visitor's account, these vague, far-off relatives of ours all seemed to have changed their characters—even Marcelline, who was no longer grasping, only provident. Eustache had inherited the paternal land and made it bear fruit; he raised children courageously. Anaïs, now, there was nobody like her for spinning the local wool and filling the cupboard with bolts of homespun. Devout she was, too, never missed her weekday mass. Uncle France had made it to a hundred, and they'd had a fine Christian birthday for him with all the children and grandchildren, of whom two were attending the seminary and three had taken vows. Family was something sacred: nothing could be as touching as the members of a single family knowing each other by their voices and opening their arms. Alas, people sometimes rejected their own flesh and blood when it turned up from afar, especially if it wasn't very clean or a particularly shining case.

This was said in a tone of resignation that made us all hang our heads, except my mother who, on the contrary, raised hers defiantly. She was sewing, a little off to one side, sticking her needle so impatiently into the cloth that she often pricked herself. Then we could hear her groan softly as she put her lips to the finger where a drop of blood was forming.

In the middle of a silence my father said: "Marcelline, now ... did she ever mention me, sometimes?"

The man assured him warmly: "Oh, for sure! She often talked about her brother ..."

"Arthur." My father completed the sentence.

"That's it, Arthur."

My father pulled up his chair until his foot almost touched the stranger's muddy boots. He lit his pipe for the fourth time and asked a question that astonished us greatly.

"Did they know back there that I'd been appointed justice of the peace?"

"They knew it," affirmed the vagabond. "Marcelline was very proud."

A happy silence followed, broken by my mother's noisy sigh.

The man turned in her direction: "What about you, cousin, which parish are you from? Maybe I know your people too ..."

My mother rose up, all round and little and trembling at this mode of address, as if the stranger's hand had touched her.

"She's from the prairies," my father hastened to explain. "I married her out here."

"What of it?" the man insisted. "I've drifted around every which way at harvest times. Maybe I knew her folks."

No one took him up on it. The man seemed hurt. A little later his pale-blue gaze grew fixed and we could see that he was close to sleep. For a second his eyelids would drop, his eyes would glaze, and before they closed you could see in them a vague smile of apology and a slightly crestfallen expression.

It had just struck eleven. But my mother was acting as if the evening had just begun. My father, for his part, kept looking at the clock, pulling out his watch and comparing the two. The stranger dozed in his chair for minutes at a time, then awoke with a start, trying to cover up by winking at each of us in turn and changing posture.

My father said suddenly: "Hey, children! It's bedtime!" Then, without waiting for my mother's approval, he suggested: "Maybe you could make up a bed, Albertine ..." He hesitated, then concluded: "... for our cousin ..."

"Gustave. After my father," explained the stranger, yawning. "Gustave, that's me."

My mother stood up without a word, took the lamp and left us in shadows and then in darkness as she went up the steps leading to the attic. We could hear her moving a cot around, opening trunks. Through the half-open trap door a cold draught swept on our shoulders, soon bearing with it the odour of fresh linen.

Later, having awakened, I could hear my mother speaking in a low voice to my father: "You always told me your brother Gustave was built like a giant, tall and broad, the strongest one in the family. This one's a puny runt ..."

"Far as that goes," my father replied, "you take any family around here. The big men don't always have the big sons. Maybe he takes after his mother," he added after a pause.

"That may be, but couldn't you see he was at a loss for an answer when you asked him for news of Marcelline and Philomène?"

"That's only natural. He's been on the road a lot. It couldn't all come back at once."

"Oh, that's the excuse, is it?" exclaimed my mother in a hostile, discouraged tone.

In the next room to theirs the man was snoring peacefully. Once he mumbled a few words in his sleep. Then I thought I heard, at the end of a jovial little laugh: "Good day! Good day, dear cousin!"

III

He stayed at our house three weeks. My mother gave him some clothes left by a former hired man, and they were about Gustave's size. Early in the morning, he used to wash in the kitchen sink, and comb his beard, and turn out quite presentable.

During the day he tried to make himself useful and took special pains to anticipate my mother's wishes. He'd bring in wood, run to the well as soon as the pail was dry, repair the traps. One day when she complained there'd been no mail for a week because of the road, he went off on foot to the village. He came back at day's end with a letter which he held out to her in the hope, no doubt, of getting a friendly word.

In spite of everything we couldn't get used to the idea that he was supposed to be our cousin. We ordered him around like a farm hand. "Better get the wood in before the rain soaks it." In the daytime we called him "you" or "the man" or "him." My mother, above all, because she was afraid of having him with us all winter, would say each morning, looking out at the road unwinding toward the dark, dank woods: "There's going to be a big snowstorm before long. A person won't even be able to get out of here."

The man seemed not to hear. In the daytime we paid little attention to him. But in the evening, as soon as the lighted lamp stood on the table, this strange creature, through what kind of spell we didn't know, became indispensable to us. Every evening he again turned into "Cousin Gustave."

He appeared sensitive to this kind of disgrace, of which we absolved him every evening. Silent the whole day long, he retained the use of words as soon as our eyes, grown softer, consented to look at him again. Then, in his quiet, unchanging voice, he would once more tell the story of Marcelline's second wedding, or Uncle France's hundredth birthday, but always adding fresh details. "Hey, you didn't mention that last time!" my father would cry. And Gustave would look at him with a vague reproach in his eyes, as if he wanted to say: The things I know are too vast, too many-sided. You can't get all that out at once.

"Well, go on," my father would hurry him.

Gustave, cut adrift from his vision, would set off again, but on a new tack.

His stories proceeded by short stages, often interrupted at the most touching or fascinating part, so that we were always inclined to give him another day of hospitality in order to hear the end. And finally we had to admit it to ourselves: if Gustave's story the previous night had been a good one, we were polite and well-disposed toward him the following day. But when he'd disappointed us, we had ways, unconsciously but cruelly, of showing him.

Well, this fellow Gustave grew very skilful. He spun his stories out. He cut them into little slices in a way that later became familiar to us through the radio. Everything was used to stretch them out. The landscape would be painstakingly described. The village teacher, the notary, and the doctor had their parts to play. Jumping from one family to the next, it might happen that he got into events that barely concerned us but livened up his story immeasurably. There was one about the son of Magloire the blacksmith who hanged himself in the barn with his own belt; and one about Fortunat, who, at the age of twenty, married a rich widow of fifty.

One evening, when I pointed out that all this had nothing to do with us, he turned toward me a look that was courageous and untamed: "Come now! Who's related to who?" There's a question: where it starts, where it stops, who knows?"

Then, as if he realized that our suspicions could be nourished by this odd remark, he gave a little strangled laugh and went patiently back to the tale that especially pleased my father, about Marcelline's second wedding. Little by little he grew lively again, and treated us to the fiddler who had made Marcelline, at fifty-five, dance for the first time in her life.

"What! She got up and danced?" asked my father.

"Yes, sir, she danced!" Gustave affirmed.

And in his eyes as pale as water we thought we saw Marcelline's cotton lustre skirt whirl and pass by.

"So she got up and danced!" repeated my father, delighted.

One night my father mentioned two of his brothers who had also settled out West, Uncle Alfred in Saskatchewan and Uncle Edouard in Alberta. In a sentimental mood, he admitted his regret that he had failed to keep in touch at least with these two.

Gustave let my father go on for some time, then he promised, in that spellbinding voice which sometimes sang through our house like the winds of the wide world: "Who knows, maybe I'll drop in and see them one of these days! You just give me the right address and if the good Lord wills, I'll give them your regards."

That was all that was said about our western uncles, whom we had seen only once. Alfred when he had started off from Montreal and stopped to see us on the way, and Edouard when he had arrived from Quebec with his family and almost settled nearby.

As Gustave could give us no news of these two, my father asked for more news from Quebec, in particular about a charlatan he had known in his youth and who, it seemed, had made a fortune.

"Oh, yes! Ephrem Brabant!" said Gustave.

And that evening he began a story that lasted almost a week.

This charlatan, Ephrem Brabant by name, had started off by handing out samples of his cough syrup to the congregation as they left the chilly church on

Sunday mornings. But the remedy that someone had taken for his cold had miraculously cured him of another much more serious illness. Thanks to an early spring, the news of the cure spread rapidly around the countryside. It was at once attributed to Ephrem, who was a "seventh son."

Now Ephrem wasn't about to belittle the powers and properties of his remedy any more than he denied the supernatural gifts attributed to him. A pious man, gentle and charitable, he was quite ready to admit that faith helped medicine along. So, as he enjoined his customers to prayer, he sold them more and more little bottles. The same herbal product with different labels and in different containers brought relief to stomach cramps, asthma and rheumatic pains.

Ephrem's renown spread beyond the limits of the village. Soon he had a little covered cart and a horse as black as night and he went from farm to farm leaving brown bottles wherever he stopped. People in perfect health tried his remedy and declared they felt none the worse, which added to Ephrem Brabant's prestige as much as the cures themselves. He had grown a beard, which he trimmed to a point, and wore a black, wide-rimmed hat. His photo appeared on the bottles of syrup. Everyone in the area called him Dr. Brabant. It was at this time that he had the notion of writing and distributing an almanac to publicize the testimonials of people cured by his attentions. It was to contain, as well, practical advice for people of various ages, the interpretation of dreams, and all the known signs of good or inclement weather. The fellow could neither read nor write, but he had immense practical knowledge based on direct observation of rural life. For the spelling and fine phrases he depended on a son he had sent to school. He moved to Montreal, to a luxurious house, and despite being hauled to court, he accumulated a tidy fortune.

This was the story Gustave told us. Or, rather, this was the version we created with the passage of time and according to our desire to draw our own conclusions. Gustave must have told it more simply, and perhaps with more indulgence. For he blamed no one, judged no one. Almost every creature found mercy before him. If some really bad ones turned up, Gustave had them die off quickly, which in the end appeased my mother.

IV

Now that I think of it, it's true he talked very little about the members of our own family, apart from saying they were fine people. The unforgettable ones he managed to dig up elsewhere. After the story of Brabant, he told us about Roma Poirier who murdered her husband by putting ground glass in his soup day after day. Oh, the strange, cruel, and fascinating beings he brought to our place in the evenings, when the pails swung and rattled on the fence posts outside and from the woodland's edge coyotes yapped incessantly.

Long after he had left, as unexpectedly as he had come, long after his features had blurred in our memories, or his gentle way of smiling as he talked of the most sinister events, it would happen that those characters—the charlatan, the murderess, the old man of a hundred and I don't know how many more— would turn up in our thoughts. A whole unconnected cohort, the friends of Gustave the tramp, who revealed them to us perhaps less through his words than through a certain slow way of pulling back his coat as he reflected on their lives, or by an occasional amused smile at the troop of them.

He knew the great wickedness of the world quite well but he neither judged it nor renounced it. Nor the great distress of the world. Of that he sometimes gave us a glimpse beneath his heavy eyelids, as he stared at a windowpane whipped by rain and branches.

But, above all, it was the great piety of the world that he had seen and recognized.

And through this, in the end, he found grace even in my mother's eyes.

One night he was telling about the pilgrims flocking to the sanctuary of Sainte-Anne-de-Beaupré. The nave appeared before us, filled with votive offerings, with longboats and schooners for lamps. Thousands of crutches hung between the stations of the Cross, as if the lame, on their march toward God, had recovered their agility and taken off for heaven through the pale openings of the stained-glass windows. A pious murmur rose in the shadows; our house was too small to contain the piety of the pilgrims, their thanksgiving, their wild hope. Gustave led us beyond all the paths we knew. We followed his blue gaze, a pool of water in the night, toward a dim region through which he led us to the sound of chants and organs.

There was always someone who sighed loudly when Gustave's voice fell silent and we came back to the reality of our house.

Of course he mixed up times and persons, but which of us, living on the prairie, far from the beaten path, could have told true from false in his accounts?

He had quickly seen that the mistress of the house appeared to listen only when he talked of miracles and pilgrimages. From that moment we could get him to speak of nothing else. He carried us to the places of prayer up and down the length of the St. Lawrence. At the very words "St. Lawrence," we were captured at once, for he had given us such a gripping vision of the river. He talked of it as a living creature, a tumultuous force, and yet at times so kind that its flow made no more than a murmur. He had described it as having its source in the Niagara cataracts (he was a little careless about geographical accuracy). Then he showed us how it fled toward the sea, encircling a great island whose name we loved: Anticosti.

Then one evening he ran out of places of prayer on the St. Lawrence. And he began to describe St. Joseph's Oratory, built stone after stone with the people's offerings. My mother (she had a special devotion for Brother André) stopped sewing and for the first time spoke directly to Gustave. She normally addressed him through the mediation of one of the children, "Ask him," she'd say, "if he's seen the hammer"; or, "Was he the one that took the shovel? See if you can find out ..." For in the process of making himself useful he mislaid things, and my mother, who would have had scruples about accusing him directly, didn't hesitate to burden him with a latent guilt.

But this time she looked him in the eye and said: "Tell me, did you ever see him? Brother André?"

Perhaps Gustave felt the full risk of a careless answer. My mother, depending on her mood, would give him a heaping plateful at dinner, or nothing but the less tasty scraps. Did he understand the thirst for spiritual adventure that lived in this serious little woman, sentimental and deprived of the joys of church? Could he conceive of her longing for "back home," she who had been born out here in the plains? And maybe, after all, he *had* seen Brother André, for had he not assured us that he'd seen the Prince of Wales and Sarah Bernhardt? In any case, he described him to us so faithfully that much later, when we received a calendar from Quebec bearing a lithograph of the saintly Brother, we all exclaimed, "that was him, sure enough!"

For greater effect he assured us at the end, after his accumulation of evidence: "I saw him the way I see you now ... Madame!"

He no longer dared to say "Cousin" to her, but could not pronounce "Madame" without a perceptible hesitation and a note of regret.

From that moment on he grew in my mother's esteem. Henceforth, she gave him an attention which if not always benevolent was at least sustained.

V

But this state of affairs didn't last long. This little devil of a man, who could down plates of porridge in the early morning and fried pork piled up on his plate at other meals without putting on a pound, this "puny runt," as my mother called him, for she still doubted at times whether he had really seen the faces of saints and sanctuaries, this tranquil old soul, perhaps he was waiting for nothing more than to tame my mother, and then away he'd go, leaving the fireside, the set table, and the lamp that shone in the window on rainy nights.

One morning we caught him at the door, staring at the scrubby copses that cut the horizon beyond the swollen coulee. The rain was still falling. Soon it was mixed with snow, and before the day's end the prairie, under its puffy vestment, seemed quite round. Only once did we see him at the door. But we knew he wanted to be on his way, as we had known three weeks before, just from seeing him sit down and sniff the smells of the house, that he wanted to stay. He was just like a big, skinny dog we'd had when we were small, who would beg to come in when the weather was bad and beg to go out when it was worse.

It was no use, my father's going back to the stories of Marcelline and France and Cousin Brault the fiddler, who left by himself for Montreal with his violin and played in orchestras there to the great shame of the family: Gustave's face had darkened. He looked at the door, nothing but the door, the one through which he had made such a joyous entrance. He looked nowhere else and seemed to be pining away each day. For we were witnesses to a strange phenomenon: the clothes my mother had given him seemed to be his own as long as he was happy to stay among us, but then we saw them collapse, hang loose about his shoulders, getting in his way. And what about the stories, the wonderful stories forever extinguished in his eyes! As the sky of our prairies is empty when all the wings have flown south, so Gustave's eyes grew bleak and, as it were, uninhabited. That was perhaps what we held against him most: not having any stories in reserve behind the farther mists of his pale smile.

One evening my father went so far as to offer him a little pay if he wanted to work. My mother showed no offence. Gustave's eyes were grateful, but he gave no other reply.

Next day he was gone. He must have slipped off at night, raising the latches cautiously. Farouche hadn't barked.

My mother flew into a rage. She ran to the silver drawer, to the relic box, to the crockery pot where the change was kept; nothing was missing anywhere. She counted the knives, the spoons, the candlesticks, but had to admit they were all there. Then she was even more humiliated.

"What did we do to make him leave like that?"

My father, for his part, inspected the barn, the granaries, the sheds. He came back discomfited. The shadows on his mute face revealed a regret that did not fade away. From time to time he sighed. At last one evening we heard him complaining, or accusing us: "We didn't receive him the way he deserved. He showed us: he went away."

But we had news of him the following year. In the mail one evening, along with the catalogue from the store in town and the weekly newspaper, was an envelope covered with an unknown handwriting, awkward and blotted with ink spots. My mother opened it at once. Leaning over her shoulder we read along with her. From the wet smell of the paper I cried out before reading a word: "It's from Gustave!"

A skip to the laborious and childish signature confirmed it. It was Gusatve's.

He'd made it to Uncle Alfred's place in Saskatchewan and said he'd been asked to send regards. He said very kind things about the three girls, Emilie,

Alma and Céline, whom my father, by the way, had described as hard to marry off: "Too fancy." From the lines a certain gaiety emanated. You could feel that Gustave was happy. No doubt he was telling his funniest stories in the evenings. A thin smell of tobacco clung to the paper. Crosses at the bottom were meant for kisses.

A little daring, this last familiarity! My mother didn't fail to be offended. My father grew cheerier and we often heard him prophesy in a satisfied tone: "You'll see, he'll be back one of these days."

The following year Gustave was in Alberta. He told us about it in a letter written at Uncle Edouard's place. Uncle Ed and Aunt Honora were working three-quarters of a section with their son. Gustave had helped with the harvest, which had been a good one. They had had him driving the truck, and he'd delivered the grain to the village. One girl was getting married this fall (he didn't say which one, and this unsettled point was the subject of many discussions among us). Another was taking orders. (My mother, to shut us up, said that could only be Paule, because of an old photo that showed her as rather scrawny, her eyes turned heavenward.) Anyway, all were well, including Gustave, except Honora who had stomach trouble. But he was sending for some of Ephrem Brabant's remedy to cure her. He didn't know yet if he'd spend the winter with the "relatives" or go and see a brother of Honora's who'd settled "across the big mountains."

My mother made a few objections, not so much to shake our convictions as to put her own to the test. Aunt Honora, who was such a cold, suspicious fish ... how could she have given Gustave a welcome like this? That remained to be seen. You'd have thought my mother felt a little resentful.

We were certainly glad to get the news, in any case. Lazy about writing, we had never, for all our good resolutions, renewed a correspondence (which in fact had never begun) with out western uncles. And it seemed that Gustave, by taking this duty over, took our bad conscience with it.

This was all very well, but my mother took the opportunity of giving a little lesson to my father, indirectly, as she well knew how to do.

Her head thrown back, shaking a mat, she remarked one day: "I must say, there's strangers that have more family feeling than ... than ..."

My father refused to take offence. He smiled the serene smile of one whose confidence is sheltered from all doubt.

And so time passed. We had another letter six months later, not from British Columbia but from the Yukon, where Gustave vaguely gave us to understand he had turned trapper. Years passed. We might even have forgotten him had he not, by coming to see us long ago, awakened that mysterious thing: interest in one's family, the bewildering affinity that makes a Marcelline, unknown though she may be, less of a stranger than any other old woman in the village. Or, above all, if he hadn't left in our house the memory of so many places and things and people that still carried us through the long evenings, when boredom was not far and we grasped at dreams to drive it off. At those times, rising behind our hazy imaginings, the slightly drawling voice of Gustave would come back from the depths of our recollections.

We no longer talked of him, but thought of him often, each of us, in the evening when a shadow grew long on the road outside.

VI

He came back on a foggy, rainy night like the first one. And Farouche was the only one that knew him, from the smell of wet leaves and mud that his clothing gave off. They recognized each other, the man and the dog, the one perhaps luckier than the other because he had obeyed the mysterious call of the roads and the moonlit nights. But the man seemed weary. Leaning over the anxious dog, patting his head, you would have said he was advising him to appreciate the comfort of his kennel and perhaps even the benevolent servitude of the chain.

He straightened up, examined with the same slow, sad smile the roof of our house and the smoking chimney.

My mother uttered a few excited words: "Good Lord! It looks like ..."

The man hesitated, then, as he had the first time, detoured around to tap on the back door.

I went to open it. He eyes, deep in their sockets, shone for a second. There was no more gaiety in those eyes, not even in their depths. The lustreless blue of water sleeping on the road after heavy storms!

But he exclaimed: "Ghislaine! I'd have known you anywhere, but my land, you've grown!"

I showed him into the big room. He followed me. He was just raising his arms in a great gesture to the reunited family when suddenly we saw him totter, then stagger against the stove and fall, his thin face turned toward us, a little spittle at his lips, his eyes fixed on the shadows like trickles of stagnant water.

My mother touched his reddened forehead. She said: "He has a high fever."

My father took Gustave's feet, my mother his shoulders, and they carried him to their bed.

Then his delirium began.

"I'm Barthélémy," he said. "Son of your brother Alcide. I come from Saint-Jerome. Yep, from Saint-Jerome."

Then he sighed.

"You've got to be friends with your folks, even if they're not always up to the mark."

Then again, in a wheezing voice, between coughing fits: "Come on! You don't know me? I'm Honoré, old man Phidime's boy, the one they thought was dead. I'm his Honoré!"

And suddenly he was muttering about tapers, the monstrance on the altar, the great piety of the world. In the middle of a brisk little laugh he exclaimed: "Good day to you, cousin Anastasie! Well, hello there!"

My father and mother exchanged a long look, then one after the other pulled the blanket over the sick man's body.

It snowed that night, and the next day too, and then another whole day. Then it blew. You could hear the coyotes that had ventured right to the doors of the barns, hear them howling and fighting over the carcass of a white hare that had fallen into their ambush. At times, from the growls that shook Farouche's kennel, we concluded that a great wolf was stalking around the house. Powerful gusts swept the prairie, piled the snow high near the stables, sheds and all the buildings of the farm, which next morning would be half-buried. Snow was already up to our windows. Suddenly a great gust hurled itself against them as if to have a try through glass at blowing out our lamp, last visible sign of life struggling against the unleashed passion of the blizzard.

"No use talking," said my father. "We'll have to try and get out before all the roads are blocked. He could die, that fellow. At least we need some medicine."

He spoke with no warmth. You could feel that his grave affection for the poor wretch had not outlasted the confessions murmured in his delirium: he was being torn by an inner tempest as powerful as the one outside.

Just then, as if mysteriously aware of our concern and his own great danger, Gustave murmured among other unintelligible phrases: "Ephrem Brabant!"

Inspired, my mother fumbled in the pockets of his old overcoat hanging on a nail in the wall. She discovered a small brown bottle. On its label, the face with the white beard, that of the charlatan of Saint-Alphonse, seemed to us familiar and reassuring.

"It can't do him any harm, anyhow," said my mother.

She gave the poor man a gulp of the elixir.

"After all, he believed in it," she added.

My father was getting ready to go out just the same. He wrapped himself in a heavy coat with a fur collar and, to calm my mother, assured her he was just going to the nearest neighbour who had a phone.

My mother calculated: "Six miles there and back. I'll be worried."

A few minutes later we heard a faint sound of sleigh bells whipped by the wind, then the horse whinnying as it plunged past the fence into an immense, tumultuous tempest.

Gustave was quieter after he had swallowed Ephrem Brabant's remedy. Soon he was sleeping deeply, his hands open on the white sheet.

"Now who'd have thought it!" my mother sighed.

Several times she went to sniff at the few drops of brown syrup left in the bottle.

"Just because he believed in it."

Her remark, however, seemed to refer less to the remedy than to a possible thought that arose in her, illuminating her solitary wonderment. She resisted it still at times, as you could see from her restive look; then, with a little shrug of her shoulders, she seemed to give in to the undeniable evidence.

The hours passed. The sick man was still asleep. My mother had finally dozed off. But, waking suddenly, she looked at the clock with growing anguish. Then she struggled to keep awake, and watched over Gustave as she had watched over us, her children, through our illnesses.

Then came the crunching of the cutter's runners in the snow, as if it were still far off, though it was in fact close by the house. A little later my father came in. He was pale, despite the cold, and in a shaking rage.

"How is he?" he asked.

My mother pointed to Gustave, sleeping, and indicated that it was all right to talk.

Then my father turned on her violently as if he were going to accuse her: "The very idea! ... Albertine ... Who'd have thought it? Do you know the police may be here tomorrow because of him?"

"What! He's not a criminal? Oh, no!" stammered my mother, her hands fluttering to her heart.

"No. Maybe worse."

"Is he crazy? Sick?" she asked, pressing her hands to her heaving breasts.

"No. But I'd just as soon it was that."

"What then? Tell me, Arthur."

My father strode across the room, darting wounded glances to one side and the other. His thick overcoat, which he had forgotten to take off, gave an impressive form to his shadow on the wall.

"Oh," he shouted, with lively rancour, "he'd be just as well off dead, that fellow. Imagine, Albertine, and you looked after him so well! Imagine, he passed himself off for a Lafrenière at the Lafrenières below the big hill. And for a Poirier at the Poiriers. And so on. He hasn't one name, that man, he has ten, twenty, as many families as he likes."

"What then?" asked my mother. She had grown strangely calm.

"An imposter!" my father exploded. "Don't you realize, Albertine? An imposter!"

He tried to control his voice: "Somebody reported him. The police have started an inquiry. When people find out he's here ..."

"What then, Arthur?"

My mother had taken up her stand at the door of the bedroom as if to forbid all entry. Tiny as she was, when she stood this way, her head high, her eyes flashing with determination, not many would have dared defy her.

"Well?" she said. "Don't we know what to say? Don't we know it?" she repeated, questioning each of us in turn with her clear, open gaze.

Suddenly the violence that had seized my father was broken. He seemed infinitely tired. Almost feeling his way, he sought out his chair in the corner by the fire and sank down in it. And at last we understood the disenchantment, worse than anger, that he had to bear. A Marcelline who could laugh and dance at her second wedding; Eustache, attached to the memory of his parents; a tender, affectionate Philomène; these characters, like a mirage that had for some time fed my father's dreams, had already disappeared from before his eyes. They were replaced by a dried-up, hardened little woman, by the bad son who had deceived his parents, by Philomène, frightful and graceless. In my father's eyes we saw the return of that absence of love with which he had had to live for so long.

"Good gracious now!" my mother said in a curiously persuasive tone. "Who's to prove it isn't true? He has to be somebody's relative. What's to prove to us it isn't true?"

Next morning Gustave awoke practically cured. He accepted the warm clothing my mother had taken from the trunks for him. He thanked her without effusiveness. You'd have thought he'd left a few of his things with us, and was grateful to get them back clean and mended. Gradually our wrath, our shame at having liked him, quieted down.

That day the sky swept the snow away with great waves of sunlight. The buildings, the cutters with their shafts pointed skyward, the buckets and barrels, all our everyday things, projected only the flimsiest of shadows in the immense plain all trembling with light. In the distance, on the hardened crust of the prairie, tiny tracks made their way toward the woods. At dawn, when the storm grew still, the wolves and coyotes had again sought the refuge of the trees.

Gustave was getting ready to go. He went to the door, downcast, but paused, his hand on the latch. My mother was preparing a splendid stew of jack rabbit and beef.

"There's no rush," she said, paying no attention to my father's silence. "You were a sick man. There's no rush at all."

Gustave made a despairing gesture with his arms. Then a shiver passed through his whole body. He seemed to be struggling against the temptation of warmth and the odour of the stew. Had some echo of our words of yesterday floated up in his memory? Or was it his old mania taking over again? He began to lift the latch.

"I suppose you have to get along to see some relatives?"

My mother had spoken in a friendly and reassuring voice. The man pricked up his ears. His stooped shoulders straightened. He looked back at the room. Greedily, as if to make a memory of it, he contemplated a ray of sunlight slanting through it, delicately lighting up the steam from the pots simmering on the stove. Finally he glanced up at my mother. His old eyes with their worn gaze were shining again.

"Yes," he said.

"Well! And which way are you heading this time?"

"I have some folks on my mother's side ... in Ontario ..." he began uncertainly.

"Would that be down Hawkesbury way?" asked my mother, with every sign of lively interest. "They say there's a lot of our people there still speak French."

She had thrown a shawl over her shoulders. She went with the man past the threshold. She encouraged him with her eyes. He went off, walking backward a few steps, as if he couldn't decide whether to give up my mother's accepting gaze. Then he turned to face the naked, empty plain.

Farouche, straining at his leash, was whining, almost choking himself in the attempt to leave with that miserable silhouette.

"Quiet. Farouche, quiet!" said my mother.

Then she did something so simple, so splendid. Cupping her hands to her mouth, she shouted loudly into the wind, her apron flying around her: "Take care! Take good care ... Cousin Gustave!"

Did he hear? Perhaps. In any case, he had cut a branch in our garden for a walking stick.

DIANE SCHOEMPERLEN

RED PLAID SHIRT

Diane Schoemperlen (b. 1954) was born in Thunder Bay, Ontario, and graduated from Lakehead University in 1976. That summer she moved to Canmore, Alberta, where she lived for ten years. Since 1986 she has lived in Kingston, Ontario, with her son Alexander. She has published five books of short fiction, including Double Exposures *(1984),* Frogs and Other Stories *(1986),* Hockey Night in Canada *(1987) and* Forms of Devotion *(1998). Her 1990 collection* The Man of My Dreams *was nominated for a Governor General's Literary Award. Her first novel,* In the Language of Love *(1994), has been translated into Swedish and German, and it has been performed as a stage play in Kingston and Toronto. As is shown by the titles above and by the story below, "Red Plaid Shirt," Schoemperlen's writing is marked by an ironic sense of humour and a knack for collecting the illuminations that hover on the peripheries of our everyday lives. "Red Plaid Shirt" also exhibits the experimentation that has marked Schoemperlen as one of Canada's chief young writers; this story won the Silver National Magazine Award for fiction in 1989.*

RED PLAID SHIRT that your mother bought you one summer in Banff. It is 100% Pure Virgin Wool, itchy but flattering against your pale skin, your black hair. You got it in a store called Western Outfitters, of the sort indigenous to the region, which stocked only *real* (as opposed to designer) blue jeans, Stetson hats, and $300 hand-tooled cowboy boots with very pointy toes. There was a saddle and a stuffed deer-head in the window.

Outside, the majestic mountains were sitting all around, magnanimously letting their pictures be taken by ten thousand tourists wielding Japanese cameras and eating ice-cream cones. You had tricked your mother into leaving her camera in the car so she wouldn't embarrass you, who lived there and were supposed to be taking the scenery for granted by now.

You liked the red plaid shirt so much that she bought you two more just like it, one green, the other chocolate brown. But these two stayed shirts, never acquiring any particular significance, eventually getting left unceremoniously behind in a Salvation Army drop-box in a grocery store parking lot somewhere along the way.

The red plaid shirt reminded you of your mother's gardening shirt, which was also plaid and which you rescued one winter when she was going to throw it away because the elbows were out. You picture her kneeling in the side garden where she grew only flowers, bleeding hearts, roses, peonies, poppies, and a small patch of strawberries. You picture her hair in a bright babushka, her bands in the black earth with her shirt-sleeves rolled up past the elbow. The honeysuckle hedge bloomed flagrantly behind her and the sweet peas curled interminably up the white trellis. You are sorry now for the way you always sulked and whined when she asked you to help, for the way you hated the dirt under your nails and sweat running into your eyes, the sweat dripping down her shirt-front between her small breasts. You kept her old shirt in a bag in your closet for years, with a leather patch half-sewn onto the left sleeve, but now you can't find it.

You were wearing the red plaid shirt the night you met Daniel in the tavern where he was drinking beer with his buddies from the highway construction crew. You ended up living with him for the next five years. He was always calling it your "magic shirt," teasing you, saying how it was the shirt that made him fall in love with you in the first place. You would tease him back, saying how you'd better hang onto it then in case you had to use it on somebody else. You've even worn it in that spirit a few times since, but the magic seems to have seeped out if it and you are hardly surprised.

You've gained a little weight since then or the shirt has shrunk, so you can't wear it anymore, but you can't throw or give it away either.

> RED: *crimson carmine cochineal cinnebar sanguine scarlet red ruby rouge my birthstone red and blood-red brick-red beet-red bleeding hearts Queen of fire god of war Mars the colour of magic my magic the colour of iron flowers and fruit the colour of meat dripping lobster cracking claws lips nipples blister blood my blood and all power.*

BLUE COTTON SWEATSHIRT that says "Why Be Normal?" in a circle on the front. This is your comfort shirt, fleecy on the inside, soft from many washings, and three sizes too big so you can tuck your hands up inside the sleeves when they're shaking or cold. You like to sit on the couch with the curtains closed, wearing your comfort shirt, eating comfort food: vanilla ice-cream, macaroni and cheese, white rice with butter and salt, white toast with CheezWhiz and peanut-butter. Sometimes you even sleep in it.

This is shirt you wore when you had the abortion three days before Christmas. They told you to be there at nine in the morning and then you didn't get into the operation room until nearly twelve-thirty. So you wore it in the waiting room with the other women also waiting, and the weight you had already gained was hidden beneath it while you pretended to read *Better Homes and Gardens* and they wouldn't let you smoke. After you came to, you put the shirt back on and waited in another waiting room for your friend, Alice, to come and pick you up because they said you weren't capable yet of going home alone. One of the other women was waiting there too, for her boyfriend who was always late, and when he finally got there, first she yelled at him briefly, and they decided to go to McDonald's for a hamburger. At home, Alice pours you tea from the porcelain pot into white china cups like precious opaque stones.

None of this has diminished, as you feared it might, the comfort this shirt can give you when you need it Alice always puts her arms around you whenever she sees you wearing it now. She has one just like it, only pink.

> BLUE: *azure aqua turquoise delft and navy-blue royal-blue cool*
> *cerulean peacock-blue ultramarine cobalt-blue Prussian-blue cyan*
> *the sky and electric a space the colour of the firmament and sapphire*
> *sleeping silence the sea the blues my lover plays the saxophone cool*
> *blue he plays the blues.*

PALE GREY TURTLENECK that you bought when you were seeing Dwight, who said one night for no apparent reason that grey is a mystical colour. You took this judgement to heart because Dwight was more likely to talk about hockey or carburetors and you were pleasantly surprised to discover that he might also think about other things. You spotted the turtleneck the very next day on sale at Maggie's for $9.99.

Your took to wearing it on Sundays because that was the day Dwight was mostly likely to wander in, unannounced, on his way to or from somewhere else. You wore it while you just happened to put a bottle of good wine into the fridge to chill and a chicken, a roast, or a pan of spinach lasagna into the oven to cook slowly just in case he showed up hungry. You suppose now that this was pathetic, but at the time you were thinking of yourself as patient and him as worth waiting for.

Three Sundays in a row you ended up passed out on the couch, the wine bottle empty on the coffee table, and supper dried out, and a black-and-white movie with violin music flickering on the TV. In the coloured morning, the pattern of the upholstery was imprinted on your cheek, and your whole head was hurting. When Dwight finally did show up, it was a Wednesday and you were wearing your orange flannelette nightie with all the buttons gone and a rip down the front, because it was three in the morning, he was drunk, and you had been in bed for hours. He just laughed and took you in his arms when you told him to get lost. Until you said you were seeing someone else, which was a lie, but one that you both wanted to believe because it was an easy answer that let both of you gingerly of the hook.

You keep meaning to wear that turtleneck again sometime because you know it's juvenile to think it's a jinx, but then you keep forgetting to iron it.

Finally, you get tough and wear it, wrinkled, grocery-shopping one Saturday afternoon. You careen through the aisles like a crazed hamster, dodging toddlers, old ladies, and other carts, scooping up vegetables with both hands, eating an apple you haven't paid for, leaving the core in the dairy section. But nothing happens and no one notices your turtleneck: the colour or the wrinkles.

Sure enough, Dwight calls the next day, Sunday, at five o'clock. You say you can't talk now you're just cooking supper: prime rib, wild rice, broccoli with Hollandaise. You have no trouble at all hanging quietly up on him while pouring the wine into the crystal goblet before setting the table for one with the Royal Albert china your mother left you in her will.

> GREY: *oyster pewter slate dull lead dove-grey pearl-grey brain my brains silver or simple gone into the mystic a cool grey day overcast with clouds ashes concrete the aftermath of airplanes gun-metal-grey granite and gossamer whales elephants cats in the country the colour of questions the best camouflage the opaque elegance an oyster.*

WHITE EMBROIDERED BLOUSE that you bought for $80 to wear with your red-flowered skirt to a Christmas party with Peter, who was working as a pizza cook until he could afford to play his sax full-time. You also bought a silken red belt with gold beads and tassels, a pair of red earrings with dragons on them, and ribbed red stockings which are too small but you wanted them anyway. This striking outfit involves you and Alice in a whole day of trudging around downtown in a snowstorm holding accessories up in front of mirrors like talismans.

You spend an hour in the bathroom getting ready, drinking white wine, plucking your eyebrows, dancing like a dervish, and smiling seductively at yourself. Peter calls to say he has to work late but he'll meet you there at midnight.

By the time he arrives, you are having a complex anatomical conversation with a intern named Fernando, who has spilled a glass of red wine down the front of your blouse. He is going to be a plastic surgeon. Your blouse is soaking in the bathtub and you are wearing only your white lace camisole. Fernando is feeding you green grapes and little squares of cheese, complimenting you on your cheekbones, and falling in love with your smooth forehead. You are having the time of your life and it's funny how you notice for the first time that Peter has an inferior bone structure.

WHITE: *ivory alabaster magnolia milk the moon is full and chalk-white pure-white snow-white moonstone limestone rime and clay marble may seashells and my bones are china bones precious porce-lain lace white magic white feather the immaculate conception of white lies wax white wine is a virtue.*

YELLOW EVENING GOWN that you bought for your New Year's Eve date with Fernando. It has a plunging neckline and a dropped sash which flatteringly accentuates your hips. You wear it with black hoop earrings, black lace stockings with seams, and black high-heels that Alice forced you to buy even though they hurt your toes and you are so unco-ordinated that you expect you will have to spend the entire evening sitting down with your legs crossed, calves nicely flexed.

You spend an hour in the bathroom getting ready, drinking pink cham-pagne, applying blusher with a fat brush according to a diagram in a women's magazine that shows you how to make the most of your face. You practise holding your chin up so it doesn't sag and look double. Alice french-braids your hair and teaches you how to waltz like a lady. Fernando calls to say he has to work late but he'll meet you there before midnight.

You go to the club with Alice instead. They seat you at a tiny table for two so that when you sit down, your knees touch hers. You are in the middle of a room full of candles, fresh flowers, lounge music, and well-groomed couples staring feverishly into each other's eyes. The meal is sumptuous: green salad, a whole lobster, home-made pasta, fresh asparagus, and warm buns wrapped in white linen in a wicker basket. You eat everything and then you get the hell out of there, leaving a message for Fernando.

You go down the street to a bar you know where they will let you in without a ticket even though it's New Year's Eve. In the lobby you meet Fernando in a tuxedo with his arm around a short homely woman in black who, when you ask, "Who the hell are you?," says, "His wife." In your black high-heels you are taller than both of them and you know your gown is gor-geous. When the wife says, "And who the hell are *you*?," you point a long finger at Fernando's nose and say, "Ask him." You stomp away with your chin up and your dropped sash swaying.

Out of sight, you take off your high-heels and walk home through the park and the snow with them in your hands, dangling. Alice follows in a cab. By the time you get there, your black lace stockings are in shreds and your feet are cut and you are laughing and crying, mostly laughing.

YELLOW: *jonquil jasmine daffodil lemon and honey-coloured corn-coloured cornsilk canary crocus the egg yolk in the morning the colour of mustard bananas brass cadmium yellow is the colour of craving craven chicken cats' eyes I am faint-hearted weak-kneed lily-livered or the sun lucid luminous means caution or yield.*

BLACK LEATHER JACKET that you bought when you were seeing Ivan, who rode a red Harley Davidson low-rider with a suicide shift, his black beard blowing in the wind. The jacket has rows of diagonal pleats at the yoke and a red leather collar and cuffs.

Ivan used to take you on weekend runs with his buddies and their old ladies to little bars in other towns where they were afraid of you: especially of Ivan's best friend, Spy, who had been hurt in a bike accident two years before and now his hands hung off his wrists at odd angles and he could not speak, could only make gutteral growls, write obscene notes to the waitress on a serviette, and laugh at her like a madman, his eyes rolling back in his head, and you could see what was left of his tongue.

You would come riding up in a noisy pack with bugs in your teeth, dropping your black helmets like bowling balls on the floor, eating greasy burgers and pickled eggs, drinking draft beer by the jug, the foam running down your chin. Your legs, after the long ride, felt like a wishbone waiting to be sprung. If no one would rent you a room, you slept on picnic tables in the campground, the bikes pulled in around you like wagons, a case of beer and one sleeping bag between ten of you. In the early morning, there was dew on your jacket and your legs were numb with the weight of Ivan's head on them.

You never did get around to telling your mother you were dating a biker (she thought you said "baker") which was just as well since Ivan eventually got tired, sold his bike, and moved back to Manitoba to live with his mother who was dying. He got a job in a hardware store and soon married his high school sweetheart, Betty, who was a dental hygienist. Spy was killed on the highway, drove his bike into the back of a tanker truck in broad daylight: there was nothing left of him.

You wear your leather jacket now when you need to feel tough. You wear it with your tight blue jeans and your cowboy boots. You strut slowly with your hands in your pockets. Your boots click on the concrete and you are a different person. You can handle anything and no one had better get in your way. You will take on the world if you have to. You will die young and in flames if you have to.

> BLACK: *ebon sable charcoal jet lamp-black blue-black bruises in a night sky ink-black soot-black the colour of my hair and burning rubber dirt the colour of infinite space speeding blackball blacklist black sheep blackberries ravens eat crow black as the ace of spades and black is black I want my baby back before midnight yes of course midnight that old black dog behind me.*

BROWN CASHMERE SWEATER that you were wearing the night you told Daniel you were leaving him. It was that week between Christmas and New Year's which is always a wasteland. Everyone was digging up recipes called Turkey-Grape Salad, Turkey Soufflé, and Turkey-Almond-Noodle Bake. You kept vacuuming up tinsel and pine needles, putting away presents one at a time from under the tree. You and Daniel sat at the kitchen table all afternoon, drinking hot rum toddies, munching on crackers and garlic sausage, playing Trivial Pursuit, asking each other questions like:

What's the most mountainous country in Europe?

Which is more tender, the left or right leg of a chicken?

What race of warriors burned off their right breasts in Greek legend?

Daniel was a poor loser and he thought that Europe was a country, maybe somewhere near Spain.

This night you have just come from a party at his friend Harold's house. You are sitting on the new couch, a loveseat, blue with white flowers, which was Daniel's Christmas present to you, and you can't help thinking of the year your father got your mother a coffee percolator when all she wanted was something personal: earrings, a necklace, a scarf for God's sake. She spent most of the day locked in their bedroom, crying noisily, coming every hour or so to baste the turkey, white-lipped, tucking more Kleenex up her sleeve. You were on her side this time and wondered how your father, who you had always secretly loved the most, could be so insensitive. It was the changing of the guard, your allegience shifting like sand from one to the other.

You were sitting on the new couch eating cold pizza and trying to figure out why you didn't have a good time at the party. Daniel was accusing you alternately of looking down on his friends or sleeping with them. He is wearing the black leather vest you bought him for Christmas and he says you are a cheapskate.

When you tell him you are leaving (which is a decision you made months ago but it took this long to figure out how you were going to manage it and it has nothing to do with the party, the couch, or the season), Daniel grips you by the shoulders and bangs your head against the wall until the picture hung there falls off. It is a photograph of the mountains on a pink spring morning, the ridges like ribs, the runoff like incisions or veins. There is glass flying everywhere in slices into your face, into your hands pressed over your eyes, and the front of your sweater is spotted and matted with blood.

On the way to the hospital, he says he will kill you if you tell them what he did to you. You promise him anything, you promise him that you will love him forever and that you will never leave.

The nurse takes you into the examining room. Daniel waits in the waiting room, reading magazines, buys a chocolate bar from the vending machine, then a Coke and a bag of ripple chips. You tell the nurse what happened and the police take him away in handcuffs with their guns drawn. In the car on the way to the station, he tells them he only did it because he loves you. The officer who takes down your report tells you this and he just keeps shaking his head and patting your arm. The police photographer takes pictures of your face, your broken fingers, your left breast which has purple bruises all over it where he grabbed it and twisted and twisted.

By the time you get to the women's shelter, it is morning and the blood on your sweater has dried, doesn't show. There is no way of knowing. There, the other women hold you, brush your hair, bring you coffee and cream and mushroom soup. The woman with the broken cheekbone has two canaries in a gold cage that she carries with her everywhere like a lamp. She shows you how the doors are steel, six inches thick, and the windows are bullet-proof. She shows you where you will sleep, in a room on the third floor with six other women, some of them lying now fully-dressed on their little iron cots with their hands behind their heads, staring at the ceiling as if it were full of stars or clouds that drift slowing westward in the shape of camels, horses, or bears. She shows you how the canaries will sit on your finger if you hold very still and pretend you are a tree or a roof or another bird.

> BROWN: *ochre cinnamon coffee copper caramel the colour of my Christmas cake chocolate mocha walnut chestnuts raw sienna my suntan burnt umber burning toast fried fricasseed sautéed grilled I baste the turkey the colour of stupid cows smart horses brown bears brown shirt brown sugar apple brown betty brunette the colour of thought and sepia the colour of old photographs the old earth and wood.*

GREEN SATIN QUILTED JACKET in the Oriental style with mandarin collar and four red frogs down the front. This jacket is older than you are. It belonged to your mother, who bought it when she was the same age you are now. In the black-and-white photos from that time, the jacket is grey but shiny and your mother is pale but smooth-skinned, smiling with her hand on her hip or your father's thigh.

You were always pestering her to let you wear it to play dress-up, with her red high-heels and that white hat with the feathers and the little veil that covered your whole face. You wanted to wear it to a Hallowe'en party at school where all the other girls would be witches, ghosts, or princesses and you would be the only mandarin, with your eyes, you imagined, painted up slanty and two sticks through the bun in your hair. But she would never let you. She would just keep on cooking supper, bringing carrots, potatoes, cabbages up from the root cellar, taking peas, beans, broccoli out of the freezer in labelled dated parcels, humming, looking out through the slats of the Venetian blind at the black garden and the leafless rose bushes. Each year, at least one of them would be winter-killed no matter how hard she had tried to protect them. And she would dig it up in the spring by the dead roots and the thorns would get tangled in her hair, leave long bloody scratches all down her arms. And the green jacket stayed where it was, in the cedar chest with the hand-made lace doilies, her grey linen wedding suit, and the picture of your father as a small boy with blond ringlets.

After the funeral, you go through her clothes while your father is outside shovelling snow. You lay them out in piles on the bed: one for the Salvation Army, one for the second-hand store, one for yourself because your father wants you to take something home with you. You will take the green satin jacket, also a white mohair cardigan with multi-coloured squares on the front, a black-and-white striped shirt you sent her for her birthday last year that she never wore, an imitation pearl necklace for Alice, and a dozen unopened packages of pantyhose. There is a fourth pile for your father's friend Jack's new wife, Frances, whom your mother never liked, but your father says Jack and Frances have fallen on hard times on the farm since Jack got the emphysema, and Frances will be glad of some new clothes.

Jack and Frances drop by the next day with your Aunt Jeanne. You serve tea and the shortbread cookies Aunt Jeanne has brought. She makes them just the way your mother did, whipped, with a sliver of maraschino cherry on top. Jack, looking weather-beaten or embarrassed, sits on the edge of the couch with his baseball cap in his lap and marvels at how grown-up you've got to be. Frances is genuinely grateful for the two green garbage bags of clothes, which you carry out to the truck for her.

After they leave you reminisce fondly with your father and Aunt Jeanne about taking the toboggan out to Jack's farm when you were small, tying it to the back of the car, your father driving slowly down the country lane, towing you on your stomach, clutching the front of the toboggan which curled like a wooden wave. You tell him for the first time how frightened you were of the black tires spinning the snow into your face, and he says he had no idea, he thought you were having fun. This was when Jack's first wife, Winnifred, was still alive. Your Aunt Jeanne, who knows everything, tells you that when Winnifred was killed in that car accident, it was Jack, driving drunk, who caused it. And now when he gets drunk, he beats Frances up, locks her out of the house in her bare feet, and she has to sleep in the barn, in the hay with the horses.

You are leaving in the morning. Aunt Jeanne helps you pack. You are anxious to get home but worried about leaving your father alone. Aunt Jeanne says she'll watch out for him.

The green satin jacket hangs in your front hall closet now, between your black leather jacket and your raincoat. You can still smell the cedar from the chest and the satin is always cool on your cheek like clean sheets or glass.

One day you think you will wear it downtown, where you are meeting a new man for lunch. You study yourself in the full-length mirror on the back of the bathroom door and you decide it makes you look like a different person: someone unconventional, unusual, and unconcerned. This new man, who you met recently at an outdoor jazz festival, is a free spirit who eats health food, plays the dulcimer, paints well, writes well, sings well, and has just completed an independent study of eastern religions. He doesn't smoke, drink, or do drugs. He is pure and peaceful, perfect. He is teaching you how to garden, how to turn the black soil, how to plant the seeds, how to water them, weed them, watch them turn into lettuce, carrots, peas, beans, radishes, and pumpkins, how to get the kinks out of your back by stretching your brown arms right up to the sun. You haven't even told Alice about him yet because he is too good to be true. He is bound to love this green jacket, and you in it too.

You get in your car, drive down the block, go back inside because you forgot your cigarettes, and you leave the green jacket on the back of a kitchen chair because who are you trying to kid? More than anything, you want to be transparent. More than anything, you want to hold his hands across the table and then you will tell him you love him and it will all come true.

> GREEN: *viridian verdigris chlorophyll grass leafy jade mossy verdant apple-green pea-green lime-green sage-green sea-green bottle-green emeralds avocadoes olives all leaves the colour of Venus hope and jealousy the colour of mould mildew envy poison and pain and snakes the colour of everything that grows in my garden fertile nourishing sturdy sane and strong.*

CAROL SHIELDS

SCENES

Carol Shields (b. 1935) was born in Oak Park, Illinois. She earned a B.A.
from Hanover College in 1957 and the same year immigrated to Canada.
"I married quite young," Shields recalls, "and had five children. So, for
maybe twelve years, I didn't do much writing. Then, I started to write
again when I was forty." Shields received her M.A. from the University of
Ottawa in 1975 and began freelance writing and editing. Her first two
books were volumes of poetry in 1972 and 1974. She soon turned to
writing novels, including Small Ceremonies *(1976),* The Box Garden
(1977), A Fairly Conventional Woman *(1982), and* Swann *(1987). Her*
writing developed Joyce's concept of the epiphany, which for Shields rep-
resents "rare transcendental moments when you suddenly feel everything
makes sense and you perceive the pattern of the universe. I think we all
get a few of these minutes. I'm very interested in finding language to
record them." In 1980 Shields became a professor at the University of
Manitoba. In 1985 Shields published her first short-story collection,
Various Miracles, *in which "Scenes" appears, and completed her second*
collection, The Orange Fish, *in 1989. The short stories Shields wrote in*
this period mark an important turning point in her career—they stand as
some of the most exciting in contemporary Canadian writing, and their
experimental verve seems also to have lent new energy to Shields's novels.
She returned to novel writing with The Republic of Love *(1992) and* The
Stone Diaries *(1993); the latter novel won the Governor General's Award*
in 1994 and the Pulitzer Prize in 1995. Larry's Party, *a Giller Prize nom-*
inee, appeared in 1997. Shields is now widely recognized as one of
Canada's most important writers.

"I love revising," Shields says. "Revising is where the pleasure is for
me in writing. I probably spend about 80% of my time revising." Her sto-
ries, often quite brief, are more experimental in form than the novels. She
says that:

> These are interesting times for a writer. The crisis of meaning,
> and we nearly died of it, has brought us a new set of options.
> The strands of reality that enter the newest of our fictions are
> looser, more random and discursive. More altogether seems pos-
> sible. The visual media, television and the cinema, have appro-
> priated the old linear set-ups, leaving fiction, by default, the

more interesting territory of the reflective consciousness, the inside of the head where nine-tenths of our lives are lived. And writers seem more happily aware of their intimate connection with readers and with other writing.

In 1974 Frances was asked to give a lecture in Edmonton, and on the way there her plane was forced to make an emergency landing in a barley field. The man sitting next to her—they had not spoken—turned and asked if he might put his arms around her. She assented. They clung together, her size 12 dress and his wool suit. Later, he gave her his business card.

She kept the card for several weeks poked in the edge of her bedroom mirror. It is a beautiful mirror, a graceful rectangle in a pine frame, and very, very old. Once it was attached to the back of a bureau belonging to Frances' grandmother. Leaves, vines, flowers and fruit are shallowly carved in the soft wood of the frame. The carving might be described as primitive—and this is exactly why Frances loves it, being drawn to those things that are incomplete or in some way flawed. Furthermore, the mirror is the first thing she remembers seeing, *really* seeing, as a child. Visiting her grandmother, she noticed the stiff waves of light and shadow on the frame, the way square pansies interlocked with rigid grapes, and she remembers creeping out of her grandmother's bed where she had been put for an afternoon nap and climbing on a chair so she could touch the worked surface with the flat of her hand.

Her grandmother died. It was discovered by the aunts and uncles that on the back of the mirror was stuck a piece of adhesive tape and on the tape was written: "For my vain little grandaughter Frances." Frances' mother was affronted, but put it down to hardening of the arteries. Frances, who was only seven, felt uniquely, mysteriously honored.

She did not attend the funeral; it was thought she was too young, and so instead she was taken one evening to the funeral home to bid goodbye to her grandmother's body. The room where the old lady lay was large, quiet, and hung all around with swags of velvet. Frances' father lifted her up so she could see her grandmother, who was wearing a black dress with a white crepe jabot, her powdered face pulled tight as though with a drawstring into a sort of grimace. A lovely blanket with satin edging covered her trunky legs and torso. Laid out, calm and silent as a boat, she looked almost generous.

For some reason Frances was left alone with the casket for a few minutes, and she took this chance—she had to pull herself up on tiptoe—to reach out and touch her grandmother's lips with the middle finger of her right hand. It was like pressing in the side of a rubber ball. The lips did not turn to dust— which did not surprise Frances at all, but rather confirmed what she had known all along. Later, she would look at her finger and say to herself, "This finger has touched dead lips." Then she would feel herself grow rich with disgust. The touch, she knew, had not been an act of love at all, but only a kind of test.

With the same middle finger she later touched the gelatinous top of a gold-fish swimming in a little glass bowl at school. She touched the raised mole on the back of her father's white neck. Shuddering, she touched horse turds in the back lane, and she touched her own urine springing onto the grass as she squatted behind the snowball bush by the fence. When she looked into her grandmother's mirror, now mounted on her own bedroom wall, she could hardly believe that she, Frances, had contravened so many natural laws.

The glass itself was bevelled all the way around, and she can remember that she took pleasure in lining up her round face so that the bevelled edge split it precisely in two. When she was fourteen she wrote in her diary, "Life is like looking into a bevelled mirror." The next day she crossed it out and, peering into the mirror, stuck out her tongue and made a face. All her life she'd had this weakness for preciosity, but mainly she'd managed to keep it in check.

She is a lithe and toothy woman with strong, thick, dark-brown hair, now starting to gray. She can be charming. "Frances can charm the bees out of the hive," said a friend of hers, a man she briefly thought she loved. Next year she'll be forty-five—terrible!—but at least she's kept her figure. A western sway to her voice is what people chiefly remember about her, just as they remember other people for their chins or noses. This voice sometimes makes her appear inquisitive, but, in fact, she generally hangs back and leaves it to others to begin a conversation.

Once, a woman got into an elevator with her and said, "Will you forgive me if I speak my mind. This morning I came within an inch of taking my life. There was no real reason, only everything had got suddenly so dull. But I'm all right now. In fact, I'm going straight to a restaurant and treat myself to a plate of french fries. Just fries, not even a sandwich to go with them. I was never allowed to have french fries when I was a little girl, but the time comes when a person should do what she wants to do."

The subject of childhood interests Frances, especially its prohibitions, so illogical and various, and its random doors and windows which appear solidly shut, but can, in fact, be opened easily with a touch or a password or a minute of devout resolution. It helps to be sly, also to be quick. There was a time when she worried that fate had pencilled her in as "debilitated by guilt," but mostly she takes guilt for what it is, a kind of lover who can be shrugged off or greeted at the gate. She looks at her two daughters and wonders if they'll look back resentfully, recalling only easy freedoms and an absence of terror—in other words, meagreness—and envy her for her own stern beginnings. It turned out to have been money in the bank, all the various shames and sweats of growing up. It was instructive; it kept things interesting; she still shivers, remembering how exquisitely sad she was as a child.

"It's only natural for children to be sad," says her husband. Theo, who, if he has a fault, is given to reductive statements. "Children are unhappy because they are inarticulate and hence lonely."

Frances can't remember being lonely, but telling this to Theo is like blowing into a hurricane. She was spoiled—a lovely word, she thinks—and adored by her parents, her plump, white-faced father and her skinny, sweet-tempered mother. Their love was immense and enveloping like a fall of snow. In the evenings, winter evenings, she sat between the two of them on a blue nubby sofa, listening to the varnished radio and taking sips from their cups of tea from time to time or sucking on a spoonful of sugar. The three of them sat enthralled through "Henry Aldrich" and "Fibber Magee and Molly," and when Frances laughed they looked at her and laughed too. Frances has no doubt that these spoonfuls of sugar and the roar of Fibber Magee's closet and her parents' soft looks were taken in and preserved so that she, years later, boiling an egg or making love or digging in the garden, is sometimes struck by a blow of sweetness that seems to come out of nowhere.

The little brown house where she grew up sat in the middle of a block crowded with other such houses. In front of each lay a tiny lawn and a flower bed edged with stones. Rows of civic trees failed to flourish, but did not die either. True, there was terror in the back lane where the big boys played with sticks and jackknives, but the street was occupied mainly by quiet, hard-working families, and in the summertime hopscotch could be played in the street, there was so little traffic.

Frances' father spent his days "at the office." Her mother stayed at home, wore bib aprons, made jam and pickles and baked custard, and every morning before school brushed and braided Frances' hair. Frances can remember, or thinks she can remember, that one morning her mother walked as far as the corner with her and said, "I don't know why, but I'm so full of happiness today I can hardly bear it." The sun came fretting through the branches of a scrubby elm at that minute and splashed across her mother's face, making her look like someone in a painting or like one of the mothers in her school reader.

Learning to read was like falling into a mystery deeper than the mystery of airwaves or the halo around the head of the baby Jesus. Deliberately, she made herself stumble and falter over the words in her first books, trying to hold back the rush of revelation. She saw other children being matter-of-fact and methodical, puzzling over vowels and consonants and sounding out words as though they were dimes and nickels that had to be extracted from the slot of a bank. She felt suffused with light and often skipped or hopped or ran wildly to keep herself from flying apart.

Her delirium, her failure to ingest books calmly, made her suspect there was something wrong with her or else with the world, yet she deeply distrusted the school librarian who insisted that a book could be a person's best friend. (Those subject to preciosity instantly spot others with the same affliction.) This librarian, Miss Mayes, visited all the classes. She was tall and soldierly with a high, light voice. "Boys and girls," she cried, bringing large red hands together, "a good book will never let you down." She went on, books could take you on magic journeys; books could teach you where the rain came from or how things used to be in the olden days. A person who truly loved books need never feel alone.

But, she continued, holding up a finger, there are people who do shameful things to books. They pull them from the shelves by their spines. They turn down the corners of pages; they leave them on screened porches where the rain and other elements can warp their covers; and they use curious and inappropriate objects as bookmarks.

From a petit-point bag she drew a list of objects that had been wrongly, criminally inserted between fresh clean pages; a blue-jay feather, an oak leaf, a matchbook cover, a piece of colored chalk and, on one occasion—on one occasion, boys and girls—a *strip of bacon*.

A strip of bacon. In Frances' mind the strip of bacon was uncooked, cold and fatty with a pathetic streaking of lean. Its oil would press into the paper, a porky abomination, and its ends would flop out obscenely. The thought was thrilling; someone, someone who lived in the same school district had had the audacity, the imagination, to mark the pages of a book with a strip of bacon. The existence of this person and his outrageous act penetrated the fever that had come over her since she'd learned to read, and she began to look around again and see what the world had to offer.

Next door lived Mr. and Mrs. Shaw, and upstairs, fast asleep, lived Louise Shaw, aged eighteen. She had been asleep for ten years. A boy across the street named Jackie McConnell told Frances that it was the sleeping sickness bug, but Frances' mother said no, it was the coma. One day Mrs. Shaw, smelling of chlorine bleach and wearing a flower-strewn housedress, stopped Frances on the sidewalk, held the back of her hand to the side of Frances' face and said, "Louise was just your age when we lost her. She was forever running or skipping rope or throwing a ball up against the side of the garage. I used to say to her, don't make such a ruckus, you'll drive me crazy. I used to yell all the time at her, she was so full of beans and such a chatterbox." After that Frances felt herself under an obligation to Mrs. Shaw, and whenever she saw her she made her body speed up and whirl on the grass or do cartwheels.

A little later she learned to negotiate the back lane. There, between board fences, garbage cans, garage doors and stands of tough weeds, she became newly nimble and strong. She learned to swear—damn, hell and dirty bastard—and played piggy-move-up and spud and got herself roughly kissed a number of times, and then something else happened: one of the neighbors put up a basketball hoop. For a year, maybe two—Frances doesn't trust her memory when it comes to time—she was obsessed with doing free throws. She became known as the queen of free throws; she acquired status, even with the big boys, able to sink ten out of ten baskets, but never, to her sorrow, twenty out of twenty. She threw free throws in the morning before school, at lunchtime, and in the evening until it got dark. Nothing made her happier than when the ball dropped silently through the ring without touching it or banking on the board. At night she dreamed of these silky baskets, the rush of air and the sinuous movement of the net, then the ball striking the pavement and returning to her hands. ("Sounds a bit Freudian to me," her husband, Theo, said when she tried to describe for him her time of free-throw madness, proving once again how far apart the two of them were in some things.) One morning she was up especially early. There was no one about. The milkman hadn't yet come, and there was dew shining on the tarry joints of the pavement. Holding the ball in her hands was like holding onto a face, it was so dearly familiar with its smell of leather and its seams and laces. That morning she threw twenty-seven perfect free throws before missing. Each time the ball went through the hoop she felt an additional oval of surprise grow round her body. She had springs inside her, in her arms and in the insteps of her feet. What stopped her finally was her mother calling her name, demanding to know what she was doing outside so early. "Nothing," Frances said, and knew for the first time the incalculable reward of self-possession.

There was a girl in her sewing class named Pat Leonard. She was older than the other girls, had a rough pitted face and a brain pocked with grotesqueries. "Imagine," she said to Frances, "sliding down a banister and suddenly it turns into a razor blade." When she trimmed the seams of the skirt she was making and accidentally cut through the fabric, she laughed out loud. To amuse the other girls she sewed the skin of her fingers together. She told a joke, a long story about a pickle factory that was really about eating excrement. In her purse was a packet of cigarettes. She had a boyfriend who went to the technical school, and several times she'd reached inside his pants and squeezed his thing until it went off like a squirt gun. She'd flunked math twice. She could hardly read. One day she wasn't there, and the sewing teacher said she'd been expelled. Frances felt as though she'd lost her best friend, even though she wouldn't have been seen dead walking down the hall with Pat Leonard. Melodramatic tears swam in to her eyes, and then real tears that wouldn't stop until the teacher brought her a glass of water and offered to phone her mother.

Another time, she was walking home from a friend's in the early evening. She passed by a little house not far from her own. The windows were open and, floating on the summer air, came the sound of people speaking in a foreign language. There seemed to be a great number of them, and the conversation was very rapid and excited. They might have been quarrelling or telling old stories; Frances had no idea which. It could have been French or Russian or Portuguese they spoke. The words ran together and made queer little dashes and runs and choking sounds. Frances imagined immense, wide-branching grammars and steep, stone streets rising out of other centuries. She felt as though she'd been struck by a bolt of good fortune, and all because the world was bigger than she'd been led to believe.

At university, where she studied languages, she earned pocket money by working in the library. She and a girl named Ursula were entrusted with the key, and it was their job to open the library on Saturday mornings. During the minute or two before anyone else came, the two of them galloped at top speed through the reference room, the periodical room, the reading room, up and down the rows of stacks, filling that stilled air with what could only be called primal screams. Why this should have given Frances such exquisite pleasure she couldn't have said, since she was in rebellion against nothing she knew of. By the time the first students arrived, she and Ursula would be standing behind the main desk, date stamp in hand, sweet as dimity.

One Saturday, the first person who came was a bushy-headed, serious-minded zoology student named Theodore, called Theo by his friends. He gave Frances a funny look, then in a cracked, raspy voice asked her to come with him later and have a cup of coffee. A year later he asked her to marry him. He had a mind unblown by self-regard and lived, it seemed to Frances, in a nursery world of goodness and badness with not much room to move in between.

It's been mainly a happy marriage. Between the two of them, they've invented hundreds of complex ways of enslaving each other, some of them amazingly tender. Like other married people, they've learned to read each other's minds. Once Theo said to Frances as they drove around and around, utterly lost in a vast treeless suburb, "In every one of these houses there's been a declaration of love," and this was exactly the thought Frances had been thinking.

She has been faithful. To her surprise, to everyone's surprise, she turned out to have an aptitude for monogamy. Nevertheless, many of the scenes that have come into her life have involved men. Once she was walking down a very ordinary French street on a hot day. A man, bare-chested, drinking Perrier at a cafe table, sang out, *"Bonjour."* Not *"bonjour, Madame"* or *"bonjour, Mademoiselle,"* just *"bonjour."* Cheeky. She was wearing white pants, a red blouse, a straw hat and sunglasses. *"Bonjour,"* she sang back and gave a sassy little kick, which became the start of a kind of dance. The man at the table clapped his hands over his head to keep time as she went dancing by.

Once she went to the British Museum to finish a piece of research. There was a bomb alert just as she entered, and everyone's shopping bags and brief-cases were confiscated and searched. It happened that Frances had just bought a teddy bear for the child of a friend she was going to visit later in the day. The guard took it, shook it till its eyes rolled, and then carried it away to be X-rayed. Later he brought it to Frances, who was sitting at a table examining a beautiful old manuscript. As he handed her the bear, he kissed the air above its fuzzy head, and Frances felt her mouth go into the shape of a kiss, too, a kiss she intended to be an expression of her innocence, only that. He winked. She winked back. He leaned over and whispered into her ear a suggestion that was hideously, comically, obscene. She pretended not to hear, and a few minutes later she left, hurrying down the street full of cheerful shame, her work unfinished.

These are just some of the scenes in Frances' life. She thinks of them as scenes because they're much too fragmentary to be stories and far too immediate to be memories. They seem to bloom out of nothing, out of the thin, uncolored air of defeats and pleasures. A curtain opens, a light appears, there are voices or music or sometimes a wide transparent stream of silence. Only rarely do they point to anything but themselves. They're difficult to talk about. They're useless, attached to nothing, can't be traded in or shaped into instruments to prise open the meaning of the universe.

There are people who think such scenes are ornaments suspended from lives that are otherwise busy and useful. Frances knows perfectly well that they are what a life is made of, one fitting against the next like English paving-stones.

Or sometimes she thinks of them as little keys on a chain, keys that open nothing, but simply exist for the beauty of their toothed edges and the way they chime in her pocket.

Other times she is reminded of the Easter eggs her mother used to bring out every year. These were real hens' eggs with a hole poked in the top and bottom and the contents blown out. The day before Easter, Frances and her mother always sat down at the kitchen table with paint brushes, a glass of water and a box of watercolors. They would decorate half-a-dozen eggs, maybe more, but only the best were saved from year to year. These were taken from a cupboard just before Easter, removed from their shoebox, and carefully arranged, always on the same little pewter cake stand. The eggs had to be handled gently, especially the older ones.

Frances, when she was young, liked to pick up each one in turn and examine it minutely. She had a way of concentrating her thoughts and shutting everything else out, thinking only of this one little thing, this little egg that was round like the world, beautiful in color and satin to the touch, and that fit into the hollow of her hand as though it were made for that very purpose.

LESLIE MARMON SILKO

STORYTELLER

Leslie Marmon Silko (b. 1948) was born in Albuquerque to parents of Pueblo and German American heritage. She grew up on the Laguna pueblo reservation, attending the Board of Indian Affairs schools. In 1969, at a time when Silko saw growing Anglo-American interest in Native literatures, she graduated with a B.A. from the University of New Mexico. After a brief stint in law, Silko turned to writing; 1974 saw the publication of both her first poems, collected in Laguna Woman *(1974), and her first short stories, which appeared in two anthologies of contemporary Native American fiction. Silko taught at colleges in New Mexico and Arizona and spent two years living in Alaska. The appearance of her internationally acclaimed novel* Ceremony *in 1977 decisively established Silko's reputation as a leading voice in modern Native American literature. Since 1978 she has been a professor of English at the University of Arizona, residing in Tucson. Silko's short fiction is represented to date in a handful of uncollected stories and in the seminal* Storyteller *(1981), a miscellany of short stories, traditional tales, poems, and anecdotes, whose title story is reprinted. She has also published a volume of correspondence,* The Delicacy and Strength of Lace *(1986), a second novel,* Almanac of Death *(1991), and most recently* Sacred Water *(1993).*

*Craig Werner notes that: "*Storyteller *juxtaposes diverse approaches to storytelling to explore the meaning of tribal traditions in an alien, and frequently hostile, world." In the narrative investments Silko makes—in how a story is told and who tells it—critics can be too quick to identify her work with the postmodern fiction of writers such as Donald Barthelme and Jorge Luis Borges. Such comparisons threaten the integrity of an entirely different order of discourse, a philosophy of the story and its power that both precedes and remains external to the postmodern turn so widely celebrated and debated in the Anglo-American culture of late capitalism. Consider, for instance, the autobiographical story Silko shares with Irmer:*

> In 1986 I stopped [writing Almanac of the Dead] for a while
> because in Arizona we had an election and a terrible, racist man
> was elected governor. I was outraged and he had been elected
> with only 35 per cent of the vote. I was having trouble with what
> was happening, so I went outside and sprayed graffiti on the side

754

of this building against this terrible man. One morning I went [to the wall] and thought 'what is going to happen with my novel' and I looked at the wall and saw a giant snake. I would paint a giant snake on the wall. This wall is very prominent in downtown Tucson. I worked for about six months and the snake came and a message came and it was in Spanish: The people are cold, the people are hungry, the rich have stolen the land, the rich have stolen freedom. The people cry out for justice, otherwise revolution. I put it on the wall. ... So there is a giant snake and he has skulls in his stomach and that's his message.

Every day the sun came up a little lower on the horizon, moving more slowly until one day she got excited and started calling the jailer. She realized she had been sitting there for many hours, yet the sun had not moved from the center of the sky. The color of the sky had not been good lately; it had been pale blue, almost white, even when there were no clouds. She told herself it wasn't a good sign for the sky to be indistinguishable from the river ice, frozen solid and white against the earth. The tundra rose up behind the river but all the boundaries between the river and hills and sky were lost in the density of the pale ice.

She yelled again, this time some English words which came randomly into her mouth, probably swear words she'd heard from the oil drilling crews last winter. The jailer was an Eskimo, but he would not speak Yupik to her. She had watched people in other cells, when they spoke to him in Yupik he ignored them until they spoke English.

He came and stared at her. She didn't know if he understood what she was telling him until he glanced behind her at the small high window. He looked at the sun, and turned and walked away. She could hear the buckles on his heavy snowmobile boots jingle as he walked to the front of the building.

It was like the other buildings that white people, the Gussucks, brought with them: BIA and school buildings, portable buildings that arrived sliced in halves, on barges coming up the river. Squares of metal panelling bulged out with the layers of insulation stuffed inside. She had asked once what it was and someone told her it was to keep out the cold. She had not laughed then, but she did now. She walked over to the small double-pane window and she laughed out loud. They thought they could keep out the cold with stringy yellow wadding. Look at the sun. It wasn't moving; it was frozen, caught in the middle of the sky. Look at the sky, solid as the river with ice which had trapped the sun. It had not moved for a long time; in few more hours it would be weak, and heavy frost would begin to appear on the edges and spread across the face of the sun like a mask. Its light was pale yellow, worn thin by the winter.

She could see people walking down the snow-packed roads, their breath steaming out from their parka hoods, faces hidden and protected by deep ruffs of fur. There were no cars or snowmobiles that day; the cold had silenced their machines. The metal froze; it split and shattered. Oil hardened and moving parts jammed solidly. She had seen it happen to their big yellow machines and the giant drill last winter when they came to drill their test holes. The cold stopped them, and they were helpless against it.

Her village was many miles upriver from this town, but in her mind she could see it clearly. Their house was not near the village houses. It stood alone on the bank upriver from the village. Snow had drifted to the eaves of the roof on the north side, but on the west side, by the door, the path was almost clear. She had nailed scraps of red tin over the logs last summer. She had done it for the bright red color, not for added warmth the way the village people had done. This final winter had been coming even then; there had been signs of its approach for many years.

She went because she was curious about the big school where the Government sent all the other girls and boys. She had not played much with the village children while she was growing up because they were afraid of the old man, and they ran when her grandmother came. She went because she was tired of being alone with the old woman whose body had been stiffening for as long as the girl could remember. Her knees and knuckles were swollen grotesquely, and the pain had squeezed the brown skin of her face tight against the bones; it left her eyes hard like river stone. The girl asked once what it was that did this to her body, and the old woman had raised up from sewing a sealskin boot, and stared at her.

"The joints," the old woman said in a low voice, whispering like wind across the roof, "the joints are swollen with anger."

Sometimes she did not answer and only stared at the girl. Each year she spoke less and less, but the old man talked more—all night sometimes, not to anyone but himself; in a soft deliberate voice, he told stories, moving his smooth brown hands above the blankets. He had not fished or hunted with the other men for many years, although he was not crippled or sick. He stayed in his bed, smelling like dry fish and urine, telling stories all winter; and when warm weather came, he went to his place on the river bank. He sat with a long willow stick, poking at the smoldering moss he burned against the insects while he continued with the stories.

The trouble was that she had not recognized the warnings in time. She did not see what the Gussuck school would do to her until she walked into the dormitory and realized that the old man had not been lying about the place. She thought he had been trying to scare her as he used to when she was very small and her grandmother was outside cutting up fish. She hadn't believed what he told her about the school because she knew he wanted to keep her there in the log house with him. She knew what he wanted.

The dormitory matron pulled down her underpants and whipped her with a leather belt because she refused to speak English.

"Those backwards village people," the matron said, because she was an Eskimo who had worked for the BIA a long time, "they kept this one until she was too big to learn." The other girls whispered in English. They knew how to work the showers, and they washed and curled their hair at night. They ate Gussuck food. She lay on her bed and imagined what her grandmother might be sewing, and what the old man was eating in his bed. When summer came, they sent her home.

The way her grandmother had hugged her before she left for school had been a warning too, because the old woman had not hugged or touched her for many years. Not like the old man, whose hands were always hunting, like ravens circling lazily in the sky, ready to touch her. She was not surprised when the priest and the old man met her at the landing strip, to say that the old lady was gone. The priest asked her where she would like to stay. He referred to the old man as her grandfather, but she did not bother to correct him. She had already been thinking about it; if she went with the priest, he would send her away to a school. But the old man was different. She knew he wouldn't send her back to school. She knew he wanted to keep her.

He told her one time, that she would get too old for him faster than he got too old for her; but again she had not believed him because sometimes he lied. He had lied about what he would do with her if she came into his bed. But as the years passed, she realized what he said was true. She was restless and strong. She had no patience with the old man who had never changed his slow smooth motions under the blankets.

The old man was in his bed for the winter; he did not leave it except to use the slop bucket in the corner. He was dozing with his mouth open slightly; his lips quivered and sometimes they moved like he was telling a story even while he dreamed. She pulled on the sealskin boots, the mukluks with the bright red flannel linings her grandmother had sewn for her, and she tied the braided red yarn tassels around her ankles over the gray wool pants. She zipped the wolf-skin parka. Her grandmother had worn it for many years, but the old man said that before she died, she instructed him to bury her in an old black sweater, and to give the parka to the girl. The wolf pelts were creamy colored and silver, almost white in some places, and when the old lady had walked across the tundra in the winter, she was invisible in the snow.

She walked toward the village, breaking her own path through the deep snow. A team of sled dogs tied outside a house at the edge of the village leaped against their chains to bark at her. She kept walking, watching the dusky sky for the first evening stars. It was warm and the dogs were alert. When it got cold again, the dogs would lie curled and still, too drowsy from the cold to bark or pull at the chains. She laughed loudly because it made them howl and snarl. Once the old man had seen her tease the dogs and he shook his head. "So that's the kind of woman you are," he said, "in the wintertime the two of us are no different from those dogs. We wait in the cold for someone to bring us a few dry fish."

She laughed out loud again, and kept walking. She was thinking about the Gussuck oil drillers. They were strange; they watched her when she walked near their machines. She wondered what they looked like underneath their quilted goosedown trousers; she wanted to know how they moved. They would be something different from the old man.

The old man screamed at her. He shook her shoulders so violently that her head bumped against the log wall. "I smelled it!" he yelled, "as soon as I woke up! I am sure of it now. You can't fool me!" His thin legs were shaking inside the baggy wool trousers; he stumbled over her boots in his bare feet. His toenails were long and yellow like bird claws; she had seen a gray crane last summer fighting another in the shallow water on the edge of the river. She laughed out loud and pulled her shoulder out of his grip. He stood in front of her. He was breathing hard and shaking; he looked weak. He would probably die next winter.

"I'm warning you," he said, "I'm warning you." He crawled back into his bunk then, and reached under the old soiled feather pillow for a piece of dry fish. He lay back on the pillow, staring at the ceiling and chewed dry strips of salmon. "I don't know what the old woman told you," he said, "but there will be trouble." He looked over to see if she was listening. His face suddenly relaxed into a smile, his dark slanty eyes were lost in wrinkles of brown skin. "I could tell you, but you are too good for warnings now. I can smell what you did all night with the Gussucks."

She did not understand why they came there, because the village was small and so far upriver that even some Eskimos who had been away to school did not want to come back. They stayed downriver in the town. They said the village was too quiet. They were used to the town where the boarding school was located, with electric lights and running water. After all those years away at school, they had forgotten how to set nets in the river and where to hunt seals in the fall. When she asked the old man why the Gussucks bothered to come to the village, his narrow eyes got bright with excitement.

"They only come when there is something to steal. The fur animals are too difficult for them to get now, and the seals and fish are hard to find. Now they come for oil deep in the earth. But this is the last time for them." His breathing was wheezy and fast; his hands gestured at the sky. "It is approaching. As it comes, ice will push across the sky." His eyes were open wide and he stared at the low ceiling rafters for hours without blinking. She remembered all this clearly because he began the story that day, the story he told from that time on. It began with a giant bear which he described muscle by muscle, from the curve of the ivory claws to the whorls of hair at the top of the massive skull. And for eight days he did not sleep, but talked continuously of the giant bear whose color was pale blue glacier ice.

The snow was dirty and worn down in a path to the door. On either side of the path, the snow was higher than her head. In front of the door there were jagged yellow stains melted into the snow where men had urinated. She stopped in the entry way and kicked the snow off her boots. The room was dim; a kerosene lantern by the cash register was burning low. The long wooden shelves were jammed with cans of beans and potted meats. On the bottom shelf a jar of mayonnaise was broken open, leaking oily white clots on the floor. There was no one in the room except the yellowish dog sleeping in the front of the long glass display case. A reflection made it appear to be lying on the knives and ammunition inside the case. Gussucks kept dogs inside their houses with them; they did not seem to mind the odors which seeped out of the dogs. "They tell us we are dirty for the food we eat—raw fish and fermented meat. But we do not live with dogs," the old man once said. She heard voices in the back room, and the sound of bottles set down hard on tables.

They were always confident. The first year they waited for the ice to break up on the river, and then they brought their big yellow machines up river on barges. They planned to drill their test holes during the summer to avoid the freezing. But the imprints and graves of their machines were still there, on the edge of the tundra above the river, where the summer mud had swallowed them before they ever left sight of the river. The village people had gathered to watch the white men, and to laugh as they drove the giant machines, one by one, off the steel ramp into the bogs; as if sheer numbers of vehicles would somehow make the tundra solid. But the old man said they behaved like desperate people, and they would come back again. When the tundra was frozen solid, they returned.

Village women did not even look through the door to the back room. The priest had warned them. The storeman was watching her because he didn't let Eskimos or Indians sit down at the tables in the back room. But she knew he couldn't throw her out if one of his Gussuck customers invited her to sit with him. She walked across the room. They stared at her, but she had the feeling she was walking for someone else, not herself, so their eyes did not matter. The red-haired man pulled out a chair and motioned for her to sit down. She looked back at the storeman while the red-haired man poured her a glass of red sweet wine. She wanted to laugh at the storeman the way she laughed at the dogs, straining against the chains, howling at her.

The red-haired man kept talking to the other Gussucks sitting around the table, but he slid one hand off the top of the table to her thigh. She looked over at the storeman to see if he was still watching her. She laughed out loud at him and the red-haired man stopped talking and turned to her. He asked if she wanted to go. She nodded and stood up.

Someone in the village had been telling him things about her, he said as they walked down the road to his trailer. She understood that much of what he was saying, but the rest she did not hear. The whine of the big generators at the construction camp sucked away the sound of his words. But English was of no concern to her anymore, and neither was anything the Christians in the village might say about her or the old man. She smiled at the effect of the subzero air on the electric lights around the trailers; they did not shine. They left only flat yellow holes in the darkness.

It took him a long time to get ready, even after she had undressed for him. She waited in the bed with the blankets pulled close, watching him. He adjusted the thermostat and lit candles in the room, turning out the electric lights. He searched through a stack of record albums until he found the right one. She was not sure about the last thing he did: he taped something on the wall behind the bed where he could see it while he lay on top of her. He was shriveled and white from the cold; he pushed against her body for warmth. He guided her hands to his thighs; he was shivering.

She had returned a last time because she wanted to know what it was he stuck on the wall above the bed. After he finished each time, he reached up and pulled it loose, folding it carefully so that she could not see it. But this time she was ready; she waited for his fast breathing and sudden collapse on top of her. She slid out from under him and stood up beside the bed. She looked at the picture while she got dressed. He did not raise his face from the pillow, and she thought she heard teeth rattling together as she left the room.

She heard the old man move when she came in. After the Gussuck's trailer, the log house felt cool. It smelled like dry fish and cured meat. The room was dark except for the blinking yellow flame in the mica window of the oil stove. She squatted in front of the stove and watched the flames for a long time before she walked to the bed where her grandmother had slept. The bed was covered with a mound of rags and fur scraps the old woman had saved. She reached into the mound until she felt something cold and solid wrapped in a wool blanket. She pushed her fingers around it until she felt smooth stone. Long ago, before the Gussucks came, they had burned whale oil in the big stone lamp which made light and heat as well. The old woman had saved everything they would need when the time came.

In the morning, the old man pulled a piece of dry caribou meat from under the blankets and offered it to her. While she was gone, men from the village had brought a bundle of dry meat. She chewed it slowly, thinking about the way they still came from the village to take care of the old man and his stories. But she had a story now, about the red-haired Gussuck. The old man knew what she was thinking, and his smile made his face seem more round than it was.

"Well," he said, "what was it?"

"A woman with a big dog on top of her."

He laughed softly to himself and walked over to the water barrel. He dipped the tin cup into the water.

"It doesn't surprise me," he said.

"Grandma," she said, "there was something red in the grass that morning. I remember." She had not asked about her parents before. The old woman stopped splitting the fish bellies open for the willow drying racks. Her jaw muscles pulled so tightly against her skull, the girl thought the old woman would not be able to speak.

"They bought a tin can full of it from the storeman. Late at night. He told them it was alcohol safe to drink. They traded a rifle for it." The old woman's voice sounded like each word stole strength from her. "It made no difference about the rifle. That year the Gussuck boats had come, firing big guns at the walrus and seals. There was nothing left to hunt after that anyway. So," the old lady said, in a low soft voice the girl had not heard for a long time, "I didn't say anything to them when they left that night."

"Right over there," she said, pointing at the fallen poles, half buried in the river sand and tall grass, "in the summer shelter. The sun was high half the night then. Early in the morning when it was still low, the policeman came around. I told the interpreter to tell him that the storeman had poisoned them." She made outlines in the air in front of her, showing how their bodies lay twisted on the sand; telling the story was like laboring to walk through deep snow; sweat shone in the white hair around her forehead. "I told the priest too, after he came. I told him the storeman lied." She turned away from the girl. She held her mouth even tighter, set solidly, not in sorrow or anger, but against the pain, which was all that remained. "I never believed," she said, "not much anyway. I wasn't surprised when the priest did nothing."

The wind came off the river and folded the tall grass into itself like river waves. She could feel the silence the story left, and she wanted to have the old woman go on.

"I heard sounds that night, grandma. Sounds like someone was singing. It was light outside. I could see something red on the ground." The old woman did not answer her; she moved to the tub full of fish on the ground beside the workbench. She stabbed her knife into the belly of a whitefish and lifted it onto the bench. "The Gussuck storeman left the village right after that," the old woman said as she pulled the entrails from the fish, "otherwise, I could tell you more." The old woman's voice flowed with the wind blowing off the river; they never spoke of it again.

When the willows got their leaves and the grass grew tall along the river banks and around the sloughs, she walked early in the morning. While the sun was still low on the horizon, she listened to the wind off the river; its sound was like the voice that day long ago. In the distance, she could hear the engines of the machinery the oil drillers had left the winter before, but she did not go near the village or the store. The sun never left the sky and the summer became the same long day, with only the winds to fan the sun into brightness or allow it to slip into twilight.

She sat beside the old man at his place on the river bank. She poked the smoky fire for him, and felt herself growing wide and thin in the sun as if she had been split from belly to throat and strung on the willow pole in preparation for the winter to come. The old man did not speak anymore. When men from the village brought him fresh fish he hid them deep in the river grass where it was cool. After he went inside, she split the fish open and spread them to dry on the willow frame the way the old woman had done. Inside, he dozed and talked to himself. He had talked all winter, softly and incessantly, about the giant polar bear stalking a lone hunter across Bering Sea ice. After all the months the old man had been telling the story, the bear was within a hundred feet of the man; but the ice fog had closed in on them now and the man could only smell the sharp ammonia odor of the bear, and hear the edge of the snow crust crack under the giant paws.

One night she listened to the old man tell the story all night in his sleep, describing each crystal of ice and the slightly different sounds they made under each paw; first the left and then the right paw, then the hind feet. Her grandmother was there suddenly, a shadow around the stove. She spoke in her low wind voice and the girl was afraid to sit up to hear more clearly. Maybe what she said had been to the old man because he stopped telling the story and began to snore softly the way he had long ago when the old woman had scolded him for telling his stories while others in the house were trying to sleep. But the last words she heard clearly: "It will take a long time, but the story must be told. There must not be any lies." She pulled the blankets up around her chin, slowly, so that her movements would not be seen. She thought her grandmother was talking about the old man's bear story; she did not know about the other story then.

She left the old man wheezing and snoring in his bed. She walked through river grass glistening with frost; the bright green summer color was already fading. She watched the sun move across the sky, already lower on the horizon, already moving away from the village. She stopped by the fallen poles of the summer shelter where her parents had died. Frost glittered on the river sand too; in a few more weeks there would be snow. The predawn light would be the color of an old woman. An old woman sky full of snow. There had been something red lying on the ground the morning they died. She looked for it again, pushing aside the grass with her foot. She knelt in the sand and looked under the fallen structure for some trace of it. When she found it, she would know what the old woman had never told her. She squatted down close to the gray poles and leaned her back against them. The wind made her shiver.

The summer rain had washed the mud from between the logs; the sod blocks stacked as high as her belly next to the log walls had lost their square-cut shape and had grown into soft mounds of tundra moss and stiff-bladed grass bending with clusters of seed bristles. She looked at the northwest, in the direction of the Bering Sea. The cold would come down from there to find narrow slits in the mud, rainwater holes in the outer layer of sod which protected the log house. The dark green tundra stretched away flat and continuous. Somewhere the sea and the land met; she knew by their dark green colors there were no boundaries between them. That was how the cold would come: when the boundaries were gone the polar ice would range across the land into the sky. She watched the horizon for a long time. She would stand in that place on the north side of the house and she would keep watch on the northwest horizon, and eventually she would see it come. She would watch for its approach in the stars, and hear it come with the wind. These preparations were unfamiliar, but gradually she recognized them as she did her own footprints in the snow.

She emptied the slop jar beside his bed twice a day and kept the barrel full of water melted from river ice. He did not recognize her anymore, and when he spoke to her, he called her by her grandmother's name and talked about people and events from long ago, before he went back to telling the story. The giant bear was creeping across the new snow on its belly, close enough now that the man could hear the rasp of its breathing. On and on in a soft singing voice, the old man caressed the story, repeating the words again and again like gentle strokes.

The sky was gray like a river crane's egg; its density curved into the thin crust of frost already covering the land. She looked at the bright red color of the tin against the ground and the sky and she told the village men to bring the pieces for the old man and her. To drill the test holes in the tundra, the Gussucks had used hundreds of barrels of fuel. The village people split open the empty barrels that were abandoned on the river bank, and pounded the red tin into flat sheets. The village people were using the strips of tin to mend walls and roofs for winter. But she nailed it on the log walls for its color. When she finished, she walked away with the hammer in her hand, not turning around until she was far away, on the ridge above the river banks, and then she looked back. She felt a chill when she saw how the sky and the land were already losing their boundaries, already becoming lost in each other. But the red tin penetrated the thick white color of earth and sky; it defined the boundaries like a wound revealing the ribs and heart of a great caribou about to bolt and be lost to the hunter forever. That night the wind howled and when she scratched a hole through the heavy frost on the inside of the window, she could see nothing but the impenetrable white; whether it was blowing snow or snow that had drifted as high as the house, she did not know.

It had come down suddenly, and she stood with her back to the wind looking at the river, its smoky water clotted with ice. The wind had blown the snow over the frozen river, hiding thin blue streaks where fast water ran under ice translucent and fragile as memory. But she could see shadows of boundaries, outlines of paths which were slender branches of solidity reaching out from the earth. She spent days walking on the river, watching the colors of ice that would safely hold her, kicking the heel of her boot into the snow crust, listening for a solid sound. When she could feel the paths through the soles of her feet, she went to the middle of the river where the fast gray water churned under a thin pane of ice. She looked back. On the river bank in the distance she could see the red tin nailed to the log house, something not swallowed up by the heavy white belly of the sky or caught in the folds of the frozen earth. It was time.

The wolverine fur around the hood of her parka was white with the frost from her breathing. The warmth inside the store melted it, and she felt tiny drops of water on her face. The storeman came in from the back room. She unzipped the parka and stood by the oil stove. She didn't look at him, but stared instead at the yellowish dog, covered with scabs of matted hair, sleeping in front of the stove. She thought of the Gussuck's picture taped on the wall above the bed and she laughed out loud. The sound of her laughter was piercing; the yellow dog jumped to its feet and the hair bristled down its back. The storeman was watching her. She wanted to laugh again because he didn't know about the ice. He did not know that it was prowling the earth, or that it had already pushed its way into the sky to seize the sun. She sat down in the chair by the stove and shook her long hair loose. He was like a dog tied up all winter, watching while the others got fed. He remembered how she had gone with the oil drillers, and his blue eyes moved like flies crawling over her body. He held his thin pale lips like he wanted to spit on her. He hated the people because they had something of value, the old man said, something which the Gussucks could never have.

They thought they could take it, suck it out of the earth or cut it from the mountains; but they were fools.

There was a matted hunk of dog hair on the floor by her foot. She thought of the yellow insulation coming unstuffed: their defense against the freezing going to pieces as it advanced on them. The ice was crouching on the northwest horizon like the old man's bear. She laughed out loud again. The sun would be down now; it was time.

The first time he spoke to her, she did not hear what he said, so she did not answer or even look up at him. He spoke to her again but his words were only noises coming from his pale mouth, trembling now as his anger began to unravel. He jerked her up and the chair fell over behind her. His arms were shaking and she could feel his hands tense up, pulling the edges of the parka tighter. He raised his fist to hit her, his thin body quivering with rage; but the fist collapsed with the desire he had for the valuable things, which, the old man had rightly said, was the only reason they came. She could hear his heart pounding as he held her close and arched his hips against her, groaning and breathing in spasms. She twisted away from him and ducked under his arms.

She ran with a mitten over her mouth, breathing through the fur to protect her lungs from the freezing air. She could hear him running behind her, his heavy breathing, the occasional sound of metal jingling against metal. But he ran without his parka or mittens, breathing the frozen air; its fire squeezed the lungs against the ribs and it was enough that he could not catch her near his store. On the river bank he realized how far he was from his stove, and the wads of yellow stuffing that held off the cold. But the girl was not able to run very fast through the deep drifts at the edge of the river. The twilight was luminous and he could still see clearly for a long distance; he knew he could catch her so he kept running.

When she neared the middle of the river she looked over her shoulder. He was not following her tracks; he went straight across the ice, running the shortest distance to reach her. He was close then; his face was twisted and scarlet from the exertion and the cold. There was satisfaction in his eyes; he was sure he could outrun her.

She was familiar with the river, down to the instant ice flexed into hairline fractures, and the cracking bone-sliver sounds gathered momentum with the opening ice until the churning gray water was set free. She stopped and turned to the sound of the river and the rattle of swirling ice fragments where he fell through. She pulled off a mitten and zipped the parka to her throat. She was conscious then of her own rapid breathing.

She moved slowly, kicking the ice ahead with the heel of her boot, feeling for sinews of ice to hold her. She looked ahead and all around herself; in the twilight, the dense white sky had merged into the flat snow-covered tundra. In the frantic running she had lost her place on the river. She stood still. The east bank of the river was lost in the sky; the boundaries had been swallowed by the freezing white. But then, in the distance, she saw something red, and suddenly it was as she had remembered it all those years.

She sat on her bed and while she waited, she listened to the old man. The hunter had found a small jagged knoll on the ice. He pulled his beaver fur cap off his head; the fur inside it steamed with his body heat and sweat. He left it upside down on the ice for the great bear to stalk, and he waited downwind on top of the ice knoll; he was holding the jade knife.

She thought she could see the end of his story in the way he wheezed out the words; but still he reached into his cache of dry fish and dribbled water into his mouth from the tin cup. All night she listened to him describe each breath the man took, each motion of the bear's head as it tried to catch the sound of the man's breathing, and tested the wind for his scent.

The state trooper asked her questions, and the woman who cleaned house for the priest translated them into Yupik. They wanted to know what happened to the storeman, the Gussuck who had been running after her down the road onto the river late last evening. He had not come back, and the Gussuck boss in Anchorage was concerned about him. She did not answer for a long time because the old man suddenly sat up in his bed and began to talk excitedly, looking at all of them—the trooper in his dark glasses and the housekeeper in her corduroy parka. He kept saying, "The story! The story! Eh-ya! The great bear! The hunter!"

They asked her again, what happened to the man from the Northern Commercial store. "He lied to them. He told them it was safe to drink. But I will not lie." She stood up and put on the gray wolfskin parka. "I killed him," she said, "but I don't lie."

The attorney came back again, and the jailer slid open the steel doors and opened the cell to let him in. He motioned for the jailer to stay to translate for him. She laughed when she saw how the jailer would be forced by this Gussuck to speak Yupik to her. She liked the Gussuck attorney for that, and for the thinning hair on his head. He was very tall, and she liked to think about the exposure of his head to the freezing; she wondered if he would feel the ice descending from the sky before the others did. He wanted to know why she told the state trooper she had killed the storeman. Some village children had seen it happen, he said, and it was an accident. "That's all you have to say to the judge: it was an accident." He kept repeating it over and over again to her, slowly in a loud but gentle voice: "It was an accident. He was running after you and he fell through the ice. That's all you have to say in court. That's all. And they will let you go home. Back to your village." The jailer translated the words sullenly, staring down at the floor. She shook her head. "I will not change the story, not even to escape this place and go home. I intended that he die. The story must be told as it is." The attorney exhaled loudly; his eyes looked tired. "Tell her that she could not have killed him that way. He was a white man. He ran after her without a parka or mittens. She could not have planned that." He paused and turned toward the cell door. "Tell her I will do all I can for her. I will explain to the judge that her mind is confused." She laughed out loud when the jailer translated what the attorney said. The Gussucks did not understand the story; they could not see the way it must be told, year after year as the old man had done, without lapse or silence.

She looked out the window at the frozen white sky. The sun had finally broken loose from the ice but it moved like a wounded caribou running on strength which only dying animals find, leaping and running on bullet-shattered lungs. Its light was weak and pale; it pushed dimly through the clouds. She turned and faced the Gussuck attorney.

"It began a long time ago," she intoned steadily, "in the summertime. Early in the morning, I remember, something red in the tall river grass. ..."

The day after the old man died, men from the village came. She was sitting on the edge of her bed, across from the woman the trooper hired to watch her. They came in to the room slowly and listened to her. At the foot of her bed they left a king salmon that had been slit open wide and dried last summer. But she did not pause or hesitate; she went on with the story, and she never stopped, not even when the woman got up to close the door behind the village men.

The old man would not change the story even when he knew the end was approaching. Lies could not stop what was coming. He thrashed around on the bed, pulling the blankets loose, knocking bundles of dried fish and meat on the floor. The hunter had been on the ice for many hours. The freezing winds on the ice knoll had numbed his hands in the mittens, and the cold had exhausted him. He felt a single muscle tremor in his hand that he could not stop, and the jade knife fell; it shattered on the ice, and the blue glacier bear turned slowly to face him.

DYLAN THOMAS

A STORY

If you can call it a story. There's no real beginning or end and there's very little in the middle. It is all about a day's outing, by charabanc, to Porthcawl, which, of course, the charabanc never reached, and it happened when I was so high and much nicer.

I was staying at the time with my uncle and his wife. Although she was my aunt, I never thought of her as anything but the wife of my uncle, partly because he was so big and trumpeting and red-hairy and used to fill every inch of the hot little house like an old buffalo squeezed into an airing cupboard, and partly because she was so small and silk and quick and made no noise at all as she whisked about on padded paws, dusting the china dogs, feeding the buffalo, setting the mousetraps that never caught her; and once she sleaked out of the room, to squeak in a nook or nibble in the hayloft, you forgot she had ever been there.

But there he was, always, a steaming hulk of an uncle, his braces straining like hawsers, crammed behind the counter of the tiny shop at the front of the house, and breathing like a brass band; or guzzling and blustery in the kitchen over his gutsy supper, too big for everything except the great black boats of his boots. As he ate, the house grew smaller; he billowed out over the furniture, the loud check meadow of his waistcoat littered, as though after a picnic, with cigarette ends, peelings, cabbage stalks, birds' bones, gravy; and the forest fire of his hair crackled among the hooked hams from the ceiling. She was so small she could hit him only if she stood on a chair; and every Saturday night at half past ten he would lift her up, under his arm, onto a chair in the kitchen so that she could hit him on the head with whatever was handy, which was always a china dog. On Sundays, and when pickled, he sang high tenor, and had won many cups.

The first I heard of the annual outing was when I was sitting one evening on a bag of rice behind the counter, under one of my uncle's stomachs, reading an advertisement for sheep-dip, which was all there was to read. The shop was full of my uncle, and when Mr. Benjamin Franklyn, Mr. Weazley, Noah Bowen, and Will Sentry came in, I thought it would burst. It was like all being together in a drawer that smelled of cheese and turps, and twist tobacco and sweet biscuits and snuff and waistcoat. Mr. Benjamin Franklyn said that he had collected enough money for the charabanc and twenty cases of pale ale and a pound apiece over that he would distribute among the members of the outing when they first stopped for refreshment, and he was about sick and tired, he said, of being followed by Will Sentry.

"All day long, wherever I go," he said, "he's after me like a collie with one eye. I got a shadow of my own *and* a dog. I don't need no Tom, Dick or Harry pursuing me with his dirty muffler on."

Will Sentry blushed, and said, "It's only oily. I got a bicycle."

"A man has no privacy at all," Mr. Franklyn went on. "I tell you he sticks so close I'm afraid to go out the back in case I sit in his lap. It's a wonder to me," he said, "he don't follow me into bed at night."

"Wife won't let," Will Sentry said.

And that started Mr. Franklyn off again, and they tried to soothe him down by saying, "Don't you mind Will Sentry." "No harm in old Will." "He's only keeping an eye on the money, Benjie."

"Aren't I honest?" asked Mr. Franklyn in surprise. There was no answer for some time; then Noah Bowen said, "You know what the committee is. Ever since Bob the Fiddle they don't feel safe with a new treasurer."

"Do you think *I'm* going to drink the outing funds, like Bob the Fiddle did?" said Mr. Franklyn.

"You *might*," said my uncle slowly.

"I resign," said Mr. Franklyn.

"Not with our money you won't," Will Sentry said.

"Who put the dynamite in the salmon pool?" said Mr. Weazley, but nobody took any notice of him. And, after a time, they all began to play cards in the thickening dusk of the hot, cheesy shop, and my uncle blew and bugled whenever he won, and Mr. Weazley grumbled like a dredger, and I fell to sleep on the gravy-scented mountain meadow of my uncle's waistcoat.

On Sunday evening, after Bethesda, Mr. Franklyn walked into the kitchen where my uncle and I were eating sardines from the tin with spoons because it was Sunday and his wife would not let us play draughts. She was somewhere in the kitchen, too. Perhaps she was inside the grandmother clock, hanging from the weights and breathing. Then, a second later, the door opened again and Will Sentry edged into the room, twiddling his hard, round hat. He and Mr. Franklyn sat down on the settee, stiff and moth-balled and black in their chapel and funeral suits.

"I brought the list," said Mr. Franklyn. "Every member fully paid. You ask Will Sentry."

My uncle put on his spectacles, wiped his whiskery mouth with a handkerchief big as a Union Jack, laid down his spoon of sardines, took Mr. Franklyn's list of names, removed the spectacles so that he could read, and then ticked the names off one by one.

"Enoch Davies. Aye. He's good with his fists. You never know. Little Gerwain. Very melodious bass. Mr. Cadwalladwr. That's right. He can tell opening time better than my watch. Mr. Weazley. Of course. He's been to Paris. Pity he suffers so much in the charabanc. Stopped us nine times last year between the Beehive and the Red Dragon. Noah Bowen. Ah, very peaceable. He's got a tongue like a turtledove. Never a argument with Noah Bowen. Jenkins Loughor. Keep him off economics. It cost us a plate-glass window. And ten pints for the Sergeant. Mr. Jervis. Very tidy."

"He tried to put a pig in the charra," Will Sentry said.

"Live and let live," said my uncle.

Will Sentry blushed.

"Sinbad the Sailor's Arms. Got to keep in with him. Old O. Jones."

"Why old O. Jones?" said Will Sentry.

"Old O. Jones always goes," said my uncle.

I looked down at the kitchen table. The tin of sardines was gone. By Gee, I said to myself, Uncle's wife is quick as a flash.

"Cuthbert Johnny Fortnight. Now there's a card," said my uncle.

"He whistles after women," Will Sentry said.

"So do you," said Mr. Benjamin Franklyn, "in your mind."

My uncle at last approved the whole list, pausing only to say, when he came across one name, "If we weren't a Christian community, we'd chuck that Bob the Fiddle in the sea."

"We can do that in Porthcawl," said Mr. Franklyn, and soon after that he went, Will Sentry no more than an inch behind him, their Sunday-bright boots squeaking on the kitchen cobbles.

And then, suddenly, there was my uncle's wife standing in front of the dresser, with a china dog in one hand. By Gee, I said to myself again, did you ever see such a woman, if that's what she is. The lamps were not lit yet in the kitchen and she stood in a wood of shadows, with the plates on the dresser behind her shining—like pink-and-white eyes.

"If you go on that outing on Saturday, Mr. Thomas," she said to my uncle in her small, silk voice, "I'm going home to my mother's."

Holy Mo, I thought, she's got a mother. Now that's one old bald mouse of a hundred and five I won't be wanting to meet in a dark lane.

"It's me or the outing, Mr. Thomas."

I would have made my choice at once, but it was almost half a minute before my uncle said, "Well, then, Sarah, it's the outing, my love." He lifted her up, under his arm, onto a chair in the kitchen, and she hit him on the head with the china dog. Then he lifted her down again, and then I said good night.

For the rest of the week my uncle's wife whisked quiet and quick round the house with her darting duster, my uncle blew and bugled and swole, and I kept myself busy all the time being up to no good. And then at breakfast time on Saturday morning, the morning of the outing, I found a note on the kitchen table. It said, "There's some eggs in the pantry. Take your boots off before you go to bed." My uncle's wife had gone, as quick as a flash.

When my uncle saw the note, he tugged out the flag of his handkerchief and blew such a hubbub of trumpets that the plates on the dresser shook. "It's the same every year," he said. And then he looked at me. "But this year it's different. *You'll* have to come on the outing, too, and what the members will say I dare not think."

The charabanc drew up outside, and when the members of the outing saw my uncle and me squeeze out of the shop together, both of us cat-licked and brushed in our Sunday best, they snarled like a zoo.

"Are you bringing a *boy*?" asked Mr. Benjamin Franklyn as we climbed into the charabanc. He looked at me with horror.

"Boys is nasty," said Mr. Weazley.

"He hasn't paid his contributions," Will Sentry said.

"No room for boys. Boys get sick in charabancs."

"So do you, Enoch Davies," said my uncle.

"Might as well bring *women*."

The way they said it, women were worse than boys.

"Better than bringing grandfathers."

"Grandfathers is nasty too," said Mr. Weazley.

"What can we do with him when we stop for refreshments?"

"I'm a grandfather," said Mr. Weazley.

"Twenty-six minutes to opening time," shouted an old man in a panama hat, not looking at a watch. They forgot me at once.

"Good old Mr. Cadwalladwr," they cried, and the charabanc started off down the village street.

A few cold women stood at their doorways, grimly watching us go. A very small boy waved goodbye, and his mother boxed his ears. It was a beautiful August morning.

We were out of the village and over the bridge, and up the hill toward Steeplehat Wood when Mr. Franklyn, with his list of names in his hand, called out loud, "Where's old O. Jones?"

"Where's old O.?"

"We've left old O. behind."

"Can't go without old O."

And though Mr. Weazley hissed all the way, we turned and drove back to the village, where, outside the Prince of Wales, old O. Jones was waiting patiently and alone with a canvas bag.

"I didn't want to come at all," old O. Jones said as they hoisted him into the charabanc and clapped him on the back and pushed him on a seat and stuck a bottle in his hand, "but I always go." And over the bridge and up the hill and under the deep green wood and along the dusty road we wove, slow cows and ducks flying by, until "Stop the bus!" Mr. Weazley cried, "I left my teeth on the mantelpiece."

"Never you mind," they said, "you're not going to bite nobody," and they gave him a bottle with a straw.

"I might want to smile," he said.

"Not you," they said.

"What's the time, Mr. Cadwalladwr?"

"Twelve minutes to go," shouted back the old man in the panama, and they all began to curse him.

The charabanc pulled outside the Mountain Sheep, a small, unhappy public house with a thatched roof like a wig with ringworm. From a flagpole by the Gents fluttered the flag of Siam. I knew it was the Flag of Siam because of cigarette cards. The landlord stood at the door to welcome us, simpering like a wolf. He was a long, lean, black-fanged man with a greased love-curl and pouncing eyes. "What a beautiful August day!" he said, and touched his love-curl with a claw. That was the way he must have welcomed the Mountain Sheep before he ate it, I said to myself. The members rushed out, bleating, and into the bar.

"You keep an eye on the charra," my uncle said, "see nobody steals it now."

"There's nobody to steal it," I said, "except some cows," but my uncle was gustily blowing his bugle in the bar. I looked at the cows opposite, and they looked at me. There was nothing else for us to do. Forty-five minutes passed, like a very slow cloud. The sun shone down on the lonely road, the lost, unwanted boy, and the lake-eyed cows. In the dark bar they were so happy they were breaking glasses. A Shoni-Onion Breton man, with a beret and a necklace of onions, bicycled down the road and stopped at the door.

"Quelle un grand matin, monsieur," I said.

"There's French, boy bach!" he said.

I followed him down the passage, and peered into the bar. I could hardly recognize the members of the outing. They had all changed colour. Beetroot, rhubarb and puce, they hollered and rollicked in that dark, damp hole like enormous ancient bad boys, and my uncle surged in the middle, all red whiskers and bellies. On the floor was broken glass and Mr. Weazley.

"Drinks all round," cried Bob the Fiddle, a small, absconding man with bright blue eyes and a plump smile.

"Who's been robbing the orphans?"

"Who sold his little babby to the gyppoes?"

"Trust old Bob, he'll let you down."

"You will have your little joke," said Bob the Fiddle, smiling like a razor, "but I forgive you, boys."

Out of the fug and babel, I heard: "Where's old O. Jones?" "Where are you old O.?" "He's in the kitchen cooking his dinner." "He never forgets his dinner time." "Good old O. Jones." "Come out and fight." "No, not now, later." "No, now when I'm in a temper." "Look at Will Sentry, he's proper snobbled." "Look at his wilful feet." "Look at Mr. Weazley lording it on the floor."

Mr. Weazley got up, hissing like a gander. "That boy pushed me down deliberate," he said, pointing to me at the door, and I slunk away down the passage and out to the mild, good cows.

Time clouded over, the cows wondered, I threw a stone at them and they wandered, wondering, away. Then out blew my Uncle, ballooning, and one by one the members lumbered after him in a grizzle. They had drunk the Mountain Sheep dry. Mr. Weazley had won a string of onions that the Shoni-Onion man had raffled in the bar.

"What's the good of onions if you left your teeth on the mantelpiece?" he said. And when I looked through the back window of the thundering charabanc, I saw the pub grow smaller in the distance. And the flag of Siam, from the flagpole by the Gents, fluttered now at half mast.

The Blue Bull, the Dragon, the Star of Wales, the Twll in the Wall, the Sour Grapes, the Shepherd's Arms, the Bells of Aberdovey: I had nothing to do in the whole wild August world but remember the names where the outing stopped and keep an eye on the charabanc. And whenever it passed a public house, Mr. Weazley would cough like a billy goat and cry, "Stop the bus, I'm dying of breath." And back we would all have to go.

Closing time meant nothing to the members of that outing. Behind locked doors, they hymned and rumpused all the beautiful afternoon. And, when a policeman entered the Druid's Tap by the back door, and found them all choral with beer, "Sssh!" said Noah Bowen, "the pub is shut."

"Where do you come from?" he said in his buttoned, blue voice.

They told him.

"I got a auntie there," the policeman said. And very soon he was singing "Asleep in the Deep."

Off we drove again at last, the charabanc bouncing with tenors and flagons, and came to a river that rushed along among willows.

"Water!" they shouted.

"Porthcawl!" sang my uncle.

"Where's the donkeys?" said Mr. Weazley.

And out they lurched, to paddle and whoop in the cool, white, winding water. Mr. Franklyn, trying to polka on the slippery stones, fell in twice. "Nothing is simple," he said with dignity as he oozed up the bank.

"It's cold!" they cried.

"It's lovely!"

"It's smooth as a moth's nose!"

"It's *better* than Porthcawl!"

And dusk came down warm and gentle on thirty wild, wet, pickled, splashing men without a care in the world at the end of the world in the west of Wales. And, "Who goes there?" called Will Sentry to a wild duck flying.

They stopped at the Hermit's Nest for a rum to keep out the cold. "I played for Aberavon in 1898," said a stranger to Enoch Davies.

"Liar," said Enoch Davies.

"I can show you photos," said the stranger.

"Forged," said Enoch Davies.

"And I'll show you my cap at home."

"Stolen."

"I got friends to prove it," the stranger said in a fury.

"Bribed," said Enoch Davies.

On the way home, through the simmering moon-splashed dark, old O. Jones began to cook his supper on a primus stove in the middle of the charabanc. Mr. Weazley coughed himself blue in the smoke. "Stop the bus!" he cried, "I'm dying of breath." We all climbed down into the moonlight. There was not a public house in sight. So they carried out the remaining cases, and the primus stove, and old O. Jones himself, and took them into a field, and sat down in a circle in the field and drank and sang while old O. Jones cooked sausage and mash and the moon flew above us. And there I drifted to sleep against my uncle's mountainous waistcoat, and, as I slept, "Who goes there?" called out Will Sentry to the flying moon.

JUDITH THOMPSON

PINK

Judith Thompson (b. 1954), a playwright and one of Canada's most powerfully dramatic writers, was born in Montreal and grew up in Connecticut and in Kingston, Ontario. She received her undergraduate degree from Queen's University and studied acting with the National Theatre School. With her first play, The Crackwalker *(1980), Thompson established herself as an important presence in Canadian theatre. Other full-length stage plays include* White Biting Dog *(1984), for which she won the Governor General's Award for English-language drama;* I Am Yours *(1987);* Lion in the Streets *(1990), winner of the Chalmers Award;* The Perfect Pie; *and* Sled *(1995). She is also the author of numerous shorter stage pieces, radio plays, screenplays, and television scripts, including the remarkable* "Life with Billy," *which won a Golden Gate Award and* "Turning to Stone," *winner of the Prix Italia. In 1989 she again won a Governor General's Award for the collection* The Other Side of the Dark.

Judith Thompson's work is "always acutely attuned to class tensions" and is characterized by a remarkable intensity. "Pink" was originally conceived as a dramatic monologue and was written for the Arts Against Apartheid Benefit in Toronto in 1986. In this piece Thompson explores, in the breathless, urgent voice of a child already sunk in the bias of her class and race, a love that does not understand itself. Judith Thompson currently lives in Toronto with her husband and children and teaches at the University of Guelph.

LUCY, *a ten-year-old white girl talking to her dead black nurse, Nellie, shot in a march, in her open coffin.*

LUCY   NELLIE NELLIE NELLIE NELLIE NELLIE NELLIE
NELLIE NELLIE NELLIE NELLIE NELLIE NELLIE
NELLIE NELLIE NELLIE NELLIE

NELLIE NELLIE NELLIE NELLIE NELLIE NELLIE
NELLIE I want you to come back, to shampoo my hair
and make a pink cake and we can sit in the back and
roll mealie pap in our hands see, I told you not to go in
those marches and I told you, I told you that what you
people don't understand, what you didn't see, is
apratheid's for YOU. IT'S FOR YOUR PEOPLE'S
FEELINGS, see, like we got separate washrooms
cause you like to spit, and if we said, 'Eww yucch,
don't spit,' it would hurt your feelings and we got
separate movies, cause you like to talk back to movie
stars and say 'amen' and 'that's the way' and stuff and
that drives us crazy so we might tell you to shut up
and then you might cry and we got separate bus stops
cause you don't like deodorant cause you say it smells
worse than people and we might tell you you stink
and the only thing I don't get is how come you get
paid less for the same job my Mummy says it's
because you people don't like money anyway, you
don't like TVs and stereo's and all that stuff cause
what you really like to do is sing and dance. And you
don't need money to sing and dance I just ... I don't
understand why you weren't happy with us, Mummy
let you eat as much sugar as you wanted, and we
never said anything to you, some days, Mummy says
it was up to a quarter-pound, but we know blacks like
sugar so we didn't mind, and we even let you take a
silver spoon, I heard Mummy say to her friends, 'there
goes another silver spoon to Soweto' but she never
called the police ... and you had your own little room
back there, and we even let your husband come once
in a while, and that's against the law, Mummy and
Daddy could have gone to jail for that, so how come
you weren't grateful? How come you stopped singing
those Zulu songs in the morning, those pretty songs
like the one that was about love and kissing, you
stopped singing, and you stopped shampooing my
hair, you said I could do it myself, and and your eyes,
your eyes used to look at me when I was little they
would look at me like they were tickling me just

tickling me all the time, like I was special, but they
went out, they went out like a light does and you
stopped making my cakes every Tuesday, every
Tuesday morning I would ask you to make me a pink
cake and you would always say, 'you ask your
mummy' and then you'd make it but you stopped
making them, you told me I was too old for pink
cakes, that the pink wasn't real, it was just food colour
anyway and then, and then, you hardly ever came
anymore, and when I saw you that day ... when I saw
you downtown with your husband and four children
all ... hanging off your arms, I just couldn't stand it! I
wanted to yell at your children and tell them you were
mine that you were more mine than theirs because
you were with me more much more so you were mine
and let go of you to get off you and I hated the way
you looked without your uniform, so brown and
plain, not neat and nice anymore, you looked so pretty
in your uniform, so pretty, but we didn't even mind
when you didn't want to wear it.

  We didn't mind, but you were still unhappy, and
when I saw you in town looking so dusty and you
didn't even introduce me to your kids and one of
them, one of them did that rude thing that
'Amandilia' thing that means black power I saw you
slap his hand but you didn't say anything, so you
must have hated me too, I saw that you hated me too
and I'd been so nice to you, I told you my nightmares
and you changed my bed when I wet it and now you
didn't even like me and it wasn't my fault it wasn't
my fault it just when I asked you why that day, you
were cleaning the stove and I said Nellie why ... don't
you like me anymore, and you said, 'you're not a child
anymore, Lucy, you're a white person now' and it
wasn't my fault I couldn't help it I couldn't help
yelling

KAFFIR, KAFFIR, DO WHAT YOU'RE TOLD, KAFFIR
OR I SLAP YOUR BLACK FACE, I SLAP YOUR
BLACK FACE AND I KICK YOUR BLACK BELLY I
KICK YOUR BLACK BELLY AND KICK IT TILL IT

CAVES RIGHT IN AND IT CAN'T HOLD MORE
BABIES EVER AGAIN. NO MORE UGLY BLACK
BABIES THAT YOU'LL ... that you'll like more than
me. Even though I'm ten years old I made you die. I
made you go in that march and I made you die. I
know that forever. I said I was sorry, I'm sorry, I'm
sorry, I'm sorry, but you never looked at me
again. You hated me. But I love you, Nellie, more than
Mummy or Daddy and I want you to come back, and
sing those songs, and roll mealie pap and be washing
the floor in your nice uniform so I can come in and ask
you make a pink cake and your eyes will tickle me.
And you will say 'yes.'
'Yes, I'll make a pink....'

ALICE WALKER

NINETEEN FIFTY-FIVE

Alice Walker (b. 1944), an African American novelist and poet, was born and raised in Eatonton, Georgia, the eighth and youngest child of poor sharecroppers. She was an excellent student and from an early age showed an interest in reading and writing, eventually winning scholarships to Spelman College and, later, to Sarah Lawrence. She has been an active member of the civil-rights movement in the United States since the 1960s, and she has travelled widely, as an exchange student in Uganda, as an aid worker delivering antibiotics to Cuba, and as an observer after the Nicaraguan revolution. With strong views on the necessity for social change, Walker uses writing as a place in which she can speak to the betrayal, the hurt, and the shame of people whose souls have been injured. She asserts: "Art is the mirror, perhaps the only one, in which we can see our true collective face. We must honour its sacred function. We must let art help us." She has spoken on behalf of the women's movement and against apartheid, nuclear issues, and female genital mutilation.

Walker is perhaps best known for her 1982 novel, The Color Purple, *for which she won the Pulitzer Prize. She began her writing career in 1968 with the publication of a collection of poetry,* Once, *and has continued to publish extensively, including several collections of poetry, novels, volumes of short stories, essays, and a memoir entitled* The Same River Twice: Honouring the Difficult *(1995). "Nineteen Fifty-Five" is from* You Can't Keep a Good Woman Down, *a collection of short stories published in 1981, and tells the story of Gracie Mae Still, a black woman who looks convention straight in the face and calls it a fool. Among those authors who have influenced her writing, Walker cites Zora Neale Hurston, Gabriel García Márquez, and Flannery O'Connor, whose home was only minutes from Walker's own birthplace.*

1955

The car is a brandnew red Thunderbird convertible, and it's passed the house more than once. It slows down real slow now, and stops at the curb. An older gentleman dressed like a Baptist deacon gets out on the side near the house, and a young fellow who looks about sixteen gets out on the driver's side. They are white, and I wonder what in the world they doing in this neighborhood.

Well, I say to J.T., put your shirt on, anyway, and let me clean these glasses offa the table.

We had been watching the ballgame on TV. I wasn't actually watching, I was sort of daydreaming, with my foots up in J.T.'s lap.

I seen 'em coming on up the walk, brisk, like they coming to sell something, and then they rung the bell, and J.T. declined to put on a shirt but instead disappeared into the bedroom where the other television is. I turned down the one in the living room; I figured I'd be rid of these two double quick and J.T. could come back out again.

Are you Gracie Mae Still? asked the old guy, when I opened the door and put my hand on the lock inside the screen.

And I don't need to buy a thing, said I.

What makes you think we're sellin'? he asks, in that heavy Southern way that makes my eyeballs ache.

Well, one way or another and they're inside the house and the first thing the young fellow does is raise the TV a couple of decibels. He's about five feet nine, sort of womanish looking, with real dark white skin and a red pouting mouth. His hair is black and curly and he looks like a Loosianna creole.

About one of your songs, says the deacon. He is maybe sixty, with white hair and beard, white silk shirt, black linen suit, black tie and black shoes. His cold gray eyes look like they're sweating.

One of my songs?

Traynor here just *loves* your songs. Don't you, Traynor? He nudges Traynor with his elbow. Traynor blinks, says something I can't catch in a pitch I don't register.

The boy learned to sing and dance livin' round you people out in the country. Practically cut his teeth on you.

Traynor looks up at me and bites his thumbnail.

I laugh.

Well, one way or another they leave with my agreement that they can record one of my songs. The deacon writes me a check for five hundred dollars, the boy grunts his awareness of the transaction, and I am laughing all over myself by the time I rejoin J.T.

Just as I am snuggling down beside him though I hear the front door bell going off again.

Forgit his hat? asks J.T.

I hope not, I say.

The deacon stands there leaning on the door frame and once again I'm thinking of those sweaty-looking eyeballs of his. I wonder if sweat makes your eyeballs pink because his are sure pink. Pink and gray and it strikes me that nobody I'd care to know is behind them.

I forgot one little thing, he says pleasantly. I forgot to tell you Traynor and I would like to buy up all of those records you made of the song. I tell you we sure do love it.

Well, love it or not, I'm not so stupid as to let them do that without making 'em pay. So I says, Well, that's gonna cost you. Because, really, that song never did sell all that good, so I was glad they was going to buy it up. But on the other hand, them two listening to my songs by themselves, and nobody else getting to hear me sing it, give me a pause.

Well, one way or another the deacon showed me where I would come out ahead on any deal he had proposed so far. Didn't I give you five hundred dollars? he asked. What white man—and don't even need to mention colored— would give you more? We buy up all your records of that particular song: first, you git royalties. Let me ask you, how much you sell that song for in the first place? Fifty dollars? A hundred, I say. And no royalties from it yet, right? Right. Well, when we buy up all of them records you gonna git royalties. And that's gonna make all them race record shops sit up and take notice of Gracie Mae Still. And they gonna push all them other records of yourn they got. And you no doubt will become one of the big name colored recording artists. And then we can offer you another five hundred dollars for letting us do all this for you. And by God you'll be sittin' pretty! You can go out and buy you the kind of outfit a star should have. Plenty sequins and yards of red satin.

I had done unlocked the screen when I saw I could get some more money out of him. Now I held it wide open while he squeezed through the opening between me and the door. He whipped out another piece of paper and I signed it.

He sort of trotted out to the car and slid in beside Traynor, whose head was back against the seat. They swung around in a u-turn in front of the house and they was gone.

J.T. was putting his shirt on when I got back to the bedroom. Yankees beat the Orioles 10–6, he said. I believe I'll drive out to Paschal's pond and go fishing. Wanta go?

While I was putting on my pants J.T. was holding the two checks.

I'm real proud of a woman that can make cash money without leavin' home, he said. And I said *Umph*. Because we met on the road with me singing in first one little low-life jook after another, making ten dollars a night for myself if I was lucky, and sometimes bringin' home nothing but my life. And J.T. just loved them times. The way I was fast and flashy and always on the go from one town to another. He loved the way my singin' made the dirt farmers cry like babies and the womens shout Honey, hush! But that's mens. They loves any style to which you can get 'em accustomed.

1956

My little grandbaby called me one night on the phone: Little Mama, Little Mama, there's a white man on the television singing one of your songs! Turn on channel 5.

Lord, if it wasn't Traynor. Still looking half asleep from the neck up, but kind of awake in a nasty way from the waist down. He wasn't doing too bad with my song either, but it wasn't just the song the people in the audience was screeching and screaming over, it was that nasty little jerk he was doing from the waist down.

Well, Lord have mercy, I said, listening to him. If I'da closed my eyes, it could have been me. He had followed every turning of my voice, side streets, avenues, red lights, train crossings and all. It gave me a chill.

Everywhere I went I heard Traynor singing my song, and all the little white girls just eating it up. I never had so many ponytails switched across my line of vision in my life. They was so *proud*. He was a *genius*.

Well, all that year I was trying to lose weight anyway and that and high blood pressure and sugar kept me pretty well occupied. Traynor had made a smash from a song of mine. I still had seven hundred dollars of the original one thousand dollars in the bank, and I felt if I could just bring my weight down, life would be sweet.

1957

I lost ten pounds in 1956. That's what I give myself for Christmas. And J.T. and me and the children and their friends and grandkids of all description had just finished dinner—over which I had put on nine and a half of my lost ten—when who should appear at the front door but Traynor. Little Mama, Little Mama! It's that white man who sings—— —— ——. The children didn't call it my song anymore. Nobody did. It was funny how that happened. Traynor and the deacon had bought up all my records, true, but on his record he had put "written by Gracie Mae Still." But that was just another name on the label, like "produced by Apex Records."

On the TV he was inclined to dress like the deacon told him. But now he looked presentable.

Merry Christmas, said he.

And same to you, Son.

I don't know why I called him Son. Well, one way or another they're all our sons. The only requirement is that they be younger than us. But then again, Traynor seemed to be aging by the minute.

You looks tired, I said. Come on in and have a glass of Christmas cheer.

J.T. ain't never in his life been able to act decent to a white man he wasn't working for, but he poured Traynor a glass of bourbon and water, then he took all the children and grandkids and friends and whatnot out to the den. After while I heard Traynor's voice singing the song, coming from the stereo console. It was just the kind of Christmas present my kids would consider cute.

I looked at Traynor, complicit. But he looked like it was the last thing in the world he wanted to hear. His head was pitched forward over his lap, his hands holding his glass and his elbows on his knees.

I done sung that song seem like a million times this year, he said. I sung it on the Grand Ole Opry, I sung it on the Ed Sullivan show. I sung it on Mike Douglas, I sung it at the Cotton Bowl, the Orange Bowl. I sung it at Festivals. I sung it at Fairs. I sung it overseas in Rome, Italy, and once in a submarine *underseas*. I've sung it and sung it, and I'm making forty thousand dollars a day offa it, and you know what, I don't have the faintest notion what the song means.

Whatchumean, what do it mean? It mean what it says. All I could think was: These suckers is making forty thousand a *day* offa my song and now they gonna come back and try to swindle me out of the original thousand.

It's just a song, I said. Cagey. When you fool around with a lot of no count mens you sing a bunch of 'em. I shrugged.

Oh, he said. Well. He started brightening up. I just come to tell you I think you are a great singer.

He didn't blush, saying that. Just said it straight out.

And I brought you a little Christmas present too. Now you take this little box and hold it until I drive off. Then you take it outside under that first streetlight back up the street aways in front of that green house. Then you open the box and see ... Well, just *see*.

What had come over this boy, I wondered, holding the box. I looked out the window in time to see another white man come up and get in the car with him and then two more cars full of white mens start out behind him. They was all in long black cars that looked like a funeral procession.

Little Mama, Little Mama, what it is? One of my grandkids come running up and started pulling at the box. It was wrapped in gay Christmas paper—the thick, rich kind that it's hard to picture folks making just to throw away.

J.T. and the rest of the crowd followed me out the house, up the street to the streetlight and in front of the green house. Nothing was there but somebody's gold-grilled white Cadillac. Brandnew and most distracting. We got to looking at it so till I almost forgot the little box in my hand. While the others were busy making 'miration I carefully took off the paper and ribbon and folded them up and put them in my pants pocket. What should I see but a pair of genuine solid gold caddy keys.

Dangling the keys in front of everybody's nose, I unlocked the caddy, motioned for J.T. to git in on the other side, and us didn't come back home for two days.

1960

Well, the boy was sure nuff famous by now. He was still a mite shy of twenty but already they was calling him the Emperor of Rock and Roll.

Then what should happen but the draft.

Well, says J.T. There goes all this Emperor of Rock and Roll business.

But even in the army the womens was on him like white on rice. We watched it on the News.

> *Dear Gracie Mae* [he wrote from Germany],
> *How you? Fine I hope as this leaves me doing real well. Before I come in the army I was gaining a lot of weight and gitting jittery from making all them dumb movies. But now I exercise and eat right and get plenty of rest. I'm more awake than I been in ten years.*
> *I wonder if you are writing any more songs?*
>
> *Sincerely,*
Traynor

I wrote him back:

> *Dear Son,*
> *We is all fine in the Lord's good grace and hope this finds you the same. J.T. and me be out all times of the day and night in that car you give me—which you know you didn't have to do. Oh, and I do appreciate the mink and the new self-cleaning oven. But if you send anymore stuff to eat from Germany I'm going to have to open up a store in the neighborhood just to get rid of it. Really, we have more than enough of everything. The Lord is good to us and we don't know Want.*
> *Glad to hear you is well and gitting your right rest. There ain't nothing like exercising to help that along. J.T. and me work some part of every day that we don't go fishing in the garden.*
> *Well, so long Soldier.*
>
> *Sincerely,*
Gracie Mae

He wrote:

> Dear Gracie Mae,
>   I hope you and J.T. like that automatic power tiller I had one of
> the stores back home send you. I went through a mountain of cata-
> logs looking for it—I wanted something that even a woman could
> use.
>   I've been thinking about writing some songs of my own but every
> time I finish one it don't seem to be about nothing I've actually lived
> myself. My agent keeps sending me other people's songs but they just
> sound mooney. I can hardly git through 'em without gagging.
>   Everybody still loves that song of yours. They ask me all the time
> what do I think it means, really. I mean, they want to know just
> what I want to know. Where out of your life did it come from?
>
>   Sincerely,
>   Traynor

1968

I didn't see the boy for seven years. No. Eight. Because just about everybody
was dead when I saw him again. Malcolm X, King, the president and his
brother, and even J.T. J.T. died of a head cold. It just settled in his head like a
block of ice, he said, and nothing we did moved it until one day he just leaned
out the bed and died.

His good friend Horace helped me put him away, and then about a year
later Horace and me started going together. We was sitting out on the front
porch swing one summer night, dusk-dark, and I saw this great procession of
lights winding to a stop.

Holy Toledo! said Horace. (He's got a real sexy voice like Ray Charles.)
Look *at* it. He meant the long line of flashy cars and the white men in white
summer suits jumping out on the drivers' sides and standing at attention. With
wings they could pass for angels, with hoods they could be the Klan.

Traynor comes waddling up the walk.

And suddenly I know what it is he could pass for. An Arab like the ones
you see in the storybooks. Plump and soft and with never a care about weight.
Because with so much money, who cares? Traynor is almost dressed like
someone from a storybook too. He has on, I swear, about ten necklaces. Two
sets of bracelets on his arms, at least one ring on every finger, and some kind of
shining buckles on his shoes, so that when he walks you get quite a few twin-
kling lights.

Gracie Mae, he says, coming up to give me a hug. J.T.

I explain that J.T. passed. That this is Horace.

Horace, he says, puzzled but polite, sort of rocking back on his heels. Horace.

That's it for Horace. He goes in the house and don't come back.

Looks like you and me is gained a few, I say.

He laughs. The first time I ever heard him laugh. It don't sound much like a laugh and I can't swear that it's better than no laugh a'tall.

He's gitting fat for sure, but he's still slim compared to me. I'll never see three hundred pounds again and I've just about said (excuse me) fuck it. I got to thinking about it one day an' I thought: aside from the face that they say it's unhealthy, my fat ain't never been no trouble. Mens always have loved me. My kids ain't never complained. Plus they's fat. And fat like I is I looks distinguished. You see me coming and know somebody's *there*.

Gracie Mae, he says, I've come with a personal invitation to you to my house tomorrow for dinner. He laughed. What did it sound like? I couldn't place it. See them men out there? he asked me. I'm sick and tired of eating with them. They don't never have nothing to talk about. That's why I eat so much. But if you come to dinner tomorrow we can talk about the old days. You can tell me about that farm I bought you.

I sold it, I said.

You did?

Yeah, I said, I did. Just cause I said I liked to exercise by working in a garden didn't mean I wanted five hundred acres! Anyhow, I'm a city girl now. Raised in the country it's true. Dirt poor—the whole bit—but that's all behind me now.

Oh well, he said, I didn't mean to offend you.

We sat a few minutes listening to the crickets.

Then he said: You write that song while you was still on the farm, didn't you, or was it right after you left?

You had somebody spying on me? I asked.

You and Bessie Smith got into a fight over it once, he said.

You *is* been spying on me!

But I don't know what the fight was about, he said. Just like I don't know what happened to your second husband. Your first one died in the Texas electric chair. Did you know that? Your third one beat you up, stole your touring costumes and your car and retired with a chorine to Tuskagee. He laughed. He's still there.

I had been mad, but suddenly I calmed down. Traynor was talking very dreamily. It was dark but seems like I could tell his eyes weren't right. It was like some*thing* was sitting there talking to me but not necessarily with a person behind it.

You gave up on marrying and seem happier for it. He laughed again. I married but it never went like it was supposed to. I never could squeeze any of my own life either into it or out of it. It was like singing somebody else's record. I copied the way it was sposed to be *exactly* but I never had a clue what marriage meant.

I bought her a diamond ring big as your fist. I bought her clothes. I built her a mansion. But right away she didn't want the boys to stay there. Said they smoked up the bottom floor. Hell, there were *five* floors.

No need to grieve, I said. No need to. Plenty more where she come from.

He perked up. That's part of what the song means, ain't it? No need to grieve. Whatever it is, there's plenty more down the line.

I never really believed that way back when I wrote that song, I said. It was all bluffing then. The trick is to live long enough to put your young bluffs to use. Now if I was to sing that song today I'd tear it up. 'Cause I done lived long enough to know it's *true*. Them words could hold me up.

I ain't lived that long, he said.

Look like you on your way, I said. I don't know why, but the boy seemed to need some encouraging. And I don't know, seem like one way or another you talk to rich white folks and you end up reassuring *them*. But what the hell, by now I feel something for the boy. I wouldn't be in his bed all alone in the middle of the night for nothing. Couldn't be nothing worse than being famous the world over for something you don't even understand. That's what I tried to tell Bessie. She wanted that same song. Overheard me practicing it one day, said, with her hands on her hips: Gracie Mae, I'ma sing your song tonight. I *likes* it.

Your lips be too swole to sing, I said. She was mean and she was strong, but I trounced her.

Ain't you famous enough with your own stuff? I said. Leave mine alone. Later on, she thanked me. By then she was Miss Bessie Smith to the World, and I was still Miss Gracie Mae Nobody from Notasulga.

The next day all these limousines arrived to pick me up. Five cars and twelve bodyguards. Horace picked that morning to start painting the kitchen.

Don't paint the kitchen, fool, I said. The only reason that dumb boy of ours is going to show me his mansion is because he intends to present us with a new house.

What you gonna do with it? he asked me, standing there in his shirtsleeves stirring the paint.

Sell it. Give it to the children. Live in it on weekends. It don't matter what I do. He sure don't care.

Horace just stood there shaking his head. Mama you sure looks *good*, he says. Wake me up when you git back.

Fool, I say, and pat my wig in front of the mirror.

The boy's house is something else. First you come to this mountain, and then you commence to drive and drive up this road that's lined with magnolias. Do magnolias grow on mountains? I was wondering. And you come to ponds and you come to deer and you come up on some sheep. And I figure these two is sposed to represent England and Wales. Or something out of Europe. And you just keep on coming to stuff. And it's all pretty. Only the man driving my car don't look at nothing but the road. Fool. And then *finally*, after all this time, you begin to go up the driveway. And there's more magnolias—only they're not in such good shape. It's sort of cool up this high and I don't think they're gonna make it. And then I see this building that looks like if it had a name it would be The Tara Hotel. Columns and steps and outdoor chandeliers and rocking chairs. Rocking chairs? Well, and there's the boy on the steps dressed in a dark green satin jacket like you see folks wearing on TV late at night, and he looks sort of like a fat dracula with all that house rising behind him, and standing beside him there's this little white vision of loveliness that he introduces as his wife.

He's nervous when he introduces us and he says to her: This is Gracie Mae Still, I want you to know me. I mean ... and she gives him a look that would fry meat.

Won't you come in, Gracie Mae, she says, and that's the last I see of her.

He fishes around for something to say or do and decides to escort me to the kitchen. We go through the entry and the parlor and the breakfast room and the dining room and the servants' passage and finally get there. The first thing I notice is that, altogether, there are five stoves. He looks about to introduce me to one.

Wait a minute, I say. Kitchens don't do nothing for me. Let's go sit on the front porch.

Well, we hike back and we sit in the rocking chairs rocking until dinner.

Gracie Mae, he says down the table, taking a piece of fried chicken from the woman standing over him, I got a little surprise for you.

It's a house, ain't it? I ask, spearing a chitlin.

You're getting *spoiled*, he says. And the way he says *spoiled* sounds funny. He slurs it. It sounds like his tongue is too thick for his mouth. Just that quick he's finished the chicken and is now eating chitlins *and* a pork chop. *Me* spoiled, I'm thinking.

I already got a house. Horace is right this minute painting the kitchen. I bought that house. My kids feel comfortable in that house.

But this one I bought you is just like mine. Only a little smaller.

I still don't need no house. And anyway who would clean it?

He looks surprised.

Really, I think, some peoples advance *so* slowly.

I hadn't thought of that. But what the hell. I'll get you somebody to live in.

I don't want other folks living 'round me. Makes me nervous.

You *don't*? It *do*?

What I want to wake up and see folks I don't even know for?

He just sits there downtable staring at me. Some of that feeling is in the song, ain't it? Not the words, the *feeling*. What I want to wake up and see folks I don't even know for? But I see twenty folks a day I don't even know, including my wife.

This food wouldn't be bad to wake up to though, I said. The boy had found the genius of corn bread.

He looked at me real hard. He laughed. Short. They want what you got but they don't want you. They want what I got only it ain't mine. That's what makes 'em so hungry for me when I sing. They getting the flavor of something but they ain't getting the thing itself. They like a pack of hound dogs trying to gobble up a scent.

You talking 'bout your fans?

Right. Right. He says.

Don't worry 'bout your fans, I say. They don't know their asses from a hole in the ground. I doubt there's a honest one in the bunch.

That's the point. Dammit, that's the point! He hits the table with his fist. It's so solid it don't even quiver. You need a honest audience! You can't have folks that's just gonna lie right back to you.

Yeah, I say, it was small compared to yours, but I had one. It would have been worth my life to try to sing 'em somebody else's stuff that I didn't know nothing about.

He must have pressed a buzzer under the table. One of his flúnkies zombies up.

Git Johnny Carson, he says.

On the phone? asks the zombie.

On the phone, says Traynor, what you think I mean, git him offa the front porch? Move your ass.

So two weeks later we's on the Johnny Carson show.

Traynor is all corseted down nice and looks a little bit fat but mostly good. And all the women that grew up on him and my song squeal and squeal.

Traynor says: The lady who wrote my first hit record is here with us tonight, and she's agreed to sing it for all of us, just like she sung it forty-five years ago. Ladies and Gentlemen, the great Gracie Mae Still!

Well, I had tried to lose a couple of pounds my own self, but failing that I had me a very big dress made. So I sort of rolls over next to Traynor, who is dwarfted by me, so that when he puts his arm around back of me to try to hug me it looks funny to the audience and they laugh.

I can see this pisses him off. But I smile out there at 'em. Imagine squealing for twenty years and not knowing why you're squealing? No more sense of endings and beginnings than hogs.

It don't matter, Son, I say. Don't fret none over me.

I commence to sing. And I sound—wonderful. Being able to sing good ain't all about having a good singing voice a'tall. A good singing voice helps. But when you come up in the Hard Shell Baptist church like I did you understand early that the fellow that sings is the singer. Them that waits for programs and arrangements and letters from home is just good voices occupying body space.

So there I am singing my own song, my own way. And I give it all I got and enjoy every minute of it. When I finish Traynor is standing up clapping and clapping and beaming at first me and then the audience like I'm his mama for true. The audience claps politely for about two seconds.

Traynor looks disgusted.

He comes over and tries to hug me again. The audience laughs.

Johnny Carson looks at us like we both weird.

Traynor is mad as hell. He's supposed to sing something called a love ballad. But instead he takes the mike, turns to me and says: Now see if my imitation still holds up. He goes into the same song, *our* song, I think, looking out at his flaky audience. And he sings it just the way he always did. My voice, my tone, my inflection, everything. But he forgets a couple of lines. Even before he's finished the matronly squeals begin.

He sits down next to me looking whipped.

It don't matter, Son, I say, patting his hand. You don't even know those people. Try to make the people you know happy.

Is that in the song? he asks.

Maybe. I say.

1977

For a few years I hear from him, then nothing. But trying to lose weight takes all the attention I got to spare. I finally faced up to the fact that my fat is the hurt I don't admit, not even to myself, and that I been trying to bury it from the day I was born. But also when you git real old, to tell the truth, it ain't as pleasant. It gits lumpy and slack. Yuck. So one day I said to Horace. I'ma git this shit offa me.

And he feel in with the program like he always try to do and Lord such a procession of salads and cottage cheese and fruit juice!

One night I dreamed Traynor had split up with his fifteenth wife. He said: *You meet 'em for no reason. You date 'em for no reason. You marry 'em for no reason. I do it all but I swear it's just like somebody else doing it. I feel like I can't remember Life.*

The boy's in trouble, I said to Horace.

You've always said that, he said.

I have?

Yeah. You always said he looked asleep. You can't sleep through life if you wants to live it.

You not such a fool after all, I said, pushing myself up with my cane and hobbling over to where he was. Let me sit down on your lap, I said, while this salad I ate takes effect.

In the morning we heard Traynor was dead. Some said fat, some said heart, some said alcohol, some said drugs. One of the children called from Detroit. Them dumb fans of his is on a crying rampage, she said. You just ought to turn on the TV.

But I didn't want to see 'em. They was crying and crying and didn't even know what they was crying for. One day this is going to be a pitiful country, I thought.

EUDORA WELTY

A WORN PATH

Eudora Welty (b. 1909) still resides in Jackson, Mississippi, where she was born. One of three children from an affectionate and close-knit family, Welty has spent most of her life in the South. Unlike such writers as William Faulkner, Richard Wright, and Flannery O'Connor, Welty's view of the South is tranquil, and her writing quietly celebrates life in a particular place, arising out of her instinct to praise. When Welty attended Mississippi State College for Women at the age of sixteen, she was already writing, but she would not publish until her midtwenties, when she began submitting stories to the Southern Review. *In 1941 she published her first collection of short stories,* A Curtain of Green, *which includes "A Worn Path." During World War II, she wrote for the* New York Times Book Review *while still living with her mother in Jackson and writing her own fiction. The* Wide Net and Other Stories *was published in 1943, and her first novel,* Delta Wedding, *appeared in 1946. Welty has published numerous collections of short stories, novels, criticism, and memoirs. In 1972 she won the Pulitzer Prize for her novel* The Optimist's Daughter, *and in 1996 she was granted the French Legion of Honor, France's highest civilian award.*

In One Writer's Beginnings *(1983), Eudora Welty says, "I am a writer who came of a sheltered life. A sheltered life can be a daring life as well. For all serious daring starts from within." This same daring motivates many of her characters. Phoenix Jackson, the old woman who is at the centre of "A Worn Path," makes her heroic journey "on foot from deep in the country into town and into a doctor's office on behalf of her little grandson," who is ill. She makes this journey periodically, and each time she succeeds in overcoming its obstacles and reaching her goal, the victory is personal. Welty sees this process as a parallel to story writing: "The way to get there is the all-important, all-absorbing problem, and this problem is your reason for undertaking the story ... [and] like Phoenix, you have to assume that what you are working in aid of is life, not death."*

It was December—a bright frozen day in the early morning. Far out in the country there was an old Negro woman with her head tied in a red rag, coming along a path through the pinewoods. Her name was Phoenix Jackson. She was very old and small and she walked slowly in the dark pine shadows, moving a little from side to side in her steps, with the balanced heaviness and lightness of a pendulum in a grandfather clock. She carried a thin, small cane made from an umbrella, and with this she kept tapping the frozen earth in front of her. This made a grave and persistent noise in the still air, that seemed meditative like the chirping of a solitary little bird.

She wore a dark striped dress reaching down to her shoe tops, and an equally long apron of bleached sugar sacks, with a full pocket: all neat and tidy, but every time she took a step she might have fallen over her shoe laces, which dragged from her unlaced shoes. She looked straight ahead. Her eyes were blue with age. Her skin had a pattern all its own of numberless branching wrinkles and as though a whole little tree stood in the middle of her forehead, but a golden color ran underneath, and the two knobs of her cheeks were illuminated by a yellow burning under the dark. Under the red rag her hair came down on her neck in the frailest of ringlets, still black, and with an odor like copper.

Now and then there was a quivering in the thicket. Old Phoenix said, "Out of my way, all you foxes, owls, beetles, jack rabbits, coons and wild animals! ... Keep out from under these feet, little bob-whites. ... Keep the big wild hogs out of my path. Don't let none of those come running my direction. I got a long way." Under her small black-freckled hand her cane, limber as a buggy whip, would switch at the brush as if to rouse up any hiding things.

On she went. The woods were deep and still. The sun made the pine needles almost too bright to look at, up where the wind rocked. The cones dropped as light as feathers. Down in the hollow was the mourning dove—it was not too late for him.

The path ran up a hill. "Seem like there is chains about my feet, time I get this far," she said, in the voice of argument old people keep to use with themselves. "Something always take a hold of me on this hill—pleads I should stay."

After she got to the top she turned and gave a full, severe look behind her where she had come. "Up through pines," she said at length. "Now down through oaks."

Her eyes opened their widest, and she started down gently. But before she got to the bottom of the hill a bush caught her dress.

Her fingers were busy and intent, but her skirts were full and long, so that before she could pull them free in one place they were caught in another. It was not possible to allow the dress to tear. "I in the thorny bush," she said.

"Thorns, you doing your appointed work. Never want to let folks pass, no sir. Old eyes thought you was a pretty little *green* bush."

Finally, trembling all over, she stood free, and after a moment dared to stoop for her cane.

"Sun so high!" she cried, leaning back and looking, while the thick tears went over her eyes. "The time getting all gone here."

At the foot of this hill was a place where a log was laid across the creek.

"Now comes the trial," said Phoenix.

Putting her right foot out, she mounted the log and shut her eyes. Lifting her skirt, leveling her cane fiercely before her, like a festival figure in some parade, she began to march across. Then she opened her eyes and she was safe on the other side.

"I wasn't as old as I thought," she said.

But she sat down to rest. She spread her skirts on the bank around her and folded her hands over her knees. Up above her was a tree in a pearly cloud of mistletoe. She did not dare to close her eyes, and when a little boy brought her a plate with a slice of marble-cake on it she spoke to him. "That would be acceptable," she said. But when she went to take it there was just her own hand in the air.

So she left that tree, and had to go through a barbed-wire fence. There she had to creep and crawl, spreading her knees and stretching her fingers like a baby trying to climb the steps. But she talked loudly to herself: she could not let her dress be torn now, so late in the day, and she could not pay for having her arm or her leg sawed off if she got caught fast where she was.

At last she was safe through the fence and risen up out in the clearing. Big dead trees, like black men with one arm, were standing in the purple stalks of the withered cotton field. There sat a buzzard.

"Who you watching?"

In the furrow she made her way along.

"Glad this not the season for bulls," she said, looking sideways, "and the good Lord made his snakes to curl up and sleep in the winter. A pleasure I don't see no two-headed snake coming around that tree, where it come once. It took a while to get by him, back in the summer."

She passed through the old cotton and went into a field of dead corn. It whispered and shook and was taller than her head. "Through the maze now," she said, for there was no path.

Then there was something tall, black, and skinny there, moving before her.

At first she took it for a man. It could have been a man dancing in the field. But she stood still and listened, and it did not make a sound. It was as silent as a ghost.

"Ghost," she said sharply, "who be you the ghost of? For I have heard of nary death close by."

But there was no answer—only the ragged dancing in the wind.

She shut her eyes, reached out her hand, and touched a sleeve. She found a coat and inside that an emptiness, cold as ice.

"You scarecrow," she said. Her face lighted. "I ought to be shut up for good," she said with laughter. "My senses is gone. I too old. I the oldest people I ever know. Dance, old scarecrow," she said, "while I dancing with you."

She kicked her foot over the furrow, and with mouth drawn down, shook her head once or twice in a little strutting way. Some husks blew down and whirled in streamers about her skirts.

Then she went on, parting her way from side to side with the cane, through the whispering field. At last she came to the end, to a wagon track where the silver grass blew between the red ruts. The quail were walking around like pullets, seeming all dainty and unseen.

"Walk pretty," she said. "This the easy place. This the easy going."

She followed the track, swaying through the quiet bare fields, through the little strings of trees silver in their dead leaves, past cabins silver from weather, with the doors and windows boarded shut, all like old women under a spell sitting there. "I walking in their sleep," she said, nodding her head vigorously.

In a ravine she went where a spring was silently flowing through a hollow log. Old Phoenix bent and drank. "Sweet-gum makes the water sweet," she said, and drank more. "Nobody know who made this well, for it was here when I was born."

The track crossed a swampy part where the moss hung as white as lace from every limb. "Sleep on, alligators, and blow your bubbles." Then the track went into the road.

Deep, deep the road went down between the high green-colored banks. Overhead the live-oaks met, and it was as dark as a cave.

A black dog with a lolling tongue came up out of the weeds by the ditch. She was meditating, and not ready, and when he came at her she only hit him a little with her cane. Over she went in the ditch, like a little puff of milkweed.

Down there, her senses drifted away. A dream visited her, and she reached her hand up, but nothing reached down and gave her a pull. So she lay there and presently went to talking. "Old woman," she said to herself, "that black dog come up out of the weeds to stall you off, and now there he sitting on his fine tail, smiling at you."

A white man finally came along and found her—a hunter, a young man, with his dog on a chain.

"Well, Granny!" he laughed. "What are you doing there?"

"Lying on my back like a June-bug waiting to be turned over, mister," she said, reaching up her hand.

He lifted her up, gave her a swing in the air, and set her down. "Anything broken, Granny?"

"No sir, them old dead weeds is springy enough," said Phoenix, when she had got her breath. "I thank you for your trouble."

"Where do you live, Granny?" he asked, while the two dogs were growling at each other.

"Away back yonder, sir, behind the ridge. You can't even see it from here."

"On your way home?"

"No sir, I going to town."

"Why, that's too far! That's as far as I walk when I come out myself, and I get something for my trouble." He patted the stuffed bag he carried, and there hung down a little closed claw. It was one of the bob-whites, with its beak hooked bitterly to show it was dead. "Now you go on home, Granny!"

"I bound to go to town, mister," said Phoenix. "The time come around."

He gave another laugh, filling the whole landscape. "I know you old colored people! Wouldn't miss going to town to see Santa Claus!"

But something held old Phoenix very still. The deep lines in her face went into a fierce and different radiation. Without warning, she had seen with her own eyes a flashing nickel fall out of the man's pocket onto the ground.

"How old are you, Granny?" he was saying.

"There is no telling, mister," she said, "no telling."

Then she gave a little cry and clapped her hands and said, "Git on away from here, dog! Look! Look at that dog!" She laughed as if in admiration. "He ain't scared of nobody. He a big black dog." She whispered, "Sic him!"

"Watch me get rid of that cur," said the man. "Sic him, Pete! Sic him!"

Phoenix heard the dogs fighting, and heard the man running and throwing sticks. She even heard a gunshot. But she was slowly bending forward by that time, further and further forward, the lids stretched down over her eyes, as if she were doing this in her sleep. Her chin was lowered almost to her knees. The yellow palm of her hand came out from the fold of her apron. Her fingers slid down and along the ground under the piece of money with the grace and care they would have in lifting an egg from under a setting hen. Then she slowly straightened up, she stood erect, and the nickel was in her apron pocket. A bird flew by. Her lips moved. "God watching me the whole time. I come to stealing."

The man came back, and his own dog panted about them. "Well, I scared him off that time," he said, and than he laughed and lifted his gun and pointed it at Phoenix.

She stood straight and faced him.

"Doesn't the gun scare you?" he said, still pointing it.

"No sir, I seen plenty go off closer by, in my day, and for less than what I done," she said, holding utterly still.

He smiled, and shouldered the gun. "Well, Granny," he said, "you must be a hundred years old, and scared of nothing. I'd give you a dime if I had any money with me. But you take my advice and stay home, and nothing will happen to you."

"I bound to go on my way, mister," said Phoenix. She inclined her head in the red rag. Then they went in different directions, but she could hear the gun shooting again and again over the hill.

She walked on. The shadows hung from the oak trees to the road like curtains. Then she smelled wood-smoke, and smelled the river, and she saw a steeple and the cabins on their steep steps. Dozens of little black children whirled around her. There ahead was Natchez shining. Bells were ringing. She walked on.

In the paved city it was Christmas time. There were red and green electric lights strung and crisscrossed everywhere, and all turned on in the daytime. Old Phoenix would have been lost if she had not distrusted her eyesight and depended on her feet to know where to take her.

She paused quietly on the sidewalk where people were passing by. A lady came along in the crowd, carrying an armful of red-, green- and silver-wrapped presents; she gave off perfume like the red roses in hot summer, and Phoenix stopped her.

"Please, missy, will you lace up my shoe?" She held up her foot.

"What do you want, Grandma?"

"See my shoe," said Phoenix. "Do all right for out in the country, but wouldn't look right to go in a big building."

"Stand still then, Grandma," said the lady. She put her packages down on the sidewalk beside her and laced and tied both shoes tightly.

"Can't lace 'em with a cane," said Phoenix. "Thank you, missy. I doesn't mind asking a nice lady to tie up my shoe, when I gets out on the street."

Moving slowly and from side to side, she went into the big building, and into a tower of steps, where she walked up and around and around until her feet knew to stop.

She entered a door, and there she saw nailed up on the wall the document that had been stamped with the gold seal and framed in the gold frame, which matched the dream that was hung up in her head.

"Here I be," she said. There was a fixed and ceremonial stiffness over her body.

"A charity case, I suppose," said an attendant who sat at the desk before her.

But Phoenix only looked above her head. There was sweat on her face, the wrinkles in her skin shone like a bright net.

"Speak up, Grandma," the woman said. "What's your name? We must have your history, you know. Have you been here before? What seems to be the trouble with you?"

Old Phoenix only gave a twitch to her face as if a fly were bothering her.

"Are you deaf?" cried the attendant.

But then the nurse came in.

"Oh, that's just old Aunt Phoenix," she said. "She doesn't come for herself—she has a little grandson. She makes these trips just as regular as clockwork. She lives away back off the Old Natchez Trace." She bent down. "Well, Aunt Phoenix, why don't you just take a seat? We won't keep you standing after your long trip." She pointed.

The old woman sat down, bolt upright in the chair.

"Now, how is the boy?" asked the nurse.

Old Phoenix did not speak.

"I said, how is the boy?'

But Phoenix only waited and stared straight ahead, her face very solemn and withdrawn into rigidity.

"Is his throat any better?" asked the nurse. "Aunt Phoenix, don't you hear me? Is your grandson's throat any better since the last time you came for the medicine?"

With her hands on her knees, the old woman waited, silent, erect and motionless, just as if she were in armor.

"You mustn't take up our time this way, Aunt Phoenix," the nurse said. "Tell us quickly about your grandson, and get it over. He isn't dead, is he?"

At last there came a flicker and then a flame of comprehension across her face, and she spoke.

"My grandson. It was my memory had left me. There I sat and forgot why I made my long trip."

"Forgot?" The nurse frowned. "After you came so far?"

Then Phoenix was like an old woman begging a dignified forgiveness for waking up frightened in the night. "I never did go to school, I was too old at the Surrender," she said in a soft voice. "I'm an old woman without an education. It was my memory fail me. My little grandson, he is just the same, and I forgot it in the coming."

"Throat never heals, does it?" said the nurse, speaking in a loud, sure voice to old Phoenix. By now she had a card with something written on it, a little list. "Yes. Swallowed lye. When was it?—January—two-three years ago—"

Phoenix spoke unasked now. "No, missy, he not dead, he just the same. Every little while his throat begin to close up again, and he not able to swallow. He not get his breath. He not able to help himself. So the time come around, and I go on another trip for the soothing medicine."

"All right. The doctor said as long as you came to get it, you could have it," said the nurse. "But it's an obstinate case."

"My little grandson, he sit up there in the house all wrapped up, waiting by himself," Phoenix went on. "We is the only two left in the world. He suffer and it don't seem to put him back at all. He got a sweet look. He going to last. He wear a little patch quilt and peep out holding his mouth open like a little bird. I remembers so plain now. I not going to forget him again, no, the whole enduring time. I could tell him from all the others in creation."

"All right." The nurse was trying to hush her now. She brought her a bottle of medicine. "Charity," she said, making a check mark in a book.

Old Phoenix held the bottle close to her eyes, and then carefully put it into her pocket.

"I thank you," she said.

"It's Christmas time, Grandma," said the attendant. "Could I give you a few pennies out of my purse?"

"Five pennies is a nickel," said Phoenix stiffly.

"Here's a nickel," said the attendant. Phoenix rose carefully and held out her hand. She received the nickel and then fished the other nickel out of her pocket and laid it beside the new one. She stared at her palm closely, with her head on one side.

Then she gave a tap with her cane on the floor.

"This is what come to me to do," she said. "I going to the store and buy my child a little windmill they sells, made out of paper. He going to find it hard to believe there such a thing in the world. I'll march myself back where he waiting, holding it straight up in this hand."

She lifted her free hand, gave a little nod, turned around, and walked out of the doctor's office. Then her slow step began on the stairs, going down.

ETHEL WILSON

MRS. GOLIGHTLY AND THE FIRST CONVENTION

Ethel Wilson (1888–1980) was born in South Africa of missionary parents and, following her mother's death, spent her early childhood in England. At the age of ten she moved to Vancouver, British Columbia, to live with her maternal grandmother. Before her marriage to a physician in 1917, she taught school. During the thirties she published a few short stories and began a series of family reminiscences; however, Wilson was almost sixty years old before she published her first short novel, Hetty Dorval *(1947). She followed this novel quickly with* The Innocent Traveller *(1949),* The Equations of Love *(1952),* Swamp Angel *(1954), and* Love and Salt Water *(1956). "Mrs. Golightly and the First Convention" is from the 1961 collection,* Mrs. Golightly and Other Stories, *the last of her published fiction. Wilson won the Canada Council Medal in 1961 and the Lorne Pierce Medal of the Royal Society of Canada in 1964. She died in Vancouver after a protracted illness.*

Wilson is a critical figure in the coming of age of Canadian fiction. Emerging like a gift in the late forties, her female, sophisticated voice was unlike anything that had been heard before. Ethel Wilson's distinctive sensibility and technical nerve have been greatly admired by many of Canada's most adventurous writers. Critics and readers also have been impressed by Wilson's delicious irony, her good humour, and her sturdy and expansive moral vision, which combines tough-mindedness with a deep compassion.

Mrs. Golightly was a shy woman. She lived in Vancouver. Her husband, Tommy Golightly, was not shy. He was personable and easy to like. He was a consulting engineer who was consulted a great deal by engineering firms, construction firms, logging firms in particular, any firm that seemed to have problems connected with traction. When he was not being consulted he played golf, tennis, or bridge according to whether the season was spring, summer, autumn or winter. Any time that was left over he spent with his wife and three small children of whom he was very fond. When he was with them, it seemed that that was what he liked best. He was a very extroverted sort of man, easy and likeable, and his little wife was so shy that it just was not fair.

At the period of which I write, Conventions had not begun to take their now-accepted place in life on the North American continent. I am speaking of Conventions with a capital C. Conventions with a small c have, of course, always been with us, but not as conspicuously now as formerly. In those days, when a man said rather importantly I am going to a Convention, someone was quite liable to ask What is a Convention? Everyone seemed to think that they must be quite a good thing, which of course they are. We now take them for granted.

Now Mr. Golightly was admirably adapted to going to Conventions. His memory for names and faces was good; he liked people, both in crowds and separately; he collected acquaintances who rapidly became friends. Everyone liked him.

One day he came home and said to his wife, "How would you like a trip to California?"

Mrs. Golightly gave a little gasp. Her face lighted up and she said, "Oh Tom ...!"

"There's a Western and Middle Western Convention meeting at Del Monte the first week of March, and you and I are going down," said Mr. Golightly.

Mrs. Golightly's face clouded and she said in quite a different tone and with great alarm, "Oh Tom ...!"

"Well, what?" said her husband.

Mrs. Golightly began the sort of hesitation that so easily overcame her. "Well, Tom," she said, "I'd have to get a hat, and I suppose a suit and a dinner dress, and Emmeline isn't very good to leave with the children and you know I'm no good with crowds and people, I never know what to say, and—"

"Well, *get* a new hat," said her husband, "get one of those hats I see women wearing with long quills on. And *get* a new dress. Get *twenty* new dresses. And Emmeline's fine with the children and what you need's a change, and I'm the only one in my profession invited from British Columbia. You get a hat with the longest feather in town and a nice dinner dress!" Mr. Golightly looked fondly at his wife and saw with new eyes that she appeared anxious and not quite as pretty as she sometimes was. He kissed her and she promised that she would get the new hat, but he did not know how terrified she was of the Convention and all the crowds of people, and that she suffered at the very thought of going. She could get along all right at home, but small talk with strangers—oh, poor Mrs. Golightly. These things certainly are not fair.

However, she got the dress, and a new hat with the longest quill in town. She spent a long time at the hairdresser's; and how pretty she looked and how disturbed she felt! "I'll break the quill every time I get into the car, Tom," she said.

"Non-*sense*," said her husband, and they set off in the car for California.

Mrs. Golightly travelled in an old knitted suit and a felt hat pulled down on her head in observance of a theory which she had inherited from her mother that you must never wear good clothes when travelling. The night before arriving at Del Monte a car passing them at high speed side-swiped them ever so little, but the small damage and fuss that resulted from that delayed them a good deal. The result was that they got late to bed that night, slept little, rose early, and had to do three hundred miles before lunch. Mrs. Golightly began to feel very tired in spite of some mounting excitement, but this did not make her forget to ask her husband to stop at the outskirts of Del Monte so that she could take her new hat out of the bag and put it on. Mr. Golightly was delighted with the way his wife was joining in the spirit of the thing. "Good girl," he said, which pleased her, and neither of them noticed that nothing looked right about Mrs. Golightly except her hat, and even smart hats, worn under those circumstances, look wrong.

How impressive it was to Mrs. Golightly, supported by her hat, to approach the portals of the fashionable Del Monte Hotel. Large cars reclined in rows, some sparkling, some dimmed by a film of dust, all of them costly. Radiant men and women, expensively dressed (the inheritors of the earth, evidently), strolled about without a care in the world, or basked on the patio, scrutinizing new arrivals with experienced eyes. Mrs. Golightly had already felt something formidably buoyant in the air of California, accustomed as she was to the mild, soft and (to tell the truth) sometimes deliciously drowsy air of the British Columbia coast. The air she breathed in California somehow alarmed her. Creatures customarily breathing this air must, she thought, by nature, be buoyant, self-confident—all the things that Mrs. Golightly was not. Flowers bloomed, trees threw their shade, birds cleft the air, blue shone the sky, and Mrs. Golightly, dazzled, knocked her hat crooked as she got out of the car, and she caught the long quill on the door. She felt it snick. Oh, she thought, my darling quill!

No sooner had they alighted from their car, which was seized on all sides by hotel minions of great competence, than her husband was surrounded by prosperous men who said, "Well Tom! And how's the boy! Say Tom this is great!" And Tom turned from side to side greeting, expansive, the most popular man in view. Mrs. Golightly had no idea that Tom had so many business friends that loved him dearly. And then with one accord these prosperous men turned their kindly attention to Mrs. Golightly. It overwhelmed her but it really warmed her heart to feel that they were all so pleased that she had come, and that she had come so far, and although she felt shy, travel-worn and tired, she tried to do her best and her face shone sweetly with a desire to please.

"Now," said the biggest of the men, "the boys are waiting for you, Tom. Up in one three three. Yes in one three three. And Mrs. Golightly I want you to meet Mrs. Allyman of the Ladies' Committee. Mrs. Allyman meet Mrs. Tom Golightly from British Columbia. Will you just register her please, we've planned a good time for the ladies, Tom ... we'll take good care of Tom, Mrs. Golightly." And Mr. Golightly said, "But my wife ..." and then a lot of people streamed in, and Tom and the other men said, "Well, well, *well*, so here's Ed! Say, Ed ..." and the words streamed past Mrs. Golightly and Tom was lost to her view.

A lump that felt large came in her throat because she was so shy, and Tom was not to be seen, but Mrs. Allyman was very kind and propelled her over to a group of ladies and said, "Oh this is the lady from British Columbia, the name is Golightly isn't it? Mrs. Golightly I want you to meet Mrs. Finkel and Mrs. Connelly and Mrs. Magnus and—pardon me I didn't catch the name— Mrs. Sloper from Colorado. Oh there's the President's wife Mrs. Bagg. Well Mrs. Bagg did you locate Mr. Bagg after all, no doubt he's in one three three. Mrs. Golightly I'd like to have you meet Mrs. Bagg and Mrs. Simmons. Mrs. Bagg, Mrs. Finkel, Mrs. Bagg, and Mrs. Sloper, Mrs. Bagg. Mrs. Golightly is all the way from British Columbia, I think that's where you come from, Mrs. Golightly?" Mrs. Allyman, speaking continually, seemed to say all this in one breath. By the time that Mrs. Golightly's vision had cleared (although she felt rather dizzy), she saw that all these ladies were chic, and that they wore hats with very long quills, longer even than hers, which made her feel much more secure. However, her exhilaration was passing; she realized that she was quite tired, and she said, smiling sweetly, "I *think* I'd better find my room." The hubbub in the hotel rotunda increased and increased.

When she reached her room she found that Tom had sent the bags up, and she thought she would unpack and lie down for a bit to get rested, and then go down and have a quiet lunch. Perhaps she would see Tom somewhere. But first she went over to the window and looked out upon the incredible radiance of blue and green and gold, and the shine of the ethereal air. She looked at the great oak trees and the graceful mimosa trees and she thought, After I've tidied up and had some lunch I'll just go and sit under one of those beautiful mimosa trees and drink in this ... this largesse of air and scent and beauty. Mrs. Golightly had never seen anything like it. The bright air dazzled her, and made her sad and gay. Just then the telephone rang. A man's strong and purposeful voice said, "Pardon me, but may I speak to Tom?"

"Oh I'm sorry," said Mrs. Golightly, "Tom's not here."

"Can you tell me where I can get him?" asked the voice very urgently.

"I'm so sorry ...," faltered Mrs. Golightly.

"Sorry to troub ..." said the voice and the telephone clicked off.

There. The Convention had invaded the bedroom, the azure sky, and the drifting grace of the mimosa tree outside the bedroom window.

"I think," said Mrs. Golightly to herself, "if I had a bath it would freshen me, I'm beginning to have a headache." She went into the bathroom and gazed with pleasure on its paleness and coolness and shiningness, on the lavish array of towels, and an uneven picture entered and left her mind of the bathroom at home, full, it seemed to her, of the essentials for cleaning and dosing a father and mother and three small children, non-stop. The peace! The peace of it! She lay in the hot water regarding idly and alternatively the soap which floated agreeably upon the water, and the window through which she saw blue sky of an astonishing azure.

The telephone rang. She dripped to the telephone. "Is that Mrs. Goodman?" purred a voice.

"No no, not Mrs. Goodman," said Mrs. Golightly, wrapped in a towel.

"I'm *so* sorry," purred the voice.

Mrs. Golightly got thankfully into the bath and turned on some more hot water.

The telephone rang.

She scrambled out, "Hello, hello?"

"There's a wire at the desk for Mr. Golightly," said a voice, "shall we send it up?"

"Oh dear, oh dear," said Mrs. Golightly, wrapped in a towel, "well ... not yet ... not for half an hour."

"Okay," said the voice.

She got back into the bath. She closed her eyes in disturbed and recovered bliss.

The telephone rang.

"Hello, hello," said Mrs. Golightly plaintively, wrapped in a very damp towel.

"Is that Mrs. Golightly?" said a kind voice.

"Yes, oh yes," agreed Mrs. Golightly.

"Well, this is Mrs. Porter speaking and we'd be pleased if you'd join Mrs. Bagg and Mrs. Wilkins and me in the Tap Room and meet some of the ladies and have a little drink before lunch."

"Oh thank you, thank you, that will be just lovely, I'd love to," said Mrs. Golightly. Away went the sky, away went the birds, away went the bath, and away went the mimosa tree.

"Well, that will be lovely," said Mrs. Porter, "in about half an hour?"

"Oh thank you, thank you, that will be lovely ...!" said Mrs. Golightly, repeating herself considerably.

She put on her new gray flannel suit which was only slightly rumpled, and straightened the tip of her quill as best she could. She patted her rather aching forehead with cold water and felt somewhat refreshed. She paid particular and delicate attention to her face, and left her room looking and feeling quite pretty but agitated.

When she got down to the Tap Room everyone was having Old-Fashioneds and a little woman in gray came up and said, "Pardon me but are you Mrs. Golightly from British Columbia? Mrs. Golightly, I'd like to have you meet Mrs. Bagg (our President's wife) and Mrs. Gillingham from St. Louis, Mrs. Wilkins from Pasadena; Mrs. Golightly, Mrs. Finkel and—pardon me?— Mrs. Connelly and Mrs. Allyman of Los Angeles."

Mrs. Golightly felt confused, but she smiled at each lady in turn, saying "How do you do," but neglected to remember or repeat their names because she was so inexperienced. She slipped into a chair and a waiter brought her an Old-Fashioned. She then looked round and tried hard to memorize the ladies nearly all of whom had stylish hats with tall quills on. Mrs. Bagg very smart. Mrs. Wilkins with pince-nez. Little Mrs. Porter in gray. Mrs. Simmons, Mrs. Connelly and Mrs. Finkel in short fur capes. Mrs. Finkel was lovely, of a gorgeous pale beauty. Mrs. Golightly sipped her Old-Fashioned and tried to feel very gay indeed. She and Mrs. Connelly who came from Chicago found that each had three small children, and before they had finished talking a waiter brought another Old-Fashioned. Then Mrs. Connelly had to speak to a lady on her other side, and Mrs. Golightly turned to the lady on her left. This lady was not talking to anyone but was quietly sipping her Old-Fashioned. By this time Mrs. Golightly was feeling unusually bold and responsible, and quite like a woman of the world. She thought to herself, Come now, everyone is being so lovely and trying to make everyone feel at home, and I must try too.

So she said to the strange lady, "I don't think we met, did we? My name is Mrs. Golightly and I come from British Columbia." And the lady said, "I'm pleased to meet you. I'm Mrs. Gampish and I come from Toledo, Ohio." And Mrs. Golightly said, "Oh isn't this a beautiful hotel and wouldn't you like to see the gardens?" and then somehow everyone was moving.

When Mrs. Golightly got up she felt as free as air, but as if she was stepping a little high. When they reached the luncheon table there must have been about a hundred ladies and of course everyone was talking. Mrs. Golighlty was seated between two perfectly charming people, Mrs. Carillo from Little Rock, Arkansas, and Mrs. Clark from Phoenix, Arizona. They both said what a cute English accent she had and she had to tell them because she was so truthful that she had never been in England. It was a little hard to talk as there was an orchestra and Mrs. Golightly and Mrs. Carillo and Mrs. Clark were seated just below the saxophones. Mrs. Golightly couldn't quite make out whether she had no headache at all, or the worst headache of her life. This is lovely, she thought as she smiled back at her shouting companions, but how nice it would be to go upstairs and lie down. Just for half an hour after lunch, before I go and sit under the mimosa tree.

But when the luncheon was over, Mrs. Wilkins clapped her hands and said, "Now Ladies, cars are waiting at the door and we'll assemble in the lobby for the drive." And Mrs. Golightly said, "Oh hadn't I better run upstairs and see whether my husband ..." But Mrs. Wilkins said again, "Now Ladies!" So they all gathered in the lobby, and for one moment, one moment, Mrs. Golightly was still.

Oh, she thought, I feel awful, and I am so sleepy, and I feel a little queer. But she soon started smiling again, and they all got into motor cars.

She got into a nice car with some other ladies whom she did not know. They all had tall quills on their hats which made it awkward. Mrs. Golightly was the smallest and sat in the middle. She turned from side to side with great politeness. Flick, flick went the quills, smiting against each other. Well, we'd better introduce ourselves, she thought. But the lady on her right had already explained that she was Mrs. Johnson from Seattle, so she turned to her left and said to the other stranger, "Do tell me your name? I'm Mrs. Golightly and I come from British Columbia."

The other lady said a little stiffly, "Well, I'm Mrs. Gampish and I come from Toledo, Ohio," and Mrs. Golightly felt awful and said, "Oh Mrs. Gampish, how stupid of me, we met in the Tap Room, of course! So *many* people!" "Oh, it's quite all right," said Mrs. Gampish rather coldly. But she and Mrs. Johnson soon found that their husbands both had gastric ulcers and so they had a very very interesting conversation. Mrs. Golightly did not join in because she had nothing to offer in the way of an ulcer, as she and Tom and the children never seemed to be ill and the ladies did not appear to need sympathy. She dodged this way and that behind Mrs. Gampish and Mrs. Johnson, interfering with their quills, and peering at gleaming Spanish villas enfolded in green, blazing masses of flowers, a crash and white spume of breakers, a twisted Monterey pine—they all rushed dazzling past the car windows—villas, pines, ocean and all. If I were courageous or even tactful, thought Mrs. Golightly, I could ask to sit beside the window where I want to be, and these ladies could talk in comfort (the talk had moved from ulcers to their son's fraternities), which is what they wish, but she knew that she was not skilful in such matters, and it would not do. Oh, she yearned, if I could ever be a woman of the world and achieve these simple matters!

Then all the cars stopped at a place called Point Lobos, and everybody got out.

Mrs. Golightly sped swiftly alone toward the cliffs. She stood on a high rock overlooking the vast ocean, and the wind roared and whistled about her. She took off her hat as the whistling, beating broken quill seemed to impede her. She looked down and could hardly believe the beauty that lay below her. Green ocean crashed and broke in towering spray on splintered rocky islets, on the cliffs where she stood, and into swirling, sucking, rock-bound bays and caves. In the translucent green waves played joyous bands of seals, so joyous that they filled her with rapture. Bellowing seals clambered upon the rocks, but the din of wind and ocean drowned their bellowing. The entrancement of sea and sky and wind and the strong playing bodies of the seals so transported Mrs. Golightly that she forgot to think, Oh I must tell the children, and how Tom would love this! She was one with the rapture of that beautiful unexpected moment. She felt someone beside her and turned. There was Mrs. Carillo with a shining face. They shouted at each other, laughing with joy, but could not hear each other, and stood arm in arm braced against the wind, looking down at the playing bands of seals.

As the party assembled again, Mrs. Golightly stepped aside and waited for Mrs. Gampish and Mrs. Johnson to get in first. Then she got in, and sat down beside the window. Conversation about Point Lobos and the seals became general, and Mrs. Johnson who was in the middle found herself turning from side to side, bending and catching her quill. They then became quiet, and the drive home was peaceful. I shall never forget, thought Mrs. Golightly, as the landscape and seascape flashed past her rather tired eyes, the glory of Point Lobos, and the strong bodies of the seals playing in the translucent water. Whatever happens to me on earth, I shall never never forget it.

When she arrived at the hotel she discovered that she was nearly dead with excitement and noise and fatigue and when Tom came in she said, because she was so simple and ignorant, "Oh darling, can we have dinner somewhere quietly tonight, I must tell you about all those seals." Tom looked shocked and said, "Seals? But darling, aren't you having a good time? I was just talking to Mr. Bagg and he tells me you made a great hit with his wife. This is a Convention, you know," he said reprovingly, "and you can't do *that* kind of thing! Seals indeed! Where's your programme? Yes, Ladies' Dinner in the Jacobean Room, and I'll be at the Men's." And Mrs. Golightly said, "Oh, Tom ... Yes, of course, I know, how stupid of me ... I'm having the *loveliest* time, Tom, and we had the *loveliest* drive, and now I'm really going to have a proper bath and a rest before I dress." And Tom said, "*Fine!* But can I have the bathroom first because ..." and then the telephone rang and Tom said, "Yes? Yes, Al, what's that? In the Tap Room? In fifteen minutes? Make it twenty, Al, I want to have a bath and change. Okay, Al ... That was Al, dear. I'll have to hurry but you have a good rest." And then the telephone rang and it was Mrs. Wilkins and she said, "Oh Mrs. Golightly, will you join Mrs. Porter and me and some of the ladies in my room one seven five for cocktails at six o'clock? I do hope it won't rush you. One seven five. Oh that will be lovely." "Oh, yes, that will be lovely," said Mrs. Golightly. She put her hands to her face and then she took out her blue dinner dress and began pressing it, and away went the bath and away went the rest and away went the mimosa tree. Tom came out of the bathroom and said, "Whyever aren't you lying down? That's the trouble with you, you never will rest! Well, so long darling, have a good time." He went, and she finished pressing her dress and put it on.

The next time Mrs. Golightly saw Tom was downstairs in the hotel lobby as she waited with some of the other ladies to go into the ladies' dinner. Tom was in the middle of a group of men who walked down the centre of the lobby. They walked almost rolling with grandeur or something down the lobby, owning it, sufficient unto themselves, laughing together at their own private jokes and unaware of anyone else. But Mr. Golightly's eyes fell on his wife. He saw how pretty she looked and was delighted with her. He checked the flow of men down the lobby and stepped forward and said, "Terry, I want you to meet Mr. Flanagan; Bill, this is my wife." A lively and powerful small man seized Mrs. Golightly's hand and held it and looked admiringly at her and said, "Well, Mrs. Golightly, I certainly am pleased to meet you. I've just got Tom here to promise that you and he will come and stay with Mrs. Flanagan and me this fall when the shooting's good up at our little place in Oregon—now, no argument, it's all settled, you're coming!" What a genial host! It would be a pleasure to stay with Mr. Flanagan.

Tom beamed in a pleased way, and Mrs. Golightly's face sparkled with pleasure. "Oh Mr. Flanagan," she said, "how kind! Tom and I will just *love* to come." (Never a word or thought about What shall we do with the children— just "We'd love to come.") "So *that's* settled," said Mr. Flanagan breezily, and the flow of men down the hotel lobby was resumed.

At dinner Mrs. Golightly sat beside a nice woman from San Francisco called Mrs. de Kay who had once lived in Toronto so of course they had a lot in common. Before dinner everyone had had one or two Old-Fashioneds, and as the mists cleared a bit, Mrs. Golightly had recognized Mrs. Bagg, Mrs. Connelly, dear Mrs. Carillo, and beautiful Mrs. Finkel. How lovely was Mrs. Finkel, sitting in blonde serenity amidst the hubbub, in silence looking around her with happy gentle gaze. You could never forget Mrs. Finkel. Her face, her person, her repose, her shadowed eyes invited scrutiny. You gazed with admiration and sweetly she accepted your admiration. While all around her were vivacious, Mrs. Finkel sat still. But now Mrs. Finkel and Mrs. Carillo were far down the table and Mrs. Golightly conversed with Mrs. de Kay as one woman of the world to another. How well I'm coming along! she thought, and felt puffed up.

During the sweet course she became hot with shame! She had not spoken a word to the lady on her left who wore a red velvet dress. She turned in a gushing way and said to the lady in the red dress who, she realized, was not speaking to anyone at the moment, "Isn't this a delightful dinner! We haven't had a chance of a word with each other, have we, and I don't believe we've met, but I'm Mrs. Golightly from British Columbia."

The lady in the red cut-velvet dress turned towards Mrs. Golightly and said clearly, "I am Mrs. Gampish, and I come from Toledo, Ohio." Their eyes met.

Mrs. Golightly remained silent. Blushes flamed over her. She thought, This is, no doubt, some dreadful dream from which I shall soon awake. And still the chatter and clatter and music went on. Mrs. Golightly could not think of anything to say. Mrs. Gampish continued to eat her dessert. Mrs. Golightly attempted to smile in a society way, but it was no good, and she couldn't say a thing.

After dinner there was bridge and what do you suppose?

Mrs. Golightly was set to play with Mrs. Magnus and Mrs. Finkel and Mrs. Gampish. Trembling a little, she stood up.

"I think I will go to bed," she said. She could not bear to think of Mrs. Gampish being compelled to play bridge with her.

"No, *I* shall go to bed," said Mrs. Gampish.

"No, do let me go to bed," cried Mrs. Golightly, "I simply insist on going to bed."

"And *I* insist on going to bed too," said Mrs. Gampish firmly. "In any case I have a headache." Mrs. Magnus and Mrs. Finkel looked on in amazement.

"No, no, I shall go to bed," said Mrs. Golightly in distress.

"No, *I* shall go to bed," said Mrs. Gampish. It was very absurd.

Mrs. Bagg hurried up. "Everything all set here?" she said in a hostess voice.

Mrs. Gampish and Mrs. Golightly said, speaking together, "I am going to bed."

"Oh, don't both go to bed," pleaded Mrs. Bagg, unaware of any special feeling. "If one of you must go to bed, do please one of you stay, and I will make the fourth."

Mrs. Golightly considered and acted quickly, "If Mrs. Gampish *really* wants to go to bed," she said, timidly but with effect, "I will stay ... a slight headache ..." she said bravely, fluttering her fingers and batting her eyelashes which were rather long.

Mrs. Gampish did not argue any more. She said good night to the ladies, and left.

"Oh do excuse me a minute," said Mrs. Golightly, flickering her eyelashes, and she caught Mrs. Gampish at the elevator. Mrs. Gampish looked at her with distaste.

"I want to tell you, Mrs. Gampish," said Mrs. Golightly with true humility, and speaking very low, "that I have never been to a Convention before, and I want to confess to you my stupidity. I am not really rude, only stupid and so shy although I have three children that I am truly in whirl. Will you be able ever to forgive me? ... It would be very kind of you if you feel that you could. Oh, please do try."

There was a silence between them as the elevators came and went. Then Mrs. Gampish gave a wan smile.

"You are too earnest, my child," she said. ("Oh how good you are," breathed Mrs. Golightly.) "I wouldn't myself know one person in this whole Convention—except Mrs. Finkel and no one could forget her," continued Mrs. Gampish, "and I never knew you each time you told me who you were *until* you told me, so you needn't have worried. If you want to know why I'm going to bed, it's because I don't like bridge and anyway, I *do* have a headache."

"Oh I'm so glad you *really* have a headache, no I mean I'm so sorry, and I think you're perfectly sweet, Mrs. Gampish, and if ever you come to Canada ..." and she saw the faintly amused smile of Mrs. Gampish going up in the elevator. "Well I never," she said, but she felt happier.

She turned, and there was Tom hurrying past. "Oh Tom," she called. He stopped.

"Having a good time darling?" he said in a hurry. "D'you want to come to the meeting at Salt Lake City next year?" and he smiled at her encouragingly.

"Oh Tom," she said, "I'd adore it!" (What a changed life. Del Monte, Mr. Flanagan's shooting lodge, Salt Lake City, all in a minute, you might say.)

"Well, well!" said Tom in surprise and vanished.

On the way to her bedroom that night Mrs. Golightly met Mr. Flanagan walking very slowly down the hall.

"How do you do, Mr. Flanagan!" said Mrs. Golightly gaily. She felt that he was already her host at his shooting lodge.

Mr. Flanagan stopped and looked at her seriously as from a great distance. It was obvious that he did not know her. "How do you do," he said very carefully and with a glazed expression. "Did we meet or did we meet? In any case, how do you do." And he continued walking with the utmost care down the corridor.

"Oh ...," said Mrs. Golightly, her eyes wide open ... "oh ..." It was probable that Mr. Flanagan invited everyone to the shooting lodge. The shooting lodge began to vanish like smoke.

When she entered the bedroom she saw that in her hurry before dinner she had not put her hat away. The quill was twice bent, and it dangled. She took scissors and cut it short. There, she thought, caressing and smoothing the feather, it looks all right, doesn't it? She had felt for a moment very low, disintegrated, but now as she sat on the bed in her blue dinner dress she thought, Mr. Flanagan isn't a bit afraid to be him and Mrs. Gampish isn't a bit afraid to be her and now I'm not a bit afraid to be me ... at least, not much. As she looked down, smoothing her little short feather, a dreamy smile came on her face. Seals swam through the green waters of her mind, Mrs. Finkel passed and repassed in careless loveliness. Mrs. Gampish said austerely, "Too earnest, my child, too earnest." The ghost of the mimosa tree drifted, drifted. Salt Lake City, she thought fondly ... and then ... where? ... anticipation ... a delicious fear ... an unfamiliar pleasure.

Mrs. Golightly was moving out of the class for beginners. She is much more skilful now (how agile and confiding are her eyelashes!) and when her husband says, "There's going to be a Convention in Mexico City" (or Chilliwack or Trois Rivières), she says with delight, "Oh *Tom* ...!"

PART II

SYMPOSIUM ON STORIES

MARGARET ATWOOD

READING BLIND

Margaret Atwood refined her thoughts on the short story in this essay written as an introduction to The Best American Short Stories 1989. *Our first stories come to us through air, she tells us. We hear voices.*

Whenever I'm asked to talk about what constitutes a "good" story, or what makes one well-written story "better" than another, I begin to feel very uncomfortable. Once you start making lists or devising rules for stories, or for any other kind of writing, some writer will be sure to happen along and casually break every abstract rule you or anyone else has ever thought up, and take your breath away in the process. The word *should* is a dangerous one to use when speaking of writing. It's a kind of challenge to the deviousness and inventiveness and audacity and perversity of the creative spirit. Sooner or later, anyone who has been too free with it will be liable to end up wearing it like a dunce's cap. We don't judge good stories by the application to them of some set of external measurements, as we judge giant pumpkins at the Fall Fair. We judge them by the way they strike us. And that will depend on a great many subjective imponderables which we lump together under the general heading of taste.

... I've recently heard it argued that writers should tell stories only from a point of view that is their own, or that of a group to which they themselves belong. Writing from the point of view of someone "other" is a form of poaching, the appropriation of material you haven't earned and to which you have no right. Men, for instance, should not write as women; although it's less frequently said that women should not write as men.

This view is understandable but, in the end, self-defeating. Not only does it condemn as thieves and imposters such writers as George Eliot, James Joyce, Emily Brontë, and William Faulkner, and, incidentally, a number of the writers in this book; it is also inhibiting to the imagination in a fundamental way. It's only a short step from saying we can't write from the point of view of an "other" to saying we can't read that way either, and from there to the position that no one can really understand anyone else, so we might as well stop trying. Follow this line of reasoning to its logical conclusion, and we would all be stuck with reading nothing but our own work, over and over; which would be my personal idea of hell. Surely the delight and the wonder come not from who tells the story but from what the story tells, and how.

... Our first stories come to us through the air. We hear voices.

Children in oral societies grow up within a web of stories; but so do all children. We listen before we can read. Some of our listening is more like listening in, to the calamitous or seductive voices of the adult world, on the radio or the television or in our daily lives. Often it's an overhearing of things we aren't supposed to hear, eavesdropping on scandalous gossip or family secrets. From all these scraps of voices, from the whispers and shouts that surround us, even from the ominous silences, the unfilled gaps in meaning, we patch together for ourselves an order of events, a plot or plots; these, then, are the things that happen, these are the people they happen to, this is the forbidden knowledge.

We have all been little pitchers with big ears, shooed out of the kitchen when the unspoken is being spoken, and we have probably all been tale-bearers, blurters at the dinner table, unwitting violators of adult rules of censorship. Perhaps this is what writers are: those who never kicked the habit. We remained tale-bearers. We learned to keep our eyes open, but not to keep our mouths shut....

Two kinds of stories we first encounter—the shaped tale, the overheard impromptu narrative we piece together—form our idea of what a story is and color the expectations we bring to stories later. Perhaps it's from the collisions between these two kinds of stories—what is often called "real life" (and which writers greedily think of as their "material") and what is sometimes dismissed as "mere literature" or "the kinds of things that happen only in stories"—that original and living writing is generated. A writer with nothing but a formal sense will produce dead work, but so will one whose only excuse for what is on the page is that it really happened....

... The uncertainty principle, as it applies to writing, might be stated: *You can say why a story is bad, but it's much harder to say why it's good.* Determining quality in fiction may be as hard as determining the reason for the happiness in families, only in reverse. The old saying has it that happy families are all happy in the same way, but each unhappy family is unique. In fiction, however, excellence resides in divergence, or how else could we be surprised? ...

From listening to the stories of others, we learn to tell our own.

MARGARET ATWOOD

AN END TO AUDIENCE?

Atwood's essay "An End to Audience?" was originally published in Dalhousie Review 60 *(1980) and was reprinted in the author's* Second Words: Selected Critical Prose *(1982). In this excerpt, Atwood explains that through the art of writing, the flesh becomes word.*

Writing can also be an art, and one of the reasons that so many writers dodge this on television talk shows is that art is hard to define or describe. Money is easier to talk about, so we talk about money. Nevertheless, art happens. It happens when you have the craft and the vocation and are waiting for something else, something extra, or maybe not waiting; in any case it happens. It's the extra rabbit coming out of the hat, the one you didn't put there. It's Odysseus standing by the blood-filled trench, except that the blood is his own. It is bringing the dead to life and giving voices to those who lack them so that they may speak for themselves. It is not "expressing yourself." It is opening yourself, discarding your *self*, so that the language and the world may be evoked through you. *Evocation* is quite different from *expression*. Because we are so fixated on the latter, we forget that writing also does the former. Maybe the writer *expresses*; but *evocation*, calling up, is what writing does for the reader. Writing is also a kind of sooth-saying, a truth-telling. It is a naming of the world, a reverse incarnation: the flesh becoming word. It's also a witnessing. *Come with me*, the writer is saying to the reader. *There is a story I have to tell you, there is something you need to know.* The writer is both an eye-witness and an I-witness, the one to whom personal experience happens and the one who makes experience personal for others. The writer *bears witness*. Bearing witness is not the same as self-expression.

JOHN BARTH

THINKING MAN'S MINIMALIST: HONORING BARTHELME

American poet Edward Hirsch, in a tribute to Donald Barthelme published in TriQuarterly 98 *(Winter 1996/97), wrote, "As a writer Barthelme could be very funny—and deadly serious—about the death of God. His favorite tactic was to take theological questions completely literally, as in 'The death of God left the angels in a strange position.'"*

Samuel Beckett's writing, Barthelme said, was an embarrassment to the void. By this he meant that good writing defeats death and illuminates life. Hirsch notes that Barthelme's fiction "tried not only to embarrass the void, but also to entertain it."

Roger Angell, Barthelme's editor at the New Yorker, *has said, "Many readers had difficulty at first cottoning to writing like this. They were put off by Barthelme's crosscutting and by his terrifying absence of explanation, and those who resisted him in the end may have been people who were by nature unable to put their full trust in humor." In explaining his intent, Barthelme wrote, "I believe that my every sentence trembles with morality in that each attempts to engage the problematic rather than present a proposition to which all reasonable men must agree."*

John Barth is a much celebrated American writer. His novels include The Sot-Weed Factor *(1960),* Giles' Goat Boy *(1966),* Tidewater Tales *(1987), and* Last Voyage of Somebody the Sailor *(1991). His single book of short stories,* Lost in the Funhouse *(1968), is generally accorded landmark status among postmodernist fiction; a critical work,* The Literature of Exhaustion *(1982), analyzes contemporary literary aesthetics.*

Barth's homage to Donald Barthelme, reprinted below, was published in the New York Times Book Review, *September 3, 1989, shortly after Barthelme's death.*

The proper work of the critic is praise, and that which cannot be praised should be surrounded with a tasteful, well-thought-out silence.

This is to praise the excellent American writer Donald Barthelme, who, in a 1981 *Paris Review* interview, cited in passing that arguable proposition (by the music critic Peter Yates).

Donald worked *hard* on that anything-but-spontaneous interview—as wise, articulate and entertaining a specimen as can be found in the *Paris Review*'s long, ongoing series of shoptalks. He worked hard on all his printed utterance, to make it worth his and our whiles. His untimely death in July at the age of 58, like the untimely death of Raymond Carver just last summer at 50, leaves our literature—leaves Literature—bereft, wham-bang, of two splendid practitioners at the peak of their powers.

Polar opposites in some obvious respects (Carver's home-grown, blue-collar realism and programmatic unsophistication, Barthelme's urbane and urban semi-Surrealism), they shared an axis of rigorous literary craftsmanship, a preoccupation with the particulars of, shall we say, post-Eisenhower American life, and a late-modern conviction, felt to the bone, that less is more. For Carver, as for Jorge Luis Borges, the step from terse lyric poetry to terse short stories was temerity enough; neither, to my knowledge, ever attempted a novel. Barthelme was among us a bit longer than Carver and published three spare, fine specimens of that genre—all brilliant, affecting, entertaining and more deep than thick—but the short story was his long suit. Without underrating either Carver's intellectuality or Barthelme's emotional range, we nevertheless associate Raymond with reticent viscerality and may consider Donald the thinking man's—and woman's—Minimalist. Opposing stars they became, in recent years, for hundreds of apprentice writers in and out of our plenteous university writing programs; one has sometimes to remind student writers that there are expansive easts and wests in their literary heritage as well as those two magnetic poles.

His writing is not the only excellent thing that Donald Barthelme leaves those who knew him personally or professionally. He was by all accounts a first-rate literary coach (most recently at the University of Houston), a conscientious literary citizen much involved with such organizations as PEN, and a gracious friend, but his fiction is our longest-lasting souvenir and the one that matters most to those of us who knew him mainly, if not only, as dedicated readers.

"We like books that have a lot of *dreck* in them," remarks one of the urban dwarfs in Barthelme's first novel, "Snow White"; and included in that novel's midpoint questionnaire for the reader is the item, "Is there too much *blague* in the narration? Not enough *blague*?" In fact the novel is *blague*-free, like all of Donald Barthelme's writing. Not enough to say that he didn't waste words; neither did extravagant Rabelais or apparently rambling Laurence Sterne. Donald barely *indulged* words—he valued them too much for that—and this rhetorical short leash makes his occasional lyric flights all the more exhilarating, like the sound of Hokie Mokie's trombone in Donald's short story, "The King of Jazz":

> You mean that sound that sounds like the cutting edge of life? That sounds like polar bears crossing Arctic ice pans? That sounds like a herd of muskox in full flight? That sounds like male walruses diving to the bottom of the sea? That sounds like fumaroles smoking on the slopes of Mt. Katmai? That sounds like the wild turkey walking through the deep, soft forest? That sounds like beavers chewing trees in an Appalachian marsh? That sounds like an oyster fungus growing on an aspen trunk? That sounds like a mule deer wandering a montane of the Sierra Nevada? That sounds like prairie dogs kissing? That sounds like witchgrass tumbling or a river meandering? That sounds like man-atees munching seaweed at Cape Sable? That sounds like coatimundis moving in packs across the face of Arkansas? That sounds like—

More characteristic is the dispatch with which he ends "Snow White": a series of chapter-titles to which it would have been *de trop* to add the chapters themselves.

THE FAILURE OF SNOW WHITE'S ARSE

REVIRGINIZATION OF SNOW WHITE

APOTHEOSIS OF SNOW WHITE

SNOW WHITE RISES INTO THE SKY

THE HEROES DEPART IN SEARCH OF A NEW PRINCIPLE

HEIGH-HO

And at his tersest, with a single comma he can constrict your heart: "I visited the child's nursery school, once."

Bright as is his accomplishment in it, the genre of the novel, even the half-inch novel, must have been basically uncongenial to a narrative imagination not only agoraphobic by disposition but less inclined to dramaturgy than to the tactful elaboration of bravura ground-metaphors, such as those suggested by his novels' titles: *Snow White, The Dead Father, Paradise*. His natural narrative space was the short story, if *story* is the right word for those often plot-less marvels of which he published some seven volumes over 20 years, from *Come Back, Dr. Caligari* in 1964 to *Overnight to Many Distant Cities* in 1983. (Most of the stories first appeared in the *New Yorker*; five dozen of the best are collected in *Sixty Stories*, published by Putnam in 1981.) These constitute his major literary accomplishment, and an extraordinary accomplishment it is, in quality and in consistency.

Is there really an "early Donald Barthelme?" Like Mozart and Kafka, he seems to have been born full-grown. One remarks some minor lengthening and shortening of his literary sideburns over the decades: The sportive, more or less Surreal, high-60s graphics, for example, tend to disappear after "City Life" (1970), and while he never forsook what Borges calls "that element of irrealism indispensable to art," there is a light shift toward the realistic, even the personal, in such later stories as "Visitors" and "Affection" (in *Overnight to Many Distant Cities*). But a Donald Barthelme story from any of his too-few decades remains recognizable from its opening line:

> "Hubert gave Charles and Irene a nice baby for Christmas."
> "The death of God left the angels in a strange position."
> "When Captain Blood goes to sea, he locks the doors and windows of his house on Cow Island personally."

I have heard Donald referred to as essentially a writer of the American 1960's. It may be true that his alloy or irrealism and its opposite is more evocative of that fermentatious decade, when European formalism had its belated flowering in North American writing, than of the relatively conservative decades since. But his literary precursors antedate the century, not to mention its 60's, and are mostly non-American. "How come you write the way you do?" a John Hopkins apprentice writer once asked him. "Because Samuel Beckett already wrote the way *he* did," Barthelme replied. He then produced for the seminar his "short list": five books he recommended to the attention of aspiring American fiction writers. No doubt the list changed from time to time; just then it consisted of Rabelais's *Gargantua and Pantagruel*, Laurence Sterne's *Tristram Shandy*, the stories of Heinrich von Kleist, Flaubert's *Bouvard and Pecuchet* and Flann O'Brien's *At Swim-Two-Birds*—a fair sample of the kind of nonlinear narration, sportive form and cohabitation of radical fantasy with quotidian detail that mark his own fiction. He readily admired other, more "traditional" writers, but it is from the likes of these that he felt his genealogical descent.

Similarly, though he tsked at the critical tendency to group certain writers against certain others "as if we were football teams"—praising these as the true "postcontemporaries" or whatever, and consigning those to some outer darkness of the passé—he freely acknowledged his admiration for such of his "teammates," in those critics' view, as Robert Coover, Stanley Elkin, William Gaddis, William Gass, John Hawkes, Thomas Pynchon and Kurt Vonnegut, among others. A few springs ago, he and wife, Marion, presided over a memorable Greenwich Village dinner party for most of these and their companions (together with his agent, Lynn Nesbit, whom Donald called "the mother of postmodernism"). In 1988, on the occasion of John Hawkes's academic retirement, Robert Coover impresarioed a more formal reunion of that team, complete with readings and symposia, at Brown University. Donald's throat cancer had by then already announced itself—another, elsewhere, would be the death of him—but he gave one more of his perfectly antitheatrical virtuoso readings.

How different from one another those above-mentioned teammates are! Indeed, other than their nationality and gender, their common inclination to some degree of irrealism and to the foregrounding of form and language, and the circumstances of their having appeared on the literary scene in the 1960's or thereabouts, it is not easy to see why their names should be so frequently linked (or why Grace Paley's, for example, is not regularly included in that all-male lineup). But if they constitute a team, it has no consistently brighter star than the one just lost.

Except for readers who require a new literary movement with each new network television season, the product of Donald Barthelme's imagination and artistry is an ongoing delight that we had looked forward to decades more of. Readers in the century to come (assuming etc.) will surely likewise prize that product—for its wonderful humor and wry pathos, for the cultural-historical interest its rich specificity will duly acquire, and—most of all, I hope and trust—for its superb verbal art.

CLARK BLAISE

TO BEGIN, TO BEGIN

Clark Blaise taught at numerous universities, including Sir George Williams (now Concordia) in Montreal, before becoming Director of the International Writer's Program at the University of Iowa. Blaise is perhaps best known in Canada for his story collection A North American Education *(1973) and his novel* Lusts *(1983); recent works include* Man and His World *(1992, stories) and* If I Were Me *(1997, a novel). "To Begin, To Begin" appears in* The Narrative Voice: Short Stories and Reflections by Canadian Authors *(1972), edited by John Metcalf. Here, he contemplates that subject fascinating to all writers, beginnings.*

"Endings are elusive, middles
are nowhere to be found, but
worst of all is to begin, to begin, to begin."
—*Donald Barthelme*

The most interesting thing about a story is not its climax or dénouement—both dated terms—nor even its style and characterization. It is its beginning, its first paragraph, often its first sentence. More decisions are made on the basis of the first few sentences of a story than on any other part, and it would seem to me after having read thousands of stories, and beginning hundreds of my own (completing, I should add, only about fifty), that something more than luck accounts for the occasional success of the operation. What I propose is theoretical, yet rooted in the practice of writing and of reading-as-a-writer; good stories *can* start unpromisingly, and well-begun stories can obviously degenerate, but the observation generally holds: the story seeks its beginning, the story many times *is* its beginning, amplified.

The first sentence of a story is an act of faith—or astonishing bravado. A story screams for attention, as it must, for it breaks a silence. It removes the reader from the everyday (no such imperative attaches to the novel, for which the reader makes his own preparations). It is an act of perfect rhythmic balance, the single crisp gesture, the drop of the baton that gathers a hundred disparate forces into a single note. The first paragraph is a microcosm of the whole, but in a way that only the whole can reveal. If the story begins one sentence too soon, or a sentence too late, the balance is lost, the energy diffused.

It is in the first line that the story reveals its kinship to poetry. Not that the line is necessarily "beautiful," merely that it can exist utterly alone, and that its force draws a series of sentences behind it. The line doesn't have go "grab" or "hook" but it should be striking. Good examples I'll offer further on, but consider first some bad ones:

> *Catelli plunged the dagger deeper in her breast, the dark blood oozed like cherry syrup....*
>
> *The President's procession would pass under the window at 12:03, and Slattery would be ready....*

Such sentences can be wearying; they strike a note too heavily, too prematurely. They "start" where they should be ending. The advantages wrested will quickly dissipate. On the other hand, the "casual" opening can be just as damaging:

> *When I saw Bob in the cafeteria he asked me to a party at his house that evening and since I wasn't doing much anyway I said sure, I wouldn't mind. Bob's kind of an ass, but his old man's loaded and there's always a lot of grass around....*

Or, *in medias res:*

> *"Linda, toast is ready! Linda, are you awake?"*

Now what's wrong with these sentences? The tone is right. The action is promising. They're real, they communicate. Yet no experienced reader would go past them. The last two start too early, (what the critics might call an imitative fallacy) and the real story is still imprisoned somewhere in the body.

Lesson One: as in poetry, a good first sentence of prose implies its opposite. If I describe a sunny morning in May (the buds, the wet-winged flies, the warm sun and cool breeze), I am also implying the perishing quality of a morning in May, and a good sensuous description of May sets up the possibility of a May disaster. It is the singular quality of that experience that counts. May follows from the sludge of April and leads to the drone of summer, and in a careful story the action will be mindful of May; it must be. May is unstable, treacherous, beguiling, seductive, and whatever experience follows from a first sentence will be, in essence, a story about the Mayness of human affairs.

What is it, for example, in this sentence from Hugh Hood's story "Fallings from Us, Vanishings" that hints so strongly at disappointment:

Brandishing a cornucopia of daffodils, flowers for Gloria, in his right hand, Arthur Merlin crossed the dusky oak-panelled foyer of his apartment building and came into the welcoming sunlit avenue.

The name Merlin? The flourish of the opening clause, associations of the name Gloria? Here is a lover doomed to loneliness, yet a lover who seeks it, despite appearances. Nowhere, however, is it stated. Yet no one, I trust, would miss it. Such openings are everywhere, at least in authors I admire:

The girl stood with her back to the bar, slightly in everyone's way. (Frank Tuohy)

The thick ticking of the tin clock stopped, Mendel, dozing, awoke in fright. (Bernard Malamud)

I owe the discovery of Uqbar to the conjunction of a mirror and an encyclopedia. (Jorge Luis Borges)

For a little while when Walter Henderson was nine years old, he thought falling dead was the very zenith of romance, and so did a number of his friends. (Richard Yates)

Our group is against the war. But the war goes on. (David Barthelme)

The principal dish at dinner had been croquettes made of turnip greens. (Thomas Mann)

The sky had been overcast since early morning; it was a still day, not hot, but tedious, as it usually is when the weather is gray and dull, when clouds have been hanging over the fields for a long time, and you wait for the rain that does not come. (Anton Chekhov)

I wanted terribly to own a dovecot when I was a child. (Isaac Babel—and I didn't even know what a dovecot was when I started reading.)

At least two or three times a day a story strikes me in the same way, and I read it through. By then I don't care if the climax and dénouement are elegantly turned—chances are they will be—I'm reading it because the first paragraph gave me confidence in the power and vision of the author.

Lesson Two: art wishes to begin, even more than end. Fashionable criticism—much of it very intelligent—has emphasized the so-called "apocalyptic impulse," the desire of fiction to bring the house down. I can understand the interest in endings—it's easier to explain why things end than how they began, for one thing. For another, the ending is a contrivance—artistic and believable, yet in many ways predictable; the beginning, however, is always a mystery. Criticism likes contrivances, and has little to say of mysteries. My own experience, as a writer and especially as a "working" reader is closer to genesis than apocalypse, and I cherish openings more than endings. My memory of any given story is likely to be its first few lines.

Lesson Three: art wishes to begin *again*. The impulse is not only to finish, it is to capture. In the stories I admire, there is a sense of a continuum disrupted, then re-established, and both the disruption and reordering are part of the *beginning* of a story. The first paragraph tells us, in effect, that "this is how things have always been," or at least, how they have been until the arrival of the story. It may summarize, as Faulkner does in "That Evening Sun":

> *Monday is no different from any other weekday in Jefferson now. The streets are paved now, and the telephone and electric companies are cutting down more and more of the shade trees....*

or it may envelop a life in a single sentence, as Bernard Malamud's often do:

> *Manischevitz, a tailor, in his fifty-first year suffered many reverses and indignities.*

Whereupon Malamud embellishes the history, a few sentences more of indignities, aches, curses, until the fateful word that occurs in almost all stories, the simple terrifying adverb: *Then*.

Then, which means to the reader: "I am ready." The moment of change is at hand, the story shifts gears and for the first time, *plot* intrudes on poetry. In Malamud's story, a Negro angel suddenly ("then") appears in the tailor's living room, reading a newspaper.

> *Suddenly there appeared ...*
> *Then one morning ...*
> *Then one evening she wasn't home to greet him ...*

Or, in the chilling construction of Flannery O'Connor:

> *... there appeared at her door three young men ... they walked single file, the middle one bent to the side carrying a black pig-shaped valise....*

A pig-shaped valise! This is the apocalypse, if the reader needs one; whatever the plot may reveal a few pages later is really redundant. The mysterious part of the story—that which is poetic yet sets it (why not?) above poetry—is over. The rest of the story will be an attempt to draw out the inferences of that earlier upheaval. What is often meant by "climax" in the conventional short story is merely the moment that the *character* realizes the true, the devastating, meaning of "then." He will try to ignore it, he will try to start again (in my story "Eyes" the character thinks he can escape the voyeurs—himself, essentially—by moving to a rougher part of town); he can't of course.

Young readers, especially young readers who want to write, should forget what they're taught of "themes" and all the rest. Stories aren't written that way. Stories are delicate interplays of action and description; "character" is that force which tries to maintain balance between the two. "Action" I equate with danger, fear, apocalypse, life itself; "description" with quiescence, peace, death itself. And the purest part of a story, I think, is from its beginning to its "then." "Then" is the moment of the slightest tremor, the moment when the author is satisfied that all the forces are deployed, the unruffled surface perfectly cast, and the insertion, gross or delicate, can now take place. It is the cracking of the perfect, smug egg of possibility.

ITALO CALVINO

CYBERNETICS AND GHOSTS

In following these excerpts from the essay "Cybernetics and Ghosts," published in The Literature Machine *(1987), it is important to bear in mind Calvino's experience as a subject of Mussolini's Italy and as a witness to the legacy of Futurism in Italian culture. The Futurist art movement, which was explicitly allied with Fascist politics, exalted automation and the machine. Calvino names the Russian Formalists and French theorists like Roland Barthes in tracing a shift in human consciousness from the "psychological" individual, inherited from the Enlightenment tradition, to a cybernetic model of "discontinuous" human subjectivity "programmed" by language. In dealing with developments in computer technology, genetic research, and linguistics, Calvino considers the similarities between literary experiment and mathematical transformation.*

Also in these excerpts, Calvino analyzes literary surrealism, an art movement begun in post-WWI France which produced a creative kind of Freudian psychoanalysis. A chief Surrealist practice was automatic writing, what André Breton called "the experimental source to which to return in order to recognize the power thought has of adopting all the modes of madness." The fiction of Barthelme, Buzzati, and Tommaso Landolfi ("Italy's Kafka") bear witness to Surrealism's enduring influence.

Primitive oral narrative, like the folk tale that has been handed down almost to the present day, is modeled on fixed structures, on, we might almost say, prefabricated elements—elements, however, that allow of an enormous number of combinations. Vladimir Propp, in the course of his studies of Russian folk tales, came to the conclusion that all such tales were like variants of a single tale, and could be broken down into a limited number of narrative functions. Forty years later Claude Levi-Strauss, working on the myths of the Indians of Brazil, saw these as a system of logical operations between permutable terms, so that they could be studied according to the mathematical processes of combinatorial analysis....

Is this true only of oral narrative traditions? Or can it be maintained of literature in all its variety of forms and complexities? ...

... Having laid down these procedures and entrusted a computer with the task of carrying out these operations, will we have a machine capable of replacing the poet and the author? Just as we already have machines that can read, machines that perform a linguistic analysis of literary texts, machines that make translations and summaries, will we also have machines capable of conceiving and composing poems and novels? ...

Let us see what my psychological reaction is when I learn that writing is purely and simply a process of combination among given elements. Well, then, what I instinctively feel is a sense of relief, of security. The same sort of relief and sense of security that I feel every time I discover that a mess of vague and indeterminate lines turns out to be a precise geometric form; or every time I succeed in discerning a series of facts, and choices to be made out of a finite number of possibilities, in the otherwise shapeless avalanche of events. Faced with the vertigo of what is countless, unclassifiable, in a state of flux, I feel reassured by what is finite, "discrete," and reduced to a system. Why is this? Does my attitude contain a hidden element of fear of the unknown, of the wish to set limits to my world and crawl back into my shell? ...

Let us attempt a thesis contrary to the one I have developed so far (this is always the best way to avoid getting trapped in the spiral of one's own thoughts). Did we say that literature is entirely involved with language, is merely the permutation of a restricted number of elements and functions? But is the tension in literature not continually striving to escape from this finite number? Does it not continually attempt to say something it cannot say, something that it does not know, and that no one could ever know? A thing cannot be known when the words and concepts used to say it and think it have not yet been used in that position, not yet arranged in that order, with that meaning. The struggle of literature is in fact a struggle to escape from the confines of language; it stretches out from the utmost limits of what can be said; what stirs literature is the call and attraction of what is not in the dictionary.

The storyteller of the tribe puts together phrases and images: the younger son gets lost in the forest, he sees a light in the distance, he walks and walks; the fable unwinds from sentence to sentence, and where is it leading? To the point at which something not yet said, something as yet only darkly felt by presentiment, suddenly appears and seizes us and tears us to pieces, like the fangs of a man-eating witch. Through the forest of fairy tale the vibrancy of myth passes like a shudder of wind.

Myth is the hidden part of every story, the buried part, the region that is still unexplored because there are as yet no words to enable us to get there....

... The unconscious is the ocean of the unsayable, of what has been expelled from the land of language, removed as a result of ancient prohibitions. The unconscious speaks—in dreams, in verbal slips, in sudden associations—with borrowed words, stolen symbols, linguistic contraband, until literature redeems these territories and annexes them to the language of the waking world.

The power of modern literature lies in its willingness to give a voice to what has remained unexpressed in the social or individual unconscious: this is the gauntlet it throws down time and again. The more enlightened our houses are, the more their walls ooze ghosts....

So here we are, carried off into an ideological landscape quite different from the one we thought we had decided to live in, there with the relays of diodes of electronic computers. But are we really all that far away? ...

The relationship between combinatorial play and the unconscious in artistic activity lies at the heart of one of the most convincing aesthetic theories currently in circulation, a formula that draws upon both psychoanalysis and the practical experience of art and letters....

It was a Freudian art historian, Ernst Kris, who first put forward Freud's study of word-play as the key to a possible aesthetics of psychoanalysis. Another gifted art historian, Ernst Gombrich, developed this notion in his essay on Freud and the psychology of art.

The pleasure of puns and feeble jokes is obtained by following the possibilities of permutation and transformation implicit in language. We start from the particular pleasure given by any combinatorial play, and at a certain point, out of the countless combinations of words with similar sounds, one becomes charged with special significance, causing laughter. What has happened is that the juxtaposition of concepts that we have stumbled across by chance unexpectedly unleashes a preconscious idea, an idea, that is, half buried in or erased from our consciousness, or maybe only held at arm's length or pushed aside, but powerful enough to appear in the consciousness if suggested not by any intention on our part, but by an objective process.

The processes of poetry and art, says Gombrich, are analogous to those of a play on words. It is the childish pleasure of the combinatorial game that leads the painter to try out arrangements of lines and colors, the poet to experiment with juxtapositions of words. At a certain moment things click into place, and one of the combinations obtained—through the combinatorial mechanism itself, independently of any search for meaning or effect on any other level—becomes charged with an unexpected meaning or unforeseen effect which the conscious mind would not have arrived at deliberately: an unconscious meaning, in fact, or at least the premonition of an unconscious meaning.

So we see that the two routes followed by my argument have here come together. Literature is a combinatorial game that pursues the possibilities implicit in its own material, independent of the personality of the poet, but it is a game that at a certain point is invested with an unexpected meaning, a meaning that is not patent on the linguistic plane on which we were working but has slipped in from another level, activating something that on that second level is of great concern to the author or his society. The literature machine can perform all the permutations possible on a given material, but the poetic result will be the particular effect of one of these permutations on a man endowed with a consciousness and an unconscious, that is, an empirical and historical man. It will be the shock that occurs only if the writing machine is surrounded by the hidden ghosts of the individual and of his society....

Myth tends to crystallize instantly, to fall into set patterns, to pass from the phase of myth-making into that of ritual, and hence out of the hands of the narrator into those of the tribal institutions responsible for the preservation and celebration of myths. The tribal system of signs is arranged in relation to myth; a certain number of signs become taboo, and the "secular" storyteller can make no direct use of them. He goes on circling around them, inventing new developments in composition, until in the course of this methodical and objective labor he suddenly gets another flash of enlightenment from the unconscious and the forbidden. And this forces the tribe to change its set of signs once more.

Within this general context, the function of literature varies according to the situation. For long periods of time literature appears to work in favor of consecration, the confirmation of values, the acceptance of authority. But at a certain moment, something in the mechanism is triggered, and literature gives birth to a movement in the opposite direction, refusing to see things and say things the way they have been seen and said until now....

Written literature is born already laden with the task of consecration, of supporting the established order of things. This is a load that it discards extremely slowly, in the course of millenia, becoming in the process a private thing, enabling poets and writers to express their own personal troubles and raise them to the level of consciousness. Literature gets to this point, I would add, by means of combinatorial games that at a certain moment become charged with preconscious subject matter, and at last find a voice for these. And it is by this road to freedom opened up by literature that men achieved the critical spirit, and transmitted it to collective thought and culture.

WILLA CATHER

ON THE ART OF FICTION

Willa Cather's On Writing: Critical Studies on Writing as an Art, *from which the two following sections were drawn, was published in 1949. Art, she says, should simplify. "Art is a concrete and personal and rather childish thing after all."*

One is sometimes asked about the "obstacles" that confront young writers who are trying to do good work. I should say the greatest obstacles that writers today have to get over are the dazzling journalistic successes of twenty years ago, stories that surprised and delighted by their sharp photographic detail and that were really nothing more than lively pieces of reporting. The whole aim of that school of writing was novelty—never a very important thing in art. They gave us, altogether, poor standards—taught us to multiply our ideas instead of to condense them. They tried to make a story out of every theme that occurred to them and to get returns on every situation that suggested itself. They got returns, of a kind. But their work, when one looks back on it, now that the novelty upon which they counted so much is gone, is journalistic and thin. The especial merit of a good reportorial story is that it shall be intensely interesting and pertinent today and shall have lost its point by tomorrow.

Art, it seems to me, should simplify. That, indeed, is very nearly the whole of the higher artistic process; finding what conventions of form and what detail one can do without and yet preserve the spirit of the whole—so that all that one has suppressed and cut away is there to the reader's consciousness as much as if it were in type on the page. Millet had done hundreds of sketches of peasants sowing grain, some of them very complicated and interesting, but when he came to paint the spirit of them all into one picture, "The Sower," the composition is so simple that it seems inevitable. All the discarded sketches that went before made the picture what it finally became, and the process was all the time one of simplifying, of sacrificing many conceptions good in themselves for one that was better and more universal.

Any first-rate novel or story must have in it the strength of a dozen fairly good stories that have been sacrificed to it. A good workman can't be a cheap workman; he can't be stingy about wasting material, and he cannot compromise. Writing ought either to be the manufacture of stories for which there is a market demand—a business as safe and commendable as making soap or breakfast foods—or it should be an art, which is always a search for something for which there is no market demand, something new and untried, where the values are intrinsic and have nothing to do with standardized values. The courage to go on without compromise does not come to a writer all at once— nor, for that matter, does the ability. Both are phases of natural development. In the beginning, the artist, like his public, is wedded to old forms, old ideals, and his vision is blurred by the memory of old delights he would like to recapture.

WILLA CATHER

LIGHT ON ADOBE WALLS

Walls are one matter, light, another.

Every artist knows that there is no such thing as "freedom" in art. The first thing an artist does when he begins a new work is to lay down the barriers and limitations; he decides upon a certain composition, a certain key, a certain relation of creatures or objects to each other. He is never free, and the more splendid his imagination, the more intense his feeling, the farther he goes from general truth and general emotion. Nobody can paint the sun, or sunlight. He can only paint the tricks that shadows play with it, or what it does to forms. He cannot even paint those relations of light and shade—he can only paint some emotion they give him, some man-made arrangement of them that happens to give him personal delight—a conception of clouds over distant mesas (or over the towers of St. Sulpice) that makes one nerve in him thrill and tremble. At bottom all he can give you is the thrill of his own poor little nerve—the projection in paint of a fleeting pleasure in a certain combination of form and colour, as temporary and almost as physical as a taste on the tongue. This oft-repeated pleasure in a painter becomes of course a "style," a way of seeing and feeling things, a favourite mood. What could be more different from Leonardo's treatment of daylight, and Velasquez'? Light is pretty much the same in Italy and Spain—southern light. Each man painted what he got out of light—what it did to him.

No art can do anything at all with great natural forces or great elemental emotions. No poet can write of love, hate, jealousy. He can only touch these things as they affect the people in his drama and his story, and unless he is more interested in his own little story and his foolish little people than in the Preservation of the Indian or Sex or Tuberculosis, then he ought to be working in a laboratory or a bureau.

Art is a concrete and personal and rather childish thing after all—no matter what people do to graft it into science and make it sociological and psychological; it is no good at all unless it is let alone to be itself—a game of make-believe, of re-production, very exciting and delightful to people who have an ear for it or an eye for it. Art is too terribly human to be very "great," perhaps. Some very great artists have outgrown art, the men were bigger than the game. Tolstoi did, and Leonardo did. When I hear the last opuses, I think Beethoven did. Shakespeare died at fifty-three, but there is an awful veiled threat in *The Tempest* that he too felt he had outgrown his toys, was about to put them away and free that spirit of Comedy and Lyrical Poetry and all the rest he held captive—quit play-making and verse-making for ever and turn his attention—to what, he did not hint, but it was probably merely to enjoy with all his senses that Warwickshire country which he loved to weakness—with a warm physical appetite. But he died before he had tried to grow old, never became a bitter old man wrangling with abstractions or creeds....

WILLIAM FAULKNER

Address upon Receiving the Nobel Prize for Literature[1]

William Faulkner's speech in acceptance of the 1952 Nobel Prize for Literature astounded people around the world, because in it this often exceptionally "dark" writer gave voice to a ringing affirmation of life—asserting that man will not only endure, but also prevail.

STOCKHOLM, DECEMBER 10, 1950

I feel that this award was not made to me as a man, but to my work—a life's work in the agony and sweat of the human spirit, not for glory and least of all for profit, but to create out of the materials of the human spirit something which did not exist before. So this award is only mine in trust. It will not be difficult to find a dedication for the money part of it commensurate with the purpose and significance of its origin. But I would like to do the same with the acclaim too, by using this moment as a pinnacle from which I might be listened to by the young men and women already dedicated to the same anguish and travail, among whom is already that one who will some day stand here where I am standing.

Our tragedy today is a general and universal physical fear so long sustained by now that we can even bear it. There are no longer problems of the spirit. There is only the question: When will I be blown up? Because of this, the young man or woman writing today has forgotten the problems of the human heart in conflict with itself which alone can make good writing because only that is worth writing about, worth the agony and the sweat.

He must learn them again. He must teach himself that the bases of all things is to be afraid; and, teaching himself that, forget it forever, leaving no room in his workshop for anything but the old verities and truths of the heart, the old universal truths lacking which any story is ephemeral and doomed—love and honor and pity and price and compassion and sacrifice. Until he does so, he labors under a curse. He writes not of love but of lust, of defeats in which nobody loses anything of value, of victories without hope and, worst of all, without pity or compassion. His griefs grieve on no universal bones, leaving no scars. He writes not of the heart but of the glands.

Until he relearns these things, he will write as though he stood among and watched the end of man. I decline to accept the end of man. It is easy enough to say that man is immortal simply because he will endure: that when the last ding-dong of doom has clanged and faded from the last worthless rock hanging tideless in the last red and dying evening, that even then there will still be one more sound: that of his puny inexhaustible voice, still talking. I refuse to accept this. I believe that man will not merely endure: he will prevail. He is immortal, not because he alone among creatures has an inexhaustible voice, but because he has a soul, a spirit capable of compassion and sacrifice and endurance. The poet's, the writer's, duty is to write about these things. It is his privilege to help man endure by lifting his heart, by reminding him of the courage and honor and hope and price and compassion and pity and sacrifice which have been the glory of his past. The poet's voice need not merely be the record of man, it can be one of the props, the pillars to help him endure and prevail.

ENDNOTE

1. The text printed here is from Faulkner's original typescript, first printed in the *New York Herald Tribune Book Review*, January 14, 1951. The version Faulkner delivered in Stockholm was slightly revised.

KEATH FRASER

FROM "NOTES TOWARD A SUPREME FICTION"

Keath Fraser won the 1996 Chapters/Books in Canada First Novel Award for Popular Anatomy *(1995); an earlier work of short stories,* Foreign Affairs *(1985), won the Ethel Wilson Fiction Prize and was shortlisted for the Governor General's Award for Fiction. Fraser's other titles include* Taking Cover *(1982), two travel books,* Bad Trips *(1991) and* Worst Journeys: The Picador Book of Travel *(1992),* Telling My Love Lies *(1996), and* As For Me and My Body: A Memoir of Sinclair Ross *(1997). "Notes Toward A Supreme Fiction," excerpted here, was commissioned by* Canadian Literature *for its one hundredth issue, published in 1984. Fraser, himself a world traveller, seeks, as did his characters in* Popular Anatomy, *"a richer, closer world against expanding odds." A different take on some of the ideas expressed here may be found in Cynthia Ozick's "Innovation and Redemption."*

The imagination is distrusted. As readers of fiction we may all be guilty at one time or another of wondering how much of what he writes "happened" to the author. The question is on the tongue of every talk-show host who has ever interviewed a novelist. Built into this naïve question is the underlying assumption that form and content are separable. This assumption leads to such meaningless, unspoken questions as How much credit should I give this writer for "making up" what he's written? How interesting is this writer, really? The question of autobiography is a fundamental one because readers, once out of childhood, do not take so easily to made-up worlds. They want their fiction rooted in a reality they recognize and can "learn" from. (Melville's English publisher had to be convinced that the travels in the South Seas related by Melville in his first novel, *Typee*, had actually happened. At least John Murray published the book. An American firm rejected it because it seemed "impossible that it could be true!")

It should be clear that I am attacking the naïve view of autobiography that pervades even our more critical thinking. Fiction of any quality above the level of Harlequin Romance and Potboiler *must be autobiographical by its very nature*. This is to say that writing fiction is an act inseparable from the mind that conceives it. The act of imagining is a real event. It happens. It happens to the author, and it happens to reveal his quality of mind, depth of vision, deftness of touch....

... The supremacy of fiction depends first and fundamentally on the thoroughness of its autobiographical voice. Hence the meaninglessness of such remarks as these in one of our national magazines: "... in his second novel, *Lusts*, Blaise begins to push the boundaries of his fiction beyond the autobiographical"—when a few lines later we read, "... if I'd been handed a page of this book without identification I'd have immediately recognized the Clark Blaise voice." Can you have it both ways? Potboilers and Harlequins are cynical and voiceless works because the author sets himself up (especially if he's only writing for money) as a mind apart from its product, instead of one *engaged in argument with itself*. No fiction worth writing has ever been undertaken, it seems to me, without the writer's doubting his ability to complete it in the way he dares hope. Every completed story or novel should be a miracle, at least to its author, if it has any chance at all of conveying the wonder of its being alive....

The fiction I am arguing for aspires to wide appeal and thus to cliché. It wants to be used up by familiarity, swallowed up as idiom, gobbled up and digested as proverb. This is its hope. This is its subversion: the unexpected resulting in the unforgettable, worn-out smile of the *Mona Lisa*, the opening bars of Beethoven's *Fifth*, Hamlet's To Be speech. It's the task of succeeding generations of artists to refurbish traditional ways of seeing, to reinvigorate worn-out idioms, to subvert the familiar. The novelist's hope is to make his own unfamiliarity dangerously familiar to the generation that succeeds him....

It must be wonderful. By what in fiction are we redeemed if it isn't the writer's love of life, growing out of his awareness of death? No fiction will be supreme unless it is haunted by Death. This is another way of saying it must be haunted by Time. We do not, as Julian Huxley argues, have memory because we are aware of civilization. We have it because we are always facing death.

Death in many forms. The kind of death affecting us least often is the death of people. Even for Charlotte Brontë, whose brother, sisters, and mother all died off like broom blossom, the fact of human death was only one death among many. She, like us, faced deaths of far less dramatic kinds: the death of holidays, the death of years, the death of seasons, the death of meals, the death of days, the death of dreams, the death of visits, the death of books, the death of flowers, the death of altruism, the death of smells, the death of enthusiasms, the death of silences. In fiction as in life an awareness of death is the measure of perspective. Maturity is having learned to appreciate the didactic nature of memory. Growing up in Death's brooding face, our imaginations are educated. This leads to compassion. It offers redemption. The more experiences we have, by which I mean simply the more we *notice* of the world, the more deaths we live through. It was patently wrong of Wittgenstein to say death is the experience we do not live through. Autobiographical (unlike Harlequin) fiction is full of death, death that is lived through, and it's in this way the novelist distinguishes himself from the historian. How to remember what he is looking at is the novelist's obsession. How to look at what he can't remember is the historian's. The perspective we value more, the perspective we *must* value more, is the novelist's. His memories are created in the face of their deaths.

In several of Wallace Stevens' early poems, writes Richard Ellmann in an essay, the poet insists "that without death, love could not exist." This is similar to saying that the way we look at something in the present is determined by how we have educated ourselves to see it simultaneously in the future. The subversion of the present is the inevitable consequence of possessing memory. What, for example, do we mean by Here and Now, and what if any are the moral, the cultural, implications of There and Then? (What is Selfishness exactly?) Our interest in fiction accrues in ratio to the wonder we feel it expressing of the Here and Now as an ideal. The supremacy of fiction resides in its capacity to inhabit Time.

The Other Worldness of great fiction makes everything happen, or so it seems, for the writer's mandate isn't to change the world but to show that within the imagination, capable of evoking both the sublime and darkness together, exists a metaphor for God. The fiction we value more is inclusive rather than exclusive. It offers no answers except the order and multiplicity of its vision, the nuances of its humblest details, the miraculousness of its language. It offers a sense of Earth. But it offers more than this, for it is a benevolent and finally human God, interested in understanding the relations of man and nature in the broadest sense of man and man. This God, this imagination, this fiction is Wonderful, for there is no getting through or around the authority of its vision and the intuitive logic of its means.

To be born without a sense of wonder, the supreme novelist tells us, is to die without knowledge. And this knowledge is finally metaphorical. "All knowledge," Kafka says in one of his stories, "the totality of all questions and all answers, is contained in the dog." ...

MAVIS GALLANT

WHAT IS STYLE?

Mavis Gallant is generally considered to be among the finest short story writers of our time. "There is no such thing as a writer who has escaped being influenced," she observes here. For more of her views on writing, of her own sense of the world, readers are encouraged to seek out the introduction she wrote for her Collected Stories *(1996).*

I do not reread my own work unless I have to; I fancy no writer does. The reason why, probably, is that during the making of the story every line has been read and rewritten and read again to the point of glut. I am unable to "see" the style ... and would not recognize its characteristics if they were pointed out to me. Once too close, the stories are already too distant. If I read a passage aloud, I am conscious of a prose rhythm easy for me to follow, that must be near to the way I think and speak. It seems to be my only link with a finished work. ...

Leaving aside the one analysis closed to me, of my own writing, let me say what style is *not*: it is not a last-minute addition to prose, a charming and universal slipcover, a coat of paint used to mask the failings of a structure. Style is inseparable from structure, part of the conformation of whatever the author has to say. What he says—this is what fiction is about—is that something is taking place and that nothing lasts. Against the sustained tick of a watch, fiction takes the measure of a life, a season, a look exchanged, the turning point, desire as brief as a dream, the grief and terror that after childhood we cease to express. The lie, the look, the grief are without permanence. The watch continues to tick where the story stops.

A loose, a wavering, a slipshod, an affected, a false way of transmitting even a fragment of this leaves the reader suspicious: What is this too elaborate or too simple language hiding? What is the author trying to disguise? Probably he doesn't know. He has shown the works of the watch instead of its message. He may be untalented, just as he may be a gifted author who for some deeply private reason (doubt, panic, the pressures of a life unsuited to writing) has taken to rearranging the works in increasingly meaningless patterns. All this is to say that content, meaning, intention and form must make up a whole, and must above all have a reason to be.

There are rules of style. By applying them doggedly any literate, ambitious and determined person should be able to write like Somerset Maugham. Maugham was conscious of his limitations and deserves appreciation on that account: "I knew that I had no lyrical quality, I had a small vocabulary ... I had little gift for metaphors; the original or striking simile seldom occurred to me. Poetic flights and the great imaginative sweep were beyond my powers." He decided, sensibly, to write "as well as my natural defects allowed" and to aim at "lucidity, simplicity and euphony." The chance that some other indispensable quality had been overlooked must have been blanketed by a lifetime of celebrity. Now, of course, first principles are there to be heeded or, at the least, considered with care; but no guided tour of literature, no commitment to the right formula or to good taste (which is changeable anyway), can provide, let alone supplant, the inborn vitality and tension of living prose.

Like every other form of art, literature is no more and nothing less than a matter of life and death. The only question worth asking about a story—or a poem, or a piece of sculpture, or a new concert hall—is, "Is it dead or alive?" If a work of the imagination needs to be coaxed into life, it is better scrapped and forgotten. Working to rule, trying to make a barely breathing work of fiction simpler and more lucid and more euphonious merely injects into the desperate author's voice a tone of suppressed hysteria, the result of what E.M. Forster called "confusing order with orders." And then, how reliable are the rules? Listen to Pablo Picasso's rejection of a fellow-artist: "He looks up at the sky and says, 'Ah, the sky is blue,' and he paints a blue sky. Then he takes another look and says, 'The sky is mauve, too,' and he adds some mauve. The next time he looks he notices a trace of pink, and he adds a little pink." It sounds a proper mess, but Picasso was talking about Pierre Bonnard. As soon as we learn the names, the blues, mauves and pinks acquire a meaning, a reason to be. Picasso was right, but only in theory. In the end, everything depends on the artist himself.

Style in writing, as in painting, is the author's thumbprint, his mark. I do not mean that it establishes him as finer or greater than other writers, though that can happen too. I am thinking now of prose style as a writer's armorial bearings, his name and address. In a privately printed and libellous pamphlet, Colette's first husband, Willy, who had fraudulently signed her early novels, tried to prove she had gone on to plagiarize and plunder different things he had written. As evidence he offered random sentences from work he was supposed to have influenced or inspired. Colette's manner, robust and personal, seems to leap from the page. Willy believed he had taught Colette "everything," and it may have been true—"everything," that is, except her instinct for language, her talent for perceiving the movement of life and a faculty for describing it. He was bound to have influenced her writing; it couldn't be helped. But by the time he chose to print a broadside on the subject, his influence had been absorbed, transmuted and—most humbling for the teacher— had left no visible trace.

There is no such a thing as a writer who has escaped being influenced. I have never heard a professional writer of any quality or standing talk about "pure" style, or say he would not read this or that for fear of corrupting or affecting his own; but I have heard it from would-be writers and amateurs. Corruption—if that is the word—sets in from the moment a child learns to speak and to hear language used and misused. A young person who does not read, and read widely, will never write anything—at least, nothing of interest. From time to time, in France, a novel is published purporting to come from a shepherd whose only influence has been the baaing of lambs on some God-for-saken slope of the Pyrenees. His artless and untampered-with mode of expression arouses the hope that there will be many more like him, but as a rule he is never heard from again. For "influences" I would be inclined to substitute "acquisitions." What they consist of, and amount to, are affected by taste and environment, preferences and upbringing (even, and sometimes particularly, where the latter has been rejected), instinctive selection. The beginning writer has to choose, tear to pieces, spit out, chew up and assimilate as naturally as a young animal—as naturally and as ruthlessly. Style cannot be copied, except by the untalented. It is, finally, the distillation of a lifetime of reading and listening, of selection and rejection. But if it is not a true voice, it is nothing.

JOHN GARDNER

TECHNIQUE

John Gardner's enduring fame will depend in part on his extraordinary novel Grendel, *the monster first introduced to readers in the famous Anglo-Saxon poem* Beowulf. *Gardner wrote many distinguished novels and stories and has influenced a large number of writers (Raymond Carver among them) through his teaching and writings. His "fiction must be moral" philosophy has been widely debated.*

In "Poetic Rhythm," Gardner insists that the rhythm of prose can matter as much as the rhythm of poetry. "A knowledge of verse scansion is no idle talent for the prose writer," Gardner tells us. The essay was published in The Art of Fiction *(1985).*

Poetic Rhythm

1. Prose, like poetry, is built of rhythms and rhythmic variations.

2. Like poetry, prose has rhythms and rhythmic variations.

3. Rhythm and variation are as basic to prose as to poetry.

4. All prose must force rhythms, just like verse.

Compare the above. Reading at the natural speed we use for prose, faster than the natural speed of verse or prose poetry, we find that item 2 is slower, more plodding, than item 1; and item 3, because of the fairly regular occurrence of stressed syllables and the number of unstressed syllables between them, runs along more lightly than either 1 or 2 and much more lightly than item 4, where the juxtaposed stresses slow the sentence to a trudge.

In good prose, rhythm never stumbles, slips into accidental doggerel, or works against the meaning of the sentence. Consider the following sentence permutations. (For my convenience, assume that the ice has been established by context and may be omitted when we like.)

1. The pig thrashed and squealed, then lay helpless on the ice, panting and trembling.

2. After thrashing and squealing, the pig lay helpless, panting and trembling.

3. Thrashing and squealing, then panting, trembling, the pig lay helpless on the ice.

4. The pig thrashed and squealed, then, panting, trembling, lay helpless.

Rhythmically, item 1 seems not entirely satisfactory. The final phrase, "panting and trembling," comes as a kind of afterthought—we don't feel propelled into it by all that has gone before—and its faint echo of the earlier rhythm, "thrashed and squealed," feels slightly awkward. Item 2 is worse: The echo of "thrashing and squealing" is now much too obvious, giving the sentence an offensive clunky symmetry. Item 3 is better. The echoing phrases have been brought together in the same part of the sentence, allowing the close of the sentence to smooth out and run free; and by dropping the word "and" from the phrase "panting and trembling," the rhythm of this segment is slowed down ("panting, trembling") and the echo is to some extent suppressed. And 4 is better yet. Slowed by the phrase "panting, trembling," the sentence winds down, like the pig, in the word "helpless." Sound now echoes sense.

By keeping out a careful ear for rhythm, the writer can control the emotion of his sentences with considerable subtlety. In my novel *Grendel*, I wanted to establish the emotion and character of the central-character monster in his first utterance. After some brooding and fiddling, I wrote:

The old ram stands looking down over rockslides, stupidly triumphant.

Part of the effect, if the sentence works, is of course the choice of words. It would be different if I'd written, "The old cow sits ..." But part of it is the handling of stresses. The opening juxtaposed stresses, intensified by near rhyme, give appropriate harshness; the alliteration of an essentially nasty sound ("*st*ands," "*st*upidly") maintains this quality; and the rhythmic hesitation of the long syllable at the end of the first phrase

rockslides

followed by the tumble into difficult-to-manage supernumerary unstressed syllables.

stupidly triumphant

gives a suggestion—I hope—of the monster's clumsiness of thought and gait. (We scan the words, I think, as

stupidly tri umphant

rather than as dactylic and amphibrachic. Thus "tri" functions—or would in metrical verse—as a rider, and, given our habits of expectation in strongly rhythmic prose as in verse, the syllables fall clumsily.)

The good writer works out his rhythms by ear; he usually has no need of the paraphernalia I've invoked here for purposes of discussion. Yet occasionally it proves helpful to scan a line with metrical analysis marks, as an aid to determining where some new, strong beat should be inserted, or some part of unstressed syllables suppressed or added. Turning sentences around, trying various combinations of the fundamental elements, will prove invaluable in the end, not just because it leads to better sentences but also because over the years it teaches certain basic ways of fixing rhythm that will work again on other, superficially quite dissimilar sentences. I don't know, myself—and I suspect most writers would say the same—what it is that I do, what formulas I use for switching bad sentences around to make better ones; but I do it all the time, less laboriously every year, trying to creep up on the best ways of getting things said....

A knowledge of verse scansion is no idle talent for the prose writer. Really good prose differs in only one way from good contemporary verse—by which one means, mainly, free verse (unrhymed and metrically irregular). Verse slows the reader by means of line breaks; prose does not. Note that these lines, by poet and fiction writer Joyce Carol Oates, could be set either as prose or as verse:

> The car plunges westward into the bluing dusk of New York State.
> There is no end to it: the snakes that writhe in the headlights,
> the scarves of snow, the veins, vines, tendrils,
> the sky a crazy broken blue
> like crockery.

Some contemporary free verse, like that of Galway Kinnell, has more compression than prose can bear; no one denies the power of Kinnell's best verse, but as Whitman proves, compression of that sort is not an absolute requirement.

WILLIAM H. GASS

THE CONCEPT OF
CHARACTER IN FICTION

William H. Gass, one of the United States' best-known writers, is a philosopher and literary essayist as well as a story writer. The collection In the Heart of the Heart of the Country *is among his many distinguished works. The following snippet on character is drawn from an essay originally appearing in* New American Review 7 *(1969).*

Enter Mr. Cashmore, who is a character in *The Awkward Age*.

> Mr. Cashmore, who would have been very red-headed if he had not been very bald, showed a single eye-glass and a long upper lip; he was large and jaunty, with little petulant movements and intense ejaculations that were not in the line of his type.

We can imagine any number of other sentences about Mr. Cashmore added to this one. Now the question is: What is Mr. Cashmore? Here is the answer I shall give: Mr. Cashmore is (1) a noise, (2) a proper name, (3) a complex system of ideas, (4) a controlling conception, (5) an instrument of verbal organization, (6) a pretended mode of referring, and (7) a source of verbal energy. But Mr. Cashmore is not a person. He is not an object of perception, and nothing whatever that is appropriate to persons can be correctly said of him. There is no path from idea to sense (this is Descartes' argument in reverse), and no amount of careful elaboration of Mr. Cashmore's single eyeglass, his upper lip, or jauntiness is going to enable us to *see* him. How many little petulant movements are there? Certainly as many as the shapes which may be taken by soft wax. If we follow Hume, we think we picture things through language because we substitute, on cue, particular visual memories of our own, and the more precisely language defines its object, the less likely we are to find a snapshot in our book to fit it. This is not a harmless error either, but a vulgar and pernicious one. Our visualizations interfere with Mr. Cashmore's development, for if we think of him as someone we have met, we must give him qualities his author hasn't yet, and we may stubbornly, or through simple lack of attention, retain these later, though they've been explicitly debarred. "On your imaginary forces work," *Henry V*'s Prologuer begs. "Piece out our imperfections with your thoughts.... Think, when we talk of horses, that you see them/ Printing their proud hoofs i' th' receiving earth," and then the audience (and the similarly situated novel reader) is praised for having done so; but this is worse than the self-congratulating pap which periodically flows from the bosom of the "creative" critic, because these generous additions destroy the work as certainly as "touching up" and "painting over." The unspoken word is often eloquent.

Well, I finally met Mr. Mulholland.

Oh, what's he like?
He has large thumbs.

Characters in fiction are mostly empty canvas. I have known many who have passed through their stories without noses, or heads to hold them; others have lacked bodies altogether, exercised no natural functions, possessed some thoughts, a few emotions, but no psychologies, and apparently made love without the necessary organs. The true principle is direct enough: Mr. Cashmore has what he's been given; he also *has* what he *hasn't*, just as strongly. Mr. Cashmore, in fact, has been cruelly scalped.

Now, is there a nose to this Mr. Cashmore? Let's suppose it—but then, of what sort? We're not told. He is an eyeglass without eyes, he has no neck or chin, his ears are unexplored. "Large"—how indefinite a word. But would it have been better to have written "sixteen stone?" Not at all, nor do we know how this weight is disposed. If it is impossible to picture Mr. Cashmore, however carefully we draw him, will it be easier to limn his soul? Or perhaps we may imagine that this sentence describes not Mr. Cashmore, out or in, but his impression—what sort of dent he makes in his surroundings. He gives the impression of a man who would have been redheaded if he hadn't been bald. Very well, what impression, exactly, is that? Will it do to think of Mr. Cashmore as a man with red eyebrows and a red fringe above his ears, but otherwise without hair? That would rephrase Mr. Cashmore, and rephrase him badly. The description of Mr. Cashmore stands as James wrote it, even if Mr. Cashmore hasn't a hair on his body.

As a set of sensations Mr. Cashmore is simply impossible; as an idea he is admirably pungent and precise.

Similarly, it is not at all correct to infer that because Mr. Mulholland has thumbs, he has hands, arms, torso, self. That inference destroys the metaphor (a pure synecdoche), since his thumbs are all he seems to be. Mr. Mulholland is monumentally clumsy, but if you fill him in behind his thumbs, clumsiness will not ensue.

So sometimes, then, we are required to take away what we've been given, as in the case of Mr. Cashmore's red hair; sometimes it's important to hold fast to what we've got and resist any inclination we may have to elaborate, as in the case of Mr. Mulholland, who I said had thumbs; and sometimes we must put our minds to the stretch, bridging the distances between concepts with other concepts, as in the two examples which follow; or we may be called upon to do all these things at once, as in what I promise will be my final misuse of poor Mulholland.

> Will, I finally met Mr. Mulholland.
> Oh, what's he like?
> A silver thimble.

> I saw Mr. Mulholland today.
> Oh, what was he doing?
> Walking his thumbs.

> Mr. Mulholland's face had
> a watchful look. Although
> its features had not yet arrived,
> they were momentarily expected.

To summarize, so far:

1. Only a few of the words which a writer normally uses to create a character can be "imaged" in any sense.
2. To the extent these images are faded sensations which we've once had, they fill in, particularize, and falsify the author's account.
3. To the degree these images are as vivid and as lively as reality is, they will very often be unpleasant, and certainly can't be "feigned." Then words would act like a mind-expanding drug.
4. To the degree these images are general schema, indistinct and vague, the great reality characters are supposed to have become less plausible, and precise writing (so often admired) will interfere with their formation.
5. Constructing images of any kind takes time, slows the flow of the work; nor can imaging keep up, in complexity, with the incredibly intricate conceptual systems which may be spun like a spiderweb in a single sentence.
6. We tend to pay attention to our pictures, and lose sight of the meaning. The novelist's words are not notes which he is begging the reader to play, as if his novel needed something more done to it in order to leap into existence.

SANDRA M. GILBERT AND SUSAN GUBAR

A FEMINIST READING
OF GILMAN'S
"THE YELLOW WALLPAPER"

Sandra M. Gilbert and Susan Gubar's "A Feminist Reading of Gilman's
'The Yellow Wallpaper'" has been frequently reprinted since its appear-
ance in their famous work, The Madwoman in the Attic: The Woman
Writer and the Nineteenth-Century Literary Imagination *(1979).*

As if to comment on the unity of all these points—on, that is, the anxiety-
inducing connections between what women writers tend to see as their parallel
confinements in texts, houses, and maternal female bodies—Charlotte Perkins
Gilman brought them all together in 1890 in a striking story of female confinement and escape, a paradigmatic tale which (like *Jane Eyre*) seems to tell *the*
story that all literary women would tell if they could speak their "speechless
woe." "The Yellow Wallpaper," which Gilman herself called "a description of
a case of nervous breakdown," recounts in the first person the experiences of a
woman who is evidently suffering from a severe post-partum psychosis. Her
husband, a censorious and paternalistic physician, is treating her according to
methods by which S. Weir Mitchell, a famous "nerve specialist," treated
Gilman herself for a similar problem. He has confined her to a large garret
room in an "ancestral hall" he has rented, and he has forbidden her to touch
pen to paper until she is well again, for he feels, says the narrator, "that with
my imaginative power and habit of story-making, a nervous weakness like
mine is sure to lead to all manner of excited fancies, and that I ought to use my
will and good sense to check the tendency."

The cure, of course, is worse than the disease, for the sick woman's mental
condition deteriorates rapidly. "I think sometimes that if I were only well
enough to write a little it would relieve the press of ideas and rest me," she
remarks, but literally confined in a room she thinks is a one-time nursery
because it has "rings and things" in the walls, she is literally locked away from

creativity. The "rings and things," although reminiscent of children's gymnastic equipment, are really the paraphernalia of confinement, like the gate at the head of the stairs, instruments that definitively indicate her imprisonment. Even more tormenting, however, is the room's wallpaper: a sulphurous yellow paper, torn off in spots, and patterned with "lame uncertain curves" that "plunge off at outrageous angles" and "destroy themselves in unheard of contradictions." Ancient, smoldering, "unclean" as the oppressive structures of the society in which she finds herself, this paper surrounds the narrator like an inexplicable text, censorious and overwhelming as her physician husband, haunting as the "hereditary estate" in which she is trying to survive. Inevitably she studies its suicidal implications—and inevitably, because of her "imaginative power and habit of story-making," she revises it, projecting her own passion for escape into its otherwise incomprehensible hieroglyphics. "This wall-paper," she decides, at a key point in her story,

> has a kind of sub-pattern in a different shade, a particularly irritating one, for you can only see it in certain lights, and not clearly then.
>
> But in the places where it isn't faded and where the sun is just so—I can see a strange, provoking formless sort of figure, that seems to skulk about behind that silly and conspicuous front design.

As time passes, this figure concealed behind what corresponds (in terms of what we have been discussing) to the facade of the patriarchal text becomes clearer and clearer. By moonlight the pattern of the wallpaper "becomes bars! The outside pattern I mean, and the woman behind it is as plain as can be." And eventually, as the narrator sinks more deeply into what the world calls madness, the terrifying implications of both the paper and the figure imprisoned behind the paper begin to permeate—that is, to *haunt*—the rented ancestral mansion in which she and her husband are immured. The "yellow smell" of the paper "creeps all over the house," drenching every room in its subtle aroma of decay. And the woman creeps too—through the house, in the house, and out of the house, in the garden and "on that long road under the trees." Sometimes, indeed, the narrator confesses, "I think there are a great many women" both behind the paper and creeping in the garden, "and sometimes only one, and she crawls around fast, and her crawling shakes [the paper] all over.... And she is all the time trying to climb through. But nobody could climb through that pattern—it strangles so; I think that is why it has so many heads."

Eventually it becomes obvious to both reader and narrator that the figure creeping through and behind the wallpaper is both the narrator and the narrator's double. By the end of the story, moreover, the narrator has enabled the double to escape from her textual/architectural confinement: "I pulled and she shook, I shook and she pulled, and before morning we had peeled off yards of that paper." Is the message of the tale's conclusion mere madness? Certainly the righteous Doctor John—whose name links him to the anti-hero of Charlotte Brontë's *Villette*—has been temporarily defeated, or at least momentarily stunned. "Now why should that man have fainted?" the narrator ironically asks as she creeps around her attic. But John's unmasculine swoon of surprise is the least of the triumphs Gilman imagines for her madwoman. More significant are the madwoman's own imaginings and creations, mirages of health and freedom with which her author endows her like a fairy godmother showering gold on a sleeping heroine. The woman from behind the wallpaper creeps away, for instance, creeps fast and far on the long road, in broad daylight. "I have watched her sometimes away off in the open country," says the narrator, "creeping as fast as a cloud shadow in a high wind."

Indistinct and yet rapid, barely perceptible but inexorable, the progress of that cloud shadow is not unlike the progress of nineteenth-century literary women out of the texts defined by patriarchal poetics into the open spaces of their own authority. That such an escape from the numb world behind the patterned walls of the text was a flight from disease into health was quite clear to Gilman herself. When "The Yellow Wallpaper" was published she sent it to Weir Mitchell whose strictures had kept her from attempting the pen during her own breakdown, thereby aggravating her illness, and she was delighted to learn, years later, that "he had changed his treatment of nervous prostration since reading" her story. "If that is a fact," she declared, "I have not lived in vain." Because she was a rebellious feminist besides being a medical iconoclast, we can be sure that Gilman did not think of this triumph of hers in narrowly therapeutic terms. Because she knew, with Emily Dickinson, that "Infection in the sentence breeds," she knew that the cure for female despair must be spiritual as well as physical, aesthetic as well as social. What "The Yellow Wallpaper" shows she knew, too, is that even when a supposedly "mad" woman has been sentenced to imprisonment in the "infected" house of her own body, she may discover that, as Sylvia Plath was to put it seventy years later, she has "a self to recover, a queen."

PATRICIA DUBRAVA KEUNING

THE SPIRITS ARE WAITING: EXCERPTS FROM AN INTERVIEW WITH ISABEL ALLENDE

The full text of Patricia Dubrava Keuning's interview with Isabel Allende may be found in The Bloomsbury Review, *June 1991. In this excerpt, Allende speaks of Chile and the military, of translations, of Latin American literature, of factors affecting the writer's point of view, of rituals, and of* The Stories of Eva Luna.

PDK: In *Of Love and Shadows*, you have a memorable, long quote from Mikhail Bakunin, which ends "One cannot love the military without detesting the people." I love that quote. Is that also Isabel Allende's belief?

IA: ... I've seen the military in all its shades and colors, and it's always exactly the same. The Nazis marching in Berlin, the Chilean soldiers marching in Santiago, the American soldiers marching, the Kuwaiti soldiers, the Iraqi soldiers, look and act the same. They play the same roles, the roles of death and destruction. There will be a point, unfortunately not in my lifetime, when we will look back and say, "Can you imagine? We paid a group of people, we trained them for death and destruction, we paid for their ceremonies, their medals, their uniforms, their deadly toys. And we spent money and energy and life on this?" We will look at it with the same shame as we now feel for slavery, or child labor, or racism. There are lots of racists, but it's always shameful, and you don't want to admit it. It's the same with women's lib. More and more people are coming to the idea that this is only natural. How didn't we think of it before? My daughter and granddaughter will live in a world where feminism is not an issue anymore as slavery is not an issue for us anymore. And my great-great-granddaughter will live in a world where she will look upon the military as an obscene, perverse thing that happened to humanity in its primitive states. *Espero que si.*

PDK: I hope so as well. Speaking of women's issues, all of your stories have strong central female characters, wonderful, dynamic characters. In *House of the Spirits* and *Eva Luna*, you have strong matriarchal systems as well, wherein wisdom and spiritual traits are handed down from mother to daughter to granddaughter. I understand that is really your experience, that you come from such a family.

IA: The previous generation of great Latin American writers of the "Boom"—García Márquez, José Donoso, Carlos Fuentes, Vargas Llosa—were all male. They belonged to this wonderful male club of Latin American literature. They were brought up in an even more segregated environment than I was, so they know much less about women than I know about men. They were never in touch with women and they had the three stereotypes—the mother, the eternal virginal fiancee, and the whore—as the only female role models. Women in that generation had to be very shrewd and had to observe men very accurately to survive in a male world with male rules. They knew much more about men than men know about them. But we lived in a world where male authors narrated women to women. And what they narrated was totally out of reality. Now the women writers have taken by assault the world of literature in Latin America. We are narrating us to ourselves. Naturally, we know much more about ourselves, and have strong realistic women characters, because that's how women are. They're not the other stereotypes. This is how we are, and we're just telling. I'm not inventing a model. I'm just talking about what I know, what I've seen. I've worked with women and for women all my life. I know them very well.

PDK: I was also thinking in terms of Virginia Woolf, who says that women have to learn to write women's sentences. And then the French feminists, who have in recent years talked about feminine writing, female writing, and distinguished that as being almost organically different from men's writing. Do you think that's the case?

IA: I have doubts. Men and women writers use the same instrument, the same tool: language. We describe the world inside and outside. That's what we do. Literature shouldn't have sex and doesn't have sex, but the writer has always a point of view that is determined by his life. If you are Black or White, old or young, male or female, healthy or sick, poor or rich, those things affect your point of view. It's determined even by the continent where you were born, by the village where you were born. Those things determine your vision of the world, your perspective, your distance, your ambiguity, and your questions. Writing is just asking questions, and those are determined by the experience of your own life. So what the French women writers have been saying is that we women ask different questions. We deal with relationships more than with achievements and goals. We are into the journey, not the end of the journey. We don't want to get anywhere. We know that it's only the process. It's just one step at a time and then one day, we die.

PDK: Do you think you'll ever go back to live in Chile?

IA: Maybe. Who knows? In the future. But now we are bringing up a family here. My husband has a job. He won't retire for many years to come. And so what we can do is have one foot there and spend some time there. But I'm a very rootless person in the sense that I don't have a landscape or a country or a family or a people or an accent of my own anymore. I don't have a homeland. I've been a foreigner for twenty years, more than twenty years, because when I was a child, I was also foreign. And I believe now that my roots are in memory. I remember people. I invent people probably. I remember my childhood, my country, and I carry all those roots with me all the time. My homeland—this sounds terribly corny—is my husband. He's my house. So wherever he is, that's home.

PDK: I would assume ... that you've started another project?

IA: Yes, I always begin my books on January 8.

PDK: Do you?

IA: Because I began *The House of the Spirits* on January 8, 1981, and it was such a lucky book that I thought I can't tempt my luck. So I started the second book and the third and the fourth on January 8. If I finish a book in the middle of the year, I wait for January 8 next year to begin another. Then I have everything prepared in a sort of superstitious ceremony: my cup of coffee, the photographs of the people I love, the works of Pablo Neruda next to the computer so that his poetry will impregnate the writing. There are flowers, you know, all the superstitious ...

PDK: Rituals.

IA: And then I turn on the computer on January 8, and I have a plan, I usually have a story that I want to tell. And something happens. I can't tell you what it is, but when I turn on the computer on that day in that ceremony, I realize that I'm not going to write that story, the one that I have planned, that something has been growing inside that I was not even aware of. And when I write the first sentence, I know what it is, and it starts unfolding slowly in a mysterious way that I can't explain. Then later, I do the real work, the correcting and editing and all that. But the first draft is like a catharsis, something that just comes out, and I just let it flow. Later I try to find the meaning to it.

PDK: Margaret Sayers Peden has done the translations for your American editions, a famous name in translation of Latin American work. Do you work with her?

IA: Oh, no. She does a perfect job, and she sends me the translation as a courtesy. What I can add or suggest is minimal. I can only say, for example, things that she wouldn't possibly know. If I say in Spanish, aguardiente, the right translation, according to the dictionary, would be "whisky." But in Latin America, whisky has a social meaning that Margaret could not know. Only the rich can drink whisky, because we don't produce whisky—we produce rum, wine—but not whisky. So I can suggest that instead of using whisky, she use rum or another local liquor. Or, there are a few words that I never use in Spanish because I don't like the sound of them. There are words in English that are the correct words, the right words, but I don't like the sound of them.

PDK: Near the end of *Eva Luna*, Rolf Carle asks Eva to tell him a story she's never told anyone and to "make it up for me." She then tells him the tale about the woman who sells stories. In the prologue to *The Stories of Eva Luna*, Carle also asks Eva to make up a story for him, and the first story, "Two Words," seems to be an extension of the other tale. Did those stories come to you as you were writing *Eva Luna*?

IA: No, no. When I finished *Eva Luna*, I thought the book was over. But then, after it was published, many people asked, "Where are the stories? She's a storyteller, and there are no stories in the book." And at that time, my life was quite hectic, really. I had just moved to this country, I didn't have a room of my own; my life was fragmented. I was teaching in Virginia, travelling, teaching in Berkeley. I didn't have space or time for a novel. A novel needs months of work, years of silence. The short stories were the natural thing to do because they allowed me to work in fragments. I had never tried that before, and I think it's a very difficult genre, much more difficult than the novel, and I don't think I will experiment with short stories for a while. With a novel, I have the feeling that it's like embroidering a patient tapestry in which you have a pattern. You have these colorful threads, you work and work and work, and then one day, you turn it over and it's ready. A short story is like an arrow. You have one shot. You need speed, tension, direction, a firm wrist, and good luck, because if you do overwork it, it shows. If you don't work it enough, it shows too. If you add a work or subtract a word. It's like poetry: everything is visible. And often language or the form is more important than the story. In a novel, you get so involved in the plot and with the characters that you forgive the mistakes.

VERA M. KUTZINSKI

THE LOGIC OF WINGS: GABRIEL GARCÍA MÁRQUEZ AND AFRO-AMERICAN LITERATURE

Robert Coover, one of North America's most original fiction writers, published some years ago in New American Review *a long, splendidly informative article entitled "His Master's Voice," in which he called Gabriel García Márquez's* One Hundred Years of Solitude *one of the best novels ever written. Coover is not alone in this view.*

While little remains on our pages from Vera M. Kutzinski's carefully reasoned article, "The Logic of Wings: Gabriel García Márquez and Afro-American Literature," we are in her debt for pointing us to "the myth of the flying Africans," and for the wonderful statement by Márquez resulting from his 1978 journey to Angola.

My grandparents were descendants of Spanish immigrants, and many of the supernatural things they told me about came from Galicia. But I believe that this taste for the supernatural, which is typical of the Galicians, is also an African inheritance. The coast of the Caribbean, where I was born, is, like Brazil, the region of Latin America where one most feels the African influence. In this sense, the trip I made to Angola in 1978 was one of the most fascinating experiences I have ever had. I believe that it divided my life into two halves. I expected to encounter a strange world, completely foreign, and from the moment I set my feet down there, from the moment I smelled the air, I found myself immediately in the world of my childhood. Yes, I found myself face to face with my entire childhood, customs and things which I had forgotten. This also included the nightmares I used to have as a child.

In Latin America we have been trained to believe that we are Spaniards. This is true in part, because the Spanish element forms part of our peculiar cultural make-up and cannot be denied. But I discovered during that trip to

Angola that we are also Africans. Or better, that we are *mestizos*. That our culture is *mestizo*, that it is enriched by diverse contributions. Never before had I been conscious of this.... In the Caribbean, to which I belong, the boundless imagination of the black African slaves mixed with that of the native pre-Columbians and then with the fantasy of the Andalucians and the supernatural cult of the Galicians. This ability to view reality in a certain magic way is characteristic of the Caribbean and also of Brazil. From there has evolved a literature, a music and a kind of painting like that of Wifredo Lam, all of which are aesthetic expressions of this part of the world.... I believe that the Caribbean has taught me to see reality in a different way, to accept supernatural elements as something that is part of our daily life. The Caribbean is a distinctive world whose first magic piece of literature is *The Diary of Christopher Columbus*, a book which speaks of fabulous plants and mythical worlds. Yes, the history of the Caribbean is full of magic....

The metaphoric link between flying and sorcery (or magic) is of vital importance to the entire Afro-American literary canon. There are numerous tales about and allusions to flight in Afro-American folklore, all of which are, in one way or another, versions of what is commonly known as the myth of the flying Africans. "Once all Africans could fly like birds; but owing to their many transgressions, their wings were taken away. There remained, here and there, in the sea-lands and out-of-the-way places in the low country, some who had been overlooked, and had retained the power of flight, though they looked like other men." In this sense, those who have retained the gift of flight are the guardians of Afro-America's cultural tradition. These keepers of traditional values and beliefs are the sorcerers and conjure-(wo)men, almost archetypal figures of notable prominence in Afro-American literature. One of those figures is that of the old man, who appears in the following version of the folktale "All God's Chillun Had Wings."

> The overseer and the driver ran at the old man with lashes ready; and the master ran too, with a picket pulled from the fence, to beat the life out of the old man who had made those Negroes fly. But the old man laughed in their faces, and said something loudly to all the Negroes in the field, the new Negroes and the old Negroes. And as he spoke to them they all remembered what they had forgotten, and recalled the power which had once been theirs. Then all Negroes, old and new, stood up together; the old man raised his hands; and they all leaped up into the air with a great shout; and in a moment were gone, flying, like a flock of crows, over the field, over the fence, and over the top of the wood; and behind them flew the old man. The men went clapping their hands, and the women went singing; and those who had children gave them their breasts; and the children laughed and sucked as their mothers flew, and were not afraid.

D.H. LAWRENCE

THE LUST OF HATE IN POE'S "THE CASK OF AMONTILLADO"

The thousand insults that Poe's character had borne were in a sense borne by Poe as well; D.H. Lawrence also received a large portion of abuse. These two pilgrims were twinned in other respects: their passion, for instance. The paragraphs that follow are from Lawrence's 1923 volume Studies in Classic American Literature.

The best [of Poe's] tales all have the same burden. Hate is as inordinate as love, and as slowly consuming, as secret, as underground, as subtle. All this underground vault business in Poe only symbolizes that which takes place *beneath* the consciousness. On top, all is fair-spoken. Beneath, there is the awful murderous extremity of burying alive. Fortunato, in "The Cask of Amontillado," is buried alive out of perfect hatred, as the lady Madeline of Usher is buried alive out of love. The lust of hate is the inordinate desire to consume and unspeakably possess the soul of the hated one, just as the lust of love is the desire to possess, or to be possessed by, the beloved, utterly. But in either case the result is the dissolution of both souls, each losing itself in transgressing its own bounds.

The lust of Montresor is to devour utterly the soul of Fortunato. It would be no use killing him outright. If a man is killed outright his soul remains integral, free to return into the bosom of some beloved, where it can enact itself. In walling-up his enemy in the vault, Montresor seeks to bring about the indescribable capitulation of the man's soul, so that he, the victor, can possess himself of the very being of the vanquished. Perhaps this can actually be done. Perhaps, in the attempt, the victor breaks the bonds of his own identity, and collapses into nothingness, or into the infinite. Becomes a monster.

ALISTAIR MacLEOD

WRITING THE KNOWN LIFE

This piece is excerpted from an article that appeared in the Globe and
Mail. *In it, MacLeod states that some of the best Canadian literature has
come from writers who have drawn on their experience of the small
towns and rural areas of the country.*

On November 27, 1976, in a piece for the *Toronto Globe and Mail*, Alistair
MacLeod wrote:

> From time to time there are writers who come riding out of the hinterlands of
> this country called Canada. And they are writing about a life that they really
> know down to its smallest detail. And it is a life that is fierce and hard and
> beautiful and close to the bone. They are not fooling around, these writers, not
> counting their phrases, not being coy. And they have not returned from an
> aimless walk through a shopping plaza "looking for something to write
> about." They both know what they want to say and how to say it and they go
> at their task with the single-mindedness of the Ancient Mariner encountering
> the wedding guest. "Look," he says, "no wedding for you today because I am
> going to tell you a story. And I am going to hold you here and not with my
> hand nor with my 'glittering eye' but by the very power of what I have to tell
> you and how I choose to tell it. I am going to show you what I saw and heard
> and smelled and tasted and felt. And I am going to tell you what it is like to be
> abandoned by God and by man and of the true nature of loneliness and of the
> preciousness of life. And I am going to do it in such a way that your life will
> never ever again be the same."

PLINIO APULEYO MENDOZA

HIS CRAFT

Translated by Ann Wright

We hear authors saying that writing is pure joy; we hear them saying that it is pure hell. Which is it? Plinio Apuleyo Mendoza posed this question to Gabriel García Márquez in 1982.

I began writing quite by chance, perhaps only to prove to a friend that my generation was capable of producing writers. After that I fell into the trap of writing for pleasure and then into the next trap of discovering there was nothing in the world I loved more than writing.

You've said writing is a pleasure. You've also said it is pure suffering. Which is it?

Both are true. At the beginning, when I was learning my craft, I wrote jubilantly, almost irresponsibly. I remember, in those days, I could easily write four, five, even ten pages of a book after I'd finished work on the newspaper around two or three in the morning. Once, I wrote a whole short story at a single sitting.

And now?

Now I'm lucky if I write a good paragraph in a whole day. With the passage of time the act of writing has become very painful.

Why? You would think the greater your skill, the easier it would be to write.

What happens is simply that your sense of responsibility increases. You begin to feel that now each word you write carries more weight, that it influences many more people....

Does a blank piece of paper distress you as it does other writers?

Yes, it's the most distressing thing I know next to claustrophobia. But I stopped worrying about it after reading some advice of Hemingway's. He said you should only break off your work if you know how you're going to go on the next day.

What is your point of departure for a book?

A visual image. For other writers, I think, a book is born out of an idea, a concept. I always start with an image....

You usually attach a lot of importance to the first sentence of a book. You told me once that at times it has taken you longer to write the first sentence than all the rest of the book together. Why?

Because the first sentence can be the laboratory for testing the style, the structure and even the length of the book.

Does it take you long to write a novel?

Not to actually write it. That's quite a rapid process. I wrote *One Hundred Years of Solitude* in less than two years. But I spent fifteen or sixteen years thinking about that book before I sat down at the typewriter....

Hemingway used to say you shouldn't write about a subject either too soon afterwards or too long afterwards. Didn't it worry you keeping a story in your head for so long without writing it?

I've never really been interested in any idea which can't withstand many years of neglect. If it's good enough to withstand fifteen years like *One Hundred Years of Solitude*, seventeen years like *The Autumn of the Patriarch*, and thirty years like *Chronicle of a Death Foretold*, then I have no option but to write it.

Do you take notes?

Never, except for a few odd jottings. I know from experience that when you take notes you end up thinking about the notes and not about the book.

Do you correct your work much?

... I correct it line by line as I go along so that at the end of the day I have a perfect page with no dirty marks or crossings out, almost ready for publication.

Do you tear many pages up?

An unbelievable amount....

Where do you think is the ideal place to write?

I've said this often before: a desert island in the morning and a big city at night. In the morning I need silence, and in the evening a few drinks and some good friends to chat to. I need to be in constant contact with people in the street and know what's going on in the world. This all fits in with what

William Faulkner meant when he said the perfect place for a writer was a brothel, because it's very quiet in the morning but there's partying every night.

Let's talk now about the craft side involved in being a writer. Can you tell me who's been the greatest help to you in your long apprenticeship.

My grandmother, first and foremost. She used to tell me about the most atrocious things without turning a hair, as if it was something she'd just seen. I realized that it was her impassive manner and her wealth of images that made her stories so credible. I wrote *One Hundred Years of Solitude* using my grandmother's method.

Was it through your grandmother that you discovered you were going to be a writer?

No, it was through Kafka, who recounted things in German the same way my grandmother used to. When I read *Metamorphosis*, at seventeen, I realized I could be a writer. When I saw how Gregor Samsa could wake up one morning transformed into a gigantic beetle, I said to myself, "I didn't know you could do this, but if you can, I'm certainly interested in writing."

Why did it attract you so strongly? Because of the freedom of being able to invent anything you like?

All of a sudden I understood how many other possibilities existed in literature outside the rational and extremely academic examples I'd come across in secondary school text books. It was like tearing off a chastity belt. Over the years, however, I discovered that you can't invent or imagine just whatever you fancy because then you risk not telling the truth and lies are more serious in literature than in real life. Even the most seemingly arbitrary creation has its rules. You can throw away the fig leaf of rationalism only if you don't then descend into total chaos and irrationality.

Into fantasy?

Yes, into fantasy.

You loathe fantasy. Why?

Because I believe the imagination is just an instrument for producing reality and that the source of creation is always, in the last instance, reality. Fantasy, in the sense of pure and simple Walt-Disney-style invention without any basis in reality is the most loathsome thing of all.... Children don't like fantasy either. What they do like is imagination. The difference between the one and other is the same as between a human being and a ventriloquist's dummy.

Which other writers, apart from Kafka, have helped you develop your craft and taught you the tricks of the trade?

Hemingway.

Whom you don't consider a great novelist.

Whom I don't consider a great novelist but an excellent short story writer. One piece of advice of his was that a short story, like an iceberg, must be supported by the part you don't see—all the thought, the study and the material collected but not used directly in the story. Yes, Hemingway teaches you a great deal, even to appreciate the way a cat turns a corner....

Why do you attach so little importance to dialogue in your books?

Because dialogue doesn't ring true in Spanish. I've always said that in this language there's a wide gulf between spoken and written dialogue. A Spanish dialogue that's good in real life is not necessarily good in a novel. So I use it very little.

Do you know exactly what is going to happen to each character before you write a novel?

Only in very general terms. Unexpected things happen in the course of the book....

What do you think inspiration is? Does it exist?

It's a word which has been discredited by the Romantics. I don't see it as a state of grace nor as a breath from heaven but as the moment when, by tenacity and control, you are at one with your theme. When you want to write something, a kind of reciprocal tension is established between you and the theme, so you spur the theme on and the theme spurs you on too. There comes a moment when all obstacles fade away, all conflict disappears, things you never dreamt of occur to you and, at that moment, there is absolutely nothing in the world better than writing. That is what I would call inspiration....

What happens when the book you're writing is almost finished?

I lose interest in it for ever. As Hemingway used to say, it's like a dead lion.

You've said that every good novel is a poetic transposition of reality. Can you explain this concept?

Yes, I think a novel is reality represented through a secret code, a kind of conundrum about the world. The reality you are dealing with in a novel is different from real life, although it is rooted in it. The same thing is true of dreams.

The way you treat reality in your books, especially in One Hundred Years of Solitude *and in* The Autumn of the Patriarch, *has been called "magical realism." I have the feeling your European readers are usually aware of the magic in your stories but fail to see the reality behind it ...*

This is surely because their rationalism prevents them seeing that reality isn't limited to the price of tomatoes and eggs. Everyday life in Latin America proves that reality is full of the most extraordinary things. To make this point I usually cite the case of the American explorer F.W. Up de Graff who made an incredible journey through the Amazon jungle at the end of the last century and saw, among other things, a river with boiling water, and a place where the sound of the human voice brought on torrential rain.... I know very ordinary people who've read *One Hundred Years of Solitude* carefully and with a lot of pleasure, but with no surprise at all because, when all is said and done, I'm telling them nothing that hasn't happened in their own lives.

So everything you put in your books is based on real life?

There's not a single line in my novels which is not based on reality.

SIGNATURES OF TIME: ALISTAIR MACLEOD AND HIS SHORT STORIES

In 1985, in Canadian Literature 107, *Colin Nicholson published "Signatures of Time: Alistair MacLeod and His Short Stories," providing an incisive view into the writer's work. Incorporated in that paper was an interview Nicholson conducted while MacLeod was writer-in-residence at Edinburgh University's Centre of Canadian Studies. Here, MacLeod speaks of his Scottish heritage and of his story "The Boat," and argues that "most of the world's great literature begins in the regional."*

[on "The Boat"]

AM: I was interested [in "The Boat"] in the idea of choice, of the price we all have to pay for the choices that we make; in the idea that sometimes people choose to do things that they don't want to do at all, somewhat like the father in that story. This is a man who is caught up in a kind of hereditary pattern, where people fish, and the only son inherits the father's boat—that kind of life. But what I was getting at with the father was that here was a person who maybe didn't want to do that at all, but who is just caught up in this inherited life. Throughout this story, nobody ever thinks of him as ever having a side to him that yearns for something else. They just see him as doing what everyone else does. Which he does. I was interested, towards the end of the story, in the son who is an ambiguous kind of person—can do things well at school as well as handle the boat. It never enters the boy's mind, until his father becomes sick, or something like that, that maybe he has to choose between this or that. And then he realizes that his father has made this choice before. So when I was writing the story, I realized that there were several things I had to do: I've got to make the father old, because if he was a thirty-eight, or even a forty-eight year old man with a son who doesn't want to fish with him, then I've got a very different kind of situation on my hands. But what you've got here is a

865

man who is fifty-six when he fathers this child, and his wife is maybe around forty-two. Six daughters before—none of whom marry local people and the mother is left alone—and this is the only son. The mother is thinking of future security and the father is thinking of other things. So that by the time the son has to make these decisions, what he's got for a father is someone who is around seventy-three. Very different indeed from a father who is thirty or forty. You've got a grandfather for a father.

[on his Scottish heritage]

AM: My parents were both from a place in Canada called Inverness County— named that for the obvious reason. When people from Scotland went over there, they went to a large extent in family groups from individual islands, like Eigg, and intermarried, and carried with them the whole body of whatever it is that people carry with them—folklore, emotional weight. Because it was all open to them, they settled pretty much where they wanted to. Cape Breton Island and Nova Scotia remained rural for a long time, and fairly isolated. And because there was no-one else to integrate with, they stayed very much to themselves almost for six generations. ... And that is why there is this felt affinity on the part of those who emigrated for those who remain. When you think that this is good you say that people were stable for several generations: when you think of it in negative terms, you could say that they were static. Although my wife has adequate Gaelic, we are really the first generation where the breakdown of that culture is beginning to occur.

[on use of the present tense]

AM: In that mode you can be tremendously intense. I just like that. I think that individuals are very interested in telling their own stories, and to adapt this persona is very effective in just riveting the listener. I do think of Coleridge's ancient mariner who, having been ordered by the wedding guest to release him—'eftsoons his hand dropt he'—fixes him with his glittering eye and just tells his story. I think, too, of David Copperfield's opening, "I Am Born," and think how basic, and arresting, that is.

[on a sense of place]

AM: I think of myself as coming from a particular place and a particular time. I do not think of myself as anything like an "instant" North American, not sure of his mother's maiden name. The idea of the melting pot, much encouraged in America, has not been encouraged in Canada; you know, the idea that people come from Scotland or Norway or wherever, and that once they're dipped in North American waters, they forget all their history and become instant

American. The cliché is that you think of America as the melting pot and of Canada as a mosaic, composed of individual areas—here are the Scots, and here are the Irish names. Here are the French-Canadians; here the Ukrainians, the Icelanders, and they're spread out like that across the country. I think of it as inhabiting a single room within a larger house; inhabiting both.

Of course, then there is the feeling that regional writing somehow is not good enough, but my own answer to this is that most of the world's great literature begins in the regional; all literature has to begin someplace. So if you look at Emily Brontë, Thomas Hardy, Charles Dickens—though that's the big city—it's still a regional world. Jane Austen is regional. A phrase much used by Flannery O'Connor is that she comes from "some place." She talks in her letters about going to conferences or whatever, meeting other writers and then saying "it seems that this afternoon I met a lot of people who were not from any place. I am from some place." A phrase that I have made use of to suggest one of the effects that this kind of writing might carry to the very different regions of a new country like Canada, is one that I borrowed from Bob Kroetsch, "the fiction makes us real." It's an issue that arises naturally with the idea, for example, of a Maritime literature; there's a current notion that this kind of writing gives people a confidence in themselves, that they can see themselves out there in the literature.

FLANNERY O'CONNOR

WRITING SHORT STORIES

One thing readers and critics often seem to forget when considering the great Flannery O'Connor is how funny she is. Despite lessons contained in the work of Ring Lardner or Stanley Elkin, among many others, the notion stubbornly persists that an artist cannot be funny and serious in the same breath—which is to say, on the same page. At the beginning of "Writing Short Stories," Flannery O'Connor says, "I have an aunt who thinks that nothing happens in a story unless somebody gets married or shot," a statement that exemplifies both her pervasive, whiplash humour and her deep seriousness. O'Connor addresses not only a thick-headedness about art, but also a disturbing appetite within North American popular culture.

Perhaps the central question to be considered in any discussion of the short story is what do we mean by short. Being short does not mean being slight. A short story should be long in depth and should give us an experience of meaning. I have an aunt who thinks that nothing happens in a story unless somebody gets married or shot at the end of it. I wrote a story about a tramp who marries an old woman's idiot daughter in order to acquire the old woman's automobile. After the marriage, he takes the daughter off on a wedding trip in the automobile and abandons her in an eating place and drives on by himself. Now that is a complete story. There is nothing more relating to the mystery of that man's personality that could be shown through that particular dramatization. But I've never been able to convince my aunt that it's a complete story. She wants to know what happened to the idiot daughter after that.

Not long ago that story was adapted for a television play, and the adapter, knowing his business, had the tramp have a change of heart and go back and pick up the idiot daughter and the two of them ride away, grinning madly. My aunt believes that the story is complete at last, but I have other sentiments about it—which are not suitable for public utterance. When you write a story, you only have to write one story, but there will always be people who will refuse to read the story you have written.

And this naturally brings up the awful question of what kind of a reader you are writing for when you write fiction. Perhaps we each think we have a personal solution for this problem. For my own part, I have a very high opinion of the art of fiction and a very low opinion of what is called the "average" reader. I tell myself that I can't escape him, that this is the personality I am supposed to keep awake, but that at the same time, I am also supposed to provide the intelligent reader with the deeper experience that he looks for in fiction. Now actually, both of these readers are just aspects of the writer's own personality, and in the last analysis, the only reader he can know anything about is himself. We all write at our own level of understanding, but it is the peculiar characteristic of fiction that its literal surface can be made to yield entertainment on an obvious physical plane to one sort of reader while the selfsame surface can be made to yield meaning to the person equipped to experience it there.

Meaning is what keeps the short story from being short. I prefer to talk about the meaning in a story rather than the theme of a story. People talk about the theme of a story as if the theme were like the string that a sack of chicken feed is tied with. They think that if you can pick out the theme, the way you pick the right thread in the chicken-feed sack, you can rip the story open and feed the chickens. But this is not the way meaning works in fiction.

When you can state the theme of a story, when you can separate it from the story itself, then you can be sure the story is not a very good one. The meaning of a story has to be embodied in it, has to be made concrete in it. A story is a way to say something that can't be said any other way, and it takes every word in the story to say what the meaning is. You tell a story because a statement would be inadequate. When anybody asks what a story is about, the only proper thing is to tell him to read the story. The meaning of fiction is not abstract meaning but experienced meaning, and the purpose of making statements about the meaning of a story is only to help you to experience that meaning more fully.

Fiction is an art that calls for the strictest attention to the real—whether the writer is writing a naturalistic story or a fantasy. I mean that we always begin with what is or with what has an eminent possibility of truth about it. Even when one writes a fantasy, reality is the proper basis of it. A thing is fantastic because it is so real, so real that it is fantastic. Grahame Greene has said that he can't write, "I stood over a bottomless pit," because that couldn't be true, or "Running down the stairs I jumped into a taxi," because that couldn't be true either. But Elizabeth Bowen can write about one of her characters that "she snatched at her hair as if she heard something in it," because that is eminently possible.

I would even go so far as to say that the person writing a fantasy has to be even more strictly attentive to the concrete detail than someone writing in a naturalistic vein—because the greater the story's strain on the credulity, the more convincing the properties in it have to be.

A good example of this is a story called "The Metamorphosis" by Franz Kafka. This is a story about a man who wakes up one morning to find that he has turned into a cockroach overnight, while not discarding his human nature. The rest of the story concerns his life and feelings and eventual death as an insect with human nature, and this situation is accepted by the reader because the concrete detail of the story is absolutely convincing. The fact is that this story describes the dual nature of man in such a realistic fashion that it is almost unbearable. The truth is not distorted here, but rather, a certain distortion is used to get at the truth. If we admit, as we must, that appearance is not the same thing as reality, then we must give the artist the liberty to make certain rearrangements of nature if these will lead to greater depths of vision. The artist himself always has to remember that what he is rearranging *is* nature, and that he has to know it and be able to describe it accurately in order to have the authority to rearrange it at all.

The peculiar problem of the short-story writer is how to make the action he describes reveal as much of the mystery of existence as possible. He has only a short space to do it in and he can't do it by statement. He has to do it by showing, not by saying, and by showing the concrete—so that his problem is really how to make the concrete work double time for him.

In good fiction, certain of the details will tend to accumulate meaning from the action of the story itself, and when this happens they become symbolic in the way they work. I once wrote a story called "Good Country People," in which a lady Ph.D. has her wooden leg stolen by a Bible salesman whom she has tried to seduce. Now I'll admit that, paraphrased in this way, the situation is simply a low joke. The average reader is pleased to observe anybody's wooden leg being stolen. But without ceasing to appeal to him and without making any statements of high intention, this story does manage to operate at another level of experience, by letting the wooden leg accumulate meaning. Early in the story, we're presented with the fact that the Ph.D. is spiritually as well as physically crippled. She believes in nothing but her own belief in nothing, and we perceive that there is a wooden part of her soul that corresponds to her wooden leg. Now of course this is never stated. The fiction writer states as little as possible. The reader makes this connection from things he is shown. He may not even know that he makes the connection, but the connection is there nevertheless and it has its effect on him. As the story goes on, the wooden leg continues to accumulate meaning. The reader learns how the girl feels about her leg, how her mother feels about it, and how the country woman on the place feels about it; and finally, by the time the Bible salesman comes along, the leg has accumulated so much meaning that it is, as the saying goes, loaded. And when the Bible salesman steals it, the reader realizes that he has taken away part of the girl's personality and has revealed her deeper affliction to her for the first time.

If you want to say that the wooden leg is a symbol, you can say that. But it is a wooden leg first, and as a wooden leg it is absolutely necessary to the story. It has its place on the literal level of the story, but it operates in depth as well as on the surface. It increases the story in every direction, and this is essentially the way a story escapes being short.

Now a little might be said about the way in which this happens. I wouldn't want you to think that in that story I sat down and said, "I am now going to write a story about a Ph.D. with a wooden leg, using the wooden leg as a symbol for another kind of affliction." I doubt myself if many writers know what they are going to do when they start out. When I started writing that story, I didn't know there was going to be a Ph.D. with a wooden leg in it. I merely found myself one morning writing a description of two women that I knew something about, and before I realized it, I had equipped one of them with a daughter with a wooden leg. As the story progressed, I brought in the Bible salesman, but I had no idea what I was going to do with him. I didn't know he was going to steal that wooden leg until ten or twelve lines before he did it, but when I found out that this was what was going to happen, I realized that it was inevitable. This is a story that produces a shock for the reader, and I think one reason for this is that it produced a shock for the writer.

Now despite the fact that this story came about in this seemingly mindless fashion, it is a story that almost no rewriting was done on. It is a story that was under control throughout the writing of it, and it might be asked how this kind of control comes about, since it is not entirely conscious.

I think the answer to this is what Maritain[1] calls "the habit of art." It is a fact that fiction writing is something in which the whole personality takes part—the conscious as well as the unconscious mind. Art is the habit of the artist; and habits have to be rooted deep in the whole personality. They have to be cultivated like any other habit, over a long period of time, by experience; and teaching any kind of writing is largely a matter of helping the student develop the habit of art. I think this is more than just a discipline, although it is that; I think it is a way of looking at the created world and of using the senses so as to make them find as much meaning as possible in things.

Now I am not so naïve as to suppose that most people come to writers' conferences in order to hear what kind of vision is necessary to write stories that will become a permanent part of our literature. Even if you do wish to hear this, your greatest concerns are immediately practical. You want to know how you can actually write a good story, and further, how you can tell when you've done it; and so you want to know what the form of a short story is, as if the form were something that existed outside of each story and could be applied or imposed on the material. Of course, the more you write, the more you will realize that the form is organic, that it is something that grows out of the material, that the form of each story is unique. A story that is any good can't be reduced, it can only be expanded. A story is good when you continue to see more and more in it, and when it continues to escape you. In fiction two and two is always more than four.

The only way, I think, to learn to write short stories is to write them, and then to try to discover what you have done. The time to think of technique is when you've actually got the story in front of you. The teacher can help the student by looking at his individual work and trying to help him decide if he has written a complete story, one in which the action fully illuminates the meaning.

Perhaps the most profitable thing I can do is to tell you about some of the general observations I made about these seven stories I read of yours. All of these observations will not fit any one of the stories exactly, but they are points nevertheless that it won't hurt anyone interested in writing to think about.

The first thing that any professional writer is conscious of in reading anything is, naturally, the use of language. Now the use of language in these stories was such that, with one exception, it would be difficult to distinguish one story from another. While I can recall running into several clichés, I can't remember one image or one metaphor from the seven stories. I don't mean there weren't images in them; I just mean that there weren't any that were effective enough to take away with you.

In connection with this, I made another observation that startled me considerably. With the exception of one story, there was practically no use made of the local idiom. Now this is a Southern Writers' Conference. All the addresses on these stories were from Georgia or Tennessee, yet there was no distinctive sense of Southern life in them. A few place-names were dropped, Savannah or Atlanta or Jacksonville, but these could just as easily have been changed to Pittsburgh or Passaic without calling for any other alteration in the story. The characters spoke as if they had never heard any kind of language except what came out of a television set. This indicates that something is way out of focus.

There are two qualities that make fiction. One is the sense of mystery and the other is the sense of manners. You get the manners from the texture of existence that surrounds you. The great advantage of being a Southern writer is that we don't have to go anywhere to look for manners; bad or good, we've got them in abundance. We in the South live in a society that is rich in contradiction, rich in irony, rich in contrast, and particularly rich in its speech. And yet here are six stories by Southerners in which almost no use is made of the gifts of the region.

Of course the reason for this may be that you have seen these gifts abused so often that you have become self-conscious about using them. There is nothing worse than the writer who doesn't *use* the gifts of the region, but wallows in them. Everything becomes so Southern that it's sickening, so local that it is unintelligible, so literally reproduced that it conveys nothing. The general gets lost in the particular instead of being shown through it.

However, when the life that actually surrounds us is totally ignored, when our patterns of speech are absolutely overlooked, then something is out of kilter. The writer should then ask himself if he is not reaching out for a kind of life that is artificial to him.

An idiom characterizes a society, and when you ignore the idiom, you are very likely ignoring the whole social fabric that could make a meaningful character. You can't cut characters off from their society and say much about them as individuals. You can't say anything meaningful about the mystery of a personality unless you put that personality in a believable and significant social context. And the best way to do this is through the character's own language. When the old lady in one of Andrew Lytle's stories says contemptuously that she has a mule that is older than Birmingham, we get in that one sentence a sense of a society and its history. A great deal of the Southern writer's work is done for him before he begins, because our history lives in our talk. In one of Eudora Welty's stories a character says, "Where I come from, we use fox for yard dogs and owls for chickens, but we sing true." Now there is a whole book in that one sentence; and when the people of your section can talk like that, and you ignore it, you're just not taking advantage of what's yours. The sound of our talk is too definite to be discarded with impunity, and if the writer tries to get rid of it, he is liable to destroy the better part of his creative power.

Another thing I observed about these stories is that most of them don't go very far inside a character, don't reveal very much of the character. I don't mean that they don't enter the character's mind, but they simply don't show that he has a personality. Again this goes back partly to speech. These characters have no distinctive speech to reveal themselves with; and sometimes they have no really distinctive features. You feel in the end that no personality is revealed because no personality is there. In most good stories it is the character's personality that creates the action of the story. In most of these stories, I feel that the writer has thought of some action and then scrounged up a character to perform it. You will usually be more successful if you start the other way around. If you start with a real personality, a real character, then something is bound to happen; and you don't have to know what before you begin. In fact it may be better if you don't know what before you begin. You ought to be able to discover something from your stories. If you don't, probably nobody else will.

ENDNOTE

1. Jacques Maritain (1882–1973), French philosopher and literary critic.

CYNTHIA OZICK

INNOVATION AND REDEMPTION: WHAT LITERATURE MEANS

Innovation and redemption. What does literature mean? Cynthia Ozick here argues what once might have been a commonly accepted notion: that literature is meant to serve humanity. She also argues for the "nimbus of meaning that envelops story"—the "corona of moral purpose: not outright in the grain of the fiction itself, but in the form of a faintly incandescent envelope around it." Muschig's "The Scythe Hand," elsewhere in this anthology, powerfully illustrates the existence of Ozick's "corona."

1. INNOVATION

A while ago, freed by a bout of flu from all responsibility, I became one of those nineteenth-century leisured persons we hear about, for whom the great novels are said to have been written. In this condition I came, for the first time, to the novels of Thomas Hardy. I began with *Tess of the D'Urbervilles*, and discovered this: it is possible first to ask the question "What is this novel *about*?" and then to give an answer. Hardy writes about—well, *life* (nowadays we are made to hesitate before daring seriously to employ this word); life observed and understood as well as felt. A society with all its interminglings and complexities is set before us: in short, knowledge; knowledge of convention and continuity; also knowledge of something real, something *there*. *Tess*, for instance, is thick with knowledge of Cow. What is a cow, how does it feel to lean against, how do you milk, what is the milkshed like, what is the life of a milker, who is the milker's boss, where does the milk go? To touch any element of Cow intimately and concretely is to enter a land, a society, a people, and to penetrate into the whole lives of human beings.

The world of Cow, or its current equivalents, is now in the possession of writers like Leon Uris and Harold Robbins—shadows of shadows of Hardy. Post-Joyce, the "real" writers have gone somewhere else. And though we may

874

not, cannot, turn back to the pre-Joycean "fundamentalist" novel, it is about time it was recognized that too much "subjectivity" has led away from mastery (which so-called "experimental" novelist tells us about Cow?) and from seriousness (to which black humorist or parodist would you entrust the whole lives of human beings?).

What is today called "experimental" writing is unreadable. It fails because it is neither intelligent nor interesting. Without seriousness it cannot be interesting, and without mastery it will never be intelligent.

The idea of the experimental derives from the notion of generations: a belief in replacement, substitution, discontinuity, above all repudiation. Who invented "generations," and when did they come into being? John Hollander, reflecting on children's literature, notes that the idea of "children" as a classification of fresh innocence is itself a remarkably short-lived fancy, squeezed into that brief pre-Freudian bourgeois moment that made Lewis Carroll possible; before the nineteenth century there *were* no children, only smaller-sized working people; and then Freud arrived to take the charm, and the purity, out of Victorian childhood.

There are, in fact, no "generations," except in the biological sense. There are only categories and crises of temperament, and these crisscross and defy and deny chronology. The concept of generations, moreover, is peculiarly solipsistic; it declares that because I am new, then everything I make or do in the world is new.

When I was a quite young child, just beginning to write stories, I had an odd idea of time. It seemed to me that because writing signified permanence, it was necessary to address not only everyone who might live afterward, but also everyone who had ever lived before. This meant one had to keep one's eye on the ancient Greeks in particular, to write for *them* too; and, knowing no ancient Greek, I got around the difficulty by employing the most archaic language the Green, Yellow, Blue, Red, and Violet Fairy Books had to offer.

Now if this belief that everything counts forever, both backward and forward, is a kind of paradisal foolishness, it is no more nonsensical than the belief that nothing counts for long—the credo that the newest generation displaces the one before it. The problem with believing in generations is not only the most obvious one—that you excise history, that you cut off even the most immediately usable past—but the sense of narrow obligation it imposes on the young, a kind of prisoner's outlook no less burdensome than all the following dicta taken together:

1. That each new crop of mass births must reinvent culture.
2. That models are unthinkable.
3. That each succeeding generation is inherently brighter and more courageous than the one before.

4. That "establishments" are irreversibly closed.
5. That whatever has won success is by definition stale.
6. That "structurelessness"—i.e., incoherence—must be understood as a paradox, since incoherence is really coherence.
7. That "experiment" is endlessly possible, and endlessly positive, and that the more "unprecedented" a thing is, the better it is.
8. That "alternative forms" are salvational.
9. That irrational (or "psychedelic") states represent artistic newness.

I could make this list longer, but it is already long enough to demonstrate the critical point that more useful cultural news inhabits the Fifth Commandment than one might imagine at first glance.

The sources of these statements are of course everywhere—they are the bad breath of the times. At best, "experimental" fiction aims for parody: it turns the tables on the old voices, it consists of allusion built upon allusion, it is a choreography of ridicule and satire. It goes without saying that no literature can live without satire; satire nourishes and cleanses and resuscitates. The great satires that have survived are majestic indictments. Our attention now is assaulted by ephemeral asterisks claiming to be satire: when you follow the dim little star to its destination, what you find is another littleness—parody. Parody without seriousness, without, in the end, irony. If the writer does not know what to do with the remnants of high culture, he parodies them; if he does not know what to do with kitsch, he simply invites it in. Twenty years hence, the American fiction of parody is going to require an addendum—complete citations of the work and tone and attitude it meant to do in. Whatever seems implicit now because of its currency as memory or tradition will have to be made explicit later, for the sake of comprehension, when tradition is forgotten and memory is dead. (Compare any annotated copy of "The Rape of the Lock.") And meanwhile, the trouble with parody is that it is endlessly reflective, one parody building on a previous parody, and so on, until eventually the goal becomes ingenuity in the varieties of derivativeness, and one loses sight of any original objective notion of what literature can be about, of the real sources of literature. Redundance is all—and in the name of escape from the redundance of convention.

One of the great conventions—and also one of the virtues—of the old novel was its suspensefulness. Suspense *seems* to make us ask "What will happen to Tess next?," but really it emerges from the writer's conviction of social or cosmic principle. Suspense occurs when the reader is about to learn something, not simply about the relationship of fictional characters, but about the writer's relationship to a set of ideas, or to the universe. Suspense is the product of teaching, and teaching is the product of mastery, and mastery is the product of seriousness, and seriousness springs not from ego or ambition or the workings of the subjective self, but from the amazing permutations of the objective world.

Fiction will not be interesting or lasting unless it is again conceived in the art of the didactic. (Emphasis, however, on *art*.) The experimental is almost never the innovative. The innovative imagines something we have never experienced before: think of Tolstoy's imagining the moment of dying in "The Death of Ivan Ilych." The experimental fiddles with what has gone before, precisely and exclusively with what has gone before; it is obsessed by precedent and predecessors. The innovative, by contrast, sets out to educate its readers in its views about what it means to be a human being—though it too can fiddle with this and that if it pleases, and is not averse to unexpected seizures and tricks, or to the jarring gifts of vitality and cunning. Innovation cannot be defined through mere *method*; the experimental can be defined no other way. And innovation has a hidden subject: coherence.

An avatar of "alternative kinds of literary coherence"[1] asks us to note how

> the criteria for measuring literacy change in time, so that the body of information and ideas that seemed "literate" in the forties may, because of the sheer increase of knowledge, seem only semi-literate now. Moreover, unless older writers' minds are open enough to recognize that what a young poet learns today may be quite different from what his predecessors know, they may miss evidences of his learning ... very rare is the literary gent over forty who can recognize, for instance, such recent-vintage ideas as say, feedback, information theory and related cybernetic concepts. This deficiency partially explains why, try as hard as we might, it is often so frustrating, if not impossible, to conduct an intelligent dialogue with older writers, the most dogmatic and semi-literate of whom are simply unable to transcend their closed and hardened ways of thought and learning. Not only do the best educated young minds seem much better educated than older intellectuals were at comparable ages, but also what a well-informed young writer knows is likely to be more relevant, not just to contemporary understanding, but also to the problems of creating literary art today.

(Surely the authors of *The Waste Land* and *Finnegans Wake*, literary and intellectual heroes of the forties, would count as "older writers"—instances, no doubt, of semi-literacy and hardened ways.)

Mindful that youth alone may not altogether make his argument, and relying on the McLuhanite vocabulary current a decade ago, the same writer offers still another variant definition of "coherence":

> A truth of contemporary avant-garde esthetics is that "formless art" is either a polemical paradox or an impossible contradiction in terms, for any work that can be defined—that can be characterized in any way—is by definition artistically coherent. It follows that just because a work fails to cohere in a linear fashion need not mean that it cannot be understood; rather, as recent literature

accustoms us to its particular ways of organizing expression, so we learn to confront a new work with expectations wholly different from those honed on traditional literature.

Or, history is bunk.

And just here is the danger and the grief—those "wholly different" expectations. If apprentice writers are trained to define away plain contradictions, bringing us at last to a skilled refinement of Orwellian doublethink (incoherence is coherence), if standardized new "information"—though no one doubts that "feedback, information theory and related cybernetic concepts" are the Cow of our time—is to take the place of the idiosyncratic cadences of literary imagination and integration, if "the criteria for measuring literacy" lead to the dumping of both cognition and recognition, if focus and possession are to be dissipated into the pointless distractions and distractibilities of "multimedia" and other devices, if becoming "wholly different" means the tedium of mechanical enmity toward and mechanical overthrow of "older writers," and if all this is to be programmed through hope of instantaneous dissolutions, then not only literature but *the desire to have a literature* will be subverted.

Culture is the continuity of human aspiration—which signifies a continuity of expectations. Innovation in art is not rupture. Innovation in art is not the consequence of the implantation of "wholly different" expectations. Innovation in art means the continuity of expectations.

Every new sentence, every new fragment of imaginative literature born into the world, is a heart-in-the-mouth experiment, and for its writer a profound chanciness; but the point of the risk is the continuation of a recognizably human enterprise. "Wholly different" means unrecognizable; unrecognizable means the breaking-off of a culture, and its supplanting. It cannot be true that the end of a culture is the beginning of art. When cultural continuity is broken off—as in the Third Reich—what happens is first the debasement, then the extirpation, of any recognizable human goals. First the violation of art (Mozart at the gas chamber's door), then the end of art.

Innovation in art is not the same as innovation in the human psyche; just the opposite. Innovation in art has as its motivation the extension of humanity, not a flow of spite against it. The difference between barbarian and civilized expectations is the difference between the will to dominate and the will toward regeneration. To dominate you must throw the rascals out; to regenerate, you have to take them with you. Spite vandalizes. Innovation redeems.

As for who the rascals are: there is no predicament that cures itself so swiftly as that of belonging to "the young." Alice, nibbling at the mushroom, shrank so quickly that her chin crashed into her shoe: *that* fast is how we go from twenty-three to fifty-four, and from fifty-five to eighty-six. *Vita brevis!* If writers are to have a program, it ought not to be toward *ressentiment*, but toward achronology. Younger writers who resent older ones will, before they are nearly ready for it, find themselves hated by someone astonishingly recently out of the pram. Older writers who envy younger ones have a bottomless cornucopia to gorge on: the baby carriages are packed with novelists and poets. The will to fashion a literature asserts the obliteration of time. The obliteration of time makes "experiment" seem a puff of air, the faintest clamor of celestial horselaugh.

2. REDEMPTION

At a party once I heard a gifted and respected American writer—a writer whose prestigious name almost everyone would recognize—say, "for me, the Holocaust and a corncob are the same." The choice of "corncob"—outlandish, unexpected, askew—is a sign of the strong and daring charge of his imagination, and so is its juxtaposition with the darkest word of our century. What he intended by this extraordinary sentence was not to shock the moral sense, but to clarify the nature of art.

He meant that there is, for art, no such element as "subject matter"; for art, one sight or moment or event is as good as another—there is no "value" or "worth" or "meaning"—because all are equally made up of language, and language and its patterns are no different from tone for the composer or color for the painter. The artist as citizen, the writer explained, can be a highly moral man or woman—one who would, if the Nazis came, hide Jews. But the artist as artist is not a moral creature. Within literature, all art is dream, and whether or not the artist is or is not in citizenly possession of moral credentials is irrelevant to the form and the texture of the work of art, which claims only the territory of the imagination, and nothing else.

For that writer, a phrase such as "a morally responsible literature" would be an oxymoron, the earlier part of the phrase clashing to the death with the latter part. To be responsible as a writer is to be responsible solely to the seizures of language and dream.

I want to stand against this view. The writer who says "For me, the Holocaust and a corncob are the same" is putting aside the moral sense in art, equating the moral impulse only with the sociologically real, or perhaps with the theologically ideal. In literature he judges the moral sense to be an absurd intrusion. He is in the stream that comes to us from Greece, through Walter Pater and Emerson: art for its own sake, separated from the moral life. He is mainly Greek.

For me, with certain rapturous exceptions, literature *is* the moral life. The exceptions occur in lyric poetry, which bursts shadowless like flowers at noon, with the eloquent bliss almost of nature itself, when nature is both benevolent and beautiful. For the rest—well, one discounts stories and novels that are really journalism; but of the stories and novels that mean to be literature, one expects a certain corona of moral purpose: not outright in the grain of the fiction itself, but in the form of a faintly incandescent envelope around it. The tales we care for lastingly are the ones that touch on the redemptive—not, it should be understood, on the guaranteed promise of redemption, and not on goodness, kindness, decency, all the usual virtues. Redemption has almost nothing to do with virtue, especially when the call to virtue is prescriptive or coercive; rather, it is the singular idea that is the opposite of the Greek belief in fate: the idea that insists on the freedom to change one's life.

Redemption means fluidity; the notion that people and things are subject to willed alteration; the sense of possibility, of turning away from, or turning toward; of deliverance; the sense that we act for ourselves rather than are acted upon; the sense that we are responsible, that there is no *deus ex machina* other than the character we have ourselves fashioned; above all, that we can surprise ourselves. Implicit in redemption is amazement, marvelling, suspense—precisely that elation-bringing suspense of the didactic I noted earlier, wherein the next revelation is about to fall. Implicit in redemption is everything against the fated or the static: everything that hates death and harm and elevates the life-giving—if only through terror at its absence.

Now I know how hazardous these last phrases are, how they suggest philistinism, how they lend themselves to a vulgar advocacy of an "affirmative" literature in order to fulfill a moral mandate. I too recoil from all that: the so-called "affirmative" is simple-minded, single-minded, crudely explicit; it belongs either to journalism or to piety or to "uplift." It is the enemy of literature and the friend of coercion. It is, above all, a hater of the freedom inherent in storytelling and in the poetry side of life. But I mean something else: I mean the corona, the luminous envelope—perhaps what Henry James meant when he said "Art is nothing more than the shadow of humanity." I think, for instance, of the literature of *midrash*, of parable, where there is no visible principle or moral imperative. The principle does not enter into, or appear in, the tale; it realizes the tale. To put it another way: the tale is its own interpretation. It is a world that decodes itself.

And that is what the "corona" is: interpretation, implicitness, the nimbus of *meaning* that envelops story. Only someone who has wholly dismissed meaning can boast that the Holocaust and a corncob are, for art, the same. The writers who claim that fiction is self-referential, that what a story is about is the language it is made out of, have snuffed the corona. They willingly sit in the dark, like the strict-constructionist Karaites who, wanting to observe the Sabbath exactly, sat in the lampless black and the fireless cold on the very day that is most meant to resemble paradise. The misuse of the significance of language by writers who most intend to celebrate the comeliness of language is like the misuse of the Sabbath by the fundamentalist Karaites: both annihilate the thing they hope to glorify.

What literature means is meaning.

But having said that, I come to something deeply perilous: and that is imagination. In Hebrew, just as there is *t'shuva*, the energy of creative renewal and turning, so there is the *yetzer ba-ra*, the Evil Impulse—so steeped in the dark brilliance of the visionary that it is said to be the source of the creative faculty. Imagination is more than make-believe, more than the power to invent. It is also the power to penetrate evil, to take on evil, to become evil, and in that guise it is the most frightening human faculty. Whoever writes a story that includes villainy enters into and becomes the villain. Imagination owns above all the facility of becoming: the writer can enter the leg of a mosquito, a sex not her own, a horizon he has never visited, a mind smaller or larger. But also the imagination seeks out the unsayable and the undoable, and says and does them. And still more dangerous: the imagination always has the lust to tear down meaning, to smash interpretation, to wear out the rational, to mock the surprise of redemption, to replace the fluid force of suspense with an image of stasis; to transfix and stun rather than to urge; to spill out, with so much quicksilver wonder, idol after idol. An idol serves no one; it is served. The imagination, like Moloch, can take you nowhere except back to its own maw. And the writers who insist that literature is "about" the language it is made of are offering an idol: literature for its own sake, for its own maw: not for the sake of humanity.

Literature is for the sake of humanity.

My conclusion is strange, and takes place on a darkling plain. Literature, to come into being at all, must call on the imagination; imagination is in fact the flesh and blood of literature; but at the same time imagination is the very force that struggles to snuff the redemptive corona. So a redemptive literature, a literature that interprets and decodes the world, beaten out for the sake of humanity, must wrestle with its own body, with its own flesh and blood, with its own life. Cell battles cell. The corona flickers, brightens, flares, clouds, grows faint. The *yetzer ba-ra*, the Evil Impulse, fills its cheeks with a black wind, hoping to blow out the redemptive corona; but at the last moment steeples of light spurt up from the corona, and the world with its meaning is laid open to our astonished sight.

In that steady interpretive light we can make distinction; we can see that one thing is not interchangeable with another thing; that not everything is the same; that the Holocaust is different, God knows, from a corncob. So we arrive, at last, at the pulse and purpose of literature: to reject the blur of the "universal"; to distinguish one life from another; to illumine diversity; to light

up the least grain of being, to show how it is concretely individual, particular-
ized from any other; to tell, in all the marvel of its singularity, the separate
holiness of the least grain.

Literature is the recognition of the particular.

For that, one needs the corona.

ENDNOTE

1. Richard Kostelanetz, "Young Writers in North America," *The American Pen*, Fall
   1971. Mr. Kostelanetz illustrates what he means by "alternative kinds of coherence," and perhaps also by literacy, in part with the following:

   > Errect, do it, do it again
   > Errect, o take me, have me, let Yourself out
   > Errect, o yes, o yess, yesss i'm Out

EDGAR ALLAN POE

THE IMPORTANCE OF THE SINGLE EFFECT IN A PROSE TALE

*Edgar Allan Poe was one of the first writers on this continent to formu-
late a definition (in 1842) of the short story as a distinct artistic form.
This attempt to define what the story does best was embedded in a lauda-
tory consideration of Nathaniel Hawthorne's tales, and had an international influence on the story's development.*

The tale proper, in our opinion, affords unquestionably the fairest field for the
exercise of the loftiest talent, which can be afforded by the wide domains of
mere prose. Were we bidden to say how the highest genius could be most
advantageously employed for the best display of its own powers, we should
answer, without hesitation—in the composition of a rhymed poem, not to
exceed in length what might be perused in an hour. Within this limit alone can
the highest order of true poetry exist. We need only here say, upon this topic,
that, in almost all classes of composition, the unity of effect or impression is a
point of the greatest importance. It is clear, moreover, that this unity cannot be
thoroughly preserved in productions whose perusal cannot be completed at
one sitting. We may continue the reading of a prose composition, from the very
nature of prose itself, much longer than we can persevere, to any good purpose, in the perusal of a poem. This latter, if truly fulfilling the demands of the
poetic sentiment, induces an exaltation of the soul which cannot be long sustained. All high excitements are necessarily transient. Thus a long poem is a
paradox. And, without unity of impression, the deepest effects cannot be
brought about. Epics were the offspring of an imperfect sense of Art, and their
reign is no more. A poem *too* brief may produce a vivid, but never an intense
or enduring impression. Without a certain continuity of effort—without a certain duration or repetition of purpose—the soul is never deeply moved. There
must be the dropping of the water upon the rock....

Were we called upon, however, to designate that class of composition which, next to such a poem as we have suggested, should best fulfill the demands of high genius—should offer it the most advantageous field of exertion—we should unhesitatingly speak of the prose tale, as Mr. Hawthorne has here exemplified it. We allude to the short prose narrative, requiring from a half-hour to one or two hours in its perusal. The ordinary novel is objectionable, from its length, for reasons already stated in substance. As it cannot be read at one sitting, it deprives itself, of course, of the immense force derivable from *totality*. Worldly interests intervening during the pauses of perusal, modify, annul, or counteract, in a greater or less degree, the impression of the book. But simple cessation in reading would, of itself, be sufficient to destroy the true unity. In the brief tale, however, the author is enabled to carry out the fullness of his intention, be it what it may. During the hour of perusal the soul of the reader is at the writer's control. There are no external or extrinsic influences—resulting from weariness or interruption.

A skillful literary artist has constructed a tale. If wise, he has not fashioned his thoughts to accommodate his incidents; but having conceived, with deliberate care, a certain unique or single *effect* to be wrought out, he then invents such incidents—he then combines such events as may best aid him in establishing this preconceived effect. If his very initial sentence tend not to the outbringing of this effect, then he has failed in his first step. In the whole composition there should be no word written, of which the tendency, direct or indirect, is not to the one pre-established design. And by such means, with such care and skill, a picture is at length painted which leaves in the mind of him who contemplates it with a kindred art, a sense of the fullest satisfaction. The idea of the tale has been presented unblemished, because undisturbed; and this is an end unattainable by the novel. Undue brevity is just as exceptionable here as in the poem; but undue length is yet more to be avoided.

We have said that the tale has a point of superiority even over the poem. In fact, while the *rhythm* of this latter is an essential aid in the development of the poem's highest idea—the idea of the Beautiful—the artificialities of this rhythm are an inseparable art to the development of all points of thought or expression which have their basis in *Truth*. But Truth is often, and in very great degree, the aim of the tale. Some of the finest tales are tales of ratiocination. Thus the field of this species of composition, if not in so elevated a region of the mountain of Mind, is a tableland of far vaster extent than the domain of the mere poem. Its products are never so rich, but infinitely more numerous, and more appreciable by the mass of mankind. The writer of the prose tale, in short, may bring to his theme a vast variety of modes or reflections of thought and expression—(the ratiocinative, for example, the sarcastic, or the humorous) which are not only antagonistical to the nature of the poem, but absolutely forbidden by one of its most peculiar and indispensable adjuncts; we allude, of course, to rhythm. It may be added, here, *par parenthèse*, that the author who aims at the purely beautiful in a prose tale is laboring at a great disadvantage. For Beauty can be better treated in the poem. Not so with terror, or passion, or horror, or a multitude of such other points....

KATHERINE ANNE PORTER

No Plot, My Dear, No Story

*In "No Plot, My Dear, No Story," Katherine Anne Porter ("Mama")
invites the reader into the writer's shop and offers sound advice to the
fledgling scribbler.*

This is a fable, children, of our times. There was a great big little magazine
with four and one half million subscribers, or readers, I forget which; and the
editors sat up nights thinking of new ways to entertain these people who
bought their magazine and made a magnificent argument to convince advertisers that $3,794.36 an inch space-rates was a mere gift at the price. Look at
all the buying-power represented. Look at all the money these subscribers must
have if they can afford to throw it away on a magazine like the one we are
talking about. So the subscribers subscribed and the readers read and the
advertisers bought space and everything went on ring-around-the-rosy like
that for God knows how long. In fact, it is going on right now.

So the editors thought up something beautiful and sent out alarms to celebrated authors and the agents of celebrated authors, asking everybody to think
hard and remember the best story he had ever read, anywhere, anytime, and
tell it over again in his own words, and he would be paid a simply appalling
price for this harmless pastime.

By some mistake a penniless and only semi-celebrated author got on this
list, and as it happened, that was the day the government had threatened to
move in and sell the author's typewriter for taxes overdue, and a dentist had
threatened to sue for a false tooth in the very front of the author's face; and
there was also a grocery bill. So this looked as if Providence had decided to
take a hand in the author's business, and he or she, it doesn't matter, sat down
at once and remembered at least *one* of the most beautiful stories he or she had
ever read anywhere.[1] It was all about three little country women finding a
wounded man in a ditch, giving him cold water to drink out of his own cap,
piling him into their cart and taking him off to a hospital, where the doctors
said they might have saved their trouble for the man was as good as dead.

The little women were just silly enough to be happy anyway that they had found him, and he wasn't going to die by himself in a ditch, at any rate. So they went on to market.

A month later they went back to the hospital, each carrying a wreath to put on the grave of the man they had rescued and found him there still alive in a wheelchair; and they were so overcome with joy they couldn't think, but just dropped on their knees in gratitude that his life was saved; this in spite of the fact that he probably was not going to be of any use to himself or anybody else for a long time if ever.... It was a story about instinctive charity and selfless love. The style was fresh and clear as the living water of their tenderness.

You may say that's not much of a story, but I hope you don't for it would pain me to hear you agree with the editors of that magazine. They sent it back to the author's agent with a merry little note: "No plot, my dear—no *story*. Sorry."

So it looks as if the tax collector will get the author's typewriter, and the dentist the front tooth, and the crows may have the rest; and all because the poor creature was stupid enough to think that a short story needed *first a theme*, and then a point of view, a certain knowledge of human nature and strong feeling about it, and style—that is to say, his own special way of telling a thing that makes it precisely his own and no one else's.... The greater the theme and the better the style, the better the story, you might say.

You might say, and it would be nice to think you would. Especially if you are an author and write short stories. Now listen carefully: except in emergencies, when you are trying to manufacture a quick trick and make some easy money, you don't really need a plot. If you have one, all well and good, if you know what it means and what to do with it. If you are aiming to take up the writing *trade*, you need very different equipment from that which you will need for the *art*, or even just the *profession* of writing. There are all sorts of schools that can teach you exactly how to handle the 197 variations on any one of the 37 basic plots; how to take a parcel of characters you never saw before and muddle them up in some difficulty and get the hero or heroine out again, and dispose of the bad uns; they can teach you the O. Henry twist; the trick of "slanting" your stuff toward this market and that; you will learn what goes over big, what not so big, what doesn't get by at all; and you will learn for yourself, if you stick to the job, *why* all this happens. Then you are all set, maybe. After that you have only to buy a pack of "Add-a-Plot" cards (free ad.) and go ahead. Frankly, I wish you the luck you deserve. You have richly earned it.

But there are other and surer and much more honest ways of making money, and Mama advises you to look about and investigate them before leaping into such a gamble as mercenary authorhood. Any plan to make money is a gamble, but grinding out "slanted" stuff takes a certain knack, a certain willingness to lose all, including honor; you will need a cold heart and a very thick skin and an allowance from your parents while you are getting started toward the big money. You stand to lose your youth, your eyesight, your self-respect, and whatever potentialities you may have had in other directions, and if the worst comes to the worst, remember, nobody promised you anything.... Well, if you are going to throw all that, except the self-respect, into the ash can, you may as well, if you wish to write, be as good a writer as you can, say what you think and feel, add a little something, even if it is the merest fraction of an atom, to the sum of human achievement.

First, have faith in your theme, then get so well acquainted with your characters that they live and grow in your imagination exactly as if you saw them in the flesh; and finally, tell their story with all the truth and tenderness and severity you are capable of; and if you have any character of your own, you will have a style of your own; it grows, as your ideas grow, and as your knowledge of your craft increases.

You will discover after a great while that you are probably a writer. You may even make some money at it.

One word more: I have heard it said, boldly and with complete sincerity by persons who should know better, that the only authors who do not write for the high-paying magazines are those who have not been able to make the grade; that any author who professes to despise or even disapprove of such writing and such magazines is a hypocrite; that he would be too happy to appear in those pages if only he were invited.

To such effrontery I have only one answer, based on experience and certain knowledge. It is simply not true.

ENDNOTE

1. "Living Water" by C. Sergeey-Tzensky *The Dial* July 1939.

KATHERINE ANNE PORTER

REFLECTIONS ON WILLA CATHER

Katherine Anne Porter, an important American short story writer, here expresses her admiration of Willa Cather and her "vein of iron."

I never knew her at all, nor anyone who did know her; do not to this day. When I was a young writer in New York I knew she was there, and sometimes wished that by some charming chance I might meet up with her; but I never did, and it did not occur to me to seek her out. I had never felt that my condition of beginning authorship gave me a natural claim on the attention of writers I admired, such as Henry James and W.B. Yeats. Some proper instinct told me that all of any importance they had to say to me was in their printed pages, mine to use as I could. Still it would have been nice to have seen them, just to remember how they looked. There are three or four great ones, gone now, that I feel, too late, I should not have missed. Willa Cather was one of them.

There exist large numbers of critical estimates of her work, appreciations; perhaps even a memoir or two, giving glimpses of her personal history—I have never read one. She was not, in the popular crutch-word to describe almost any kind of sensation, "exciting"; so far as I know, nobody, not even one of the Freudian school of critics, ever sat up nights with a textbook in one hand and her works in the other, reading between the lines to discover how much sexual autobiography could be mined out of her stories. I remember only one photograph—Steichen's—made in middle life, showing a plain smiling woman, her arms crossed easily over a girl scout sort of white blouse, with a ragged part in her hair. She seemed, as the French say, "well seated" and not very outgoing. Even the earnestly amiable, finely shaped eyes, the left one faintly askew, were in some mysterious way not expressive, lacking as they did altogether that look of strangeness which a strange vision is supposed to give to the eye of any real artist, and very often does. One doesn't have to be a genius absolutely to get this look, it is often quite enough merely to believe one is a genius; and to have had the wild vision only once is enough—the afterlight stays, even if, in such case, it is phosphorescence instead of living fire.

Well, Miss Cather looks awfully like somebody's big sister, or maiden aunt, both of which she was. No genius ever looked less like one, according to the romantic popular view, unless it was her idol, Flaubert, whose photographs could pass easily for those of any paunchy country squire indifferent to his appearance. Like him, none of her genius was in her looks, only in her works. Flaubert was a good son, adoring uncle of a niece, devoted to his friends, contemptuous of the mediocre, obstinate in his preferences, fiercely jealous of his privacy, unyielding to the death in his literary principles and not in the slightest concerned with what was fashionable. No wonder she loved him. She had been rebuffed a little at first, not by his astronomical standards in art—none could be too high for her—but by a certain coldness of heart in him. She soon got over that; it became for her only another facet of his nobility of mind.

Very early she had learned to reverence that indispensable faculty of aspiration of the human mind toward perfection called, in morals and the arts, nobility. She was born to the idea and brought up in it: first in a comfortable farmhouse in Virginia, and later, the eldest of seven children, in a little crowded ranch house in Nebraska. She had, as many American country people did have in those times and places, literate parents and grandparents, soundly educated and deeply read, educated, if not always at schools, always at their own firesides. Two such, her grandmothers, taught her from her infancy. Her sister, Mrs. Auld, in Palo Alto, California, told it like this:

"She mothered us all, took care of us, and there was a lot to do in such a big family. She learned Greek and Latin from our grandmothers before she ever got to go to school. She used to go, after we lived in Red Cloud, to read Latin and Greek with a little old man who kept a general store down the road. In the evenings for entertainment—there was nowhere to go, you know, almost nothing to see or hear—she entertained us, it was good as a theater for us! She told us long stories, some she made up herself, and some were her versions of legends and fairy tales she had read; she taught us Greek mythology this way, Homer, and tales from the Old Testament. We were all story tellers," said her sister, "all of us wanted to be the one to tell the stories, but she was the one who told them. And we loved to listen all of us to her, when maybe we would not have listened to each other."

She was not the first nor the last American writer to be formed in this system of home education; at one time it was the customary education for daughters, many of them never got to school at all or expected to; but they were capable of educating their grandchildren, as this little history shows. To her last day Willa Cather was the true child of her plain-living, provincial farming people, with their aristocratic ways of feeling and thinking; poor, but not poverty-stricken for a moment; rock-based in character, a character shaped in an old school of good manners, good morals, and the unchallenged assumption that classic culture was their birthright; the belief that knowledge of great art and great thought was a good in itself not to be missed for anything; she subscribed to it all with her whole heart, and in herself there was the vein of iron she had inherited from a long line of people who had helped to break wildernesses and to found a new nation in such faiths. When you think of the whole unbelievable history, how did anything like this survive? Yet it did, and this life is one of the proofs.

CONSTANCE AND LEON ROOKE

CONVERSATION WITH RUSSELL BANKS

Constance and Leon Rooke interviewed Russell Banks at his home in Keene, New York, in March 1997.

ROOKE: We hear that you recently climbed the biggest live volcano in the world, Mt. Cotopaxi in Ecuador. How does a decision to embark on an adventure like that connect with the kind of fiction you write? In short, what possessed you?

BANKS: Oh, Lord, what possessed me, indeed. It's a useful metaphor, I suppose. Middle-aged novelist attempts to defy gravity. But not a very original metaphor. I think the case is that in recent years I've acquired the life I always wanted, a life defined and shaped purely by my desire to read and write, and it terrifies me. Be careful, or you might get what you want, et cetera. So climbing high mountains (taking what my brother calls *el viaje estupido*) may simply be my expression of a perverse need to sabotage that satisfaction, to undercut and challenge the lifelong desire that generated it, to test it, discover its limits, and maybe thereby come to know its rewards truly, if there are any. This may be connected to my fiction, insofar as nearly every book I've written has sabotaged the previous book, tested its achievement, defined its limits, and thereby declared its virtues (and vices) forthrightly. Well, not forthrightly. Aslant.

ROOKE: When asked by *Brick* magazine in Toronto what you would be if you were not a writer you said: "Dead." It's such a wonderfully succinct response that I hesitate to ask you to elaborate—but will you?

BANKS: I think I added, "... in a parking lot behind a bar in Lakeland, Florida," or something like that. So it wasn't all that succinct. Anyhow, what I was implying was that story-telling saved my life. In my late teens and early twenties, I was literally on my way to being killed. I drank and fought and ran in front of moving cars. When I started telling stories, I calmed down some. I had run away from my New England hometown at eighteen and ended up in mid

Florida, turbulent, angry, and ignorant, an abandoned boy who'd abandoned what had been left him, like Lee Harvey Oswald or Gary Gilmore or all those other American white boys who end up either killing somebody or themselves in a bar or gas station or book repository. Except that I started telling stories to myself, and then began to attend to the craft of telling stories, to make them more interesting to myself than mere fantasies could be, and before I knew it I was a writer. The discipline of storytelling, of turning my needs over to its needs, saved me from myself, who was a killer.

ROOKE: You were a charter member of the Fiction Collective, responsible for bringing new and innovative work into print. For a decade or so you and poet William Matthews helped to bring along a generation of new writers with your magazine and press, Lillabulero. What impact have that work and your own early experimental fiction had on the sort of writing you are doing now?

BANKS: That early work as editor and collaborator taught me my craft. I paid attention to other people's work in a way that no other activity permitted. Certainly not writing on my own, and not my work as an academic or as a scholar or critic. It was only as an editor, with Matthews, trying to understand what my peers were capable of doing, and as a collaborator, with the Fiction Collective, trying to put the best of my peers' work into the public ear, that I was able to see and hear clearly what it was I both wanted to do myself and wanted not to do.

ROOKE: I'm always interested in the most urgent messages that established writers have for beginners. What do you tell your writing students at Princeton? What do they tell you?

BANKS: Mainly, I try to help them distinguish in a lifelong way between their work and their careers, and show them that they can control the first and not the second, and therefore that the only one worth paying any close attention to is the first. What my students tend to tell me is that I'm different than they, I'm old, I'm a man writing more from memory than desire, which of course makes me think that I'm much more interesting than they are, which brings me back to the first part of the question, since one's work inevitably springs from memory and one's career springs from desire. I could lie and say that my students keep me young, but they don't; they keep me old, which is why I love them and love teaching.

ROOKE: You are married to a superb American poet, Chase Twichell. Are you each other's first reader? Does her poet's eye see things in your work that help you in the process of revision? What can you tell us about the process of revision generally?

BANKS: Fact is, Chase is the best reader of fiction I know, and not because she's a poet. It's because she's honest and she's smart as hell and doesn't really want to write fiction or think she could if she only had the time, like just about every lawyer I've ever met, and it's because being a poet, she can give herself over to the dream of fiction with no critical or professional inhibitions. So she gets very angry when that dream is interrupted by a dopey break in tone or by insecurity or defensiveness or simple incompetence. And she reads so much fiction, she has context. I can't fool her. In life or in art. You absolutely cannot survive as an honest person without someone you cannot fool.

ROOKE: Canadian filmmaker Atom Egoyan has filmed an adaptation from your novel *The Sweet Hereafter*. What can you tell us about that? Is it hard to let go?

BANKS: I've been very, undeservedly, lucky to have someone as gifted and competent as Atom Egoyan make a film from my book. He wrote an extraordinary screenplay adaptation of the novel that reorganized the fictional elements of the novel in cinematic terms, and yet he retained the same moral universe that drives the novel. What more can a fiction writer ask of a film adaptation? It wasn't at all hard to give the novel over to him, after I'd seen his films and come to know him personally. He is in a sense my Ideal Reader: he made the novel his own, and didn't shrink its implications. Visiting the sets, watching the film being made, and finally viewing the finished film—that was like dreaming a dream based on a dream, seeing a triple overlay of what I'd only seen in a dream in the first place. Nabakov says somewhere that what a filmmaker does with a novel is what a novelist does with the world. That's the case with Egoyan, certainly. He did with my novel what I tried to do with my world. No complaints. Same with Paul Schrader's version of *Affliction*, and pretty much for the same reasons.

ROOKE: About thirty years ago a woman said to me, "Why must you writers always write about good-looking people?" I said, "We don't. You must be thinking of the movies." Now along comes "Sarah Cole," the love story about an extremely attractive man and a very unattractive woman. Readers are always asking writers where they get their ideas. Where did you get this one?

BANKS: That old story, "The Frog Prince," only told from the woman's point of view. John Gardner advised retelling the old stories, probably the best of all the advice he gave, and he gave plenty. That was for me the genesis of the story, a sort of formal "what if ...?" I simply plugged into the story the details of the world I happened to live in at the time, and of course reversed the gender dynamic of the story, and wrote it to see not what my story meant, but what the old "original" story meant. It's how we come to know ourselves finally— by figuring out what our old stories really mean. It's amused and pleased me over the years that the readers most sensitive to and intelligent about that story have been women, not men. I think it embarrasses most men.

ROOKE: This is a very risky story. What do you really think of this guy? Or, indeed, of Sarah herself?

BANKS: I don't know what I think about the story or the characters, since I wrote it. People keep re-reading it, so there must be some truth in it that matters, but I honestly don't know what it is. Maybe it helps people know what it is to be human.

CONSTANCE AND LEON ROOKE

CONVERSATION WITH
RICHARD FORD

Constance and Leon Rooke first spoke to Richard Ford about this interview when he was in Rome promoting the Italian edition of his award-winning novel Independence Day. *Later conversations found him in Paris and New York. The interview was finally nailed down in January 1997, when Ford was home again in New Orleans.*

ROOKE: I'm struck by how beautifully the basic ingredients of this story—even the smallest details—are integrated. In many ways, it's an unlikely assembly. We have (1) the Montana setting; (2) the defective stolen car; (3) the monkey and its astonishing fate; (4) the trailer community and the excellent Negro woman with her brain-damaged grandson; (5) the gold mine; (6) the old, disgruntled cabbie; (7) Rock Springs as boomtown with its "B-girls" run by men in pink Cadillacs wearing big hats; (8) the motel; (9) the parking lot and the family car—and, of course, lots more. Which of these ingredients were discovered in the process of writing the story, and which did you have in mind from the moment you entered the story? Was there ever a version that didn't end in the parking lot with that extraordinary set of questions?

FORD: I can't very reliably remember which raw materials came out of my notebook or were on hand when I started the story, and which turned up in the writing. It's usual for me to plan until I can't plan any more and then to rely on providence. I had once been stranded in Rock Springs, Wyoming, in 1980; but nothing remotely similar happened to me as happened to my characters. I seem to remember thinking there was a gold mine outside the town, but I'm not sure now if it was a gold mine or a coal mine. Gold mine certainly seemed more, well, dramatic. Truthfully, once a story's finished the details and particulars seem so permanent as to have all come from the same reliable source, and ultimately to adhere only to the story and not to their more provisional sources in life. Generally, my way of making stories is to collect and use pretty disparate materials—events, random lines, names, occupations, locations—and to forge them into a narrated whole which is plausible. I think that makes my stories rich—makes them innately dramatic at a primary level due to all the unusual things that are put into context—and I think this way of making sense of life is very much like life as we live and negotiate it daily.

As to the last scene, it is in the story almost word-for-word as I wrote it in long-hand in my heatless apartment in SoHo in New York in February 1981. Those questions are, I believe, untouched.

ROOKE: We're told that the car Earl has stolen, the cranberry Mercedes, is owned by an ophthalmologist—one who studies the diseases of the eye. This is the sort of innocent-seeming detail that writers often tuck into a story to alert readers to an issue of importance to the writer. There are many other references to seeing, as well. But where is the blindness, the defective vision, in this story? Is Earl the one who has trouble seeing things as they really are? I certainly do not myself think of him as being by any measure unreliable, but other readers might. Would you?

FORD: I maintain the innocence of my choice of ophthalmologist. I also never thought once about the issue of defective vision—moral or physical—at least not in those terms. I suppose Earl has his limitations as a narrator, though only as do all first-person narrators. Such tellers of stories are always submissive to a reader's larger field of vision, are always to be assessed, are always in some ways not completely reliable. But that lack of total reliability seems a quality they share with humans. Our task as readers and as simple listeners to the stories of others is to find the truth. I hope Earl's life and story reveal a useful truth without sacrificing goodwill the reader might have for him. I like him.

ROOKE: I love him. I love Edna, too. Can you say something about the gold mine? How that relates to dreams, or the American dream, or things that are hidden, or materialism, or easy solutions, or anything at all?

FORD: I certainly chose a gold mine for Rock Springs in the awareness of a gold mine's simple significance as an emblem (even if a slightly absurd emblem) of success and riches. I was moved by both the absurdity and the obviousness. But about the "American Dream," I don't know. I've never been moved by the peculiar "American-ness" of dreams and success. That's pretty much of a cliché to me, and certainly it's conventional wisdom which art should question and seek to redefine or explode or otherwise refurbish. It seems to me every person might dream about a gold mine, in some form or other—somebody in Saskatchewan, maybe. Or Prague.

ROOKE: What resonance do you hope the title, "Rock Springs," will have for the reader?

FORD: I really just called the story "Rock Springs" because that's where it mostly took place. Maybe in some subliminal way I was attracted to the dramatic juxtaposition of a soft, life-giving spring emerging from an adamant and irreducible rock. But I didn't know it at the time; and although those juxtaposed images appeal to me now, I don't know precisely what they have to do with this story. I really just try to use simple images, finally, though I'm willing to invent complex contexts for them within a story.

ROOKE: Each time I read this story I'm riveted by the following small detail: Edna with her bare feet on the dash before she tells the story of the monkey. Later on, the car hidden in the bush, she turns off the parking lights, and turns on the radio, with her naked feet—much like a monkey! Would you care to comment on this?

FORD: No. The monkey is just the monkey. Edna is meant to bear no freight of that sort. It's overtaxing the story to draw connective lines between these two. At least, it is overtaxing the story as far as the author is concerned. The image of Edna putting her feet on the dash is probably something I saw somebody do once, and felt that it portrayed a sort of relaxed, free feeling. I think that when Edna and Earl are first on the road, she feels pretty liberated. She feels good. It's only later that a sense of consequence visits her, and she changes her plans and leaves him.

ROOKE: Earl is a likeable guy, feckless, maybe, but chipper. He wants things to be pleasant and upbeat. What do you like about Earl? How do you think liking Earl and judging him might fit together for readers of the story?

FORD: Earl is a small-time crook, at least in this one instant he is—perhaps defensibly, on behalf of his daughter. My wish is to write a story that provides the reader all the evidence necessary to make a good and sympathetic judgment of Earl and his action—thus, instead and in place of conventional wisdom and morality as rationals for judging Earl. Fiction might well teach us to think for ourselves and to be more exacting and sympathetic in collecting and assessing evidence of our fellow man's character and moral worth.

ROOKE: Has Earl learned anything in the course of this story? There are numerous references here to fresh starts, to starting a new life.

FORD: Earl's learned, of course, about Edna; and he's at least admitted or re-admitted that his intentions don't always comply with his acts. He's learned implicitly what he's willing to do for his daughter and therefore what is the measure of his care and affection for her. And he's, at the end, faced the evidence of his life's being materially different from what he might imagine as the ordinary citizen's life—although in doing this last, I hope he's stressed to the reader's satisfaction how fundamentally similar his life and dilemmas are to most everyone's, even if we're not outside the law ourselves. In doing this I hope the story helps the reader realize what we all have in common with those we might feel we have little in common with.

ROOKE: What are we to make of the fact that the story is told in the past tense?

FORD: I understand the fictive present to be a time later than the narrated events and that this separation in times suggests that all these events have been survived sufficient for Earl to be able to tell them. It's rather smally optimistic in that way.

CONVERSATION WITH THOMAS KING

The Rooke's describe their interview with Thomas King:
This discussion took place on October 31, 1996, in Eden Mills,
Ontario, during the winter's first snowfall. It was supposed to
have happened the previous day, over lunch at the Bookshelf
Cafe in Guelph, surrounded by books, but instead King threw
onto the table an idea for a stage play. So we found ourselves
exploring the possibilities of that project. The author was
expecting to complete the draft of a new novel over the
weekend, and because of this was in exceedingly high spirits.
The play talk carried him higher. Thus, when we met again the
following day, he openly welcomed weighty questions about his
story "The One About Coyote Going West"—a story far less
simple than its comic mode suggests.

ROOKE: Creation myths are of course common to a great many cultures and are often remarkably similar despite vast geographical spread. But do the many—five or six?—North American Indian groups whose mythology has divined Coyote, have the copyright on the Trickster, the prankster, as the figure responsible for their origins?

KING: Actually, in Native creation stories, there are a great many creators. Normally they act in concert rather than as omnipotent individuals (Genesis). Coyote is only one of these creative forces. Sometimes he/she is involved in creation and sometimes he/she is not. But Native people don't have a copyright on this figure. African stories feature a trickster figure, as do stories from other cultures. The figure of the trickster is rather widespread. Our problem in North America is that we don't pay much attention to other cultures and so we assume that the little we do see is unique, when, in fact, it is most likely simply a piece of a larger mosaic.

ROOKE: In some North American Indian mythologies Coyote has existed from the beginning of time into the present day. But is your story the lone one in which "creation," the fixing and refixing of the universe, continues into current time?

KING: Most stories about Coyote are part of what we like to call "oral literature," the idea being that these stories are part of an ancient tradition. But since storytellers borrow shamelessly from other storytellers, we should expect to see story strategies and characters come from the past to the present. And, in fact, this is exactly what happens. There are a number of Coyote stories told by contemporary storytellers that bring Coyote from the past to the present or which combine elements from the traditional past and link them with elements from the present. Jeannette Armstrong does it. Gerald Vizenor does it. Simon Ortiz does it. Leslie Silko does it. Actually, much contemporary Native poetry is full of contemporary visions of Coyote. My story is only one of many.

ROOKE: In several Native mythologies the creator or culture hero is accompanied by a wise grandmother. Just as Coyote can traditionally assume other skins, so can your grandmother become grandfather. The gender switch is so overt that one might concede the author has ulterior purposes. Care to elaborate?

KING: The gender switch in "The One About Coyote Going West" is certainly overt. But it is not simply a nod to the sensibilities of the day. Many traditional stories have Coyote changing gender. In one story, Coyote turns himself into a woman so he can marry the chief of a tribe and have children. All I'm doing is playing off those earlier suggestions. That's the beauty of using Coyote as a character in prose and poetry. The range that Coyote can travel is enormous. Whatever you can imagine, Coyote can do it.

ROOKE: "If I think, I am."

KING: "Sink or swim, I am."

ROOKE: The difficulties some readers will have with the story is in the relationship between Coyote and the grandmother/grandfather.

KING: A good many will see this as a relationship between a mentor and an assistant/student/trainee, etc., and not, as it is, a relationship between equals. Coyote's voice and the grandmother/grandfather's voice are mirrors of each other—that is, the voices are equal parts of one complete voice. The one voice cautions, the other listens or does not listen. The one acts, the other reacts. Things happen that are not necessarily predictable. Yeats, in saying that the centre will not hold, probably was thinking of Coyote and the complexities of voice.

ROOKE: Your Coyote is consistently a she. Is she a she in most Coyote tales?

KING: In most Coyote stories that I know, Coyote is a "he." I don't know if that was always true and I suspect that it was not. Don't forget, most of the traditional stories that we have were collected and translated by non-Natives. A powerful figure such as Coyote would have, almost certainly, been converted into a "he" whether or not he/she was to begin with. But Coyote defies gender and is free to roam the imagination.

ROOKE: Your second sentence tells us Coyote is going west? Any significance in this?

KING: In terms of global politics, no. In non-Native western literature, the idea of going west is linked with the notion of escaping the strictures of civilization and returning to a more basic and elemental existence *and* with the idea of death (the setting sun). In much of literature (and culture), movement through the four directions starts in the east, goes to the south, then to the west, and finally to the north. In many Coyote stories, the storyteller simply says, "Coyote was going west," to indicate that the story proper (of creation) has already started and that Coyote, as a character, is heading out, looking for new adventures, looking for new things to fix.

ROOKE: The first thing your Coyote makes in her making of the world is a big mistake. The mistakes pile up. The beautiful river that runs both ways is remade to run just one way. If the river had continued to run both ways the exploration of North America, I think we can say—the continent's westward expansion—would certainly have been slowed. Looking for Indians, your Coyote finds toaster ovens. If the river had continued to run both ways, would she right away have found Indians?

KING: Who knows what might have been found? The difference between rivers that run in one direction and rivers that run both ways or roses with thorns and roses with no thorns is the question of balance. Piles and piles of good things may look appealing, just as piles and piles of nasty things may look troublesome, but, in fact, either would be disastrous. Coyote knows this, and the give and take, good and bad, silly and serious wanderings of the story are a search, not so much for Indians or toaster ovens, as it is a search for balance. Besides, Europeans didn't find Indians. We found them. It's true. You can trust me on this one.

ROOKE: Coyote spends a long time singing the song (of early history) through her butt-hole. She likes it and keeps on singing. For how long? A thousand years? Until a voice calling for "reform" is heard?

KING: Coyote is of two voices, the voice we hear coming out of her mouth and the voice we hear coming out of her butt-hole. Their "conversation" is neither historical nor reform, though these elements are certainly present. It is, once again, that attempt at balance by disparate parts of a particular character (or a culture). We have these voices within ourselves though we don't normally present them to our friends and colleagues in the same way that Coyote does. To silence either of these voices would be to court disaster.

ROOKE: The ducks, tired of waiting for their creator, create themselves. Are there political, social, and/or religious implications intended with this neat, quick, and wonderfully decisive line?

KING: Ah, the ducks. Yes. And, yes, there are those implications residing in this particular moment. In my mind (at least), standing around waiting for things to happen is problematic. It may feel safe (tell me how to vote, tell me what to do, tell me who to worship), but it also provides scoundrels (of which there are many), opportunities to upset the balance we need to establish and maintain in our lives. The ducks decide to take on that responsibility themselves. Had they waited for Coyote, they would have been ducks that Coyote imagined rather than ducks that they themselves imagined.

ROOKE: As Cynthia Ozick argues in her essay "What Literature Means," they may now improve—change!—their lives.

KING: Right. Because they have taken on that responsibility and that power, they may now, as they do, choose to imagine themselves as Indians. Neat trick. Personally, I would rather imagine myself than allow someone else to do that for me.

ROOKE: Now. A crucial question. Coyote, out to create the world, falls into a hole. A big mistake. More "mistakes" ensue. An Indian cannot be found. Then the dance, duck eggs, and—*voila!*—Indians all over the place. And very unhappy ducks. "Ugg," the ducks say, "What happened to our beautiful feathers, our beautiful feet?" So unhappy are they that they stomp Coyote flat. Yet at the end we have this intriguing passage, so placed as to be seen as the writer's departing message to the reader: "This world is pretty good all by itself. Best to leave it alone. Stop messing around with it?" Why? Because "fixers" are "coyotes"? Are there other explanations?

KING: One way of regarding the world is to see the world as unformed and in need of guidance. The forests are too dense, the mountains are too high, the rivers tend to flood, etc. It is a world in which things need to be fixed and organized. Another way of looking at the world is to see it as perfect in all respects and to conclude that it doesn't need any help and that it is best left alone. Guess which one North American culture most subscribes to. So, yes, on one level all "fixers" are Coyotes. But if we are concerned with balance, I guess Coyotes are what we need, like it or not. In one story I know, Coyote makes a bet with Old Woman and because of the bet death comes into the world. Our first reaction is, what a screw-up. But as Old Woman points out, if the world had continued to be "perfect" and no one died, then no one could be born or the world would soon run out of room. A mistake that we constantly make is to believe that "perfection" is something worth having. Coyote knows better. At the same time, there is a level of "fixing" that transcends balance, a level at which Coyote likes to work. It is this level of gratuitous fixing that concerns the grandfather/grandmother figure. Coyote, of course, like most of us, doesn't always know the difference.

ROOKE: Any parting words?

KING: Coyote speaks. Coyote say, "Hey, you!"

DIANE SCHOEMPERLEN IN CONVERSATION

Constance and Leon Rooke interviewed Diane Schoemperlen in March 1997.

ROOKE: The green satin quilted jacket sequence closing this story is more important than the red plaid shirt section that opens it. Did you think about calling this story "Green Satin Jacket?" and decide that this was a tactical disadvantage?

SCHOEMPERLEN: I always called it "Red Plaid Shirt." It was that first section that set the rest of the story in motion. The shirt had great resonance for me from the beginning and so it never occurred to me to call it anything else. When I began writing the story, I knew where I was starting from but not exactly where I was headed. Or maybe, unconsciously, I wanted the story to build from that point and so did not want to give the ending away. Or maybe this choice of title was a purely practical reason: when I began writing, I like to have the title already decided. It helps me to feel focused. I am especially fond of titles; they come to me by the dozen, often with no accompanying story ideas. For the last twenty years I've kept a file of these titles—it now numbers 519! Of these, about 60 have actually been used for one thing or another, most of them by me but a few by other people too. I'm happy to give one away to anyone who needs one.

ROOKE: Some stories invite an autobiographical reading. Would one find among Diane Schoemperlen's favourite articles of clothing a red plaid shirt, a blue cotton sweatshirt, a yellow evening gown, and so forth? Would you care to talk about your approach to making use of autobiographical material in fiction and where and why one chooses to embroider and invent?

SCHOEMPERLEN: Yes, indeed, there is an autobiographical component to this story. I have owned, at various times, a red plaid shirt, a white embroidered blouse, a black leather jacket, and a green satin quilted jacket which originally belonged to my mother. The other items of clothing in the story are made up (except for the yellow evening gown which was, in fact, green).

I am often asked if my writing is autobiographical and I've never denied it. I suppose the real question here is not which of these clothes I may have really owned, but which of these incidents may have happened to me. Well ... some of them did and some of them didn't and I'm not going to tell you which is which! For the purposes of the story, of course, it doesn't really matter. As the American writer Jayne Anne Phillips said in the disclaimer to her short-story collection *Black Tickets,* "Characters and voices in these stories began in what is real, but became, in fact, dreams. They bear no relation to living persons, except that love or loss lends a reality to what is imagined."

Much as many of my stories begin from an autobiographical point, once I begin to transfigure reality into fiction, my sense of these people and these incidents as "real" becomes merely a shadow behind the story I want to tell. The characters become just that, characters who take on their own fictional lives, and I feel free to use them in whatever ways the story may dictate. As soon as I call them "fiction," they become more real to me than the "reality" from which they may have originally sprung. As the years go by and the pages pile up, even I am not always sure what really happened and what I made up!

In my more recent work I find that I am moving away from the autobiographical. The significance of this will no doubt make itself clear eventually.

ROOKE: Would you care to say something about the "tone" employed in "Red Plaid Shirt"?

SCHOEMPERLEN: "Red Plaid Shirt" is written in the second person. I chose this point of view because it offered some measure of detachment and distance. Early on in the writing, I tried switching to the first person and found it didn't work. The "I" voice sounded whiny and a little petulant. And it was too intimate. I needed the second person to be able to write the more painful sections of the story. I felt the second person offered just the right level of detachment between first and third. And it seemed also to bring with it just the right undercurrent of irony that I was aiming for.

ROOKE: A good many lives intersect with your narrator's in "Red Plaid Shirt," but a large part of the story's power accrues from the contrast drawn—with minimal strokes—between your protagonist's shifting relationships and the more rooted or "settled" one of her mother. Comment?

SCHOEMPERLEN: Although I didn't consciously set up the contrast between the narrator's shifting relationships with men and the more settled one of her parents, in the end I think this contrast does add power to the story as it unfolds. This is an example, I think, of one of the great and marvellous mysteries of fiction—how the material sometimes forms itself in ways that the writer may not originally have intended and yet it may be these largely unconscious themes and images which give the story a broader and deeper resonance than it could have achieved otherwise. These moments when the material comes together on its own and shows you things you didn't know were there, things you didn't know you were looking for, are pure gift. They can only be appreciated afterwards, never predicted or planned in advance.

ROOKE: How important to our understanding of the parents' marriage is that one short paragraph describing the mother's behaviour after the father had given her a coffee percolator rather than the earrings she wanted?

SCHOEMPERLEN: That paragraph is quite central in understanding the parents' relationship. The mother wanted a personal gift. The father thought she would just love a coffee percolator. This is meant to show the lack of communication between them, how little one person may know of another despite having been married for many years. It raises important questions. Why didn't the father know that she wanted something for herself, not something for the house? Why didn't the mother just tell him beforehand what she wanted? (This, I will tell you, is an autobiographical incident. I remember that disastrous Christmas very well!) This incident is mostly significant because, as I wrote, it "was the changing of the guard," the first time the narrator began to understand her mother (representative here of all women) and to see that her father (representative here of all men) was not perfect.

ROOKE: In the indented paragraphs on colour a more playful, poetic personality is heard, and a more zingy style employed. How important to you was it to have these bridges in the story?

SCHOEMPERLEN: Oh, very important. Their function is something akin to that of the chorus in theatre. They were purposely written in a different style and set off from the text to give them more impact. Essentially they are disembodied voices meant to comment wisely and poetically on the events of the story. They are intended to be both evocative and provocative. Colours, both historically and in everyday life, have great power and complicated symbolic overtones. Each article of clothing is of a different colour, allowing me to bring in the whole spectrum of this suggestive symbolism.

ROOKE: The beautifully resonant ending focuses on a green satin jacket that was the mother's when the mother was the same age as the story's central character is. Your narrator wanted to play "dress-up" with this jacket when she was a kid. Now, grown-up, she thinks of it as the perfect apparel to wear when meeting "the new man" in her life who is "too good to be true." When she goes to meet him she deliberately leaves the jacket hanging on a chair. Would you care to discuss that decision?

SCHOEMPERLEN: She first intends to wear the green satin jacket because she thinks it makes her look like a different person, as if she needs to be a different person before someone could possibly love her. She thinks this jacket is just the sort of thing this man will love. She thinks that if she wears it, he'll love her too, and she really wants him to love her because he's not a loser like the others. But then she leaves the jacket behind and goes to meet him naked, figuratively speaking. She doesn't want any more to try and create a particular impression just to please and/or catch a man. She wants him to see her real self. The implication here is that she will stop trying to be what some man wants her to be. She will be transparent. No more pretending. No more playing dress-up in her very own clothes. No more games just to get a man.

MAKEDA SILVERA

AN INTERVIEW WITH DIONNE BRAND: IN THE COMPANY OF MY WORK

The following excerpts are from Makeda Silvera's 1995 interview with Dionne Brand, published by Toronto's Sister Vision Press.

BRAND: ... I have always been influenced by Marxism and feminist ideas. I don't see Marxism and feminism as theories I need to graft onto people, I see them as living things. Analysis is supposed to work, to be living, growing. And I don't mind saying I belonged to the Communist Party—even though certain communist states have fallen and the ideas of communism seem to have come into disrepute, I don't think there's anything different going on in the world since those communist states fell. I don't think people have stopped being exploited. I don't think poverty has suddenly disappeared. I don't think corporate capital is our salvation and answer.

I still think there is a need for a socialist vision. And I honestly do not mind saying that that is what my work is about. I think that is where my work differs—in its explicitness about that idea....

I think that my positioning as a woman in my work—and I can only say this now in retrospect, it's not like I was doing it consciously or anything like that—has always been to question what it means to be female. I don't mean *that* one is female, but what it means to be that. I'm remembering writing about my grandmother's life.

The poems about my grandmother's life are always poems tinged not just with her difficulties but with her departures from male life, departures from where men had a role in defining her. What I saw in her life were those departures—notwithstanding her relationship to men, or to my grandfather—and I rejected that construct that also constructs women. I read in my work my distance from certain constructs of womanhood.

909

And I'm not talking simplistically about asserting myself as a female. I'm talking about distancing myself as a human being from concepts or constructs of womanhood that are laid down....

I'm not talking about super-repressed women, I'm not talking about women who have conformed to the idea of femininity as weak. I'm talking about the strong women I saw all my life on the streets and in my house: they were buried in those constructs of womanhood. When I look back at some of the work I've written I can see myself wanting to get away from that radically, so radically as to not ever allow those constructs to determine even how I wrote a love poem. I can see myself making that distance, not getting buried by those constructs, whether it's the woman super-exploited through her femininity or the woman who doesn't conform to those rules of femininity but nevertheless is caught in them. I also didn't see myself carrying on a dialogue with men about anything.... I've always felt in myself that a woman has another life apart from the male construct of a woman's life, that she has a derisive kind of eye, an eye of cynicism, an eye that notices its own oppression but resists it, not openly, but just by having that other way of seeing the world, a way that doesn't engage itself with the male vision. So possibly, I don't engage men in my work. In a funny way, they don't exist in my work....

SILVERA: ... You came to Canada at seventeen. To do what?

BRAND: To run away. To escape.

SILVERA: Okay, let's talk about that.

BRAND: I left because of the really limited possibilities for me as a girl at that point in Trinidad. It was an ex-colonial country with few possibilities for anybody, truly. Especially girls. What was a girl going to do? Become a wife and a mother? And mother, mostly. And then what? Or do what was called a "commercial course" and not even actually become a typist because there wasn't that much work. And some jobs were based a lot on the nexus of race and class, and I wasn't fair-skinned enough to get a job in a bank, or connected enough....

... When my generation came along—when that whole exodus of people left for Canada or the United States or wherever—the stakes were smaller. They were going away to fill in the cheap labour spots. So it wasn't the élite going off to become doctors, lawyers and so forth. My generation was more of the masses—maybe lower working-class to upper working-class—and we were saving up money and going away. And going away to find a job to send back money.

And I have to say that when I left I was also running from femininity. I can't say I did that consciously, but I know I felt something on my shoulder: the possibility that staying there meant finding some boy to get pregnant for....

SILVERA: Who would you say had the most influence on you?

BRAND: In what sense?

SILVERA: While growing up. Your grandmother?

BRAND: Please, let's not get into my grandmother again. I loved the woman and I want to leave her alone now.

SILVERA: Do you think she had any influence on you becoming a writer at all?

BRAND: Only by being a kind of subject for notice. I loved her a lot and I looked at her a lot—and she did tell stories really well and really nice. But I suppose everybody had some grandmother who did that.

SILVERA: But was she an influence on any other aspect of your life?

BRAND: I think by the time I met her she was a loving kind of woman. That's what I remember, though her children may not remember her that way. That was her gift to me: she encouraged ambition in all the little children because she didn't want us to end up in ways she thought she ended up. So that's what I got from her. She didn't tell us we were going to suffer. She didn't like the idea of us suffering. She told us: if you don't want to suffer, do this. And it was mostly girl grandchildren that she had.

SILVERA: Do you think that when reading your poetry—and particularly when reading your collection of short stories—that readers or reviewers think of it as autobiographical? Have you come across anything like that?

BRAND: Only to the extent that I think people think women writers write that way.

SILVERA: Do you think it's women writers? Do you think that for women of colour writers it's even more? That readers and reviewers usually think it's autobiographical? That women of colour usually write in that way?

BRAND: I don't think that people think that Tony Morrison writes autobiographically. I don't think that they think that Toni Cade Bambara does. No, I don't think so. But we tend to get reviewed sociologically or anthropologically, as ethnography.

SILVERA: So they don't ask you, "Now did this really happen?"

BRAND: Not so far; I haven't gotten that at all. But I think the writing that comes out of feminist presses is prone to being asked these questions.

SILVERA: So why do you think that is?

BRAND: Because of all kinds of levels of misunderstanding about feminist thinking, feminist consciousness, and about the feminist principle of the personal being political and the political being personal. And also, to some extent, because some feminists have reinforced this notion that the personal is political in the narrowest sense.

And what always get popularized about radical movements is the most simplistic vision, and sometimes it happens from within too. So I think that that's the reason for that kind of thinking. I think there are also some feminist writers who really think that every word they write is sacred and that they don't need an editor to say that's not important, and so on. That's just naïveness and youthfulness—it's not feminist consciousness, it's not the personal is political. It's just naïveté....

SILVERA: What I want you to talk about is what you mean by being ruthless about writing and about the space you need.

BRAND: It just means that a long time ago I decided—I was twenty-four—and I decided I would have no children because I thought children took the time and the same energy from the same place as writing. I decided that I loved to write, that it made me happy to write. And I would actually sit in my room at two a.m. and feel really nice about what I wrote. And it was not that I was going to get it published, but I would be in the company of my work—and I don't mean just my individual work, I was also reading. I think writing is also reading: reading massive amounts of all kinds of people through all times is necessary....

The only thing that tore me from writing was political work, was community work, whether I was going to go and join some revolution and live by my convictions. That was the only thing that tore me. So then my whole life was then organized and geared toward how to make room for writing, where to find money or a job for six months and then take off six months to write. I'm lucky....

SILVERA: You get up in the morning. Then do you always write?

BRAND: Yeah, I have to....

Each piece of work is a piece of my life. It is my life's work. The writing is not a career thing. It's a vocation. It can't be put off. If I didn't do this novel this year—if I don't finish it this year or at least make a major dent in it this year, or if I hadn't started it when I did—I would forget it. I wouldn't be able to stretch my thoughts to it any other time. I would miss it completely.

Writing is the outcome of your ruminations, your logic, your reasoning, and it reflects your growth as a person too. So if you don't catch it at the moment it comes, you're going to miss it. It's more than putting out a book, it's the possibility for growth for yourself too. With every piece of writing I can see I moved.

FERNANDO SORRENTINO

BORGES IN CONVERSATION

Translated by Clark M. Zlotchew

The excerpt that follows is from a 1973 interview that Argentine story writer Fernando Sorrentino conducted with Jorge Luis Borges, to be found in full in Seven Conversations with Jorge Luis Borges *(1982).*

SORRENTINO: When and where was Jorge Luis Borges born?

BORGES: I was born on August 24, 1899. I'm very happy about this because I like the nineteenth century very much, although it could be said to the detriment of the nineteenth century that it led to the twentieth century, which I find less admirable....

I believe that a writer should never attempt a contemporary theme nor a very precise topography. Otherwise people are immediately going to find mistakes. Or if they don't find them, they're going to look for them, and if they look for them, they'll find them. That's why I prefer to have my stories take place in somewhat indeterminate places and many years ago. ... The other day I came upon a young fellow who told me he was going to write a novel about a café called "El Socorrito," at the corner of Juncal and Esmeralda: a contemporary novel. I told him not to say the café was "El Socorrito" and not to say the time is the present, because if he did someone was going to tell him, "The people in that café don't talk that way" or, "The atmosphere is phoney." So I think a certain distance in time and space is appropriate. Besides, I believe that the idea that literature should treat contemporary themes is relatively new. If I'm not mistaken, the *Iliad* was probably written two or three centuries after the fall of Troy. I think that freedom of imagination demands that we search for subjects which are distant in time and space, or if not, on other planets, the way those who write science-fiction are doing right now. Otherwise, we are somewhat tied down by reality, and literature already seems too much like journalism.

SORRENTINO: Do you mean you don't believe in psychological literature somehow?

BORGES: Yes, of course I believe in psychological literature, and I think that all literature is fundamentally psychological. The acts performed by a character are facets of or ways of describing that character.

ELEANOR WACHTEL

An Interview with Cynthia Ozick

Eleanor Wachtel's "An Interview with Cynthia Ozick" is excerpted from Writers and Company (1996), and was originally conducted by Wachtel on CBC Stereo's literary arts program "Writers and Company."

WACHTEL: You're a writer who believes that ideas are emotions. What do you mean by that?

OZICK: Oh yes. That's a principle that I certainly don't want to relax. Literary critics tend to make a distinction between psychological realism and what they call the literature of ideas, but it strikes me that nothing is more participatory, more allied to psychological realism, than ideas. Ideas make your heart beat; ideas turn your stomach upside down; ideas are the most emotional stimuli there are.

The world may be divided between writers who believe in experience as stimulus and writers for whom ideas are the stimulus. In other words, do you start with a character, and the event is your germ, to use the Jamesian phrase: is your germ an experience or is your germ an idea? Very often for me the germ is an idea, and the idea creates the character, and the character and the idea are fused—they cannot be pried apart. The psychological and the idea are entwined. But then you may say, well, which comes first? For me, the idea comes first. There's nothing more emotional than certain notions....

WACHTEL: You have written a novella, a book called *The Shawl*, about a Holocaust survivor who lives in a perpetual and wretched state of mourning, dreaming of her lost daughter, writing letters to her, imagining the life her daughter might have had, had she survived, and rejecting any attempts to live a life now. I've heard that this is a book you're not happy with, even though it's a very powerful, strong book. Why are you no longer comfortable with it?

OZICK: I suppose I was not comfortable with it even before I wrote it, during, and certainly after. The reason is that I did undertake to turn this event, this cataclysm, this great destruction, into a lyrical piece of writing, into a poetic artifact. I turned it into fiction and at least an attempt at making art, and it seems to me I did it because I couldn't help myself; it was done to me, so to speak. That doesn't mean that I approve of it, because I believe that if we spent five hundred, a thousand years simply ploughing through the documents of the Holocaust, there still wouldn't be enough time to learn in every detail what happened.

I don't believe that the Holocaust was a mysterious event. I believe that it's an event comprised of known and knowable data, and these data are in a thousand, two thousand, a million books. These books are growing generation by generation, decade by decade, and it seems to me that our responsibility is to pay attention to the documents and not to indulge in myth-making. I believe that's what I did, in a sense, in *The Shawl*; I approached the mythopoetic. I also believe that it is becoming dangerous to write Holocaust fiction. When we are surrounded by people of depraved imagination who say that the data are false, that what happened never happened, that what happened is in fact fiction, and we ourselves then participate in making these events into fiction, in some way we become complicit in that depravity.

ALICE WALKER

The Same River Twice: Honouring the Difficult

In saying "let art help us," Alice Walker is stepping onto the writer's path established also in Cynthia Ozick's "Innovation and Redemption."

I belong to a people so wounded by betrayal, so hurt by misplacing their trust, that to offer us a gift of love is often to risk one's life, certainly one's name and reputation. I do not mean only the Africans, sold and bought, and bought and sold again; or the Indians, who joyfully fed those who, when strong, gleefully starved them out. I speak as well of the shadowy European ancestry, resentfully denied, except that one cannot forget the thatched one-room hovels of old Europe, put to the torch by those who grabbed the land; and the grief of the starving, ashen ancestor, forced to seek his or her lonely fortune in a land that seemed to demand ruthlessness if one intended to survive.

I belong to a people, heart and mind, who do not trust mirrors. Not those, in any case, in which we ourselves appear. The empty mirror, the one that reflects noses and hair unlike our own, and a prosperity and harmony we may never have known, gives us peace. Our shame is deep. For shame is the result of soul injury. Mirrors, however, are sacred, not only because they permit us to witness the body we are fortunate this time around to be in, but because they permit us to ascertain the condition of the eternal that rests behind the body, the soul. As an ancient Japanese proverb states: when the mirror is dim, the soul is not pure.

Art is the mirror, perhaps the only one, in which we can see our true collective face. We must honour its sacred function. We must let art help us.

EUDORA WELTY

IS PHOENIX JACKSON'S GRANDSON REALLY DEAD?

Eudora Welty discusses here a frequent misreading (as she—and we—would see it) of her story "A Worn Path." The essay is from her 1977 book, The Eye of the Story.

A story writer is more than happy to be read by students; the fact that these serious readers think and feel something in response to his work he finds life-giving. At the same time he may not always be able to reply to their specific questions in kind. I wondered if it might clarify something, for both the questioners and myself, if I set down a general reply to the question that comes to me most often in the mail, from both students and their teachers, after some classroom discussion. The unrivaled favorite is this: "Is Phoenix Jackson's grandson really *dead*?"

It refers to a short story I wrote years ago called "A Worn Path," which tells of a day's journey an old woman makes on foot from deep in the country into town and into a doctor's office on behalf of her little grandson; he is at home, periodically ill, and periodically she comes for his medicine; they give it to her as usual, she receives it and starts the journey back.

I had not meant to mystify readers by withholding any fact; it is not a writer's business to tease. The story is told through Phoenix's mind as she undertakes her errand. As the author at one with the character as I tell it, I must assume that the boy is alive. As the reader, you are free to think as you like, of course: The story invites you to believe that no matter what happens, Phoenix for as long as she is able to walk and can hold to her purpose will make her journey. The *possibility* that she would keep on even if he were dead is there in her devotion and its single-minded, single-track errand. Certainly the *artistic* truth, which should be good enough for the fact, lies in Phoenix's own answer to that question. When the nurse asks, "He isn't dead, is he?" she speaks for herself: "He still the same. He going to last."

The grandchild is the incentive. But it is the journey, the going of the errand, that is the story, and the question is not whether the grandchild is in reality alive or dead. It doesn't affect the outcome of the story or its meaning from start to finish. But it is not the question itself that has struck me as much as the idea, almost without exception implied in the asking, that for Phoenix's grandson to be dead would somehow make the story "better."

It's *all right*, I want to say to the students who write to me, for things to be what they appear to be, and for words to mean what they say. It's all right, too, for words and appearances to mean more than one thing—ambiguity is a fact of life. A fiction writer's responsibility covers not only what he presents as the facts of a given story but what he chooses to stir up as their implications; in the end, these implications, too, become facts, in the larger, fictional sense. But it is not all right, not in good faith, for things *not* to mean what they say.

The grandson's plight was real and it made the truth of the story, which is the story of an errand of love carried out. If the child no longer lived, the truth would persist in the "wornness" of the path. But his being dead can't increase the truth of the story, can't affect it one way or the other. I think I signal this, because the end of the story has been reached before old Phoenix gets home again: she simply starts back. To the question "Is the grandson really dead?" I could reply that it doesn't make any difference. I could also say that I did not make him up in order to let him play a trick on Phoenix. But my best answer would be: "*Phoenix* is alive."

The origin of a story is sometimes a trustworthy clue to the author—or can provide him with the clue—to its key image; maybe in this case it will do the same for the reader. One day I saw a solitary old woman like Phoenix. She was walking; I saw her, at middle distance, in a winter country landscape, and watched her slowly make her way across my line of vision. That sight of her made me write the story. I invented an errand for her, but that only seemed a living part of the figure she was herself: What errand other than for someone else could be making her go? And her going was the first thing, her persisting in her landscape was the real thing, and the first and the real were what I wanted and worked to keep. I brought her up close enough, by imagination, to describe her face, make her present to the eyes, but the full-length figure moving across the winter fields was the indelible one and the image to keep, and the perspective extending into the vanishing distance the true one to hold in mind.

I invented for my character, as I wrote, some passing adventures—some dreams and harassments and a small triumph or two, some jolts to her pride, some flights of fancy to console her, one or two encounters to scare her, a moment that gave her cause to feel ashamed, a moment to dance and preen—for it had to be a *journey*, and all these things belonged to that, parts of life's uncertainty.

A narrative line is in its deeper sense, of course, the tracing out of a meaning, and the real continuity of a story lies in this probing forward. The real dramatic force of a story depends on the strength of the emotion that has set it going. The emotional value is the measure of the reach of the story. What gives any such content to "A Worn Path" is not its circumstances but its *subject*: the deep-grained habit of love.

What I hoped would come clear was that in the whole surround of this story, the world it threads through, the only certain thing at all is the worn path. The habit of love cuts through confusion and stumbles or contrives its way out of difficulty, it remembers the way even when it forgets, for a dumbfounded moment, its reason for being. The path is the thing that matters.

Her victory—old Phoenix's—is when she sees the diploma in the doctor's office, when she finds "nailed up on the wall the document that had been stamped with the gold seal and framed in the gold frame, which matched the dream that was hung up in her head." The return with the medicine is just a matter of retracing her own footsteps. It is the part of the journey, and of the story, that can now go without saying.

In the matter of function, old Phoenix's way might even do as a sort of parallel to your way of work if you are a writer of stories. The way to get there is the all-important, all-absorbing problem, and this problem is your reason for undertaking the story. Your only guide, too, is your sureness about your subject, about what this subject is. Like Phoenix, you work all your life to find your way, through all the obstructions and the false appearances and the upsets you may have brought on yourself, to reach a meaning—using inventions of your imagination, perhaps helped out by your dreams and bits of good luck. And finally too, like Phoenix, you have to assume that what you are working in aid of is life, not death.

But you would make the trip anyway—wouldn't you—just on hope.

PART III

CASEBOOKS

Casebook 1:
Anton Chekhov and
Raymond Carver

In a letter to Gorky, Chekhov gave this advice: "If I write, 'A man sat down on the grass,' it is understandable because it is clear and doesn't require a second reading. But it would be hard to follow and brain-taxing were I to write, 'A tall, narrow-chested, red-bearded man of medium height sat down noiselessly, looking around timidly and in fright, on a patch of green grass that had been trampled by pedestrians.'" Raymond Carver was one among many authors who took to heart Chekhov's advice: "work on your sentences. You must, you know. That's what makes art."

In this casebook, another wizard of the carefully honed sentence, Vladimir Nabokov, offers exacting commentary on one of the world's most celebrated stories: Chekhov's "The Lady with the Little Dog." Also included are penetrating observations on the genius of Chekhov written by a number of well-known writers on the occasion of the Ecco Press publication of a fourteen-volume edition of Chekhov's stories and letters.

The painter Konstantine Korovin is here, as well, with a charming, insightful portrait of Chekhov as a young man, in which we hear Chekhov cheerfully remarking, "I have no ideology and no convictions." Carver often stated the affinity he felt with the Russian master. Nowhere is that affinity better demonstrated that in Carver's story of Chekhov's final hours, "Errand," which originated in Carver's reading of Henri Troyat's biography of Chekhov. The dialogue included in "Errand" is taken from the Troyat biography, but the vivid and marvellously interior rendering of the scene is pure Carver—and pure Chekhov. The story won first prize in the 1990 O. Henry Prize Awards.

In "On Writing," Carver describes the "artistic delight" that he seeks in fiction, both as reader and as writer. The casebook concludes with Michael Schumacher's 1987 interview with Carver.

VLADIMIR NABOKOV

A Reading of Chekhov's
"The Lady with the Little Dog"

Chekhov comes into the story "The Lady with the Little Dog" without knocking. There is no dilly-dallying. The very first paragraph reveals the main character, the young fair-haired lady followed by her white Spitz dog on the waterfront of a Crimean resort, Yalta, on the Black Sea. And immediately after, the male character Gurov appears. His wife, whom he has left with the children in Moscow, is vividly depicted: her solid frame, her thick black eyebrows, and the way she has of calling herself "a woman who thinks." One notes the magic of the trifles the author collects—the wife's manner of dropping a certain mute letter in spelling and her calling her husband by the longest and fullest form of his name, both traits in combination with the impressive dignity of her beetle-browed face and rigid poise forming exactly the necessary impression. A hard woman with the strong feminist and social ideas of her time, but one whom her husband finds in his heart of hearts to be narrow, dull-minded, and devoid of grace. The natural transition is to Gurov's constant unfaithfulness to her, to his general attitude toward women—"that inferior race" is what he calls them, but without that inferior race he could not exist. It is hinted that these Russian romances were not altogether as light-winged as in the Paris of Maupassant. Complications and problems are unavoidable with those decent hesitating people of Moscow who are slow heavy starters but plunge into tedious difficulties when once they start going.

Then with the same neat and direct method of attack, with the bridging formula "and so ..." (or perhaps still better rendered in English by that "Now" which begins a new paragraph in straightforward fairy tales), we slide back to the lady with the dog. Everything about her, even the way her hair was done, told him that she was bored. The spirit of adventure—though he realized perfectly well that his attitude toward a lone woman in a fashionable sea town was based on vulgar stories, generally false—this spirit of adventure prompts him to call the little dog, which thus becomes a link between her and him. They are both in a public restaurant.

> He beckoned invitingly to the Spitz, and when the dog approached him, shook his finger at it. The Spitz growled; Gurov threatened it again.
> The lady glanced at him and at once dropped her eyes.
> "He doesn't bite," she said and blushed.

"May I give him a bone?" he asked; and when she nodded he inquired affably, "Have you been in Yalta long?"

"About five days."

They talk. The author has hinted already that Gurov was witty in the company of women; and instead of having the reader take it for granted (you know the old method of describing the talk as "brilliant" but giving no samples of the conversation), Chekhov makes him joke in a really attractive, winning way. "Bored, are you? An average citizen lives in ... (here Chekhov lists the names of beautifully chosen, super-provincial towns) and is not bored, but when he arrives here on his vacation it is all boredom and dust. One could think he came from Granada" (a name particularly appealing to the Russian imagination). The rest of their talk, for which this sidelight is richly sufficient, is conveyed indirectly. Now comes a first glimpse of Chekhov's own system of suggesting atmosphere by the most concise details of nature, "the sea was of a warm lilac hue with a golden path for the moon"; whoever has lived in Yalta knows how exactly this conveys the impression of a summer evening there. This first movement of the story ends with Gurov alone in his hotel room thinking of her as he goes to sleep and imagining her delicate weak-looking neck and her pretty gray eyes. It is to be noted that only now, through the medium of the hero's imagination, does Chekhov give a visible and definite form to the lady, features that fit perfectly with her listless manner and expression of boredom already known to us.

> Getting into bed he recalled that she had been a schoolgirl only recently, doing lessons like his own daughter; he thought how much timidity and angularity there was still in her laugh and her manner of talking with a stranger. It must have been the first time in her life that she was alone in a setting in which she was followed, looked at, and spoken to for one secret purpose alone, which she could hardly fail to guess. He thought of her slim, delicate throat, her lovely gray eyes.
>
> "There's something pathetic about her, though," he thought, and dropped off.

The next movement (each of the four diminutive chapters or movements of which the story is composed is not more than four or five pages long), the next movement starts a week later with Gurov going to the pavilion and bringing the lady iced lemonade on a hot windy day, with the dust flying; and then in the evening when the sirocco subsides, they go on the pier to watch the incoming steamer. "The lady lost her lorgnette in the crowd," Chekhov notes shortly, and this being so casually worded, without any direct influence on the story—just a passing statement—somehow fits in with that helpless pathos already alluded to.

Then in her hotel room her awkwardness and tender angularity are delicately conveyed. They have become lovers. She was now sitting with her long hair hanging down on both sides of her face in the dejected pose of a sinner in some old picture. There was a watermelon on the table. Gurov cut himself a piece and began to eat unhurriedly. This realistic touch is again a typical Chekhov device.

She tells him about her existence in the remote town she comes from and Gurov is slightly bored by her naiveté, confusion and tears. It is only now that we learn her husband's name: von Dideritz—probably of German descent.

They roam about Yalta in the early morning mist.

> At Oreanda they sat on a bench not far from the church, looked down at the sea, and were silent. Yalta was barely visible through the morning mist; white clouds rested motionlessly on the mountaintops. The leaves did not stir on the trees, the crickets chirped, and the monotonous muffled sound of the sea that rose from below spoke of the peace, the eternal sleep awaiting us. So it rumbled below when there was no Yalta, no Oreanda here; so it rumbles now, and it will rumble as indifferently and hollowly when we are no more. ... Sitting beside a young woman who in the dawn seemed so lovely, Gurov, soothed and spellbound by these magical surroundings—the sea, the mountains, the clouds, the wide sky—thought how everything is really beautiful in this world when one reflects: everything except what we think or do ourselves when we forget the higher aims of life and our own human dignity.
>
> A man strolled up to them—probably a watchman—looked at them and walked away. And this detail, too, seemed so mysterious and beautiful. They saw a steamer arrive from Feodosia, its lights extinguished in the glow of dawn.
>
> "There is dew on the grass," said Anna Sergeievna, after a silence.
>
> "Yes, it's time to go home."

Then several days pass and then she has to bo back to her home town.

"Time for me, too, to go North," thought Gurov as he returned after seeing her off." And there the chapter ends.

The third movement plunges us straight into Gurov's life in Moscow. The richness of a gay Russian winter, his family affairs, the dinners at clubs and restaurants, all this is swiftly and vividly suggested. Then a page is devoted to a queer thing that has happened to him: he cannot forget the lady with the little dog. He has many friends, but the curious longing he has for talking about his adventure finds no outlet. When he happens to speak in a very general way of love and women, nobody guesses what he means, and only his wife moves her dark eyebrows and says: "Stop that fatuous posing; it does not suit you."

And now comes what in Chekhov's quiet stories may be called the climax. There is something that your average citizen calls romance and something he

calls prose—though both are the meat of poetry for the artist. Such a contract
has already been hinted at by the slice of watermelon which Gurov crunched in
a Yalta hotel room at a most romantic moment, sitting heavily and munching
away. This contract is beautifully followed up when at last Gurov blurts out to
a friend late at night as they come out of the club: If you knew what a
delightful woman I met in Yalta! His friend, a bureaucratic civil servant, got
into his sleigh, the horses moved, but suddenly he turned and called back to
Gurov. Yes? asked Gurov, evidently expecting some reaction to what he had
just mentioned. By the way, said the man, you were quite right. That fish at the
club was decidedly smelly.

This is a natural transition to the description of Gurov's new mood, his
feeling that he lives among savages where cards and food are life. His family,
his bank, the whole trend of his existence, everything seems futile, dull, and
senseless. About Christmas he tells his wife he is going on a business trip to St.
Petersburg, instead of which he travels to the remote Volga town where the
lady lives.

Critics of Chekhov in the good old days when the mania for the civic
problem flourished in Russia were incensed with his way of describing what
they considered to be trivial unnecessary matters instead of thoroughly examining and solving the problems of bourgeois marriage. For as soon as Gurov
arrives in the early hours to that town and takes the best room at the local
hotel, Chekhov, instead of describing his mood or intensifying his difficult
moral position, gives what is artistic in the highest sense of the word: he notes
the gray carpet, made of military cloth, and the inkstand, also gray with dust,
with a horseman whose hand waves a hat and whose head is gone. That is all:
it is nothing but it is everything in authentic literature. A feature in the same
line is the phonetic transformation which the hotel porter imposes on the
German name von Dideritz. Having learned the address Gurov goes there and
looks at the house. Opposite was a long gray fence with nails sticking out. An
unescapable fence, Gurov says to himself, and here we get the concluding note
in the rhythm of drabness and grayness already suggested by the carpet, the
inkstand, the illiterate accent of the porter. The unexpected little turns and the
lightness of the touches are what places Chekhov, above all Russian writers of
fiction, on the level of Gogol and Tolstoy.

Presently he saw an old servant coming out with the familiar little white
dog. He wanted to call it (by a kind of conditional reflex), but suddenly his
heart began beating fast and in his excitement he could not remember the dog's
name—another delightful touch. Later on he decides to go to the local theatre,
where for the first time the operetta The Geisha is being given. In sixty words
Chekhov paints a complete picture of a provincial theatre, not forgetting the
town-governor who modestly hid in his box behind a plush curtain so that
only his hands were visible. Then the lady appeared. And he realized quite

clearly that now in the whole world there was none nearer and dearer and more important to him than this slight woman, lost in a small-town crowd, a woman perfectly unremarkable, with a vulgar lorgnette in her hand. He saw her husband and remembered her qualifying him as a flunkey—he distinctly resembled one.

A remarkably fine scene follows when Gurov manages to talk to her, and then their mad swift walk up all kinds of staircases and corridors, and down again, and up again, amid people in the various uniforms of provincial officials. Neither does Chekhov forget "two schoolboys who smoked on the stairs and looked down at him and her."

> "You must leave," Anna Sergeievna went on in a whisper. "Do you hear, Dmitri Dmitrich? I will come and see you in Moscow. I have never been happy; I am unhappy now, and I never, never shall be happy, never! So don't make me suffer still more! I swear I'll come to Moscow. But now let us part. My dear, good, precious one, let us part!"
>
> She pressed his hand and walked rapidly downstairs, turning to look round at him, and from her eyes he could see that she really was unhappy. Gurov stood for a while, listening, then when all grew quiet, he found his coat and left the theatre.

The fourth and last little chapter gives the atmosphere of their secret meetings in Moscow. As soon as she would arrive she used to send a red-capped messenger to Gurov. One day he was on his way to her and his daughter was with him. She was going to school, in the same direction as he. Big damp snowflakes were slowly coming down.

The thermometer, Gurov was saying to his daughter, shows a few degrees above freezing point (actually 37° above, Fahrenheit), but nevertheless snow is falling. The explanation is that this warmth applies only to the surface of the earth, while in the higher layers of the atmosphere the temperature is quite different.

And as he spoke and walked, he kept thinking that not a soul knew or would ever know about these secret meetings.

What puzzled him was that all the false part of his life, his bank, his club, his conversations, his social obligations—all this happened openly, while the real and interesting part was hidden.

> He had two lives, an open one, seen and known by all who needed to know of it, full of conventional truth and conventional falsehood, exactly like the lives of his friends and acquaintances; and another life that went on in secret. And through some strange, perhaps accidental, combination of circumstances, everything that was of interest and importance to him, everything that was essential to him, everything about which he felt sincerely and did not

deceive himself, everything that constituted the core of his life, was going on concealed from others; while all that was false, the shell in which he hid to cover the truth—his work at the bank for instance, his discussions at the club, his references to the "inferior race," his appearances at anniversary celebrations with his wife—all that went on in the open. Judging others by himself, he did not believe what he saw, and always fancied that every man led his real, most interesting life under cover of secrecy as under cover of night. The personal life of every individual is based on secrecy, and perhaps it is partly for that reason that civilized man is so nervously anxious that personal privacy should be respected.

The final scene is full of that pathos which has been suggested in the very beginning. They meet, she sobs, they feel that they are the closest of couples, the tenderest of friends, and he sees that his hair is getting a little gray and knows that only death will end their love.

> The shoulders on which his hands rested were warm and quivering. He felt compassion for this life, still so warm and lovely, but probably already about to begin to fade and wither like his own. Why did she love him so much? He always seemed to women different from what he was, and they loved in him not himself, but the man whom their imagination had created and whom they had been eagerly seeking all their lives; and afterwards, when they saw their mistake, they loved him nevertheless. And not one of them had been happy with him. In the past he had met women, come together with them, parted from them, but he had never once loved; it was anything you please, but not love. And only now when his head was gray he had fallen in love, really, truly—for the first time in his life.

They talk, they discuss their position, how to get rid of the necessity of this sordid secrecy, how to be together always. They find no solution and in the typical Chekhov way the tale fades out with no definite full-stop but with the natural motion of life.

> And it seemed as though in a little while the solution would be found, and then a new and glorious life would begin; and it was clear to both of them that the end was still far off, and that what was to be most complicated and difficult for them was only just beginning.

All the traditional rules of story telling have been broken in this wonderful short story of twenty pages or so. There is no problem, no regular climax, no point at the end. And it is one of the greatest stories ever written.

THE ECCO PRESS HOMAGES
TO CHEKHOV

HAROLD BRODKEY

Chekhov is a supreme artist. Maybe in our poor, mad, dumb, ambitious country this cannot be said. Instead, it can be announced that Chekhov is soulful and sad and deeply human and wise. What nonsense: all great artists are wise. All great artists are all those things he is said to be. Modern art, perhaps, should be measured against his accomplishment; we perhaps should read only him.

And he is a great thinker. I offer one example: in him the nineteenth century discovery of the melodramatic nature of life (in an industrial society) is brought forward from Baudelairean spleen (the aesthetic of the bed of burning pitch) to a knowledge of social reality and to a patience and with in regard to that reality such that we ought, indeed, to be instructed by it.

Chekhov is not difficult or particularly gloomy, but it is true that he is utterly disruptive because he is so masterly. Consider his powers of description: night, day, horses, men, buildings, smiling women all are more brilliantly present in him than in Tolstoy.

And from Chekhov flow the most interesting twentieth century notions of what a dramatic action is. The balance in his work between melodramatic reality and contemplative truth is so profound that this balance is both a depth and an elevation.

The excellence of his judgment echoes in the justness of the proportions and wording and pace of his sentences and in his power to convey meaning in that realm just beyond definition which is said to be what the music of poetry is. He has conferred more meaning on us than any other artist of the century. He is the founding master and tutelary spirit of democratic realism.

CYNTHIA OZICK

"Chekhovian." It's clear that this adjective had to be invented for the new voice Chekhov's genius breathed into the world—elusive, inconclusive, flickering; nuanced through an underlying disquiet, though never morbid or disgruntled; unerringly intuitive, catching out of the air vibrations, glittering motes, faint turnings of the heart, tendrils thinner than hairs, drift. But Chekhov's art is more than merely Chekhovian. It is dedicated to explicit and definitive portraiture and the muscular trajectory of whole lives. Each story, however, allusive or broken-off, is nevertheless exhaustive—like the curve of a shard that implies not simply the form of the pitcher entire, but also the thirsts of its shattered civilization.

And yet it is an odd misdirection that we have come to think of Chekhov mainly as a writer of hints and significant fragments, when so much of his expression is highly colored and abundant, declaratively open, bold, even noisy. He is not reticent, and his people are often charged with conviction, sometimes ludicrously, sometimes with the serious nobility of Chekhov himself. But even when his characters strike us as unwholesome, or exasperating, or enervated, or only perverse (especially then), we feel Chekhov's patience, his clarity, his meticulous humanity; there isn't a grain of malevolence or spite. Chekhov is, for his own remote generation and for our needy time even more, quintessentially a writer who has flung his soul to the side of pity, and sees into the holiness and immaculate fragility of the human spirit. Perhaps this is why we know that when we are with Chekhov, we are with a poet of latency. He is an interpreter of the inner life, even when his characters appear to be cut off from inwardness. At the same time he is an artist of solidity and precision, as much a master of the observed as he is of the unobserved.

SUSAN SONTAG

Chekhov is one of the few indispensable writers. One cannot seriously follow both Dostoyevsky and Tolstoy (as one can't be both a Platonist and an Aristotelian), but one must have Chekhov: his swiftness as a writer, his perfect moral pitch, his freedom from all forms of demagoguery provide essential solace, pleasure, inspiration. With Chekhov I gladly forgo the excesses that make some writers indispensable for me—spiritual odyssey, intellectual extravaganza, formal playfulness. For the most part working in a comparatively young literary form generally conceived as a minor effort, and within the minor, modern emotional register, that of irony and melancholy, he irradiated modest conventions with a redemptive sanity, truthfulness, and tact. In these stories there is no hysteria or compensatory solipsism of distress, no disrespect for the sensual, no improving judgments, no detachment. Chekhov's stories, which deluge us with feeling, make feeling more intelligent; more magnanimous. He is an artist of our moral maturity.

Although Chekhov did not write about himself (in a letter he mentions his "autobiographophobia"), his stories seem to mirror unaffectedly their author's soul, as they appeal directly to the reader's. I revere the truly good human being disclosed in his letters, and find exemplary his defense of the rights of the individual—"it's odd," he observed, "how people fear freedom"—and of the rights of literature, against even the best-intentioned claims of politicizers and moralists. In another letter Chekhov wrote: "My holy of holies is the human body, health, intelligence, talent, inspiration, love and the most absolute freedom imaginable, freedom from violence and lies, no matter what form the latter two take." He is not only a great writer but, even rarer, a liberating one; and everything finally depends on one's relation to freedom.

WILLIAM TREVOR

Of all literary forms, the short story belongs most unequivocally to the twentieth century. It is true that there are antique examples of the modern art ("Susanna and the Elders" is sometimes cited) but they are rare. It is also true that the told stories of the distant past, leading listeners into a realm of marvels and drama, have a contemporary counterpart. Somerset Maugham, who performed brilliantly in bringing that particular mode fashionably up to date, asserted that the test of a good short story was that it could be endlessly retold as an after-dinner yarn. When he came to read Chekhov he was taken aback—and not impressed. Because Chekhov it was who had already turned these antique values inside out: just as the genius of Giotto and the obsessional strivings of Uccello had by chance scattered the seeds of the Italian Renaissance, so Chekhov noticed that there was something the novel could not do: inspired, he fashioned the art of the glimpse. The blustering nineteenth-century novel had seized upon the heroics and plot patterns that for so long had distinguished the fiction of the European myths; after Chekhov, the short story at its best reflected a view of life in which the mundane and what appeared to be the inconsequential never ceased to matter. Truth, like a hard beam of light, was the new storyteller's favorite instrument, shredding the very skin of the characters it scrutinized. "Lice consume the grass," Chekhov wrote, "rust consumes the iron, and lying the soul." And again: "Art ... does not tolerate a lie. You can tell lies in love, politics, medicine ... but you cannot practise deception in art."

In story after story, explosions of truth make his point for him. Escapism has no place; all human sentiment, however humble its manifestation, is worthy of investigation. With subtlety and with passion he wrote what he believed. His voice is unique; his art timeless.

KONSTANTIN KOROVIN
MY ENCOUNTERS WITH CHEKHOV

It all took place, if I'm not mistaken, in 1883.

On the corner of Dyakovskaya and Sadovaya Streets in Moscow there was a hotel called Oriental Rooms, though no one knew what was Oriental about it. It had very shabby furnished rooms. Three bricks hanging on a rope were attached to the front door to help it close more securely.

Anton Pavlovich Chekhov lived on the first floor. ...

As we went into the hotel, Levitan said to me, "Let's stop in at Antosha's [i.e. Chekhov's]."

Anton Pavlovich's room was filled with smoke. There was a samova on the table, surrounded by bread, sausages, and beer. The couch was strewn with papers and lecture notebooks: Anton Pavlovich was preparing for the final examinations at the university, after which he would become a doctor.

He was sitting on the edge of the couch wearing a gray jacket of the type many students wore at the time. Some young men whom we didn't know were in the room with him. They were university students.

The students were talking heatedly—there was an argument going on—drinking tea and beer, and eating sausage. Anton Pavlovich sat quietly, only occasionally answering the questions put to him.

He was extremely handsome. He had a large, open face with kind, laughing eyes. When talking with someone, he would sometimes fix his eyes on him for a moment, only to lower them immediately and smile his own special shy smile. His whole appearance—his open face, his broad chest—inspired in people a special sort of confidence. It was as if he emanated waves of warmth and protection. Despite his youth, despite his adolescent appearance, he even then made you think of a kind old man whom you could approach and ask about the meaning of life, tell of your sorrows, and confess something very important, the kind of secret everyone has somewhere down deep. Anton Pavlovich was simple and natural; he was unpretentious and lacked the least bit of affectation or self-admiration. Innate modesty, his own special sense of measure, even timidity were always a part of his character.

It was a sunny spring day. Levitan and I asked Anton Pavlovich to come to Sokolniki Park with us.

We told him about the medals we had received. One of the students present asked, "Well, are you going to wear them around your neck the way doormen do?"

It was Levitan who answered. "No, they're not meant to be worn. They aren't used for anything. They're awarded at graduation as a sign of distinction."

"Like the ribbons dogs get at dog shows," added another student.

The students were different from Anton Pavlovich. They loved to argue, and they were in some peculiar way opposed to just about everything.

"If you have no convictions," said one student turning to Chekhov, "you can't be a writer."

"No one can say, 'I have no convictions,'" said another. "I can't understand how anyone could not have convictions."

"I have no convictions," replied Chekhov.

"You claim to be a man without convictions, but how can you write a work of literature without any ideology? Don't you have an ideology?"

"I have no ideology and no convictions," answered Chekhov.

These students had an odd way of arguing. They were apparently displeased with Anton Pavlovich. It was clear that they could not fit him into the didactic turn of their outlook or into their moralizing ideology. They wanted to guide, to instruct, to lead, and to influence. They knew everything. They understood everything. And Anton Pavlovich was plainly bored by it all.

"Who needs your stories? Where do they lead? They don't oppose anything. They contain no ideas. The *Russian Bulletin*, say, would have no use for you. Your stories are entertaining and nothing else."

"Nothing else," answered Anton Pavlovich.

"And why, may I ask, do you sign your stories Chekhonte? What's the point of such an outlandish pen name?"

Chekhov laughed.

"And when you get to be a doctor," the student added, "you'll be ashamed of having written without ideology or protest."

"You're right," answered Chekhov, still laughing. Then he added, "Let's go to Sokolniki. It's a beautiful day. The violets will be in bloom by now. We can breathe fresh air and enjoy spring."

RAYMOND CARVER

ERRAND

Chekhov. On the evening of March 22, 1897, he went to dinner in Moscow with his friend and confidant Alexei Suvorin. This Suvorin was a very rich newspaper and book publisher, a reactionary, a self-made man whose father was a private at the battle of Borodino. Like Chekhov, he was the grandson of a serf. They had that in common: each had peasant's blood in his veins. Otherwise, politically and temperamentally, they were miles apart. Nevertheless, Suvorin was one of Chekhov's few intimates, and Chekhov enjoyed his company.

Naturally, they went to the best restaurant in the city, a former town house called the Hermitage—a place where it could take hours, half the night even, to get through a ten-course meal that would, of course, include several wines, liqueurs, and coffee. Chekhov was impeccably dressed, as always—a dark suit and waistcoat, his usual pince-nez. He looked that night very much as he looks in the photographs taken of him during this period. He was relaxed, jovial. He shook hands with the maître d', and with a glance took in the large dining room. It was brilliantly illuminated by ornate chandeliers, the table occupied by elegantly dressed men and women. Waiters came and went ceaselessly. He had just been seated across the table from Suvorin when suddenly, without warning, blood began gushing from his mouth. Suvorin and two waiters helped him to the gentlemen's room and tried to stanch the flow of blood with ice packs. Suvorin saw him back to his own hotel and had a bed prepared for Chekhov in one of the rooms of the suite. Later, after another hemorrhage, Chekhov allowed himself to be moved to a clinic that specialized in the treatment of tuberculosis and related respiratory infections. When Suvorin visited him there, Chekhov apologized for the "scandal" at the restaurant three nights earlier but continued to insist there was nothing seriously wrong. "He laughed and jested as usual," Suvorin noted in his diary, "while spitting blood into a large vessel."

Maria Chekhov, his younger sister, visited Chekhov in the clinic during the last days of March. The weather was miserable, a sleet storm was in progress, and frozen heaps of snow lay everywhere. It was hard for her to wave down a carriage to take her to the hospital. By the time she arrived she was filled with dread and anxiety.

"Anton Pavlovich lay on his back," Maria wrote in her *Memoirs*. "He was not allowed to speak. After greeting him, I went over to the table to hide my emotions." There, among bottles of champagne, jars of caviar, bouquets of flowers from well-wishers, she saw something that terrified her: a freehand drawing, obviously done by a specialist in these matters, of Chekhov's lungs. It was the kind of sketch a doctor often makes in order to show his patient what he thinks is taking place. The lungs were outlined in blue, but the upper parts were filled in with red. "I realized they were diseased," Maria wrote.

Leo Tolstoy was another visitor. The hospital staff were awed to find themselves in the presence of the country's greatest writer. The most famous man in Russia? Of course they had to let him in to see Chekhov, even though "nonessential" visitors were forbidden. With much obsequiousness on the part of the nurses and resident doctors, the bearded, fierce-looking old man was shown into Chekhov's room. Despite his low opinion of Chekhov's abilities as a playwright (Tolstoy felt the plays were static and lacking in any moral vision. "Where do your characters take you?" he once demanded of Chekhov. "From the sofa to the junk room and back"), Tolstoy liked Chekhov's short stories. Furthermore, and quite simply, he loved the man. He told Gorky, "What a beautiful, magnificent man: modest and quiet, like a girl. He even walks like a girl. He's simply wonderful." And Tolstoy wrote in his journal (everyone kept a journal or a diary in those days), "I am glad I love ... Chekhov."

Tolstoy removed his woollen scarf and bearskin coat, then lowered himself into a chair next to Chekhov's bed. Never mind that Chekhov was taking medication and not permitted to talk, much less carry on a conversation. He had to listen, amazedly, as the Count began to discourse on his theories of the immortality of the soul. Concerning that visit, Chekhov later wrote, "Tolstoy assumes that all of us (humans and animals alike) will live on in a principle (such as reason or love) the essence and goals of which are a mystery to us. ... I have no use for that kind of immortality. I don't understand it, and Lev Nikolayevich [Tolstoy] was astonished I didn't."

Nevertheless, Chekhov was impressed with the solicitude shown by Tolstoy's visit. But, unlike Tolstoy, Chekhov didn't believe in an afterlife and never had. He didn't believe in anything that couldn't be apprehended by one or more of his five senses. And as far as his outlook on life and writing went, he once told someone that he lacked "a political, religious, and philosophical world view. I change it every month, so I'll have to limit myself to the description of how my heroes love, marry, give birth, die, and how they speak."

Earlier, before his t.b. was diagnosed, Chekhov had remarked, "When a peasant has consumption, he says, 'There's nothing I can do. I'll go off in the spring with the melting of the snows.'" (Chekhov himself died in the summer, during a heat wave.) But once Chekhov's own tuberculosis was discovered he continually tried to minimize the seriousness of his condition. To all appearances, it was as if he felt, right up to the end, that he might be able to throw off the disease as he would a lingering catarrh. Well into his final days, he spoke with seeming conviction of the possibility of an improvement. In fact, in a letter written shortly before his end, he went so far as to tell his sister that he was "getting fat" and felt much better now that he was in Badenweiler.

Badenweiler is a spa and resort city in the western area of the Black Forest, not far from Basel. The Vosges are visible from nearly anywhere in the city, and in those days the air was pure and invigorating. Russians had been going there for years to soak in the hot mineral baths and promenade on the boulevards. In June, 1904, Chekhov went there to die.

Earlier that month, he'd made a difficult journey by train from Moscow to Berlin. He traveled with his wife, the actress Olga Knipper, a woman he'd met in 1898 during rehearsals for "The Seagull." Her contemporaries describe her as an excellent actress. She was talented, pretty, and almost ten years younger than the playwright. Chekhov had been immediately attracted to her, but was slow to act on his feelings. As always, he preferred a flirtation to marriage. Finally, after a three-year courtship involving many separations, letters, and the inevitable misunderstandings, they were at last married, in a private ceremony in Moscow, on May 25, 1901. Chekhov was enormously happy. He called Olga his "pony," and sometimes "dog" or "puppy." He was also fond of addressing her as "little turkey" or simply as "my joy."

In Berlin, Chekhov consulted with a renowned specialist in pulmonary disorders, a Dr. Karl Ewald. But, according to an eyewitness, after the doctor examined Chekhov he threw up his hands and left the room without a word. Chekhov was too far gone for help: this Dr. Ewald was furious with himself for not being able to work miracles, and with Chekhov for being so ill.

A Russian journalist happened to visit the Chekhovs at their hotel and sent back this dispatch to his editor: "Chekhov's days are numbered. He seems mortally ill, is terribly thin, coughs all the time, gasps for breath at the slightest movement, and is running a high temperature." This same journalist saw the Chekhovs off at Potsdam Station when they boarded their train for Badenweiler. According to his account, "Chekhov had trouble making his way up the small staircase at the station. He had to sit down for several minutes to catch his breath." In fact, it was painful for Chekhov to move: his legs ached continually and his insides hurt. The disease had attacked his intestines and spinal cord. At this point he had less than a month to live. When Chekhov spoke of his condition now, it was, according to Olga, "with an almost reckless indifference."

Dr. Schwöhrer was one of the many Badenweiler physicians who earned a good living by treating the well-to-do who came to the spa seeking relief from various maladies. Some of his patients were ill and infirm, others simply old and hypochondriacal. But Chekhov's was a special case: he was clearly beyond help and in his last days. He was also very famous. Even Dr. Schwöhrer knew his name: he'd read some of Chekhov's stories in a German magazine. When he examined the writer early in June, he voiced his appreciation of Chekhov's art but kept his medical opinions to himself. Instead, he prescribed a diet of cocoa, oatmeal drenched in butter, and strawberry tea. This last was supposed to help Chekhov sleep at night.

On June 13, less than three weeks before he died, Chekhov wrote a letter to his mother in which he told her his health was on the mend. In it he said, "It's likely that I'll be completely cured in a week." Who knows why he said this? What could he have been thinking? He was a doctor himself, and he knew better. He was dying, it was as simple and as unavoidable as that. Nevertheless, he sat out on the balcony of his hotel room and read railway timetables. He asked for information on sailings of boats bound for Odessa from Marseilles. But he *knew*. At this stage he had to have known. Yet in one of the last letters he ever wrote he told his sister he was growing stronger by the day.

He no longer had any appetite for literary work, and hadn't for a long time. In fact, he had very nearly failed to complete *The Cherry Orchard* the year before. Writing that play was the hardest thing he'd ever done in his life. Toward the end, he was able to manage only six or seven lines a day. "I've started losing heart," he wrote Olga. "I feel I'm finished as a writer, and every sentence strikes me as worthless and of no use whatever." But he didn't stop. He finished his play in October, 1903. It was the last thing he ever wrote, except for letters and a few entries in his notebook.

A little after midnight on July 2, 1904, Olga sent someone to fetch Dr. Schwöhrer. It was an emergency: Chekhov was delirious. Two young Russians on holiday happened to have the adjacent room, and Olga hurried next door to explain what was happening. One of the youths was in his bed asleep, but the other was still awake, smoking and reading. He left the hotel at a run to find Dr. Schwöhrer. "I can still hear the sound of the gravel under his shoes in the silence of that stifling July night," Olga wrote later on in her memoirs. Chekhov was hallucinating, talking about sailors, and there were snatches of something about the Japanese. "You don't put ice on an empty stomach," he said when she tried to place an ice pack on his chest.

Dr. Schwöhrer arrived and unpacked his bag, all the while keeping his gaze fastened on Chekhov, who lay gasping in the bed. The sick man's pupils were dilated and his temples glistened with sweat. Dr. Schwöhrer's face didn't register anything. He was not an emotional man, but he knew Chekhov's end was near. Still, he was a doctor, sworn to do his utmost, and Chekhov held on to life, however tenuously. Dr. Schwöhrer prepared a hypodermic and administered an injection of camphor, something that was supposed to speed up the heart. But the injection didn't help—nothing, of course, could have helped.

Nevertheless, the doctor made known to Olga his intention of sending for oxygen. Suddenly, Chekhov roused himself, became lucid, and said quietly, "What's the use? Before it arrives I'll be a corpse."

Dr. Schwöhrer pulled on his big moustache and stared at Chekhov. The writer's cheeks were sunken and gray, his complexion waxen; his breath was raspy. Dr. Schwöhrer knew the time could be reckoned in minutes. Without a word, without conferring with Olga, he went over to an alcove where there was a telephone on the wall. He read the instructions for using the device. If he activated it by holding his finger on a button and turning a handle on the side of the phone, he could reach the lower regions of the hotel—the kitchen. He picked up the receiver, held it to his ear, and did as the instructions told him. When someone finally answered, Dr. Schwöhrer ordered a bottle of the hotel's best champagne. "How many glasses?" he was asked. "Three glasses!" the doctor shouted into the mouthpiece. "And hurry, do you hear?" It was one of those rare moments of inspiration that can easily enough be overlooked later on, because the action is so entirely appropriate it seems inevitable.

The champagne was brought to the door by a tired-looking young man whose blond hair was standing up. The trousers of his uniform were wrinkled, the creases gone, and in his haste he'd missed a loop while buttoning his jacket. His appearance was that of someone who'd been resting (slumped in a chair, say, dozing a little), when off in the distance the phone had clamored in the early-morning hours—great God in Heaven!—and the next thing he knew he was being shaken awake by a superior and told to deliver a bottle of Moët to Room 211. "And hurry, do you hear?"

The young man entered the room carrying a silver ice bucket with the champagne in it and a silver tray with three cut-crystal glasses. He found a place on the table for the bucket and glasses, all the while craning his neck, trying to see into the other room, where someone panted ferociously for breath. It was a dreadful, harrowing sound, and the young man lowered his chin into his collar and turned away as the ratchety breathing worsened. Forgetting himself, he stared out the open window toward the darkened city. Then this big imposing man with a thick moustache pressed some coins into his hand—a large tip, by the feel of it—and suddenly the young man saw the door open. He took some steps and found himself on the landing, where he opened his hand and looked at the coins in amazement.

Methodically, the way he did everything, the doctor went about the business of working the cork out of the bottle. He did it in such a way as to minimize, as much as possible, the festive explosion. He poured three glasses and, out of habit, pushed the cork back in to the neck of the bottle. He then took the glasses of champagne over to the bed. Olga momentarily released her grip on Chekhov's hand—a hand, she said later, that burned her fingers. She arranged another pillow behind his head. Then she put the cool glass of champagne against Chekhov's palm and made sure his fingers closed around the stem. They exchanged looks—Chekhov, Olga, Dr. Schwöhrer. They didn't touch glasses. There was no toast. What on earth was there to drink to? To death? Chekhov summoned his remaining strength and said, "It's been so long since I've had champagne." He brought the glass to his lips and drank. In a minute or two Olga took the empty glass from his hand and set it on the nightstand. Then Chekhov turned onto his side. He closed his eyes and sighed. A minute later, his breathing stopped.

Dr. Schwöhrer picked up Chekhov's hand from the bedsheet. He held his fingers to Chekhov's wrist and drew a gold watch from his vest pocket, opening the lid of the watch as he did so. The second hand on the watch moved slowly, very slowly. He let it move around the face of the watch three times while he waited for signs of a pulse. It was three o'clock in the morning and still sultry in the room. Badenweiler was in the grip of its worst heat wave in years. All the windows in both rooms stood open, but there was no sign of a breeze. A large, black-winged moth flew through a window and banged wildly against the electric lamp. Dr. Schwöhrer let go of Chekhov's wrist. "It's over," he said. He closed the lid of his watch and returned it to his vest pocket.

At once Olga dried her eyes and set about composing herself. She thanked the doctor for coming. He asked if she wanted some medication—laudanum, perhaps, or a few drops of valerian. She shook her head. She did have one request, though: before the authorities were notified and the newspapers found out, before the time came when Chekhov was no longer in her keeping, she wanted to be alone with him for a while. Could the doctor help with this? Could he withhold, for a while anyway, news of what had just occurred?

Dr. Schwöhrer stroked his moustache with the back of a finger. Why not? After all, what difference would it make to anyone whether this matter became known now or a few hours from now? The only detail that remained was to fill out a death certificate, and this could be done at his office later on in the morning, after he'd slept a few hours. Dr. Schwöhrer nodded his agreement and prepared to leave. He murmured a few words of condolence. Olga inclined her head. "An honour," Dr. Schwöhrer said. He picked up his bag and left the room and, for that matter, history.

It was at this moment that the cork popped out of the champagne bottle; foam spilled down onto the table. Olga went back to Chekhov's bedside. She sat on a footstool, holding his hand, from time to time stroking his face. "There were no human voices, no everyday sounds," she wrote. "There was only beauty, peace, and the grandeur of death."

She stayed with Chekhov until daybreak, when thrushes began to call from the garden below. Then came the sound of tables and chairs being moved about down there. Before long, voices carried up to her. It was then a knock sounded at the door. Of course she thought it must be an official of some sort—the medical examiner, say, or someone from the police who had questions to ask and forms for her to fill out, or maybe, just maybe, it could be Dr. Schwöhrer returning with a mortician to render assistance in embalming and transporting Chekhov's remains back to Russia.

But, instead, it was the same blond young man who'd brought the champagne a few hours earlier. This time, however, his uniform trousers were neatly pressed, with stiff creases in front, and every button on his snug green jacket was fastened. He seemed quite another person. Not only was he wide awake but his plump cheeks were smooth-shaven, his hair was in place, and he appeared anxious to please. He was holding a porcelain vase with three long-stemmed yellow roses. He presented these to Olga with a smart click of his heels. She stepped back and let him into the room. He was there, he said, to collect the glasses, ice bucket, and tray, yes. But he also wanted to say that, because of the extreme heat, breakfast would be served in the garden this morning. He hoped this weather wasn't too bothersome; he apologized for it.

The woman seemed distracted. While he talked, she turned her eyes away and looked down at something in the carpet. She crossed her arms and held her elbows. Meanwhile, still holding his vase, waiting for a sign, the young man took in the details of the room. Bright sunlight flooded through the open windows. The room was tidy and seemed undisturbed, almost untouched. No garments were flung over chairs, no shoes, stockings, braces, or stays were in evidence, no open suitcases. In short, there was no clutter, nothing but the usual heavy pieces of hotel-room furniture. Then, because the woman was still looking down, he looked down, too, and at once spied a cork near the toe of his shoe. The woman did not see it—she was looking somewhere else. The young man wanted to bend over and pick up the cork, but he was still holding the roses and was afraid of seeming to intrude even more by drawing any further attention to himself. Reluctantly, he left the cork where it was and raised his eyes. Everything was in order except for the uncorked, half-empty bottle of champagne that stood alongside two crystal glasses over on the little table. He cast his gaze about once more. Through an open door he saw that the third glass was in the bedroom, on the nightstand. But someone still occupied the bed! He couldn't see a face, but the figure under the covers lay perfectly motionless and quiet. He noted the figure and looked elsewhere. Then, for a reason he couldn't understand, a feeling of uneasiness took hold of him. He cleared his throat and moved his weight to the other leg. The woman still didn't look up or break her silence. The young man felt his cheeks grow warm. It occurred to him, quite without his having thought it through, that he should perhaps suggest an alternative to breakfast in the garden. He coughed, hoping to focus the woman's attention, but she didn't look at him. The distinguished foreign guests could, he said, take breakfast in their rooms this morning if they wished. The young man (his name hasn't survived, and it's likely he perished in the Great War) said he would be happy to bring up a tray. Two trays, he added, glancing uncertainly once again in the direction of the bedroom.

He fell silent and ran a finger around the inside of his collar. He didn't understand. He wasn't even sure the woman had been listening. He didn't know what else to do now; he was still holding the vase. The sweet odor of the roses filled his nostrils and inexplicably caused a pang of regret. The entire time he'd been waiting, the woman had apparently been lost in thought. It was as if all the while he'd been standing there, talking, shifting his weight, holding his flowers, she had been someplace else, somewhere far from Badenweiler. But now she came back to herself, and her face assumed another expression. She raised her eyes, looked at him, and then shook her head. She seemed to be struggling to understand what on earth this young man could be doing there in the room holding a vase with three yellow roses. Flowers? She hadn't ordered flowers.

The moment passed. She went over to her handbag and scooped up some coins. She drew out a number of banknotes as well. The young man touched his lips with his tongue; another large tip was forthcoming, but for what? What did she want him to do? He'd never before waited on such guests. He cleared his throat once more.

No breakfast, the woman said. Not yet, at any rate. Breakfast wasn't the important thing this morning. She required something else. She needed him to go out and bring back a mortician. Did he understand her? Herr Chekhov was dead, you see. *Comprenez-vous?* Young man? Anton Chekhov was dead. Now listen carefully to me, she said. She wanted him to go downstairs and ask someone at the front desk where he could go to find the most respected mortician in the city. Someone reliable, who took great pains in his work and whose manner was appropriately reserved. A mortician, in short, worthy of a great artist. Here, she said, and pressed the money on him. Tell them downstairs that I have specifically requested you to perform this duty for me. Are you listening? Do you understand what I'm saying to you?

The young man grappled to take in what she was saying. He chose not to look again in the direction of the other room. He had sensed something was not right. He became aware of his heart beating rapidly under his jacket, and he felt perspiration break out on his forehead. He didn't know where he should turn his eyes. He wanted to put the vase down.

Please do this for me, the woman said. I'll remember you with gratitude. Tell them downstairs that I insist. Say that. But don't call any unnecessary attention to yourself or to the situation. Just say that this is necessary, that I request it—and that's all. Do you hear me? Nod if you understand. Above all, don't raise an alarm. Everything else, all the rest, the commotion—that'll come soon enough. The worst is over. Do we understand each other?

The young man's face had grown pale. He stood rigid, clasping the vase. He managed to nod his head.

After securing permission to leave the hotel he was to proceed quietly and resolutely, though without any unbecoming haste, to the mortician's. He was to behave exactly as if he were engaged on a very important errand, nothing more. He *was* engaged on an important errand, she said. And if it would help keep his movements purposeful he should imagine himself as someone moving down the busy sidewalk carrying in his arms a porcelain vase of roses that he had to deliver to an important man. (She spoke quietly, almost confidentially, as if to a relative or a friend.) He could even tell himself that the man he was going to see was expecting him, was perhaps impatient for him to arrive with his flowers. Nevertheless, the young man was not to become excited and run, or otherwise break his stride. Remember the vase he was carrying! He was to walk briskly, comporting himself at all times in as dignified a manner as possible. He should keep walking until he came to the mortician's house and stood before the door. He would then raise the brass knocker and let it fall, once, twice, three times. In a minute the mortician himself would answer.

This mortician would be in his forties, no doubt, or maybe early fifties— bald, solidly built, wearing steel-frame spectacles set very low on his nose. He would be modest, unassuming, a man who would ask only the most direct and necessary questions. An apron. Probably he would be wearing an apron. He might even be wiping his hands on a dark towel while he listened to what was being said. There'd be a faint whiff of formaldehyde on his clothes. But it was all right, and the young man shouldn't worry. He was nearly a grown-up now and shouldn't be frightened or repelled by any of this. The mortician would hear him out. He was a man of restraint and bearing, this mortician, someone who could help allay people's fears in this situation, not increase them. Long ago he'd acquainted himself with death in all its various guises and forms; death held no surprises for him any longer, no hidden secrets. It was this man whose services were required this morning.

The mortician takes the vase of roses. Only once while the young man is speaking does the mortician betray the least flicker of interest, or indicate that he's heard anything out of the ordinary. But the one time the young man mentions the name of the deceased, the mortician's eyebrows rise just a little. Chekhov, you say? Just a minute, and I'll be with you.

Do you understand what I'm saying, Olga said to the young man. Leave the glasses. Don't worry about them. Forget about crystal wineglasses and such. Leave the room as it is. Everything is ready now. We're ready. Will you go?

But at that moment the young man was thinking of the cork still resting near the toe of his shoe. To retrieve it he would have to bend over, still gripping the vase. He would do this. He leaned over. Without looking down he reached out and closed it into his hand.

RAYMOND CARVER
On Writing

Back in the mid-1960s, I found I was having trouble concentrating my attention on long narrative fiction. For a time I experienced difficulty in trying to read it as well as in attempting to write it. My attention span had gone out on me; I no longer had the patience to try to write novels. It's an involved story, too tedious to talk about here. But I know it has much to do now with why I write poems and short stories. Get in, get out. Don't linger. Go on. It could be that I lost any great ambitions at about the same time, in my late twenties. If I did, I think it was good it happened. Ambition and a little luck are good things for a writer to have going for him. Too much ambition and bad luck, or no luck at all, can be killing. There has to be talent.

Some writers have a bunch of talent; I don't know any writers who are without it. But a unique and exact way of looking at things, and finding the right context for expressing that way of looking, that's something else. *The World According to Garp* is, of course, the marvelous world according to John Irving. There is another world according to Flannery O'Connor, and others according to William Faulkner and Ernest Hemingway. There are worlds according to Cheever, Updike, Singer, Stanley Elkin, Ann Beattie, Cynthia Ozick, Donald Barthelme, Mary Robison, William Kittredge, Barry Hannah, Ursula K. Le Guin. Every great or even every very good writer makes the world over according to his own specifications.

It's akin to style, what I'm talking about, but it isn't style alone. It is the writer's particular and unmistakable signature on everything he writes. It is his world and no other. This is one of the things that distinguishes one writer from another. Not talent. There's plenty of that around. But a writer who has some special way of looking at things and who gives artistic expression to that way of looking: that writer may be around for a time.

Isak Dinesen said that she wrote a little every day, without hope and without despair. Someday I'll put that on a three-by-five card and tape it to the wall beside my desk. I have some three-by-five cards on the wall now. "Fundamental accuracy of statement is the ONE sole morality of writing." Ezra Pound. It is not everything by ANY means, but if a writer has "fundamental accuracy of statement" going for him, he's at least on the right track.

I have a three-by-five up there with this fragment of a sentence from a story by Chekhov: "... and suddenly everything became clear to him." I find these words filled with wonder and possibility. I love their simple clarity, and the hint of revelation that's implied. There is mystery, too. What has been unclear before? Why is it just now becoming clear? What's happened? Most of all—what now? There are consequences as a result of such sudden awakenings. I feel a sharp sense of relief—and anticipation.

I overheard the writer Geoffrey Wolff say "No cheap tricks" to a group of writing students. That should go on a three-by-five card. I'd amend it a little to "No tricks." Period. I hate tricks. At the first sign of a trick or a gimmick in a piece of fiction, a cheap trick or even an elaborate trick, I tend to look for cover. Tricks are ultimately boring, and I get bored easily, which may go along with my not having much of an attention span. But extremely clever chi-chi writing, or just plain tomfoolery writing, puts me to sleep. Writers don't need tricks or gimmicks or even necessarily need to be the smartest fellows on the block. At the risk of appearing foolish, a writer sometimes needs to be able to just stand and gape at this or that thing—a sunset or an old shoe—in absolute and simple amazement.

Some months back, in the *New York Times Book Review*, John Barth said that ten years ago most of the students in his fiction writing seminar were interested in "formal innovation," and this no longer seems to be the case. He's a little worried that writers are going to start writing mom-and-pop novels in the 1980s. He worried that experimentation may be on the way out, along with liberalism. I get a little nervous if I find myself within earshot of somber discussions about "formal innovation" in fiction writing. Too often "experimentation" is a license to be careless, silly, or imitative in the writing. Even worse, a license to try to brutalize or alienate the reader. Too often such writing gives us no news of the world, or else describes a desert landscape and that's all—a few dunes and lizards here and there, but no people; a place uninhabited by anything recognizably human, a place of interest only to a few scientific specialists.

It should be noted that real experiment in fiction is original, hard-earned and cause for rejoicing. But someone else's way of looking at things—Barthelme's, for instance—should not be chased after by other writers. It won't work. There is only one Barthelme, and for another writer to try to appropriate Barthelme's peculiar sensibility or mise en scène under the rubric of innovation is for that writer to mess around with chaos and disaster and, worse, self-deception. The real experimenters have to Make It New, as Pound urged, and in the process have to find things out for themselves. But if writers haven't taken leave of their senses, they also want to stay in touch with us, they want to carry news from their world to ours.

It's possible, in a poem or a short story, to write about commonplace things and objects using commonplace but precise language, and to endow those things—a chair, a window curtain, a fork, a stone, a woman's earring—with immense, even startling power. It is possible to write a line of seemingly innocuous dialogue and have it send a chill along the reader's spine—the source of artistic delight, as Nabokov would have it. That's the kind of writing that most interests me. I hate sloppy or haphazard writing whether it flies under the banner of experimentation or else is just clumsily rendered realism. In Isaac Babel's wonderful short story, "Guy de Maupassant," the narrator has this to say about the writing of fiction: "No iron can pierce the heart with such force as a period put just at the right place." This too ought to go on a three-by-five.

Evan Connell said once that he knew he was finished with a short story when he found himself going through it and taking out commas and then going through the story again and putting commas back in the same places. I like that way of working on something. I respect that kind of care for what is being done. That's all we have, finally, the words, and they had better be the right ones, with the punctuation in the right places so that they can best say what they are meant to say. If the words are heavy with the writer's own unbridled emotions, or if they are imprecise and inaccurate for some other reason—if the words are in any way blurred—the reader's eyes will slide right over them and nothing will be achieved. The reader's own artistic sense will simply not be engaged. Henry James called this sort of hapless writing "weak specification."

I have friends who've told me they had to hurry a book because they needed the money, their editor or their wife was leaning on them or leaving them—something, some apology for the writing not being very good. "It would have been better if I'd taken the time." I was dumbfounded when I heard a novelist friend say this. I still am, if I think about it, which I don't. It's none of my business. But if the writing can't be made as good as it is within us to make it, then why do it? In the end, the satisfaction of having done our best, and the proof of that labor, is the one thing we can take into the grave. I wanted to say to my friend, for heaven's sake go do something else. There have to be easier and maybe more honest ways to try and earn a living. Or else just do it to the best of your abilities, your talents, and then don't justify or make excuses. Don't complain, don't explain.

In an essay called, simply enough, "Writing Short Stories," Flannery O'Connor talks about writing as an act of discovery. O'Connor says she most often did not know where she was going when she sat down to work on a short story. She says she doubts that many writers know where they are going when they begin something. She uses "Good Country People" as an example of how she put together a short story whose ending she could not even guess at until she was nearly there:

> When I started writing that story, I didn't know there was going to be a Ph.D. with a wooden leg in it. I merely found myself one morning writing a description of two women I knew something about, and before I realized it, I had equipped one of them with a daughter with a wooden leg. I brought in the

Bible salesman, but I had no idea what I was going to do with him. I didn't know he was going to steal that wooden leg until ten or twelve lines before he did it, but when I found out that this was what was going to happen, I realized it was inevitable.

When I read this some years ago it came as a shock that she, or anyone for that matter, wrote stories in this fashion. I thought this was my uncomfortable secret, and I was a little uneasy with it. For sure I thought this way of working on a short story somehow revealed my own shortcomings. I remember being tremendously heartened by reading what she had to say on the subject.

I once sat down to write what turned out to be a pretty good story, though only the first sentence of the story had offered itself to me when I began it. For several days I'd been going around with this sentence in my head: "He was running the vacuum cleaner when the telephone rang." I knew a story was there and that it wanted telling. I felt it in my bones, that a story belonged with that beginning, if I could just have the time to write it. I found the time, an entire day—twelve, fifteen hours even—if I wanted to make use of it. I did, and I sat down in the morning and wrote the first sentence, and other sentences promptly began to attach themselves. I made the story just as I'd make a poem; one line and then the next, and the next. Pretty soon I could see a story, and I knew it was my story, the one I'd been wanting to write.

I like it when there is some feeling of threat or sense of menace in short stories. I think a little menace is fine to have in a story. For one thing, it's good for the circulation. There has to be tension, a sense that something is imminent, that certain things are in relentless motion, or else, most often, there simply won't be a story. What creates tension in a piece of fiction is partly the way the concrete words are linked together to make up the visible action of the story. But it's also the things that are left out, that are implied, the landscape just under the smooth (but sometimes broken and unsettled) surface of things.

V.S. Pritchett's definition of a short story is "something glimpsed from the corner of the eye, in passing." Notice the "glimpse" part of this. First the glimpse. Then the glimpse given life, turned into something that illuminates the moment and may, if we're lucky—that word again—have even further-ranging consequences and meaning. The short story writer's task is to invest the glimpse with all that is in his power. He'll bring his intelligence and literary skill to bear (his talent), his sense of proportion and sense of the fitness of things: of how things out there really are and how he sees those things—like no one else sees them. And this is done through the use of clear and specific language, language used so as to bring to life the details that will light up the story for the reader. For the details to be concrete and convey meaning, the language must be accurate and precisely given. The words can be so precise they may even sound flat, but they can still carry; if used right, they can hit all the notes.

MICHAEL SCHUMACHER

AFTER THE FIRE, INTO THE FIRE: AN INTERVIEW WITH RAYMOND CARVER

You've published more volumes of poetry than short fiction. How did your career as a poet evolve?

Back when I began to write and send things out, I gave an equal amount of time to short stories and poems. Then, in the early Sixties, I had a short story and a poem accepted on the same day. The letters of acceptance, from two different magazines, were there in the box on the same day. This was truly a red-letter day. I was writing both short fiction and poetry in a more or less hit-or-miss fashion, given the circumstances of my life. Finally I decided, consciously or otherwise, that I was going to have to make a decision as to where to put the energy and strength I had. And I came down on the side of the short story.

You continued to write poetry, though.

Yes. For many years, I was an occasional poet, but that, to me, was better than being no poet at all. I wrote a poem whenever I could, whenever I had the chance and wasn't writing stories....

For the last couple of years, you've been more than an occasional poet. Your output of poems during this period has been prodigious. How did that come to be?

After the publication of *Cathedral* and the attendant hubbub, I couldn't seem to find any peace and quiet or a place to work. We were living in Syracuse. Tess was teaching and there was a lot of traffic in the house, the phone kept ringing, people were showing up at the door. And there was her school business, and some socializing. But there was little time to work. So I came out to Port Angeles, to find a quiet place to work. I came here to this little house with the intention of writing fiction. I had not written any poems in well over two years and, so far as I knew, I felt it was conceivable I might not ever write another poem. But after I'd gotten out here and had just sat still and was quiet for about six days, I picked up a magazine and read some poems, and they were poems I didn't care for. And I thought: Jesus, I could do better than this. *(laughs)* It may not have been a good motive to begin writing poems, but whatever the motive, I wrote a poem that night and the next morning I got up and wrote another poem. And this went on, sometimes two or even three

948

poems a day, for sixty-five days. I've never had a period in my life that remotely resembles that time. I mean, I felt like it would have been all right, you know, simply to have died after those sixty-five days. I felt *on fire....*

Do you think it's a good idea for aspiring writers to attend schools or work-shops?

Yes, I do. Obviously, it's not for everybody, but I can't think of any writers or musicians who have just sprung full-blown without some kind of help. De Maupassant was helped by Flaubert, who went over all his stories and criti-cized them and gave him advice. Beethoven learned his business from Haydn. Michelangelo was an apprentice for a long while to someone else. Rilke showed his poems to someone early on. Same with Pasternak. Just about any writer you can think of. Everybody, whether it's a conductor or composer or microbiologist or mathematician—they've all learned their business from older practitioners; the idea of the maestro–apprentice relationship is an old and dis-tinguished relationship. Obviously, this is not going to guarantee that it's going to make a great—or even a good—writer out of anybody, but I don't think it's going to hurt the writer's chances, either....

Do you encourage your students to read a lot? How important do you see reading being to the writer?

I think writers—especially young writers—should want to read all the books they can get their hands on. To this extent, that's where it's helpful to have some instruction as to what to read and who to read, from somebody who knows. But a young writer has to make a choice somewhere along the line whether he's going to be, finally, a writer or a reader. I've known good, bright, young, putative writers who felt they couldn't begin to write until they had read *everything* and, of course, you simply can't read everything. You can't read all the masterpieces, all the people that you hear people talking about—you just don't have the time. I mean, I wish there were two of me—one to read and one to write—because I love to read....

What do you encourage your students to read?

Flaubert's letters—that's one book I'd recommend. Every writer should read those letters. And Chekhov's letters, and the life of Chekhov. I'll recommend a great book of letters between Lawrence Durrell and Henry Miller, which I read some years back. What a book! But writers should read other writers, yes, to see how it's done, for one thing, how the others are doing it; and there's also the sense of shared enterprise, the sense that we're all in this together....

John Gardner was my teacher. He hadn't published anything at the time, but he seemed to know everything. He was directing me to authors—people I *should* read, books I *had* to look at.... I suppose the influence on my fiction would be the early stories by Hemingway. I can still go back, every two or three years, and reread those early stories and become excited just by the cadences of his sentences—not just by what he's writing about, but the *way* he's writing....

When you have that first line in your head, do you know right away whether it's going to be in a poem or a short story?

I'm not making a conscious decision to use a line in a poem or story. When I'm writing poems, it's invariably, inevitably going to become a poem; when I'm writing stories, it's going to become part of a story. Some writers write poetry and fiction at the same time, they can move easily from this to that, but I don't seem to be able to work that way. When I'm writing fiction, I'm in a period of writing fiction; when I'm writing poetry, everything I touch seems to turn to poetry.... Most of my stories and poems have a starting point in real life, in reality, but I'm not writing autobiography. It's all subject to change—everything is—in a story or a poem. Whatever seems to suit the work best, that's the direction I'll go in....

In addition to this interest in the short story itself, there has been a growing interest, even on the part of literary elitists, in tales of survivors, whether they're found in the stories by writers such as yourself, Richard Ford, Barry Hannah, Charles Bukowski, Tobias Wolff, and so forth, or in the music of Bruce Springsteen, John Cougar Mellencamp, and Tom Waits. Why do you think that is?

Well, in part, of course, it simply has to do with the fact that these people are bearing witness to what they have experienced; they're able to talk about it. There's a fascination with somebody who's been there and come back—lived to talk about it, as it were. You know: "I'll tell you what it's like. This is my song, this is my poem or short story. Make of it what you will." ...

... Can you explain how your blue-collar background helped you with your writing, both in terms of subject and approach?

For certain I had a *subject*, something to write about, people and events that I knew well. I never had to go around looking for material. Also, I think that blue-collar life put a premium on directness and being straightforward. In that life, there wasn't a whole lot of room for, or patience with, the Henry Jamesian kind of indirection.... There are significant moments in everyone's day that can make literature. You have to be alert to them and pay attention to them. That's what you ought to write about....

In discussing technique in your Introduction to The Best American Short Stories 1986, *you listed the five elements you consider important in the short story: choices, conflict, drama, consequence, and narrative. Do you have these things mapped out in your head before you start writing?*

No. I begin the story and it takes a natural course. Most often I'm not aware, when I start a poem or story, of where it's going until I get there. Not while I'm writing it.... I read a little essay by Hemingway called "Monologue to the Maestro," in which somebody asked him if he knew where he was going with a story, and Hemingway answered that he never knew, that he just wrote and the situation developed and unfolded....

Very often, when reading one of your short stories, I get the impression that something very, very important has happened just before the story begins—or will happen after the story ends. Your stories, like Hemingway's, really deal with the tip of the iceberg. When it works, it's wonderful, but a lot of beginning writers have problems in this area. They assume that their readers know what's going on—occurrences that are never mentioned in their stories. What's the cutting edge to you? How do you teach that to your students?

Well, you can't keep necessary information from the reader. You can assume that the reader can put a face on some of these characters—you don't *have* to describe the color of their eyes, and so forth. Insofar as the stories are concerned, you have to presuppose some kind of knowledge on the part of the readers, that they're going to fill in some of the gaps. But you can't leave them drifting around without enough information to make them care about these people; you can't obfuscate what's going on.... I'm much more interested in stories and poems that have some bearing on how we live and how we conduct ourselves and how we work out the consequences of our actions. Most of my stories start pretty near the end of the arc of the dramatic conflict. I don't give a lot of detail about what went on before; I just start it fairly near the end of the swing of the action.

Your stories begin at crisis point.

Yes, I think so. I don't have a lot of patience for the other, I guess. But there is a fine line—the cutting edge, as you put it—where you have to give the reader enough, but you don't want to give him too much. I don't want to bore the reader, or bore myself.

Kurt Vonnegut wrote that short story writers should just write their stories and then toss out the first few pages when they were done.

There's something to that. D.H. Lawrence made a remark to the effect that you finish your story and when it's all finished, you go back and shake the branches of the tree, prune it again....

When you're revising, what are you looking for? What do you tend to change?

I want to make the stories interesting on every level and that involves creating believable characters and situations, along with working on the language of the story until it is perfectly clear, but still a language capable of carrying complex ideas and sophisticated nuances....

Point of view is so important to a story. I've heard of people who have changed from first to third person in a story after it's been written.

Well, my friend Richard Ford changed the point of view of one of his novels. He worked on it for two years, and he felt it wasn't right, so he spent another year changing the entire point of view.... I don't know how many books a person's going to take to the grave with him, but you want to have it right, or else what's the point? ...

Do you prefer to write a story from beginning to end in one sitting?

Yes. I'm afraid of interruption and losing the story—whatever it was that made me want to write the story in the first place. I don't think I've ever spent longer than two days writing the first draft of a story. Usually only one day. I spend lots of time after that typing it up and reworking it, but I think it's good to try to get that story down before you lose sight of it....

Your survival as a writer has been a source of inspiration to a lot of struggling writers.

... After I got sober and had quit drinking entirely, there was a period of time, for a year or so, when I didn't write anything and it wasn't even important for me to write anything. It was so important for me to have my health back and not be brain-dead any longer that whether I wrote or not didn't matter any longer. I just felt like I had a second chance at my life again. But for about a year or so, I didn't write anything. And then, when things were right, when I was well again, I taught for a year in El Paso, and then, suddenly, I began to write again. And that was just a great gift, and everything that has happened since then has been a great gift.

CASEBOOK II: "THE DROVER'S WIFE"

Henry Lawson's classic Australian story "The Drover's Wife" has spawned a fascinating cluster of other works—including a famous painting by Russell Drysdale and the two irreverent contemporary stories reprinted in this casebook. The Murray Bail and Frank Moorhouse stories must be read as commentaries on Lawson's story; they are included in the casebook, rather than with the other stories, for that reason. Both are works of fiction, although Moorhouse's purports to be an academic paper, which provides readers with an intriguing example of the playful crossing of genre boundaries that we find in contemporary writing. Most importantly, both pieces illustrate intertextuality, which has always been a reality in literature but is increasingly being brought to the foreground in contemporary fiction.

Bail's version of "The Drover's Wife" takes off from the image of the long-suffering and ever faithful wife in Lawson's story, an image that some readers have regarded as destructively stereotypical, at least in the way that it has registered in the Australian imagination. Lawson clearly admires the wife in his story. Readers like Bail, however, have found that her willingness to accept whatever life has dealt her and to never complain or seek to be anything other than "the drover's wife" offers a model that contemporary women would do well to resist. This model is accommodating of womanhood; its counterpart is the unaccommodating figure of the "macho" Australian male, who is prepared to tolerate and even to praise women, but only on condition that women not disturb male equanimity with any "silly" female business. In Bail's story, we see both the moment of woman's rebellion and, in the comically unattractive figure of the aggrieved dentist husband who narrates the story, a spoof of the Australian male who, it turns out, is not even remotely like Crocodile Dundee (a recent and more cheerful version of the drover). Bail's decision to have the wife leave her dentist husband for the drover is a masterful piece of fun; the silent drover, at least, has an appeal that contemporary men who loudly boast of masculinity do not. "If we see Lawson as a figurative artist," Bail has written, "then I am more attracted to abstract expressionists or 'surrealists' like Kafka."

In the Frank Moorhouse piece, we find a spoof not only of the Australian male whose "wife," according to the young Italian cultural critic, is really a sheep, but also of academic criticism. Like the critic who speaks at the end of Margaret Atwood's novel The Handmaid's Tale, *this one (for all his ingenuity and pompous self-assurance) has simply got it wrong. At the same time, the critic's silliness allows Moorhouse to satirize important issues of Australian identity politics.*

Bail, born in Adelaide in 1941, and Moorhouse, born in 1938 and raised on the south coast of New South Wales, are among Australia's best-known and most inventive short-story writers.

MURRAY BAIL

THE DROVER'S WIFE

Sir Russell Drysdale. *The Drover's Wife*. 1945, oil on canvas. 50.8 cm x 61 cm. Reproduced by permission of Lady Maisie Drysdale.

There has perhaps been a mistake—but of no great importance—made in the denomination of this picture. The woman depicted is not "The Drover's Wife." She is my wife. We have not seen each other now ... it must be getting on thirty years. This portrait was painted shortly after she left—and had joined him. Notice she has very conveniently hidden her wedding hand. It is a canvas 20 x 24 inches, signed l/r "Russell Drysdale."

I say "shortly after" because she has our small suitcase—Drysdale has made it look like a shopping bag—and she is wearing the sandshoes she normally wore to the beach. Besides, it is dated 1945.

It is Hazel alright.

How much can you tell by a face? That a woman has left a husband and two children? Here, I think the artist has fallen down (though how was he to know?). He has Hazel with a resigned helpless expression—as if it was all my fault. Or, as if she had been a country woman all her ruddy life.

Otherwise the likeness is fair enough.

Hazel was large-boned. Our last argument I remember concerned her weight. She weighed—I have the figures—12st. 4 ozs. And she wasn't exactly tall. I see that she put it back on almost immediately. It doesn't take long. See her legs.

She had a small, pretty face, I'll give her that. I was always surprised by her eyes. How solemn they were. The painting shows that. Overall, a gentle face, one that other women liked. How long it must have lasted up in the drought conditions is anybody's guess.

A drover! Why a drover? It has come as a shock to me.

"I am just going round the corner," she wrote, characteristically. It was a piece of butcher's paper left on the table.

Then, and this sounded odd at the time: "Your tea's in the oven. Don't give Trev any carrots."

Now that sounded as if she wouldn't be back, but after puzzling over it, I dismissed it.

And I think that is what hurt me most. No "Dear" at the top, not even "Gordon." No "love" at the bottom. Hazel left without so much as a goodbye. We could have talked it over.

Adelaide is a small town. People soon got to know. They ... shied away. I was left alone to bring up Trevor and Kay. It took a long time—years—before, if asked, I could say: "She vamoosed. I haven't got a clue to where."

Fancy coming across her in a painting, one reproduced in colour at that. I suppose in a way that makes Hazel famous.

The picture gives little away though. It is the outback—but where exactly? South Australia? It could easily be Queensland, West Australia, the Northern Territory. We don't know. You could never find that spot.

He is bending over (feeding?) the horse, so it is around dusk. This is borne out by the length of Hazel's shadow. It is probably in the region of 5 p.m. Probably still over the hundred mark. What a place to spend the night. The silence would have already begun.

Hazel looks unhappy. I can see she is having second thoughts. Alright, it was soon after she had left me; but she is standing away, in the foreground, as though they're not speaking. See that? Distance = doubts. They've had an argument.

Of course, I want to know all about him. I don't even know his name. In Drysdale's picture he is a silhouette. A completely black figure. He could have been an Aborigine; by the late forties I understand some were employed as drovers.

But I rejected that.

I took a magnifying glass. I wanted to see the expression on his face. What colour is his hair? Magnified, he is nothing but brush strokes. A real mystery man.

It is my opinion, however, that he is a small character. See his size in relation to the horse, to the wheels of the cart. Either that, or it is a ruddy big horse.

It begins to fall into place.

I had an argument with our youngest, Kay, the other day. Both she and Trevor sometimes visit me. I might add, she hasn't married and has her mother's general build. She was blaming me, said people said mum was a good sort.

Right, I nodded.

"Then why did she scoot?"

"Your mother," I said thinking quickly, "had a silly streak."

If looks could kill!

I searched around—"She liked to paddle in water!"

Kay gave a nasty laugh, "What? You're the limit. You really are."

Of course, I hadn't explained properly. And I didn't even know then she had gone off with a drover.

Hazel was basically shy, even with me: quiet, generally non-committal. At the same time, I can imagine her allowing herself to be painted so soon after running off without leaving even a phone number or forwarding address. It fits. It sounds funny, but it does.

This silly streak. Heavy snow covered Mt. Barker for the first time and we took the Austin up on the Sunday. From a visual point of view it was certainly remarkable. Our gum trees and stringy barks somehow do not go with the white stuff, not even the old Ghost Gum. I mentioned this to Hazel but she just ran into it and began chucking snowballs at me. People were laughing. Then she fell in up to her knees, squawking like a schoolgirl. I didn't mean to speak harshly, but I went up to her, "Come on, don't be stupid. Get up." She went very quiet. She didn't speak for hours.

Kay of course wouldn't remember that.

With the benefit of hindsight, and looking at this portrait by Drysdale, I can see Hazel had a soft side. I think I let her clumsiness get me down. The sight of sweat patches under her arms, for example, somehow put me in a bad mood. It irritated me the way she chopped wood. I think she enjoyed chopping wood. There was the time I caught her lugging into the house the ice for the ice chest—this is just after the war. The ice man didn't seem to notice; he was following, working out his change. It somehow made her less attractive in my eyes, I don't know why. And then of course she killed that snake down at the beach shack we took one Christmas. I happened to lift the lid of the incinerator—a black brute, its head bashed in. "It was under the house," she explained.

It was a two-roomed shack, bare floorboards. It had a primus stove, and an asbestos toilet down the back. Hazel didn't mind. Quite the contrary; when it came time to leave she was downcast. I had to be at town for work.

The picture reminds me. It was around then Hazel took to wearing just a slip around the house. And bare feet. The dress in the picture looks like a slip. She even used to burn rubbish in it down the back.

I don't know.

"Hello, missus!" I used to say, entering the kitchen. Not perfect perhaps, especially by today's standards, but that is my way of showing affection. I think Hazel understood. Sometimes I could see she was touched.

I mention that to illustrate our marriage was not all nit-picking and argument. When I realized she had gone I sat for nights in the lounge with the lights out. I am a dentist. You can't have shaking hands and be a dentist. The word passed around. Only now, touch wood, has the practice picked up to any extent.

Does this explain at all why she left?

Not really.

To return to the picture. Drysdale has left out the flies. No doubt he didn't want Hazel waving her hand, or them crawling over her face. Nevertheless, this is a serious omission. It is altering the truth for the sake of a pretty picture, or "composition." I've been up around there—and there are hundreds of flies. Not necessarily germ carriers, "bush flies" I think these are called; and they drive you mad. Hazel of course accepted everything without a song and dance. She didn't mind the heat, or the flies.

It was a camping holiday. We had one of those striped beach tents shaped like a bell. I thought at the time it would prove handy—visible from the air—if we got lost. Now that is a point. Although I will never forget the colours and the assortment of rocks I saw up there I have no desire to return, none. I realized one night. Standing a few yards from the tent, the cavernous sky and the silence all round suddenly made me shudder. I felt lost. It defied logic. And during the day the bush, which is small and prickly, offered no help (I was going to say "sympathy"). It was stinking hot.

Yet Hazel was in her element, so much so she seemed to take no interest in the surroundings. She acted as if she were part of it. I felt ourselves moving apart, as if I didn't belong there, especially with her. I felt left out. My mistake was to believe it was a passing phase, almost a form of indolence on her part.

An unfortunate incident didn't help. We were looking for a camp site. "Not yet. No, not there," I kept saying—mainly to myself, for Hazel let me go on, barely saying a word. At last I found a spot. A tree showed in the dark. We bedded down. Past midnight we were woken by a terrifying noise and lights. The children all began to cry. I had pitched camp alongside the Adelaide-Port Augusta railway line.

Twenty or thirty miles north of Port Augusta I turned back. I had to. We seemed to be losing our senses. We actually met a drover somewhere around there. He was off on the side making tea. When I asked where were his sheep, or the cattle, he gave a wave of his hand. For some reason this amused Hazel. She squatted down. I can still see her expression, silly girl.

The man didn't say much. He did offer tea though. "Come on," said Hazel, smiling up at me.

Hazel and her silly streak—she knew I wanted to get back. The drover, a diplomat, poked at the fire with a stick.

I said:

"You can if you want. I'll be in the car."

That is all.

I recall the drover as a thin head in a khaki hat, not talkative, with dusty boots. He is indistinct. Is it him? I don't know. Hazel—it is Hazel and the rotten landscape that dominate everything.

FRANK MOORHOUSE

THE DROVER'S WIFE[*]

The writing of a story called *The Drover's Wife* by Henry Lawson, published in the great Australian magazine, *The Bulletin*, in 1893, the painting of a picture called *The Drover's Wife* by Russell Drysdale in 1945, and the writing of another story by the same name in 1975 by Murray Bail, also published in *The Bulletin*, draws our attention to what, I will argue in this paper, is an elaborate example of a national culture joke, an "insider joke." Each of these works has the status of an Australian classic and each of these works, I will show, contains a joking wink in the direction of the Australian people. The joke draws on the colloquial Australian humour surrounding the idea of a drover's "wife."

First, a few notations of background for those who are unfamiliar with Australian folklore and the occupation of drover, which is a corruption of the word "driver." A drover or driver of sheep literally drove the sheep to market. The sheep, because of health regulations governing strictly the towns and cities of Australia, were kept many kilometres inland from the sea market towns. The sheep had then to be "driven" by the driver or drover from the inland to the towns, often many thousands of kilometres, taking many months. I am told that this practice has ceased and the sheep are now housed in the cities.

The method of driving sheep was that each sheep individually was placed in a wicker basket on the backs of bullock-drawn wagons known as the woollen wagons. This preserved the sheep in good condition for the market. These bullocks, it is said, would pull the sheep to the coast without human guidance, being able, of course, to smell the sea. But the sheep had to be fed and the drover or driver would give water and seed to the sheep during the journey. The wagon in the Drysdale painting is horse-drawn, denoting a poorer peasant class of drover. The wagon in the painting would probably hold a thousand sheep in wicker baskets.

Now the length of the journey and the harshness of conditions precluded the presence of women and historical fact is that for a century or more there were no women in this pioneering country. This, understandably, led to a close relationship growing between the drover or driver and his sheep. Australian historians acknowledge the closeness of men under this condition of pioneering and have described it as mateship or a pledging of unspoken alliance between two men, a marriage of silence.

---

[*] This is a transcription of a paper on Australian culture given, excitedly, by an Italian student, Franco Casamaggiore, at a recent conference on Commonwealth Writing in Milan.

But the other outlet for emotional and physical drives unacknowledged by historians for reasons of national shame, but widely acknowledged by the folk culture of Australia, was the relationship between the drover or driver and the sheep. Interspecies reciprocity. Hence the joke implicit in the use by the two writers and the painter of the title *The Drover's Wife* and the entry of this unacceptable historical truth from the oral culture into high culture via coded humour.

I illicited the first inklings of this from answers received to questions asked of Australian visitors to Italia about the sheep droving. First, I should explain. Unfortunately I am a poor student living in a humble two-room tugurio. It is a necessity for me to work in the bar of the Hotel Principe e Savoia in Milano and, for a time before that, in the Gritti Palace Hotel, Venezia. But this experience gave to me the opportunity on many occasions to talk and question visiting Australians, although almost always men.

There is an Australian humour of the coarse peasant type not unknown in Italia. Without becoming involved in these details it is necessary for me to document some of the information harvested from contact with the Australian, not having been to the country at first hand although my brother Giovanni is living there in Adelaide but is not any help in such matters, knowing nothing of the droving or culture and knowing only of the price of things and the Holden automobile. Knowing nothing of the things of the spirit. You are wrong, Giovanni.

Yes, but to continue. A rubber shoe or boot used when hunting in wet weather called the gun boot was used by the drovers or drivers and found to be a natural love aid while at the same time a ritualistic symbol used in a gesture of voluntary submission by the drover before his charge. The boots were put on the hind legs of the sheep. The drover would then be shoeless like the sheep and the sheep would "wear the boots" (cf "wearing the pants" in a domestic household). The toe of the boots would be turned towards the drover who would stand on the toes of the boot thus holding the sheep close to him in embrace. These details suffice.

According to my Australian informants the sheep often formed an emotional attachment to the drover who reciprocated. But the journey to the coast had its inherent romantic tragedy. The long journey and shared hardship, the kilometres of companionship, daily took other men he met at GMH factory but he has a head that is too full of materialism to concern himself with exploration of the human condition. How was the sheep chosen? But as in all matters of the human emotion the answer comes blindingly plain. It was explained to me that it is very much like being in a crowded lift, or in a prison, or on board a ship. In a situation of confinement or limitation it is instinctive for people to single out one another from the herd. There is communication by eye, an eye-mating, the same it is with the sheep, I am told. In the absence of human contact the eyes wander across species, the eyes meet, the eyes and ewes.

Yes, and the question comes, was I being fooled about by these Australian visitors and their peasant humour? Or "taken in" as they, the Australian, say. I ask in return—were the Australian visitors telling more than they knew or wanted to tell? The joking is a form of truth telling, a confession. They were also, by joking with my questions, trying to make me look away from my inquiry. But they were also telling me what they did not wish me to know, for the confession is precisely this, and brings relief. I let them joke at me for it was the joke to which I listened. This is the manoeuvre of the national joke, the telling and the not telling at the same time.

We are told that humour has within it the three dialogues. The dialogue between the teller and the listener. The dialogue between the unconscious mind of the teller and his voice. The dialogue between the joker teller and the racial memory which is embodied in the language and the subject of his joking. Humour is the underground route that taboo material—or material of shame—must travel and it is the costume it must wear.

Today such relations between sheep and men are, of course, rare in Australia. However the racial memory of those stranger and more primitive days, and its guilt, still lingers. It is present in a number of ways. As illustrated, it is present in the elaborate cultural joke of High Art. The art which winks. It is there in the peasant humour of the male Australian, the joke which confesses. And further, I am told, it is present in a national artefact—the sheep skin with the wool attached is now often used as a seat cover in the automobile. That today a driver or drover of a car now sits (or lies) with sheep, as it were, under him, while driving not a flock of sheep but a family in a modern auto. It gives comfort through racial memory far exceeding the need for warmth. The car sheep skin covering is an emotional trophy from the sexual underworld of the Australian past. The artefact which remembers.

Naturally all this is still not an open subject for academic explicitness in Australia and only an older culture such as Italia and its perspective of centuries on these newer cultures can reveal it. But I say, Australia—be not ashamed of that which is bizarre, seek not always the genteel. Remember that we, the older cultures, have myths which also acknowledge such happenings of interspecies reciprocity (cf Jason and the Search for the Golden Fleece). See in these happenings the beginnings of your own mythology. See it as an affirmation of the beautiful truth—that we share the planet with animals and we are partners, therefore, in its destiny.

So, in Lawson, Drysdale and Bail, we see how a High Art admits a message of unspeakable truth (albeit, in a coded and guilty way), this being a ploy of all great national cultures.

Thus is the magic of the imagination.

CASEBOOK III:
ALICE MUNRO

This Casebook gathers some of Alice Munro's most interesting remarks about her own practice of the art of fiction. It includes Munro's essay "What is Real?," written in 1982 for John Metcalf's Making It New: Contemporary Canadian Stories; excerpts from Geoff Hancock's 1987 interview; and excerpts from a more recent interview conducted by Eleanor Wachtel for CBC Radio's program "Writers & Company."

GEOFF HANCOCK

INTERVIEW WITH ALICE MUNRO

[on Eudora Welty's "The Worn Path" and the importance of plot]

MUNRO: What happens as event doesn't really much matter. When the event becomes the thing that matters, the story isn't working too well. There has to be a feeling in the story. I said I think "The Worn Path" is a perfect story. It's about an old woman going into town to get medicine for her grandchild. At each successive stage nothing happens. She doesn't come home to find her child dead. She doesn't fail to get the medicine. Nothing happens. I don't feel it's important what happens in my stories. Sometimes, when I have a story that doesn't work, I've made something happen. I've made too much happen....

[on how a story might begin and the "climate" of a story]

MUNRO: I observed a figure of a woman ... and she's wearing a nice striped summer dress, the sort of dress a nice woman wears. A sort of self-effacing, good-taste kind of dress. I saw this woman wearing this, and a huge straw hat with fabric roses on it which was a southern belle's romantic notion of herself. The woman was middle-aged and tall and skinny and very happy. That's what started the story. I was thinking about what might have happened to her. Why she was dressed like that. If she was going to meet her lover. Then other things attached themselves to this story. Material comes from all over. Something someone tells me will attach itself.... I want the characters and what happens subordinated to a climate.

HANCOCK: How do you create that climate?

MUNRO: That's what the whole story is trying to do. You don't do it by passages of descriptive writing or anything like that. It's the writer's angle of vision that will do it.... I have to work at it scene by scene. Oh yes, yes.... Then other things came to me that seemed to fit this climate. And I worked at them.... If I've got a good hold on the mood, I don't have any trouble keeping it growing. In me, it's there. Now, how to keep it growing in the story or how to sustain it or how to make the story work is what I never know from one story to the next. I just keep trying. I just keep trying! I write it! And then I see it's wrong and I write it again.... I change things but I never can tell you why. You know, I might think something was too long-winded or too pointed. Things like that.... What I like is not to really know what the story is all about. And for me to keep trying to find out.

HANCOCK: What makes a story interesting for you?

MUNRO: The thing that I don't know and that I will discover as I go along.... I'll discover things about the characters that I didn't know when I started out. Or just ambiguities in the situation. I will be interested because of the picture, the image, and then I will just keep finding out more and more about it....

[on "Royal Beatings" and whether her writing is a way of making a better world]

MUNRO: As far as I am a normal political person, the kind of person who contributes money and gets involved in causes and thinks about things, I would say I am trying to make a better world. But as a writer, I don't think that way at all. I just get excited by looking at bits of the world here and there and trying to pull a story out of them. Take the story that begins *Who Do You Think You Are?* "Royal Beatings" contains, among many other things, a child being beaten by her father. There is no way I started out to write a story to alleviate the lot of children who are beaten by fathers. As a person this is a cause that would concern me very much. As a writer I just want to see what's there. I just want to write about it. Then, when I transform back into my ordinary liberal, maternal self, I would immediately want such things stopped.... Many writers know exactly what they're doing and have thought things out. Whereas I go into this peculiar limbo and this kind of shady area to look for the story and this takes up a lot of my time and I don't think very clearly about it....

[on setting and the fact that her more recent stories sometimes employ international settings]

MUNRO: To me, that kind of geography is very unimportant. I don't think that a story in which the characters go through their actions in, say Tokyo, is somehow a deeper story with a kind of meaning in it you can't have if the characters do those things in Moose Jaw. I don't think the setting matters at all. A lot of people think I'm a regional writer. And I use the region where I grew up a lot. But I don't have any idea of writing to show the kind of things that happen in a certain place....

[on the development of understanding over time and the gaps in time that occur within her stories]

MUNRO: I like looking at people's lives over a number of years, without continuity. Like catching them in snapshots. And I like the way people relate, or don't relate, to the people they were earlier. This is the sense of life that interests me a lot.... I think this is why I'm not drawn to writing novels. Because I don't see that people develop and arrive somewhere. I just see people living in flashes. From time to time. And this is something you do become aware of as you move into middle age.... You meet people who were a certain kind of character ten years ago and they're someone completely different today. They may tell you a story of what their life was like ten years ago that is different again from what you saw at the time. None of these stories will seem to connect. There are all these realities. The reality a person presents in the narrative we all tell about our own lives. And there's the reality that you observe in the person as a character in your life. And then there's God knows what else....

I don't think I have a sense of time as brutally diminishing or hurting people. My feeling is probably too random for that. That we are liable to get hurt at any time and that things can get better at any time too.

Mostly in my stories I like to look at what people don't understand. What we don't understand. What we think is happening and what we understand later, and so on....

[on residents of Southwestern Ontario who wrote threatening letters to Munro because they were appalled by the implication in one of her stories that incest could happen in their neck of the woods]

MUNRO: It's very understandable really. Because this is the way most people view their lives. You edit your life as you go along. That's one of the things I was talking about. The different editions people make of their lives. So people who could remember these things were editing them out....

[on her characters]

MUNRO: People sometimes criticize my characters. They will say that my characters don't find proper fulfillment, or don't find much of anything. I think critics expect, perhaps, something different from a female writer's characters, or maybe, female characters. The questing male is familiar but the female is not. There's still some expectation that the woman will find a solution to her life. The solution used to be marriage. Then in recent years, it's been walking out on your husband. You know, living on your own; finding yourself. I don't have these resolutions because they seem quite ridiculous to me. What I have is people going on. Just as if every day had its own pitfalls and discoveries and it doesn't make much difference whether the heroine ends up married or living in a room by herself. Or how she ends up at all. Because we finally end up dead.

There are just flashes of things we know and find out. I don't see life very much in terms of progress. I don't feel at all pessimistic. I rather like the idea that we go on and we don't know what's happening and we don't know what we'll find. We think we've got things figured out and then they turn around on us. No state of mind is permanent. It just all has to be there....

[on images and story-building]

HANCOCK: When you write down an image, does that generate a series of other images?

MUNRO: Yes. That's what I started to tell you about how I write stories. I have this picture. It generates some other images and attracts them like a magnet. Things stick to it. Anecdotes and details. I just feel that so much of it is dark. The structure of the story is building up, and you don't see the final shape at all.

HANCOCK: And yet you know it's there and you are moving toward it. That image that is there somewhere.

MUNRO: Audrey [Thomas] said a nice thing to me once in a letter. She was writing a novel and it was like a jig-saw puzzle but she didn't even have all the pieces yet. Or she didn't have the outside pieces. And that is exactly what it's like. You just take the pieces and put them here and there....

[on style]

MUNRO: What I want to get changes with different stories. It's got to be dictated by the story itself. And sometimes I want to get something that is very grainy and I don't want any artifice at all. I don't want the choice of words to seem anywhere elegant. I want awkwardness. I want to get a kind of plainness. And then I would be doing another story with different material and I want it to be, I feel that it should be, well, lush isn't the word I mean. But there should be a kind of luxuriance. Things level upon level. And this means the writing has to change completely.

I don't do this consciously. I'm talking about it now and I know it's what I do. But I don't say I'm going to write a very sort of deadpan (deadpan's the wrong word) dogged kind of prose. Or I'm going to write a fancier prose here. I don't say that but it's what I do. It's not that I want a different effect. The story is different and has to be told a different way.... I want to go with the story the way it has to be. I do feel a kind of inner bell that rings when something is okay.

HANCOCK: The grandmother in "Marrakesh" says that there is in everything something to be discovered.

MUNRO: Oh, yes. Everything. Even totally commonplace things like a shopping centre and a supermarket and things like that are just sort of endlessly interesting in their physical reality. I find them that way. That they seem to mean something way beyond themselves. But I can't explain it much more than that. But I know I can get very excited by ordinary things—things like a bus or something, and I won't really know why. And sometimes this leaves me. Everything, all the physical objects in the world begin to look as if they are just constructed out of material. They don't mean anything but what they seem to mean. You know, a bus is just a conveyance for getting people around. Then I'm greatly depressed. With me this is a sign of depression. When I can't see things with this rim around them.

But usually I do. And it has nothing to do with judgment about things being beautiful or ugly. Which is why, in a way, I don't get as upset as I might about ugly things. There again, there's a difference between the person and the writer. The person that I am, living in a house across from a beautiful wood, would get upset when the bulldozers came in and knocked all the trees down and put up a Texaco station. The person would hate to see that such things are happening in the world. But the writer wouldn't mind at all. The writer would start watching what went on at the Texaco station. It's going back to what I said about how, in the story about the child being beaten, I didn't make any judgments about whether beating children was a horrifying thing.

I just wanted to look at it and think about it and it was a drama in my mind. And I feel the same way about ugly things.

[on her background]

MUNRO: I feel, myself, that I have this enormously good background for a writer. Part of that was not being a member of the middle class. And not living in a neighbourhood where people were more or less the same. And, perhaps not having to carry the burden of expectation that's put on the middle-class child. You make a living and your parents aren't going to be embarrassed if you make that living as a waitress. So you're free....

[on realistic detail and ugly things]

MUNRO: The way people live. The way houses are furnished and all the objects in them. I am crazy about doing this. I have to stop myself. I just love doing everything in the room and everything in the cupboard. You know those things Salinger used to do where he told you everything in the bathroom cabinet.... I love that kind of thing. I like people's clothes, too. I like doing that. I do a lot of surface things. Then I read with great admiration the stories where nothing is described. And I think how wonderful. To go straight to the heart of the matter like that and not bother about what they are wearing! Or what the lampshade was like or anything. I think that's great but I don't do it.... When I was a kid.... I just felt the whole world was seething around me. And everything was to be noted. An object was to be just as important as an animal.

I remember in one of the stories I used a roll of linoleum that was in the attic.

HANCOCK: Someone said that was actually a key word in your work.

MUNRO: What? Linoleum? Well, yes. That's part of being poor, you see. We didn't have any rugs. We had linoleum on the floor. It's as simple as that....

[on endings]

MUNRO: I know the ending when I start a story. But that sometimes changes as I go through it. I don't have any worry, ever, about the end. It may change a bit or something may be substituted but the ending is one of the things that is there very early. Almost as early as that kernel I was talking to you about, in the center of the story. It's just a lot of stuff in between I don't know. I don't know how we get there.

ALICE MUNRO

WHAT IS REAL?

Whenever people get an opportunity to ask me questions about my writing, I can be sure that some of the questions asked will be these:

"Do you write about real people?"

"Did those things really happen?"

"When you write about a small town are you really writing about Wingham?" (Wingham is a small town in Ontario where I was born and grew up and it has often been assumed, by people who should know better, that I have simply "fictionalized" this place in my work. Indeed, the local newspaper has taken me to task for making it the "butt of a soured and cruel introspection.")

The usual thing, for writers, is to regard these either as very naïve questions, asked by people who really don't understand the difference between autobiography and fiction, who can't recognize the device of the first-person narrator, or else as catch-you-out questions posed by journalists who hope to stir up exactly the sort of dreary (and to outsiders, slightly comic) indignation voiced by my home-town paper. Writers answer such questions patiently or crossly according to temperament and the mood they're in. They say, no, you must understand, my characters are composites; no, those things didn't happen the way I wrote about them; no, of course not, that isn't Wingham (or whatever other place it may be that has had the queer unsought-after distinction of hatching a writer). Or the writer may, riskily, ask the questioners what is real, anyway? None of this seems to be very satisfactory. People go on asking these same questions because the subject really does interest and bewilder them. It would seem to be quite true that they don't actually know what fiction is.

And how could they know, when what it is, is changing all the time, and we differ among ourselves, and we don't really try to explain because it is too difficult?

What I would like to do here is what I can't do in two or three sentences at the end of a reading. I won't try to explain what fiction is, and what short stories are (assuming, which we can't, that there is any fixed thing that it is and they are), but what short stories are to me, and how I write them, and how I use things that are "real." I will start by explaining how I read stories written by other people. For one thing, I can start reading from anywhere; from beginning to end, from end to beginning, from any point in between in either direction. So obviously I don't take up a story and follow it as if it were a road, taking me somewhere, with views and neat diversions along the way. I go into it, and move back and forth and settle here and there, and stay in it for a while. It's more like a house. Everybody knows what a house does, how it encloses space and makes connections between one enclosed space and another and presents what is outside in a new way. This is the nearest I can come to explaining what a story does for me, and what I want my stories to do for other people.

So when I write a story I want to make a certain kind of structure, and I know the feeling I want to get from being inside that structure. This is the hard part of the explanation, where I have to use a word like "feeling," which is not very precise, because if I attempt to be more intellectually respectable I will have to be dishonest. "Feeling" will have to do.

There is no blueprint for the structure. It's not a question of, "I'll make this kind of house because if I do it right it will have this effect." I've got to make, I've got to build up, a house, a story, to fit around the indescribable "feeling" that is like the soul of the story, and which I must insist upon in a dogged, embarrassed way, as being no more definable than that. And I don't know where it comes from. It seems to be already there, and some unlikely clue, such as a shop window or a bit of conversation, makes me aware of it. Then I start accumulating the material and putting it together. Some of the material I may have lying around already, in memories and observations, and some I invent, and some I have to go diligently looking for (factual details), while some is dumped in my lap (anecdotes, bits of speech). I see how this material might go together to make the shape I need, and I try it. I keep trying and seeing where I went wrong and trying again.

I suppose this is the place where I should talk about technical problems and how I solve them. The main reason I can't is that I'm never sure I do solve anything. Even when I say that I see where I went wrong, I'm being misleading. I never figure out how I'm going to change things, I never say to myself, "That page is heavy going, that paragraph's clumsy, I need some dialogue and shorter sentences." I feel a part that's wrong, like a soggy weight, then I pay attention to the story, as if it were really happening somewhere, not just in my head, and in its own way, not mine. As a result, the sentences may indeed get shorter, there may be more dialogue, and so on. But though I've tried to pay attention to the story, I may not have got it right; those shorter sentences may be an evasion, a mistake. Every final draft, every published story, is still only an attempt, an approach, to the story.

I did promise to talk about using reality. "Why, if Jubilee isn't Wingham, has it got Shuter Street in it?" people want to know. Why have I described somebody's real ceramic elephant sitting on the mantelpiece? I could say I get momentum from doing things like this. The fictional room, town, world, needs a bit of starter dough from the real world. It's a device to help the writer—at least it helps me—but it arouses a certain baulked fury in the people who really do live on Shuter Street and the lady who owns the ceramic elephant. "Why do you put in something true and then go and tell lies?" they say, and anybody who has been on the receiving end of this kind of thing knows how they feel.

"I do it for the sake of my art and to make this structure that encloses the soul of my story, which I've been telling you about," says the writer. "That is more important than anything."

Not to everybody, it isn't.

So I can see there might be a case, once you've written the story and got the momentum, for going back and changing the elephant to a camel (though there's always a chance the lady might complain that you made a nasty camel out of a beautiful elephant), and changing Shuter Street to Blank Street. But what about the big chunks of reality, without which your story can't exist? In the story "Royal Beatings," I use a big chunk of reality: the story of the butcher, and of the young men who may have been egged on to "get" him. This is a story out of an old newspaper; it really did happen in a town I know. There is no legal difficulty about using it because it has been printed in a newspaper, and besides, the people who figure in it are all long dead. But there is a difficulty about offending people in that town who would feel that use of this story is a deliberate exposure, taunt, and insult. Other people who have no connection with the real happening would say, "Why write about anything so hideous?" And lest you think that such an objection could only be raised by simple folk who read nothing but Harlequin Romances, let me tell you that one of the questions most frequently asked at universities is, "Why do you write about things that are so depressing?" People can accept almost any amount of ugliness if it is contained in a familiar formula, as it is on television, but when they come closer to their own place, their own lives, they are much offended by a lack of editing.

There are ways I can defend myself against such objections. I can say, "I do it in the interests of historical reality. That is what the old days were really like." Or, I do it to show the dark side of human nature, the beast let loose, the evil we can run up against in communities and families." In certain countries I could say, "I do it to show how bad things were under the old system when there were prosperous butchers and young fellows hanging around livery stables and nobody thought about building a new society." But the fact is, the minute I say *to show* I am telling a lie. I don't do it to show anything. I put this story at the heart of my story because I need it there and it belongs there. It is the black room at the centre of the house with all other rooms leading to and away from it. That is all. A strange defence. Who told me to write this story? Who feels any need of it before it is written? I do. I do, so that I might grab off this piece of horrid reality and install it where I see fit, even if Hat Nettleton and his friends were still around to make me sorry.

The answer seems to be as confusing as ever. Lots of true answers are. Yes and no. Yes, I use bits of what is real, in the sense of being really there and really happening, in the world, as most people see it, and I transform it into something that is really there and really happening, in my story. No, I am not concerned with using what is real to make any sort of record or prove any sort of point, and I am not concerned with any methods of selection but my own, which I can't fully explain. This is quite presumptuous, and if writers are not allowed to be so—and quite often, in many places, they are not—I see no point in the writing of fiction.

ALICE MUNRO

WACHTEL: Is that part of writing stories? To try to figure something out? Do you ever write stories where you already know everything at the beginning and you just put them together?

MUNRO: I don't usually bother to write that kind of story any more because it doesn't interest me enough. It works, but it doesn't give me enough pleasure. Now when I write a story I'm always trying to figure out what the story is all about—not how it will work, but what it's really about. This to me is the pleasure of writing.

WACHTEL: Many traditional stories lead to a moment of insight, an epiphany, that sort of thing. Your stories have moments of insight—

MUNRO: Yes, and then they're proved wrong!

WACHTEL: Or there's something that in one instance happens, a moment of accidental clarity, then it evaporates; they're that ephemeral.

MUNRO: The moment evaporates, or the insight leads to something else. That's what I meant when I said flippantly that they're wrong. I want the stories to keep going on. I want the story to exist somewhere so that, in a way, it's still happening, or happening over and over again. I don't want it to be shut up in the book and put away.

WACHTEL: That kind of open-endedness also implies that things don't necessarily improve or get better, that there isn't really—as in the title of one your books—a progress of love.

MUNRO: I haven't lived a whole life yet, so I can't tell you. We'll do an interview sometime later! But that doesn't depress me, the idea that things don't "improve." If you ask me what I believe as a person, I'd say that life gets better, or one's ability to put up with it gets better. But things change. One of the things that interests me so much in writing and in observing people is that things keep changing. Cherished beliefs change. Ways of dealing with life change. The importance of certain things in life changes. All this seems to me endlessly interesting—that is the thing that doesn't change or that I certainly hope doesn't change. If you find life interesting, it just goes on being so.

WACHTEL: Some critics have found *Friend of My Youth* sad, elegiac, that sort of thing. Is it misguided to expect happiness in modern fiction?

MUNRO: I'd like to think that there are lots of periods of happiness in the stories. It's all muddled up: happiness, sadness, depression, elation. As I said, the constant happiness is curiosity. I wouldn't set out to write a story that I thought was depressing, because that would depress me. But I notice that sometimes other people's stories that I like very much are criticized as being depressing. And I feel very puzzled about the person who's making this judgment and what they like to read or what their lives are like. Maybe a lot of people are happy all the time.

WACHTEL: I want to try out a theory on you. One of the ways you exhibit your craft as a writer is that you give us in these stories a profound sense of absence. There are absences everywhere: deaths, vanished worlds, missing spouses, broken marriages, one character even has a missing eye. What do you think?

MUNRO: I can't deal with theories very well. But yes, absences certainly interest me. Loss, which everyone experiences all the time. We keep losing ourselves and the worlds we used to live in. Whether this is more a factor in modern life, I don't know. I think maybe it is. Nowadays people do go from one sort of life to another. It's not uncommon now to go from one marriage to another or from being one sort of person to being an entirely different kind of person. So you've got all these rooms in your head that you've shut off but that you can remember. I think some people don't really bother much with remembering; it seems a useless activity. But most writers are addicted to it. I suppose I am, too.

WACHTEL: Your stories are getting very, very complex. It's a bit like a three-dimensional chess game sometimes. There are so many layers of things going on and crosscutting in time and memory. Or it's like a pile of snapshots that are all shuffled up. Why do you do that?

MUNRO: I just like to. I can't get a grasp on what I'm trying to talk about unless I do that. I don't do it to make things difficult. You might think it's the challenge of writing this way, but I don't think that's true. It's that I see things now in this way, and there is absolutely no other way I can deal with the material of fiction. You'll have something that is awkward, that is difficult to work in, and you think, I can cut this, I can streamline this, and it doesn't work. It's got to go in somehow.

WACHTEL: At the beginning of one of your stories a character taking a creative writing course is told not to try to put in too many things at once, so she makes this long list of all the things she wants to make sure she gets in there, and hands it in as an appendix to her story.

MUNRO: Of course I haven't done that and don't know of anybody who has, but it seems to me that if you wrote the sort of story she is advised to write, you'd be very worried afterwards, thinking, But I didn't mention that and that was also part of what was going on at the time, and I didn't say that afterwards, and so on. To me, what you have when you pull all these things out is not the story. I suppose this is a kind of anti-minimalist way of writing. I can enjoy minimalist stories. They seem to me to have a singular force, but I couldn't enjoy writing one.

WACHTEL: That's because yours have a multiple force. In a story in *Friend of My Youth* called "Hold Me Fast, Don't Let Me Pass" the narrator ponders questions like: What makes a man happy? What makes a woman happy? Do you know what makes you happy? Are you happy?

MUNRO: Yes. It's as I said, it's being interested. This is the thing I hope will never leave me—a very high level of interest most of the time. When that vanishes, which it sometimes does temporarily, I think it would be awful to live like this, going through the motions of life. But we all experience times like that. It's also very important to me to love certain human beings and be loved by them—then what happens in their lives is very important. But underneath, the thing that would help me survive anything, I think, is this interestedness.

WACHTEL: In your fiction there is often sex without guilt. In fact, given the complexity and the attentiveness of all the characters, I am surprised at how little guilt there is generally.

MUNRO: That's part of being interested. If you find something interesting— really interesting—it's very hard to regret it. You may think, Oh, that was frivolous behaviour, that was selfish behaviour, that was perhaps damaging behaviour—but wasn't it interesting. Why would a person who feels this way now about something have felt that way then? Regret fades away in the face of interest.

WACHTEL: Why are you so interested in adultery?

MUNRO: Adultery is like modern theatre in the adventure it offers in ordinary people's lives. I suppose it always did, but much more in men's lives than in women's in days gone by, and more in rich, idle people's lives than in ordinary people's lives. The opportunities have become much greater. The guilt about it may be less, but it's still there. It's a way of expressing themselves, perhaps, for people who have no other way, because people get boxed in and there's this role it's possible to play, very briefly, which gives people a sense of still existing. Then, of course, it leads into all kinds of other things. It's a drama in people's lives that I think a writer is naturally attracted to.

WACHTEL: Like your earlier books, *Friend of My Youth* has been enormously successful. Do you allow yourself to enjoy this success or do you still cling to feelings of insecurity?

MUNRO: I do both: I enjoy it and I'm insecure at the same time.

September 1990

interview prepared in collaboration
with Richard Handler
and Sandra Rabinovitch

PART IV

APPENDIXES

A BRIEF NOTE ON THE HISTORY OF THE SHORT STORY

Prose fiction became an important branch of literature only in the eighteenth century, and the novel came before the story. The modern short story is often said to have begun in the nineteenth century, with writers like Washington Irving, Nathaniel Hawthorne, and Edgar Allan Poe in the United States, or Nikolai Gogol in Russia. But the history of the story is, in fact, far older and geographically more diverse, reaching into all cultures and beginning in prehistoric times. The comments that follow should be understood both as being particularly Western in their orientation and as barely scratching the surface of the rich and complex history of the short story.

The earliest known stories were oral and were concerned with explaining how human beings and the world began. These creation myths, occurring in virtually all tribal cultures, have been among the most potent of human stories. Many written stories in all historical periods—think of *Genesis*, for example, or some recent science fiction—are a part of this tradition. Both the huge questions such stories addressed and the marvellous shapes of the stories themselves have continued to be important to us and to inspire writers to produce more of such stories.

Two other early forms of the story are the beast fable and the religious parable. In beast fables, animals are made to conduct themselves in ways that illuminate human behaviour and teach a moral lesson. Aesop, a Greek slave in the fifth or sixth century B.C., gave us some of the earliest and still most famous examples of the beast fable; more recent examples include the Uncle Remus stories of Joel Chandler Harris, which recount the humorous escapades of Br'er Rabbit and Br'er Fox,[1] and George Orwell's satirical novel *Animal Farm*. Religious parables, such as the biblical story of the prodigal son or the tale of the wise and foolish virgins, also invite the reader to reflect on a religious or moral lesson. Both the beast fable and the religious parable have a consciousness-altering intent, relying for their effect on a kind of jolt or gradual awakening whereby we are made to recognize ourselves—or some application to us—in the story being told. Like most stories, they may be said to work by example. But here the force of the revelation, mirroring and overcoming our slowness to see a particular truth, is engineered by the author's choice of an example that strikes us at first as being more unlike us. These two early forms of the story illustrate the craftily induced sense of recognition that is fundamental to the story, and both remain within the repertoire of fictional types.

Most narrative art (that is, story telling) in ancient Greece and Rome took the form of poetry or drama rather than prose fiction, and its subject matter was largely historical and mythological. Although some prose fiction was written in the classical period, such as Petronius's *The Satyricon*, the literary developments that would turn out to be most important for the subsequent history of the story occurred in poetry, with the rise of the epic and pastoral traditions, and in poetic drama. Greek tragedy, in particular, which was brilliantly analyzed by Aristotle in *The Poetics*, greatly influenced later understandings of how plot and character operate in fiction. That Petronius's great satirical work was written in prose, however, is of interest, given the later importance of satire in the prose tradition generally.

In the medieval period, narrative art remained primarily poetic, with prose being reserved primarily for instructional and devotional writing. Of particular note for the history of the story are the French comic tales of "low" life, called *fabliaux*, the romance tradition associated with courtly love, Boccaccio's *Decameron* in Italy (a cycle of prose tales), and Chaucer's *Canterbury Tales* in England. Chaucer's great work, which was strongly influenced by Boccaccio, is a cycle of "tales" told in both verse and prose, incorporating such literary forms as the romance, the religious parable, and the fabliau.

The distrust of fiction, or the tendency to regard fiction as ungodly falsehood and as being self-indulgent and dangerous in its powerful appeal to the human imagination, goes back to Plato in ancient Greece and was especially pronounced in the medieval period. Chaucer is careful to insist on the moral value and, therefore, the respectability of the tale. But an unresolved tension between morality (or instruction) and art for art's sake (pleasure or entertainment) lies at the heart of *The Canterbury Tales*.

At work here are two distinct attitudes, held by different groups of people, against which prose fiction would have to struggle over time. The first was a distrust, fed by Christian theologians such as St. Thomas Aquinas, of imaginative writing, including poetry and drama; and the second, amongst those who did value imaginative writing, was a belief that prose was a lower form. Poetry offered the elevated language that was considered more stirring and appropriate for large subjects and noble human figures. In the Renaissance, prose fiction continued as a minor branch of literary production; stories, of which a great many were recycled, including many from the East, were typically told in verse, whether dramatic or not, and the majority of prose work was nonfiction.

Then, in the eighteenth century, with increasing secularization and the rise of the middle class, fiction began to come into its own. Both the distrust of imaginative writing, which had been based largely in the power of the church, and the disdain of prose were lessening. Why prose became more respectable at this time is an interesting question, one explanation of which may be the more practical or prosaic attitude of this emerging middle class. Epic poetry and drama had been associated primarily with telling the stories of elevated figures such as kings and queens, whereas the novel, essentially a new form developed in the eighteenth century, would at last bring to centre stage the less elevated figures who for centuries had been threatening to have their say (as, for example, the "low" characters of Greek drama or the fabliau or Shakespeare). The novel also would serve to mirror the lives of the middle class, to tell their stories. Realism is thus strongly linked with the rise of the novel.

At the same time, the attraction of literature was that it gave scope for the repressed imagination and relief from the too prosaic quality of daily life. In the eighteenth and nineteenth centuries, audiences were attracted by both the real and the marvellous (or the romantic). Thus, the "oriental" tale and the gothic novel were both popular literary forms. But the essential point is that the audience, and therefore the market, for literature was expanding greatly. More and more people had the education, the leisure, and the money necessary to read. Particularly important in this period were the periodicals, which published novels in serial form, aimed at keeping the middle classes in eager anticipation of the instalment in the next issue, as well as short tales and sketches. The demand for stories short enough to be published in their entirety in a single issue increased over time, and professional writers could make money producing them.

Short fiction appearing in the early periodicals was often conventionally sentimental or sensationalist. Much of it was published anonymously, and much was aimed largely at producing an income for its authors. But several things converged to increase the quality and respectability of the short story. French mid-eighteenth century satirical writers such as Voltaire and Diderot were critical of easy, "escapist" effects, which they saw as means of evading serious social, moral, and philosophical issues, and the romantic writers at the beginning of the nineteenth century revealed that the heightened realm of fancy and the imagination could be approached with a passionate seriousness. German writers such as Goethe, Hoffmann, Kleist, and the Grimm brothers (authors of the fairy tales, based on folk materials, that became known around the world) were particularly important in developing the romantic or marvellous strain of short fiction. Another important influence on the story at this time was a fascination with psychology and with the abnormal, including criminal behaviour, which can be found both in escapist stories and in the increasing number of serious examples of short fiction. Fictional treatments of the abnormal often present an interesting mix of the realistic and the romantic.

The modern short story generally is said to have arisen in the nineteenth century. That the story itself is often said to have been born at this time may be explained by the new seriousness with which the form was being taken. The short story began to be seen as a serious literary genre, something distinct from other literary types and worthy of respect. Previously, a kind of "bastard" form—a product of indiscriminate cominglings, emerging without regard for law, and unacknowledged by its family—the short story could now be regarded as a legitimate form of literary art. The first phase of its legitimacy came in the romantic era, roughly the first half of the nineteenth century, and the second phase began in the mid century with the rise of realism.

These two basic strains—the romantic and the realistic—are often mixed in a particular story, both in the nineteenth century and today, and neither the laws or the conventions of romance nor the laws of realism could properly be said to determine legitimacy. The true legitimacy of the story as a genre begins with a recognition of its power to achieve greatness. Ironically, such legitimacy depends on a kind of return to bastard status, for the story, like other respectable literary genres, is in fact promiscuous—it goes where it likes and establishes its own rules. The story rests on a rich multiplicity of antecedents, on which practitioners continue to build, and on the open range of its possibilities in the future.

In the United States, a country that has been especially important for the development of the short story, principal figures of the romantic era include Washington Irving, Nathaniel Hawthorne, and Edgar Allan Poe. Irving, in tales such as the familiar "Rip Van Winkle," built on the folk tradition, as the brothers Grimm had in Germany. Hawthorne's stories, dealing with serious moral issues and questions about the relationship of art and life, were romantic particularly in their use of dramatically heightened situations and fantastical elements. Edgar Allan Poe picked up the European interest in the gothic and the abnormal and greatly influenced the history of the story through his "unity of effect" theory. Poe saw the special genius of the story as a function of the story's brevity, which allowed each brushstroke to count toward some single lasting impression of the whole. If subsequent writers have been less sure about unity of effect, arguing that a story is often more multifaceted and less compressed than that term suggests, they have nonetheless agreed that every detail should count toward the whole. On one level, what Poe was defending was simply the art of the story.

Writers such as Hawthorne and Poe, or the Russian Gogol, wrote stories they called "tales." The great Canadian literary critic Northrop Frye defined the *tale* as being close in kind to the prose romance of the middle ages; its characters are stylized figures that stand for basic human types, in contrast to the particularity and complexity sought after for the characters of realistic fiction.

Realism in the American short story began approximately with Herman Melville, and became dominant at the end of the century with the work of Henry James, Edith Wharton, Stephen Crane, and Willa Cather—all of these writers being associated particularly with *psychological* realism and with complexity of characterization.

The "local colour" movement in the United States was another significant part of the realist impulse in the mid-to-late nineteenth century. Its special concern was realism of place or setting; characters were made to speak and behave in ways that would express the "colour" or texture of life in some particular region of the country. This movement was of limited duration and was important mainly for raising the profile of place or locale as an ingredient for fiction. Writers like William Faulkner and Flannery O'Connor, who attempt so much more than an evocative description of the American South, would never be called local colourists. It is worth noting here that the felt atmosphere of place is generally, though not always, important in both realistic stories and romantic tales. Even in realistic fiction, however, the writer need not be confined to places that actually exist whereas for local colourists the wish to convey the feel of an actual place is the central goal.

Two fathers of the modern short story are Guy de Maupassant in France and the great Anton Chekhov in Russia. Like the American O. Henry, de Maupassant often wrote very tidy stories ending with an ironic twist, but his principal and relentless concern was to see life as it really is, including most particularly the material conditions of our lives. *Irony*, which involves some disparity between appearance or aspiration and reality, is an important part of the realistic vision. Irony is important also in Chekhov, who has probably been more influential than any other writer in the development of the short story. Chekhov's stories are less plot driven than de Maupassant's and more subtle. Chekhov is a kind of sympathetic moralist, working away with great delicacy at the nuances of his characters' lives—their feelings and impressions, as well as their attempts to find meaning in existence.

Nearly all of the great modernist writers of the short story were strongly influenced by the interior impressionism of Chekhov. Among these writers, the Irish writer James Joyce built directly on Chekhov in designing his stories around what he called an "epiphany"—the moment of revelation at which a character attains some sudden insight. This strategy of working toward an epiphany which has dominated the recent history of the story, can be linked to the moment of "recognition" that Aristotle described in his analysis of Greek tragedy. But for Chekhov, Joyce, and their descendents, the epiphany or recognition is likely to occur in quite ordinary people and can itself constitute the climax of the action. Plot is usually quite a modest affair. It is interesting to note here that in contemporary stories the moment of insight is often reserved for the reader.

Other modernist giants of the short story include Joseph Conrad, D.H. Lawrence, Franz Kafka, and Katherine Mansfield, and, in the United States, Sherwood Anderson, William Faulkner, and Ernest Hemingway. Although these writers have very distinct voices and concerns, all are modernist in the sense that they are part of a critical phase of the story's development in which the discovery of new ways of getting at the interior or "felt" quality of our lives was paramount.

The experimental impulse is still strong in the contemporary story, but where the story is now, with the advent of postmodernism, is hard to say. Writers often borrow from their predecessors, reinventing their stories as in "The Drover's Wife" or in Raymond Carver's revisiting of Chekhov's final hours. The traditional "well-made" story, with a recognizable beginning, middle, and end, continues to compete for magazine space as well as for readers with more experimental work, as has been the case for the past fifty years. But the experimental impulse itself often takes the form of "playing" with the old; this is indeed a large part of what is meant by postmodernism.

Among the many contemporary developments in the story are the stripped-down minimalism especially popular in the United States; the "magic realism" associated primarily with South America; the "metafictional" self-consciousness of the story as story; the interest in unreliable or multiple narrators; and the transgression of genre boundaries (a story, for instance, that "pretends" to be an essay). All of these developments reveal an awakened interest in the formal construction or rearrangement of story and in the very concept of what short fiction is and can be.

Among the most important developments in the contemporary story is its increasing internationalism—an awareness on the part of writers in one country of work being done in another. Both within and between countries, writers are travelling more and more widely, and their work is travelling too. The widespread practice of writers giving public readings of their work is one factor contributing to an increased sense of the community of writers, or what the Canadian novelist Margaret Laurence called her "tribe." Such cross-fertilization has contributed immensely to the health and vitality of the short story form, and indeed to the development of national literatures. Donald Barthelme's statement (*Paris Review, 80*) that "Beckett, I suppose, made it possible for me to write" is representative of the claims made so frequently by writers themselves as to the critical importance of other writers' work. Writers are fed promiscuously by other writers both at home and far away, by living writers, and by those who are alive only on the page.

ENDNOTE

1. Uncle Remus, *His Songs and Sayings*. n.p.: Appleyard, 1935.

DEFINING THE SHORT STORY

Numerous attempts have been made to identify the characteristics of the short story that define it as a genre and distinguish it from the novel. Edgar Allan Poe's discussion of unity of effect is perhaps the most important of these attempts. But in any strict sense such attempts are doomed; the best one might hope for is to say that "usually" or "often" the story does this or that. In fact, the term *short story* is itself about as close to a definition that would cover all particular examples of the genre as we can get: it is a story, or a work of fiction, and it is short, meaning shorter than a novel.

But there is no magic number of words or pages at which point a work of fiction ceases to be a story and becomes a novel, or indeed a novella. *Novella* is the intermediate term often used to describe fiction that seems too long to call a story and too short to call a novel. The average length of a novella might be around thirty thousand words, but there is no settled rule and no necessity to use the term novella—one writer, critic, or publisher might choose to use the term novella for a work of fiction that someone else decides to call a story if it's fairly short, or a novel if it's long. There is also no established minimum length for a short story; some have been only a single sentence long. Very short stories (up to a thousand or possibly two thousand words) are now often called *short-shorts*.

If a short story is a (more or less) short work of fiction, all that would seem to remain in defining it is to distinguish fiction from nonfiction and then from poetry and drama, as the other traditional forms of what we call "imaginative writing." Usually the category into which a work falls—nonfiction, fiction, poetry, or drama—will be self-evident. But increasingly in our time, the boundaries between these genres are consciously transgressed. We have, for example, genres we now identify as the "prose poem" and "creative non-fiction"; we also may have a story that purports to be something else, such as an interview or a speech. A story might adopt the voice of an expert in some area of knowledge and incorporate something of the flavour and devices of nonfiction; Borges, one notes, is notoriously fond of using footnotes.

The basic meaning of story is "narrative," meaning an account of certain events. However, many contemporary novels and short stories seem to do everything possible to flout this equation of story with plot, as if to show what else a story can be or do. It seems impossible to dispense with plot altogether:

something has to happen, some movement has to occur over time. But in some stories the events recounted might be experienced simply as a sequence of feelings, ideas, or observations; the trick here, as always, is to maintain some form of narrative or dramatic tension. The reader wants to know what happens next, where this thing is going. In certain stories it is hard to distinguish narrative tension from curiosity about what the form or language of the story will do next: part of the "story" is what *story* can do. Narrative tension—and not dramatic tension (a term borrowed from drama)—would be the correct term in this case.

The Elements of Fiction

Plot and Structure

The plot of a story is what happens in it, or the events that are recounted. Because the short story is short, its plot often involves a single episode, or a small number of related events, and a brief time frame. But this is not always the case. A short story can take on the whole of a person's life—even the history of planet Earth—or it may speak of events that conclude within just a few minutes, or even seconds. The length of the story itself, however, will not depend on the temporal frame of the events recounted. Lengthy action can be radically compressed, so that the story of Earth is told in a page, and brief action can be drawn out, as, for example, in a long story that treats the moment before death.

A crucial distinction needs to be made between the order of events as they are supposed to have occurred in the lives of the characters (following the distinction made by Aristotle, this is sometimes called the "action") and the order in which these events are recounted in the story. Sometimes there is no apparent difference: what happens is told in strict chronological order. But often the time line is disrupted. Flashbacks are an obvious example, whereby a narrative that is proceeding linearly is suddenly interrupted to recall something that happened earlier. Thus, a character in old age whose last days constitute the forward motion or apparent "story" of the story might recall or "flash back" to something she witnessed as a child.

Either a character or the narrator can take us into the past. The temporal interruption may consume only a few lines and may or may not be of major importance. Sometimes the most dramatic action and the most significant events occur entirely in the past; telling this, however, could take up only a small portion or nearly all of the story's words. If the present time of the story is primarily a site from which to recall the past and largely disappears from view once the story gets underway, that present portion of the story is usually called the *frame*. This term suggests that the story, the picture or the thing we are really interested in, exists inside it. Usually, we return to the frame at the end. Sometimes the frame can be quite sizable and richly detailed, and often it is more important than is immediately apparent. Thus, the frame should always be inspected with great care.

Plot is often held to be the most fundamental element of fiction. Something has to happen as the story moves through time or from beginning to end. The story has to *go* somewhere. Indeed, we might think of plot (though it is only one element of fiction) as the path the story takes. But the main point here is that the story cannot be static; change of some kind must occur. The situation changes, or characters change, or the reader's understanding changes.

Plot is sometimes understood as the major things that happen in a story, a kind of outline of significant events; plot in this sense is the skeleton upon which the rest of the living organism of the story is hung. Thus, we sometimes speak of the "bare bones" of the plot. But we might also say that everything that happens in a story—including, for example, the sudden appearance of a hawk in the sky, whether or not that hawk swoops down to attack the central character—is actually part of the plot. We might say of a certain story that "not much happens in it," meaning that the events described are not particularly dramatic, but a story, by definition, always has a plot of some kind. And even very small events—is she or isn't she going to burn her husband's toast?—can be made to feel surprisingly dramatic.

Conflict in a story generates dramatic tension for the reader. A conflict may develop between individuals or groups, between the individual and nature (a storm at sea, for example), between competing ideas or conceptions of reality, or between parts of (that is to say, within) a person. We want to know not only what happens next, but, more specifically, which of the competing forces will prevail. There can, of course, be more than one sort of conflict going on, or there may be conflicts within conflicts. Because plots are steered by conflict, going this way or that along the story's path as the struggle develops, conflict is a primary driver of plot.

The beginning, middle, and end of stories can usually be analyzed in terms of this developing conflict. The beginning sets up the conflict, the middle complicates it, and the ending resolves it, at least to some degree. The *exposition* is a term often used for the first phase of the story, in which we are introduced or "exposed" to the characters, the setting, and the initial situation in which some conflict is either latent or explicit. In the modern story, exposition draws far less attention to itself than is evident in much of our earlier literature. Next comes the *rising action*, in which this conflict is complicated and intensified; the action of this phase of the story is called "rising" because our tension mounts. The rising action is the "middle" of the story and is generally its longest phase. The third phase is the *climax*, the most dramatic moment of the story. This is what the story has been working up to; it is a kind of explosion generated by the friction of opposing forces. The climax or third phase is also sometimes called the "turning point" of the plot. The fourth phase is the *falling action*, in which the story starts to wind down. The fifth and final phase is the *conclusion*, which in a short story is often the last paragraph. The resolution of the conflict occurs in these last two phases and may also be implicit in the climax. The conclusion is the final and often very complex emotional "note" on which the story comes to rest.

This five-part linear analysis of plot goes back to Aristotle and Greek tragedy; it applies well to some stories, and much less well to others. While it can help the reader to see the underlying design of a great many stories, it should not become a straitjacket into which all stories are forced. In any case, an ability to locate these phases in a particular story may not take the reader very far into an understanding of how plot works. Perhaps the most important thing we can do in trying to understand plot is to ask ourselves what each event in the story contributes to the whole, keeping in mind that everything is there for a reason.

An important question having to do with the relationship between events may be suggested by the term *juxtaposition*. The writer decides not only what events to include in the story, but what to put them next to or close to. Because two things are close together in the text, the first is still fresh in our minds and possibly still visible on the page when we come to the second. Juxtaposition, the writer hopes, will cause the two things to "mix" in the reader's mind. The relationship between these two events may in fact be causal, meaning something happens because something else did. Or it may be that one thing helps us to understand something in the other. Thus, if an event (a detail or an episode) seems extraneous to the story, the reader should pause to think about why it is in the story at all and why the writer has placed it *here*. Is there something in the vicinity that provides a clue to the usefulness of this puzzling piece of the story?

Coming to terms with plot and with the story itself is a matter of understanding how the pieces fit together. Juxtaposition helps us to connect things that are close to one another, but we must also stretch our minds to connect things that are farther apart. The *repetition* of some element (for example, the sound of a child weeping) may signal to us that a connection between two widely separated scenes is worth exploring. Consider, also, foreshadowing: something happens, possibly an episode in the plot or just a small detail, that anticipates or sets us up for a subsequent event. Foreshadowing attempts to put us in an appropriate frame of mind for our encounter with this later event; it builds tension and increases our sense of "rightness" or inevitability when at last we come to the foreshadowed event. We may or may not be conscious of such foreshadowing in a first reading, and usually the writer takes care not to be heavy handed. But in subsequent readings, when we are trying to understand how the story is made and how it has achieved its effects, this is one of the things to look for.

The term *foreshadowing* is often reserved for things such as a gun we might see lying casually on the mantlepiece in the opening scene, a "shadowy" gun that takes on real substance for us when it kills someone at the climax of the story. But a story is full of shadows cast in all directions, shadows that take on greater substance when seen in the light of something else, and it is important to understand that the process is not simply linear. Our minds move around in—or should move in—the space the story makes. We do not simply proceed from the first word to the last. We do that, of course, and the sequence is important, but we also remember; and we stop to reflect and connect. And so things that happen later may give substance to, or shed an entirely new light on, earlier events.

This capacity we have to let our minds play or move around within the thing the writer has made also helps to explain why action (the chronological order of events) and plot (the ordering of those events by the writer) are not identical. Plot often differs from action so as to unleash that power of intellectual movement in us. Episodes are arranged by the writer in a way that allows us to go beyond a simple apprehension of events to a more complex understanding of what lies behind them.

The term *structure* may be introduced here, in relation to plot, because plot—as the "skeleton," we said earlier, on which everything else hangs—is closely identified with structure. For example, movement from exposition to rising action to climax to falling action to conclusion suggests a five-part structure. But a story with this structure, told in three scenes, might also have a more apparent three-part structure. A story can be structured in any number of ways, not all of which involve plot, and there are always structures within or overlapping other structures. A story as a whole might be structured by the use of alternating points of view, time periods, or levels of reality (for example, dream sections written in a markedly different style may be interspersed throughout a narrative)—or by any number of other factors.

To approach the concept of literary structure, it may be helpful to think about what we mean when we say that a plot or a story is circular. The story starts at point "A" and circles back to it. Plot is what happens along the way; we may say that the plot is circular, but in doing so we are addressing an issue of structure. We are looking at the abstract quality of circularity, the form of the circle, along which this particular plot moves.

Structure is the basic shape or design that underlies any particular entity. For example, we may speak of the structure of a sentence by pointing out that it begins with a participial phrase or by saying that its basic pattern is simple, compound, or complex. Paragraphs also have a structure of some kind. Individual scenes have a structure, or a way in which they are organized or built, and so has the story as a whole. A building might be designed in three sections; similarly, a story may have a tri-partite structure. Lots of individual buildings, or individual stories, are built using this basic structure.

Certain basic story types—the Cinderella story, let's say—can also be used to structure or to suggest the basic shape of other stories. Similarly, character types that are used repeatedly in fiction, such as the wise old woman, may provide a kind of skeleton or structural model that is fleshed out or played upon in new ways with a particular wise old woman in a certain story. These examples—Cinderella and the wise old woman—suggest yet another level of the meaning of structure, which is a particularly complex and important literary concept.

CHARACTER

Characters are the actors in the plot. A story must have characters. If we have a murder, for example, someone has to do the killing, and someone has to die. But how important those characters are—how large a part of the writer's purpose is vested in the attractions or believability of the characters—will vary from one kind of story to another. Similarly, some stories depend more on plot than other stories do. Most often, however, the link between character and plot is very strong and is causal; that is, certain things happen because of who the characters are, and to understand why certain things occur we look to the characters. Indeed, in order to believe certain events we must satisfy ourselves that there is something in the "character" of the character that could account for this behaviour. At the same time, we should always be wary of psychoanalyzing fictional characters as if they were real people. Characters are not people, but are literary constructs or beings made out of words, existing only within the larger construct that is the story itself. Characters do not even always purport to be human beings; animals, too, quite often function as characters. Even pieces of furniture might serve as characters in an occasional experimental story!

All this being said, the ability to create memorable or compelling characters—including characters about whom we are made to care, almost as if they were people we knew in life—is one of the greatest gifts the writer of fiction can possess. Characters are created out of some interplay between two impulses in the writer's imagination: those "touches" that typify, or remind us of a particular kind of person, and those that individualize, or make us feel that this person is somehow unique. Both of these impulses are important; and the mix is important, especially in realistic fiction. Characters are called *stereotypical* when the typifying impulse is borrowed directly from everyday life and repeats certain lazy and inaccurate habits of generalization; they are called *archetypal* when the type that is embodied by the character is experienced as some universal truth. Although many characters are neither stereotypical nor archetypal, all contain certain typifying features that help us to recognize them as a certain kind of person. The individualizing touches—the peculiar way a person speaks, perhaps—are often a source of great delight, in fiction as in life, as they provide relief from the typical and can make the characters come alive.

It is important to understand that in some stories the writer is not interested in creating what are often referred to as *rounded* characters. All, some, or none of the characters in a particular story might be "rounded," a term suggesting the complexity, three-dimensionality, or many sides of real people. So-called *flat* characters—"one-note" characters or characters with few sides, who have not been endowed with depth or three-dimensionality—often serve the writer's purpose better, since they can be extremely funny or chilling, and as memorable as a rounded character, or they can simply function to perform some required action.

The rounding out of a character generally takes some time to produce, and would not always be time well spent. It is generally more effective even in realistic fiction to sketch in some characters quickly, so as not to distract the reader from more pressing matters. In some stories, none of the characters may be rounded. The emphasis is intended to be on plot or atmosphere or ideas, and the characters are there primarily to enact that plot, to create that atmosphere, or to express those ideas. Psychological realism could obscure, slow down, or utterly defeat what the writer is attempting to achieve.

Sometimes, however, a character is flat that was intended to be round; the impression of depth, even perhaps after a considerable expenditure of words devoted to that purpose, has not been successfully achieved by the writer. (Readers, of course, may well disagree on the question of whether a character is or was intended to be flat or round.) Another pair of terms often used to describe fictional characters, *static* and *dynamic*, presents a similar difficulty. We might suppose that a static character, meaning one that does not seem to change in the course of a story, is less compelling to the reader and less meritorious on the writer's part than a *dynamic* character. In fact, a character may be static either because that is what the story calls for—or because the writer has failed to convey an intended impression of that character changing over time. Again, readers may disagree on these points. A final observation to be made about these terms is that characters can be more or less rounded or flat, and more or less dynamic or static; we are not by any means obliged to consign them to one category or the other, or indeed to use these terms at all.

Characterization is the term used to describe how a writer goes about the job of creating a character. What tools are available to the writer? What can the writer use to create a particular character in our minds? Just words, of course, but words can convey what the character does, says, and thinks, as well as what the character looks like, and how other characters react to him or think or talk about him. How a character speaks, or the particular way she uses language—as opposed simply to what she says—helps to establish and distinguish a character in our minds and can also reveal a good deal about her. Important information about the character, such as snippets of family history, may be provided by the narrator or worked into dialogue or into the character's own thoughts. Sometimes a story will have a narrator who makes judgments about the sort of person this is, who analyzes the "character" of the character. Most often, however, the writer's aim is to show rather than tell.

Keep in mind here that the writer usually works with a number of characters at once, creating them in relation to one another and to certain ideas or themes that are being explored in the story. Characters are not a series of individuals to be approached by the reader in isolation from one another. Rather, they are something like an "ensemble" that combines to fulfill the writer's purpose. They shed light on one another, and not only in an obvious way through their interaction in the story, but also because the reader is being silently urged by the writer to compare and contrast them. Perhaps two people are seated next to each other on a bus. One may have been invented primarily to deepen our understanding of the other, rather than simply to perform some necessary piece of business in the plot. Parallels of various kinds may be established between two characters (both, for example, have lost their mothers at an early age) in order to make us reflect on the ways in which these characters are alike and not alike. We can perhaps apply some insight extracted from our contemplation of one to the other, who is of greater interest. Such parallels or repetitions work like juxtaposition (putting those two people next to each other on the bus) to make us connect them, and perhaps to see what the writer wants us to see.

The main character of a story is called its *protagonist*; the less common term *antagonist* may be used to describe an opponent of the main character in some struggle being depicted. Sometimes the protagonist is also called the *hero*, but this term can only be used in place of protagonist if, in spite of whatever faults the protagonist may possess, we regard him or her as essentially admirable and wish to emphasize that fact. The term hero also tends to direct attention to some struggle in which we regard the protagonist as being on the right side.

POINT OF VIEW

The term *point of view* refers to the perspective from which the story is told. This is one of the most critical decisions a writer makes: how will I approach the story? Who will tell it and how much will I permit that person (or those persons or that disembodied voice) to know?

The writer's decision on point of view is a technical decision establishing some of the basic rules for the telling of a particular story. These rules, varying from one story to another and self-imposed by the writer, can sometimes be rather complicated; a number of technical terms, the most basic of which are defined below, have been developed to help explain them. Before looking at these terms, however, we should be clear that point of view is much more than a *device* for telling a story. The "rules" of point of view do not just stand outside of the story to govern it; rather, they go right to the heart of what kind of thing a story *is*.

Decisions about point of view take the fiction writer into her own version of a branch of philosophy called epistemology, which concerns the theory of knowledge. The fundamental question of epistemology is "How do we know?" Stories are "about" knowledge, existing in some sense to deepen our understanding of life, and they are "about" perspective, partly in the sense that they allow us to get out of our own skins and to inhabit other lives, in which things may be looked at differently. This is not to say that we "know" only what the point of view delivers for our inspection. Point of view determines what gets on the page, not what we do with it. Readers may distrust the chosen point of view or may find other ways of knowing within the angled mirrors of the tale, and the writer may have anticipated such divergence.

The writer may choose to employ for a story one or another of certain established ways of telling a story—in the first person, for example. The words on the page have to come from *somewhere*, don't they? And the reader has to orient himself the point of view: "Oh, I see—some guy is telling me what happened to him when he was a kid." Point of view establishes what sort of occasion this is. Perhaps the words on the page "pretend" to be a diary someone wrote, and I the reader am getting a chance to read it. Maybe all the words on the page are dialogue; in this case it seems I am being allowed to overhear some conversation. Things get more complicated if, in addition to this dialogue, some other voice is telling me what things look like or maybe what one or more of the people are thinking. "Who is that? What's happening here? What have I gotten myself into?"

As we ask what we have gotten ourselves into, we are essentially moving from our own reality into another world. And so we look around to figure out what the basic rules are: "Oh, I see. This is like a story where some godlike voice knows everything and tells you about it." That first time we ask "What's happening here?" we may not be asking what is happening in the story, but what *kind* of thing this story is—what sort of planet it is we have landed on. There is not just one planet called Fiction; there are a great many such planets, and like space travellers we try to get oriented as quickly as possible upon arrival. It's a magic moment, or perhaps a magic split-second, when we enter into another kind of world. We may, of course, be scarcely aware of it if we have been to places like this before.

The term *narrator* refers to the person or voice telling a story. The two most basic forms of narration, or point of view, are *first person*, in which the narrator is an "I," or a person speaking to us, and *third person*. The third-person narrator is a voice using third-person pronouns like "he," "she," and "they" to tell us a story. This narrator may seem to have a kind of person-ality—for example, a humorous or judgmental character—but cannot, for example, be said to have a gender. The third-person narrator doesn't "exist" within the story itself. Whereas the first-person narrator is at least to some fractional degree a participant in the story, whether a minor or a major char-acter, the third-person narrator is only a disembodied voice. Occasionally, a story will be told in the second person: "You move to the window, and what you see there...." This point of view can produce interesting effects, but it is difficult to sustain over a lengthy piece of fiction. An individual story or novel also may employ more than one point of view: perhaps there will be several first-person narrators, or sections alternating between first person and third.

We are inclined—until something makes us disinclined—to trust whoever is telling us a story. This tendency is something to watch out for with first-person narrators, who may be biased or *unreliable*. The artfulness of the story, in this case, depends on our being helped to "see through" the narrator and also to "see around" him. The unreliable narrator distorts the story for pur-poses of his own or because of certain limitations, and those purposes or limi-tations are part of what the writer's story is about. Using a first-person narrator is often a risky business for the writer, as should be clear if we con-sider the case of a flagrantly sexist first-person narrator. The writer may intend us to reject this narrator's point of view, to be appalled by it—in fact, that could be the whole point of the story. But how are we to know? A narrator also may be essentially reliable and yet limited, as all human beings are, by what he or she is capable of seeing; in other words, the line between reliable and unreliable narration is often unclear.

A piece of advice often given to beginning writers is "Show, don't tell." A similar and equally familiar piece of advice, addressed by D.H. Lawrence to readers, is "Trust the tale, not the teller." In the case of the sexist narrator described above, the writer must rely on showing the reader, through the tale, not the teller, that something abhorrent is afoot. But doing so also involves placing a good deal of trust in the reader. The subtlety of the writer who refuses to stand on a platform within the story to say "Not me; I don't believe this" must be matched by the subtlety of the reader. The reasons for taking such a risk are complex and always worth exploring.

Third-person narration, involving that disembodied voice, falls into three categories: objective, omniscient, and limited omniscient. An *objective* nar-rator offers a detached perspective, reporting only what can be seen or heard. An *omniscient* or all-knowing narrator can see into the minds of all the charac-ters. A narrator with *limited omniscience* can enter the mind of a single char-acter, or perhaps two.

Omniscient narrators, according to the rules of this kind of narration, may move around with perfect freedom, going into characters' minds at will, describing the world they inhabit, philosophizing, and offering judgments on characters and behaviour. Not all of these liberties may be exercised, but none is forbidden. We see such narrators as being something like the voice of the author, and we are meant to trust them. A possible hazard associated with this form of narration for the writer is the temptation to tell rather than to show or demonstrate through the action. The art of fiction is generally dependent on the writer's leading the reader with some degree of subtlety to a sense of the story's meaning; the impact is greater when the reader's mind has been obliged to work, and it may be less when the reader is simply told what to think. "Telling" does not always mean moral commentary; it may also refer to action that is simply recounted rather than dramatized or cast into scenes. This recounting is indeed one of the principal things that is meant when writers are advised to "Show, don't tell." All this being said, a certain amount of "telling" and of generalizing or moralizing statements can be very effective.

Limited omniscience often involves what Henry James described as the *central intelligence* (also called the *central consciousness*). In this form of narration, the writer has recourse again and again to the consciousness of a single character, who may or may not be the central character of the story. This person responds to and interprets the action of the story, and because so much is filtered through him, this central intelligence may almost feel to the reader like a first-person narrator. Frequently in such stories, the growth in understanding of this character is an important part of what the story is about.

A technique called *stream-of-consciousness*, in which a "stream" of ideas, impressions, memories, and associations moves freely through the mind of a character, can be employed in either first-person or third-person narration.

There are advantages and disadvantages to any point of view. For this reason, writers will often use several points of view within a single story; this can work very well, but sometimes a shift in point of view will feel to the reader like a sudden violation of an agreement she had unconsciously made with the writer. The artful handling of point of view is one of the writer's greatest challenges. The reader should always give close consideration to the way that point of view has been managed and to the reasons that a story has been told in this way rather than another.

SETTING, VOICE, STYLE, AND TONE

The *setting* of a story is its place, time, and milieu—or the physical environment in which the characters move and the actions of the story take place. The words devoted to a description or evocation of setting help us see the world in which the story takes place; they serve to create that three-dimensional space in the reader's imagination. Though a writer will sometimes devote many words to creating this dramatic illusion, setting can also sometimes be established successfully with very few words. In any case, those same words almost always accomplish other things as well; most obviously, perhaps, they are aimed at creating a mood. For example, vivid descriptions of a river's murky depths or of sunlight sparkling on a river help us to visualize a scene, but these descriptions also work to point us in very different emotional directions.

The importance of setting varies greatly from one story to another. In some stories, the action is closely related to the setting, which is then likely to be rendered in considerable detail. What happens in these stories, and even who the characters are, may have a great deal to do with the physical circumstances of where and when the action takes place. In other stories, setting scarcely matters at all. The illusion of reality, or *verisimilitude*, if that is what the writer is after, can be created in other ways—through the compelling specificity of voice, for example.

Voice in fiction is a rather slippery concept. In life, the way a person sounds and uses language is one of the most potent ways in which the identity of that particular person is established; it is a large part of how we recognize that person. When an actor attempts to imitate a famous living person, getting the voice right is often as important as getting the look right. Voice can cast a spell; it can seem to make a cohesive world of its own, and for this reason it may be as important as visual detail in creating the dramatic illusion of reality. In fiction, voice can refer both to dialogue and to the voice of the narrator. Much of the artistry of fiction is concerned with sustaining a particular voice or with orchestrating a range of voices, since "false notes" can break the spell that the story attempts to cast over the reader.

Style is the general term used to describe the way a writer uses language. We may speak of a plain or an ornate style, a colloquial or a formal style. The characteristic ways that sentences or paragraphs are formed, the presence or absence of irony, and a minimal or heavy reliance on adjectives or on metaphor are all issues of style. Voice and style are closely related terms. Perhaps the best way of distinguishing between them is to say that voice is a product of style—it is the human signature (a sense of individuality) that emerges from some particular way of using language.

Tone is a literary term that refers primarily to the writer's implied attitude to the subject matter, and it too is an aspect of style. We may speak, for example, of an ironic, a sympathetic, or a critical tone. Tone, in a slightly different sense, is an aspect of the voice of characters as well as the narrator, and may be said to pervade all of the language of the story. It speaks to an angle of vision. Pedestrian language can be toneless, but in a good story tone is operative from the very first sentence, orienting us to the sensibility, or the way of thinking, that the writer wants the reader to pursue.

IMAGERY AND SYMBOLISM

Our five senses—sight, hearing, smell, touch, and taste—make us feel alive. Fictional worlds also become more real or more alive through an appeal to the senses, perhaps especially to our sense of sight; words that evoke sensations (for example, a velvet cheek, the sharp, clean smell of lemons) transport us viscerally into the world of the story. When details appeal to one of the senses and stand out in some way, they are called *images*—a term referring specifically to the visual, which has been generalized to include all of the five senses so that we may speak, for example, of the "velvet cheek" as a tactile image.

The term *image*—when it is distinguished from *detail*—may suggest some special impact on our imaginations—something that should remain with us to crystallize or encapsulate a certain feeling. Thus, a coating of grease on all the surfaces of a small, depressing hotel room may be the image that remains with us after a lengthy description both of that room and of the depressing things that transpire there. The distinction between detail and image is not absolute; neither is the distinction between image, which may suggest something more than itself, and symbol, which clearly does. A literary *symbol* is anything in the story that carries some general or abstract significance in addition to its literal meaning. For example, a mountain might be simply a detail helping us to visualize the setting, or it may be an image that summarizes for us the hero's birthplace, or a symbol of the hero's aspiration.

Like poems, stories often work with patterns of imagery. It may be helpful to think about how such patterns typically come into being for the writer. Early in the story a bird may appear, and, later, another bird is introduced, probably because that first bird is still lingering in the writer's mind. This time, perhaps, some meaning that might be associated with the bird becomes more clear; other birds may follow, and taken together these birds may convey some more or less subtle dimension of the story's meaning. If that meaning can be abstracted, we might say that the birds are symbolic. What the birds symbolize should emerge from the story itself; it may well be something we conventionally associate with birds, like freedom, or just something that has been associated with birds in this particular story—hysteria, let's say. It should be remembered, also, that detail, image, and symbol form a kind of continuum, so the point at which an image becomes a symbol is not always clear: if the idea of freedom or hysteria is very strongly linked to the birds we might prefer the term symbol.

All kinds of things in a story might be called symbolic: images, characters, settings, actions. A story that is structured around a series of symbolic equivalencies, and that operates more at the level of moral parable than of realistic fiction, is called an *allegory*. Each element has a fixed meaning—for example, one setting represents hell, another heaven; one character represents courage, another humility, and so on. (A story might also have some allegorical elements without being a full-scale allegory.) In realistic fiction, characters may possess the qualities of courage or humility; in allegory, they *stand for* these qualities, and the abstract concept is more important than the person who embodies it. Similarly, in realistic fiction, a setting might be "hellish" without actually representing hell; in allegory, the whole point is lost if we do not recognize that this is hell.

The continuum running between detail and symbol may be said to have allegory as its extreme fourth term: detail–image–symbol–allegory. This continuum reflects a gradual "hardening" or fixity of meaning; with detail we have the thing itself, with image the beginning of an association of this thing with something beyond itself, with symbol a strengthening of that association, and with allegory a recognition that this other thing is what really counts. Symbolism is more complex than allegory. Meaning is not so fixed because the complex real thing from which the meaning arises still matters and complicates the meaning to be extracted from it. Symbols can often be understood on several levels or in a number of different ways.

THEME

The *theme* of a story is a generalization about its meaning or subject; a story might also have several themes—being concerned, for instance, with both death and violence. Often the term "theme" refers to something like the "message" of the story, or the lessons it may be said to teach. The danger of thematic analysis is that the particulars of the story may get lost, and the nature of fiction itself may be forgotten. Stories are, of course, concerned with making sense of life, but the warning issued by Flannery O'Connor (a story writer with very strong moral and religious concerns) is well worth heeding: "A story is a way to say something that can't be said any other way, and it takes every word in the story to say what the meaning is.... When anybody asks what a story is about, the only proper thing is to tell him to read the story."

ADVICE ON ESSAY WRITING

CHOOSING A TOPIC

Assuming that your goal is to write an excellent essay (one that has a chance of earning an A grade), and that you are making up your own topic, I would recommend that you build an essay around some exciting idea (or set of ideas) you have had or (if you haven't had any exciting ideas yet) something that is bothering you about the text. Either of these approaches can lead to a first-class essay. Either should mean that you are interested in the task at hand—and that is surely the crucial point. What you want to avoid is a topic that does not challenge you, or one that is unlikely to take you into rewarding areas of investigation.

Particularly if you choose something that is bothering you, something you still haven't figured out, you may find that it doesn't work out. If you find yourself floundering, ask yourself whether this is a good time to abandon ship and switch over to another topic. It's often a good idea to try out more than one topic for an essay. This may seem like a waste of time, but it isn't if your goal is to find something really good.

If you are choosing from a list of assigned topics, again you should look for something that challenges you to think for yourself. The main thing to avoid is a topic that you know will just mean rehashing ideas you have picked up in class.

Generally, you should avoid topics that are too big or that will lead you too far away from the text. Remember that the success of your essay will depend to a large extent on the intelligent analysis of detail in the text.

You may be reluctant to choose a small (narrowly defined) topic because you fear that it will not give you an opportunity to get into the heart of the text. Usually, that fear is mistaken. Since elements of a literary text are interrelated, almost any small topic will allow you to get into the big questions. In fact, this is often a problem: you choose one small thread and keep pulling, and find that the whole fabric of the text is on the table. Instead of finding that you don't have *enough* to say, you may discover that you have too much, and that you don't know how to organize it all in a manageable structure. But at least the choice of a supposedly small topic will help you to *enter the text* with some degree of specificity.

To *try out* a topic, go back to the text and see if you can find the textual evidence for an interesting argument. Remember that you don't want to use just the detail that has been discussed in class, unless you can use it in a new way. If you don't find anything, try another topic.

When you are working with an assigned topic, or choosing from a list of assigned topics, you should keep in mind several things. In most cases the topic does not give you the thesis; that is, it does not state a position. Topics often begin with words like "examine" or "consider." Such words do not mean that you should wander around in a topic; they are a polite way of asking you to articulate an *opinion* about something, and to demonstrate the validity of that opinion by using logic and evidence. To "discuss" effectively you must decide *what it is you are going to show* and fit it together under a thesis. Sometimes the topic simply identifies a general area of investigation, like the "setting" of a story. Sometimes it asks you explicitly to take a stand on some question, such as whether race is an important issue in the story "A Worn Path." However the topic is posed, it is your responsibility to find something *interesting* in it and to develop a worthwhile thesis.

CREATING A THESIS

Once you have selected a topic, you must narrow it down and find a workable *thesis*. The thesis is the argument; it is your opinion about some aspect of the text. But this opinion cannot be plucked out of the air, or adapted from your own repertoire of opinions and then imposed upon the text. A good thesis—that is to say, a sustainable argument—must be consistent with the details of the text, which you will go on to analyze in the body of the essay. As you did in selecting a topic, choose a thesis that is small enough (focused and particular enough) to invite that detailed level of analysis.

Remember that a good thesis is not self-evident; it is debatable, inspiring you to rise to its defence. If your essay just states the obvious, it will not be interesting; your reader will wonder why you bothered to write it in the first place.

Take note: Many English teachers require students to include a thesis statement in the introduction of the essay. Sometimes teachers ask students to submit a thesis statement before submitting the essay itself, so that they can see whether you have embarked on a sensible path. The thesis statement is simply a condensed statement of the argument—your essay's *big idea*. Whether or not your teacher explicitly requires a thesis statement, it's always a good idea to try to state your thesis in one sentence before you begin to write the essay itself. It may turn out to be just the sentence you want for the end of the first paragraph! But even if this version of the thesis statement does not survive, it will help you to see for yourself whether you've got an appropriately focused and unified idea.

To show you the differences between a weak thesis and a strong one, I will take a terrible thesis statement, explain its weaknesses, and move it through a couple of revisions.

TOPIC:
Discuss Phoenix's relationship to nature in "A Worn Path."

THESIS 1:
In "A Worn Path," Phoenix has a good relationship with nature.

The problem here is that the word "good" is vague. What does it mean to have a good relationship with nature? The answer to that question needs to be part of the thesis.

THESIS 2:
In "A Worn Path," Phoenix treats nature with respect.

This thesis is stronger than the previous one because it identifies what is meant by "good." But the thesis still doesn't explain why Phoenix treats nature with respect. Furthermore, because this respect for nature is obvious in the text, the thesis is neither interesting nor debatable.

THESIS 3:
In "A Worn Path," Phoenix treats nature with respect because she sees it as God's creation.

This gets at the reason for Phoenix's respect for nature. It draws a connection between her response to nature and her spirituality, which takes us into the heart of the story. Most importantly, the thesis can be supported by interesting *details*—references to nature that have a spiritual quality (e.g., the bird that flies by and is associated with "God watching me the whole time").

There are many possible thesis statements for every topic. Here are some examples of thesis statements I've created for a single topic.

TOPIC:
Examine Silas's relationship with the alligator in *Crawl*.

THESIS 1:
In *Crawl*, Silas treats the alligator as an ally in his battle against the adult world.

THESIS 2:
In *Crawl*, the alligator represents the realm of childhood fantasy, which, at the end of the novel, Silas realizes he must leave behind.

THESIS 3:
The alligator, because it lives in the sewer and appears in Silas's night-mares, represents the protagonist's deepest fears.

Being a Teacher/Lawyer

Just as we want a literary work to do something to us, to change how we see things, so a really good essay about literature should surprise the reader. Think of yourself as a teacher: your job is to teach the teacher. In this context, you can surprise and instruct the reader (your instructor) by convincing her (or him) of the merits of ideas she hasn't had herself, or by providing new support for familiar ideas. Say that in fact you don't come up with an idea the instructor hasn't thought of, or evidence she hasn't seen; you can still surprise her if you don't just repeat or rehash what has been said in class. One of the fatal mistakes students make is to assume that a rehash is what their teachers really want.

Notice that I said the *merits* of the idea; the instructor's job is to determine whether you've made a good case (not the only possible case). Think of yourself as a defence lawyer arguing a case to a jury. Just as the lawyer doesn't have to prove *absolutely* the innocence of the client, so you are not obliged to prove the undeniable truth of your thesis. The lawyer's job is to prove that the client could be innocent, that the scenario offered to the jury by the defence could quite easily be correct. (Notice that this involves disposing of any possibly damning evidence on the other side.) This analogy is a bit problematic, how-ever, since you should believe in your thesis. You haven't been landed with it, after all (as a lawyer might be landed with a client); you have *chosen* this thesis because you think it is worth defending. Therefore, avoid taking on a bizarre, wildly improbable case just for the hell of it. (You want to be original; you do not want to be crazy.) Ideally, you want to be the kind of lawyer who believes passionately in a client who is not *obviously* innocent; and you want to convince the jury that your defence is sound, so that you win the case.

Getting the Ideas

There is no one way, of course, but I'll tell you how I often do it. I catch wind of a possible idea, and then I mark up my text to track it down. I notice some-thing—say, that there is something interesting going on with birds in a text, or that the narration switches between present and future tense to good effect but for no immediately apparent reason, or that every now and again I am offended by a seemingly admirable character's behaviour or manner of speech—and I start marking each occurrence of the thing I'm interested in. I might have several things like that going. Sometimes I jot down questions and possible answers in the margin as I go along; sometimes I take notes elsewhere, using a separate page for each thing I'm pursuing. Then I go back and look at my notes and everything I've marked in the text to see if I can make anything of it. Perhaps the germ of an idea will occur to me only when I have finished reading, in which case I'll go back as soon as possible (while the germ is still active) to mark up the text and check it out.

I make more notes, getting down fast whatever occurs to me, without censoring myself too much. (I call this stage *brainstorming*.) Then I get critical. Does this make *sense*? What of all this is good, and what must I discard because it is almost certainly rubbish? Can I shape a worthwhile thesis out of what is left? What fits together? What ideas are so intriguing to me that—even though they don't obviously fit my thesis—I will try to work them in? (Sometimes in the act of writing a perfect opportunity will miraculously appear, so that it turns out the idea *does* fit after all.)

At this point, I usually write down a preliminary thesis statement (what it is I'm trying to prove). My next step is to ask myself whether I've gathered enough evidence. If not, it's back to the text. I also try to look really hard once more at each passage I think I might use, to see if there is something in it that I might have missed. This approach *often* pays off, providing me with the most interesting points in my argument.

In pushing harder for ideas, I rely heavily on the question *why* to prod me. I ask myself *why* the writer put this scene next to that one, *why* I respond a certain way, *why* this language is so formal or so flat, *why* this or that detail has been included, and so on. Whenever I come up with an idea, I try to resist breathing a sigh of relief or patting myself on the back. Instead, I try to push the idea, to keep on thinking about it. I mention this because in my experience the worst mistake students make is to quit thinking too soon; there is a tendency to give up when you think you might have rounded up enough material to fill up the pages assigned.

Another mistake that students make quite often is to get so hooked on an exciting, original idea that they refuse to let it go, even when the opposing evidence mounts and the interpretation really cannot be sustained. We all take pleasure in making discoveries on our own, and it is sometimes very hard to let that exhilaration go. But if you're wrong you have to let go! There is a fine but crucial line between not pushing far enough and pushing too far, or imposing your own ideas on the text and ignoring urgent, contradictory signals. How do you know when you've gone too far? Ask yourself as honestly as you can whether this *feels* right. Is it consistent with or does it contradict an interpretation that is obviously valid? Does it limit too far the appeal of the text's meaning?

Once you have followed all of the trails that you think are interesting and that have led in fruitful directions, you need to start thinking about what your thesis will be. Sometimes the paths you have followed will seem to converge around a *big idea*—an overriding question that has been posed and answered in the course of all your brainstorming and questioning and re-reading. Once this idea begins to take shape, you will see that some of the lines of inquiry you have pursued are off the track—and you can let those go. Now the question is how to organize what remains. To help you make your essay as effective as possible, I give advice in the next section on how to organize ideas within the body of your essay.

Organizing the Ideas

In this section I discuss ways to organize ideas into paragraphs, as well as the organization of ideas within paragraphs. I recommend that you try using a paragraph outline—essentially a plan for an argument. A big part of the job here is to figure out what goes with what. Remember that each paragraph represents a *phase* of your argument; each is a part of what you need to accomplish in order to prove your thesis. Each phase should be distinct; thus, each paragraph should have its own *topic* to which every sentence relates.

Think of prospective paragraphs as *files*; the task at this point is to sort the ideas and the evidence into the appropriate files, and to be sure that nothing is misfiled or left out in the cold. (If I've got some especially appealing idea that doesn't seem to fit anywhere, I jot it down in the margin—so that I'll remember it in case it turns out that I can use it after all.) Later, each file will become a paragraph. If the file gets too bulky, it will eventually have to be broken down into two or more paragraphs. If it is too skimpy, it will have to be combined with another in some logical way. So try to be sure now that each file is of a manageable size.

What is a manageable size? How long should a paragraph be? Half of a typed page is an average length for a paragraph. You will want to vary the length of paragraphs, but avoid too many short paragraphs and try not to have a page on which there is no paragraph break at all. Very short paragraphs typically occur when you fail to develop ideas or to combine related ideas. Very long paragraphs are hard on the reader, and can usually be avoided.

At this stage, you should also try to discover the best possible order for the paragraphs. Sometimes this is easy; sometimes it's hard. Remember that your paragraphs are stages in an argument or a lesson. You need to figure out what things the reader needs to be shown prior to being shown something else; an essay is a developmental learning curve that you control. You need to think about logical progression. Remember that you are trying to keep the reader with you on a clearly marked trail; the reader must trust that you know where you are going, and that your moves make sense.

You might also try thinking of your essay as theatre, which typically begins with exposition (setting up the situation), continues through various developments and complications, and ends with a dramatic climax and resolution. The point here is that you want to keep the reader interested. The theatrical model of essay-writing suggests that each act should be stronger and more compelling than the one before. One trouble with this model is the requirement that you state your thesis at the beginning of the paper. Is this like telling who did it in the opening scene of a mystery? If so, go ahead and do it anyway! There can still be some element of surprise in the way you manage the ending, and you can still choose to save your most satisfying examples for the end.

You want to achieve order *within* each paragraph as well. Again, proceed in a *logical* manner (moving from A to B to C) through the phases of an idea. It may be possible to proceed in a *dramatic* manner as well, leaving the most important or surprising point for the end. But if you have to choose between logic and drama, go for logic.

In some circumstances another kind of order will suggest itself strongly— chronological order, for instance. But do spend some time *thinking* about the order of material within paragraphs and the order of the paragraphs themselves. Do this thinking at the outline stage, and do it again once you have written a draft of the essay.

Paragraph outlines can begin just as clusters of related ideas that you think might take shape as paragraphs. Eventually, though, you will probably want to have something that looks like an outline—with the paragraphs themselves in an effective order, under headings to indicate the topic of each paragraph, and the points and the evidence you intend to use for each paragraph briefly indicated (again in a likely order) under each paragraph heading. This skeleton helps you to see the bones of the essay. It helps you to see the transitions that will be needed as you move from one phase of the argument to the next.

A few of you, however, may find that to begin with an outline is counterproductive. For some people, at least on some occasions, an outline seems to make the ideas go dead on the page. When they get to the writing stage, the life is gone. You will have to experiment to see what is best for you; when you get stuck one way, you can try another. Sometimes you can just start writing, with very little idea of where you are going, and find ideas through something like free fall. *Warning:* You may want to try this method, but you shouldn't trust it. You should always stand back afterward and examine what you have written very carefully. If it has not, by some special dispensation of the gods, come out in a perfect order, now is the time to make an outline. Treat what you have written as raw material; keep the relevant good bits, and toss out the junk. But be sure that whatever you are tempted to turn in to your instructor looks like something that has a *solid outline beneath the flesh*; if it doesn't (and it probably won't) don't stop. Make that outline now, and adjust the text to fit it. Do not quit because you have come up with the requisite number of words.

Even when you are working from a very detailed outline, you will find that *as you write* new (and sometimes better) ideas occur to you. Sentences will appear on your page that suggest new possibilities for development and new connections. This is a major part of the pleasure of writing. Don't be afraid to take advantage of insights that arrive in this way. Just be sure that you make the necessary adjustments to your essay plan, so that the structure of your essay is clear. (I find that I almost always make some adjustments in my paragraph outline when I get down to the job of writing.)

How do I know how to organize the ideas I have? In the next section, I suggest two possible ways of organizing ideas on *The Last Savages* (a novel I have invented for the sake of this example).

TOPIC:

Examine the depiction of Native people in William Smith's *The Last Savages.*

THESIS:

Basing his assumptions about culture on a white, Western European model, William Smith in *The Last Savages* reinforces negative stereotypes of Native people.

Now consider the pieces of this thesis.

1. The book contains stereotypes of Native people.
2. The stereotypes are negative.
3. The stereotypes follow from Smith's white, Western European view of the world.

Let's assume that Smith relies on five basic stereotypes about Native people. The question then is how to order the five stereotypes. In a good essay, the order would not be simply random. It might, for example, be the case that some of the stereotypes *seem* positive while others are obviously negative. Remember that part of what you are arguing in this essay is that the stereotypes are negative. You could use your introduction to discuss the sense in which all stereotypes have damaging consequences, though some appear to be complimentary. In this case, you might move from the apparently positive to the most obviously negative—or the other way around. Either way, you are dealing with the issue of *negative* stereotypes at the same time that you are moving through the examples.

Another way of organizing this paper might be to assign a paragraph to each of Smith's cultural assumptions, and to fit the stereotypes that follow from those assumptions into those paragraphs.

Two Common Modes of Organization

In this section, I want to say a few words about two modes of organization that are often appropriate for an English essay: organization by *classification* and by *comparison/contrast*. One or another of these may make obvious sense as the basic organizational mode for a particular essay. The choice of one of these basic organizational modes does not preclude the internal use of the other. Thus, you may need to use comparisons in a classification essay, or to classify items in a comparison/contrast essay.

CLASSIFICATION

In literary criticism, classification—putting items into categories—is often a valuable tool. For example, you might classify something as a tragedy, or as a romance, or as a feminist text. You might classify a character as heroic. These terms, which refer to literary tradition, can illuminate aspects of the particular text at hand *and* show how literary texts grow out of similar preoccupations and conventions. In this style of classification, you would first define your term (tragedy, for example) and then, using textual evidence, show why the text you are analyzing belongs in this category. This might be an interesting thing to do if the text in question is not obviously a tragedy.

Another useful kind of classification essay seeks to classify items from the text into different categories. For example, you might classify the kinds of imagery in a text. When you are using classification, always keep your purpose in mind. What do you *learn* about the text by putting textual items into categories? Say you are looking at the kinds of humour used in a text. What do these uses reveal about the characters? What do they reveal about the themes of the text? Classification can be an important tool for revealing patterns within a text. And that's one of the main things that literary criticism is about: rising above the trees to see the forest, and to see how carefully the paths are laid out.

Suppose you notice that the character Morgan is strangely silent during many of the scenes in the novel *Twelve Angry Women* (another text I have invented!). You might begin to take notes classifying *according to the reasons for her silence* all those occasions on which Morgan is silent. You discover that she is silent for one of three reasons: she is angry, or guilty, or afraid. You observe that each of these types of silence seems to be accompanied by a particular gesture or behaviour. For instance, when Morgan is silent and afraid she wrings her hands. You decide that a discussion of the three kinds of silence would make an interesting essay. This is probably not yet reason enough to write the essay. *So what* if there are three different kinds of silence with three different accompanying gestures? Why is this an important discovery? It may be—but always ask yourself this question. Say that in looking for these different kinds of silence, you reread the final courtroom scene—and find that you have to read it in a new way! Morgan's silence in the court has been interpreted by your teacher and classmates (or by some famous critic) as evidence of her guilt. You notice, however, that her gesture in this scene is not the one that signifies guilt. You can reinterpret the final scene in a convincing way; the *evidence* you have assembled shows that Morgan's real emotion here is fear.

THESIS:
Morgan is not guilty: she remains silent in the final courtroom scene because she is afraid.

Paragraph 1 (introduction):
Give the usual interpretation of the ending. Disagree and state thesis. Point out that she is often silent—when angry, guilty, or afraid—and that specific gestures associated with these silences signal to the reader the reason for her silence in any given case. (Don't tell what the gestures are yet—I want to surprise my reader!—but end the paragraph with the idea that Morgan's gesture in the final scene proves she's innocent.)

Paragraph 2:
Morgan's silence when she is angry. Three examples, moving from the one in which she is obviously furious to the one in which her anger is least clear; in each case she fiddles with her ears.

Paragraph 3:
Morgan's silence when she is feeling guilty. Four clear examples. Each time she fans herself, as if shooing away a mosquito.

Paragraph 4:
Morgan's silence when she is afraid. Two examples; each time she's wringing her hands. (Don't use the courtroom scene yet.)

Paragraph 5 (conclusion):
The final courtroom scene. Again challenge the interpretation that Morgan is guilty. She is wringing her hands; she is not fanning herself.

COMPARISON/CONTRAST

This mode of organization allows you to show how two items (themes, characters, images, outcomes, scenes, etc.) are alike and/or different from each other. Sometimes the thrust of your paper will be to show how alike the items are, and sometimes the point will be how dissimilar they are. But a likeness is *interesting* only if it surprises us; thus, you will be pointing out that despite obvious differences (contrasts), A and B are, with respect to X, surprisingly alike (comparison). In the same way, a difference (contrast) is interesting only if we might have thought that A and B are very much alike (comparison). Keep in mind that there has to be a *reason* for comparing the two items: some illumination of the text that occurs as a result.

There are two obvious models for a comparison/contrast essay. Say you're comparing two texts, and your discussion involves nine points of comparison. One way of organizing the essay is to discuss text A first, going through all nine features; then you move on to text B, discussing the same nine features in the same order. The danger of this approach is that the essay falls into two very separate halves. To reduce the risk, be sure to refer frequently to text A in your discussion of text B, and use the introduction to establish some good reason for thinking of these two texts together.

The second obvious model for a comparison/contrast essay involves moving through the *features* (the nine points of comparison) one by one. Each feature gets a paragraph of its own, in which both texts are discussed. The danger of this approach is that you will be moving back and forth between texts so rapidly that the essay may feel both choppy and incoherent.

To solve these problems, a paper will often mix models one and two. You might do this by taking the nine features and sorting them into three categories. That way, you can discuss category 1 (including three related features) as these appear in text A and then in text B; then category 2 (involving three related features) for text A and then text B; and finally category 3 (involving three related features) for text A and then text B. It won't always be as tidy as this, but I hope you get the idea!

Now for more imaginary texts that I will use to suggest a means of organizing ideas for a comparison/contrast essay.

TOPIC:
Compare and contrast images of the sea in "The Gale" and "Under Polaris."

THESIS:
Both stories draw upon literary archetypes of the sea in ways that intensify reader response.

INTRODUCTION:

Introduce the three archetypes: the sea as creator/destroyer, as testing ground for the hero, and as an arena for change. (Mention Shakespeare's *The Tempest*—say it's alluded to in both stories: "There is nothing but doth suffer a sea-change into something rich and strange.") State thesis.

Paragraph 1:

Creator/destroyer. In "Under Polaris," while sailing alone across the Atlantic, Eliza falls into the sea. Though terrified, she floats: "The sea carried her like a mother." Later she loses the main mast in a storm and nearly loses the ship.

Paragraph 2:

Creator/destroyer. In "The Gale," the captain's son has his first swimming lesson off the bowsprit. Compare the childish joy of the son to Eliza's joy upon floating. Later the son is killed in the storm.

Paragraph 3:

Testing ground for hero. In both stories, the heroes are tested by the storm. Eliza faces "the challenge that would determine whether she could ever believe in herself again." The storm in "The Gale" shows the captain his "mortality." He is compared to Ulysses.

Paragraph 4:

Arena of change. Both texts allude to the final scenes of *The Tempest* where Prospero's right to the Dukedom of Milan is asserted. Like Prospero, Eliza wins the championship sailing title that was stolen from her. The captain regains the respect of his crew. These victories may not seem like allusions to *The Tempest*, but given the odd references to pearls in both stories (compare Shakespeare's "These are pearls that were his eyes") as well as more obvious allusions to *The Tempest*, they probably are.

Conclusion:

The references to *The Tempest* and Ulysses, as well as the three associated archetypes of the sea, make the reader aware of an ancient tradition to which these contemporary stories belong. At the same time, we recognize with a deep sense of satisfaction the departure from tradition (a "sea-change"!) these stories represent: thus Eliza, a young woman, can be an archetypal hero.

INTRODUCTION

The introduction (usually the first paragraph of the essay) is very important. Some writers feel that they cannot go on until they get the introduction exactly right; others hurry through it in a first draft because they have learned from experience that what they actually write in the body of the essay will often require significant changes in the introduction by the time they're done. In either case—whether you have slaved over the introduction or not—you should *always* go back at the end to see whether the introduction (and in particular the thesis statement) still works.

You may have been taught the "funnel" model for an introduction. This involves starting off with something broad and funnelling down to the narrowly defined thesis of your essay at the end of the paragraph. Funnelling, or zeroing in on the topic in the introduction, often works extremely well. But it is not the only possible model, and not always the best.

Students often get the *tone* of an introduction wrong. You should avoid being stuffy or pretentious, and you should not waste time offering compliments to the author. An introduction should not contain puffery or *filler*. You cannot afford to waste time with filler anywhere in the essay, but I mention this here because introductions are often guilty of this crime—especially at the broad part of the funnel. Whatever the broad portion of the funnel contains (assuming that you employ this useful model), remember that it has to *count*; it should be necessary to the argument that follows.

The introduction should give your reader some idea of where the paper is going, what its thesis is, and perhaps how you are going to proceed—but don't feel that you have to give away all your secrets at the start. In a short essay, the introduction usually takes just one paragraph. In a longer essay, the introduction is often longer, and the first *paragraph* is sometimes used to provide a kind of background to the argument, so that the thesis appears a bit later.

In a short and relatively uncomplicated essay, you should be wary of using the introduction to tell the reader exactly what you are going to say in the body of the essay and in what order. (Avoid "First I will show X; then I will show Y; finally I will show Z.") This leads to unnecessary repetition and a dull essay. Often, in a good short essay, the introduction indicates the stages of the argument more subtly. For example, the introduction might say that "The author accomplishes this through X, Y, and Z," and the body of the essay is then committed to dealing with X, Y, and Z *in that order*.

Incidentally, it may be perfectly all right to use the first person ("I") in an English essay, but you should do so only for a good reason. Ask your instructor if you are uncertain. (A good reason might be that you are tracking the stages of your own response or the reasons for that response.)

Every essay must have a thesis. Usually, the thesis is contained in a sentence or two near the end of the introduction. (This portion of the introduction is called the *thesis statement.*) Be sure that you understand the difference between a topic and a thesis. The topic is what the essay is about (setting, let's say); the thesis is what you are trying to *prove* about the topic (for example, that the physical setting of a certain story establishes a mood of stagnation, which is critical to the reader's understanding of the main character).

Using the thesis about setting that I have proposed, the body of the essay might go on to present and *analyze* (probably in chronological order) carefully selected examples of stagnation—a swamp, mould growing on things in a refrigerator, etc.—and to connect these with the growth of the reader's awareness of a comparable stagnation in the life of the protagonist.

The introduction itself might look something like this:

> Alex Sutherland, the narrator of "In the Swamp," clearly thinks he
> is a man of purpose, a man on the go. His constant activity and fre-
> quent praise of his own energy may convince an unwary reader
> that this is so. However, details of the physical setting confirm the
> message of the title, that Alex is stuck in a kind of swamp. These
> images of stagnation should help the reader to understand that
> Alex is not the man he thinks he is.

This introduction does not seem to follow the funnel model, but in a way it does. The student moves from something that may seem evident in a hasty, broad view of the story to something more subtle and particular (the images of stagnation, which provide the thesis of the essay). Using a more obvious funnel, the student might have begun like this: "A wary reader should always be alert to the possibility that the narrator is deceiving us, or that he deceives himself. Alex Sutherland ...," etc. Now the lip of the funnel extends beyond the limits of this particular story, to make a general claim. But either of these two versions is fine.

THE BODY OF THE ESSAY

Avoid plot summary. The essay should make some sense even to someone who doesn't know the text you are discussing, but don't waste time retelling the plot. The trick here is to orient your reader to the action while *at the same time* proceeding with your argument. This is one of the hardest things for students to learn. And excessive plot summary is one of the most common—and fatal—shortcomings of student essays. Check to see that you are not wasting time in this way. To put the matter bluntly, a sentence that merely tells the story contributes nothing to the merit of the essay or to the grade you receive.

Here's an example of a paragraph that is almost entirely plot summary. Be *very* careful not to fall into this trap.

> Alex is just stagnating. Flora isn't interested in him, and he just won't give up. He goes to her house, he rings the bell, he is carrying chocolates and flowers, and he is wearing those silly plaid pants left over from grade eight. Flora tries to shut the door on him, but he falls down "weeping at her feet" (83). "He grabs her ankles, he cries, he pleads" (84). Alex can't understand that she doesn't like him. She threatens to call the police, but he still can't get the message.

Use present tense. In general, when you refer to the present time of the text, use the *present* tense: "Alex Sutherland, the narrator of 'In the Swamp,' *thinks* he *is* a man of purpose" (*not* "thought he was"). This is the basic tense, from which you depart as the need arises: "As a child, Alex had feared that he would die young; now he fears that he will not."

Analyze evidence. Don't fill your essay up with quotations on which you offer no comment. Before or after the quotation, *analyze* it—or at least be sure that the *point* of the quotation (how *you* are using it) is clear to the reader. Remember that the reader cannot read your mind.

Select examples carefully. In most cases, there will be more evidence than you can use. Don't feel that you have to give it all. Choose the most persuasive as well as the most subtle and interesting examples. Although you should not be afraid of using important examples cited in class, you should always try to find fresh examples of your own. Avoid using too many examples that make exactly the same point.

Control the flow. Check for paragraph unity. Each paragraph should have a general topic, and everything in the paragraph should relate to that topic. Be sure that your reader remains aware of what the topic is, but don't beat him over the head with it. Each sentence should lead into the next in an easy and logical manner. Place signposts along the trail, so that the reader can keep track of your argument (and can be confident that *you* are on track). If you change direction, provide a signal to that effect—a word such as "however"; if you want to be sure that the reader knows that the next bit follows from the last, consider a word like "thus" or "therefore," but don't become excessively reliant on such devices. Your reader shouldn't feel that you are being too stiff or too bossy, or that you think he hasn't got a brain in his head. Be sure too that you have achieved an effective or natural transition as you move from one paragraph to the next. Remember that you want to keep the reader with you every step of the way. The reader should not be frustrated and confused *or* irritated and bored. The reader's journey through the words of your essay is *in your hands*, the hands that have written the words. Remember that the reader can read only the words on the page. *The reader cannot read your mind.*

CONCLUSION

In a short essay, the conclusion should avoid an extensive repetition of points already made. A good conclusion may remind us of those points, however. Often it returns to the thesis (of which we should *always* be reminded at the end) in a slightly different way. A good conclusion often goes beyond what was said in the body of the paper, to assess the larger implications of the thesis.

Students are sometimes told that the argument should be completed prior to the conclusion, and that new evidence and new ideas should not appear in the conclusion. That advice seems to me just a bit suspect, especially for a short essay. Certainly you want to have completed the basic argument before you get to the conclusion. Your case should be secure before that point. But you might still pull a rabbit or two out of the magician's hat in the last paragraph.

A good conclusion provides *the sense of an ending*. Have you ever been to a play and been unsure whether it's time to clap? That uncertainty in the reader is what you want to avoid. In a very short essay, you may have so much to pack into a few paragraphs that you cannot afford to have a final paragraph that is bereft of new ideas. In that case, just be sure that the last paragraph reminds the reader of the thesis and that it provides the sense of an ending.

REMARKS ON STYLE

In talking about how to write a good essay, I have used the analogy of a path or a trail. One of the main things you *don't* want on a trail is *deadwood*. This obscures the trail and slows your reader down. What do I mean by the term *deadwood*? I mean words that are dead because they serve no function; they just take up space. I mean *wordiness*, which is one of the most common and deplorable characteristics of bad writing.

There are two principal (and often overlapping) types of wordiness. In one kind, the words just take up space, trying to sound impressive and failing to say anything—perhaps even for a full paragraph, or a full essay. Usually you know when you're doing this; this kind of bad writing is often a handy but ill-advised substitute for the hard job of *thinking*. The sentences may sound all right, but there's nothing at all behind them; the words are just puffed up with hot air. In the second kind of wordiness, there is meaning in there somewhere. But the live wood—the real structure of thought—is obscured by the deadwood, the *useless words* that the writer may have stuck in out of a mistaken sense that they sound good. Sometimes, students are afraid their ideas sound too simple, so they haul in the deadwood. (Wordiness is a disease that has also—and unpleasantly but aptly—been likened to diarrhea.)

Many common expressions are wordy and should be avoided. The meaning they contain can be expressed much more concisely. Thus, for example, "on account of the fact that" really means "because"; "at this point in time" really means "now"; and "in spite of the fact that" really means "although."

Getting rid of wordiness can mean choosing exact nouns, verbs, adjectives, and adverbs (not "She ran as quickly as she could down the street" but "She sprinted down the street"); replacing inexact adverbs (such as "really," "rather," "somewhat," "very") with a more precise word (not "really happy" but "ecstatic"); eliminating redundancies (not "cooperating together" but "cooperating"; not "the two twins" but "the twins"); and condensing phrases to single words (not "in the event that" but "if").

I'm going to take a sentence through several versions now, clearing away the deadwood:

1. Because of the work he did in the 1940s and 1950s, Humphrey Bogart could, by some, be considered legendary in terms of his film career.
2. Because of his work in the 1940s and 1950s, Humphrey Bogart is considered by some to be legendary in terms of his film career.
3. Humphrey Bogart is considered legendary in terms of his film career.
4. Humphrey Bogart is considered a film legend.
5. Humphrey Bogart is a film legend.

This sentence keeps getting stronger. Has anything been lost since the first version? Probably not, although we would have to know more about the context to establish that. But even if you do need to specify his work in the 1940s and 1950s, the first version of this sentence is very bad. You could say this instead:

> Because of his work in the 1940s and 1950s, Humphrey Bogart is a film legend.

Observe that the phrase "in terms of his film career" has to go!

Don't take simple points and try to make them sound complicated. The true struggle is to take a complicated thought and express it in a sentence that is as simple and clear as possible. I'll give you another example now of a wordy sentence, with a revision that is much stronger:

1. One of the most disturbing types of possible tendencies that occurs when we begin the act of writing is an inability of sorts to suitably render into concise and wholly efficient language our multidimensional ranges of various ideas.
2. A major problem in writing is the inability to express our ideas concisely.

Two good things happen when you move from the first to the second version. You make the point easier to follow, *and* you take up less space, so that now there is more room in the essay for the other things you want to say. You should be ruthless with yourself. If a word or phrase isn't doing anything, if you don't *need* it, get rid of it. *Be concise.*

Let's do some more. Say I have a sentence like this one:

> It could be said that the poets from the Romantic time period were interested in issues concerning our place in the natural world.

Let's think about the opening clause, "It could be said that the poets from the Romantic time period." What do I mean? Well, I really mean "the Romantic poets." So that's what I should say. The sentence is now much stronger—

> The Romantic poets were interested in issues concerning our place in the natural world.

How much do we lose if the sentence is stripped down further? Does the author really mean something more than "The Romantic poets were interested in nature"? Perhaps so ...

Here's another:

> Margaret Atwood, a Canadian writer, has thus far in her career written in four genres: she has written novels, short stories, poetry, and criticism.

The most obvious things to take out are "thus far in her career," because that fact is implied, and "she has written," because it is redundant. This would leave the following:

> Margaret Atwood, a Canadian writer, has written in four genres: novels, short stories, poetry, and criticism.

Beyond that, your changes will depend on context. If for some reason you wanted to emphasize that she is Canadian, you would keep "a Canadian writer" in the sentence. But this is probably just filler. If you really wanted to stress the range of her work you might get away with saying that she has written in four genres. But it's probably more filler. If you aren't particularly concerned about the issue of genre, then "Margaret Atwood has written novels, short stories, poetry, and criticism" is surely sufficient.

Think about some of the filler we all use from time to time. What does "it is my opinion that" contribute to a sentence? The fact that you are making your point in the first place is evidence enough that this is what you think. Start right in with your point. You don't need to say, for example, "It is my opinion that Hamlet is an existentialist." Just say "Hamlet is an existentialist," and then go on to explain why you think so. Similarly, the expression "it can be seen that" adds nothing to the meaning of a sentence. Instead of saying "It can be seen that Thomas King is drawing upon oral tradition in *Green Grass, Running Water*," just say "Thomas King draws upon oral tradition in *Green Grass, Running Water*."

Sometimes wordiness is more difficult to fix. Even if there's a good idea hidden under the deadwood, it can be very hard to find. To show you what I mean, here's a sentence that demonstrates extreme wordiness.

> By way of conclusion, I would like to posit that with regard to colonization and granting the fact that the negatively affecting characteristics of the colonial mentality are complex, Jean Rhys makes the point astutely.

What am I trying to say here? It's hard to say, but the sentence might mean something like this:

> In her novel, Jean Rhys analyzes the complexity of colonization and its overwhelmingly negative effects.

Probably the hardest part of writing is the struggle for clarity. It's also the most exciting part. You may think of this as the struggle to translate what you think into words, but often it's more than that. Often, you *find out* what you think in the struggle of writing, or you find out that what you thought isn't quite right—now that you're staring at it, naked on the page—and that you are going to have to think some more. There are two good reasons for writing: to communicate something to the *reader*, and to communicate something to *yourself*. That second reason is not as obvious or as widely understood as the first, but it is a very potent reason all the same. We clarify our own thoughts by writing well; and when we do succeed in getting those thoughts down clearly on paper, we possess them much more thoroughly than we did when they were just buzzing around inside our brains. (When we write badly, we get frustrated—because we suspect that the makings of something much better is lurking in our heads. We just can't get it *out*!)

The struggle to be concise and clear occurs at the level of the sentence. You fight to make *each sentence* as tight and as clear as possible. You may sometimes feel that these are competing claims: you think that in order to be *clear*, you will have to be less *concise* (taking more time to say what you mean). *That may well be true.* But what often happens in the writing process is that you don't quite hit on what you mean in one whack (one sentence), so you take a few more whacks (more sentences)—trying to zoom in on the point you want to make. That's O.K. for a rough draft. But in the revision process, you should step back and ask yourself whether *now* you are in a position to say this thing more quickly. Reduce the total numbers of words as far as you can without sacrificing clarity.

Be concrete. Be precise. In choosing your words, prefer the particular to the general wherever possible. Consider this sentence: "Here one sees his lack of emotion." What exactly is meant by "lack of emotion"? This *could* mean any number of things, like indifference, or iciness, or impartiality; each of these words is more particular, more precise than "lack of emotion." And any one of these, if it succeeds in capturing your idea, would be preferable to "lack of emotion," since that term gives the reader only a general idea of what you might mean. Now consider this sentence: "The clown's part in *Othello* is very small." There is nothing wrong with that sentence, but this one is better: "The clown in *Othello* speaks only thirty lines." You have still spent only eight words on the sentence, and the general idea (that the part is very small) is still there; but now the sentence is more concrete and more precise. The reader gets a bigger return on the time that was spent in reading these eight words—a more precise picture, and a piece of hard information—and loses nothing.

Choose the right word. Sometimes a *thesaurus* will help you to find exactly the right word; it will give you possible synonyms (words that mean more or less the same thing) from which to choose the word that says it best. (In fact, few words are *really* synonymous; there are usually shades of meaning that make one word more appropriate than another in a particular context.) The best word is often the most particular word. To achieve precision, you choose the word that narrows the field. Is skiing "enjoyable" or "exhilarating"? It may well be enjoyable, but so are lots of things. You want the word that scores a bull's-eye. You want the word to land in the precise location of the thing you are describing, rather than on one of the outer circles.

When you look up a word in the thesaurus, you are often given a number of possible synonyms. Some are so imprecise that you can discard them immediately, while others seem fine. Before you use any of the ones you think are fine, look up each one in the dictionary. There is no point in using a thesaurus if you are trying only to find the biggest and fanciest word you can and are not interested in the precision of your language. Often you are given a list of other words to see; it doesn't hurt to look them up as long as you follow the same procedure before you use them.

Consider level of diction. Has X been incarcerated, thrown in the slammer, or sent to prison? The first is too highfalutin or stiff, the second is too low or colloquial, and the third is fine. Don't be afraid of saying things simply. "Exhilarating" is better than "enjoyable" in the example given previously, not because it is fancier but because it is more precise. In most situations, for example, I would use the word "use" where others might (as they would say) *employ* the word "employ"—because it sounds fancier. I like "use" better because I don't see any good reason for using the fancier word. The best writers in my experience are not afraid of using striking or unusual words *or* of using good, strong, simple words. And the mix is most pleasing to most readers.

Because you will be writing formal academic essays, the level of diction is important. One of the things that determines the level you should use is your target audience. For academic essays, your target audience is your professor, so your tone should be formal and professional.

Prefer the active voice. The great advantage of the active voice—"I broke the window"—over the passive voice—"The window was broken"—is that the active voice requires you to take or assign responsibility; in the passive voice the actor of the verb is obscured. For that very reason, politicians are fond of the passive voice. Certainly, there are occasions when your meaning will require that you use the passive. These would include scientific experiments (*example:* The beaker was filled with water, and a flame was placed beneath it) and cases in which the agent of the action is understood, unimportant, or unknown (*example:* It was said at the meeting that the new development would interfere with the wildlife). If you have a choice, though, prefer the active. Writing that overuses the passive voice tends to be abstract, stuffy, and weak.

Vary sentence structure. You should provide variety both in the *length* and in the *structure* of sentences. Too many short or long sentences in a row should be avoided. A short sentence can be very effective, especially after a long one. However, more than a couple of short sentences in a row can sound choppy— and juvenile. Learn how to *combine* sentences effectively. Make effective use of introductory elements—starting with a dependent clause, a participial phrase, etc. You should be concerned if nearly all your sentences start with the subject of the main clause. Don't be afraid to use parallel construction, semicolons, and colons; it is important to learn how to use these well. Use the full range of conjunctive adverbs and conjunctions, not just a few like "but."

Here are some examples of ways to combine sentences:

> Phoenix is an old woman. She travels the same path over and over. She must get her grandson his medicine. Her journey is a long one.

1. Though she is an old woman, Phoenix travels the same long path over and over to get the medicine for her grandson.

2. Travelling the same long path over and over, old Phoenix must get medicine for her grandson.

3. In spite of the long journey and her old age, Phoenix must travel the same path over and over to get her grandson his medicine.

Notice that the emphasis of the sentence changes with the change in openings. What was once a choppy group of sentences becomes, by combining sentences, a smooth, unified statement.

Here is an example of a paragraph I can improve by combining sentences:

> Spenser's poetry reflects the attitudes of the Royal Court. Queen Elizabeth used her private life as a tool for foreign policy. Therefore, the private message of the love poems written by her court poet, Spenser, was also a tool of foreign policy. You can see this in the poems' description of the lover. The descriptions are unlike descriptions in love poems by other poets. They do not reveal the intimate self of a lover. They reveal a courtly persona.

This paragraph says a lot. But it says it inefficiently and without making adequate connections between the ideas of the sentences. Combining sentences forces you to subordinate some ideas to others; the ideas are put together in a way that suggests their relationship to one another.

> Spenser's poetry reflects Queen Elizabeth's use of her private life as a tool of foreign policy. That the private messages of the love poems are also tools of foreign policy is revealed in the descriptions of the lover, which suggest a courtly persona rather than the intimate self of a lover described by other love poets.

CHECK YOUR WORK!

This is a critical factor in the success or failure of your essay. You must leave time to check your work *very* carefully; to omit this task or to spend only a few minutes on it can be costly. Remember that your purpose here is to find out what's wrong, and what could be improved, *not* to convince yourself that the essay is fine as it stands. Two things can lull you into a false sense of security: the lovely sight of a cleanly typed page, and the flattering sound of your own voice reading the essay out loud. I strongly recommend both things—clean copy and reading aloud—but you must maintain a critical perspective. I'll give you now a list of things to check for, and I recommend that you *use* this list (going down it point by point, checking for each thing before you proceed to the next).

THE ESSAY AS A WHOLE

1. Does the thesis come out clearly?
2. Is the organization of the essay clear?
3. Is each paragraph unified? Is there anything in any of the paragraphs that doesn't belong?
4. Do the transitions work well within and between paragraphs?
5. Are arguments properly supported? Do I need to go back to the text for further evidence?
6. Does the introduction need to be rewritten to fit the body of the essay?
7. Is the conclusion effective?

SENTENCE BY SENTENCE

1. Check each sentence for deadwood, wordiness. Is each sentence clear? Is it concise?
2. Check for credibility. Do I believe this? Can I reasonably claim this? Watch out for hasty generalizations.
3. Run-ons and fragments. Have I written as a sentence something that is *more* than a sentence? *Less* than a sentence?
4. Agreement errors. Consciously identify the subject and verb of each sentence. Am I sure that the verb agrees with the *subject* of the sentence and not with some other noun that intervenes between subject and verb? Do my pronouns agree with their antecedents in gender and in number?
5. Parallelism and placement of modifiers. Have I messed up parallel constructions? Have I placed my modifiers as close as possible to the words they modify?
6. Punctuation. Check each sentence *very* carefully. Have I chosen the correct mark of punctuation? Have I set things off on both sides? Have I left out any necessary punctuation? Have I committed any intrusive comma errors?
7. Apostrophes. Have I used them properly?
8. Spelling. Have I checked for all possible spelling errors? Software spell-checkers are good, but they cannot catch some of the more insidious spelling errors, nor do they catch problems like using "are" for "our," or accidentally dropping the "t" from "this" so that it reads "his." Proofread for these types of errors and always use a dictionary if you are uncertain of any spelling.
9. Handling and accuracy of quotations. Have I punctuated quotations correctly? Have I integrated them effectively into my own prose? Have I quoted accurately? *(Go back to the text to double-check.)*
10. Can I improve word choice?
11. How might I improve this essay by changing (and varying) sentence structure?

APPENDIX V

SAMPLE ESSAY

There is an analogy I like to use when I'm trying to explain how I arrive at a grade. Try thinking of your essay as a dive: you attempt a dive of a particular level of difficulty—it might be a simple dive or an extraordinarily difficult one—and then you *perform* it more or less well. To evaluate your performance fairly, I must take into consideration how challenging the task is that you have set yourself. On the one hand, an easy dive perfectly executed will obviously not be as impressive as a complex dive perfectly executed, or even as impressive as a complex dive performed with minor imperfections. On the other hand, a badly botched dive, no matter how tough it is, gets a lower score than an impeccably performed dive of moderate difficulty.

A paper that earns a grade of A can contain errors; an F paper can contain brilliant insights. There is no such thing really as a typical A, B, C, D, or F essay in an English course, since these grades are arrived at by weighing a number of factors:

1. grammar, punctuation, etc. (technical correctness)
2. quality of analysis
3. organization
4. use of evidence
5. style (effectiveness, precision, elegance)

A paper that gets top marks will be strong in all of these areas, though it will always (theoretically, at least) be possible to make the essay even better. But an essay that earns a C, for example, might be C-like in all five areas cited above, or A-like in one, F-like in another, and C-like in the remaining three. (I should acknowledge that in practice it is often impossible to un-tangle these factors from one another: strong analysis, for instance, cannot occur without appropriate evidence and will be unclear if the argument is poorly organized or if the sentences are so grammatically mangled that their meaning is unclear.)

What I'm going to do now is take a failing sample essay (probably worth no more than 40 percent) that is based on Eudora Welty's famous story "A Worn Path," and show you how it can be improved until after several versions it deserves an A grade.

"A Worn Path" is printed in Part I of this anthology (see page 793). Read Welty's story with great care before proceeding through the versions of our sample essay.

VERSION 1

- sp = spelling
- FRAG = sentence fragment
- CS = comma splice

Is she senile? Phoenix appears to inavertly wander [split infinitive] — *sp*

up and down her chosen path. ⌊A path she has on FRAG

numerous occassions worn down through the years.⌋ *sp*

Her destination is apparent, when she leaves her

country home. Phoenix is going to collect the med-

ication for her beloved grandson,/during her journey

- verb = verb form incorrect

she encounter many obstacles and finally ends up at *CS* — *verb*

the town, only to forget why she came.

Is she senile? The reader must wonder about the

old woman travelling such a great distance alone.

⌊Dreaming of marble-cake and momentarily thinking it FRAG

- Q = quotation inaccurate or mishandled

is reality.⌋ '. . . "That would be acceptable", she said,

'but when she went to take it there was just her own | Q

hand in the air." (p.9) Is she senile? The people

Phoenix meets denote her as inferior, a grandma,

- ∂ = delete punctuation

granny, and old woman. The white man⌿with the gun

says to her, after inquiring her where-abouts and desti- *about* ∧ *sp*

nation, . . . "Now you go home granny.". . . "I know you

old coloured people wouldn't miss going to town to see | Q

Santa Claus." (p.10) Phoenix stops a nice white lady in

town. She wants this woman to tie her shoelaces, for

Phoenix is too old and cannot with a cane in hand. The

woman asked . . . "What do you want grandma ?" | Q

(p.11)

Phoenix speaks to herself and anything that moves

on her path, even the imaginary creatures. 'Now and

then there was a quivering in the thicket'. . . "Out of

my way, all you foxes, owls, beetles, jack rabbits, coons

and wild animals"... (p.8) ... "up through the pines",

she said at length,", "Now down through the oaks."

(p.8) Her <u>illussive</u> mind causes the reader to question
sp

her behavior. Is she senile? Phoenix has a mission,

- **poss =**
  possessive
  apostrophe

but <u>has forgot</u> what it was once at the <u>doctors</u> office.
verb   poss

She remembers the clinic, with the document in the
poss

gold frame with the gold seal. Still Phoenix <u>has forgot</u>
           verb

her appointed calling. "My grandson. It was my

memory that left me"... (p.12) she answered, after | Q

much <u>persuassion</u> from the nurse and attendant at the
    sp

clinic.

   Is she senile? No, I do not believe so. Phoenix

- **pc = parallel**
  construction

makes excuses because she is old. <u>Yey</u>, she is <u>niether</u>
            sp   sp pc

- **c.a.c. =**
  "comma and
  construction"
  between
  independent
  clauses

senile <u>nor</u> a scared old woman. Phoenix is cautious

and anticipates that whatever she confronts on the

worn path will not stall her journey. Phoenix has

taken the path <u>often and</u> she encounters the same
       c.a.c.

external conditions. Yet her eyes <u>decieve</u> her "... old
             sp | Q

eyes thought you was a pretty little green bush"...

(p.8) you scarecrow she said "my senses is gone. I too | Q

old" (p.9) Phoenix depends on her feet, not her eyes to

- **pronoun =**
  wrong pro-
  noun form

direct <u>herself</u>. "Where she walked up and around and | Q
   pronoun

around, until her feet knew to stop." (p 11)

   I believe that Phoenix's heart is what guides her

feet. She loves her grandson dearly and believes that

"We is the only two left in the world". (p.12) The only FRAG

two <u>that</u> <u>counts</u> in her life. Phoenix is not afraid to
 pronoun verb

take the nickel that fell from the white <u>mans</u> pocket.
                                        poss
Nor is she scared to ask for five pennies, which is

another <u>nickle</u>, from the attendant. Now the coins are
         sp
worth a dime. ⌊Enough money to buy a paper windmill   FRAG

from the store.⌋ "He going to find it hard to believe   ⎤
                                                              ⎥ Q
there is such a thing in the world" (p12) The journey   ⎦

this time was <u>not</u> for just medication, from a doctor,
                 pc
<u>but</u> love, the ultimate medicine. Is this senile?

COMMENT

This essay is obviously very weak. In order to address the problems of argumentation and so on, I will provide a cleaned-up version. This Version 2 corrects the errors in grammar, punctuation, and spelling marked on Version 1. It
also corrects the quotations, every one of which was faulty! Please remember
that you *must* quote exactly. In proofreading your essay, *always* go back to the
text to ensure that you've got every word and every mark of
punctuation exactly as it was in the original. There is no excuse for making
errors of this kind. Also learn how to handle quotation marks, page numbers,
and punctuation with quotations. Errors remaining in Version 2 (and marked
on this otherwise clean copy) are one redundant phrase and four words that
were incorrectly chosen.

VERSION 2

#1   Is she senile? Phoenix appears to wander inadver-

tently up and down her chosen path, which she has

• < > = omit,   worn down⟨on numerous occasions⟩through the
  redundant
years. Her destination is apparent when she leaves

her country home. Phoenix is going to collect the

medication for her beloved grandson. During her

journey she encounters many obstacles and finally

ends up at the town, only to forget why she came.

#2   Is she senile? The reader must wonder about the

old woman travelling such a great distance alone,

dreaming of marble-cake and momentarily thinking it

is reality. "'That would be acceptable,' she said, but

when she went to take it there was just her own hand

in the air" (9). Is she senile? The people Phoenix meets

• ww = wrong   <u>denote</u> her as inferior, a grandma, granny, and old
  word   ww

woman. The white man with the gun says to her, after

inquiring about her <u>whereabouts</u> and destination,
                                       ww

"'Now you go on home, Granny! . . . I know you old

coloured people! Wouldn't miss going to town to see

Santa Claus!'" (10). Phoenix stops a nice white lady in

town. She wants this woman to tie her shoelaces, for

Phoenix is too old and cannot with a cane in hand. The

woman asks, "'What do you want, Grandma?'" (11).

#3   Phoenix speaks to herself and anything that moves

on her path, even imaginary creatures. "Now and then

there was a quivering in the thicket. Old Phoenix said,

'Out of my way, all you foxes, owls, beetles, jack rab-

bits, coons and wild animals!'" (8). "'Up through the

pines,' she said at length. 'Now down through oaks'"

(8). Her <u>illusive</u> mind causes the reader to question
              ww

her behaviour. Is she senile? Phoenix has a mission but

forgets what it is once at the doctor's office. She

remembers the clinic with the document in the gold

frame with the gold seal. Still Phoenix forgets her

appointed calling. "'My grandson. It was my memory

that left me'" (12), she answers, after much persuasion from the nurse and attendant at the clinic.

#4   Is she senile? No, I do not believe so. Phoenix makes excuses because she is old. Yet she is neither senile nor scared. Phoenix is cautious and <u>anticipates</u>
                                                                          ww
that whatever she confronts on the worn path will not

• ww = wrong word

stall her journey. Phoenix has taken the path often, and she encounters the same external conditions. Yet her eyes deceive her: "'Old eyes thought you was a pretty little green bush'" (8). "'You scarecrow,' she said. . . . 'My senses is gone. I too old'" (9). Phoenix depends on her feet, not her eyes, to direct her: "she walked up and around and around until her feet knew to stop" (11).

#5   I believe that Phoenix's heart is what guides her feet. She loves her grandson dearly and believes that "'We is the only two left in the world'" (12). They are the only two who count in her life. Phoenix is not afraid to take the nickel that fell from the white man's pocket. Nor is she scared to ask for five pennies, which is another nickel, from the attendant. Now the coins are worth a dime, which is enough money to buy a paper windmill from the store. "'He going to find it hard to believe there such a thing in the world'" (12). The journey this time was not just for medication from a doctor, but for love, the ultimate medicine. Is this senile?

COMMENT

I would say that Version 2 is worth around 60 percent. But I find this version hard to grade because it would be extremely unusual to find an essay so free of technical errors that is also so weak in argumentation. In the versions that follow, I will not introduce any further technical errors. You should not conclude, however, that the 20-percent spread between 40 percent in Version 1 and 60 percent in Version 2 represents the amount that technical errors can count in an assessment of your work. The correction of the errors in this case raises the mark by 20 percent, but if you were to *commit* errors as serious and plentiful as these in an essay that might otherwise have earned 85 percent, your essay would still fail. Technical errors can make the difference between an A and an F, but an essay that is totally free of technical errors could still be a failing essay.

Argumentation. The cleaned-up copy of Version 2 makes it easier for us to see what the writer of the essay might be trying to say and how the argument can be improved. Notice that I have used the word "argument"—but what *is* the argument of this essay? What is the writer trying to prove? The repeated question ("Is she senile?") and the answer given in paragraph 4 ("No, I do not believe so.") suggest that the writer's purpose is to convince the reader that Phoenix is not senile. One of the oddities of this essay is that although it lacks a clear thesis statement, the reader knows from the repeated rhetorical questions what the essay is about. The *topic* is senility, and the implicit *thesis* is that Phoenix is not senile.

Most English instructors insist that the introductory paragraph of the essay contain a thesis statement. I am relatively flexible on this point, since I find that in superb essays by professional literary critics it is often impossible to find a sentence at the start of the essay that sums up the author's thesis. Still, I advise students to formulate a thesis and state it clearly near the beginning. In almost all cases, to do so will strengthen your work. In this case, if the writer had attempted to develop a thesis statement, the inadequacy of the project might have become apparent, and the project might at that stage have been redefined. Remember that the goal of a critical essay is to convince the reader that the thesis is *worth* defending and that it has been defended well.

My criticism of Version 2 is not so much that the essay lacks a thesis as that the implicit thesis is not sufficiently interesting from a literary point of view, and not properly worked out. The writer's attempt at diagnosis on this matter seems a bit peculiar. Does the writer know enough about symptoms of senile dementia (the technically correct term) to assess whether Phoenix is senile? Isn't senility a degenerative disorder, which gets worse over time (so that a person could be a bit senile but not totally so)? Does a defence of

Phoenix require us to establish the truth or falsehood of this diagnosis? How important is this question? Is that really what the writer wants to work out? If so, we might expect a definition of senility and a list of symptoms to be found (or not found) in Phoenix.

Here is what I think might have gone on in the mind of the student who submitted Version 1. (I'll assume that the student was female.) In reading the story, she noticed that this very old woman was doing some peculiar things— talking to shrubs, hallucinating about marble-cake, and so on. Not surprisingly, she wondered whether Phoenix might be senile. To begin with, remember, she would have had no idea where Phoenix was going or whether this journey along the worn path made any sense. By the end of the story, her respect for Phoenix had naturally increased. She wanted in some way to account for her own earlier suspicions, while at the same time expressing admiration for Phoenix Jackson. But she didn't think the problem through before she began. She relied on the repeated question ("Is she senile?") to establish an easy structure for the essay. The technical carelessness of Version 1 is a symptom of the student's hurried approach to the task at hand; it is matched by her lack of care with the argument.

Now let's look at the function of each of the paragraphs in Version 2.

Please reread each paragraph of Version 2 before reading my analysis of it!

Paragraph 1

The student states incorrectly that "Her destination is apparent when she leaves her country home." In fact, Phoenix's destination and purpose are not revealed to the reader until the end of the story. But in the previous sentence the student seems to be recounting the experience of a reader who doesn't know the ending yet, when she says that "Phoenix appears to wander inadvertently up and down her chosen path ..." I find myself confused. Is Phoenix just wandering "inadvertently" (without choice or conscious purpose), or is she consciously pursuing a "chosen path"? The two points contradict each other. I think the confusion arises because the student is not distinguishing between what she thought at the beginning and what she learned later. Or she may be reproducing a confusion she felt all along, since Phoenix might well have seemed determined *and* befuddled. (Notice also that the phrase "on numerous occasions" is redundant. It should be omitted, since "worn down" and "through the years" make the point by themselves.)

This paragraph asks the question ("Is she senile?") and does not answer it. On dramatic grounds, I could defend the student's decision not to answer the question (or state her thesis) in the first paragraph. She sets up the problem by offering one sample piece of evidence opposing the senility idea (Phoenix has a rational purpose: "medication for her beloved grandson") and another piece supporting it ("only to forget why she came"). These bits of evidence are well chosen because they serve another purpose too: they orient us to the story, giving a kind of miniature plot summary in an economical way. The main thing that is wrong with this paragraph is the confusion I describe above.

Paragraph 2 (Reread it first.)
Probably the intention of this paragraph (and the next) is to set out evidence that might lead the reader to think Phoenix is senile. But how well does the student *analyze* this evidence? Can I be sure that she intends it as evidence that Phoenix might be senile? Mainly, it feels like plot summary. If it were not for the repeated question ("Is she senile?"), the reader would have no idea that it formed any part of an argument. The first attempt at evidence is not too bad: the reader "must wonder" about the old woman travelling so far alone and about the cake dream. But the references to the hunter and the lady do not in any clear way show that Phoenix might be senile, and the student does not tell us why she thinks they do. She fails to analyze the evidence.

These two references are introduced by the statement that the people Phoenix meets "denote her as inferior"—presumably *because* she is old, since the student goes on to say "a grandma, granny, and old woman." Can you see that "denote" is the wrong word here? The people do not "denote" or (a better word) *call* her "inferior," though they do use the other three terms— "Granny," "Grandma," and "old colored people" (rather than "old woman"—so that's another error!). Try *regard* or *see* to cover all four cases: "The people Phoenix meets *see* her as inferior, *calling* her grandma, granny, and old woman." But note that the student has put these terms in the wrong order; they *should* occur in the order of their appearance in the quotations that follow. In Version 3 I change this to "a granny, an old coloured person, a grandma." (Incidentally, the word "whereabouts" is marked as wrong because what the hunter actually asks is where she *lives*; her "whereabouts" is her present location, which is a ditch!)

But what does any of that have to do with evidence of *senility*? Has the student switched topics here? If so, has she switched from senility to *old age* (failing to make a distinction between the two) or has she switched from senility to *inferiority*? Could it be that she's less interested in whether Phoenix is senile than in the larger question of what might lead us into the error of thinking that Phoenix is a person unworthy of our respect? (This worries me. Does she think old people or people suffering from senility are generally unworthy of respect? Couldn't Phoenix be afflicted by senility *and* be a heroine?)

I can't tell whether the student has detected and is trying to demonstrate through the quoted dialogue the racial condescension of the hunter and the lady. If she doesn't recognize the racial condescension, can we trust her understanding of the quoted material? The student is right in indicating that the hunter and the lady regard Phoenix as an inferior. But is that just because she's old or because she's black? Since the student hasn't given any interpretation of the dialogue she quotes, I don't know whether she has considered the latter possibility. (The dialogue suggests to me that they condescend for both reasons. Terms like "Granny" were used in the South only for blacks, unless the person in question really was your grandmother.) If race is part of what she is getting at here, how does it connect with the topic of old age and senility? In the beginning of this paragraph the idea of inferiority was tied to old age, but the issue of race complicates this. (You must always be certain that the *point* of a quotation is clear.)

Paragraph 3 (Reread it first.)
In this paragraph, the student points out (in a good topic sentence) that "Phoenix speaks to herself and anything that moves on her path, even imaginary creatures." She then supplies some good textual evidence, and offers a comment on it: "Her illusive mind causes the reader to question her behaviour. Is she senile?" (The word "illusive" is a rarely used adjective; "illusory" has the same meaning and is much more common. It means that the thing it modifies—in this case, Phoenix's mind—is an illusion. This is obviously not what the student intends. She might say instead that "Phoenix's illusions cause the reader to question her behaviour." But is it really her *behaviour* that comes into question? What the student means, I think, is simply this: "Phoenix's illusions cause the reader to think she may be senile.")

I wonder why the marble-cake hallucination doesn't come here (rather than in the second paragraph). Another problem with paragraph unity is that the student now leaves the subject of illusion and returns to the fact that when Phoenix gets to the doctor's office she forgets her mission. Also, the detail here feels too much like plot summary.

Paragraph 4 (Reread it first.)
Now nearing the end of the essay, the student tells us that she doesn't believe Phoenix is senile. She doesn't dispose of the evidence to the contrary that she has assembled in the previous paragraphs, except by saying that Phoenix must make excuses because she is old. (And I wonder if that's true. Does Phoenix really try to make excuses for herself? I would say rather that she acknowledges the infirmity that comes with age. The student does not tell us what excuses she makes.) As evidence against senility, she offers this comment: "Phoenix is cautious and anticipates that whatever she confronts on the worn path will not stall her journey." (Notice that the word "anticipates" is wrong. Do you see how this sentence snaps into focus if you substitute the adjective "determined"?)

In the second half of the paragraph, the student seems to return to the infirmity of old age, as she points out that Phoenix's "eyes deceive her"—even though "she encounters the same external conditions" whenever she walks on this path. (But that isn't true; the dangers and pleasures vary with the seasons, as Phoenix herself points out.) The scarecrow is mentioned without apparent purpose, although the quotation goes on to supply further evidence that Phoenix acknowledges the infirmity of age. The final quotation ("her feet knew to stop") shows that she can rely on her feet even if her eyes fail.

Paragraph 5 (Reread it first.)
The concluding paragraph begins with an excellent transition from paragraph 4: "I believe that Phoenix's heart is what guides her feet." The general topic of this paragraph is love. The student establishes the intense focus of Phoenix's love with the quotation "'We is the only two left in the world,'" and goes on to say that Phoenix is "not afraid" to steal and beg the money to buy the paper windmill. The student does not state that love gives Phoenix this courage, though I'm sure that's what she means. She might also point out that love makes Phoenix determined and resourceful.

The lovely quotation describing the grandson's predicted wonder over the gift helps to provide a feeling of intensity for the conclusion of the essay. (But what it actually *says* hasn't been analyzed or used.) The next sentence—about love as "the ultimate medicine"—is also dramatically effective. But what does she mean by this exactly? Does love (as the ultimate medicine) cure the grandson or Phoenix? Remember that love is being offered as the final argument against senility, so it would seem that it "cures" Phoenix. But the student doesn't indicate this because she hasn't thought through her own analogy (love = medicine). And why is the journey undertaken "this time" for love, rather than for ordinary medicine? Haven't all of Phoenix's previous journeys demonstrated her love? The difference this time is that she also brings back the windmill. Certainly that is a gift of love, but so is the medicine. (Actually, I'm not sure whether the student *means* me to connect the windmill and "this time ... for love.")

The final sentence varies the refrain slightly: "Is this senile?" The answer is supposed to be self-evident. The student thinks that Phoenix's love and the gift of the windmill prove that she isn't senile, so she rests her case there.

Now I will improve the quality of analysis, the organization, and the use of evidence for Version 3. First, though, let's think about a refinement of the implicit thesis from Version 2 *(Phoenix is not senile)*. I suggest the following: *Especially before they get to the end of the story, readers may wonder if Phoenix is senile. But in the end it seems that Phoenix's love and determination are so strong that even if she is a little senile, old age cannot defeat her.* It's helpful to write down a statement like this, even if you don't end up using it in exactly that form once you get down to the job of writing.

In the version that follows I use little more than was provided in the original essay. The improvements come from testing and then revising or omitting certain statements in the original essay, from looking harder at the quotations used, and *most of all* from refining the argument and presenting it in a logical order.

Here now is a brief outline for Version 3:

> *Paragraph 1. Introduction*
> – set up situation
> – effect on reader of not knowing P's goal until end
> – thesis
>
> *Paragraph 2. Evidence of possible senility (illusions)*
> – talking to herself
> – marble-cake
> – scarecrow (but turn toward P's awareness of problem)
>
> *Paragraph 3. More evidence? (other characters)*
> – hunter ("Granny" & "old colored people")
> – lady ("Grandma")
> – *but* note racism too & P's success in dealing w/it (fit in nickel from
>   hunter somewhere); thus she comes out on top.
>
> *Paragraph 4. Conclusion (love triumphs over age)*
> – "too old"
> – eyes fail her, but feet take over
> – heart guides feet
> – gets what she came for even though she forgets
> – also money for windmill
> – her love is what seems really "hard to believe"
> – love is ultimate medicine, for him & her

VERSION 3

Is Phoenix senile? As she travels along her chosen

path, Phoenix knows what her destination is. She is

going to collect medicine for her beloved grandson.

But we don't know this. To us, her journey may
seem foolish and without purpose. Phoenix often
seems out of touch with reality, and the other characters she meets see her as incompetent. Finally,
she gets to town, only to forget why she came. But
by this time, it is clear to the reader that Phoenix's
love and determination are so strong that even if
she is a little senile, old age cannot defeat her.

Phoenix speaks to herself and anything that moves
on her path, even imaginary creatures. "Now and then
there was a quivering in the thicket. Old Phoenix said,
'Out of my way, all you foxes, owls, beetles, jack rabbits,
coons and wild animals!'" (8). At one point, she has a
hallucination about a little boy serving her a slice of
marble-cake: "'That would be acceptable,' she said, but
when she went to take it there was just her own hand
in the air" (9). At another point, she talks to a scarecrow she has mistaken for a ghost. All of this might be
taken as evidence of senility. However, in her speech to
the scarecrow, it is clear that Phoenix is aware of the
problem: "'I ought to be shut up for good,' she said with
laughter. 'My senses is gone. I too old'" (9).

The people Phoenix meets regard her as an inferior, a granny, an old coloured person, a grandma. The
white man with the gun, who lifts her up when she
falls on the path, seems to think Phoenix is too old to
be out alone, and that she has entered her second
childhood: "'Now you go on home, Granny! . . . I know

you old colored people! Wouldn't miss going to town to see Santa Claus!'" (10). When she gets to town, Phoenix cannot tie her own shoes because of the cane in her hand. The white lady who ties them for her also speaks to Phoenix in a condescending way, asking, "'What do you want, Grandma?'" (11) even though "Grandma" has already told her. These characters look down on Phoenix because of her age and her race, but readers may not want to follow their example. What we notice most is that she is determined to get what she needs (including the nickel that the hunter drops) and is not ashamed to ask for help. In fact, Phoenix seems to come out on top in these scenes.

Is Phoenix senile? Perhaps she is a bit, but that doesn't stop her. Since Phoenix is "'the oldest people I ever know'" (9), her eyes may deceive her: "'Old eyes thought you was a pretty little green bush'" (8). But Phoenix depends on her feet, not her eyes, to achieve her goal: "she walked up and around and around until her feet knew to stop" (11). I believe that Phoenix's heart is what guides her feet. At the end of the story, just as Phoenix achieves her goal, she forgets why she came. But she does finally remember: "'My grandson. It was my memory that left me'" (12). She gets the medicine, and she also cleverly gets another five pennies from the attendant, so that now she has enough money to buy a paper windmill as a Christmas present for her grandson: "'He going to find it hard to believe there such a thing in the world'" (12). At this point,

the reader may find it hard to believe that there can be

love as strong as Phoenix's in this world. Love, the

ultimate medicine, triumphs over the sickness of old

age and—along with the medicine and the windmill—

goes home with Phoenix to her grandson.

COMMENT

This essay is probably worth an A. It is entirely free of technical errors, it has a reasonable thesis, and it is clear and beautifully organized. However, it doesn't contain any surprises, except for the last sentence, which is very sophisticated. Try to imagine Version 3 with a few technical errors and without that great last sentence, and you'll have an essay in the B range.

In the next and final version, I show you what happens when the student comes up with truly exciting ideas about the text. Version 4 would certainly be a high A+. In fact, it would be extremely unusual to find an essay as sophisticated and as polished as this one in an introductory English course. (It would be good work coming from a graduate student, so please don't be alarmed!) However, it is *not* unusual for a first-year essay to contain some great ideas. Real insights about the text can have a considerable impact upon your grade; it may be possible for an essay that contains such ideas to falter a bit on the organizational and technical side and *still* get an A.

VERSION 4

Readers of "A Worn Path" may question whether

Phoenix Jackson is a senile and incompetent wan-

derer or a heroic old woman who is in charge of her

life's journey. Only at the end of the story do we

learn that she travels her long and difficult path in

pursuit of medicine for her beloved grandson. It is

interesting that the strongest evidence of senility

also comes at this point, when her heroism is most clearly revealed. Phoenix forgets for a moment the thing that is most important to her: her grandson and the purpose of her long walk. This juxtaposition may cause the reader to reflect upon the connection between such setbacks and the triumph of Phoenix. I would argue that the difficulties this extraordinary individual has experienced through her long life as an impoverished black woman in the South, to which are now added the humiliations of old age, have actually served to strengthen her spirit.

Phoenix talks to herself and to animals who may or may not be there: "Now and then there was a quivering in the thicket. Old Phoenix said, 'Out of my way, all you foxes, owls, beetles, jack rabbits, coons and wild animals!'" (8). Tired out, she has a vision of marble-cake being served to her by a little boy, "but when she went to take it there was just her own hand in the air" (9). She also mistakes a scarecrow for a ghost. We might be tempted to condescend to Phoenix and to see such occasions as indicating a loss of contact with reality or as evidence of senility, but these examples could also suggest that old Phoenix is extraordinarily sensitive to the natural and supernatural worlds. The other characters in the story seem to look down on Phoenix and are ready to dismiss her, partly because she is so old. The hunter tries to send her home, exclaiming, "'I know you old colored people! Wouldn't

miss going to town to see Santa Claus!'" (10). The
irony is that he is dead wrong, because Phoenix has a
serious reason for going to town. The hunter is clearly
guilty of racism and ageism in applying this infantile
stereotype to Phoenix. Ironically too, Phoenix manages
to get a coin he claimed he didn't have, and she will
use it to buy a Christmas present for someone who
really is a child.

"'What do you want, Grandma?'" asks the lady
who eventually bends to tie Phoenix's shoes, making
her repeat a clear request, and treating her like an
incompetent child: "'Stand still then, Grandma'" (11).
In this second example too, stereotypes of race and age
strive to make the real Phoenix invisible, but the
careful and sympathetic reader should not succumb.
Ironically, black Phoenix takes advantage of her age to
manipulate the white woman into kneeling before <u>her</u>.

Phoenix has presumably had trouble all her life
because she is black, and now she is looked down upon
also because she is old. But she triumphs in spite of
that. Interestingly, despite their condescension and her
failing senses, Phoenix can see and hear and speak her
desires much more clearly than the young white people
in the story. This recognition may cause us to think
again about Phoenix's supposed senile hallucinations.
Perhaps at this late stage in her life, Phoenix is able
not only to operate successfully in the reality she is

confronted with (a racist society), but also to glimpse the supernatural reality that awaits her. In heaven, Phoenix will rest and be served her reward of marble-cake by angels or by the child she has loved so tenderly in this world.

The scarecrow she has danced with all her life is the racism that attempts to scare off needy and insistent black creatures like Phoenix (and the crow); the scarecrow she (an old crow) is dancing with in her old age is death. Phoenix knows that her senses are failing—knows that soon she will be "'shut down for good'" and that she is "'too old'" (9)—but she laughs in the face of death, dances, and perseveres. If her eyes fail, she can depend on her feet: "she walked up and around and around until her feet knew to stop" (11). If her memory fails, she can depend on the extraordinary power of her determined heart, which takes Phoenix infallibly along the worn path to the doctor's office and earns her the reward she seeks above all.

This simple medication can soothe the throat of a child who has swallowed lye, as people like Phoenix and her grandson have been made to swallow all kinds of hardship, because it represents love, life's ultimate medicine. Hardships, we may conclude, such as racial prejudice and the infirmity of old age, may be overcome through the power of love—which is tested and strengthened by adversity.

COMMENT

This essay is remarkable because it has attempted a very hard dive and accomplished it almost perfectly. The style is now more elegant, more polished; the structure is more complex because more ideas are being developed. Notice some of the new things that are here.

Paragraph 1
A sophisticated *literary* point is made in the first paragraph, concerning the "juxtaposition" of the strongest evidence of senility and the revelation of Phoenix's heroism. Seeing that these things are next to each other in the text, the writer asks *why*—and comes up with a good answer. The thesis (last sentence) goes beyond arguing that old age cannot defeat Phoenix. It now argues something much more difficult: that hardships such as old age and racism have actually *strengthened* her spirit.

Paragraph 2
This paragraph (now in a new position within the essay) makes the interesting suggestion that Phoenix's illusions may hint at a spiritual strength.

Paragraph 3
The irony of the hunter's remark about Santa Claus has been pointed out. We are also led to see the much more subtle irony of the fact that the hunter's nickel will buy some "Santa Claus" for a real child. (Attention to irony is often a mark of *literary* sophistication.)

Paragraph 4
The issue of racism is skilfully interwoven with ageism in this paragraph about the lady (now split off from the hunter because the essay has more to say about each). Another subtle irony is pointed out: that a white woman is manipulated into kneeling before a black woman. You might object that she doesn't necessarily *kneel*, or that this is probably not Phoenix's aim. But the point is still quite a nifty one, and it may very well be that the author wanted us to appreciate this tableau.

Paragraph 5
The idea that Phoenix comes out on top has now been extended to make the interesting suggestion that her failing senses are nonetheless stronger than those of the hunter and the lady. This point is valid, but it would be nice to have some examples. (They have been left out because the essay was getting too long; the writer is struggling hard to be concise because she has a great deal to say.) Notice how the essay tracks the effect of certain observations on the

reader—if we notice that Phoenix's senses are actually quite strong, we may then "think again" about her senile hallucinations. The essay returns to the marble-cake (discussed in an earlier paragraph) now that the groundwork has been laid for a more interesting suggestion (that the little boy might be the grandson in heaven). The connection of race and age becomes even more sophisticated as the essay associates racism with this world and suggests that old age will deliver Phoenix into a better world hereafter.

Paragraph 6

The essay also returns to the scarecrow now that more groundwork has been laid. Having paused to think a little about scarecrows, the writer has taken note of the fact that crows are black and hungry, and that people who own land set up straw men to scare them off. She can therefore make a fascinating and persuasive connection between crows and black people, and between scarecrows and racism. (She might also have recalled the "Jim Crow" laws, which protected segregation.) She has remembered that old people are sometimes called old crows, and she is apparently aware of the traditional literary images of death as a scarecrow and of dancing with death. Thus, she is able to use this scarecrow to confirm her sense that the issues of racism and old age are deeply intertwined in this story.

Paragraph 7

The conclusion of the essay builds on the idea of love as the ultimate medicine and takes account of its effect on Phoenix, as Version 3 failed to do. Particularly striking is the fact that the writer has stopped to think about the lye swallowed by the grandson, and has *used* that (lye = hardship; think of a throat and the terrible things each has had to "swallow") to show that love (the ultimate medicine) eases the tortured path of life for both Phoenix and her grandson. The analogy is concisely expressed, and it works well.

The final sentence reminds us of the claim made in the thesis statement: that Phoenix's spirit has been strengthened by adversity. This conclusion has been prepared for by the writer's insistence on how well Phoenix manages in the circumstances of her age and race. But now in a *very* concise statement (the last sentence of Version 4) she shows how the idea works. Ideally, the writer takes more time to make this point. I will elaborate, so that you can take in the logic of what she is saying in this last sentence.

(1) Hardships can be "overcome through the power of love." That is, love can keep her going in very difficult circumstances. Thus, Phoenix's love for her grandson is such that in her eyes "'We is the only two left in the world'" (12); because she focuses on the intensity of her love for him, she can brush off insults and threats from bigots like the hunter. Thus, too, she can travel a path

that ought to be impossible for an extremely old woman because she loves her grandson too much to let him down. The hardships of "racial prejudice and the infirmity of old age" are in this way "overcome through the power of love."

(2) Love is "tested and strengthened by adversity." Obviously she is tested by adversity, but so is her love. Love keeps her going, and a failure in love would stop her. The weights that her love must push hard against in this life-long test are "adversity"; because her love is exercised so thoroughly, because it contends with such heavy weights, it is "strengthened" (as any muscle is strengthened by exercise).

(3) Phoenix's "spirit" (to return to the term used in the thesis statement) is "strengthened by adversity" because love is strengthened by it (as shown above) *and* because other qualities—courage, determination, cleverness—are also called into play and strengthened by the powerful insistence of her love. Together, these qualities make up her spirit. She needs these things if she is "'going to last'" (12)—as her grandson, with his "'sweet look'" of love, is also going to last.

FINAL COMMENTS

Original ideas. I have assumed in assigning grades to the four versions of the sample essay that the ideas contained in them have not simply been recycled from lectures and tutorials. This does not mean that you cannot use such ideas; it *does* mean that your essay should go beyond them. Consider the new ideas that are introduced in Version 4. If the ideas about the scarecrow, for example, had been given in the lecture, there would be no merit in simply repeating them in an essay. If nothing had been said about the scarecrow, the essay would be particularly impressive; if something had been pointed out—perhaps that the scarecrow is an image of death or that crows (like Phoenix) are black—the essay would still be impressive because it extends these ideas and situates them within an argument.

Titles. I have not so far given a title to any of these essays. However, you should always provide a title. Your instructor may wish you to indicate in some way which topic you are addressing, if you are choosing from an assigned list. But only rarely will the exact wording of the topic provide you with a good title. For example, "The Extent to Which Old Age and Racism Are Related Issues in 'A Worn Path'" is a poor title for Version 4; "Old Age and Racism in 'A Worn Path'" is better, and perfectly satisfactory—but you may find it a little dull. The title should give the reader some idea of what the essay is about. If I wanted a more imaginative title for Version 4—let's say, "Phoenix and the Scarecrow"—I could *combine* that with a more obvious signal of the essay's content by using a colon.

Phoenix and the Scarecrow:
Old Age and Racism in "A Worn Path"

"Phoenix and the Scarecrow" would have been a fine title all by itself if the essay had been primarily focused on the scarecrow. In the case of Version 4, "Phoenix and the Scarecrow" could not be used alone; as *half* the title, however, it serves the useful purpose of directing the reader's attention to how the scarecrow encapsulates (for this essay) the two themes of old age and racism.

Works cited. I have so far left out the Works Cited section of the essay, which comes at the end. In a short essay, you may choose to put this on the last page—if there is enough room. This saves trees. For all versions of the sample essay, you would type a dividing line (row of equal-signs or hyphens) and write as follows:

Works Cited

Welty, Eudora. "A Worn Path." Reading Our World: The Guelph
   Anthology. Eds. Constance Rooke, Renée Hulan, and Linda
   Warley. Needham Heights: Ginn, 1990. 8–12.

COPYRIGHT ACKNOWLEDGMENTS

To the owner of this book

We hope that you have enjoyed *The Writer's Path* and we would like to know as much about your experiences with this text as you would care to offer. Only through your comments and those of others can we learn how to make this a better text for future readers.

School _____   Your instructor's name _____

Course _____   Was the text required? _____

Recommended? _____

1. What did you like the most about *The Writer's Path?*

_____

_____

_____

2. How useful was this text for your course?

_____

_____

_____

3. Do you have any recommendations for ways to improve the next edition of this text?

_____

_____

_____

4. In the space below or in a separate letter, please write any other comments you have about the book. (For example, please feel free to comment on reading level, writing style, terminology, design features, and learning aids.)

_____

_____

_____

Optional

Your name _____   Date _____

May ITP Nelson quote you, either in promotion for *The Writer's Path* or in future publishing ventures?

Yes _____   No _____   *Thanks!*

You can also send your comments to us via e-mail at
college_arts_hum@nelson.com

PLEASE TAPE SHUT. DO NOT STAPLE.

- - - TAPE SHUT - - -

- - - - - - - - - FOLD HERE - - - - - - - - -

MAIL ⟩ POSTE
Canada Post Corporation
Société canadienne des postes
Postage paid   Port payé
if mailed in Canada si posté au Canada
Business Reply   Réponse d'affaires
0066102399   01

Nelson

0066102399-M1K5G4-BR01

```
ITP NELSON
MARKET AND PRODUCT DEVELOPMENT
PO BOX 60225 STN BRM B
TORONTO ON M7Y 2H1
```